ROGER R. MARTELLA, JR. AND J.

International Environmental Law

The Practitioner's Guide to the Laws of the Planet

AMERICAN BAR ASSOCIATION
Section of Environment,
Energy, and Resources

Printed in the United States of America

18 17 16 15 14   5 4 3 2 1

Library of Congress Cataloging-in-Publication Data

International environmental law / edited by Roger R. Martella Jr. and J. Brett Grosko. — First edition.
    pages cm
Includes bibliographical references and index.
    ISBN 978-1-62722-737-7 (print : alk. paper)
    1. Environmental law, International. 2. Environmental law. I. Martella, Roger Romulus, editor. II. Grosko, J. Brett, editor.
    K3585.I5773 2014
    344.04'6—dc23

                                                                            2014017915

CONTENTS

CHAPTER 7

Handling, Treatment, Transportation, and Disposal of Hazardous Materials

Tzvi Levinson and Jennifer Wills

CHAPTER 8

Waste and Site Remediation
Bradley M. Campbell

CHAPTER 9

Emergency Response.
Jamon L. Bollock and David O. Chang

CHAPTER 10

Natural Resource Management and Protection.
Robert L. Glicksman

CHAPTER 11

Natural Resource Damages 179
Kim Smaczniak

CHAPTER 12

Protected Species 189
Andrew Long

CHAPTER 13

Environmental Review and Decision Making 217
Edward (Ted) Boling

CHAPTER 14

Transboundary Pollution 235
Michael G. Faure

CHAPTER 21

Angeles Murgier and Guillermo Malm Green

CHAPTER 22

Luiz Fernando Henry Sant'Anna and Marise Hosomi Spitzeck

CHAPTER 29

Germany **547**
Dr. Bettina Enderle

CHAPTER 30

United Kingdom **581**
Owen Lomas, Douglas Bryden, and Carl Boeuf

CHAPTER 34

Armen Khachaturyan and Oleh Furmanchuk

CHAPTER 35

Irina O. Krasnova

CHAPTER 44

Tonbofa Eva Ashimi, Tolulope Abimbola Moseli, and Francis Etivieya

CHAPTER 45

John Taberner

CHAPTER 46

New Zealand.. **909**

Robert Makgill

CHAPTER 47

Arctic Region **933**

Peter H. Oppenheimer and Brian Israel

ABOUT THE EDITORS

Roger Martella is an international environmental attorney with Sidley Austin LLP in Washington, D.C., focusing on assisting multinational corporations with environmental compliance, sustainable development, and litigation across the globe. Prior to joining Sidley Austin, Mr. Martella was the General Counsel of the U.S. Environmental Protection Agency and the Principal Counsel for Complex Litigation for the Justice Department's Natural Resources Section. Mr. Martella is the co-chair of the International Bar Association's Climate Change Justice and Human Rights Task Force, vice chair of the American Bar Association's Sustainable Development Task Force, and vice chair of the ABA's World Justice Forum committee. Mr. Martella also is the founder of the U.S. EPA's China Environmental Law Initiative. He is listed as one of the ten leading environmental lawyers globally by the International Who's Who of Environmental Lawyers. Mr. Martella graduated from Vanderbilt Law School, where he was Editor in Chief of the Vanderbilt Law Review, and Cornell University.

J. Brett Grosko is a Trial Attorney in the U.S. Department of Justice Environment and Natural Resources Division. He previously served as an attorney-advisor at the National Oceanic and Atmospheric Administration Office of General Counsel and an international litigation associate at Holland & Knight LLP, and clerked at the U.S. Court of International Trade. Prior to attending law school, he researched environmental law enforcement on a Fulbright scholarship. For the ABA Section of Environment, Energy, and Resources, Mr. Grosko is a vice chair of the Environmental Rule of Law Task Force and a former co-chair and current vice chair of the International Environmental and Resources Law Committee. He graduated from the George Washington University Law School, the Johns Hopkins University School of Advanced International Studies, and Georgetown University. The views expressed in the Introduction and East and South Asia Overview are those of Mr. Grosko and do not necessarily reflect the views of the U.S. Department of Justice or the United States. The views expressed in the other chapters of this volume are those of the respective authors.

ABOUT THE CONTRIBUTORS

Tonbofa Eva Ashimi is the Managing Partner of the Nigerian law firm of Edward Ekiyor & Co., based in Bayelsa and Lagos States. She holds a Bachelor of Laws degree from the University of Lagos, Nigeria, and a Masters in Law from Harvard Law School. She is licensed to practice in New York and in Nigeria. Ms. Ashimi's practice spans Nigeria's energy, oil, gas, environmental, and finance laws. She works closely with regulators in these sectors and has been part of teams drafting rules guiding operations in these sectors, such as the Nigerian Electricity Supply Industry Standards. She also advises corporations sponsoring projects in the energy and natural resources sectors on Nigerian law issues. Ms. Ashimi is involved in ensuring the enforcement of environmental laws through Nigerian Courts.

Başak Başoğlu is a member of the Law Faculty at Istanbul Bilgi University. She received her law degree and JD from Istanbul University and her LLM in business law from Istanbul Bilgi University. She specializes in the field of tort law, environmental law, contract law, international sales law, and family law. She has various publications, including two books in Turkish, *Specific Performance under Turkish Law and Comparative Law* and *Civil Liability for Environmental Damages*. She was admitted to the Istanbul Bar Association in 2005.

Daniel Basurto González is Founding Partner of the Environmentally Sustainable Development Initiative (Iniciativa para el Dessarrollo Ambiental y Sustentable, S.C., or IDEAS) law firm in Mexico City and graduated from the Universidad Anahuac Mexico Norte, 1983. He has been awarded specialized diplomas and recognitions in environmental law and has practiced in this field since 1987. He developed and coordinated the Environmental Law Diploma Program of the Universidad Panamericana from 2000 to 2006 and was a member of the Teaching Staff for Postgraduate Studies of the Escuela Libre de Derecho and the Universidad Panamericana. He has mainly advised the private sector, basically in industrial activities and tourist and real estate developments. In his participation with the industrial and service sectors, he has acted as Chairman of COPARMEX's and CONCAMIN's Ecology Commissions. Mr. González was the Coordinator of the Environmental Law Commission of the Mexican Bar Association for five years, currently chairs the Environment and Energy International Environmental Matters Commission of the International Chamber of Commerce (ICC-MEXICO), and is a member of its Executive Board. He is also an active member of the ANADE. As to NAFTA, he has been a dynamic participant, representing private sector entities, and has been a member of the Joint Public Advisory Committee (JPAC) and NAFTA's Decade Revision Committee (TRAC). At the international level, he is an active member of the American Bar Association and of the International Bar Association.

Shephali Mehra Birdi is a Principal Associate at the Gurgaon office of Kochhar & Co. Her areas of expertise include environment and natural resource law, life sciences, and drugs and pharmaceutical law. Ms. Birdi regularly advises clients on complex environmental issues and compliance matters, including environmental pollution, environment impact assessment, commercial utilization of biological resources, forests clearance, law and policy on gene technology, and genetically modified products, including food articles and seeds. She works on areas concerning regulation of hazardous wastes, hazardous chemicals, dangerous goods, electronic wastes, medical wastes, and various industry-specific licensing, approval, reporting, mitigation, product recall, and related aspects. She has also been involved in several environmental due diligence exercises. Ms. Birdi is co-author of the *Environmental Law Reporter (ELR) India Update*, a quarterly brief of Indian environmental law and policy updates, published by Environment Law Institute, USA. She has co-authored the EIATRACK India pages for the website http://www.eiatrack.org.

Carl Boeuf is an Associate in the Environment & Operational Regulatory Group at Travers Smith LLP, London. Mr. Boeuf specializes in environmental, health and safety, and product stewardship matters. He advises at EU and UK level, providing support on transactions, crisis management response (including in relation to environmental, product safety and workplace incidents), commercial litigation, regulatory compliance, and defense. Mr. Boeuf also advises on environmental, social, and governance (ESG) issues, including in relation to corporate reporting. He has written a number of articles on environmental law for UK legal publications, is co-author of the UK Environment chapter of *Getting the Deal Through*, and is an active member of the UK Environmental Law Association.

Edward (Ted) Boling is Deputy Solicitor for Parks & Wildlife at the U.S. Department of the Interior, where he supervises the work of the Solicitor's Office in support of programs of the National Park Service and the U.S. Fish and Wildlife Service. Mr. Boling joined the Department in August of 2010 as Counselor to the Assistant Secretary for Land and Minerals Management, where he focused on land management planning and renewable energy development, and was Deputy Solicitor for Land Resources from April of 2011 to July of 2013. Before Interior, he served ten years at the President's Council on Environmental Quality (CEQ) as Deputy General Counsel beginning in August of 2000, General Counsel beginning in January of 2008, and Senior Counsel from September of 2009. He went to CEQ from the Environment and Natural Resources Division of the U.S. Department of Justice, where he was a senior trial attorney. Mr. Boling joined the Department of Justice in 1990 through the Attorney General's Honor Program. At the Department of Justice he was a trial attorney in three Sections of the Division: Law and Policy, Wildlife and Marine Resources, and Natural Resources.

Jamon L. Bollock is a Senior Associate in the global Energy and Natural Resources Practice Group of Reed Smith LLP. Mr. Bollock represents energy companies, manufacturers, and transportation companies in all aspects of environmental law, including litigation and compliance matters involving hazardous waste, air pollution, water quality, and natural resource protection. Previously, he was an Attorney-Advisor with the National Oceanic and Atmospheric Administration (NOAA) Office of General Counsel. During his time at NOAA, Mr. Bollock served as a special assistant on the federal government's response to the BP Deepwater Horizon oil spill disaster. He was also Trial Attorney in the Environmental Enforcement Section of the U.S. Department of Justice's Environment and Natural Resources Section, where he represented the federal government in civil enforcement litigation and cost-recovery actions under the Clean Water Act, Oil Pollution Act, and CERCLA. He also clerked for Judge Procter Hug of the U.S. Court of Appeals for the Ninth Circuit. He received his JD from Stanford Law School and a BA from Bowdoin College.

Douglas Bryden is Partner and Head of Environment & Operational Regulatory at Travers Smith LLP, London. Mr. Bryden specializes in UK, EU, and international environment, energy, and regulatory law and policy. In addition to dealing with such risks in major projects and transactions, Mr. Bryden has defended clients in the Crown Court and regularly advises more generally on complex compliance and risk management issues. Mr. Bryden has worked on a number of high-profile mandates, including for Trafigura on the UK's largest environmental case to date and on one of the first onshore unconventional oil and gas developments in the UK. The legal directories list him as one of the UK's leading environmental lawyers. Mr. Bryden is also the General Editor of *Commercial Environmental Law & Liability* (Sweet & Maxwell) and lectures widely on environmental and other operational regulatory matters.

Bradley M. Campbell is president of an independent national law practice (Bradley M. Campbell, LLC) focused on energy, environment, entrepreneurship, and science; and president of an energy development firm (Swan Creek Energy LLC) focused on innovative and alternative power generation projects. Mr. Campbell brings to these firms broad experience in public policy and law enforcement, and he has been the lead attorney in numerous matters involving transboundary pollution. He served as the Commissioner of

New Jersey's Department of Environmental Protection (2002–2006), where he was central to developing the Regional Greenhouse Gas Initiative (RGGI) and other climate change programs. Earlier, he served as a Regional Administrator of the United States Environmental Protection Agency (1999–2001), implementing and enforcing federal environmental law in the Mid-Atlantic region; as an Associate Director of the White House Counsel on Environmental Quality (1995–1999); and as a trial attorney with the United States Department of Justice (2002–2005). An alumnus of Amherst College and the University of Chicago Law School, Mr. Campbell has offices in Trenton, New Jersey, and Washington, D.C.

Antonella Capria heads the Environmental Law team of the Italian law firm Gianni, Origoni, Grippo, Cappelli & Partners. She has more than 30 years of experience in advising domestic and international clients on the full range of administrative, environmental, and health and safety matters. She has particular experience in the energy sector, environmental liability, compliance with EU and Italian environmental regulatory requirements, negotiation with public authorities, settlements, and environmental disputes. She also developed significant experience in permitting issues connected to the development of offshore terminals and energy and oils infrastructures projects. She has coordinated research projects for the European Union, the Italian Ministry of Environment, and the Italian National Research Council. Ms. Capria has authored a number of books and journal articles on EU and Italian environmental law, and she regularly lectures in several postgraduate environmental law courses. She is listed in the International Who's Who of Environment Lawyers. In 2013, Ms. Capria was recognized as "Professional of the Year in the field of Administrative law" by Top Legal Italy.

David O. Chang is an Associate at Reed Smith LLP and previously advised AAA on legal and regulatory affairs. Mr. Chang has also served in senior positions at GlaxoSmithKline and Well Fargo. He received his JD from the University of California, Hastings College of Law, where he served as an editor of the *Hastings Law Journal* and a co-chair of the Hastings Moot Court Team. He also received an MBA from Thunderbird School of Global Management and a BS from Pepperdine University.

Eduardo Del Valle Mora is an associate with Brigard & Urrutia Abogados in Bogotá, Colombia. He received his JD from the Pontificia Universidad Javeriana and LLM (Environmental Law) from McGill University. He also has done postgraduate studies in administrative law and environmental law at Universidad del Rosario. He also obtained merit-based scholarships from McGill University Scholar and Colfuturo. Mr. Del Valle Mora is a Lecturer at the Law School of Universidad Javeriana and the Law School of Universidad del Rosario and a member of the Colegio de Abogados Javerianos and of the Graduate Law Students Association of McGill University. He advises local and foreign companies in environmental (regulatory, environmental liability, management of community affairs, and management of governmental affairs), mining (exploration, exploitation, and commercialization of minerals), and oil and gas matters (exploration, exploitation, transportation, and distribution of hydrocarbons). Recently, he published *Aplicación de los Principales Principios Constitucionales y Legales en el régimen sancionatorio ambiental colombiano (Application of the principal constitutional and legal principles to the Colombian Environmental Sanction regime)* (Brigard & Urrutia, 2014).

David Desforges is a partner at Genesis Avocats (France) where he heads the firm's environmental law practice from the Paris office. He advises and defends essentially industrial companies on site and product-related issues. His experience with industrial and mining activities is acknowledged both in France and internationally. Formerly the partner in charge of the environmental practice at Gide Loyrette Nouel until 2010, he subsequently joined Jones Day in Paris and is listed as one of the leading environmental lawyers in France by *Chambers Europe*, the *Legal 500-EMEA, PLC Which Lawyer?*, the *International Who's Who of Environment Lawyers*, and *Best Lawyers*. Mr. Desforges received a diploma of the Institut d'Etudes Politiques de Paris with *Lauréat* honors in 1991, his LLM from Northwestern University in 1994, a Public Services Certificate Degree from the Graduate School of Public Services of Paul University in 1994, and a postgraduate law degree from the Université Paris II–Assas Law School in 1997. He is a lecturer in law at the Université Paris Sud Law School.

Charles E. Di Leva (Part I Editor and author of chapter 3, "How to Approach an International Environmental Law Question") is Chief Counsel and manager of the Environmental and International Law practice group of the World Bank Legal Department. His work covers all geographic regions, specializing on environmental and social risk management and compliance in project finance, as well as climate law and carbon finance. He represents the Bank in a range of international treaty negotiations. From 1999 until 2001, he was Director of the Environmental Law Program of the International Union for the Conservation of Nature, while based in Bonn, Germany, and also served as Senior Program Officer with the Environmental Law Unit for the U.N. Environment Program in Nairobi, Kenya. Mr. Di Leva also served as Trial Attorney for four years with the U.S. Department of Justice Environment and Natural Resources Division and for five years with the State of Rhode Island as Legal Counsel with the Department of Environmental Management and the Attorney General's office. Mr. Di Leva is an adjunct professor at the George Washington University School of Law, teaching trade and sustainable development, and at the American University Washington College of Law, teaching project finance and the environment.

Gil Dror received his LLB degree from the Haifa University Law School. He has academic background in the field of environmental sciences. His bachelor's degree (B.Sc.Agr) is from the Faculty of Agriculture of the Hebrew University in Jerusalem, and his master's degree (M.Sc) is from the Department of Environmental Sciences and Energy Research at the Weizmann Institute for Sciences. Currently Mr. Dror is a PhD student at the Porter School of Environmental Studies in Tel Aviv University. He is a partner in The Levinson Environmental Law Firm. Before joining the firm, ten years ago, he acquired practical experience in various environmental fields, including as Hazardous Materials Inspector at the Western Galilee Township Association for Environmental Protection and as Environmental Engineer in the field of monitoring and rehabilitation of polluted rivers at the Kishon River Authority.

Alexandra Dapolito Dunn is Executive Director and General Counsel of the Environmental Council of the States (ECOS), the national nonprofit, nonpartisan association of U.S. state and territorial environmental commissioners. Ms. Dunn has two decades of experience in environmental law and policy, with extensive work on water quality, treatment, and implementation of the Clean Water Act. Ms. Dunn is a member of the bar in Washington, D.C., Maryland, and New York, the U.S. Supreme Court, and federal courts. She has represented parties, intervenors, or amicus curiae in over 25 environmental cases. Ms. Dunn is the immediate past Chair of the American Bar Association's Section of Environment, Energy, and Resources, and serves on the Board of the Environmental Law Institute. She is a Lecturer in Law at Columbus School of Law, Catholic University of America, and an Adjunct Professor at American University's Washington College of Law. She earned her JD, magna cum laude, at the Columbus School of Law, Catholic University of America, where she was Editor in Chief of the *Law Review*. She received a BA, cum laude, in political science, from James Madison University, VA.

Bettina Enderle, PhD, is Counsel in the Environmental Law Group at Allen & Overy LLP, Germany. She has 15 years' experience in environmental matters, advisory, and litigation, and in M&A or financing transactions. Her focus areas are permit procedures and compliance issues of industrial plants, energy, and infrastructure projects. She advised in the planning of the Fixed Femernbelt Link, the biggest infrastructure project in Europe, connecting a Danish and a German island via a submarine 19km tunnel combining a motorway with high-speed rail tracks. Her industry clients are active in the refinery, paper and pulp, electronics, and waste recycling as well as (renewable) energy sectors (power plants, solar, wind, geothermal). Currently she represents several clients in challenges against the allocation of greenhouse gas emissions allowances under the EU Emissions Trading Scheme. She represents her clients in proceedings before German and EU authorities and courts, including the European Court of Justice. She publishes and presents in her areas of expertise in Europe and the Americas (e.g., ABA, Salt Lake City 2012) and is a member of the German-American Lawyers Association.

Francis Etivieya is an Associate in the Nigerian law firm of Edward Ekiyor & Co. based in Lagos and Bayelsa States. He holds a Bachelor of Laws degree from Niger Delta University, Nigeria. He is licensed to practice in Nigeria and is a member of the Nigerian Bar Association. Mr. Etivieya's legal practice spans Nigeria's energy, oil and gas, property, and finance indsutries. He has been working with the Nigerian Bar Association Yenagoa branch, Bayelsa State through the Energy and Environmental Law Committee to ensure environmental sanity in the Niger Delta, as well as making efforts to see that lawyers benefit from the oil and gas resources in the region.

Francesca Libera Falco is an associate in the Environmental team of the law firm Gianni, Origoni, Grippo, Cappelli & Partners. Ms. Falco has gained experience in working on environmental and administrative law issues with particular focus on the environmental regulatory matters on air, water and waste management, EU Emissions Trading System, clean-up procedures of contaminated sites as well as the liability for environmental damage. She regularly speaks on marine pollution at environmental law training courses organized by a leading energy company. Previously, she attended a training program at the Italian Ministry of Foreign Affairs, Embassy in Tehran, Iran, where she dealt in particular with oil and gas matters. She has been a Blue Book trainee at the EU Commission, Foreign Policy Instrument Service. Ms. Falco graduated cum laude at Bocconi University, Milan (2008), and completed a master's program in International and European Law at the Geneva University, Switzerland (2010). She speaks Italian, French, and English and is conversant in Persian.

Dr. Michael G. Faure, LLM, became academic director of the Maastricht European institute for transnational legal research (METRO) and professor of Comparative and International Environmental Law at the law faculty of Maastricht University in September 1991. Professor Faure still holds both positions today. In addition, he is academic director of the Ius Commune Research School and member of the board of directors of Ectil. Since the first of February 2008, he is half-time professor of comparative private law and economics at the Rotterdam Institute of Law & Economics (RILE) of the Erasmus University in Rotterdam and academic director of the European Doctorate in Law and Economics (EDLE) programme. Since 1982 he has also been an attorney at the Antwerp Bar. He publishes in the areas of environmental (criminal) law, tort and insurance and economic analysis of (accident) law.

Luiz Fernando Henry Sant'Anna has been a partner in Demarest Advogados since 1993, and currently is responsible for its Environmental Law Department, acting in the administrative, judicial, and extrajudicial areas comprising civil and criminal aspects of environmental law. In addition to his activities in the environmental area, he is the partner responsible for the civil and business consultancy practice in Demarest Advogados. He graduated from Universidade Católica de São Paulo Law School in 1986, and earned a LLM from the University of Illinois College of Law in 1990. He was assistant professor at Civil Law at Universidade Católica de São Paulo Law School from 1987 to 2006.

Andrew Fitanides is an Associate in Baker & McKenzie's Ho Chi Minh office. As a member of the Dispute Resolution Practice Group, Mr. Fitanides managed a major commercial litigation effort in Vietnamese courts and has assisted with several litigation efforts involving foreign and domestic Vietnamese parties. Mr. Fitanides also advises clients on Vietnamese information, technology, and communications (IT/C), advertising, and pharmaceutical and environmental regulations as well as the Foreign Corrupt Practices Act (FCPA) and other anti-corruption law compliance. Prior to joining Baker & McKenzie in 2010, Mr. Fitanides clerked in the Massachusetts Superior Court's Special Business Litigation Session and worked for one of Vietnam's largest real estate developers. Mr. Fitanides is a graduate of Cornell University (BA, 1990), Columbia University's School of International and Public Affairs (MIA, 1998), and Northeastern University School of Law (JD, 2008). He is a member of the Massachusetts Bar (2008). Mr. Fitanides speaks English and French and is conversant in Japanese.

Tad Ferris is Partner and Co-Chair of the Greater China Regulatory Practice at Foley & Lardner LLP, General Counsel and Founder of the China EHS Roundtable, Vice Chairman of the Board of the International Fund for China's Environment, and Chair of the China Committee and China-Environment Task Force of the U.S. Council for International Business. Mr. Ferris also served as Chair (2002–2004) and Vice Chair (2004–2006) of the International Environmental Law Committee of the ABA Section on Environment Energy and Resources. In his role as attorney, Mr. Ferris advises companies on compliance, risk management, and international trade and stakeholder engagement in China and elsewhere in Asia. Mr. Ferris has acted as a comparative law expert for United Nations organizations, development banks, and foreign government institutions and agencies. He is a graduate of the Duke University School of Law, with a JD and a masters of law in comparative and international legal studies.

Russell Fraker is an Associate in the Washington, D.C., office of Beveridge & Diamond, P.C., where he advises clients on environmental regulatory issues associated with facilities and products, both domestically and internationally. He has experience with the environmental laws of most Latin American countries, with a particular focus on Brazil. Before studying law, Mr. Fraker worked as a consultant to the petroleum, forestry, fisheries, and telecommunications industries. He received his law degree from Vanderbilt Law School, where he was Managing Editor of the *Vanderbilt Law Review* and Co-founder and Managing Editor of the *Environmental Law & Policy Annual Review*. He also holds degrees in philosophy and political science from Reed College, and in international relations from Yale University.

Glory Francke is an associate in the Environmental Practice Group at Sidley Austin LLP, where she provides compliance and product stewardship advice on EU chemical and climate change legislation. More generally, she helps multinational clients understand the practical functioning of EU environmental law and policy, from how decisions are made in Brussels to the implementation of EU law in the Member States. Prior to joining Sidley, Ms. Francke was in-house counsel for the Brussels office of GE's Corporate Environmental Programs where she counseled the GE businesses on EU chemical legislation and climate change regulation and advocated for GE's interests before the EU Institutions. Ms. Francke graduated with a *Juristexamen* from the University of Stockholm and holds an LLM in energy and environmental law from the Catholic University of Leuven, Belgium. She moved with her family to Seattle, Washington, in 2012 and will graduate with her JD from the University of Seattle School of Law in 2015.

Oleh Furmanchuk is an Associate at Asters, Kiev, Ukraine. Mr. Furmanchuk has a broad experience in advising Ukrainian and foreign clients on regulatory and environmental legal matters, including environmental legal due diligences, environmental permits and licensing, compliance with regulatory requirements, inspections of environmental authorities, sanctions for environmental pollution, and others. Mr. Furmanchuk advised on environmental legal aspects of liquidation of Ukrainian industrial enterprises and analyzed environmental legal compliance at numerous Ukrainian companies. His areas of practice also include banking and finance, employment, M&A, and general corporate advice. He received his LLM degree from University of Amsterdam (the Netherlands) and master's degree (law) from the National University of Ostroh Academy (Ukraine). He also contributes to Ukrainian and international publications.

Robert L. Glicksman is the J.B & Maurice C. Shapiro Professor of Environmental Law at the George Washington University Law School, where he focuses on environmental, natural resources, and administrative law. A graduate of the Cornell Law School, Mr. Glicksman taught at the University of Kansas School of Law before joining the GW faculty. He has practiced and consulted on environmental issues, including for the Commission for Environmental Cooperation. He is co-author of *Environmental Protection: Law and Policy* (6th ed. Aspen); *Administrative Law: Agency Action in Legal Context* (Foundation Press); *Public Natural Resources Law* (2d ed. West); *Risk Regulation at Risk: Restoring a Pragmatic Approach* and *Pollution Limits and Polluters' Efforts to Comply: The Role of Government Monitoring and Enforcement*, both published by Stanford University Press; and *Modern Public Land Law in a Nutshell* (4th ed. West). He has written extensively on environmental and natural resources law topics, concentrating recently on climate change, federalism issues, federal land management, and environmental enforcement. Mr. Glicksman is a member scholar and Board member for the Center for Progressive Reform.

Hana Heineken is a Policy Advisor at Global Witness, an international NGO that seeks to prevent natural resource-related conflict and corruption and associated environmental and human rights abuses. Her areas of expertise include the trade in illegal or unsustainable timber, the international financing of environmentally destructive activities, and associated violations of human rights. Her work focuses on Japanese government policy and the responsibilities of Japanese companies. Prior to joining Global Witness, Ms. Heineken worked as a consultant for the Center for International Environmental Law on climate change, hazardous waste, and international finance. She also worked for a number of years as a policy aide to members of the Japanese Parliament on matters relating to the environment and human rights. She graduated cum laude from Pace Law School with certificates in international law and environmental law, served as a research fellow at the Tokyo University Graduate School for Law and Politics, and holds an A.B. from Princeton University. She is a member of the ABA Section of Environment, Energy, and Resources World Justice Project (WJP) Task Force.

Brian Israel is an Attorney-Adviser at the U.S. Department of State in the Office of the Legal Adviser for Oceans, International Environmental, and Scientific Affairs where he is presently responsible for the Arctic portfolio, among others. In this capacity he headed the United States delegations to the Arctic Council Task Force on Institutional Issues and Task Force on Arctic Marine Oil Pollution Prevention. Mr. Israel also teaches international law as an adjunct professor at George Mason University School of Law. Mr. Israel is a graduate of the University of California, San Diego, and the University of California, Berkeley, School of Law, where he was Editor in Chief of the *Berkeley Journal of International Law* and founded *Publicist*, an online international law publication.

Madeleine B. Kadas is a Shareholder in the Austin office of Beveridge & Diamond, P.C., and the founder and chair of the Firm's Latin American Practice Group. She advises clients on environmental laws affecting industrial facilities and products throughout Latin America, with a focus on Mexico. She was the first Managing Director of the Austin office (2005–2009) and maintains a significant domestic environmental law practice focusing on air and waste compliance issues in Texas. She received her law degree from the University of Texas and holds a graduate law degree from La Escuela Libre de Derecho, Mexico's premier law school. Before studying law, Ms. Kadas was a U.S. Peace Corps Volunteer in Guatemala. She speaks Spanish fluently.

Armen Khachaturyan is a Senior Partner at Asters, Kiev, Ukraine. He has extensive experience in the wide spectrum of practices, including environmental law, advising a large number of Ukrainian and foreign public and private clients in different industries on such matters as environmental permits and licensing, land-fills, emissions, and compliance with regulatory requirements. Mr. Khachaturyan's expertise includes cross-border legal planning and legal

regime of foreign investment, banking and finance, M&A, general corporate advice, energy, privatization, and restructuring. He is consistently recognized as a highly recommended lawyer in *Chambers Global and Chambers
Europe, IFLR1000, The Legal 500: EMEA, Who's Who Legal, Best Lawyers,
Expert Guide,* and *Ukrainian Law Firms.* Mr. Khachaturyan received his LLM
degree from Yale Law School, PhD (private international law) and master's
degree (international law) from the Kiev National University, and diploma
from the International Law Institute, Washington, D.C. Mr. Khachaturyan is
frequently involved in legislative and regulatory initiatives, speaks at professional conferences and seminars, and contributes to Ukrainian and international publications.

Kyoung Yeon Kim is a partner at Yulchon, LLC, Seoul, Korea. Ms. Kim's
area of practice covers antitrust, M&A, corporate general, environment and
energy, data privacy, and other regulatory matters. Ms. Kim joined Yulchon
as an associate in 2001 and became a partner in 2009. She served as a counsel
for the Korean Ministry of Environment (MOE) from 2010 to 2013 and for
the Ministry of Justice since 2011. As the counsel for the MOE, she has provided advice on interpretation of various laws and regulation of the environment as well as in the government's policymaking process. She also served
as the legal counsel for the 2012 IUCN World Conservation Congress in Jeju,
Korea, and the counsel for National Institute for Ecology from 2012. She
received her LLB from Seoul National University in 1998 and LLM from the
University of Michigan Law School in 2007. She is a member of the bars of
the Republic of Korea (2001) and New York (2008).

John H. Knox is the Henry C. Lauerman Professor of International Law at
Wake Forest University, where he teaches international trade law, international environmental law, and human rights law. His recent scholarship
includes "A Presumption Against Extrajurisdictionality," published in the
American Journal of International Law; "Climate Ethics and Human Rights," in
the *Journal of Human Rights and the Environment*; and "Neglected Lessons of
the NAFTA Environmental Regime," in the *Wake Forest Law Review*. As an
attorney-adviser at the Department of State from 1988 to 1994, he participated in the negotiation of the North American Agreement on Environmental
Cooperation. Between 1999 and 2005, Mr. Knox chaired the National Advisory Committee to U.S. EPA on North American environmental cooperation.
In 2012, he was appointed by the United Nations Human Rights Council to a
three-year term as its first Independent Expert on human rights and the environment. He graduated with honors from Stanford Law School in 1987 and
clerked for Judge Joseph Sneed on the Ninth Circuit Court of Appeals.

Irina O. Krasnova is the Head of the Department of Land Use and Environmental Law of the Russian Academy of Justice and a Professor of Environmental and Natural Resources Law of the Moscow State University of Law
(MSAL). In 1997 she was awarded a doctorate degree from the Institute of

Legislation and Comparative (Moscow, Russia) and in 1995 an LLM in environmental law by the Pace University School of Law (New York, USA). In addition to teaching environmental and land use law, Ms. Krasnova is an expert on the Scientific and Consultative Committee of the Supreme Court of the Russian Federation, a member of the Higher Ecological Council of the State Duma (parliament), and an expert of the Higher Attestation Commission of the Ministry of Education. She has gained a great deal of experience in international environmental law by working as environmental affairs officer at the United Nations Environment Programme Regional Office for Europe, as a legal consultant in various EU and UN projects dealing with transboundary rivers, biodiversity protection, Caspian Sea marine environment protection, and environmental standards.

K. Russell LaMotte is a Principal in the Washington, D.C., office of Beveridge & Diamond P.C., and co-chair of the Firm's International Environmental Law practice group. His practice focuses on advocacy in the major multilateral environmental agreements and multijurisdictional product compliance matters relating to environmental and human rights issues, in sectors ranging from chemicals and GMOs to IT equipment. Prior to joining the firm, he served as Deputy Assistant Legal Adviser at the U.S. Department of State and as a law clerk to Hon. Judith Rogers on the U.S. Court of Appeals for the D.C. Circuit. He is an adjunct professor at the American University Washington College of Law, a member of the Executive Council of the American Society of International Law, a member of the Governing Board of the Washington Foreign Law Society, and a magna cum laude graduate of Harvard Law School.

Seung Min Lee is an associate at Yulchon, LLC, Seoul, Korea. Mr. Lee practices primarily in the areas of antitrust, TMT, construction/real estate disputes, environment and energy, and administrative disputes. Mr. Lee received his LLB, MA (administrative law), and PhD (administrative law) from Seoul National University and lectured at Seoul National University School of Law (2011) and Konkuk University Law School (2012–2013). He is a member of the Korean Bar Association.

Tzvi Levinson is the founding partner of the Levinson Environmental Law Firm. Mr. Levinson received his LLB degree from the Hebrew University Law School in Jerusalem. He has built the leading practice in Israel specializing in legal counsel and representation in the fields of environmental, health, and safety (EHS) laws to industries and businesses. The largest firms in the market use his services. Mr. Levinson is uniquely experienced in providing day-to-day "preventive" counsel and representation in legal proceedings (civil, administrative, and criminal) in a variety of EHS issues. He lectures at the Haifa University on environmental law, at the Institute for Advanced Studies for Attorneys, and in many other Israeli and international fora, and has published numerous articles on various EHS law issues. Mr.

Levinson formerly chaired the Environmental Law Committee of the Central Board of the Israeli Bar.

Owen Lomas is Consultant with the Environment & Operational Regulatory Group at Travers Smith LLP, London. He was previously a partner and Head of Global Environmental Law Services at Allen & Overy LLP for over 20 years. Mr. Lomas has wide experience in advising on environmental and climate change law issues both on a standalone basis and in the context of business transactions. A leading writer and commentator on environmental law, his publications include *Commercial Environmental Law and Liability* (Sweet & Maxwell) (joint editor), *Frontiers of Environmental Law* (Chancery), *Packaging Waste Recycling Obligations—a business guide to British regulations* (Pira), and numerous papers and articles on environmental law and policy. He is a member of the board of trustees of the UK Environmental Law Foundation; a member of the editorial boards of *Water Law, The Utilities Law Review*, and *Environmental Law and Management;* and former Editor of the *Journal of Environmental Law* (FT Law & Tax 1989–1997). He was a founding member of the UK Environmental Law Association and served as Chairman of the Law and Policy Working Group of the Environmental Industries Commission from 2000 to 2004.

Andrew Long is a Visiting Associate Professor of Law at the University of Missouri Kansas City School of Law. His research focuses on environmental governance, with an emphasis on regulatory approaches to global challenges such as climate change and biodiversity loss. He is particularly interested in the linkage of environmental issues with human well-being and the interaction of multiple levels of governance. Mr. Long has published a dozen research articles in law reviews and peer-reviewed journals, as well as book chapters and shorter works. He is currently writing a book that analyzes the significance of issue-linkage as an element of international environmental governance effectiveness, drawing on polycentric governance and complexity theories. Professor Long holds an LLM from New York University School of Law and a JD from Willamette University College of Law. He also is the co-chair for newsletters for the ABA Section of Environment, Energy, and Resources International Environmental and Resources Law and Endangered Species Committees.

Robert Makgill is a barrister who specializes in environmental, natural resources, and public law. He regularly appears before the Environment Court and courts of general jurisdiction in New Zealand. In 2010, he was legal counsel in the International Law for the Sea Tribunal's (ITLOS) historic advisory opinion on deep sea mining in the High Seas. In 2011, he chaired the legal working group for the International Seabed Authority's international workshop on "Environmental Management Needs for Exploration and Exploitation of Deep Sea Minerals." In 2012, he advised the Secretariat of the Pacific Community on the European Union-funded deep sea minerals project, which aims to establish deep sea regulatory frameworks for Pacific Island member states. In 2013, he was appointed an exclusive economic zone (EEZ) Hearing Commissioner for the New Zealand Environmental Protection Authority, and assisted in advising a party to the ITLOS advisory proceedings on illegal fishing activities within the EEZs of third-party states. Mr. Makgill is doctoral researcher at the University of Ghent, and research fellow with the Faculty of Environment, Society, and Design at Lincoln University, New Zealand.

Guillermo Malm Green is a partner at the Brons & Salas law firm in Buenos Aires, Argentina. He chairs the Environmental Law Practice and co-chairs the corporate and M&A Practice. He graduated, with honors, from Buenos Aires University Law School in 1989. In 1993 he took a postgraduate course on International Environmental Law at the Southwestern University School of Law Summer Law Program. In 1994 he attended a course at the Academy of American and International Law, Center for American and International Law (formerly Southwestern Legal Foundation), University of Texas, Dallas. He is a member of the International Bar Association, American Bar Association, New York State Bar Association, Buenos Aires Bar Association, and San Isidro Bar Association. He is Vice President of the Environmental Committee of the United States Chamber of Commerce in Argentina. He is also the Country Chair (Argentina) of the New York State Bar Association, Vice Chair of the International Environmental Law Committee of the American Bar Association Section of International Law, and former Co-Chair of the Latin America & Caribbean Committee (2006–2009).

Tolulope Abimbola Moseli is a Senior Associate in the Nigerian law firm of Edward Ekiyor & Co. based in Lagos and Bayelsa States. She holds a Bachelor of Laws from Obafemi Awolowo University, Nigeria, and a Masters in Law from the University of London (Queens Mary College), United Kingdom. She is licensed to practice in Nigeria and is a member of the Nigerian Bar Association. Ms. Moseli has advised various companies in the construction sector on their compliance with the relevant Nigerian environmental laws and communities in pollution abatement civil actions.

Angeles Murgier is a senior attorney at Brons & Salas law firm in Buenos Aires, Argentina. Since she joined the firm her practice has been focused on both environmental and corporate law. She graduated from the Argentine Catholic University in March 2000. She has additionally completed a number of training programs in environmental and international environmental law at the American University Washington College of Law, the University of California, San Diego Graduate School of International Relations and Pacific Studies, the American Law Institute, and the ABA Committee on Continuing Professional Education. She is a member of the ABA Section of Environment, Energy, and Resources, was appointed the first International Liaison Vice Chair for 2008–2011 of the International Environmental Law Committee, and is currently Vice Chair at Large of that committee. She is also a member of the International Bar Association (Vice Chair of the Environment, Health and Safety Committee of the Section on Energy, Environment, Natural Resources and Infrastructure Law), and the Bar Association of the Buenos Aires City.

Peter J. Murtha is a self-employed attorney in Silver Spring, Maryland, who advises on environmental and criminal litigation matters. Mr. Murtha retired from the federal government after over 30 years of service, the majority of which was with the Environment and Natural Resources Division (ENRD) of the U.S. Department of Justice. At ENRD he was a prosecutor handling both environmental crimes and wildlife and marine resources matters, and tried numerous cases. After leaving DOJ, Mr. Murtha headed U.S. EPA's criminal enforcement program where he directed an organization of approximately 375 individuals including criminal investigators, attorneys, and forensic scientists across EPA's ten regions. Upon leaving the criminal director's position in 2008, he spent his final years of government service working on climate change and international environmental law issues with a focus on ensuring compliance with commitments. Mr. Murtha writes on climate change compliance issues and has been active with nongovernmental organizations in promoting the need for limits upon carbon pollution and a transition to clean renewable energy. He graduated from Bucknell University and the George Washington University law school.

Peter H. Oppenheimer is the Chief of the NOAA Office of General Counsel International Section. He oversees an office that provides legal counsel to NOAA and other federal agencies on international environmental and oceans law, particularly the UN Convention on the Law of the Sea. Mr. Oppenheimer has participated in the negotiation, amendment, or implementation of numerous international agreements that address vessel pollution, shipwrecks, ocean dumping, seabirds, and marine scientific research, among others. He currently serves as the principal legal adviser on the U.S. delegation to the Arctic Council's Working Group on the Protection of the Arctic Marine Environment (PAME). Mr. Oppenheimer graduated in 1992 with joint degrees from the Yale Law School (JD) and Tuft University's Fletcher School of Law and Diplomacy (MA in law and diplomacy). He received his BA in history summa cum laude from Yale University in 1986.

Nilüfer Oral is a member of the Law Faculty at Istanbul Bilgi University and Deputy Director of the Marine Research Center for the Law of the Sea. She is Chair of the IUCN Academy on Environmental Law, Councilor on the IUCN Council, and co-chair of the IUCN Specialist Group on Oceans, Coasts and Coral Reefs for the IUCN World Commission on Environmental Law. She is also a member of the Environmental and Social Advisory Council for the European Bank for Reconstruction and Development. Dr. Oral has served as legal advisor to the Turkish Foreign Ministry on law of the sea and climate change and has participated as a climate change negotiator with the Turkish

Delegation (2009–2013). She is a Distinguished Senior Visiting Scholar at the Law of the Sea Institute, University of California School of Law, Berkeley (2011–2014), and has lectured on several occasions at the Rhodes Academy for the Law of the Sea.

LeRoy C. (Lee) Paddock is Associate Dean for Environmental Law Studies at the George Washington University Law School. His work focuses on environmental compliance and enforcement; environmental governance with particular emphasis on integrating the regulatory system with economic and values-based drivers; and governance in the context of emerging technologies, environmental justice, public participation, and energy efficiency. Associate Dean Paddock is a member of the American Bar Association's Task Force on Sustainable Development. He also serves on the George Washington University Sustainability Implementation Team. Prior to coming to George Washington University, Mr. Paddock was Director of Environmental Law Programs at Pace University School of Law for five years. Before Pace, he served for 20 years in the Minnesota Attorney General's Office, including 13 years as Director of Environmental Policy for Minnesota Attorney General Hubert H. Humphrey III. Mr. Paddock holds a BA from the University of Michigan and a JD with high honors from the University of Iowa. He clerked for Judge Donald Lay of the U.S. Court of Appeals for the Eighth Circuit Court.

Robert V. Percival is the Robert F. Stanton Professor of Law and Director of the Environmental Law Program at the University of Maryland Francis King Carey School of Law. He received a BA summa cum laude from Macalester College and a JD/MA from Stanford University, where he was named the Nathan Abbott Scholar for graduating first in his law school class. Mr. Percival served as a law clerk for Judge Shirley M. Hufstedler of the U.S. Court of Appeals for the Ninth Circuit and for U.S. Supreme Court Justice Byron R. White. A former senior attorney at the Environmental Defense Fund, Mr. Percival is internationally recognized as a leading environmental law scholar and has lectured in 28 countries. For more than two decades he has been the principal author of the most widely used casebook on U.S. environmental law, *Environmental Regulation: Law, Science and Policy*, now in its seventh edition. Mr. Percival has served as a visiting professor of law at Harvard Law School, the Georgetown University Law Center, the China University of Political Science and Law, and Comenius University.

Iván Poklepovic is Partner and Head of the Regulated Markets and Natural Resources Practice at Morales & Besa, Abogados, Santiago, Chile (ipoklepovic @moralesybesa.cl). He focuses his practice on environmental and regulatory matters and has a significant experience in environmental litigation and environmental administrative proceedings. He is also well versed in environmental regulation applicable to investment projects and issues relating to energy and natural resources. He founded and led the Environmental Unit of the State Defense Council of Chile (Consejo de Defensa del Estado de Chile) for more than 10 years, where he implemented and developed the environmental liability system for environmental damage under the Chilean environmental law. He also worked on matters relating to environmental law enforcement at the Environmental Compliance Office of the U.S. EPA in Washington, D.C. He was a Fulbright grantee in 2003 and obtained his LLM in environmental law from Pace University Law School in 2004.

Arnold W. Reitze, Jr., has been an environmental lawyer for 50 years, Professor of Law at the University of Utah since 2008, and a member of the University's Institute for Clean and Secure Energy. He is the J.B. and Maurice C. Shapiro Professor Emeritus of Law at the George Washington University School of Law where he was the director of the program in environmental law for 38 years. For nine years he was the faculty editor of the ABA's *Environmental Lawyer*. Professor Reitze is the author of three books on environmental law, four books on air pollution and climate change, and more than 50 law review articles on air pollution. He has extensive experience as an environmental lawyer with an emphasis on air pollution and climate change issues and has been Of Counsel with a number of law firms. He represented the automobile industry in the U.S. Supreme Court in *Massachusetts v. EPA* (2007) and *Engine Manufacturers Ass'n v. South Coast Air Quality Management District* (2003). The author is available at arnold.reitze@law.utah.edu.

Héctor Rodríguez Molnar is the founding partner of Rodríguez Molnar & Asociados, a corporate and environmental law firm in Madrid, Spain. In addition to his corporate and commercial practices, he is a specialist in industrial environment and a member of the Madrid Bar Association, entitled to practice in all Spanish jurisdictions. He is a frequent speaker at International Bar Association (IBA) Conferences and other fora. He holds an Argentine LLB in law and an LLM degree in law from the University of Pennsylvania; currently, he is Vice Chair of the IBA Environmental Health & Safety Law Committee for the period 2013/2014. He can be reached at h.rodriguezmolnar@rm-as.com.

Edward Ruggeri is an associate in the Environmental team of the law firm Gianni, Origoni, Grippo, Cappelli & Partners. Mr. Ruggeri has developed his experience in the fields of environmental, health and safety, and energy law. This experience includes issues concerning asbestos, air emissions, water discharges, waste management, clean-up procedures, and authorization procedures for industrial plants fueled by traditional and renewable energy sources. In addition, he was seconded to a leading international oil and gas company, dealing with regulatory, environmental, and safety issues related to building and management of a regasification terminal. Moreover, he has written various articles on environmental governance and regularly lectures at environmental law training courses organized by a leading energy company.

Mr. Ruggeri graduated in law at the Florence University (2005). During his academic career, he was Junior Editor for the *Journal of Environmental Law* (Oxford University Press) and an assistant at the Siena Summer School "Environmental Law: International and European Perspectives." He obtained an LLM in European and environmental law at University College London (2006). He is bilingual in English and Italian.

Noah M. Sachs is a professor at the University of Richmond School of Law and directs the Robert R. Merhige, Jr. Center for Environmental Studies. He teaches both domestic and international environmental law, and his research focuses on climate change, toxic substance regulation, and European Union law. His work has appeared in the *UCLA Law Review*, *Vanderbilt Law Review*, and *University of Illinois Law Review*, among other venues, and his co-authored text, *Regulation of Toxic Substances and Hazardous Waste*, is the leading casebook on toxic substances regulation. Professor Sachs was awarded the University of Richmond's Distinguished Educator award in 2013, the highest recognition for teaching and scholarship for the faculty. In 2007, he was awarded a fellowship through the EU Visitors Program to study EU environmental lawmaking in Brussels, and in 2014, he was a Fulbright scholar at the National Law School of India University in Bangalore, India.

Jose Pablo Sanchez is senior attorney at VS Abogados in charge of the firm's Environmental, Natural Resources and Energy Practice. With over 10 years of experience in the field, Mr. Sanchez has acquired expertise in all aspects of environmental and energy law with particular strengths in regulatory, due diligence, and project development while advising clients in sophisticated cross-border transactions. He advises leading electronics and consumer products companies on product take-back and recycling requirements across Central America and energy companies including financial institutions for energy and oil transactions. He has been as a foremost practitioner in his fields of practice by recognized international publications such as Chambers & Partners and Who's Who Legal. Mr. Sanchez is also an Associate Professor of Environmental Law at the University of Costa Rica. JD, University of Costa Rica; LLM, American University Washington College of Law.

Yee Chung Seck is a partner in the Ho Chi Minh City office of Baker & McKenzie LLP. Mr. Seck has extensive experience in foreign investment, corporate/commercial, and mergers and acquisitions, and is recognized a leading lawyer for corporate/M&A in Vietnam by Chambers Global and Chambers Asia. He has dealt with a wide range of investment projects and major M&A deals, and advised on corporate, commercial, and regulatory compliance matters, including foreign direct investment, licensing, and market access including numerous environmental matters. Mr. Seck has experience working with entities from a diverse range of industries, including agribusiness, cosmetics, pharmaceuticals and medical devices, food and beverages, manufacturing, property, software, information technology, media and telecommunication, and aviation, both in Vietnam and regionally. He is Vice President of the

Singapore Business Group (HCMC Chapter) and an active participant in the Vietnam Business Forum through its Advisory Council on Administrative Reform and Manufacturing & Distribution Working Group. Mr. Seck graduated from the Law School of the National University of Singapore (1996) and was admitted to the Singapore Bar (1997).

Jung Pyo Seo is an associate at Yulchon, LLC, Seoul, Korea. He practices primarily in the areas of banking/general finance, project finance and lease, transportation finance, and environment and energy. Mr. Seo received his LLB from Korea National Police University. He is currently a member of the Korean Bar Association.

Krishna Vijay Singh is a Senior Partner in the law firm Kochhar & Co and heads the firm's practice at its Gurgaon office. He also is in charge of the infrastructure, life sciences, and environment law practice of the firm. Though he primarily practices corporate law, he has over 17 years of experience in litigation and arbitration and is involved in several prominent domestic and international contentious matters. He has advised clients on a range of complex environmental issues including issues concerning developmental projects and forests and environmental laws, environmental pollution, environmental clearances and licenses, law and policy on gene-technology and genetically modified products, hazardous wastes, and product recall issues, among others. He is co-author of *Environmental Law Reporter India Update*, published by Environment Law Institute, USA, a quarterly briefing that discusses Indian environmental law issues and provides policy updates. He has also co-authored the EIATRACK India pages for the website http://www.eiatrack.org.

Kim Smaczniak (Part II Editor and author of chapter 8, "Natural Resource Damages") is counsel at the United States Senate Committee on Environment and Public Works and previously served as a trial attorney at the United States Department of Justice, Environmental Natural and Resources Division, Environmental Defense Section. She is an adjunct professor at Howard University Law School and is the co-chair of the ABA Section for Environment, Energy, and Resources' International Environmental and Resources Law Committee and the ABA Section for International Law's International Environmental Law Committee.

Eugene E. Smary is a partner with the Grand Rapids, Michigan, office of Warner Norcross & Judd LLP. He has been practicing environmental and resources law for over 30 years. Much of his practice currently focuses on cross-border environmental, natural resource, and infrastructure issues, and on metallic mineral mining. He is the past Chair of the Section of Environment, Energy, and Resources of the American Bar Association. Mr. Smary is also the immediate past Chair of the International Bar Association's Environment Health and Safety Law Committee and was recently elected to serve as Secretary of the IBA's Section of Energy, Environment, Resources and Infrastructure Law. He served as an Adjunct Associate Professor of Law at the University of Notre Dame Law School. He holds his JD and MA degrees from the University of Notre Dame, and his BA from Aquinas College. Following his graduation from law school, he served as a judicial clerk to the Hon. John A. Danaher of the United States Court of Appeals for the District of Columbia Circuit.

Marise Hosomi Spitzeck is an Associate at Demarest Advogados. She graduated from Universidade de São Paulo Law School in 1999 and was admitted to the Brazilian Bar the following year. She has taken specialization courses in economy and company law from Fundação Getúlio Vargas and environment and society from Fundação Escola de Sociologia e Política. Ms. Spitzeck earned an LLM degree at the University of California in 2007. She is a member of the New York Bar Association. At Demarest, she has been a member of the Environmental Department since 2009.

John Taberner is a Consultant in Herbert Smith Freehills' Sydney office, where he was a partner for 20 years between 1988 and 2008. He has over 30 years' experience exclusively in environmental law. He is recognized as a leading practitioner in the field. He has acted for a number of significant government, semi-government, and private clients in a wide variety of matters involving environmental legal issues, including greenhouse issues. Mr. Taberner has leading-edge skills in all practice areas of environmental law (including greenhouse law). He was named by the *Australian Financial Review* in March 2008 as Best Lawyer in the greenhouse field. He served as Secretary of the National Environmental Law Association of Australia for the first four years after its establishment, and as a member of the Executive Committee of the International Bar Association's Committee on Environmental Law for four years in the late 1980s. Mr. Taberner also served as a member of the Advisory Board of the Commonwealth Environment Protection Authority while that Authority existed. He is a Life Patron and a Director of the Australian Chamber Orchestra.

Gray E. Taylor is co-leader of Bennett Jones LLP's climate change and emission trading practice. His practice focuses on climate change and related corporate issues affecting businesses in Canada and abroad. Mr. Taylor is a past chair of the National Environmental, Energy and Resources Law Section of the Canadian Bar Association, a director of the International Emissions Trading Association and the co-Chair of IETA's Canadian Working Group and is recognized in *Chambers Global* and *Lexpert*. He is qualified to practice in Ontario and New York.

Kirk Tracy is an associate at Paladin Law Group LLP's Walnut Creek, California, office with an environmental litigation practice. Mr. Tracy counsels clients on a variety of federal and state environmental laws, including RCRA, CERCLA, and the Clean Water Act. He received his JD with an environmental certificate from Tulane University Law School, where he was Editor in Chief of the *Tulane Environmental Law Journal* and was a student attorney in the Environmental Law Clinic, where he presented oral argument at the United States Court of Appeals for the Fifth Circuit in a Clean Water Act Citizen Suit. Mr. Tracy previously worked as an environmental engineer. He received an MS in environmental engineering from the University of Michigan and a BS in civil engineering with an environmental focus from the University of Iowa. He is currently a Vice Chair of eCommunications for the ABA's Section of Environment, Energy, and Resources Water Resources Committee and the Vice Chair of Social Media for the Pesticides, Chemical Regulation, and Right to Know Committee.

Juta Wada is the managing director of Wada Law Firm, located in Osaka, Japan. He has represented many companies and individuals in civil, criminal, and administrative litigations, including various environmental cases. Mr. Wada is a member of Japan Federation of Bar Associations, Environmental Protection Committee, and served as the Chair of Global Warming Measures Project Team of that Committee from 2008 to 2012. He was a member of Japan International Cooperation Agency, Advisory Council of Environmental and Social Considerations Review from 2004 to 2006. He also has taught environmental law in Kobe College from 2008 and in Kwansei Gakuin University from 2010 to 2013, and is a co-author of *Preventive Measures for Global Warming in the World* (written in Japanese). Mr. Wada received a master's degree in environmental law, cum laude, from Vermont Law School; a master's degree in human rights and education for peace from University for Peace in Costa Rica; and a BA in law from the University of Tokyo.

Scott Watson is a Partner at Warner Norcross & Judd LLP in Grand Rapids, Michigan. Mr. Watson concentrates his practice in environmental law and the energy industry. He advises clients on complex regulatory and litigation matters involving federal and state environmental law. He is currently a member of Environmental Law Section Council of the Michigan State Bar, where he is also chair of the Technology Committee, and he is a co-author of the Part 201 (state Superfund law) chapter of the *Michigan Environmental Law Deskbook.* He obtained a BS, with honors, in ecology and evolutionary biology from the University of Michigan, and a JD and MSEL, both magna cum laude, from Vermont Law School, where he was Senior Managing Editor of the *Vermont Law Review* and a Production Coordinator on the *Vermont Journal of Environmental Law.* He previously clerked in the Region 3 Office of Regional Counsel for the U.S. Environmental Protection Agency, and he served as a judicial law clerk to the Honorable Robert J. Jonker, U.S. District Court, Western District of Michigan.

Jessica Wentz is a Visiting Associate Professor and Environmental Law Fellow at George Washington University Law School for 2012–2014. Professor Wentz received her JD from Columbia Law School in 2012, where she studied environmental law, participated in clinical programs, and conducted independent research on issues related to climate change and energy policy. She was designated a Harlan Fiske Stone Scholar for each of her three years at Columbia and was awarded the Alfred A. Forsyth Prize for her dedication to the field of environmental law. During her time as a law student, Professor Wentz worked on a range of issues including the atmospheric impact of livestock production systems, geothermal energy development, and alternative modes of international climate governance. She interned with the Center for Climate Change Law in New York and clerked at the Earthjustice regional office in California. Professor Wentz received her BA in international development from the University of California, Los Angeles.

Jennifer Wills is an attorney with the U.S. Environmental Protection Agency in Washington, D.C., where she counsels on the regulation of industrial chemicals and pesticides. Since joining EPA in 2003, she has provided legal advice on issues related to a number of environmental and administrative statutes including Superfund, Toxic Substances Control Act, and the Federal Insecticide, Fungicide, and Rodenticide Act. She has participated extensively in the development and implementation of chemical regulatory matters, including work on the use of chemicals in hydraulic fracturing and in consumer products. Ms. Wills's previous experience includes a Brookings Fellowship in the office of Senator Frank R. Lautenberg, where she advised on energy and environmental policy issues, including legislation on the testing and prioritization of chemicals in commerce. She clerked for the Kentucky Supreme Court and the United States Court of Appeals for the Sixth Circuit. Ms. Wills earned a JD from the University of Kentucky College of Law. She is a vice chair and former co-chair of the ABA Section of Environment, Energy, and Resources International Environmental and Resources Law Committee.

Steve Wolfson coordinates the U.S. EPA Office of General Counsel (OGC) international capacity-building activities on environmental law; has trained environmental lawyers in Africa, Asia, and Latin America; and leads the OGC's China Environmental Law Initiative, which works with China's Environment Ministry to help strengthen Chinese environmental law and institutions. Mr. Wolfson has represented EPA in environmental and trade treaty negotiations and at World Trade Organization dispute settlement proceedings concerning environmental issues. He has taught international environmental law as an adjunct professor at Howard University Law School and U.S.-Chinese comparative environmental law as an adjunct professor in the Vermont Law School summer program. Mr. Wolfson is a member of the IUCN Commission on Environmental Law, served as Vice Chair for Programs of the International Environmental Law Committee in the ABA Section of Environment, Energy, and Resources, and is a graduate of UCLA School of Law.

Tseming Yang is Professor of Law and the Faculty Director of Graduate Legal Programs at Santa Clara University School of Law. His teaching and research focus on international and comparative environmental law, environmental governance, and China's environmental governance system. From 2010 to 2012, Professor Yang served as Deputy General Counsel of the U.S. Environmental Protection Agency, where he supervised the legal aspects of the Agency's international work, including on multilateral environmental agreements. From 2007 to 2010, he led the establishment of the U.S.-China Partnership for Environmental Law, a U.S. AID and State Department-funded initiative to build China's institutional capacity in environmental law and governance. Professor Yang has previously been a member of the National Environmental Justice Advisory Council and was a Fulbright Lecturer at the Tsinghua University School of Law in Beijing. He currently serves on the Board of Trustees of Earthjustice and is a member of the American Law Institute, the IUCN Commission on Environmental Law, and the National Committee on United States-China Relations.

Yong Hee Yoon is an Associate at Yulchon LLC, Seoul, Korea. Mr. Yoon practices primarily in the areas of antitrust, TMT, construction/real estate, environment and energy, and administrative disputes. Mr. Yoon received his LLB and MA (environmental law) from, and is a PhD candidate (environmental law) at Seoul National University. He is currently a member of the Korean Bar Association.

Duk Guen Yun is an Associate at Yulchon LLC, Seoul, Korea. Mr. Yun practices primarily in the areas of general corporate, mergers and acquisitions, antitrust, and environment and energy. Mr. Yun received his LLB and MA (administrative law) from Korea University. He is currently a member of the Korean Bar Association.

ACKNOWLEDGMENTS

The editors sincerely appreciate the tireless efforts of the following editors: Charles Di Leva (Part I), Kim Smaczniak (Part II, Nigeria), Betsy Baker (Arctic Region), Jessica R. Bell (Costa Rica), Lea Colasuonno (Germany, China), Richard Emory (Civil and Criminal Enforcement), Bettina Enderle (European Union Overview: The Shift of Power in the European Union and Its Consequences for Energy and the Environment; The European Union), Thekla Hanson-Young (Colombia), Tammy Hui (Canada, Argentina, Chile, India), Margret Kim (Brazil, Italy, Spain, Vietnam), Jane Luxton (Handling, Treatment, and Disposal of Chemicals and Hazardous Materials), Brittany Meyer (Russia), Angeles Murgier (Central and South America Overview: Emerging Trends in Latin America), Dania Nasser (France, Turkey), Lee Paddock (Civil and Criminal Enforcement), Luigi Iacobi Pontones (Mexico), James Rubin (Key Environmental Law Treaties and Agreements; The Role of International Standards), Andrew Schatz (Air and Climate Change), Justin Smith (Transboundary Pollution), Odin Smith (Mexico), Brandy K.M. Toelupe (Israel, New Zealand), and Steve Wolfson (How to Approach an International Environmental Law Question).

INTRODUCTION

Increasingly, every environmental lawyer is becoming an international environmental lawyer.

Until recently, international environmental law was largely the focus of diplomatic discussions, treaty negotiations, and academic debates of interest to a particular group of passionate and patient attorneys working for governments and international non-governmental organizations. Unlike the rapid and real time implementation of federal and state environmental laws and regulations, the success of international environmental laws was frequently measured in decades or generations, not years. And the topics at issue largely concerned obligations and commitments of sovereign nations, with only indirect interest or impact on specific companies responsible for much of the environmental issues being addressed.

Recent developments, however, have thrust international environmental law issues from strictly a foreign arena onto the front doorstep of attorneys practicing environmental law from regional cities to small manufacturing towns. The rapid globalization of developing world economies, the increasingly international nature of energy markets, and growing concern over global environmental challenges such as climate change are driving fundamental changes to the practice of environmental law.[1] Companies—and, in turn, the clients we represent—are almost necessarily multinational by nature and are confronting a rapidly emerging and confusing regime of international environmental laws here, there, and everywhere in between. Meanwhile, nations who have prioritized growing their economies without protecting their environment along the way are waking up to dangerous skies, polluted water, rapid resource depletion, and the struggles of climate change adaptation. While some nations have been lax in developing and enforcing environmental law regimes so far, the trends are all toward more rigorous requirements being implemented.

Thus, every environmental lawyer increasingly must become an international environmental lawyer, regardless of where they practice and who they represent, to be positioned to fully represent their clients on matters that are as fundamental, if not more so, to their interests as any domestic environmental law. In upcoming years, multinational companies are likely to face more rapidly developing, rigid, complex, and confusing environmental requirements abroad than they do in the United States and the European Union. It will be critical for attorneys to understand not only the substance of the laws, but also the context in which international environmental law problems uniquely must be addressed.

Recognizing the need to present a pragmatic "what you need to know" approach to what until now has largely been an academic endeavor, the American Bar Association's Section of Environment, Energy, and Resources is proud to present this practitioner-oriented toolkit for understanding comparative and international environmental law issues. The overarching goal of this book is to be a one-stop reference for an attorney anywhere in the United States or in the world to understand not only the substance of environmental laws in nations where our clients are most likely to operate, but also, importantly, the unique process and framework for addressing international environmental law issues more generally.

The four parts of this volume provide practitioners with a comprehensive analytical framework for meeting this demand.

Part I provides insight into several key overarching issues to orient attorneys to the current state of play of international environmental law generally and the framework for approaching an international environmental law issue. Chapter 1, "Globalization of Environmental Law," explains how countries are increasingly borrowing standards from international treaties and other nations' environmental regimes. The author notes that some of the most important innovations in United States environmental law, including environmental impact assessment and the establishment of national parks, have now been widely adopted globally. But in other areas, such as chemical regulation, the rest of the world is now following the lead of the European Union (EU) in requiring extensive pre-market testing of chemicals. The result is the emergence of a kind of "global environmental law" hybrid blending elements from traditional international and domestic environmental law. Chapter 2, "The Relationship between Domestic and International Environmental Law," describes how different governments translate international environmental treaties into domestic law. It helpfully distinguishes, for example, between dualist and monist systems. In the former, international treaties must be incorporated into the domestic system according to the constitutional rules of that system. In contrast, when a purely monist state ratifies an international treaty, it automatically incorporates the treaty into national law, rendering it immediately operative.

Chapter 3 provides useful guidance on how to research an international or comparative environmental law question in "How to Approach an International Environmental Law Question." The author notes the necessity of determining at the outset the relevant jurisdictions in which legal obligations might arise. The author goes on to describe the importance of delving into the character of any international law obligations at issue and how the previously identified jurisdictions view those obligations. The chapter also describes how practitioners should consider requirements flowing from other sources, such as soft law obligations. Chapter 4 then describes the top ten trends in international environmental law. These include a focus on oceans and fisheries, climate change and energy policy, biodiversity, the rise of the developing world, the role of the environment in the development of international economic law, and chemicals and substance management.

Part II provides a template for considering comparative and international environmental law questions. These chapters cover 11 subtopics: (1) air and climate change; (2) water; (3) the handling, treatment, transportation, and disposal of hazardous materials; (4) waste and site remediation; (5) response to emergencies; (6) natural resource management and protection; (7) the management and recovery of natural resource damages; (8) the protection of particular species of flora and fauna; (9) environmental review and decision making; (10) transboundary pollution; and (11) civil and criminal enforcement and penalties. Together, the Part II chapters help lawyers categorize the subparts of an issue for ease of analysis.

Part III then uses this eleven-subtopic template to digest the environmental and natural resource legal regimes in 26 key markets. These chapters cover the top fifteen nations in terms of gross domestic product, including Brazil, Russia, India, and China. They also include key developing and developed nations such as Turkey, Ukraine, Argentina, Israel, and the Netherlands.[2] Part III also describes the trends and legal systems in place in four crucial regions: North America (especially NAFTA-inspired institutions); South and Central America; the EU (two separate chapters on institutions and trends, respectively); and the Arctic. The EU has become a key driving force in the development of environmental law globally through its Regulation on Registration, Evaluation, Authorisation and Restriction of Chemicals (REACH) and Restriction of the Use of Certain Hazardous Substances in Electrical and Electronic Equipment (RoHS) directives governing chemical and electronic waste management, respectively. The Arctic has, for its part, become increasingly important as the reduction in sea ice extent due to climate change has led to greater interest in the region for shipping, conservation, and resource extraction purposes.

Finally, Part IV addresses global and cross-border issues. First, Chapter 48, "Mechanisms for Global Agreements," explains the primary instruments and vehicles through which international environmental law is developed, memorialized, and implemented. The chapter usefully differentiates between hard and soft law regimes and bilateral, regional, and global agreements. It also highlights the importance of Conferences of the Parties and protocols to refining legal obligations that governments may originally undertake. Chapter 49 identifies the most important environmental law treaties that practitioners should be aware of, from the Stockholm Declaration to the recently concluded Minamata Convention on Mercury, which bans the trade of certain mercury-containing products. Finally, Chapter 50 sensitizes practitioners to the existence of international standards such as those promulgated by the International Organization for Standardization (ISO), and the role that they play in international environmental law development, respectively.

Finally, we would like to recognize the extraordinary effort of the authors who contributed to this unprecedented effort. Some 58 authors located in 26 nations, each well-known leaders in their established areas and countries, collaborated on this project over an 18-month period, volunteering to write on cutting-edge developments internationally and domestically. This project could not have even started without the enthusiastic commitment of this diverse group of authors from the outset, and we were humbled by the opportunity to get to work with them directly on completing this first of its kind project.

In addition to the many leading authors and experts who contributed to this book both domestically and around the world, we would like to specifically express our appreciation to Peter Wright, who embraced this project from the earliest moment and whose constant support and leadership was critical to this daunting idea becoming reality. We also would like to thank the 22 section and chapter editors. Without their tireless effort, this book would not have been possible.

Together, the collective effort of these authors and editors provide environmental attorneys with the means to assess environmental and resource law questions in many of the places of the globe where they might arise. We hope that this becomes a useful resource not only in assisting attorneys and their clients in complying with emerging environmental laws around the world, but along the way, that it also furthers opportunities for nations to promote a stronger and healthier environment both domestically and globally.

Dedication

The editors, who are fathers of young children, dedicate this book to the children of the developing world with the hope that the contributions of the authors here will assist attorneys around the world in promoting the healthiest possible environment for youth as these nations grow their economies.

Notes

1. For example, the value of world merchandise exports alone has increased nearly fivefold since 1993. *See* http://www.wto.org/english/res_e/statis_e/its2013_e/its13_world_trade_dev_e.pdf at tbl.I.5 (last visited February 15, 2014).

2. *See* http://data.worldbank.org/data-catalog/GDP-ranking-table (2012 data) (last visited February 15, 2014).

PART I

Approaching International Environmental Regimes

CHAPTER 1

The Globalization of Environmental Law

ROBERT V. PERCIVAL*

Globalization is profoundly affecting the development of environmental law throughout the world. As countries increasingly borrow law and regulatory innovations from one another, there is growing convergence around a few principal approaches to environmental regulation. Although this is not an entirely new phenomenon, it is occurring at an unprecedented pace as the growth of global trade and multinational enterprises has increased pressure on nations to harmonize regulatory standards. Increased cross-border collaboration between governments, non-governmental organizations (NGOs), and multinational corporations also is significantly influencing the development of environmental law. Private actors are helping to expose environmental problems, to coordinate responses to them, and to mobilize informed consumers to harness market forces on behalf of environmental protection. These developments are blurring traditional distinctions between public and private law and domestic and international law.

These trends are resulting in the emergence of what I have called "'global environmental law'—a field of law that is international, national, and transnational in character all at once."[1] This chapter begins by explaining the concept of global environmental law. It then explores the principal forces that are contributing to its development. After discussing several examples of this phenomenon, the chapter concludes by examining its implications for the practice of environmental law.

I. The Concept of Global Environmental Law

Global environmental law is a term used to describe the reality of how transplantation, convergence, integration, and harmonization are influencing the development of environmental law today throughout the world. It includes

(1) public international environmental law, commonly used to refer to the set of treaties and customary international legal principles governing the relations between nations;

*The author would like to thank Zoe Fullem (Macalester College '12) for research assistance with this chapter.

3

(2) national environmental law, which describes the principles used by national governments to regulate the behavior of private individuals, organizations, and subnational governmental entities within their borders; and

(3) transnational law, which describes the set of legal principles used to regulate the cross-border relationships between private individuals and organizations.[2]

Public international environmental law governs relations between nations. It includes treaties and other agreements between states and norms governing their conduct that have become so universal as to be considered customary international law. But so much of the law that shapes environmental policy around the world today no longer is a direct product of these sources of international law.

As the forces of globalization bind the world more closely together than ever before, environmental law is developing throughout the world in important new ways. Increased scientific understanding of the health effects of pollution and other threats to the planet are contributing to a surge of global environmental concern. People and their governments are seeking whatever works to protect them against environmental harm and nations are borrowing law from one another, even from countries with very different legal or political traditions.

Some of the most important innovations in U.S. environmental law, including environmental impact assessment and the creation of national parks, have now been almost universally adopted throughout the world. But in other areas of environmental law, such as chemical regulation, the rest of the world is now following the lead of the European Union (EU) in requiring extensive pre-market testing of chemicals, a concept the United States has eschewed to date.

Environmental law is not the only field in which "global law" is developing. A similar phenomenon is occurring in fields such as patent law, antitrust, and securities regulation as authorities recognize the need for global coordination of regulatory policy toward multinational enterprises.[3] Regulators from different countries are cooperating with one another as never before. NGOs are forming global networks as civil society throughout the world becomes increasingly interconnected. Today no company can damage the environment in a remote corner of the world without fear that its actions will be exposed to the public in its home country. As a result, norms concerning what is acceptable corporate behavior are converging even in jurisdictions that have not formally updated their regulatory standards.

Transnational regulatory norms to protect the environment are no longer being developed primarily in a top-down manner through multilateral consensus agreements. This is reflected in global efforts to respond to climate change. The United Nations Framework Convention on Climate Change (UNFCCC), adopted in 1992, contemplated a regime of international law to require countries to control their greenhouse gas (GHG) emissions.[4] This approach was embodied in the 1997 Kyoto Protocol to the UNFCCC, which entered into force in 2005.[5] But the world's leading emitter of GHGs—China—was not required by the Kyoto Protocol to control its emissions, and the second-leading emitter—the United States—refused to ratify it. Both countries instead have endorsed the Copenhagen Accord, negotiated at the 15th Conference of the Parties (COP-15) to the Kyoto Protocol, which commits countries only to make their own voluntary commitments to control emissions of GHGs.[6]

To be sure, multilateral environmental agreements are not entirely a thing of the past. In January 2013, 140 nations reached agreement on the Minimata Convention to control emissions of mercury.[7] The International Civil Aviation Organization (ICAO) is considering a global regime to control GHG emissions from aviation. This was spurred by the EU requiring airlines flying to or from its member nations to pay a fee based on all the GHG emissions these flights generate. After vehement opposition from non-EU nations, the EU agreed temporarily to suspend enforcement of its emissions fees on foreign airlines to give the ICAO time to make meaningful progress on a global regime.

II.   Forces Driving the Rise of Global Environmental Law

Several forces are driving the emergence of global environmental law. One is the growth of global trade and multinational corporate enterprises, which is increasing pressure for harmonization of environmental standards. Another is the tremendous global growth of public concern for the environment. A third is the increased global collaboration between NGOs, environmental officials, and multinational enterprises.

Companies who want to sell their products throughout the world have a natural incentive to push for greater harmonization of environmental standards. To simplify compliance some companies even are deciding to adhere to the highest standards applicable to them in the various countries where they operate. Trade liberalization has not been the one-way street to relaxed environmental standards that some environmentalists once feared. Some countries are upgrading their environmental laws to ensure that lax standards will not be used as an excuse to eschew trade with them. The fact that U.S. automakers already were selling cars in other countries that require automakers to meet much higher fuel efficiency standards helped ease the way for substantial increases in fuel economy standards in the United States.

Another force contributing to the emergence of global environmental law is the globalization of environmental concerns. Virtually every country that has revised its constitution in the last few decades has written into the constitution some provision for protection of the environment.[8] According to a count by Professor James May, about 130 countries now have constitutions with environmental provisions.[9]

Another factor contributing to the development of global environmental law is increased global collaboration among and between NGOs and government officials. Several informal global networks have formed to help improve the implementation and enforcement of environmental law. In the past when developed countries would ban or restrict particular toxic substances, the companies manufacturing such products would redouble their efforts to sell them to the developing world. That happened with respect to both tobacco products and asbestos. But now most countries are banning asbestos with the blessing of the World Trade Organization. The World Health Organization has negotiated its first treaty ever, the Framework Convention on Tobacco Control, to educate all countries about the dangers of tobacco use. Even in countries where large portions of the population smoke, restrictions on tobacco use are inexorably growing.

Greenpeace, one of the first and best-known international NGOs, helped expose incidents where developed countries sought to surreptitiously dump toxic waste in the developing world. Due to the work of such global NGOs, we now live in a world where companies from the developed world no longer can engage in environmentally damaging practices in remote areas of the developing world without fear of discovery. Environmental NGOs are now opening offices around the world.

An important example of informal global collaboration among government officials is the International Network of Environmental Compliance and Enforcement (INECE).[10] This organization regularly sponsors conferences where environmental enforcement officials from all over the world share strategies for improving enforcement of the environmental laws. As regulators increasingly coordinate their policies, multinational corporations no longer can play off countries against each other, reducing any "race to the bottom."

Government environmental agencies from different countries also are engaging in regular dialogue concerning common environmental concerns. The U.S. Environmental Protection Agency (EPA) has been collaborating with China's Ministry of Environmental Protection on a variety of projects, and the EPA maintains a website to provide information about the state of environmental law in China.[11]

III. Examples of the Evolution of Global Environmental Law

A. Transnational Environmental Regulatory Reforms

Countries increasingly are learning from one another and borrowing regulatory standards. This is illustrated by the global growth of bans on unreasonably dangerous products such as asbestos and gasoline lead additives. Even in the absence of a comprehensive international treaty, 175 countries in the world have now banned gasoline lead additives,[12] and the enormous benefits of such action to public health and the environment are now widely acknowledged. Most developed countries also have banned asbestos,[13] though its use unfortunately is increasing in China and India. As countries learn from the experience of others, regulatory innovations with diffuse pedigrees are spreading more rapidly around the globe.

In addition to transplantation of legal norms, disparate legal systems are evolving toward similar regulatory standards through increased dialogue among regulatory officials in different countries, mutual recognition or regulatory equivalence agreements, and formal and informal efforts to harmonize regulatory standards. Regional approaches also are being pursued to address significant transboundary pollution problems. When the International Maritime Organization failed to adopt global standards to control pollution from ocean vessels, the United States and Canada were allowed to promulgate standards to protect the west coast of North America. These standards require ships to reduce the air pollution they generate by more than 80 percent.[14] Outside of the environmental arena, an unusual example of regulatory harmonization is the Cooperative Patent Classification project between the European Patent Office and the U.S. Patent and Trademark Office. This project seeks to harmonize disparate patent classification systems to reduce search costs and to harmonize recognition of intellectual property rights.[15]

B. Transnational Liability Litigation

The growth of transnational liability litigation is another source of emerging global environmental law. For decades litigation has been underway between residents of the oil-polluted Oriente region of Ecuador and the Chevron Corporation. In February 2011 this litigation, which initially had been filed in the United States during the early 1990s, ultimately produced the largest environmental judgment in history—an $18 billion judgment against Chevron issued by a court in Ecuador. Chevron has challenged this decision in U.S. federal district court and international fora. Transnational liability litigation also was brought by workers in Central American banana plantations who allegedly were rendered sterile by exposure to Dibromo-3-Chloropropane, a pesticide banned in the United States because of its reproductive toxicity. A lawsuit brought in London by those harmed from the British trading firm Trafigura's dumping of toxic waste on a beach in the Ivory Coast resulted in a $48.7 million settlement.[16] Each of these cases reflects a new global legal landscape where poor plaintiffs from developing countries are seeking to hold accountable corporate wealth and power that previously would have been immune from challenge.

C. Private Transnational Transparency Initiatives

Emerging quasi-public/quasi-private global transparency and disclosure initiatives are being championed by NGOs and private enterprises in collaboration with regulatory authorities. These include the Equator Principles, which govern funding of development projects by multinational banks;[17] the Roundtable on Sustainable Palm Oil;[18] and the Sustainable Apparel Coalition.[19]

These initiatives, as well as the Dodd-Frank Wall Street Financial Reform legislation's disclosure provisions concerning conflict minerals and payments to foreign governments, are promoting a new corporate ethic for assessing the environmental implications of development projects and greening the supply chains of multinational enterprises.

Companies that adhere to high environmental and worker safety standards while operating in the developed world may not be as scrupulous when operating in developing countries. In some cases large companies claim to be unaware of environmental or worker safety problems in the companies that are part of their supply chain.[20] In recent years NGOs have worked to highlight these problems in an effort to encourage companies to "green" their supply chains.[21] These efforts have the potential to improve environmental and working conditions in developed countries even when regulatory standards do not require such improvements.

In January 2011, a coalition of 23 Chinese NGOs led by the Beijing-based Institute of Public and Environmental Affairs released a report assessing the environmental health and safety records of Chinese companies that supply 29 multinational technology companies.[22] The suppliers of Apple Corporation placed last because of industrial pollution and exposure of workers to health risks.[23] In response to this pressure from Chinese NGOs, Apple agreed to become the first technology company to join the Fair Labor Standards Association and to have independent auditors conduct annual audits of its suppliers' labor and environmental practices. Apple also joined the Public-Private Alliance for Responsible Minerals Trade to ensure that it was not using conflict minerals. Apple now publishes an annual supplier responsibility report disclosing the results of these audits and the actions it has taken to improve compliance by its suppliers.[24]

In March 2011, a group of clothing manufacturers, retailers, and environmental groups formed the Sustainable Apparel Coalition to assess the environmental impact of every element of apparel production in order to provide consumers with "sustainability scores" for each product.[25] The 30 founding members of the coalition include major retailers such as Wal-Mart and J.C. Penney, the Environmental Defense Fund, and the EPA.[26] The chairman of the new coalition is former mountain climber Rick Ridgeway, who runs Patagonia's sustainability efforts.[27] The focus of the coalition is on assisting companies in "greening" their supply chains.[28]

Some large retailers, such as Wal-Mart, have pioneered their own form of "retail regulation" by refusing to carry products that do not meet various environmental criteria, for example, by containing certain toxic substances.[29] But the latest initiatives go a significant step further by requiring companies to make affirmative inquiries concerning conditions at their suppliers in developing countries. These efforts could be bolstered by provisions in the Dodd-Frank Wall Street Reform and Consumer Protection Act (Dodd-Frank Act). Section 1502 of the Act added a subsection to the Securities Exchange Act of 1934 regarding conflict minerals.[30] The new provision requires disclosure to the U.S. Securities and Exchange Commission (SEC) of whether minerals used by companies originated in the Democratic Republic of Congo or an adjoining country.[31]

In addition to privately led initiatives, new laws increasingly are taking into account transnational environmental considerations. For example, on December 15, 2010, the SEC proposed regulations regarding conflict mineral disclosures.[32] The four primary metals covered by the legislation that are widely used by electronics manufacturers are tin, tungsten, tantalum, and gold.[33] It is hoped that these regulations will help mobilize companies to pay more attention to the sources of the raw materials they use.[34] Section 1504 of the Dodd-Frank Act requires companies in extractive industries to disclose to the SEC payments made to foreign governments for the purpose of commercial development of oil, natural gas, or minerals. This provision is designed to help make it harder for corrupt foreign government officials to seek bribes because they would have to be publicly disclosed by the company paying them.

IV. Conclusion

Globalization is having a profound impact on legal systems throughout the world and environmental law is a field in which this impact is most prominent. International law traditionally governs only relations between states, but relations between states and private multinational enterprises are becoming of central importance in a globalized world. In an effort to control more effectively risks generated by multinational enterprises, countries are borrowing regulatory innovations from one another at a rapid rate and increasing efforts to coordinate regulatory policy. Distinctions between domestic and international law and between private and public law are diminishing in force.

The traditional top-down approach of negotiating multilateral international agreements is giving way to a variety of bottom-up initiatives that often involve greater participation by NGOs. The result is the emergence of global environmental law, which is not a set of globally harmonized regulatory standards, but rather a more complex set of phenomena also occurring in other fields of law.

The path by which global environmental norms are emerging is changing. Even as efforts to achieve global consensus on a successor to the Kyoto Protocol have faltered, regional responses to climate change are alive and well. The movement to ban leaded gasoline and the remaining uses of asbestos has made global strides, and regional efforts to control air pollution from ships are progressing.

In response to perceived harm caused by the operations of multinational corporations, plaintiffs are bringing transnational liability litigation both in their own countries and in countries where such corporations have their headquarters. Even when transnational litigation fails to win a judgment, it can shine a global spotlight on environmentally destructive practices that companies would be wise to abandon.

Finally, transparency initiatives promoted by coalitions of NGOs and corporations also are a new and vibrant part of the complex architecture of global environmental law. In an interconnected world, multinational enterprises no longer can claim ignorance of occupational and environmental conditions in their supply chains even in remote parts of the world. Transparency can work precisely because of the emergence of global environmental norms against exposing the residents of developing countries to risks no longer tolerated in the developed world. The clear implication of these trends is that today's savvy lawyer cannot be content to master purely domestic or purely international law. He or she must be prepared to venture into the complexities of the brave new world of global environmental law.

Notes

1. T. Yang & R. Percival, *The Emergence of Global Environmental Law*, 36 ECOLOGY L.Q. 615, 616 (2009); R. Percival, *The Globalization of Environmental Law*, 26 PACE ENVTL. L. REV. 451 (2009); R. Percival, *Liability for Environmental Harm and Emerging Global Environmental Law*, 25 MD. J. INT'L L. 101 (2010).

2. Yang & Percival, *supra* note 1, at 617.

3. *See, e.g.*, M. Sunder, *IP3*, 59 STAN. L. REV. 257, 263 (2006); E. ELHAUGE & D. GERADIN, GLOBAL ANTITRUST LAW AND ECONOMICS (2007); B. Kingsbury et al., *The Emergence of Global Administrative Law: Foreword: Global Governance as Administration—National and Transnational Approaches to Global Administrative Law*, 68 LAW & CONTEMP. PROBS. 1 (2005); H. Hansmann & R. Kraakman, *The End of History for Corporate Law*, 89 GEO. L.J. 439, 468 (2001).

4. U.S. EPA, UN Framework Convention on Climate Change, http://epa.gov /climatechange/policy/international_unfccc.html).

5. UNFCC, Kyoto Protocol, http://unfccc.int/kyoto_protocol/items/2830.php.

6. United Nations, Report of the Conference of the Parties on its Fifteenth Session, held in Copenhagen from 7 to 19 December 2009, *available at* http://unfccc.int/resource /docs/2009/cop15/eng/11a01.pdf.

7. U.N. Env't Programme, Minimata Convention Agreed by Nations (Jan. 19, 2013), http://www.unep.org/newscentre/default.aspx?DocumentID=2702&ArticleID=9373.

8. For example, in September 2008, Ecuador adopted a new constitution designed to grant inalienable rights to nature, including "the right to exist, persist, maintain and regenerate its vital cycles, structure, functions and its processes in evolution." CONSTITUCIÓN DE LA REPÚBLICA DEL ECUADOR 2008, tit. II, ch. 1, art. 10, *available at* http://www .oas.org/juridico/PDFs/mesicic4_ecu_const.pdf.

9. J. May, *Constituting Fundamental Environmental Rights Worldwide*, 23 PACE ENVTL. L. REV. 113, 129 (2005–06).

10. *See* http://www.inece.org.

11. *See* U.S. EPA, EPA–China Environmental Law Initiative, http://www.epa.gov /ogc/china/initiative_home.htm.

12. P. Lehner, *Global Phase-out of Lead in Gasoline Succeeds: Major Victory for Kid's Health*, SWITCHBOARD: NAT'L RES. DEF. COUNCIL STAFF BLOG, Oct. 27, 2011, http://switch board.nrdc.org/blogs/plehner/global_phase-out_of_lead_in_ga.html.

13. *See* International Ban Asbestos Secretariat, http://ibasecretariat.org/alpha_ban _list.php.

14. Int'l Mar. Org., Marine Env't Prot. Comm., Report of the Marine Environment Protection Committee on its Sixtieth Session, MEPC 60/22 (Apr. 12, 2010), http://www.uscg.mil/imo/mepc/docs/mepc60-report.pdf.

15. *See* Cooperative Patent Classification, http://www.cooperativepatentclassification.org/index.html.

16. G. Chazen, *Firm to Pay $48.7 Million in Ivory Coast Pollution Case*, Wall St. J. (Sept. 21, 2009).

17. *See* http://www.equator-principles.com.

18. *See* http://www.rspo.org.

19. *See* http://www.apparelcoalition.org.

20. D. Barbosa, *In Chinese Factories, Lost Fingers and Low Pay*, N.Y. Times (Jan. 5, 2008), http://www.nytimes.com/2008/01/05/business/worldbusiness/05sweatshop.html.

21. M. Betsill & E. Corell, *NGO Influence in International Environmental Negotiations: A Framework for Analysis*, 1 Global Envtl. Politics 65 (2001).

22. Inst. of Pub. & Envtl. Affairs, The Other Side of Apple: Investigative Report into Heavy Metal Pollution in the I.T. Industry (Phase IV): Special Apple Inc. Edition (Jan. 25, 2011), http://www.ipe.org.cn/En/about/notice_de.aspx?id=9693.

23. *Id.* at 27.

24. Apple Inc., Supplier Responsibility, http://images.apple.com/supplier-responsibility/pdf/Apple_SR_2013_Progress_Report.pdf. Apple's 2013 Supplier Responsibility Report discloses that a record 393 audits were conducted on the company's supply chain in 2012, a 72 percent increase over 2011. These included 55 focused environmental audits and 40 process safety assessments.

25. Sustainable Apparel Coal., 1. The Higg Index, http://www.apparelcoalition.org/higgindex/ (last visited June 19, 2014).

26. T. Zeller Jr., *Clothes Makers Join to Set "Green Score,"* N.Y. Times (Mar. 1, 2011), http://www.nytimes.com/2011/03/01/business/01apparel.html.

27. Leon Kaye, *Clothing Industry Giants Launch Sustainable Apparel Coal.*, The Guardian, Mar. 1, 2011, http://www.theguardian.com/sustainable-business/clothing-industry-supply-chain-coalition.

28. *Id.*

29. L. Layton, *Wal-Mart Turns to "Retail Regulation" to Ban Flame Retardant*, Wash. Post, Feb. 27, 2011, at A4.

30. Dodd-Frank Wall Street Reform and Consumer Protection Act, Pub. L. No. 111-203, 124 Stat. 1376 (2010) [hereinafter Dodd-Frank Act].

31. Dodd-Frank Act § 1502(b).

32. Conflict Minerals, Exchange Act Release No. 34-63547, 17 C.F.R. pts 229 & 249 (Dec. 15, 2010), http://www.sec.gov/rules/proposed/2010/34-63547.pdf.

33. M. Thwing Eastman & J. Shoemaker-Hopkins, *Dodd-Frank Not Just About Banks: Conflict Minerals Reporting Requirements Will Affect Chipmakers, Other Electronics Firms*, RiskMetrics Group (Jan 18, 2011), http://www.msci.com/insights/responsible_investing/dodd-frank-conflict-minerals.html.

34. D. Meyer, *Using Materiality Analysis to Drive Corporate Social Responsibility & Sustainability in the Supply Chain*, Dave Meyer's Green Supply Chain Blog Cmty. (Jan. 18, 2011), https://community.kinaxis.com/people/DRMeyer/blog/2011/01/18/using-materiality-analysis-to-drive-corporate-social-responsibility-sustainability-in-the-supply-chain. Meyer is a Consultant at EORM, an environmental, health, safety, and sustainability consulting firm out of Portland, Oregon, and was formerly an Adjunct Professor at the University of California San Diego teaching Business Accounting and Management.

CHAPTER 2

The Relationship between Domestic and International Environmental Law

TSEMING YANG*

The connections between domestic and international law have proliferated in the last few decades as a direct result of the explosive growth of international environmental law. Yet most environmental lawyers remain relatively unaware of the effects of this trend even though it is increasingly affecting the practice of environmental law itself.[1] Where most of the rest of this book provides background on the specific substantive content of global environmental laws, both international regimes as well as the environmental law systems of other countries, this chapter addresses the formal legal relationship between international environmental law and U.S. domestic law and questions of implementation.

I. Relationship of International Environmental Law to U.S. Domestic Law

The rapid growth of international environmental law in the past four decades has been driven primarily by the proliferation of environmental treaties and agreements, the predominant source of new international environmental law. In their substantive scope, they have covered the gamut of environmental and natural resource issues, including climate change,[2] ozone depletion,[3] biodiversity conservation,[4] hazardous waste trade,[5] trade in endangered species,[6] migratory species conservation,[7] chemicals management,[8] desertification,[9] marine pollution,[10] and whaling.[11] Their participation levels range from multilateral agreements that have universal or near universal membership to regional[12] or bilateral treaties.[13] Details about the substantive content of these agreements are left to subsequent chapters.

Given the broad and growing scope of international environmental law, how then does it connect with domestic law? With respect to treaties, domestic legal processes are relevant in the treaty-making process, in the incorporation of treaties into the U.S. law, and the domestic application/

*I am grateful to Charles Lane for excellent research assistance and to David Gravallese for his valuable comments on an earlier draft of the chapter.

implementation of treaty commitments. With respect to customary law, the rules are deemed to be part of the common law.

A.   General Relationship

The U.S. system is traditionally referred to as a dualist system. In dualist systems, international and domestic laws are seen as operating in separate spheres. National legal systems are "separate and discrete"[14] from the international counterpart, and "international law is generally not thought to be able to make itself effective in a domestic legal order [but rather] depends on the constitutional rules of the municipal system itself" for its application.[15]

The competing approach to dualism is monism. The monist approach "views the international legal order and all national legal orders as component parts of a single 'universal legal order' in which international law has a certain supremacy."[16] Theoretically, when a monist state ratifies an international treaty it immediately incorporates the treaty into national law.[17] Customary rules of international law are also treated as part of national law.[18] This single unified system is binding on a state's legislature, courts, and individuals.[19]

The differences between dualist and monist systems become clearer when obligations under international and national laws conflict.[20] A dualist system would treat national sources of law as superior to international sources of law.[21] A monist system would treat national sources as subordinate to international sources.[22] Moreover, a monist system might allow international sources to override national ones. This means that a national or "municipal" court could invalidate a national law that contradicts an international law, or an individual could invoke rights under international law, just as if it were national law.[23]

In practice, the general consensus is that the relationship between international and national law is predominantly dualist.[24] That is, "[m]ost states and most courts . . . presumptively view national and international legal systems as discrete entities and routinely discuss in a dualist fashion the incorporation of rules from one system to the other."[25]

Within the United States, dualism is manifested through domestic processes such as Senate advice and consent or the enactment of congressional legislation to implement a treaty. Upon approval by the Senate, the president then usually deposits an instrument of ratification, an international step signifying ratification that is distinct from the domestic process, and which then makes treaty membership effective as an international matter.

Conversely, international law has traditionally not concerned itself with a state's internal laws, and internal matters including domestic laws do not usually affect international treaty obligations.[26] Yet the practical connection between international and domestic affairs in international environmental law has grown significantly over the decades. Because most environmental degradation is the result of private activity rather than direct government actions, the affirmative regulatory engagement and assistance of national and subnational governments are usually critical in accomplishing a treaty's environmental protection objectives. In other words, member states have a relationship with the treaty system that is analogous to that of a coregulator or regulatory delegatee, much like what is seen in the U.S. environmental federalism structure, than of a "regulated entity," as may be more common in the fields of arms control, humans rights, or trade regulation.

1.   *Types of International Agreements in U.S. Law*

Apart from international agreements that have been approved by the U.S. Senate via the treaty clause and that have coequal status to congressional statutes, there are two other broad categories of international agreements. First, congressional-executive agreements require approval only by a simple majority of both houses of Congress.[27] Such agreements have been utilized most frequently with respect to international trade agreements, although some of these agreements have also included environmental issues, such as the North American Agreement on Environmental Cooperation. They are usually negotiated by the executive branch, often with negotiation parameters provided by Congress through special legislation. The final agreement is enacted by Congress as if it were ordinary domestic legislation.

A second category of agreements is sole executive agreements. They may be entered into by the president pursuant to his own constitutionally enumerated powers, such as his position as commander-in-chief of the armed forces and his foreign affairs power, or as authorized by Congress. Such executive agreements are usually not subject to formal congressional approval, although informal consultations occur in the due course of ordinary executive-congressional interactions and congressional oversight.

2.   *Oversight and Control over Treaty-Making Process*

Oversight over the treaty-making process occurs both at the congressional level as well as within the executive branch itself. Within the U.S. system, the president may be formally in charge of treaty negotiations. As a practical matter, however, treaty making is a collaborative process involving usually the Senate and oftentimes also the House of Representatives.

The Constitution requires Senate advice and consent by two-thirds of the senators for treaties to be approved.[28] Moreover, Congress is constitutionally assigned authority over foreign commerce and may exercise its oversight, appropriations, and other authorities to ensure its involvement in foreign policy processes.[29] In fact, consultation and consideration of interests by Congress occurs on a regular basis before and during the negotiation process, especially when it is expected that Congress will ultimately need to enact legislation to implement a treaty domestically.

Within the executive branch, oversight and control over treaty-making processes is largely vested in the State Department. Such oversight and control occurs primarily through the Circular 175 procedure (C-175), which applies to internal State Department as well as interagency coordination of negotiation of international agreements.[30] The State Department describes the procedure as intended to make sure that the making of treaties and other international agreements for the United States is carried out within constitutional and other appropriate limits, and with appropriate involvement by the State Department.[31] As a practical matter, the C-175 also ensures that agencies and officials of the federal government do not make legal commitments on behalf of the U.S. government internationally, whether by informal memoranda of understandings or formal contracts, without involvement of the State Department.

The substance of the C-175 is designed to inform and address considerations ranging from "[t]he policy benefits to the United States" to whether an environmental impact assessment is needed.[32] The State Department's Office of the Legal Adviser usually provides a "memorandum of law discussing thoroughly the legal bases for the agreement."[33]

Within the U.S. government, participation in negotiations for a multilateral environmental agreement may not commence absent authority provided through the C-175 process. Such C-175 authority may also provide authority to sign the resulting agreement.[34]

II.   How Is International Environmental Law Implemented?

Before official ratification of an international agreement occurs, and thus before the United States becomes a party, the question of domestic implementation must be resolved.

A.   Congressional Implementing Legislation

It has been the general treaty practice for the United States to ratify international agreements, including environmental agreements, only when it is in a position to implement the obligations under such agreements (such as by having in place necessary domestic legal authorities).[35] Frequently, this has meant that Congress must enact executing legislative authority or provide appropriate funding for the U.S. Environmental Protection Agency (EPA) or other federal agencies to fulfill new treaty commitments. On some occasions, new treaty obligations can be implemented with existing statutory authority.

At times, existing legislation or constitutional authority already vests a particular federal agency or the president with all the necessary powers to carry out U.S. obligations under the new treaty. However, in either situation, whether implementation occurs through existing or new congressional authority, implementing agencies are likely to have to promulgate new regulations or revise their existing ones.

B.   Self-Executing and Non-Self-Executing Agreements

While national implementation through legislatively delegated authority is the most common path for environmental agreements, when a treaty is deemed self-executing, it can be judicially enforced and thus become legally effective upon ratification. Professor Fred Kirgis has described whether a treaty is self-executing or not as a question focusing primarily on the

> *intent—or lack thereof—*that the provision become effective as judicially-enforceable domestic law without implementing legislation. For the most part, the more specific the provision is and the more it reads like an act of Congress, the more likely it is to be treated as self-executing.[36]

Given the need for treaty mandates to be tailored to the circumstances of specific sectors of the economy, whether industry, agriculture, or natural resources, as well as integrated into the existing regulatory scheme so as to ensure effective implementation, environmental agreements have generally been interpreted as non-self-executing. However, this has also led to delay in the ability of the United States to ratify and participate in international environmental agreements.[37]

Once a treaty or agreement has passed through the necessary channels of ratification and implementing authority is in place, then the president must issue a proclamation that the treaty has entered into force.[38] The president's proclamation puts the domestic legal community on notice and triggers the implementation process.[39]

C. Adjustments of International Agreements and Domestic Linkage

The growing influence of environmental agreements on domestic regulatory systems is also casting a spotlight on processes used to change and adjust international agreements. Ordinarily, amendments of environmental agreements require the same adoption and ratification process as the underlying agreement. Increasingly, however, environmental agreements are including processes to allow for the revision or modification of a treaty in a simplified or expedited manner, such as tacit amendment procedures.[40]

At the same time, it has become more common for U.S. environmental statutes to directly incorporate or reference international treaty requirements. The Marine Protection, Research, and Sanctuaries Act specifically requires application of standards and criteria that are binding under the 1972 Convention on the Prevention of Marine Pollution by Dumping of Wastes and Other Matter (London Convention).[41] Likewise, Title VI of the Clean Air Act makes its provisions contingent on being "consistent with the Montreal Protocol [on Substances that Deplete the Ozone Layer]" and sets out that in the event of conflict, "the more stringent provision shall govern."[42]

Tighter linkage of parts of domestic regulatory schemes to their international counterparts has ultimately furthered integration and effectiveness of U.S. regulatory efforts with respect to its international commitments. Unfortunately, tighter linkage has also raised concerns about the alleged loss of sovereignty due to a perceived delegation of legislative and regulatory authority to international organizations.[43]

D.   The Growing Practice of International Environmental Law

The practice of international environmental law used to be almost exclusively confined to international lawyers providing legal counsel, support for treaty negotiations, participation in international organizations, and representation of the United States before international tribunals. However, as the field has matured and implementation processes have become more important, so has the range of lawyers who are engaged in this field and the scope of the legal practice.[44]

International environmental law is now practiced not only as a specialty in the State Department's Legal Adviser's Office, but also as a subject matter by lawyers in the EPA, the Interior Department, the National Oceanographic and Atmospheric Administration, the Coast Guard, the Justice Department, and the Department of Defense. Their work addresses the promulgation of regulations, legislative drafting of implementing treaty commitments, and other domestic legal work. It includes interpretation of relevant treaty provisions that arise in civil and criminal enforcement actions designed to implement treaty requirements and scrutinizing treaty commitments to determine compliance. Finally, the practice can involve providing technical assistance and capacity building in other countries to help promote compliance.

Lawyers in the environmental non-governmental organization (NGO) community and the commercial bar have also become more engaged in this field. For example, NGO lawyers have raised environment and human rights issues in Alien Tort Act claims in U.S. courts or in petitions to international human rights tribunals, such as the Inter-American Commission on Human Rights. They have filed submissions under Article 14 of the North American Agreement on Environmental Cooperation regarding a North American Free Trade Agreement (NAFTA) party's failure to effectively enforce its environmental laws. The commercial bar has filed investor claims related to environmental regulatory issues under chapter 11 of NAFTA and represented corporate clients' interests by influencing the internal processes of international organizations. Further, private lawyers (and consultants) are assisting their clients with navigating international administrative regulatory schemes and processes, such as the Clean Development Mechanism.

Undoubtedly, many of these practice areas are still small compared to traditional and more established areas of environmental regulation and litigation. As globalization continues to shrink the planet, link communities and environments, and grow economic activities and ecological pressures on the Earth, however, the need for regulatory approaches and legal solutions that integrate or harmonize national, subnational, and international efforts will only grow. And with this trend, the volume and scope of this part of environmental law practice will grow as well.

III. Contemporary Issues

As international environmental law has gained prominence, the difficult political climate in the United States for the ratification of environmental treaties presents a serious contemporary challenge. Among the major multilateral environmental agreements that the United States has signed, but not ratified, are the 1989 Basel Convention on the Transboundary Movement of Hazardous Wastes, the 1992 Convention on Biological Diversity, the 1997 Kyoto Protocol to the U.N. Framework Convention on Climate Change, the 1997 Protocol to the London Convention, the 1998 Rotterdam Convention on Prior Informed Consent, and the 2001 Stockholm Convention on Persistent Organic Pollutants.

Political opposition to ratification of international agreements is not unique to the environmental area, nor is opposition to new environmental legislation.[45] But these domestic political challenges do undermine the ability of the United States to effectively engage or play a leadership role within these multilateral environmental regimes—simply because the United States is a non-party. Even though ordinarily permitted to participate as an observer, the United States has no vote or formal voice in such treaty proceedings. The ability of its representative to fully protect U.S. interests and concerns, including of U.S. civil society organizations as well as industry, is undoubtedly greatly weakened.

A separate issue of contemporary significance has been the extraterritorial application of U.S. environmental laws. When such instances have arisen, they have on occasion given rise to international disputes such as the Tuna-Dolphin General Agreement on Tariffs and Trade (GATT) case and other trade and environment matters before the World Trade Organization (WTO) dispute resolution mechanism, particularly those trade law challenges to fisheries and wildlife-related legislation.

Unilateral, extraterritorial action remains tempting because of the opportunity to recruit the weight of the United States economic influence for environmental purposes. In contrast, treaty making entails significant resource and personnel demands, faces challenges in terms of consensus building, requires time for negotiation, and oftentimes leads ultimately to an agreement of limited effectiveness. Until these issues are better addressed, unilateral, extraterritorial application of U.S. law is likely to remain an option of interest for environmentalists.

Notes

1. For a general discussion, see T. Yang, *The Emerging Practice of Global Environmental Law*, 1 TRANSNATIONAL ENVTL. LAW 53 (2012).

2. U.N. Framework Convention on Climate Change, 1771 U.N.T.S. 107 (1992); Kyoto Protocol, 37 ILM 22 (1997).

3. Vienna Convention on the Protection of the Ozone Layer, 1513 U.N.T.S. 293 (1985); Montreal Protocol on Ozone Depleting Substances, 1522 U.N.T.S 3 (1987).

4. Convention on Biological Diversity, 1760 U.N.T.S. 79 (1992); Cartagena Biosafety Protocol, 39.I.L.M. 1027 (2000); Nagoya Protocol on Access to Genetic Resources and the Fair and Equitable Sharing of Benefits Arising from their Utilization (2010), *available at* http://www.cbd.int/abs/text/default.shtml.

5. Basel Convention on the Control of Transboundary Movements of Hazardous Wastes and Their Disposal, 1673 U.N.T.S. 57 (1989).

6. Convention to Regulate International Trade in Endangered Species of Flora and Fauna, 993 U.N.T.S. 243, 12 I.L.M. 1085 (1973).

7. Convention on the Conservation of Migratory Species of Wild Animals, 19 I.L.M. 15 (1979).

8. Stockholm Convention on Persistent Organic Pollutants, 40 I.L.M. 532 (2001); Rotterdam Convention on Prior Informed Consent, 38 I.L.M. 1 (1999).

9. U.N. Convention to Combat Desertification in Countries Experiencing Serious Drought and/or Desertification, Particularly Africa, 1954 U.N.T.S. 3 (1994).

10. MARPOL, 2 I.L.M. 1319 (1973); Convention on the Prevention of Marine Pollution by Dumping of Wastes and Other Matter, 11 I.L.M. 1294 (1972).

11. International Convention for the Regulation of Whaling, 161 U.N.T.S. 72, 10 U.S.T. 952 (1946).

12. North American Agreement on Environmental Cooperation, 32 I.L.M. (1993).

13. Boundary Waters Treaty, Jan. 11, 1909, U.S.-Gr. Brit., 36 Stat. 2448.

14. M. JANIS, INTERNATIONAL LAW 87 (2012).

15. *Id.*

16. *Id.* at 88 (citing H. KELSEN, PRINCIPLES OF INTERNATIONAL LAW 553–88 (2d ed. 1966)).

17. D. Sloss, *Domestic Application of Treaties, in* THE OXFORD GUIDE TO TREATIES 375 (Duncan B. Hollis ed., Oxford Univ. Press 2012).

18. J.G. STARKE, STARKE'S INTERNATIONAL LAW 65, 74, 76 (11th ed. 1994).

19. *Id.* at 65.

20. *Id.* at 66.

21. JANIS, *supra* note 14, at 88.

22. STARKE, *supra* note 18, at 77 (discussing, for example, "article 25 of the Basic Law for the Federal Republic of Germany which lays down that the general rules of public international law shall form part of federal law, and shall take precedence over the laws of and create rights and duties directly for the inhabitants of the federal territory").

23. *Id.*

24. JANIS, *supra* note 14, at 88.

25. *Id.* Like most other relationships, the one between international law and national law is complex. Generally speaking, it is rare to see a legal system that is purely monist or dualist; most countries take a mixed approach. A dualist state may allow domestic courts to apply customary international law in judicial decisions—a monist norm; while a monist state may require formal treaty-approval processes—a dualist norm. Therefore, it is necessary for the practitioner to consider the source of international law to determine its place in the state's domestic legal system.

Additionally, a practitioner may consider that the relationship between international law and national law often reflects a state's political history. For example, "countries that have experienced dictatorships or foreign occupation often generally reveal greater receptivity to international law, often incorporating or referring to specific international texts in their post-repression constitutions." INTERNATIONAL LAW AND DOMESTIC LEGAL SYSTEMS: INCORPORATION, TRANSFORMATION, AND PERSUASION 2 (D. Shelton ed., Oxford Univ. Press 2011). In contrast, "[c]ountries that have not had such experiences, like France and the

United States . . . appear less likely to adhere to international agreements or to incorporate and apply customary international law in judicial decisions." *Id.*

Notably, membership in the European Union (EU) creates a unique situation for a state's domestic legal system since "member states must now implement and apply the legal norms issued by EU institutions and also the international commitments undertaken at the regional level." *Id.* at 6.

With these considerations in mind, the following list reflects general categories of monist and dualist countries:

Dualist: Australia, Canada, Colombia, India, Israel, Italy, New Zealand, Nigeria, United Kingdom, United States, Vietnam.

Monist: Argentina, Brazil, Chile, China, Costa Rica, France, Germany, Japan, Kenya, South Korea, Netherlands, Russia, South Africa, Spain, Thailand.

26. *See, e.g.,* Vienna Convention, art. 27.

27. F. Kirgis, *International Agreements and U.S. Law,* ASIL INSIGHTS (May 1997), *available at* http://asil.org/insights/volume/1/issue/5/international-agreements-and-us-law.

28. U.S. CONST. art II, § 2, cl. 2.

29. *See* R. F. GRIMMETT, CONG. RES. SERV., FOREIGN POLICY ROLES OF THE PRESIDENT AND CONGRESS (June 1, 1999), *available at* http://fpc.state.gov/6172.htm.

30. Case-Zablocki Act (1972), 1 U.S.C. § 112b.

31. U.S. Dep't of State, Circular 175 Procedure, http://www.state.gov/s/l/treaty /c175/.

32. *Id.*

33. *Id.*

34. *See* U.S. Dep't of State, Chapter 2: Overview of the C-175 Process, http://www .state.gov/e/oes/rls/rpts/175/1265.htm.

35. *See, e.g.,* Susan Biniaz, Deputy Legal Adviser, U.S. Dep't of State, Remarks at the American Approach to Treaties, Panel, American Society of International Law Annual Meeting (Apr. 6, 2013) (stating that if provisions of a treaty go beyond existing U.S. laws, U.S. joining of the treaty would need to await additional congressional implementing legislation).

36. Kirgis, *supra* note 27 (emphasis added). The inquiry into intent usually focuses on the participants in the treaty creation and ratification process.

37. In the most extreme of examples, the Basel Convention on the Transboundary Movement of Hazardous Wastes and Their Disposal received Senate advice and consent in 1993, but the United States has not yet ratified the agreement because of its position that implementing legislation is necessary. As of this writing, Congress has yet to act on proposed implementing legislation.

38. CONG. RES. SERV., SPRT 106-71, TREATIES AND OTHER INTERNATIONAL AGREE-MENTS: THE ROLE OF THE UNITED STATES SENATE 12 (2001), *available at* http://www.gpo .gov/fdsys/pkg/CPRT-106SPRT66922/pdf/CPRT-106SPRT66922.pdf.

39. *Id.*

40. Modern agreements have sought to introduce innovations that have departed from the traditional rule of unanimous consent, such as article 2(9) of the Montreal Protocol.

41. Marine Protection, Research, and Sanctuaries Act of 1972, § 102(a), 33 U.S.C. 1412(a).

42. Clean Air Act § 614.

43. NRDC v. EPA, 464 F.3d 1 (D.C. Cir. 2006).

44. *See, e.g.,* Yang, *supra* note 1.

45. The U.N. Convention on the Law of the Seas has been languishing for decades in spite of consistent executive branch support for ratification.

CHAPTER 3

How to Approach an International Environmental Law Question

CHARLES E. DI LEVA

This chapter is intended to explain some key steps a practitioner should follow when addressing an international environmental law (IEL) question. First and foremost is the need to determine the relevant jurisdictions in which legal obligations might arise or policy considerations may be relevant. This exercise alone may be complex, as exemplified by the U.S. Supreme Court's decision in *Kiobel v. Royal Dutch Petroleum*, which addresses the applicability of laws to multinational corporations with headquarters outside the United States.[1] Second, once the relevant jurisdictions are identified, it is necessary to delve into the character of the international law obligations at issue and how said jurisdictions view those obligations. Third, the breadth of international law encompasses obligations that might fall outside a traditional domestic realm, and therefore should include obligations flowing from institutions themselves, such as from internal compliance obligations, or from soft-law obligations, or beyond, such as reputational issues that arise in the perceived court of public opinion. All three steps are discussed below.

I. The Context for Approaching an IEL Question

The approach to questions concerning IEL will depend on a multiplicity of factors. Broad categories of questions might be divided into those pertaining to public versus private law matters; treaty versus statute; or binding versus nonbinding hortatory measures; as well as categories of information reasonably available to the practitioner such as legal and regulatory measures available in the ordinary course of business as opposed to those that immediately launch one into a world of foreign law firms, consultants, and translators.

At the outset, this vast body of law stretches across all nation-states. Indeed, it is generally assumed that by now all sovereign states and their territories have some body of environmental law as part of their legal framework, albeit with significant differences in approach, completeness, and stringency. Moreover, as is clear in this chapter and other parts of this

23

volume, the environmental and corporate social responsibility movements have led numerous global and regional public and private institutions—be they financial, industrial, or resource-based—to develop their own environmental standards and codes, and to develop accountability systems to address noncompliance with those provisions. In addition, governments have taken seriously the negotiation of a wide range of so-called soft instruments, that is, those instruments that are considered nonbinding under international law but that retain important political and moral commitments.

The massive growth in environmental law at the international level began with the U.N. Conference on the Human Environment in 1972 (Stockholm Conference), but particularly accelerated in the days leading up to the U.N. Conference on Environment and Development in 1992 (Rio Conference).[2] This growth has been particularly dramatic in developing countries and emerging economies. Some of this growth in developing countries has been informed and aided by the international and bilateral development community, such as the United Nations Environment Programme (UNEP) and international development aid and financial institutions, such as the World Bank and the Asian Development Bank. The U.S. Agency for International Development and the European Union (EU) have also been heavily involved. However, it would be an inaccuracy to indicate that the growth in environmental law at the international level is a result of donor country impetus alone—developing countries have been taking a major oar to move this field forward on their own as witnessed in many of the chapters in this volume.

Given this remarkable growth, what is IEL? At the inception of this field, IEL encompassed the literally hundreds of multilateral environmental agreements (MEAs) that are binding on the member states that have ratified them. Such treaties represent a classic example of "hard law"—that is, binding as a matter of *international law* on the actors that ratify them. As IEL began its significant growth, some commentators distinguished "hard law" and "soft law" for international legal instruments.[3] As noted below, that distinction still has utility.

However, in recent years, it has been understood that IEL should be approached through a wider lens.[4] This wider focus has emerged as lawyers facing environmental issues that go beyond their borders frequently find legal or quasi-legal implications emanating not only from treaties, but also from a wide array of legal instruments. Moreover, another recent phenomenon is that international and regional organizations have been consistently promulgating environmental or environment-related standards, codes, and practices to which their members have agreed to be bound. Such agreements lend IEL status to these measures, including those emanating from organizations with mandates as widely different as the International Maritime Organization and Codex Alimentarius and those emanating from regional trade agreements such as the North American Free Trade Agreement (NAFTA), especially in its side agreement on Environmental Cooperation, and the Central American Free Trade Agreement (CAFTA). Both NAFTA and CAFTA contain their own environmental requirements and fact-finding bodies capable of addressing certain types of claims by civil society of environmental noncompliance by their member states. Indeed, key guidance for many of the IEL questions that the practitioner must approach can be provided by the website location of the organizational code or standard to which the client's issue is connected. (See the appendix to this chapter for a list of IEL-related websites.)

Another factor to take into account is the steady growth over the past 20 years in the decision making by tribunals associated with the environment. This jurisprudence goes beyond the slow and relatively scant but important inclusion of environmental law issues in rulings of the International Court of Justice (ICJ). A wide range of international financial institutions (IFIs) have developed their own tribunals capable of determining whether IFI activities have complied with their environmental policies and procedures. The World Bank's Independent Inspection Panel, for example, has been issuing determinations about the bank's compliance with bank policies for almost 20 years.[5] Many of its findings deal with environmental compliance, particularly related to environmental impact assessment. The panel preceded the development of similar mechanisms in almost all IFIs, and these mechanisms publish their findings. Now, in addition to what IFIs have established, a wide range of U.N. agencies operating in support of environmental activities are also developing tribunals that can make findings on compliance with agency environmental policies.

Also critical to the scope of IEL is the environmental law of, and within, foreign nations. Indeed, while addressing environmental issues for clients working internationally, many practitioners may never have to look beyond the laws of another nation or consider environmental treaty issues. Instead, the focus may be on the extremely wide array of domestic environmental law issues, be they new national environmental law requirements in Brazil, China, or Egypt, or subsovereign mandates in Sao Paolo, Jiangsu Province, or Cairo, or be they published in Portuguese, Mandarin, or Arabic. While some of these national-level laws may indeed be enacted in order to satisfy the requirements of environmental treaties for executing legislation, they are not "international" per se, and may be viewed as framed under the domain of "comparative environmental law," a field that was first introduced in law schools in the early 1990s and that has steadily grown. This chapter focuses chiefly on IEL; readers interested in the law of other nations are encouraged to look to the other chapters of this book.

II. Checklist of IEL Issues to Consider

A. Has an Environmental Agreement Become Binding?

The Vienna Convention on the Law of Treaties (Vienna Convention) codifies the generally accepted principles of international law on how treaties become binding on states. The Vienna Convention principally recognizes states as having the power to bind themselves through international treaties. If and when binding international law obligations can include entities beyond states, it is only because those states have expressly set forth an agreement to the extension. This has occurred, for instance, for certain treaties in which states have agreed that international or regional organizations (such as the EU) can bind themselves. The EU has acceded to several MEAs through individual member states as well as through the EU as an entity.

Negotiating states can determine when and how a negotiated instrument can become binding on states that ratify or accede to the agreement. For example, they can establish the number of countries that must ratify an agreement before it enters into force. They can also establish whether a treaty can have any reservations. Some treaties enter into force soon after their negotiation. Some do not, like the 1997 Convention on the Law of Non-Navigational Use of International Watercourses, which will not enter into force until August 2014.

B.   What Is "Hard" and "Soft" Law, and What Is the Basis for the Distinction?

"Hard law" has generally been viewed as including treaties, "general principles of law," and customary international law. Disputes over hard law between U.N. member states are justiciable before the ICJ, provided the states agree to the assumption of jurisdiction over the dispute. One scholar explained the distinction between hard and soft law as follows:

> Hard law represents law in its traditional meaning; it is compulsory ("shall"); it reflects a real obligation that "must" be fulfilled; if it is violated the perpetrator incurs international responsibility, which implies compensation for any loss or repair of any damage caused by the actor's behaviors. Soft law is a relatively new notion; it is of a recommendatory nature ("should"). If it is violated it entails criticism and the qualification as an unfriendly act. But even these relatively weak consequences of misbehavior can be damaging for the perpetrator; his/her reputation are at stake, which again has a certain impact on the educated and alert public opinion in our open societies.[6]

Thus, soft law may be described as the type of instrument to which states and other actors agree, but that does not require the act of ratification or other means to be bound as set out under the Vienna Convention. This method of adoption led to the coinage of "soft law" representing a sort of "second tier" of legal instrument. Because it is not binding, states or other parties can agree to follow it without fear of legal consequences. However, in many instances, parties that agree to soft-law instruments may expressly or implicitly agree that the soft-law instrument may ripen into a hard-law instrument, such as a treaty. A classic recent example is the Non-Legally Binding Instrument on All Types of Forests.[7] This instrument was negotiated for many years, with a number of parties hoping it would ripen into a treaty. When a consensus that it should become legally binding did not materialize, the leading advocate states agreed to enshrine the instrument with a clearly nonbinding status. At the same time, they still held out hope that it might someday be converted to a binding treaty. At the time of the negotiation of that instrument, it was reported that "non-legally binding instruments can have a major impact on the behaviour of Governments and international organizations, but that, in order to be effective, they must satisfy certain criteria. Typical characteristics of successful non-legally binding instruments include clarity, credibility, commitment and consensus and continuity."[8]

Other examples of soft-law instruments may take the form of codes of conduct, declarations, resolutions, and guidelines. Having listed these various terms, the cardinal point remains that the status of any instrument depends on the express terms of the instrument, the powers of the actors that agree to the instrument, and the degree to which they are willing to be bound, or not.

C. Steps to Take to Offer Counsel on IEL Issues When a Client Is About to Embark on Operations in a Foreign Jurisdiction

Once it is clear where the client is operating, including the states in which it might be required to assume some responsibility for its operations or materials, and once counsel understands the relevant subject matters that are implicated by the operation, counsel can begin to try to identify the various legal instruments that might be relevant and that should be reviewed to provide advice. Steps to take include the following:

1. Using one or more of the websites that provide the requisite treaty information, determine the international, regional, and bilateral environmental treaties/agreements/conventions to which the relevant country has become a party or that may be pending ratification in the requisite legislative bodies.[9] (Of course, many other agreements may be relevant, such as participation in bilateral investment treaties, but the array of possible agreements makes listing all such possible subjects beyond the scope of this chapter.

2. Determine whether the relevant implementing legislation required for the agreement has been enacted and the language in which the legislation is available. Some international conventions, and some international organizations offer translated copies of relevant treaties and relevant legislation.

3. Determine whether the country is a member of other international, regional, or bilateral organizations. Membership in such organizations may also mean that there are obligations that will affect the manner in which domestic legal obligations are to be carried out. For example, membership in some organizations may result in binding obligations, while others may only call upon aspirational goals. Thus,

for example, the La Plata River is governed by an agreement that requires reporting obligations ahead of certain proposed activities, and moreover specifically allowed the parties to submit disputes to the ICJ.[10] Demonstrating the justiciable nature of treaty disputes, a claim by Argentina against Uruguay for having violated the treaty was adjudicated by the ICJ. Conversely, a different approach toward riparian agreements evolved along the Mekong River. There, countries moved away from an agreement that gave power to riparian states to veto certain activities that were inimical to their interest, and in 1995 revised the arrangements to make the goals of the treaty aspirational in nature.[11]

4. Determine the hierarchy of law obligations within the nation. While most countries recognize that international law obligations may be superior when they are adopted as part of national law, there may be some situations where it is important to research the views of national courts on such issues. Recent issues within the EU have also raised questions about the supremacy of international law.[12] As well, there may be instances where obligations under different international obligations may result in actual or perceived conflict, as evident in the trade and environment disputes.[13]

5. Determine whether the activity generating the IEL issue is one that comes under the jurisdiction or influence of an international agency and, if so, which rules of those organizations might control or influence the activities. The types of activities are almost limitless. The financing agreements entered into between sovereign states and IFIs take on a status of international law. Thus the environmental conditions incorporated in these agreements are binding on the respective states. Moreover, commercial financial organizations have increasingly been willing to commit themselves when they operate in developing countries to apply a set of environmental and social provisions known as the Equator Principles[14] that make these principles a kind of de facto international environmental instrument. The great reach of the environmental provisions of the World Bank are reflected in their role as antecedents for the World Bank Group's International Finance Corporation development of their Environmental and Social Performance Standards, upon which the Equator Principles are based. Moreover, the World Bank Group has adopted environmental, health, and safety guidelines for more than 60 industrial sectors.[15]

6. Determine the extraterritorial impact, that is, not necessarily from a legal standpoint, of the domestic environmental legislation. Increasing numbers of countries are adopting environment-related laws and regulations that may affect their ability to engage in commerce outside domestic borders. A classic example of this was the EU adoption of its Registration, Evaluation, Authorization, and Restriction of Chemicals (REACH) legislation.[16] The chemicals industry has also noted that REACH was just the start of domestic regulation that affects imported or manufactured chemicals.[17] Many other major mar-

kets have begun to adopt legislation influenced by REACH.[18] The EU has also adopted requirements that limit the kinds of emission reductions that can be credited under the EU Emissions Trading System (EU ETS).[19] Under the EU ETS, European companies are allowed to trade emission reduction allowances within the member countries and to purchase a certain amount of emission reductions from outside the EU. This scheme requires the emission reduction activities abroad to meet certain requirements, and has a goal to eventually link up on a worldwide carbon market.[20]

D.   Assessing the Legal Status of Decisions by Treaty Bodies

Once a treaty has been adopted, parties to that treaty generally meet on some regular basis at a Conference of the Parties (COPs) to decide on further actions needed to help achieve the objectives of that treaty.[21] A potentially confusing aspect of treaty law is the status of the decisions that are adopted by such COPs. Each treaty instrument needs to be consulted to determine the status of such decisions. In addition, the status of such decisions needs to be considered under the domestic law of the country in which a question might arise. Because COP decisions are generally not subject to the ratification process set forth under the Vienna Convention, decisions are generally not seen as binding under international law. However, there are notable exceptions such as under the Montreal Protocol on Substances That Deplete the Ozone Layer.[22] In any event, COP decisions apply to the states that are parties to the treaty, and do not directly affect private sector conduct until transformed into national law in those countries.

E.   The Distinction between Signing and Ratifying a Treaty

The Vienna Convention provides that signatory states are "obliged to refrain from acts that would defeat the object and purpose of a treaty" when "it has signed the treaty or otherwise indicated it has exchanged instruments constituting the treaty subject to ratification" or "when it has expressed its consent to be bound by the treaty, pending the entry into force."[23] Accordingly, while activities within states that have not ratified a relevant environmental treaty do not need to be tested for compliance with the treaty, the question might still need further analysis. That analysis could include whether the activities would be seen to frustrate the objectives of the treaty.

F.   Potential Sanctions for Noncompliance with IEL

This issue brings us back to the distinction between hard law and soft law and the variety of mechanisms to address compliance with IEL. Even in the case of IEL hard law, most treaties rarely require sanctions from state parties that fail to comply with terms of the treaty.[24] However, there are some notable exceptions, such as the trade sanctions that can be imposed on parties that fail to comply with provisions of the Montreal Protocol and the

Convention on the International Trade in Endangered Species. Moreover, even if the Basel Convention did not directly impose trade sanctions, it did require state parties to not allow trade in hazardous wastes with non-parties and it stated that transboundary movements of hazardous wastes carried out in contravention of the convention are to be considered illegal traffic and a criminal act. In addition, all parties are to introduce national legislation to prevent and punish illegal traffic in hazardous wastes. To this end, the Basel Convention Secretariat has worked closely with Interpol and the World Customs Organization in seeking to pursue violators of the Basel Convention provisions, and to help seek prosecution pursuant to relevant domestic law. The growth of efforts to enforce environmental law at the international level are well documented through the work of a growing number of organizations. One, in particular, the International Network for Environmental Compliance and Enforcement (INECE) maintains a database of information for environmental prosecutors,[25] and Interpol has increasingly worked with INECE and UNEP to strengthen efforts against both environmental crime and wildlife crime.

III.   Useful References on IEL

As noted above, there are several important categories of IEL as laid out in this publication. The sources of information for the practitioner will vary from the easily accessible to those that are likely to require translation or those that are outdated.

As it pertains to international treaties, practitioners can usually begin to locate relevant treaty material at several different sources. The U.S. State Department keeps all relevant information on treaty status for the United States.[26] In addition, United Nations Treaty Series keeps an up-to-date listing of all treaties.[27] In addition, most major treaties have websites established and maintained by their secretariats.[28] Moreover, there are several databases that focus on assembling IEL materials beginning with their cataloging of environmental treaties. These databases often include relevant environmental law and judicial decision making.[29]

As it pertains to domestic law of foreign nations, national gazettes are increasingly useful[30] and sometimes offer translated material.[31] And, of course, when it comes to the relevant environmental measures applicable to activities in various environment-related fields, websites of U.N. specialized agencies such as the International Maritime Organization, Food and Agriculture Organization, UNEP, and the World Bank (and member organizations of the World Bank Group) all maintain materials on their website.

IV.   Conclusion

This chapter has introduced the types of issues and considerations that might arise upon confronting a question related to IEL. It has to be remembered that "environment" is often read more broadly in certain regions than in others and the approach is constantly evolving. Related laws and regulations in the field of agriculture, mining, and trade are only some of the areas that might pose challenges to the practitioner.

Notes

1. Kiobel v. Royal Dutch Petroleum, 133 S. Ct. 1659 (2013).

2. D. HUNTER, J. SALZMAN & D. ZAELKE, INTERNATIONAL ENVIRONMENTAL LAW AND POLICY 1518 (2009) (noting the observation by E. Brown Weiss of the growth of environmental treaties from approximately 40 at Stockholm to 900 by the time of Rio (citing E. Brown Weiss, *International Environmental Law: Contemporary Issues and the Emergence of a New World Order*, 81 GEO. L J. 675 (1993)).

3. *See* C. DI LEVA, INTERNATIONAL FINANCIAL INSTITUTIONS AND INTERNATIONAL LAW 343 (D. Bradlow & D. Hunter eds., 2010).

4. *See, e.g.*, HUNTER, SALZMAN & ZAELKE, *supra* note 2, at 344–45.

5. *See* http://www.inspectionpanel.org.

6. W. Lang, Treaties as a Source of International Law, *available at* http://www.eolss .net/Sample-Chapters/C14/E1-36-05.pdf.

7. *See* http://www.un.org/esa/forests/pdf/ERes2007_40E.pdf.

8. United Nations Forum on Forests Open-ended Ad Hoc Expert Group on the consideration of the content of the Non-Legally Binding Instrument on all types of forests (New York, 11–15 Dec. 2006), *available at* http://www.un.org/esa/forests/pdf/aheg /nlbi/ahegnlbi-report.pdf.

9. In some countries, ratification can proceed by an act of the executive. It can be time consuming in some countries to clarify the necessary process for treaty ratification.

10. Treaty between Uruguay and Argentina concerning the Rio de la Plata and the Corresponding Maritime Boundary 19 November 1973, *available at* http://www.un.org /Depts/los/LEGISLATIONANDTREATIES/PDFFILES/TREATIES/URY-ARG1973MB .PDF.

11. *See* M. Traisawasdichai Lang, *Management of the Mekong River Basin: Contesting Its Sustainability from a Communication Perspective* (Working Paper, Aalborg Univ. 2005), *available at* http://vbn.aau.dk/files/33966688/workingpaper_130.pdf.

12. A. Nollkaemper, *Rethinking the Supremacy of International Law* (Amsterdam Ctr. for Int'l Law Working Paper, Feb. 3, 2009), *available at* SSRN: http://papers.ssrn.com /sol3/papers.cfm?abstract_id=1336946.

13. The United States and other World Trade Organization member countries challenged the EU measures to restrict biotech products from entering the EU. Among other grounds that the EU raised in its defense was that their actions were consistent with the Biosafety Protocol of the Convention on Biological Diversity. This argument failed in the view of the WTO Appellate Body because, at a minimum, the United States was not a party to the CBD or the Biosafety Protocol, and could not be required to comply with that treaty's obligations. *See* World Trade Org., European Communities—Measures Affecting the Approval and Marketing of Biotech Products, http://www.wto.org/english /tratop_e/dispu_e/cases_e/ds291_e.htm.

14. "The Equator Principles is a credit risk management framework for determining, assessing and managing environmental and social risk in project finance transactions." Equator Principles, http://www.equator-principles.com/. The Principles cover over 70 percent of international project finance debt in emerging markets. "Equator Principles Financial Institutions (EPFIs) commit to not providing loans to projects where the borrower will not or is unable to comply with their respective social and environmental

policies and procedures." *Id.* "The EPs have become the industry standard for environmental and social risk management and financial institutions, clients/project sponsors,
other financial institutions, and even some industry bodies refer to the EPs as good practice." *Id.*

15. *See* Int'l Fin. Corp., General Environmental, Health, and Safety Guidelines,
https://www1.ifc.org/wps/wcm/connect/topics_ext_content/ifc_external_corporate
_site/ifc+sustainability/sustainability+framework/environmental,+health,+and+safety
+guidelines/ehs+guidelines+technical+revision/generalehs_1-2.

16. Under REACH, manufacturers and importers are obliged to register substances
they produce or import in quantities over one ton per year. REACH foresees a restriction
process to regulate the manufacture, placing on the market, or use of certain substances,
either on their own or in mixtures or articles, within the EU territory if they pose an unacceptable risk to health or the environment. Such activities may be limited or even banned,
if necessary. The restriction is designed to manage risks that are not addressed by the
other REACH processes or by other European Community legislation. European Comm'n,
Enterprise and Industry, Restrictions, http://ec.europa.eu/enterprise/sectors/chemicals
/reach/restrictions/index_en.htm.

17. http://ec.europa.eu/enterprise/sectors/chemicals/documents/reach/review
2012/index_en.htm.

18. ICIS, Reach-Like Regulations Enacted Globally, http://www.icis.com/Articles
/2010/05/31/9362538/reach-like-regulations-enacted-globally.html.

19. *See* European Comm'n, Climate Action, The EU Emissions Trading System,
http://ec.europa.eu/clima/policies/ets/index_en.htm.

20. As the European Commission has noted: "The number of emissions trading systems around the world is increasing. Besides the EU ETS, national or sub-national systems are already operating in Australia, Japan, New Zealand and the United States, and
are planned in Canada, China, South Korea and Switzerland." *See* European Comm'n,
Climate Action, International Carbon Market, http://ec.europa.eu/clima/policies/ets
/linking/index_en.htm.

21. *See* chapter 48, Mechanisms for Global Agreements, in this volume.

22. Article 2.9 of the Montreal Protocol allows the parties to make binding decisions
on reduction levels of ozone-depleting substances. However, the status such decisions
have as a matter of domestic law has been the subject of some debate. *See, e.g.,* Duncan
Hollis, *NRDC v. EPA: Are IO Decisions Really Only Political Commitments?*, OPINIO JURIS
(Sept. 5, 2006), http://opiniojuris.org/2006/09/05/nrdc-v-epa-are-io-decisions-really
-only-political-commitments/.

23. *See* Vienna Convention on the Law of Treaties, https://treaties.un.org/doc/Pub
lication/UNTS/Volume%201155/volume-1155-I-18232-English.pdf.

24. *See, e.g.,* LEGAL RESPONSE INITIATIVE, SANCTIONS AND PENALTIES IN ENVIRONMEN-
TAL TREATIES (Briefing Paper No. BP 14 E, July 19, 2010), http://legalresponseinitiative
.org/legaladvice/sanctions-and-penalties-in-environmental-treaties/.

25. *See* http://inece.org/.

26. *See* U.S. Dep't of State, Treaty Affairs, http://www.state.gov/s/l/treaty/.

27. *See* http://treaties.un.org/Pages/UNTSOnline.aspx?id=1.

28. *See, e.g.,* UNFCCC, http://www.unfccc.int.

29. *See, e.g.,* appendix 1 to this chapter.

30. *See, e.g.,* S. Africa Gov't Online, http://www.gov.za/documents/index.php?term
=&dfrom=&dto=&tps.

31. For translated legal instruments from China, see the resources at the Internet
Chinese Legal Research Center, http://law.wustl.edu/chinalaw/intersou.html.

APPENDIX I

Sample of Public Interest
Web-Based Sources of International
Environmental Law

Website	Organization/ Entity	Purpose and Fields	Related Links
CIEL http://www.ciel.org *(Center for International Environmental Law)*	CIEL	A nonprofit law firm focusing on strengthening and developing international and comparative environmental law, policy, and management.	

(continued)

Website	Organization/ Entity	Purpose and Fields	Related Links
CIESIN http://www.ciesin.org *(Center for International Earth Science Information Network)*	Columbia University's Earth Institute	Focuses on applying information technology to interdisciplinary data, information, and research problems related to human interactions in the environment. CIESIN's website contains the text of more than 140 international environmental agreements.	**ENTRI** (Environmental Treaties and Resource Indicators) (http://sedac.ciesin .columbia.edu/entri/) allows searches for treaties by date, keyword, and other fields. **The Country Explorer** (http:// sedac.ciesin.columbia .edu/entri/partySearch .jsp) provides access to national-level data on more than 200 countries, such as which treaties a country, organization, or territory has signed or ratified. **Decision search tool** (http://sedac .ciesin.columbia.edu /gsametasearch/cop _start.jsp) searches a complete collection of decision documents from selected multilateral environmental agreements.

Website	Organization/ Entity	Purpose and Fields	Related Links
ECOLEX http://www.ecolex .org/start.php	Jointly developed by the FAO, UNEP, and IUCN Environmental Law Center	Provides information on treaties, international soft-law and other nonbinding policy and technical guidance documents, national legislation, judicial decisions, and law and policy literature. Users have direct access to the abstracts and indexing information about each document, as well as to the full text of most of the information provided.	
E-LAW http://www.elaw.org *(Environmental Law Alliance Worldwide)*		E-LAW is a worldwide network of public interest attorneys, scientists, and other advocates interested in international and domestic environmental law. The advocates exchange information concerning international environmental issues, with the aim of building local environmental law expertise. Most of these exchanges occur through e-mail and electronic conferencing. The website features environmental law cases from around the world, mostly in English.	

(*continued*)

Website	Organization/ Entity	Purpose and Fields	Related Links
E-Law's Legal & Scientific Resources http://www.elaw.org /resources/	E-Law	Provides access to foreign environmental legislation, including court decisions from around the world.	
FAOLEX http://faolex.fao.org /faolex/	FAO	Contains a large collection of national laws and regulations on food, agriculture, and renewable natural resources. This database includes abstracts and indexing information about each text, as well as the full text of most legislation contained in the database.	In addition to Ecolex and FAOLEX, FAO also offers WaterLex and FishLex.
GIWA http://www.unep.org /dewa/giwa/areas /giwamap.asp *(Global International Waters Assessment)*	UNEP Global Waters Program	A draft map divides the world's waters into regions. By clicking on the region, one can see the major international agreements, actors, research, state of the environment, and other useful information.	
GLIN http://www.glin.gov/ *(Global Legal Information Network)*	GLIN	Contains statutes, regulations, court decisions, and related national materials from over 50 countries in the Americas, Europe, Africa, and Asia with more than 60,000 references of national laws. Relevant subject terms include biological diversity, environment, pollution, sustainable development, UNEP, and water.	

Website	Organization/ Entity	Purpose and Fields	Related Links
Globalex Guide http://www .nyulawglobal.org /Globalex /International _Environmental _Legal_Research1 .htm#Blogs	New York University Law School	Useful table of subtopics in international environmental law with a list of treaties and relevant research websites.	
Globelaw http://www.globelaw .com/index.html	GLOBE	Includes the text of several conventions, several decisions of international and national tribunals along with summaries and parties' arguments, selected UN resolutions, and links to other sites containing multilateral conventions and international environmental law and policy documents.	

(*continued*)

Website	Organization/ Entity	Purpose and Fields	Related Links
IELRC http://www.ielrc.org/ *(International Environmental Law Research Centre)*	IELRC	The IELRC, located in Geneva and New Delhi, serves as a forum for the development of legal and institutional frameworks that foster equitable and sustainable environmental management at local/ national/international level. The website provides access to articles, working papers, briefing papers, and more on a variety of environmental topics, including biosafety, biodiversity, climate change, intellectual property, justice and human rights, and water.	
IISD http://www.iisd.org/ *(International Institute for Sustainable Development)*		Promotes sustainable development in decision making internationally and within Canada.	Publishes the Internet periodical Earth Negotiations Bulletin (http://www .iisd.ca/linkages/) and hosts the Linkages site (http://www.iisd .ca/linkages), a multimedia resource providing timely coverage of conferences and updates re ongoing negotiations.

Website	Organization/ Entity	Purpose and Fields	Related Links
International Environmental Law http://www.asil.org /erg/?page=ienvl	ASIL (*American Society for International Law*)	This research guide is part of the American Society for International Law (ASIL) Guide to Electronic Resources for International Law.	**ASIL: Interest Group in International Environmental Law** (http://www.asil .org/interest-groups -view.cfm?groupid=20) focuses on the role of law in addressing international environmental issues.
International Environmental Law Research Guide http://www.law .georgetown.edu /library/research /guides/International EnvironmentalLaw.cfm	Georgetown Law School	This is an in-depth guide to researching international environmental law.	
IPCC http://www.ipcc.ch/ (*Intergovernmental Panel on Climate Change*)	IPCC	The IPCC is a scientific body under the auspices of the United Nations. It reviews and assesses the most recent scientific, technical, and socioeconomic information produced worldwide relevant to the understanding of climate change.	

(*continued*)

Website	Organization/ Entity	Purpose and Fields	Related Links
Multilaterals Project http://fletcher.archive .tusm-oit.org /multilaterals/	The Fletcher School at the Tufts University	Designed to make available the texts of international multilateral conventions and other instruments. Although the database now includes treaties in other fields, the major subject headings still reflect the emphasis on environmental agreements: they include "Atmosphere and Space," "Flora and Fauna— Biodiversity," "Marine and Coastal," and "Other Environmental instruments." NOTE: This site has been archived and is no longer regularly maintained. Information may be outdated.	
UNEP http://www.unep.org/ *(United Nations Environment Programme)*		Full-text publications of treaties.	UNEP offers links to specific UNEP programs headquartered in Geneva (http://www .unep.ch/) and to other UNEP programs, including those at UNEP headquarters in Nairobi.

Website	Organization/ Entity	Purpose and Fields	Related Links
UNTS http://www.un.org /Depts/Treaty	United Nations Treaty Department	Provides information on the status of over 500 major multilateral instruments deposited with the Secretary-General of the United Nations (including the texts of reservations, declarations, and objections).	
WHO http://www .who.int/en/ *(The World Health Organization)*	WHO	WHO is the directing and coordinating authority for health within the United Nations system. It is responsible for providing leadership on global health matters, shaping the health research agenda, setting norms and standards, articulating evidence-based policy options, providing technical support to countries and monitoring and assessing health trends.	The public-health section of this website contains reports and other WHO publications on environmental health addressing such topics as indoor and outdoor pollution, chemical safety, children's environmental health, and global environmental change (http://www.who.int /phe/en/).
WMO http://www.wmo.ch *(World Meteorological Organization)*	WMO	The World Meteorological Organization (WMO) is a specialized agency of the United Nations. It is the UN system's authoritative voice on the state and behavior of the Earth's atmosphere, its interaction with the oceans, the climate it produces, and the resulting distribution of water resources.	

REGIONAL WEBSITES AND SPECIAL ORGANIZATIONS

Website	Organization/ Entity	Purpose and Fields	Related Links
The Association of Southeast Asian Nations (ASEAN) http://www.asean .org/	ASEAN	Promotes economic cooperation and the welfare of southeast Asian nations. Although the focus thus far has been on economic cooperation, the member states have concluded several agreements on the environment.	The website includes links to ASEAN environmental agreements and other publications (http://www.asean .org/links).
Council of Europe http://www.coe.int	Council of Europe	Contains numerous documents, including international agreements.	Environmental conventions can be located using the website's full-text searching function (http://conventions.coe.int/). Examples of environmental conventions in the context of the Council of Europe are Convention on the Conservation of European Wildlife and Natural Habitats and Convention on Civil Liability for Damage Resulting from Activities Dangerous to the Environment. More information about the Council of Europe's environmental work can be found on the **Culture and Nature** web page, which includes topics such as biological diversity, sustainable development, and climate change (http://www.coe.int/lportal/web /coe-portal/what-we-do/culture -and-nature).
The Department of Sustainable Development and Environment http://www.oas.org /usde/	Organization of American States (OAS)	This department is responding to the needs of member states of OAS on issues relating to sustainable development within an economic development context.	

Website	Organization/ Entity	Purpose and Fields	Related Links
European Union Environment http://europa.eu/pol /env/index_en.htm	The European Union	This website provides access to legislation, reports, and publications.	**European Environmental Law Homepage** (http://www .eel.nl) provides access to European Environmental Treaties and case law with cases of the European Court of Justice of the EU (jurisdiction within the EU) along with cases of the ECHR (jurisdiction within the Council of Europe), draft legislation, and other environmental documents, including selected national court decisions along with special national developments on environmental issues. The legal documents of the EU are available through **EUR-Lex,** http://eur-lex.europa.eu /en/index.htm **European Environment Policy Page** (http://ec.europa .eu/environment/index_en.htm) provides access to press releases, environmental action programs, studies, reports, environment fact sheets, speeches, and information about member states' implementing legislation. The Commission has also published a number of **Communications on Climate Change** (http://ec .europa.eu/environment/climat /future_action_com.htm). The **Directorate-General for the Environment** is responsible for the European Commission work on the Environment (http://ec.europa .eu/dgs/environment/index_en .htm).

(continued)

Website	Organization/ Entity	Purpose and Fields	Related Links
			The website contains a selection of recent Environment Directorate-General proposals, fact sheets on air quality and waste, and numerous newsletters. It also includes information about the EU's **Eco-label Programme,** which serves the primary purpose of stimulating the supply and demand of products with reduced environmental impact (http://ec.europa.eu /environment/ecolabel/index _en.htm).
			The **European Environmental Agency** assists EU institutions and EEA members in making decisions and formulating policies on environmental issues. Relevant information can be found under "Environmental Topics" and "Data and Maps" (http://www .eea.europa.eu/).
			The **EC Biodiversity Clearing-House Mechanism** facilitates the exchange of biodiversity information between EU institutions. Clearing-House provides a biodiversity thesaurus, directory of information sources on biodiversity, and numerous links to full-text documents maintained on other EU sites (http://biodiversity-chm.eea .europa.eu/).
			European Union Delegation in the United States covers developments in the Transatlantic Action Plan and contains numerous full-text documents (http://www .eurunion.org).

Website	Organization/ Entity	Purpose and Fields	Related Links
GATT & the World Trade Organization (WTO) http://docsonline .wto.org/	WTO	A WTO Committee on Trade and Environment works on incorporating environmental and sustainable development issues into trade rules. The website contains the official documentation of the WTO, including the legal texts of the WTO agreements, documents from dispute settlement panels, and more.	The WTO's environmental work is discussed and updated on a daily basis at http://www .wto.org/english/tratop_e /envir_e/envir_e.htm.
The North American Agreement for Environmental Cooperation http://www.cec.org /Page. asp?PageID =1226&SiteNodeID =567	NAFTA	In 1993, the three NAFTA member states (Canada, Mexico, and the United States) also entered into a complementary agreement to address shared environmental concerns.	The **Commission for Environmental Cooperation (CEC)** was created to address regional environmental concerns. It works to prevent trade and environmental conflicts and to promote the enforcement of environmental law (http://www.cec.org). This website provides documents from the CEC's governing body, the **CEC Council,** as well as a Summary of Environmental Law in North America, including links to the texts of several international agreements and relevant national laws in NAFTA member countries (Canada, Mexico, and the United States) (http://www .cec.org/Page.asp?PageID=1226 &SiteNodeID=207).
OECD's Environment Directorate http://www.oecd .org/env/	OECD	This website includes environment-related documents under the heading "Publications and Documents" and provides links to related OECD materials.	**OECD Environment** (http:// www.oecd.org/environment/)

CHAPTER 4

The Top Ten Trends in International Environmental Law

TSEMING YANG*

Given the multitude of international environmental issues, the choice of the top ten trending issues is to some extent arbitrary. A better description of such a list may be as the top matters on the minds of environmental lawyers, diplomats, and policy makers.

I.   Global Climate Change and Energy Policy

In any inventory like this, climate change must be at the very top. With its global scope, both in terms of contributions and effects, the warming of the Earth's surface and atmosphere from rising concentrations of greenhouse gases (GHGs) is unquestionably the greatest environmental challenge for humanity. Within just the last four decades, the total global anthropogenic carbon emissions into the atmosphere have doubled. The increase has been tenfold over the last century. Temperatures and sea levels are expected to rise, with more frequent and intense storms, floods, droughts, and other extreme weather events; changes in ecosystems; and adverse effects on human health.

Of course, the international community has not stood still. The call has been for the widest possible cooperation by all countries to limit carbon emissions. Policy and legal responses have come not only from national governments and international organizations but also triggered efforts by subnational and local entities as well as businesses and civil society organizations. While there is too much to discuss in detail, there have been notable initiatives at the international, regional, national, and subnational level.

Among the most visible international activities have been (1) the work of the Intergovernmental Panel on Climate Change (IPCC) to assess the state of the science and potential effects of climate change and (2) the 1992 United Nations Framework Convention on Climate Change (UNFCCC), which

---

*The author is grateful to Shana Inspektor for her excellent research assistance.

promotes global cooperation to devise and implement appropriate policy responses. Designed with the goal to "limit average global temperature increases" and to cope with the inevitable impacts of climate change, the UNFCCC has served primarily as a forum for cooperation and dialogue. Quantitatively defined GHG emission reduction commitments are contained only in a subsidiary agreement, the 1997 Kyoto Protocol. Under the Kyoto Protocol, most of the wealthiest nations agreed to reach on average 5 percent emission reductions from 1990 levels by the end of 2012. One of the notable exceptions was the United States, which signed the Kyoto Protocol but did not ratify it.

The aggregate emission reduction target of the Kyoto Protocol parties as a whole is expected to be met, largely due to reduced economic activity from the breakup of the Soviet Union in the 1990s and the global economic slowdown during the 2008–2012 first commitment period. However, compliance by individual country parties with their Kyoto-assigned reduction targets has varied significantly. Some nations have missed their individual targets by significant amounts.

Since 1992, the parties to the UNFCCC have also made progress in other ways. Among these have been efforts to encourage developing countries to engage in voluntary emission reduction activities, especially through the Clean Development Mechanism (CDM), addressing the role of deforestation and other land use-related contributors to climate change, and creating a new financial entity to support the work of the developing world, the Green Climate Fund. Most recently, the 2012 Doha negotiations created a second commitment period to last from 2013 to 2020. Doha also set out a plan for more significant post-2020 long-term reductions to be negotiated by 2015, with the ultimate goal of ensuring "that global temperature increases are limited to below 2 degrees Celsius."[1]

At the regional level, the European Union's efforts, especially its Emissions Trading System (EU ETS), has been noteworthy. Designed to control the "carbon dioxide emissions from more than 11,000 power stations and industrial plants in 30 participating countries," the EU ETS covers a total of "40% of the European Union's total greenhouse gas emissions."[2] When the EU took the controversial step of expanding coverage of EU ETS to the aviation sector, including non-EU airlines flying in and out of virtually any EU airport, many non-EU states, including the United States, voiced their opposition. As a result, the European Parliament temporarily suspended the aviation measure put on hold at this time by the European Parliament.

At the national level, governments are active in virtually every single country. Within the United States, efforts have accelerated since the U.S. Supreme Court's 2007 decision in *Massachusetts v. EPA*.[3] The Environmental Protection Agency's (EPA) 2009 finding that "greenhouse gases constitute a threat to public health and welfare" under section 202(a) of the Clean Air Act triggered a number of regulatory actions, such as new emission standards for new motor vehicles, "expected to save more than 6 billion barrels of oil through 2025 and reduce more than 3,100 million metric tons of carbon dioxide emissions" in car emissions alone.[4] Most recently, in January and June 2014, the

Agency published proposed regulations addressing GHG emissions from new and existing fossil fuel fired power plants, respectively.[5]

Finally, activity at the subnational level has also been progressing rapidly. Within the United States, California has been a leader. Through its Global Warming Solutions Act of 2006, often referred to as Assembly Bill 32 (AB 32), it mandated statewide GHG emission reductions to 1990 levels by 2020. AB 32's emission reduction requirements as well as its most visible implementing feature, a cap-and-trade system administered by the California Air Resources Board, became legally enforceable as of 2013.[6]

II. Globalization of Environmental Law

As international and global environmental problems have grown in importance over the last couple of decades, environmental law has evolved to meet these needs and given rise to global environmental law. As the opening chapter of this book describes, global environmental law is the amalgam of international, national, and transnational environmental law that is being produced by active efforts of environmental law transplantation, convergence of law and governance systems, and integration and harmonization of international regulatory systems among themselves and with national systems.

Global environmental law is thus the manifestation of complementary trends of proliferation of environmental treaties and other international legal instruments, rapid development of national environmental law and governance systems across the world, and the growing importance of transnational law. It represents the inevitable realization that effective solutions to global environmental problems require not only government-to-government legal commitments, but also the development of law and governance institutions at the national and subnational level. Such institutions are critical not only for engaging national governments but also for effective intervention into the contributions of the private sector and individuals in environmental degradation. The critical importance of such governance and capacity necessities cannot be assumed away, especially in developing countries.

While globalization continues to contribute to environmental pressures across the world, it is also promoting convergence, integration, and harmonization in international, national, and transnational environmental regimes, both legal rules as well as in the underlying environmental governance institutions and mechanisms. Just as the environment is ultimately interconnected, humanity's response to the global range of environmental problems will also force increasingly integrated and comprehensive institutional regulatory response. Whether these trends will eventually lead to the emergence of a globally integrated, or at least coordinated, regime of environmental governance remains to be seen.

III. Sustainable Development and Law

"Sustainable development" has been around as a buzzword at least since the Brundtland Commission's 1987 report *Our Common Future*.[7] Its prospects have enjoyed a significant revival in recent years, however. As a concept, it embraces notions of temporal balance by providing for "development that meets the needs of the present without compromising the ability of future generations to meet their own needs"[8] as well as substantive balance between economic development and social and environmental considerations, such as eradication of poverty and conservation of natural resources. As a key framework through which global issues, especially maintenance of the health of the Earth's ecosystems, are being evaluated, sustainable development was the focus of the recent 2012 U.N. Conference on Sustainable Development. Also referred to as Rio+20, the conference centered on two thematic issues: a "green economy" and institutional frameworks for sustainable development.[9]

Rio+20 made evident that the concept is of broad significance across many different sectors and levels of government, private business, and civil society. It showcased both government initiatives as well as innovations by civil society organizations such as farmers, women's groups, the scientific community, indigenous peoples, and many others.[10] Rio+20 demonstrated that creative projects are advancing the cause of natural resource conservation and environmental protection as well as helping to alleviate poverty, create jobs, and grow the economy. Its "framework for action and follow-up" will likely spur further developments. Whether Rio+20's vision of how the "green economy may help achieve sustainable development" will ultimately be realized remains to be seen.[11]

At the national level in the United States, the concept of sustainable development has enjoyed varying levels of attention, including as a subject of White House study through the President's Council on Sustainable Development during the Clinton administration. However, EPA's decision to commission a study for a new "Green Book," a "management system framework to accelerate incorporation of sustainability into the operational activities of the EPA,"[12] is the most substantive exploration yet of how sustainability can be operationalized. The "Green Book" calls for nine sustainability principles to guide EPA's work: (1) environmental protection, (2) the precautionary approach, (3) intergenerational equity, (4) internalization of environmental costs, (5) participation of all concerned citizens, (6) regeneration, (7) substitutability, (8) assimilation, and (9) avoiding irreversibility.[13] Such consideration remains ongoing, though it has not been without controversy.

Finally, the private sector has been developing and implementing its own sustainability initiatives. Motivated in part by the cost savings that can be achieved as well as consideration of good corporate citizenship and public opinion, such efforts have given rise to progressive corporate policies and programs.[14] In the banking industry specifically, the Equator Principles have attracted a significant international following and come to be seen as the leading set of voluntary guidelines for "determining, assessing and managing environmental and social risk in projects."[15] Unfortunately, significant public relations and marketing efforts accompanying and supporting such sustainability initiatives have made it difficult to distinguish between what are substantively progressive and green corporate policies and commitments and what is just "green-washing."

IV.   The Rise of the Developing World

Rapid economic growth in many developing countries has not only raised standards of living but also increased their environmental footprint correspondingly. Most prominent examples of this trend have been the emerging economies in East Asia and South America where standards of living comparable to North America, Western Europe, and Japan have been achieved in at least substantial parts of society. And even if countries like China and India still have some ways to go in their development trajectories, their sheer population size and prospective global environmental impact have made them important players in international environmental cooperation and diplomacy.

In the past, poverty alleviation and other societal needs made such countries reluctant to prioritize pollution control and other environmental issues over economic growth. Furthermore, the notion of "common but differentiated responsibilities" under Rio Principle 7, based on "the different contributions to global environmental degradation," has provided a key argument that industrialized countries bear the primary responsibility for addressing environmental problems.[16]

Rio Principle 7 remains foundational for much of modern international environmental law. It is referenced in the UNFCCC and in the Stockholm Convention on Persistent Organic Pollutants, and was reaffirmed most recently in Rio+20's outcome document *The Future We Want*. But with the growing environmental footprint of the developing world, the practical application of Principle 7 has become increasingly difficult and controversial. For example, in the context of international climate negotiations, industrialized countries are putting increasing pressure on countries with large carbon footprints, such as China, to make meaningful emission reduction commitments.

There will undoubtedly be resistance by the developing world, especially emerging economies, to taking on greater environmental commitments, especially given its increasing clout and role in shaping international environmental negotiations. However, there also seems little doubt that changes will ultimately have to come, not only in the developing world's active contribution to environmental problem solving, but ultimately also the structure of international cooperation on environmental issues.

V.   Environmental Institutions, Governance Mechanisms, and the Rule of Law

The rise of global environmental law and proliferation of environmental treaties and legislation at the national and subnational level has highlighted one important bottleneck in the development of effective systems to protect the environment. While legal rules and environmental standards are necessary elements, they are not sufficient conditions for such systems to be effective. In other words, successful international, national, and local environmental governance systems require both well-designed legal rules and standards as well as effective governance mechanisms and institutions.

At the international level, discussions of enhanced and more effective governance have revolved around the internal structures and external relationships of multilateral environmental agreements with each other, the United Nations, especially the United Nations Environment Programme and the other specialized agencies of the U.N., as well as non-U.N.-affiliated multilateral organizations such as the WTO. Reform efforts have been controversial and centered in part on initiatives to restructure and enhance the status of UNEP.[17] They did not find much traction in the preparations for the 2012 Rio+20 Conference, although the long-term goal of reform remains an important international objective.

Efforts to enhance environmental governance at the national level have had less visibility, although appreciation of its critical importance is spreading. Effective national governance systems are critical to the implementation of international commitments on the environment and turning policy aspirations into on-the-ground reality. They require not only well-designed legislation, but also mechanisms and institutions concerned with the environment. As articulated by Scott Fulton and Antonio Benjamin, such systems must include mechanisms that allow civil society to participate in environmental decision making, ensure accountability of both private and governmental actors in regard to the environment, provide access to fair and responsive dispute resolution, and make environmental information available to the public. At the same time, environmental institutions must be well designed and operate efficiently and with maximum integrity.[18]

The need for effective international and national governance systems has been recognized in international conferences such as Rio+20 and the concurrent World Congress on Justice, Governance, and Law for Environmental Sustainability,[19] as well as through the work of transnational networks, such as the International Network on Environmental Compliance and Enforcement,[20] the IUCN Commission on Environmental Law, and the World Resources Institute's Access Initiative. Without more progress on developing effective governance systems, however, this issue will likely be a limiting factor in making significant further progress on international environmental initiatives.

More importantly, to the extent that efforts to strengthen environmental governance systems are successful, they also help to make the rule of law in such systems more robust. Conversely, the work of organizations like the International Development Law Organization and the 2012 U.N. High Level Meeting on the Rule of Law[21] suggest that a robust rule of law will make environmental governance more effective. Ultimately, strengthening environmental institutions and governance benefits not only the environment and public health, it also strengthens the rule of law and produces other collateral benefits for human rights and democratic governance.

VI.   Human Rights and the Environment

While the connection to public health has arguably been one key motivation for public attention to environmental protection, explicit recognition of the linkage between human rights and environmental protection is increasingly also attracting broader support in recent years. Thus, traditional human rights advocacy organizations have become increasingly engaged in environmental matters, and environmental organizations in human rights matters.

In the United States, this connection has manifested itself in the rise of the environmental justice (EJ) movement. Based in large part on the 1960s civil rights movement, the EJ movement's primary focus has been on environmental discrimination. Its aims, however, have been broader in raising concern about fundamental entitlement and equal rights to clean air, clean water, and other environmental goods. Since its rise in the 1980s and 1990s, however, the EJ movement has lost much visibility.

What the U.S. national EJ movement has lost in attention, however, is increasingly being made up by growing international interest in environmental human rights issues. For example, in recent years, the Inter-American Commission on Human Rights has received petitions related to the impact of climate change on the Inuits in Alaska as well as claims of environmental discrimination against racial minority communities in Louisiana.[22] On July 28, 2010, the U.N. General Assembly explicitly recognized the human right to clean drinking water and sanitation and called upon states and international organizations to provide financial resources and technology to countries where access to clean drinking water is limited.[23] And in 2012, the U.N. Human Rights Council appointed an independent expert on human rights and the environment to study and report on the connection between these fields.[24] These developments will not only continue to enhance understanding about this relationship but also maintain international attention.

VII.   The Growing Role of the Environment in International Economic Law

The evolution and growing scope of international economic law and institutions, ranging from international trade law to multilateral financial institutions such as the World Bank, has led to the inevitable collision with environmental issues. In one of the most visible early instances, Mexico filed a legal challenge under the General Agreement on Tariffs and Trade (GATT) against the United States for a ban on tuna imports caught by methods that resulted in excessive dolphin mortality. While the import ban sought to promote dolphin protection, Mexico asserted that the ban violated GATT requirements, a contention that the United States eventually lost.

Since then, environmental issues have proliferated in number and scope in this area. International investment regimes routinely must confront regulatory takings claims by investors with respect to environmental regulations restricting business activities. In the intellectual property context, environmentalists see concerns about bioprospecting activities by pharmaceuticals companies and the inadequate protection of the interests of indigenous and other local communities. And finally, financing support by international financial institutions for large infrastructure developments, such as hydro-dam projects, in developing countries has raised serious questions about potential environmental harm to local ecosystems, extinction of endangered species, and displacement of local residents from their homes and communities.

The international response to such issues has been the creation of environmental safeguards and further study. For example, the World Bank and other international financial institutions have created internal mechanisms, such as the World Bank's Inspection Panel, to ensure compliance with bank directives imposing environmental safeguards and public participation requirements in projects supported by such institutions. As interest in and attention to the relationship between the policies and objectives of international economic regimes and the environment grows, the legal and institutional mechanisms can also be expected to continue adjusting.

VIII.   Increased Attention to Biodiversity

According to the 2010 Global Biodiversity Outlook 3, biological diversity in all of its manifestations, genes, species, and ecosystems continues to decline across the world.[25] Natural habitats in many forms, ranging from freshwater wetlands and sea ice habitats to coral and shellfish reefs, have deteriorated significantly. With humanity's ecological footprint exceeding the Earth's biological capacity, the resulting pressures from habitat change, overexploitation, pollution, invasive alien species, and climate change have decreased biodiversity substantially. For example, many amphibians, coral species, and almost a quarter of plant species are declining and facing extinction.

As with other global environmental challenges, the international community has responded with broad-based cooperative efforts, foremost the Convention on Biological Diversity (CBD). Through the CBD, parties have encouraged national efforts to conserve national ecosystems and species. These include the creation of national strategies and strengthening of enabling governance systems, as well as enhancing international financial support. Its comprehensive subject matter scope and near universal membership have made the CBD arguably the most important international treaty regime focused on nature conservation. It is also the only agreement to address the commercial benefits that could arise out of biodiversity conservation, including biotechnology and pharmaceuticals. In the short two decades of its existence, its parties have already managed to negotiate and adopt three subsidiary protocols: the Cartagena Biosafety Protocol, the supplemental Biosafety Liability Protocol, and in 2010 the Nagoya Access and Benefit Sharing Protocol.

Yet the Biodiversity Convention is neither the first nor the only major forum for nature conservation and resource management. Its predecessors range from the turn-of-the-century Migratory Bird Treaties and the 1946 International Whaling Convention to the 1972 Convention on International Trade in Endangered Species and the Bonn Convention on Migratory Species. These treaty regimes continue as focal points for particular issues such as whale conservation or endangered species trade. However, as understanding of the broader importance of biodiversity to human well-being grows, so will legal and regulatory interest in the broader area.

IX.   Chemicals and Hazardous Substances Management

Since the 1992 Rio Earth Summit, management of chemicals and hazardous substances has gained significantly in international visibility. Starting with the Basel Convention on the Transboundary Movement of Hazardous Wastes and Substances in 1989, four primary global environmental agreements focusing on this set of issues have been concluded in the last 25 years, with a fifth nonbinding policy framework system, the Strategic Approach to International Chemicals Management, created in 2006 at the International Conference on Chemicals Management. The newest of these, the Minamata Convention on Mercury, joins the Rotterdam Convention on Prior Informed Consent Procedure for Chemicals and the Stockholm Convention on Persistent Organic Pollutants, concluded in 1998 and 2001, respectively. While the Minamata Convention's legal effectiveness still has to await formal entry into force, the other three conventions enjoy near universal membership and have been in effect for some time. Both the Rotterdam and the Stockholm Conventions entered into force in 2004. The Basel Convention has been in force since 1992.

This proliferation of international agreements addressing chemicals and hazardous wastes has come primarily in response to their dramatically increased ubiquity. In the last 40 years alone, the global chemicals industry has more than tripled its output in inflation-adjusted dollars and shifted production increasingly from Organisation for Economic Co-operation and Development nations toward the emerging economies.[26] In fact, according to UNEP's 2012 Global Chemicals Outlook, China is now the world's leader in chemicals production.[27] Yet such international activity has also been tracking growing awareness and regulatory activity at the national level in the United States and Western Europe as well as highly visible dumping incidents, such as of Italian hazardous waste in Koko Island, Nigeria, and growing exports of chemicals to the developing world.[28]

In spite of the growing number of international agreements, over 40 by one count, such efforts remain collectively inadequate because of their piecemeal approach. They either focus on individual or a limited set of hazardous substances or address only a subset of the issues that impede proper regulation. The European Union's Registration, Evaluation, Authorization, and Restriction of Chemicals (REACH) regulation offers a recent governmental response to these growing risks by providing a clearer picture of the significant number of chemicals that are produced in significant quantities and present serious concerns to public health.[29] However, regulatory systems in many other countries, including in the United States, remain outdated.

Efforts to increase the effectiveness of international agreements remain ongoing and have included initiatives to ensure close coordination of the Basel, Rotterdam, and Stockholm Conventions through a joint secretariat. Broadening the scope of these agreements in terms of substances covered and issues addressed remains an unresolved issue, suggesting that international pressure for more comprehensive approaches will arise again in the future.

X.   Oceans and Fisheries

The oceans remain a key agenda item for the management of the global environment. Of interest have been the ocean's natural resources, both fisheries and ecosystems such as coral reefs, as well as the connection to broader ocean governance matters, especially the U.N. Convention on the Law of the Sea (UNCLOS).

The oceans might have seemed capable of providing a limitless bounty of food for the world just a few decades ago. Now, overfishing and pollution have dramatically increased the need for management of marine resources. Just as the increasingly intense whaling activities a little less than a century ago led to the international management of whaling, first under the auspices of the League of Nations and then in the form of the present-day International Whaling Commission, a number of regional fisheries management organizations have been created to oversee the exploitation of various fish stocks and to reign in unsustainable fisheries practices. In addition, pollution and climate change, including ocean acidification and temperature rise effects, have forced increasing attention to the degradation of the marine ecosystem, including coral reefs, as places critical for maintenance of marine biodiversity and habitat.

One critical aspect of ocean and marine resource management has been the UNCLOS, especially the question of the U.S. government's relationship to it. UNCLOS was concluded over three decades ago.[30] Unfortunately, the United States remains the only major nation outside of this treaty regime. Successive presidents from both major political parties, as well as the military and foreign policy establishment, have supported ratification. Yet, Senate advice and consent remains outstanding. Nevertheless, the United States has continued to remain engaged in the work of UNCLOS. And with sea-level rise and the expectation that the Arctic region will in the future become available for regular marine passage due to climate change, the questions about marine jurisdiction and governmental claims over areas of the sea floor are likely to increase in importance and require greater attention and engagement by the United States.

XI. Conclusion

There remain many more important developments in international environmental law that this chapter cannot address. Nevertheless, the trends discussed here are among the most important and will arguably be the ones to dominate the discourse among international and environmental lawyers, diplomats, industry stakeholders, and interested members of civil society in the coming years.

Notes

1. *See* http://unfccc.int/essential_background/items/6031.php.

2. *See* http://www.edf.org/climate/eu-emissions-trading-system-report.

3. 549 U.S. 497 (2007).

4. *See* http://epa.gov/climatechange/EPAactivities/regulatory-initiatives.html.

5. Standards of Performance for Greenhouse Gas Emissions From New Stationary Sources: Electric Utility Generating Units, 79 Fed. Reg. 1430 (proposed Jan. 8, 2014); Carbon Pollution Emission Guidelines for Existing Stationary Sources: Electric Utility Generating Units, *available at* http://www2.epa.gov/sites/production/files/2014-05/documents /20140602proposal-cleanpowerplan.pdf.

6. *See* http://www.arb.ca.gov/cc/ab32/ab32.htm.

7. WORLD COMM'N ON ENVT. & DEV., OUR COMMON FUTURE (G. Brundtland ed., 1987) (Brundtland Report).

8. *Id.* at ¶ 27.

9. The Future We Want, U.N. General Assembly resolution, A/RES/66/288 (Sept. 11, 2012), at 9, http://www.un.org/en/sustainablefuture/ (click on The Future We Want: Outcome Document).

10. *See* T. Yang, *ASIL Insight: The UN Rio+20 Conference on Sustainable Development— What Happened?* (Sept. 2012), http://www.asil.org/insights/volume/16/issue/28/un-rio 20-conference-sustainable-development%E2%80%94what-happened.

11. *See id.*

12. *See* http://www.epa.gov/region9/science/seminars/2012/green-book.pdf; http:// epa.gov/sciencematters/april2011/truenorth.htm.

13. *See* http://www.epa.gov/region9/science/seminars/2012/green-book.pdf at 42.

14. General Electric's "Ecomagination" program, which has engaged the company in "build[ing] innovative solutions to today's environmental challenges while driving economic growth," according to its company literature, is among the most visible of such corporate initiatives. *See* http://www.ge.com/about-us/ecomagination. Under this program, the company has built the GE38 Turboshaft Engine. Compared to its predecessor, it provides "57 percent more power, . . . eighteen percent better fuel consumption, with 63 percent fewer parts." *See* http://www.geaviation.com/engines/military/ge38/.

15. *See* http://www.equator-principles.com/index.php/about-ep/about-ep.

16. Rio Declaration on Environment and Development, Principle 7 ("developed countries acknowledge the responsibility that they bear in the international pursuit to sustainable development in view of the pressures their societies place on the global environment and of the technologies and financial resources they command"), http://www .un.org/documents/ga/conf151/aconf15126-1annex1.htm.

17. T. Yang, *ASIL Insight: The UN Rio+20 Conference on Sustainable Development—What Happened?*, http://www.asil.org/insights/volume/16/issue/28/un-rio20-conference-sustain able-development%E2%80%94what-happened.

18. C. S. Fulton & A. H. Benjamin, *Foundations of Sustainability*, 28 Envtl. Forum (Nov.–Dec. 2011).

19. *See* http://www.asil.org/insights/volume/16/issue/28/un-rio20-conference -sustainable-development%E2%80%94what-happened.

20. For example, during the IUCN World Conservation Congress in Jeju, the INECE provided a workshop on "facilitating responses to environmental crime through a global network of environmental prosecutors in order to effectuate the rule of law and good gover-nance." *See* http://inece.org/resource/facilitating-collaborative-responses-to-environmental -crime-through-a-global-network-of-environmental-prosecutors/.

21. Declaration of the High-Level Meeting of the General Assembly on the Rule of Law at the National and International Levels, at para. 30, http://www.unrol.org/files /Declaration%20HLM_A%20RES%2067%201.pdf.

22. P. Revkin, *Inuit Climate Change Petition Rejected*, N.Y. Times, Dec. 16, 2006, http:// www.nytimes.com/2006/12/16/world/americas/16briefs-inuitcomplaint.html?_r=0; Inter-American Commission on Human Rights, Report No. 43/10 (2010), Pet. 242-05, Mossville Environmental Action Now.

23. U.N. Resolution 64/292, http://www.un.org/waterforlifedecade/human_right _to_water.shtml.

24. A/HRC/RES/19/10. *See also* http://www.ohchr.org/EN/Issues/Environment /IEEnvironment/Pages/IEenvironmentIndex.aspx.

25. Secretariat of the Convention on Biological Diversity, Global Biodiversity Out-look 3, http://www.cbd.int/publications/gbo/gbo3-final-en.pdf.

26. Ctr. for Int'l Envtl. L. (CIEL), Paths to Global Chemical Safety: The 2020 Goal and Beyond 9 (2013).

27. UNEP, Global Chemicals Outlook 9 (2012).

28. For a general overview, see Carmen G. Gonzalez, *Beyond Eco-Imperialism: An Environmental Justice Critique of Free Trade*, 78 Denv. U. L. Rev. 981 (2001).

29. CIEL, *supra* note 26, at 10.

30. United Nations Convention on the Law of the Sea, Dec. 10, 1982, 1833 U.N.T.S. 397.

PART II

Topics in International Environmental Law

CHAPTER 5

Air and Climate Change

ARNOLD W. REITZE, JR.

I. Introduction

The international law of air pollution has had little effect on domestic practitioners and their clients. Some of the legal principles that have developed
in international law, however, have become part of domestic law. Moreover,
when international attention is directed at an environmental problem, it soon
becomes the focus of domestic legislative efforts. Developments on the international front, therefore, are important because they may foreshadow the
emergence of additional domestic regulatory controls over air pollutants.

The international climate change regime exemplifies this kind of relationship between emerging international law and domestic air pollution
laws. International efforts to address climate change during the past two
decades have had limited success in reducing greenhouse gas (GHG) emissions into the atmosphere. But the failure of international law and the efforts
of environmental organizations have helped create the conditions that are
leading to domestic laws and regulations to address this issue.

A. Local and Regional Air Pollutants

Air pollutants that have lasting effects can be divided into three categories.
First, we have pollutants that have adverse health effects and are released in
large quantities. The primary pollutants of concern are particulates, sulfur
oxides, and nitrogen oxides. Second, we have hazardous air pollutants that
are harmful to persons in low concentrations. These pollutants are usually
controlled through chemical-specific requirements. Finally, we have pollutants that may or may not adversely affect human health but are subject to
controls because of their serious impact on ecosystems. Two of the classes of
chemicals that have no direct effects on human health but are subject to
international treaties because of ecosystem impacts are chlorofluorocarbons
and carbon dioxide, which are discussed *infra*.

B.   Common Air Pollution Regulatory Controls.

There are a finite number of ways to abate pollution, and international agreements must of necessity adopt one or more of them. The common measures to control air pollution at the national level include (1) caps on emissions from sources in order to meet ambient air quality standards;[1] (2) emission limits for source categories;[2] (3) economic incentives or disincentives, often called market-based mechanisms, such as pollution taxes or cap-and-trade programs;[3] (4) work or operational practice requirements;[4] and (5) bans on products or activities that pollute. International agreements use caps on emissions, but caps have not been used to meet ambient air quality standards in the international context. Emission limits are commonly used, but they are usually based on achieving national reductions from the emissions of a base year. Emission limits for specific sources are based on domestic law. Operational requirements to minimize pollution are found in some of the regional international agreements. Finally, bans are a major part of the Montreal Protocol's program to limit the release of ozone-depleting substances.

II.   Transboundary Air Pollution Litigation

International case law concerning air pollution is limited to a single 1941 case, the *Trail Smelter* arbitration, but the principles embodied in that decision are reflected throughout customary international law.[5] The case began in 1928 after sulfur dioxide emissions from a zinc and lead smelter in Trail, British Columbia, Canada, owned by Teck Cominco Metals, damaged private agricultural and forest properties in the State of Washington. The United States and Canada governments responded by referring the issue to the International Joint Commission (IJC).[6] In 1931, the IJC found the smelter had caused damage and awarded $350,000.[7]

In 1933, damages were continuing. Canada implicitly accepted liability, and an ad hoc arbitral tribunal awarded damages of $78,000 to the U.S. government attributable to the smelter's operation from 1932 to October 1937.[8] The tribunal based its holding on "the principles of international law, as well as the law of the United States.[9] The precedential value of this case is minimal because it involved a tribunal, not the International Court of Justice. Moreover, the case appears to be based primarily on U.S. law. In the years following this decision, international case law has not materialized concerning air pollution or climate change. But because of the paucity of case law, this case continues to be cited for the proposition that a nation has a duty to protect other nations and their citizens from injurious acts by individuals from within its jurisdiction when the case is of serious consequences and the injury is established by clear and convincing evidence.[10]

Two later international law cases, not involving air pollution, are frequently cited for the proposition that a state should not allow its transboundary pollution to cause significant damage in another country.[11] But case law is not a significant factor in the control of transboundary air pollution.

The world's governments paid little attention to air pollution until the Council of Europe Committee of Ministers, on March 26, 1971, adopted its Resolution on Air Pollution in Frontier Areas, which included the recommendation "that the member States of the Council of Europe ensure for the inhabitants of regions beyond their frontiers the same protection against air pollution in frontier areas as is provided for their own inhabitants."[12] In 1972 the United Nations Conference on the Human Environment produced the Stockholm Declaration on the Human Environment, which included Principle 21. Principle 21 states that nations have "the responsibility to ensure that the activities within their jurisdiction or control do not cause damage to the environment of other States or of areas beyond the limits of national jurisdiction."[13] The Stockholm Declaration was endorsed by the United Nations General Assembly on December 15, 1972,[14] and Principle 21 is now generally viewed as customary international law.[15] In addition, Principles 22 and 13 encourage the development of international and national law to compensate victims of pollution and other environmental damage.

In 1974 the Organisation for Economic Co-operation and Development (OECD)[16] recommended that countries "should endeavour to prevent any increase in transfrontier pollution."[17] In 1977 the OECD recommended that any person injured by transfrontier pollution should receive treatment by a country of origin of the pollution that is equivalent to the treatment provided for those impacted by domestic pollution.[18]

In 1987, the Second International North Sea Conference declared that a "precautionary approach is necessary which may require action to control inputs of such substances even before a casual link has been established by absolutely clear scientific evidence."[19] Some contend that this principle has crystallized into customary international law and thus become an accepted part of international environmental law.

III.   Conventional and Toxic Air Pollutant Agreements

During the 1970s, environmental protection became a concern in many developed nations. Most of the international environmental law developments involved water pollution or hazardous chemical disposal. International law does not appear to play a significant role in the control of conventional or toxic air pollutants. The more important regional approaches, however, are discussed next.

A.   U.S./Canada/Mexico

The primary international air pollution issue in North America is emissions of sulfur oxides and nitrogen oxides, which often lead to rain or snow with a low pH, called acid rain, although there are multiple pathways for these emissions to impact downwind ecosystems.[20] Since the 1970s, Canadian emissions have damaged land and aquatic environments in the United States, while the greater emissions released in the United States caused damage in

Canada. On August 5, 1980, a Memorandum of Intent on Transboundary Air Pollution committed both nations to work toward a bilateral agreement on air quality.[21] The Reagan administration, however, had little interest in addressing this issue, which led to the unsuccessful litigation discussed below.

In *New York v. Thomas*, northeastern states and national organizations sued to prevent air emissions that caused acid rain in Canada.[22] The U.S. Clean Air Act (CAA) section 115 provides that if the U.S. Environmental Protection Agency's (EPA) administrator finds that air pollution released in the United States may reasonably be anticipated to endanger public health or welfare in a foreign country, and the administrator determines the foreign country has essentially the same air pollution limits as are applicable in the United States, then the EPA must promulgate rules to prevent the harm.[23] On January 13, 1981, EPA Administrator Douglas Costle found that Canada gave essentially the same rights to the United States as the United States affords Canada. EPA's reciprocity finding resulted in the federal district court granting summary judgment and ordering EPA to force states to act to protect Canada from the effects of acid rain, if reciprocity still existed.[24] On October 22, 1985, EPA Administrator Lee Thomas found that reciprocity continued to exist.

The district court's decision was appealed, and the U.S. Court of Appeals for the D.C. Circuit remanded the case to the district court with instructions to dismiss, because Administrator Costle, in making his findings, had failed to comply with the Administrative Procedure Act's (APA)[25] notice and comment procedures.[26]

In 1990, the D.C. Circuit upheld EPA's refusal to promulgate endangerment and reciprocity findings in *Her Majesty the Queen in Right of Ontario v. EPA*.[27] The court held that EPA was not obliged to make findings until it was able to determine specific pollution sources. The court accepted EPA's claim that the endangerment could not be correlated to sources of pollution. However, Congress made such a connection in the 1990 CAA Amendments. Its section 404(e) requires 110 specified electric power plants to reduce emissions of SO_2.[28] Moreover, the 1990 subchapter IV sulfur and nitrogen oxides reduction provisions were enacted to control both interstate and international air pollution from domestic stationary sources.[29]

The U.S. and Canada continued to work on pollution problems along their border. On March 13, 1991, the United States and Canada announced an agreement on air quality that called for reductions of sulfur dioxide and nitrogen oxides.[30] The agreement created a bilateral Air Quality Committee and assigned implementation responsibilities to the IJC. On December 7, 2000, Canada and the United States signed the Ozone Annex to the Canada-U.S. Air Quality Agreement.[31] This agreement commits both the United States and Canada to reductions in nitrogen oxides and volatile organic compounds. It designates a transboundary area that includes central and southern Ontario, southern Quebec, and 18 U.S. states and the District of Columbia for regional action. In addition to the ozone issue, the joint actions address particulates, mercury and other persistent toxics, and sulfur dioxide.[32] The 2010 Progress Report concluded that both Canada and the United States were meeting their obligations under the agreement, and significant progress was being made in reducing the emissions of pollutants that cause acid rain and the formation of smog.[33]

The United States and Mexico jointly address pollution problems in their border area. On August 14, 1983, the Agreement between the United States of America and the United Mexican States on Cooperation for the Protection and Improvement of the Environment in the Border Area was concluded.[34] The agreement, known as the La Paz Agreement, calls for cooperation but has little in the way of mandates.[35] Annex IV covers transboundary air pollution caused by copper smelters along the common border and calls for each nation to impose more stringent domestic legal requirements on smelters within their borders.[36] Annex V of October 3, 1989, deals with international transport of urban air pollution from the cities of Ciudad Juarez, Chihuahua, and El Paso, Texas, and Dona Ana County, New Mexico. It calls for study, monitoring, modeling, development of an emissions inventory, and the harmonization of standards. Implementation is dependent upon the availability of sufficient funding.[37] On February 28, 2012, the United States and Mexico released the High-Level Regulatory Cooperation Council Work Plan, which is primarily concerned with reducing the burden of regulation, including environmental regulations, in order to improve the economic well-being of both nations.[38]

On August 8, 2012, the United States and Mexico signed the Border 2020 U.S.-Mexico Environmental Program Agreement.[39] It replaces the Border 2012 Agreement and will be implemented under the U.S.-Mexico La Paz Agreement. It is aimed at improving environmental quality, and among its five areas of specific concern is reducing air pollution in binational air sheds by promoting vehicle inspection programs, road paving, and anti-idling technologies such as diesel truck electrification at ports of entry.[40] Another objective is to "approach attainment of respective national ambient air quality standards" by 2020.[41] The agreement calls for completion of a climate action plan for each of the six northern Mexican border states by 2015 and build the capacity to implement the plans.[42] It calls for reducing emissions and the associated impacts by 2020 through "energy efficiency and/or alternative/renewable energy projects."[43]

B.   Agreements Primarily Involving European Nations

The Convention on Long-Range Transboundary Air Pollution (LRTAP) is the first legally binding international agreement to address air pollution on a broad regional basis.[44] It was approved November 13, 1979, and entered into force on March 16, 1983.[45] Its 51 parties are primarily the European nations, but in 1981 Canada ratified it, and the United States accepted it with qualifications.[46] The LRTAP's goal is to facilitate environmental protection among nations, primarily through cooperative programs for monitoring and evaluation of long-range transmission of air pollutants in Europe.

The development of this convention was primarily motivated by concern over the impacts of acid rain, but the agreement calls for reductions in air pollution generally and is not limited to transboundary air pollution. Article 6 calls for new and rebuilt installations to control air pollution by using the best available technology that is economically feasible. However, the Convention does not have specific commitments. It requires plans to be developed, but it has no requirements for implementation. Moreover, it calls for air pollution control measures that are compatible with balanced development. It has no enforcement mechanism or provision for funding its operations. Implementation is delegated to the U.N. Economic Commission for Europe (UNECE), and is administered by its Executive Body, which operates within the Commission.[47] The LRTAP was followed by the European Communities Council Directive No. 80/779, which provided more direction for establishing sulfur dioxide and suspended particulate emissions limitations and the conditions for their application.[48] That directive has been updated and replaced by Directive 2001/80/EC, which entered into force on November 27, 2001.[49]

The LRTAP has been expanded by eight protocols. The 1984 Protocol on Long-term Financing of the Cooperative Programme for Monitoring and Evaluation of the Long-range Transmission of Air Pollutants in Europe provides for the support of the LRTAP program.[50] An annex establishes the details concerning international cost sharing.[51] Canada is one of the 44 nations that ratified this protocol; the United States accepted the protocol.

The 1985 Protocol on the Reduction of Sulfur Emissions or Their Transboundary Fluxes by at Least 30 Per Cent (September 2, 1987), as the name implies, seeks to reduce sulfur emissions by 30 percent below 1980 levels.[52] European nations and Canada ratified this protocol; the United States, the United Kingdom, and the European Union did not.[53] The United States objected to the 1980 baseline, because U.S. emissions already had been reduced by 1980 as mandated by the CAA of 1970.[54]

The 1988 Protocol Concerning the Control of Emissions of Nitrogen Oxides or Their Transboundary Fluxes (February 14, 1991) calls for emissions not to exceed each party's 1987 emissions, or any other year selected by a party, by December 31, 1994.[55] It also requires major new or substantially modified stationary sources to use the best available technologies (BAT) economically feasible, but no deadline is specified. New mobile sources are required to meet a BAT requirement. Major existing sources are to utilize control measures based on factors set forth in Article 2(3a). In addition, the protocol seeks to regulate lead in fuel.[56] However, the protocol has no specific enforcement provision. The 34 parties are mostly European nations, but Canada ratified it; the United States accepted it with qualifications.

The 1991 Protocol Concerning the Control of Emissions of Volatile Organic Compounds (VOCs) or Their Transboundary Fluxes (September 29, 1997) provides several options for countries to reduce VOC emissions and requires technology-based controls for stationary sources, motor vehicles, and products that emit VOCs.[57] The protocol seeks to reduce VOC emissions by 30 percent by 1999 from a 1988 baseline (or another date between 1984 and 1990 selected by a party).[58] The protocol applies to 24 nations, primarily in Europe; Canada and the United States have signed but not ratified it.[59]

The 1994 Protocol on Further Reduction of Sulphur Emissions modifies the 1985 Sulphur Protocol (August 5, 1998).[60] The 29 parties, including the European Union, are primarily European nations, but Canada is a party, while the United States is not.[61] Article 2 requires the parties to make use of the most effective measures for the reduction of sulfur emissions, including (1) measures to increase energy efficiency; (2) increasing the use of renewable energy; (3) reducing the sulfur content of particular fuels and to encourage the use of fuel with a low sulfur content; and (4) applying best available control technologies not entailing excessive cost, including stringent controls on major new stationary combustion sources. In addition, the parties may apply economic instruments to encourage the adoption of cost-effective approaches to the reduction of sulfur emissions. The emission levels for each party to the protocol were adjusted in amendments in December 2007.[62]

The 1998 Aarhus Protocol on Heavy Metals (December 29, 2003) seeks to reduce emissions from stationary sources of heavy metals, particularly cadmium, lead, and mercury, below their 1990 levels. It requires lead to be phased out of gasoline and regulates heavy metal emissions from products containing the regulated metals.[63] There are no enforcement mechanisms or sanctions beyond review by its Implementation Committee. Thirty-one nations ratified the protocol, including Canada; the United States accepted the protocol.[64]

The 1998 Protocol on Persistent Organic Pollutants (POPs) (October 23, 2003) is aimed at 16 organic pollutants that resist degradation and include 11 pesticides, two industrial chemicals, and three by-products/contaminants.[65] The parties are to reduce their annual emissions of listed pollutants and impose best available techniques on major stationary sources.[66] However, there is no enforcement provisions or sanctions for failure to meet the obligations of the protocol. Thirty-six nations signed this protocol and 31 have ratified it (including the EU). Canada ratified it on December 12, 1998; the United States signed but did not ratify it.[67] Amendments were adopted on December 18, 2009, but they are not yet in force.[68]

The 1999 Gothenburg Protocol to Abate Acidification, Eutrophication, and Ground-level Ozone (May 17, 2005) calls for reductions in emissions by 63 percent for sulfur, 41 percent for NO_x, 40 percent for VOCs, and 17 percent for ammonia, based on 1990 emissions.[69] The protocol also sets emission limits for combustion sources, electric power plants, dry cleaning operation, motor vehicles, and other sources.[70] The 25 parties are primarily European nations, but the United States accepted the protocol on November 22, 2004; Canada signed the protocol on January 12, 1999, but has not yet ratified it.[71] On May 4, 2012, the U.N. Economic Commission for Europe released a draft of amendments.[72]

C.   Agreement Primarily Involving Asian Nations

In 2002 the Association of Southeast Asian Nations (ASEAN) Environmental Ministers agreed to an ASEAN Agreement on Transboundary Haze Pollution to address transboundary atmospheric pollution.[73] The agreement identified actions that would reduce the problem, including forest fire prevention and restrictions on burning biomass during dry seasons. However, there are no specific standards or binding obligations included in the agreement.[74] The issue of primary concern was smoke created by forest fires caused by land clearing on the island of Sumatra in Indonesia.[75] Indonesia, which is a primary source of transboundary air pollution, had not ratified the agreement as of 2012.

IV.   Protection of Stratospheric Ozone

Ozone in the stratosphere shields the planet from harmful ultraviolet radiation, but chlorofluorocarbons (CFCs) released into the environment migrate to the stratosphere where through chemical reactions ozone is depleted.[76] Other chemicals including carbon tetrachloride, methyl chloroform, halons, and hydrochloroflurocarbons (HCFCs) also deplete the ozone layer, which allows more UV-B radiation to reach the surface of the Earth.[77]

On March 22, 1985, the Vienna Convention for the Protection of the Ozone Layer was adopted.[78] It expresses only general aspirations, based on the use of a precautionary approach, to prevent activities that have or are likely to have adverse effects on the environment.[79] It provides for an annual Conference of the Parties, which has resulted in the approval of protocols having more focused requirements.[80]

A.   The 1987 Montreal Protocol

In 1987, the protection of stratospheric ozone was significantly enhanced when 24 nations, including the United States, signed the Montreal Protocol on Substances that Deplete the Ozone Layer.[81] It entered into force in 1989 after being ratified by more than the required 11 signatory states that represented at least two-thirds of the estimated global consumption of the controlled substances.[82] The protocol covers 95 ozone-depleting substances and requires a phased reduction, based on 1986 production and consumption, of specified CFCs as well as a freeze that began in 1989 on the production and consumption of specified halons.[83] Since 1987 many amendments and modifications to the protocol have resulted in an accelerated phased reduction for ozone-depleting substances (ODSs).

Acknowledging the developmental needs of developing countries, the protocol generally requires developed nations to phase out the production and consumption of various ODSs 10–20 years prior to developing nations.[84] Subject to possible essential use exemptions, signatories must phase out ODS consumption and production in accordance with Table 5.1.

Table 5.1. Termination Dates for Ozone-Depleting Substance Production and Consumption

Ozone-Depleting Substance	Developed Nations	Developing Nations
CFCs	January 1, 1996	January 1, 2010
Halons	January 1, 1994	January 1, 2010
Other fully halogenated CFCs	January 1, 1996	January 1, 2010
Carbon tetrachloride	January 1, 1996	January 1, 2010
Methyl chloroform	January 1, 1996	January 1, 2015
HCFCs	January 1, 2030	January 1, 2040
Hydrobromofluorocarbons (HBFCs)	January 1, 1996	January 1, 1996
Bromochloromethane	January 1, 2002	January 1, 2002
Methyl bromide	January 1, 2005	January 1, 2015

Source: Montreal Protocol, pmbl., arts. 2, 2A-2I; *see also* UNEP, Summary of Control Measures under the Montreal Protocol, http://ozone.unep.org/new_site/en/Treaties/treaties_decisions-hb.php?nav_id=44 (last visited Nov. 18, 2012).

The Montreal Protocol is considered to be a very effective agreement, but its success is difficult to transfer to other environmental problems. CFCs were produced by a very small number of facilities, less damaging technology was available, and the industry supported the protocol—all factors which allowed an effective regime to be put in place to control ODS production.

B.   The Meetings of the Parties

The annual Meeting of the Parties (MOPs) to the Montreal Protocol[85] provides an opportunity for a two-thirds majority of the parties to the protocol who are present and vote to amend the protocol, but each party must sign and ratify each amendment before becoming obligated to abide by the amendment.[86] However, once an amendment to the protocol is adopted each party loses its right to avoid what are known as "adjustments." Adjustments are changes that are considered minor, but they include changes in the phase-out schedules of all controlled chemicals and determinations of the ozone depletion potential of regulated chemicals.[87] Adjustments are determined by a two-thirds majority vote of the parties present and voting that represent at least 50 percent of the developed nations and 50 percent of the developing nations.[88]

The MOPs are of particular importance to entities regulated by the CAA because the CAA provides that in the case of a conflict between the CAA's subchapter VI and any provision of the Montreal Protocol, the more stringent provision shall apply.[89] In 1990, the CAA was more stringent than the Montreal Protocol, but as more stringent provisions are adopted under the Montreal Protocol, they become applicable domestically based on the provisions of CAA § 614.

In 2012 the 24th MOP was held in Geneva, but no significant policy changes occurred.[90] Only six meetings resulted in adjustments and/or amendments to the Montreal Protocol. They are MOP-2 (London, 1990), MOP-4 (Copenhagen, 1992), MOP-7 (Vienna, 1995), MOP-9 (Montreal, 1997), MOP-11 (Beijing, 1999), and MOP-19 (Montreal, 2007).[91] The details of the numerous changes to the protocol that resulted from the annual MOPs are beyond the scope of this chapter, but the most significant changes were to accelerate the phase-out of the regulated chemicals and to increase the number of regulated substances.[92]

The MOPs are becoming less important now that the Montreal Protocol passed its 25th anniversary. Much of the work of the parties now occurs at meetings of experts in the various issues that need adjustment because the protocol is a mature program.

V.   Control of Greenhouse Gases

In 1992, 178 nations attended the United Nations Conference on Environment and Development (UNCED) in Rio de Janeiro, Brazil, which produced the U.N. Framework Convention on Climate Change (UNFCCC), the first international agreement to address climate change.[93] On March 21, 1994, the UNFCCC entered into force after the required 50 countries, including the United States, ratified it. By 2012, the UNFCCC had been ratified by 195 countries.[94] Developed countries, on a nonbinding basis, were to lower emissions of GHGs.[95] Developing countries have few obligations.[96]

After the UNFCCC entered into force, the parties to the agreement began to meet each year at a Conference of the Parties to strengthen the UNFCCC.[97] The most important meeting was the 1997 Third Conference of the Parties, held in Kyoto, Japan, which resulted in the Kyoto Protocol to the UNFCCC.[98]

The Kyoto Protocol divides nations into Annex I and non-Annex I categories. Developed nations are designated as Annex I nations, which includes the OECD nations as of 1992, the nations of Eastern and Central Europe, and the European states of the former Soviet Union. The Annex I nations agreed to reduce their anthropogenic emissions of six GHGs listed in Annex A.[99] Reductions are to be implemented using domestic laws of the ratifying nations.[100] Non-Annex I nations, which are developing nations, have no obligations to reduce emissions during the covered period that ended in 2012.[101]

The Kyoto Protocol in Article 3 establishes emissions targets for developed (Annex I) countries that aimed for an average reduction of 5.2 percent from 1990 emissions during the years 2008–2012. The reduction requirement for each Annex I nation is found in Annex B of the protocol. In 1998, the United States signed the Kyoto Protocol.[102] However, because the protocol is strongly opposed by many senators, the United States never ratified it.

To enter into force, the protocol had to be ratified (or adopted, approved, or acceded to) by 55 parties to the UNFCCC, including Annex I parties accounting for 55 percent of carbon dioxide emissions from this group in 1990. On February 16, 2005, the Kyoto Protocol entered into force after Russia became the 127th nation to ratify it.[103]

A. The Meeting of the Parties 1999–2011

Many of the details concerning program development and compliance were left for future determination at the annual meetings of the parties. The details of these meetings are beyond the scope of this chapter, but a brief discussion of the most important developments follows. At the 2001 COP-7 meeting in Marrakesh, Morocco, the parties adopted the Marrakesh Accords, which concerned emission credits for various actions involving third parties.[104] COP-7 also resulted in the establishment of the Least Developed Countries Fund (LDCF), which addresses the needs of the 48 least developed countries.[105] COP-8, in New Delhi, India, in 2002, produced the Delhi Declaration.[106] It reaffirmed "that economic and social development and poverty eradication are the first and overriding priorities in developing country Parties." However, it did not call for specific actions.[107]

The COP-11 and the first meeting of the parties to the Kyoto Protocol (MOP-1) were held in Montreal in 2005.[108] The work of the conference was routine, but it ended with an agreement to begin discussions on post-2012 commitments.[109] COP-13 and the MOP-3 meetings were held in 2007 in Bali, Indonesia.[110] A significant development was the agreement on the process to be used for the climate change adaptation fund. The fund is administered by the Global Environment Facility (GEF), which is the financial mechanism for the UNFCCC and the Montreal Protocol, with the World Bank acting as trustee.[111] The GEF has become the largest public funder of projects to improve the global environment, with over $10 billion in grants for over 2,700 projects in 165 countries as of 2011.[112]

The meeting led to developing nations, for the first time, agreeing to consider taking "measurable, reportable and verifiable" mitigation actions. COP-13 also produced the Bali Action Plan, which provided a roadmap of how negotiations for a new convention would proceed.[113] However, the parties did not agree to specific emission reduction targets or to binding reduction commitments. There was also no agreement to impose requirements on developing countries.[114]

The primary topic discussed in 2008 at COP-14 and MOP-4 was the content of a treaty to replace Kyoto after 2012.[115] At COP-15 and MOP-5, held in Copenhagen, Denmark, in 2009, the major issues were the need to limit emissions from both developing and developed countries and how financial support would be provided to developing countries to mitigate the effects of GHG emissions.[116] As developing countries expand their gross domestic product, the potential increase in carbon emissions is tremendous. China, however, would not agree to reduce GHG emissions.[117] COP-15 ended with a nonbinding accord that calls for limiting the global temperature rise to below two degrees Celsius, and commits developed countries to help developing countries with mitigation actions.[118] Each country is to develop reduction targets, but there are no mandates or GHG reduction targets.[119] The accord calls for a $30 billion Green Climate Fund to support mitigation efforts in poor countries between 2010 and 2012, and the fund is to increase to $100 billion a year by 2020.[120]

COP-16 and MOP-6, held in Cancun, Mexico, in 2010, failed to achieve the commitments needed to slow the increase in atmospheric GHG concentrations or to make meaningful progress in creating a replacement for the Kyoto Protocol.[121] The parties created a Green Climate Fund (GCF) to be the operating entity of the financial mechanism under Article 11 of the Convention, but left the details concerning its implementation to be the subject of subsequent meetings. The GCF had a target of raising $100 billion a year by 2020, but as of September 2011, only $11.3 billion had been transferred to an account in the GCF.[122]

COP-17 and MOP-7 was held in Durban, South Africa, in 2011.[123] The parties agreed to develop "a protocol, another legal instrument or an agreed outcome with legal force" by 2015 that can be implemented beginning in 2020, and they agreed to temporarily extend the Kyoto Protocol for another five to eight years through amendments to be adopted at the 2012 meeting in Doha, Qatar.[124] However, the developed nations and the developing nations are so divided in their views that a binding agreement to reduce emissions is unlikely to be produced anytime in the foreseeable future. The Durban Platform does not mention the 2007 Bali Action Plan, which called for separate negotiations for developed and developing nations, and it says almost nothing about the content of what is to be included in a new agreement. Moreover, it does not appear that the current positions of the parties would limit global warming to no more than two degrees Celsius. Even if a commitment was included in a new agreement, there does not appear to be any mechanism for assuring effective compliance.[125]

The Durban Conference did result in approval of a governing agreement needed to launch the GCF to help poorer countries adapt to climate change and to acquire clean energy technologies.[126] The GCF will operate under the UNFCCC through a board with 24 national representatives plus one private sector representative of a developed country and one private sector representative of a developing country. In addition, two civil society representatives will be active observers. The fund plans to raise $100 billion a year by 2020.[127] It receives about $3 billion a year from the United States, but the funding in 2012 is inadequate to accomplish a great deal.[128]

B. 2012 Actions

The 18th COP to the UNFCCC met from November 26 to December 7, 2012, in Doha, Qatar. A preliminary meeting in Bonn, Germany, ended May 25, 2012, with the delegates approving an outline of the agenda for a treaty to reduce GHGs beginning in 2020.[129] A rough draft of a second Kyoto Protocol commitment period was produced on September 5, 2012, at a meeting in Bangkok, but little progress was made.[130] The parties in Doha approved a second commitment period to run from 2013 through 2020. The meeting approved amendments to continue legally binding GHG targets, but they only encompass about 15 percent of global emissions. Moreover, Japan, Russia, and Canada will not participate. Even this limited agreement will not enter into force until ratified by three-quarters of the parties.[131]

On June 20–22, 2012, the U.N. Conference on Sustainable Development took place in Rio de Janeiro.[132] This conference, known as Rio+20, resulted in a seven-part document that sets out a "common vision" that is strong on aspirations, but makes few commitments.[133] The outcome document reaffirms the principle of "common but differentiated responsibilities," which has been a major contributor to the failure of the Kyoto Protocol.[134] Issues concerning climate change were a minor part of Rio+20, which was focused more broadly on sustainability efforts.[135] The United States pledged $2 billion to support sustainable development and clean energy projects, but such funding may or may not materialize.[136]

Most environmental organizations consider Rio+20 to be a failure.[137] The most important weakness of the outcome document is its avoidance of any serious discussion of the role of population growth in driving climate change. The document recognizes that the world's population is projected to exceed nine billion by 2050, but its recommendation is to "increase our efforts to achieve sustainable development."[138] The discussion of population related issues is limited to calling for "universal access to reproductive health, including family planning."[139]

The document reaffirms that "climate change is one of the greatest challenges of our time."[140] But it provides only aspirational platitudes rather than guidance for those dealing with the issue. Finally, the document fails to address the exacerbation of climate change created when populations living in poverty that collectively have small GHG emissions industrialize and begin to rapidly increase their GHG emissions.

VI.   International Efforts to Control Black Carbon

Black carbon is not regulated by the Kyoto Protocol or by any other international law because it is an aerosol, not a GHG.[141] EPA estimates that black carbon deposited on snow and ice has a larger impact on climate change than methane, but is not as important as carbon dioxide.[142] Black carbon is formed by the incomplete combustion of fossil fuels, biofuels, and biomass."[143] In the United States, black carbon is estimated to be about 12 percent of the fine particulate ($PM_{2.5}$) emissions.[144] Black carbon has climate effects that are more regional and have a shorter duration than most GHGs, which means that strategies to reduce black carbon emissions can provide benefits in the next several decades.[145]

Unlike CO_2, more than 75 percent of black carbon emissions come from developing countries in Asia, Latin America, and Africa. In these regions, most black carbon emissions result from the use of cookstoves and open biomass burning.[146] In developed nations, most emissions come from mobile diesel engines.[147]

The U.S. Department of State, on February 16, 2012, announced the Climate and Clean Air Coalition to Reduce Short-Lived Climate Pollutants.[148] The United States, Bangladesh, Canada, Ghana, Mexico, and Sweden are working with the United Nations Environment Programme in an international effort to target short-lived climate pollutants.[149] The targeted pollutants are black carbon, methane (a primary component of natural gas), and hydrofluorocarbons.[150] Black carbon control efforts are primarily directed at the stoves widely used in Africa, Asia, and Latin America for cooking.[151] The initiative seeks to develop national action plans to build capacity among developing nations to deal with these pollutants.

VII.   Conclusion

Case law is unlikely to have a meaningful role in the development of an international response to air pollution or climate change. The release of air pollutants usually provides benefits to a polluter because the atmosphere can be used as a low-cost disposal site for the unwanted residuals created by their economic activity. Nations protect their citizens and their economy by using claims of sovereignty to allow injury from air pollutants to downwind countries and to the planet. The possibility of using courts to prevent nations from releasing air pollutants and GHGs is remote.

The development of international agreements to deal with conventional and toxic air pollutants has not been an important factor in dealing with these substances. This is unlikely to change. But, at least in developed nations, sustained progress in controlling these substances has been and continues to be made through the application of domestic legislation. The most important success by the international community in dealing with air pollutants has been the reduction in emissions that adversely affect the ozone layer based on the requirements imposed by the Montreal Protocol. This success is unlikely to be duplicated in the efforts to address climate change. The Montreal Protocol had to deal primarily with a small number of companies producing chemicals that deplete stratospheric ozone, and alternative chemicals were available that can be substituted for some of the most harmful chemicals regulated under the protocol.

Dealing with climate change is much more complex than dealing with stratospheric ozone depletion, and requires the participation of many nations. Development of international law on this subject will evolve slowly as nations negotiate and participate in international agreements. The pace of international legal developments is hampered by the unwillingness of nations to limit their options or their sovereign powers. Moreover, the structure of the U.N. negotiating process allows a relatively small number of nations to prevent agreements because the system's decision making is consensus based. The Kyoto Protocol and the many agreements to modify or interpret it have not arrested the growth of GHG emissions. Unless a catastrophic event occurs, international law is unlikely to result in enforceable GHG restrictions being imposed.

Notes

1. Japan, for example, has adopted legislation intended to target emissions of nitrogen oxide that are a particular problem around large cities. The law imposes requirements on certain classes of motor vehicles and authorizes a local authority to take necessary measures to address the pollution. *See* chapter 39, Japan, in this volume. Similarly, China's air pollution law mandates that operations in areas exceeding ambient standards, known as "control" areas, must obtain emissions permits. *See* chapter 37, China.

2. The Netherlands is one country where emission limitations are imposed based on the source category. *See* chapter 32, Netherlands, section II (discussing the Environmental Management Act of 2004).

3. The EU Emissions Trading System (ETS) is a prime example. *See* chapter 31, Italy, section I.B (discussing Italy's implementation of a cap-and-trade system limiting GHG emissions). As a further example under domestic law, South Korea is slated to implement a domestic GHG emissions trading scheme in 2015. *See* chapter 40, South Korea, section II.

4. For example, EU Directive (IED) 2010/75/EC on Industrial Emissions requires implementation of "best available techniques" as a condition to permit certain operations. The requirement is incorporated into domestic implementing legislation. *See* chapter 29, Germany, section II (Air and Climate Change).

5. 3 U.N.R.I.A.A. 1905 (1941) reprinted at 35 Am. J. Int'l L. 684 (1941).

6. *See* Treaty between the United States and Great Britain Relating to Boundary Waters, and Questions Arising between the United States and Canada, 36 Stat. 2448 (entered into force May 5, 1910), *available at* http://www.ijc.org/rel/agree/water.html (last visited Aug. 29, 2012).

7. Trail Smelter Case, 3 U.N. Rep. Int'l Awards, 1905, 1945–46 (1949).

8. J. Read, *The Trial Smelter Dispute*, Canadian Y.B. Int'l L. 213 (1963), reprinted in David Hunter, James Salzman, & Durwood Zaelke, International Environmental Law and Policy 544 (3d ed. 2007).

9. United States v. Canada, Arbitration Tribunal 1941, 3 U.N. Rep. Int'l Arb. Awards (1941).

10. *Id.*

11. Corfu Channel (United Kingdom v. Albania), 1949 I.C.J. 4 (Judgement Apr. 9, 1949); Lac Lanoux (France v. Spain) 24 I.L.R. 101 (1957).

12. C/E Res. 71(5), 19 E.Y.B. 263 (Mar. 26, 1971).

13. Report of the U.N. Conference on the Human Environment, U.N. Doc. A/CONF: 48/14/Rev.1 at 3 (1973), U.N. Doc. A/CONF:48/14 at 2 and Corr. 1 (1972), 11 I.L.M. 1416 (1972).

14. UNGS Res. 2994 (Dec. 15, 1972).

15. Edith Brown Weiss et al., International Environmental Law and Policy 282 (2d ed. 2007).

16. *See* http://www.oecd.org (last visited Sept. 28, 2012).

17. OECD Council, Recommendation on Principles Concerning Transfrontier Pollution (with Annex), adopted 14 November 1974, 1974 O.E.C.D. C224, O.E.C.D. 142, *reprinted in* 14 I.L.M. 242 (1975).

18. OECD Council Recommendation for the Implementation of a Regime of Equal Right of Access and Nondiscrimination in Relation to Trans-Frontier Pollution (with Annex), adopted 17 May 1977. 1977 O.E.C.D. C(77)28, O.E.C.D. 150; *reprinted in* 16 I.L.M. 977 (1977).

19. Second International Conference on the Protection of the North Sea, London, 24–25 November 1987.

20. *See generally* ARNOLD W. REITZE, JR., AIR POLLUTION CONTROL LAW: COMPLIANCE AND ENFORCEMENT 252 (2001).

21. The U.S.–Canada Memorandum of Intent Concerning Transboundary Air Pollution, Aug. 5, 1980, 32 U.S.T. 2521 with annex (entered into force Aug. 5, 1980). T.I.A.S. No. 9856, *reprinted in* 20 I.L.M. 690 (1981).

22. 613 F. Supp. 1472, 1476 (D.D.C. 1985).

23. 42 U.S.C. § 7415.

24. Thomas v. New York, 802 F.2d 1443, 1446 (D.C. Cir. 1986), *cert. denied*, 482 U.S. 919 (1987).

25. 5 U.S.C. § 551(4).

26. 802 F.2d at 1447.

27. 912 F.2d 1525 (D.C. Cir. 1990).

28. 42 U.S.C. § 7651c.

29. 42 U.S.C. §§ 7651–7651g.

30. Canada–United States Air Quality Agreement (Mar. 13, 1991), *reprinted in* 30 I.L.M. (1991), *available at* http://www.ec.gc.ca/Air/default.asp?lang=En&n=1E841873-1 (last visited June 25, 2012).

31. *Available at* http://www.ec.gc.ca/air/default.asp?lang=En&n=FA26FE79-1 (last visited Oct. 14, 2012).

32. *Id.*

33. Environment Canada, Canada–United States Air Quality Agreement: 2010 Progress Report ISDM-444 (2010). *See also* U.S. Dep't of State, Progress under United States-Canada Air Quality Agreement to Reduce Emissions of Pollutants in Border Region (Nov. 19, 2009), http://www.state.gov/r/pa/prs/ps/2009/nov/132173.htm (last visited Aug. 29, 2012).

34. This agreement entered into force on February 16, 1984, *reprinted in* 22 I.L.M. 1025 (1983).

35. *Available at* http://www.epa.gov/border2012/docs/LaPazAgreement.pdf (last visited Aug. 22, 2012).

36. *Id.*

37. *Id.*

38. *Available at* http://www.whitehouse.gov/sites/default/files/omb/oira/irc/united-states-mexico-high-level-regulatory-cooperation-council-work-plan.pdf (last visited Aug. 22, 2012).

39. *Available at* http://www.epa.gov/border2020/ (last visited Sept. 28, 2012).

40. U.S. Envtl. Prot. Agency, U.S.-Mexico Border 2020, Goals and Objectives, http://www2.epa.gov/border2020/ (last visited Sept. 28, 2012).

41. *Id.*

42. *Id.*

43. *Id.*

44. UNECE, The 1979 Geneva Convention on Long-range Transboundary Air Pollution, http://www.unece.org/env/lrtap/lrtap_h1.html (last visited Aug. 20, 2012).

45. 13 U.N.T.S. 10,541, *reprinted in* 18 I.L.M. 1442 (1979).

46. UNECE, Status of Ratification of the 1979 Geneva Convention on Long-range Transboundary Air Pollution as of 24 May 2012, http://www.unece.org/env/lrtap/status/lrtap_st.html (last visited Aug. 20, 2012).

47. LRTAP art. 11.

48. Adopted at Brussels, 15 July 1980, L229 O.J.E.C. 30 (1980).

49. Directive 2001/80/EC of the European Parliament and of the Council of 23 October 2001 on the limitation of emissions of certain pollutants into the air from large combustion plants.

50. *Available at* http://www.unece.org (last visited Oct. 14, 2012).

51. *Id.*

52. *Reprinted in* 27 I.L.M. 707 (1988).

53. UNECE, Status of the Convention on Long-range Transboundary Air Pollution and its Related Protocols as of 15 May 2012, http://www.unece.org/fileadmin/DAM /env/documents/2012/air/Status_of_the_Covention.pdf (last visited Oct. 14, 2012).

54. EDITH BROWN WEISS ET AL., INTERNATIONAL ENVIRONMENTAL LAW AND POLICY 513 (2d ed. 2007).

55. Protocol to the 1979 Convention on Long-Range Transboundary Air Pollution Concerning the Control of Emissions of Nitrogen Oxides or Their Transboundary Fluxes Concluded at Sofia 31 October 1988. Entered into force February 14, 1991. EB.Air/21; *reprinted in* 28 I.L.M. 212 (1989).

56. Protocol Concerning the Control of Emissions of Nitrogen Oxides or Their Transboundary Fluxes art. 4 (Feb. 14, 1991).

57. Protocol on the Control of Emissions of Volatile Organic Compounds or Their Transboundary Fluxes, 31 I.L.M. (1992).

58. The Protocol Concerning the Control of Emissions of Volatile Organic Compounds (VOCs) or Their Transboundary Fluxes (Sept. 29, 1997), http://www.unece.org /fileadmin/DAM/env/lrtap/full%20text/1991.VOC.e.pdf (last visited Aug. 17, 2012).

59. UNECE, Status of Ratification of the 1991 Geneva Protocol Concerning the Control of Emissions of Volatile Organic Compounds or Their Transboundary Fluxes As of 24 May 2012, http://www.unece.org/env/lrtap/status/91v_st.html (last visited Aug. 20, 2012). Note that some UNECE documents say there are 23 parties, other documents say there are 24.

60. UNECE, The 1994 Oslo Protocol on Further Reduction of Sulphur Emissions, 33 I.L.M. 1540 (1994), http://www.unece.org/env/lrtap/fsulf_h1.html (last visited Aug. 15, 2012).

61. The status of ratification as of May 11, 2012, is available at http://www.unecc .org/env/lrtap/status/94s_st.html (last visited Aug. 15, 2012).

62. Adjustments to Annex II to the 1984 Oslo Protocol on Further Reduction of Sulfur Emissions, Annex II, Sulphur Emission Ceilings and Percentage Emission Reductions (amended Dec. 2007).

63. *Available at* http://www.unece.org/env/lrtap/hmt_h1.html (last visited Oct. 14, 2012).

64. UNECE, Status of Ratification of the 1998 Aarhus Protocol on Heavy Metals as of 14 May 2012.

65. EB.AIR/1998/2; *reprinted in* 37 I.L.M.505 (1998).

66. UNECE, Protocol on Persistent Organic Pollutants (POPs) art. 3(5), http://www .unece.org/env/lrtap/pops_h1.html (last visited Aug. 20, 2012).

67. UNECE, Status of Ratification of the 1998 Aarhus Protocol on Persistent Organic Pollutants (POPs) as of 14 May 2012, http://www.unece.org/env/irtap/status/98pop _st.html (last visited Aug. 20, 2012).

68. UNECE, Protocol on Persistent Organic Pollutants (POPs), http://www.unece .org/env/lrtap/pops_h1.html (last visited Aug. 20, 2012).

69. Protocol to the 1979 Convention on Long-Range Transboundary Air Pollution to Abate Acidification, Eutrophication and Ground-Level Ozone, http://www.unece.org /fileadmin/DAM/env/lrtap/full%20text/1999%20Multi.E.Amended.2005.pdf (last visited Aug. 19, 2012).

70. UNECE, The Protocol to Abate Acidification, Eutrophication and Ground-level Ozone, http://www.unece.org/env/lrtap/multi_h1.html (last visited Aug. 20, 2012).

71. Status of Ratification of the 1999 Gothenburg Protocol to Abate Acidification, Eutrophication and Ground-level Ozone as of 24 May 2012, http://www.unece.org/env/lrtap/status/99multi_ST.HTML (last visited Aug.18, 2012).

72. UNECE, Draft decision on amending the text of and annexes II to IX to the Gothenburg Protocol to Abate Acidification, Eutrophication and Ground-level Ozone and the addition of new annexes X and XI, http://www.unece.org/fileadmin/DAM/env/documents/2012/EB/ECE_EB_AIR_2012_L2_E.pdf (last visited Aug. 19, 2012).

73. ASEAN, Agreement on Transboundary Haze Pollution, June 10, 2002, http://haze.asean.org?page_id=185 (last visited Aug. 30, 2012).

74. *Id.*

75. Liz Gooch, *Malaysia Haze Points to a Regional Problem*, N.Y. TIMES, June 23, 2012, http://www.nytimes.com/2012/06/24/world/asia/smoky-haze-over-malysia-signals-a-regional-problem.html?_r=1 (last visited Aug. 30, 2012).

76. Edith Brown Weiss, *Substances That Deplete the Ozone Layer* (Sept. 16, 1987), http://legal.un.org/avl/pdf/ha/vcpol/vcpol_e.pdf (last visited Aug. 30, 2012).

77. UNEP, ENVIRONMENTAL EFFECTS OF OZONE DEPLETION 1998 ASSESSMENT (1998).

78. The Vienna Convention for the Protection of the Ozone Layer, Mar. 22, 1985, 1513 U.N.T.S. 323 (1988); 26 I.L.M. 1529 (1987). This convention entered into force on Sept. 22, 1988.

79. *Id.* art. 2(a) & (b).

80. *Id.* art. 6 & 8.

81. 26 I.L.M. 1550 (1987).

82. Montreal Protocol art. 16.

83. Montreal Protocol art. 2.

84. Montreal Protocol, pmbl., arts. 2, 2A-2I.

85. Vienna Convention for the Protection of the Ozone Layer art. 6, 1513 U.N.T.S. 323 (1988).

86. Vienna Convention for the Protection of the Ozone Layer art. 9(3), 9(4), 26 I.L.M. 1529 (1987).

87. *Id.* art. 2(9)(a).

88. Montreal Protocol art. 2(9)(c), 26 I.L.M. 1550 (1987).

89. CAA § 614, 42 U.S.C. § 7671m.

90. UNEP, Twenty-Fourth Meeting of the Parties to the Montreal Protocol on Substances That Deplete the Ozone Layer (Nov. 22, 2012).

91. UNEP, HANDBOOK FOR THE MONTREAL PROTOCOL ON SUBSTANCES THAT DEPLETE THE OZONE LAYER 3 (9th ed. 2012).

92. For the list of the MOPs and the reports see http://ozone.unep.org/new_site/en/committee_documents.php?committee_id=1 (last visited Sept. 2, 2012).

93. U.N. Framework Convention on Climate Change, 1771 U.N.T.S. 164 (1992), *reprinted in* 31 I.L.M. 849.

94. UNFCCC, Background on the UNFCCC: The International Response to Climate Change, http://unfccc.int/essential_background//items/6031.php (last visited Sept. 9, 2012).

95. U.N. Framework Convention on Climate Change, *supra* note 93, art. 4.2(b).

96. *Id.* art. 4.7.

97. The annual meetings are discussed in more detail at Arnold W. Reitze, Jr., *Global Warming*, 32 ENVTL. L. 369 (ELI) (2002), and Arnold W. Reitze, Jr., *Federal Control of Greenhouse Gas Emissions*, 40 ENVTL. L. (ELI) 1261 (2011).

98. United Nations, Conference of the Parties to the Framework Convention on Climate Change, Kyoto Protocol to the United Nations Framework Convention on Climate Change, U.N. Doc. FCCC/CP/1992/L.7/Add.1 (1997), *reprinted in* 37 I.L.M. 22. Amend-

ments to the FCCC are allowed as provided in articles 15 and 16 of the UNFCCC; protocols may be adopted as provided by article 17 of the UNFCCC.

99. *Id.* art. 3.1. The GHGs are CO_2, CH_4, N_2O, HFCs, PFCs, and SF_6.

100. *Id.* arts. 4, 6, 12, and 17, 37 I.L.M. 34, 35, 38, and 40.

101. Kyoto Protocol to the United Nations Framework Convention on Climate Change, adopted Dec. 10, 1997, U.N. Doc. FCCC/CP/1997/7/Add.237 I.L.M. 22 (hereinafter Kyoto Protocol).

102. U.N. Framework Convention on Climate Change, *Report of the Conference of the Parties on its fourth session, Held at Buenos Aires from 2 to 14 November 1998* (Jan. 25, 1999), http://unfccc.int/2860.php (search for report COP-4) (last visited Sept. 10, 2012).

103. John R. Justus & Susan R. Fletcher, Cong. Res. Serv., Global Climate Change (summary, Oct. 29, 2004).

104. UNFCCC, The Marrakesh Accords & the Marrakesh Declaration, http://unfccc .int (last visited Sept. 10, 2012).

105. *See* UNFCCC, Global Environment Facility (May 22, 2009) [GEF/LDCF/SCCF.6 /Inf.3], http://unfccc.int (last visited Sept. 10, 2012).

106. UNFCCC, *Report of the Conference of the Parties on its eighth session, Held at New Delhi From 23 October to 1 November 2002*, http://unfccc.int (last visited Sept. 10, 2012).

107. *Id.* at 3; *see also Summary of the Eighth Conference of the Parties to the U.N. Framework Convention on Climate Change 23 October-1 November 2002*, 12 Earth Negotiations Bull. 209:1, 13 (Int'l Inst. for Sustainable Dev. Nov. 4, 2002).

108. UNFCCC, *Report of the Conference of the Parties on its eleventh session, Held in Montreal from 28 November to 10 December 2005*, http://unfccc.int (last visited Sept. 11, 2012).

109. Eric J. Lyman, *U.N. Conference Agrees to Open Discussions on What Will Follow Initial Five-Year Period*, 36 Env't Rep. (BNA) 2565 (Dec. 16, 2005). *See also* Eric J. Lyman, *Conference Participants Note Increasing Attention on Adaptation as Weather Worsens*, 36 Env't Rep. (BNA) 2566 (Dec. 16, 2005); Eric J. Lyman, *Agreement on Carbon Capture, Storage May Set Stage for Formal U.N. Recognition*, 36 Env't Rep. (BNA) 2567 (Dec. 16, 2005).

110. UNFCCC, *Report of the Conference of the Parties on its thirteenth session, held in Bali from 3 to 15 December 2007*, http://unfccc.int (last visited Sept. 11, 2012).

111. *Deal on Adaptation Funds Hailed as Key "Breakthrough" of Bali Talks*, XVIII Clean Air Rep. (Inside EPA) 26:12 (Dec. 27, 2007).

112. *See* http://www.thegef.org/gef/whatisgef (last visited Oct. 14, 2012).

113. COP-13, *supra* note 110, Decision 1/CP.13.

114. Daniel Pruzin, *Intergovernmental Panel Elects New Board, Adopts Program for Next Assessment Report*, 39 Env't Rep. (BNA) 1823 (Sept. 12, 2008).

115. UNFCCC, *Report of the Conference of the Parties on its fourteenth session, held in Pozan from 1 to 12 December 2008*, http://unfccc.int (last visited Sept. 11, 2012).

116. UNFCCC, *Report of the Conference of the Parties on its fifteenth session, held in Copenhagen from 7 to 19 December 2009*, http://unfccc.int (last visited Sept. 11, 2012).

117. COP15 Agreement, http://unfccc.int (last visited Sept. 13, 2012).

118. UNFCCC, *Report of the Conference of the Parties on its fifteenth session, held in Copenhagen from 7 to 19 December 2009*, http://unfccc.int (last visited Sept. 13, 2012).

119. Ctr. for Climate & Energy Solutions, http://www.c2es.org/search/common ?text=COP15 (last visited Sept. 28, 2012).

120. *Id.*

121. UNFCCC, *Report of the Conference of the Parties on its sixteenth session, held in Cancun from 29 November to 10 December 2010*, http://unfccc.int (last visited Sept. 13, 2012).

122. UNFCCC, Cancun Agreements, http://unfccc.int/meetings/cancun_nov_2010 /items/6005.php last visited Sept. 19, 2012).

123. UNFCCC, *Draft report of the Conference of the Parties on its seventeenth session*, Dec. 7, 2011, http://unfccc.int.

124. Doug Obey, *Negotiators in Durban Buy Time for Future Climate Change Deal*, 22 CLEAN AIR REP. (Inside EPA) 26:29 (Dec. 22, 2011). The reports may be accessed at http://unfccc.int/meetings/durban_nov_2011/session/6294/php/view/reports.php (last visited Sept. 13, 2012).

125. D. Bodansky, *The Durban Platform Negotiations: Goals and Options*, HARV. PROJECT ON CLIMATE AGREEMENTS (July 2012).

126. Dean Scott, *Divisions Remain Over Kyoto Extension In Upcoming U.N. Climate Talks, Stern Says*, 42 Env't Rep. (BNA) 2665 (Nov. 25, 2011).

127. Eric J. Lyman, *U.N. Talks in Bonn Aim to Make Progress on Unfinished Work From Durban Summit*, 43 ENV'T REP. (BNA) 1279 (MAY 18, 2012).

128. Dean Scott, *International Shipping Seen as Potential Source of Funding for Climate Adaptation*, 43 Env't Rep. (BNA) 1404 (June 1, 2012).

129. Lyman, *Talks in Bonn, supra* note 127.

130. Eric J. Lyman, *Bangkok Talks Yield Draft for Post-2012 Period in Preparation for Doha Summit*, 43 Env't Rep. (BNA) 2256 (Sept. 7, 2012).

131. CTR. FOR CLIMATE & ENERGY SOLUTIONS, OUTCOMES OF THE U.N. CLIMATE CHANGE CONFERENCE IN DOHA, QATAR (2012).

132. United Nations, *Report of the United Nations Conference on Sustainable Development Rio de Janeiro, Brazil, 20–22 June 2012*, http://www.uncsd2012.org (last visited Sept. 19, 2012).

133. Murray Griffin & Michael Kepp, *Rio+20 Summit Defines Global To-Do List But Ends with Few Solid Commitments*, 43 Env't Rep. (BNA) 1702 (June 29, 2012).

134. *Id.* ¶ 15.

135. Michael Kepp, *Organizations Pledge $513 Billion to Finance Sustainability Efforts, Rio+20 Official Says*, 43 Env't Rep. (BNA) 1703 (June 29, 2012).

136. Avery Fellow, *U.S. Government Pledges $2 Billion to Global Sustainability Efforts at Rio+20*, 43 Env't Rep. (BNA) 1704 (June 29, 2012).

137. Michael Kepp, *While Some Criticize Rio+20 as Toothless, Others Praise Idea-Sharing, Commitments*, 43 Env't Rep. (BNA) 1705 (June 29, 2012).

138. *Id.* ¶ 21.

139. *Id.* ¶¶ 145 & 241.

140. *Id.* ¶ 190.

141. Steven Ferry, *The Failure of International Global Warming Regulation to Promote Needed Renewable Energy*, 37 B.C. ENVTL. AFF. L. REV. 67, 103 (2010).

142. U.S. ENVTL. PROT. AGENCY, EPA-450/R-12-001, REPORT TO CONGRESS ON BLACK CARBON 4 (Mar. 2012) [hereinafter BLACK CARBON].

143. *Id.* at 1.

144. *Id.*

145. *Id.* at 5.

146. *Id.* at 6.

147. BLACK CARBON, supra note 142, at 6.

148. *See* http://www.state.gov/r/pa/prs/ps/2012/02/184055.htm (last visited Sept. 17, 2012).

149. BLACK CARBON, supra note 142, at 7.

150. *Id.* at 3.

151. Tina Casey, *In Fight Against Global Warming, U.S. Declares War on Cook Stoves*, TPM (Feb. 21, 2012), http://idealab.talkingpointsmemo.com/2012/02/in-fight-against-global-warming-us-declares-war-on-cook-stoves.php (last visited Sept. 17, 2012).

CHAPTER 6

Water

ALEXANDRA DAPOLITO DUNN AND KIRK TRACY

I. Introduction

The next war may well be over water, not oil.[1] This speaks of the essential nature of water to global society. Seventy percent of the Earth's surface is covered by water; our bodies are 60 percent water.[2] And yet there is a finite supply of water on Earth. Of all the water on the planet, less than 4 percent is freshwater (most of which is frozen in glaciers or otherwise inaccessible).[3] The remainder is salt water, which supports many ecosystems but generally is not fit for drinking or agricultural purposes. While desalination plants are on the rise around the world,[4] the process can be controversial due to its energy intensity, high cost, ecosystem impacts, and waste stream management issues.[5]

Water law and regulation in most nations attempts to balance and manage many competing interests and uses for surface water and groundwater—including human consumption, agricultural applications, recreational uses, navigation, waste assimilation, and ecosystem support. Managing water requires analysis and control of pollutant levels through modeling and monitoring, study and management of instream flows and diversions, and assessment of impacts to aquatic life and human health—often over decades. In many nations, laws and regulations addressing human consumption of water are public health oriented, while water resource and quality laws are more focused on ecosystem health. As such, legal practitioners generally must identify and become familiar with diverse systems, protocols, and governmental authorities to fully embrace water law and regulation.[6]

This chapter sets forth foundational water law guideposts that will help practitioners ask the right questions and identify legal and regulatory structures that define a nation's approach to water governance. This chapter covers four broad topics in international water law: water quality, water quantity, management and use, and water rights and equity. This chapter also lists the key international laws and policies relative to water quality and quantity. This chapter discusses both surface water and groundwater topics, with recognition that legal systems treat them separately based on historical, scientific, administrative, and other factors.

II. Water-Quality-Based Approaches
to Water Governance

Many nations manage water in terms of its quality,[7] and through water quality regulation the impacts on ecosystems and public health can be mitigated and addressed. The quality of water is impacted by a variety of pollutants, the most common of concern being sediment,[8] nitrogen and phosphorus,[9] pathogens,[10] toxics, bioaccumulatives,[11] and synthetics.[12] The types of pollutants most likely to be found in a nation's waters, or those pollutants most likely to adversely impact humans or the aquatic ecosystem, drive the method of regulation. Regulatory approaches may focus on the pollutant(s), the sources and industries most likely to discharge them, special requirements to protect high-quality waters or unique regional or national water resources, or a combination of these and other factors.

Some of the primary approaches to protecting water quality are the use of prohibitions, permitting, and liability. For example, under the United States' Clean Water Act (CWA), all discharges of pollutants to waters of the United States are prohibited unless authorized via a permit that delineates permissible discharges and related conditions. The system is implemented via a cooperative federalism approach where states are delegated the federal program and carry it out under state law that mirrors the federal law—and that can be more stringent.[13] The U.S. system combines strict liability with an authorization mechanism. Another approach is a non-permitting-based liability system. Legislation in China in 2008 established individual liability for companies and company officials for water pollution and toxic spills. The law shifted economic liability for actual damage and cleanup costs to corporate polluters who previously would have faced only administrative penalties, which were largely unrelated to the severity of the pollution.[14] This Chinese law follows the polluter pays principle, a widely accepted doctrine that puts liability for pollution on the entity emitting the pollution into the environment; it is one of the primary principles of environmental law in the European Union.[15] However, recent studies and examples have shown that the polluter pays principle alone has only had a slight impact on pollution behaviors. Instead, alternative pollution control approaches, including the use of a combination of methods (e.g., beneficiary pays, subsidies, and targeted enforcement), should be—and are being—considered.[16]

Another fundamental guidepost in the water quality area is the state (subnational)/federal (national) relationship. For example, in the United States, the CWA's water quality programs are driven by a careful balance between state and federal authorities. In Australia, the Commonwealth has passed national legislation and developed federally led programs, but successful implementation of integrated water management programs has also required state legislation.[17] South Africa, however, has a more federally focused approach, with a system grounded on a constitutional right to water. In this system, the constitution more closely guides the actions of municipal water services authorities and the judiciary has played a strong role in developing the normative jurisprudence of the country's water laws.[18] Mexico also utilizes a strong national approach in addressing water quality issues. There, the National Water Law of 1992 set forth a legal framework for all water usage and hence all water policy.[19] This legislation authorizes the federal government to develop and enforce environmental regulations and technical standards pertaining to water pollution.[20]

Economics play a significant role in the area of water quality. In the United States, the first level of water pollution control is set in terms of technology—expressed and applied through the U.S. Environmental Protection Agency's (EPA) development of effluent limitation guidelines (ELGs), which are one of the few places the law allows costs to be explicitly considered in determining the most accessible baseline technology by the applicable industry sector.[21] Economic factors are also used to regulate water pollution in other ways, such as water quality trading, which creates a market for pollutant (nontoxic) exchanges, allowing sources that can more cost-effectively reduce discharges exchange with others whose reduction comes at a higher cost.[22]

Since not all water pollution comes from industrial sources, many nations have regulatory approaches to managing and controlling diffuse sources of water pollution such as urban storm runoff, snow melt, and agricultural runoff. For example, in the United States under the CWA, municipal stormwater generally is subject to best management practice controls, such as street sweeping, catch basins, and settlement ponds.[23] The United States also requires states to implement management plans for nonpoint source pollution.[24] In the European Union (EU), all water pollution is covered under the EU Water Directive, also known as the Water Framework Directive (WFD). The WFD was passed in 2000 as a combined approach of both pollution control at the source and environmental quality standards. The WFD is a cross-border approach to water protection organized around river basin districts, is applicable to point and diffuse sources, and uses a combination of best available technology (BAT) requirements, emission limits, or, for diffuse impacts, best practices requirements.[25] The WFD incorporated preexisting directives, such as the 1991 directive concerning urban wastewater treatment and the 1991 Nitrates Directive concerning agricultural sources.[26] Under the Nitrates Directive, which is still operative under the WFD, EU member states are required to develop and implement action programs for managing the application of nitrogen fertilizers.[27] In Brazil, a substantial increase in agricultural activity has driven increased use of fertilizer and pesticides. A 2012 UNEP overview on nutrient management addressed the nutrient runoff problem in Latin America, taking a specific look at Brazil, one of the two Latin American countries with the highest fertilizer use (Mexico is the other).[28] Though current legislation in Brazil seeks to prevent contaminants in fertilizers, there is no policy in place to regulate the excessive use of fertilizers themselves, thus leaving open the issue of excessive nutrient runoff in that country.[29]

Water quality law can also incorporate mechanisms intended to prevent degradation of clean water, remediate poor water quality, and ensure that pollutants do not exceed a water body's assimilative capacity. The U.S. CWA requires states to include as a component of their water quality standards an antidegradation policy to maintain the quality of waters classified as high quality.[30] As a component of broader water quality standards—which aim to both remediate and protect—antidegradation policy is implemented through state plans for protecting water quality based on protection of existing uses, when evaluating activities that may impact water quality.[31] The U.S. CWA also includes an assimilative capacity tool called a total maximum daily load (TMDL), which allocates a set amount of pollutant loading across sources as a way to remediate a water body that has been negatively impacted by water pollution.[32] The Quantity Regulation in South Korea similarly sets a water quality standard for a body of water and then grants a cap on the quantity of point source contaminants in the respective area, to protect against pollution on a watershed scale.[33] Another comparable regulation is the EU Nitrates Directive, which provides a framework for managing fertilizer application rates based on a total amount of nitrogen applied per hectare depending on categories of agricultural activity.[34] The Nitrates Directive has a general goal of protecting water quality in both rivers and coastal waters through reduction of nitrogen fertilizer application across the EU.[35] This broad regulation, if implemented as intended, would result in both remediation of polluted waters and protection of high-quality water bodies.

III.   Water Quantity

Another foundational element of water law is water quantity and supply. Given the finite supply of water, most nations, states/provinces, and localities govern surface water and groundwater withdrawals, water usage for industrial activities, and water impoundments such as dams and reservoirs. Until the past century or so, water management has historically focused on quantity and not quality, due in part to a lack of scientific understanding, but also due to the fact that access to water and the right to control diversions were historically of primary concern in water-scarce nations.[36] The earliest water laws were focused on rights to use water and to control diversions sufficiently to avoid flooding neighbors.[37] Even where water was scarce, commercial interests including navigation and agricultural uses predominated over water quality concerns, and in arid regions water was often treated as a communal good to be used to benefit society.[38] As a result, countries that have shifted to a water quality focus without adapting their water governance structures have struggled to morph a quantity-focused regulatory framework into a quality-focused system.[39] Thus, a historical perspective must be kept in mind when assessing the varied legal frameworks for water quantity management.[40]

In the United States, regulation of water quantity historically relates to a right to put the water to a consumptive use—water rights are property rights protected by the U.S. Constitution.[41] Two basic systems of defining the right to use water establish the pillars under which water rights are analyzed, with numerous variants on the two themes existing across the nation and in other countries.[42] The first concept is known as riparianism, based on the English rule of "natural flow," which entitles riparian owners (owners of land that border a water body) to equally share in use of the water.[43] Under the traditional English rule, no change to the quantity or quality of the flow was permitted. Land was not a good to be used, but instead was a private estate to enjoy (although from the earliest days there were allowances for domestic uses). Once consumptive uses became more prevalent—especially during the industrial revolution—the riparian system began to be modified and has more modernly adapted to variants such as reasonable-use riparianism.[44] Depending on the state or nation regulating the body of water, various rules on permissible and reasonable uses have been adopted, including a crucial question of what uses are classified as reasonable.[45] South Africa's National Water Act of 1998 sought to fundamentally reform the existing riparian distribution system in favor of a more equitable and sustainable allocation of water resources.[46] The Act imposes a licensing requirement for water use, placing authority for allocation in the hands of the Minister of Water.[47] Exceptions to licensed use under the Act include both reasonable domestic use and the continuation of existing lawful uses.[48] However, the implementation of the Act has yet to gather significant momentum, and thus South Africa's water use remains primarily determined by adjacent land use.[49]

The other basic concept in the U.S. governance of water rights is the system of prior appropriation—a system where the right is based on use of water, not on ownership of the land.[50] This system dominated the landscape of the western United States starting in the mid-1800s, initially serving mining demands for water, and later as a way to encourage settlement by granting water usage rights on a first-come, first-served basis.[51] Under the system of prior appropriation, instream natural flow is unowned initially and is held by the state for acquisition by users. Users acquire the right by taking the water and putting it to beneficial use, often requiring a nonwasteful diversion out of stream.[52] Chile's 1981 Water Code, a leading example of a free-market approach to water law and economics, created a similar system of consumptive use allocations based on establishing a property right at a certain point in time and added the authority to freely trade those water rights.[53] The water code fully severed water rights from land ownership and deemed them to be freely tradable, similar to real estate. Under this policy, the free market determines use and allocation of water.[54] Although the Chilean system may not identically match the prior appropriation system of the western United States, it generally represents the same concept of a right to consumptive use that takes precedence over other users.

It is worth noting that groundwater has historically been treated separately, based on lacking scientific understanding of the hydraulic connection between ground and surface waters.[55] Groundwater may be governed under a wide variety of legal systems, from the English Rule of Capture, under which the first user to control the water could put it to whatever use they want, to numerous variations of prior appropriation, riparianism, and concepts of reasonable use designed to share the resource among multiple possible users.[56] As more and more scientific evidence has arisen to show the connection between groundwater and surface waters—and thus a connection between groundwater and total water supply—legal systems of governing water rights have struggled to adapt, often retaining seemingly archaic notions of separate rights over the two water sources because of inability to change the legal system. Perhaps the most extensive use of groundwater occurs in India, home to roughly 30 million groundwater extraction structures.[57] Historically, the common law property system in India considered groundwater as an easement connected to the land.[58] In 1970, the Indian Central Government created the "Model Bill" as a pathway to the reformation of Indian water law.[59] The bill acknowledges the need for a statutory framework that gives the states more control to address groundwater depletion via the establishment of a groundwater authority.[60] In recent years, revisions to the bill have failed to incorporate a modern scientific understanding of the challenges involved in sustainable groundwater management and therefore have failed to stem worsening supply issues.[61] In practice, states have been slow in following the model bill and adopting their own groundwater legislation, thus India stands to face significant challenges in the upcoming years as groundwater extraction and depletion continue to rise.[62] In contrast, Australia has instituted a more aggressive groundwater management strategy in recognition of the importance of protecting this fragile resource. Most state agencies in Australia allocate entitlements based on existing supply, which is determined and updated through continual scientific observation.[63] This method aims to avoid overextraction of groundwater resources by ensuring that entitlements correspond to the actual availability of water resources.[64]

The impact of human activity on water flows is significant, as there is not a nation in the world without dams or impoundments. The allocation of water from these structures is governed by local, state, or national policy, and often has far-reaching impacts on patterns of societal development. The largest use of freshwater worldwide is irrigation, which accounts for 70 percent of total freshwater withdrawals.[65] In the western United States, major dam construction has been federally financed under the Reclamation Act of 1902,[66] which targeted delivering irrigation water to farmers, thus encouraging settlement of lands previously viewed as unusable, promising water to farmers under the prior appropriation system. The reclamation program supplies over 20 percent of the water for irrigated land in the western 17 states and for over 50 percent of the land in those states irrigated by surface water.[67] The reclamation program was designed to have water users repay the costs of the dams through rate payments, but the farmers have never repaid the full cost of the projects and some estimates put the total federal subsidies at 75 to 81 percent.[68] Federal spending policy and support for the prior appropriation doctrine have heavily influenced both water and land use in the western United States. Similarly, Ethiopia's plan to construct the Grand Ethiopian Renaissance Dam embodies that nation's determination to harness the Blue Nile through aggressive dam-building policy to compensate for the significant energy shortage facing its population.[69] The project has its fair share of controversy as the Nile's downstream riparian users may suffer impeded flows as a result of the project.[70] China has also pursued an aggressive dam-building policy. Since 1950, China has constructed over half of the world's large dams.[71] The world's leading producer of hydroelectricity, China shows no signs of slowing dam construction as they plan to expand dam-building activities to transboundary rivers and far distant countries. These aspirations have faced little obstruction from environmental or political concerns.[72]

As competing uses have continued to struggle for water rights and various nations have recognized the ecological benefits of maintaining a quantity of water instream, water quantity management in many locations has become an issue of scale—maintaining flow in a single stream, or managing large-scale diversions. Different governance systems have been developed to manage instream flows and diversions. These can be either state-based (e.g., New York State Department of Environmental Conservation rules to establish a permitting, registration, and reporting system for water withdrawals of 100,000 gallons or more per day[73]), regional (e.g., the Canada-United States Great Lakes agreements that make ecosystem use a top priority over consumptive uses[74]); or national (e.g., the Chinese government's management of everything from design, finance, and construction to environmental impacts and population resettlement of the Three Gorges Dam on the Yangtze River in China[75]).

Water quantity is also managed through water conservation efforts. In the United States, conservation efforts are promoted in concept at the federal level, but the actual development of policies and regulations to achieve such conservation is implemented by the states and localities. Mechanisms to address water conservation include building codes for water-efficient buildings, irrigation protocols, and reclaimed/recycled water initiatives and projects. To address indoor water use, the Energy Policy Act, enacted in 1992, establishes minimum water efficiency standards for faucets, toilets, urinals, and other fixtures.[76] EPA's WaterSense program enables partnerships with utilities, state and local governments, and nonprofit organizations to promote water efficiency through informative labeling of water-efficient products, financial incentives (discounts and rebates), and certifications of newly built homes.[77] Although U.S. federal laws also address stormwater runoff, some issues remain for localities to manage and regulate directly. Following examples from Germany and parts of Switzerland, U.S. state and municipal laws have been established requiring or encouraging green roofs, which reduce stormwater runoff while adding energy and aesthetic benefits to the building.[78] Other innovative municipal ordinances around the country have been implemented in efforts to reduce water used for irrigating laws, promote groundwater recharge, and requiring on-site management of stormwater.[79] As consciousness has been raised about water shortages, concepts of sustainable, equitable, and reasonable use of water have emerged and can impact water law. Local conditions often force such an increase of awareness. Australian water law, for example, has been heavily influenced by impacts of drought and climate change. For decades, attempted intergovernmental water management arrangements failed to prevent problems such as salinity, overallocation of water resources, and environmental degradation.[80] In the 1990s, reform efforts used a basin-wide management approach, including the sharing of water between states, interstate transfers of water entitlements, caps on water allocations, water pricing reform, and allocation of water sufficient for environmental purposes[81]—many of these regulatory tools promote conservation. Subsequent regulations have built on these initial reforms and the country is now moving toward an integrated management approach that "optimises economic, social and environmental outcomes."[82] The concepts surrounding the right to use water (a water quantity issue) are slowly changing to systems of water management, as discussed in the following section.

Population growth will have a tremendous impact on water quantity in the future and is already stressing supplies in many nations. Nations are working together in new ways to deal with water supply issues, such as in the recent Colorado River agreement between Mexico and the United States.[83] Under the agreement, the two nations agreed to a new system of sharing water during both high- and low-flow periods to better accommodate the needs of each nation.[84] Current population growth estimates project that India will overtake China as the world's most populous country by the year 2025.[85] This substantial growth will engender further dependency on India's already strained freshwater resources. Amidst this backdrop, India's Supreme Court has sought to prioritize allocation of water for basic needs by reading into the Indian Constitution an individual's right to "pollution-free water" and "safe drinking water."[86] This policy acknowledges a paucity of water resources and commands that these rights be met even at the cost of other development programs.[87] However, the state governments of India ultimately determine the water supply function, so actual rights-based water allocation based on the Supreme Court's directive may lack a concrete remedy for the individual to pursue.[88] China expects demand for water to parallel population growth in its arid north region.[89] To ensure that the northern region's quantity needs will be met, China has implemented the South-North Water Transfer Project (SNWTP), designed to transfer approximately 45 billion cubic meters of water per year from China's more water-rich areas to meet the growing demand around the Beijing-Tianjin region.[90] The project represents an audacious attempt to evenly distribute China's bountiful yet asymmetrically dispersed freshwater supplies.

IV.   Management and Use

Another significant aspect of water law is a nation's approach to water system management, which envelopes water quality and quantity concerns within a larger management framework. More sophisticated water laws tend to shift away from a fragmented approach (e.g., management of a single water body, or a single regulatory parameter) toward the goal of managing water comprehensively. The most common approach used today is watershed management, in which the focal point is the entire land area that drains to a common water source. Watershed management is a challenging approach because watershed boundaries often differ from political boundaries. An emerging and prevailing management concept is that of integrated water resource management (IWRM). IWRM seeks to manage water in a broader societal context, taking into account goals of economic efficiency, social equity, and sustainability.[91] It tends to adopt a more participatory approach to management of water, and often entails implementation through land use controls.[92] A primary feature of IWRM is that any new demands for water must be viewed as a potential constraint on existing uses to meet environmental and social equity demands.[93] This largely European philosophy is making its way into North America and the rest of the world,[94] in part because European donor nations have required countries to implement IWRM as the price for aid.[95]

The EU Water Framework Directive[96] is an "ecosystem approach," based on IWRM principles,[97] which requires EU members to analyze ecological characteristics of different water types, review the impact of human activity on the status of surface waters and groundwater, and to conduct an economic analysis of water use.[98] The WFD "necessitates a river basin management approach and calls for cross-border cooperation."[99] This comprehensive approach was implemented in Holland through a management system of water boards responsible for water quality, including wastewater treatment, in addition to their core responsibility of flood protection.[100]

In 2008, the government of India published the Common Guidelines for Watershed Development Projects to provide a fresh framework for the next generation of watershed programs.[101] The guidelines eschew a top-down approach to watershed management in favor of community participation and organizational restructuring at the national, state, district, and project levels.[102]

The financing of water and wastewater infrastructure is a significant issue in water law, particularly because the source of funding can lead to ownership and equity issues. In the United States, for example, the federal government maintains, and states implement, revolving loan funds authorized by the CWA,[103] which allow communities to borrow funds for water and wastewater infrastructure projects on local government-friendly terms. In other nations, where massive capital investment is needed to build facilities and transportation systems, governments lacking such funds have turned to private capital. While some have hailed privatization as the wave of the future, it has often created equity issues for the poor (discussed further in the next section).[104] Various finance mechanisms have been utilized to encourage private investment. In the Philippines, for example, to better finance water development goals, the Philippine government, along with the U.S. Agency for International Development and its Japanese counterpart, JICA, set up the Philippines Water Revolving Fund (PWRF) to convince private banks to lend to water projects.[105] The fund has helped finance various water projects, many of which have been exclusively paid for by private financial institutions.[106]

Another evolving aspect of water management and use is regulation of the quantity of water used in industrial applications.[107] Increasingly, nations are struggling to adopt laws, policies, and regulations concerning the volume of water that can be diverted or compromised to produce energy, such as at nuclear power plants or for natural gas extraction.[108] In the United States, for example, Colorado is currently leading the way in adapting laws and regulations to adjust to the unique water resource pressures by the oil and gas industry. Colorado's efforts to focus broadly on the hydrologic impacts of water produced from all types of oil and gas development have led to industry investment in compliance resources.[109] Canada lays claim to the largest reserves of bitumen (heavy crude oil) in the world, spurring the fast-growing oil sands industry. Extracting bitumen from the oil sands can be a water-intensive operation.[110] As a result, strict water usage regulations apply, including daily limits for withdrawals and the regular monitoring of surface water and groundwater.[111] In China, the government has set specific targets on the quantity of water to be used by industries in order to limit excessive consumption. A 2012 new water management decree issued by the State Council will set quotas on individual industries; an industrial user exceeding its quota may have its business permit revoked.[112] This policy has the capacity to significantly affect China's coal industry. Producing one ton of coal can take upwards of 3,000 gallons of water, and most of China's coal plants are located in the arid north.[113] Disclosure of an industry's consumptive use of water is also bringing societal and purchasing pressure to bear on this subject around the world.[114]

V.   Water Rights and Equity

Life cannot exist without water. In light of that basic fact, a framework for treating access to water as a human right and matter of equity has emerged at both the international and national levels. Although it is a foundational principle of international law that water is a sovereign national resource, nations have put into practice, in a variety of ways, the principle that all people have a fundamental right to water. Over 60 constitutions around the world refer to environmental obligations, although only the South African Bill of Rights explicitly grants a right to access to sufficient water to live.[115] Where there is a lack of environmental provisions in a nation's constitution, international courts have relied on a basic right to life (found in most constitutions) to impart some level of environmental rights, including a right to water.[116] In addition to constitutional interpretations, some scholars argue that an obligation to provide adequate domestic water supplies can be found in several international treaties, including the 1989 Convention on the Rights of the Child, the 1979 Convention on the Elimination of All Forms of Discrimination Against Women, and the 1949 Geneva Convention.[117]

Alternatively, countries have turned to policy measures to ensure accessible water for their citizens. In Bolivia, for example, the government, in cooperation with financial institutions such as the International Monetary Fund and the World Bank, launched a nationwide project to privatize water systems in an effort to inject much needed capital into a system that suffered from high costs and access issues (although the effort was quickly scrapped by the government in the face of protests over hefty price increases).[118] Similar privatization efforts have struggled with issues of inequity; in a context in which demand does not often reflect a willingness to pay, but instead an ability to pay, water purveyors face difficulty recovering the full cost of delivering water while meeting social objectives of universal access to water.[119] In other places around the world, people continue to drink contaminated water, despite the availability of clean tap water, because the privatized systems deliver clean water at an unaffordable market rate. There continues to be a large discrepancy between drinking water treatment and sanitation in the developing versus the developed world. A 2008 WHO report estimated that only 53 percent of the population in developing countries in 2006 had access to improved sanitation facilities.[120] The report also noted that, as of 2006, 16 percent of the population in developing countries gets drinking water from unimproved sources as compared to only 1 percent of people in developed regions.[121] Funding constraints and policy are the main drivers for these statistics.

Viewing access to water as a human right raises the question of who can own water. In some nations, such as Israel, water is held in the commons and cannot be owned.[122] Instead, the government manages and allocates usage rights.[123] In others, such as the western United States, entities can have rights to use water in certain amounts, sometimes to the detriment of downstream users, with the right to use often considered a property right.[124] As discussed in section III, above, the right to own water implies the right to consume water to the detriment of another. In nations where water is scarce, this can quickly lead to basic human rights and equity issues.

The human rights framework also raises the question of prioritization of water uses. Water law can embody important policy choices, such as prioritization of drinking water and related human consumptive uses over other types of water uses such as agriculture or the volume of water needed to support key ecosystems. As discussed in section III, water management approaches like IWRM attempt to take a holistic view of the hydrological cycle and allocate water based on considerations of environmental and social equity.

As population growth and climate change continue to rise as key water stressors, their impacts adversely affect water equity.[125] Climate change will leave poor communities highly vulnerable to water shortages as they lack the ability to adapt quickly.[126] As regions of low income and high population growth become exposed to more extreme weather events, significant shifts in water resource availability may be expected and patterns of human migration could be affected.[127]

VI.   Relevant International Law and Policy[128]

A.   Harmon Doctrine

The Harmon Doctrine is synonymous with the doctrine of "absolute territorial sovereignty," in which upstream users have the right to do whatever they want with water in their territory, regardless of downstream impacts. The name originates from an 1895 opinion prepared by the U.S. attorney general, Judson Harmon, regarding a dispute with Mexico over the use of waters of the Rio Grande.[129] The doctrine has been repudiated and replaced by the principle of limited territorial sovereignty, in which "All states bordering a watercourse have a right to participate in the use of the resource."[130]

B.   Helsinki Rules and Berlin Rules

The Helsinki Rules are a series of general principles of international water law, summarized by the International Law Association (ILA).[131] The most basic principle of the Helsinki Rules is that each state in an international drainage basin is entitled to a reasonable and equitable share in the beneficial uses of the waters of that basin.[132] The Helsinki Rules have no legal force of their own, but have widely been recognized as having substantial influence on international water law and disputes between nations.[133] Article V, section II of the rules provides a list of relevant factors for determining what is a "reasonable and equitable" share. The rules cover surface water and groundwater that is hydrologically connected.[134] In 1986, the ILA adopted the Seoul Rules on the Law of International Groundwater Resources, to extend the principle of equitable use to international aquifers not connected to international surface waters.[135] In 2004, the ILA updated and incorporated the Helsinki Rules and the Seoul Rules into the Berlin Rules, most of which are applicable to all surface waters and groundwater, other than marine waters, regardless of whether they are found in an international drainage basin.[136]

C.   U.N. Global Agreements

In 1997, the U.N. General Assembly adopted the Convention on the Law of the Non-navigational Use of International Watercourses.[137] This agreement urged Watercourse states to utilize international watercourses in an equitable and reasonable manner.[138] Although the Convention has not yet entered into force,[139] its principles primarily reflect customary international law and its provisions "can be instructive in assessing the sufficiency of other international watercourse agreements."[140] This includes recommending a holistic approach to using an international watercourse that mandates consideration of the needs and dependencies of other users.[141]

On August 3, 2010, the United Nations General Assembly adopted Resolution 64/292 on the human right to water and sanitation. The resolution calls on states and international organizations to provide financial resources and technology in order to aid efforts to provide safe, clean, accessible, and affordable drinking water and sanitation especially.[142]

Also of recent significance is the globalization of the U.N. Economic Commission for Europe's Convention on the Protection and Use of Transboundary Watercourses and International Lakes.[143] The Convention requires parties to "prevent, control and reduce transboundary impact, use transboundary waters in a reasonable and equitable way and ensure their sustainable management," including provisions requiring bordering parties to work cooperatively.[144] The Convention was initially negotiated in 1992 as a regional instrument, but was amended in 2003 to allow all United Nations member states to join.[145] The amendments entered into force on 6 February 2013, making the Convention a "global legal framework for transboundary water cooperation."[146]

Notes

1. *See* STEVEN SOLOMON, WATER: THE EPIC STRUGGLE FOR WEALTH, POWER, AND CIVILIZATION (2010); *see also* Peter H. Gleick, *Water Conflict Chronology*, Global Policy Forum, http://www.globalpolicy.org/images/pdfs/Security_Council/conflictchronology .pdf (last updated Nov. 10, 2008) (inventory of water conflicts going back to 3000 BC).

2. U.S. Geological Surv., How Much Water Is There on, in, and Above the Earth?, http://water.usgs.gov/edu/earthhowmuch.html (last modified May 10, 2013); U.S. Geological Surv., The Water in You, http://water.usgs.gov/edu/propertyyou.html (last modified Apr. 30, 2013).

3. U.S. Geological Surv., How Much Water Is There on, in, and Above the Earth?, http://water.usgs.gov/edu/earthhowmuch.html (last modified May 10, 2013).

4. Vaughan Scully, *Desalination, for a World Short of Water*, BLOOMBERGBUSINESS-WEEK (May 21, 2008), http://www.businessweek.com/stories/2008-05-21/desalination -for-a-world-short-of-waterbusinessweek-business-news-stock-market-and-financial -advice. See desalination statistics at Int'l Desalination Ass'n, Desalination by the Numbers, http://www.idadesal.org/desalination-101/desalination-by-the-numbers/(last visited May 12, 2013).

5. ROBERT GLENNON, UNQUENCHABLE: AMERICA'S WATER CRISIS AND WHAT TO DO ABOUT IT 155 (2009) (noting large amounts of energy required for desalination); KEN MIDKIFF, NOT A DROP TO DRINK: AMERICA'S WATER CRISIS (AND WHAT YOU CAN DO ABOUT IT) 138 (2007) (discussing high costs of desalination and various environmental harm caused by desalination waste discharges); Matthew C. Lewis, Comment, *Thirsty for Change: Desalination as a Practical and Environmentally Friendly Answer to California's Growing Water Shortage*, 44 U.S.F. L. REV. 933, 937 (2010) (discussing impingement and entrainment of large and small organisms, respectively, by desalination water intakes); Robin Kundis Craig, *Water Supply, Desalination, Climate Change, and Energy Policy*, 22 PAC. MCGEORGE GLOBAL BUS. & DEV. L.J. 225, 242 (2010) (noting challenges with the waste brine stream from desalination).

6. In the United States, the term "water quality" often refers to criteria for non-drinking uses, and is mostly regulated under the Clean Water Act (CWA), while drinking water standards are established and governed under the Safe Drinking Water Act (SDWA).

7. *See, e.g.*, Env't Can., Water Quality Objectives and Guidelines, http://www.ec .gc.ca/eau-water/default.asp?lang=En&n=F77856A7-1 (last modified Nov. 1, 2010) ("In Canada, governments use various measures to protect water quality."); David N. Cassuto

& Rômulo S. R. Sampaio, *Water Law in the United States and Brazil—Climate Change & Two Approaches to Emerging Water Poverty*, 35 WM. & MARY ENVTL. L. & POL'Y REV. 371,401 (discussing Brazil's national water management system goals of preserving both water quality and quantity); Dep't Water Aff. & Forestry, WQM in SA, http://www.dwa.gov .za/Dir_WQM/wqmFrame.htm (last visited May 12, 2013) (discussing South Africa's water quality management framework).

8. "Water quality is affected by changes in nutrients, sedimentation, temperature, pH, heavy metals, non-metallic toxins, persistent organics and pesticides, and biological factors, among many other factors." UNEP, CLEARING THE WATERS: A FOCUS ON WATER QUALITY SOLUTIONS 11 (2010), http://www.unep.org/PDF/Clearing_the_Waters.pdf.

9. "Globally, the most prevalent water quality problem is eutrophication, a result of high-nutrient loads (mainly phosphorus and nitrogen), which substantially impairs beneficial uses of water." UNESCO, THE UNITED NATIONS WORLD WATER DEVELOPMENT REPORT 3: WATER IN A CHANGING WORLD 138 (2009), http://webworld.unesco.org/water /wwap/wwdr/wwdr3/pdf/WWDR3_Water_in_a_Changing_World.pdf.

10. WORLD HEALTH ORG., ANIMAL WASTE, WATER QUALITY AND HUMAN HEALTH, at vii-x (Al Dufour et al. eds., 2012), *available at* http://www.zaragoza.es/ciudad/medio ambiente/onu/en/detallePer_Onu?id=487.

11. The EU Water Framework Directive of 2000 requires the identification of priority hazardous substances, based on persistence, bioaccumulation, and toxicity. Council Directive 2000/60/EC, 2000 O.J. (L 327) arts. 2(29), (30), 16(3) (EC) [hereinafter WFD], *available at* http://eur-lex.europa.eu/LexUriServ/LexUriServ.do?uri=OJ:L:2000:327:0001:0072:en: PDF; *Report from the Commission to the European Parliament and the Council on the outcome of the review of Annex X to Directive 2000/60/EC of the European Parliament and of the Council on Priority Substances in the Field of Water Policy* 3, COM (2011) 875 final (Jan. 31, 2012), *available at* http://ec.europa.eu/environment/water/water-dangersub/pdf/com_2011_875.pdf. Mercury and pesticides are two well-known bioaccumulating, toxic, and highly persistent substances, which accumulate in fish and other organisms high on the food chain. *See* UNESCO, *supra* note 9, at 139, 144.

12. Pharmaceuticals and personal care products present a new challenge for water quality management. U.N. WATER, POLICY BRIEF: WATER QUALITY 2 (2011), http://www .unwater.org/downloads/waterquality_policybrief.pdf.

13. JOEL M. GROSS & KERRI L. STELCEN, CLEAN WATER ACT 27–38 (2d ed. 2012).

14. *Water Pollution: New Chinese Law Will Hold Companies, Officials Financially Liable for Water Pollution*, 31 BNA Int'l Env't Rep. 212 (Mar. 5, 2008).

15. Directive 2004/35/CE of the European Parliament and of the Council of 21 April 2004 on Environmental Liability with Regard to the Prevention and Remedying of Environmental Damage, 2004 O.J. (L 143) 56, 56.

16. UNESCO, *supra* note 9, at 62, 140, 145; *see generally* JANIS D. BERNSTEIN, ALTERNATIVE APPROACHES TO POLLUTION CONTROL AND WASTE MANAGEMENT (1993).

17. Paul Kildea & George Williams, *The Constitution and the Management of Water in Australia's Rivers*, 32 SYDNEY L. REV. 595, 598–99 (2010); Louis J. Kotze & Rebecca Bates, *Similar But Different: Comparative Perspectives on Access to Water in Australia and South Africa*, 15 U. DENV. L. REV. 221, 255 (2012).

18. Kotze & Bates, *supra* note 17, at 236–37, 242–45, 266–67.

19. Vivienne Bennett & Lawrence A. Herzog, *U.S.-Mexico Borderland Water Conflicts and Institutional Change: A Commentary*, 40 NAT. RES. J. 973, 981 (2000).

20. Keith Pezzoli, *Environmental Management Systems (EMSS) and Regulatory Innovation*, 36 CAL. W. L. REV. 335, 343 (2000).

21. U.S. EPA, Industrial Regulations, http://water.epa.gov/scitech/wastetech/guide /industry.cfm (last updated Apr. 20, 2013).

> Effluent guidelines are national standards for wastewater discharges to sur-face waters and publicly owned treatment works (sometimes called munici-pal sewage treatment plants). [EPA] issue[s] effluent guidelines for catego-ries of existing sources and new sources under Title III of the Clean Water Act. The standards are technology-based (i.e. they are based on the perfor-mance of treatment and control technologies); they are not based on risk or impacts upon receiving waters.

Id.

22. *See* Alexandra Dapolito Dunn & Elise Bacon, *Doing Water Quality Credit Trading Right*, Nat. Res. & Env't, Summer 2005, at 43; Alexandra Dapolito Dunn, *Water Quality Trading: Bringing Market Forces to Bear in Watersheds*, Nat. Res. & Env't, Fall 2002, at 137.

23. CWA § 402(p), 33 U.S.C. § 1342(p); U.S. EPA, National Menu of Stormwater Best Management Practices, http://cfpub.epa.gov/npdes/stormwater/menuofbmps/ (last updated Apr. 03, 2012 5:01 PM).

24. CWA §§ 208, 319; 33 U.S.C. §§ 1288, 1329.

25. Council Directive 2000/60/EC, 2000 O.J. (L 327) 40 & art. 10 (EC), *available at* http://eur-lex.europa.eu/LexUriServ/LexUriServ.do?uri=OJ:L:2000:327:0001:0072:en:PDF.

26. WFD art. 10.

27. European Comm'n, EU Nitrates Directive (Jan. 2010), http://ec.europa.eu/envi-ronment/pubs/pdf/factsheets/nitrates.pdf.

28. M.A. Sutton et al., Our Nutrient World: The Challenge to Produce More Food and Energy with Less Pollution 80–82 (2013), http://www.scopenvironment .org/Latest%20News/ONW.pdf.

29. *Id.* at 81.

30. CWA § 304(d)(4)(b); *see also* U.S. EPA, Water Quality Standards Handbook—Chapter 4: Antidegradation (40 C.F.R. § 131.12), http://water.epa.gov/scitech/swguidance /standards/handbook/chapter04.cfm (last updated Oct. 24, 2012).

31. *Id.*

32. CWA § 303(d); *see* Oliver A. Houck, *TMDLs III: A New Framework for the Clean Water Act's Ambient Standards Program*, [1998] 28 Envtl. L. Rep. (Envtl. L. Inst.) 10,415, 10,419–20.

33. *See* chapter 40, South Korea, section III (discussing South Korea's water pollu-tion control laws).

34. Council Directive 91/676/EEC, 1991 O.J. (L 375), *available at* http://eur-lex .europa.eu/LexUriServ/LexUriServ.do?uri=CELEX:31991L0676:EN:NOT.

35. European Comm'n, EU Nitrates Directive (Jan. 2010), *available at* http:// ec.europa.eu/environment/pubs/pdf/factsheets/nitrates.pdf.

36. Joseph L. Sax et al., Legal Control of Water Resources: Cases and Materi-als 15 (4th ed. 2006); History, Water and Air Pollution, http://www.history.com/topics /water-and-air-pollution (last visited May 14, 2013); *see* Peter H. Gleick, *Water Conflict Chronology*, Global Policy Forum, http://www.globalpolicy.org/images/pdfs/Security _Council/conflictchronology.pdf (last updated Nov. 10, 2008) (inventory of water con-flicts going back to 3000 BC).

37. Itzchak E. Kornfeld, *Mesopotamia: A History of Water and Law, in* The Evolution of the Law and Politics of Water 21, 23 (Joseph W. Dellapenna & Joyeeta Gupta eds., 2008) (discussing some of the earliest written laws, which were about water).

38. Joyeeta Gupta & Joseph W. Dellapenna, *The Challenges for the Twenty-First Century: A Critical Approach*, *in* THE EVOLUTION OF THE LAW AND POLITICS OF WATER 391, 393 (Joseph W. Dellapenna & Joyeeta Gupta eds., 2008) (discussing the origins of water law in Mesopotamia, Islamic law, and Hindu law, and the need for early laws to promote cooperation for agriculture and development).

39. *See, e.g.*, Charles F. Wilkinson, *The Headwaters of the Public Trust*, 19 ENVTL. L. 425, 469 (1989) ("[A]lthough western water law has been modernized in some respects, prior appropriation presents a classic example of how the passage of time and a changed social consciousness can make legal rules archaic."); Christine A. Klein et al., *Modernizing Water Law: The Example of Florida*, 61 FLA. L. REV. 403, 468–71 (2009) (discussing challenges across the United States adapting state water laws to accommodate new uses).

40. Joseph W. Dellapenna & Joyeeta Gupta, *The Evolution of Global Water Law*, *in* THE EVOLUTION OF THE LAW AND POLITICS OF WATER 3, 9 (Joseph W. Dellapenna & Joyeeta Gupta eds., 2008) ("History shows that water law has developed in a highly contextual manner reflecting the historical, geographical and political contexts of the countries concerned.").

41. SAX ET AL., *supra* note 36, at 139.

42. *Id.* at 12–13.

43. *Id.* at 37–39.

44. *Id.* at 29, 32–33.

45. *Id.* at 29, 32–33.

46. National Water Act 36 of 1998 § 2 (S. Afr.), *available at* http://www.info.gov.za /view/DownloadFileAction?id=70693.

47. *Id.* § 3.

48. *Id.* § 4.

49. Lee Godden, *Water Law Reform in Australia and South Africa: Sustainability, Efficiency and Social Justice*, 17 J. ENVTL. L. 181, 201 (2005).

50. SAX ET AL., *supra* note 36, at 124.

51. *See id.* at 330–35.

52. *Id.* at 124–26; *see also* Carl J. Bauer, *Dams and Markets: Rivers and Electric Power in Chile*, 49 NAT. RES. J. 583, 596, 601 (2009) (discussing Chile's system of consumptive use allocations).

53. Bauer, *supra* note 52, at 596, 598–99.

54. *Id.* at 600.

55. SAX ET AL., *supra* note 36, at 393–94.

56. *Id.* at 415–17.

57. PHILIPPE CULLETT ET AL., WATER CONFLICTS IN INDIA: TOWARDS A NEW LEGAL AND INSTITUTIONAL FRAMEWORK 58 (2012), *available at* http://soppecom.org/pdf/3 Water%20conflicts%20in%20India.pdf.

58. *Id.* at 59.

59. *Id.* at 62.

60. *Id.*

61. *Id.* at 63.

62. *Id.* at 64.

63. Rebecca Nelson, *Instituting Integration: Findings of the Comparative Groundwater Law & Policy Program's Workshop 1*, at 4 (Water in the West, Working Paper No. 3, 2012), http://waterinthewest.stanford.edu/sites/default/files/RNelsonWorkingPaper3.pdf.

64. *Id.*

65. U.N. WATER, Statistics: Graphs & Maps: Water Use, http://www.unwater.org /statistics/statistics-detail/en/c/211204/ (last visited May 15, 2013).

66. 32 Stat. 388.

67. SAX ET AL., *supra* note 36, at 747.

68. *Id.* at 747–48.

69. Michael Hammond, *The Grand Ethiopian Renaissance Dam and the Blue Nile: Implications for Transboundary Water Governance* 1 (Global Water Forum, Discussion Paper No. 1307, 2013), http://www.globalwaterforum.org/wp-content/uploads/2013/02/The-Grand-Ethiopian -Renaissance-Dam-and-the-Blue-Nile-Implications-for-transboundary-water-governance -GWF-1307.pdf.

70. *Id.* at 2.

71. Peter H. Gleick, *Three Gorges Dam Project, Yangtze River, China, in* PETER H. GLEICK ET AL., THE WORLD'S WATER 2008–2009: THE BIENNIAL REPORT ON FRESHWATER RESOURCES 129 (2009), *available at* http://www.worldwater.org/data20082009/WB03.pdf.

72. *Id.*

73. Gerald B. Silverman, *New York Environment Department Issues Rules for Large Water Withdrawals*, BloombergBNA Daily Env't Report, Nov. 30, 2012 (on file with author).

74. A. Dan Tarlock, *Four Challenges for International Water Law*, 23 TUL. ENVTL. L.J. 369, 390–92 (2010).

75. Gleick, *supra* note 71, at 139.

76. Pub. L. No. 102-486, 106 Stat. 2776 (1992).

77. Alexandra Dapolito Dunn, *Water Use and Management in Buildings, in* THE LAW OF GREEN BUILDINGS: REGULATORY AND LEGAL ISSUES IN DESIGN, CONSTRUCTION, OPERA-TIONS, AND FINANCING 249, 253–54 (J. Cullen Howe & Michael B. Gerrard eds., 2010).

78. *Id.* at 259.

79. *Id.* at 263–64.

80. Paul Kildea & George Williams, *The Constitution and the Management of Water in Australia's Rivers*, 32 SYDNEY L. REV. 595, 598 (2010).

81. *Id.* at 598–99. Many of these reforms were implemented through state legislation, encouraged by financial incentives for states to do so. *Id.*

82. *Id.* at 599 (citing Water Act 2007 (Cth) ss 3, 20 (Austl.)).

83. Press Release, U.S. Dep't of Interior, Secretary Salazar Joins U.S. and Mexico Del-egations for Historic Colorado River Water Agreement Ceremony (Nov. 20, 2012), http:// www.doi.gov/news/pressreleases/secretary-salazar-joins-us-and-mexico-delegations-for -historic-colorado-river-water-agreement-ceremony.cfm.

84. Press Release, Int'l Boundary and Water Comm'n: United States and Mexico, Commission Signs Colorado River Agreement (Nov. 20, 2012), http://www.ibwc.state .gov/Files/Press_Release_112012.pdf.

85. *India Population "To Be Biggest,"* BBC NEWS (Aug. 18, 2004, 11:26 AM), http:// news.bbc.co.uk/2/hi/3575994.stm.

86. Videh Upadhyay, *Water Rights and the "New" Water Laws in India: Emerging Issues and Concerns in a Rights Based Perspective, in* INFRASTRUCTURE DEV. FIN. CO., INDIA INFRA-STRUCTURE REPORT 2011: WATER: POLICY AND PERFORMANCE FOR SUSTAINABLE DEVELOP-MENT 56, http://www.idfc.com/pdf/report/IIR-2011.pdf.

87. *Id.* at 57.

88. *Id.* at 58.

89. Scott Moore, *Issue Brief: Water Resource Issues, Policy and Politics in China*, BROOK-INGS (Feb. 12, 2013), http://www.brookings.edu/research/papers/2013/02/water-politics -china-moore.

90. *Id.*

91. *See* Tarlock, *supra* note 74, at 405–06.

92. Alfred R. Light, *The Intergovernmental Relations of Water Policy and Management: Florida-Holland Parallels*, 23 TUL. ENVTL. L.J. 279, 302 (2010); Tarlock, *supra* note 74, at 404

("Integrated Water Resource Management (IWRM) has been progressively adopted as the international water management standard.").

93. Tarlock, *supra* note 74, at 406.

94. *See* Light, *supra* note 92, at 291–93 (comparing Dutch water boards to Florida water management districts).

95. Tarlock, *supra* note 74, at 405.

96. Council Directive 2000/60/EC, 2000 O.J. (L 327), *available at* http://eur-lex.europa.eu/LexUriServ/LexUriServ.do?uri=CELEX:32000L0060:EN:HTML.

97. Tarlock, *supra* note 74, at 406 ("The 2000 European Union Water Framework Directive adopts IWRM. . . ."). *But see* Muhammad Mizanur Rahaman et al., *EU Water Framework Directive vs. Integrated Water Resources Management: The Seven Mismatches*, 20 Water Res. Dev. 565 (2004) (highlighting seven key discrepancies between IWRM and the WFD).

98. Victor N. de Jonge, *From a Defensive to an Integrated Approach*, *in* Water Policy in the Netherlands: Integrated Management in a Densely Populated Delta 36–37 (Stijn Reinhard & Henk Folmer eds., 2009).

99. World Wildlife Found., Rivers at Risk: Dams and the Future of Freshwater Ecosystems 36, http://assets.panda.org/downloads/riversatriskfullreport.pdf. All water pollution in the EU is covered under the WFD. *Id.* The WFD was a tool to streamline legislation in Europe, by replacing seven previous directives on different water pollution issues with one single directive that incorporated all of the provisions from those directives. European Comm'n, Introduction to the New EU Water Framework Directive, http://ec.europa.eu/environment/water/water-framework/info/intro_en.htm (last updated Sept. 21, 2012).

100. Light, *supra* note 92, at 291–92.

101. Gov't of India, Common Guidelines for Watershed Development Projects 5–6 (2008), http://dolr.nic.in/CommonGuidelines2008.pdf.

102. *Id.* at 10–11.

103. U.S. EPA, Clean Water State Revolving Fund, http://water.epa.gov/grants_funding/cwsrf/cwsrf_index.cfm (last updated July 31, 2012); U.S. EPA, Drinking Water State Revolving Fund (DWSRF), http://water.epa.gov/grants_funding/dwsrf/index.cfm (last updated Mar. 4, 2013).

104. Alexandra Dapolito Dunn & Erin Derrington, *Investment in Water and Wastewater Infrastructure: An Environmental Justice Challenge, a Governance Solution*, Nat. Res. & Env't, Winter 2010, at 3.

105. *Philippines Water Fund Revolves and Evolves*, 13(8) Global Water Intelligence (Aug. 2012), http://www.globalwaterintel.com/archive/13/8/general/philippines-water-fund-revolves-and-evolves.html.

106. *Id.*

107. *See* Jeffrey Rothfeder, Every Drop for Sale: Our Desperate battle Over Water in a World about to Run Out 8 (2001) (estimating that individual humans use less than 10 percent of the planet's freshwater, irrigation uses 60 to 70 percent, and industry consumes the rest); U.N. Water, Statistics: Graphs & Maps: Water Use, http://www.unwater.org/statistics/statistics-detail/en/c/211204/ (last visited May 15, 2013) (providing similar estimates). Paper, food production, textiles, and chemicals are among the most water-intensive (amount of water used per amount of product produced) industries. UNESCO, *supra* note 9, at 116.

108. *See* Christopher L. Thorne & William H. Caile, *Produced Water Extraction from Oil and Gas Wells: Implications for Western Water Rights*, Nat. Res. & Env't, Winter 2013, at 16 (discussing the need for states in the western U.S. to address water quantity ramifications

of oil and gas production and the historical struggle for water between farmers, miners, and growing cities).

109. *Id.* at 17.

110. *See generally* Gov't of Can., Natural Resources Canada, Oil Sands: A Strategic Resource for Canada, North America and the Global Market (Aug. 2011), http://www.nrcan.gc.ca/sites/www.nrcan.gc.ca/files/energy/pdf/eneene/pubpub/pdf/OS-brochure-eng.pdf.

111. *Id.*

112. *Government Issues Stark Warning*, China Water Risk (Mar. 13, 2012), chinawater risk.org/resources/analysis-reviews/government-issues-stark-warning/.

113. Scott Moore, *Issue Brief: Water Resource Issues, Policy and Politics in China*, Brookings (Feb.12, 2013), http://www.brookings.edu/research/papers/2013/02/water-politics-china-moore.

114. *See* Carbon Disclosure Project, Water Program, https://www.cdproject.net/water (last visited June 7, 2013).

115. Svitlana Kravchenko & John E. Bonine, Human Rights and the Environment: Cases, Law, and Policy 114 (2008).

116. *Id.; see* Dinah Shelton, *Human Rights, Health & Environmental Protection: Linkages in Law & Practice* 16 (World Health Org., Health & Human Rights Working Paper Series No. 1, 2002), http://www.who.int/hhr/information/en/Series_1%20%20Human_Rights_Health_Environmental%20Protection_Shelton.pdf.

117. Kravchenko & Bonine, *supra* note 115, at 118.

118. *Id.* at 123.

119. *Id.*

120. World Health Organization & U.N. Children's Fund Joint Monitoring Programme (JMP) for Water Supply and Sanitation, Progress on Drinking Water and Sanitation: Special Focus on Sanitation 7 fig. 2 (2008), http://www.who.int/water_sanitation_health/monitoring/jmp2008.pdf.

121. *Id.* at 23 fig. 20.

122. Richard Laster et al., *The Sound of One Hand Clapping: Limitations to Integrated Resources Water Management in the Dead Sea Basin*, 22 Pace Envtl. L. Rev. 123, 137 (2005).

123. *Id.*

124. Sax et al., *supra* note 36, at 330–35.

125. It should be noted that a 2009 UNESCO report indicates that while population growth is the major driver during early stages of development, rapid economic growth in a country that already has a large population is the largest driver of water demand growth because it coincides with improving lifestyles that demand more water. UNESCO, *supra* note 9, at 14.

126. *Id.* at 18.

127. *Id.*

128. *See also* chapter 49, Key Environmental Law Treaties and Agreements.

129. Stephen C. McCaffrey, *The Harmon Doctrine One Hundred Years Later: Buried, Not Praised*, 36 Nat. Res. J. 725, 727 (1996).

130. Dan Tarlock, Law of Water Rights and Resources § 11:4 (2013).

131. Int'l Law Ass'n, Report of the 52d Conference, Helsinki Rules on the Use of the Waters of International Rivers (1996).

132. Helsinki Rules art. IV; *see* Joseph Sax et al., Legal Control of Water Resources: Cases and Materials 891 (4th ed. 2006).

133. Sax et al., *supra* note 132, at 891 n.1.

134. Helsinki Rules art. II.

135. Int'l Law Ass'n, Report of the 62d Conference, Seoul Rules on International Groundwaters art. I (1986).

136. *Berlin Rules on Water Resources, in* Int'l L. Ass'n, Fourth Report of the Berlin Conference: Water Resources Law (2004), http://internationalwaterlaw.org /documents/intldocs/ILA_Berlin_Rules-2004.pdf; Sax et al., *supra* note 132, at 892.

137. World Wildlife Fed'n, Everything You Need to Know about the UN Watercourses Convention 1 (Jan. 2009), http://www.unwater.org/downloads/wwf _un_watercourses_brochure_for_web_1.pdf.

138. Convention on the Law of the Non-navigational Uses of International Watercourses, G.A. Res. 51/229, art. 5, U.N. Doc. A/51/869 (May 21, 1997), *available at* http:// www.undemocracy.com/A-51-869.pdf.

139. At the time of writing, the Convention had been ratified by 30 countries, five short of what is required for it to come into force. *Convention on the Law of the Non-Navigational Uses of International Watercourses*, U.N. Treaty Collection, http://treaties .un.org/Pages/ViewDetails.aspx?src=TREATY&mtdsg_no=XXVII-12&chapter=27& lang=en (last visited June 7, 2013, 5:30 PM).

140. Megan Matthews, *The Volta Convention: An Effective Tool for Transboundary Water Resource Management in an Era of Impending Climate Change and Devastating Natural Disasters?*, 41 Denv. J. Int'l L. & Pol'y 273, 297–98 (2013).

141. Convention on the Law of the Non-navigational Uses of International Watercourses, G.A. Res. 51/229, art. 6, sec. 1, U.N. Doc. A/51/869 (May 21, 1997), *available at* http://www.undemocracy.com/A-51-869.pdf.

142. G.A. Res. 64/292 ¶ 2, U.N. Doc. A/RES/64/292 (Aug. 3, 2010).

143. United Nations Convention on the Protection and Use of Transboundary Watercourses and International Lakes, Mar. 17, 1992, 1936 U.N.T.S. 269, *available at* http:// www.unece.org/fileadmin/DAM/env/water/pdf/watercon.pdf.

144. UNECE, Water Convention, http://www.unece.org/env/water/ (last visited July 23, 2013).

145. *Id.*

146. *Id.*

CHAPTER 7

Handling, Treatment, Transportation, and Disposal of Hazardous Materials

TZVI LEVINSON AND JENNIFER WILLS

I. Introduction

Chemicals are used throughout every sector of society and in greater quantities each year, particularly in developing countries and countries with economies in transition.[1] Chemicals benefit society but can harm human health and the environment if not handled, used, and disposed of properly. Countries of all development levels realize the economic benefits from chemicals. Since chemical use will continue to grow, governments will continue to focus on reducing their environmental and human impacts.[2]

The regulation of chemicals and hazardous substances on a domestic level or international level is complicated due to the number of chemicals in commerce and their vast global supply chain.[3] In understanding domestic regulation of chemicals, a primary issue is how the regulating country (e.g., country of import or manufacture) defines the chemical or substance at issue. For example, is it classified as a "hazardous chemical substance,"[4] "hazardous waste,"[5] "dangerous good,"[6] "substance,"[7] or pesticide? These definitions vary from country to country, and when exporting, it is important to know the importing country's approach.

Against this backdrop, this chapter seeks to sensitize practitioners to some of the most important international approaches, norms, and legal instruments governing chemical and hazardous waste management globally. Section II covers various treaties and agreements governing chemicals and hazardous substances that merit attention. Section III covers principles that may be embedded in various countries' domestic laws. Finally, section IV discusses the key features of domestic chemical and hazardous substance regulation, and certain substances and materials that have increasingly been the focus of new chemicals regulation.

II.   Treaties and Agreements Governing Chemicals and Hazardous Materials

A number of treaties establish certain norms and methods for cooperating in the management of chemicals and hazardous materials.

A.   NAFTA Commission for Environmental Cooperation (CEC)

In 1994 Mexico, the United States, and Canada negotiated the North American Free Trade Agreement (NAFTA).[8] The Sound Management of Chemicals program sets forth the goals of chemicals management in NAFTA member countries, and provides a mechanism for coordination among NAFTA chemical regulators. Goals of the program include developing better data and tools to monitor chemicals (e.g., developing an inventory in Mexico of industrial chemicals) and reducing the risks posed by certain chemicals of concern, such as mercury. In May 2012, the CEC convened the Chemicals Management Forum, which discussed the progress and future of the CEC Sound Management of Chemicals program and provided a medium for information sharing among participants.[9]

B.   Rotterdam Convention on the Prior Informed Consent Procedure for Certain Hazardous Chemicals and Pesticides in International Trade

The Rotterdam Convention is an agreement concerning the prior notification and consent to the international trade of hazardous chemicals and pesticides. The convention was adopted in 1998 and came into force in February 2004. As of August 2013, 153 states have joined the Rotterdam Convention.[10]

The Rotterdam Convention currently applies to a list of 43 substances (32 pesticide materials and 11 industrial materials). For each of the listed chemicals, parties receive a guidance document containing information about the risks of handling and use of the substance. Each party must then decide whether to allow, prohibit, or restrict the import of the listed chemical. All parties are obligated to ensure chemicals subject to the convention are not exported contrary to the decision of an importing party.[11] For chemicals that are not listed, parties are nonetheless obligated to inform the Convention Secretariat if a chemical is banned or restricted under national regulation, and such notifications are shared regularly with the other parties.[12] Such notifications play an important role in disseminating information on hazardous chemicals, and identifying candidates for listing under the convention.

C.   Stockholm Convention on Persistent Organic Pollutants

In 2001, under the Stockholm Convention on Persistent Organic Pollutants, countries agreed to reduce or eliminate a category of substances known as persistent organic pollutants (POPs) that are harmful to human health and the environment.[13] POPs are found all over the world and accumulate in living organisms, causing harmful and irreversible results. Various studies have found that POPs persist in the environment and are present in varying levels in human beings all over the world. These substances are not degradable, and over time they migrate from one environment to another. They accumulate both on land and in water, both in the place of their origin and in places around the world, remote from their areas of origin. Exposure to even low levels of these materials may trigger the development of cancer; damage the nervous, immune, and reproductive systems; and impede development.[14]

The Stockholm Convention originally targeted 12 chemicals, set forth in three separate lists. The convention proscribed different controls for those chemicals listed in each Annex:

- Parties are required to eliminate the production and use of chemicals listed Annex A, unless a specific exemption applies.[15] The import and export of Annex A chemicals is also restricted.
- Parties are required to restrict the production, use, import and export of chemicals listed in Annex B. Annex B sets forth the limited acceptable purposes for which listed POPs may be produced or used.[16]
- Unlike other POPs, Annex C chemicals are formed and released unintentionally. Parties agree to take measures to reduce or eliminate such releases of Annex C POPs.[17]

The Stockholm Convention instructs member states to prepare detailed action plans to minimize or eliminate releases of Annex C chemicals, including steps to inventory sources and releases of the chemicals; identification of priority source categories; and promoting best available technologies and best environmental practices.[18] The convention also requires parties to develop, endeavor to implement, and periodically update, as appropriate, a national implementation plan (NIP) to achieve the removal or the reduction of POPs created intentionally or unintentionally.[19]

The list of chemicals subject to control under the convention has expanded over time. Nine additional substances, including various chemicals used in insecticides and flame retardants, were added by amendment to the convention in 2009; another was added in 2011.[20] Five more substances are currently candidates for listing under the Convention.[21]

D. Basel Convention on the Control of Transboundary Movements of Hazardous Wastes and Their Disposal

The Basel Convention on the Control of Transboundary Movements of Hazardous Wastes and Their Disposal (Basel Convention) is an agreement that is intended to protect human and environmental health from the negative effects of hazardous waste.[22] It applies to a large variety of hazardous waste material, defined on the basis of the source of the waste, its chemical composition, and its dangerous features. There are also types of wastes with specific definitions, such as household waste and incinerator ash. The convention does not address radioactive waste. The Basel Convention was opened for signature on March 22, 1989 and came into force on May 5, 1992. As of February 2014, 180 states and the European Union are parties to the Convention. The United States has signed the convention but not ratified it.

It has three principle aims: reduction of waste and sound management of waste in home countries; restrictions on the transboundary movement of wastes; and implementation of a permitting system to control the flow of waste based on the principle of prior informed consent.

1. Reduction

The convention aspires, ultimately, to reduce the movement of hazardous wastes between states. To that end, the convention promotes environmentally sound waste management at the site that is closest to the place of the creation of the waste and building the capacity of developing states to properly manage waste.[23]

2. Restrictions

The convention restricts the transboundary conveyance of hazardous wastes between states, and in particular seeks to prevent the shipment of hazardous wastes from developed states to developing states. It prohibits the export of hazardous wastes to states that are not parties to the convention, to Antarctica, and to states that have prohibited the import of hazardous wastes.[24] A party may, however, export to a non-party state if a bilateral or multilateral agreement "no less environmentally sound" than the Basel Convention is in place.

3. Permits

If certain criteria are met, permits may be granted for the transboundary shipment of hazardous wastes. Both exporting and importing national authorities are required to ensure compliance with convention obligations. The main criteria, inter alia, are:

- Parties shall prohibit or shall not permit the export of hazardous wastes and other wastes to the parties that have prohibited the import of such waste.[25]
- The export of hazardous wastes can only take place after advance written notice of the sending state and prior informed consent of the transit and target states.[26]
- Hazardous waste is designated for recovery (i.e., it is not for disposal).[27]
- The recipient of the waste and countries of transit have all necessary information regarding the category of waste and its composition.[28]
- The importing, transport, storage, maintenance, and use of the hazardous waste do not endanger the health of the public or the environment.

The convention encourages, but does not require, importing members to require the exporting and importing entities to carry insurance, bonds, or other form of guarantee.

4. *Additional Tools*

The convention has a number of tools that have been developed over the years. The Basel Protocol on Liability and Compensation for Damage Resulting from Transboundary Movements of Hazardous Wastes and their Disposal of 1999[29] is intended to regulate the payment of compensation for damage caused to a person and the environment in the course of transboundary movement or transportation of hazardous waste. The protocol has not come in force, because it has not yet been ratified by 20 states.

In the sixth meeting of the Conference of the Parties to the Basel Convention, a mechanism for promoting implementation and compliance was established.[30] The mechanism operates via a committee of 15 nominated member states. Members can make a submission to the committee (1) stating it will not be able to comply, despite its best efforts with its obligations, or (2) identifying another member state whose noncompliance with the convention obligation is a cause for concern. The committee facilitates compliance by providing advice, nonbinding recommendations, and information to noncomplying states. Where necessary after such facilitation, the committee may recommend the Conference of the Parties provide further support or issue a cautionary statement in response to a submission.

In 1995, an amendment was added known as the Basel Ban Amendment[31] that prohibits the export of any hazardous waste for any purpose whatsoever from member states of the European Union (EU) or the Organisation for Economic Co-operation and Development (OECD) to states that are not members (Appendix VII). The amendment will come into effect after being ratified by 75 percent of the states that have endorsed it. This amendment has not yet come into effect.

E. Strategic Approach to International Chemicals Management

The Strategic Approach to International Chemicals Management (SAICM) is a global initiative for a policy framework to promote chemical safety around the world.

The SAICM was developed by a multistakeholder and multisectoral preparatory committee. The SAICM supports the goal of ensuring that, by the year 2020, chemicals are produced and used in ways that minimize significant adverse impacts on the environment and human health.[32] This approach was implemented, as a voluntary agreement, during the first session of the International Conference on Chemicals Management held in Dubai, United Arab Emirates, from February 4–6, 2006.[33]

The first session of the conference and the process to develop the Strategic Approach to International Chemicals Management were co-convened by the United Nations Environment Program (UNEP), the Inter-Organization Program for the Sound Management of Chemicals (IOMC) and the Intergovernmental Forum on Chemical Safety (IFCS). The participating organizations of IOMC are the U.N. Food and Agriculture Organization (FAO), the International Labor Organization, the OECD, UNEP, the United Nations Industrial Development Organization, the United Nations Institute for Training and Research, and the World Health Organization (WHO). The Global Environment Facility, the United Nations Development Program, and the World Bank joined the IOMC participating organizations and IFCS in a steering committee established to oversee the development of the SAICM.

SAICM objectives are grouped under five themes: (1) risk reduction; (2) knowledge and information; (3) governance; (4) capacity building and technical cooperation; and (5) illegal international traffic.

The SAICM contains a global plan of action. In general, it was decided that priority in the action plan should be given to activities that

- Focus on narrowing the gap between developed countries and developing countries and countries with economies in transition in their capacities for the sound management of chemicals;
- Facilitate the implementation of existing agreements and work areas;
- Target issues not currently addressed in existing agreements and work areas;
- Ensure that by 2020 (1) chemicals or chemical uses that pose an unreasonable and otherwise unmanageable risk to human health and the environment based on a science-based risk assessment and taking into account the costs and benefits as well as the availability of safer substitutes and their efficacy are no longer produced or used for such uses; and (2) the risks from unintended releases of chemicals that pose an unreasonable and otherwise unmanageable risk to human health and the environment based on a science-based risk assessment and taking into account costs and benefits are minimized;
- Target chemicals that pose unreasonable and unmanageable risks;
- Promote the generation of adequate science-based knowledge on health and environmental risks of chemicals and make it available to all stakeholders.

In order to make the development of the SAICM successful, the governments, meeting in advance of the ninth special session of the UNEP Governing Council/Global Ministerial Environment Forum, also gave support to a multimillion-dollar fund called the "Quick Start" Program and a trust fund aimed at giving financial support to national action plans, especially in least developed countries and small island developing states.

UNEP, which helped organize the Dubai meeting along with other U.N. bodies and organizations and which involved participation from industry, business, trade unions, and other civil society groups, will house the SAICM Secretariat.

III.   Principles Related to Regulation of Chemicals and Hazardous Substances

Several principles have been incorporated into treaties and customary international law that could impact a particular country's regulatory framework. These include several interrelated principles (polluter pays, cradle to grave, and extended producer responsibility), approaches to evaluating environmental, social, and economic impacts (life-cycle assessment and life-cycle sustainability analysis), policies regarding when a government should regulate based on the available knowledge (precautionary principle/approach and preventive principle), and expectations for informing foreign governments of shipments prior to export (prior informed consent). Most of these principles reflect a growing trend toward assessing the overall environmental impact of a product or process and placing responsibility for those impacts at the beginning of the value chain rather than on the consumer or municipality dealing with waste at the end of the product's life cycle.

A.   Polluter Pays; Cradle to Grave; Extended Producer Responsibility

Developed by the OECD in the early 1970s, the polluter pays principle has evolved to hold the polluter responsible for the costs of preventing and controlling pollution it creates and the damages caused by that pollution.[34] It was one of the principles in the 1992 Rio Declaration on Environment and Development, which was reaffirmed at the United Nations Conference on Sustainable Development in 2012.[35]

The polluter pays principle has been categorized as weak (i.e., governments must not subsidize polluters) or strong (i.e., polluters must internalize pollution costs).[36] The principle can be implemented as a liability framework so that the manufacturer or importer of a substance is responsible for resulting pollution even if the company was not responsible for the ultimate release of the substance into the environment.[37] In such circumstances, liability for cleanup rests with the original manufacturer. (See chapter 8, Waste and Site Remediation, for more on cleanup responsibilities.)

Under the cradle-to-grave concept, a substance is regulated from the beginning of its existence (e.g., manufacture or import) to the end of its life (e.g., export, disposal, or recycling) and everything in between (e.g., transportation and storage). In the United States, the cradle-to-grave concept is embodied in the Resource Conservation and Recovery Act (RCRA).[38]

There is some movement in the international community toward extended producer responsibility (EPR). This principle holds that producers of products should have some responsibility for the end-of-life environmental impacts of their products.[39] As such, EPR incorporates the polluter pays principle.[40] EPR is meant to encourage design changes to products to reduce adverse impacts, such as by eliminating or reducing the use of hazardous substances in the products, thereby lessening hazardous waste, requiring manufacturers to manage recycling of products or both.[41]

EPR requirements may include take-back programs for electrical equipment and electronics containing hazardous substances in which the manufacturer or importer accepts the product from the consumer or otherwise provides for recycling of the products.[42] EPR will continue to grow in popularity as countries seek solutions for electronic waste and other used products such as tires and batteries. See discussion *infra* regarding electronic waste.[43]

B.   Life-Cycle Assessment and Life-Cycle Sustainability Analysis

The term life-cycle assessment (LCA) refers to measuring the environmental impact of a product, process, or service.[44] With respect to chemicals, it could include "research and development; extracting and processing raw materials; manufacturing, transportation and distribution; use, reuse, and maintenance; and recycling and final disposal."[45] ISO 14040 has formalized a framework for LCAs.[46]

A trend in the area of LCA is a shift toward the life-cycle sustainability analysis (LCSA).[47] This is a broader assessment combining several different models and includes analysis of environmental, economic, and social impacts.[48] Sustainability has been defined as undertaking development in a way that "meets the needs of the present without compromising the ability of future generations to meet their own needs."[49]

Performing an LCA or LCSA could be very useful in identifying opportunities in the process or product's life cycle for reducing the use of hazardous materials or generation of hazardous waste.

C.   Precautionary Principle/Approach and Preventive Principle

The precautionary approach is described in the 1992 Rio Declaration on Environment and Development: "Where there are threats of serious or irreversible damage, lack of full scientific certainty shall not be used as a reason for postponing cost-effective measures to prevent environmental degradation."[50] There is no universal agreement on the meaning of "precaution,"[51] and although the general concept has taken root in the international community, its application remains a matter of debate.[52]

Some jurisdictions have adopted the precautionary approach as a formal principle. The EU and Canada have made precaution a statutory requirement.[53] The EU Regulation on the Registration, Evaluation, and Authorization of Chemicals (REACH) is one example of chemicals regulation that incorporates the precautionary principle.[54] REACH requires companies to register chemicals before they can be produced or placed on the market in the EU. Registration must include information on the use and toxicity of chemicals. For certain substances that are particularly dangerous, authorization is required for specific uses. In essence, REACH requires companies to prove that their substances will not present unacceptable risk.

The OECD Guidelines for Multinational Enterprises provide principles for businesses to use in implementing the precautionary approach.[55] The guidelines include recommendations for training employees on environmental safety and being proactive to prevent irreversible environmental damage.

The preventive or prevention principle holds that damage to the environment should be prevented as a first course of action.[56] This differs from the precautionary approach in that the preventive principle aims to eliminate risk and uncertainty at the outset.[57]

IV. Types of Regulation

Chemicals and hazardous materials are regulated in a variety of ways, including registration; labeling, tracking, record-keeping, and reporting; import and export notifications; restrictions on use, import, export, manufacture; and requirements regarding disposal or recovery. This section also highlights pesticides because they are used around the globe and the regulation of these chemicals tends to be separate from other chemicals and hazardous substances. Finally, this section describes three issues that will continue to grow in importance: nanomaterials, mercury, and electronic waste.

A. Inventories and Registration

Some countries have inventories listing chemicals already in use. For example, Korea and Australia have such inventories of chemicals.[58] Notification prior to manufacture is required only for chemicals not on the list.[59] Notification may be as straightforward as identifying the chemical to the regulatory body. The regulatory body may or may not affirmatively approve the manufacture of the chemical.

In contrast to notification, some jurisdictions require registration of a chemical prior to its use. Registration is more comprehensive than notification because registration typically requires more information (e.g., safety studies) and an affirmative act on the part of the regulatory body. A well-known example is REACH. This regulatory regime aspires to unify the European Inventory of Existing Commercial Chemical Substances and European List of Notified Chemical Substances in one database of registered substances. As another example, numerous countries require registration of pesticides prior to sale or use.[60]

B. Labeling, Tracking, Record-Keeping and Reporting

The Globally Harmonized System for Classification and Labeling of Chemicals (GHS) is a system for developing standard criteria for the classification of chemicals based on hazards and creating uniform hazard communications including labeling and safety data sheets.[61] Hazard communications include pictograms such as skull and crossbones, statements about hazards, and precautionary statements.[62]

There are several benefits to creating a uniform system of labeling and classifying chemicals, including facilitation of trade, decreasing the need for testing chemicals, and increasing protection of human health and the environment.[63] These requirements are not enforceable unless incorporated into domestic legislation.

The U.N. Economic Commission for Europe (UNECE) has established a website that shows importing and exporting countries' regulations on labeling.[64] Under the GHS, these would ideally be the same.[65] When they are not, there may be conflicts between the importing and exporting countries' labels that can lead to legal issues. For example, one issue that can arise is whether a particular product is mislabeled.

Related to the transport of hazardous substances are safety data sheets and manifests. The GHS has guidance for safety data sheets, which are hazard communication devices used to provide hazard information and storage, handling, and disposal information.[66] Manifests are used to track hazardous materials or hazardous wastes as the materials are transported from site of generation to other destinations.[67] This is based on the cradle-to-grave concept in some countries such as the United States.[68]

Record-keeping and reporting requirements on the manufacture, shipment, and use of hazardous substances is another way countries regulate these materials. For example, in Japan, manufacturers and importers of chemical substances must report annually on their use of certain substances.[69] Reporting requirements include the quantities being manufactured, imported, and shipped within and outside the country.

C. End of Life (Disposal and Resource Recovery)

As noted *supra* in section II.D, the Basel Convention restricts the transboundary transportation of hazardous waste for disposal. Regional conventions may be more stringent than the Basel Convention. One such convention is the Bamako Convention. African nations adopted the Bamako Convention in 1991 to ban the import of hazardous waste from non-party countries.[70] Another such convention is the Waigani Convention, under which parties ban the import of hazardous and radioactive wastes.[71]

Domestic laws govern the disposal of hazardous wastes. Requirements may include landfilling and incineration of hazardous waste.[72] The EU discourages landfilling with the objective of preventing waste, where possible, and encourages recycling and reusing materials if prevention cannot be achieved.[73]

D. Import and Export Requirements

1. Notice of Export to Importing Country

Under RCRA, exports of hazardous waste from the United States are subject to U.S. Environmental Protection Agency (EPA) notification requirements. EPA then sends notice to the importing country. If it concurs, EPA sends an acknowledgment to the exporting entity.[74]

The OECD's Control of Transboundary Movement of Wastes Destined for Recovery Operations decision governs movement of wastes for recycling in OECD countries.[75] OECD countries are expected to implement the decision through domestic regulations.[76] The decision has been aligned with the Basel Convention. (See section II.D, *supra*.) Recognizing that most OECD member countries and the European Community have become parties to the Basel Convention, the OECD established procedures that should be implemented among OECD countries.

The United States' Toxic Substances Control Act (TSCA)[77] also requires notification of export to a receiving country for chemicals or mixtures regulated under certain provisions of the statute.[78] TSCA addresses the production, importation, use, and disposal of specific chemicals including polychlorinated biphenyls (PCBs), asbestos, radon, and lead-based paint. The process is similar to that under RCRA: the exporter notifies EPA of the export, and EPA then notifies the importing country of the TSCA regulatory status of the chemical being exported.[79]

2. Import Certification Requirements

TSCA requires U.S. importers of chemical substances and mixtures to certify that their shipments comply with TSCA.[80] Normally, the certification requirement does not apply to products or articles containing chemicals, but if a particular TSCA regulation so states, the import certification would apply to articles.[81]

Import requirements under RCRA are fairly minimal. They require modification of the manifest to make clear that the waste was generated outside the United States. There is no requirement for the importer to obtain EPA consent to import the waste.

3. Bilateral Agreements

Bilateral agreements between the United States and Canada and the United States and Mexico provide for the transboundary shipment of wastes, including requirements for notification and manifests.[82] Without these bilateral agreements, the United States would not be able to exchange hazardous wastes with Canada or Mexico because the United States is not a party to the Basel Convention.

E. Restrictions

Some international instruments have identified specific chemicals or categories of chemicals the manufacture, import, sale, or use of which is restricted or banned. For example, the Stockholm and Rotterdam Conventions list chemicals that are restricted in some way.[83]

Some countries identify specific chemicals and restrict the manufacture, import, sale, or use of those chemicals. For instance, Norway has such restrictions on lead shot, PCBs, and chemicals known as short-chain chloro-paraffins, to name a few.[84]

F.   Pesticides, Nanomaterials, Mercury, and E-Waste

1.   Pesticides

The FAO is the lead international organization engaged in ensuring safe use and handling of pesticides. The FAO issued the International Code of Conduct on the Distribution and Use of Pesticides (FAO Code of Conduct) to establish voluntary standards of conduct for the pesticide industry, governments, and others dealing with pesticides to ensure the use of pesticides does not result in unacceptable adverse effects.[85] The voluntary standards include measures to promote the effective and efficient use of pesticides; assistance to countries in addressing potential risks associated with use of pesticides; consideration of the life cycle of the pesticide; and implementation of integrated pest management (IPM).

The FAO defines IPM as "the careful consideration of all available pest control techniques and subsequent integration of appropriate measures that discourage the development of pest populations and keep pesticides and other interventions to levels that are economically justified and reduce or minimize risks to human health and the environment."[86] In addition to the FAO, the World Bank encourages IPM and permits the financing of agricultural pesticides under an IPM approach.[87]

Besides the FAO Code of Conduct, there are several international instruments and systems that relate directly or indirectly to pesticides. These include the Stockholm, Rotterdam and Basel Conventions, and the GHS.[88]

While there are many aspects to the regulation of pesticides, one common element is that they must be registered for sale and use. Registration of pesticides is highly encouraged by the FAO and WHO as a critical part of any national legislation governing the regulation of pesticides.[89]

2.   Nanomaterials

Nanomaterials are an emerging issue and have been identified by SAICM as such.[90] Nanomaterial can generally be described as "a material that is made up of nanometer-scale particles or otherwise includes nanometer-scale structures."[91] Nanomaterials have varied applications including energy efficiency, pesticides, agriculture, and consumer products.[92] The market for nanomaterials will continue to grow, as will the regulation of these materials as government policies catch up with the technology.

Nano versions of chemicals have the same chemical makeup as their conventional counterparts, yet may be subject to different regulatory requirements. One consideration for practitioners is whether the nanoscale version of a chemical is listed separately on the chemical inventory, or whether it would be covered by the listing of the non-nano chemical.

3. Mercury

One chemical that has been identified in recent years for special focus is mercury. The UNEP Mercury Programme is working toward a global legally binding instrument to reduce the supply and demand of mercury, reduce waste containing mercury, lower or eliminate emissions of mercury, and develop storage solutions.[93] More than 120 countries have participated in the negotiating meetings to date.[94] In January 2013, governments agreed to a global, legally binding treaty on mercury: the Minamata Convention on Mercury. The convention bans the production, import, and export of certain mercury-containing priducts by 2020.[95]

In the United States, the Mercury Export Ban Act prohibits the export of elemental mercury beginning in 2013 unless EPA grants a party an essential use exemption.[96]

4. Electronic Waste

An emerging issue regarding chemicals is the concern about the impacts of chemicals contained in products or articles.[97] Electronic waste, or e-waste, is a type of waste that contains hazardous substances that has received considerable attention in recent years.[98] E-waste is often shipped between countries, particularly from developed to developing countries.[99] The demand for old electronics can be attributed mainly to two factors: the electronics can be (1) refurbished and reused in other countries and (2) disassembled and the various metals and materials recycled. This disassembly and recycling takes place under unsafe conditions in many countries, resulting in human health and environmental impacts such as releases of mercury, cadmium, and lead.[100]

One regional directive addressing e-waste is the EU Waste Electrical and Electronic Equipment (WEEE) Directive.[101] Its main purposes are to encourage the reuse and recycling of electronics and avoid their diversion to waste streams.[102] The directive incorporates the producer responsibility principle to encourage design of electrical and electronic equipment that takes into consideration the reuse and recycling of their products.[103]

A working group of the Basel Convention is in the process of negotiating guidelines on trade in e-waste.[104] While the guidelines would not be binding, they will be a useful tool for companies seeking to transport electronics (whether e-waste or non-waste) to other countries.

5. The RoHS Directive

The EU Restriction of Hazardous Substances directive (2002/95/EC) (RoHS) is a European guideline restricting the use of six dangerous substances commonly seen in the production of various categories of electric and electronic equipment. The six substances are lead, mercury, cadmium, chrome +6, and two substances that are fire retardants for plastic materials: polybrominated biphenyls (PBBs) and polybrominated diphenyl ethers (PBDEs).

The RoHS directive is not directly binding upon EU member states; rather, it obligates EU member states to formulate domestic legislation as well as domestic policy for its enforcement. The RoHS directive was published in January 2003, and enactment of national domestic implementing legislation was required by August 2004.

In June 2011, a comprehensive recast was published for the RoHS directive.[105] The directive repealed the prior RoHS directive and replaced it with a new framework. The "RoHS recast" or "RoHS 2" retained the basic prohibition on the six materials listed above. It changed significantly, however, the network of duties and obligations under the program. First, the scope of the directive was changed. The new directive increased coverage from 8 to 11 categories, namely large domestic tools; small domestic tools; communication and telecommunication equipment; consumption products; lighting products; electric and electronic tools; toys and leisure/sport equipment; medical equipment; tools for supervision and monitoring, including supervision and notice tools for industrial monitoring and supervision; automatic distribution machines; and "other electric and electronic tools . . . not covered by the other categories."

Second, whereas the original directive explicitly excluded from its application spare parts, this exception has now been eliminated. Under the new directive, all exclusions expire after a predetermined period of time unless a decision is adopted to retain them. Consequently, cases of delay or lack of authority will ultimately cause the cancellation of the exclusion and not its continued existence, as was the case in the original directive. In addition to this, a new, revised list of exclusions from the RoHS directive—2011/65/EU—appears in Appendix III of the directive, including the expiration dates for each exclusion.

At the same time, certain products were removed from the scope of the directive, for example, equipment urgently required for the protection of the essential security needs of EU members states, including ammunition and weaponry intended for combat purposes.

The responsibility of entities in the supply chain was also altered. The original version of the RoHS directive placed most compliance responsibilities on the manufacturer. This resulted in a lack of obligations on some parts of the supply chain (e.g., distributors). The amended RoHS directive specified duties throughout the supply chain.

- *The authorized representative* is responsible for examining the obligations of the manufacturer such as preparing a conformity declaration.
- *The distributor* bears various obligations such as ensuring the product contains a "European Community" or "CE" (for the French "Communauté Européenne") marking, and keeping records of defective products.
- *The economic operator* may be the manufacturer, the authorized representative, the importer, or the distributor.

CE marking is a mandatory conformity marking for products placed on the market in the European Economic Area. The RoHS Recast mandates the addition of the CE mark to electric and electronic equipment, and creates a legal presumption that the product was found to conform to the legal requirements of European legislation requiring the embossment of that mark.

The conformity declaration is a document that attests to the conformity of the electric or electronic equipment with the provisions of the RoHS directive. The manufacturer is obliged to prepare and transfer it to the next entity in the supply chain. The significance of the conformity declaration lies in manufacturer's assumption of responsibility for fulfillment of the provisions of the directive.

V. Conclusion

New chemicals are being manufactured every year, and products containing chemicals are being shipped internationally at an ever-increasing rate. While lawmakers strive to develop laws balancing environmental and health concerns with the benefits those chemicals and products provide, keeping pace with the development of new technologies and chemicals can be challenging. At the same time, multinational corporations face a diversity of regulatory approaches across jurisdictions, in addition to a multiplicity of international agreements. Practitioners in this field thus must contend with a dynamic legal landscape and ever evolving challenges in advising their clients.

Notes

1. *See, e.g.,* UNEP, Global Chemicals Outlook: Towards Sound Management of Chemicals, at 13-14, Job No.: DTI/1543/GE, (2012) (describing OECD and American Chemistry Council predictions of increases in chemical production).

2. *See, e.g., id.* (describing the usefulness of chemicals in society and the harms that can arise).

3. There are estimated to be over 100,000 chemicals in commerce in the United States over the past 30 years and approximately 100,000 chemicals marketed in Europe between 1971–1981. D. Muir & P. Howard, *Are There Other Persistent Organic Pollutants? A Challenge for Environmental Chemist*, 40 ENVTL. SCI. & TECH. 7157, 7158 (2006).

4. Unified Text of Secondary Legislation of the Environment Ministry (Ecuador), Book VI, Title V, Regulation for the Prevention and Control of Contamination by Hazardous Chemical Substances, Hazardous Wastes, and Special Wastes (2011), http://www .efficacitas.com/efficacitas_in/default2.php?siteid=26 and http://www.efficacitas.com /efficacitas_in/assets/Desechos%20peligrosos.pdf.

5. The definition of "hazardous waste" varies among countries. J. Krueger, *The Basel Convention and the International Trade in Hazardous Wastes, in* YEARBOOK OF INTERNATIONAL CO-OPERATION ON ENVIRONMENT AND DEVELOPMENT 2001/2001, at 43–51 (Olav Schram Stokke & Øystein B. Thommessen eds., 2001).

6. For example, Australian law regulates the transport of dangerous goods in the Australian Code for the Transport of Dangerous Goods by Road and Rail, 2007 (as amended by Corrigendum 1, 2011), *available at* http://www.ntc.gov.au/filemedia/Publi cations/ADG7October2011.pdf.

7. *See* Regulation (EC) No. 1907/2006 of the European Parliament and of the Council of December 18, 2006 concerning the Registration, Evaluation, Authorisation and Restriction of Chemicals (REACH), ch. 2, art. 3, 2006 O.J. (L 396) 47, 53.

8. See chapter 16, North America Overview: NAFTA, the CEC, and Other Bilateral/Trilateral Institutions, in this volume.

9. Commission for Environmental Cooperation Chemicals Management Forum, 15–16 May 2012, Meeting Summary, http://www.cec.org/Storage/142/16814_CEC_Chemicals_Management_Forum_Meeting_Summary_en.pdf, last visited Dec. 16, 2012.

10. http://www.pic.int/Countries/Statusofratifications/tabid/1072/language/en-US/Default.aspx.

11. http://www.pic.int/Home/tabid/855/language/en-US/Default.aspx.

12. Rotterdam Convention art. 5.

13. *See* http://chm.pops.int/default.aspx (last visited Oct. 25, 2013).

14. P.O. Darnerud, *Toxic Effects of Brominated Flame Retardants in Man and in Wildlife*, ENVIRONMENT INT'L 29(6), 841–53 (2003); L.S. Birnbaum, & D.F. Staskal, (2004). *Brominated Flame Retardants: Cause for Concern?*, ENVIRONMENTAL HEALTH PERSPECTIVES 112(1), 9 (2004).

15. Stockholm Convention art. 3.1(a). The original Appendix A chemicals include aldrin, alpha hexachlorocyclohexane, beta hexachlorocyclohexane, chloradane, chlordecone, dieldrin, endrin, endosulfan, heptachlor, hexabromobiphenyl, hexabromodiphenyl ether, heptabromodiphenyl ether, hexachlorobenzene, lindane, mirex, pentachlorobenzene, polychlorinated biphenyls (PCB), tetrabromodiphenyl ether, pentabromodiphenyl ether, and toxaphene.

16. Stockholm Convention art. 3.1(b), 2. Annex B chemicals include DDT, perfluorooctane sulfonic acid and its salts, and perfluorooctane sulfonyl fluoride.

17. Stockholm Convention, Art 5. Annex C chemicals include polychlorinated biphenols or PCBs, hexachlorobenzene, dioxins, and furans.

18. Stockholm Convention art. 5(a) (requiring a national plan to identify, characterize, and address the release of the chemicals listed in Annex C).

19. Stockholm Convention art. 7.

20. In 2009: hexachlorocyclohexane, beta hexachlorocyclohexane, chlordecone, hexabromobiphenyl, hexabromodiphenyl ether and heptabromodiphenyl ether, lindane, pentachlorobenzene, perfluorooctane sulfonic acid, its salts and perfluorooctane sulfonyl fluoride and tetrabromodiphenyl ether and pentabromodiphenyl ether. In 2011, endosulfan was added to the list, bringing the total chemical regulation under the Convention to 22.

21. Hexabromocyclododecane, short-chained chlorinated paraffins, chlorinated naphthalenes, hexachlorobutadiene, pentachlorophenol.

22. For more information on the historical context in which the Basel Convention was developed and some of the challenges in its implementation, *see* chapter 8, Waste and Site Remediation.

23. Basel Convention art. 4.

24. Basel Convention art. 4.1(b), 4.5, 4.6.

25. Basel Convention art. 4(b).

26. Basel Convention art. 6(1).

27. Basel Convention art. 4(9)(b).

28. Basel Convention art. 6(2).

29. Decision V/29 (1999).

30. Decision VI/12 (2002).

31. Decision III/1 (1995). *See* http://www.basel.int/implementation/legalmatters/banamendment/tabid/1484/default.aspx last visited Oct. 24, 2013).

32. This goal was elaborated at the 2002 Johannesburg World Summit on Sustainable Development.

33. *See* http://www.saicm.org/index.php?option=com_content&view=article&id=80:iccm-1&catid=88:iccm-1&Itemid=518.

34. *See* OECD Joint Working Party on Trade and the Environment, *Polluter-Pays Principle as It Relates to International Law*, COM/ENV/TD(2001)44/FINAL, at 6 (2002); *see also* O. Vicha, *The Polluter-Pays Principle in OECD Recommendations and its Application in International and EC/EU Law*, 2 Czech Y.B. Pub. & Private Int'l L. at 60 (2011), *available at* http://www.cyil.eu/contents-cyil-2011/.

35. Rio Declaration on Environment and Development, United Nations Conference on Environment and Development, U.N. Doc. A/CONF. 151/5/Rev.1 (1992), *reprinted in* 31 I.L.M. 874, 878 (1992); The Future We Want, U.N. General Assembly resolution, A /RES/66/288 (Sept. 11, 2012).

36. Jonathan Remy Nash, *Too Much Market? Conflict between Tradable Pollution Allowances and the "Polluter Pays" Principle*, 24 Harv. Envtl. L. Rev. 465, 473–77 (2000).

37. In the United States, the Comprehensive Environmental Response, Compensation, and Liability Act, 42 U.S.C. §§ 9601 *et seq.*, is one such law.

38. 42 U.S.C. §§ 6901 *et seq.* For further discussion of RCRA's implementation of "cradle to grave" regulation of substances, see *infra* note 56.

39. *See* OECD Working Group on Waste Prevention and Recycling, EPR Policies and Product Design: Economic Theory and Selected Case Studies, ENV /EPOC/WGWPR(2005)9/FINAL (2006), http://search.oecd.org/officialdocuments/displ aydocumentpdf/?doclanguage=en&cote=env/epoc/wgwpr(2005)9/final.

40. P. Pak, *Haste Makes E-Waste: A Comparative Analysis of How the United States Should Approach the Growing E-Waste Threat*, 16 Cardozo J. Int'l & Comp. L. 241, 258–59 (2008).

41. *See* OECD Working Group on Waste Prevention and Recycling, *supra* note 39.

42. *See* Catherine K. Lin et al., *Globalization, Extended Producer Responsibility and the Problem of Discarded Computers in China: An Exploratory Proposal for Environmental Protection*, 14 Geo. Int'l Envtl. L. Rev. 525, 536–37 (2002).

43. Pak, *supra* note 40, at 258–59 (e-waste requirements are based on extended producer responsibility concept).

44. U.S. EPA, EPA/600/R-06/060, Life Cycle Assessment: Principles and Practice 2 (2006).

45. G. Wiser & D. Magraw, Jr., Ctr. for Int'l Envtl. L. (CIEL), Principles and Approaches of Sustainable Development and Chemicals Management for a Strategic Approach to International Chemicals Management (SAICM) 14 (2005), http:// www.ciel.org/Publications/SAICM_PrinciplesStudyFinal_July05.pdf. For an example of the difference between a life-cycle assessment and an environmental risk assessment, see Sanne & Widheden, Akzo Nobel, Environmental Risk Assessment (ERA) and Life Cycle Assessment (LCA) of the Same Product (2005), http://www.dantes.info/Publi cations/Publication-doc/LCA%20and%20ERA%20of%20the%20same%20product%20 -%20report.pdf.

46. Life Cycle Assessment of PVC and of Principal Competing Materials 22 (commissioned by the European Commission, 2004), http://ec.europa.eu/enterprise /sectors/chemicals/files/sustdev/pvc-final_report_lca_en.pdf (referencing ISO 14040: Environmental management—Life cycle assessment—Principles and framework, International Standard Organization (2006)).

47. *See, e.g.*, UNEP, Towards a Life Cycle Sustainability Assessment: Making Informed Choices on Products.

48. *See also* http://www.ncbi.nlm.nih.gov/pubmed/20812726. Many of the more recent developments were initiated to broaden traditional environmental LCA to a more comprehensive life-cycle sustainability analysis (LCSA). Recently, a framework for LCSA was suggested linking life-cycle sustainability questions to knowledge needed for

addressing them, identifying available knowledge and related models, knowledge gaps, and defining research programs to fill these gaps. LCA is evolving into LCSA, which is a transdisciplinary integration framework of models rather than a model in itself. LCSA works with a plethora of disciplinary models and guides selecting the proper ones, given a specific sustainability question.

49. WORLD COMM'N ON ENVT. & DEV., OUR COMMON FUTURE (G. Brundtland ed., 1987) (Brundtland Report).

50. United Nations Conference on Environment and Development, Rio de Janeiro, Brazil, June 3–14, 1992, Rio Declaration on Environment and Development, U.N. Doc. A/CONF.151/5/Rev.1 (Aug. 12, 1992), *reprinted in* 31 I.L.M. 876 (1992).

51. *See generally* M. G. Puder, *The Rise of Regional Integration Law (RIL): Good News for International Environment Law (IEL)?*, 23 GEO. INT'L ENVTL. L. REV. 165 (2011).

52. *See* Markus Wagner, *Taking Interdependence Seriously: The Need for a Reassessment of the Precautionary Principle in International Trade Law*, 20 CARDOZO J. OF INT'L & COMP. L. 713, 724–30 (2012).

53. *See Communication from the Commission on the Precautionary Principle*, COM (2000) 1 final (Feb. 2, 2000); and Canadian Environmental Protection Act, 1999, S.C. 1999; *see also* Puder, *supra* note 51.

54. *See* Regulation (EC) No. 1907/2006 of the European Parliament and of the Council (Dec. 18, 2006), ch. 1, art. 1, 2006 O.J. (L 396) 47, ("This Regulation is based on the principle that it is for manufacturers, importers and downstream users to ensure that they manufacture, place on the market or use such substances that do not adversely affect human health or the environment. Its provisions are underpinned by the precautionary principle.").

55. OECD, OECD Guidelines for Multinational Enterprises (2011).

56. For a list of examples of preventive principle in international agreements, see RESEARCH HANDBOOK IN INTERNATIONAL ENVIRONMENTAL LAW 183 (M. Fitzmaurice et al. eds., 2010), *available at* http://www.tradevenvironment.eu/uploads/papers/Research HandbookOnInternationalEnvLawChap9.pdf.

57. Wagner, *supra* note 52, at 731.

58. *See, e.g.*, Toxic Chemicals Control Law (Existing Chemicals Inventory published pursuant to TCCL) (Korea); Industrial Chemicals (Notification and Assessment) Act, 1989 (Austl.).

59. For example, Australia requires notification prior to introduction of a new chemical. Industrial Chemicals (Notification and Assessment) Act, 1989 (Austl.).

60. *See, e.g.*, Hazardous Substance Act (No. 3) B.E. 2551 (2008) (Thailand); Agricultural Chemicals Regulation Law (Law No. 82 of July 1, 1948) (2007) (Japan).

61. GLOBALLY HARMONIZED SYSTEM FOR CLASSIFICATION AND LABELLING OF CHEMICALS, sec. 1.1.2.1 (3d rev. ed. 2009), *available at* http://www.unece.org/fileadmin /DAM/trans/danger/publi/ghs/ghs_rev03/English/01e_part1.pdf.

62. For a list of hazard communications, see http://www.epa.gov/oppfead1/inter national/globalharmon.htm.

63. GLOBALLY HARMONIZED SYSTEM FOR CLASSIFICATION AND LABELLING OF CHEMICALS, *supra* note 61.

64. For the implementation status by country, see the UNECE website at http:// www.unece.org/trans/danger/publi/ghs/ghs_welcome_e.html.

65. OECD has compiled a table of some OECD countries, regions, and international organizations that shows whether each has implemented GHS in categorizing and labeling chemicals and whether those that have implemented GHS have made GHS classifications publicly available. *See* http://www.oecd.org/env/chemicalsafetyandbiosafety/assess mentofchemicals/publicavailabilityofnationalregionalghsclassifications.htm.

66. GLOBALLY HARMONIZED SYSTEM FOR CLASSIFICATION AND LABELLING OF CHEMICALS, *supra* note 61.

67. For example, Canada requires that a manifest accompany hazardous waste and hazardous recyclable materials as they are transported through the country. *Interprovincial Movement of Hazardous Waste Regulations (2002)*, SOR/2002-301.

68. *See* U.S. Department of Transportation regulations at 49 C.F.R. § 172.205 (2005); *see also* U.S. EPA, Frequently Asked Questions, http://www.epa.gov/osw/hazard/trans portation/manifest/faqs.htm (RCRA "requires that all hazardous waste shipped off-site be tracked from 'cradle-to-grave' using a manifest that provides information about the generator of the waste, the facility that will receive the waste, a description and quantity of the waste (including the number and type of containers), and how the waste will be routed to the receiving facility.").

69. Act on the Evaluation of Chemical Substances and Regulation of Their Manufacture, etc. (Act No. 117 of October 16, 1973) (Chemical Substances Control Law) (Japan), as amended 2009.

70. Bamako Convention on the Ban of the Import of all Forms of Hazardous Wastes into Africa and the Control of Trans-boundary Movements of Such Wastes Generated in Africa, adopted January 30, 1991, 2101 U.N.T.S. 177, entered into force April 22, 1998.

71. The Convention to Ban the Importation into Forum Island Countries of Hazardous and Radioactive Wastes and to Control the Trans-boundary Movement and Management of Hazardous Wastes within the South Pacific Region, Waigani, Sept. 16, 1995, in force Oct. 21, 2001, 2161 U.N.T.S. 93.

72. *See, e.g.,* Directive 2008/98/Ec of the European Parliament and of the Council of November 19, 2008 on waste and repealing certain Directives, 2008 O.J. (L 312) 3, at 5–6.

73. *See, e.g., id.* at 4.

74. *See* 42 U.S.C. § 6938 (RCRA § 3017).

75. *Control of Transboundary Movement of Wastes Destined for Recovery Operations*, OECD, C(2001)107/FINAL (May 2002).

76. The guidance manual on implementation of Decision C(2001)107/FINAL can be found at http://www.oecd.org/environment/resourceproductivityandwaste/42262259 .pdf. The manual provides the following examples of domestic regulation implementing the OECD Decision. For example, in the member states of the European Union, the OECD Decision is implemented through the EC Waste Shipment Regulation No. 1013/2006 as from July 12, 2007. In Canada, the Export and Import of Hazardous Waste and Hazardous Recyclable Material Regulations fully implement the requirements of the OECD Decision, the Basel Convention, and the Canada-U.S. Agreement on Transboundary Movement of Hazardous Waste. In Switzerland, the OECD Decision is translated into national legislation through the Swiss Ordinance on the Movements of Waste of June 22, 2005, which entered into force on January 1, 2006. In Japan, the National Law for the Control of Export, Import of Specified Hazardous Wastes and other Wastes was revised and entered into force on 16 December 2001 as an ordinance titled Ordinance Designating Materials to be Controlled by the OECD Decision C(2001)107/FINAL Concerning the Control of Transboundary Movements of Wastes Destined for Recovery Operations. In Korea, the requirements of the OECD Decision have been transposed into the Act on the Control of Transboundary Movements of Hazardous Wastes and their Disposal. Guidance Manual for the Control of Transboundary Movements of Recoverable Wastes (2009), at 10.

77. 15 U.S.C. §§ 2601 *et seq.* (1976).

78. 15 U.S.C. § 2611. Chemicals regulated under TSCA sections 4, 5, 6, or 7, including asbestos and PCBs, are subject to export notification requirements. *Id.* Export notification is not required for articles containing chemicals, except articles containing PCBs, unless specifically required by a rule under TSCA. 40 C.F.R. § 707.60(b).

79. 40 C.F.R. pt. 707, subpt. D (2006).

80. 15 U.S.C. § 2612.

81. TSCA Import certification regulations are at 19 C.F.R. §§ 12.118 through 12.127 and 127.28.

82. Agreement between the United States of America and the United Mexican States on Cooperation for the Protection and Improvement of the Environment in the Border Area, Aug. 14, 1983, U.S.-Mex., T.I.A.S. No. 10,827; Agreement between the Government of the United States of America and the Government of Canada Concerning the Transboundary Movement of Hazardous Waste, Oct. 28, 1986, U.S.-Can., T.I.A.S. No. 11,099 (entered into force Nov. 8, 1986; amended Nov. 4 & 25, 1992).

83. A list of restricted chemicals from 2010 can be found at http://www.chem.unep .ch/Legal/ECOSOC/UNEP%20Consolidated%20List%2010%20May%202010.pdf.

84. Regulations relating to restrictions on the manufacture, import, export, sale, and use of chemicals and other products hazardous to health and the environment (2012) (Norway); an unofficial English translation available at http://www.klif.no/38637#24.

85. Food & Agric. Org. of the United Nations, International Code of Conduct on the Distribution and Use of Pesticides.

86. *Id.* art. 2.

87. *See* THE WORLD BANK OPERATIONS MANUAL, OPERATIONAL POLICY 4.09, PEST MANAGEMENT (Dec. 1998), http://siteresources.worldbank.org/OPSMANUAL/Resources /EntireOM_External.pdf.

88. J. VAPNEK ET AL., FOOD & AGRIC. ORG. OF THE UNITED NATIONS, DESIGNING NATIONAL PESTICIDE LEGISLATION 12 (2007), *available at* ftp://ftp.fao.org/docrep /fao/010/a1467e/a1467e.pdf.

89. WORLD HEALTH ORG. & FOOD & AGRIC. ORG. OF THE UNITED NATIONS, WHO/ HTM/NTD/WHOPES/2010.7, INTERNATIONAL CODE OF CONDUCT ON THE DISTRIBUTION AND USE OF PESTICIDES: GUIDELINES FOR THE REGISTRATION OF PESTICIDES 9 (2010), *available at* http://whqlibdoc.who.int/hq/2010/WHO_HTM_NTD_WHOPES_2010.7_eng.pdf.

90. *Report of the International Conference on Chemicals Management on the work of its third session*, International Conference on Chemicals Management Third session, Nairobi, 17–21 September 2012, SAICM//ICCM.3/24, at 20.

91. D. Fiorino, *Voluntary Initiatives, Regulation, and Nanotechnology Oversight: Charting a Path* 10 (Woodrow Wilson Int'l Ctr. for Scholars Project on Emerging Nanotechnologies, 2010), http://www.nanotechproject.org/process/assets/files/8347/pen-19.pdf.

92. JOHN F. SARGENT JR., CONG. RES. SERV., RL34401, THE NATIONAL NANOTECHNOLOGY INITIATIVE: OVERVIEW, REAUTHORIZATION, AND APPROPRIATIONS ISSUES 3–4 (2012). For a searchable database of nanomaterials in consumer products, see http://www.nano techproject.org/inventories/consumer/.

93. UNEP, *Report of the Governing Council*, Twenty-fifth session, A/64/25, ISSN 0252-2055 (2009).

94. *See, e.g., Report of the intergovernmental negotiating committee to prepare a global legally binding instrument on mercury on the work of its third session*, Intergovernmental negotiating committee to prepare a global legally binding instrument on mercury Third session, Nairobi, 31 October–4 November 2011, UNEP(DTIE)/Hg/INC.3/8 (2011), at Section II.C. (Attendance list).

95. *See* http://www.unep.org/chemicalsandwaste/Portals/9/Mercury/Documents /INC5/press_release_mercury_Jan_19_2013.pdf.

96. *See* 15 U.S.C. § 2611(c).

97. *See, e.g.*, UNEP, GLOBAL CHEMICALS OUTLOOK: TOWARDS SOUND MANAGEMENT OF CHEMICALS 15 (2012) (noting that "articles are important vehicles of the global transport of chemicals with potentially significant impacts at every stage of the product life cycle").

98. *See Report of the International Conference on Chemicals Management on the work of its third session, supra* note 90, at 19–20 (identifying e-waste as an emerging issue).

99. *See* Biennium Conference of the Global Partnership on Waste Management Osaka, Japan, 5 and 6 November 2012, *Background paper on electrical and electronic waste*, UNEP(DTIE)/GPWM/BC.1/INF/5, at 2.

100. L. Luther, Cong. Res. Serv., R40850, Managing Electronic Waste: Issues with Exporting E-Waste 3–4 (2010).

101. Directive 2012/19/EU of the European Parliament and of the Council of 4 July 2012 on waste electrical and electronic equipment (WEEE), 2012 O.J. (L 197) 38.

102. *Id.* at 38–39.

103. *Id.* at 39.

104. Open-ended Working Group of the Basel Convention on the Control of Transboundary Movements of Hazardous Wastes and Their Disposal, Eighth meeting, Geneva, 25–28 September 2012, *Technical guidelines on transboundary movements of electronic and electrical waste (e-waste), in particular regarding the distinction between waste and non-waste*, UNEPCHW/OEWG.8/INF/9/Rev.1.

105. Directive 2011/65/EU on the restriction of the use of certain hazardous substances in electrical and electronic equipment (recast) (June 8, 2011). *See also* http://ec.europa.eu/environment/waste/rohs_eee/ (last visited Oct. 23, 2013).

CHAPTER 8

Waste and Site Remediation

BRADLEY M. CAMPBELL

I. Introduction

Disparities among nations in establishing and enforcing public health and environmental protections are perhaps nowhere more evident than in the treatment of solid and hazardous waste and in the management of sites at which there has been a release or spill of hazardous substances or oil. These disparities have been reflected in four prevalent patterns: the direct transfer of hazardous waste from developed to less developed countries (LDCs) lacking sufficient capacity for treatment or regulation; the relocation of hazardous waste-producing industrial and extraction activities to LDCs; the abandonment of former industrial, military, and extraction sites in LDCs without adequate remediation; and limited institutional and juridical capacity in the LDCs to enforce environmental standards and protections.

The response to these disparities over the past 30 years has been the development of numerous multilateral agreements and institutions, the strengthening of domestic environmental standards in the LDCs; and, to a much lesser extent, development of environmental regulatory and enforcement capacity among LDC governments. These responses have tempered or eliminated some stark disparities between the developed nations and the LDCs, and have established broad consensus on certain principles of international environmental governance—most notably the principle that transshipment of hazardous waste should require receiving country consent.

But progress in many areas has been stymied by uneven country participation at the international level, including in particular the limited participation of the United States in the development of strong international agreements and institutions. The persistent lack of adequate juridical capacity among the LDCs also has rendered both international and domestic regulatory regimes less effectual in the LDCs. These limiting factors have resulted in the persistence of wide disparities in environmental governance between the developed world and the LDCs with respect to oil and hazardous waste management, and in mostly unsuccessful attempts to use courts in more developed countries to address environmental claims arising in the LDCs.

Concurrently, the dramatic pace of trade expansion and globalization have made these disparities of ever greater importance as waste-generating industries and processes have proliferated, and natural resource extraction (oil, gas, minerals) has intensified in the nations least able to regulate hazardous substance storage, treatment, and disposal.

Consequently, despite a high degree of consensus on the normative standards that should govern hazardous waste and oil storage, treatment, disposal, and remediation, disparities remain, and are likely to persist in the absence of significant new investments in the technical and juridical capacity of LDC governments.

II. The Basel Moment

The development of stricter controls on storage, treatment, and disposal of oil, hazardous substances, and hazardous waste in the United States and other developed countries in the 1970s and early 1980s was at least partly the impetus for a new and toxic international trade, as firms in developed countries identified waste transfer to LDCs as a means of reducing treatment and disposal costs. This trade achieved international notoriety as LDCs began to reject waste shipments originating overseas in the late eighties. In 1986, the barge *Khian Sea* spent 16 months trying to unload its cargo of municipal incinerator ash from Philadelphia in the Caribbean. After being rejected by several countries, the barge ultimately dumped its cargo partly in Haiti and partly in the Indian Ocean.[1] A year later, the *Mobro 4000*, a garbage barge from Long Island, made a similar and similarly unsuccessful quest for Caribbean disposal sites before returning to New York still laden with its original cargo.[2] Another nautical pariah grabbed headlines in 1988, when the *Karin B.* shipped hazardous PCB-laden waste from Italy to a dumpsite in Koko, Nigeria. Complaints from the Nigerian government and environmental groups forced Italy to take the waste back.[3]

Largely in response to the international spectacle of these orphan waste ships, a series of multilateral and bilateral agreements to reduce the shipment of hazardous wastes from the developed world to LDCs established the principle of informed consent by the receiving country prior to shipment. Foremost among these, the Basel Convention on the Transboundary Movement of Hazardous Wastes and their Disposal[4] was adopted in 1989, soon after the *Karin B.* and other controversies, and entered into force in 1992. The Basel principle of informed consent as to waste shipments from developed countries was then adopted by other international organizations, including the Commonwealth of Independent States and the Organisation for Economic Co-operation and Development,[5] and regional pacts extended the principle to waste shipments between and among LDCs.[6] These legal developments were reinforced by an extensive literature decrying the pattern of waste shipments to the LDCs, either in economic terms as inefficient,[7] or in normative terms as racist.[8]

Despite the apparent international consensus reflected in the Basel Convention and its progeny, implementation of the Basel Convention is incomplete in both the developed world and the LDCs. While a signatory, the United States has yet to ratify the convention, although the U.S. Environmental Protection Agency does conform its rules to the convention's requirements. There has been no serious interest by either the White House or the Congress in ratification or the enactment of implementing legislation in at least a decade, no matter which political party is in charge of the respective branch. And indifference or ambivalence concerning the Basel Convention's principles has extended beyond the U.S. government, with the chief economist of the World Bank suggesting as late as 1991 that, on efficiency grounds, there should be more, not less migration of waste and dirty industries to the LDCs.[9]

The loss of momentum behind the Basel Convention is reflected in the fate of a 1995 Basel Convention amendment banning hazardous waste shipments from developed countries to LDCs, which after 18 years has not been ratified by the number of countries required for the amendment to go into force.[10] The convention also does not provide for liability for harm from waste dumping,[11] and such a liability regime under the auspices of the Basel Convention is not even a prospect. So transfers from the United States of waste and waste-generating industries to LDCs—such as the transfer for scrapping of decommissioned ships containing hazardous substances and the increasing volume of electronic or e-waste shipped to LDCs—have survived the Basel Convention.[12] Moreover, the Basel Convention never purported to establish liability for contamination, or require remediation or restoration at sites where oil or hazardous waste has been dumped—even where such dumping occurs in violation of the Basel Convention's strictures. So no international agreement currently provides recourse for legacy disposal sites.

A second and later multilateral effort to stem exposure to hazardous substances, specifically directed to those substances that bioaccumulate in the food web, culminated in the 2001 Stockholm Convention on Persistent Organic Pollutants (POPS),[13] which went into force in 2004. Now ratified by 178 states and the European Union (EU), the Stockholm Convention on POPs prohibits or restricts the production or use of enumerated chemicals like dioxins and PCBs, a list that has grown to include 22 organic hazardous substances. The United States, however, has not ratified or implemented the convention.

Further impediments to achieving the goals advanced by Basel lie in the failure of many LDCs to develop adequate domestic capacity—for want of adequate laws, want of expertise and personnel, want of political will, or the presence of corruption—to enforce the restrictions in either the Basel or Stockholm conventions. This has been illustrated by incidents as notorious as those of the orphan waste ships of the 1980s. In 1998, a Taiwanese company shipped and disposed of tons of mercury- and PCB-laden waste at a site near Sihanoukville, Cambodia. The dumping had been approved by local officials, who were later arrested for corruption, and resulted in numerous reports of illnesses and deaths linked to the waste.[14] In 2006, a British trading firm arranged for the disposal of highly toxic petrochemical wastes in Cote d'Ivoire. Hundreds of tons of sludge from the ship, the *Probo Koala*, were unloaded into tanker trunks that dumped the sludge at 18 or more sites, resulting in 17 deaths and tens of thousands of illnesses.[15] These are just two examples of how both Basel's promise of strengthened environmental governance with respect to hazardous waste has been compromised by corruption or gaps in enforcement in the LDCs.

III. Domestic Law Developments in the LDCs

The Basel Convention and the Stockholm Convention on POPs comprised a broad aspiration as well as a set of concrete regulatory prohibitions and requirements: the aspiration that multilateral agreements and new international institutions could begin to eliminate wide disparities in the regulation of oil and hazardous substances, with concomitant benefits to public health and natural resource protection in the LDCs. As seen in Cambodia and Cote d'Ivoire, this aspiration necessarily depended on the adoption of environmental laws and regulations, and the development of adequate technical expertise and enforcement capacity, in the LDCs, including meaningful access to competent courts.

This requirement has been only half satisfied. As to formal adoption of statutes and regulations, the same forces that animated the Basel Convention did indeed lead to a proliferation of new or revised laws in the LDCs to protect the environment and natural resources from oil and hazardous substance spills and unregulated disposal. For example, following the international notoriety attached to the *Karin B.* incident, Nigeria established a new regulatory structure for regulating oil and hazardous substances, beginning with a series of decrees issued shortly after that incident. On the other side of the world, Ecuador put in place comprehensive environmental management statutes to address oil and hazardous substance spills and remediation, with specific provisions for oil and gas production sites. More recently, in 2008, Ecuador broke new legal ground when it gave "Rights of Nature" explicit protection in a new constitution ratified by popular referendum.

But these new laws have only been effective where the rule of law is otherwise honored, and traditional jurisprudential doctrines do not bar enforcement. In Nigeria, to continue the example, property owners and environmental activists have complained not only that the country's pollution laws are simply not enforced, but also that the government has conspired with a Royal Dutch Petroleum Company (Shell) subsidiary in the murderous suppression of protests against oil development.[16]

Nigeria is concededly the extreme case, but failures in enforcement and lack of governmental integrity and accountability persist in countries of diverse circumstance, including those with greater political stability and legal maturity. In cases first filed in the Southern District of New York nearly 20 years ago, numerous Ecuadorian plaintiffs sought a federal court forum for claims arising from an alleged failure by Texaco, later acquired by Chevron, to remediate sites it polluted in Ecuador's Lago Agrio oil field. The district court considered and rejected evidence that Ecuador's courts were corrupt and could not provide a fair forum for the suit.[17] A decade later, the tables turned: despite Texaco having prevailed in its motion to remit the case to Ecuador's courts,[18] and despite Texaco having consented in writing to Ecuadorian court jurisdiction,[19] Chevron sought relief from courts of the United States and other developed countries effectively to bar enforcement of the $18.2 billion judgment awarded by the Ecuadorian court after trial.[20] Chevron argues that the judgment is infected by corruption,[21] a contention given credence by numerous federal district courts.[22]

The litigation saga in the Chevron cases demonstrates the enormous and continued complexity of resolving oil and hazardous waste spill or dumping claims through a patchwork of national and international jurisdictions.

IV.   Foreign Claims, Foreign Courts

Uncertainty concerning both technical and juridical capacity and integrity in the LDCs has caused plaintiffs and some defendants to seek a competent forum in the United States or Europe to hear claims arising overseas from oil or hazardous substance releases or hazardous waste disposal. In U.S. courts, such claims often face insurmountable substantive and jurisdictional barriers to successful litigation, and many of these barriers are present as well in the legal systems of other developed countries.

Foremost among these barriers in courts of the United States has been the presumption or canon against extraterritorial application of U.S. law: "That canon provides that '[w]hen a statute gives no clear indication of an extraterritorial application, it has none.'"[23] Invoking this presumption, the Ninth Circuit dismissed claims by Philippine plaintiffs seeking relief under the Comprehensive Environmental Response, Compensation, and Liability Act (CERCLA)[24] for contamination at the former Clark and Subic Bay military bases in their country, finding no evidence that Congress intended CERCLA to apply outside the United States.[25] A federal district court reached the same conclusion with respect to the hazardous waste requirements of the Resource Conservation and Recovery Act (RCRA),[26] dismissing claims seeking relief under RCRA for conduct occurring in the United Kingdom.[27]

The same presumption has been fatal to invoking international law to oil or hazardous waste management claims arising outside U.S. territory. Such claims relied in many cases on the Alien Tort Statute (ATS),[28] part of the Judiciary Act of 1789,[29] which provides jurisdiction and a remedy for torts "committed in violation of the law of nations" but which the U.S. Supreme Court narrowed significantly in *Kiobel v. Royal Dutch Petroleum Co.*[30] In *Kiobel*, Nigerian plaintiffs who had been given asylum in the United States alleged that Shell had conspired with the Nigerian government to deprive them of their human rights in retribution for their protests against Shell's oil and hazardous waste disposal practices in the Niger Delta.[31] The Court, unanimous in its judgment but divided in its reasoning, affirmed the Second Circuit's dismissal of the entire case.[32] The Court held that the ATS bears no evidence of congressional intent to apply the ATS overseas sufficient to overcome the presumption against extraterritorial application of U.S. law and extend jurisdiction to the alleged human rights violations, let alone to the underlying pollution case (which was not before the Court), when the conduct at issue occurred entirely on Nigerian soil.[33]

Even before *Kiobel* foreclosed application of the ATS to claims arising wholly extraterritorially, federal and state courts had generally declined to hear tort claims arising overseas that involved oil or hazardous waste handling or disposal on a variety of grounds. The ATS provides a limited mechanism for review of tort claims alleged to have been "committed in violation of the law of nations." Courts have struggled to find international legal norms related to hazardous waste disposal or exposure that are so clearly established as to meet that high bar, and consequently many cases arising from such disposal have been dismissed.[34] More often, courts do not reach the substantive merits of such claims by declining to exercise jurisdiction under the prudential, discretionary doctrines of forum non conveniens[35] and the law of comity of nations.[36]

Courts in the EU and the United Kingdom have been more receptive to adjudicating claims arising from the management or disposal of oil, hazardous waste, or hazardous substances in the LDCs. One plaintiff from the Niger Delta, among many that tried, has prevailed in bringing environmental claims against a Shell subsidiary in a Dutch court,[37] and more claims by other Nigerian plaintiffs against Shell and its subsidiary were presented to British courts. In the Ecuador case, Chevron successfully established jurisdiction in an arbitral forum in The Hague, and has had an interim award by that tribunal (barring enforcement of the Ecuador judgment) enforced in federal district court.[38]

With regard to abandoned sites or discontinued operations, there are further headwinds to compelling remediation or seeking compensation for hazardous substance spills and hazardous waste (and ready protection for potentially responsible parties) even in those countries that do boast technical environmental expertise and capacity and competent courts committed to the rule of law. Foremost among these are the corporate veil and the doctrine of sovereign immunity.

Multinational firms operating in other nations often do so through separately incorporated subsidiaries, whose assets are limited to those necessary for the operations in each country or for a subset of activities in each country. They are well advised to do so. When operations cease in, or a firm otherwise disinvests from, a given country, the corporate entity operating in that country is likely to have few if any assets left in that country to satisfy alleged liabilities for hazardous waste spills or disposal, and traditional principles of limited corporate liability—as applied in much of the developed world—set a high bar for piercing the corporate veil to reach parent or affiliate corporate entities that may have the assets to satisfy a remedial obligation or a damages judgment. So it was that the Niger Delta farmers suing Shell in the Nether-lands failed in their case to establish liability against the corporate parent to Shell's operating entity in Nigeria.[39]

Sovereign immunity has proved an especially significant bar to compel-ling potentially responsible parties to remediate or compensate for oil, haz-ardous substance, or hazardous waste spills or disposal in other countries due to the global reach of the developed nations' militaries, and the legacy of improper disposal practices endemic to military bases throughout the world. Bermuda, for example, sought for years to hold the United States to account for contamination left behind at the former Naval Air Station Ber-muda, an issue that was resolved diplomatically without payment by the United States for the estimated $50 million in cleanup required at the base. Vietnam, similarly, has for 40 years sought to hold the United States accountable for dioxin contamination left behind in the country from the use of Agent Orange during the Vietnam War. In this case, exceptionally, a diplomatic overture has resulted in at least the start of cleanup at the for-mer Da Nang Airport.[40] In both the Bermuda and Vietnam cases, sovereign immunity would have been an insurmountable bar to securing a remedy through litigation in both cases, particularly after courts had rejected appli-cation of CERCLA and RCRA (each of which includes a waiver of sover-eign immunity) to sites overseas by invoking the presumption against extraterritoriality.[41]

V.   Trade, Globalization, and Hazardous Waste

Beginning shortly after the Basel Convention entered into force, the pace of trade liberalization and resulting globalization through multilateral organi-zations accelerated rapidly. While the nexus between trade and environmen-tal protection is considered more fully elsewhere in this volume, free trade institutions like the World Trade Organization and multilateral pacts like the North American Free Trade Agreement (NAFTA) have a number of distinct impacts on hazardous waste management and disputes arising over hazard-ous waste regulation.

First, despite provisions of some trade pacts to ameliorate the adverse environmental consequences of expanded trade, such as the environmental side agreements to NAFTA, trade liberalization has dramatically increased the scale and number of waste-producing manufacturing, extraction, and other industrial processes in the LDCs, the very nations least able to regulate these activities.

Second, there has been incipient use of trade agreements to challenge local land use control of proposed or existing hazardous waste sites. In one case, a California company, Metalclad, acquired an uncontrolled hazardous waste landfill in Mexico's City of Guadalcazar with the intention of operat-ing a hazardous waste disposal facility there. Mexico's federal government issued Metalclad an operating permit, conditioned on remediation of the existing waste dump, but local officials denied Metalclad a required building permit. In response, Metalclad sued Mexico under the foreign investment protections conferred by chapter 11 of NAFTA—in essence seeking compensation from Mexico for expropriation by asserting that the local permit denial was "tantamount to expropriation"—that is, a regulatory taking. Metalclad prevailed in arbitration,[42] and the courts of British Columbia largely upheld the arbitral award of more than $15 million, which ultimately prompted a settlement between the parties. This outcome raises the prospect that hazardous waste regulators in the LDCs, already hobbled by limited technical and juridical capacity, will be further hampered in their work by the in terrorem effect of possible takings claims like those in *Metalclad*.

The third impact of trade agreements, evident in *Metalclad*, is the tendency to shift cases involving otherwise local decisions concerning oil, hazardous substance, and hazardous waste disputes to multilateral trade arbitration panels. On the one hand, such a shift may subordinate local environmental regulatory objectives to the given mandate of these tribunals to protect trade and investment. On the other hand, as in the case of Chevron's dispute with Ecuador, such tribunals may offer a needed and competent extranational forum in cases where domestic juridical processes in the LDCs are of dubious integrity, and U.S. courts are legally unavailable for the reasons discussed. At this writing, there have been too few cases to discern a trend or reach firm conclusions about whether this development is salutary or pernicious.

VI. Domestic Legal Frameworks for Waste Remediation

In the absence of a framework for international liability, domestic laws continue to provide the primary impetus for cleanup of contaminated sites. While waste regulations seek to limit future exposure to contamination by controlling the use, transport, and disposal of chemicals and hazardous wastes (see chapter 7, Handling, Treatment, Transportation, and Disposal of Hazardous Materials, in this volume), waste and site remediation laws provide the vehicle for cleaning up waste sites at which contamination levels pose a risk to public health or the environment. Remedial laws achieve this goal through three general mechanisms: (1) a designated government authority may order the potentially responsible party (PRP) to clean up the site;[43] (2) the government authority may clean up the site itself and then seek to impose liability for its costs on PRPs;[44] or (3) private parties (such as a property owner or municipality) may conduct a cleanup and then seek to recover costs from PRPs. The United States' CERCLA uses a combination of all three measures to realize its goal of site cleanup. Governments commonly develop inventories of contaminated sites and may establish a list of high-priority sites, in order to assess the scope of the problem and best utilize limited agency resources.[45] In Italy, for example, the Environmental Ministry retains authority to clean up "sites of natural interest" that pose a particularly severe risk, while regional or local authorities remediate less seriously contaminated sites.[46] In some cases, a remedial law establishes a dedicated fund to advance cleanup goals.[47]

The key parameters of domestic waste and site remediation laws are discussed next.

A. Who Is a PRP?

The definition of a PRP generally includes the party who releases pollution contaminating a site, but may be much broader than the owner or operator of the polluting facility.[48] As mentioned above, the laws governing corporate liability often limit a parent or successor corporation's responsibility for cleanup of contamination, effectively passing remedial costs on to the public. Some lawmakers have responded to the difficulties posed by limited corporate liability. Under German law, for example, the corporate veil may be pierced to establish liability of a parent corporation in certain exceptional cases, such as where there is intentional undercapitalization of a company that owns contaminated sites.[49]

Remediation laws vary as to whether they include landowners (or tenants) that did not contribute to the contamination in the definition of a PRP. Excluding landowners categorically creates incentives for polluters to sell contaminated land cheaply to avoid cleanup liability, passing along a potential windfall to developers and burdening the public with the costs of cleanup. On the other hand, holding "innocent" landowners liable strikes many as unjust, and furthermore creates barriers to redevelopment of brownfields (land formerly used for industrial/commercial activities) and thus indirectly contributes to development of greenfields (undeveloped land). Lawmakers have formulated a number of approaches to resolving these competing interests. Italian law, for example, does not impose liability on innocent landowners unless the competent authority is unable to recover from a PRP. Even where the landowner faces liability for cleanup costs, recovery is limited based upon the fair market value of the remediated property.[50] Similarly, in the United Kingdom, innocent landowners are typically not PRPs, though they may face liability if established to be "knowing permitters" of contamination.[51] In the Netherlands, innocent landowners constitute PRPs but lawmakers provided additional programs to combat the disincentives of such liability to brownfield redevelopment. For example, the law provides flexibility for cleanup to occur in phases or only partially, and the central government offers financial support to private sector cleanups.[52]

B. What Liability Does a PRP Face?

Liability under waste and site remediation laws runs the gamut from strict liability and joint and several liability where more than one party contributes to contamination, to fault-based liability and proportionate liability among joint tortfeasors.[53] Belgian law combines both types of liability, depending upon when the contamination occurred. PRPs who contaminated a site prior to the enactment of the law are liable only if negligent, while PRPs contaminating after its enactment face strict liability.[54] Like Belgium, a number of other jurisdictions limit retroactive liability, in whole or part.[55] Typically, liability under remediation laws includes the cost of investigating a site and assessing the scope of contamination, in addition to any remedial costs.

C.   What Contamination Triggers Liability?

The type and degree of contamination that triggers an obligation to remediate a site are likely to vary across jurisdictions. The selection of such thresholds entail complex scientific and policy judgments regarding the appropriate degree of risk to public health and the environment, and their development marks an important step toward an effective legal framework for waste remediation.[56] Under the United States' CERCLA, liability is triggered by the release in any amount of a "hazardous substance," a defined term that includes a substantial list of substances specifically identified by the U.S. Environmental Protection Agency, as well as any substance meeting particular characteristics (e.g., meeting a defined "toxicity" characteristic).[57] Italian law sets forth a list of contamination threshold values whose exceedance triggers legal obligations, while Mexico has developed national standards identifying maximum permissible levels of certain contaminants.[58] Rather than setting thresholds, the United Kingdom's Environmental Protection Act uses a risk-based approach. A site is considered contaminated where a contaminant is present, there is a pathway for exposure to the contaminant, and there is "a significant possibility of significant harm" or pollution of controlled waters is occurring or likely to occur.[59]

D.   How Much Cleanup Is Required?

Site cleanup objectives are closely related to the thresholds triggering cleanup obligations, as the latter identifies an unacceptable risk, and the former sets out the parameters to reduce that risk. Cleanup objectives are commonly driven by risk assessment, taking into account the future use of the land.[60] Considerations of costs in determining acceptable cleanup goals and methods vary. The United Kingdom law requires consideration of the likely costs of remediation, alongside the severity of the risk posed by the contamination, in determining a reasonable remediation plan.[61] Under U.S. law, on the other hand, the regulator enjoys a strong presumption that the costs it incurs for cleanup are recoverable.[62] Waste and site remediation laws have at times been subject to criticism for failing to require remediation to be cost justified or to compel selection of the most cost effective.[63]

Ultimately, even where such laws are on the books, successful remediation of waste sites depends on the resources and technical capacity of the competent authority. While many laws provide flexibility for PRPs to take a lead in funding and managing site assessments and proposed remediation plans, regulator oversight is essential to ensure the remediation responds to the risk posed by site contamination. Indeed, until the competent authority begins the task of identifying contaminated sites, there is likely to be little understanding of the risks posed by contaminated sites, and little real enforcement of cleanup obligations against PRPs.

Notes

1. *Ship Operators Face Jail in Ocean Dumping*, N.Y. TIMES (Oct. 7, 1993); *Ship Dumps Philadelphia Ash, but Where?*, N.Y. TIMES (Nov. 10, 1988).

2. J. PICHTEL, WASTE MANAGEMENT PRACTICES: MUNICIPAL, HAZARDOUS, AND INDUSTRIAL 3 (2005).

3. *Toxic Waste Boomerang: Ciao Italy!*, N.Y. TIMES (Sept. 3, 1988).

4. Basel Convention on the Control of Transboundary Movements of Hazardous Wastes and Their Disposal, Mar. 22, 1989, art. 2(14), 1673 U.N.T.S. 57.

5. Commonwealth of Independent States (CIS), *The intergovernmental agreement of the participating states of the CIS about control of cross-border transportation of dangerous and other waste* (Apr. 12, 1996); Organisation on Economic Co-operation and Development (OECD), *Decision on the control of transboundary movements of waste destined for recovery operations*, C(2001)107/FINAL (2201), *amended by* C(2004)20; C(2005)141; and C(2008)156.

6. *E.g.*, Bamako Convention on the Ban on the Import into Africa and the Control of Transboundary Movement and Management of Hazardous Wastes within Africa (entered into force 1991) (prohibition of waste imports among 24 parties), *available at* http://www.au.int/en/content/bamako-convention-ban-import-africa-and-control-trans boundary-movement-and-management-hazard (last visited Oct. 15, 2013).

7. ENVIRONMENTAL ECONOMICS IN THEORY AND PRACTICE 163 (N. Hanley et al. eds., 1997).

8. *E.g.*, D. PELLOW, RESISTING GLOBAL TOXICS 9 (2007).

9. Memorandum to Distribution from Lawrence H. Summers (Dec. 12, 1991), *quoted in Furor on Memo at the World Bank*, N.Y. TIMES, Feb. 7, 1992. Summers and the staff member who drafted the memorandum later recanted the suggestion.

10. *See* http://archive.basel.int/ratif/ban-alpha.htm. The European Union has codified the so-called Basel Ban by regulation applicable to its member countries. European Union, Reg. (EC) No. 1013/2006 of the European Parliament and of the Council of 14 June, 2006, *available at* http://eur-lex.europa.eu/LexUriServ/LexUriServ.do?uri=CELEX :32006R1013:EN:NOT.

11. *See generally* R. Percival, *Global Law and the Environment*, 86 WASH. L. REV. 579, 621 (2011).

12. M. Clayton, *Aged Ships a Toxic Export*, CHRISTIAN SCI. MONITOR (Mar. 19, 2008).

13. Stockholm Convention on Persistent Organic Pollutants (POPS), May 22, 2001, 2256 U.N.T.S. 119.

14. *Tests Show High Mercury at Cambodia Dump Site*, N.Y. TIMES (Dec. 26, 1998).

15. *Global Sludge Ends in Tragedy for Ivory Coast*, N.Y. TIMES (Oct. 2, 2006); Percival, *supra* note 11, at 621 (discussing Cote d'Ivoire case).

16. *See, e.g.*, Kiobel v. Royal Dutch Petroleum Co., 133 S. Ct. 1659 (2013).

17. Aguinda v. Texaco, Inc., 142 F. Supp. 2d 534 (S.D.N.Y. 2001), *aff'd*, 303 F.3d 470 (2d Cir. 2002).

18. *Id.*

19. Of the $18.2 billion award, half comprises punitive damages imposed because Chevron did not apologize by a specific deadline. Republic of Ecuador v. Chevron Corp., 638 F.3d 384, 390 (2d Cir. 2011).

20. Chevron Corp. v. Donziger, No. 11-0691, slip op. at n.8 (S.D.N.Y. Jan. 7, 2013).

21. Chevron has prevailed in securing an interim award in arbitration at The Hague to prevent enforcement of the judgment; a prominent consulting firm retained by the plaintiffs has recanted its expert reports and testimony in the Ecuadorian proceeding, and one Ecuadorian judge has accused the judge who issued the judgment with corruption. *Consultant Recants in Chevron Pollution Case in Ecuador*, N.Y. TIMES (Apr. 12, 2013).

22. Chevron has secured an injunction preventing two of the Ecuadorian plaintiffs and the attorney in the case from enforcing or otherwise profiting from the Ecuadoran judgment. Chevron Corp. v. Donzinger, 974 F. Supp. 2d 362 (S.D.N.Y. 2014), *modified* in No. 11-0869 (S.D.N.Y. April 25, 2014). At least six other federal courts have found prima facie evidence of fraud in the Ecuadorian judgment against Chevron. Chevron Corp. v. Donziger, No. 11-0691 (S.D.N.Y. Mar. 15, 2013); Chevron Corp. v. Camp, 2010 WL 3418394, at *6 (W.D.N.C. Aug. 28, 2010) ("While this court is unfamiliar with the practices of the Ecuadorian judicial system, the court must believe that the concept of fraud is universal, and that what has blatantly occurred in this matter would in fact be considered fraud by any court. If such conduct does not amount to fraud in a particular country, then that country has larger problems than an oil spill."); Chevron Corp. v. Page, No. RWT-11-0395 (D. Md. Jan 25, 2013) ("there is ample evidence of the existence of a fraudulent scheme"); *In re* Chevron Corp., No. 11-24599-CV (S.D. Fla. June 12, 2012) (denoting a "large scale" fraud); *In re* Chevron Corp., No. 10-cv-1146-IEG (WMC) (S.D. Cal. Sept. 10, 2010) ("ample evidence" of fraud); *In re* Chevron Corp., Nos. 1:10-mc-00021-22 ((JH/FLG) (D.N.M. June 11, 2010); *In re* Chevron Corp., No. cv-10-2675 (SRC) (D.N.J. June 11, 2010 (concluding there was a "fraud upon the tribunal"). The Ecuadorian Lago Agrio plaintiffs and their lawyers continue to dispute these findings and Chevron's claims generally, while seeking to enforce their judgment in countries other than the United States where Chevron has assets.

23. Kiobel v. Royal Dutch Pet. Co., 133 S. Ct. 1659, 1664 (2013) (quoting Morrison v. Nat'l Australia Bank Ltd., 130 S. Ct. 2869, 2878 (2010)).

24. 42 U.S.C. §§ 9601 *et seq.* (CERCLA).

25. Arc Ecology v. U.S. Dep't of the Air Force, 411 F.3d 1092 (9th Cir. 2005).

26. 42 U.S.C. §§ 9601 *et seq.*

27. Amlon Metal, Inc. v. FMC Corp. 775 F. Supp. 668, 672–76 (S.D.N.Y. 1991).

28. 28 U.S.C. § 1350.

29. Act of Sept. 24, 1789, § 9, 1 Stat 77; *see* Moxon v. Fanny, 17 F. Cas. 942 (No. 9,895) (D.C. Pa. 1793).

30. Kiobel v. Royal Dutch Petroleum Co., 133 S. Ct. 1659 (2013).

31. *Id.* at 1662–63.

32. *Id.* at 1669–71.

33. *Id.* at 1665–69. An earlier ATS case originating in the same district court, *Wiwa v. Royal Dutch Petroleum Co.*, No. 96 Civ. 8386 (KMW) (HBP), 2009 BL 97569 (S.D.N.Y. Mar. 18, 2009), survived dismissal long enough to yield a settlement in which Shell paid $15.5 million to resolve allegations of its complicity in the military regime's hanging of Nigerian environmentalist Ken Saro-Wiwa. *Shell to Pay $15.5 Million to Settle Nigerian Case*, N.Y. TIMES (June 8, 2009).

34. *E.g.*, Beanal v. Freeport-McMoran, Inc., 197 F.3d 161, 167 (5th Cir. 1999) (no rule of international law applicable to disposal of mine tailings); Flores v. S. Peru Copper Corp., 253 F. Supp. 2d 510, 519 (S.D.N.Y. 2002) ("plaintiffs have not demonstrated that high levels of environmental pollution, causing harm to human life, health, and sustainable development within a nation's borders violate any well-established rules of customary international law"); Presbyterian Church of Sudan v. Talisman Energy, 244 F. Supp. 2d

289, 340 (S.D.N.Y 2003) ("[I]t is well-established that environmental damage, without more, generally does not violate international law" (citations omitted)).

35. *E.g., In re* Union Carbide Corp. Gas Plant Disaster at Bhopal 809 F.2d 195, 199–202 (2d Cir. 1987).

36. Sequihua v. Texaco, 847 F. Supp. 61 (S.D. Tex. 1994).

37. David Jolly & Stanley Reed, *Mixed Decision for Shell in Nigeria Oil Spill Suits*, N.Y. TIMES (Jan. 30, 2013); *Dutch Court Says Shell Responsible for Nigeria Spills*, REUTERS (Jan. 30, 2013) http://www.reuters.com/article/2013/01/30/us-shell-nigeria-lawsuit-idUSBRE90 S16X20130130.

38. Chevron Corp. v. Republic of Ecuador, No. 12-1247 (JEB), 2013 BL 148362 (D.D.C. June 06, 2013); Mercedes Alvaro, *U.S. District Court Confirmed $96 Million Award to Chevron in Ecuador Case*, WALL ST. J. (June 12, 2013).

39. Jolly & Reed, *supra* note 37.

40. T. Fuller, *4 Decades On, U.S. Starts Cleanup of Agent Orange in Vietnam*, N.Y. TIMES (Aug. 9, 2012).

41. *See* notes 28 and 29, *supra*. The U.S. Circuit Court of Appeals for the D.C. Circuit, in a challenge to food-waste incineration in Antarctica under the National Environmental Policy Act, 42 U.S.C. §§ 4321 *et seq.* (NEPA), has allowed NEPA challenges to U.S. activities in Antarctica, declining to apply the presumption against extraterritoriality. Envtl. Def. Fund v. Massey, 986 F.2d 528, 531–35 (D.C. Cir. 1993). After *Kiobel*, it seems unlikely that *Massey* remains good law.

42. Metalclad Corp. v. United Mexican States, ICSID Case No. ARB(AF)/97/1, Award ¶ 131 (Aug. 30, 2000), 5 ICSID Rep. 212 (2002), *available at* http://naftaclaims .com/Disputes/Mexico/Metalclad/MetalcladFinalAward.pdf.

43. *See, e.g.*, chapter 42, Israel, section VI (discussing authority to issue orders under the "Maintenance of Cleanliness Law").

44. The EU Environmental Liability Directive (ELD) calls on national competent authorities, which conduct cleanup themselves, to ensure its costs are recovered from a PRP (in the language of the directive, the "operator" of a site). Directive 2004/35 of the European Parliament and the Council of April 21 2004 on Environmental Liability with Regard to the Prevention and Remedying of Environmental Damage, art. 8, at 62.

45. For example, laws in Argentina and Mexico mandate a national inventory of contaminated sites. Brazil, Chile, Columbia, and Peru do not require inventories, but have made preliminary efforts toward identifying contaminated sites. M. Kadas et al., *Emerging Environmental Regimes for Contaminated Land in Latin America*, 31 INT'L ENV'T. REP. (BNA) (2008).

46. Chapter 31, Italy, section IV.B; *see also* chapter 33, Spain, section V (law requires regional authorities to identify contaminated sites). Interestingly, Japan maintains a public register of lands at risk of soil contamination, by requiring landowners to report the results of soil inspections. *See* chapter 39, Japan, section V.

47. *See, e.g.*, chapter 42, Israel, section VI. The United States' CERCLA formerly imposed a "Superfund" tax on certain chemical companies that supported a cleanup trust fund. The tax expired in 1995 and has not been reinstated.

48. For example, the ELD, *supra* note 44, defines a liable "operator" as including the entity "whom has economic power over the technical functioning of [a facility]," which may include the holder of a permit authorizing the activity. For further discussion, see chapter 9, Emergency Response. As another example, the United States' CERCLA holds liable parties who "arrange" for the disposal of wastes, that is, parties who do not directly dispose of the waste but convey the waste to another party with the intent that it be disposed.

49. Chapter 29, Germany, section II.A.2.

50. Chapter 31, Italy, section IV.B.

51. Chapter 30, United Kingdom, section IV.

52. Chapter 32, Netherlands, section V.

53. *See, e.g.*, chapter 46, New Zealand, section V (under Resource Management Act polluters liable for cleanup); chapter 32, Netherlands, sections IV, V (strict liability imposed on owners and operators of sites); chapter 33, Spain, section V (joint and several liability may be imposed); chapter 29, Germany, section II.A.2 (strict and joint and several liability). While the majority of EU member states appear to have adopted joint and several liability, some (including Denmark, Finland, France, Slovakia, and Slovenia) have adopted proportionate liability. R. Percival, *CERCLA in a Global Context*, 41 Sw. L.J. 727, 733 (2012).

54. Percival, *supra* note 53, at 735.

55. *See, e.g.*, chapter 46, New Zealand, section V (court ruling limits retroactive liability).

56. *See, e.g.*, Kadas, *supra* note 45, at 9 (discussing evolution of Peruvian remediation laws, including eventual proposal to establish soil cleanup levels).

57. 42 U.S.C. § 9601(14).

58. Chapter 31, Italy, section IV.B.2.; chapter 19, Mexico, section V.

59. Chapter 30, United Kingdom, section IV; *see also* part IIA of the U.K. Environmental Protection Act 78A (2).

60. *See, e.g.*, chapter 28, France, section XII.

61. Chapter 30, United Kingdom, section IV.

62. 42 U.S.C. § 9607(a)(4)(A).

63. *See, e.g.*, J.T. Hamilton & W. Kip Viscusi, Calculating Risks? The Spatial and Political Dimensions of Hazardous Waste Policy (MIT 1999) (arguing that the costs per cancer case averted at U.S. Superfund sites are excessive).

CHAPTER 9

Emergency Response

JAMON L. BOLLOCK AND DAVID O. CHANG

Recent environmental disasters illustrate how local pollution events can take on global importance by threatening to become disasters of international scope. The radiation leak at the Fukishima Daichi nuclear reactor in Japan, for example, created fears of radiation pollution in neighboring countries and even as far away as the U.S. State of Hawaii. The BP Deepwater Horizon oil spill in the U.S. Gulf of Mexico appeared to threaten international waters, as uncertainty over the spread of oil from the spill led some to predict that spilled oil would reach Cuba and the Atlantic Gulf Stream. In fact, oil spills have frequently been international concerns, because sea currents transport oil slicks to other nearby countries' shores, and the vessels causing the spills are usually owned by corporations that are not located in the country where the spill has occurred and are usually flagged in a third country.[1]

A recent environmental disaster that actually became an international problem was the accident at the Ajkai Timflödgyár alumina plant in Hungary on October 4, 2010.[2] When a portion of the dam holding toxic waste in a reservoir ruptured,[3] a wave of 35 million cubic feet of slightly radioactive sludge flooded more than 15 square miles.[4] The sludge eventually reached the Danube River and forced the downriver countries of Slovakia, Croatia, Serbia, Romania, Bulgaria, and Ukraine to develop emergency response plans.[5] The release killed 10 people, injured hundreds of residents, and contaminated waterways.[6] Economically, the International Commission for the Protection of the Danube River estimated that the costs for removal of the sludge, decontamination, and compensation were between US$100 to US$200 million.[7]

The rapid industrialization of formerly undeveloped areas globally, along with the inability or unwillingness of some local authorities to impose restrictions on the international corporations leading that development, increases the likelihood that similar accidents will occur in the future.[8] In response to international environmental disasters of the past, including the *Torrey Canyon* spill[9] and Chernobyl nuclear accident, nations have worked together to develop mechanisms for addressing environmental disasters. Much of this work has focused on either prevention of pollution or liability and compensation after disasters have already occurred. There is at the moment little legal guidance for responding to environmental disasters affecting multiple countries.

This chapter provides an overview of the legal frameworks pertaining to responses to international environmental emergencies. It further identifies some basic steps to develop a pre-emergency response plan and response strategies for companies and organizations that potentially face the need to respond to such emergencies.

I.   Determining the Scope of the Response: International, Regional, and Domestic Legal Considerations

The first step in planning for an international environmental emergency response is to understand the laws and requirements of the affected jurisdictions and international institutions. When working with transnational environmental disasters such as industrial accidents and hazardous waste or oil spills, an organization must consider the applicable international, regional, and domestic legal frameworks before it can determine how to properly respond to an environmental disaster.

A.   International Legal Considerations

Well-publicized environmental emergencies have provided the impetus for international agreements and coordination by international institutions to foster accident prevention and preparedness and to develop frameworks for responding to emergencies.[10] These agreements typically focus on either providing information about emergencies[11] or on specific types of hazards, such as radioactive pollution or oil spills at sea.[12] Additionally, bilateral treaties between particular nations also address transboundary emergency preparedness and prevention.[13] The United States and Mexico, for example, have entered into an agreement[14] on the discharge of hazardous substances along their border. It establishes a joint contingency plan and provides for joint responses to transboundary pollution incidents, as well as a joint response team with the authority to provide advice on response actions needed in individual emergency events and to take steps to coordinate response resources.[15]

More broadly, international institutions also undertake the coordination of responses to international environmental disasters throughout the world. The nation in which a pollution event occurs has a duty under international law to minimize the damage from the incident, and nations that are in a position to help alleviate the damage have a duty to provide assistance.[16] The duty to minimize damage includes an obligation to notify other countries that might be affected and to provide information about the incident so that other countries may take their own steps to minimize the damage.[17] There is also a developing duty under international law to cooperate with other states in responding to disasters, as reflected in the growing number of bilateral and multilateral agreements addressing disaster response between particular nations.[18]

To achieve the goals of minimizing damage from international environmental disasters and providing assistance in responding to disasters, organizations like the United Nations have established agencies and programs to foster cooperation among states. The Joint Environment Unit (JEU) of the U.N. Environment Programme (UNEP) and U.N. Office for the Coordination of Humanitarian Affairs (OCHA) facilitates the provision of assistance between affected countries and those nations willing to donate resources, including environmental expertise and mobile laboratories, to conduct rapid assessments, and to help national authorities in developing strategies to respond.[19] Similarly, UNEP's Disasters and Conflicts Sub-Programme supports early postdisaster recovery from environmental disasters by rapidly mobilizing teams of international and national environmental experts to conduct detailed environmental assessments based on field investigations and laboratory analyses.[20] The JEU also sponsors an Advisory Group on Environmental Emergencies to bring together environmental responders from all over the world to share information and encourage cooperation.[21] Additionally, UNEP's Awareness for Emergencies at the Local Level Programme (APELL) produces technical reports and other materials to assist disaster prevention and response planning in vulnerable areas, specifically by assisting in the development of local communities' emergency response plans.[22]

Beyond the U.N., the International Labor Organization's Code of Conduct on Major Industrial Accidents[23] and Convention on the Prevention of Major Industrial Accidents[24] establish responsibilities for companies regarding the conduct of industrial activities and for government authorities concerning the preparation of emergency preparedness arrangements.[25] Meanwhile, the Organisation for Economic Co-operation and Development's (OECD) Working Group on Chemical Accidents has issued several guidance documents related to addressing chemical emergencies. Most importantly, the OECD Guiding Principles for Chemical Accident Prevention, Preparedness, and Response[26] provides information to public authorities, industry, and communities worldwide for the development and implementation of laws, regulations, policies, and practices to prevent and prepare for accidents involving hazardous substances.[27]

In the context of oil and chemical spills, 14 international and regional conventions and protocols provide a framework for responding to threats to the marine environment. First, the 1969 Intervention Convention[28] and 1973 Intervention Protocol[29] authorize affected coastal states to take action on the high seas to prevent, mitigate, or eliminate threats from pollution and other hazardous substances. The 1989 Salvage Convention[30] creates incentives for salvors to prevent or mitigate damage from pollution. The 1990 Convention on Oil Pollution Preparedness, Response, and Cooperation[31] (OPRC Convention) commits parties to take all appropriate measures to respond to pollution from oil spill incidents.[32] The 2000 Protocol to the OPRC Convention on

Preparedness, Response, and Cooperation to Pollution Incidents by Hazardous and Noxious Substances[33] (2000 HNS Protocol) extends the same obligations to a list of chemicals covered by other international conventions and codes.[34] Together, these agreements provide a global framework for responding to pollution disasters involving oil and other hazardous substances.

Several important international agreements also address responses to oil and chemical spills at the regional level. Nine of the UNEP Regional Seas Conventions contain protocols that cover emergency response and preparedness for areas under the jurisdiction of the conventions.[35] The agreements include similar provisions that, inter alia, provide for international cooperation and information exchange, require the development of emergency contingency plans and monitoring programs, ensure reporting of accidents, and authorize response actions.[36] In the North Sea, the 1969 and 1983 Bonn Agreements[37] require parties to assess and observe spillage and provide information to other parties.[38] In the Mediterranean Sea, the Protocol for the Protection of the Mediterranean Sea against pollution resulting from exploration and exploitation of the continental shelf and the seabed and its subsoil[39] provides for contingency planning, development of safety measures, notification, and mutual assistance in the case of emergencies resulting from offshore exploration and drilling activities.[40]

Beyond oil and chemical spills, other regional instruments establish rules applicable to a wide range of potentially hazardous and dangerous activities. The European Union's (EU) Seveso Directive,[41] originally adopted in 1982 in response to the major industrial disaster in Seveso, Italy, and amended in 1996, is intended to prevent major accidents involving dangerous substances. To that end, the directive requires member states to ensure that facility operators take necessary measures to prevent accidents, notify public authorities of certain activities, and implement an emergency policy, accident prevention policy, and safety policy.[42] Also, the U.N. Economic Commission for Europe's (UNECE) Convention on the Transboundary Effects of Industrial Accidents, adopted in 1992, follows the Seveso Directive in fostering international cooperation in preventing industrial accidents, reducing their frequency and severity, and mitigating their effects.[43] Party states must identify hazardous activities within their jurisdictions and ensure notification of other affected states.[44] Individual operators are also required to demonstrate the safety of hazardous activities performed at their facilities.[45]

B. Liability Considerations

Companies and organizations engaged in activities that could potentially lead to an environmental emergency should also understand the possible liability resulting from such an emergency. For oil spills, one of the major conventions overseen by the International Maritime Organization (IMO) is the International Convention on Civil Liability for Oil Pollution Damage (CLC).[46] The CLC was adopted in 1969[47] to ensure that "adequate compensation is available to persons who suffer oil pollution damage resulting from maritime casualties involving oil-carrying ships."[48] The convention imposes a strict liability regime on ship owners.[49] If a ship owner is at fault for oil pollution, the CLC does not cap the amount of liability that may ultimately arise.[50] If the ship owner is not at fault, the CLC caps liability at 3 million special drawing rights (SDR)—an international reserve asset created by the International Monetary Fund (IMF)[51]—for a ship not exceeding gross tonnage of 5,000.[52] The CLC caps liability at 59.7 million SDR rights for ships that exceed a gross tonnage of 140,000.[53] The SDR limits under the CLC equate to about US$3.8 million for ships not exceeding a gross tonnage of 5,000 to US$76.5 million for larger ships.[54] Originally, the CLC only applied to oil tankers.[55] The International Convention on Civil Liability for Bunker Oil Pollution Damage (Bunker Convention) changed this when it extended the basic tenets of civil liability under the CLC for oil pollution damage to all ships.[56] The Bunker Convention also requires ships over 1,000 gross tonnage to maintain insurance or other financial security.[57] Today, oil pollution caused by all ships is subject to civil liability under the CLC.

Some areas of the world have regional instruments that establish civil liability for environmental disasters. Entities working in such a region must consider their legal responsibilities under these agreements.

Europe is one such region. The EU has adopted Directive 2004/35/CE on environmental liability with regard to the prevention and remedying of environmental damage (ELD Directive).[58] The ELD Directive was established with the purpose of ensuring that "an operator whose activity has caused environmental damage or the imminent threat of such damage [should] be held financially liable, in order to induce operators to adopt measures and develop practices to minimize the risks of environmental damage so that their exposure to financial liabilities is reduced."[59] Under the ELD Directive, the person or group responsible for causing the environmental damage is the party responsible for the damages and costs of the disaster.[60] The responsible party is also accountable for the costs of assessing the damage or assessing the "imminent threat of such damage."[61] To facilitate recovery of such costs, the ELD Directive provides its member states with the authority to collect the costs associated with the environmental disaster "via security over property or other appropriate guarantees from the [responsible party]."[62] The ELD Directive defines a liable "operator" to include the person "whom has economic power over the technical functioning of" an occupational activity.[63] The definition of an "operator" is not uniform among all members of the ELD Directive, however, as the ELD Directive allows a member state to broaden its own definition of the term.[64] Currently, all but one of the EU member countries has opted to broaden the scope of "operator."[65] The ELD Directive has authority over both land-based and maritime environmental disasters. The ELD Directive's maritime reach is limited to coasts and territorial seas;[66] however, there are currently efforts aimed at expanding the reach of the ELD Directive so that it would cover "all marine waters under the jurisdiction of the Member States."[67] The proposed changes to the ELD

Directive would add liability for operators who cause environmental damage through their offshore oil and gas activities.[68]

The ELD Directive establishes two liability schemes. Under the first scheme, strict liability applies to the activities that have been listed in Annex III.[69] Annex III includes waste and waste management, mining and other extractive industries, operations that discharge water, and the transport of hazardous materials.[70] Operators who engage in activities listed under Annex III may be held liable for damage from a release, regardless of fault.[71] The second liability scheme is a fault-based scheme.[72] This scheme only applies to the occupational activities that are not listed in Annex III.[73] Under the fault-based scheme, the operator is only liable if it is found to be at fault or negligent.[74]

Outside of those addressing oil spills and nuclear accidents, no major international civil liability treaties have entered into force for transboundary environmental disasters.[75] Typically, domestic laws have governed transboundary environmental disasters. However, suits under domestic laws for international or transboundary environmental damage have been very difficult to prosecute because of the procedural hurdles involved with transboundary tort litigation.[76] These challenges often include difficulty in exercising personal jurisdiction over foreign firms, challenges in executing extraterritorial service of process, difficulties in resolving choice of law issues, overcoming motions to dismiss based on forum non conveniens, and enforcing judgments.[77]

C.   Domestic Legal Considerations

In addition to international frameworks for responding to environmental disasters and establishing liability, many nations have implemented domestic legal frameworks for responding to environmental emergencies. While a discussion of domestic legal regimes throughout the world is beyond the scope of this chapter, an examination of the response framework in the United States is helpful in highlighting the legal factors that a corporation or organization should consider when faced with an international emergency.

In the United States, there are two major sets of laws that deal with environmental disasters: the Oil Protection Act of 1990 (OPA) and the Comprehensive Environmental Response, Compensation, and Liability Act (CERCLA). The OPA prohibits the discharge of oil or hazardous substances into the navigable waters of the United States.[78] CERCLA establishes a national program that addresses the release of hazardous substances.[79] The federal government has also established the National Oil and Hazardous Substance Contingency Plan (National Contingency Plan or NCP), the government's "blueprint" for responding to pollution emergencies.[80] The National Contingency Plan was expanded and enhanced by CERCLA and OPA to set forth extensive and comprehensive procedures for responding to oil spills and releases of other hazardous substances.

Under the NCP, the U.S. government's preparedness efforts and response to disasters is coordinated by the National Response Team and teams at the regional level.[81] The coordinated response is directed by the Federal On-Scene Coordinator (FOSC), which directs all response activities at the site of discharge[82] through the unified command structure for managing responses to discharges.[83] Facility operators are required to notify the National Response Center of any discharge or release of oil or hazardous substances.[84] In the case of oil spills, the FOSC directs the coordinated response by determining the threat posed by the incident, classifying the size and type of the release, notifying the regional response team and the National Response Center, and supervising removal actions.[85] In responding to oil spills under the NCP, the FOSC may enlist the assistance of other federal entities.[86] In the case of a release of a hazardous substance, the NCP authorizes the lead agency to initiate appropriate actions to mitigate or remove the release of hazardous substances.[87] Under the NCP, responsible parties—that is, the owners or operators of the facilities where the discharge occurred—may participate in the response effort, as determined by the FOSC. The OPA and CERCLA also establish liability for responsible parties for compensating the government for its response efforts and for damages to natural resources.[88]

Rather than simply focusing on response and liability, however, OPA also requires preventive measures.[89] To prevent future oil and hazardous chemical spills, regulations issued under section 311(j) require facilities that store large amounts of oil and hazardous chemicals to prepare spill prevention plans and prevent accidental releases of oil and hazardous chemicals from reaching navigable waters.[90] Facilities with a high likelihood of accidents that release oil or hazardous chemicals are also required to develop plans for quickly responding to spills.[91]

D. Summary

When environmental disasters occur in other nations or transcend national boundaries, it is difficult to craft a response that addresses the requirements of every jurisdiction impacted by the disaster. While some international and regional frameworks provide for cooperation among nations in responding to environmental emergencies, most countries have their own sets of laws for responding to environmental disasters. Additionally, provinces or regions within countries may also have additional rules pertaining to environmental disaster response. Each jurisdiction creates a new potential set of responsibilities that organizations must recognize and follow.

II. Planning and Implementing Emergency Responses
A. Developing a Pre-Emergency Response Plan

There are four basic principles that apply to any emergency response: prevent, prepare, respond, and recover.[92] To minimize financial and legal liabilities, companies and organizations that engage in hazardous activities should work to prevent accidents and develop pre-emergency response plans.

Relying on the authorities discussed above, a company that engages in hazardous activities should develop and implement a pre-emergency response plan to guide its efforts in responding to an environmental emergency. Pre-emergency response plans will reduce the likelihood of an incident and mitigate the effects if an accident occurs.[93]

There are six elements to an effective pre-emergency response plan: risk assessment, environmental sensitivities assessment, response strategy, equipment types and quantity, stakeholder management, and transboundary issues.[94] First, organizations engaging in hazardous activities should conduct a comprehensive risk assessment.[95] The risk assessment forms the foundation of the emergency response plan because it provides the information necessary to develop a systematic approach for the identification, management, and reduction of the risk.[96] An effective risk assessment should establish the probability of an accident occurring and develop a baseline for assessing the adequacy of current preparedness and response capabilities.[97] The risk assessment should also include a scientific analysis. The scientific analysis should detail the types of chemicals or oils that could be discharged.[98] The risk assessment should also include an analysis of possible intervention measures and equipment.[99] Finally, the assessment should also contain an analysis modeling the spread of potential discharges.[100] This will help organizations determine the geographic extent of a potential emergency.

Second, a pre-emergency response plan should include an environmental sensitivities analysis that estimates the probability that an accident will occur and the time necessary for the environment to recover from the potential damage.[101] Environmental sensitivities (also referred to as resource mapping) are the natural resources in an area that could be impacted by a discharge or release of a hazardous substance.[102] An environmental sensitivities analysis goes hand in hand with the risk assessment.[103]

In developing a pre-emergency response plan, a company that engages in hazardous activities should also use the risk assessment and environmental sensitivities analysis to develop an overall response strategy. It is important to optimize the response to ensure that it is efficient and effective, for example by targeting the key areas where an accident is most likely to occur.[104] As part of the overall response strategy, it is important to identify, acquire, and properly locate the materials and equipment needed for a quick response. The type and amount of equipment required will depend on the type of discharge and how long it will take for additional resources to arrive after the initial response.[105]

Finally, if the potentially hazardous activity occurs close to an international or local border, it is important to preemptively address a potential transboundary situation by setting up a combination of liaison contacts, lines of reporting between regions or countries, and estimates of the limits of transboundary contamination, and to recognize the need for rapid cooperation.[106] Ideally, the countries will agree on and establish communication processes and emergency protocols, as in the case of the United States and Mexico, so that there can be seamless transitions between the countries during the emergency.[107]

B.   Responding to the Emergency

An operator's response to an environmental emergency should follow its pre-emergency response plan to the extent possible.[108] During the response, it is important to have clear procedures in place to notify, assess, and initiate the response, and to establish a reliable way to receive accurate information.[109] During the emergency, it is also very important for the operator to assist public authorities in determining the extent and movement of the discharge.[110] Real-time aerial observations and global positioning system capture tools are the most effective ways to track a discharge in order to predict its movement.[111] Finally, in responding to a discharge, an operator must also identify and target the highest priority areas that could be affected by the emergency.[112] To do this, the pre-emergency plan should provide a method for the quick integration of local knowledge and stakeholder feedback to guide the response and establish priority areas.[113] Once the priority areas have been selected, response efforts should focus on containing high-priority areas to prevent the discharge from reaching sensitive resources. The next step for the operator is to execute cleanup efforts, beginning with the high-priority areas if necessary.

Once the response phase has ended, an operator should either make a final assessment of the affected area or assist public authorities in making a final assessment[114] and implement an environmental management plan to monitor the recovery of the area.[115] Options for monitoring plans include short, medium, and long-term studies to evaluate the health of the damaged locations, and which plan to implement will generally be dictated by the jurisdiction's legal requirements.[116]

III.   Conclusion

International environmental disasters require large-scale emergency responses,[117] resulting in significant financial and legal ramifications for the responsible organizations. When these disasters cross international borders, an additional layer of complexity is added to the response process.[118] The best way to address international environmental emergencies is to prevent them from occurring in the first place, but preparation is necessary in case an accident occurs. A pre-emergency response plan is essential to responding quickly and in a manner that is consistent with an operator's responsibilities under international and national laws. While there are some examples of harmonization of emergency response requirements regionally, in large part operators continue to face multiple, overlapping legal frameworks when such disasters arise.

Notes

1. Marissa Smith, *The Deepwater Horizon Disaster: An Examination of the Spill's Impact on the Gap in International Regulation of Oil Pollution from Fixed Platforms*, 25 EMORY INT'L L. REV. 1477, 1477–78 (2011).

2. *Hungarian Chemical Sludge Spill Reaches the Danube*, BBC News (Oct. 7, 2010), http://www.bbc.co.uk/news/world-europe-11491412; *One Year to Clean Toxic Spill in Hungary*, BBC News (Oct. 6, 2010), http://www.bbc.co.uk/news/world-europe-11481740. Alumina is a form of aluminum oxide.

3. *One Year to Clean Toxic Spill in Hungary*, BBC News (Oct. 6, 2010), http://www.bbc.co.uk/news/world-europe-11481740.

4. *Id.*

5. *Hungarian Chemical Sludge Spill Reaches the Danube*, BBC News (Oct. 7, 2010), http://www.bbc.co.uk/news/world-europe-11491412.

6. Stefan Bos, *Six Months On, Chemical Spill Still Haunts Hungary*, Deutsche Welle (Apr. 4, 2011).

7. ICPDR, The Red Sludge Tragedy (Mar. 2010), http://www.icpdr.org/main /publications/red-sludge-tragedy-danube-basin.

8. Edith Brown Weiss, *Environmental Disasters in International Law*, Anuario Juridico Interamerican 1986, at 141 (1988), *reprinted in* Edith Brown Weiss et al., International Environmental Law and Policy 398 (2007).

9. The *Torrey Canyon* oil spill took place in 1967, the largest oil spill of its time, and is still harming wildlife today. Patrick Barkham, *Oil Spills: Legacy of the Torrey Canyon*, Guardian (June 23, 2010).

10. Philippe Sands & Jacqueline Peel, Principles of International Environmental Law 517 (3d ed. 2012).

11. *See, e.g.*, OECD Council Decision on Exchange of Information Concerning Accidents Capable of Causing Transfrontier Damage (July 8, 1988), 8 ILM 247 (1989); OECD Council Decision/Recommendation on Provision of Information to Public and Private Participation in Decision Making Processes Related to the Prevention of, and Responses to, Accidents Involving Hazardous Substances (July 8, 1988), 28 I.L.M., 277 (1989).

12. Sands & Peel, *supra* note 10, at 517.

13. *Id.*

14. Agreement of Cooperation between the United States of America and the United Mexican States Regarding Pollution of the Environment Along the Inland International Boundary by Discharges of Hazardous Substances (July 18, 1985, in force November 29, 1985), 26 ILM 19 (1987).

15. Sands & Peel, *supra* note 10, at 517.

16. Weiss, *supra* note 8, at 401.

17. *Id.* at 402–03.

18. *Id.* at 403.

19. U.N. Office for the Coordination of Humanitarian Affairs, Environmental Emergencies, http://www.unocha.org/what-we-do/coordination-tools/environmental-emergencies.

20. UNEP, Disasters and Conflicts Sub-Programme, http://www.unep.org/disasters andconflicts.

21. U.N. Office for the Coordination of Humanitarian Affairs, Advisory Group on Environmental Emergencies, http://www.unocha.org/what-we-do/coordination-tools /environmental-emergencies/events.

22. UNEP, APELL Programme, http://www.unep.org/resourceefficiency/Business /CleanerSaferProduction/SaferProduction/APELL/APELLProgramme/tabid/78883 /Default.aspx.

23. Prevention of Major Industrial Accidents: An ILO Code of Practice (1991).

24. Convention No. 174 on the Prevention of Major Industrial Accidents (June 22, 1993, in force January 3, 1996).

25. Sands & Peel, *supra* note 10, at 517.

26. OECD, Guiding Principles for Chemical Accident Prevention, Preparedness, and Response (2003), http://www.oecd-ilibrary.org/environment/oecd-guiding-principles-for -chemical-accident-prevention-preparedness-and-response_9789264101821-en.

27. U.S. EPA, Emergency Management: Multilateral Programs, http://www.epa .gov/osweroe1/content/multilateral.htm.

28. International Convention Relating to Intervention on the High Seas in Cases of Oil Pollution Casualties (Nov. 29, 2969, in force May 6, 1975), 9 ILM 25 (1970).

29. Protocol on Intervention on the High Seas in Cases of Marine Pollution by Substances Other Than Oil (Nov. 2, 1973, in force Mar. 30, 1983).

30. International Convention on Salvage (Apr. 28, 1989).

31. 1990 London Convention on Oil Pollution Preparedness, Response, and Cooperation (Nov. 30, 1990, in force May 13, 1995), 30 ILM 753 (1991).

32. Sands & Peel, *supra* note 10, at 393.

33. Protocol to the OPRC Convention on Preparedness, Response, and Cooperation to Pollution Incidents by Hazardous and Noxious Substances (Mar. 15, 2000).

34. Sands & Peel, *supra* note 10, at 393.

35. *See* http://www.unep.ch/regionalseas/main/hconlist.html (last visited Oct. 1, 2013); *see also* Sands & Peel, *supra* note 10, at 394–95.

36. Sands & Peel, *supra* note 10, at 395.

37. 1969 Bonn Agreement for Cooperation in Dealing with Pollution of the North Sea by Oil (June 9, 1969); 1983 Agreement for Cooperation in Dealing with Pollution of the North Sea by Oil and Other Harmful Substances (Sept. 13, 1983, in force Sept. 1, 1989), *available at* http://www.bonnagreement.org.

38. *See* Sands & Peel, *supra* note 10, at 394.

39. Barcelona Convention for the Protection of the Marine Environment and the Coastal Region of the Mediterranean (1975, amended 1995), Protocol concerning Pollution Resulting from Exploration and Exploitation of the Continental Shelf (Oct. 14, 1994).

40. *See* http://eurlex.europa.eu/LexUriServ/LexUriServ.do?uri=OJ:L:2013:004:0015 :0033: EN:PDF (last visited Oct. 1, 2013); Tullio Scovazzi, *Maritime Accidents with Particular Emphasis on Liability and Compensation for Damage from the Exploitation of Mineral Resources from the Seabed, in* Andrea de Guttry et al., International Disaster Response Law 297–99 (2012).

41. Council Directive 96/82/EC on the control of major-accident hazards involving dangerous substances (Jan. 14, 1997).

42. Sands & Peel, *supra* note 10, at 519.

43. Convention on the Transboundary Effects of Industrial Accidents (1992), http:// www.unece.org/env/teia/welcome.html.

44. Sands & Peel, *supra* note 10, at 519–20.

45. *Id.* at 520.

46. Int'l Mar. Org., International Convention on Civil Liability for Oil Pollution Damage (CLC), http://www.imo.org/About/Conventions/ListOfConventions/Pages /International-Convention-on-Civil-Liability-for-Oil-Pollution-Damage-(CLC).aspx (last visited June 5, 2013).

47. The United States is not a signatory to the CLC. *See* Int'l Mar. Org., Status of Conventions, http://www.imo.org/About/Conventions/StatusOfConventions/Documents /status-x.xls (last visited June 6, 2013).

48. Int'l Mar. Org., International Convention on Civil Liability for Oil Pollution Damage (CLC), *supra* note 46.

49. *Id.*

50. *Id.*

51. Int'l Monetary Fund, Special Drawing Rights Factsheet, http://www.imf.org /external/np/exr/facts/sdr.htm (last visited June 5, 2013).

52. *Id.*

53. *Id.*

54. *Id.*

55. Int'l Mar. Org., International Convention on Civil Liability for Oil Pollution Damage (CLC), *supra* note 46.

56. Int'l Mar. Org., International Convention on Civil Liability for Bunker Oil Pollution Damage (BUNKER), http://www.imo.org/about/conventions/listofconventions /pages/international-convention-on-civil-liability-for-bunker-oil-pollution-damage -(bunker).aspx.

57. *Id.*

58. Directive 2004/35, of the European Parliament and of the Council of April 21 2004 on Environmental Liability with Regard to the Prevention and Remedying of Environmental Damage, pmbl. 2, 2004 O.J. (L143) 56(EC), *available at* http://eur-lex.europa .eu/LexUriServ/LexUriServ.do?uri=OJ:L:2004:143:0056:0075:en:PDF.

59. *Id.*, pmbl., at 56.

60. *Id.*, art. 6, at 61–62.

61. *Id.*, pmbl. 18, at 57–58.

62. *Id.*, art. 8, at 62.

63. *Id.*, art. 2, at 60.

64. Report from the Commission to the Council, the European Parliament, the European Economic and Social Committee and the Committee of the Regions, Under Article 14(2) of Directive 2004/35/CE on the Environmental Liability with Regard to the Prevention and Remedying of Environmental Damage, (COM) 581 final, 3–4 (Dec. 10, 2010), *available at* http://eurlex.europa.eu/LexUriServ/LexUriServ.do?uri=COM:2010:0581:FIN :EN:PDF.

65. *Id.*

66. Proposal for a Regulation of the European Parliament and of the Council on Safety of Offshore Oil and Gas Prospection, Exploration and Production Activities, EUR. PARL. DOC. (COM 688) at 3, *available at* http://eurlex.europa.eu/LexUriServ/LexUriServ .do?uri= COM:2011:0688:FIN:EN:PDF.

67. *Id.*, art. 37, at 39–40.

68. *Id.*, art. 7, at 25.

69. *See* 2004 Directive, *supra* note 58, at 70.

70. EU Environmental Liability Directive 101, AON, http://eur-lex.europa.eu/legal -content/EN/TXT/PDF/?uri=CELEX:32004L0035&from=EN.

71. *Id.*, art. 3 ¶ 1(a), at 60.

72. *Id.*, art. 3.

73. *Id.*

74. *Id.*

75. Noah Sachs, *Beyond the Liability Wall: Strengthening Tort Remedies in International Environmental Law*, 55 UCLA L. REV. 837, 839 (2009).

76. Hague Conference on Private International Law, Apr. 2000, Civil Liability Resulting From Transfrontier Environmental Damage: A Case for the Hague Conference? 5–16, Preliminary Doc. 8 (prepared by Christophe Bernasconi), *available at* http://www.hcch .net/upload/wop/gen_pd8e.pdf.

77. *See id.*, at 40–44, 50–53; XUE HANQIN, TRANSBOUNDARY DAMAGE IN INTERNATIONAL LAW 104–05 (2003).

78. U.S. EPA, Office of Enforcement & Compliance Assurance, Civil Penalty Policy for Section 311(b)(3) and Section 311(j) of the Clean Water Act 1 (1998), http://www2.epa.gov/sites/production/files/documents/311pen.pdf.

79. Robert Percival, *CERCLA in a Global Context*, 41 Sw. L.J. 727, 727 (2012).

80. U.S. EPA, National Oil and Hazardous Substances Pollution Contingency Plan Overview, http://www.epa.gov/osweroe1/content/lawsregs/ncpover.htm.

81. NCP §§ 300.110, 300.115.

82. NCP §§ 300.120, 300.135(a).

83. NCP § 300.135(d).

84. NCP § 300.125(a).

85. NCP § 300.320.

86. NCP § 300.322.

87. NCP § 300.415.

88. Percival, *supra* note 79, at 727.

89. U.S. EPA, Civil Penalty Policy, *supra* note 78, at 1 (citing Spill Prevention, Control, and Countermeasure (SPCC) Regulation, 40 C.F.R. Part 112).

90. *Id.*

91. *Id.*

92. Ecosystem Mgmt. & Assocs., Inc., Criteria for Evaluating Oil Spill Planning and Response Operations 4 (2008).

93. *Id.* at 3.

94. Joselito Guevarra, Soc'y of Petroleum Eng'rs, Managing Oil Spill Risks of Transnational Onshore Pipelines 2 (2010).

95. *Id.*

96. *Id.*

97. Ecosystem Mgmt. & Assocs., *supra* note 92, at 4.

98. Guevarra, *supra* note 94, at 2 (2010).

99. *Id.*

100. *Id.*

101. *Id.*

102. *Id.;* Ecosystem Mgmt. & Assocs., *supra* note 92, at 4.

103. *Id.*

104. *Id.*

105. *Id.*

106. E. Owens, E. Taylor & D. Dickens, Final Expert Response Baku-Tbilisi-Ceyhan (BTC) Pipeline Project (2005).

107. Guevarra, *supra* note 94, at 11.

108. Ecosystem Mgmt. & Assocs., *supra* note 92, at 4.

109. *Id.*

110. *Id.* at 31.

111. *Id.*

112. *Id.* at 32.

113. *Id.*

114. *Id.* at 34.

115. *Id.*

116. *Id.*

117. Guevarra, *supra* note 94, at 2.

118. Owens et al., *supra* note 106.

CHAPTER 10

Natural Resource Management and Protection

ROBERT L. GLICKSMAN

"The scale and complexity of our requirements for natural resources have increased greatly with the rising levels of population and production. Nature is bountiful, but it is also fragile and finely balanced."— Report of the World Commission on Environment and Development: Our Common Future

I. Introduction

Natural resources are essential to human survival and prosperity. While it once may have seemed as if natural resources were limitless, it is abundantly clear that careful management is necessary to preserve our ability to continue to benefit from the ecosystem services that nature supplies. This chapter addresses four categories of natural resources from which people derive economic value: timber, minerals, fisheries, and range (or grasslands). It also covers recreational use of natural resources and preservation of natural resources. It addresses the laws that govern use of natural resources for each of these purposes. These laws are typically designed to allow recovery of the benefits, economic and otherwise, that natural resources provide, while simultaneously promoting complementary goals or accommodating conflicting goals. These other goals include avoiding environmental degradation, controlling the pace of development to avoid waste, reconciling potentially conflicting uses of the same resource, and assuring equitable distribution and continued availability of natural resource benefits in the future.

For each of the resource use categories covered, the chapter first addresses public international laws and then provides a comparative law perspective by briefly describing key natural resource management laws adopted in the United States and selected other countries that reflect different approaches to management of each aspect of natural resource development and use. The comparative law sections are not meant to be exhaustive. Rather, the discussion provides examples of some of the alternatives to natural resource management and protection reflected in domestic law.

II. Timber Management

The annual commercial value of wood and wood products is measured in the trillions of dollars. The value of forests, however, extends beyond the timber harvested from them. Forests provide a host of important ecosystem services, including fostering biological diversity, sequestering carbon to mitigate climate change, and protecting water quality. Developing countries often regard exploitation of their timber resources as essential to their economic development, while the developed world tends to place greater emphasis on sustainable management and forest conservation.[1] The emphasis on the exploitation of timber resources or the conservation of forest ecosystems differs from country to country. In the United States, for example, the emphasis on ecological sustainability of the national forests has taken on increased importance, with concomitant reductions in allowable timber harvests. Some developing nations place a higher priority on economic development, and may agree to restrictions on timber clearing only if they are subsidized by developed nations.

A. International Laws Governing Timber Resources

While it has proven impossible to date to negotiate a successful comprehensive, binding global agreement to promote forest conservation, international agreements address various aspects of forest use and conservation. The 1992 UNCED (Rio) principles begin with the proposition that all nations have the sovereign right to exploit their own resources (including timber resources) pursuant to their own environmental policies. They also have the responsibility, however, to ensure that activities within their jurisdiction or control do not cause damage to the environment of other states or to areas beyond the limits of national jurisdiction.[2] These principles recognize the sovereign right to manage and develop forests in accordance with their development needs and level of socioeconomic development.[3] They state that forest resources should be sustainably managed to meet the social, economic, ecological, cultural, and spiritual needs of present and future generations for uses that include wood products, water, food, medicine, fuel, shelter, recreation, wildlife habitat, landscape diversity, and carbon sinks.[4] The UNCED principles recognize the importance of forests to the cultures of indigenous peoples and the provision of renewable energy resources.[5] They support the sustainable management and use of natural forests and the integration of forest conservation and sustainable development policies with economic and trade policies.[6] The 1992 Rio conference also produced Agenda 21, which includes provisions to prevent deforestation.[7]

More recently, the U.N. General Assembly passed a nonbinding resolution in 2008 dealing with forest use and management. It provides that each state is responsible for the sustainable management of its forests.[8] It identifies shared global objectives on forests that include reversing the loss of forest cover through sustainable forest management; enhancing forest-based economic, social, and environmental benefits; and reversing the decline in development assistance for sustainable forest management.[9]

Nations have entered binding international agreements of a more limited scale. The International Tropical Timber Agreement, for example, began as an effort to enhance profits for timber-producing countries in the tropics, but over time has incorporated sustainable development and forest conservation objectives.[10] Another agreement relating to use of tropical forests in Africa, the Yaounde Declaration on the Conservation and Sustainable Management of Tropical Forests,[11] has not yet entered into force. Several measures are designed to protect forest resources more indirectly, such as by promoting trade in products from sustainably managed forests. These include a trade agreement between the European Union and Central American states[12] and the United States-Peru Free Trade Agreement.[13] The EU's Forest Law Enforcement, Governance, and Trade[14] seeks to combat illegal logging by encouraging timber-producing countries that export to EU markets to enter voluntary agreements to implement licensing programs to keep illegally harvested timber out of the EU.[15]

B.   Comparative Law Perspectives on Timber Resources

Domestic laws concerning forest management may apply differently to publicly and privately owned forests. In the United States, state laws govern the management of private forest lands.[16] The principal federal statute is the National Forest Management Act (NFMA), which applies to forests and grasslands managed by the U.S. Forest Service.[17] The NFMA requires the Forest Service to adopt plans for managing units of the National Forest System and then requires that site-specific projects, such as timber sales, conform to the applicable plan. Each plan must provide for multiple use and sustained yield of the products and services obtained from the forest, including coordinated use of the forest for outdoor recreation, range, timber, watershed, wildlife and fish, and wilderness preservation.[18] Sustained yield means "achievement and maintenance in perpetuity of a high-level annual or regular periodic output" of the renewable forest resources without impairment of productivity of the land.[19] Forest plans must provide for the diversity of plant and animal communities. The NFMA restricts timber harvesting so that soil and watershed conditions are not irreversibly damaged, there is assurance that lands can be adequately restocked within five years after harvest, and clear-cutting and similar harvesting techniques are used only in limited circumstances and with appropriate protective conditions. The Forest Service may not select a harvesting system primarily because it will provide the greatest dollar return or the greatest unit timber output.[20] Over the years, the Forest Service, which has considerable discretion in implementing the NFMA, has shifted the balance between emphasizing economic productivity and ecological sustainability.

The domestic forest management and timber production laws of other nations vary in terms of scope of coverage and the nature of the restrictions placed on timber removal. In Argentina, federal law prohibits the destruction or irrational use of forest resources, but exploitation of public forests is allowed on payment of a fee, preparation of a plan, and issuance of a permit. The nature of the restrictions contained in a permit will depend on whether the forest is classified as protective, permanent, experimental, special, or productive.[21] Some countries regulate timber harvesting on private as well as public land. In Brazil, for example, the Forest Code requires that even private landowners leave a minimum percentage of trees standing on their property. The Code also creates permanent conservation zones (such as on hillsides with steep slopes) in which timber harvesting is restricted.[22]

In India, most timber is owned by the national government so that trade in timber and other forest produce is largely managed by the government. India's Forest Conservation Act, enacted in 1980, tightly restricts both deforestation and use of forests for nonforestry purposes (such as mining).[23] Kenya's laws also base the degree of restrictions on timber production on the ownership of the land and the categorization of a particular forest. The Forest Act prohibits timber cutting, grazing, or removal of flora in areas designed by the Minister of Environment and Natural Resources as "nature reserves" without government authorization, which will be provided only if the activities are consistent with conservation of the natural flora and amenities of the reserve. Separate legislation governs private forest land, which prohibits wasteful destruction of trees. Ukrainian laws also provide different levels of protection of forest lands based on a use classification system.[24] In 2011, Indonesia banned forest clearing, for which the nation's palm oil and mining industries had been largely responsible, for two years as part of an agreement with Norway. The ban was extended in 2013.[25]

In some countries, laws provide special protections for indigenous peoples.[26] India's Recognition of Forest Rights Act, for example, affords special access, use, and both individual and community ownership rights to "traditional forest dwellers."[27]

III. Mineral Exploration and Development

Outside of Antarctica, mining activities other than deep seabed mining are subject to relatively few international treaty restrictions. Instead, international law addresses mining largely indirectly through agreements concerning protection of flora and fauna, pollution, and impact assessment.[28] There does not appear to be significant momentum toward new multilateral agreements on mining. On the domestic front, there is no clear trend in the regulation of mining. In some countries, environmental restrictions on mineral extraction have increased, while in others, the economic benefits resulting from the development of these resources trumps environmental protection goals. The discovery of new techniques for extracting fossil fuels, such as hydraulic fracturing, has provided another context in which this clash of interests will play out.

A.   International Laws Governing Mineral Resources

1.   *Onshore Mining in Antarctica*

Antarctica is free of the exercise of territorial sovereignty. The 1988 Convention on the Regulation of Antarctic Mineral Resources Activities (CRAMRA) would have prohibited any mining activity that caused significant pollution, caused significant changes in atmospheric, terrestrial, or marine environments or in flora and fauna, or resulted in the degradation of areas of special biological, scientific, historic, aesthetic, or wilderness significance. CRAMRA also would have allowed mining only if the capacity existed to respond effectively to environmental accidents.[29] The treaty never went into effect following rejection by France and Australia, among others. The Protocol on Environmental Protection to the Antarctic Treaty,[30] however, entered into force in 1998. The parties to the protocol committed themselves to "the comprehensive protection of the Antarctic environment"[31] and the protocol prohibits any activity relating to mineral resources, other than scientific development.[32] The protocol includes a "walk-out" clause, however, which allows any signatory to withdraw after 50 years from the date the protocol entered into force. Two years later, that nation could conduct mining notwithstanding the protocol.[33] The protocol therefore effectively imposes a 50-year moratorium on mining in Antarctica.[34]

2.   *Mining Regulation under UNCLOS*

The U.N. Convention on the Law of the Sea (UNCLOS),[35] which the United States has signed but not ratified, is the principal international law regime governing deep seabed mining. UNCLOS provides that the sovereignty of a coastal state extends beyond its land and inland waters to an adjacent belt, the territorial seas, which may extend up to 12 nautical miles.[36] UNCLOS also defines an exclusive economic zone that may extend up to 200 nautical miles beyond the territorial sea. A coastal state has sovereign rights to explore, conserve, and manage the natural resources of the seabed within the exclusive economic zone.[37] The continental shelf of a coastal state includes the seabed and subsoil of areas that extend up to 200 nautical miles beyond the territorial sea, and the coastal state exercises sovereign rights over the continental shelf for the purpose of exploring it and exploiting its natural resources. No one may engage in these activities without the consent of the coastal state,[38] which has the exclusive right to authorize and regulate drilling on the continental shelf.[39]

No state may claim or exercise sovereign rights over the seabed or ocean floor beyond the limits of national jurisdiction or over appropriate mineral resources located there. Instead, mineral resources in these areas are declared by UNCLOS to be the common heritage of mankind.[40] U.S. refusal to ratify UNCLOS has been based on opposition to these restrictions on exploitation of seabed mineral resources.[41]

UNCLOS created the International Seabed Authority (ISA) to oversee mining interests in international waters. The treaty prohibits exploration for or exploitation of mineral resources without a license from the ISA, which requires licensed parties to set aside reserved areas in which an entity authorized by the ISA may engage in mining operations in competition with private entities licensed by the ISA.[42] In addition, the ISA requires miners to pay fees, which are handed over to nonmining states. A mining venture must be sponsored by a member state and demonstrate the capacity to meet financial and technology standards.[43] To date, despite the presence of extensive hard mineral deposits, significant deep seabed mining has not occurred, largely because of the high cost of mineral recovery.[44] Deep seabed mining activities in the Arctic region would be subject to UNCLOS.[45]

B.   Comparative Law Perspectives on Timber Resources

Domestic laws governing the exploration for and production of mineral resources often create different regulatory regimes depending on factors such as the identity of the owner of the land containing the resources and the nature of the mineral resource. Mining on private lands in the United States is governed largely by state laws that establish property and contract rights and may impose regulatory restrictions. Surface coal mining, however, is subject to a federal statute, the Surface Mining Control and Reclamation Act (SMCRA),[46] even when the mining takes place on private lands. SMCRA's goals include protecting the environment from the adverse effects of surface coal mining operations and the appropriate reclamation of areas that have been mined. The Act requires compliance by surface coal mining operations with performance standards, including provisions that govern waste disposal and reclamation, that are applied through a permit program administered by the Office of Surface Mining within the U.S. Interior Department. Special restrictions apply to mining on prime farmland and in vulnerable areas such as steep slopes.[47]

An array of U.S. laws governs mineral production on public lands. The oldest of these laws is the 1872 General Mining Law (GML).[48] The GML is a holdover from an era in which federal land and resource policy was dominated by efforts to transfer title to federally owned lands and resources into private hands. It allows any citizen to enter federal lands that have not been withdrawn from mineral entry, stake a claim, and upon discovering valuable deposits of qualifying minerals, take title to the minerals free of charge.[49] Although the GML has long been subject to heavy criticism for not demanding that miners pay fair market value for publicly owned minerals found on federal lands, efforts to amend and modernize it have failed to date. The two agencies that manage the federal lands on which mining claims may be located, however, have adopted environmental protection regulations for activities under the GML.[50]

Those seeking to develop other minerals located on federal public lands generally must pay for the right to do so. Onshore oil and gas exploration and production, for example, are governed by a system of competitive leasing under the Federal Onshore Oil and Gas Leasing Act of 1987.[51] The statute and implementing regulations provide eligibility requirements for bidders, impose acreage restrictions on lease holders, and authorize environmental regulation by the U.S. Forest Service and the Bureau of Land Management (BLM).[52] Offshore oil and gas exploration and development in areas beyond the territorial seas are governed by the Outer Continental Shelf Lands Act of 1978,[53] which also establishes a competitive leasing program and mandates comprehensive environmental reviews at several stages of the leasing process. Surface coal mining on federal lands is subject to the Federal Coal Leasing Act Amendments of 1976,[54] which established another competitive bidding lease program. Sale prices must reflect fair market value.[55] Surface coal mining on federal lands, like surface mining on privately owned land, is also subject to SMCRA's requirements, including bonding requirements and regulatory performance standards. SMCRA requires the Secretary of the Interior to determine whether there are areas of federal lands that are unsuitable for mining or for which special restrictions are appropriate.[56] While oil, natural gas, coal, and oil shale are governed by leasing programs established under the Mineral Leasing Act or amendments to that law, other resources, such as geothermal resources and so-called common varieties (which include sand, stone, gravel, pumice, and clay) are subject to separate statutory sale or leasing programs.[57]

In some other nations, the distinction between minerals found on public and private lands is irrelevant because title to all subsurface resources is vested in the government. Kenya's 1987 Mining Act, for example, vests title to unextracted surface or subsurface minerals in the government, subject to limited private property rights. The Commissioner of Mines may grant exclusive prospecting permits that are subject to conditions designed to protect forests and water supplies. The holder of a prospecting permit may apply for a lease, which provides the exclusive right to mine upon payment of rental fees. As in the United States, certain areas are not open to prospecting or mining, including burial sites and trust lands.[58] Leasing regimes such as those established under U.S. mining laws have been created in other countries, including the Russian Federation.[59] These regimes sometimes apply to precious minerals such as diamonds, as in Nigeria. Laws may regulate minerals after they have been extracted. Nigeria's Minerals and Mining Decree of 1999, for example, prohibits the export of raw gold without a Treasury receipt for the royalty paid or until the receipt is endorsed by a collector of customs with the amount of the raw gold to be exported.[60]

Some countries have tried to govern the pace of mining activities to achieve intergenerational equity. The Russian Federation's Code on Mineral Resources, for example, seeks to conserve depletable resources in the interests of present and future generations.[61] Environmental regulation of mining activities is common. In Hungary, miners must limit the burden of mining activities on natural areas to the least possible extent. They must make continuous efforts to restore the damaged surface of abandoned mining areas and, where possible, to reestablish near-natural conditions.[62] Environmental impact assessment requirements are also common.[63]

IV.   Fisheries

Global production of fish and other aquatic animals reached 148.5 million tons in 2010, about 90 million of which resulted from oceanic capture as opposed to aquaculture. About 86 percent of total fishery production in 2010 was used for direct human consumption, with the rest devoted to nonfood products, including the manufacture of fishmeal and fish oil.[64] Fishing takes its toll on ocean ecosystems, however. The U.N. Food and Agriculture Organization estimated recently that only about 20 percent of the world's marine fish populations are not depleted, overexploited, or fully exploited.[65] Fisheries management laws therefore strive to allow harvesting to meet demand for fish for food and other purposes, while maintaining sustainable fisheries capable of providing a source of nourishment and economic value in the future. The depletion or collapse of oceanic fisheries for many species, resulting from increases in population and in the demand for fish as food, has prompted increasing concern over the state of fisheries for many species and in efforts to conserve and restore them. Section A below addresses the major international legal regimes that govern fisheries management, including UNCLOS, the Straddling Stocks Treaty, and regional fisheries management organizations. Section B summarizes the principal fisheries management in the United States, the Magnuson-Stevens Fisheries Conservation Act, and similar laws in other nations heavily engaged in fishing.

A.   International Laws Governing Fisheries

Traditionally, fish and other living marine aquatic life within a state's territory belonged to the nation, while such resources in the high seas were common resources available to be taken by anyone under the law of capture (the first-come, first-served principle).[66] International disputes arose when coastal states claimed more extensive exclusive fishing zones, and high seas vessels from other nations refused to recognize these claims. The International Court of Justice decided in 1974 that coastal and high seas states share responsibility for conserving living marine resources and that "the former *laissez faire* treatment of the living resources of the sea in the high seas has been replaced by a recognition of a duty to have due regard to the rights of other States and the needs of conservation for the benefit of all."[67]

UNCLOS addresses fisheries management more comprehensively in a manner consistent with the ICJ decision. Under Article 2, coastal states have exclusive sovereignty to regulate ocean fisheries within the territorial sea.[68] Within the exclusive economic zone, a coastal state has sovereign rights to exploit, conserve, and manage living natural resources of the waters superadjacent to the seabed, but such a state "shall have due regard to the rights of other States."[69] More specifically, a coastal state shall determine the allowable catch of the living resources in its exclusive economic zone, and shall, taking into account the best available scientific evidence, ensure through proper conservation and management measures that the maintenance of these resources is not endangered by overexploitation. Management measures must maintain or restore populations of harvested species at levels capable of producing the maximum sustainable yield, "as qualified by relevant environmental and economic factors, including the economic needs of fishing communities and the special requirements of developing States."[70] If a coastal state does not have the capacity to harvest its entire allowable catch, UNCLOS requires it to enter agreements allowing other states access to the surplus, particularly landlocked and economically disadvantaged states.[71]

UNCLOS includes provisions that address four categories of fish whose management has proven troublesome under international law.[72] States must agree upon measures to coordinate and ensure the conservation and development of straddling stocks, which occur within the exclusive economic zones of two or more coastal states or within an exclusive economic zone and the high seas.[73] Coastal states and other states whose nationals fish for highly migratory species must cooperate through appropriate international organizations to ensure conservation and promote optimal utilization of those species, both within and beyond the exclusive economic zone.[74] States with rivers containing anadromous stocks (which are born and spawn in fresh water but spend most of their lives in salt water) have the primary interest in and responsibility for those stocks, and must ensure their conservation through the adoption of regulatory measures for fishing in waters landward of the outer limits of the exclusive economic zone. The state of origin may establish total allowable catches for its anadromous stocks, after consultation with other states in which economic dislocation may result from these measures and states into whose waters anadromous stocks that originate elsewhere migrate.[75] A coastal state with waters in which catadromous stocks (such as eels that are born and spawn in salt water but otherwise live in fresh water) spend most of their life cycle are responsible for managing those stocks and must ensure ingress and egress of migrating fish. If catadromous fish migrate through the exclusive economic zone of another state, the management and harvesting of those fish must be regulated by agreement between the affected states.[76]

The high seas are open to all states, and UNCLOS recognizes freedom of navigation and fishing there, subject to applicable rules of international law and UNCLOS itself.[77] All states have the right for their nationals to engage in fishing on the high seas, subject to treaty obligations and the interests of coastal states recognized under UNCLOS.[78] In addition, all states have a duty to take, both themselves and in cooperation with other states, measures necessary for conservation of living resources of the high seas.[79] UNCLOS parties must cooperate to establish subregional or regional fisheries organizations to conserve and manage these resources.[80] In determining the allowable catch and establishing other conservation measures for the high seas, states must take measures designed to maintain or restore populations of harvested species at levels that can produce the maximum sustainable yield, "as qualified by relevant environmental and economic factors, including the special requirements of developing States."[81]

UNCLOS created the International Tribunal for the Law of the Sea to adjudicate disputes arising out of the interpretation and application of the Convention. Part XV of UNCLOS established a system for the settlement of disputes concerning interpretation and application of the Convention. It requires parties to settle their disputes by peaceful means indicated in the U.N. Charter, but if parties to a dispute fail to do so, they must resort to the compulsory dispute settlement procedures contained in the Convention.[82] The Tribunal's decisions are easily accessible on its website.[83]

The provisions of UNCLOS proved to be inadequate to resolve disputes over straddling stocks and highly migratory fish.[84] In 1995, the Straddling Stocks Agreement[85] was opened for signature, and the agreement entered into force in November 2001. The agreement's goal is to ensure the long-term conservation and sustainable use of straddling fish stocks and highly migratory fish stocks.[86] The agreement limits freedom of fishing on the high seas through a series of conservation mandates implemented by regional organizations. Among other things, parties must adopt measures to ensure long-term sustainability of straddling fish stocks and highly migratory fish stocks and promote their optimum utilization, ensure that such measures are based on the best scientific evidence available and are designed to maintain or restore stocks at levels capable of producing maximum sustainable yield (with the same kinds of qualifications found in UNCLOS), protect biodiversity in the marine environment, take measures to prevent or eliminate over-fishing to ensure that levels of fishing effort do not exceed those commensurate with the sustainable use of fishery resources, and implement and enforce conservation and management measures through effective monitoring, control and surveillance.[87] In addition, the agreement requires that states "apply the precautionary approach widely to conservation, management and exploitation of straddling fish stocks and highly migratory fish stocks in order to protect the living marine resources and preserve the marine environment."[88] More specifically, states must "be more cautious when information is uncertain, unreliable or inadequate," and "[t]he absence of adequate scientific information shall not be used as a reason for postponing or failing to take conservation and management measures."[89]

As envisioned by the Straddling Stocks Agreement, a series of regional organizations have been formed to manage and conserve fisheries. One such organization is the Northwest Atlantic Fisheries Organization, whose 17 members meet each year to agree on the total allowable catch for commercially important species and allocate quotas to each member state's fishing fleet.[90] As of about 2011, there were 20 regional fisheries management organizations.[91] Five regional organizations, for example, have been formed to manage tuna fisheries, including the Commission for the Conservation of Southern Bluefin Tuna, Inter-American Tropical Tuna Commission, the International Commission for the Conservation of Atlantic Tunas, the Indian

Ocean Tuna Commission, and the Western and Central Pacific Fisheries Commission.[92] According to one observer, these organizations "all balance conservation, management, or utilization objectives and are guided by the Precautionary Approach and Ecosystem-Based-Management Approach. The extent to which these are realized is another question."[93]

B.   Comparative Law Perspectives on Fisheries

Individual nations have adopted their own laws to govern fisheries. The primary U.S. law is the Magnuson-Stevens Fishery Conservation and Management Act,[94] which was initially adopted in 1976, while UNCLOS was being negotiated. The Act reflects the need for government action to address the tragedy of the commons posed when individuals have incentives to maximize their own use of common resources, even though the result is overexploitation that conflicts with the broader public interest. Congress adopted the Act "to conserve and manage the fishery resources found off the coasts of the United States, and the anadromous species and Continental Shelf fishery resources of the United States, by exercising (A) sovereign rights for the purposes of exploring, exploiting, conserving, and managing all fish, within the exclusive economic zone ... and (B) exclusive fishery management authority beyond the exclusive economic zone over such anadromous species and Continental Shelf fishery resources."[95] Additional goals include encouraging implementation and enforcement of international fishery agreements for the conservation and management of highly migratory species, promoting domestic commercial and recreational fishing under sound conservation and management principles, providing for the preparation and implementation of fishery management plans to achieve and maintain the optimum yield from each fishery, and promoting the protection of essential fish habitat in the review of projects conducted under federal permits or licenses that affect or have the potential to affect such habitat.[96] Congress was careful to include in the Act a commitment to a policy of maintaining without change the existing territorial or other ocean jurisdiction of the United States for all purposes other than the conservation and management of fishery resources.[97]

The Magnuson Act established a series of Regional Fishery Management Councils to supervise fishery management plans that will achieve and maintain the optimum yield from each fishery within their jurisdiction.[98] Each plan must meet a series of minimum standards, including that it contain the conservation and management measures, applicable to foreign fishing and fishing by vessels of the United States, which are necessary and appropriate for the conservation and management of the fishery, to prevent overfishing and rebuild overfished stocks, and to protect, restore, and promote the long-term health and stability of the fishery.[99] A plan also must comply with regulations implementing recommendations by international organizations in which the United States participates (including but not limited to closed areas, quotas, and size limits).[100] It must assess and specify the present and probable future condition of, and the maximum sustainable yield and optimum yield from, the fishery; specify the capacity and the extent to which U.S. fishing vessels, on an annual basis, will harvest the optimum yield, and the portion of that yield that can be made available for foreign fishing; specify measurable criteria for identifying when the fishery to which the plan applies is overfished and contain conservation and management measures to prevent overfishing or end overfishing and rebuild the fishery; allocate any harvest restrictions or recovery benefits fairly and equitably among the commercial, recreational, and charter fishing sectors in the fishery; and establish a mechanism for specifying annual catch limits at a level such that overfishing does not occur in the fishery, including measures to ensure accountability.[101] The Secretary of Commerce (acting through the National Marine Fisheries Service) may adopt federal management measures if a regional Council fails to do so within a reasonable time.[102] Essentially, the Act allows harvesting of only "that portion of the fish that represents interest. That is called the maximum sustainable yield."[103] The Act prevents harvesting of the "principal," the amounts in excess of the maximum sustainable yield. Plans must rebuild depleted fish populations as quickly as possible, during a period not to exceed 10 years, to a biomass level that allows the fishery to produce maximum sustainable yield on a continuing basis.[104]

Other nations that rely heavily on fish as a food source also have adopted fishery management measures. The European Union collaboratively manages its fisheries under the Common Fisheries Policy (CFP), first adopted in 1983.[105] The CFP seeks to achieve sustainable fisheries and aquaculture in a healthy marine environment, which can support an economically viable industry providing employment and opportunities for coastal communities.[106] It aims to promote sustainable fishing through restrictions on the size of the fleets and the amount of time they are allowed to spend fishing, the quantities of fish that may be caught, and measures to prevent damage to the marine environment. In addition, like the Magnuson-Stevens Act, the CFP authorizes the adoption of measures governing the manner of permissible fishing, such as minimum mesh sizes for nets, closed areas and seasons, limits on by-catches (catches of unwanted or nontarget species), and a requirement to use more selective fishing gear to reduce unwanted bycatch).[107] The EU Fisheries Council, composed of ministers responsible for fisheries from all EU member states, is charged with, among other things, setting catch limits (called total allowable catches) for all regulated species.[108]

As initially adopted, the CFP was "designed to assure a minimum income to fishermen as well as allowing a continuous supply of fishery products to the market, [but the] policy took no account of environmental or ecosystem factors."[109] In 1992, Regulation 3760/92 allowed the establishment of limits on exploitation levels based on biological, technical, or socioeconomic considerations.[110] Notwithstanding these changes, the policy has proven inadequate according to the European Commission's own assessment:

Europe's fisheries policy is in urgent need of reform. Vessels are catching more fish than can be safely reproduced, thus exhausting individual fish stocks and threatening the marine ecosystem. Today too many stocks are overfished: 80% of Mediterranean stocks and 47 % of Atlantic stocks. The fishing industry is experiencing smaller catches and facing an uncertain future. It is time to make fishing environmentally, economically, and socially sustainable.[111]

In short, the current CFP has failed to adequately address overfishing, fleet overcapacity, perverse subsidies, low economic resilience, and a decline in the volume of fish caught by European fishermen.[112] These problems may be the result of the establishment of catch limits "through political negotiations dominated by short-term interests, [which] has led to overfishing."[113] The Council has consistently established total allowable catches and quotas in excess of those suggested on the basis of scientific evidence.[114] Efforts to reform the CFP therefore continue.[115]

Japanese coastal fisheries are governed by fishery cooperative associations (FCAs), whose jurisdictional boundaries are defined geo-politically, rather than on the basis of the biological characteristics of the targeted species. FCAs comprise mostly fishing households and companies that fall below a certain number of employees by the number and tonnage of the vessels owned, and are usually associated with coastal communities with a history of dependence on fisheries resources. Offshore and high-sea fisheries are typically governed by a license system managed by the central or prefectural government. FCAs may impose controls involving resource management, fishing ground management, and fishing effort control. Among the problems with the Japanese system are discrepancies between the area in which a fish species reproduces and migrates and the jurisdictional boundaries of the FCAs, and the inadequacy and lack of reliance on scientific information.[116]

In Korea, the Fishery Resources Management Act[117] governs the management of fisheries. The Act's purpose is "to contribute to the continuous development of fishery resources and to the increase in income by fishery personnel by establishing plans for the management of fishery resources and by efficiently managing fishery resources through the prescription of matters necessary for the protection, recovery, formation, etc. of fishery resources."[118] The Act requires the minister for Food, Agriculture, Forestry, and Fisheries, in conjunction with a Central Fishery Resources Management Committee, to establish and implement plans for the management of fishery resources. A plan should establish total catch quotas, establish measures for the recovery of fishery resources in danger of reduction or exhaustion, and provide for the management of fishery resource habitat.[119] To protect fishery resources, the minister may designate areas and times in which the capture and gathering of fishery resources are prohibited.[120] The minister also may prohibit the sale, possession, and distribution of illegal catches;[121] restrict the number and tonnage of fishing vessels in operation;[122] and prohibit the use of certain fishing gear.[123] The Act authorizes the minister to establish and allocate total catch quotas for particular fish species and sea areas as a means of conserving and recovering fishery resources.[124] The Act also further provides for the designation and management of protected waters for the spawning of fishery resources. The Act also authorizes restrictions or prohibitions on the installation of structures that may obstruct the passage of anadromous fish.[125]

V.   Rangeland Management

Overgrazing by cattle, sheep, and goats can contribute to desertification of rangelands when the animals allowed to graze exceed the carrying capacity of the land. Excessive grazing causes loss of vegetation cover when the animals eat or trample vegetation. Loss of vegetation, in turn, facilitates soil erosion. Soil compaction that results from trampling of the ground by animals can also contribute to erosion by reducing the ability of soil to absorb water.[126] As climate change increases the incidence of drought, especially in already arid climates, one can expect greater attention to and recognition of the need for international agreements and domestic regulatory measures to prevent grazing and similar activities to control desertification.

A.   International Laws Governing Range Resources

The United Nations Convention to Combat Desertification in Countries Experiencing Serious Drought and/or Desertification, Particularly in Africa was executed in 1994 and went into force in December 1996.[127] The Convention's purpose is "to combat desertification and mitigate the effects of drought in countries experiencing serious drought and/or desertification, particularly in Africa."[128] It defines desertification to mean land degradation in arid, semi-arid, and dry subhumid areas resulting from climatic variations and human activities.[129] Land degradation includes loss of biological or economic productivity of cropland, range, pasture, forests, and woodlands resulting from human activities and habitation patterns.[130]

The Convention requires the parties to develop national action programs to combat desertification and mitigate the effects of drought.[131] The purpose of these programs is to identify the factors contributing to desertification and practical measures to combat it. Programs must be integrated with national policies for sustainable development. They also must include, as appropriate given a party's circumstances and requirements, measures to promote alternative livelihoods and improve national economic environments with a view to strengthening programs aimed at the eradication of poverty and at ensuring food security. Plans also must promote sustainable management of natural resources and agricultural practices, and development and efficient use of various energy sources.[132] The Convention emphasizes the process of preventing desertification more than it does the prescription of substantive measures for achieving that goal. In particular, it encourages opportunities for participation in decision making by local communities and land users,

and it creates mechanisms for developing partnerships that link these communities to international institutions, states, and NGOs. The Convention
commits developed country parties to provide grants and loans to assist
developing nations in combating desertification.[133]

Other bilateral and multilateral treaties address conflicts that have arisen
from cross-border grazing, especially by tribal communities. These include
the Treaty of Jeddah, which governs tribal grazing rights along the Yemeni-
Omani-Saudi borders;[134] treaties that govern the rights of the Lapps to graze
their herds in Sweden, Norway, and Finland;[135] agreements that govern grazing along the Ethiopian-Somali border;[136] and the Treaty of Guadalupe-
Hidalgo between the United States and Mexico.[137] Other agreements, such as
the Protocol on the Implementation of the Alpine Convention Relating to
Mountain Forests, restrict grazing of hoofed animals in mountainous areas
to facilitate reforestation.[138]

B.   Comparative Law Perspectives on Range Resources

Most of the federally owned land in the United States that is open to grazing
is managed by the BLM or the U.S. Forest Service. Both agencies manage
their lands under a multiple-use, sustained-yield mandate that recognizes
that these lands may be suitable for many purposes. The Federal Land Policy
and Management Act (FLPMA) authorizes the BLM to issue grazing permits
for ten-year terms under such conditions as the agency deems appropriate.[139]
Permits specify the number of cattle or sheep that the permit holder is
allowed to graze on BLM lands, as expressed in animal-unit-months (AUMs).
Although the federal government charges fees for the privilege to graze on
federal lands, there is general agreement that the fees are less than fair market value, so that the government subsidizes private grazing on public
lands.[140] Permit holders who graze in excess of the designated AUMs are
liable to the government for having committed a trespass.[141]

Critics of BLM grazing practices have attacked not only the subsidies
provided to ranchers through below-market value grazing fees, but also the
agency's failure to halt overgrazing and the environmental degradation it
can cause. The BLM strengthened its environmental controls in regulations
issued in 1994. These regulations seek to promote sustainable rangeland ecosystems, accelerate restoration of public rangelands to properly functioning
conditions, and provide for the sustainability of the western livestock industry and communities that depend on productive, healthy rangelands.[142]
Among other things, grazing regulations are supposed to ensure that watersheds are in properly functioning physical condition, ecological processes
are adequate to support healthy biotic populations, water quality complies
with applicable water quality standards, and habitats are suitable for endangered and threatened species.[143] BLM regulations issued in 2006 that would
have weakened these protective requirements were invalidated as a result of
violations of FLPMA, the National Environmental Policy Act (the United
States' environmental impact assessment law), and the Endangered Species

Act.[144] The Forest Service regulates grazing under FLPMA and the NFMA largely through the planning process described in the discussion of U.S. timber management legislation above.[145]

Other nations also restrict use of rangelands in ways that contribute to environmental degradation. Australia's rangelands cover three-quarters of its land area, and overgrazing has caused degradation of grasslands and loss of biodiversity.[146] Although Australia lacks legislation limiting grazing to sustainable levels, its legislation protecting biodiversity could be used to constrain overstocking of grasslands.[147]

Desertification in China, which is extensive, is caused partly by overgrazing and harvesting of wild vegetation that contribute to soil erosion. According to some sources, the Grassland Law of 1985 regulates land tenure in grasslands. It grants ownership of rangelands to the state or collectives, which may grant to households 50-year contracts that specify seasonal pasture allocations and stocking rates that are enforceable by Animal Husbandry Bureaus. Contract holders must pay pasture use fees and abide by a duty to sustain rangeland production. In practice, however, stocking rates appear to be poorly enforced. In addition, provincial policies sometimes conflict with the objectives of the Grassland Law, such as by encouraging nomads to settle and take up grazing. The 2001 Law of the People's Republic of China on Desert Prevention and Transformation, which seeks to implement the U.N. Convention to Combat Desertification, was an attempt to strengthen the 1985 law. It relies on both traditional regulation and market-based incentives to rehabilitate desertified areas and promote sustainable rangelands use. The 2001 legislation authorizes local animal husbandry departments to promote rotational grazing and control the number of animals grazed. The law also allows local governments to provide financial incentives to those engaged in desertification prevention and control on government lands.[148]

VI.   Recreational Use and Preservation

Preservation of natural areas is important to the continued provision of ecosystem services and the protection of biological diversity. Natural areas also provide an important source of economic value, not least because of their attractiveness as tourist destinations. Both international and domestic laws have sought to ensure that sufficient land is available for recreational use. In some places, such as portions of the western United States, the value of public lands for recreation has outstripped the value of those lands for traditional extractive uses, fueling new constraints on economic uses that may interfere with recreation. At the same time, more and less intensive recreational uses have clashed, with no clear winner emerging. In addition, more sophisticated understanding of the value of the ecosystem services provided by unimpaired natural resources may provide the basis for more protective preservation laws.

A. International Laws Governing Recreation and Preservation

Regional multilateral treaties seek to preserve important natural features. The Convention on Nature Protection and Wildlife Preservation in the Western Hemisphere[149] committed the parties to exploring the possibility of establishing in their territories national parks, national reserves, nature monuments, and wilderness reserves. It provides that where feasible, establishment of these areas shall begin as soon as possible after the effective date of the Convention.[150] The Convention prohibits the exploitation of the resources of these areas for commercial profit, and the parties agreed to restrict hunting, killing, or capturing of fauna in national parks. They also agreed to provide facilities for public recreation.[151] The parties committed to the maintenance of wilderness reserves inviolate as far as practical, except for scientific investigations and uses consistent with the purposes for which the area was established, and to the adoption of laws to protect and preserve natural scenery, striking geological formations, and regions and natural objects of aesthetic interest or historic or scientific value.[152]

Other regions have adopted similar agreements. The African Convention on the Conservation of Nature and Natural Resources[153] requires the parties to establish and maintain conservation areas, which include wilderness areas, national parks, natural monuments, and protected landscapes. Wherever possible, the parties must designate such areas to ensure the long-term conservation of biological diversity.[154] The Convention describes the goals of each type of conservation area. Wilderness areas are supposed to ensure that future generations have the opportunity to experience and enjoy areas largely undisturbed by human action, and to enable local communities living at low density and in balance with available resources to maintain their lifestyle. National parks should be managed to protect the ecological integrity of the affected areas for present and future generations, exclude exploitation or occupation inimical to the purposes of designation, and provide a foundation for spiritual, scientific, educational, and recreational opportunities. Natural monuments are established to protect or preserve outstanding natural features because of their national significance, unique or representational quality, or spiritual connotations. Protected landscapes or seascapes should maintain the harmonious interaction of nature and culture and support lifestyles and economic activities that are in harmony with nature and the preservation of the social and cultural fabric of concerned communities.[155] Similarly, the Association of South East Asian Nations Agreement on the Conservation of Nature and Natural Resources, enacted in 1985 but not yet in force, would require the parties to establish terrestrial, freshwater, coastal, or marine protected areas to safeguard ecological and biological processes essential to the functioning of regional ecosystems. These would include national parks dedicated to conservation, scientific, educational, and recreational uses.[156]

Nature preservation is among the aims of the Convention for the Protection of the World Cultural and Natural Heritage of 1972 (the World Heritage

Convention).[157] The agreement seeks to create a list of irreplaceable natural sites to preserve and protect for future generations. At the same time, each party to the Convention is responsible for preserving sites within its territory.[158] Each party is responsible for submitting to a World Heritage Committee an inventory of property within its territory that forms part of its cultural and natural heritage. The Committee maintains a World Heritage List, which includes properties having outstanding universal value under criteria established under the Convention. No site may be listed without the consent of the state in which it is located. In addition, the Committee maintains a List of World Heritage in Danger, composed of sites whose conservation requires major operations and for which assistance has been requested under the Convention. This list is limited to properties forming part of the cultural and natural heritage that are threatened by activities such as large-scale public or private projects, rapid urban or tourist development, changes in ownership or land use, abandonment, calamities or cataclysms, or changes in water level, floods, or tidal waves.[159] A party may request international assistance for properties on the List of World Heritage in Danger from the Committee.[160]

B.   Comparative Law Perspectives on Recreation and Preservation

The United States has long been a leader in nature preservation and the establishment of areas for recreational use. The concept of the national park has been described as the "best idea" America ever had.[161] Congress created the first national park, Yellowstone, in 1872, followed by Yosemite in 1890. In 1916, Congress passed what has become known as the National Park Service Organic Act.[162] That statute created the National Park Service (NPS), which now operates within the Department of the Interior, to manage the national parks and monuments for the dual purposes of conserving the scenery, natural and historic objects, and wildlife within those areas and of providing for the enjoyment of these areas "in such manner and by such means as will leave them unimpaired for the enjoyment of future generations."[163] Although the creation of the National Park System was designed both to preserve natural and historic resources and provide recreational opportunities, these two objectives may conflict, and different forms of recreational use (such as backpacking or bird watching and motorized vehicle use) may clash. It is generally agreed that Congress intended the preservation purpose to take priority over the recreation purpose. Activities that may conflict with preservation or recreational goals are tightly restricted. Thus, hunting is generally forbidden in the national parks, as are most commercial uses (such as mining, grazing, and timber cutting).

National monuments, which the NPS also administers, are created by presidential designation under the Antiquities Act of 1906.[164] The 1906 Act authorizes the president to designate as national monuments historic landmarks and structures and "other objects of historic or scientific interest" found on federal lands. Although the statute restricts such monuments "to the smallest area compatible with the proper care and management of the objects to be protected,"[165] various presidents have included large areas within national monuments, including President Carter's designation of 17 monuments totaling 56 million acres of land in Alaska.[166] The use of presidential authority under the Antiquities Act has been politically controversial, as critics of the statute have claimed that presidential designations have ignored local sentiments. Every designation that has been challenged in court has been upheld, however. The management standards and restrictions that apply to national monuments are the same as the ones that apply to national parks under the National Park Service Organic Act. Congress on occasion has endorsed presidential designations by changing the status of a national monument to a national park. The NPS now manages more than 80 million acres of parks, monuments, and historic sites.

Preservation of wildlife refuges began when Theodore Roosevelt reserved Pelican Island as a bird refuge in 1903. In 1966, Congress consolidated areas previously set aside for wildlife preservation into the National Wildlife Refuge System, and charged the U.S. Fish and Wildlife Service (FWS), another agency within the Interior Department, with the responsibility to manage it. The National Wildlife Refuge System Improvement Act[167] declares the FWS's mission in managing the system to be conservation, management, and restoration of fish, wildlife, and plant resources and their habitats for the benefit of present and future generations of Americans.[168] The conservation of fish, wildlife, plants, and their habitats is the preeminent use of the national wildlife refuges. The Act prohibits any human use of a refuge that is not compatible with such preservation.[169] Wildlife-dependent recreational uses that are compatible with the preservation goal are afforded secondary priority within the system. These include hunting, fishing, wildlife observation and photography, and environmental education.[170] All other uses have the lowest priority. As a result, activities such as grazing, mineral development, nonwildlife-related recreation, water development, and timber harvesting are prohibited if they conflict with the preservation function of the National Wildlife Refuge System or of an individual unit, or if they would materially interfere with wildlife-dependent recreational uses.[171]

The most protective of all the U.S. preservation statutes is the Wilderness Act of 1964.[172] The Act defines wilderness as "an area where the earth and its community of life are untrammeled by man, where man himself is a visitor who does not remain" and as "an area of undeveloped Federal land retaining its primeval character and influence, without permanent improvements or human habitation, which is protected and managed so as to preserve its natural conditions" because of its outstanding recreational opportunities or its "ecological, geological, or other features of scientific, educational, scenic, or historic value."[173] Congress may designate wilderness within any of the principal federal lands systems—the national parks, forests, or wildlife refuges, or the lands managed by the multiple-use agencies, the Forest Service, and the BLM. The Wilderness Act declares a policy of securing for present and future generations the benefits of the enduring resource of wilderness and mandates that wilderness areas be managed "in such manner as will leave them unimpaired for future use and enjoyment as wilderness, and so as to provide for the protection of these areas [and] the preservation of their wilderness character."[174] By 2012, Congress had designated nearly 110 million acres of wilderness. These areas must be devoted to recreational, scenic, scientific, educational, conservation, and historical use.[175] With limited exceptions, the Act prohibits all commercial activities and permanent roads within wilderness areas, and most temporary roads and motorized vehicles.[176]

Other nations have followed the lead of the United States in enacting laws to protect natural resources, often to fulfill their responsibilities under the international agreements discussed in section VI.A above. The Commonwealth Government of Australia manages sites listed on the World Heritage List and has created a national park system that includes the Great Barrier Reef Marine Park.[177] In South Australia, the National Parks and Wildlife Act of 1972 divides national parks into several categories, including game reserves, regional reserves, recreation parks, national parks, conservation parks, and wilderness protection areas. Each area is governed by a management plan that is designed to preserve natural features and wildlife and encourage public use.[178] In France, the national government has the authority to create national parks, while local authorities, in conjunction with the Minister of the Environment, may create regional parks.[179] In Hungary, 1996 legislation prohibits the alteration of natural areas, which include national parks, landscape protection reserves, nature conservation areas, and natural monuments, unless the alteration is in the interests of nature conservation. As in Argentina, buffer zones may be created to protect natural areas from outside activities.[180]

In Nigeria, the 1991 National Parks Service Act/Decree established a National Parks Governing Board to manage national parks. Each park has its own management committee, which is subject to the supervision of the Governing Board. Committees must ensure that the park is set aside exclusively for the propagation, protection, conservation, and management of vegetation and wild animals in the parks, and ensure that hunting and destruction or collection of plants are prohibited, except for scientific or management purposes. They also may regulate access to the parks and must prohibit, with limited exceptions, agriculture, grazing, mining, drilling, work that alters soil configuration or vegetation character, and any act likely to disturb fauna and flora. It is illegal to kill or maim any animal or plant within a park without a permit.[181]

VII.   Conclusion

Practitioners representing many different kinds of interests may encounter the laws discussed in this chapter. Attorneys representing a timber company, for example, should understand the laws that govern the execution of timber contracts on public lands and the constraints that those contracts may include to protect forest natural resources. An attorney representing a supplier of timber products should be familiar with international and domestic laws that make the sale and purchase of improperly harvested timer illegal. Mining activities are often conducted by companies with operations that span the globe. Knowledge of the laws that govern mineral extraction in different parts of the world is essential to advising a client which country is likely to provide the most profitable venture opportunities. Similarly, an attorney advising a company that wants to become involved in oil and gas development in international waters needs to know how international law affects the rights of countries and private businesses to become involved in such development. Knowledge of laws affecting the use of rangelands may be important to an attorney representing a client that wants to develop cattle or sheep herds for sale of the meat, wool, or other products derivable from these animals. It is also essential for a practitioner advising commercial fishing clients to be familiar with international and domestic laws that govern the availability of fishing licenses or other permissions and that constrain fishing activities as a means of providing sustainable fisheries. A business that provides commercial recreational opportunities (such as the rental of snowmobiles, canoes, or other outdoor recreational opportunities) will seek out an attorney capable of providing advice on the permissible uses of public lands for commercially provided recreation.

Attorneys representing other kinds of clients also need to be familiar with the laws addressed in this chapter. Attorneys representing environmental non-government organizations (NGOs) need to understand the laws that constrain economic development that involves the use of natural resources. These laws may provide tools for attorneys representing such NGOs to prevent or limit timber harvesting, mining, grazing, or fishing that threatens ecosystem integrity or sustainable resource use. They also may determine the extent to which public lands are available for recreational use and provide the basis for prioritizing different kinds of recreational use that may or may not be compatible with each other.

Notes

1. David Hunter, James Salzman & Durwood Zaelke, International Environmental Law and Policy 1145 (4th ed. 2011).

2. Non-Legally Binding Authoritative Statement of Principles for a Global Consensus on the Management, Conservation and Sustainable Development of All Types of Forests, Principle/Element 1(a), A/CONF.151/26 (Vol. III) (1992), *reprinted in* 31 I.L.M. 881.

3. *Id.* Principle/Element 2(a).

4. *Id.* Principle/Element 2(b).

5. *Id.* Principles/Elements 5(a), 6(a).

6. *Id.* Principles/Elements 6(e), 13(d).

7. United Nations Conference on Environment & Development, June 3–14, 1992, Agenda 21 Programme of Action for Sustainable Development, Chapter 11, P8.28, U.N. Doc. A/CONF.151/26 (1992).

8. Non-Legally Binding Instrument on All Types of Forests art. 2(b), UNGA Res. No. 62/98 (Jan. 21, 2008).

9. *Id.* art. 5.

10. International Tropical Timber Agreement art. 1(c), Geneva, 2006, Doc/TD/TIM-BER.3/12. *See* Hunter et al., *supra* note 1, at 1164.

11. Summit of Central African Heads of State on the Conservation and Sustainable Management of Tropical Forests: The Yaounde Declaration, Mar. 17, 1999, *reprinted in* 38 I.L.M. 783.

12. *See* Elisa Morgera, *Bilateralism at the Service of Community Interests? Non-judicial Enforcement of Global Public Goods in the Context of Global Environmental Law*, 23 Eur. J. Int'l L. 743, 757 (2012).

13. U.S.-Peru Trade Promotion Agreement, U.S.-Peru, Dec. 14, 2007, *available at* http://www.ustr.gov/Trade_Agreements/Bilateral/Peru_TPA/Final_ Texts/Section_Index .html.

14. EU's Forest Law Enforcement, Governance, and Trade (FLEGT), http://www .euflegt.efi.int/portal/.

15. Hunter et al., *supra* note 1, at 1167.

16. Blake Hudson, *Climate Change, Forests, and Federalism: Seeing the Treaty for the Trees*, 82 U. Colo. L. Rev. 363, 391 (2011).

17. 16 U.S.C. §§ 1600–1687.

18. *Id.* § 1604(a), (e), (i).

19. 16 U.S.C. § 531(b).

20. 16 U.S.C. § 1604(g)(3).

21. Comparative Environmental Law and Regulation § 2:33 (Nicholas A. Robinson et al. eds., 2012); Law No. 13.273, Nov. 13, 1995, arts. 5, 11, 30; B.O. Nov. 24, 1995; Decree 710/95, *available at* http://www.bcn.cl/carpeta_temas/temas_portada.2005-10 -27.5914140963/pdf/13273argentina.pdf (in Spanish).

22. Comparative Environmental Law and Regulation, *supra* note 21, § 12:44; Lei No. 12.651, de 25 de Maio de 2012, arts. 3, 12, *available at* http://www.planalto.gov.br /ccivil_03/_Ato2011-2014/2012/Lei/L12651.htm (in Portuguese).

23. Shephali Mehra Birdi, *Environmental Law, in* Corporate Counsel's Guide to Doing Business in India § 17:7 (3d ed.); The Forest (Conservation) Act, No. 69 of 1980, art. 2, *available at* http://indiacode.nic.in.

24. Comparative Environmental Law and Regulation, *supra* note 21, § 53:31; Forest Code of Ukraine, No. 3853-XII, art. 39 (Jan. 21, 1994), *available at* http://zakon1 .rada.gov.ua/laws/show/3852-12 (in Ukrainian).

25. *Nation Extends Ban on Tree Clearing*, Greenwire, May 13, 2013.

26. Comparative Environmental Law and Regulation, *supra* note 21, § 33:24.

27. The Scheduled Tribes and Other Traditional Forest Dwellers (Recognition of Forest Rights) Act, No. 2 of 2007, art. 3, *available at* http://indiacode.nic.in; Danielle M. Conway, *Promoting Indigenous Innovation, Enterprise, and Entrepreneurship through the Licensing of Article 31 Indigenous Assets and Resources*, 64 SMU L. Rev. 1095, 1114 (2011); Prashant Bhushan, *Sacrificing Human Rights and Environmental Rights at the Altar of "Development,"* 41 Geo. Wash. Int'l L. Rev. 389, 399 (2009).

28. Philippe Sands, Principles of International Environmental law 667 (2d ed. 2003).

29. Jonathan D. Weiss, *The Balance of Nature and Human Needs in Antarctica: The Legality of Mining*, 9 Temp. Int'l & Comp. L.J. 387, 398–99 (1995).

30. 30 I.L.M. 1461 (1991).

31. *Id.* art. 2.

32. *Id.* art. 7.

33. *Id.* art. 25.

34. Weiss, *supra* note 29, at 398–401.

35. 1833 U.N.T.S. 397 (Dec. 10, 1982) (entered into force in 1994).

36. *Id.* arts. 2, 3.

37. *Id.* arts. 55, 56(1), 57.

38. *Id.* arts. 76, 77.

39. *Id.* art. 81.

40. *Id.* arts. 136–37.

41. Ryan Hugh O'Donnell, Comment, *Staking a Claim in the Twenty-First Century: Real Property Rights on Extraterrestrial Bodies*, 32 U. DAYTON L. REV. 461, 479 (2007).

42. Matthew Johnshoy, Note, *The Final Frontier and a Guano Islands Act for the Twenty-First Century: Reaching for the Stars without Reaching for the Stars*, 37 J. CORP. L. 717, 723 (2012).

43. Eric A. Posner & Alan O. Sykes, *Economic Foundations of the Law of the Sea*, 104 AM. J. INT'L L. 569, 587–88 (2010).

44. Benjamin David Landry, *A Tragedy of the Anticommons: The Economic Inefficiencies of Space Law*, 38 BROOK. J. INT'L L. 523, 538–39 (2013).

45. Marta Kolcz-Ryan, Comment, *An Arctic Race: How the United States' Failure to Ratify the Law of the Sea Convention Could Adversely Affect its Interests in the Arctic*, 35 U. DAYTON L. REV. 149, 170 (2009).

46. 30 U.S.C. §§ 1201–1328.

47. *Id.* § 1265.

48. 30 U.S.C. §§ 22–47.

49. *See* 4 GEORGE CAMERON COGGINS & ROBERT L. GLICKSMAN, PUBLIC NATURAL RESOURCES LAW ch. 42. (West 2d ed. 2007).

50. *Id.* §§ 42:31–42:36.

51. Pub. L. No. 100-203, 101 Stat. 1330.

52. 4 COGGINS & GLICKSMAN, *supra* note 49, at ch. 39.

53. 43 U.S.C. §§ 1331–1343.

54. Pub. L. No. 94-377, 90 Stat. 1083.

55. *See* 4 COGGINS & GLICKSMAN, *supra* note 49, §§ 38:18–38:32.

56. 30 U.S.C. § 1272.

57. *See* 4 COGGINS & GLICKSMAN, *supra* note 49, at ch. 40.

58. COMPARATIVE ENVIRONMENTAL LAW AND REGULATION, *supra* note 21, § 33:33; The Mining Act, (1987) Cap. 306 §§ 4, 7(1), 13, 18, 39, 44, 47, *available at* http://www.kenyalaw.org.

59. COMPARATIVE ENVIRONMENTAL LAW AND REGULATION, *supra* note 21, § 45:24; Federal Law on Subsoil, No. 27-FZ (Mar. 3, 1995), *available at* http://www.systema.ru/.

60. Minerals and Mining Decree No. (34) (1999), §§ 147–158, 162(1), *available at* http://www.nigeria-law.org/MineralsAndMiningDecree1999.htm.

61. COMPARATIVE ENVIRONMENTAL LAW AND REGULATION, *supra* note 21, § 45:8; Fundamentals of Legislation of the USSR and Union Republics on Minerals, Ved. Verkh, SSSR, No. 29, item 435; amended in 1979, Ved. Verkh, SSSR, No. 39, item 643.

62. 1996 évi LIII. Törvény a Természet Védelmér?l (Act LIII of 1996 on Nature Conservation) art. 20(1), *available at* http://www.asser.nl/upload/eel-webroot/www/documents/HUN/hungary%20Nature%20Conservation%20law.htm (in English) *and* http://faolex.fao.org/ (in Hungarian).

63. *E.g.*, COMPARATIVE ENVIRONMENTAL LAW AND REGULATION, *supra* note 21, § 33:33 (Kenya); The Environmental Management and Co-ordination Act, No. 8 (1999) § 58(1), *available at* http://www.kenyalaw.org/.

64. Food & Agric. Org., *Overview: Major Trends and Issues* at xvi–xvii, *available at* http://www.fao.org/fishery/statistics/153320/en.

65. HUNTER ET AL., *supra* note 1, at 761.

66. *Id.* at 768.

67. Icelandic Fisheries Case (United Kingdom v. Iceland), 1974 I.C.J. 3 (1974).

68. UNCLOS, *supra* note 35, art. 2.

69. *Id.* art. 56.

70. *Id.* art. 61(1)–(3).

71. *Id.* art. 62.

72. HUNTER ET AL., *supra* note 1, at 769.

73. UNCLOS, *supra* note 35, art. 63.

74. *Id.* art. 64.

75. *Id.* art. 66.

76. *Id.* art. 67.

77. *Id.* art. 87(1).

78. *Id.* art. 116.

79. *Id.* art. 117.

80. *Id.* art. 118.

81. *Id.* art. 119(1).

82. International Tribunal for the Law of the Sea, The Tribunal, http://www.itlos.org/index.php?id=15&L=0.

83. International Tribunal for the Law of the Sea, Cases, http://www.itlos.org/index.php?id=10&L=0.

84. HUNTER ET AL., *supra* note 1, at 782.

85. The United Nations Agreement for the Implementation of the Provisions of the United Nations Convention on the Law of the Sea of 10 December 1982 relating to the Conservation and Management of Straddling Fish Stocks and Highly Migratory Fish Stocks, U.N. Doc. A/CONF.164/37 (1995).

86. *Id.* art. 2.

87. *Id.* art. 5.

88. *Id.* art. 6(1).

89. *Id.* art. 6(2). For analysis of the Agreement, *see generally* Eric Franckx, *Pacta Tertiis and the Agreement for the Implementation of the Straddling and Highly Migratory Fish Stocks Provisions of the United Nations Convention on the Law of the Sea*, 8 TUL. J. INT'L & COMP. L. 49 (2000); Giselle Vigneron, *Compliance and International Environmental Agreements: A Case Study of the 1995 United Nations Straddling Fish Stocks Agreement*, 10 GEO. INT'L ENVTL. L. REV. 581 (1998).

90. *See* Nw. Atl. Fisheries Org., http://www.nafo.int.

91. Howard S. Schiffman, *The Evolution of Fisheries Conservation and Management: A Look at the New South Pacific Regional Fisheries Management Organization in Law and Policy*, 28 T.M. COOLEY L. REV. 181, 182 (2011).

92. *See* http://www.tuna-org.org/.

93. Schiffman, *supra* note 91, at 183. *See also* Elise Anne Clark, *Strengthening Regional Fisheries Management—An Analysis of the Duty to Cooperate*, 9 N.Z. J. PUB. & INT'L L. 223 (2011); Howard S. Schiffman, *Moving from Single-Species Management to Ecosystem Management in Regional Fisheries Management Organizations*, 13 ILSA J. INT'L & COMP. L. 387 (2007).

94. 16 U.S.C. §§ 1801–1882. *See generally* Roger Fleming, Peter Shelly & Priscilla M. Brooks, *Twenty-Eight Years and Counting: Can the Magnuson-Stevens Act Deliver on Its Conservation Promise?*, 28 VT. L. REV. 579 (2004); Marian Macpherson, *Integrating Ecosystem Management Approaches into Federal Fishery Management Through the Magnuson-Stevens Fishery Conservation and Management Act*, 6 OCEAN & COASTAL L.J. 1 (2001).

95. 16 U.S.C. § 1801(b)(1).

96. *Id.* § 1801(b).

97. *Id.* § 1801(c)(1).

98. *Id.* § 1804(b)(4).

99. *Id.* § 1853(a)(1) (A).

100. *Id.* § 1853(a)(1)(C).

101. *Id.* § 1853(a).

102. *Id.* § 1854(c)(1).

103. 141 Cong. Rec. H10232 (daily ed. Oct. 15, 1995).

104. 16 U.S.C. § 1854(e)(4)(A). For further description of the Act and the fishery management plans that it requires, see Pac. Coast Fed'n of Fishermen's Ass'ns v. Blank, 693 F.3d 1084, 1086–88 (9th Cir. 2012); Yakutat, Inc. v. Gutierrez, 407 F.3d 1054 (9th Cir. 2005).

105. The Common Fisheries Policy, European Fisheries Comm'n (Sept. 15, 2011), http://ec.europa.eu/fisheries/cfp/index_en.htm; Regional Policy, European Comm'n http://ec.europa.eu/regional_policy/what/index_en.cfm.

106. European Comm'n, The Common Fisheries Policy: A User's Guide 8 (2009), *available at* http://ec.europa.eu/fisheries/documentation/publications/pcp2008_en.pdf.

107. European Comm'n, Fishing Rules, http://ec.europa.eu/fisheries/cfp/fishing _rules/index_en.htm (last visited May 24, 2013).

108. Council Regulation 2371/2002, art. 20, 2002 O.J. (L 358) 59, 61 (EC).

109. Gwenaële Proutière-Maulion, *From Resource Conservation to Sustainability: An Assessment of Two Decades of the European Union's Common Fisheries Policy*, 11 Ocean & Coastal L.J. 37, 38 (2005–2006).

110. Council Regulation 3760/92, Establishing a Community System for Fisheries and Aquaculture, 1992 O.J. (L 389) 1.

111. European Comm'n, Fisheries, http://ec.europa.eu/fisheries/reform/background /index_en.htm (last visited May 24, 2013).

112. Comm'n of the European Cmtys., Green Paper, *Reform of the Common Fisheries Policy*, Brussels, 22.4.2009, COM(2009)163 final, at 4–5, *available at* http://eur-lex.europa .eu/LexUriServ/LexUriServ.do?uri=COM:2009:0163:FIN:EN:PDF.

113. Stijn van Osch, *Save Our Sharks: Using International Fisheries Laws within Regional Fisheries Management to Improve Shark Conservation*, 33 Mich. J. Int'l L. 383, 394 (2012).

114. Proutière-Maulion, *supra* note 109, at 40.

115. *See, e.g.*, European Comm'n, Reform of the Common Fisheries Policy, http:// ec.europa.eu/fisheries/reform/index_en.htm (last visited May 24, 2013).

116. H. Uchida & M. Makino, Japanese Coastal Fishery Co-Management: An Overview (2008), *available at* ftp://ftp.fao.org/docrep/fao/010/a1497e/a1497e20.pdf. *See also* Tadashi Yamamoto, *Development of a Community-Based Fishery Management System in Japan*, 10 Marine Res. Econ. 21 (1995).

117. Act. No. 9627, Apr. 22, 2009, as amended, *available at* http://faolex.fao.org/docs /pdf/kor108399.pdf.

118. *Id.* art. 1.

119. *Id.* arts. 7, 54–55.

120. *Id.* arts. 14–15.

121. *Id.* arts. 16–17.

122. *Id.* arts. 20–21.

123. *Id.* arts. 23–24.

124. *Id.* arts. 36–37.

125. *Id.* art. 43.

126. Hunter et al., *supra* note 1, at 1174–75.

127. United Nations Convention to Combat Desertification in Countries Experiencing Serious Drought and/or Desertification, Particularly in Africa, June 17, 1994, 1954 U.N.T.S. 3 (entered into force Dec. 26, 1996).

128. *Id.* art. 2.

129. *Id.* art. 1(a).

130. *Id.* art. 1(f).

131. *Id.* art. 9.

132. *Id.* art. 10.

133. HUNTER ET AL., *supra* note 1, at 1177–78.

134. Askar Halwan Al-Enazy, *"The International Boundary Treaty" (Treaty of Jeddah) Concluded between the Kingdom of Saudi Arabia and the Yemeni Republic on June 12, 2000*, 96 AM. J. INT'L L. 161, 165 (2002).

135. Barry A. Feinstein, *Permeable Fences Make Good Neighbors: Improving a Seemingly Intractable Border Conflict between Israelis and Palestinians*, 16 AM. U. INT'L L. REV. 1, 107 n.582 (2000).

136. Michael Reisman, Comment, *Protecting Indigenous Rights in International Adjudication*, 89 AM. J. INT'L L. 350, 358 n.40 (1995).

137. Harold J. Krent, *Monitoring Governmental Disposition of Assets: Fashioning Regulatory Substitutes for Market Controls*, 52 VAND. L. REV. 1705, 1731 n.107 (1999). *See also* A. Dan Tarlock, *Environmental Protection: The Potential Misfit between Equity and Efficiency*, 63 U. COLO. L. REV. 871, 880 (1992) ("Hispanics also developed a thriving sheep industry which was dependent on communal grazing privileges protected by the Treaty of Guadalupe de Hidalgo.").

138. http://www.ecolex.org/ecolex/ledge/view/RecordDetails?id=TRE-001240&index =treaties (art. 2(b)).

139. 43 U.S.C. § 1752(a).

140. 3 COGGINS & GLICKSMAN, *supra* note 49, §§ 33:7, 33:15.

141. *Id.* § 33:18.

142. 43 C.F.R. § 4100.0-2(a).

143. *Id.* § 4180.1.

144. W. Watersheds Project v. Kraayenbrink, 632 F.3d 472 (9th Cir. 2011).

145. *See* 3 COGGINS AND GLICKSMAN, *supra* note 49, §§ 33:31–33:40.

146. Rebecca Nelson, *Regulating Grassland Degradation in China: Shallow-Rooted Laws?*, 7 ASIAN-PAC. L. & POL'Y J. 385 (2006).

147. *Id.*

148. *Id. See also* Grassland Law of the People's Republic of China (promulgated by the Standing Comm. Nat'l People's Cong., June 18, 1985, effective as of October 1, 1985), *available at* http://faolex.fao.org/; Law of the People's Republic of China on Desert Prevention and Transformation (promulgated by the Standing Comm. Nat'l People's Cong., Aug. 31, 2001, effective as of Jan. 1, 2002), *available at* http://faolex.fao.org/.

149. UN Registration: 03/03/53 No. 485, Vol. 161 (1940, entered into force in 1942).

150. *Id.* art. 2.

151. *Id.* art. 3.

152. *Id.* arts. 4–5.

153. 1001 U.N.T.S. 4 (Sept. 15, 1968).

154. *Id.* art. 12(1).

155. *Id.* at Annex 2.

156. Association of South East Asian Nations Agreement on the Conservation of Nature and Natural Resources art. 13, July 9, 1985, *reprinted in* 15 ENVTL. POL'Y & L. 64 (1985) (not yet in force).

157. 27 U.N.T.S. 37, 1037 U.N.T.S. 151. *See generally* Natasha Affolder, *Mining and the World Heritage Convention: Democratic Legitimacy and Treaty Compliance*, 24 PACE ENVTL. L. REV. 35 (2007); William C.G. Burns, *Belt and Suspenders?: The World Heritage Convention's Role in Confronting Climate Change*, 17 SE. ENVTL. L.J. 359 (2009); Edward J. Goodwin, *The World Heritage Convention, the Environment, and Compliance*, 20 COLO. J. INT'L ENVTL. L. & POL'Y 157 (2009).

158. World Heritage Convention, *supra* note 157, art. 3; HUNTER ET AL., *supra* note 1, at 1129.

159. World Heritage Convention, *supra* note 157, art. 11.

160. *Id.* arts. 19–20.

161. *See* Joseph L. Sax, *Ownership, Property, and Sustainability*, 31 UTAH ENVTL. L. REV. 1, 8 (2011) (quoting Wallace Stegner).

162. 16 U.S.C. §§ 1–18f.

163. *Id.* § 1.

164. 16 U.S.C. §§ 431–433.

165. *Id.* § 431.

166. 2 COGGINS & GLICKSMAN, *supra* note 49, § 14:4.

167. 16 U.S.C. §§ 6668dd to 668ee.

168. *Id.* § 668dd(a)(2).

169. *Id.* § 668dd(d)(3)(A)(i).

170. *Id.* § 668ee(2).

171. *See* 3 COGGINS & GLICKSMAN, *supra* note 49, § 24:5.

172. 16 U.S.C. §§ 1131–1136.

173. *Id.* § 1131(c).

174. *Id.* § 1131(a).

175. *Id.* § 1133(b).

176. *Id.* § 1133(c).

177. COMPARATIVE ENVIRONMENTAL LAW AND REGULATION, *supra* note 21, § 6:23.

178. *Id.* § 48:14; National Parks and Wildlife Act 1972 (SA) pt. 3.

179. COMPARATIVE ENVIRONMENTAL LAW AND REGULATION, *supra* note 21, § 21:20; Code de l'environnement, arts. L331-1, L333-1, *available at* http://www.legifrance.gouv.fr/Traductions/en-English/Legifrance-translations/.

180. COMPARATIVE ENVIRONMENTAL LAW AND REGULATION, *supra* note 21, § 26:30; 1996 évi LIII. Törvény a Természet Védelmér?l (Act LIII of 1996 on Nature Conservation) arts. 28, 30, 31, *available at* http://www.asser.nl/upload/eel-webroot/www/documents/HUN/hungary%20Nature%20Conservation%20law.htm (in English) *and* http://faolex.fao.org/ (in Hungarian).

181. COMPARATIVE ENVIRONMENTAL LAW AND REGULATION, *supra* note 21, § 40:161; National Parks Service Act/Decree No. (46) (1999) §§ 2, 21–23, 30; *available at* http://faolex.fao.org/.

CHAPTER 11

Natural Resource Damages

KIM SMACZNIAK

I. What Are Natural Resource Damage Laws?

A number of jurisdictions have laws that provide for separate liability for harms caused to natural resources. While tort law and other civil liability tend to focus on the impairment of private rights over such resources, natural resource damage (NRD) laws broaden the scope of liability to include harm to the public value of the affected natural resource. NRD laws also tend to be distinct from laws that focus on alleviating a current or threatened harm to human health or the environment. NRD law seeks to restore a natural resource to its functionality prior to the harm. In contrast, many emergency response and remediation laws focus on containing and eliminating exposure to the harm (e.g., the contamination) without necessarily restoring the environment to its original state. For example, liability for an oil spill under many legal regimes includes the cost to contain and remove the oil from the environment. It also may include an NRD component: a separately assessed cost to restore the impacted ecosystem to its prespill status. NRD laws thus serve an important, complementary function to other environmental and natural resource laws. They provide additional deterrence to environmentally harmful activities and, in most jurisdictions, a dedicated source of funding to assess and restore ecological damage resultant from such activities.

In jurisdictions that have not yet developed laws explicitly providing for NRD, in some cases liability may nonetheless be imposed under background civil liability. For example, in 2004, the Canadian Supreme Court held that the federal government may recover damages for harm to a public forest under a theory of public nuisance and other common law torts. This decision has been hailed as opening the door for other NRD claims by the Canadian government.[1] Such civil liability mechanisms, however, typically lack a mechanism by which damages are allocated to natural resource restoration efforts.

While the principle underlying NRD laws has a venerable origin in Roman and English public trust doctrine, the relatively recent emergence of statutory frameworks for NRD liability is a significant trend.[2] This chapter can only begin to describe the rich variability among modern NRD laws and similar liability mechanisms that have emerged in international law.

II.   Key Components of Natural Resource Damage Laws

While NRD statutes reflect a common goal of deterring harm to and spurring restoration of natural resources, the kind and degree of liability can vary greatly across jurisdictions. The statutory or regulatory definitions often provide key parameters of the scope of liability. Given that assessment of NRD entail complicated scientific and technical judgments, the backdrop rules of evidence (e.g., admissibility of expert testimony), civil procedure (e.g., burden of proof), and administrative law (e.g., deference to a government agency's assessment of environmental damages) at play within a jurisdiction are also likely to impact the evaluation of liability. The difficulty in assessing the public value of a natural resource and the uncertainty in the cost to restore the full functionality of the public resource can create barriers to efficient resolution of liability claims. Such problems can also limit the effectiveness of these laws in deterring and compensating for environmental harm to public resources.[3]

A.   Which Resources Are Covered?

A growing number of jurisdictions have adopted generally applicable liability regimes for environmental damage. Such laws typically incorporate a broad definition of the covered natural resources, including air, soils, waters, flora, and fauna. For example, the European Commission contemplated, in the course of evaluating a then-proposed directive on environmental liability, adopting a definition that included biodiversity. The proposed definition would have valued not only the species and habitats, but also the degree of variability among living organisms.[4] Ultimately, the Commission concluded that measuring harm to biodiversity was too difficult and adopted a more conventional definition of the covered resources based on language used in other, existing environmental directives.[5]

In some jurisdictions, NRD claims are limited to harm to publicly owned natural resources.[6] NRD claims are also commonly limited to the public value of natural resources, while harm to private rights to natural resources is addressed by alternative civil liability mechanisms. Thus, following the massive British Petroleum (BP) Deepwater Horizon oil spill in the Gulf of Mexico in 2010, the U.S. government had the authority to pursue a remedy for harm to the marine environment under federal environmental statutes. However, affected commercial fishermen and other classes whose private rights were impaired by the oil spill largely retained the ability to pursue civil suits against BP.

It is also common to find natural resource damage provisions in laws that cover only specific forms of pollution. The scope of covered resources under such media-specific laws are correspondingly narrower. Oil pollution liability regimes stemming from a number of sources, including international conventions and national legislation, tend to include natural resource damage provisions that apply exclusively to oil spills. For example, the 1992 International Convention on Civil Liability for Oil Pollution Damage and corresponding Convention on the Establishment of an International Fund for Compensation for Oil Pollution Damage together provide a mechanism to compensate governments for the "costs of reasonable measures of reinstatement" of the environment impacted by an oil tanker spill.[7] Similarly, the United States' Oil Pollution Act provides for recovery of "[d]amages for injury to, destruction of, loss of, or loss of use of, natural resources, including the reasonable costs of assessing the damage" caused by discharge of oil.[8] These media-specific liability regimes often incorporate other particularized limitations on liability, such as overall liability caps and limits on damages that are recoverable.

B.   What Kind of Liability Applies?

Another key parameter that varies across jurisdictions is the type of liability imposed. These span a continuum from strict to fault-based liability. Like traditional civil liability, there are significant differences in the stringency of liability regimes, depending on whether defenses to liability apply (e.g., exemptions for contamination caused while operating within the terms of a permit) and the duty of care imposed under fault-based rules. Strict liability may apply to a subset of industries or activities (e.g., "inherently dangerous" activities). In its 2004 Directive on Environmental Liability, the European Commission adopted this approach. Operators of specific listed activities, including installations subject to an environmental permit; waste management facilities; authorized water abstraction and impoundment; or manufacture, use, storage, processing, and transport of dangerous substances and products or genetically modified organisms, are strictly liable for any damage to covered resources. Operators of other types of facilities may only be liable for NRD that arise from operator negligence.[9] An "operator" of a facility is defined by reference to national laws, but may include the entity who operates, controls, or has "decisive economic power over the technical functioning" of the activity (including a permit holder).[10]

Liability under some regimes is triggered only where there is a threshold level of environmental injury. For example, the European Commission's Environmental Liability Directive imposes liability for injury to covered habitat or species only if it causes "significant adverse effects on reaching or maintaining the favourable conservation status" of the habitats or species concerned.[11] While the "favourable conservation status" of a species and habitat are defined terms,[12] the directive does not further define "significant adverse effects." National authorities retain discretion to define the threshold triggering liability. To highlight one approach, Scotland's implementing regulations and guidance provide that "a 'significant' effect is more than simply a measurable one."[13] While the guidance provides a series of factors that may be measured to determine the significance of the effect, including, among others, the number of individuals in the species affected, the rarity of the species, and the capacity for propagating the species, the determination that an impact is significant is ultimately a qualitative judgment.[14]

C.   Who Has Standing to Sue?

One of the interesting questions to emerge on the landscape of natural resource damage law is the question of who should have standing to sue. Traditionally, the role of enforcing laws for the public good falls to governments, be they central or local. Under the U.S. Comprehensive Environmental Response, Compensation, and Liability Act (CERCLA), particular federal and state agencies are designated as trustees. These trustees have exclusive authority to initiate suit to recover damages to publicly owned or managed natural resources.[15] In contrast, some jurisdictions enable public interest organizations or individuals to file such suits. Brazil's Law on Public Civil Action (LPCA) is one such law. When coupled with the National Policy for the Environment, for example, the LPCA has been utilized to bring successful suits for damage to publicly owned resources. It explicitly grants civil associations the ability to bring lawsuits concerning environmental damage.[16] That said, even where such a right is not provided generally within a jurisdiction, laws granting standing in narrower circumstances may apply. For example, legislation in Denmark provides that non-governmental parties may sue for the cost of restocking waters with fish.[17]

Closely linked to the matter of who has standing is the question of whether that entity's interests are properly aligned with the goals of deterrence, recovery, and restoration of NRD. Some commentators have criticized the U.S. trustee model, arguing that trustees have failed to adequately pursue natural resource damage cases or apply recovered funds toward effective environmental restoration. Trustees may have conflicts of interest that lead them to settle for much less than the cost of fully restoring the environmental harm. They may also mismanage funds or fail to coordinate with trustees that share concurrent jurisdiction.[18] Trustees also face significant barriers to bringing NRD suits. The costs of assessing the environmental damage and developing a restoration plan that are sufficiently robust to support a claim can be prohibitively high for many underfunded trustees. Furthermore, there is evidence that some trustees have turned to contingency fee arrangements to pursue claims, thereby diverting millions of dollars away from environmental restoration to private sector fees.[19] In light of these alleged deficiencies, some commentators have proposed modifications to current laws, such as adopting a stricter fiduciary model that would hold trustees accountable for inaction or mismanagement of funds,[20] or amending the underlying statutes to provide that trustees may recover their attorneys' fees.[21]

Such critiques of the U.S. trustee model, whether warranted or not, highlight the importance of balancing the power of enforcement agencies to pursue NRD with certain checks on that special authority. Under U.S. statutes, the restoration plans proposed by trustees are subject to public notice and comment, and settlements are subject to judicial approval only if "fair, reasonable, and in the public interest, with particular consideration of the adequacy of the settlement to restore, replace, rehabilitate, or acquire the equivalent of the injured natural resources and services."[22] Such procedures, combined with the active participation of civil society, can serve as an important check on government authority to resolve natural resource damage claims. Such procedures do not, however, address the challenge of a government failure to bring claims in the first instance. The European Commission's Environmental Liability Directive addressed the latter issue by granting non-governmental organizations (NGOs) the right to request the competent authority to take action.[23] Like its U.S. counterpart, the EC's directive did not grant NGOs the right to pursue compensation against potentially responsible parties (PRPs) directly where the competent authority fails to act.[24]

D.   Which Kinds of Damages Are Recoverable?

The most uncertain and challenging aspect of NRD laws is the assessment of the harm to the covered natural resources, otherwise known as the natural resource damage assessment (NRDA). As a matter of economics, assessment of the public value of natural resources is problematic because no free market exists for such goods and services, and therefore no ready market value to provide benchmarks. NRDA may include both use values, such as aesthetics (e.g., the value not only of recreating in a public forest, but of landscape views of the forest), and nonuse values, such as existence value (e.g., the value to individuals of knowing that a given species has not gone extinct), that are inherently variable and difficult to measure reliably.[25] Further, the NRDA depends on the availability of information about baseline environmental conditions, as parties are generally not liable for preexisting environmental harms. In many cases, limited information is available regarding the baseline status of the resource. This, in turn, opens the door to disputes regarding the incremental impacts caused by the PRP's activities. From an ecological perspective, NRDA involves uncertainty to the extent that assessing the best methods to restore a damaged ecosystem or impacted species remains an imperfect science. Moreover, interactions among ecosystems and many ecosystem services remain poorly understood. While scientists and economists continue to improve our understanding of how to effectively undertake such valuations, for now NRDA techniques remain a topic of dispute.[26]

It is beyond the scope of this chapter to present in detail the various methods of NRDA. In general, damages may be monetary, the actual undertaking of a restoration project, or a combination of both. Under many NRD laws, the costs of assessing damages and remedial options are also recoverable. In addition to primary restoration, aimed at restoring the natural resource to its baseline condition, damages often include compensatory restoration, which compensate for the interim harm to the natural resource until it is fully restored. A rich body of legal and economic literature describes a variety of methods to monetize the value of natural resources, and the strengths and weaknesses of each.[27] The acceptability of any such methods as the basis of a resolution of liability will vary across jurisdictions.

NRDA requirements may be established by law or regulation. Alternatively, particular methods of assessment may be discretionary—in which case the party seeking to recover damages will be guided by background procedural rules. Under CERCLA, a trustee who follows applicable regulations is granted a "rebuttable presumption," which shifts the burden to the defendant to establish that the assessment is inaccurate.[28] If the trustee selects an assessment methodology different from that established in applicable regulations, the trustee may proceed with the suit, but faces the normal procedural burdens to establish the claim. In practice, trustees have faced significant obstacles to meeting their burden of proof to establish the degree of damage to covered natural resources without the benefit of the rebuttable presumption.[29] The complexity and expense of NRDA has led to a number of proposals for simplified methodologies, such as predefined categories of damage and use of approximate values. Though less accurate, simplified methodologies would offer the benefit of clarifying liability ex ante, reducing the burden on entities conducting NRDAs, and leading to greater efficiencies in resolving liability. They do so by facilitating (1) the creation of effective insurance, (2) the streamlined settlement of claims, and (3) the reduction of administrative burdens associated with conducting NRDAs.[30]

Another variable across jurisdictions is the extent to which cost-benefit analysis and cost-effectiveness analysis play a role in NRDA.[31] Cost-benefit analysis involves a comparison of (1) the benefits provided by the proposed restoration and (2) the estimated cost of completing the restoration. In contrast, cost-effectiveness assesses the least costly method of attaining the same benefit. Even if cost benefit or cost effectiveness is not explicitly called for by law or regulation, such considerations may play a factor in evaluating the reasonableness of the proposed restoration plan.

E.   Is It Better to Litigate or Cooperate?

Litigation of natural resource damage claims can be costly and uncertain, leading some enforcement entities to conclude that a more cooperative model of resolving liability is desirable. In the United States, which has a comparatively long history of implementation of natural resource damage laws, trustees have turned to more cooperative models of resolution of these claims.[32] PRPs, too, often perceive advantages to cooperating with government entities to conduct studies of the damages and develop a restoration plan.[33] Cooperating with the governmental agency can offer a PRP a greater voice in the NRDA process. Similarly, it can have a positive impact on public relations and may ultimately result in a more cost-effective resolution. On the other hand, PRPs may forgo certain litigation advantages by participating in studies of NRD and restoration plans. Cooperation with the enforcement agency expedites a process that is otherwise prolonged; NRD claims take years to develop and then litigate. By working with the enforcement agency to develop a plan to study and restore ecological harm, a PRP diminishes its ability to credibly challenge the data generated or the scope of the restoration efforts. By agreeing to a streamlined, and more cost effective, study of environmental conditions, the PRP may limit the development of evidence necessary to its defense. Moreover, mistrust between the parties may ultimately derail cooperative efforts.

III. NRD Principles in International Law

A concept of liability similar to that embodied in municipal natural resource damage statutes has emerged in international civil liability regimes as well. For example, the 1993 Convention on Civil Liability for Damage Resulting from Activities Dangerous to the Environment (Lugano Convention) provides for strict liability for, among other harms, loss or damage by impairment of the environment, including "any reasonable measures aiming to reinstate or restore damaged or destroyed components of the environment, or to introduce, where reasonable, the equivalent of these components into the environment."[34] The 1996 International Convention on Liability and Compensation for Damage in Connection with the Carriage of Hazardous and Noxious Substances by Sea (HNS Convention), which is largely modeled on the International Convention on Civil Liability for Oil Pollution Damage mentioned above, and the 1999 Basel Protocol on Liability and Compensation for Damage Resulting from Transboundary Movements of Hazardous Wastes and their Disposal (Basel Convention) likewise provide for liability for the costs of reasonable measures to restore the environment to the status quo ante.

Beyond international civil liability regimes, natural resource damages caused by international conflict have at times been addressed through discrete mechanisms. For example, the United Nations Compensation Commission (UNCC), established by the U.N. Security Council following Iraq's invasion of Kuwait, provided a compensation mechanism for six comprehensive categories of environmental harm. International organizations and governments could seek compensation from the UNCC for (1) monitoring and assessment of the environmental damage, (2) monitoring and assessment of public health impacts (3) abatement and prevention of environmental harm (4) restoration measures, (5) recovery for interim and permanent environmental damage and (6) damage or depletion of natural resources.[35] Ultimately, the Commission received approximately 170 claims for damages falling within these categories, seeking over $80 billion in compensation.[36]

These international legal regimes remain largely ineffective as a means to impose liability for damages to natural resources, deter environmental injuries, and restore damaged natural resources absent corresponding national implementing laws and expert institutions. They nevertheless demonstrate the growing acceptance of the polluter pays principle. While such laws remain far from universal today, the adoption of natural resource damage statutes is a trend that is likely to continue around the globe, driven by a growing awareness of the vital role that ecosystems play in the provision of basic human needs such as drinking water, food, and sanitation, and the enormous economic value of protecting natural resources.

Notes

1. British Columbia v. Canadian Forests Prods. Ltd., 2004 SCC 38. *See also* Nicholas Hughes, *Supreme Court of Canada Rules on Natural Resource Damages Claims: Expanding the Scope of Environmental Liability* (June 21, 2004), http://mccarthy.ca/article_detail.aspx ?id=1622.

2. The public trust doctrine considered certain resources, particularly the seashore, fisheries, and navigable waters, to be held in trust for the benefit of the public. H. Kennison et al., *State Actions for Natural Resource Damages: Enforcement of the Public Trust*, 17 ENVTL. L. REP. NEWS & ANALYSIS 10,434 (1987); *see also* Sax, *The Public Trust Doctrine in Natural Resource Law: Effective Judicial Intervention*, 68 MICH. L. REV. 471 (1970).

3. *See, e.g.*, Itzchak Kornfeld, Symposium Article, *Of Dead Pelicans, Turtles, and Marshes: Natural Resource Damages in the Wake of the BP Deepwater Horizon Oil Spill*, 38 B.C. ENVTL. AFF. L. REV. 317 (2011) (arguing that the U.S. National Oceanic and Atmospheric Administration's assessment of the damages from the BP oil spill under the Oil Pollution Act was "piecemeal" and failed to account for the value of the ecosystem as a whole).

4. Comm'n of the European Cmtys., *Proposal for a Directive of the European Parliament and Council on Environmental Liability with regard to the Prevention and Restoration of Environmental Damage*, COM (2002) 17 at 17–18. Note that the Convention of Biological Diversity has struggled with the matter of how to measure damage to biodiversity for the purposes of determining liability and redress. *See, e.g.*, Liability and Redress in the Context of Paragraph 2 of Article 14 of the Convention on Biological Diversity: An Analysis of Pertinent Issues (UNEP/CBD/EG-L&R/1/2/Rev.1 (Aug 9, 2005)).

5. For example, all natural resources covered by the Wild Birds and Habitats Directives are covered by the Environmental Liability Directive. For further discussion of the European Commission Liability Directive, see E.H.P. Brans, *Liability for Damage to Public Natural Resources under the 2004 EC Environmental Liability Directive*, 7 ENVTL. L. REV. 91 (2005).

6. The United States' primary environmental cleanup statute, the Comprehensive Environmental Response, Compensation, and Liability Act (CERCLA) is a key example. Ohio v. U.S. DOI, 880 F.2d 432, 460 (D.C. Cir. 1989) (Congress deliberately excluded private property from ambit of CERCLA's NRD provisions). Note that public ownership may include ownership or control of resources by local and tribal government. Under CERCLA, natural resources are defined to include those "belonging to, managed by, held in trust by, appertaining to, or otherwise controlled by the United States . . . any State or local government, any foreign government, [or] any Indian tribe." 42 U.S.C. § 9601(16).

7. UN Counsel on Trade & Dev., *Liability and Compensation for Ship-Source Oil Pollution* (Studies in Transport Law and Policy Series, 2012). *See also* Int'l Oil Pollution Compensation Fund, Claims Manual (Dec. 2008); 33 U.S.C. § 2702(b)(2)(A).

8. 33 U.S.C. § 2702(b)(2)(A).

9. European Commission Environmental Liability Directive, 2004/35/EC, art. 3(1), Annex III.

10. *Id.* art. 2(6).

11. *See* Brans, *supra* note 5, at 94.

12. This is defined by reference to the EU Habitats Directive (92/43/EEC) art. 1(e), (i). The conservation status of a natural habitat will be taken as "favourable" when (1) its natural range and areas it covers within that range are stable or increasing; (2) the specific structure and functions that are necessary for its long-term maintenance exist and are likely to continue to exist for the foreseeable future; and (3) the conservation status of its typical species is favorable. A conservation status is "favourable" when (1) population dynamics data on the species concerned indicate that it is maintaining itself on a long-term basis as a viable component of its natural habitats; (2) the natural range of the species is neither being reduced nor is likely to be reduced for the foreseeable future and (3) there is, and will probably continue to be, a sufficiently large habitat to maintain its populations on a long-term basis.

13. Scotland Environmental Liability Regulations 2009 Draft Guidance, at para. 32 (Aug 2009), *available at* http://www.scotland.gov.uk/Topics/Environment/waste-and -pollution/Pollution-1/ELD/ELDGuidance.

14. *Id.* at paras. 30–31.

15. 42 U.S.C. § 9607(f)(2).

16. Recovered damages are paid into a "Fund for the Defense of Diffuse Interests," with the goal of restoring the harmed environmental resource. S. Vieira, *Environmental Damage Evaluation in Brazil, in* ENVIRONMENTAL DAMAGE IN INTERNATIONAL AND COMPARATIVE LAW: PROBLEMS OF DEFINITION AND VALUATION 298–301 (M. Bowman & A. Boyle eds., 2002). Despite the ability of NGOs to pursue lawsuits, much of the environmental enforcement in Brazil is led by state and federal prosecutors. *See* C. Crawford, *Rainforests and Regulation: New Direction in Brazilian Environmental Law and Legal Institutions,* 40 GEO. WASH. INT'L L. REV. 649, 652–53 (2009).

17. European Comm'n, *White Paper on Liability,* COM(2000) 66 final, at 35 (2000).

18. K. Murray et al., *Natural Resource Damage Trustees: Whose Side Are They Really On?,* 5 ENVTL. LAW. 407 (1998).

19. J. Steiner, *The Illegality of Contingency Fee-Arrangements When Prosecuting Public Natural Resource Damage Claims and the Need for Legislative Reform,* 32 WM. & MARY ENVTL. L. & POL'Y REV. 169, 176–81 (2007).

20. L. Rowley, *NRD Trustees: To What Extent Are They Truly Trustees?,* 28 ENVTL. AFF. L. REV. 459 (2001).

21. Steiner, *supra* note 19, at 206–07.

22. 15 C.F.R. §§ 990.25, 990.61–62.

23. Directive 2004/35/EC of the European Parliament and of the Council of April 21, 2004, on environmental liability with regard to the prevention and remedying of environmental damage establishes a framework based on the polluter pays principle to prevent and remedy environmental damage. *See* http://ec.europa.eu/environment/legal /liability/ (last visited July 12, 2013). The ELD defines "environmental damage" as damage to water, soil, protected species, and natural habitats. Member EU states transposed the ELD into national law by July 2010. *Id.*

24. Brans, *supra* note 5, at 97–98.

25. Note, *"Ask a Silly Question . . . ": Contingent Valuation of Natural Resource,* 105 HARV. L. REV. 1981 (1992).

26. *See, e.g.,* P. Tolan, *Natural Resource Damages under CERCLA: Failures, Lessons Learned, and Alternatives,* 38 N.M. L. REV. 409, 419 (2008) (arguing, inter alia, that U.S.

Department of the Interior regulations proscribing methodologies for NRDAs are "deficient in a number of respects"); A. Ando & P. Wallapak, *Envelope Backs or the Gold Standard? Choosing the Accuracy of Natural Resource Damage Assessment Methods*, 83 LAND ECON. 424 (2006) (arguing that existing assessment methods are too complex, and that simplified methods would be preferable in some cases); M. Rutherford et al., *Assessing Environmental Losses: Judgments of Importance and Damage Schedules*, 22 HARV. ENVTL. L. REV. 51 (1998) ("Current valuations are, for the most part, limited in scope and accuracy and, in addition to being expensive, may well be misleading."); Idaho v. S. Refrigerated Transp., Inc., No. 88-1279, 1991 U.S. Dist. LEXIS 1869, at *55–56 (D. Idaho Jan. 24, 1991) (rejecting contingent valuation survey results measuring the existence value of a certain fish population as too speculative a measure of damages).

27. *See, e.g.*, S. Doshi, *Making the Sale on Contingent Valuation*, 21 TUL. ENVTL. L.J. 295 (2008) (arguing that certain methods of contingent valuation are more reliable than others); U.S. Department of the Interior Natural Resource Damage Assessment and Restoration Federal Advisory Committee, FINAL REPORT TO THE SECRETARY (May 2007) (report advising on how best to optimize NRDA and restoration activities, and proposing areas where further research and guidance needs to be developed); N. Flores & M. Thatcher, *Money, Who Needs It? Natural Resource Damage Assessment*, 20 CONTEMPORARY ECONOMIC POLICY 171 (2002) (analyzing and rejecting proposal that it is better to avoid monetary assessment in a natural resource damage assessment).

28. 43 C.F.R. § 11.10.

29. Tolan, *supra* note 26 (describing the state of New Mexico's unsuccessful suit to recover natural resource damages, Mexico v. Gen. Elec. Co., 335 F. Supp. 2d 1157 (D.N.M. 2003), due to its failure to present sufficient evidence to support its alleged damages); Idaho v. S. Refrigerated Transp., Inc., *supra* note 26, at *32–63 (rejecting much of the State of Idaho's evidence on the population of fish present in a river, the number of fish killed by a spill of fungicide, and the value of the loss of those fish).

30. Ando et al., *supra* note 26; Rutherford et al., *supra* note 26.

31. *See* Study on the Valuation and Restoration of Damage to Natural Resources for the Purpose of Environmental Liability, European Commission Directorate-General Environment (B4-3040/2000/265781/MAR/B3 (May 2001)) at 33, 36–37, 50 (discussing role of cost-benefit analysis and cost-effectiveness in NRDA).

32. NOAA, Cooperative Assessment Project Framework (Oct. 2003), http://www.darrp.noaa.gov/partner/cap/relate.html (describing framework for cooperation developed with input from multiple federal agencies); D. Helton, *The Benefits of Cooperative Natural Resource Damages Assessment*, BALTIC INT'L MAR. COUNCIL (BIMCO) REVIEW (2000).

33. *See, e.g.*, AD-HOC INDUSTRY NATURAL RESOURCE DAMAGE GROUP INDUSTRY/ TRUSTEE STANDING COMMITTEE, COOPERATIVE NATURAL RESOURCE DAMAGE ASSESSMENT AGREEMENTS GUIDING PRINCIPLES AND SAMPLE PROVISIONS (May 2009, rev. Sept. 2011); B. Israel, *Natural Resources Damages, in* ENVIRONMENTAL LAW PRACTICE GUIDE § 32B.09 The Cooperative Advantage (2012).

34. Lugano Convention art. 2 § 7. The Lugano Convention is a regional European treaty that, as of the drafting of this chapter, has not entered into force.

35. R. Juni & E. Eder, *Ecosystem Management and Damage Recovery in International Conflict*, 14 NAT. RES. & ENV'T 193 (2000).

36. *See* http://www.uncc.ch/claims/f_claims.htm (last accessed Jan. 5, 2013).

CHAPTER 12

Protected Species

ANDREW LONG

I. Introduction

This chapter alerts practitioners to relevant international environmental law concerning species protection and explains the evolution of international species protection law. Species protection is among the oldest goals of international environmental law, and remains among the most significant challenges within the field. Since early efforts to resolve economically motivated conflicts over allocation of rights to harvest species, such as the Pacific fur seal arbitration case, species protection law has evolved into the leading edge of the broader field of "biodiversity law." Thus, species protection law embodies both the oldest and the most cutting-edge elements of international environmental law.

Biodiversity preservation is also among the most pressing and challenging policy issues encompassed in the field.[1] "Biodiversity" can be defined as "the variability among living organisms from all sources ... this includes diversity within species, between species and of ecosystems."[2] This diversity of life is essential to sustaining the well-being of humanity, but human activities have created severe pressures on species that result in an ongoing extinction crisis. Unlike ozone protection or climate change, which result from emissions that are essentially fungible throughout the world, species extinction results from a vast array of forces, many of which are closely tied to national or local circumstances. Yet international law and policy is necessary to address the threat because of the global significance of biodiversity, the low regulatory capacity of many highly biodiverse nations, and global market incentives that tend to undermine species protection. Thus, although the aggregate value of global biodiversity makes its protection a high international priority, achieving better species protection on the ground will often require improving local or regional regulation, enforcement, and economic incentives. Therefore, international species protection law (like much of international environmental law) seeks to address a global problem by promoting or requiring national and subnational regulatory measures.

In addition, legal efforts to achieve more effective preservation of biodiversity (of which species protection is an integral part) at the global scale must necessarily affect an extensive array of human activities in virtually every sector. Agricultural practices, legal and illegal trade, industrial pollution, greenhouse gas emissions and climate change, poverty, and national governance failures are some of the more significant causes of biodiversity loss. The challenges involved with regulating the harmful effects of such a diverse array of causal factors are complex. The international legal instruments and institutions in this area are well developed. But they are far from effective in solving the problem of biodiversity loss. They also appear paradoxical: ad hoc, yet including several complex and interrelated regimes; extensive, yet with gaping policy holes that remain underregulated or virtually untouched. Thus, practitioners need to have a firm grasp on the larger context of species protection law when handling a matter implicating this area to avoid overlooking potentially important legal requirements and to maximize opportunities for participation in relevant programs that may provide significant opportunities for reputational or economic benefit.

II. Biodiversity Loss and International Regulation
A. The Extinction Crisis: Natural and Policy Complexity of Biodiversity Loss

The issues that species protection law seeks to address involve some of the world's most complex natural and human systems. Species are interdependently connected in ecosystems that produce a wide variety of goods and services underlying most economic and social activity. Over a decade ago, the annual economic value of ecosystem services was estimated at $33 trillion.[3] As high as this figure is, it arguably does not even begin to capture the importance of ecosystem services to humanity. Ecosystem services underlie the building blocks of human society, such as clean water, productive soil, and a stable climate. These essential elements of human well-being arise naturally and, apparently, for free.[4] One well-known illustration of how policymakers can draw upon ecosystem services to benefit humanity is New York City's decision to purchase development rights in the Lower Hudson Valley in order to ensure a safe and clean drinking water supply.[5] This decision was reached after conducting a cost-benefit comparison with the alternative of constructing water treatment facilities. In that instance, the value of ecosystem services became clear to policymakers. Unfortunately, it is far more common for the value of ecosystem services to go unrecognized by decision makers until the loss of such services causes negative impacts.

Although ecosystem services are "free" in the sense that they are public goods, the real cost of ensuring their sustainability lies in the challenge of preserving biodiversity. Biodiversity promotes resilience of natural systems, which is the essential characteristic necessary for continual "healthy" functioning of these systems over time and in the face of significant stressors such as pollution, land development for human habitation and agriculture, and global climate change. Species protection is perhaps the most visible and well-developed element of biodiversity preservation. Despite decades of attention, however, species are continually pushed toward extinction at an alarmingly high rate.

The current rate of extinction is 1,000 to 10,000 times higher than the background rate of extinction over the past 450 million years.[6] Many scientists, therefore, characterize the current extinction crisis as one of only five "mass extinction" events in the last 600 million years. After a mass extinction event, it takes 5 to 10 million years for diversity to recover to pre-crisis levels. The most recent comparable event was the mass extinction that ended the reign of the dinosaurs. Never has one species impacted others as extensively as humanity is currently impacting the other forms of life.[7]

The roots of human-caused extinction are varied and complex. The drivers of biodiversity loss are often described by the acronym HIPPO, coined by renowned biologist Edward O. Wilson to represent habitat loss, invasive species, human overpopulation, pollution, and overexploitation.[8] We might add to this list a sixth factor that is becoming increasingly important: climate change, which could produce the acronym CHIPPO.[9] Midrange estimates suggest that roughly one-third of all species will be at risk of extinction from climate-related impacts within the next few decades. Overall, as many as half of all currently extant species may be extinct by 2050.

Responding to the CHIPPO drivers of extinction presents an enormously complex policy challenge at the global level.[10] The vast majority of terrestrial biodiversity is concentrated in the tropics and, thus, faces massive risks from forces such as agricultural and urban expansion (especially in tropical forest regions), rapidly growing human population in many developing countries, inefficient and unsustainable natural resource use driven by poverty and/or economic globalization, poor governance caused by lack of capacity or corruption, and a range of other issues at the intersection of human development and environmental policy. Moreover, biophysical challenges, many of which are complicated by uncertainty—such as the increasing spread of invasive species due to globalization and climate change, or the incompletely understood risks to marine biodiversity that result from ocean acidification[11]—present their own complex policy challenges. Combined, the human and natural systems challenges involved in global biodiversity policy make it one of the most vexing or "wicked" problems facing humanity.[12]

B.   Approaches to Species Protection in International Law

The complexity of biodiversity preservation and the relatively long history of "wildlife law" have served as primary forces in shaping the current field of international species protection law.[13] A wide variety of species protection treaties exist at bilateral, regional, and global-multilateral scales. The approaches vary from those concerned primarily with ensuring a sustainable harvest of a single species for its economic value to those that attempt to affect a broad array of activities throughout the planet to conserve and enhance biodiversity.[14] Likewise, some treaties represent a classic international law approach of regulating the conduct of nations, while others reflect the increased importance of non-state actors or incorporate strategies designed to support development of domestic biodiversity policy within nations.

Perhaps the oldest and most traditional approach to international species protection, which is evident in treaties signed in the early 20th century and some of the agreements signed within the last 20 years, focuses on identifying sustainable harvest levels of economically valuable species. The key innovation of this approach lies in the creation of institutions and formal processes for incorporating scientific information into legal standards or rules. The many regional fisheries management organizations (RFMOs) provide examples of this approach.[15] They also illustrate both the wide range of legal authority that can be incorporated into this management structure. Some RFMOs possess authority to establish binding rules and to enforce compliance. Others are empowered only to assess stock levels and promulgate unenforceable harvest guidelines. Like RFMOs, another example of an entity with an institutional structure that establishes harvest level targets based on a scientific assessment of species populations is the International Convention for the Regulation of Whaling (ICRW).[16] The ICRW, discussed *infra*, also illustrates the increasing impact of environmental protection objectives on species management. Its primary institution, the International Whaling Commission (IWC), operated for nearly 30 years by setting harvest levels that sought to ensure the sustainability of whales as an economic resource. It also did so, to some extent, to maintain the industry that developed to harvest them. As scientific information and, more importantly, global public opinion coalesced around protection of whales as sentient creatures and an ecologically significant species (that is, as intrinsically valuable regardless of their instrumental economic value), the IWC adopted a complete moratorium on whaling. This moratorium has all but eliminated the whaling industry. Thus, the IWC illustrates that a management approach grounded in creation of institutions and process is inherently flexible. This flexibility enables the IWC to respond to changing social values even to the extent of pursuing a purpose that is radically different from the goals it was created to meet.

A more complex process-based species protection approach is the "listing" of a species as a trigger for preestablished protective measures tied to specific implementation obligations agreed to by the parties. The Convention on the International Trade in Endangered Species of Fauna and Flora (CITES) employs this structure to regulate any species imperiled by international trade anywhere on the planet.[17] CITES' Conference of the Parties, which meets biannually, decides whether to list species when petitioned to do so by parties. Parties are required to implement CITES through the designation of a scientific authority and a management authority in the national government. National governments are then obligated to comply with CITES requirements for regulating the trade in listed species or items derived from them. These include the requirement and specifications for issuance of permits for the trade in listed species. The listing approach is also evident in the

Bonn Convention on the Conservation of Migratory Species and in various regional treaties.[18]

Another approach to species protection focuses not on the species themselves, but on the protection of habitats. Habitat protection occurs either through the international designation of specific protected areas or through more general international regulation of particular habitat types. The UNESCO Convention Concerning the Protection of the World Cultural and Natural Heritage (World Heritage Convention) illustrates the protected areas approach.[19] This approach is also evident in the national law of many states, where it is often supported by international organizations or transnational non-governmental organizations. This approach arguably represents one of very few bright spots in global species protection policy because an increasing amount of land has come under some form of protection in recent years.[20] However, its effectiveness varies widely depending on a number of factors, including the authority under which the protective designation is made. General regulation of habitat types remains only partially realized as a legal approach to species protection. The Convention on Wetlands of International Importance (Ramsar Convention), for example, provides overarching guidance on regulation of a particular habitat type—wetlands—but also employs elements of the protected areas approach in that it applies only to wetlands that are designated as wetlands of international importance.[21] A number of efforts have been made to adopt generally applicable ecosystem protection regulations according to habitat type, but none has produced a robust regime. The U.N. Convention to Combat Desertification (UNCCD) regulates arid regions, but only through weak international commitments and processes.[22] Other attempts to enshrine the approach in international law have failed, such as the effort to negotiate a global forest protection regime.[23] A more complex example of a broad effort to regulate a habitat type can be found in some portions of the U.N. Convention on the Law of the Sea (UNCLOS). UNCLOS includes habitat-based protective provisions along with modest species-based protection obligations in the context of extensive regulation of the economic aspects of resource control.[24]

Most recently, species protection has been included as a component of biodiversity preservation law in the Convention on Biological Diversity (CBD), which can be understood as the most comprehensive and far-reaching species protection effort to date. The general approach emphasizes support for development of national species protection law and development of new approaches to affecting the activities that cause biodiversity loss. It encompasses a wide variety of approaches to species protection, including cutting-edge programs that may suggest the direction of future international species protection law development. These include traditional approaches such as protected areas designation, as well as emerging approaches such as the creation of incentives for species protection (such as payment for ecosystem services, mitigation banking, and economic development based on sustainable use), and voluntary arrangements involving the private sector such as the Global Platform for Biodiversity and Business. Further, two protocols to the

CBD that have been negotiated (the Cartagena Protocol, which is in force, and the Nagoya Protocol, which is not). They suggest that international agreements targeting the economic forces affecting species exploitation and protection will likely be the primary focus of efforts to strengthen and expand the impact and effectiveness of international species protection law in the near term.

The brief survey above illustrates the approaches, or general methods, employed in international law designed to protect species. One axis for evaluating specific laws in this area is the degree to which a particular treaty is binding. Treaties that concentrate on ensuring sustainability of specific populations or that target specific activities causing harm to species tend to be the more legalistic and top-down approaches. Broader efforts to preserve ecosystems or affect general incentives are often "softer" and serve to strengthen national protections rather than create new international obligations.[25]

III.   International Species Protection: From Wildlife Law to Biodiversity Governance

The oldest environmental laws, such as Egyptian nature reserves of 1370 BCE, suggest the foundational importance of protecting species and their habitats to human societies.[26] Indeed, these issues entered the international political agenda as early as the 1300s, with many fisheries treaties in existence before 1800.[27] By the late 19th century, species and habitat protection agreements were beginning to take a shape that we now recognize as the roots of international environmental law.[28] At that time, species protection law addressed the need for allocation of rights to harvest and restrictions to preserve specific species of economic value for a limited number of nations undertaking exploitation in defined geographic areas.[29] Over the course of the 20th century, species protection law became increasingly complex as it continued to serve economic ends in an increasingly diverse and dense international political and legal system. It also increasingly embraced broader goals reflecting increased scientific and public understanding of species' value as part of a complex web of life that supports the ecosystem services necessary for most human social and economic activities. This section highlights that evolution, with an emphasis on the legal structure of treaties that remain effective or otherwise shape the current legal landscape. It then turns to more recent efforts to promote species protection as a part of broad global biodiversity preservation goals.

A.   Species Protection and the Origins of International Environmental Law

As the technological advances of the 19th century began to imperil resources through industrialization and mineral extraction, states began to respond to the need to create law to preserve dwindling populations of economically important species. Thus, long before the environmental movement became a significant force in international politics, a body of law protecting species (often referred to as "wildlife law") emerged through allocative natural resources agreements that served property law purposes as much as conservation purposes.

Early treaties regulating a single species to preserve economic value frequently arose from "political pressure to serve some particular, narrowly conceived human interest."[30] They were "ad hoc, sporadic, and limited in scope."[31] These agreements serve as precursors to the main body of current international environmental law in some ways, as with an 1867 oyster conservation treaty that limited exploitation to certain dates in an early example of an international fishing season.[32] At the same time, many were often "deficient in a structural sense" because they lacked institutional or other mechanisms to facilitate implementation.[33] Thus, while they may highlight the economic foundation of most conservation law, most treaties from this period do not provide direct models for later agreements.

Among the most important events to mark the beginning of international species protection law was the 1892 *Bering Sea Fur Seals* arbitration between the United States and Great Britain (for Canada), which followed several unsuccessful bilateral attempts at regulation of that economically valuable fishery.[34] Within two decades, the United States, the United Kingdom, Russia, and Japan established one of the earliest multiparty species protection agreements, the 1911 Convention for the Preservation and Protection of Fur Seals.[35] The treaty banned pelagic sealing and sought to combat the illegal seal pelt trade through a certification system.[36] The original treaty was replaced several years after its expiration by a 1957 treaty that functioned similarly, which itself ultimately expired in 1984. Although no active antisealing regime is operative today, seal regulation signals, for many, the beginning of the era of species protection law and, more broadly, international environmental law.

Another early example of international regulation to protect species is the Convention for the Protection of Migratory Birds in Canada and the United States between the United States and Great Britain (on behalf of Canada).[37] This treaty, which remains important, informed the constitutional basis for early U.S. federal wildlife legislation.[38] Justice Holmes' well-known opinion in *Missouri v. Holland* described preservation of migratory birds as "a national interest of very nearly the first magnitude."[39]

B. Species-Specific Regimes: International Agreements Responding to Pressing Economic and Environmental Needs

Although treaties regulating fur seals and migratory birds demonstrate the origins of modern species protection law in relatively narrow agreements of limited geographic scope involving a few parties,[40] species protection law evolved toward the development of treaties with a broader scope in terms of geographic applicability, species coverage, or both. Nonetheless, a number of species-specific treaties remain an important component of current international species protection law. These agreements tend to be relatively simple and address either exploitation of economically significant species or species that are found primarily in geographic areas outside of national jurisdiction. Some species-specific treaties may be effectively (if not formally) superseded by regulation under other more developed international governance arrangements. This is particularly true where the issues affecting the regulated species change.[41] Yet in other cases, the initial treaty arrangements have ripened into active regimes on the leading edge of significant political issues. The ICRW, mentioned *supra*, provides the most important example of the latter type.

The ICRW is among the oldest operative international environmental treaties. It was created in 1946 to replace earlier agreements that regulated the whaling industry. It applies globally (wherever whaling occurs) and to essentially all forms of whaling and all practices necessary to sustain it. However, enforcement authority for violation of the IWC lies entirely with the parties. The ICRW did not create any international enforcement power.

The IWC is the primary institution of the ICRW. Consisting of one member from each party, the IWC serves as the regulatory body for the convention through the creation of what is known as the "Schedule." The Schedule identifies the specific species covered by the ICRW and sets forth the regulatory controls on whaling deemed necessary by the IWC. IWC retains authority to amend the Schedule based on scientific findings.[42] Most of the legal and political controversies under the ICRW have to do with amendments to the Schedule. For example, the ICRW includes a monitoring requirement. There was, however, great controversy over the creation of an observer program under the Schedule to ensure compliance.

Without question, the most important amendment to the Schedule was the passage of a moratorium on whaling in 1982. It took effect in 1986 and has since been extended. Despite the ban, three nations—Iceland, Norway, and Japan—continue to conduct whaling. Iceland withdrew from the ICRW completely in 1993 to continue its whaling practices. Norway effectively objected to the moratorium and, therefore, is not subject to it. Japan took neither of these steps and, therefore, contends that its whaling complies with the ban. Japan relies on Article VIII of the ICRW, which authorizes parties to grant their nationals "a special permit" allowing whaling conducted "for the purposes of scientific research." Japan's reliance on the scientific purposes exception has created significant controversy, including a currently pending case before the International Court of Justice.[43] The ICRW nevertheless leaves the ultimate authority to determine compliance to the parties themselves.

The lack of IWC authority to monitor or enforce compliance has, at times, undermined the effectiveness of the ICRW. For example, from the 1950s and 1980s, the Soviet Union was systematically violating IWC restrictions on hunting humpback whales—taking more than 100,000 excess whales over 30 years—without the knowledge of the international community. This systematic violation was not revealed until the 1990s, when the Soviet Union collapsed and records of the violations became available.[44] Thus, although the ICRW is an important species protection agreement, its effect may be limited by overreliance on national self-policing.

C. Regional Regimes for Species Protection

Another category of wildlife treaties are those that protect species in a given region. Some such treaties are focused on a specific species, such as the various regimes applicable to the vicuna in Latin America.[45] However, many regional treaties go beyond traditional wildlife law approaches and advance more comprehensive biodiversity conservation, but not on a global level. An example of such a comprehensive regional treaty is the Convention on the Conservation of European Wildlife and Natural Habitats, which was signed in 1982.[46] Similar agreements exist in other regions.[47] Regional approaches, however, vary widely. In contrast with the European Union's (EU) well-developed regional species protection agreements, Asian nations have perhaps the least developed biodiversity law of any region, with only one agreement. That agreement only encompasses southern Asian countries and is, in any event, not in force.[48]

One of the better-known illustrations of evolution in regional treaty arrangements has occurred in Africa. European colonial powers initiated one of the earliest regional wildlife conservation regimes in 1900 to protect agricultural interests. This regime became the first in a chain of conventions leading to the currently operative conventions adopted by African states.[49]

IV. Global Species Protection and Biodiversity Preservation Treaties

As scientific understanding and public interest in biodiversity and its connection to ecosystem services developed, the inadequacy of bilateral and regional management agreements became apparent. Combined with greater scientific and public understanding of the biodiversity crisis, the broad development of environmental norms laid the groundwork for the negotiation of species protection agreements that reach beyond prior geographically limited or species-specific agreements. These species protection treaties, the earliest of which date to the 1970s, are truly global biodiversity preservation treaties. They establish a framework for the preservation of any species threatened with extinction anywhere on the globe.

A. Protecting Species through Listing: CITES and the Bonn Convention on the Conservation of Migratory Species (CMS)

Building off of prior wildlife law treaties, several modern environmental treaties are designed to protect specific species, sometimes only from specific threats. What makes these treaties different from their predecessors, other than their global scope, is that a treaty body is empowered to determine which species warrant protection and, generally, what level of protection is required. Without question, the most significant treaty to use this approach is CITES. A less widely discussed treaty using this approach is the CMS. These two regimes may be the only significant examples of the "listing" approach with global reach, but they illustrate an approach to species protection that is widely used at other levels of governance. Each of the treaties is discussed briefly below.

1.   CITES

CITES aims to protect species threatened by international trade. Although this goal limits its efficacy for combating biodiversity loss overall, CITES has proven valuable in the protection of a number of specific species. For example, CITES has had success in the preservation of rhinos, tigers, and elephants in Asia and Africa, although its effectiveness in some countries containing these species is hotly debated.[50] More than 40 years after being opened for signature, the CITES regime has proven durable and currently includes 180 parties. Of potentially greater significance, CITES has been highly influential in the development of species and environmental protection law at the international and national levels. CITES is also noteworthy as a turning point in species protection law in that it was the first global agreement to invert the traditional regulation of species for economic benefit by regulating international trade for the benefit of protected species. Moreover, CITES is simultaneously among the oldest international environmental law regimes and one of the most cutting-edge treaties in that its provisions may effectively regulate states or private entities within them without explicit state consent.

CITES applies to "specimens of species," which include "any readily recognizable part or derivative thereof," once the species has been listed in one of the CITES appendices.[51] Listing on Annex I or II occurs only by a two-thirds majority vote of parties present and voting (which usually occurs at the Conference of the Parties meetings). Any party may unilaterally list a species on Annex III if certain criteria are met.[52]

Species may be listed on Appendix I if the species is threatened with extinction and may be affected by trade.[53] There are over 800 species, subspecies, and populations listed on Appendix I.[54] Species can be listed on Appendix II when it is not yet threatened with extinction, but may become so threatened if trade in the species is not strictly monitored and controlled.[55] So-called look alike species, those that are morphologically similar to Appendix I species, may also be listed on Appendix II to prevent harm to the relevant Appendix I species. Appendix II contains the most species of any CITES appendix, with over 30,000 species listed to date.[56] Species may be listed on Appendix III by a party where the species is native to the country, is protected under its domestic law, and the party desires assistance from other parties to limit trade in the species.[57]

Any trade in Appendix I species requires permits from both exporting and importing parties' management authorities and scientific authorities.

The latter must confirm that the trade will not be detrimental to the species' survival.[58] The exporting party's management authority must also confirm that the specimen to be traded was not obtained in violation of law, along with other confirmations regarding the safety of the shipping method. Finally, the importing party's management authority must confirm that the specimen will not be used for "primarily commercial purposes."[59] This last requirement has been a point of some controversy and has generally been interpreted at the international level to favor species protection. The COP has decided that a use will be considered primarily commercial whenever the "non-commercial aspects do not clearly predominate."[60]

Listing of a species on Appendix II imposes the same export permit requirements as those imposed under Appendix I.[61] However, there are no import permit requirements under Appendix II. Because many developing countries that may export species lack capacity to effectively assess the potential detriment of trade in Appendix II species, this type of listing is generally far less protective in practice than an Appendix I listing.

Appendix III provides the least protection of listed species. Trade in Appendix III species requires only that the exporting party's management authority issue an export permit certifying that the specimen was not obtained illegally and the method of shipment minimizes risk to the species.[62] Import of any species listed on Appendix III requires a certificate of origin, regardless of whether the country of origin is the party that listed the species.[63] Thus, although only the listing party is required to provide export permits for specimens of the species that enter international trade from its territory, all parties must comply with the certificate of origin requirement once any party lists the species.[64] Accordingly, this is one of the relatively rare instances in international law where a country may be formally bound without giving specific consent.

The specific application of CITES' international trade rules can vary by country, however, because the agreement's exceptions and reservations provisions may enable parties to avoid the obligations that would otherwise be imposed.[65] In addition, CITES may be relevant to business transactions involving countries that are not parties to the agreement because it generally requires that parties trading with non-parties follow similar requirements to those required for trade between parties.[66] In this way, private entities may be compelled to comply with CITES regardless of whether their home country has consented to be bound by the agreement.

To promote compliance, CITES imposes a number of detailed and specific implementation actions to be undertaken domestically by parties. For example, after a party specifies its scientific authority and management authority, these authorities must make the determinations required for trade of listed species in compliance with CITES.

CITES contains significant penalty provisions that, together with its detailed implementation obligations, distinguish it as among the most "binding" agreements in international environmental law. At the international level, countries in violation of CITES—including non-parties—may face trade suspension measures.[67] Further, CITES obligates parties to "take appropriate measures" to prohibit trade in species listed in accordance with its requirements and to enforce its provisions through penalties and confiscation of specimens traded in violation thereof.[68]

CITES is often characterized as a successful agreement, at least when compared with many other species protection agreements.[69] This relative success must be understood, however, in the context of the narrow scope of actions that CITES regulates (international trade), the identifiable points of accountability at which violations may occur (mainly, import and export), the obligation to designate responsible national actors (the scientific and management authorities), and clear statements of such actors' duties (primarily consisting of determinations regarding permits, inspection regimes, and similar easily observable actions). Despite CITES' successful implementation in some areas, it must be remembered that enforcement of its specific provisions depends heavily on national actors and thus varies according to the capabilities of parties' national governments and wildlife agencies. On the whole, "compliance and enforcement remain enormous challenges to the effectiveness of the Convention" and shortcomings in this area have been the subject of several Conference of the Parties and CITES Secretariat actions.[70]

2.   CMS

The CMS was adopted in 1979 with the aim of encouraging and supporting parties to "individually or in co-operation [adopt] appropriate and necessary steps to conserve [migratory] species and their habitat."[71] "Migratory species" is defined as "the entire population or any geographically separate part of the population of any species or lower taxon of wild animals, a significant proportion of whose members cyclically and predictably cross one or more national jurisdictional boundaries."[72] Despite its global scope and over 115 parties, the significance of the CMS for species protection is limited by its focus on migratory species and fairly shallow obligations.

Like CITES, the CMS operates through appendices. The CMS imposes obligations upon parties to conserve specific species based upon their status as listed on one of its two appendices. Appendix I lists endangered migratory species. The CMS requires parties to prohibit the taking of Appendix I species and "endeavor to" take steps to conserve the species and protect its habitat.[73] Appendix II lists species that would benefit from international agreements to promote their conservation. Parties are obligated to "endeavor to conclude agreements" that will enhance the conservation of Appendix II species.[74] CMS provides further guidance on such agreements, including requirements that the agreement seek to return the species to "favourable conservation status" and be open to all countries whose territory includes a portion of the species' range (regardless of the country's status as a CMS party).

The CMS has had limited success. The most significant value of CMS may lie in its coordinating function, both through its role as a potential catalyst for regional agreements and partnerships with private actors, and through collaboration between the CMS, CITES, and CBD Secretariats in cooperative implementation programs. Given its limitations compared with CITES and the CBD, the CMS appears to be emphasizing this coordinative function as its potential niche.[75]

B.   Habitat-Based Treaties

Along with treaties that provide for protection of individually listed species, there are several regimes that seek to protect types of habitat, such as wetlands and forests. This section briefly highlights several of the most significant regimes.

1.   *The Ramsar Convention*

The 1971 Convention on Wetlands of International Importance (the Ramsar Convention) is the only major, globally applicable convention that protects a specific type of ecosystem. Although the original parties were primarily concerned with preserving the habitat of migratory waterfowl, Ramsar now protects a wide range of wetlands, from mangroves to rice paddies.[76] It currently has 163 parties and applies to over 100 million hectares.[77]

The Ramsar Convention operates through "three pillars": designating wetlands for the List of Wetlands of International Importance and ensuring their effective management; national implementing law and policy designed to ensure "wise use" of these wetlands, including the incorporation of nature reserves within the designated wetland;[78] and international cooperation to address cross-border issues related to wetlands and the reasons for their designation.[79]

Ramsar's provisions apply only to designated wetlands.[80] Parties to the convention may submit wetlands for listing, which must then be approved by the Ramsar Secretariat. Wetlands submitted for designation under Ramsar are evaluated for international importance based on several factors, including the zoological significance, especially for waterfowl.[81]

2.   *The World Heritage Convention*

The 1972 UNESCO Convention for the Protection of World Cultural and Natural Heritage, known as the World Heritage Convention, entered into force in 1975 and currently includes 191 parties. It operates through listing specific sites considered to be of "outstanding universal" natural or cultural value on the World Heritage List and, where appropriate, the World Heritage in Danger List. Two of the listing criteria are based solely on biodiversity value. Listing obligates the party within which the site is located to manage and preserve the site.[82] While, in some cases, World Heritage List designation provides an international incentive for biodiversity conservation and the convention is frequently considered as one of the global biodiversity conventions, the World Heritage Convention offers only limited protection for species.

C.   A Framework for Global Biodiversity Preservation to Address the Economics of Extinction: The CBD

The CBD was signed at the Rio Earth Summit in 1992 and is seen as a framework convention for biodiversity issues because of its breadth and because it anticipates significant further substantive development of the regime it creates.[83] The CBD is a conservation treaty, but it is also a treaty that reflects the negotiation of economic development issues between the global north (developed countries) and global south (less developed countries (LDCs)). In this latter point lies the key to understanding the CBD as an evolutionary step in species protection, as well as the likely direction of future species protection law development.

The overarching theme of the CBD is the effort to preserve biodiversity in the context of tension between the economic wealth of developed countries and the resource wealth (but economic poverty) of many LDCs. Over the course of their industrial development, the developed countries of the global north have severely degraded significant environmental resources, including biodiversity, in pursuit of their current high standard of living and economic wealth. The environmental concern motivating negotiation of the CBD related to the global south's proclivity to take a similarly destructive path to economic development. The CBD regime is the most significant and complex legal effort to begin shifting economic incentives to favor species protection, primarily in LDCs. It contains only qualified species protection commitments, but is designed to operate as a framework convention spurring further legal and policy development to achieve its goals.

1.   Overview

The CBD must be viewed in light of the three core issues (or approaches) that it seeks to address: (1) the conservation of biodiversity; (2) sustainable use of biodiversity's components, which essentially seeks to end overexploitation; and (3) equitable sharing of benefits derived from genetic resources.[84] The latter concept refers primarily to the concerns of LDCs that multinational corporations seek to hoard profits derived from information or resources gained in LDCs.

The CBD is broad, but not necessarily deep. While the CBD seeks to enlist national activities in the effort to preserve species, it does so primarily through voluntary or procedural provisions. Although it contains sweeping goals for biodiversity conservation, its "requirements" are highly qualified by the phrase "as far as possible and as appropriate," which appears no less than eight times in the CBD text and is infused into nearly every conservation-related provision. Indeed, the CBD's conservation provisions may be seen as primarily aspirational and hortatory, providing encouragement for conservation but lacking "teeth."[85] Given the extremely wide range of activities that affect biodiversity loss, including most aspects of land use in highly biodiverse countries, it is unlikely that a firm, binding agreement to broadly protect all biodiversity could have been reached. Thus, the CBD may be understood as a policy choice to favor breadth of coverage over countries' depth of commitment.

In addition to the specific CBD provisions discussed below, the CBD regime—including the treaty and other instruments, as well as various institutions created thereunder—is actively engaged in promoting awareness and education on biodiversity-related issues, as well as significant research and development support.[86] Its Global Biodiversity Outlook reports are among the most important sources of information and influential policy documents on the status of global biodiversity and species protection. Further, the CBD Secretariat has recently engaged national and international business communities through its Global Platform on Business and Biodiversity Platform.[87] The Platform includes associations, certifications, best practices, and other informational or potentially incentivizing activities aimed at mitigating the impact of businesses on biodiversity.

2. *CBD Conservation Provisions*

The specific conservation obligations imposed by the CBD are relatively nonbinding, or "soft," in the sense that they are highly qualified and are generally not designed to make national conservation failures a violation of the convention. Instead, the CBD largely encourages national measures to protect species and other components of biodiversity. The CBD Conference of the Parties has specifically encouraged parties to embrace an "ecosystem approach" to management. The CBD regime, as a whole, has undertaken significant steps to promote biodiversity conservation on the ground in developing countries.[88]

The CBD's approach to conservation is epitomized by its requirement for national conservation plans and the integration of biodiversity conservation considerations into all areas of national policy and decision making.[89] Furthermore, the CBD imposes specific (albeit qualified) monitoring and identification requirements upon countries to promote conservation and sustainable use of biodiversity.[90] For example, parties are instructed to identify components of biodiversity warranting conservation, identify activities that affect them, and monitor changes in the components or activities. The CBD also encourages cooperation among parties, the development of incentive measures, and training of national officials to promote conservation and sustainable use.

The CBD recognizes two types of conservation: in- and ex-situ. It gives preference to in-situ conservation.[91] Further, Article 8 provides that parties "shall, as far as possible and as appropriate" secure in-situ conservation through 13 specific measures, including establishment of protected areas and development of national legislation to protect threatened species.[92]

Subsequent COP decisions have illuminated the ways in which the CBD can help to promote conservation on the ground. For example, Decision VI/23 includes rather extensive principles for limiting the impact of invasive species, a pervasive and exceedingly difficult problem in many regions. In this and other areas, the CBD has proven of some value as a framework conservation treaty—its breadth allows the regime to begin addressing conservation issues that require attention but are left unaddressed by other species protection laws.

3. CBD's Endorsement of Sustainable Use

Throughout the CBD, sustainable use is treated alongside conservation, such that most of the measures required to promote conservation are also required to promote sustainable use. The CBD defines "sustainable use" as

> the use of components of biological diversity in a way and at a rate that does not lead to the long-term decline of biological diversity, thereby maintaining its potential to meet the needs and aspirations of present and future generations.[93]

These "components" can be understood to include "biological resources," defined broadly as "genetic resources, organisms or parts thereof, populations, or any other biotic component of ecosystems with actual or potential use or value for humanity."[94] Article 10 of the CBD broadly encourages national measures that ensure use of biological resources proceeds in a sustainable manner that minimizes risk to overall biodiversity.[95]

The provisions on sustainable use illustrate the balance that the CBD, as an agreement and as a regime, promotes. It encourages strategies that support economic development in LDCs in a way that will maintain their natural biodiversity. It therefore seeks to balance global environmental and economic development priorities.

4. The CBD: Benefit Sharing

The economics of biotechnology development was a major topic during negotiations leading to the signing of the CBD, arguably to the detriment of conservation.[96] Many LDCs were concerned about being cut out of profits derived from products—mostly pharmaceuticals—derived from biological resources taken from their territory. Most LDCs, reflecting concerns of multinational corporations and others, were concerned about protection of intellectual property rights and ensuring access to biological information. The resulting CBD language strengthens the sovereign rights of LDCs over resources within their territory, while encouraging access to such resources on equitable terms negotiated to include benefit sharing.

Article 15 of the CBD reaffirms countries' sovereignty over their natural resources and requires parties to "endeavor to create conditions to facilitate access to genetic resources for environmentally sound uses" by other parties, further requiring that "[a]ccess, where granted, shall be on mutually agreed terms" and "subject to prior informed consent."[97] Further, Article 15(7) calls upon parties to take measures "with the aim of sharing in a fair and equitable way the results of research and development and the benefits arising from the commercial and other utilization of genetic resources . . . upon mutually agreed terms."[98] Article 16 identified "access to and transfer of technology," which explicitly includes biotechnology, as "essential elements for the attainment of the objectives" of the CBD.[99] Although littered with the qualification "as appropriate," the remainder of Article 16 sets out the parameters of biotechnology prospecting envisioned by the CBD.[100] It is a delicate balance designed to protect and benefit developing countries while enabling access to the resources found within their borders and protecting the intellectual property rights associated with products derived therefrom. The Bonn Guidelines, adopted by the COP in Decision VI/24, clarify many details of the arrangements envisioned. To a large extent, the 2010 Nagoya Protocol on Access and Benefit Sharing (Nagoya Protocol)—adopted in 2010 but not in force—builds further upon these terms.[101]

5. *CBD: Continuing Evolution*

The CBD is very much an active and evolving regime. As suggested above, much of the ongoing activity by the CBD institutions involves programs aimed at creating economic incentives in favor of conservation or realigning the economics of biodiversity use to promote sustainable economic development. However, the CBD also plays a role in other major issue areas affecting biodiversity.

The Cartagena Protocol on Biosafety (Biosafety Protocol), which entered into force in 2003, is an example of the CBD regime's regulation of economically significant issues that may affect biodiversity indirectly.[102] The Biosafety Protocol provides for a precautionary approach to managing the trade in genetically modified organisms, designed primarily to minimize the risk presented by such organisms to species and ecosystems.

The adoption of the Nagoya Protocol signals the continued importance of the benefit-sharing objective of the CBD. Regardless of whether the Nagoya Protocol enters into force, the CBD is likely to remain the seat of international environmental law development affecting the economic arrangements entered into by corporations doing business involving the biological resources located in the LDCs.

Overall, the CBD cannot claim quantifiable success in preventing extinction and does not create the same type of penalty risks that CITES imposes. However, the CBD provides an institutional setting for the continued development of policies that balance the interests of economically wealthy northern countries (including both their interest in global environmental protection, and in protecting the intellectual property rights of transnational corporations) with LDCs' interests in economic development and their need for support to establish and implement effective biodiversity conservation policies. In that sense, the CBD has achieved a measure of success by providing a forum and set of processes through which these issues may be more effectively addressed over time.

V.   Other Public International Law Affecting Species Protection

Because of the wide variety of activities that affect species protection, it is important to consider a range of international law instruments not directly focused on species when working with a species protection issue. These agreements may be considered part of the biodiversity "regime complex."[103]

A.   UNCLOS

Perhaps the single most important treaty regime for protecting species that is not designed primarily for biodiversity conservation is UNCLOS.[104] UNCLOS settled key jurisdictional questions involving resource exploitation in the oceans and imposed a number of significant environmentally protective obligations on parties. Many of its provisions also represent customary international law that binds non-parties, such as the United States, except where they successfully resisted the imposition of such obligations. UNCLOS is important because it essentially established a legal framework for the ocean. As a result, any enhancement of current biodiversity protections in the ocean would ideally be implemented through UNCLOS.[105]

UNCLOS imposes obligations on states to sustainably manage marine and coastal resources within their jurisdiction, including the exclusive economic zone extending 200 nautical miles off of each state's coast. This includes an obligation to manage the fisheries and other species that constitute biological resources, as well as the habitats necessary to sustain them. Specifically, UNCLOS provides a general requirement that states have "the obligation to protect and preserve the marine environment."[106] Additionally, it provides for the states to combat pollution and take measures "necessary to protect and preserve rare or fragile ecosystems as well as the habitat of depleted, threatened or endangered species and other forms of marine life."[107]

Although UNCLOS could serve as an effective way to eventually implement stronger biodiversity protection on the high seas, currently it does not accomplish a great deal concerning species preservation in these areas, besides providing general guiding principles for species conservation. For example, only 1 percent of the world's oceans are currently designated as marine protection areas, and the majority of these areas fall under countries' national jurisdiction.[108]

B.   U.N. Framework Convention on Climate Change (UNFCCC)

The UNFCCC does not directly provide for species protection, nor do any other elements of the climate change regime. However, the climate change regime is particularly important to species protection law for at least two reasons. First, the massive threat that climate change poses to many species means that efforts to reduce the extent of climate change may have significant species protection benefits by reducing a force likely to drive extinction. Second, and more directly relevant, decisions related to climate change—including efforts to mitigate climate change and adapt to its effects—could have significant implications for species protection. Thus, it may be important in many instances to consider whether species protection obligations imposed by other treaties or by national law are implicated by specific policies or projects being advanced as a response to climate change.

One relatively clear example is the Clean Development Mechanism (CDM) of the Kyoto Protocol to the UNFCCC.[109] Hydroelectric projects designed to prevent carbon dioxide emissions from coal-fired power plants can have significant impacts on species and their habitats. Examples of this concern can be found in China and elsewhere.[110] Also, the creation of afforestation and reforestation CDM projects may have significant and complex effects on species protection in the countries where they are undertaken. Beyond the CDM, other types of carbon offsetting schemes, such as the emerging "REDD+" mechanism (which stands for "reducing emissions from deforestation and forest degradation" "plus" conservation, that is, the sustainable management of forests and enhancement of forest carbon stocks), have significant potential to affect species protection beneficially or detrimentally. The UNFCCC parties also work on various on-the-ground climate change activities, among which is the Rio Bravo Climate Action Project. This project focuses on the preservation of rainforest areas to combat climate change and preserve biodiversity.[111]

Beyond carbon offsetting, the climate change regime may have important effects on species protection efforts to the extent that it affects the mix of energy sources employed. Biofuels, in particular, present a significant risk of harmful impacts on species and ecosystems because of the extensive land use required for their production.[112] In some situations, solar and wind projects may also affect species detrimentally, although such effects need to be considered against the effects of the pollution generated by the fossil-fuel-based sources of energy that renewable projects replace.

C. Desertification

The UNCCD was negotiated to address desertification, one of the greatest challenges to sustainable development in Africa, at the Rio Summit in 1992.[113] It evolved from the 1978 U.N. Conference to Combat Desertification.[114] The convention provides that the parties may take into account, among other things, "conservation and sustainable use of biodiversity in accordance with the provisions of the [CBD]" when formulating plans on a national level for combating desertification.[115]

D. Other International Law Settings Important to Species Protection

A variety of other international law topics play a role in species protection. Perhaps the most significant policy area in this regard is agriculture.

Conversion of land for agricultural use is among the most important drivers of extinction. Yet changes in agricultural practice can significantly reduce the harmful effects of agriculture on biodiversity. Thus, agricultural law and policy intersects with species protection law in many instances.[116] Perhaps not surprisingly, the CBD has developed a work program specifically targeting agriculture as an area where improved compliance with international species protection law could have significant benefits for species.[117]

Another area of law that regularly intersects with species protection is finance and trade law. Decisions of institutions such as the International Monetary Fund and World Bank can have significant effects on species survival. The World Trade Organization (WTO) (and its predecessor, the General Agreement on Tariffs and Trade) had significant impacts in the *Tuna-Dolphin* and *Shrimp-Turtle* cases.[118] Notably, in the 1998 *Shrimp-Turtle* WTO Appellate Body decision, the WTO Appellate Body recognized that WTO members may adopt regulations to protect natural resources beyond the national jurisdiction, provided that doing so gives effect to a multilateral conservation agreement.[119]

A third area of international law warranting consideration is human rights law. The right to a healthy environment, found in many regional human rights agreements, as well as several other economic and social rights, can provide a tool for advancing environmental protection that is beneficial to species—particularly through the preservation of habitats. For example, observers have linked the right to clean water and biodiversity protection.[120] In addition, some have called for a broader approach linking the right to livelihood with biodiversity conservation.[121] Livelihood includes a right to the basic necessities needed to live, including food, clothing, shelter, and medical treatment.[122] Scholars have suggested that conservation of biodiversity should be viewed as a necessary condition to achieve the right to livelihood.[123] More generally, although humans are the main drivers of biodiversity loss, biodiversity is essential to human well-being.[124] Without adequate biodiversity, the Earth's life giving systems would not function properly and human quality of life and longevity would be diminished.[125]

E.   Non-Governmental Approaches

Beginning in the early 1990s with the formation of the Forest Stewardship Council (FSC), non-state approaches to environmental governance have become increasingly important. The FSC was, and continues to be, an influential organization in biodiversity protection. After the 1992 Earth Summit in Rio, a coalition of NGOs and other actors established the FSC to combat deforestation through the creation of market incentives for sustainably produced forest products.[126] The FSC has had only mixed success since its inception. Although it operates in over 80 countries, the FSC enjoys the greatest influence in the developed countries' forestry industries and has not significantly affected deforestation in the tropics (the region most in need of improved forest governance).[127]

The International Union for the Conservation of Nature (IUCN) and its annual Red List of endangered species illustrate the role that NGOs play in advancing awareness of species protection issues and disseminating knowledge gained from experiences with various regulatory approaches.[128] The IUCN Red List is "widely recognized as the most comprehensive, objective global approach for evaluating the conservation status of plant and animal species."[129] This list is produced by a network of scientists and organizations from countries all over the world. The list is used by governments, NGOs, and various other institutions.[130] The IUCN prepares the list to provide a comprehensive tool that may further effective species protection.[131] Thus, the list includes baselines for species monitoring, identifies global conservation priorities, and directly monitors representative members of species worldwide.[132]

Other NGOs, such as the Nature Conservancy, advance biodiversity conservation through privately managed protected areas.[133] This can be the best option in countries that lack adequate resources to establish publicly protected areas.[134]

Non-state-based species protection has arisen from frustration with the slow pace and often nonbinding outcomes of multilateral negotiations. In the context of forests, the failure to negotiate a meaningful protective treaty led to an innovative effort to create a wholly separate form of governance, which has established some significance in the international market. Although far from a panacea, and arguably not even particularly effective, the FSC and similar organizations are important because they represent an expansion in what "species protection law" entails. The approach represented by the FSC, as well as other NGO-sponsored efforts, is likely to remain an important component of international species protection. Thus, practitioners should be alert to potential opportunities to effectively advance their clients' interests within these "private governance" systems.[135]

VI. Conclusion: The Direction of Species Protection Law

This brief examination of species protection law indicates that significant further development is both necessary (given continued high rates of extinction) and likely (in light of the extensive international institutional development in recent decades). CITES, an agreement from the 1970s, provides some of the most binding requirements, creating a need for careful compliance, but affecting only a limited area of practice. Other agreements, most notably the CBD, highlight the trend toward consideration of economic incentives in species protection that is likely to continue. Although new, firm mandates like those in CITES are unlikely to arise in the near future, international species protection law remains highly dynamic. Most of the development is occurring not through the formal negotiation of new treaties (although that remains possible), but through the development of programs under the CBD, including partnerships involving private entities like those created through the CMS, and at the linkages among the various institutions and, importantly, among biodiversity and other environmental and nonenvironmental issues. In this respect, the development of market-related programs, by both international and civil society organizations—particularly through certification of products and services, but also through development of payment for ecosystem services and information dissemination—is likely to offer the greatest opportunities for transnational corporations and other non-state international actors to engage international species protection law in a way that is both economically beneficial and environmentally sustainable. If the goals of international species protection law are to be achieved, the challenge for international institutions, and for the practitioners who engage with them, lie in identifying or creating opportunities to enhance the connection between economic and environmental benefits.

Notes

1. *See, e.g.*, Philippe Sands & Jacqueline Peel, Principles of International Environmental Law 511 (3d ed. 2012) ("The conservation of biodiversity presents enormous regulatory challenges to international law").

2. Convention on Biological Diversity § 2 (defining "biological diversity"). The text of the CBD is available at http://www.cbd.int/convention/text/.

3. R. Costanza et al., *The Value of the World's Ecosystem Services and Natural Capital*, 387 Nature 253 (1997).

4. Ecosystem services are "free" in that no market exists to price them, except where one is created by environmental regulation. This insight underlies the "market failure" rationale for environmental law.

5. *E.g.*, Rasband et al., Natural Resources Law, at 1209–10 (discussing New York City's acquisition of development rights as "the best known example of payment for forest ecosystem services").

6. E.O. Wilson, The Future of Life 98–102 (2002).

7. This massive impact on species is one of several reasons that some scientists describe the current geological period as the "Anthropocene Epoch." *See, e.g.*, Jan Zalasiewicz et al., *The New World of the Anthropocene*, 44 Envtl. Sci. Tech. 2228 (2010).

8. Wilson, *supra* note 6, at 50–51.

9. Wilson's HIPPO acronym is designed to cover extinction pressure over most of human history and, in that context, it makes sense to consider climate change as habitat destruction. However, for purposes of considering current policy options, climate change arguably warrants separate attention. The significance of climate change as a driver of biodiversity loss is discussed at length in Climate Change & Biodiversity Loss (Lovejoy & Hannah eds. 2006). For additional discussion of the policy significance of this linkage, see A. Long, *Developing Linkages to Preserve Biodiversity*, 21 Y.B. Int'l Envtl. L. 1 (2012).

10. Within these policy changes are a host of novel and complex legal issues. For example, some scholars suggest that quarantine controls could be an effective way to help limit the invasive species problem. However, the WTO has discouraged countries from utilizing quarantine controls to control invasive species due to concerns this could turn into a disguised regulation on trade. *See* S. Riley, *Invasive Alien Species and the*

Protection of Biodiversity: The Role of Quarantine Laws in Resolving Inadequacies in the International Legal Regime, 17(3) J. ENVTL. L. 323–59 (2005).

11. Ocean acidification causes coral bleaching and destruction of entire coral reef communities, but also threatens to interfere with the ability of phytoplankton and other species that create calcium carbonate shells, along with other incompletely understood impacts. R.K. Craig, *Ocean Governance for the 21st Century: Making Marine Zoning Climate Change Adaptable*, 36 HARV. ENVTL. L. REV. 305, 233–23 (2012).

12. The concept of a "wicked" problem was developed in social science literature, but has recently been used by some legal scholars to discuss environmental problems that are particularly difficult to define and for which the potential solutions involve irreversible impacts. *See, e.g.,* H. Doremus, *Constitutive Law and Environmental Policy*, 22 STAN. ENVTL. L.J. 295, 331–33 (2003); R. J. Lazarus, *Super Wicked Problems and Climate Change: Restraining the Present to Liberate the Future*, 94 CORNELL L. REV. 1153 (2009).

13. *See, e.g.,* SANDS & PEEL, *supra* note 1, at 449 (noting that "[u]ntil the 1980s, international instruments tended to address 'wildlife' or 'wild fauna and flora,' and focused on species and habitats" and that "biodiversity" is a "more inclusive term" that includes the focus of these earlier instruments).

14. *Id.* at 452 (providing a list of ten "key international regulatory techniques" applied in biodiversity protection law).

15. RFMOs governing the regulation of the tuna fishing industry include the International Commission for the Conservation of Atlantic Tunas (ICCAT), http://www.iccat .org; Indian Ocean Tuna Commission, http://www.iotc.org; Western and Central Pacific Fisheries Commission, http://www.wcptc.int; Inter-American Tropical Tuna Commission, http://www.iattc.org; and Commission for the Conservation of Southern Bluefin Tuna, http://www.ccsbt.org. RFMOs managing fish stocks by geographical area include the North-East Atlantic Fisheries Commission, http://www.neafc.org; Northwest Atlantic Fisheries Organization, http://www.nafo.int; North Atlantic Salmon Conservation Organisation, http://www.nasco.int; South-East Atlantic Fisheries Organisation, http://www .seafo.org; South Pacific Regional Fisheries Management Organisation, http://www .southpacificrfmo.org; Convention on Conservation of Antarctic Marine Living Resources, http://www.ccamlr.org; General Fisheries Commission for the Mediterranean, http:// www.gfcm.org; and Convention on the Conservation and Management of the Pollock Resources in the Central Bering Sea, http://www.afsc.noaa.gov/refm/cbs/convention _description.htm. *See also* Food & Agric. Org. of the United Nations, Fisheries and Aquaculture Department, http://www.fao.org/fishery/rfb/ccbsp/en. *See generally* http:// ec.europa.eu/fisheries/cfp/international/rfmo/; SANDS & PEEL, *supra* note 1, at 411–18.

16. International Convention on the Regulation of Whaling, http://iwc.int/convention (last visited Sept. 12, 2013).

17. CITES, http://www.cites.org.

18. Bonn Convention on the Conservation of Migratory Species, http://www.cms .int (last visited Sept. 12, 2013).

19. World Heritage Convention, http://whc.unesco.org/en/conventiontext/ (last visited Sept. 12, 2013).

20. *See* Secretariat of the Convention on Biological Diversity, Global Biodiversity Outlook, at 3, tbl.2 (2010) (providing data on indicators of biodiversity preservation and decline, of which only two show unqualified progress in recent years—increasing land area within protected areas and increasing official development aid for biodiversity protection—in contrast to indicators of habitat quality and native species viability, which indicate significant deterioration).

21. Ramsar Convention, http://www.ramsar.org.

22. UNCCD, http://www.unccd.int.

23. This effort produced only institutions that one scholar aptly describes as "'decoys' deliberately designed to preempt governance." R. S. Dimitrov, *Hostage to Norms: States, Institutions and Global Forest Politics*, 5 Global Envtl. Politics 1 (2005).

24. The text of UNCLOS is available at http://www.un.org/depts/los/convention _agreements/texts/unclos/UNCLOS-TOC.htm (last visited Sept. 12, 2013).

25. Separately, some of the most innovative quasi-regulatory development in species protection law is occurring not in public international law, but in voluntary non-governmental market-based certification systems, such as those that affect forestry and the forest products industry or trade in coffee. On forestry certification as a regulatory approach to habitat preservation, see, for example, Confronting Sustainability: Forest Certification in Developing and Transitioning Countries 7 (B. Cashore et al. eds., 2006).

26. *See* M. Bowman et al., Lyster's International Wildlife Law: An Analysis of International Treaties 88 (2d ed. 2010).

27. *See* Andonova & Mitchell, *The Rescaling of Global Politics*, 35 Annual Rev. Env't & Res. 255, 259 (2010).

28. Sands & Peel, *supra* note 1, at 23 (observing that "[e]arly attempts to develop international environmental rules focused on the conservation of wildlife (fisheries, birds and seals) and, to a limited extent, on the protection of rivers and seas," while also noting the mid-18th century recognition that deforestation affected freshwater availability).

29. The narrow economic rationale for early species protection agreements is perhaps best illustrated by the 1902 Convention for the Protection of Birds Useful to Agriculture, which prescribed protection of certain species beneficial to agriculture and called for the destruction of species deemed pests. *See* Bowman et al., *supra* note 26, at 5.

30. Bowman et al., *supra* note 26, at 5 (discussing early agreements by colonial powers to protect African agricultural interests).

31. Sands & Peel, *supra* note 1, at 24.

32. *Id.*

33. Bowman et al., *supra* note 26, at 5.

34. *Id.* at 4; Elli Louka, International Environmental Law: Fairness, Effectiveness, and the World Order 42–43 (2006).

35. Bowman et al., *supra* note 26, at 4.

36. Louka, *supra* note 34, at 339.

37. Convention for the Protection of Migratory Birds in Canada and the United States, *available at* http://iea.uoregon.edu/pages/view_treaty.php?t=1916-ProtectionMigratoryBirds CanadaUnitedStates.EN.txt&par=view_treaty_html (last visited Sept. 13, 2013).

38. Notably, although United States environmental and natural resources law now derives its authority primarily from the Commerce Clause of the U.S. Constitution, other nations employ a treaty-based constitutional rationale for species protection similar to that articulated by Justice Holmes in *Missouri v. Holland*, 252 U.S. 416 (1920). The Australian Supreme Court, for example, has upheld national regulatory action as an implementation of the World Heritage Convention in the absence of other national constitutional authority. Commonwealth v. State of Tasmania, 158 C.L.R. 1 (1983).

39. 252 U.S. 416, 435 (1920).

40. The Fur Seal Treaty of 1911, *available at* http://docs.lib.noaa.gov/noaa_documents /NOS/ORR/TM_NOS_ORR/TM_NOS-ORR_17/HTML/Pribilof_html/Documents /THE_FUR_SEAL_TREATY_OF_1911.pdf (convention between the United States, Great Britain, Russia, and Japan); The Migratory Bird Treaty of 1918, *available at* http://www .law.cornell.edu/uscode/text/16/chapter-7/subchapter-II (convention between the U.S. and Great Britain), discussed *supra*.

41. In the case of the polar bear, climate change is likely to dominate consideration of future protection efforts. Given that the 1973 Agreement on Conservation of Polar

Bears creates no institutions and has only rarely given rise to consultation among the parties, whereas the climate change regime is among the most extensively developed international environmental law regimes, it is unclear whether the polar bear agreement will play a significant role in future decisions regarding international regulatory action regarding polar bears.

42. International Convention for the Regulation of Whaling, 62 Stat. 1716, TIAS No. 1849, 161 UNTS 72, Art V (Dec. 2, 1946).

43. Australia has even commenced an ICJ case seeking to have Japan's whaling declared illegal. *See, e.g.*, A. Geary, *Australia's Case in the International Court of Justice against Japan for Violations of International Conventions through Japan's Scientific Whaling Program*, 14(3) INT'L ENVTL. L. COMM. NEWSL. (ABA) (Aug. 2012), *available at* http://apps.americanbar.org/dch/comadd.cfm?com=NR350500&pg=3.

44. D. BODANSKY, THE ART AND CRAFT OF INTERNATIONAL ENVIRONMENTAL LAW 225–26 (2010).

45. The vicuna, which is closely related to the llama, is covered by a number of bilateral and multilateral treaties in Latin America, including the Convention for the Conservation of Vicuna (Argentina, Bolivia, Chile, Peru, and Ecuador); the Convention for the Conservation and Management of Vicuna (Bolivia, Chile, Ecuador, and Peru); and the Agreement between the Bolivian and Argentinian Governments for the Protection and Conservation of Vicuna. BOWMAN ET AL., *supra* note 26, at 88.

46. *Id.* at 297.

47. For extensive discussion of regional instruments, *see* BOWMAN ET AL., *supra* note 26, at 241–400. A more concise discussion is presented in LOUKA, *supra* note 34, at 323–34.

48. *See* SANDS & PEEL, *supra* note 1, at 490.

49. The first of these was the 1900 London Convention for the Protection of Wild Animals, Birds, and Fish in Africa, which was adopted by Great Britain, Italy, Portugal, Spain, and France. It was later replaced by the 1933 London Convention Relative to the Preservation of Flora and Fauna in Their Natural State. In 1968, the Convention was again superseded by the African Convention on the Conservation of Nature and Natural Resources, which was adopted by African nations. The African nations have also adopted the 1994 Lusaka Agreement on Co-operative Enforcement Operations Directed at Illegal Trade in Wild Flora and Fauna. SANDS & PEEL, *supra* note 1, at 480–83.

50. UNEP, Activity Report of the CITES Secretariat, http://www.cites.org/eng/disc/sec/ann_rep/2008-09.pdf; For a discussion of CITES effectiveness for conservation of the elephant, see A. J. Heimert, *How the Elephant Lost His Tusks*, 104 YALE L.J. 1473, 1483 (1995).

51. CITES art. I.

52. CITES art. XV.

53. *Id.*

54. BOWMAN ET AL., *supra* note 26, at 495; *see also* Convention on Trade in Endangered Species Appendixes, http://www.cites.org/eng/app/appendices.php.

55. CITES art. XV.

56. BOWMAN ET AL., *supra* note 26, at 495; *see also* Convention on Trade in Endangered Species Appendixes, http://www.cites.org/eng/app/appendices.php.

57. CITES art. XVI.

58. CITES art. III.

59. *Id.*

60. COP Resolution 5.10 (1985), *available at* http://www.cites.org/eng/cop/15/doc/E15-18A01.pdf.

61. CITES art. IV.

62. CITES art. V.

63. *Id.*

64. CITES art. V(3). This results in the rare situation where one nation may unilaterally adjust the international obligations of several others. *See* HUNTER ET AL., INTERNATIONAL ENVIRONMENTAL LAW AND POLICY 1071 (3d ed. 2006).

65. CITES art. VII & XXII.

66. CITES art. X.

67. Notably, CITES utilizes suspension of trade as a compliance mechanism. In 2009 there were "thirty-two trade suspensions in effect under CITES, for failure to provide the required annual report on illegal trade, for failure properly to implement CITES in domestic law and for significant trade in Appendix II species. This total includes trade suspensions against four states which are not parties to CITES." BOWMAN ET AL., *supra* note 26, at 652.

68. CITES art. VIII. However, 30 years after its entry into force, more than half of the parties had not enacted implementing legislation that fully satisfies CITES requirements. BODANSKY, *supra* note 44, at 225–26.

69. BOWMAN ET AL., *supra* note 26, at 484 ("CITES is arguably the most successful of all international treaties concerned with the conservation of wildlife.").

70. SANDS & PEEL, *supra* note 1, at 479.

71. Convention on Migratory Species art. II, *available at* http://www.cms.int/documents/convtxt/cms_convtxt.htm.

72. *Id.* art. I(a).

73. *Id.* art. III.

74. *Id.* art. IV.

75. *See, e.g.* Elizabeth M. Mrema, *CMS Networking for Migratory Species: The Way Forward*, IISD BIODIVERSITY POLICY & PRAC. (2011), http://biodiversity-l.iisd.org/guest-articles/cms-networking-for-migratory-species-the-way-forward/. Mrema is Executive Secretary, Convention on the Conservation of Migratory Species of Wild Animals.

76. The text of the convention is available at http://www.ramsar.org/cda/en/ramsar-documents-texts-convention-on/main/ramsar/1-31-38^20671_4000_0__.

77. *See* Contracting Parties to the Ramsar Convention on Wetlands, http://www.ramsar.org/cda/en/ramsar-about-parties-parties/main/ramsar/1-36-123^23808_4000_0__.

78. BOWMAN ET AL., *supra* note 26, at 405.

79. *Id.* at 403–50.

80. The convention encourages an "ecosystem approach" very much in line with the approach advocated by the CBD. BOWMAN ET AL., *supra* note 26, at 403–50.

81. Ramsar serves as a primary implementation body for the CBD under a joint work program related to wetlands. The Joint Work Programme (JWP) between the CBD and the Ramsar Convention: Progress with Implementation and Development of the Fifth JWP, Doc. UNEP/CBD/COP/10/INF/38 (2010), *available at* http://www.cbd.int/doc/meetings/cop/cop-10/information/cop-10-inf-38-en.pdf.

82. BOWMAN ET AL., *supra* note 26, at 465.

83. The latter point—that the CBD anticipates further development of biodiversity law—is among the reasons that the United States did not ratify the convention. *See* J. Brunnée, *The United States and International Environmental Law: Living with an Elephant*, 15 EUR. J. INT'L L. 617, 641 (2004) (discussing objections of U.S. senators based on the concern that the CBD COP would have authority to expand parties' obligations).

84. Convention on Biological Diversity art. 1.

85. For example, the 193-member UN Convention on Biological Diversity instated a de facto moratorium on geoengineering, which built upon the 2008 moratorium on ocean fertilization. *See* ETC Group, Press Release, Geoengineering Moratorium at UN Ministerial in Japan: Risky Climate Techno-fixes Blocked (Oct. 29, 2010), http://www.etcgroup.org/content/news-release-geoengineering-moratorium-un-ministerial-japan. However,

despite this moratorium, in October of 2012 Canada was found to be in violation of this provision by failing to prevent a corporation and indigenous people from participating in geoengineering. As of yet, there is no information on any action by the Conference of the Parties to pursue this violation. Helena Paul, EcoNexus, *Canada Found to Be in Violation of International Obligations to the CBD . . .*, 44(10) Eco. 1 (October 19, 2012), http://www.ukabc .org/eco@cop11-10.pdf.

86. The CBD Secretariat, for example, was closely involved in "UN Decade on Biodiversity," the "Year of Biodiversity," and the assessment of progress toward U.N. Millennium Development Goals pertaining to biodiversity. *See* UN Decade on Biodiversity, https://www.cbd.int/2011-2020/; The International Year on Biodiversity, *available at* http://www.cbd.int/2010/welcome/.

87. Global Platform on Business and Biodiversity, http://www.cbd.int/business/.

88. Decision V/6; *see also* Long, Developing Linkages to Preserve Biodiversity, 21 Y.B. Int'l Envtl. L.1 (2011).

89. Convention on Biological Diversity art. 6.

90. *Id.* art. 7.

91. "In situ conservation" is defined as "the conservation of ecosystems and natural habitats and the maintenance and recovery of viable populations of species in their natural surroundings and, in the case of domesticated or cultivated species, in the surroundings where they have developed their distinctive properties." Convention on Biological Diversity art. 2.

92. Convention on Biological Diversity art. 8.

93. Convention on Biological Diversity art. 2.

94. Convention on Biological Diversity art. 10.

95. *Id.*

96. Hunter et al., *supra* note 64, at 1008–09.

97. Convention on Biological Diversity, http://www.cbd.int/convention/text/.

98. Convention on Biological Diversity art. 15, http://www.cbd.int/convention/text/.

99. Convention on Biological Diversity art. 16, http://www.cbd.int/convention/text/.

100. *Id.*

101. http://www.cbd.int/abs/ (last visited Sept. 13, 2013).

102. http://bch.cbd.int/protocol/ (last visited Sept. 13, 2013).

103. *See* Robert O. Keohane & David G. Victor, *The Regime Complex for Climate Change,* 9 Perspectives on Politics 7 (2011).

104. *See also* chapter 41 in this volume, Arctic Region.

105. Marine Biological Diversity Beyond Areas of National Jurisdiction: Legal and Policy Framework, http://www.un.org/Depts/los/biodiversityworkinggroup/webpage _legal%20and%20policy.pdf.

106. United Nations Convention on the Law of the Sea art. 192, http://www.un.org /Depts/los/convention_agreements/texts/unclos/closindx.htm.

107. *Id.*

108. Sharelle Hart, *Elements of a Possible Implementation Agreement to UNCLOS for the Conservation and Sustainable Use of Marine Biodiversity in Areas beyond National Jurisdiction,* IUCN Environmental Policy and Law Papers Online--Marine Series No. 4 (2008), *available at* https://portals.iucn.org/library/efiles/edocs/EPLP-MS-4.pdf.

109. http://unfccc.int/documentation/document_lists/items/2960.php (last visited Sept. 13, 2013).

110. For an example see the Xiaogushan Hydropower Project in People's Republic of China, information available at http://cdm.unfccc.int/Projects/DB/JCI1145495919.5.

111. *Interlinkages between Biological Diversity and Climate Change; Advice on the integration of biodiversity considerations into the implementation of the UNFCCC and its Kyoto Protocol* (CBD Technical Series No. 10, Secretariat of the Convention on Biological Diversity, 2003),

http://unfccc.int/files/meetings/workshops/other_meetings/application/pdf/exec
sum.pdf.

112. Additionally, biofuels have the potential to exacerbate the problem invasive species pose to biodiversity loss. *See* Charles Chimera et al., *Biofuels: The Risks and Dangers of Introducing Invasive Species*, 1 BIOFUELS 785 (Sept. 2010).

113. United Nations Convention to Combat Desertification, http://www.unccd.int /en/about-the-convention/Pages/About-the-Convention.aspx.

114. United Nations Conference on Desertification, http://www.ciesin.org/docs/002 -478/002-478.html; *see also* United Nations Convention to Combat Desertification, http:// www.unccd.int/en/about-the-convention/Pages/About-the-Convention.aspx.

115. United Nations Convention to Combat Desertification art. 4(j), http://www .unccd.int/en/about-the-convention/Pages/About-the-Convention.aspx.

116. For example, the UNEP and the FAO have adopted nonbinding agreements on "the use of environmental impact assessment on agricultural activities, and other environmental aspects of agricultural practices." Additionally, the WTO Agreement on Agriculture exempts environmental programs from rules limiting government subsidies. SANDS & PEEL, *supra* note 1, at 551.

117. For a discussion of the Work Programme, see Convention on Biological Diversity: Agricultural Diversity, http://www.cbd.int/agro/whatneedstobedone.shtml.

118. BOWMAN ET AL., *supra* note 26, at 653.

119. *Id.* at 654.

120. Sullivan et al., *Global Threats to Human Water Scarcity and River Biodiversity*, http://limnology.wisc.edu/personnel/mcintyre/publications/vorosmarty_etal_2010 _nature_global_threats.pdf.

121. Ryan Hartzell C. Balisacan, *Harmonizing Biodiversity Conservation and the Human Right to Livelihood: Towards a Viable Model for Sustainable Community-Based Ecotourism Using Lessons from the Donsol Whale Shark Project*, 57 ATENEO L.J. 423 (2012), *available at* http:// papers.ssrn.com/sol3/papers.cfm?abstract_id=2189234.

122. *Id.*

123. *Id.*

124. Tim Hayward, *Biodiversity, Human Rights and Sustainability*, 1(22) ROOTS (July 2001), http://www.bgci.org/education/article/0423.

125. *See id.*

126. Forest Stewardship Council, https://us.fsc.org/our-history.180.htm.

127. *Id.* On the ability of FSC and similar programs to affect tropical programs, see generally Benjamin Cashore et al., *Introduction, in* CONFRONTING SUSTAINABILITY: FOREST CERTIFICATION IN DEVELOPING AND TRANSITIONING COUNTRIES 7 (B. Cashore et al. eds., 2006); Peter Dauvergne & Jane Lister, *The Prospects and Limits of Eco-Consumerism: Shopping Our Way to Less Deforestation?* 23 ORG. & ENV'T 132, 138–40 (2010).

128. *See* http://www.iucn.org (last visited Sept. 13, 2013).

129. The IUCN Red List of Threatened Species, http://www.iucnredlist.org/about /red-list-overview.

130. *Id.*

131. *Id.*

132. *Id.*

133. J. Langholz & W. Krug, *New Forms of Biodiversity Governance: Non-State Actors and Private Protected Area Action Plan* (2004), *available at* http://www.asiconservachile.cl /fileadmin/templates/data_users/Publicaciones/APs_Voluntarias/Langholz_04_.pdf.

134. *Id.*

135. *See generally infra*, chapter 51 in this volume, International Standards.

CHAPTER 13

Environmental Review and Decision Making

EDWARD (TED) BOLING

I. Introduction

Environmental impact assessment (EIA) has been described as a legally binding "process for institutionalizing *foresight*."[1] This description focuses on the end result of the EIA process: decisions that are better than they might have been had they not undergone a public process of scrutiny into their environmental consequences. However, an equally important aspect of the EIA process may be its support for "environmental democracy."[2] By informing and facilitating public involvement in government decisions on actions that affect communities, EIA processes can help establish community support necessary to ensure that development decisions are both politically and environmentally sustainable. As such, EIA has been shown to provide a procedural framework that, where necessary, has strengthened substantive laws for sustainable development.

Requirements for environmental impact assessment take myriad forms, but generally have elements in common with the U.S. National Environmental Policy Act of 1969 (NEPA). NEPA was enacted with sweeping and transformative goals: to "declare a national policy which will encourage productive and enjoyable harmony between man and his environment; to promote efforts which will prevent or eliminate damage to the environment and biosphere and stimulate the health and welfare of man; to enrich the understanding of the ecological systems and natural resources important to the Nation; and to establish a Council on Environmental Quality."[3] Since the U.S. Congress enacted NEPA, more than 75 nations[4] have enacted some form of EIA law. EIA has also been adopted by multilateral development banks and international organizations, and as part of international agreements to ensure deliberate and transparent analysis of the consequences of their decision making. The European Union (EU) required that its members enact legislation for EIA in 1985[5] and Principle 17 of the 1992 Rio Declaration on Environment and Development provided that "Environmental impact assessment, as a national instrument, shall be undertaken for proposed activities that are likely to have a significant adverse impact on the environment and are subject to a decision of a competent national authority."[6]

In the course of adoption and application of EIA principles, EIA has been adapted to a wide variety of legal, social, political, and cultural traditions. While EIA is typically focused upon site-specific projects—particularly project compliance with environmental standards and mitigation of projects' adverse impacts—programmatic approaches, described as strategic environmental assessment (SEA), have been employed to advance sustainability goals as an objective of development programs. SEA refers to a range of "analytical and participatory approaches that aim to integrate environmental considerations into policies, plans and programmes and evaluate the interlinkages with economic and social considerations."[7] SEA has been used to address changes in policies, institutions, laws, and regulations required to achieve reform of economic sectors in a manner that is sensitive to political processes often driven by economic interests.

This chapter discusses the development, variations, and current trends in EIA and SEA. National EIA requirements are addressed in subsequent chapters, though notable trends are addressed in this chapter as well.

II.   The Development of EIA

As its title indicates, the EIA procedures of NEPA were enacted to implement a general statement of the environmental policy of the United States:

> [I]t is the continuing policy of the Federal Government, in cooperation with State and local governments, and other concerned public and private organizations, to use all practicable means and measures, including financial and technical assistance, in a manner calculated to foster and promote the general welfare, to create and maintain conditions under which man and nature can exist in productive harmony, and fulfill the social, economic, and other requirements of present and future generations of Americans.[8]

This policy statement codified, for the United States, what became during the 1970s and 1980s an international trend to adopt EIA mandates designed to address a wide range of development effects, such as biophysical, biodiversity, social, economic, and human health risks and uncertainties. The trend also expanded its focus from NEPA's policy of cooperation with affected interests and jurisdictions to a broader "environmental democracy" movement that seeks to open up decisions that affect the environment by "widening the range of voices heard and improving the quantity and quality of policy choices available to society."[9] While these EIA processes seek to legitimize government decisions by grounding them in public review, EIA processes can also provide the basis for partnerships with affected communities that facilitate implementation of decisions with the specialized knowledge of local conditions and capacities for mitigating impacts.[10] Thus, EIA processes benefit the governments that adopt them by helping governments supplement or save resources through accessing the local environmental, financial, governmental, and other information that is necessary for governmental planning processes.[11]

Experience with EIA-led consideration of cumulative effects and an emerging interest in integrating environmental, social, and economic effects at the policy level was documented by the 1987 report of the World Commission on Environment and Development (the Brundtland Report), which provided the most quoted definition of "sustainable development."[12] Closely tied with its strategy for sustainable development is the report's call for integration of economic and ecological factors into the law and decision-making systems at the national and international levels.[13] The report documented, based on EIA-led experience, that sustainable development requires changes in the legal and institutional frameworks that enforce the common interest in integrated consideration of the environment and economics in decision making. According to the Brundtland Report, this goal is best achieved by giving communities an effective say over the use of resources upon which the communities depend, promoting citizen initiatives, empowering people's organizations, and strengthening local democracy.[14] With regard to large-scale projects, particularly those that entail high environmental impacts, the report calls for public inquiries, free access to relevant information, and availability of alternative sources of technical expertise to provide an informed basis for public discussion.[15] Moreover, the report predicted growth in fuel and material uses that increase direct physical linkages between ecosystems of different countries with heightened economic and ecological interdependence. It addressed this trend by calling for integration of environmental objectives into taxation, prior approval procedures for investment and technology choice, foreign trade incentives, and development policy.[16]

Public participation became a generally accepted principle of international environmental law with the 1992 Rio Declaration and its Agenda 21. Agenda 21 stated that one of the

> fundamental prerequisites for the achievement of sustainable development is broad public participation in decision-making. . . . This includes the need of individuals, groups, and organizations to participate in environmental impact assessment procedures and to know about and participate in decisions, particularly those which potentially affect the communities in which they live and work.[17]

At Rio, 172 nations adopted, inter alia, Principle 10 of the Rio Declaration, with its statement that "each individual shall have appropriate access to information concerning the environment that is held by public authorities . . . and the opportunity to participate in decision-making processes."[18]

These principles are reflected in several multilateral environmental agreements, including the United Nations Economic Committee for Europe (UNECE) Convention on Environmental Impact Assessment in a Transboundary Context (Espoo Convention).[19] The Espoo Convention obliges parties to assess the environmental impact of their activities at an early stage of planning and states the general obligation of states to notify and consult with each other on all major projects that are likely to have a significant adverse impact across boundaries. In recognition of the importance of including the concerned public on all sides of the borders, the Espoo Convention includes provisions for public participation in relevant decision making.

The Convention is supplemented by the high water mark for the international development of EIA: the UNECE's Convention on Access to Information, Public Participation in Decision-making, and Access to Justice in Environmental Matters known popularly as the Aarhus Convention. U.N. Secretary General Kofi Annan described it as "by far the most impressive elaboration on principle 10 of the Rio Declaration" and, although regional in scope, "the Convention will be open to accession by non-ECE countries, giving it the potential to serve as a global framework for strengthening citizens' environmental rights."[20] Also, building on judicial recognition that the health of generations to come is represented by the environment,[21] the Aarhus Convention has been described as the first international legal instrument to recognize the rights of future generations.[22]

The Aarhus Convention is based on three organizational "pillars": access to information, public participation in decision making, and access to justice. Access to information is the first pillar because effective public participation in decision making depends on full, accurate, and up-to-date information.[23] Article 4 provides for "passive" rights to seek information from public authorities and the obligation of public authorities to provide information upon request. Article 5 provides for "active" access to information with the obligation of authorities to collect and disseminate information of public interest without a specific request.

Article 6 provides for public participation in decision making regarding "specific activities with a possible significant environmental impact." An annex to the Convention provides a list of such activities, including the siting, construction, and operation of various industrial facilities. The Convention also incorporates any activity that is subject to EIA under the national legislation of a party. Article 7 addresses public participation in the strategic environmental assessment of "plans, programmes and policies relating to the environment." This article requires parties to "make appropriate practical and/or other provisions for the public to participate during the preparation" of land use and sectoral plans, environmental action plans, and environmental policies. Article 8 reaches public participation in the promulgation of laws and rules with potentially significant environmental impact. The article comes closest to directing substantive changes to national laws by committing parties to "promote effective public participation at an appropriate stage, and while options are still open, during the preparation by public authorities of executive regulations and other generally applicable legally binding rules that may have a significant effect on the environment."

Access to justice is addressed in the Convention as a matter of the parties' obligations toward their own citizens, not only as a matter of parties' rights and obligations to each other. This aspect, supported by oversight of the Aarhus Convention Compliance Committee, makes the Convention unique among multilateral environmental agreements.[24] The Committee is made up of individuals nominated by parties to serve only in their individual capacities. They may review submissions about a party's compliance from parties, the secretariat, or any member of the public (including nongovernmental organizations).[25] The Committee must "take into account whether available and effective domestic remedies have been exhausted" and cannot consider "anonymous, manifestly ill-founded and abusive communications or those incompatible with the provisions of the Convention." Rights accorded to the "public" in general are not limited by standing doctrine, though some obligations under Article 6 may be referred only by "the public affected or likely to be affected by, or having an interest in, the environmental decision-making: for the purposes of this definition, non-governmental organizations promoting environmental protection and meeting any requirements under national law shall be deemed to have an interest."[26]

The Aarhus Convention has been adopted by 44 countries, which is a substantial majority of the 55-member UNECE. Other UNECE members, including the United States and Canada, have EIA laws that meet or exceed the provisions of the Aarhus Convention but have not joined the convention. The U.S. legal system already provides for public access to environmental information, participation in public decision making, and access to justice. However, on the Convention's provisions for a Compliance Committee, the United States objected to the participation of non-state, non-party actors in the membership of, and communications to, the Committee.[27] Russian participation was a major focus of the negotiations leading up to the Aarhus Convention, but withdrew its participation in 1998 and has not signed the Convention.[28]

Building on the impetus of the Rio Summit, there has been greater emphasis on efforts to integrate assessment, planning, and decision making in support of sustainable development. The Rio Summit and its Agenda 21, the 17th Session of the United Nations Environment Programme (UNEP) Governing Council, and the second and third meetings of the United Nations Commission on Sustainable Development, for example, not only gave new impetus to the use of EIA, but also encouraged the development of SEA, sustainability impact assessment (SIA) or sustainability appraisal (SA), and integrated assessment (IA). The call for an integrated approach was renewed in the Plan of Implementation of the World Summit on Sustainable Development (WSSD 2002), where frequent reference is made to the importance of taking a "holistic and inter-sector approach." Particular importance is given to addressing the relationship among poverty, development, and the environment at all levels and across key sectors to deliver the Millennium Development Goals (MDGs) and particularly MDG7: "to ensure environmental sustainability . . . integrating the principles of sustainable development into country policies and programmes and reverse the loss of environmental resources." As international development activities have been refocused around a new modus operandi of broad-based policies and strategies for poverty reduction, the demand for a holistic, integrated approach is increasing significantly. These goals have promoted the development of various other related assessment tools, including social impact assessment, health assessment, technology assessment, poverty assessment, risk assessment, and biodiversity impact assessment.

III.   Common Elements and Variations in EIA

The basic elements of EIA have been described as (1) screening; (2) scoping; (3) impact analysis and report preparation; (4) public and agency participation; (5) final decision; and (6) follow-up.[29] Within that structure, EIA encompasses a range of variations that have adapted its elements to the legal and social contexts in which it is applied. For example, the World Bank procedures for EIA follow a six-step process that is coordinated with major project decisions: screening a proposal; preparing an initial executive project summary; preparing Terms of Reference for an environmental assessment; preparing the environmental assessment; reviewing the assessment and incorporating its findings into the project; and conducting postproject evaluation.[30] For purposes of this summary, EIA processes can be broadly categorized into those that have a narrow application (e.g., NEPA's application to only "major Federal actions significantly affecting the quality of the human environment") and those with a broader scope (e.g., the EU Directive 85/337, as amended by Directive 97/11/EC to widen the scope, strengthen the procedural stages and integrate the changes provided by the Espoo Convention).

A.   Screening for Actions with Significant Environmental Impacts

Most international agreements are based on a threshold standard of "significant" environmental effects for implementation of their EIA standards.[31] This standard is drawn from domestic EIA standards and, as such, reflects an application of the international standard of nondiscrimination in the nondifferentiation between domestic and international impacts as a basis for EIA obligations.[32] The use of a standard in common with domestic EIA requirements also facilitates the implementation of international commitments through existing EIA regimes based on familiar standards.

The threshold identification of "significant" environmental effects for determination of impact significance may be a function of a technical approach, a collaborative approach, or through reasoned argumentation. The technical approach to impact significance determination is based on expert and technical data, analyses, and opinion to aggregate impact significance determination considerations into regulatory definitions of impacts of importance at a national, regional, state or provincial, or territorial level.[33] In a collaborative approach, parties collectively determine the impacts that are acceptable and unacceptable, important and unimportant, and how much importance to attach to potential impacts.[34] The reasoned argumentation model builds on a long history of reasoned argumentation in judicial and social science models, and has become a major element of the "conceptual foundation of EIA."[35] The reasoned argumentation approach expresses significance qualitatively, supported by quantitative data and analyses, as a reasoned judgment supported by evidence.[36]

The Espoo Convention reflects a technical approach in its use of both lists of activities and criteria for determining the application of its threshold significance standard for EIA obligations. Under this approach, the originating state is required to carry out an EIA for a list of public or private sector activities listed at Appendix I to the Convention that are "likely to cause a significant adverse transboundary effect."[37] The Convention also maintains a list of general criteria for determining whether nonlisted activities are significant for EIA purposes. For activities that are not listed in Appendix 1, the Convention relies on the procedural requirement of the initiation of discussions between parties to determine whether a particular activity is likely to have a significant adverse transboundary impact. If the parties disagree regarding the initial assessment of significance by the originating state, the affected party may require the exchange of information and either party may submit the question of whether the threshold has been met to an independent inquiry commission.[38] The inquiry procedure is designed to provide a nonbinding recommendation based on a technical and scientific assessment. Thus, the Espoo Convention relies on the parties' appeals to scientific norms and community pressure to obtain compliance with its terms.[39]

Other international EIA obligations recognize the significance determination as the product of a political process that reflects its origins in domestic EIA.[40] A leading example of this is found in NEPA. Under NEPA, any major federal action in the United States "significantly affecting the quality of the human environment" triggers an obligation to prepare a detailed environmental impact statement (EIS).[41] Rather than define, by criteria or list of actions, the threshold consideration for significance of any proposed federal action, the Council on Environmental Quality (CEQ), established by NEPA, defines "significantly" as a requiring consideration of the context and intensity of the environmental effects of a federal agency action.[42] Under the CEQ regulations implementing NEPA, each federal agency must establish its own NEPA procedures that are tailored to the agency's own authorities, programs, and decision-making processes.[43] These agency-specific procedures identify agency actions that normally require an EIS, those actions that are normally excluded from the EIS requirement because their effects are not significant, and those intermediate actions that require some environmental assessment to assist the agency in determining whether a particular proposal for agency action may have significant effects or not.[44] The federal judiciary has construed NEPA's provisions to be limited to federal agencies, thereby excluding executive actions by the president of the United States, and limit their requirements to be proportional to the federal agency role in the proposed action.[45] Congress has further constrained the NEPA process for some actions and exempted others from NEPA analysis or judicial review of the adequacy of agency implementation of NEPA. Thus, under NEPA, what is characterized as a "screening" process in many EIA procedures involves the application of agency rules, judicial interpretation, and legislative actions implementing or modifying NEPA.

Within the agency-specific screening system established in NEPA regulations, the identification of a "significant" environmental effect is typically an action-specific analysis that depends on reasoned argumentation and public review processes for its standardization. Agencies must identify those actions that "normally" have significant impacts on the human environment and those that do not, either individually or cumulatively.[46] In identifying actions that do not normally have significant impacts, the agency must describe its basis for concluding that the environmental effects of a given action are not individually or cumulatively significant.[47] This "categorical exclusion" finding may be based on prior environmental analyses of the actions, other agencies' experience with similar actions, and expert assessment.[48] The agency must also identify parameters for the application of the categorical exclusion, both in the definition of the action to be excluded from environmental analysis and the definition of "extraordinary circumstances" that may require the agency to conduct an action-specific environmental analysis.[49] To encourage the use of categorical exclusions that avoid unnecessary environmental analysis and focus environmental analysis on actions that may have significant environmental effects, CEQ has advised federal agencies to consider further definition of categories to address physical, temporal, and environmental conditions that should constrain the use of a categorical exclusion.[50]

The effects of other actions not specifically identified in agency NEPA procedures as normally significant or excluded as insignificant are evaluated for significance in a concise, public document known simply as an environmental assessment. Agencies may use an environmental assessment to assist in the preparation of a full EIS. However, in the great majority of cases the agencies use their environmental assessment as a basis for finding that the action will have no significant impacts.

B.   Scoping the Action for EIA

International EIA obligations have largely relied on domestic requirements of their parties to determine the scope and content of EIA reports.[51] The Espoo Convention, for example, contains a list of minimum requirements that leave elements such as the range of alternatives and inclusion of a "no action" alternative to the discretion of the source state "where appropriate."[52] Contrast that approach with NEPA, where the components of the "detailed statement" known today as an EIS are defined in the statute as follows:

 (i) the environmental impact of the proposed action;
 (ii) any adverse environmental effects which cannot be avoided should the proposal be implemented;

(iii) alternatives to the proposed action;

(iv) the relationship between local short-term uses of man's environment and the maintenance and enhancement of long-term productivity, and

(v) any irreversible and irretrievable commitments of resources which would be involved in the proposed action should it be implemented.[53]

Under NEPA, analysis of alternatives to the proposed action is the "heart" of the analysis of environmental consequences and available mitigation. The "no action" alternative establishes the environmental baseline against which the consequences of various alternatives are compared. This approach to alternatives is typical in EIA systems in a variety of legal and social contexts.

At the international level, the relative absence of substantive environmental standards makes the analysis of alternatives particularly important to the function of the EIA regime. The analysis of alternatives can serve as both a measure of the effects of a particular action and of the parties' implementation of their international obligations.[54] In this context, the evaluation of alternatives demonstrates the reasonableness of state activity by showing the considerations involved in the selection among alternatives with differing consequences for the environment of other states. International obligations may also expand the range of considerations in EIA. For example, under the Convention on Biological Diversity (CBD), parties must identify activities that are likely to have significant adverse impacts on the conservation and sustainable use of biological diversity, and monitor their effects.[55] The CBD calls on parties to evaluate alternatives such as including "no net biodiversity loss" or "biodiversity restoration" alternatives that may not be readily identifiable at the outset of impact study.[56] Therefore, the CBD calls on parties to structure their EIA as an iterative process of assessing impacts, redesigning alternatives and comparison of effects on biological diversity in ways that may expand upon domestic EIA practice.

C. Impact Analysis and Report Preparation

The United Nations Environment Programme EIA Goals and Principles document the generally accepted minimum requirements of an EIA.[57] At the heart of these requirements is the assessment of the "likely or potential environmental impacts of the proposed activity and alternatives, including direct, indirect, cumulative, short-term and long-term effects."[58] Cumulative effects refers to the effects of an action that are additive to the effects of past, present, and reasonably foreseeable future actions.[59] The Supreme Court of the United States has construed NEPA's requirement to consider the environmental impacts of a proposed action as including its cumulative effects, subject to a rule of reason to bind the scope of the analysis.[60] Consistent with EIA's predictive purposes, CEQ interprets NEPA and CEQ's NEPA regulations on cumulative effects as requiring analysis and a "concise description of the identifiable present effects of past actions to the extent that they are relevant and useful in analyzing whether the reasonably foreseeable effects of the agency proposal for action and its alternatives may have a continuing, additive and significant relationship to those effects."[61] While the CEQ definition notes that individually minor effects may be cumulatively significant, in evaluating the U.S. Department of Transportation's analysis of the effects of lifting a moratorium on cross-border trucks from Mexico, the U.S. Supreme Court has construed CEQ's definition of cumulative effects as requiring the consideration of individually minor actions in the context of their "incremental" impact.[62]

Given its reliance on domestic EIA standards, the adequacy of cumulative effects analysis is particularly important for implementation of international commitments regarding transboundary issues such as effects on migratory species, the oceans, and climate change. Early in the development of EIA, the Organisation for Economic Co-operation and Development (OECD) recommended that the principle of nondiscrimination be applied through national laws that assess transboundary impacts on an equal footing with domestic impact, and that foreign nationals within an affected state should be extended the same rights of access to information and administrative or judicial review.[63] However, the Convention fails to mention the assessment of the cumulative effects of proposed actions. This is a significant deviation from the domestic EIA rules of many of its parties.[64]

A different approach was taken in the United States, where the president addressed the obligations of federal agencies to consider the extraterritorial effects of their actions in an executive order that provided for EIA regarding significant effects on foreign nations and the global commons.[65] Later, in the context of negotiations undertaken with the governments of Mexico and Canada to develop an agreement on transboundary EIA in North America, CEQ resolved ambiguities regarding the application of NEPA to transboundary effects through guidance that found that agencies must include analysis of reasonably foreseeable transboundary effects of proposed actions in their analysis of proposed actions in the United States.[66] In its guidance, CEQ underscored that its interpretation of NEPA did not expand the scope of actions that are subject to NEPA analysis or apply to "U.S. actions that take place in another country or otherwise outside the jurisdiction of the United States."[67] CEQ based its guidance on its construction of the text and purposes of NEPA as consistent with long-standing principles of international law.[68]

D.   Public and Agency Participation

While the heart of the EIA analysis may be its comparison of alternatives, the participation of affected interests is the soul of the EIA process. In the international setting, notifications that may be regularized in a domestic setting require a different set of rules to cover a new set of actors. The Espoo Convention approaches this problem from a principle of nondiscrimination with designated points of contact for the receipt of notifications in the same time and manner as domestic agencies.[69] These notification provisions require notice to the affected public as well as direct communications between states. To address the information needs of the state conducting the EIA, the Convention requires affected states to provide information that can be reasonably obtained in response to the party conducting the EIA.[70]

While most domestic EIA systems provide for multiple notifications at significant stages of the EIA process, the duty to consult under the Convention arises only after the completion of the EIA.[71] This approach misses the opportunity to engage in an iterative process of impact assessment of mitigation that is the goal of many domestic EIA processes[72] and is reflected in the provisions for EIA processes in international agreements on particular environmental impacts.[73] Following principles of nondiscrimination, states that consult with the public during scoping or other points earlier in the EIA process will afford these same opportunities to other states and their citizens. By requiring communications at both the state-to-state level and the level of a state communicating with foreign individuals, the Convention supports environmental democracy as a means of ensuring the quality of EIA analysis and the identification of mitigation opportunities. In its support of transparency in decision making and conflict resolution, the political purposes of EIA are themselves supported.

While the Espoo Convention achieves these purposes indirectly, the Aarhus Convention provides a significant supplement of minimum standards for access to information and opportunities for public participation. The Aarhus Convention provides a broader list of covered activities and a broader focus on participation in environmental decision making by all concerned members of the public. Thus, like NEPA, the Aarhus Convention addresses environmental impacts without regard to national boundaries.[74] Moreover, the Aarhus Convention brings a human rights dimension to the conduct of national EIA processes by member states by their recognition that "every person has the right to live in an environment adequate to his or her health and well-being."[75] Rather than limit its provisions to a threshold of significance, however determined in domestic EIA systems, the Aarhus Convention broadens the invitation to participate to the entire "public affected or likely to be affected by, or having an interest in, the environmental decision-making."[76]

The human rights elements of the Aarhus Convention broaden to all persons the guarantee of rights that have been particularly focused on environmentally vulnerable indigenous persons. Public participation and impact assessment requirements implement Principle 22 of the Rio Declaration in its recognition of the "vital role in environmental management and development" for indigenous people and other local communities.[77] Principle 22 calls on states to support the identity, culture, and interests of indigenous communities and "enable their effective participation in the achievement of sustainable development."[78] In 2007, the U.N. Declaration on the Rights of Indigenous Persons restated this principle in its recognition "that respect for indigenous knowledge, cultures and traditional practices contributes to sustainable and equitable development and proper management of the environment."[79] Though it lacks explicit references to EIA as a means of implementing its provisions, many of its 46 Articles provide for informed consultation and participation in decision making that characterize the goals of EIA processes.[80]

E.   Final Decision

The culmination of domestic EIA processes is a decision document that explains the agency choice among the alternatives considered. Under NEPA, this Record of Decision serves to identify the trade-offs between alternatives and the application of decision-making standards such as essential policy considerations and a related cost-benefit analysis.[81] The policy goals of NEPA are reinforced by requiring the agency to identify the "environmentally preferable alternative," explain why if that alternative is not selected, and explain its decision with regard to the adoption or rejection of mitigation measures.[82] The final agency decision is subject to judicial review under a deferential review for agency action that is "arbitrary, capricious, and abuse of discretion or otherwise not in accordance with law."[83]

International EIA obligations follow the same model, but in the absence of an international system for judicial review, the documentation of the reasons for selection of an alternative serves as the sole measure of the state's adherence to its international obligations. For example, the Espoo Convention does not act as a prohibition on the selection of an alternative that will have significant transboundary impact. Rather, compliance with Article 2 of the Convention serves to ensure that the harms entailed and interests affected are fully considered by the parties. The parties demonstrate compliance by taking "due account" of the analysis and interests articulated by the affected states and the affected public.[84] This reliance on documentation of the state's reasons and countervailing considerations as a means of enforcement is supplemented, but not materially affected, by the Aarhus Convention provisions for investigation of the state's reasoning by an independent panel upon petition by a party member of the public concerned.[85]

F.   Decision Implementation and Follow-Up

EIA regimes are frequently criticized for relying on predictive analyses without ensuring verification and adaptation to the actual environmental consequences of the decision making that EIA is intended to inform.[86] The Espoo Convention addresses this tendency by providing for continuing disclosure of relevant information that becomes available after the decision.[87] The obligations of disclosure apply to both the originating and affected states until the activity is commenced.[88] While this new information may provide the basis for a new round of consultations, the Convention lacks provisions for supplementation that would require the originating state to reconsider its decision.

This approach contrasts with NEPA, which has been construed to require consideration of EIS supplementation while the agency action remains substantially incomplete.[89] Supplementation is required if the agency makes "substantial changes in the proposed action that are relevant to environmental concerns" or it finds that there are "significant new circumstances or information relevant to environmental concerns and bearing on the proposed action or its impacts."[90] Even a completed action can be subject to a monitoring and enforcement program, which NEPA's implementing regulations require as an element of the Record of Decision "where applicable for any mitigation."[91] Mitigation and other conditions established in the EIS, or during its review, and committed to as part of the Record of Decision must be implemented by the lead agency or "other appropriate consenting agency."[92] The lead agency must also inform cooperating or commenting agencies on progress in carrying out their proposed mitigation measures that were adopted in the Record of Decision and "make available to the public the results of relevant monitoring."[93] CEQ has also advised that when agencies premise their environmental analysis on a commitment to mitigate the environmental impacts of a proposed action, they should adhere to those commitments, monitor how they are implemented, and monitor the effectiveness of the mitigation in public reports.[94]

IV.   EIA and SEA

In 1978, when CEQ promulgated regulations implementing procedural provisions of NEPA, CEQ sought to address criticism of the NEPA process as an after-the-fact documentation of the environmental consequences of decisions that had effectively been made before that EIA process commenced. CEQ addressed this criticism directly, by requiring agencies to commence preparation of an EIS as close as possible to the time the agency is developing or is presented with a proposal so that preparation can be completed in time for the final statement to be included in any recommendation or report on the proposal and "early enough so that it can serve practically as an important contribution to the decision-making process and will not be used to rationalize or justify decisions already made."[95] CEQ also provided for EISs for "broad [f]ederal actions," such as the adoption of new agency programs or regulations, and required EISs on broad actions so that they are "relevant to policy and are timed to coincide with meaningful points in agency planning and decisionmaking."[96] Federal agencies typically use these broad, "programmatic" EISs to make strategic decisions regarding actions occurring in the same general location or actions having relevant similarities, such as common timing, impacts, alternatives, methods of implementation, media, technology, or subject matter.[97]

Similarly, the Espoo Convention encourages its parties to apply EIA to "policies, plans, and programmes" in addition to its project-specific EIA requirements.[98] By 2001, when the European Commission adopted its directive on SEA, this approach to EIA had developed into an important element of domestic environmental decision-making processes.[99] In 2003, the parties to the Convention adopted a SEA protocol that is not limited to transboundary effects, but requires the parties to conduct SEA for specified plans and programs that are likely to have significant environmental effects wherever those effects occur.[100] In 2005, the World Bank established a pilot program to test and promote SEA by applying institution-centered SEA approaches in policy and sector reform.[101] These SEA programs seek greater integration of EIA processes at the level and time where broader social and economic policy decisions are made.

Notes

1. Nicholas A. Robinson, *The 1991 Bellagio Conference on U.S.-U.S.S.R. Environmental Protection Institution: International Trends in Environmental Impact Assessment*, 19 B.C. Envtl. Aff. L. Rev. 591 (1991–1992).

2. Joseph Foti et al., Voice and Choice: Opening the Door to Environmental Democracy, at ix (2008), http://www.wri.org/publication/voice-and-choice.

3. 42 U.S.C. § 4321.

4. *See* https://www.elaw.org/node/5986.

5. Council Directive 85/337 of June 27, 1985, on the Assessment of the Effects of Certain Public and Private Projects on the Environment. 1985 O.J. (I.175). "Member States shall adopt all measures necessary to ensure that, before consent is given, projects likely to have significant effects on the environment by virtue, inter alia, of their nature, size or location are made subject to an assessment with regard to their effects." *Id.* art. 2.1.

6. UN Doc. A/CONF.151/26, 31 I.L.M. 874 (1992).

7. OECD DAC SEA Guidance (2006), http://www.seataskteam.net/guidance.php.

8. 42 U.S.C. § 4331(a).

9. Foti et al., *supra* note 2, at 3.

10. Biodiversity Conservation Ctr., Main Benefits of Public Participation, http://www.biodiversity.ru/coastlearn/pp-eng/benefits.html.

11. Marianne Dellinger, *Ten Years of the Aarhus Convention: How Procedural Democracy Is Paving the Way for Substantive Change in National and International Environmental Law*, 23 Colo. J. Int'l Envtl. L. & Pol'y 314 (2012).

12. *See* http://www.un-documents.net/ocf-02.htm.

13. World Comm'n on Envt. & Dev., Our Common Future, ch. 2 ¶ 80 (1987), *available at* http://www.un-documents.net/ocf-02.htm.

14. *Id.* at ¶ 77.

15. *Id.* at ¶ 78.

16. *Id.* at ¶¶ 79–80.

17. United Nations Conference on Environment and Development, Rio de Janeiro, Brazil, June 3–14, 1992, *Agenda 21*, ¶ 23.2, U.N. Doc. A/CONF.151/26 (Vol. III) *available at* http://sustainabledevelopment.un.org/content/documents/Agenda21.pdf.

18. *Id.* at ¶ 10.

19. Convention on Environmental Impact Assessment in a Transboundary Context art. 2(6), Feb. 25, 1991, 1989 U.N.T.S. 309, *available at* http://www.unece.org/env/eia/eia.html. *See also* art. 4, para. 2 regarding public participation.

20. *Foreword, in* Aarhus Convention Implementation Guide (2000), http://www.unece.org/fileadmin/DAM/env/pp/ppdm/Aarhus_Implementation_Guide_second_edition_-_text_only.pdf.

21. *Id.* at 15 (citing *Case concerning the Gabčíkovo-Nagymaros Project* (Hungary/Slovakia).

22. *Id.* at 6.

23. *Id.* at 6.

24. Dellinger, *supra* note 11, at 322.

25. The "public" is defined to include "natural or legal persons, and, in accordance with national legislation or practice, their associations, organizations or groups." Aarhus Convention art. 3.

26. Aarhus Convention art. 2(5).

27. Dellinger, *supra* note 11, at 357.

28. *Id.*

29. Craik, The International Law of Environmental Impact Assessment 27 (2010). *See also* J. Holder, Environmental Assessment: The Regulation of Decision Making (2004); Christopher Wood, Environmental Impact Assessment: A Comparative Review (2d ed. 2002).

30. Robinson, *supra* note 1, at 603.

31. Craik, *supra* note 29, at 133 (citing UNEP EIA Goals and Principles, the Espoo Convention, the Convention on Biological Diversity, the U.S.-Canada Air Quality Agreement, and the regional seas agreements).

32. *Id.*

33. D.P. Lawrence, *Impact Significance Determination—Designing and Approach*, 27 Envtl. Impact Assessment Rev. 730, 731 (2007).

34. *Id.* at 736–37. This approach presupposes a decision-making model that is interactive, with government agencies focused on facilitating the direct and ongoing involvement of interested and affected parties in impact significance determinations. *Id.* at 737. This approach can facilitate public understanding and involvement, integrate community and traditional knowledge, and contribute to dialogue, mutual learning, and creative problem-solving that foster local and regional empowerment and democratic decision making. *Id.* at 742. It can also be inefficient, particularly where it involves multiple parties with limited potential for consensus. *Id.* at 738.

35. *Id.* at 745.

36. *Id.*

37. Espoo Convention, *supra* note 17, art. 2(3).

38. *Id.* art. 3(7).

39. Craik, *supra* note 29, at 136.

40. *See* Convention on Biological Diversity EIA guidelines, Biodiversity in Impact Assessment, Background Document to Decision VIII/28 of the Convention on Biological Diversity: Voluntary Guidelines on Biodiversity-Inclusive Impact Assessment, http://www.cbd.int/doc/publications/cbd-ts-26-en.pdf [hereinafter CBD EIA Guidelines].

41. 42 U.S.C. § 4332(2)(C).

42. 40 C.F.R. § 1508.27. While "NEPA requires considerations of both context and intensity" under the CEQ regulations, the responsible agency official may use a technical, collaborative, or rational argumentation model in analyzing the significance of an action's context (societal, regional, the affected interests, and the locality) and intensity (the severity of impacts), as appropriate to the substantive and procedural requirements of other applicable laws.

43. 40 C.F.R. § 1505.1, 1507.3.

44. 40 C.F.R. § 1501.4.

45. DOT v. Pub. Citizen, 541 U.S. 752, 769–70 (2004).

46. 40 C.F.R. § 1501.4.

47. This "categorical exclusion" from more detailed action-specific environmental analysis is defined as "a category of actions which do not individually or cumulatively have a significant effect on the human environment and which have been found to have no such effect in procedures adopted by a [f]ederal agency in implementation of these regulations [40 C.F.R. § 1507.3] and for which, therefore, neither an environmental assessment nor an environmental impact statement is required." 40 C.F.R. § 1508.4.

48. Memorandum from Nancy H. Sutley, Chair, CEQ, to Heads of Fed. Dep'ts & Agencies, Establishing, Applying, and Revising Categorical Exclusions under the National Environmental Policy Act (Nov. 23, 2010), at 7–8, http://ceq.hss.doe.gov/ceq_regula tions/NEPA_CE_Guidance_Nov232010.pdf.

49. 40 C.F.R. § 1508.4.

50. CEQ Memorandum, *supra* note 48, at 5.

51. Craik, *supra* note 29, at 139.

52. Espoo Convention, *supra* note 17, art. II.

53. 42 U.S.C. § 4332(2)(C).

54. Craik, *supra* note 29, at 140; Int'l Law Comm'n, *Draft Articles on Prevention of Transboundary Harm from Hazardous Activities, in* Report of the International Law Comm'n, Fifty-Third Session, UN GAOR 56th Sess. Supp. No. 10, UN Doc. A/56/10 (2001) 370, art. 10.

55. *See* CBD EIA Guidelines, *supra* note 40.

56. *Id.* at 27–28.

57. UNEP, Goals and Principles of Environmental Impact Assessment, UNEP Res. GC14/25, 14th Sess. (1987).

58. *Id.*

59. 40 C.F.R. § 1508.7.

60. Kleppe v. Sierra Club, 427 U.S. 390, 413–14 (1976).

61. CEQ Guidance on the Consideration of the Cumulative Effects of Past Actions, http://ceq.hss.doe.gov/nepa/regs/Guidance_on_CE.pdf.

62. DOT v. Pub. Citizen, 541 U.S. 752, 769–70 (2004).

63. OECD, Recommendations on the Implementation of a Regime of Equal Access and Non-discrimination in Relation to Transfrontier Pollution, C(77)28 Final (May 17, 1977), http://acts.oecd.org/Instruments/ShowInstrumentView.aspx?InstrumentID=17&L ang=en&Book=False.

64. *See, e.g.,* Canadian Environmental Assessment Act, SC 1997, c.37, s.16(1).

65. Exec. Order 12,114, 3 C.F.R. § 356.

66. Memorandum from Kathleen A. McGinty, Chair, CEQ, to Heads of Agencies, Application of the National Environmental Policy Act to Proposed Federal Actions in the United States with Transboundary Effects (July 1, 1997), http://ceq.hss.doe.gov/nepa /regs/transguide.html.

67. *Id.*

68. *Id.* at n.20 (citing *Trail Smelter Arbitration,* United States v. Canada, 3 UN Rep. Int'l Arbit. Awards 1911 (1941)).

69. Espoo Convention art. 3.

70. *Id.* art. 3(6).

71. *Id.* art. 5.

72. *See* 40 C.F.R. § 1501.7 ("There shall be an early and open process for determining the scope of issues to be addressed and for identifying the significant issues related to a proposed action."), § 1506.6 (public involvement).

73. *See* CBD EIA Guidelines, *supra* note 40.

74. Craik, *supra* note 29, at 149.

75. Aarhus Convention, pmbl.

76. Aarhus Convention art. 2(5).

77. UNCED, Rio Declaration on Environment and Development, June 14, 1992, UN Doc. A/Conf.151/5/Rev.1, Principle 22.

78. *Id.*

79. United Nations Declaration on the Rights of Indigenous Peoples, 61/295 (Sept. 13, 2007), *available at* http://www.un.org/esa/socdev/unpfii/documents/DRIPS_en.pdf.

80. *See, e.g., id.* art. 32(2) ("States shall consult and cooperate in good faith with the indigenous peoples concerned through their own representative institutions in order to obtain their free and informed consent prior to the approval of any project affecting their lands or territories and other resources, particularly in connection with the development, utilization or exploitation of mineral, water or other resources.").

81. 40 C.F.R. § 1505.2.

82. *Id.*

83. 5 U.S.C. § 706(a)(2).

84. Espoo Convention art. 6(1).

85. Aarhus Convention art. 6(9).

86. Craik, The International Law of Environmental Impact Assessment 27 (2010). *See also* J. Holder, Environmental Assessment: The Regulation of Decision Making (2004); Christopher Wood, Environmental Impact Assessment: A Comparative Review (2d ed. 2002).

87. Espoo Convention art. 6(3).

88. *Id.*

89. Marsh v. Or. Nat. Res. Council, 490 U.S. 360, 374 (1988). *See also* Norton v. S. Utah Wilderness Alliance, 542 U.S. 55, 73 (2004).

90. 40 C.F.R. § 1502.9(c).

91. 40 C.F.R. § 1505.2(c).

92. 40 C.F.R. § 1505.3.

93. 40 C.F.R. § 1505.3(c), (d).

94. *See* Memorandum from Nancy H. Sutley, Chair, CEQ, to Heads of Fed. Dep'ts & Agencies, Appropriate Use of Mitigation and Monitoring and Clarifying the Appropriate Use of Mitigated Findings of No Significant Impact (Jan. 14, 2011), http://ceq.hss.doe .gov/current_developments/docs/Mitigation_and_Monitoring_Guidance_14Jan2011.pdf.

95. 40 C.F.R. § 1502.5.

96. 40 C.F.R. § 1502.4(b).

97. 40 C.F.R. § 1502.4(c). *See, e.g.,* Dep'ts of Energy & Interior, Project Summary, http://solareis.anl.gov/ ("The Office of Energy Efficiency and Renewable Energy (EERE), Department of Energy (DOE); and the Bureau of Land Management (BLM), Department of the Interior (DOI), have prepared a Programmatic Environmental Impact Statement to evaluate utility-scale solar energy development, to develop and implement agency-specific programs or guidance that would establish environmental policies and mitigation strategies for solar energy projects, and to amend relevant Bureau of Land Management (BLM) land use plans with the consideration of establishing a new BLM Solar Energy Program.").

98. Espoo Convention art. 2(7).

99. Assessment of the Effects of Certain Plans and Programmes on the Environment, EC Council Directive 01/42, OJ 2001 L197/30.

100. UNECE, Protocol on SEA, http://www.unece.org/env/eia/sea_protocol.html.

101. World Bank, Strategic Environmental Assessment in Policy and Sector Reform (2011).

CHAPTER 14

Transboundary Pollution

MICHAEL G. FAURE

I. Introduction

The central theme of this volume is undoubtedly the globalization of environmental law. This globalization of legal instruments and institutions is driven by the increasingly transboundary nature of pollution. As a result, domestic practitioners are increasingly confronted with problems whose solutions require navigating laws across multiple jurisdictions. This chapter wishes to contribute to the understanding of international environmental regimes by identifying some of the key issues that will arise if a practitioner is confronted with a transboundary pollution case. The objective of this chapter is hence not to indicate the details on how to resolve a particular case, because this will very often be domain specific (depending on whether it, for example, constitutes water pollution, air pollution, or transboundary waste). The goal is rather to guide the practitioner through the complexity of international and national environmental laws and to explain their relationship and overall structure. To be most useful, this chapter should be read in connection with the other chapters in this volume.

We will explain how the transboundary character of a particular pollution problem may affect the way in which the problem has to be approached. Specific attention will be paid to the relationship between international environmental conventions and national law. To an important extent, as we will argue, transboundary pollution cases will rely on national (tort) law, but there are particular ways in which international law can (increasingly) influence adjudication by national courts. There is indeed a trend, at least in particular jurisdictions, to take into account obligations under international law even in adjudicating domestic pollution cases.

Multilateral treaties dealing with transboundary pollution are, of course, relevant to resolving such cases. U.S.-based practitioners should be aware, however, that the United States has not joined a number of key international regimes, and has instead drafted its own legislation (which, incidentally, often provides better protection to pollution victims than the international

235

regime). Some international treaties may hence be less relevant in a U.S. environmental practice than in Europe or elsewhere.

This chapter discusses in detail a number of cases—both at the international level as well as in Europe and in the United States—that dealt with transboundary pollution. While not directly applicable beyond a particular jurisdiction, the cases illustrate general issues that come up when dealing with transboundary pollution cases.

Though most transboundary cases involve private clients in a national court (in the United States or abroad), transboundary pollution cases can also play out between states. Under the traditional paradigm, international law was limited to providing obligations and rights to states and hence does not affect rights and obligations of actors in national jurisdictions. Yet review of case law suggests the blurring of such previously strict boundaries between international law and national law. Indeed, some national courts increasingly are willing to infer obligations from international law, which could equally be applicable within the national legal context. Some of these, admittedly rather revolutionary, trends come from the Netherlands, a rather small European country in which there are nonetheless a remarkably high number of adjudicated cases dealing with transboundary pollution. The Dutch cases indicate the kind of legal issues that come up when dealing with a transboundary pollution case and hence add to the checklist to be followed when dealing with transboundary pollution cases in practice. The experience of the Netherlands may also suggest potential directions in which practice in other jurisdictions may develop as transboundary pollution issues become more prevalent.

The remainder of this chapter is set up as follows: We briefly sketch why transboundary pollution occurs and how transboundary pollution should be viewed from an economic perspective (section II). Next, we assess various possible approaches to transboundary pollution, distinguishing between the role of national courts in resolving transboundary pollution conflicts and the resolution of transboundary environmental dispute between states (section III). The remainder of the contribution will focus on the role of national courts in resolving transboundary pollution conflicts. A first issue that arises in that respect is to what extent international law will also affect the adjudication of a case in a national court (section IV); next, unavoidably, questions of the competent forum and applicable law will arise (section V), as well as the actors, legal bases and potential remedies (section VI). The chapter concludes by providing a tentative checklist that a practitioner confronted with a transboundary pollution case could follow when he/she is presumably consulted by a victim of transboundary pollution (section VII).

II.   Why Transboundary Pollution?

It seems like pushing at an open door to argue that one way in which environmental problems have "gone global" is that pollution problems have increasingly become transboundary.[1] To a large extent, this may be the result of an increased awareness of the transboundary character of environmental pollution.[2] Environmental pollution probably always had a transboundary character, but increased technological abilities better allow pollution's effects to be traced across borders to its source.[3] Environmental awareness originally focused on so-called point source pollution coming from particular identifiable sources (such as emissions by factories), the immediate harms such pollution caused to workers and then, later, the impacts of such pollution to local soil and surface or ground waters.[4] But even during the early stages of industrialization, emissions by particular factories may have caused transboundary air and water pollution. At that time, however, there was not the necessary technical ability to trace the sources of that pollution. In the second half of the last century, as a result of an increasing awareness that many environmental problems have a transboundary character, attention shifted to the impacts of long-range air pollution and acid rain.[5]

From an economic perspective, the basic problem is that local industry exports environmental pollution, leading to a de facto "externalization" of pollution problems. Economists have often argued that the reasons for the transboundary character of environmental pollution problems are well known: local politicians will not have many incentives to act strongly against polluters who may be able to export large quantities of pollution outside the borders of the national territory. Thus the polluting activity could result in socioeconomic benefits for the nation (increased tax revenues and job security), whereas the negative effects (referred to as externalities by economists) are exported to the neighboring countries.[6] Because politicians need to be reelected by the citizens within their particular state, their primary concern may not be with the transboundary effects of pollution caused by factories within their nation. Seen in this context, it is unsurprising that such an externalization of pollution to other countries takes place.

Just as within the national context externalities are considered a market failure to which the law should react, the same is true for transboundary environmental harm. In the absence of legal rules that force countries to take into account the transboundary pollution they cause, states will have no incentives to do so. The primary goal of international environmental law should, therefore, from this simple economic perspective, be no other than the internalization of the transboundary externality caused by pollution.

Of course, some economists may argue that it is not necessary to use legal rules to internalize externalities: Ronald Coase taught that as long as transaction costs are zero, an efficient internalization, of both domestic and transboundary externalities, could take place via bargaining between the parties.[7] Some economists have indeed suggested that, for example, as far as small-scale pollution is concerned, this type of bargaining may result in an efficient internalization of the harm.[8] However, experience shows that so far very few transboundary pollution cases have been solved through efficient bargaining. Even in cases where there are only two parties involved (for example, an upstream polluting state and a downstream victim state) bargaining leading to the victim state paying the polluter state to install efficient pollution reduction mechanisms is rare. Even though transaction costs are low, there may be a variety of reasons why efficient bargaining does not take place, one of them being strategic behavior by the states or political failures as a result of which states would be insufficiently willing to represent the interests of those (small number of) victims actually suffering the harm. Moreover, as soon as the transboundary pollution passes the boundaries of multiple states, complicated causation issues arise and multiple parties must engage in negotiation, and it becomes clear that bargaining is unlikely to generate efficient results.

Economists argue that the transboundary character of an externality, like environmental pollution, is one of the primary reasons in favor of shifting powers to a higher level of government.[9] Hence, there are strong arguments from an economic perspective that shifting powers to a higher level of government is an efficient reaction to transboundary pollution. That explains why larger or federal government entities, such as the European Union (EU) or the U.S. government, tend to focus more closely on transboundary pollution problems. Likewise, a central goal of international treaties at the core of international environmental law is this internalization of transboundary environmental externalities.

III.   Various Approaches to Transboundary Pollution

The problem of transboundary pollution may be addressed in two distinct legal fora: (1) disputes between non-state actors before courts of national jurisdiction applying national law or (2) disputes between states before courts of international jurisdiction.

A.   Extraterritoriality of National Tort Law

1.   Applying National Law to Transboundary Pollution

The most likely way in which most practitioners will be confronted with a transboundary pollution case is when, for example, a victim in the United States claims to have suffered harm coming from Canada. The question that arises in that respect is whether national law (in this example U.S. law) can be applied to this transboundary pollution case. To some extent, this amounts to an extraterritorial application of national tort law, because the national tort law of (usually) the victim's state will be applied to pollution, which has its origin in the polluter's state.

The approach of applying national tort law to transboundary pollution cases has some serious limits. If the number of polluters becomes very large or the damage very widespread, complicated causation issues may arise and the scope for applying national tort law may become more limited. For those cases, the argument in favor of regulation through international conventions becomes stronger.[10] Nevertheless, there are many who argue that national tort laws can also be used to tackle even complicated problems where many causation questions arise. In this respect, applying liability law has even been suggested in the literature as a remedy for damage caused by climate change.[11] Given the many weaknesses in international treaties in remedying transboundary pollution (more particularly the well-known problems of compliance and enforcement),[12] there may be ample reasons not to exclude the possibility to apply national tort law to transboundary pollution cases.

2.   A Few Cases

Many countries in Europe, and more particularly the Netherlands, have developed considerable experience with the application of national liability law to transboundary pollution cases. Here, we provide a brief overview of the cases that have arisen in the Netherlands, in order to illuminate the type of questions that arise in the use of liability to remedy transboundary pollution problems.[13]

In an important decision—the *Bier* case[14]—the European Court of Justice held in 1976 that by European treaty,[15] a victim of interstate pollution may sue either in the courts of the country where the damage occurred, or in the courts for the place of the event that gives rise to and is at the origin of that damage.[16] A series of Dutch cases decided under the authority of *Bier*[17] established within Europe (where federal judicial powers do not exist) a regime under which transboundary pollution disputes are resolved through a de facto extraterritorial application of national law to foreign polluters. The substantive content of the interstate pollution entitlement emerging from these decisions is one that involves a balancing of the value of the polluting activity against the harm to downstream victims. In *Bier* itself (a suit by Dutch market gardeners against a French mining company), the Supreme Court of the Netherlands held that in deciding the liability of the upstream polluter, the seriousness and the duration of the damage inflicted on the downstream users has to be taken into account as well as the gravity of the interests served by the discharges.

Similarly, in the decision of the Hoge Raad (the Netherlands Supreme Court), the Dutch court held that "it should be borne in mind that on weighing these mutual interests a special weight accrues to the interests of the user downstream in so far that in principle he may expect that the river is not excessively polluted by large-scale discharges."[18] A second Dutch case that is equally interesting was launched by an environmental non-governmental organization (NGO), Reinwater, against a Belgian polluter, Sopar. The plaintiffs demanded and received an injunction against Sopar to discontinue or at least limit the discharges of Polycyclic Aromatic Hydrocarbons on the basis of best available technical means. Reinwater asserted that Sopar's discharges into the Gent-Terneuzen Channel, just over the Dutch border, constituted a wrongful act. Because Sopar grossly disregarded the conditions of its Belgian permit, the Dutch Court of Appeal of The Hague had no difficulty in allowing Reinwater's claim for compliance with the permit. In a decision of November 19, 1992, the court ordered Sopar to fully comply with all conditions of its permit under a penalty of 50,000 Dutch guilders[19] for each day that it remained in noncompliance.[20]

Another case illustrating such extraterritorial pollution control is a suit that pitted an NGO named Rhine Water (in the Netherlands) against Cockerill NV, a large manufacturing company situated in Belgium in the neighborhood of Liège. Cockerill NV emitted directly into the river Meuse. In determining the lawfulness of Cockerill's discharges, the president of the Court of Maastricht (the Netherlands) asked whether Cockerill's discharges exceeded a "reasonable limit," and to determine what might constitute such a limit, looked to Dutch regulatory standards for emissions like Cockerill's.[21] Because the president of the court held that this was not the case, the emissions were not considered unlawful.

B.   Dispute Resolution between States

Formal dispute resolution between states formerly took place via the Permanent Court of International Justice. Today, such dispute resolution occurs via international tribunals such as the International Court of Justice (ICJ) (to the extent that the states where the dispute occurs have accepted jurisdiction of the court). However, the number of international environmental disputes between states settled through formal adjudication is small. Sands reports that the ICJ established a seven member chamber for environmental matters in 1993 but that it had in 2003 not yet been utilized.[22] Because the ICJ Chamber for Environmental Matters in the 13 years of its existence never received any case, the court decided in 2006 not to reconstitute this chamber.[23]

In resolving transboundary environmental disputes between states, parties often avoid the formal approach of going (at the time) to the Permanent Court of International Justice and (today) to the International Court of Justice. For example, the Dutch government instituted proceedings before the Permanent Court of International Justice in 1936 related to water diversions from the river Meuse only after more than 20 years of negotiations with Belgium led nowhere.[24] Strategic behavior by the lobbies of the Rotterdam and Antwerp harbors blocked any initiative that might benefit either party.[25] The general (not surprising) tenet in the literature reviewing the resolution of transboundary environmental justice is that parties will basically first try all diplomatic means available. Dispute resolution through courts is only sought when bargaining through diplomatic channels has (for a variety of reasons) failed. And even if formal dispute resolution is sought it is often by way of arbitration.

A few cases can illustrate the resolution of transboundary environmental disputes between states.

1.   The Trail Smelter Arbitration

One of the most cited environmental disputes is the *Trail Smelter* arbitration.[26] It concerned a dispute between Canada and the United States resulting from air pollution emanating from a private company in British Columbia (Canada) and causing damage to private property in the U.S. State of Washington. Extensive diplomatic negotiations between the parties led to the conclusion of an ad hoc arbitration convention.[27] In the final judgment of March 11, 1941, the arbitrators came to the often quoted sentence that

> Under principles of international law, as well as the law of the United States, no state has the right to use or permit the use of its territory in such a manner as to cause injury by fumes in or on to the territory of another or the properties or persons therein.[28]

On that basis, the tribunal held Canada responsible under international law for the conduct of the smelter. More interesting is that after this uncertainty had been clarified, the *Trail Smelter* dispute was satisfactorily settled.[29] Romano argues that the arbitrators were mostly concerned with finding practical solutions satisfactory to all parties rather than stating the broad legal principle for which they later became famous.[30] Recently Knox has criticized this decision, arguing that the arbitration was before the wrong tribunal, between the wrong parties, and applied the wrong law. Instead of an international body, a national court should have been used, primarily applying domestic and not international law, by private litigants rather than by states.[31] Moreover, recently there was a second trail smelter case, now concerning leachate of heavy metals from the deposited tailings, which caused harm to the environment and human health. The plaintiff was an affected member of an Indian tribe living in the United States. The recent cases addressed plaintiff's attempt to enforce a U.S. Environmental Protection Agency (EPA) unilateral administrative order to remediate the contamination under the Comprehensive Environmental Response, Compensation, and Liability Act (CERCLA).[32] The U.S. courts held in that case that the plaintiffs—Mr. Pakootas, other members of the Indian tribes, and the State of Washington—had adequately alleged a claim under CERCLA against the Canadian polluter (Teck Cominco), though the contamination originated from the Canadian smelter. Some argue that these decisions constitute an important first extraterritorial application of CERCLA.[33]

2. *Iceland Fisheries and Bluefin Tuna*

In some cases, the court does not specify the entitlements in a clear and defined way, but rather sheds light on a few issues and subsequently sends the parties back to the negotiating table. One such case is the Icelandic fisheries jurisdiction dispute (sometimes referred to as the cod war), an incident between Iceland on the one hand and the United Kingdom (and partially Germany) on the other hand concerning fishing rights.[34] The dispute itself related to the question of whether only Iceland had fishing rights in its coastal waters, more particularly in a fishery zone around Iceland, or whether others (such as the United Kingdom) could enjoy fishing rights as well.[35] In its judgment of July 25, 1974, the court found that regulations of 1972 extending

Icelandic fisheries jurisdiction limits to 50 miles were not applicable to the United Kingdom (and Germany) and that accordingly Iceland could not unilaterally exclude British (and German) fishing vessels from the zone between 12 and 50 miles from Icelandic coasts. More importantly, the court held that parties were under a mutual obligation to negotiate a settlement of the dispute that would take into consideration not only Iceland's entitlement to a preferential share of the fishing resources in the area, and the United Kingdom's and Germany's established rights over the resources, but also the interests of third-party states in the conservation and equitable exploitation of these resources.[36]

Commentators argued that the court's resolution of the entitlements in the Iceland fisheries jurisdiction case was intentionally ambiguous. The court specifically refrained from touching the issue of the precise width of exclusive fishing zones, and from stating that a 50-mile limit would be contrary to international law. Romano notes that the judgment of the court came at the time when many parties were negotiating the U.N. Convention on the Law of the Sea where many participants were claiming fisheries jurisdiction limits equal if not wider than those claimed by Iceland. Hence, Romano contends, the court had an interest in formulating the entitlement in a rather ambiguous way to avoid interfering with negotiations at the U.N. conference or risk being proven wrong by the majority of the states at the U.N. conference.[37]

In the aftermath of the case, an agreement was reached between Iceland and Germany and with the United Kingdom as well. Later, many jurisdictions agreed to establish a joint fisheries commission charged with fixing species catch quotas.[38]

A second noteworthy case again concerned fish, but this time southern bluefin tuna. The dispute arose between Australia and New Zealand against Japan, and was decided by the International Tribunal for the Law of the Sea (ITLOS).[39] The case dealt (again) with a conflict between coastal and long-distance fishing states and resulted in a provisional measures order on August 27, 1999. The tribunal ordered all parties to ensure no action is taken that might aggravate or extend the dispute pending the constitution of the arbitral tribunal. It also prescribed that all parties refrain from conducting an experimental fishing program, unless by consensus and unless the experimental catch is counted against national annual allocations. The tribunal moreover recommended explicitly that negotiations be resumed without delay with a view to reaching an agreement on the conservation and management of the southern bluefin tuna.[40] Thus, the tribunal again consciously decided only a set of defined aspects of the dispute that was before it, with the goal of prompting negotiation.

3. Gabcikovo-Nagymaros

A third case illustrative of the tendency of courts or arbitrators to encourage negotiations rather than providing final determinations of entitlements is the well-known dispute between Hungary and Slovakia concerning the Gabcikovo-Nagymaros project. The dispute arose over a 1977 treaty providing for the construction and joint operation of the Gabcikovo-Nagymaros barrage system. This provided that Hungary and (at the time) Czechoslovakia agreed to build a dam and a reservoir. Several years later, the Hungarian parliament (as a result of public pressure) held that ecological interests should take priority over economic considerations and prompted the government to order a reevaluation of the project. This led to the suspension of the construction work on the barrage. The Czechoslovak government, however, decided to continue to work on the construction. In 1992, following the failure to settle the dispute, Hungary filed its original application with the ICJ and later Czechoslovakia diverted a significant proportion of the Danube into a by-pass canal.[41]

Hungary declared a "state of ecological necessity" to justify its refusal to continue the dam project. The ICJ, however, found in its decision that the perils invoked by Hungary were not sufficiently established, nor were they "imminent" because they were long term in nature and uncertain. Next, the ICJ also considered whether the diversion of the Danube carried out by Czechoslovakia was a lawful countermeasure and held that this was not the case because it was not proportional.

As far as the merits of the case are concerned, the ICJ held:

> The parties should look afresh at the effects on the environment of the operation of the Gabcikovo power plant. In particular they must find a satisfactory solution for the volume of water, to be released into the old bed of the Danube and into the side arms of both sides of the river.[42]

Remarkably, the ICJ considered that it was not for the court to determine the final result of the negotiations between the parties. The ICJ instructed the parties "to find an agreed solution that takes account of the objectives of the treaty, which must be pursued in a joint and integrated way, as well as the norms of international environmental law and the principles of the law of international water courses."[43]

This brief overview of the resolution of environmental disputes between states shows not only that the number of cases that is formally adjudicated is quite small, but also that courts will often not provide a final allocation of the entitlements, but rather provide the framework within which states can further negotiate a settlement. Though at first blush less relevant to domestic practitioners, international law cases can play a role and be called upon as a source of law in transboundary pollution cases in the domestic legal context. The remainder of this chapter examines what particular questions come up when dealing with such a transboundary pollution case before a domestic court.

IV. International Law in a Transboundary Liability Case

A. General: Monism versus Dualism

Many potential problems of transboundary pollution are now subject to international regulations in the form of treaties. States are parties to these treaties and the regime of the particular treaty will determine how the treaty is enforced and what sanctions may apply in case of noncompliance. Because, under classic international law, only states enjoy the benefits or face responsibility under a treaty, these instruments appear to be in a separate world from liability cases.[44] The reality, however, is a bit more complex. Typically non-state entities are confronted by the terms of a treaty through the national laws that implement that treaty. For example, the Paris Convention concerning civil liability in the domain of nuclear energy of July 29, 1960 (as many times amended), creates obligations for the licensee of a nuclear power plant in the ratifying states to obtain compulsory insurance coverage up to the amount specified in the convention. It also grants specific rights to victims to obtain compensation in case of a nuclear accident up to the limits specified in the convention.[45] These particular obligations or rights are made enforceable for individuals through national implementing legislation. What happens, however, if such treaty provisions have not been adequately implemented in national law or if, more generally, a state were to violate obligations (other than those arising from treaties) under international law? Suppose that the victim's *own state* fails to implement obligations under a treaty and that the victim claims to suffer damage as a result of the violation of treaty obligations. The question that interests us here is, of course, not whether such an omission gives rise to responsibility of the state under international law, but whether a particular individual could call on this violation of international law in a domestic court? The answer turns on whether the state of the victim adopts a "monistic" or a "dualistic" approach to international legal obligations.

In countries where a monistic approach is followed (such as the Netherlands, France, and Belgium), international law automatically becomes part of internal law and, provided that the obligations imposed upon the state in the treaty are sufficiently clear and precise (the typical wording in this respect is "self-executing") the victim can call directly on these provisions even if the state failed to take measures in national law to implement the obligations. This is not true in legal systems that have a dualistic approach (e.g., Germany).[46] In those systems, citizens cannot rely directly on international law as long as it has not been transposed into national law.

B.   Chernobyl Case: District Court of Bonn

A second, more interesting, question arises where a victim alleges harm as a result of a violation of international law by a foreign (not the victim's own) state. Suppose that a convention (or obligation of international customary law) were to oblige states to warn neighboring states and their citizens if a major nuclear incident took place as a result of which a nuclear cloud could come in the direction of the neighbors, necessitating preventive measures (e.g., putting cattle in the stables) in the neighboring states. Could a victim in the neighboring state rely on the liability of the polluter state if this obligation were violated and the victim suffered harm as a result? This was the question that had to be answered by the Civil Court of First Instance of Bonn in a claim filed by a gardener in Germany against the Soviet Union. The gardener argued that the Soviet Union had violated its obligation of early notification.[47] The German court held, not surprisingly, that there is no direct liability of the Soviet Union vis-à-vis the German gardener. If the Soviet Union had an obligation under international law to notify Germany and had not done so, this could only have amounted to liability under international law of the Soviet Union vis-à-vis Germany. The German court therefore adhered to the classic view that international norms cannot be called upon by one individual in a victim state to hold a polluter state liable.[48]

C. MDPA Case: Direct Application of International Law

Nevertheless, there can be situations where norms of international law do clearly play a role in transboundary liability suits.[49] In a case already mentioned, launched by various gardeners in the Netherlands in the 1970s against the Mines de Potasse d'Alsace (MDPA), the market gardeners contended that MDPA, by discharging salt in the Rhine, increased the salt burden of the water of the Rhine to such an extent that they could not make use any more of the water of the Rhine and suffered damage. This MDPA case has been extensively discussed in the literature[50] and has given rise to many judgments, even of the Supreme Court of the Netherlands.[51] The cases are noteworthy for their discussion of the relationship between international law and the rights of individuals suffering harm.

The most far-reaching approach[52] was provided by the District Court of Rotterdam handling the case in first instance.[53] The court held that because no rule of national law could be found to decide this case, it had to turn to unwritten international law and applied the principle that no state can use its territory for activities that cause harm to another state. The court referred to the well-known *Trail Smelter* case, which explicitly stated the principle of good neighborliness.[54] The court of appeals of The Hague, however, reversed this ruling.[55] The court held that direct effects of rules of international law applied exclusively to treaties and not to unwritten rules of international law. Professor Nollkaemper, however, argues that general principles of law can also satisfy the "self-executing test" and that, moreover, these general principles often find their origin in national law, where they do generally apply to individuals. He therefore concludes that the court of appeals

> did not expressly overrule (nor did it need to do so) the part of the judgment that sanctioned violation of the norm on the basis of international law. To that extent, this construction of direct application and enforcement of international law can still be said to exist in Dutch law.[56]

The MDPA case discusses another interesting aspect of the relationship between international law and national liability law. The attorney for the defendant argued that the lawfulness of the emissions by MDPA had to be seen in light of the Bonn Salt Treaty.[57] The defendant argued that the Netherlands and

France accession to this treaty, which aimed at reducing transborder pollution of the Rhine to acceptable levels for Dutch users, barred claims against MDPA for its discharges. MDPA claimed that this international treaty was determinative on matters relating to salt discharges from France into the Rhine. The Hoge Raad explicitly discusses this argument and rejects it on the following grounds:

> The argument of the count cannot be accepted as correct. Leaving aside that fact that the Treaty only became operative in 1985, while damages in this action are demanded as from 1974, it follows from the text and the purport of the Treaty that it only intends to impose obligations on the States that enter into the Treaty. There is no indication at all that the Treaty—which came into being when the action in question was already running—should also have in view the regulation of the internal relations of the subjects of that States entering into the Treaty, nor also that in this manner the judge in one of these States should be held to have to decide an action between those subjects on the basis of the Treaty.

The Supreme Court held, in other words, that the treaty was not relevant to determining the wrongfulness of the discharges by the French defendant because the treaty would only cover the relationship between parties to the treaty and not between private persons.[58]

D.   Nuclear and Oil Pollution Conventions

We already referred to the fact that in some cases, like for nuclear liability, international conventions create specific rights for victims on which victims can rely if the treaty has been properly implemented into national law. The United States, though often an active participant in international negotiations preceding the conclusion of a convention, commonly does not sign the convention. Instead, the United States relies on its own domestic legislation to address the subject of the international agreement. Two cases in point can illustrate this approach and make clear why from a U.S. perspective, domestic law is often preferred to international conventions.

1.   Nuclear Liability

As we already mentioned, in the 1960s international conventions were drafted with respect to nuclear liability under the auspices of the Nuclear Energy Agency (NEA) and the International Atomic Energy Agency (IAEA). The NEA drafted the Paris and Brussels Convention and was originally regionally confined to Western Europe, Slovenia, and Turkey. The IAEA drafted the Vienna Convention, which was worldwide in scope. These conventions contain a number of principles, such as strict liability, and exclusive operator liability, financial security, and exclusive jurisdiction.

Interestingly, the nuclear liability conventions were in fact initiated by the United States. At that time, the United States possessed a de facto monopoly of nuclear technology. The American nuclear industry feared potential liability for nuclear accidents in Europe, and two reports published in the United States advocated for exclusive imposition of liability on nuclear operators.[59] By limiting liability to the (European) operators, (American) suppliers and contractors would be exempted from liability.

This international regime has, however, been seriously criticized in the literature for several reasons: the limitation on liability seriously limits the victim's rights to compensation and public funding (by the operator's state and all contracting parties) lead to a de facto subsidization of the nuclear industry. Moreover, because nuclear operators are not fully exposed to the costs of nuclear accidents, this could negatively affect their incentives for prevention.[60] The financial cap on the liability of the operators means that operators are not liable to pay all costs but also up to the limit. Hence, not only has liability been shifted from suppliers to operators; the operators are, moreover, not held to compensate the total damage suffered by the victim.

Even as the United States helped shape international nuclear liability conventions (clearly serving the interests of U.S. suppliers of nuclear material and technology), its legislature passed the Price Anderson Act in 1957. That statute provides a much broader (and admittedly better), protection to victims of a nuclear accident than the international conventions. For example, the Price Anderson Act does not limit liability to operators and has a system of two tiers of compensation: the first relies on the liability of the nuclear operator, but the second consists of retrospective premiums to be paid by all operators active in the United States. Following the most recent amendments to the Act, the two-tier system provides for a total potential compensation of $12.2 billion.[61] Comparatively, the Price Anderson Act therefore generates much higher amounts of compensation. This compensation is, moreover, financed by the nuclear sector itself (and not, as in the international regime) through public funds.[62]

2. *Oil Pollution*

A similar story can be told as far as oil pollution is concerned.[63] The International Convention on Civil Liability for Oil Pollution Damage 1969 (known as the CLC 1969) addresses vessel-based pollution, and is supplemented by the International Fund for Compensation for Oil Pollution Damage 1971 (Fund Convention 1971).

The CLC 1969 embodies principles that are similar to those found in the nuclear liability conventions: it imposes strict liability exclusively on the tanker owner. Moreover, it requires compulsory financial guarantees and it puts a financial limit on the liability of the ship owner (a so-called cap). The Fund Convention 1971 established an International Oil Pollution Compensation fund (IOPC Fund) to provide a second tier of compensation. However, several serious oil spills occurring afterward, such as the Amoco Cadiz spill in 1978, showed the inadequacy of the regime and triggered the revisions of the original conventions.

The U.S. sent delegations to the negotiations of the 1969 CLC and the 1971 Fund Conventions. However, due to some characteristics of the conventions, such as the preemption of state laws, low liability limits and the channeling of liability to ship owners, the United States declined to ratify the conventions.[64] In response to the Exxon Valdez accident in 1979, the U.S. Congress rapidly passed the Oil Pollution Act 1990 (OPA 1990). OPA is similar in some ways to the international regime, each contains provisions on strict liability, limited liability and a compulsory financial guarantee. However, in other ways it is substantially different as well: the scope of compensable damage is much wider, liability is not limited to operators, and there are higher liability limits in general as well as a greater risk potential that responsible parties will face liability beyond those limits. OPA does not preempt state laws, which means U.S. states can still impose additional liability or financial responsibility.[65]

In sum, for some important domains of transboundary pollution, such as nuclear liability and oil pollution, the United States did not join the international conventions, but created its domestic laws. These domestic U.S. laws often provide more protection to victims of transboundary pollution than the international regime and are from that perspective to be preferred. Note also that, with a view on the Deepwater Horizon incident, there is no international convention whatsoever dealing with damage resulting from offshore oil and gas activities.[66] OPA (as well as several state laws that are not preempted by OPA) does apply to damage resulting from offshore oil and gas activities and hence to incidents like the Deepwater Horizon oil spill.[67]

These examples also make clear that international conventions do not always (as is sometimes wrongly assumed) provide better protection to pollution victims than domestic law. In some cases these international conventions emerge as a result of lobbying by industry, therefore better reflecting interests of industry than interests of pollution victims.

E.   Lessons

The lesson from this legal doctrine and case law seems to be that individuals cannot directly call on a violation of norms of international law by another state (as exemplified in the District Court of Bonn, see section IV, *supra*) but at least some case law bases liability in tort of a foreign polluter on a violation of international law (for example, in the District Court of Rotterdam case, see section IV, *supra*). Moreover, because treaties in principle only govern the relationship between states, compliance with a treaty by the polluter state does not necessarily have a justificatory effect for individual polluters (Supreme Court in the MDPA case, see section IV, *supra*). Moreover, even though the decision of the District Court of Rotterdam—whereby an individual polluter was basically held directly liable for violating international law—may be debated, international law can of course play another role in transboundary pollution disputes between individuals: it can be used as an aid to interpret open norms in national law.[68] In this respect, it should not be forgotten that the basic norm of tort law in many legal systems is today still rather open-ended and contextual, for example requiring that a defendant behaved with "reasonable care." In interpreting whether, in a transboundary pollution case, a defendant took reasonable care, a judge could also consider whether treaty obligations or unwritten norms of international law have been violated. Even though the defendant would then not be held directly liable for violating international law, the norms of international law can assist in making vague obligations under national tort law more specific and concrete.[69]

V.   Forum and Applicable Law

In any case, the preliminary questions arise: in what court can the case be brought and what is the applicable law?

A.   Forum

For victims, it will usually be far more attractive to bring a liability suit before their own courts. Intuitively, one can understand why this would be the case. First of all, there is a simple argument of costs: when the victim would have to sue a polluter in the polluter state, he would probably need to seek counsel in the polluter state, would have to pay the costs of travel, and so on, which can be substantially higher than when a suit can be brought in the place where the harm is suffered by the victim. Second, the choice of jurisdiction will often also have a decisive influence on the choice of law. It will usually be the lex fori that will determine the rules on conflicts of law. Having the possibility to sue in the victim state will hence often result in the application of the victim's national law and the reverse may be the case when the victim has to sue in the polluter state. The latter issue is of course crucially related to a third element: one can expect the judiciary in the victim state to be far more sympathetic toward the case of the victim than the judiciary in the polluter state. This has all to do with the issues mentioned above:[70] even if in most European states, judges are not elected, but are professional, appointed judges, a judge in a polluter state may, far away from where the harm occurred, have more sympathy for the difficulties that a polluter has in applying (costly) pollution reducing measures and may fear negative socioeconomic consequences of liability cases and vice versa. Conversely, a judge in the victim state will primarily be concerned with the harm suffered on his territory and be less inclined to worry about socioeconomic consequences of a finding of liability in the polluter state. As a result, success of transboundary pollution cases will often depend upon the ability of the victim to bring a claim in his own state. Of course, it is also crucial whether, if the victim obtains a positive judgment, he can subsequently obtain recognition and enforcement of the judgment in the polluter state. If enforcement of an award is not possible, starting legal proceedings in a victim state would be pointless.

There is abundant literature on jurisdiction issues in international conflicts, which goes far beyond the limited scope of this contribution. We should, however, remember that a common and universally accepted jurisdiction ground is the so-called forum rei: the place of the defendant's domicile. The main argument for it is the protection of the defendant. Because the defendant did not initiate the proceedings, he should not be forced to go abroad and defend himself. The opposite, the place of domicile of the plaintiff (forum actoris) is therefore rather the exception. The result is that to constitute a rule of jurisdiction allowing a plaintiff to bring a claim in the state where the harm occurred will usually require an explicit legal basis in a convention. Within the European context, for a long time the relevant convention was the Brussels Convention of September 27, 1968, on jurisdiction and the enforcement of judgments in civil and commercial matters.[71] This document provided the context for deciding the jurisdiction in a few of the Dutch cases, which we provide a central place in this volume, but of course in other continents other bilateral or multilateral treaties with the same goal (providing rules on jurisdictions) apply.

Article 5(3) of this Brussels Convention provides that a person domiciled in a member state may, in any other member state, be sued "in matters relating to tort, delict or quasi-delict, in the courts for the place where the harmful event occurred."[72] Because pollution cases are of course usually cases of noncontractual liability, this rule could provide victim courts with jurisdiction over transboundary pollution cases. However, the problem is that the expression "place where the harmful event occurred" in Article 5(3) is ambiguous. It is not clear whether this refers to the place where the damage occurs (the so-called *Erfolgsort* in German) or the place where the emission took place (the so-called *Handlungsort* in German) or to both. This problem arose also in the already-discussed case of the Dutch gardeners against the French potassium mines.[73] Uncertainty arose concerning the interpretation of Article 5(3) because the District Court of Rotterdam in a first judgment held that it had no jurisdiction. In its view, Article 5(3) only created jurisdiction for the courts of the place where the emission took place.[74] The latter would have meant that the victims could only bring a claim in France. On appeal, the court of appeals of The Hague referred the question of the interpretation of this provision to the European Court of Justice (ECJ).[75] The court ruled as follows in its well-known ruling in the *Bier* case:

> Where the place of the happening of the event which may give raise to liability in tort, delict or quasi-delict and the place where that event results in damage are not identical, the expression "place where the harmful event occurred" in Article 5(3) of the [Brussels] Convention . . . must be understood as being intended to cover both the place where the damage occurred and the place of the event giving raise to it. The result is that the defendant may be sued, at the option of the plaintiff, either in the courts for the place where the damage occurred or in the court for the place of the event which gives raise to and is at the origin of that damage.[76]

The major advantage for victims of transboundary pollution in the European context is hence that they can bring a suit in their own state against foreign polluters who are based in another EU member state.[77]

B. Applicable Law

The question of which law will govern the dispute had been at issue in the two Dutch cases already discussed. Once it has been established that a Dutch court is competent to adjudicate the transnational dispute the question arises—given the international character of the case—which law the court will apply: Dutch or foreign (tort) law? Potentially complex litigation about this issue may be prevented by a choice of law provision agreed to by the parties. This may be in the interest of both parties, including the non-Dutch based one, as application of foreign law is not reviewable before the Dutch Supreme Court. For that reason, that is, to be able to fully pursue litigation before three courts, the French defendant in the French potassium mines litigation concerning pollution of the river Rhine opted for a choice of Dutch law. In its first (interlocutory) judgment on the merits, the District Court of Rotterdam decided as follows:[78]

> [C]oncerning the applicable law:
>
> the plaintiffs regard their actions as being governed by Dutch law, whereas MDPA in principle prefers the dispute to be adjudged by French law but agreed at the hearing that the court shall apply Dutch law, because—if French law were to be applied—the misapplication of foreign law by the lower courts could not be pleaded in cassation; the court acknowledges this subsequent choice of law "as a choice of current Dutch law."

Here one can hence notice the acceptance of party autonomy with respect to applicable tort law: if all parties agree that Dutch law applies, that agreement will be accepted by the court.

Also in the *Sopar* case, an interesting issue concerning applicable law arose.[79] Even though it was not discussed in much detail, the question whether there was unlawfulness was apparently decided on the basis of Dutch law by the Dutch courts (District Court of Middelburg and Court of Appeals of The Hague).[80] However, the plaintiff (the NGO Reinwater) had also challenged Sopar's discharge permit, arguing that it would not have been legal. In that respect, the court of appeals held: "The Belgian discharge permit (of which for the moment it has to be accepted that it is valid according to Belgian law) cannot in a summary proceedings be tested by a Dutch judge according to Dutch norms, unless there would be a violation of international norms, which has not appeared in this particular case."

VI. Actors, Legal Basis, and Remedies
A. Actors

Another important question in a transboundary pollution case is the matter of who can bring suit. Many legal systems require that the plaintiff suffer a personal harm in order to bring suit. For certain plaintiffs like the market gardeners in the *Bier* case with a clear and direct interest at stake, this is not a problem. The *Bier* plaintiffs could argue that they were completely dependent on drainage water for the spraying of the crops that they cultivated. As a result of the emissions of salt waste into the river Rhine, the total salt burden increased and the gardeners suffered a diminution of the cultivated crops.[81]

However, it is well known that in many cases of (transboundary) environmental pollution, the damage may be so widespread that no individual victim has a sufficient incentive to bring a liability suit. Often, it is the public at large or a large group that suffers harm as a result of the transboundary pollution. In those cases, the question arises whether either environmental organizations or public authorities have standing in court.[82] The answer will vary across domestic legal contexts, and a court must first decide the law that applies to determine the transnational locus standi of the NGO. Because this admissibility issue is a procedural question, usually the lex fori, hence the domestic law of the court will apply to this standing issue. In a transboundary pollution case, this may mean that a foreign NGO will have standing to sue in a domestic court.

Another issue related to actors concerns not the plaintiffs, but the potential defendant. What if a state is being sued before a civil court of another state: will it be able to rely on state immunity as a defense? This follows from a basic principle of international law, the equality of sovereignty of states.[83] Immunity is not absolute nor does the court take it into account the fact that the foreign state can waive immunity; appearance before a court without raising the defense constitutes such a waiver. In addition, immunity only covers acts of state (acta iure imperii), and not acts of a commercial nature (acta iure gestiones).[84] Ultimately, it will again depend upon the national legal system whether state immunity is available as a defense.

B. Legal Basis

The court faced with a transboundary pollution case must further decide what norms apply in determining whether the defendant emission of pollution is wrongful and subject to liability.[85] Until recently, there was no strict liability for transboundary environmental pollution in the sense that the polluter would be liable for any damage resulting from his activity, irrespective of his behavior. Because almost any industrial activity creates risk of emissions, a broadly interpreted strict liability rule potentially leads to far-reaching liability for any industrial activity. Especially in the transboundary context, this may be problematic. In most transboundary pollution cases, one could therefore see the application of (a variation of) the negligence/nuisance rule. While the specific formulation varies across jurisdictions, the legal test typically hinges upon whether the behavior of the defendant was such that the pollution passed a certain threshold. Similarly, state responsibility under international law depends upon a balancing of various factors.[86] For example, in the *Trail Smelter* case the tribunal held that "under the principles

of international law no State has the right to use or permit the use of territory in such a manner as to cause injury by fumes in or to the territory of
another or the properties or persons therein, when the case is of serious consequence and the injury is established by clear and convincing evidence."[87]
Inherent in the passage is a balancing approach, wherein liability is triggered
only where "the case is of serious consequence." A certain level of pollution
must be accepted by the victim; only when that threshold is passed is liability triggered.

A finding of liability in a negligence regime supposes that the plaintiff
proves that the defendant violated a standard of due care. In most legal systems, a distinction is made between two situations: on the one hand, the
situation where a specific regulatory regime exists (for example, emission
standards in a permit) that has been violated and, on the other, the situation
where no such regulatory regime is at hand. In most legal systems, the first
situation is the relatively easy one: many legal systems hold that as soon as
a defendant violates a specific regulatory standard prescribing or prohibiting
a certain behavior, wrongfulness is automatically established. It is sometimes
referred to as a per se rule of liability.[88]

This type of liability rule was in fact applied in *Sopar*, discussed *supra*.
The Court of Appeal of The Hague established that the defendant, Sopar,
violated the norms laid down in the Belgian license: Reinwater argued that
Sopar discharged more than 100 micrograms of polycyclic aromatic hydrocarbons (PAH) per liter, whereas the permissible quantities as set forth in the
discharge permit were 30 micrograms per liter. Considering that Sopar
grossly disregarded the conditions of its Belgian permit, the Court of Appeal
of The Hague had no difficulty in allowing Reinwater's claim for compliance
with the permit.

The Bier case against the Alsatian Potassium Mines nicely shows the
type of elements that have to be taken into account when judging the unlawfulness of the defendant's discharges. The Hoge Raad held:

> The criterion should be that whether a party who discharges substances
> into a river fails to observe its duty of care towards those using the
> river-water downstream depends on the nature, seriousness and dura-
> tion of the damage caused to the latter and on the other circumstances
> of the case, among the factors to be considered here are, on the one
> hand, the nature and importance of the interests served by the dis-
> charges and, on the other hand, the interests served by the use of the
> water downstream and the extent to which this use is liable to be
> affected by the substances discharged. It should be borne in mind that
> in weighing up the respective interests, special importance must be
> attributed to the interests of the user downstream and that such a user
> may in principle expect the river not to be polluted excessively by large
> discharges.

As far as the duty of care of the defendant is concerned, the Hoge Raad
repeats the considerations held by the Court of Appeal:

In order to answer the question whether MDPA acted in breach of this duty of care, it is necessary to weigh its interests against those of the market gardeners. It has to be borne in mind in this connection that the mutual interests are of a similar kind in that of the interests of both parties are of a financial and commercial nature.

The Court of Appeal and subsequently the Hoge Raad therefore held that the MDPA violated its duty of care toward the market gardeners and held the defendant liable.

C.   Remedies

The type of remedy sought by a plaintiff in these type of pollution cases is often related to the nature of the plaintiff. When the plaintiff is a traditional victim suffering personal injury or economic losses, the plaintiff can, depending upon the rules in his national legal system, obtain damages that should in principle aim at restoring the victim in the status quo ante. NGOs can request either an injunction aimed at preventing further harm by ordering the defendant to stop the polluting discharges or to restore harm done. In practice, there may be overlap between the reparation in kind and the injunction.[89]

In principle, NGOs do not have the right to claim damages for the damage to the environment itself.[90] The NGO can, on the basis of its interest as defined in its purpose, have standing to ask for an injunction, which may lead to prohibiting actions that may endanger the interests it serves. But because the NGO does not own the environment of which it purports to protect the interests, it cannot claim damages for the harm that would be caused. There is, however, one important exception to this rule where an NGO expends resources to, for example, clean birds if that would be the stated interest of the particular NGO. There is a 1991 Dutch first instance judgment confirming the availability of this kind of remedy.[91]

Let us now briefly address how the NGO right of action and more particularly its remedies would be dealt with under some international conventions. At first blush, an NGO's damages claim would appear to not be allowed under the Council of Europe's Lugano Convention addressing civil liability for certain environmentally harmful activities.[92] Article 18 deals with "Requests by Organisations" and entitles NGOs to bring the following actions:

- a prohibition of an unlawful, dangerous activity posing a grave threat of damage to the environment;
- an order to require the operator to take measures to prevent damage, before or after an incident;
- an order to require the operator to take measures of reinstatement.

These are three actions for an injunction; the provision does not include damages. However, the rules on locus standi are not the final answer: we must also look at the definition of compensable loss to get the complete picture on possible actions by NGOs and then we see a different picture. That is to say that—just as noted above under Dutch law—the Lugano Convention includes the availability of a claim to recover the costs of preventive measures. It defines them in Article 2(9), which reads as follows:

> "Preventive measures" means any reasonable measures taken by any person, after an incident has occurred to prevent or minimise loss or damage as referred to in paragraph 7, sub-paragraphs a to c of this Article.

This definition is a widely adopted formulation of the concept of recoverable costs of preventive measures;[93] it first appeared in the maritime law sector, from which it has been copied.[94] The same definition has subsequently been adopted in numerous other conventions, including the so-called HNS Convention,[95] the 1997 Vienna Convention on Civil Liability for Nuclear Damage[96] and the 1999 Basel Protocol on Liability for Damage resulting from the Transboundary Movement of Hazardous Waste.[97]

Because these provisions grant the right to claim the costs of preventive measures taken by "whomsoever" or by "any person," public interest groups are entitled to a claim for reimbursement if they have incurred such costs. This view is supported by the "case law" of the International Oil Pollution Compensation Fund (IOPC Fund), where it decides on claims under the 1969 Oil Pollution Convention.[98] With respect to "preventive measures" it has recognized that "cleanup measures by voluntary groups . . . satisfy the requirements for consideration as preventive measures" and are thus recoverable in the context of the IOPC Fund.[99] Comparable to the cited Dutch *Borcea* case, the IOPC Fund has ruled in the *Braer* case that the costs of caring for "injured wildlife" by environmental protection groups are recoverable, provided that they were reasonably incurred.[100]

In conclusion, the availability of damage claims by NGOs has been accepted by most states in the context of relevant international conventions, that is, those dealing with civil liability of operators for activities causing damage to the environment such as nuclear incidents, oil spills, and other hazardous substances. Provided NGOs are legally capable of carrying out remedial actions, they will be able to claim the costs thereof from those responsible for the damage.

D. U.S. Citizen Suits: The *Pakootas* Case[101]

We have already referred, *supra*, to the *Trail Smelter* matter, the most famous case concerning transboundary air pollution in public international law. The events leading up to the international tribunal's rulings occurred between 1925 and 1941. Both prior to and after the dispute, the smelter also discharged hazardous materials including heavy metals such as cadmium (forming slag) into the Columbia River. The slag travelled downstream from Canada into the United States, where it accumulated over the years in the sediment of the river and Lake Roosevelt. Leachate of the heavy metals from the deposited slag caused harm to the environment and human health; there is ample evidence that the main source of the pollution is Teck Cominco's plant in Trail, Canada.[102] Particularly affected are the Indian tribes who live in the Colville and Spokane reservations, which use these waters for fishing and recreation.[103] To date no cleanup action has been undertaken. In this section, we examine a civil liability follow-up of *Trail Smelter*, which provides an important illustration of the use of citizen suits in a transboundary scenario.

1.   Action by EPA

CERCLA, otherwise known as the "Superfund" statute, is the chief federal U.S. statute in the field of environmental liability.[104] Among other things, it imposes strict, retrospective, and joint and several liability on potentially responsible parties for releases of hazardous substances, including on those who arranged the disposal of the substances. It does not contain any regulatory standards such as emission norms; instead it focuses on remediation and cleanup of hazardous waste sites in the United States.[105] EPA is the public entity empowered to implement and enforce the statute. On the request of the Colville Tribes, EPA conducted preliminary assessments of a particular section of the Upper Columbia River. It concluded that the section was a highly contaminated site eligible for inclusion on the Superfund National Priorities List. EPA opened informal negotiations with the American subsidiary of Teck Cominco so as to persuade it to conduct a remedial investigation and feasibility study of the site.[106] Because no settlement could be reached, EPA then issued a unilateral administrative order for a remedial/feasibility study to Teck Cominco (Canada) under CERCLA § 9606. The addressee refused to comply and enlisted the support of the Canadian government, arguing that CERCLA cannot be relied upon against a Canadian-based company. EPA has not enforced the order. However, members of the Colville tribes took up the case as a matter of private enforcement pursuant to CERCLA's citizen suit provision.

2.   Judgment

For the first time, U.S. courts applied CERCLA in a cross-border context. In July 2006, the U.S. Court of Appeals for the Ninth Circuit affirmed the key findings of the U.S. District Court for the Eastern District of Washington.[107] However, as further examined next, some aspects of the reasoning of the two courts differ; notably about the key issue of whether CERCLA had been applied extraterritorially or not. The judgments on appeal as well as at the district court level do not deal with any legal proceedings by EPA itself. Instead, they concern a civil action by the plaintiff, Mr. Pakootas and other members of the Colville tribes and the State of Washington—which intervened against Teck Cominco Metals Ltd.—a Canadian company, before the competent U.S. district courts as designated by CERCLA's citizen suit provision,

CERCLA § 9659. The latter empowers "any person [to] commence a civil action on his own behalf . . . against any person [including the United States and other public authorities] who is alleged to be in violation of any standard, regulation, condition, requirement, or order that has become effective pursuant to this chapter." Jurisdiction lies with the local federal district court of the place where the violation occurred—locus delicti. The court may issue injunctions and/or impose civil penalties. Citizens must first provide 60 days notice to the violator as well as relevant public authorities as a condition for admissibility of the action; the U.S. government and individual states have the right to intervene.

The key legal issues decided by the U.S. Court of Appeals for the Ninth Circuit (Ninth Circuit) in this civil action to enforce the EPA order are that the river site from which the leaching of the substances took place constitutes a "facility" and a "release" within the meaning of CERCLA; the foreign corporation (operator) comes within the ambit of CERCLA's notions of "any person" and is liable as an "arranger" of the release; and no extraterritorial application of CERCLA had occurred. The last conclusion is based on the analysis that the site from which the substances leached was situated entirely within the United States and that it did not matter that the substances had originated in Canada and were transported by the river stream across the border. Whether a suit would be characterized as domestic or extraterritorial is determined not by where the operator had initially arranged for the emission of the slag but by the locus of the actual (or threatened) damaging release of the heavy metals, and so on. The latter took place in the United States, not in Canada. The international jurisdiction of the U.S. court over the Canadian operator was based on the generally applicable venue rules for international torts (personal jurisdiction found on place of the harmful event).

We now focus on those aspects with wider implications for transboundary environmental liability suits, rather than questions of interpretation of CERCLA.

3. *Extraterritoriality or Not?*

The relevant statute, CERCLA, does not explicitly contemplate its application to sites beyond the United States. Is that an indication that the territorial scope cannot reach beyond the U.S. borders? Not necessarily, because normally neither regulatory statutes nor liability rules include provisions on their spatial scope; generally speaking, it is a matter of interpretation of the · rules in a cross-border setting within the framework of the conflict of laws (notably jurisdiction and choice of law) and/or public international law. Under U.S. law, a presumption exists that legislation applies only within U.S. territorial borders; however, the presumption is merely a canon of interpretation and the U.S. legislator has the power to extend the application of its laws beyond its borders if it intends to do so. Congressional intent may be express or implied.

Application of the law of the forum poses difficulty where a defendant's action occurred beyond the forum's borders, and the defendant is subject to its own local law. In that case, the court would hence not apply its own law extraterritorially, but would apply the domestic law of the defendant. Such an application is particularly problematic where the defendant's conduct is permissible under its local law, but prohibited under the law of the forum (a so-called true conflict of law). In such a case, the legislatures of both states have expressed an interest in protecting the conduct of either the plaintiff or the defendant (by adopting strong or relaxed regulation), but those interests are in conflict. However, the picture is quite different where no such conflict arises and effects of the foreign conduct are having an impact in the forum state; normally, sufficient connecting factors would be present to justify the exercise of jurisdiction over the foreign-based defendant.[108]

There is no bright line rule between a domestic and extraterritorial application of CERCLA. Indeed, while the Ninth Circuit concluded it need not reach the question of whether CERCLA applies extraterritorially because the release of the pollutants addressed in plaintiff's complaint occurred within the United States, the lower court took the contrary position on this point, that is, that the suit required extraterritorial application of CERCLA and such application is permissible. This confusion is not surprising given the somewhat nebulous nature of the concept of extraterritoriality and its rather less relevant impact in the sphere of liability rules than in the context of regulatory norms. To a certain extent, all cross-border disputes involving noncontractual liability inevitably involve the application of one state's tort rules to a party based abroad; such application in itself cannot be disparaged as unacceptable extraterritorial application of laws. Quite rightly, the Ninth Circuit emphasized that the case did not involve the regulation of foreign discharges, that is, the court was not engaged in proscribing conduct in Canada, but rather the assessment of the legal effects of discharges in the United States where harm ensued. The nature of the legislation—liability rather than regulation—is determinative in this regard. CERCLA is not a regulatory statute; it creates liability for remediation (costs) where hazardous substances are released into the environment.[109] Accordingly, the Ninth Circuit could convincingly hold that because the harm was caused by the release of the substances through leachate and that all of this occurred entirely on U.S. territory, a domestic application of CERCLA was obtained so that there was no need to consider the presumption against extraterritoriality. Teck Cominco is not caught in any conflict of norms with, for example, Canadian law obliging it to act differently from U.S. law.[110] Notably, no different emission limits are set because CERCLA simply does not cover emission limits; Teck Cominco is only subject to Canadian regulatory law.[111]

CERCLA focuses on the release of substances with ensuing contamination as the trigger for remediation action so that the relevant connecting factor rightly is the place where that happens rather than the place where the operator initially emitted the substances. There is a clear parallel here with EU civil jurisdiction law under which "place of the harmful event" has been construed, in situations where the impact of the damaging actions are felt in a different state than where the operator had acted, to cover both places with courts having jurisdiction.[112] Because the statute (CERCLA) had already made the choice between the two possible places for triggering liability, the Ninth Circuit's decision is convincing.

E.   Recognition and Enforcement

A final but crucial issue in any transboundary (also pollution) case is of course recognition and enforcement. In the Dutch cases that we often discussed, plaintiffs won their case against foreign polluters. The crucial next question will obviously be how they are able to execute such a judgment abroad. If a judgment obtained in a domestic court would not be recognized abroad, enforcement would be impossible and the whole exercise would have been pointless.

Again, many international conventions, both bilateral and multilateral, deal with recognition and enforcement and often provide for automatic recognition of a judgment rendered in one of the member states without any special procedure being required.[113] Refusing recognition is then an exception, for example, when the judgment would violate public policy in the member state in which recognition is sought. Those international conventions usually also provide foreign automatic enforcement of a judgment and explicitly hold that the foreign judgment may not be reviewed as to its substance.

Because in the European context, the already mentioned Brussels Convention on jurisdiction and the recognition and enforcement of judgments in civil and commercial matters of 1968 applied[114] the successful plaintiff in the Dutch cases we discussed could enforce its judgment subsequently in the polluter's state.

VII.   Conclusion: A Checklist

In sum, the following checklist identifies issues that may play a role when dealing with a transboundary pollution case at the practical level:

- Does your legal system apply a monistic or a dualistic approach to international conventions and can citizens in principle call directly on provisions in a treaty that are considered "self-executing"?[115]
- Is there an international convention that is applicable to this case of transboundary pollution and does it grant clear and precise rights to the pollution victims?
- Has the convention entered into force (i.e., have sufficient ratifications been acquired) and has it been correctly implemented in the domestic legislation of your jurisdiction?
- Is there any international convention, legal principle, or domestic rule allowing the victim to sue the foreign polluter in the victim's state?

- Are there international conventions, legal principles, or domestic legal rules specifying the applicable law to the specific aspects of the transboundary pollution case?
- Is the judge in the domestic court of the victim allowed to apply domestic law to the transboundary pollution case?
- Did the victim suffer a personal and direct harm as a result of the transboundary pollution?
- To the extent that the plaintiff is an NGO/public authority or trustee, does the applicable law allow standing to one of those actors as plaintiff and do these actors comply with the requirements for standing?
- If the suit is directed against a foreign state as defendant: can the defendant/state rely on state immunity as a defense, or is there a bilateral or multilateral treaty limiting the right of the state to rely on its immunity?
- Can, on the basis of applicable law, strict liability or a similar standard (like public nuisance) be applied to the transboundary pollution case?
- To the extent that a negligence/fault regime would be applicable, did the defendant violate a specific regulatory standard or a due care standard as a result of which his behavior can be considered negligent or wrongful?
- Is it possible under applicable law to claim damages for the (both pecuniary and nonpecuniary) loss suffered by the victim? Is it equally possible to claim compensation for purely economic loss?
- To the extent that the plaintiff is an NGO/public authority/trustee, does the law allow the plaintiff to recover the costs of preventive measures?
- Does the law allow any plaintiff to claim an injunction (either aiming at restoration of harm done or prevention of future harm) in addition to the claim for damages?
- Is there any applicable bilateral or multilateral convention allowing the recognition of the judgment of the domestic court in the foreign court where executing and enforcement of the judgment will be sought?

Obviously, the questions mentioned in this checklist have to be adapted to the specific national law in the domestic legal system and could hence be further refined. The checklist is meant as an overview of the type of questions that will, in some form or another, undoubtedly arise in any transboundary pollution case before a domestic court. The way in which some of those questions will be answered has to some extent been dealt with in other chapters in this volume.

Notes

1. *See, e.g.*, P. Lemke, *Dimensions and Mechanisms of Global Climate Change*, in MULTI-LEVEL GOVERNANCE OF GLOBAL ENVIRONMENTAL CHANGE. PERSPECTIVES FROM SCIENCE, SOCIOLOGY AND THE LAW 37–66 (G. Winter ed., 2006).

2. For a fuller account of the importance of transboundary impacts, see J. Handl, *Transboundary Impacts, in* THE OXFORD HANDBOOK OF INTERNATIONAL ENVIRONMENTAL LAW 531–49 (D. Bodansky, J. Brunnée & E. Hey eds., 2007).

3. *See* IN DEFENSE OF GLOBALIZATION (J. Bhagwati ed., 2007) (arguing that globalization has been driven in an important way by technological change).

4. Note that environmental law in many countries originated from a shift in attention from safety at work to the so-called external safety around the factory.

5. *See, e.g.,* the 1979 Geneva Convention on Long-Range Transboundary Air Pollution (LRTAP) and the subsequent protocols.

6. *See* M. Faure & G. Betlem, *Applying National Liability Law to Transboundary Pollution: Some Lessons from Europe and the United States, in* CHINA AND INTERNATIONAL ENVIRONMENTAL LIABILITY. LEGAL REMEDIES FOR TRANSBOUNDARY POLLUTION 129–91 (M. Faure & Y. Song eds., 2008).

7. R.A. Coase, *The Problem of Social Cost*, J.L. & ECON., 1960, 1–44.

8. *See* M. Cohen, *Commentary, in* LAW AND ECONOMICS OF THE ENVIRONMENT 167–71 (E. Eide & R.J. Van den Bergh eds., 1996).

9. *See, e.g.,* D. Esty, *Revitalizing Environmental Federalism*, 95 MICH. L. REV. 625 (1996); C. Kimber, *A Comparison of Environmental Federalism in the United States and the European Union*, 54 MD. L. REV. 1658–90 (1995); W. Oates & R. Schwab, *Economic Competition among Jurisdictions: Efficiency Enhancing or Distortion Inducing?*, 35 J. PUB. ECON. 333–54 (1988).

10. This complies with the general economic argument made by Steven Shavell that regulation should be used when the deterrent effect of tort rules may be weaker. S. Shavell, *Liability for Harm versus Regulation of Safety*, J. LEGAL STUDIES 357–74 (1984); S. Shavell, *A Model of the Optimal Use of Liability and Safety Regulation*, RAND J. ECON. 271–80 (1984).

11. *See, e.g.,* M. Allen, *Liability for Climate Change. Will It Ever Be Possible to Sue Anyone for Damaging the Climate?*, 421 NATURE, 2003, 891–92; M. Faure & A. Nollkaemper, *International Liability as an Instrument to Prevent and Compensate for Climate Change*, STAN. ENVTL. L.J. (26A)/STAN. J. INT'L L. (43A), Symposium Issue June 2007, 123–79; CLIMATE CHANGE LIABILITY (M.G. Faure & M. Peeters eds., 2011); D.A. Grosman, *Warming Up to a Not-So-Radical Idea: Tort-Based Climate Change Litigation*, 28 COLUM. J. ENVTL. L. 1–61 (2003); J. Gupta, *Who's Afraid of Climate Change?*, Inauguration address, Free University of Amsterdam, 2005; R. VERHEYEN, CLIMATE CHANGE DAMAGE AND INTERNATIONAL LAW: PREVENTION, DUTIES AND STATE RESPONSIBILITY (2005).

12. With respect to the problems of enforcement and compliance in international law, see, for example, H.K. Jacobsen & E. Brown Weiss, *Strengthening Compliance with International Environmental Accords: Preliminary Observations, from a Collaborative Project*, 1 GLOBAL GOVERNANCE 119–48 (1995); R.B. Mitchell, *Compliance Theory: An Overview, in* IMPROVING COMPLIANCE WITH INTERNATIONAL ENVIRONMENTAL LAW 3–28 (J. Cameron, J. Werksman & P. Roderick eds., 1996); M. Faure & J. Lefevere, *Compliance with Global Environmental Policy, in* THE GLOBAL ENVIRONMENT. INSTITUTIONS, LAW AND POLICY 163–80 (R.S. Axelrod, D.L. Downie & N.J. Vig eds., 2d ed. 2004).

13. For an overview of the different cases of transboundary pollution that arose in Europe, see C.P.R. ROMANO, THE PEACEFUL SETTLEMENT OF INTERNATIONAL ENVIRONMENTAL DISPUTES. A PRAGMATIC APPROACH (2000). In the 1980s, many victims of water pollution suffered downstream in the Netherlands started lawsuits against upstream polluters in Belgium. Many victims of water pollution suffered downstream and environmental NGOs in the Netherlands started legal proceedings against polluters in Belgium.

14. Case 21/76 *Bier v. Mine de Potace d'Alsace*, [1976] E.C.R. 1735.

15. The Brussels Convention of 27 September 1968 on jurisdiction and the enforcement of judgments in civil and commercial matters. This convention stipulates in Article

5 (3) that "a person domiciled in a contracting state may, in another contracting state, be sued: in matters relating to tort, delict or quasi-delict, in the courts for the place where the harmful event occurred." Today, jurisdiction within the European Union is defined by council regulation 44/2001 of 22 December 2000 on jurisdiction and the recognition and enforcement of judgments in civil and commercial matters. 2001 O.J. (L12/1). The new regulation has overtaken article 5 (3) of the Brussels Convention.

16.   The case involved Dutch-based plaintiffs suffering harm as a result of emissions of chloride by the Alsatian potassium mines in France. More precisely, the ECJ was faced with the interpretation of the phrase "place of the harmful event," and held that "where the place of the happening of the event which may give rise to liability in tort, delict, or quasi-delict, and the place where that event results in damage are not identical, the expression 'place where the harmful event occurred' in Article 5 (3) of the convention . . . must be understood as being intended to cover both the place where the damage occurred and the place of the event giving rise to it."

17.   For a discussion of these cases, see G. Betlem, Civil Liability for Transfrontier Pollution, Dutch Environmental Tort Law in International Cases in the Light of Community Law (1993).

18.   The defendant MPDA argued that it could not be held liable because it held and complied with the terms of its French license. The Court of Appeals held that this license "does not have the purport that all eligible interests are weighed to such an extent that the licence holder should be shielded from liability in tort" (Court of Appeals of The Hague, 10 September 1986, Netherlands Y.B. Int'l L., 1988, Vol. 19, 469). In the *Hoge Raad* decision, the Netherlands Supreme Court affirmed the judgment holding the MPDA liable for the wrongful emissions (Supreme Court of the Netherlands, 23 September 1988, *Tijdschrift voor Milieuaansprakelijkheid* (Environmental Liability Review), 1993, 137.

19.   Today this would be approximately 25,000 euros.

20.   Court of Appeal of The Hague, 19 November 1992, *Tijdschrift voor Milieuaansprakelijkheid* (Environmental Liability Review), 1993, 132 with case note by L.J.A. De Vries; (Belgian) *Tijdschrift voor Milieurecht* (Environmental Law Review), 1993, 153 with case note by Faure. The defendant appeal in cassation was unsuccessful, see Dutch Supreme Court (Hoge Raad) 25 February 1994, Nederlandse Jurisprudentie, 1996, 362 (Rütgers/Sopar v. Stichting Reinwater). For a commentary see Faure & Betlem, *supra* note 6, at 142.

21.   Apparently due to an error in calculating Cockerill's emissions, the president held that there was no direct evidence that the discharges were exceeding "every reasonable limit," and ordered Cockerill simply to meet applicable wastewater treatment standards under the Belgium Surface Water Act and to inform the NGO Rhine water of these results under a penalty of NLG 10 000 (President of the Court of Maastricht, 3 Feb. 1993), *Tijdschrift voor MilieuAansprakelijkheid* (Environmental Liability Review), 1993, 137. For a commentary see Faure & Betlem, *supra* note 6, at 162–63.

22.   Philippe Sands, Principles of International Environmental Law 215 (2d ed. 2003).

23.   On the website of the ICJ one can read, "With respect to the formation of a chamber pursuant to article 26, par. 1, of the statute, it should be noted that, in 1993, the court created a Chamber for Environmental Matters, which was periodically reconstituted until 2006. In the chamber's thirteen years of existence, however, no state ever requested that a case be dealt with by it. The court consequently decided in 2006 not to hold elections for a bench for the said chamber."

24.   For a description of the dispute, see *Diversion of Water from Meuse* (Neth. v. Belg.), 1937 P.C.I.J. (ser. A/B) No. 70 (June 28).

25. Romano, *supra* note 13, at 236.

26. For a detailed discussion see, for example, Romano, *supra* note 13, at 261–78, and Sands, *supra* note 22, at 318–19.

27. Romano, *supra* note 13, at 266.

28. The decision is available at http://legal.un.org/riaa/cases/vol_III/1905-1982 .pdf (last visited Oct. 27, 2013).

29. By compensating the parties who had suffered damage. For details see Romano, *supra* note 13, at 272.

30. Romano, *supra* note 13, at 276.

31. *See* J.H. Knox, *The Flawed Trail Smelter Procedure: The Wrong Tribunal, The Wrong Parties and the Wrong Law, in* Transboundary Harm in International Law: Lessons from the Trail Smelter Arbitration (R.M. Bratspies & R.A. Miller eds., 2003). Other contributions in this volume also discuss the *Trail Smelter* arbitration.

32. For a discussion of these cases see G. Betlem, *Trail Smelter II: Transnational Application of CERCLA*—Pakootas v. Teck Cominco Metals Ltd., 452 F.3d 1066 (9th Cir. 2006), 19(3) J. Envtl. L. (2007); M.J. Robinson-Dorn, *The Trail Smelter: Is What's Past Prologue? EPA Blazes a New Trail for CERCLA*, 14 N.Y.U. Envtl. L.J. 233–21 (2006).

33. See the studies cited in the previous footnote. We will come back to the *Pakootas* case, *infra*.

34. For a detailed discussion of the case see Romano, *supra* note 13, at 151–76, and Sands, *supra* note 22, at 567–68. The first—interlocutory—judgment of 2 February 1973 is published in the reports of judgments, advisory opinions, and orders of the ICJ, 1973.

35. The legal issues involved were of course far more complicated, but are less relevant for the current purpose of this chapter. We refer the reader to the judgment or the discussion in the literature cited in the previous footnote for further details.

36. In the decision the court held:

> (3) holds that the Government of Iceland and the Government of the United Kingdom are under mutual obligations to undertake negotiations in good faith for the equitable solution of their differences concerning their respective fishery rights in the areas specified in subparagraph 2; (4) holds that in these negotiations the Parties are to take into account, *inter alia*:
>
> a. that in the distribution of the fishing resources in the areas specified in subparagraph 2 Iceland is entitled to a preferential share to the extent of the special dependence of its people upon the fisheries in the seas around its coasts for their livelihood and economic development;
>
> b. that by reason of its fishing activities in the areas specified in subparagraph 2, the United Kingdom also has established rights in the fishery resources of the said areas on which elements of its people depend for their livelihood and economic well-being;
>
> c. The obligation to pay due regard to the interests of other States in the conservation and equitable exploitation of these resources;
>
> d. that the above-mentioned rights of Iceland and of the United Kingdom should each be given effect to the extent compatible with the conservation and development of the fishery resources in the areas specified in subparagraph 2 and with the interests of other States in their conservation and equitable exploitation;
>
> e. Their obligation to keep under review those resources and to examine together, in the light of scientific and other available information, such measures as may be required for the conservation and development,

and equitable exploitation, of those resources, making use of the machinery established by the North-East Atlantic Fisheries Convention or such other means as may be agreed upon as a result of international negotiations.

Judgment of 25 July 1974 in the Fisheries Jurisdiction Case at 34–35, no. 79.

37. ROMANO, *supra* note 13, at 169–70.

38. *Id.* at 173.

39. For details, see *id.* at 196–217.

40. The International Tribunal for the Law of the Sea prescribed inter alia the following measure: "Australia, Japan and New Zealand should resume negotiations without delay with a view to reaching agreements on measures for the conservation and management of southern blue fin tuna." *See also* ROMANO, *supra* note 13, at 207–08.

41. For a detailed discussion of the case see ROMANO, *supra* note 13, at 246–60, and SANDS, *supra* note 22, at 469–77).

42. Case concerning the Gabcikovo-Nagymaros project (1997) ICJ reports 7, para. 140.

43. *Id.*, para. 141.

44. *See generally* P.W. BIRNIE & A. BOYLE, INTERNATIONAL LAW AND THE ENVIRONMENT chs. 3–5 (2d ed. 2002).

45. For details on nuclear liability see, for example, Ch. Degros, *La responsabilité civile nucléaire: un état des lieux*, in LES RESPONSABILITÉS ENVIRONNEMENTALES DANS L'ESPACE EUROPÉEN. POINT DE VUE FRANCO-BELGE 303–74 (G. Viney & B. Dubuisson eds., 2006); J. LIU, COMPENSATING ECOLOGICAL DAMAGE. COMPARATIVE AND ECONOMIC OBSERVATIONS 207–30 (2013), and T. Vanden Borre, *Shifts in Governance in Compensation for Nuclear Damage, 20 Years after Chernobyl*, in SHIFTS IN COMPENSATION FOR ENVIRONMENTAL DAMAGE 261–311 (M. Faure & A. Verheij eds. 2007).

46. *See also* chapter 2, The Relationship between Domestic and International Environmental Law.

47. See a discussion of this decision of 29 September 1987 by A. Rest, *International Environmental Liability Law before German Courts, Tijdschrift voor Milieuaansprakelijkheid* (Environmental Liability Review), 1997, 116–22; and A. Nollkaemper *How Public International (Environmental) Law Can Furnish a Rule of Decision in Civil Litigation, Tijdschrift voor Milieuaansprakelijkheid*, ENVIRONMENTAL LIAB. REV. 3–4 (1998).

48. Nollkaemper adds that this a fortiori means that if the German farmer would not have sued the Soviet Union but the private corporation in the Soviet Union liable for the nuclear cloud the principle of notification would then certainly also not have had any effects between two individuals (Nollkaemper (1998)).

49. For a detailed discussion of this see Nollkaemper, *supra* note 47.

50. *See, e.g.*, BETLEM, *supra* note 17, at 393–401;, TRANSBOUNDARY POLLUTION AND LIABILITY: THE CASE OF THE RIVER RHINE (J.M. Van Dunné, ed., 1991).

51. Supreme Court of the Netherlands, 23 September 1988, *Tijdschrift voor Milieuaansprakelijkheid* (Environmental Liability Review), 1989, 15–18.

52. According to Nollkaemper, *supra* note 47.

53. Handelskwekerij G.J. Bier B.V. and Stichting Reinwater v. Mines de Potasse d'Alsace sa (MDPA), District Court of Rotterdam NJ 1979, 113, NETHERLANDS Y.B. INT'L L., 1980, vol. 11, 326 and District Court of Rotterdam, 16 December 1983, NJ 1984, 341, NETHERLANDS Y.B. INT'L L., 1984, vol. 15, 471.

54. Trail Smelter Arbitration Tribunal (United States v. Canada), 33 AJIL 182 (1939) and 35 AJIL 684 (1941); *see generally* Bratspies & Miller, *supra* note 31; SANDS, *supra* note 22, at 241–42 & 318–19.

55. Court of Appeals of The Hague, 10 September 1986, *Tijdschrift voor Milieuaansprake-lijkheid* (Environmental Liability Review) 1987, 15 with case note by Vandermeer, Netherlands Y.B. Int'l L., 1988, vol. 19, 496.

56. *See* Nollkaemper, *supra* note 47. The Supreme Court did not express itself on this particular issue.

57. An agreement of 3 December 1976 concerning the protection of the Rhine against pollution by chloride.

58. Nollkaemper rightly argues that this opinion can have very far-reaching consequences because in this way a Dutch judge could theoretically prohibit all discharges from France and could thus disregard the rights of France under international law on the basis of a Treaty. Nollkaemper considers it doubtful whether the Hoge Raad intended such a radical gap between international and domestic law. Nollkaemper, *supra* note 47.

59. *See* Vanden Borre, *supra* note 45, at 261–62.

60. *See* M. Trebilcock & R.A. Winter, *The Economics of Nuclear Accident Law*, 17 Int'l Rev. L. & Econ. 215–43 (1997); M.G. Faure & K. Fiore, *An Economic Analysis of the Nuclear Liability Subsidy*, 26(2) Pace Envtl. L. Rev. 419–47 (2009).

61. *See* Liu, *supra* note 45, at 244–45.

62. For a comparison of the nuclear liability regime in the international conventions and in the U.S. Price Anderson Act, see M. Faure & T. Vanden Borre, *Compensating Nuclear Damage: A Comparative Economic Analysis of the U.S. and International Liability Schemes*, 32 William & Mary Envtl. L. & Pol'y Rev. 219–87 (2008).

63. For details, see H. Wang, Civil Liability for Marine Oil Pollution Damage: A Comparative and Economics Study of the International, US and Chinese Compensation Regime (2011).

64. *See* H. Wang & M. Faure, *Civil Liability and Compensation for Marina Pollution—Lessons to be learnt for offshore oil spills*, 8(3) Oil, Gas, Energy L. Intelligence 1–27 (2010).

65. 33 U.S.C. § 2718.

66. The CLC 1969 is only applicable to vessel-based pollution and not to pollution resulting from offshore oil and gas activities. The International Maritime Organization does not even consider itself competent to draft a convention dealing with damage resulting from offshore oil and gas activities, because it is only responsible for maritime affairs.

67. *See, e.g.,* R. Force, M. Davies & J.S. Force, *Deepwater Horizon: Removal Costs, Civil Damages, Crimes, Civil Penalties, and State Remedies in Oil Spill Cases*, 85 Tul. L. Rev. 889–82 (2011).

68. Nollkaemper, *supra* note 47, at 9.

69. That is hence different from what the District Court of Rotterdam did when it held the French defendant liable because the company had violated a norm of international law.

70. See section II, *supra*.

71. *See* http://curia.europa.eu/common/recdoc/convention/en/c-textes/brux-idx .htm (last visited Oct. 27, 2013).

72. *See* http://curia.europa.eu/common/recdoc/convention/en/c-textes/brux-idx .htm (last visited Oct. 27, 2013).

73. *See supra* note 53.

74. District Court of Rotterdam, 12 May 1975, Netherlands Y.B. Int'l L., 1976, vol. 7, 344, Netherlands Int'l L. Rev., 1975, 203 with case note by Verheul.

75. *See* http://europa.eu/about-eu/institutions-bodies/court-justice/ (last visited Oct. 25, 2013).

76. Case 21/76 *Bier v. Mine de Potace d'Alsace*, [1976] E.C.R. 1735, 1748–49.

77. For a more detailed discussion of the consequences and reasoning in this *Bier* decision of the ECJ see BETLEM, *supra* note 17, at 92 *et seq.* & 146–49.

78. District Court of Rotterdam, 8 Jan. 1979, NETHERLANDS Y.B. INT'L L. 1980, vol. 11, 326, *Netherlands Int'l L. Rev.*, 1981, 63 with case note by Duintjer Tebbens, *Nederlandse Jurisprudentie*, 1979, 113, *Ars Aequi*, 1980, 788 with case note by D'Olivera.

79. *See* section III.A.2, *supra.*

80. Because it concerns a summary proceeding, the judgment did not refer explicitly to the choice of law issue. *See* BETLEM, *supra* note 17, at 174.

81. *Id.* at 394–95.

82. For a detailed discussion of these issues, see BETLEM, *supra* note 17, at 305–48; M. WILDE, CIVIL LIABILITY FOR ENVIRONMENTAL DAMAGE. A COMPARATIVE ANALYSIS OF LAW AND POLICY IN EUROPE AND THE US, chs. 7–8 (2d ed. 2013).

83. *See generally* I. Brownlie, Principles of Public International Law 321 & chs. 14–16 *passim* (6th ed. 2003).

84. L. STRIKWERDA, INLEIDING TOT HET NEDERLANDSE INTERNATIONAAL PRIVAA-TRECHT (8th ed. 2005) (citing HR 25 November 1994, *NJ* 1995, 660 *Morocco v. De Trappenberg*).

85. For a discussion of this unlawfulness issue, see BETLEM, *supra* note 17, at 349–442.

86. For a discussion of the evaluation of State responsibility under international law see SANDS, *supra* note 22, at 134 *et seq.*; N.L.J.T. Horbach, *Liability versus responsibility under international law. Defending strict State responsibility for transboundary damage*, diss. Leiden, 27 June 1996; R. LEFEBRE, TRANSBOUNDARY ENVIRONMENTAL INTERFERENCE AND THE ORIGIN OF STATE LIABILITY (1996).

87. *See* section III.B.1, *supra.*

88. On the interferences between liability law and regulation, see the contributions in TORT LAW AND REGULATORY LAW (W.H. Van Boom, M. Lukas & C.H.R. Kissling eds., 2007).

89. *See* BETLEM, *supra* note 17, at 491–93.

90. *But see* chapter 11, Natural Resource Damages, section II.7, discussing the emergence of laws providing a cause of action to recover costs to restore the harm to the environment. Potentially, in some jurisdictions, NGOs may have the ability to bring such claims.

91. District Court of Rotterdam 15 Mar. 1991, (1992), 23, NETHERLANDS Y.B. INT'L L., 513.

92. Convention on Civil Liability for Damage resulting from Activities Dangerous to the Environment, Lugano, 21 June 1993, *European Treaty Series* 150 (http://conventions.coe.int), 32 *International Legal Materials* (I.L.M. 1993); not in force; signed by Cyprus, Finland, Greece, Iceland, Italy, Liechtenstein, Luxembourg, the Netherlands and Portugal. Concerning the Council of Europe, see http://hub.coe.int (explaining that the Council of Europe is an international organization in Strasbourg, France, comprising 47 European countries and that it was set up to promote democracy and protect human rights and the rule of law in Europe).

93. *See generally* M.-L. LARSSON, THE LAW OF ENVIRONMENTAL DAMAGE: LIABILITY AND REPARATION 172 *et seq.* (1999); P. Kottenhagen-Edzes, *De begrippen milieu-aantasting en milieuschade in enkele internationale verdragen, bezien vanuit privaatrechtelijk perspectief, in* GRENSOVERSCHRIJDENDE MILIEUPROBLEMEN: UITDAGINGEN VOOR DE NATIONALE EN INTERNATIONALE RECHTSORDE 207–23 (K. Deketelaere et al. eds., 1998).

94. *See* art. I(7) of the 1969 International Convention on Civil Liability for Oil Pollution Damage, Brussels, 29 November 1969, *Tractatenblad* 1970, 196; 9 I.L.M. 45 (1970), as amended.

95. International Convention on Liability and Compensation for Damage in connection with the Carriage of Hazardous and Noxious Substances by Sea, London, 3 May 1996, 35 I.L.M. 1406 (1996), http://www.imo.org/About/Conventions/ListOfConventions /Pages/International-Convention-on-Liability-and-Compensation-for-Damage-in -Connection-with-the-Carriage-of-Hazardous-and-Noxious-.aspx.

96. Consolidated text of the Vienna Convention on Civil Liability for Nuclear Damage of 21 May 1963 as amended by the Protocol of 12 September 1997, 36 I.L.M. 1454 (1997), http://www.iaea.org/Publications/Documents/Conventions/liability.html.

97. Basel, 10 December 1999, http://www.basel.int for the text and signatures /ratifications; *see generally* French, D.A., *The 1999 Protocol on Liability and Compensation for Damage Resulting from the Transboundary Movements of Hazardous Wastes and their Disposal,* ENVTL. LIAB. 3 (2000).

98. See on that convention *supra* section IV.D.2.

99. G. GAUCI, OIL POLLUTION AT SEA. CIVIL LIABILITY AND COMPENSATION FOR DAMAGE 36 (1997) (referring to FUND/EXC.34/9, 12 March 1993, § 3.28).

100. C. WU, POLLUTION FROM THE CARRIAGE OF OIL BY SEA: LIABILITY AND COMPENSATION 291 (1996) (referring to FUND/EXC.34/5/Add.1, 1 March 1993, p. 9).

101. This section is based on Faure & Betlem, *supra* note 6, at 175–81.

102. Robinson-Dorn, *supra* note 32, at 265–67.

103. Pakootas v. Teck Cominco Metals, Ltd., 452 F.3d 1066 (9th Cir. 2006).

104. 42 U.S.C. §§ 9601 *et seq.*

105. Robinson-Dorn, *supra* note 32, at 275).

106. *Id.* at p. 268.

107. *Pakootas,* 452 F.3d at 1069, *aff'g* 2004 WL 2578982 (E.D. Wash. Nov. 8, 2004).

108. 2004 WL 2578982, at *5–10 (citing cases).

109. 452 F.3d at 1073–74.

110. Even Canadian courts had ruled along these lines in cases about the enforcement of U.S. judgments in Canada, see Robinson-Dorn, *supra* note 32, at 295.

111. *Id.* at 272.

112. Case 21/76 *Bier v. Mines de Potasse d'Alsace* [1976] E.C.R. 1735; [1977] 1 CMLR 284.

113. Take, for example, the Brussels convention on jurisdiction and recognition and enforcement of judgment in civil and commercial matters (also referred to as Rome I).

114. Now replaced by the council regulation 44/2001 of 22 December 2000.

115. *See* section IV.A, *supra,* and chapter 2, The Relationship between Domestic and International Environmental Law.

CHAPTER 15

Civil and Criminal Enforcement and Penalties

I. Introduction

In assessing the topic of civil and criminal environmental enforcement and penalties across the globe, it is fair to say that there is considerable variability in nearly every respect. There is variability in available enforcement tools, potential severity of penalties, and robustness of the institutions undertaking enforcement efforts. This means that specific, localized knowledge will be the key to an attorney's success. Nonetheless, for broad advisory purposes there are clearly ways of minimizing risk. As a general matter, environmental enforcement tends to be strongest and most consistent in countries with a mature rule of law, a well-established environmental statutory and regulatory framework, and the economic resources to provide essential environmental oversight by government regulators and prosecutors.

Based on a review of official government environmental websites and news sites, it appears that dating back to at least the 1970s the United States has had the most comprehensive system of environmental enforcement of any country. It continues to be the leader in terms of the breadth of its enforcement tools and the severity of penalties associated with findings of environmental noncompliance. Thus, if one were to conduct business activities in foreign countries as if under the watchful eye of U.S. environmental regulators—though, naturally, with regard to the particular environmental standards and procedures required by that country—one would expect to generally avoid precipitating a vigorous enforcement action or more extreme penalties. While the United States may not necessarily have in place the most stringent environmental standard of any nation with respect to the regulation of a particular activity, it is much more likely to compel a business to comply with the requirements that it has in place and apply sanctions if they have not.

It is not remotely possible within the confines of this chapter to provide a detailed roadmap to this subject that will permit one to navigate across the globe. There are far too many complexities and distinctions among the environmental enforcement and judicial systems of the various countries to permit that. However, it is realistic to identify some of the questions an attorney will want to consider in assessing the potential for an enforcement action.

These questions include

1. What are the "prohibited acts" that can subject a regulated party to the possibility of an enforcement action?
2. Which media (air, water, waste, toxics, etc.) are most likely to be subject to enforcement actions?
3. Which environmental enforcement processes are available to government officials with respect to those prohibited acts? (That is, are administrative, civil,[1] and criminal tools provided, as in the United States?)
4. What are the penalties and remedies that the government may seek under a particular law? (Are there additional tools not utilized in the United States, for example, cutting off utilities to the offending business?)
5. Does a particular enforcement approach dominate? (It is growing increasingly rare for a country to rely predominantly on criminal enforcement. Yet criminal enforcement would likely mean a very different approach and set of actors than would a regulatory action directed by an environmental agency.)
6. Which level of government primarily oversees the activity for which there are environmental requirements? (Are there national, state/provincial, and local regulators? How do those various levels of government mesh together?)
7. Apart from the various levels of government, is there more than one governmental agency that might assert jurisdiction over a particular activity?
8. Which entity is subject to the enforcement action—the business entity, responsible individuals at the business entity, or both? (In a number of countries, corporations are either not criminally liable or are subject to more limited liability than in the United States.)
9. Does the government need to demonstrate "state of mind" or "intent" in order to prove its case? (This is typically a consideration only in a criminal case, and the "knowing" or "willful" conduct that typifies criminal liability in the United States is not necessarily required to gain a conviction in other countries.)
10. What is the standard of proof required to prevail in an enforcement proceeding? (With respect to criminal proceedings, do not count on a defendant being protected by the presumption of innocence or the government needing to meet its proof beyond a reasonable doubt unless you are in a common law country.)[2]
11. Does the country have an adversarial or inquisitorial system of justice or a combination of the two? (As a general matter, adversarial systems tend to be associated with common law countries, while inquisitorial

systems—where the judge actively participates in the fact-finding—tend to occur in civil law countries.) Inquisitorial systems outnumber adversarial systems, and are common in continental Europe (e.g., France), Asia (e.g., Japan), and South America (e.g., Brazil).

This is by no means intended to be an exhaustive list of issues that should be considered at an early stage of engagement, but simply a starting point. We will further consider some of these and related issues next.

II. Which Enforcement Tools Exist within the Environmental Compliance and Enforcement Scheme?

As will be made clear later in this volume, comprehensive national environmental statutes covering air, water, waste, and toxic substances have become the norm in developed countries and emerging economies, and this is increasingly so in less developed countries. National legislation is accompanied by national regulatory schemes of varying comprehensiveness and complexity, but typically includes discrete pollution standards and a permitting system. In many countries, as in the United States, this national scheme runs in parallel with state or local environmental legislative and regulatory requirements. The existence of complementary state or local environmental schemes may, as in the United States, create the possibility of conflicts with the national scheme. As detailed environmental regulatory systems become relatively commonplace, it may be that the greater distinction from one country to the next will lie in how those environmental requirements are enforced and the consequences for failing to comply with them.

The United States would appear to pursue enforcement of environmental laws with a zeal that is unmatched elsewhere in the world, though some other countries (especially certain nations within the European Union) clearly put considerable effort and resources into ensuring broad compliance with the law.[3]

The enthusiasm with which U.S. federal officials enforce environmental requirements is displayed in a number of very public ways.[4] For example, the U.S. Environmental Protection Agency (EPA) issues an annual report that catalogs its efforts in this regard. For 2012, EPA touts the following broad statistics:

(a) $252 million in criminal fines and civil penalties assessed to deter pollution;
(b) 6.6 billion pounds of pollution and hazardous waste reduced, eliminated, properly disposed of or treated; and
(c) $44 million in additional investments for supplemental environmental projects that benefit communities.[5]

During that year, 1,760 administrative complaints were filed,[6] as well as 115 civil complaints filed in federal court, and, additionally, 231 defendants (the substantial majority of which were individual defendants, but also including a significant number of corporations) criminally charged, and a combined 79 years of imprisonment imposed upon individual defendants.[7]

There are three things immediately striking about EPA's enforcement results. The first is that enforcement officials clearly utilize all of the many tools that have been provided to them. Regulated parties are subject to a flexible range of enforcement actions, generally ranging from administrative action for the least serious violations, to criminal prosecution for the most egregious.[8] (The individual states within the United States generally have a similar range of enforcement options.) Not only are government officials provided a variety of enforcement pathways, but also multiple tools are available within each pathway. To take one example, corporations convicted of environmental crimes are often subject to a procedure known as contractor debarment, where they may lose the ability the enter into potentially lucrative contracts with the federal government. Another example is the court's power to grant restitution to "make whole" the "victims" of an environmental crime. By contrast, most foreign jurisdictions are limited to monetary fines or penalties and, possibly, incarceration of convicted individuals.

The second observation is that the U.S. enforcement accomplishments—as measured by frequency and severity—would appear to substantially exceed those of other countries.[9] However, it is hard to know that with absolute certainty because many other countries do not necessarily publicize their accomplishments in a readily accessible public manner. By contrast, not only does EPA make certain that the public has access to a comprehensive listing of its enforcement statistics on an annual basis, but nearly every significant enforcement action, whether civil or criminal, is accompanied by press releases by EPA or its prosecutorial partner, the U.S. Department of Justice (DOJ). This is done often at multiple stages of the action (e.g., at the time the complaint is filed, again when liability has been proven or admitted to, and finally when the penalty has been imposed). As a result of its aggressive promotion of its enforcement activities, EPA is able to raise awareness of its regulatory requirements and the penalties for noncompliance. The publicity surrounding enforcement actions undoubtedly contributes to U.S EPA's goal of deterring regulated parties from disobeying environmental requirements, both through raising consciousness of regulatory requirements and fear of the negative publicity that is likely to stem from publicizing the violation. While the EPA's aggressive use of publicity may also suggest a more confrontational and less collaborative approach to gaining environmental compliance than is the case in other countries, the approach is rules-based, with little favoritism.

Another element of transparency and fairness is that the results of all enforcement cases in the United States are publicly available on the EPA website. This means that regulators anywhere in the world can determine by its public record whether a company operating in the United States is likely to be law-abiding and deserve a permit in another country, or whether the applicant should receive special scrutiny and even be met with suspicion if it is a repetitive and serious violator of U.S. environmental requirements.[10]

The third observation is that national enforcement tools cover an extremely wide range of environmental activities. All of its major environmental statutes—covering air pollution, water pollution, the handling of hazardous waste, and the manufacture and distribution of pesticides or other toxic chemicals—permit most violations to be pursued with any tool, assuming that the required level of "intent" can be proven.[11] This is quite significant because the possibility of prison time for environmental violations may encourage widespread compliance, even though a relatively small percentage of cases are handled criminally.

With respect to criminal enforcement, prosecutors in the United States are not limited to environmental statutes, and frequently rely on generally applicable criminal statutes including prohibitions on conspiracy, false statements, fraud, and even money laundering. In a relatively limited number of federal cases, the government may initiate both criminal and civil (or administrative) actions against a single entity, which are known as "parallel proceedings." This is typically done only in cases where one or the other enforcement mechanism is inadequate to fully vindicate the range of the government's interests, for example, when justice requires both that individuals be subject to imprisonment but legal authorities under the criminal law are inadequate to implement necessary corrective action.

It is beyond the purview of this chapter to discuss in any detail which legal authorities are available in any particular country. Suffice it to say that in many instances environmental protections are broadly "on the books." Most countries also provide for the possibility of criminal prosecution for certain serious environmental violations. What is probably most significant is that the emerging global trend appears to be toward greater reliance upon administrative enforcement tools, at least for violations that are not especially egregious in terms of environmental harm or wrongful conduct (e.g., deliberate misconduct for financial gain). Thus, for example, administrative environmental enforcement now predominates in countries such as Australia, Canada, Mexico, and the United Kingdom. In a large and growing number of countries, administrative action is possible with respect to most violations (including failure to abide by permits, meet discrete pollution standards, or report required information to regulatory officials), and can result in significant fines. This likely reflects the greater flexibility, ability to take action more quickly, and lower resource intensity of administrative compared with criminal enforcement.[12] The shift toward greater reliance on administrative authority is probably best viewed as the evolution of legal systems to deal more efficiently with regulating businesses, is not limited to environmental regulation, and does not indicate a de-emphasis of environmental protections. Indeed, criminal prosecution remains available for those cases where administrative sanctions are inadequate.

By way of contrast to the United States, most countries do not have a civil enforcement option—generally considered a stronger tool than administrative action—which means that enforcement officials must choose between administrative and criminal enforcement. The absence of the civil enforcement option may have contributed to the fact that Germany has criminally prosecuted a surprisingly large number of violations—approximately 4,300 offenders per year for environmental violations, out of 26,000 reported violations.[13] With nearly 17 percent of violations being pursued criminally, this appears to represent a higher percentage of cases being pursued criminally as compared to the United States.[14] The reliance by U.S. federal environmental officials on civil enforcement, especially for large, complex actions with the potential for significant environmental harm, such as lawsuits against power plants and chemical manufacturers for violation of clean air regulations, is a major distinction with most other nations. These cases sacrifice the relative speed, limited rights for the defendants, and efficiency of administrative actions in favor of more thorough investigation through extensive discovery, and the enhanced penalties and wide range of remedies available in court.

III.   At What Levels of Government Is Enforcement Being Undertaken?

An important consideration in conducting business operations in any country is determining the relevant regulatory requirements for the particular activity being engaged in. Those who practice in the United States are quite familiar with the need to consider regulatory officials at all levels of government: national, state, and local. It is generally no different in other nations—avoiding the prospect of enforcement means carefully assessing the full range of potential regulatory requirements at all levels of government and being diligent in complying with all requirements.

In the United States, states and localities are primarily responsible for inspecting a wide range of regulated entities and ensuring compliance through routine enforcement actions. To put this in some perspective, in 2012 U.S. states brought more than 10 times as many enforcement actions as EPA did.[15] That said, the U.S. government plays a leading role in terms of bringing the most complex and significant enforcement actions both civilly and criminally.

One aspect of environmental enforcement that may distinguish the United States from many other countries is the close cooperation generally found between the national environmental regulatory agency—EPA—and the prosecutorial officials—DOJ—whose attorneys pursue both civil and criminal judicial cases.[16] Given the complexity of environmental law, the combination of well-trained regulatory personnel and criminal investigators working with experienced environmental litigators has been instrumental in the success of the environmental enforcement program in the United States.

Contrary to the strong role of national-level enforcement in the United States, in many developed countries, especially those with federated systems of government (for example, Australia, Canada, and Germany), as well as the emerging economies, the primary enforcement activities occur at the state (or provincial) level. National policy, but little enforcement, proceeds from the central environmental ministry. This is the situation, for example, in India, where the State Pollution Control Boards (SPCBs)—rather than the Central Pollution Control Board—are responsible for the great majority of compliance monitoring and enforcement activity.[17] In reviewing India's environmental enforcement capacity, the Organisation for Economic Co-operation and Development (OECD) noted that while many of the SPCBs conducted numerous inspections—for example, the SPCB in Andhra Pradesh (India's fifth-largest state by population) conducted over 8,000 per year—enforcement was weakened by the cursory nature of the inspections, a failure to inspect medium and small businesses, and the regulators' inability to impose fines absent filing the rare judicial case.[18]

The slow-moving nature of the judicial system in India and the lack of prosecutorial resources available to environmental officials results in penalties that are few and far between, and, at least as of 2006, a compliance rate that was decreasing rather than improving. Given these impediments, it is not surprising that regulatory officials there frequently resort to methods that they are in a position to implement without resorting the judicial system, such as cutting off power and water to noncomplying businesses as one practical and direct way to stop polluting.[19] India in 2010 created a National Green Tribunal, a specialized court for providing environmental compensation, relief, and restoration, which may improve the speed at which cases are heard and could signal a heightened commitment to environmental protection.[20]

China has a similarly decentralized system of environmental enforcement. There are signs—including elevating the national-level State Environmental Protection Administration to ministry status as the renamed Ministry of Environmental Protection and recent central government responses to the air pollution crises in major municipalities such as Beijing—that environmental protection is gaining some added political support and resources.[21] Environmental enforcement in China is complicated by the fact that approximately 2,000 Environmental Protection Bureaus (EPBs) at the provincial and municipal levels are responsible for a great majority of the enforcement, and vary considerably in their level of assertiveness concerning important local economic activities.[22] With roughly 50,000 EPB environmental inspectors, most at the local level, the size of the workforce is impressive, as is the reported number of site visits, which in 2006 reportedly averaged over eight per entity per year for a total of over two million visits, although this figure might not include all types of polluting facilities.[23] Unlike in India, regulatory officials in China can issue fines, and some have not hesitated to do so, while others exhibit a pattern of deference to interests with strong local economic or political influence. According to the OECD, in 2004 Chinese environmental officials brought nearly 80,000 enforcement actions totaling approximately $75 million in fines (however, these fines were on average relatively small, at an average of less than $1,000 per action).[24] While these figures make clear that environmental enforcement has been employed widely in China, given its ongoing and severe pollution problems, incomplete environmental law framework, low penalties, and considerable variation in enforcement capacity and rigor, it is difficult to say that it can be considered successful in ensuring compliance with environmental standards.

Despite the decentralized enforcement efforts described previously, it is important not to overgeneralize. Countries with a unitary system of government—the substantial majority of countries in the world—may have only a national-level judicial system and thus environmental enforcement will be centrally controlled, as there are no subnational sovereigns with whom such power is shared. This includes, for example, some major European nations such as France and Italy, as well as important Asian nations such as South Korea and Indonesia. However, even in unitary systems, the environmental regulation may be delegated to subnational levels of government, so from a practical perspective it is more important to focus upon how enforcement is implemented functionally rather than upon legalistic form.

IV.   Potential Environmental Penalties

Often much attention is given to the types of sanctions available for environmental violations. Certainly that is a very significant consideration, as the absence of sufficient legal authorities to impose penalties will thwart regulators from their goal of ensuring compliance through deterring environmental violations. However, the actual penalties imposed, and the timeliness, appropriateness, and consistency of their imposition, are very likely more important than the maximum fines or term of imprisonment that theoretically could be imposed.

With respect to the severity of penalties actually imposed, the United States has to be considered the leader. One need only look at the recent criminal plea agreement between the U.S. Department of Justice and BP for the Deepwater Horizon oil rig catastrophic explosion and oil spill. The plea resulted in the imposition of $4 billion in criminal fines and penalties, the company being barred from government contracts and criminal charging of three BP employees who are subject to lengthy prison terms and fines.[25] Moreover, quite apart from the criminal case against BP, the United States continues to pursue a civil action for civil penalties and natural resource damages that are said to exceed $10 billion.

While the criminal penalties already imposed and likelihood of massive penalties in the Deepwater Horizon case are extraordinary—given the magnitude of the environmental damage created by the blowout, as well as the death of 11 workers—the fact remains that there are now dozens (if not hundreds) of EPA noncriminal cases with multimillion-dollar penalties.[26] By way of comparison penalties of such magnitude in other countries appear to be quite unusual, even in the European Union where environmental oversight is considered strong. For example, the Scottish Environment Protection Agency (SEPA) imposed a monetary penalty of £2.8 million (approximately $4.5M) in 2011 after ExxonMobil failed to report 33,000 tons of carbon dioxide emissions from a chemical plant and thus failed to procure necessary carbon allowances—the largest environmental fine in the history of the United Kingdom.[27] In contrast to the emphasis on publicity in the United States, SEPA did nothing to publicize its record fine, and merely included it in its end of year report. A review of recent environmental fines publicized by the Environment Agency of the United Kingdom shows that the highest penalty was approximately $100,000. Notwithstanding this general trend of more modest penalties beyond the United States, prosecutors in some countries have displayed the ambition to impose much more substantial fines. Prosecutors in Brazil, for example, are seeking to impose an over $10 billion fine on Chevron for an oil spill that took place in November 2011 (and have additionally charged 17 individuals, including a U.S. citizen who was in charge of operations).[28] While such efforts have not yet borne fruit, they are worth noting as potential developments at the national enforcement level.

The distinction between the United States and the rest of the world with respect to criminal penalties is much the same. Most environmental violations in the United States are punishable by up to five years of imprisonment, and "knowing endangerment" violations—where individuals put others in danger of serious bodily injury or death as a result of statutorily specified environmental malfeasance—are punishable by up to 15 years of imprisonment. As a practical matter, the Federal Sentencing Guidelines (Part Q, Environmental Offenses), though only advisory to the sentencing judge (and apply only to individuals, not corporations), nonetheless exert great influence on the sentence to be handed down. The guidelines set up an elaborate system of factors to consider in sentencing (specific offense characteristics) such as whether the violation is repetitive, results in the substantial likelihood of death or bodily injury, requires a cleanup or disrupted a public utility, among other items and assigns a point system that ultimately yields a recommended sentencing range. For many "routine" environmental crimes without particularly severe environmental consequences (e.g., repetitive, knowing discharge of a pollutant into a navigable water) the guidelines recommend between one and two years in jail, though in aggravated cases the sentences can be far longer.

For example, a federal judge sentenced the owner of a fertilizer manufacturing company to serve 17 years in prison for the illegal treatment of hazardous waste that left an employee with permanent brain damage from cyanide poisoning, and the judge ordered the owner to pay $6 million in restitution to the victim and his family.[29] While that was a record sentence at the time, it did not take too long for another defendant to be sentenced to 25 years in prison for a series of crimes in which he illegally removed and disposed of asbestos insulation, while exposing his employees to the same.[30] While environmental crimes sentences in excess of five years of imprisonment remain relatively unusual in the United States, it is not unusual for those convicted of environmental crimes to be sentenced to two or more years of jail and substantial fines.

It is difficult to find instances in other countries where environmental criminals receive jail sentences of this length. In the United Kingdom, for example, the longest sentence ever handed out for a waste crime was to an organized crime boss who was imprisoned for nearly six years for running a massive illegal building waste site and committing money laundering with millions of pounds in profits.[31] The European Commission sought to strengthen and create greater uniformity in the pursuit of environmental crimes through the implementation of Directive 2008/99/EC, which requires member states no later than 2010 to implement changes in their laws including specifying a broad range of conduct as criminal if done "intentionally or through serious negligence" and imposing minimum penalties. One self-imposed limitation is that many of the acts criminalized (e.g., unlawful discharges into the air, soil, or water) require proof that the act "causes or is likely to cause death or serious injury to any person or substantial damage to the environment."[32] It is too early to determine whether the implementation of this directive will meet the stated goal of encouraging the prosecution of environmental crimes.

In China occasionally an environmental violation results in sufficient environmental degradation and adverse publicity and is sufficiently attributable to a particular business to result in significant criminal penalties. For example, in 2009 Biaoxin Chemical Co. discharged toxic chemicals on multiple occasions to the body of water serving as a city's drinking water supply resulting in 200,000 people being without water for three days. The chairman of the company was sentenced to 11 years in jail and a second defendant to six years.[33] In 2010 in China a wastewater leak from a gold mine caused extensive environmental damage including a large fish kill, and resulted in the imposition of a $4.6 million fine to Zijin Mining and five individuals, including the plant vice-president and the environmental compliance officer, being sentenced to between three and three and one-half years in jail.[34] While the sentences in these two cases appear to be exceedingly rare, one needs to be cautious evaluating enforcement in a country where the death sentence has been imposed for adulterating milk (resulting in the death of six infants) and where the "spreading of poison" is a capital offense. In contrast, while India uses criminal prosecution as an environmental enforcement tool, this writer could find no examples of large fines or significant terms of imprisonment being imposed.

V. Conclusion

This introductory section has overviewed some of the environmental enforcement landscape across the globe. The purpose has been to describe some of the similarities and differences in environmental enforcement with the United States being the primary reference point. On a structural level the systems have more similarities than differences. After all, they generally parallel the legislative taxonomy, in many cases supplemented by implementing regulations (of greater or lesser effectiveness), inspectors to check on whether businesses are complying with their environmental obligations, and two or more enforcement options, generally including administrative fines and criminal prosecution for serious violations. However, in implementation there are vast differences, with the maturity of the regulatory system and the availability of resources—including training, staffing, access to monitoring equipment and other technical resources, responsive and well-trained prosecutors, and adequate access to the courts—being key factors in whether environmental enforcement is effective.

One could probably fairly conclude that the United States stands alone in terms of the robustness of its environmental enforcement program as reflected by the reach and sophistication of its program, the number of enforcement actions it brings and the yield of the program in terms of pollution prevented, fines paid, convictions obtained, and defendants incarcerated. But these "outputs," while impressive, do not conclusively prove the ultimate effectiveness of environmental enforcement in the United States. It remains an open question whether highly robust environmental enforcement, in contrast with more collaborative approaches, best protect human health and the environment, encourage regulated parties to comply with environmental requirements, and deter potential violators from "crossing the line" to noncompliance. Moreover, in at least some other countries, a less robust approach may reflect that less enforcement is necessary than in the United States to deter environmental violations, perhaps due to the strong environmental values and highly cohesive or collaborative culture of those other countries. In such other countries, businesses may be adequately influenced to obey environmental requirements with a less confrontational and pervasive enforcement approach.

Finally, and at the risk of stating the obvious, by pointing out that other countries may not necessarily employ the same emphasis on environmental enforcement is not to suggest that any business based in the United States should operate with less stringent environmental safeguards than they would at home. Even if the prospect of environmental enforcement may be more remote or lacking the severity in some other countries, the best way to avoid the prospect of an unwanted, costly, and potentially embarrassing enforcement action is to operate a facility with the equivalent internal safeguards as those designed to avoid compliance problems under the vigilant enforcement found in the United States.

Notes

1. To be clear, throughout this chapter regarding enforcement, "civil" means a noncriminal judicial proceeding in a court of general jurisdiction (and not simply an action that is noncriminal in nature).

2. To take one example, in China the standard of proof in a criminal trial is "the facts are clear and the evidence is reliable and sufficient." Ira Belkin, *China's Criminal Justice System: A Work in Progress*, 6 Wash. J. Modern China 21 (Fall 2000).

3. The EU's Industrial Emissions Directive 2010 is a good example of its push toward more stringent enforcement. *See* Bettina Enderle, *Is the Grass Greener? The EU Industrial Emissions Directive: Implications for Environmental Permit Holders*, 14 Int'l L. Comm. Newsl. 2 (2012).

4. The author wishes to make clear from the very start that this is not an endorsement of how well the United States protects its or the global environment nor a criticism of how other countries do it. Indeed, many would object to the United States' lack of action on climate change, energy efficiency, lack of investment in public transportation, protection of public lands, relative ease with which new chemicals can be marketed or rapid embrace of hydraulic fracturing. Rather, it is simply to say that when an environmental law or regulation is enacted in the United States, chances are good, relative to most other countries, that it will be vigorously enforced.

5. U.S. EPA, Enforcement Annual Results for Fiscal Year 2012, http://www2.epa.gov/enforcement/enforcement-annual-results-fiscal-year-2012.

6. This total only includes formal administrative proceedings that are to be heard by administrative law judges—EPA is also responsible for numerous informal administrative actions, which can nonetheless result in fines.

7. Contrary to some misperceptions of the criminal justice system in the United States, the years of imprisonment imposed by a federal judge may generally only be reduced by up to 15 percent of the sentence imposed, and thus is generally quite close to the amount of time actually served by the defendants.

8. To be sure, many violations that have serious pollution consequences are not necessarily subject to criminal prosecution because the burden of proving criminal intent cannot be met (i.e., no party can be shown to have acted in a "knowing" manner). In other cases, the technical requirements of the regulations are particularly complex, as in certain air pollution requirements, making them too difficult to successfully explain to a jury. Thus, for example, violations involving excess emissions from power plants may have significant human health consequences, but typically have been pursued civilly due to the challenge of proving guilt beyond a reasonable doubt.

9. I have reached this conclusion through a variety of sources, including reviewing the websites of the environmental agencies in a number of leading countries, searching key newspapers throughout the world, and surveying additional enforcement literature available on the Internet.

10. *See* Enforcement and Compliance History Online (ECHO), http://www.epa-echo.gov/echo/stateperformance/dashboard.php?media=water&state=National&view=activity. This exceptionally powerful database of enforcement activity contains the permit, inspection, and enforcement histories of over 800,000 regulated facilities, including both federal and state data, and permits the user to manipulate data in a variety of ways including the creation of reports and maps showing enforcement actions and trends. It appears to have no counterpart in other countries.

11. Criminal cases naturally require the highest level of intent. Though there is some variation, most environmental statutes require that a criminal defendant has acted "knowingly."

12. The Macrory Review, which has been very influential in the United Kingdom's transition to principally relying on regulatory penalties from criminal prosecution, details numerous reasons why that evolution is beneficial from the standpoint of greater environmental protection, efficiency, and leveling the playing field for businesses. OFFICE OF THE BETTER REGULATION EXECUTIVE (U.K.), REGULATORY JUSTICE: MAKING SANCTIONS EFFECTIVE (1996), http://www.berr.gov.uk/files/file44593.pdf.

13. Christian Almery & Timo Goeschly, *Environmental Crime and Punishment: Empirical Evidence from the German Penal Code*, 86 LAND ECON. 707, 711 (2010).

14. For example, in 2012 U.S. EPA brought a total of 1,494 formal and informal (noncriminal) enforcement actions under its three primary statutes covering air, water, and hazardous waste (but not covering less actively enforced programs such as pesticides and toxics) versus 232 criminal defendants indicted under all statutes. ECHO, *supra* note 10. Note that the actual number of criminal cases brought by EPA would be far less than 232

as in most cases multiple defendants are criminally charged, so the figure probably represents less than 100 distinct cases, which would suggest a rate of criminal prosecution of roughly five percent.

15. According to U.S. EPA's ECHO data base, *supra* note 10, the 50 states brought a total of 19,479 formal and informal enforcement actions under air, water, and hazardous waste statutes in 2012 compared with 1,494 such actions brought by U.S. EPA. ECHO shows a corresponding disparity in the number of inspections conducted.

16. U.S. DOJ's Environment and Natural Resources Division (ENRD) is entirely dedicated to pollution, conservation, and related matters. The U.S. Attorney's Offices in the majority of the 94 judicial districts also have experienced environmental attorneys litigating these cases, either with or without the support of ENRD.

17. OECD, Environmental Compliance and Enforcement in India: Rapid Assessment 13 (2006), http://www.oecd.org/env/outreach/37838061.pdf (last visited Sept. 8, 2013). This report provides excellent detail concerning environmental enforcement in India and is highly recommended for anyone seeking an in-depth view of the challenges facing the strengthening of the system.

18. *Id.* at 18.

19. The West Bengal PCB cut off power to businesses 222 times in a 12-month period during 2005–2006. *Id.* at 13.

20. World Wildlife Fund (India), http://www.wwfindia.org/about_wwf/enablers/cel /national_green_tribunal/ (last visited Mar. 28, 2013).

21. Rainer Quitzow, Holger Bär & Klaus Jacob, *Asia at a Crossroads: New Trends in Environmental Governance in India, China, Vietnam and Indonesia* 5 (Envtl. Policy Research Ctr. (FFU), Freie Universität Berlin, 2011).

22. OECD, Environmental Compliance and Enforcement in China: An Assessment of Current Practices and Ways Forward 17 (2006), http://www.oecd.org /environment/outreach/37867511.pdf.

23. *Id.* at 26.

24. *Id.* at 26—27.

25. Dep't of Justice Press Release, Nov. 15, 2012, http://www.justice.gov/opa/pr /2012/November/12-ag-1369.html.

26. *See* U.S. EPA, Civil Cases and Settlements, http://cfpub.epa.gov/compliance/cases /index.cfm?templatePage=12&ID=3&sortby=TITLE.

27. *Oil Giant Exxonmobil Pays Record Fine for Greenhouse Gas Emissions*, Times (U.K.), Feb. 20, 2012. http://www.thetimes.co.uk/tto/news/uk/scotland/article3325291.ece.

28. *Chevron, Transocean Charged in Brazilian Oil Spill*, Reuters, May 22, 2012, http:// www.reuters.com/article/2012/03/22/us-chevron-spill-idUSBRE82K0PL20120322.

29. U.S. DOJ press release, Apr. 29, 2000, http://www.justice.gov/opa/pr/2000 /April/239enrd.htm.

30. U.S. DOJ press release, Dec. 23, 2004, http://www.justice.gov/opa/pr/2004 /December/04_enrd_803.htm.

31. Emily Gosden, *Jail for Boss of Illegal Waste Site "the Size of Five Football Pitches,"* Telegraph, June 24, 2011, http://www.telegraph.co.uk/news/uknews/crime/8597855 /Jail-for-boss-of-illegal-waste-site-the-size-of-five-football-pitches.html.

32. Europa, Protection of the Environment through Criminal Law, http://europa .eu/legislation_summaries/justice_freedom_security/fight_against_organised_crime /ev0012_en.htm (last visited Mar. 28, 2013).

33. *A New Era of Environmental Crimes in China?*, China Envtl. L. (Aug. 20, 2009), http://www.chinaenvironmentallaw.com/2009/08/20/a-new-era-of-environmental -crimes-in-china/.

34. *Zijin Mining Fined 4.6m Over Toxic Spill*, China Daily (May 4, 2011).

PART III

International Environmental Law Digest

CHAPTER 16

North America Overview: NAFTA, the CEC, and Other Bilateral/Trilateral Institutions

JOHN H. KNOX

The United States, Canada, and Mexico have entered into many international environmental agreements with one another.[1] Most are bilateral, but all three countries belong to one regional environmental agreement, the North American Agreement on Environmental Cooperation (NAAEC).[2] This chapter describes first the agreements between the United States and Canada, then the U.S-Mexico agreements, and finally the NAAEC.

I. Agreements between the United States and Canada

The United States and Canada have a long history of environmental cooperation, which has resulted in agreements concerning (1) the lakes and rivers along their long boundary; (2) transboundary air pollution; (3) cross-border trade in hazardous and solid waste; and (4) conservation of species of mutual interest.

A. Boundary Waters

The oldest North American environmental agreement is the 1909 Boundary Waters Treaty, which is principally directed at establishing reciprocal freedom of navigation in, and regulating diversions from, the Great Lakes and other border water bodies.[3] Under the treaty, obstructions and diversions on either side of the boundary that affect the level or flow of waters on the other side may occur only with the approval of an independent, binational body, the International Joint Commission (IJC).[4] The countries have also negotiated agreements on the development of particular border water resources, such as the Columbia River.[5]

The 1909 Boundary Waters Treaty includes a general prohibition on harmful transboundary water pollution,[6] but it leaves implementation entirely to the governments; unlike diversions of the boundary waters, transboundary

285

pollution may occur without IJC approval. In the decades after the Boundary Waters Treaty entered into force, the level of pollution in the Great Lakes greatly increased.

In response, the United States and Canada entered into an agreement aimed at improving Great Lakes water quality. First signed in 1972, the agreement has been amended several times, most recently in September 2012.[7] In its current form, the agreement does not commit the parties to particular emissions reductions. Instead, it sets out general objectives for the Great Lakes (including that they should be a source of safe, high-quality drinking water and free from pollutants at levels that could be harmful to human health or wildlife), provides for the joint development of more specific objectives, and states that the parties shall use their best efforts to ensure that their regulatory standards and requirements are consistent with all of the objectives. It also requires that the parties monitor environmental conditions and report on the extent to which the objectives are being met, provides for reciprocal notification of planned projects that could cause harmful pollution, extends the role of the IJC in monitoring water quality, and includes annexes with more detailed commitments in specific areas, including nutrients, discharges from vessels, and invasive species.[8]

B.   Transboundary Air Pollution

Spurred by Canadian complaints over the contribution by U.S. industrial sources to acid rain in Canada, the United States and Canada entered into an Air Quality Agreement in 1991.[9] The agreement requires each party to establish specific objectives for limitations or reductions of transboundary air pollutants, and sets out such objectives for sulfur dioxide and nitrogen oxides. An annex added in 2000 establishes similar objectives for precursors to ground-level ozone,[10] and since 2007 the parties have engaged in talks aimed at objectives for particulate matter.[11] The United States generally carries out its emissions reduction commitments under the treaty through existing domestic law, including in particular the Clean Air Act.[12]

More generally, the Air Quality Agreement requires the parties to undertake environmental impact assessment, prior notification, and, as appropriate, mitigation measures, in accordance with domestic law, for proposed projects likely to cause significant transboundary air pollution.[13] It provides for cooperative scientific and technical activities and research, as well as the exchange of information regarding air pollution, monitoring, and control technologies.[14] It also establishes an Air Quality Committee, composed of government appointees, which publishes biannual progress reports on implementation of the agreement.[15]

C.   Cross-Border Trade in Hazardous and Solid Waste

In 1986, Canada and the United States entered into an agreement to regulate the shipment of hazardous waste across their common border.[16] The agreement requires the environmental agency (in the United States, EPA; in Canada, the Department of the Environment) of the exporting country to notify its counterpart in the country of import of proposed transboundary shipments of hazardous waste.[17] Under the agreement, the term "hazardous waste" refers to such waste as defined in the respective national laws of the two countries.[18] In 1992, the scope of the agreement was widened to include municipal solid waste sent for final disposal or incineration, again as defined in national laws.[19]

The notice may be of just one shipment or of a series of shipments taking place over a period of time up to one year. The notice must provide certain information, including the names and contact information of the exporter, transporter, and consignee; a description of the waste to be exported and the means of transportation; and a description of "the manner in which the waste will be treated, stored or disposed of in the importing country."[20] The country of import has 30 days to indicate its approval or disapproval of the proposed import.[21] The parties also agree to cooperate in monitoring transboundary shipments of waste to ensure, to the extent possible, that the shipments conform to the applicable legal requirements.[22]

D. Conservation of Species

The United States and Canada have entered into several treaties on the conservation of species. In 1916, they signed an agreement that generally prohibits the taking of listed migratory birds with the exception of certain game birds, such as wild ducks and pigeons, for which it requires specific closed seasons.[23] In the United States, the treaty is implemented through the Migratory Birds Treaty Act.[24] In 1995, the parties agreed to amend the treaty to: add a general commitment to use their authority to protect the environment of the migratory birds, including through pollution control, habitat conservation, and protection against invasive species; allow indigenous groups in Alaska and Canada to hunt covered birds for subsistence purposes; and provide for regular meetings to review progress in implementing the agreement.[25]

The two countries have also entered into bilateral agreements on fisheries. In order to conserve stocks of fish that straddle or move between their jurisdictions, fisheries agreements typically include restrictions on allowable catches, provide for allocation of fishing rights between the parties, and establish binational institutions to facilitate implementation of the commitments. A leading example is the Pacific Salmon Treaty, which was signed in 1985 and has been substantially amended several times, including in 1999 and 2008.[26] Other agreements address halibut and Pacific hake.[27]

The United States and Canada also negotiated an agreement on conservation of the Porcupine (River) caribou herd, whose range includes territory in Alaska and northwestern Canada and that migrates annually more than 700 miles to and from its calving grounds on the Arctic coastal plain.[28] The 1987 agreement calls for various cooperative measures, including assessment of activities likely to cause adverse effects on the herd or its habitat, and notification and consultation when an action in either country is determined to be a likely cause of long-term adverse impact on the herd or its habitat.[29]

II.   Agreements between the United States and Mexico

The environmental agreements between the United States and Mexico are similar in some respects to those between the United States and Canada, but they also have substantial differences. The United States and Mexico have entered into agreements on boundary waters, air quality, hazardous waste, and conservation of species, but they have also devoted attention to the general environmental quality of their border region, including by establishing mechanisms for financing wastewater treatment plants and other environmental infrastructure projects. The following sections describe the U.S.-Mexico agreements concerning: boundary waters; border environmental protection; border infrastructure; and conservation of migratory species.[30]

A.   Boundary Waters

A 1944 agreement known as the Water Treaty allocates the water of the Colorado River and the Rio Grande between the two countries and provides for the construction of facilities to maximize the amount of water available.[31] The treaty authorizes the International Boundary and Water Commission (IBWC) to develop and operate specified dams, reservoirs, and other public works.[32] The IBWC has two national sections, each of which is headed by a commissioner.[33] The sections make joint decisions through "minutes" signed by the commissioners and approved by the governments. Through these minutes, the governments have approved a number of projects in addition to those listed in the 1944 Water Treaty.

B.   Border Environmental Quality

In 1983, Mexico and the United States entered into an Agreement on Cooperation for the Protection and Improvement of the Environment in the Border Area, known as the "La Paz Agreement" after the city in which it was signed.[34] The La Paz Agreement requires each party to adopt appropriate measures to prevent, reduce, and eliminate sources of transboundary pollution, and to assess "as appropriate in accordance with their respective national laws, regulations and policies," projects with significant effects on the border environment, so that "appropriate measures may be considered to avoid or mitigate adverse environmental effects."[35]

More concretely, the La Paz Agreement establishes a forum for addressing border environmental issues. Under the agreement, two "national coordinators" oversee cooperation between the governments on a wide variety of issues, including air pollution, water pollution, and hazardous waste. The governments have adopted a series of border programs that set long-term goals to be implemented by working groups and task forces, which are composed of representatives from the local and regional as well as the national levels.[36]

Five annexes to the La Paz Agreement include more specific provisions on particular topics. Annex I, concluded in 1985, calls for cooperation in addressing wastewater treatment in the Tijuana-San Diego area.[37] In Annex II, also signed in 1985, the United States and Mexico agree to establish a joint contingency plan to deal effectively with polluting incidents in the border region.[38]

Annex III addresses the transboundary shipment of hazardous waste and hazardous substances.[39] Like the U.S.-Canada agreement on hazardous and other waste, it requires prior notification of transboundary shipments. Specifically, it requires each party to notify the other 45 days in advance of transboundary shipments (which may be of an individual shipment or of a series of shipments lasting up to one year), when the consent of the country of import is required by the laws of the country of export.[40] The notification must include the name and contact information for the exporter, transporter, and consignee; the means of transportation; and a description of the planned disposal of the waste.[41] The country of import has 45 days to indicate its approval or disapproval of the proposed shipment.[42] In addition, each country is required to notify the other when it bans or severely restricts a pesticide or chemical.[43]

In Annex IV, concluded in 1987, the United States and Mexico agree to restrict sulfur dioxide emissions from copper smelters in the border area.[44] Annex V, signed in 1989, concerns air pollution more generally.[45] It provides that with respect to designated "study areas," the two countries will identify the magnitude of emissions of selected pollutants, the sources of the pollutants, and the steps necessary to control the emissions.[46] It also provides that the parties will monitor and issue periodic reports on air pollution in the study areas.[47] The only study area named in the agreement is El Paso/Ciudad Juárez.[48]

C. Border Infrastructure

In 1979, the governments agreed that the IBWC has the authority to identify and propose solutions to problems of transboundary water pollution, including through the development of wastewater treatment facilities.[49] Since then, the IBWC has overseen the construction of a number of such facilities in border cities. Despite these efforts, however, it became clear by the early 1990s that billions of dollars in new investment would be needed to build sufficient water treatment, wastewater, and solid waste infrastructure to meet the needs of the rapidly growing population in the border region.

In response, Mexico and the United States decided in 1993 to establish two new institutions to facilitate financing for border environmental infrastructure.[50] The Border Environment Cooperation Commission (BECC) provides technical expertise to communities for projects within the border region (and, with the approval of the two governments, for projects outside the border region that would remedy a transboundary environmental problem), and it certifies projects that meet certain environmental and technical requirements. The North American Development Bank (NADBank) prepares funding packages for projects certified by the BECC.[51]

The BECC began receiving applications for assistance and certification in 1995. Through September 2012, it has certified 201 projects (110 in Mexico and 91 in the United States), and the NADBank has provided over $700 million in loans to support the implementation of the projects.[52] In addition, the NADBank has disbursed over $500 million in grants from funding provided by the EPA Border Environment Infrastructure Fund.[53] While the NADBank principally supports water, wastewater, and solid waste facilities, it can finance a broader array of projects designed to reduce pollution and protect the environment.[54]

D. Species Conservation

In 1936, the United States and Mexico signed a convention on the protection of migratory birds, which is similar but not identical to the 1916 migratory birds treaty with Canada. The U.S.-Mexico treaty commits the parties to limit hunting of listed birds to no more than four months in a year, to establish refuge zones in which takings of the birds are completely prohibited, and to generally ban the taking of insectivorous birds.[55] In addition, the parties agree to prohibit the transportation over their common border of migratory birds and game mammals.[56] In 1972, the parties added to the list of birds, and in 1997, they adjusted the closed season on taking wild ducks to allow subsistence hunting by indigenous groups in Alaska.[57] Like the U.S.-Canada treaty, the U.S.-Mexico treaty is implemented in the United States by the Migratory Birds Treaty Act.[58]

In 1989, the U.S. National Park Service and the Mexican environmental agency entered into a memorandum of understanding (MOU) on cooperation in management and protection of national parks, in which they agreed to meet regularly and to exchange information and personnel. The MOU does not set out substantive obligations, but instead identifies potential areas of cooperation, including establishment of natural and cultural heritage areas, monitoring of protected areas, especially those contiguous to the border, and technical cooperation to protect flora and fauna within shared ecosystems protected by one or both countries.[59]

III.   The North American Agreement on Environmental Cooperation

The three North American countries negotiated the NAAEC in 1993, during the debate over approval of NAFTA. Environmental critics of NAFTA were concerned that by lowering barriers to international trade and investment, NAFTA would lead U.S. companies to move to Mexico in search of lower-cost environmental standards. They generally acknowledged that on paper, Mexican environmental laws were comparable to those of the United States and Canada, but argued that the laws were ineffectively enforced. In response, the three countries adopted a supplemental agreement, the NAAEC, aimed at ensuring effective enforcement of environmental laws.[60]

The NAAEC does far more than promote effective enforcement, however. As the following sections describe, the agreement (1) sets out binding obligations; (2) creates a regional environmental organization, the Commission for Environmental Cooperation; (3) provides for cooperative programs; (4) creates a mechanism for intergovernmental dispute resolution; and (5) establishes a citizen submissions procedure.

A. Obligations

The NAAEC sets out several obligations that apply to each of the parties. Two of the obligations are aimed at discouraging countries from lowering their environmental standards to attract foreign investment. Article 5 requires each party to "effectively enforce its environmental laws."[61] To prevent countries from achieving effective enforcement of the laws by weakening the laws as written, Article 3 requires each party to "ensure that its laws and regulations provide for high levels of environmental protection," and "strive to continue to improve those laws and regulations."[62]

In addition, the NAAEC includes more specific obligations, including requiring each of the parties to: periodically publish reports on the state of the environment; promote environmental education; notify the other parties whenever it prohibits or severely restricts the use of a pesticide or other toxic substance; promptly publish its environmental laws; and ensure that its environmental enforcement proceedings are "fair, open and equitable" and before "impartial and independent" tribunals.[63]

None of these obligations appears to have required changes in domestic laws. Instead, the parties have viewed these commitments as being met by their existing environmental laws and policies. No party has accused another of failing to comply with any of these obligations in the years since they were agreed.

B. Commission for Environmental Cooperation

The NAAEC created a new international institution, the Commission for Environmental Cooperation (CEC), which has three components: a Council made up of the environmental ministers (or their designates); a secretariat of international civil servants; and a joint public advisory committee (JPAC) composed of 15 individuals, five from each country.[64]

The Council serves as a forum for the parties to discuss issues of shared interest on a cooperative basis.[65] The secretariat is composed of international civil servants headed by an executive director, who is appointed by the Council to a three-year term.[66] In addition to supporting the Council, the secretariat has some independent functions: it administers the citizen submissions procedure described below, and it has limited authority to prepare independent reports on its own initiative.[67] The JPAC, which meets several times a year, serves as an avenue for public concerns and questions to reach the Council.[68] While each government appoints five members from its own country, the JPAC has generally acted as a unified body in preparing recommendations for the Council.[69]

C.   Cooperative Programs

The NAAEC sets out a long list of topics for possible consideration by the Council, but the list is not exhaustive and in practice the Council can take on virtually any environmental issue it chooses.[70] The Council has established working groups to address issues on a continuing basis, and some of these cooperative endeavors have resulted in concrete changes to environmental policy. For example, the working group on the sound management of chemicals has helped to phase out the use of certain toxic chemicals, including DDT, in Mexico, and the CEC's cooperative work on pollutant releases and transfers is credited with helping Mexico establish its first national toxic release inventory.[71] Nevertheless, the CEC's limited budget— only about $9 million per year—has limited its ability to influence North American environmental policy.

D.   Dispute Resolution

Part Five of the NAAEC sets out a detailed intergovernmental dispute resolution procedure, through which any party to the agreement may accuse another party of engaging in "a persistent pattern of failure . . . to effectively enforce its environmental law."[72] If requested by a party, the Council may decide by a two-thirds vote to convene an arbitral panel to hear the complaint, where the alleged pattern of failure to enforce relates to goods or services traded between the territories of the parties or in competition with goods or services of one another.[73] Under certain circumstances, the panel has the authority to establish an "action plan" to remedy the problem and to impose fines on a recalcitrant party.[74] If the party does not pay, the complaining party may suspend NAFTA benefits.[75]

It seems highly doubtful, however, that Part Five will ever result in sanctions. In the 20 years after the negotiation of the NAAEC, no government has ever brought a complaint under it. Indeed, the parties have never even negotiated the rules of procedure for the arbitral panels. To some degree, this is likely due to the reluctance of the parties to accuse one another of failing to effectively enforce their environmental laws. It may also be due to the realization, as shown by a number of post-NAFTA studies, that companies rarely if ever shift operations in search of lower environmental standards.[76]

E.   Citizen Submissions

Articles 14 and 15 of the NAAEC create a procedure through which any person or non-governmental organization in North America may complain that a party is failing to effectively enforce its environmental law. Unlike the Part Five procedure, there is no requirement of a link to trade or competition between the parties. The submission goes to the secretariat, which decides in the first instance whether it meets admissibility criteria set out in the NAAEC.[77] If the secretariat determines that the submission is admissible, then it decides whether it merits requesting a response from the party concerned, in light of four factors, including whether "the submission . . . raises matters whose further study in this process would advance the goals of this Agreement," and "private remedies available under the Party's law have been pursued."[78] In light of the response from the party, the secretariat may inform the Council that further investigation is warranted. In that case, the Council decides by a two-thirds vote whether to instruct the secretariat to prepare a "factual record" on the issues raised by the submission.[79] Factual records are not binding, and they do not include legal conclusions on whether a party has failed to effectively enforce its laws. Nevertheless, by providing an objective investigative description, they may give a basis for others to draw their own conclusions on that question.

In contrast to the moribund Part Five procedure, the citizen submissions procedure has been active. Through 2012, the secretariat has received 80 submissions. Half (40) of the submissions have been against Mexico, 31 against Canada, and only ten against the United States.[80] The secretariat has dismissed 26 submissions on admissibility grounds, declined to proceed with another 17 after receiving the party's response, and recommended factual records in 26 cases.[81] Of the 26 secretariat recommendations for factual records, the Council has approved 21 and declined only two,[82] although it has sometimes narrowed the scope of the secretariat recommendations in ways that have drawn criticisms from submitters and outside observers.[83] The procedure has resulted in 17 factual records to date, almost all of which have concerned Canada or Mexico.

Notes

1. The focus of this chapter is on agreements only among the North American countries. The countries also belong to many international environmental agreements with broader membership, such as the Framework Convention on Climate Change and the Montreal Protocol on Substances that Deplete the Ozone Layer.

2. North American Agreement on Environmental Cooperation (NAAEC), Sept. 14, 1993, 32 I.L.M. 1480.

3. Treaty between the United States and Great Britain Relating to Boundary Waters between the United States and Canada, Jan. 11, 1909, 36 Stat. 2449.

4. *Id.* arts. III, IV. Each government appoints three of the six IJC commissioners. The website of the IJC is http://www.ijc.org/.

5. Treaty relating to Cooperative Development of the Water Resources of the Columbia River Basin, Jan. 17, 1961, 15 U.S.T. 1555, 16 U.S.T. 1263.

6. 1909 Boundary Waters Treaty, *supra* note 3, art. IV ("the waters herein defined as boundary waters and waters flowing across the boundary shall not be polluted on either side to the injury of health or property on the other").

7. Great Lakes Water Quality Agreement of 2012, *available at* http://www.epa.gov /glnpo/glwqa/.

8. *Id.* arts. 3, 4, 6, 7, annexes.

9. Agreement on Air Quality, Mar. 13, 1991, 30 I.L.M. 676 (1991).

10. Annex 3: Specific Objectives Concerning Ground-level Ozone Precursors, *available at* http://www.ec.gc.ca/air/default.asp?lang=En&n=9992B080-1.

11. Joint Statement by the Governments of Canada and the United States of America on Bilateral Cooperation to Improve Air Quality, Apr. 12, 2007, *available at* http://www .epa.gov/usca/jointstatement.html.

12. 42 U.S.C. §§ 7401 *et seq.*

13. Agreement on Air Quality, *supra* note 9, art. V.

14. *Id.* arts. VI, VII.

15. The 2012 report is available at http://www.epa.gov/airmarkets/progsregs /usca/docs/2012report.pdf.

16. Agreement concerning the Transboundary Shipment of Hazardous Waste, Oct. 28, 1986, 2120 U.N.T.S. 97.

17. *Id.* art. 3(a).

18. *Id.* art. 1(b). For the United States, the definition only includes "hazardous waste subject to a manifest requirement in the United States," as defined by U.S. law. *Id.*

19. *Id.* art. 1(h).

20. *Id.* art. 3(b).

21. *Id.* art. 3(d).

22. *Id.* art. 5.

23. Convention for the Protection of Migratory Birds, Aug. 16, 1916, 39 Stat. 1702.

24. 16 U.S.C. §§ 703–712.

25. Protocol Amending the 1916 Convention for the Protection of Migratory Birds, Dec. 14, 1995, T.I.A.S. No. 12,721.

26. Treaty concerning Pacific Salmon, Jan. 28, 1985, 1469 U.N.T.S. 357. A version including the more recent amendments is available from the Pacific Salmon Commission, the organization established to assist in implementing the treaty, at http://www.psc.org /publications_psctreaty.htm.

27. *E.g.*, Convention for the preservation of the halibut fishery of the Northern Pacific Ocean and Bering Sea, Mar. 2, 1953, 5 U.S.T. 5, amended Mar. 29, 1979, 32 U.S.T. 2483; Agreement on Pacific Hake/Whiting, Nov. 21, 2003, S. Treaty Doc. No. 108-24 (2004).

28. Agreement on the conservation of the Porcupine Caribou Herd, July 17, 1987, 2174 U.N.T.S. 267.

29. *Id.* art. 3.

30. These sections cover virtually all of the bilateral environmental agreements between the countries, with the exception of a handful of agreements that call for cooperation in addressing certain problems but do not contain substantive requirements. *See, e.g.*, Agreement on Cooperation for the Protection and Improvement of the Environment in the Metropolitan Area of Mexico City, Oct. 3, 1989, 2191 U.N.T.S. 269; Agreement regarding Pollution of the Marine Environment by Discharge of Hydrocarbons and Other Hazardous Substances, July 24, 1980, 32 U.S.T. 5899.

31. Treaty Relating to the Utilization of Waters of the Colorado and Tijuana Rivers and of the Rio Grande, Feb. 3, 1944, 59 Stat. 1219. An earlier agreement had allocated

water of the Rio Grande between El Paso and Fort Quitman. Convention Providing for the Equitable Distribution of the Waters of the Rio Grande for Irrigation Purposes, May 21, 1906, 34 Stat. 2953.

32. *Id.* arts. 5, 6, 7.

33. The IBWC website is http://www.ibwc.state.gov/.

34. La Paz Agreement on Cooperation for the Protection and Improvement of the Environment in the Border Area, Aug. 14, 1983, 22 I.L.M. 1025 (1983).

35. *Id.* arts. 2, 7.

36. The most recent program, Border 2020, was adopted in September 2012. Its home page is http://www2.epa.gov/border2020.

37. Annex I: Agreement of cooperation for solution of the border sanitation problem at San Diego, California/Tijuana, Baja, California, July 18, 1985, T.I.A.S. No. 11,269.

38. Annex II: Agreement of cooperation regarding pollution of the environment along the inland international boundary by discharges of hazardous substances, July 18, 1985, T.I.A.S. No. 11,269.

39. Annex III: Agreement of Cooperation Regarding the Transboundary Shipments of Hazardous Wastes and Hazardous Substances, Nov. 12, 1986, 26 I.L.M. 25. The Annex defines "hazardous waste" as "any waste, as designated or defined by [the United States or Mexico] pursuant to national policies, laws or regulations, which if improperly dealt with in activities associated with them, may result in health or environmental damage." *Id.* art. I(2). It defines "hazardous substance" as "any substance, as designated or defined by the applicable national policies, laws or regulations, including pesticides or chemicals, which when improperly dealt with in activities associated with them, may produce harmful effects to public health, property or the environment, and is banned or severely restricted by [the United States or Mexico]." *Id.* art. I(3).

40. In general, U.S. law requires such consent. Resource Conservation and Recovery Act § 3017(a), 42 U.S.C. § 6938(a).

41. Annex III, *supra* note 39, art. III.

42. *Id.*

43. *Id.* art. V.

44. Annex IV: Agreement of cooperation regarding transboundary air pollution caused by copper smelters along their common border, Jan. 29, 1987, T.I.A.S. No. 11,269.

45. Annex V: Agreement of Cooperation Regarding International Transport of Urban Air Pollution, Oct. 3, 1989, T.I.A.S. No. 11,269.

46. *Id.* art. II.

47. *Id.* arts. II, IV.

48. *Id.* app.

49. Minute 261 concerning Recommendations for the Solution to the Border Sanitation Problems, Sept. 24, 1979, 31 U.S.T. 5099.

50. Agreement Concerning the Establishment of a Border Environment Cooperation Commission and a North American Development Bank, Nov. 16–18, 1993, T.I.A.S. No. 12,516. The agreement establishing the BECC and NADBank was amended in 2004. Protocol of Amendment to the Agreement Concerning the Establishment of a Border Environment Cooperation Commission and a North American Development Bank, app. 1, Nov. 25–26, 2002, *available at* http://www.becc.org/uploads/content/images/BECC-NADB -Charter.pdf. The border region was initially defined as the area within 100 kilometers of the border, but the 2004 amendment extended it to include the area within 300 kilometers of the border on the Mexican side. *Id.* ch. V, art. II.

51. The two institutions were initially governed by two separate boards of directors, but the 2004 amendment created one unified ten-member board, composed of three federal officials, one border state official, and one resident of the border region, from each country. *Id.* ch. I, art. III, § 3.

52. BECC/NADBank Quarterly Status Report 16, 19 (Sept. 2012), available at the website of the NADBank, http://www.nadbank.org.

53. *Id.* at 19.

54. The agreement defines "environmental infrastructure project" as "a project that will prevent, control or reduce environmental pollutants or contaminants, improve the drinking water supply, or protect flora and fauna so as to improve human health, promote sustainable development, or contribute to a higher quality of life." BECC/NADBank Agreement, *supra*, ch. V. art. II. For example, the BECC has certified, and the NADBank has approved financing for, pilot projects aimed at improving energy efficiency and renewable energy, including a biodiesel production plant in El Paso, a methane capture project for a dairy farm in Chihuahua, and a solar-panel program in Baja, California. NADBANK ANNUAL REPORT 2008, at 12, 14 (2008), http://www.nadbank.org/pdf/publications/2008AnnualReport .pdf.

55. Convention for the Protection of Migratory Birds and Game Mammals, Feb. 7, 1936, art. II, 50 Stat. 1311.

56. *Id.* arts. III, V.

57. Agreement supplementing the Convention of February 7, 1936, for the Protection of Migratory Birds and Game Mammals, Mar. 10, 1972, 23 U.S.T. 260; Protocol amending the Convention for the Protection of Migratory Birds and Game Animals art. I, May 5, 1997.

58. 16 U.S.C. §§ 703–712.

59. Memorandum of Understanding on Cooperation in Management and Protection of National Parks and Other Protected Natural and Cultural Heritage Sites, Nov. 30, 1988 & Jan. 24, 1989, 2304 U.N.T.S. 357.

60. *See* John H. Knox & David L. Markell, *The Innovative North American Commission for Environmental Cooperation, in* GREENING NAFTA: THE NORTH AMERICAN COMMISSION FOR ENVIRONMENTAL COOPERATION 1 (David L. Markell & John H. Knox eds., 2003).

61. NAAEC, *supra* note 2, art. 5.

62. *Id.* art. 3.

63. *Id.* arts. 2, 4, 6, 7.

64. CEC, http://www.cec.org.

65. NAAEC, *supra* note 2, art. 9.

66. *Id.* art. 11.

67. *Id.* art. 13. For example, it announced in February 2012 that it would conduct an article 13 report into the environmental and health issues associated with the transboundary movement and recycling of spent lead-acid batteries. *See* CEC, Environmental Hazards of the Transboundary Movement and Recycling of Spent Lead-Acid Batteries, at http://www.cec.org/Page.asp?PageID=751&SiteNodeID=1075&AA_SiteLanguageID=1.

68. NAAEC, *supra* note 2, art. 16.

69. *See* John D. Wirth, *Perspectives on the Joint Public Advisory Committee, in* GREENING NAFTA, *supra* note 60, at 199.

70. NAAEC, *supra* note 2, art. 10.

71. *See* Mark S. Winfield, *North American Pollutant Release and Transfer Registries: A Case Study in Environmental Policy Convergence, in* GREENING NAFTA, *supra* note 60, at 38.

72. NAAEC, *supra* note 2, art. 22(1).

73. *Id.* art. 24(1).

74. *Id.* art. 34.

75. *Id.* art. 36.

76. *See, e.g.,* KEVIN P. GALLAGHER, FREE TRADE AND THE ENVIRONMENT: MEXICO, NAFTA, AND BEYOND (2004).

77. For example, the submission must "clearly identif[y] the person or organization making the submission," and provide "sufficient information to allow the Secretariat to review the submission." NAAEC, *supra* note 2, art. 14(1).

78. *Id.* art. 14(2).

79. *Id.* art. 15(2).

80. One of the submissions was against Canada and the United States jointly. *See* Devils Lake, SEM-06-002 (filed Mar. 30, 2006). The submissions may be found at the CEC Registry of Submissions, at http://www.cec.org/Page.asp?PageID=924&SiteNodeID=250.

81. Of the other 11, two were consolidated with other submissions and two were withdrawn before final decision by the Secretariat. Seven are still pending Secretariat decision.

82. Of the remaining three, the Council consolidated one with another submission and two were withdrawn by the submitters after being submitted to the Council.

83. *See, e.g.*, Chris Wold et al., *The Inadequacy of the Citizen Submission Process of Articles 14 & 15 of the North American Agreement on Environmental Cooperation*, 26 Loy. L.A. Int'l & Comp. L. Rev. 415 (2004).

CHAPTER 17

United States

EUGENE E. SMARY AND SCOTT WATSON

I. Introduction

This chapter provides a brief summary of U.S. environmental law. It is a starting point for the interested practitioner or student. U.S. environmental law is constantly evolving. Environmental statutes and regulations rarely remain static, and even when they do, the law evolves through application in specific cases. Accordingly, statements of general principles do not always completely reflect the competing positions behind the often complex and sometimes nuanced resolution of issues decided by agencies and courts. The general framework set out in this chapter is only the first step. The reader is encouraged to supplement study of this chapter with review of current versions of the statutes regulations and cases that put flesh on specific issues in the skeleton outlined here.

II. Air and Climate Change
A. Air Pollution Control

At its core, the federal Clean Air Act (CAA) is intended to regulate the emission of pollutants into the ambient air in the United States.[1] It is a maddeningly complex statute, with specificity rarely seen in legislative acts and ostensibly clarified by perhaps the most voluminous set of regulations in the Code of Federal Regulations.[2] There are many important provisions in the CAA, but at the highest level of generality the CAA understood as consisting of four key parts: NAAQS, PSD, stationary source requirements, and mobile source requirements.

The first key part of the Clean Air Act is the National Ambient Air Quality Standards (NAAQS).[3] The NAAQS guarantee that ambient air across the United States is protective of public health and welfare.[4] Primary NAAQS protect public health within a predetermined appropriate margin of safety.[5] Secondary NAAQS protect public welfare.[6] The pollutants subject to the NAAQS are usually referred to as "criteria pollutants" because Congress directed EPA to establish the NAAQS after identifying and publishing air quality criteria for the pollutants and their impact on public health and welfare. There are currently six criteria pollutants: ozone, particulate matter, carbon monoxide, nitrogen oxides, sulfur dioxide, and lead.[7] Ground-level ozone is not emitted directly but is formed through the interaction of VOCs, nitrous oxides, and sunlight. Particulate matter is regulated in two standards, one for particulates of 10 micrometers or less, and one for particulates of 2.5 micrometers or less.[8]

State governments are primarily responsible for attaining the NAAQS. To that end, states must submit and implement a state implementation plan (SIP) to attain the NAAQS as expeditiously as possible.[9] States are generally free to adopt whatever standard they choose to meet the NAAQS, but to ensure that the NAAQS are eventually achieved throughout the country, onerous standards apply to states with "nonattainment areas."[10] In this way, EPA administers the CAA through its state counterparts.[11]

The second key part of the CAA is prevention of significant deterioration (PSD).[12] The PSD program protects areas of the country that are already in compliance with the NAAQS. It is designed to prevent the air quality in those so-called attainment areas from deteriorating to levels that would otherwise be allowed under the NAAQS. PSD increments, which are the key to the PSD program, represent the maximum allowable increase in the concentration of criteria pollutants in attainment areas. Thus, the total allowed pollution in an attainment area is not necessarily the NAAQS but is an increment beyond a baseline established when the first major emitting facility is located in the regulated area.[13] The NAAQS remain a hard limit such that even if it would otherwise be allowed by the increment, the emission of additional criteria pollutants is prohibited if it will cause an exceedance of a NAAQS.[14] Major new sources of air pollution in a PSD area must comply with special permitting requirements, including the requirement to utilize the best available control technology (BACT).[15]

Nonattainment New Source Review is essentially the opposite side of the PSD coin. New or modified major emitting facilities in attainment areas must obtain a PSD permit and utilize BACT while not exceeding an increment or NAAQS; major new or modified stationary sources in nonattainment areas must, among other things, obtain a permit requiring the source to comply with the lowest achievable emissions rate (LAER), and offset emissions by obtaining permanent reductions in emissions from other sources in the area.[16] Given that areas are classified as attainment or nonattainment for each of the six criteria pollutants, it is therefore possible that a particular source could be required to obtain a PSD permit and comply with BACT for some pollutants, and to comply with nonattainment's LAER and offset requirements for other pollutants.

The third key part of the CAA is the stationary source requirements. Title V of the CAA requires every source regulated under the CAA to have a permit.[17] This includes, for example, major stationary sources, regulated hazardous air pollutant sources, and sources subject to New Source Performance Standards (NSPS). Title V permits contain enforceable emission limits and require monitoring to demonstrate compliance.[18]

Another stationary source requirement is section 111's NSPS program.[19] New sources that fall within categories or classes identified by rules promulgated under section 111 must comply with the regulatory standards of performance applicable to that category or class. Standards of performance are promulgated by EPA to reflect the degree of emission limitations achievable through the application of the best technological system of continuous emission reduction that EPA determines has been adequately demonstrated, taking into account the cost of achieving those reductions, as well as other factors.[20] Classes and categories subject to NSPS vary greatly, from lead smelters to residential indoor wood furnaces.

There are also pollutant-specific requirements that apply to stationary sources. These requirements include section 111's "designated pollutants," and the "hazardous air pollutants" listed with unusual specificity for an act of Congress in section 112.[21] New and existing sources must meet the emission limits established for the applicable NSPS class or category for each "designated pollutant" established for that class or category. New and existing sources must also meet the standards for the approximately 200 hazardous air pollutants (HAPs) listed in section 112.[22] Section 112 requires emission standards for HAPs to be set under a two-step process. Step one sets technology-based standards for categories and classes of sources that emit a HAP.[23] Those standards are known as the maximum achievable control technology (MACT) standards. Under step two, EPA must impose more-stringent-than-MACT standards if the residual risk of cancer to the most exposed individual for a HAP is greater than one in one million after implementation of the MACT standards.[24] Application of MACT standards is generally limited to "major sources," which are sources that emit 10 tons per year of any single HAP or 25 tons per year of any combination of HAPs.[25]

Title IV of the CAA established a novel, market-based cap-and-trade exchange for sulfur dioxide (SO_2) emissions referred to as the Acid Rain Program.[26] The program imposes a national cap on utilities' SO_2 emissions and grants allowances, which can be traded, to utilities to emit specific amounts of SO_2. This program has been heavily litigated with the U.S. Court of Appeals for the District of Columbia requiring EPA to reform the program and set additional standards under the Clean Air Interstate Rule (CAIR) and later the Cross-State Air Pollution Rule (CSAPR), and the U.S. Supreme Court then reversing the Court of Appeals and holding that CSAPR is a permissible implementation of the Clean Air Act.[27] There is a similar trading program for mercury, called the Clean Air Mercury Rule (CAMR), which the court has also required EPA to reform.[28] In early 2012, the EPA modified CAMR to include new standards referred to as the Mercury and Air Toxic Standards (MATS) that limit mercury and other heavy metals, acid gases, and other toxic emissions from utilities, and the U.S. Court of Appeals recently upheld MATS.[29] These programs remain in flux, however, as litigation and program reevaluation are ongoing.

Similarly tumultuous is the program to regulate CO_2 emissions in response to concerns and political pressures regarding climate change.[30] Although CO_2 is still not considered a criteria pollutant, the climate change initiative establishes CO_2 emission standards for utilities and sets up a trading program. Whether and how to address climate change remains controversial and, as a result, climate change regulation is ever-changing and increasingly complex. The current approach includes several programs to address the issue of climate change from various angles, including monitoring emissions, encouraging federal, state, and local governments to work together to reduce CO_2 emissions, and conducting ongoing climate research. There are tailoring rules that apply to sources of CO_2 emissions, depending on the nature and size of the source and its *potential* to emit CO_2.[31] A stationary source that has the potential to emit over the applicable threshold amount must report to EPA.[32] In addition, the EPA has proposed regulating CO_2 emissions from power plants under Section III.

The fourth key part of the CAA is the mobile source requirements. Title II of the CAA sets tailpipe emission standards for motor vehicles.[33] Manufacturers must produce vehicles that comply with those standards or face significant penalties designed to both deter noncompliance and to eliminate any competitive advantage of noncompliance.[34] The standards also require the use of certain formulations of gasoline (e.g., unleaded gasoline), and they specifically regulate certain toxic pollutants in motor vehicle emissions (e.g., benzene).[35]

B.   Climate Change

Climate change is addressed not only at the federal level through the CAA, but also at the local, state, and international level. State and local governments have created a patchwork of programs, including energy regulation and direct regulation of greenhouse gas (GHG) emissions at the state and regional level, to address climate change.[36]

International agreements are also part of the story. The United States participated in the United Nations Framework Convention on Climate Change (UNFCCC).[37] The UNFCCC is only a framework for more specific future action to achieve the general objective of stabilizing GHG concentrations in the atmosphere at a level that would prevent dangerous interference with the climate. It does not set binding limits for GHG emissions.

The Kyoto Protocol was developed to implement the general framework established by the UNFCCC.[38] Unlike the UNFCCC, the Kyoto Protocol does set binding emissions limits.[39] Parties to the Kyoto Protocol have broad discretion to develop programs to meet those limits. The limits were initially applicable only through 2012, but they were subsequently extended through at least 2017. The United States is a party to the UNFCCC, but has not ratified the Kyoto Protocol.

Another significant round of negotiations under the UNFCCC occurred in Copenhagen in December 2009. The result was the Copenhagen Accord.[40] The Copenhagen Accord introduced nonbinding emission pledges designed to limit global warming to two degrees Celsius above preindustrial temperatures. The United States formally indicated its conditional association with the targets in the Copenhagen Accord.[41] A United Nations decision in the 2010 Cancun Agreements formalized certain elements of the Copenhagen

Accord, and the Durban Outcomes in 2011, the Doha Climate Gateway in 2012, and the Warsaw Decisions in 2013 further operationalized this still-developing global framework for addressing climate change.

III. Water
A. Clean Water Act (CWA)

In many ways the statutory structure of the CWA mirrors that of the CAA. For example, the CAA's focus on the quality of the ambient air through the NAAQS and implementation through SIPs is analogous to the Clean Water Act's water quality standards and state implementation plans. The CAA's stationary source standards are akin to the Clean Water Act's effluent limitations for point sources. And just as the CAA singles out certain chemicals deemed especially dangerous and worthy of regulation (i.e., HAPs), the Clean Water Act specifically targets toxic water pollutants for special consideration and regulation. The EPA and the U.S. Army Corps of Engineers (Corps), jointly administer the CWA.

The CWA focuses primarily on using permits to limit point source emissions.[42] Under the CWA, there can be no discharge of a pollutant from a point source to a water of the United States without a permit.[43] Permits, particularly National Pollutant Discharge Elimination System (NPDES) permits, are thus the central focus of the CWA. Permitted discharges are subject to technology-based effluent limits, which may be supplemented by more stringent water-quality-based standards if water quality standards are not met using technology-based limits alone.[44]

Because of its focus on discharges to certain regulatory waters, the CWA continually presents vexing questions regarding the extent of its application. The statute applies to "navigable waters," which means "waters of the United States," which has generally been interpreted broadly—though not without limits—to cover nearly any water body with a connection to interstate commerce at any time in the past, present, or if there is potential for use in the future.[45] The most significant limits on that broad interpretation have come from the U.S. Supreme Court's decisions in *Solid Waste Agency of Northern Cook County v. Army Corps of Engineers*[46] (*SWANCC*) and *Rapanos v. United States*.[47] In *SWANCC*, the Court invalidated the so-called migratory bird rule by holding that Congress's reach under the CWA did not extend to waters whose only connection to interstate commerce was their use as habitat by migratory birds.[48] In *Rapanos*, the Court crafted an even more incomprehensible standard intended to establish the outside bounds of the CWA's application. *Rapanos* states that the CWA's authority extends to all waters that have a "significant nexus" to a navigable water. A significant nexus is interpreted as a "relatively permanent, standing or continuously flowing bodies of water" that are connected to a traditional navigable water or as "a wetland with a continuous surface connection" to such relatively permanent waters.[49] On April 21, 2014, the EPA and Army Corps published a proposed rule to attempt to clarify the scope of the waters subject to the CWA under

SWANCC and *Rapanos*. At the time of writing, that rule was still subject to comment and was not yet final.

The CWA also regulates stormwater discharges and is administered by EPA through delegated state programs in 45 states and directly by the EPA in the remaining states and U.S. territories.[50] Stormwater discharges that fall into one of the following categories will require a permit: industrial activity, facility with wastewater effluent limitations, hazardous waste treatment, storage, or disposal facilities, landfills, steam electric plants, wastewater treatment works (1 million gallon+ per day flow), or construction activity that disturbs more than one acre.[51] A stormwater permit will establish pollutant monitoring and reporting requirements and will outline conditions and effluent limitations for a permitted discharge. Once a facility obtains a general or a specific discharge permit, the facility must develop a stormwater pollution prevention plan.[52] Although the point source will determine the proper NPDES permitting jurisdiction, many of the stormwater regulations are designed to protect against nonpoint source runoff.[53]

Part 404 of the CWA specifically regulates the discharge of dredge or fill material into waters of the United States, including wetlands.[54] CWA section 404(f) exempts from regulation discharges associated with certain specified activities, provided the discharges do not convert an area of waters of the United States to a new use, and do not impair the flow or circulation of waters of the United States or reduce the reach of waters of the United States.[55] Normal farming and harvesting activities that are part of established, ongoing farming or forestry operations are generally exempt.[56]

B.   Rivers and Harbors Act of 1899 (RHA)

Among the oldest environmental laws in the United States, the Rivers and Harbors Act regulates dredge and fill activity in waters of the United States.[57] The CWA and the RHA overlap in many respects, but the Corps independently administers section 10, the primary provision of the RHA. Specifically, section 10 of the RHA makes it illegal to dredge, fill, construct a bridge or dam, or alter the navigable waters of the United States without first obtaining a permit.[58] The RHA's permitting requirements continue to apply to any alteration to the navigable waters of the United States, which includes hydroelectric generation and other technological advances. In addition, the RHA also establishes permit criteria for the discharge of refuse into navigable waters and establishes criteria for temporary use of a sea wall, levee, wharf, or similar structure built by the United States.[59]

C.   Safe Drinking Water Act (SDWA)

The United States regulates every public water system in the country under the Safe Drinking Water Act, which establishes national standards for drinking water by identifying contaminants and setting limits for these contaminants based on scientific research on human health.[60] If a state government can show EPA that it will enforce drinking water standards at least as stringent as those set by the SDWA, then EPA will allow the state to administer the program.[61] SDWA efforts to protect drinking water include source water protection, treatment, ensuring the integrity of water distribution systems, and providing updated information to the public about the quality of its drinking water.[62]

The federal Underground Injection Control (UIC) Program is a component of the Safe Drinking Water Act.[63] It is a delegated program in many states, but it is a federally implemented and enforced program in a handful of states, such as Michigan.

As a general matter, the UIC program regulates construction, operation, and closure of injection wells that store or dispose of fluids underground. Under the UIC program, a person generally must obtain a permit for an underground injection, which means that a person needs a UIC permit from EPA if the person will put fluids into position underground through bored, drilled, or driven shafts, dug holes, improved sink holes, or subsurface fluid distribution systems.[64] There are six classes of wells, each requiring a permit, although some classes are issued a permit by rule.[65]

D. Marine Protection, Research, and Sanctuaries Act of 1972 (Ocean Dumping Act)

The MPRSA implements the London Convention, an international treaty governing ocean dumping. In general, the MPRSA prohibits ocean dumping of material leaving the United States, prohibits ocean dumping by any U.S. agency or vessel, and prohibits anyone from dumping material into the U.S. territorial seas.[66] To conduct any of these activities, the MPRSA requires a permit.[67] The standard for obtaining a permit for such activities is whether the dumping will unreasonably degrade or endanger human health, welfare, the marine environment, ecological systems, or related economic potential.[68] The EPA and the Corps have developed criteria to administer the permit programs and evaluate permit applications.[69] There are also MPRSA provisions that specifically address marine sanctuaries that are administered by the National Oceanic and Atmospheric Administration (NOAA)[70] and a coastal monitoring system administered by the U.S. Coast Guard.[71]

IV. Handling, Treatment, Transportation, and Disposal of Chemicals and Hazardous Materials

A. Resource Conservation and Recovery Act (RCRA)

To the extent that Comprehensive Environmental Response, Compensation, and Liability Act (CERCLA), discussed *infra*, can be considered a backward-looking statute focused on the cleanup of contaminated property, RCRA can be considered a forward-looking statute focused on regulating the generation and disposal of wastes to ensure that new contaminated properties are not created.[72] Its regulatory requirements impact a broad swath of ongoing businesses that generate regulated wastes.

RCRA's detailed waste management framework is often referred to as a "cradle to grave" program. RCRA itself applies to solid waste, hazardous waste, and underground storage tanks, but the core focus of its onerous regulatory requirements is hazardous waste.[73] RCRA broadly defines hazardous waste and regulates the generation, transport, treatment, storage, disposal, and cleanup of those wastes.[74]

Subtitle C of RCRA regulates hazardous wastes.[75] The definition of hazardous waste is both simple and complex. A hazardous waste is a solid waste that meets certain criteria. Assuming that a material is a "solid waste" under RCRA, it is also a hazardous waste if it exhibits a characteristic (i.e., ignitability, corrosivity, reactivity, or toxicity), or if it is a specifically listed waste in the Code of Federal Regulations.[76] A solid waste can also be a hazardous waste if it is mixed with a listed waste or if it is derived from the treatment, storage, or disposal of a listed waste.

Generators of hazardous waste must provide notification of their hazardous waste activities, obtain a generator identification number, and comply with applicable storage requirements, including the requirement to accumulate waste on-site in only certain areas and for no more than a certain amount of time.[77] They must properly manifest waste shipments, and they must retain all required records.[78] More lenient requirements apply to small generators (Small Quantity Generators and Conditionally Exempt Small Quantity Generators) than to Large Quantity Generators.[79]

Transporters of hazardous waste are subject not only to RCRA but also to hazardous materials requirements enforced by the U.S. Department of Transportation.[80] Transporters must obtain identification numbers, transport waste in proper containers, properly use and maintain waste manifests, and maintain appropriate records.[81]

Unless an exemption applies, a facility that treats, stores, or disposes of a hazardous waste must obtain a permit.[82] The RCRA permitting requirements are exceptionally onerous, and unless a person is actively in the business of treating, storing, or disposing of hazardous wastes, RCRA's regulatory program is an exceptionally effective incentive for unpermitted businesses to take great effort to avoid treating, storing, or disposing of hazardous waste.[83] Generally, a treatment, storage, or disposal facility must obtain a permit, obtain an identification number, conduct waste analyses, comply with security and inspection requirements, provide training, utilize appropriate waste management techniques and precautions, locate facilities in approved areas, implement required preparedness and prevention measures, implement a groundwater monitoring program, comply with significant financial assurance requirements, comply with detailed equipment and technical standards, treat disposed-of wastes to comply with the so-called land ban, and implement corrective action to address releases from solid waste management units.[84]

Apart from hazardous wastes, RCRA also regulates nonhazardous solid waste and underground storage tanks. Subtitle I of RCRA regulates underground storage tanks (USTs) containing regulated substances, including petroleum and CERCLA hazardous substances.[85] UST owners who are not exempt must provide notification of tanks, design and construct them to comply with technical requirements, install leak detection equipment and report leaks, take corrective action to clean up releases, and demonstrate financial responsibility.[86]

Subtitle D of RCRA regulates nonhazardous solid wastes.[87] In general, it requires states to develop solid waste management plans, eliminate open dumping of solid waste, and ensure that landfills comply with design and management criteria.[88] Certain wastes, such as used oil, are specifically regulated or exempted from regulation even as solid waste.

B.   Federal Insecticide, Fungicide, and Rodenticide Act (FIFRA)

FIFRA (and the federal Food, Drug, and Cosmetics Act) regulates pesticides.[89] It generally requires that pesticides be registered before they are sold.[90] The type of registration governs who may use the pesticide.[91]

FIFRA broadly defines pesticide as, among other things, a substance intended to prevent, destroy, repel, or mitigate a "pest," which is also broadly defined.[92] To be registered it must be shown that a pesticide will perform as claimed, will be properly labeled, and generally will not cause unreasonable adverse effects on the environment.[93] If those criteria can all be met without restrictions on use or user, then the pesticide can be registered as a "general pesticide" and made readily available to the public (on shelves in hardware stores, for example).[94] If the criteria cannot be met without restricting the use or users of the pesticide, then the pesticide will be registered as a "restricted pesticide."[95] If the criteria cannot be met in any circumstances, then registration will be denied. EPA implements FIFRA.

Restricted-use pesticides may be applied only by or under the supervision of certified applicators, or under whatever other restrictions EPA imposes.[96] Applicators of restricted-use pesticides must generally be certified by federal certification or approved state certification, but there are exemptions for private applicators who use restricted-use pesticides without compensation or only on property owned or rented by the applicator.[97]

C.   Toxic Substances Control Act (TSCA)

TSCA comprehensively regulates chemical substances and mixtures. It also targets certain specific chemicals and substances: asbestos in schools, indoor-air radon, lead-based paint, and polychlorinated biphenyls (PCBs).[98]

Despite its broad application with respect to substances, TSCA has a narrow, in many ways specialized, application with respect to persons subject to the act. Administered by EPA, TSCA broadly regulates "chemical substances," but most of its requirements apply only to manufacturers, which by definition includes importers.[99] Under TSCA, manufacturers and processors must generally test new or existing chemical substances and mixtures for their effects on human health and the environment.[100] Most new chemical substances must be reviewed, approved, and subject to regulation by EPA before they can be distributed for commercial use.[101] And manufacturers and processors must generally collect, maintain, and submit data and records regarding the chemical and its effects on human health and the environment.[102] TSCA also regulates in detail the manufacture, processing, use, and disposal of certain identified chemicals, such as PCBs.[103] And it has specific requirements that apply to import and export of certain chemical substances.[104] There is currently an effort to amend TSCA.

V. Waste and Site Remediation
A. CERCLA

CERCLA is an amalgam of at least three related but distinct, and sometimes contradictory, policy desires: a desire to allow EPA to clean up contaminated properties and to pay for that cleanup with federal funds (i.e., the "superfund"); a desire to allow parties to recover cleanup costs from polluters such that "polluters pay" first, with allocation among potentially responisble parties (PRPs) to follow; and a desire to impose strict, generally joint and several liability as a cost of doing business on contaminated property.[105] The almost exclusive focus of CERCLA is on identification and cleanup of contaminated real property.

CERCLA is triggered when there has been a "release" or "threat of release" of a "hazardous substance" from a "facility" to the environment.[106] Each of those terms is broadly defined, and the prima facie case necessary to trigger CERCLA is generally relatively easy to establish. Once triggered, CERCLA imposes liability on four classes of parties: owners, operators, arrangers, and transporters.[107] These so-called potentially responsible parties (PRPs) are generally jointly and severally liable for the cost of cleaning up the release.[108] They are also liable for natural resource damages to "restore, replace, or acquire the equivalent of . . . natural resources" harmed by the release of hazardous substances.[109]

Two sections of CERCLA impose liability. Section 106 of CERCLA authorizes EPA to issue administrative orders and initiate lawsuits to require PRPs to abate imminent and substantial endangerments caused by the release of a hazardous substance.[110] There is generally no pre-enforcement review available to recipients of 106 orders, so EPA's authority to issue what are essentially unreviewable orders, backed up by daily, per-violation penalties and the threat of treble damages for noncompliance, is an especially powerful enforcement tool for EPA.[111]

Section 107 of CERCLA allows the United States, a state, and a private party to bring a federal claim to recover costs spent responding to a release or threat of release of a hazardous substance.[112] PRPs in such actions are generally jointly and severally liable, although in rare circumstances a PRP is able to establish divisibility of harm and thereby apportion liability among all PRPs. In instances where liability remains joint and several, contribution claims under section 113 generally result in an equitable allocation of damages among liable parties.[113]

Persons wishing to purchase a CERCLA facility and to avoid status liability as an owner of that facility may qualify as a Bona Fide Prospective Purchaser (BFPP) of that property and thereby be exempt from CERCLA liability.[114]

A person achieves BFPP status by performing all appropriate inquiries (AAI), which is generally accomplished by performing an ASTM-compliant Phase I Environmental Site Assessment, and by complying with continuing obligations to, among other things, not exacerbate contamination, cooperate with cleanup efforts, and not impede the performance of a response action at the property.[115] Purchasers with BFPP status are not subject to status liability as owners of a facility, but their property can be affected by a so-called windfall lien in favor of EPA if EPA determines that a government-funded response action had the effect of increasing the value of the property.[116]

Other narrow defenses to liability are also available in certain circumstances under CERCLA. For example, the owner of a contiguous property contaminated or threatened by contamination from an adjacent property is generally not liable as an owner or operator of a facility. And there is no liability if it can be established that a property is a facility solely because of an act of god, act of war, or an act or omission of a third party (i.e., a person with whom the owner is not contractually related through, for example, a deed, land contract, or other instrument transferring title.[117]

VI. Emergency Response
A. Oil Pollution Act

The Oil Pollution Act (OPA) was passed in 1990 to improve the United States' ability to prevent and respond to oil spills by establishing provisions that expand the federal government's ability to respond to oil spills and that provide the money and resources necessary to so respond.[118] As part of this effort, the OPA authorized use of the Oil Spill Liability Trust Fund, which is a national fund financed by a tax on oil and made available to provide up to one billion dollars per spill incident.[119]

The OPA also imposed new requirements for government and industry-wide contingency planning.[120] The National Oil and Hazardous Substances Pollution Contingency Plan (NCP) has a three-tiered approach: (1) the federal government must direct all public and private response efforts for certain types of spill events; (2) regionally, area committees, composed of federal, state, and local government officials, must develop detailed, location-specific area contingency plans; and (3) owners or operators of vessels and certain facilities that pose a serious threat to the environment must prepare and submit facility response plans.[121]

To further serve its purpose, the OPA increased penalties for noncompliance, expanded the federal government's response and enforcement authority, and preserved state authority to establish laws governing oil spill prevention and response.[122]

B. Emergency Planning and Community Right-to-Know Act

Amendments to Title III of CERCLA, referred to as the Superfund Amendments and Reauthorization Act (SARA), enacted the Emergency Planning & Community Right-to-Know Act (EPCRA) to address community safety.[123] In general, this law is designed to help local communities protect public health, safety, and the environment from hazardous substances by planning for potential emergencies. EPCRA requires each state to appoint a State Emergency Response Commission (SERC) to divide the state into emergency planning districts and to name a Local Emergency Planning Committee (LEPC) for each district.[124] Ideally, each SERC and LEPC will include a spectrum of firefighters, health officials, emergency managers, and representatives from government, media, community groups, and industrial facilities to ensure that each SERC and LEPC is equipped to consider all necessary elements of the planning process.[125] EPCRA further requires that people who store hazardous substances regularly submit reports on the amount, type, and condition of the hazardous substance stored.[126] Any release of a hazardous substance must be reported.[127] Information submitted to comply with EPCRA will be made available to the public.[128]

In addition to the emergency planning and release notification requirements, sections 311–313 require reporting of hazardous chemical storage and toxic chemical releases. Specifically, section 311 of EPCRA requires that the owner or operator of a facility must submit a material safety data sheet (MSDS) for each hazardous chemical, or a list of MSDS chemicals, which meets or exceeds a specified threshold quantity at the facility, to the SERC, LEPC, and the local fire department.[129] Any facility required under the Occupational Safety and Health Administration (OSHA) to prepare or have an MSDS available for a hazardous chemical must comply with sections 311 and 312 of EPCRA. Section 311 is a one-time reporting requirement unless there are significant changes that affect the information already submitted, at which point a facility must submit an update within three months of the significant change.

Section 312 of EPCRA includes a two-tiered reporting approach. Tier I is required by federal law and involves aggregating information, such as maximum amount of hazardous chemicals at the facility during preceding year, estimate of average daily amount of hazardous chemicals at the facility, and the general location be aggregated and reported by hazard category based on federal law.[130] Tier II requires the information from Tier I in addition to information on the specific location and storage information for each chemical. Section 312 applies to the same owners and operators as section 311. However, under section 312, if a facility manufactures, processes, or otherwise uses less than (1) 10,000 pounds of a hazardous chemical and/or (2) 500 pounds of an extremely hazardous substance, then the facility has no reporting requirements under section 312.[131] When applicable, reporting under section 312 is due on or before March 1 of each calendar year. A Tier II report under section 312 can be used in place of a section 311 MSDS list.

Section 313 of EPCRA establishes the Toxic Release Inventory (TRI) to track the management of certain toxic chemicals that pose a threat to human health and the environment. A facility must report how much of each chemical they managed through recycling, energy recovery, treatment, and environmental releases. TRI reporting forms must be submitted by July 1 each year and are made available to the public.[132] The North American Industry Classification System, available online, outlines which industries must complete TRI reporting under section 313.

VII. Protected Species
A. Endangered Species Act (ESA)

The ESA is a unique environmental law. It is narrowly focused on a particular resource—listed species of plants and animals. And it has teeth. It requires virtually all other federal laws, and private activities, to yield to its mandate.[133] The ESA's mandate is clear and straightforward. Under the ESA, no person may "take" a listed species.[134] "Take" includes not only physical interference with the species itself, but also destruction of a species' critical habitat.[135] Any activity that would negatively impact a species or its critical habitat is prohibited unless it has been authorized under an incidental take permit.[136] NOAA and FWS jointly administer the ESA.[137]

B. Migratory Bird Treaty Act of 1918 (MBTA)

Designed to end the commercial trade of native birds and their feathers that decimated native bird populations in the early 1900s, the MBTA imposes complete protection for all migratory birds and bird parts (eggs, feathers, nests).[138] The MBTA implements four international conventions that protect migratory birds.[139] There are currently more than 800 species on the protected migratory bird list, which is administered by FWS.

C. Marine Mammal Protection Act of 1972

The Marine Mammal Protection Act declared a moratorium on the taking of or commerce in marine mammals.[140] "Taking" is defined as the act of hunting, killing, capturing, and/or harassing any marine mammal; or the attempt at such."[141] "Harassment" is defined to include any annoyance to or disturbance of a marine mammal.[142] The act is jointly administered by NOAA and FWS and established a Marine Mammal Commission to consider and study the human impact on marine mammals.[143] Permits are available for commercial fisheries with "incidental" takings of marine mammals and violators may be prosecuted.[144]

VIII. Natural Resource Management and Protection
A. Federal Land Policy and Management Act (FLPMA)

FLPMA aims to allow a variety of uses on public land while preserving the natural resources that exist on those lands—a concept known as "multiple use" that includes diverse activities from recreation to mining.[145] FLPMA directs the agencies that manage public lands to "take any action necessary to prevent unnecessary or undue degradation of public lands" and to pre-serve "the quality of scientific, scenic, historical, ecological, environmental, air and atmospheric, water resource, and archeological values" of the lands.[146] As a result, anyone wishing to mine or otherwise operate on and disturb public lands must obtain authorization from the Bureau of Land Management (BLM), which administers FLPMA along with the National Forest Service (USFS) and the National Park Service (NPS).[147] BLM has the authority to postpone any activity on public lands until the agency has com-plied with its duty to take any action necessary to prevent unnecessary or undue degradation.[148] As such, BLM has broad authority to delay projects on public lands.

B.   General Mining Act of 1872 (Hardrock Mining Act)

This Act governs prospecting and mining for economically valuable minerals such as gold, silver, and platinum on federal public lands.[149] The law exem-plified the practices of prospectors who expanded west to California and Nevada in the mid-1800s in search of gold and other minerals. Under the Act, any U.S. citizen who is at least 18 years old has a right to discover and locate a lode (hard rock) or placer (gravel) mining claim on federal public land that has been approved for such entry or a mill site.[150] To establish a claim, a claimant must simply demonstrate physical exposure or proper use, exclude others from the claim or site, and perform at least $500 worth of improvements on each (i.e., stake a claim).[151] Once these steps are completed, the claimant has title superior to everyone except the United States. BLM administers the act and, in the past, once a claimant staked a claim, the claim-ant could submit an application under the act for a mining patent and could then pay the required processing fee, purchase the subject land, and obtain title even against the United States.[152] However, as of October 1, 1994, Con-gress imposed a budget moratorium on BLM preventing BLM from accept-ing any new mineral patent applications. Until the moratorium has been lifted, BLM cannot accept any mineral patent applications.

C.   Multiple-Use Sustained Yield Act

The MUSYA directs the secretary of Agriculture to administer the renewable surface resources of the national forests for "multiple use" and "sustained yield" of the products and services obtained from them and to give "due consideration" to the relative values of the various resources in particular areas and how they can be used to best meet the needs of the people of the United States.[153] To direct this effort, the MUSYA establishes a policy that the national forests be administered for five different purposes of equal importance: (1) outdoor recreation; (2) range; (3) timber; (4) watershed; and (5) wildlife and fish purposes.[154] BLM and the USFS work together for this purpose as directed by the FLPMA.[155] Upon implementation, both agencies consider current and future potential uses for the land for economic use and for the five purposes outlined by MUSYA.

D. National Forest Management Act (NFMA)

The NFMA is the primary statute governing the national forest system that includes more than 190 million acres. USFS is directed to prepare plans for the national forests that effectively manage the renewable resources within the forest system.[156] NFMA imposes a series of restraints on the National Forest Service's discretion to cut timber, imposes additional oversight on the USFS, and creates new land and resource planning procedures for the national forest system.[157] It also prohibits USFS from selling timber from the national forests for less than its appraised value.[158]

E. Submerged Lands Act

This act grants states the right to submerged land within their boundaries, including within navigable waterways and the continental shelf, for three geographical miles from the states' coastline.[159]

F. Surface Mining Control and Reclamation Act (SMCRA)

SMCRA is primarily directed at coal strip-mining on public and private lands.[160] The act establishes a program for the regulation of surface mining activities and the reclamation of coal-mined lands overseen by the Department of the Interior.[161] SMCRA sets minimum standards for all coal surface mining, including exploration activities and the surface effects of underground mining. Mine operators must minimize disturbances and adverse impacts on fish, wildlife, and the environment and enhance such resources where practicable. SMCRA also requires mine operators to restore land and water resources and to focus on such concerns when creating a plan for reclamation.

G. Coastal Zone Management Act (CZMA)

The CZMA is a voluntary program for states and tribes to receive federal financial assistance for developing and implementing a comprehensive coastal management program.[162] The CZMA is designed to encourage states and tribes to preserve, protect, develop, restore, or enhance valuable natural coastal resources, including wetlands, floodplains, beaches, dunes, barrier islands, coral reefs, and the fish and other wildlife using those habitats.[163] Amendments to the CZMA identified nonpoint source pollution as a major factor in the continuing degradation of coastal waters.[164] As a result, states and tribes with coastal management programs are charged to develop and implement coastal nonpoint pollution control programs, administered by EPA and NOAA.[165]

H.   Antiquities Act of 1906

The Antiquities Act gives the president of the United States the authority to issue an executive order to restrict the use of particular public land to preserve historic and scientific interests.[166] Often controversial, sitting presidents have used this authority over 100 times to ensure the preservation of Native American ruins and artifacts and even prehistoric ruins. When the president makes such a restriction, the result is a national monument.

I.   Wilderness Act

The Wilderness Act was an effort to review open areas of federal land of more than 5,000 acres to determine whether the area was suitable for inclusion in the National Wilderness Preservation System (NWPS), which focuses on conservation efforts.[167] The act established criteria for reviewing these areas and authorized the federal government to receive gifts of land for conservation purposes.[168] To date, over 25 million acres of land and water (many in Alaska) have been reviewed under this mandate, nearly seven million acres of which have been designated for conservation in the NWPS.[169] The FWS, BLM, NPS, and USFS work together to administer the Wilderness Act.

J.   Magnuson-Stevens Fishery Conservation and Management Act (MSA)

Originally enacted in 1976 under a different name, this law has been amended many times to adapt to overfishing and new technology available in the commercial fishing industry.[170] The MSA establishes regional councils to manage fish stocks and promotes the United States' fishing industries optimal use of coastal fisheries.[171] The law intends to conserve fish resources, maximize those resources for use by the states, establish fishery management plans, and protect fish habitats, among other goals.[172] NOAA administers the MSA, which specifically calls for the reduction of bycatch and the development of fishery information monitoring systems.[173]

K.   National Historic Preservation Act (NHPA)

The National Historic Preservation Act (NHPA), like the National Environmental Policy Act, discussed *infra*, applies only to federal actions, and it is strictly a procedural statute—only an agency's compliance with appropriate procedures, not its ultimate substantive decision to go forward with a project, is subject to judicial review.[174] Activities that require federal permits are generally undertakings subject to the NHPA.

The NHPA requires federal agencies issuing permits to consider whether the permitted federal undertaking will adversely affect a historic property.[175]

If the agency determines that the undertaking will adversely affect a historic property, the agency must consider ways to avoid, minimize, or mitigate those adverse effects.[176] Generally, as long as the agency has identified all relevant historic properties, avoidance alternatives, and mitigation measures, and consulted with relevant parties, it has complied with the NHPA.[177] The Advisory Council on Historic Preservation oversees the implementation of the NHPA.[178]

NHPA is often a vehicle for the involvement of Native American tribes. If a project involves a federal undertaking subject to NHPA, then the agencies must generally afford an affected tribe the opportunity to participate in the NHPA process as interested persons.[179] In fact, the NHPA regulations focus heavily on the importance of consulting with tribes that attach religious or cultural significance to historic properties.[180] This importance reflects the sensitivity to tribes' unique government-to-government relationship with the United States.

IX. Natural Resource Damages

A handful of federal statutes authorize recovery of "natural resource damages" (NRD) intended to compensate the public for damages caused by pollution to natural resources. In general, natural resource damages are paid to a trustee and must be used to restore or replace the resources or the ecosystem services provided by the harmed resources.

NRD trustees are appointed governmental entities. They include designated federal, tribal, and state agencies and officials, such as the U.S. Department of Interior and NOAA.[181] NRD trustees oversee the process of assessing natural resource harm, bringing suit to recover NRD, and using recovered NRD to restore harmed natural resources.

The best-known NRD provision is section 107(f) of CERCLA, which provides that CERCLA potentially responsible parties are liable for the cost of "restor[ing], replac[ing], or acquir[ing] the equivalent of . . . natural resources" harmed by the release of hazardous substances.[182]

The CWA also provides for NRD liability. Specifically, under the CWA, NRD liability attaches to the discharge of oil or a hazardous substance "into or upon the navigable waters of the United States, adjoining shorelines, or into or upon the waters of the contiguous zone."[183] The same regulations govern NRD actions under CERCLA and the CWA.[184]

Like CERCLA, OPA extends liability to "injury to, destruction of, loss of, or loss of use of, natural resources."[185] The definitions of "natural resources" in CERCLA and OPA are essentially identical.[186]

The Ocean Dumping Act also establishes NRD liability for causing harm to certain federal marine resources.[187] And there is also NRD liability for harming national park system resources.[188]

X. Environmental Review and Decision Making

The chief statute governing environmental review in the United States is the National Environmental Policy Act (NEPA). NEPA is primarily a procedural statute. NEPA does a number of things, but the heart of NEPA is the requirement that federal agencies prepare an environmental impact statement (EIS) before taking a major federal action that significantly affects the quality of the human environment.[189] The requirement applies to federal agencies, not private parties or states.[190] But in practice private parties, such as applicants for a federal permit, often prepare the EIS in cooperation with the federal agency.[191] And even if a private party is not involved in preparing an EIS, private parties are invariably affected by the EIS process, and the major federal actions subject to NEPA. NEPA also established the Council on Environmental Quality.[192]

All agencies of the federal government are subject to NEPA, but an agency need not prepare an EIS every time that it takes an action. The only federal actions subject to NEPA are "major federal actions."[193] And the only "major federal actions" subject to NEPA are those that significantly affect the quality of the human environment.[194]

The question of whether a federal action is a major federal action that significantly affects the quality of the human environment is often answered by preparing an environmental assessment (EA).[195] If the EA concludes that a major federal action significantly affects the quality of the human environment, then the agency must prepare an EIS.[196] If, on the other hand, the EA concludes that there is no major federal action significantly affecting the quality of the human environment, then the agency memorializes that conclusion by issuing a finding of no significant impact (FONSI).[197]

In determining whether there is a major federal action significantly affecting the quality of the human environment, agencies and the courts generally interpret NEPA broadly. An EIS is often required when a project will cause significant "degradation," or if it will "arguably" have a "potentially" significant adverse effect.[198] The federal action cannot be viewed in isolation, but rather must be considered alongside other related actions that, while separately might be insignificant, when considered cumulatively are significant. Whether the action is short term or long term, and whether it is small-scale or large-scale are also relevant to the inquiry. The scope of federal, relative to private, monetary involvement and decision-making control can also be relevant, especially when determining the scope of the "federal action" to identify whether what could otherwise be considered a private project is federalized such that the entire project is subject to NEPA's EIS requirement.[199]

Importantly, an EIS need only consider the effect of the proposed federal action on the quality of the human environment. It must identify impacts and explore all reasonable alternatives, including the no action alternative.[200] But it need not result in selection of the most environmentally protective alternative. As long as an agency properly conducts an EIS, it may proceed with its preferred alternative, even if that alternative is the least protective of the environment.[201] In that way, NEPA is a purely procedural statute: it is the National Environmental *Policy* Act, not the National Environmental *Protection* Act.

XI. Transboundary Pollution

Air emissions and water discharges are not contained by national borders. Through the natural currents of air and water, countries both send and receive pollution. Such transboundary pollution is difficult to regulate and compensate for solely at the domestic level. It is inherently international.

One method for addressing transboundary pollution is through the use of multinational and bilateral agreements. Arguably the best-known multinational treaty addressing transboundary pollution in North America is the North American Agreement on Environmental Cooperation between the United States, Canada, and Mexico, a side agreement of the North American Free Trade Agreement.[202] This agreement expresses a hope that the liberalization of trade and economic growth in North America would be accompanied by improvement in environmental protection provided by each country.[203] Among other things, the treaty established the intergovernmental Commission for Environmental Cooperation to address intercontinental environmental concerns.[204] The Commission has broad powers, including the right to establish standing committees and working groups, issue reports, and issue opinions on whether member states are effectively enforcing their environmental laws.[205]

In addition to multinational agreements, there are several examples of bilateral agreements intended to address transboundary pollution between the United States and Canada,[206] and the United States and Mexico.[207] These agreements tend to focus on unique issues or particular areas of concern between the countries. For example, the United States and Canada have entered into bilateral agreements regarding the Great Lakes and the boundary waters between the two countries.[208] A specific example of such an agreement is the Boundary Waters Treaty, executed in 1909. The Boundary Waters Treaty imposes a strict obligation on the United States and Canada not to pollute boundary waters, and it prevents either country from using or diverting boundary waters in a way that would affect the natural level or flow of the water.[209] The Boundary Waters Treaty also created the International Joint Commission, which both conducts binding arbitral adjudication and produces nonbinding investigative reports and studies.[210] In response to a report issued from the International Joint Commission, the United States and Canada signed the Great Lakes Water Quality Agreement, demonstrating the countries' ongoing commitment to the Great Lakes.[211]

Even with agreements and international organizations in place, disputes sometimes are resolved outside of any dedicated international dispute resolution mechanism. Perhaps the best-known transboundary pollution dispute was ultimately resolved by a specially commissioned arbitral panel. The dispute, often referred to as the *Trail Smelter* case, involved a privately owned smelting plant in Trail, British Columbia. SO_2 from the smelter's smoke stacks was harming farms in Stevens County, Washington. But the farmers in Washington were not able to take the smelter to court—the "boundary between Canada and the United States was not as porous to private litigation as it was to the winds that carried the fumes."[212] The private dispute eventually evolved into an international arbitration, with a specially appointed tribunal holding Canada liable for property damage in the United States.[213]

Transboundary environmental issues, and related jurisdictional difficulties, associated with the trail smelter continue to evolve and have presented a renewed source of litigation in U.S. courts. The most recent dispute centered on a CERCLA cleanup to address hazardous substances (i.e., slag discharged from the smelter) in the Columbia River, which flows from British Columbia into Washington.[214]

In addition to the latest iteration of the *Trail Smelter* dispute, there have been other attempts to try transboundary disputes in U.S. courts. For example, the Canadian Province of Manitoba has twice involved itself in litigation in U.S. courts regarding allegations of transboundary pollution. In one lawsuit, *Province of Manitoba v. Norton*, the U.S. government wished to divert 3.5 billion gallons of the Missouri River annually into communities in North Dakota for their water supply.[215] The water received by the communities would eventually drain into the Hudson Bay Basin, which includes several lakes and bays in Canada.[216] Canada was concerned that this drainage could introduce foreign bacteria and viruses that could devastate fisheries.[217] Ultimately, Manitoba sued the secretary of the Interior and the Bureau of Reclamation under the Administrative Procedure Act (APA) for not preparing an EIS under NEPA.[218] After a remand, the district court entered an injunction to allow North Dakota to finish work on a water treatment plant, but continued to enjoin it from building any pipelines or entering any new pipeline contracts until a full EIS is complete.[219]

In another lawsuit, Manitoba, several U.S. states, and various environmental groups challenged EPA's water transfer rule.[220] That rule categorically exempts "discharges from a water transfer" from CWA permitting requirements.[221] Manitoba argued that transfers made in North Dakota as part of water supply projects should be subject to permitting and that EPA's water transfer rule prohibited them from commenting on ongoing and future water transfers that would impact their waterways.[222] The case was consolidated with several other similar challenges in various states. At the time of this writing, a final decision has not been issued.

Political pressure is also exerted in the United States in an attempt to influence foreign decisions regarding perceived transboundary issues. For example, some groups are mounting increasingly fierce political—in addition to legal—opposition in the United States in an attempt to influence Canada's decision to develop its domestic oil sands resource.[223]

XII.   Civil and Criminal Enforcement and Penalties

A.   Assumed Programs and Concurrent Jurisdiction in U.S. Courts

Most federal environmental laws provide for joint enforcement by both the federal and state government.[224] In some circumstances, the legislature or enforcing administrative agency will require a state to direct its own program or will authorize a state to do so once it receives federal approval.[225] A state program will only be approved if its requirements are at least as stringent as the federal requirements, although a state may choose to impose more stringent requirements as well.

The U.S. court system consists of a series of ascending federal courts with jurisdiction to hear federal claims and related state law claims. Each state has its own court system with jurisdiction to hear state law claims and, occasionally, federal claims. Concurrent jurisdiction exists when both state and federal courts have authority to hear a particular claim.[226] For most claims arising under environmental laws, state and federal courts have concurrent jurisdiction.[227] However, there are some environmental claims that can only be heard by a federal court even when a state has assumed responsibility for a program pursuant to federal approval.[228]

B.   Citizen Suits

Some environmental laws, such as the CWA, include a specific provision that authorizes private citizens to file a lawsuit against alleged violators to enforce the environmental law.[229] A citizen may only file a lawsuit if he or she has standing explicitly granted by statute or as defined by the U.S. Supreme Court in *Lujan v. Defenders of Wildlife*.[230] *Lujan* defines standing as an injury in fact (i.e., an injury that is (1) concrete and particularized and (2) actual or imminent as opposed to conjectural or hypothetical) that is fairly traceable to the challenged action and that is likely to be redressed by a decision in the citizen's favor.[231]

The purpose of a citizen suit is to prevent environmental harm by allowing private citizens who are closer to the effects of such harm to file a lawsuit in response to the harm sooner than an agency is able. These provisions effectively create private attorneys general who, if they comply with notice requirements to alleged violators and the appropriate oversight agency, can file a lawsuit against those same parties to enforce the environmental law.[232] If successful, these private citizens can recover the attorneys' fees incurred in bringing the lawsuit to enforce the law.[233]

Because costs of bringing the suit may be covered by the alleged violators, there is little incentive for private citizens to forgo bringing such a lawsuit. As a result, citizen suit provisions are seen by some as a huge drain on the resources of courts and agencies required by law to respond to private citizens' demands.[234] In particular, states with delegated programs, which have exclusive authority to enforce those programs, have experienced strains on available resources.[235]

C.   Civil Administrative and Judicial Enforcement

As evidenced above, environmental laws are enforced by administrative agencies like EPA and others with authority delegated by the legislature in the text of the law itself.[236] These agencies have the authority to enforce the laws by issuing administrative orders requiring compliance and imposing civil penalties for failure to comply. An administrative agency has the authority to request information, order compliance, impose civil penalties, and/or sue to enforce compliance with the agency's order. Because of the structure of the administrative agency system and the separation of powers in the United States, it is very difficult, if not impossible, to obtain judicial review of an administrative order prior to the agency's attempt to enforce the order. For this reason, if an administrative order is issued, a person's only options in response are to comply with the order or risk being sued by the agency for failure to comply. If sued, the person will finally have the opportunity to argue that the order is improper before a court, although the ensuing litigation is necessarily costly and time-consuming.

Some environmental statutes create agency obligations without any enforcement authority at all. NEPA and FLPMA are procedural statutes that impose oversight obligations on the respective administrative agencies.

In the absence of specific authority to enforce a statute, enforcement litigation only arises under the APA, a statute specifically enacted to address the activity of administrative agencies.[237] A court will only overturn an agency's decision, when challenged, if the person bringing suit can establish that the agency decision making was "arbitrary and capricious, an abuse of discretion, or otherwise not in accordance with the law."[238]

D.   Criminal Enforcement

Most environmental laws of the United States provide potential criminal sanctions against polluters. These sanctions are serious and carry the potential for imprisonment and substantial fines. Even so, the mens rea (or mental state) requirement for an environmental violation is very high. In most circumstances, criminal sanctions for environmental liability only result in the United States when there is a proven specific intent to cause harm to the environment in a specific way.[239]

E.   Common Law

In addition to laws created by statute, U.S. law also consists of common law, a constantly evolving system of rules and interpretations established by the federal and state courts based on specific cases and rooted in hundreds of years of court precedent.[240] Certain causes of action arise out of the common law and still exist today, for instance, trespass, nuisance, negligence. Prior to Congress implementing environmental statutes, traditional common law causes of action were the only method by which to seek relief for any sort of environmental harm.[241] Whether or not common law is preempted by the passage of environmental statutes remains controversial.[242] The consideration becomes more complex with the possibility of both state common law and potentially conflicting federal common law. Although it remains controversial, federal courts ultimately determined that there technically is no federal common law, leaving only common law established by the states.[243] Even so, the consideration of which law applies remains complex when, for instance, a state wishes to use common law (either state common law or resurrected federal common law) to enjoin the activities of a foreign (i.e., out-of-state) company.[244]

Notes

1. Clean Air Act, 42 U.S.C. §§ 7401 *et seq.* (1990) (originally passed in 1970).
2. 40 C.F.R. pts. 50–87.
3. 42 U.S.C. §§ 7408–7410; 40 C.F.R. pt. 50.
4. 42 U.S.C. § 7409, 40 C.F.R. § 50.2.
5. 42 U.S.C. § 7409, 40 C.F.R. § 50.2.
6. 42 U.S.C. § 7409, 40 C.F.R. § 50.2.
7. 40 C.F.R. §§ 50.4–50.18.
8. 40 C.F.R. §§ 50.6–.7.
9. 42 U.S.C. § 7410; 40 C.F.R. pts. 51–52.
10. 42 U.S.C. § 7509.
11. 40 C.F.R. pts. 51–52.
12. 42 U.S.C. §§ 7470–7492.
13. *Id.* § 7473
14. *Id.*
15. *Id.* § 7475
16. *Id.* § 7503
17. 42 U.S.C. § 7661a.
18. *Id.* § 7661c.
19. 42 U.S.C. § 7411.
20. *Id.*
21. 42 U.S.C. § 7412.
22. *Id.*
23. *Id.* § 7412.
24. *Id.* § 7412(f).
25. *Id.* § 7412(a).
26. *Id.* §§ 7651–7651o; 40 C.F.R. pts. 72–78.
27. Clean Air Interstate Rule, 70 Fed. Reg. 25,162 (May 12, 2005); Cross-State Air Pollution Rule, 40 C.F.R. pts. 52, 97 (2011); EPA v. EME Homer City Generation, 134 S. Ct. 1584 (2014).
28. Standards of Performance for New and Existing Stationary Sources: Electric Utility Steam Generating Units (CAMR), 70 Fed. Reg. 28,606 (May 18, 2005); New Jersey v. EPA, 517 F.3d 574 (D.C. Cir. 2008).

29. Mercury and Air Toxic Standards, 77 Fed. Reg. 9304 (Feb. 16, 2011); White Stallion Energy Center, LLC v. EPA, No. 12-2200 (D.C. Cir. Apr. 19, 2014).

30. *See* President's Climate Action Plan (June 2013), http://www.whitehouse.gov /sites/default/files/image/president27sclimateactionplan.pdf (last visited Oct. 8, 2013); U.S. EPA, Carbon Pollution Standards, 2013 Proposed Carbon Pollution Standard for New Power Plants, http://www2.epa.gov/carbon-pollution-standards/2013-proposed -carbon-pollution-standard-new-power-plants (EPA proposing on September 20, 2013, a new source performance standard for emissions of carbon dioxide for certain new fossil fuel-fired electric utility generating units); 2017 and Later Model Year Light-Duty Vehicle Greenhouse Gas Emissions and Corporate Average Fuel Economy Standards, 77 Fed. Reg. 62,624 (Oct. 15, 2012) (EPA and National Highway Transportation Safety Administration (NHTSA) issuing final rules to reduce GHGs and improve fuel economy for light-duty vehicles for model years 2017 and beyond); Greenhouse Gas Emissions Standards and Fuel Efficiency Standards for Medium- and Heavy-Duty Engines and Vehicles, 78 Fed. Reg. 57,106 (Sept. 15, 2011) (EPA and NHTSA finalizing rules designed to reduce GHG emissions and fuel consumption for on-road heavy-duty vehicles); Prevention of Significant Deterioration and Title V Greenhouse Gas Tailoring Rule, 75 Fed. Reg. 31,514 (June 3, 2010) (EPA's rule designed to tailor the applicability of criteria that determine which stationary sources and modification projects become subject to permitting requirements for GHG emissions under the CAA PSD and title V programs); Final Rule, Endangerment and Cause or Contribute Findings for Greenhouse Gases Under Section 202(a) of the Clean Air Act, 74 Fed. Reg. 66,496 (Dec. 15, 2009) (EPA endangerment finding); Massachusetts v. EPA, 549 U.S. 497 (2007) (U.S. Supreme Court finding that GHGs are air pollutants covered by CAA and requiring EPA administrator to make endangerment finding); A. Liptak, *Supreme Court to Hear Challenge to E.P.A. Rules on Gas Emissions*, N.Y. Times (Oct. 15, 2013) (reporting on Supreme Court's agreement to hear challenge to EPA's regulations of GHG emissions from stationary sources, such as power plants). Separately, California aims to reduce GHG emissions within the State to 1990 levels by 2020, and then 80 percent by 2050. *See* http://www.arb.ca.gov/cc/cc.htm (last visited Oct. 8, 2013).

31. 40 C.F.R. pt. 82.

32. *Id.*

33. 42 U.S.C. §§ 7521–7590.

34. *Id.* § 7524; 40 C.F.R. pt. 86.

35. *See* 42 U.S.C. §§ 7545–7554.

36. *E.g.*, AB 32 (Cal. 2006); Clean, Renewable, and Efficient Energy Act, Mich. Comp. Laws §§ 460.1001–.1195; A Progress Report on the City of Portland and Multnomah County Local Action Plan on Global Warming 1, 3–4 (June 2005); Regional Greenhouse Gas Initiative, Memorandum of Understanding, http://www.rggi.org/docs/mou _final_12_20_05.pdf.

37. U.N. Framework Convention on Climate Change, Annex I, *concluded* May 9, 1992, 1771 U.N.T.S. 107.

38. U.N. Framework Convention on Climate Change, Kyoto Protocol, *concluded* Dec. 11, 1997, 37 I.L.M. 22.

39. *Id.* art. 3.

40. UNFCCC, Report of the Conference of the Parties, Fifteenth Session, Dec. 18, 2009, Copenhagen Accord UN Doc. FCCC.CP.2009.11/Add.1 (Mar. 30, 2010).

41. Letter from Todd Stern, U.S. Special Envoy for Climate Change, U.S. Dep't of State, to Mr. Yvo de Boer, Exec. Sec'y, UNFCCC (Jan. 28, 2010), *available at* http://unfccc .int/files/meetings/cop_15/copenhagen_accord/application/pdf/unitedstatescphaccord _app.1.pdf.

42. Clean Water Act, 33 U.S.C. § 1251 *et seq.* (1972).

43. *Id.* §§ 1311, 1341–1342.

44. *Id.* §§ 1311–1313.

45. 33 U.S.C. § 1342–1346; 531 U.S. 159, 169, 173 (2001).

46. 531 U.S. 159 (2001).

47. 547 U.S. 715 (2006).

48. *SWANCC*, 531 U.S. 159.

49. *Rapanos*, 547 U.S. 715, 739, 742; Proposal Rule: Definition of Waters of the United States under the Clean Warter Act, 79 Fed. Reg. 22,188 22,192 (Apr. 21, 2014).

50. 33 U.S.C. § 1342(p); 40 C.F.R. pt. 123.

51. 40 C.F.R. § 122.26.

52. E.g., National Pollutant Discharge Elimination System General Permit for Discharges from Construction Activities 38 (Feb. 16, 2012).

53. *See* 40 C.F.R. § 122.26.

54. 33 U.S.C. § 1344.

55. *Id.* § 1344(f).

56. *Id.*

57. 33 U.S.C. § 401 *et seq.* (1899).

58. *Id.* § 403; 33 C.F.R. pt. 323.

59. 33 U.S.C. §§ 407–408.

60. Safe Drinking Water Act, 42 U.S.C. § 300f *et seq.* (1996).

61. *Id.* § 300g-2; 40 C.F.R. pts. 141–143.

62. 42 U.S.C. §§ 300g-300g-1.

63. 40 C.F.R. pts. 144–148.

64. *Id.* § 146.3.

65. *See id.* §§ 146.1–146.95.

66. Marine Protection, Research, and Sanctuaries Act, 33 U.S.C. §§ 1401–1445, 16 U.S.C. §§ 1431–1447f, 33 U.S.C. §§ 2801–2805 (1992).

67. 33 U.S.C. §§ 1411–1421 (1988).

68. *See id.* §§ 1411–1414c; 40 C.F.R. pts. 220–229.

69. *See* 33 U.S.C. §§ 1411–1421 (1988).

70. 16 U.S.C. §§ 1447–1447f (1988).

71. 33 U.S.C. §§ 2801–2805 (1992).

72. Resource Conservation and Recovery Act, 42 U.S.C. § 6901 *et seq.* (1976).

73. *Id.*

74. 42 U.S.C. §§ 6921–6939e.

75. *Id.*

76. *Id.*, 40 C.F.R. pts. 260–261.

77. 40 C.F.R. pt. 262.

78. *Id.*

79. 42 U.S.C. § 6921.

80. 40 C.F.R. §§ 263.10–263.31.

81. *Id.*

82. *Id.* pts. 264–265.

83. *Id.*

84. 42 U.S.C. §§ 6924–6925; 40 C.F.R. pts. 264–265.

85. 42 U.S.C. §§ 6991–6991i; 40 C.F.R. pts. 280–282.

86. 40 C.F.R. pt. 280.

87. 42 U.S.C. §§ 6941 *et seq.*

88. 40 C.F.R. pts. 268–272.

89. Federal Insecticide, Fungicide & Rodenticide Act (FIFRA), 7 U.S.C. §§ 136–136y (1996).

90. *Id.* § 136a.

91. *Id.* § 136a; 40 C.F.R. pts. 152, 155, 158.

92. 7 U.S.C. § 136.

93. *Id* § 136a.

94. *Id* § 136a(d).

95. 7 U.S.C. § 136a(d); 40 C.F.R. pts. 154, 167.

96. 7 U.S.C. § 136i; 40 C.F.R. pt. 171.

97. 7 U.S.C. § 136i; 40 C.F.R. pts. 166, 171.

98. Toxic Substance Control Act (TSCA), 15 U.S.C. §§ 2601–2629 (1976).

99. *Id.* §§ 2602–2605

100. *See id.* § 2604.

101. *Id.* §§ 2606–2607

102. *Id.* § 2608.

103. 15 U.S.C. § 2606(e).

104. *Id.* §§ 2612–2613.

105. Comprehensive Environmental Response, Compensation, and Liability Act, 42 U.S.C. § 9601 *et seq.* (1980).

106. *Id.* § 9601, 9607.

107. *Id.* § 9607.

108. *Id.*

109. *Id.* § 9607(f).

110. *Id.* § 9606.

111. *Id.*

112. *Id.* § 9607.

113. *Id.* § 9613.

114. *Id.* §§ 9601(40), 9607(q)(1)(C).

115. *Id.* § 9601(35)(B); 40 C.F.R. pt. 312.

116. 42 U.S.C. § 9607(r).

117. *See id.* § 9607(b).

118. Oil Pollution Act, 33 U.S.C. § 2701–2762 (1990).

119. Internal Revenue Code, 26 U.S.C. § 9509; 40 C.F.R. pt. 300 (2012).

120. 40 C.F.R. pt. 300.

121. *Id.* §§ 300.1–300.1105.

122. 33 U.S.C. §§ 2701–2762; 40 C.F.R. pt. 370.

123. Emergency Planning & Community Right-to-Know Act, 42 U.S.C. §§ 11001–11050 (1986).

124. 40 C.F.R. pts. 355, 370.

125. *See* 42 U.S.C. § 11001.

126. *Id.* §§ 11001–11005.

127. *Id.* §§ 11021–11023.

128. *See id.* § 11044.

129. *Id.* § 11021

130. 42 U.S.C. § 11022. Hazard categories include immediate health hazard, delayed health hazard, fire hazard, sudden release of pressure hazard, and reactive hazard. See the Occupational Safety and Health Administration for more detail on the hazard categories and who must submit MSDS(s). There are approximately 500,000 products that require an MSDS.

131. 40 C.F.R. pt. 370. Note that there are additional thresholds to exempt reporting by retail gas stations that have complied with the underground storage tank (UST) requirements for the preceding year and store less than 75,000 gallons of gasoline and less than 100,000 gallons of diesel fuel. 40 C.F.R. § 370.10.

132. U.S. EPA, Toxic Release Inventory Program, http://www2.epa.gov/toxics
-release-inventory-tri-program.

133. Endangered Species Act, 16 U.S.C. §§ 1531–1544 (1973).

134. *See id.* § 1538.

135. *See id.* § 1536(a)(2); 50 C.F.R. § 17.3.

136. *Id.* § 1539.

137. 50 C.F.R. pts. 17, 401–453.

138. Migratory Bird Act, 16 U.S.C. §§ 703–712 (1918).

139. The original Act of 1918 implemented a treaty between the United States and
Great Britain, with later amendments implementing treaties between the United States
and Mexico, Japan, Russia.

140. Marine Mammal Protection Act, 16 U.S.C. §§ 1361–1421a (1972).

141. *Id.* § 1362(13).

142. *Id.* § 1362(18).

143. *Id.* §§ 1401–1407.

144. *Id.* § 1374.

145. Federal Land Policy Management Act, 43 U.S.C. §§ 1701–1784 (1976).

146. *Id.* §§ 1701, 1732.

147. *Id.* §§ 1731–1748b.

148. *Id.* §§ 1731–1732.

149. General Mining Act, 30 U.S.C. § 29 (1872); 43 C.F.R. pt. 3860 *et seq.*

150. 30 U.S.C. § 29.

151. *Id.*

152. 43 C.F.R. pts. 3861–3864.

153. Multiple-Use Sustained Yield Act, 16 U.S.C.A. §§ 528–531 (1960), as amended
(1996).

154. *See id.* § 528.

155. *Id.* §§ 529–530.

156. National Forest Management Act, 16 U.S.C. §§ 1600–1614 (1976).

157. *See id.* §§ 1601, 1604.

158. 16 U.S.C. §§ 472a, 1611.

159. Submerged Lands Act, 43 U.S.C. §§ 1301–1356a (1953).

160. Surface Mining Control and Reclamation Act, 30 U.S.C. §§ 1201–1328 (1977).

161. 30 C.F.R. pt. 700 *et seq.*

162. Coastal Zone Management Act, 16 U.S.C. §§ 1451–1465 (1972).

163. *Id.* §§ 1451–1452; 15 C.F.R. pts. 921–933.

164. Coastal Zone Act Reauthorization Amendments (CZARA), 16 U.S.C. § 1455b
(1990) (commonly referred to as section 6217).

165. *Id.* §§ 1455a-b.

166. Antiquities Act, 16 U.S.C. §§ 431–433 (1906).

167. Wilderness Act, 16 U.S.C. §§ 1131–1136 (1964).

168. *Id.*

169. U.S. Fish & Wildlife Serv., Digest of Wilderness Act, http://www.fws.gov/laws
/lawsdigest/wildrns.html (last visited Nov. 10, 2012).

170. Magnuson-Stevens Fishery Conservation and Management Act, 16 U.S.C. § 1801
et seq. (2006).

171. *Id.* § 1852.

172. *Id.* § 1801.

173. *Id.* §§ 1891, 1893.

174. National Historic Preservation Act, 16 U.S.C. §§ 470 *et seq.* (1966).

175. *Id.* § 470f.

176. 36 C.F.R. pt. 800 *et seq.*

177. *Id.*

178. 36 C.F.R. § 800.2.

179. *Id.*

180. 36 C.F.R. §§ 800.2–800.4.

181. 40 C.F.R. § 300.600.

182. 42 U.S.C. § 9607(f).

183. 33 U.S.C. § 1321(b)(1).

184. 43 C.F.R. §§ 11.10, 11.14(u).

185. 33 U.S.C. § 2702(b)(2)(A).

186. 33 U.S.C. § 2701(20); 42 U.S.C. § 9601(16).

187. 16 U.S.C. § 1443(a)(1).

188. 16 U.S.C. § 19jj-1(a).

189. National Environmental Policy Act, 42 U.S.C. §§ 4321 *et seq.* (1970).

190. *Id.* § 4332.

191. 40 C.F.R. §§ 1501.4, 1502.

192. 42 U.S.C. § 4342; 40 C.F.R. pts. 1500–1508.

193. 40 C.F.R. § 1506.1.

194. *Id.* § 1508.18.

195. *Id.* § 1501.3.

196. *Id.* § 1501.4.

197. *Id.*

198. *See* 40 C.F.R. pts. 1500–1508.

199. *Id.*

200. *Id.* pt. 1502.

201. *Id.*

202. 32 I.L.M. 1480 (1993).

203. *Id.*

204. *Id.*

205. *Id.*

206. *E.g.*, U.S.-Canada Air Quality Agreement 30 I.L.M. 676 (1991).

207. *E.g.*, International Boundary and Water Commission, 22 U.S.C. §§ 277 *et seq.* (authorizing appointment of American Commissioner to the Commission and discussing scope of involvement); Border Environment Cooperation Commission 19 U.S.C. § 3473 (authorizing U.S. participation in the Commission).

208. Boundary Water Treaty, U.S.-Gr. Brit. (for Can.), Jan 11, 1909, 36 Stat. 2448.

209. *Id.* at 2449–50.

210. Noah D. Hall, *Bilateral Breakdown: U.S.–Canada Pollution Disputes*, 21 Nat. Res. & Envt. 18 (2006).

211. Noah D. Hall, *Centennial of the Boundary Waters Treaty: A Century of United States–Canadian Transboundary Water Management*, 54 Wayne L. Rev. 1417, 1431 (2008).

212. DD Caron, Transboundary Harm in International Law: Lessons from the Trail Smelter Arbitration, at xxi (2006).

213. United States v. Canada (Trail Smelter Arbitration), 3 R.I.A.A. 1905 (1938), *further proceedings* 3 R.I.A.A. 1938 (1941).

214. Pakootas v. Teck Cominco Metals, Ltd., 452 F.3d 1066 (9th Cir. 2006); Pakootas v. Teck Cominco Metals, Ltd., 646 F.3d 1214 (9th Cir. 2011); *see* Noah D. Hall, *Bilateral Breakdown: U.S.–Canada Pollution Disputes*, 21 Nat. Res. & Env't 18 (2006).

215. Province of Manitoba v. Norton, 398 F. Supp. 2d 41 (D.D.C. 2005).

216. *Id.* at 45.

217. *Id.*

218. *Id.* at 50.

219. Province of Manitoba v. Salazar, 926 F. Supp. 2d 189, 193 (D.D.C. 2013).

220. Catskill Mountains Chapter of Trout Unlimited, Inc. v. U.S. EPA, 630 F. Supp. 2d 295 (S.D.N.Y. 2009); New York v. U.S. EPA, No. 08-CV-8430 (S.D.N.Y. 2008).

221. NPDES Water Transfer Rule, 73 Fed. Reg. 33,697, 33,699 (June 13, 2008).

222. *Catskill Mountains,* 630 F. Supp. 2d 295; *New York,* No. 08-CV-8430.

223. *See, e.g.,* Brandon D. Cunningham, *Border Petrol: U.S. Challenges to Canadian Tar Sands Development,* 19 N.Y.U. ENVTL. L.J. 489 (2012).

224. E.g., 33 U.S.C. § 1319; C. WRIGHT, A. MILLER, E. COOPER, & R. FREER, FED. PRAC. & PROC. § 3531.8 (3d ed. 2008).

225. *See, e.g.,* 40 C.F.R. § 52.21; 30 C.F.R. §§ 250.302, 303.

226. 28 U.S.C. § 1441.

227. *See* WRIGHT & MILLER, *supra* note 225, § 3561, p. 163.

228. For instance, federal courts have exclusive jurisdiction to review decisions by administrative agencies and to review other government actions when challenged.

229. *See, e.g.,* 33 U.S.C. § 1365.

230. 504 U.S. 555 (1992).

231. *Id.* at 560–61; *see, e.g.,* Friends of the Earth, Inc. v. Laidlaw Envtl. Servs. (TOC), Inc., 528 U.S. 167, 180–84 (2000).

232. Among other provisions, see 42 U.S.C. §§ 4321, 4332, 6959, 6972, 7604; 33 U.S.C. § 1365.

233. *See, e.g.,* 42 U.S.C. §§ 300j-8, 6972, 7604, 8435, 11046; 33 U.S.C. §§ 1319, 1365; 15 U.S.C. § 1640.

234. *See* Lynda L. Butler, *State Environmental Programs: A Study in Political Influence and Regulatory Failure,* 31 WM. & MARY L. REV. 823 (1990).

235. *See, e.g.,* Bragg v. W. Va. Coal Ass'n, 248 F.3d 275, 297 (4th Cir. 2001) (applying state law to delegated program under SMCRA).

236. Other than the EPA, these agencies include NOAA, FWS, NMFS, Department of the Interior, Minerals Management Service, Corps, ACHP, Council on Environmental Quality, USFS, NPS, and BLM, as described throughout this chapter.

237. 5 U.S.C. §§ 500 *et seq.*

238. 5 U.S.C. § 706(2)(A).

239. *See* D. R. Hodas, *Enforcement of Environmental Law in a Triangular Federal System: Can Three Not Be a Crowd When Enforcement Authority is Shared by the United States, the States, and Their Citizens?,* 54 MD. L. REV. 1552 (1995).

240. *See* WRIGHT & MILLER, *supra* note 225, § 4514.

241. *See, e.g.,* Anderson v. Am. Smelting & Ref. Co., 265 F. 928 (D. Utah 1919) (plaintiffs complained of sulfur dioxide, arsenic, and other chemical residuals from the smelting factory were damaging their health and their crops by alleging nuisance).

242. *See* WRIGHT & MILLER, *supra* note 225, § 4514.

243. *See* Erie R.R. Co. v. Tompkins, 304 U.S. 64 (1938).

244. *See, e.g.,* Native Vill. of Kivalina v. ExxonMobil Corp., No. 09-17490, 2012 U.S. App. LEXIS 19870 (9th Cir. Sept. 21, 2012); Am. Elec. Power v. Connecticut, 131 S. Ct. 2527 (2011); *see also* Georgia v. Tenn. Copper Co., 206 U.S. 230 (1907) (finding that the state of Georgia could protect its trees despite the needs of the timber industry which would otherwise be regulated as interstate commerce under federal law).

CHAPTER 18

Canada

GRAY E. TAYLOR

I. Overview and Structure
A. Geography and History

Canada's vast geography, stretching from the Atlantic Ocean to the Pacific Ocean and from its long border with the United States to the Arctic, encompasses multiple ecological regions including fresh and salt water coastlines, mountains, forests, prairies, Arctic and sub-Arctic tundra and island archipelagos, and fertile river valleys as well as large and small population centers. On this stage the growth of a modern economy has taken place, strongly based in resource extraction but participating in industrial and technological development on a relatively even footing with those of the United States, European countries, Japan, Australia, New Zealand, and other prosperous economies.

The environmental challenges encountered in Canada, not surprisingly, are not different from those of other modern economies with increasing impacts to air, water, and land as well as the ecological web that ties them together. And as is the case for many other countries, the specific challenges of natural resource development add a frequently challenging set of issues for Canadians. Canada's evolution as a country has been strongly influenced by the political drama that has played out immediately to the south in the United States, with the choice of British parliamentary institutions and a constitutional monarchy by Canada over republicanism and an elected executive being a critical difference. Yet the example of U.S. institutions, policy, and approach is never far from Canadian consciousness, particularly as Canada's approximately 35 million people (about one-tenth of the U.S. population) are strung along the southern border of a land mass slightly larger than the United States with more than 25 percent of Canadians living within 161 kilometers of the United States.[1] That most of Canada and the United States share the same language and, importantly for lawyers, a commitment to the common law, makes that situation, with both attraction and rejection on the Canadian side, a key determinant in Canadian practice on many issues, including the environment.

That said, Canada includes a strong French-speaking minority (approximately 23 percent), which comprises the vast majority of citizens in one of Canada's largest provinces, Québec. In Québec, the civil law remains the law of the land, similar (but on a much less important scale) to the manner in which Louisiana has retained a civil law approach in the United States.

1.   *The Canadian Constitution*

Canada is, as indicated above, a parliamentary and constitutional monarchy. It is also a confederation, composed of the federal government and ten provinces of widely varying geographical and population sizes. The federal government is responsible for three very large territories in Canada's north, each sparsely populated but with great natural resource potential and many Aboriginal citizens (in the territory of Nunavut, an overwhelming majority of its citizens are Aboriginal).

Canada's constitution does not include the word "environment," and responsibility and authority for environmental issues are thus not allocated directly to the federal government of Canada or to the provinces and territories.[2] Rather, the exclusive right to legislate with respect to certain "classes of subjects" (frequently called "heads of power" in Canada) is allocated in the constitution[3] to the federal or provincial government (neither territories nor municipalities are mentioned in the constitution; a territory receives only those powers devolved onto it by the federal government and municipalities receive their authority from provinces) and those heads of power provide the federal and provincial governments with the ability to legislate and otherwise deal with environmental matters related to those heads of power.

The provinces are granted the right to legislate exclusively with respect to, among other things, "property and civil rights within the province," most "local works and undertakings," and "all matters of a merely local or private nature in the province."[4] In a 1982 amendment, each province was given the exclusive right to legislate in relation to the exploration for nonrenewable natural resources in the provinces and the development, conservation, and management of nonrenewable natural resources and forestry resources in the province and of sites and facilities for the generation and production of electricity in the province, and the provinces were granted some ancillary rights.[5]

On the other hand, the federal government has the exclusive right to legislate with respect to, among other things, "fisheries," "Indians, and lands reserved for Indians," "the criminal law," "trade and commerce," and "for the peace, order and good government of Canada in relation to all matters not coming within the classes of subjects ... assigned exclusively to the ... provinces" (this last category being referenced to frequently as POGG).[6] There is a shared responsibility for agriculture,[7] with federal laws overriding provincial laws if the provincial law is repugnant to a federal law.

That environmental matter can readily be described as falling within the classes of subjects assigned exclusively to the federal government *and* the provincial governments at the same time is apparent. The prima facie rule is that where that is the case, legislation of both the federal government and the provincial government is valid unless it is impossible to comply with both pieces of legislation or would frustrate the federal government's legislative purpose, in which case federal legislation will be held to be the only valid legislation under the doctrine of "federal paramountcy."[8] It may be open to courts to "read down" provincial legislation to make it capable of being complied with along with federal legislation, rather than invalidating the provincial legislation completely.[9]

An interesting case that illustrates the manner in which the constitutional validity of federal legislation can be upheld is the *Hydro Québec*[10] case. There the applicability of requirements of the federal government's centerpiece legislation, the Canadian Environmental Protection Act, 1999 (CEPA),[11] with respect to polychlorinated biphenyls (PCBs) contamination was challenged on constitutional grounds by Hydro Québec, the Quebec-based electricity generation transmission corporation. Clearly PCBs and PCB contamination can be seen as a matter of a local nature and as dealing with property and civil rights. Nevertheless, the Canadian Supreme Court held in a 5–4 decision that the federal power to legislate as it did in CEPA was valid in this instance as a proper exercise of the criminal law power. As criminal law must be aimed at eliminating and punishing criminal behavior, not regulating behavior of a normal nature, the extensive provisions of CEPA relating to appropriate behavior and reporting were characterized as being necessary to identify those evidencing behaviors in a manner requiring criminal sanctions, thus permitting the characterization of CEPA as a statute founded on the criminal law head of power allocated to the federal government.

A challenge is the need to coordinate these jurisdictions with national efforts, a difficult task in light of the different stages of development each of the provinces and territories is in. The federal and provincial Minister of the Environment have caused the Canadian Council of Minister of the Environment (CCME) to be formed[12] in an effort to coordinate in a nonbinding way environmental policies, legislation, and activities by governments across Canada. Thus, efforts to develop common standards across Canada for the cleanup of contaminated lands as well as for emissions of contaminants into the environment have found a home at CCME.

Provincial legislation that is not impossible to comply with while complying with federal legislation (e.g., provincial reporting regulations and cleanup requirements) is not invalid in these circumstances. In light of the nationalist aspirations of Quebec and both the maturity and wealth of some of Canada's provinces, provinces have resisted (or threatened to resist) the intrusion of federal laws into matters within the province, thus leading to both actions designed to coordinate federal activities with provincial law and programs without a conflict.

Municipalities are not mentioned in the constitution at all and are created and empowered by the provinces. Nevertheless, municipalities frequently tackle environmental issues, which is permissible if authorized by the province and valid as provincial legislation.

2. Federal Legislation

While numerous pieces of legislation exist at the federal level that relate to environmental matters, the principal statute is CEPA. CEPA, while very broad in its application, is largely devoted to the gathering of information and the authorization of federal participation in environmental matters, particularly where national (including in the sense of interprovincial) issues arise or an interface with the international community and/or international environmental issues is in play. For example, the National Pollutant Release Inventory (NPRI), the Canada-wide reporting system imposed on facilities (over 8,000 in 2011) using or emitting quantities of substances above a NPRI-established threshold, is created in CEPA.[13] Some specific substances deemed to be worthy of special treatment, including PCBs,[14] ozone-depleting substances (ODS),[15] and the quality of fuels,[16] are also regulated under CEPA. The interprovincial movement of hazardous waste,[17] the import into Canada and the export out of Canada of hazardous waste,[18] assessment requirements for new substances that are imported or manufactured in Canada, restrictions on prescribed toxic substances,[19] impacts to marine environments,[20] federal and Aboriginal lands[21] and the use of market-based approaches[22] are all covered by CEPA.

3. Aboriginal Rights and Issues

An important factor in the treatment of environmental issues in Canada is the set of rights of Aboriginal peoples. Canada's constitution, when repatriated from Britain in 1982, clearly preserved the existing treaty and nontreaty rights of Aboriginals in Canada,[23] without specifying what those rights are. Given that a broad range of relationships exist, including some Aboriginals (frequently called First Nations) that have entered into treaties, some that have comprehensive land claim settlements, and some that have no treaty and no settlement but do have outstanding land claims, and given that Canadian courts have held that, depending on the particular circumstances, both federal and provincial governments in Canada (i.e., the Crown in right of Canada or of a province) have a duty to consult with, and to accommodate the interests of, Aboriginals, even where treaties exist,[24] Aboriginal issues are frequently encountered in the Canadian environmental law context, particularly for the development of natural resources.

For example, the numerous environmental issues with respect to the exploration for and development of shale gas in Canada have interacted with Aboriginal rights, resulting in litigation on behalf of Aboriginal groups alleging failure to take into account the rights of Aboriginals and the Crown's duty to consult and accommodate, an aspect of the litigation relating to shale gas development that makes Canada different from the United States.

4. International Environmental Law as a Part of Canadian Environmental Law

Canadian courts have moved far down the road of accepting international laws, particularly treaties, ratified or not, and customary international laws into the body of laws applicable in Canada. One aspect of this can be seen in *114957 Canada Ltd. (Spraytech, Sprinkler Company) v. Hudson (Town)*,[25] where the Supreme Court of Canada referred to the precautionary principle, a principle found in customary international law, to support its judgment.

5. *The Canadian Judiciary*

A system of federal courts does exist in Canada. However, their jurisdiction is limited to matters with respect to which the federal government can legislate under the constitution, where there is applicable federal law, and where the federal court is given jurisdiction. That includes matters relating to environmental impact assessment, CEPA, and claims against the government, including by Aboriginals or alleging a failure to enforce laws. As a result, the system of courts established in each province of Canada is more likely to deal with environmental issues. Provinces all have a court with general jurisdiction (often called superior court or supreme court) that provides most of the trial functions, including hearing significant criminal matters, while there is also a provincial court that acts as a court of first instance, particularly with respect to regulatory offenses; decisions from those courts are applicable to the general jurisdiction courts. The decisions of the court of general jurisdiction are subject to review by a court of appeal in each province and there is the right to appeal decisions from a court of appeal to the Supreme Court of Canada, but generally only with the approval of the Supreme Court.[26]

In addition to the traditional court system, most jurisdictions have created tribunals to deal with environmental matters. In Ontario, for example, the Environmental Review Tribunal (ERT)[27] hears appeals of steps (such as the issuance of approvals or orders) taken by the provincial government and, while their decisions are reviewable by the Ontario Superior Court, significant deference is given to the decisions of the ERT except where matters of law are being decided.[28]

II. Air and Climate Change
A. Air Pollution Control

Most Canadian provinces and territories have legislation designed to regulate emissions to the atmosphere. In Ontario, for example, the Environmental Protection Act (OEPA) requires an environmental compliance approval be issued by the Ministry of Environment (MOE) before an entity may use, operate, construct, alter, extend, or replace a plant, structure, equipment, or other thing that may discharge a contaminant into any part of the natural environment except water.[29] As well, discharges of contaminants that cause or may cause an adverse effect are prohibited.[30] Depending on the particular circumstances, the OEPA provides the MOE with the ability to issue certain orders requiring the control or cessation, investigation, and/or remediation of impacts from the emission of contaminants into the natural environment.[31] Similar provisions exist in most Canadian provinces and territories.[32] There are many issues and nuances related to these provisions that are beyond the scope of this chapter.

Air pollution, however, does not stop at provincial borders. CEPA contains provisions that, depending on the circumstances, may permit action to be taken by a department of the federal government (such as Environment Canada), including enacting regulations, if a substance released from a source in Canada may reasonably be anticipated to be contributed to air pollution in a country other than Canada, or air pollution that is likely to violate an international agreement binding on Canada in relation to the prevention, control, or connection of pollution.[33] Prior to acting, the federal government is required to consult with the government of the province or territory in which the source is located and give it an opportunity to act. As well, the federal government arguably has the ability to legislate with respect to cross-border air pollution, even where the boundary in question is one between provinces.

A current initiative of CCME is the development of a nationwide Air Quality Management System (AQMS)[34] that has a similar purpose to the Clean Air Act (CAA) in the United States but that is premised on the recognition that federal authority over air emission matters is likely limited so that provincial action, coupled with federal support, is likely to produce a better result than efforts focused only at the provincial or federal level. The AQMS contemplates the creation of Canadian air quality standards to establish targets for outdoor air quality across the country, base-level industrial emission requirements (BLIERS) that set a minimum performance standard for major industries in Canada, coordinated actions in regional air sheds where air pollution crosses a border, and intergovernmental collaboration to reduce transportation emissions. It is notable that Quebec will not participate directly in AQMS as it considers AQMS duplicative of its own efforts; Quebec apparently will collaborate with the AQMS initiative, however, on air zone and air shed provisions of the system. It is believed by some industrial sections that AQMS, and in particular BLIERS, may have a profound effect on their operations, not unlike the impact some CAA requirements have had in the United States.

B.   Climate Change

An earlier federal government (Liberal) took the step of subjecting the traditional Kyoto Protocol greenhouse gases (GHGs) to the process designed to determine if they are "toxic substances" for purposes of CEPA; the result was positive and these GHGs have been declared to be "toxic."[35] The current government (Conservative) has relied on that determination in connection with its own GHG emission control policies and legislation. It has collected GHG emission data from facilities across the country[36] in concert with many provincial reporting systems, some of which apply to emitters of smaller annual quantities of GHGs.[37] As well, although the federal government withdrew Canadian participation in the Kyoto Protocol as of December 2012 (notice was given a year earlier), Canada has made a commitment under the Copenhagen Accord and later the Cancun Agreements to reduce its annual GHG emissions in 2020 to 17 percent or more below its 2005 emissions "to be aligned with the final economy-wide emission reduction target of the United States of America in enacted legislation."[38]

It appears to be valid Canadian law that only the federal government of Canada can enter into treaties with foreign nations,[39] although that view is not necessarily shared completely by all. However, the fact that only the federal government can enter into treaties binding Canada does *not* give the federal government the right to legislate in areas of exclusive provincial jurisdiction; arguably, though, the existence of a treaty helps support the "national nature" of legislation that is more likely to fall within the jurisdiction of the federal government.

The federal government's legislation to date has all been made under CEPA. Those actions include setting emissions standards for passenger automobiles and light trucks[40] that are, for practical purposes, identical to those imposed by the United States and a regulation requiring coal-fired electricity-producing facilities generally to meet the emissions standards associated with combined-cycle natural gas electricity generation on and after July 1, 2015, if they are new or have reached the "end of their useful life," usually 45 years after the commissioning date.[41] This approach is part of the federal government's announced intention to proceed "sector by sector" with performance-based standards,[42] which it plans to continue with draft regulations expected to be announced at the time of this writing for the oil and gas sector and later for chemicals, cement, and other major emitting sectors. As will be seen below, this is inconsistent with some provincial approaches, particularly those in Alberta, British Columbia, and Quebec that are economy-wide and incorporate market mechanisms such as emissions trading or a carbon tax. Under CEPA, the federal government has successfully legislated with respect to vehicles and their efficiency before and with respect to ODS, but the argument has been made that the sector-by-sector approach of the federal government does not meet the requirements for federal legislation to be valid, as it trenches on matters of clear provincial authority, and this may be ultra vires (i.e., beyond the power of) the federal government.

Provinces have enacted GHG reporting requirements and in some cases have put in place GHG emission control systems. The Western Climate Initiative (WCI) that once featured California and seven U.S. states as well as four Canadian provinces (Ontario, British Columbia, Manitoba, and Quebec) has now been reduced by the departure of the seven U.S. states other than California. Only Quebec joined California on January 1, 2013, in implementing a cap-and-trade system applicable to facilities emitting more than 25,000 metric tons of GHG (measured on a CO_2e basis) per annum and to be extended in 2015 to distributors of fossil fuels (other than aviation fuel) with respect to the CO_2 to be emitted on the combustion of those fuels; the Quebec system, like California, will permit the use of some offsets produced using government-approved protocols. Alberta has implemented the Specified Gas

Emitters Regulation (SGER) under its Climate Change and Emissions Management Act requiring emission intensity reductions from large (100,000 CO_2e metric tons per annum) emitters and permitting the use of offsets produced using government-approved offset protocols as well as compliance payments to a government controlled "technology fund" (which invests in GHG emission reduction projects) in lieu of making reductions. British Columbia has imposed a carbon tax equal to $30 per metric ton of CO_2e on fossil fuels combusted in that province.

CEPA includes a historically little-used provision permitting the federal government to make a regulation enacted under CEPA not enforceable in a specific province if that province and the federal government enter into an "equivalency agreement" premised on the province having its own legislation that is "equivalent" to that in the federal regulation.[43] The province of Nova Scotia and the federal government have negotiated an equivalency agreement with respect to the coal-fired electricity GHG regulation referred to above[44] and there are strong suggestions from the federal government and some provinces that additional equivalency agreements and nonenforcement orders may follow for federal government sectoral GHG emission regulations, although only time will tell if that can be politically and legally achieved.[45]

III.   Water

With lengthy coast lines on three oceans and major rivers and lake systems, including large freshwater Great Lakes shared with the United States and the rivers like the Columbia, Red, and St. Croix that cross the Canada/U.S. boundary, and a sense that an essential element of Canada's uniqueness is its relationship to nature, including oceans, lakes, and rivers, efforts to protect those waters by legislation and legal principles are abundant in Canada.

While provinces have historically taken the lead in implementing protective legislation, the international and interprovincial nature of the water resources has drawn the federal government into this area as well. Federal engagement is premised on its jurisdiction over criminal law (in addition to CEPA, there are criminal code provisions that arguably apply to serious environmental offenses such as the possession or deposit of an offensive volatile substance; common nuisance endangering the life, safety, or health of the public; criminal negligence causing death or bodily harm; and mischief in relation to property), fisheries (relevant to the quality of water and fish habitat and a strong basis for the federal Fisheries Act), Aboriginals and lands reserved for Aboriginals (which topic, as mentioned above, is of growing importance), and POGG.

Under CEPA, the federal government has enacted regulations dealing with such matters as pulp and paper mill effluent and disposal of substances at sea. Under the Shipping Act, the discharge of prescribed pollutants at sea is prohibited while the Fisheries Act makes it an offense to deposit or permit the deposit of a "deleterious substance" (a very broadly defined term) in water frequented by fish or in any place under any conditions where a deleterious substance might enter such waters.[46] Moreover, any work, undertaking, or activity that results in any harmful alteration, destruction, or disturbance of any fish habitat is illegal;[47] this is being changed by a controversial amendment[48] to prohibit serious harm to fish (i.e., death of a fish or permanent alteration to, or destruction of, fish habitat) that are part of a commercial, recreational, or Aboriginal fishery. Specific regulations are made under the Fisheries Act for, among other things, the discharge of liquid effluent from chlor-alkali mercury operations, meat and poultry plants, metal mining facilities, petroleum refineries, potato processing plants, and pulp and paper plants; as well, regulations relating to fish farming and other fishing related topics are in place under the statute.

Provinces, relying on their constitutional rights to legislate with respect to property and civil rights and matters of a local concern, have included water protection in their legislation. For example, Ontario's Environmental Protection Act (OEPA) contains similar protections for water as it does for the atmosphere. Ontario also has other statutes designed to specifically protect water, including the Ontario Water Resources Act (OWRA),[49] which regulates the taking of water as well as groundwater and surface water quality. The OWRA also regulates the management and disposal of sewage (a broad term that includes stormwater).[50] Ontario's Clean Water Act, 2006[51] and the Nutrient Management Act, 2002[52] regulate matters relating to the source protection of drinking water in the province and agricultural waste management, respectively; these issues are particularly topical in light of the tragedy that struck the Town of Walkerton in Ontario in 2000 when farm waste found its way into the municipal drinking water system and was passed through, untreated, resulting in seven deaths and many others whose health was adversely affected. Ontario also has a Safe Drinking Water Act, 2002[53] to deal with aspects of that same issue.

An important additional issue relating to water is the cross-border character of many water bodies and the potential for the need for regulation of water on an international and interprovincial basis. International agreements relating to water are referred to elsewhere in this book. They include the Great Lakes Water Quality Agreement between Canada and the United States, most recently updated and expanded in 2012,[54] and the nonbinding Great Lakes St. Lawrence River Basin Sustainable Water Resources Agreement between Ontario, Quebec, and the eight states bordering the Great Lakes, most recently updated in 2005.[55] It is appropriate to note that provinces have regulated the withdrawal of large quantities of water (e.g., the OWRA requires a permit to withdraw more than 50,000 liters/day from surface or groundwater[56]) and the transfer of large amounts of water out of a watershed, even if into another regulated watershed.[57]

IV. Handling, Treatment, Transportation, and Disposal of Hazardous Materials

The day-to-day management of the use, handling, and storage of chemicals, hazardous materials, and wastes is primarily regulated by the provinces, including by general and some more specific environmental legislation; this includes legislation with respect to the environmental aspects of chemical use (including storage, release, and disposal) as well as the health and safety aspects of chemical use (including labeling, exposure, and training). The federal government also has a significant regulatory role in this area, particularly with respect to the regulation of what chemicals and other substances may be manufactured, imported, or sold in Canada.

This section discusses the regulation of chemicals and other substances and products in Canada. Section V discusses the regulation of waste, including hazardous waste and recyclable materials. CEPA contains important provisions with respect to the regulation of substances in Canada. Part 5 of CEPA provides a regulatory regime that prohibits a person from manufacturing or importing a "new" substance in or into Canada unless the federal government is notified and has completed a risk assessment on the substance to identify any risks that may be associated with the substance. A substance will be considered "new" to Canada if it is not listed on the Domestic Substances List (DSL), which is a list that is intended to identify all substances that are known to have been in commerce in Canada prior to 1984 or authorized under CEPA thereafter.

Of particular importance to CEPA are those substances that are determined to be a "toxic substance," which is any substance that has or may have an immediate or long-term harmful effect on the environment or its biological diversity; that constitutes or may constitute a danger to the environment on which life depends; or that constitutes or may constitute a danger in Canada to human life or health. Substances that are determined to be toxic under CEPA are added to a list of toxic substances in Schedule 1 of the Act and will generally have some form of risk management measure imposed. Risk management measures typically consist of regulations regarding some aspect of the manufacture, import, use, handling, or disposal of the substance, depending on the nature of the risk, but could also include an obligation to prepare and implement a pollution prevention plan or an environmental emergency plan, or the creation by the federal government of a code of practice or a guideline. Substances may also be identified for "virtual elimination" with regulations prescribing stringent release limits and other preventive measures. The federal government is currently in the midst of a significant review, on a staged and prioritized basis, of those substances that are already listed on the DSL to determine whether any of them (many of which were in commerce in Canada prior to 1984 and then not subjected to the regulatory scrutiny of the current notification and assessment regime) should be considered toxic substances and subject to risk management measures.

The federal government establishes safety standards for consumer products through the Canada Consumer Product Safety Act. This Act is used, among other things, to prohibit products that pose an unreasonable risk to consumers, to impose mandatory reporting obligations with respect to safety incidents, and to authorize the government to issue product-related orders, including product recalls and safety testing. The federal government also regulates products under the Hazardous Products Act,[58] which is directed primarily at the sale, importation, and use of controlled products used in work places in Canada, and requires, among other things, proper labeling and the use of Material Safety Data Sheets for such products.

The federal government legislates with respect to specific chemical products, such as pesticides under the Pest Control Products Act[59] and fertilizers under the Fertilizers Act.[60] These Acts generally require a federal government registration prior to the sale or import of the product in Canada. The federal government also has specific legislation with respect to the safe handling and transportation of dangerous goods under the Transportation of Dangerous Goods Act, 1992.[61]

Provinces have the ability to regulate many of the matters referred to above as subject to federal regulation, a situation that can result in the imposition of regulatory requirements from both levels of government. For example, with respect to the regulation of pesticides, the federal Pest Control Products Act requires the registration of a pesticide prior to its manufacture, importation, handling, or distribution within Canada.[62] Provincial legislation, such as the Pesticides Act[63] in Ontario, primarily regulates the licensing of persons involved in the sale and application of pesticides within a province. Municipalities, despite having only those powers delegated to them by provinces, also have the ability to regulate many environmental matters, including the use of pesticides, within the municipal boundaries. Many municipalities in Canada have enacted bylaws banning the cosmetic application of certain pesticides. As long as the municipality is properly exercising its powers provided under municipal legislation and such a bylaw is not incompatible with federal and provincial legislation, it will be a valid exercise of municipal authority.[64]

V.   Waste and Site Remediation

Site remediation is primarily (and typically) dealt with under provincial legislation. Most provincial legislation contains remedial (investigation, remediation, monitoring, etc.) obligations premised, at least in theory, on the "polluter pays" principle, which has been endorsed by the CCME. Some jurisdictions, such as Ontario, also authorize the imposition of remedial obligations on property owners, regardless of whether they caused or contributed to the contamination. Remedial obligations can be enforced by the issuance of governmental orders.

In British Columbia, the contaminated sites legislation creates a scheme similar to U.S. Superfund legislation, including the allocation of liability when more than one person is named on a cleanup order and the right to recover from "responsible persons" if a party incurs "remediation costs" (whether voluntarily or as a result of an order).[65] While provincial cleanup laws can apply on sites subject to federal legislation (banks, railways, airports, nuclear facilitations, Indian reservations, defense facilities, etc.) if they do not overly interfere with federal jurisdiction, the federal government has taken the responsibility to deal with the cleanup of contaminated sites in a number of those situations.

The regulation of waste and hazardous waste is a shared federal and provincial responsibility with federal jurisdiction focused on international and interprovincial aspects. Federal regulations under CEPA deal with the import and export of hazardous waste and hazardous recyclable materials[66] and the interprovincial movement of hazardous waste.[67] Provincial statutes typically provide detailed requirements with respect to all aspects of the generation, handling, and disposal of waste within a province, including hazardous wastes and recyclable materials. For example, under the OEPA, certain materials are expressly designated as wastes and some materials such as prescribed recyclable materials are exempted from the regulatory requirements. Activities involving the transportation, handling, and disposal of waste generally require an environmental compliance approval, and subject wastes (a term that includes hazardous wastes and liquid industrial wastes) are subject to additional regulatory requirements including generator registration and the use of waste manifests for off-site shipments. Where waste has been unlawfully disposed of in Ontario, the OEPA authorizes the issuance of orders requiring the removal of the waste and/or remediation of the site.[68]

In recent years there have been significant regulatory developments in Canada with respect to waste diversion and extended producer responsibility. Many jurisdictions in Canada now have mandatory obligations on producers or "stewards" of products such as blue box materials (glass, metal, paper, etc.), paper and packaging, electronic and electrical equipment, and tires. These programs require the stewards to either operate or be part of a diversion program that collects and manages the wastes in a responsible manner, or pay a fee to the government or an agent of the government to fund the diversion of their products from the waste stream.

VI.   Emergency Response

The Emergency Management Framework for Canada[69] provides for the cooperative approach by federal and provincial governments to the preparation for and response to a broad range of emergencies, including chemical, biological, radiological, and nuclear events. It recognizes the local nature of most emergencies and explicitly allocates responsibility to the municipalities and the provinces and territories but also recognizes the potential to transcend boundaries and thus the role of the federal government in coordinating the efforts of others while providing leadership where it has exclusive jurisdiction or where the lands and properties involved are the responsibility of the federal government.

CEPA contains provisions permitting the federal government to regulate with respect to the prevention and response to environmental emergencies relating to the release of substances into the natural environment.[70] Persons in Canada who own or manage prescribed substances above concentration and quantity thresholds are required to notify the federal government of their substances and to prepare and implement environmental emergency response plans.[71]

Most provinces also have emergency response legislation that sets out responsibilities and authorizations that may be exercised as part of a provincial response to an emergency. For example, Ontario has passed the Emergency Management and Civil Protection Act, which clearly could be applied in the event of an environmental emergency.[72]

VII. Natural Resource Management and Protection

As a result of the addition of section 92A to Canada's constitution, the exclusive jurisdiction to legislate with respect to renewable natural resources and forests and the sites relating to the generation of electricity is allocated to the provinces. In addition, the provinces have ownership of most natural resources, subject to grants made to private citizens, with some exceptions where the Canadian constitution grants ownership to the federal government and of course to Aboriginal rights. Consequently, the provinces have taken the primary role in regulating environmental matters related to natural resource development. Many provinces have adopted land use planning requirements that determine or guide the development of natural resources. For example, British Columbia has implemented a series of regional land use plans that inform regulators in making decisions as to permitting an environmental assessment (EA).

A number of matters under the exclusive jurisdiction of the federal government are frequently involved in natural resource development and extraction including fisheries, navigable waters, and occasionally Indians and Indian lands. As a result, both the federal and provincial EA statutes have been put in place to force the review and mitigation of adverse environmental impact (or occasionally the abandonment of) the proposed development (see section X below).

VIII. Natural Resource Damages

Unlike the United States, where a substantial and growing body of law has grown around litigation relating to natural resource damages, the concept of natural resource damages is not a readily recognizable part of Canadian law.[73] However, in the Canfor[74] case, the Supreme Court explains that damages could have been allowed if properly pleaded with respect to damage to environmentally protected forests, despite the fact that no individuals suffered direct damage.

IX. Protected Species

Endangered species are, like many other environmental matters, subject to joint jurisdiction of the federal and provincial governments with the federal government drawing its jurisdiction from international matters (migrating birds), its responsibility for fisheries, trade, and commerce (an international concern) and other international and interprovincial aspects of this issue. Consequently, Canada has a Species at Risk Act (SARA), pursuant to which species can be listed as endangered so that protection of the species and its habitat becomes mandatory in some cases. The activities of the federal government under SARA have been controversial because of the generally perceived reluctance by the federal government to include species on the endangered species list where commercial interests could be limited.

At the same time, provinces often have endangered species legislation dealing with those species within the province that are at risk. Ontario, for example, has its own Endangered Species Act, 2007.[75] SARA can be deployed where the federal government is of the opinion that the laws of a province do not effectively protect the species.[76]

X.   Environmental Review and Decision Making

The Canadian government made major changes to its EA legislation with the Canadian Environmental Assessment Act, 2012[77] (CEAA 2012). Generally, CEAA 2012 is intended to eliminate matters where assessments were not required, make assessments more efficient, and limit the burden, delay, and overlap with provincial EAs that the government perceived to exist under the previous regime. This may permit natural resources and other projects to proceed with a higher degree of certainty, while at the same time ensuring that environmental impacts are considered before projects are undertaken. In that regard, CEAA 2012 is part of the federal government's Responsible Resource Development initiative that included changes to the Fisheries Act.

CEAA 2012 reflects an intention to defer to provincial EA processes unless there is a matter within federal competency (such as projects that may impact fisheries, federal lands, migratory birds, and Aboriginals). This is designed to prevent overlap with provincial assessments. Those conducting federal EAs are required to consult and cooperate with other jurisdictions (including provinces, foreign states, international organizations and their institutions, and certain Aboriginal self-government bodies or a body that is established under an Aboriginal land claims agreement) that have EA powers, duties, or functions. Where there is a provincial EA and the province so requests, the provincial EA will be substituted for the federal EA if the federal Ministry of the Environment is satisfied, based upon prescribed criteria, that the substitution would be appropriate. This is intended to preclude the need for joint or parallel EAs at the provincial and federal levels, a result frequently seen before CEAA 2012 became law.

Under CEAA 2012, certain prescribed types of projects are potentially subject to EAs; this includes fossil fuel electricity-generating stations, hydroelectric facilities, transmission lines, water diversion structures, oil sands mines and processing facilities, offshore oil and gas production facilities, petroleum refineries (and certain other coal, oil, and gas facilities), pipelines, mines, pulp and paper mills, steel production facilities, other metal working facilities, chemical and pharmaceutical facilities, some wood processing facilities, canals, railways, and waste treatment facilities in addition to nuclear facilities and mines and asbestos facilities. Under CEAA 2012, other projects can be designated for assessment.

An initial screening of projects for which the Canadian Environmental Assessment Agency is responsible is to be done within 45 days of the notice of the project being posted. An assessment will be done only if the federal government decides that it is required, based upon prescribed factors, and can be done either as a "standard" assessment or as a panel review (which would include a hearing, with witnesses, etc.).

The government has attempted to deal with a problem of lengthy delays caused by EAs by imposing timelines (usually one or two years for completion), but even these can be extended in certain circumstances.

Most Canadian provinces have their own provincial EA legislation requiring environmental assessment of a range of proposed activities.

In Ontario, for example, the Environmental Assessment Act applies to certain activities undertaken by the government (provincial and municipal governments and their agencies), as well as designated activities (such as certain electricity and waste projects, whether by private or public sector entities), and other private sector developments that are designated or where the proponent chooses to be subject to an Ontario EA. The Ontario EA process includes the development of terms of reference for approval by the government. Where an EA is required, a development cannot proceed without the EA having been completed and a decision having been made that does not preclude it being implemented. Procedures for Class EAs conducted by proponents exist for routine, predictable, and manageable types of projects with known impacts; those Class EAs can be "bumped up" to full assessment in certain circumstances.

Some federal legislation requires permitting, or meeting specified requirements, before facilities can be constructed; for example, nuclear facilities are subject to a permitting system, as are certain projects impacting fish, fish habitat, species at risk, aeronautics, and other matters within federal jurisdiction. CEAA 2012 includes "substitution" and "equivalency" provisions, which can result in deferring a matter to provincial EA processes. While "substitution" and "equivalency" details are being worked out between provinces and the federal government, it seems clear that the intention is that the provincial processes would produce the information necessary for the federal government to issue (or decline to issue) specific permits and licenses.

The legislation of almost every province contains an obligation to obtain permits where a development is to take place that could discharge contaminants into the environment that could have an adverse effect. The process of obtaining a permit involves an application and a review by the government but also involves posting for review by the public, for example, in Ontario, on the Environmental Registry, so that opportunity for public comment is available, again depending on the circumstances. The granting of permits is subject to review by the Environmental Review Tribunal in Ontario.

XI.   Transboundary Pollution

As indicated above, CEPA contains provisions dealing with international water and air pollution, permitting the federal government to deal with those matters, subject to discussions and an opportunity to act for any province that serves as a source for such contamination. Marine pollution has been determined to have a sufficiently "national" element so as to justify federal legislation under POGG.[78] Canada is a signatory to many international environmental agreements, including the 1991 Canada-United States Air Quality Agreement, the United Nations Framework Convention on Climate Change, the Montreal Protocol on Substances That Deplete the Ozone Layer, and agreements with the United States dealing with boundary waters. Canada participates in the Arctic Council, which frequently deals with transboundary pollution issues.[79]

XII.   Civil and Criminal Enforcement and Penalties

Environmental statutes in Canada provide a broad range of remedies for provincial and federal governmental authorities, including the issuance of orders[80] and administrative penalties as well as the laying of charges. Convictions for environmental offenses in Canada generally carry significant maximum penalties (in some jurisdictions, maximum penalties include fines in the range of several million dollars per day that an offense occurs, as well as the imposition of imprisonment). Some jurisdictions also have minimum statutory penalties imposed, which is generally reserved for more serious environmental offenses.[81] Environmental offenses in Canada are considered to be strict liability offenses (unless a contrary intent is clearly expressed), which means that they are subject to a defense of due diligence. To establish due diligence a defendant must prove, on a balance of probabilities, that he or she (1) took all reasonable care in the circumstances to prevent the events giving rise to the offense or (2) had a reasonable belief in a mistaken set of facts, which, if true, would have rendered the act or omission innocent.[82]

Those potentially subject to being charged include directors and officers who, under CEPA and the OEPA, are given a positive duty to take all reasonable care to avoid having the corporation commit offenses; in other provinces, generally directors and officers must participate in or acquiesce to the activity that constituted the prohibited act to be charged.

In addition to regulatory offenses, administrative monetary penalties are increasingly being adopted in environmental statutes. An administrative penalty is an administrative fine (i.e., it does not involve the laying of a charge and proof of an offense) that is available in respect of specific offenses.[83] Administrative penalties can often be issued on an absolute liability basis (where there is no defense of due diligence available).

Provisions of the Canadian Criminal Code[84] are available but are not typically used with respect to environmental matters, likely because any such provision requires the Crown to prove mens rea, that is, a mental element indicating recklessness or intent.

Citizen suits seeking enforcement of environmental statutes are rare, with the lack of a statutory right to bring such suits and the restrictive interpretation of statutory and other litigation rules to deny standing being significant obstacles.

Statutory remedies for those harmed by the emission of contamination are also rare; however, Ontario created a civil cause of action under the OEPA to recover the damage caused by a spill.[85] Ontario also passed the Environmental Bill of Rights, which creates a cause of action related to harm to a public resource. British Columbia's contaminated sites legislation also creates the right to recover damages from a person who is involved with the pollution in some circumstances.[86] Under the Fisheries Act, a private charge laid by an individual that results in a conviction can result in 50 percent of any fine imposed paid to the person laying the charge;[87] this has traditionally been of limited significance because the government will often take over the prosecution and, more often than not, settle the matter short of a fine.

Canadian courts recognize the traditional environmental torts that are common in the United States, including trespass, negligence, nuisance, and strict liability. Canadian courts have accepted the possibility of regulatory negligence pursuant to which government agencies can be held liable.[88] Tort class actions have been used to seek a remedy for environment-related damages, although this is still very much an emerging development.

Notes

1. *See* http://www.nationalgeographic.com/travel/countries-facts/.

2. Friends of the Oldman River Soc'y v. Canada (Minister of Transport), [1992] S.C.J. No. 1.

3. Constitution Act, 1867 (as amended).

4. *Id.* § 92.

5. *Id.* § 92A.

6. *Id.* § 91.

7. *Id.* § 95.

8. Multiple Access v. McCutcheon, [1982], 2 S.C.R. 191.

9. Canadian W. Bank v. The Queen in Right of Alberta, [2007], 2 S.C.R. 3.

10. R v. Hydro Canada, [1997] S.C.J. No. 76.

11. Canadian Environmental Protection Act, 1999, S.C. 1999, C. 33.

12. *See* http://www.ccme.ca.

13. Canadian Environmental Protection Act, 1999, S.C. 1999, c.33, secs. 48–50.

14. PCB Regulations (2008) and other CEPA regulations.

15. Ozone-Depleting Substances Regulations, 1998 (SOR/99-7), as amended.

16. Canadian Environmental Protection Act, 1999, secs. 139, 140, 148, and Schedule 1.

17. Interprovincial Movement of Hazardous Waste Regulations (SOR/2002-301).

18. Export and Import of Hazardous Waste and Hazardous Recyclable Material Regulations (SOR/2005-149).

19. Canadian Environmental Protection Act, 1999, pt. 5—Controlling Toxic Substances.
20. *Id.* secs. 120–121.
21. *Id.* pt. 9.
22. *Id.* § 322.
23. Constitution Act, 1867, sec. 35.
24. Haida Nation v. British Columbia (Minister of Forests), 2004 S.C.C. 73.
25. [2001], 2 R.S.C. 241.
26. http://www.scc-csc.gc.ca/court-cour/role-eng.aspx.
27. Environmental Review Tribunal Act, 2000, S.O. 2000, S.26, S.C.H.F.
28. *Id.*
29. Environmental Protection Act, R.S.O. 1990, ch. 19, S. 9.
30. *Id.* at sec.14.
31. *Id.* at secs. 7, 8, 10, 11, 17, 18.
32. For example, in Alberta, the Environmental Protection and Enhancement Act, R.S.A. 2000, C.E. 12.
33. Canadian Environmental Protection Act, 1999, § 166.
34. http://www.ccme.ca/ourwork/air.html?cateogry_id=46.
35. Order Adding Toxic Substances to Schedule 1 to the Canadian Environmental Protection Act, 1999, SOR/2005-345.
36. http://www.ec.gc.ca/indicateurs-indicators/default.asp?lang=En&n=BFB1B398-1.
37. For example, Ontario's threshold is 25,000 metric tons CO_2e per annum.
38. http://www.climatechange.gc.ca/default.asp?lang=En&n=D6B3FF2B-1.
39. http://www.parl.gc.ca/content/lop/researchpublications/2008-45-e.htm.
40. Passenger Automobile and Light Truck Greenhouse Gas Emission Regulations, http://laws-lois.justice.gc.ca/eng/regulations/SOR-2010-201/page-1.html.
41. Reduction of Carbon Dioxide Emissions from Coal-fired Generation of Electricity Regulations, http://www.gazette.gc.ca/rp-pr/p2/2012/2012-09-12/html/sor-dors167-eng.html.
42. http://climatechange.gc.ca/default.asp?lang=En&n=4FE85A4C-1.
43. http://laws-lois.justice.gc.ca/eng/acts/C-15.31/page-5.html#h-8.
44. http://www.ec.gc.ca/lcpe-cepa/default.asp?lang=En&n=1ADECEDE-1.
45. Land use changes can also impact the level of a country's GHG emissions. Canada has recently determined that it will report on the sequestration and emission consequences of land use, land use changes, and forestry with respect to its greenhouse gas targets. CANADIAN EMISSION TRENDS 35–40 (2012). Canada had earlier suggested that it might take that position but the unfortunate consequences of a number of events and actions in Canada, including the effects of the infestation of forest by the mountain pine beetle in British Columbia and more recently Alberta, adversely affected the sequestration/emission balance. With Canada's new target under the Copenhagen Accords and Cancun Agreements using 2005 as the baseline as opposed to 1990 under the Kyoto Protocol, and a variety of changes to the sequestration US emissions balance in Canada, Canada is again in a position where land use, land use changes, and forestry do have a beneficial effect on emissions by reducing them and increasing sequestration.
46. Fisheries Act, R.S.C., c. F-14, § 36.
47. *Id.* § 35.
48. S.C. 2012, c. 19, § 142(2).
49. R.S.O., 1990, c. O.40.
50. OWRA §§ 1, 53–62.
51. S.O. 2006, c. 22.
52. S.O. 2002, c. 4.

53. S.O. 2002, c. 32.

54. http://www.ec.gc.ca/grandslacs-greatlakes/default.asp?lang=En&n=45B79BF 9-1.

55. http://www.mnr.gov.on.ca/en/Business/Water/2ColumnSubPage/STEL02 _164560.html.

56. OWRA § 34.

57. OWRA §§ 34.3, 34.4.

58. R.S.C. 1985, c. H-3.

59. R.S.C. 1985, c. 28.

60. R.S.C. 1985, c. F-10.

61. S.C. 1992, c. 34.

62. S.C. 2002, c. 28.

63. R.S.O. 1990, c. P.11.

64. 114957 Canada Ltd. (Spraytech, Sprinkler Co.) v. Hudson (Town), [2001], 2 RSC 241.

65. Environmental Management Act, SBC, c. 53, pt. 4, § 47.

66. Export and Import of Hazardous Waste and Recyclable Hazardous Waste.

67. Interprovincial Movement of Hazardous Waste Regulations, SOR/2002-301.

68. OEPA, secs. 43, 44.

69. http://www.publicsafety.gc.ca/cnt/rsrcs/pblctns/mrgnc-mngmnt-frmwrk/index -eng.aspx.

70. CEPA, pt. 8.

71. Environmental Emergency Regulations, SOR/2003-307.

72. R.S.O. 1990, c. E.9.

73. A related field is land management. As a local matter, and one that deals with property and civil rights, land management is almost entirely a provincial responsibility. Environmental matters assist in guiding provincial decision making. For example, in Ontario, the Planning Act has as one of its purposes "to promote sustainable development in a healthy natural environment" and requires inclusion of the effects on the social, economic, and natural environment in an official plan. R.S.O. 1990, c. P.13. Land use planning by municipalities includes consideration of environmental matters including traffic nuisance and sunlight access. In Ontario, under the Green Energy Act, S.O. 2009, c. 12, Schedule A, municipalities were prohibited from applying land use planning requirements to the sites for provincially approved renewable energy facilities, with the entire obligation to deal with environmental matters delegated to the Ministry of the Environment under the Renewable Energy Approval process. OEPA, pt. V.0.1. An exception to the general rule that provincial governments deal with land use (and therefore planning) matters occurs in the City of Ottawa, Canada's national city, where the federal government's National Capital Commission has broad authority to deal with planning matters. Munro v. Nat'l Capital Comm'n, [1966] S.C.R. 663.

74. British Columbia v. Canadian Forest Prods. Ltd., [2004] 2 SCR 74.

75. S.O. 2007, c. 6.

76. SARA S 34.

77. S.C. 2012, C. 19, S 52.

78. R v. Crown Zellerbach, 49 D.L.R. (4th), 161.

79. *See* chapter 47, Arctic Region, in this volume.

80. *See, e.g.,* OEPA, secs. 7, 8, 17, 18, 43, 44.

81. Environmental Enforcement Act, S.C. 2009, c. 14.

82. *Supra* note 3.

83. Environmental Enforcement Act, S.C. 2009, c. 14; OEPA § 182.1(6).

84. Criminal Code, R.S.C. 1985, C-46, § 178, 180, 219–221, 428–430.
85. OEPA § 99.
86. Environmental Management Act § 47.
87. Fisheries (General) Regulation, SOR/93-53, § 62.
88. Taylor v. Canada (Attorney General), 2012 ONCA 479.

CHAPTER 19

Mexico

DANIEL BASURTO GONZÁLEZ*

I. General Overview of the Environmental Law of Mexico

A. Constitutional Legal Framework

Mexico's legal system stems from the civil law tradition and therefore is a system of positive law. Thus, the Mexican legal system is based in written laws, regulations, and other legal provisions, created by the legislature (Federal Congress) and applicable in the Mexican territory. After the entry into force of the North American Free Trade Agreement (NAFTA), a third-party verification system[1] and system of conformity assessment were incorporated into the Mexican legal system.

The constitutional supremacy doctrine governs the Mexican legal system. Under Article 133 of the Political Constitution of the United Mexican States, the constitution is the supreme law in the Mexican territory, along with the laws enacted by the Federal Congress and all treaties consistent with the constitution.[2] The Mexican Constitution establishes that all individuals located in the Mexican territory are entitled to a list of guarantees, including the right to a healthy environment.[3] This right to a healthy environment was the result of one of the many reforms of the Mexican Constitution, a living document.

B. Constitutional Provisions on Environmental Law

As the supreme governing legal instrument, all existing general and federal legal provisions flow from the Mexican Constitution. Thus, the Mexican Constitution establishes the constitutional grounds from which all the environmental legal provisions in force in the Mexican territory derive. These constitutional grounds include Article 4, regarding the right to a healthy environment; Article 27, regarding rules regarding natural resources conservation; Article 73, regarding the prevention and control of pollution,

---

*The author appreciates the contribution of Regina Gallegos Triana on this chapter.

349

specifically in subsection XVI, fourth part; and Article 25, regarding environmental protection of productive resources when incentivizing private sector development.

The standards of environmental protection in the Mexican Constitution have increased over the years in response to developments from several international summits. Three major reforms have significantly shaped the constitutional bases of Mexican environmental law.

The first reform took place in 1987, with the inclusion of the federal government's duty to preserve and restore ecological balance in Article 27, and the grant to the Federal Congress of the power to legislate on environmental matters in Article 73, paragraph 29(c). The second reform took place in 2010, with the recognition in Article 17 of "collective actions" (class actions), which are expected to have significant impacts on environmental regulation. The most recent reform took place in 2012, when Article 4 was rephrased to recognize the right to a healthy environment and the right of access to water and sanitation, and to establish the federal government's duty to guarantee these rights and take actions to achieve these ends.[4]

C.   International Environmental Instruments

In international fora, Mexico is one of the most active and prolific nations in terms of instruments signed and ratified. To date, Mexico is party to more than 70 international environmental treaties. In some of these treaties, such as the United Nations Framework Convention on Climate Change (UNFCCC), and the Basel Convention on the Control of Transboundary Movements of Hazardous Wastes and Their Disposal (Basel Convention), among others, Mexico has participated quite actively.

According to the Mexican Constitution, international treaties must be consistent with it as the supreme law and must be approved and ratified by the Senate. According to public international law, treaties bind state parties, but not individuals (i.e., citizens). As a result, once a state has signed a treaty, it is that state's obligation to enact pertinent laws to implement the provisions agreed to in a given treaty.

Mexico is party to various bilateral and multilateral international environmental instruments. In the bilateral sphere, NAFTA is one of the most influential in environmental matters. Although it is a trade agreement in principle, it includes relevant environment provisions to be fulfilled by the parties. Additionally, it creates a Commission for Environmental Cooperation (CEC) consisting of a council, a secretariat, and a Joint Public Advisory Committee (JPAC). The objective of the CEC is to increase cooperation among the parties (United States, Canada, and Mexico). However, in practice the CEC has served only to monitor what is occurring in the three member countries, without any further significant accomplishments to date.

Multilateral treaties, such as the Basel Convention, the Vienna Convention for the Protection of the Ozone Layer and its Protocol on Substances That Deplete the Ozone Layer, the Stockholm Convention on Persistent Organic Pollutants, Rotterdam Convention on the Prior Informed Consent

Procedure for Certain Hazardous Chemicals and Pesticides in International Trade, the Convention on Biological Diversity and its protocols, UNFCCC, and the Kyoto Protocol to the UNFCCC, have significant influence over Mexican policies as the federal government takes actions to comply with the obligations contained in these instruments.

D. General and Federal Laws

Derived from the constitutional reform of 1987, in January 1988 the General Law of Ecological Balance and Environmental Protection (LGEEPA) was enacted. The LGEEPA sets out the distribution of authorities and responsibilities of the three levels of government (federal, state, and municipal), along with environmental policy instruments, remedies, and sanctions.

A prolific year for environmental law was 1992, when the Federal Congress created and/or modified several laws regarding natural resources. To date, 11 federal laws enacted in 1992 form part of the environmental legal framework: the LGEEPA, General Law for the Prevention and Management of Waste, General Wildlife Law, National Waters Law, General National Assets Law, Federal Law on Fisheries and Aquaculture, General Law on Human Resettlement, Law on the Biosafety of Genetically Modified Organisms, Federal Law on Fees, General Law on Sustainable Forestry Development, and the recently enacted Climate Change Law.[5]

E. Environmental Management in Mexico

Environmental management is the set of human activities that are undertaken in order to build an environmental framework. Its main components are policies, laws, and environmental administration.[6] Before 1986, the environmental management regime in Mexico was predominantly centralized. However, with the constitutional reform of the Article 73, a system was established allowing the decentralization of authorities and, in principle, the "concurrence," or overlapping jurisdiction, of the federation, states, and municipalities.[7]

In this regard, we believe that there is actually a lack of "concurrence" in environmental law because a clear distribution of authority between the three levels of government—federal, state, and municipal—exists in the environmental legal framework. For instance, in terms of atmospheric emissions, there is a specific list establishing whether an activity falls under federal jurisdiction; those activities not included in that list fall under state jurisdiction; normally, those activities from services and smaller establishments are under municipal jurisdiction.[8] The same situation occurs regarding waste management, in which each type of waste is the responsibility of a different level of government.

On the federal level, the Ministry of Environment and Natural Resources (SEMARNAT) is the government agency in charge of the protection, restoration, and conservation of ecosystems, natural resources, and environmental services of Mexico, with the purpose of fostering their use and sustainable development.[9] SEMARNAT contains several subagencies, including (1) the Federal Attorney for Environmental Protection (PROFEPA), responsible for monitoring legal compliance; (2) the National Water Commission (CONAGUA); (3) the National Institute of Ecology (INE), which soon will be the National Institute of Ecology and Climate Change, as required by a recently enacted law;[10] (4) the Mexican Institute of Water Technology (IMTA); (5) the National Forestry Commission (CONAFOR), created to develop and promote the productive activities, protection, conservation, and restoration of forest resources; and (6) the National Commission of Natural Protected Areas (CONANP), responsible for conserving the natural heritage of Mexico through natural protected areas and other forms of preservation.

F.   Environmental Policy Instruments

Environmental policy instruments are an important element in the Mexican environmental law regime subject, of course, to their adequate implementation. In Mexico, environmental policy instruments tend to have more of a preventive, rather than corrective, nature. These instruments are related to economic matters, include policies based on economic incentives, and mainly put a price on the damage caused to the environment, or to be paid by those who contaminate the environment. We briefly describe two of the most common instruments that are derived from LGEEPA (environmental impact assessment, a third instrument, is discussed in section IX, *infra*):

1.   Ecological Settlement of the Territory

The ecological settlement of the nation's territory is an instrument located at the second section of the LGEEPA, which concerns environmental planning, from articles 19 to 20 BIS 7. The intent of this instrument is to characterize and permit the uses of land and natural resources, utilizing a rational and diverse approach and after obtaining public consensus.

In principle, this instrument should be one of the most important public policy tools used by the federal government. If all general policies on development, such as forestry and marine development, were derived from this policy instrument, there would be a better control of activities across the country. Unfortunately, this instrument remains largely unimplemented to date.

2.   Self-Regulation and Environmental Audits

These two innovative instruments were introduced for the first time in Mexico as a result of the LGEEPA reform of 1996.[11] They came to revolutionize the way environmental management is performed, by including a new voluntary compliance scheme. In this context, the term "self-regulation" is used to define the process by which entities subject to regulation establish their own standards by including requirements more stringent than those in the current regulations or by filling the gaps in such regulations. In terms of their compliance, this implies an improvement in their environmental performance.[12]

The environmental audit is a process carried out on a voluntary basis by a business in which a methodological examination of the pollution and risk of its operations is conducted, along with an analysis of environmental regulations and international parameters, to define preventive and corrective measures, which are set forth in an entity-specific action plan for environmental protection.[13]

In practice, the Environmental Audit Sub-Attorney (EASA) of the Federal Attorney for Environmental Protection (PROFEPA) is the office in charge of leading, implementing, and operating this program, known as the National Environmental Audit Program (NAPA). The EASA recognizes those companies that voluntarily participate in the program and comply with an action plan by granting them a Clean Industry Certificate (CIC).[14]

Currently, the CIC is only issued within the industrial sector, although efforts have been made to extend the scope of the NAPA to other sectors. There are several considerations to the real effectiveness of this instrument. For instance, this certificate is awarded only after fulfillment of the action plan, which may or may not include other performance activities and their environmental impacts, for example, soil contamination remediation. Indeed, there are some organizations that have obtained a CIC even when their works on site remediation are still ongoing.

These processes of self-regulation and auditing have been positively impacted by the development of environmental development systems.[15] There is currently a need to improve standards of protection and Mexico is trying to import from other countries their best practices in this regard. In the particular case of International Organization for Standardization (ISO) 14000,[16] some in the industrial sector have been supporting its implementation. That said, greater consensus is needed with all environmental stakeholders.

G. Access to Mexican Courts to Achieve Environmental Justice

In general, Mexican environmental law has been developing at a rapid pace. Since the creation of LGEEPA in 1988, appropriate laws and institutions, such as PROFEPA, were created and in subsequent years more than 20 states, and more recently, the Federal District (i.e., Mexico City), have created their own local environmental prosecutor offices. Despite this growth and consolidation, however, there remains a jurisprudential gap in recognition of, and a lack of full access to, environmental justice.

Currently, there is no procedural law that allows a full and effective access to environmental justice. All environmental matters are subject to administrative proceedings; thus, substantive environmental law is limited by those administrative law procedures. Several vehicles for obtaining a remedy in environmental matters, however, bear mentioning.

First, regarding judicial remedies, the *amparo* (regulated by the Mexican Constitution Articles 103 and 107) is a judicial writ available to protect constitutional rights and challenge unconstitutional actions. It was necessary, nevertheless, to develop a new legal concept enabling individuals to file complaints against those governmental actions that affect their environmental rights. These "citizen complaints" have been very effective in deterring activities that are illegal and harmful to the environment.[17]

Second, the constitutional reform of 2011 to Article 17 allows the creation of the "collective action" (akin to the class action of the common law system), to allow a group of people to challenge those actions that contravene their fundamental rights.

Finally, the Mexican legal system provides a remedy of judicial review called revocation, or vacatur, as a tool to challenge actions that result from the exceedance of authority or illegal acts of the government. Such actions are, however, rarely effective.

Alternatively, as the applicable procedural law in environmental matters is administrative procedural law, an entity can challenge a governmental act or decision through the Federal Court of Fiscal and Administrative Justice. Such actions typically request an injunction of the governmental action. This type of court exists in each level of government (federal, state, and municipal).

II.   Air and Climate Change
A.   Air Pollution

Since 1988, protection of the atmosphere has been regulated by the LGEEPA. This law includes legal provisions on the prevention and control of air pollution, and it defines which stationary sources of air pollution are subject to federal jurisdiction, along with a short list of industries that are also under federal jurisdiction.[18]

In 1988, the federal government issued the LGEEPA Regulations on Prevention and Control of Pollution of the Atmosphere. In these regulations, the subsectors of the original list of industries under federal jurisdiction were specified. Additionally, the regulation sets out the obligations of those responsible for stationary sources that emit gases or solid particles into the atmosphere. These include (1) monitoring and accounting for emissions; (2) maintaining a log of the operation and maintenance of the process and control equipment, (3) submitting an annual report of emissions through the Annual Operation Certificate (COA), and (4) complying with the maximum permissible limits established by the applicable mandatory technical regulations, known as Official Mexican Standards (NOMs).[19]

At the state level, the framework is similar to the federal regime. Those responsible for stationary sources under state jurisdiction have to comply with the obligations derived from state legislation. It is important, though, to note that stationary sources are defined within a specific jurisdiction, and cannot be subject to both jurisdictions.

With regard to mobile sources of air pollution, the regulations define them as those that—due to their operation—generate or may generate emissions of pollutants into the atmosphere, such as cars or airplanes.[20] These mobile sources shall not exceed the maximum permissible emission levels established in the catalog of the appropriate NOMs. Newly built cars that are located at the auto plant are considered to be part of the stationary source, and thus are subject to federal jurisdiction.

B. Climate Change

Mexico, as a proactive participant in the international arena, has been very engaged in the climate change negotiations since they began. As party to the UNFCCC and the Kyoto Protocol, it was obliged to regulate domestically on the matter. Therefore, in 2010 a Climate Change Bill was presented to the Mexican Senate, and after several consultations with relevant stakeholders, the General Law on Climate Change (Climate Change Law) was approved and enacted on the 6th of June, 2012.[21]

The main objective of the Climate Change Law is to create a legal framework on climate change by distributing the legal authority to create public policies for adaptation and mitigation on climate change upon the three levels of government. Moreover, the law seeks to (1) regulate the greenhouse gas (GHG) emissions in the Mexican territory; (2) regulate a mitigation and adaptation actions framework; (3) reduce the population-level and ecosystem vulnerability to the effects of climate change; and (4) promote the transition toward a competitive, sustainable, and low-carbon economy.[22]

Additionally, the Climate Change Law established the National Climate Change System in order to create mechanisms that will foster internal communication, collaboration, and coordination of the various entities involved in the climate change issue.[23] A climate change fund was created, with the intention of capturing and channeling financial resources, both public and private, national and international, along with a national emissions registry. The latter will provide Mexico with adequate tools to participate more in the reducing emissions from deforestation and forest degradation mechanism (REDD+). Finally, some aspirational goals in reducing GHG emissions were included within the transitional articles of the statute.[24] Mexico has the main goal of reducing GHG emissions by 30 percent by the year 2020 and by 50 percent by 2050. In civil protection matters, one goal is to establish a program that will be integrated and published with the national risk atlas, the state atlases, and local atlases of those human settlements in Mexico that are most vulnerable to the effects of climate change.

III. Water

At the domestic level, the Mexican Constitution states that the national territory includes the islands, reefs, keys and adjacent seas, the continental shelf, and the waters of the territorial seas as established by international law. In principle, the Mexican Constitution does not allow the sale of national waters, as they belong to the nation.[25] Therefore, the national authority on water issues, the National Water Commission (CNA), is only entitled to issue "concession titles" to individuals to use and exploit those waters.

The applicable laws regarding the prevention and control of water pollution are the LGEEPA and the National Water Law. The LGEEPA, which does not contain a special chapter on water, has some provisions on the sustainable use of continental waters and marine ecosystems, with corresponding provisions on the prevention of pollution.[26] The National Water Law was published in 1992; however, in 1994 the regulations of this law were created with provisions that supplanted the ones included in the law, thereby creating confusion that remains today. In 2004, the National Water Law was modified, but the regulations were not modified accordingly, leaving the legal confusion in place.

The Mexican water authority, CNA, as mentioned before, is entitled to issue "concession titles." However, as paradoxical as it may seem, the CNA does not have sufficient authority to monitor the pollutants discharged into water bodies, even though the concession-holder must report what it has been discharging at the time that fees for water exploitation are paid. Therefore, the CNA remains more of a revenue-raising tax entity, acting on behalf of the community, instead of an authentic water authority. A reform on this matter is urgently needed to promote the effective use of the water concession titles.

Recently, the water authority issued a new regulation to establish a guarantee fee for the nonforfeiture of national water rights,[27] with the intention to prevent individuals from hoarding unused volumes of water. Finally, it is important to distinguish between federal waters and those that are the responsibility of the states or municipalities, which are chiefly conveyed in pipes.

The issue of international waters has been a controversial issue in Mexico, as it is in many countries. However, a recent international agreement has been signed between the Mexican government and the United States, known as Minute 319 to the 1944 Treaty for the Utilization of the Waters of the Colorado and Tijuana Rivers and the Rio Grande. There, Mexico agreed to "siphon less water from the river during dry periods but will be permitted to store water in Lake Mead to use when there is a surplus of water in the system."[28] It is anticipated that this agreement can serve as a model for other countries confronted with similar circumstances.

IV. Handling, Treatment, Transportation, and Disposal of Hazardous Materials
A. Waste Management, Generally

The regulation of hazardous materials and wastes is governed by the LGEEPA, the General Law for the Prevention and Management of Waste (LGPGIR) and its regulations,[29] and the NOMs issued by SEMARNAT, as well as prior opinions of the Ministries of the Interior (Secretaría de Gobernación), Economy, Health, Energy, Transportation and Communications, and Marine Affairs.

LGPGIR defines waste as a material or product, discarded by the owner or holder, that may be susceptible to being valued as something useful (e.g., recycled or used as raw material in another context) or required to be subject to treatment or disposal.[30] LGPGIR distinguishes three types of waste: (1) hazardous waste (subject to federal jurisdiction), (2) special treatment waste (subject to state jurisdiction), and (3) urban solid waste (subject to municipal jurisdiction).[31] Additionally, the LGPGIR specifies the obligations that must be met by those generating the waste, such as the obligation to have a management plan. This instrument is used to minimize the generation and maximize the recovery of the three types of waste. The positive aspect of this new instrument is that it puts into practice the valuation principle, where an item does not formally become waste until its owner determines that it cannot be put to use and have value in another context.

In the case of hazardous waste, a criterion to classify waste as hazardous has been included since 1998 in the LGEEPA. This criterion is known as the CRETI criterion, after the acronym in Spanish for corrosivity, reactivity, explosivity, toxicity, and flammability. If a waste possesses one of these characteristics, or contains dangerous infectious agents, it is classified as hazardous waste.[32]

B. Highly Risky Activities

There are, unfortunately, few provisions that regulate highly risky activities within LGEEPA.[33] Nonetheless, it can be inferred from LGEEPA's provisions that risky activities are those that can have severe effects on ecosystems or the environment, for example, the management of hazardous substances such as nitric oxide in its gaseous state, phosphorus zinc in its solid state, and ethylene oxide in its liquid state.

In 1990 and 1992, the Interior Ministry published, in conjunction with the Ministry of Urban Development and Ecology (which ceased to exist in 1992) a list that helps to determine whether an activity should be considered risky.[34] Currently, the Federal Regulatory Commission (COFEMER) has prepared a draft of the regulations in this matter; however, there are economic interests that could be influencing its approval.[35]

V. Waste and Site Remediation

Contaminated sites are regulated under the LGPGIR and its regulations. Site remediation is defined as the set of measures that contaminated sites must undergo to eliminate or reduce pollutants to a level safe for human health and the environment, or to prevent dispersal into the environment without modification.[36]

In 2005, the government published a nonbinding national program with guidelines to describe the risk analysis for site remediation, and through which the federal government seeks to specify the technologies and methods for developing remediation plans, and where necessary make appropriate proposals.[37] Additionally, there are two NOMs related to site remediation: NOM-138-SEMARNAT/SS-2003 and NOM-147-SEMARNAT/ SSA1-2004, which determine the maximum permissible levels of hydrocarbons and certain metals and metalloids, respectively.[38] These current regulations, however, are insufficient to allow objectivity and accuracy in remediation programs.

Regarding bioremediation, in the past there were many projects that were developed with this method, and it is still possible to propose this method as the methodology to be developed in a remediation plan. Today, however, there are no legal provisions establishing a mandatory requirement to use it.

VI.   Emergency Response

For information about Mexican law concerning emergency response for oil or chemical spills, see section V, *supra*, and NOM-138-SEMARNAT/SS-2003.

VII.   Natural Resource Management and Protection

Mexico is a country with an extraordinary diversity of ecosystems and the Mexican environmental legal framework includes provisions on each type of natural resources. Accordingly, we briefly address the legal framework for biodiversity, natural protected areas (ANPs), and forestry.

Mexico is one of the 12 countries in the world that, together, account for approximately 65 percent of the planet's biological diversity.[39] The legal framework regarding biodiversity consists of the LGEEPA, the Wildlife Law, its regulations, and appropriate NOMs. LGEEPA includes provisions on policy criteria regarding the protection of wildlife.[40] The Wildlife Law allocates jurisdiction between the three levels of government regarding the conservation and sustainable use of wildlife and their habitat.[41] The Wildlife Law's regulations, inter alia, regulate Management Units for Wildlife Conservation.[42] An example, in which the natural resources damage liability is regulated, is Article 60 *ter*, in which mangroves are protected from any removal, transplanting, and pruning, or any work or activity affecting the integrity of the hydrological flow of the mangrove ecosystem and its zone of influence of natural productivity.[43]

One response to the disappearance and degradation of ecosystems has been the creation of ANPs, which are areas of land or water that have not been significantly altered by human activity, that protect flora and fauna, and that are natural resources of special importance for representative ecosystems.[44] Undoubtedly, ANPs are one of the most significant elements in Mexican environmental policy. Currently, the CONANP manages 176 federal ANPs representing more than 25,387,972 hectares of the Mexican territory.[45]

However, there are some failures in the ANP framework. These weaknesses correspond to the lack of particular regulations to provide legal certainty regarding certain matters, such as identifying the status of each ANP, identifying its core area, its buffer zone, and its possible development. Although LGEEPA has some provision on ANPs, and its own regulations on the matter, these have not proven sufficient to fulfill the purpose of ANPs.[46]

Forestry is regulated under the LGEEPA, the General Law on Sustainable Forestry Development,[47] the Biosafety Law on Genetically Modified Organisms,[48] and these statutes' respective regulations.

To be sure, forestry is a controversial issue in Mexico. In recent years, CONAFOR and PROFEPA have worked very hard to create a clear, unified, and effective framework on the use and exploitation of forest lands. However, problems remain.[49]

The issues of deforestation and reforestation are important tools for forestry conservation in Mexico. Although Mexico is still in the process of developing carbon markets, there are some projects underway seeking to take advantage of the REDD+ mechanism agreed to as part of the Bali Action Plan to the UNFCCC. These projects are intended to represent an important mitigation response to climate change.

VIII. Natural Resource Damages

For information about Mexican law concerning compensation for natural resource damages, see section XI, *infra*, and section VI, *supra*.

IX. Protected Species

Mexico occupies the fourth or fifth place worldwide in terms of biological and ecological diversity. A significant part of the world's biodiversity— 10 percent—is found exclusively in Mexico.[50] The legal framework for the protection of species is found in LGEEPA, the General Wildlife Law, and implementing regulations for both statutes. The loss of species is an irreversible fact that needs to be regulated and protected. Article 56 of the General Wildlife Law requires the Ministry of Environment and Natural Resources to identify through lists those species or populations at risk in accordance with the provisions of the relevant NOM, NOM-059-SEMAR-NAT-2010, published March 6, 2002. This NOM deals primarily with the listing of species that are in danger. There are 89 protected species by law, and there are different categories in which the species are categorized. The categories are the following:

1. *Probably extinct in the wild (E):* those native species that have disappeared, as far as documentation and studies show, but that are known to exist in confinement or outside of Mexican territory.
2. *Endangered (P):* those species whose area of distribution or size of population in the national territory have decreased dramatically, threatening their biological viability throughout their natural habitat due to factors such as the destruction or drastic modification of their habitat, unsustainable harvesting, disease, or predation, among others.
3. *Threatened (A):* those species who may become in danger of disappearing in the short or medium term, if there are factors operating to adversely affect their viability, to cause the deterioration or modification of habitat, or directly decrease the size of their populations.

4. *Subject to special protection (Pr):* those species that could potentially be threatened by factors that adversely affect their viability, as determined by the need to facilitate their recovery and preservation or restoration and conservation of stocks of associated species.

The General Directorate of Inspection and Monitoring of Wildlife and Marine and Coastal Ecosystems of PROFEPA ensures compliance with environmental legislation applicable to the preservation and protection of turtles, marine mammals, and aquatic species at risk, and marine protected areas, among others.

The government agencies responsible for these species are the PROFEPA, the Department of the Navy, SEMARNAT, the CONANP, the National Commission of Aquaculture and Fisheries (CONAPESCA), and state governments.

X.   Environmental Review and Decision Making

Environmental impact assessment (EIA) is one of the oldest policy instruments in Mexico's environmental regime. The EIA is an administrative procedure by which any covered construction or other type of project is subject to review by the Environmental Impact and Risk General Office (DGIRA).[51] Project proponents receive through DGIRA an authorization or denial to proceed with the activity, or a list of conditions that must be followed.[52] Whether a given activity or construction project is subject to federal or state jurisdiction is determined by the nature of the project at issue.[53]

XI.   Transboundary Pollution

Transboundary pollution is an increasingly important issue. Pollution originating in other countries can cause damage in a neighboring country's environment through water, air, or ground pollution. Because of these issues, Mexico has made a series of agreements, programs, and regulations for preserving, protecting, and improving its environment, and to control the environmental damage that pollution occurring in Mexico can cause to its territorial neighbors.

In Mexico, this issue began to be regulated in 1988 in LGEEPA's regulation in matters of prevention and control of atmosphere pollution at Article 3, where the prevention and control of atmospheric pollution is established as a federal concern. This is especially true with respect to pollution originating in other countries affecting the environmental equilibrium within the national territory, and also pollution originating in Mexico affecting other countries.[54]

Since 1969, Mexico has signed different bilateral and multilateral international treaties in relation to the prevention and treatment of transboundary pollution. The first, signed in 1969, was the International Convention Relating to Intervention on the High Seas in Cases of Oil Pollution Casualties. In 1972, Mexico signed the Convention on the Prevention of Marine Pollution by Dumping of Wastes and Other Matter, followed by the 1973 International Convention for the Prevention of Pollution from Ships. In the 1980s Mexico became a party to various bilateral agreements with the United States. The first was the Agreement of Cooperation between the United States of America and the Mexican States regarding Pollution of the Marine Environment by Discharges of Hydrocarbons and Other Hazardous Substances. Similarly, in 1983, Mexico signed the Agreement on Cooperation for the Protection and Improvement of the Environment in the Border Area. This agreement was signed in La Paz, Baja California Sur, and is known as the La Paz Agreement. The La Paz Agreement established the general normative framework through which Mexico and the United States agreed to prevent, reduce, and eliminate water, air, and land pollution sources. The La Paz Agreement has been implemented through a series of environmental programs, the latest of which is Border 2020. This program has five main goals: to reduce air pollution; to improve access to clean and safe water; to promote materials management, waste management, and clean sites; to enhance joint preparedness for environmental response; and to implement compliance assurance and environmental stewardship.

Two additional relevant agreements are (1) the 1989 Agreement on Cooperation for the Protection and Improvement of the Environment in the Metropolitan Area of Mexico City and (2) the 1993 North American Agreement on Environmental Cooperation.

XII. Civil and Criminal Enforcement and Penalties
A. Civil Enforcement

On April 25, 2013, the Federal Law of Environmental Liability (LFRA) was approved in Mexico. This law establishes the liability that results from damage to the environment, as well as its repair and compensation. Article 2, subsection III, defines environmental damage as: "Loss, change, deterioration, or impaired or measurable adverse modification of habitat, ecosystems, natural resources and elements, their chemical, physical or biological conditions, the relationships of interaction that exist between them and the environmental services they provide." This definition is subject to the provisions of Article 6 of the LFRA.[55] Any natural or legal person whose act or omission causes direct or indirect damage to the environment will be responsible, and will be obliged to remedy all the damages caused.[56] Repairing this damage means that the environment will have to be restored to its baseline condition.[57] The LFRA establishes an environmental liability fund for the payment of the damages established in Article 2, and establishes that the financial penalty is secondary to the remedying or compensation for the damage caused to the environment. The payment consists of payment in an amount equal to 300 to 50,000 days of the general minimum wage (Mex$19,428 to Mex$3,238,000) when the offender is a natural person, and 1,000 to 600,000 days of the general minimum wage (Mex$64,760 to Mex$38,856,000) when the offender is a legal entity, with the amount determined based on the damage caused.[58] Any person who has knowledge of any crime against the environment is required to denounce such crime directly to the public ministry.[59]

B.   Criminal Enforcement

In general, Mexican environmental crimes are located in the criminal code from articles 414 to 423. The first chapter deals with those criminal acts relating to dangerous activities, from articles 414 to 416. The second chapter establishes criminal norms concerning biodiversity at articles 417 to 420 *bis*. The third chapter concerns biosecurity-related crimes, from articles 420 *ter* to 423.

Penalties for environmental crimes include monetary fines and/or prison time. Prison sentences typically range from six months to ten years.

Notes

1. The third-party verification system is the system in which compliance with the Mexican Official Standards (NOM) (technical regulations) and Mexican Standards (NMX) (voluntary standards and guidelines) is evaluated by a third party (individuals or corporations). This verification includes the characteristics and specifications for products, processes, and services that must be evaluated when they may constitute a danger to human safety, human, animal, plant health, or the environment in general. The main difference between these two standards is that the NOMs are obligatory and are published in the Federal Official Diary (*Diario Oficial de la Federación,* DOF). The DOF is the instrument that is used for the publication of laws, standards, and regulations. In contrast, the NMX do not have the force of law by themselves. The basis for this standardization system is the Federal Law of Metrology and Normalization, http://www.diputados.gob.mx/Leyes Biblio/pdf/130.pdf.

2. Constitución Política de los Estados Unidos Mexicanos art. 133.

3. *Id.* art. 4.

4. *Id.* art. 4, § 5 ("Everyone has the right to a healthy environment for their development and welfare. The Federal government shall ensure that this right is respected. Environmental deterioration and damage shall result in legal liability for those who cause it, as set forth by law"); § 6 ("Everyone has the right to access water and sanitation for personal and household consumption that is sufficient, safe, acceptable and affordable. The Federal government shall guarantee this right and the law will define the bases and arrangements for access to and equitable and sustainable use of water resources, and establish the participation of the Federation, the states and municipalities, and the participation of citizens to achieving these ends."

5. The texts of these statutes and associated regulations are available on the official website of the Ministry of Environment and Natural Resources (SEMARNAT), http://www.semarnat.gob.mx/leyes-y-normas/leyes-federales.

6. Raúl Brañes, Manual de Derecho Ambiental Mexicano 117 (2d ed. 2000).

7. State laws can be found at SEMARNAT's website, http://www.semarnat.gob.mx/leyes-y-normas/leyes-estatales.

8. General Law of Ecological Balance and Environmental Protection Regulations on Prevention and Control of Pollution of the Atmosphere, Transitional Third Article. Executive Agreement that determines the list of substances subject to Federal jurisdiction report to the Registry of Emissions and Pollutant Transfer, published in the Federal Official Gazette on the 31 of March, 2005.

9. Organic Law of the Federal Public Administration, published in the Federal Official Gazette on the 29 of December of 1976, art. 32*bis.*

10. General Law on Climate Change art. 13.

11. Law of Ecological Balance and Environmental Protection (LGEEPA), published in the Federal Official Gazette on the 28 of January, 1988, art. 38.

12. Brañes, *supra* note 6, at 240.

13. LGEEPA art. 38 *bis*.

14. General Rules of Law of Ecological Balance and Environmental Protection for Self-Regulation and Environmental Audits, published in the Federal Official Gazette on the 29 of April, 2010, arts. 38–39 *bis*.

15. This system is a cyclical process of planning, implementation, revision, and improvement in the actions and processes that organizations execute in their activities and guaranteeing the accomplishment of their environmental objectives. http://www .revistafuturos.info/futuros_3/gestion_amb.htm.

16. The ISO 14000 family of standards addresses various aspects of environmental management. It provides practical tools for companies and organizations looking to identify and control their environmental impact and constantly improve their environmental performance. *See* ISO official website, http://www.iso.org/iso/iso14000.

17. LGEEPA arts. 189–204.

18. LGEEPA arts. 110 to 116, art. 11 *bis*. "For the purposes referred to in this Law, facilities engaged in the following types of industries are considered point sources under federal jurisdiction: the chemical, oil and petrochemical, paints and inks, automotive, pulp and paper, metals, glass, electric power generation, asbestos, cement and lime kiln and hazardous waste treatment."

19. General Law of Ecological Balance and Environmental Protection Regulations on Prevention and Control of Pollution of the Atmosphere art. 17.

20. *Id.* art. 6.

21. General Law on Climate Change Decree, 19 April 2012. Mexican Senate Chamber.

22. General Law on Climate Change art. 2.

23. *Id.* arts. 38–44.

24. For example, Mexico's goal for emissions reductions is 30 percent from the baseline by 2020 and 50 percent by 2050. *See* General Law on Climate Change, Second Transitional Article.

25. Political Constitution of the United Mexican States art. 42, §§ II–V.

26. LGEEPA arts. 117–133.

27. Regulation for the determination of the guarantee fee of nonforfeiture of National Waters Rights, 2009.

28. April Reese, *U.S., Mexico Officials Sign "Historic" Colorado River Pact*, Greenwire, Nov. 21, 2012, http://eenews.net/Greenwire/2012/11/21/archive/7?terms=mexico+color ado+pact.

29. General Law for the Prevention and Management of Waste (LGPGIR), published in the Federal Official Gazette on the 8 of October of 2003, and its Regulations published on the 30 of November of 2006.

30. LGPGIR art. 5, § XXIX.

31. LGPGIR art. 5.

32. LGEEPA art. 5, § XXXII.

33. LGEEPA art. 5, § V; art. 7, § IV; art. 145.

34. It is a highly risky activity to handle any of the substances contained in the First List of High-Risk Activities, published March 28, 1990, or in the Second High-Risk Activities List, published May 7, 1992, in amounts equal to or greater than those which are defined in the listings. See SEMARNAT, http://www.semarnat.gob.mx/temas/gestion ambiental/materiales-y-actividades-riesgosas/actividades-altamente-riesgosas.

35. Noise and light pollution are regulated in Mexico. In 1982, the regulation for environmental protection against pollution caused by the emission of noise was published, in consistence with Article 1 of the LGEEPA, related to noise from artificial sources. The regulation defines "noise" as any undesirable sound that upsets or harms people.

Regulations for the environment protection against pollution caused by the emission of noise, published in the Federal Official Gazette on the 6 of December, 1982. *See* LGEEPA art. 5. This regulation has not been updated since. However, the NOM-081-SEMARNAT -1994 was created to establish the maximum permissible noise emission from stationary sources (which is 68 decibels during the day and 65 decibels at night) and the prescribed measurement method. Mexico lacks a regulation on the control and prevention of light pollution. Several bills on the matter have been presented to local governments, but never adopted.

36. LGPGIR art. 5, § XXVIII.

37. National Programme on polluted sites remediation, published by SEMARNAT, 2005.

38. NOM-138-SEMARNAT/SS-2003 establishes maximum permissible levels of hydrocarbons in soil and specifications for their characterization and remediation; NOM -147-SEMARNAT/SSA1-2004 establishes criteria for determining the concentrations of contaminated soil remediation for arsenic, barium, beryllium, cadmium, hexavalent chromium, mercury, nickel, silver, lead, selenium, thallium, and vanadium.

39. BRAÑES, *supra* note 6, at 302.

40. LGEEPA art. 79–87*bis*.

41. Wildlife Law, published in the Federal Official Gazette on 3 of July of 2000, art. 1.

42. Wildlife Law's Regulations, published in the Federal Official Gazette on the 30 of November of 2006.

43. Wildlife Law art. 60*ter*, http://www.diputados.gob.mx/LeyesBiblio/ref/lgvs /LGVS_ref04_01feb07.pdf.

44. LGEEPA art. 3, § II.

45. Comm'n of Natural Protected Areas, http://www.conanp.gob.mx.

46. Regulations on Natural Protected Areas, published in the Federal Official Gazette on the 28 of December of 2004.

47. General Law on Sustainable Forestry Development, published in the Federal Official Gazette on the 16 of November 2011.

48. Biosafety Law on Genetically Modified Organisms, published in the Federal Official Gazette on the 18 of March of 2005.

49. General Law on Sustainable Forestry Development Regulations, published in the Federal Official Gazette on the 21 of February of 2005.

50. Nat'l Comm'n for the Knowledge and Use of Biodiversity (CONABIO), Two Decades of History: 1992–2012, http://www.conabio.gob.mx/web/pdf/Two_Decades _synthesis_web.pdf.

51. Dirección General de Impacto y Riesgo Ambiental (DGIRA).

52. General Law of Ecological Balance and Environmental Protection Regulations on Self-Regulation and Environmental Audits, published in the Federal Official Gazette on the 29 of April of 2010.

53. See LGEEPA art. 28 & LGEEPA Regulation art. 5.

54. LGEEPA Regulation art. 3, §§ IV–V.

55. Federal Law of Environmental Liability (LFRA) art. 2, § III.

56. LFRA art. 10.

57. LFRA art. 13.

58. LFRA art. 19.

59. LFRA art. 54.

CHAPTER 20

Central and South America Overview: Emerging Trends in Latin America

MADELEINE B. KADAS AND RUSSELL FRAKER

I. Introduction

As a result of rapid industrialization, enormous population growth, increased economic power, and compelling environmental and natural resources challenges, environmental law in Latin America has never been more dynamic or perhaps important. Although framework laws have existed in many countries for decades, most have mandated aspirational standards marked by sparse enforcement, leaving adrift their potential for meaningful impact. The past decade has been one of extensive regulatory evolution and implementation, a trend not likely to reverse. Several jurisdictions, especially among the more developed economies, now boast mature environmental regimes supplemented by complex technical standards, robust licensing and enforcement mechanisms, and new or expanded private remedies for the redress of environmental harms. The region's legislative activity and standardization in the fields of climate change and product stewardship rivals that of Europe and surpasses the United States. This chapter provides an overview of the landscape of environmental law in Latin America, with brief accounts of its legal and institutional structure and selected substantive areas of interest in the region.

II. Constitutional Underpinnings of Environmental Laws

Latin American countries are civil law systems, and provisions governing the environment are set forth in national constitutions.[1] The range of constitutional rights and protections is diverse in scope and substance, with some constitutions guaranteeing a right to a healthy environment and others simply establishing state jurisdiction over natural resources.[2] The overall trend is increased environmental protections and guarantees. Bolivia is a global leader, recently adopting Mother Earth (*Pachamama*) protections into its constitution and environmental laws.[3]

The constitutional underpinnings of environmental legal systems in Latin America have practical implications. First, several constitutions establish shared jurisdiction over natural resources between national and local (state, municipal, or regional) bodies. In many cases, subnational jurisdictions can impose more stringent requirements than those of the national government, leading to separate and significant layers of environmental law, licensing, and potential enforcement.[4] Second, the constitutional foundations of environmental laws usually provide for redress of environmental harms and protection of the environment as constitutional claims (e.g., *amparo*);[5] the use of these claims is increasing.[6] Third, as a matter of constitutional law, patrimony over natural resources is often reserved to the nation and private rights to use natural resources are accorded through concessions systems.[7] Negotiation of private resource concessions, in particular for water use,[8] will likely become significant to future regional development.

III.   Laws, Regulations, and Technical Standards

Constitutional environmental provisions are implemented through a variety of legal instruments. Although the hierarchy of laws and their nomenclature varies from country to country, a typical environmental legal structure will include a governing law (adopted by a legislative body); implementing regulations (adopted by a government agency, sometimes in multiple layers, issued at different organizational levels within agencies); and technical standards (adopted by agencies, but in many countries developed and issued by a separate, non-governmental technical standards organization). For example, Mexico[9] has in place a comprehensive waste law governing solid urban, special management, and hazardous waste;[10] an implementing regulation to that law;[11] and a set of technical standards that provide significant definitional contours including, among many others, hazardous waste listings and definitions of hazardous waste characteristics;[12] hazardous waste landfill siting requirements;[13] and hydrocarbon remediation standards.[14]

In many jurisdictions, there are also framework environmental laws that cover a wide range of environmental media, jurisdictional, licensing, and enforcement provisions.[15] Many of these framework laws were the first environmental or natural resources legislation adopted in these countries, or their successors.[16] While the general regional trend is toward media-specific laws, these framework laws continue to remain important to the regulatory landscape and are often cited as authority for subsequent laws, regulations, and agency actions.

It bears emphasis that states and municipalities, especially in heavily industrialized areas, are typically active in exercising jurisdiction over environmental matters. In many places, local environmental laws either augment or implement provisions of national laws. For example, Brazil has a national waste law, the National Solid Waste Policy Act, adopted in 2010;[17] however, the State of São Paulo has long regulated the field and developed one of the most advanced site remediation regimes in the region.[18] Other particularly active states and municipalities include the Federal District of Mexico; Buenos Aires Province and the Autonomous City of Buenos Aires, Argentina; City of Santiago, Chile; City of Bogotá, Colombia; and in Brazil, the States of São Paulo, Paraná, Rio Grande do Sul, and Rio de Janeiro, and the City of São Paulo.

Public participation in the development of environmental legal standards is increasing in Latin America. Bills in many national legislatures can be monitored electronically.[19] Administrative procedure and government transparency laws usually require that agency draft regulations be published in official registers for public comments prior to finalization. Many legislators and regulators in most Latin American countries are receptive to input from environmentalists and the regulated community alike; technical standards are often developed by working groups that involve the private and public sectors.

The role and sophistication of environmental technical standards has increased as legal regimes mature. The development of technical standards can be less transparent than for laws and regulations, though they typically provide concrete operating rules and regulatory thresholds. For example, the Brazilian Technical Standards Association, a private, nonprofit institution, develops numerous environmental rules, including hazardous waste standards, of general reference in Brazil.[20] In Peru a discrete governmental organization is charged with developing technical standards.[21] Some of these standards are issued as binding law,[22] while others are voluntary,[23] and still others have an intermediate status as nonbinding but "normative"[24] or, more commonly, are made binding by law or practice. Such formally nonbinding technical standards may become binding in the following ways: (1) by setting industry standards of care; (2) by being incorporated by reference into binding regulations; (3) by filling a regulatory gap (i.e., incorporated by inference); or (4) by being referenced in environmental licenses. While it is common in the region for technical standards to be adopted directly from international technical bodies such as the International Standards Organization and ASTM International,[25] many national standardization institutions also create their own unique technical standards. More often than not, international harmonization is the exception rather than the rule.

IV.   Agencies with Environmental Jurisdiction

National environmental agencies in Latin America have increasing prominence and sophistication. Historically, authority over environmental matters was often housed in the departments of other agencies, such as health or social development agencies.[26] Agency structure has changed significantly in the last decade, and the trend is for environmental agencies to be established as stand-alone institutions with broad jurisdiction to oversee policy development, standard-setting, permitting, and enforcement of most environmental

laws. Several countries now have in place national cabinet-level environmental administrative bodies, for example, Argentina,[27] Brazil,[28] Chile,[29] and
Mexico.[30] Enforcement is sometimes conducted through separate prosecutorial bodies or attorneys general.[31] Some key states and municipalities have
highly sophisticated and progressive environmental agencies, some of such
import that they drive the policies of their national agencies.[32]

Even with the advent of dedicated environmental agencies, total or partial jurisdiction over certain environmental subject matter may belong to
other agencies. For example, health agencies may have jurisdiction over the
regulation of chemical substances and wastes;[33] agriculture agencies over
registration and control of pesticides and fertilizers;[34] and transportation
agencies over transportation of hazardous products and substances.[35] Overlapping jurisdiction tends to complicate regulation and oversight of subject
matter and can prolong permit approval processes.

V.   Agency Licensing and Enforcement

Environmental regulatory programs in Latin America are license-intensive.
In most cases, industrial operations must obtain concessions for the use of
natural resources and licenses to construct and operate a facility that will
emit or discharge pollutants.[36] Concessions and licenses frequently must be
listed in publicly available registries.[37] General requirements for concessions
and licenses are typically set forth in media-specific regulations and application forms, some of them quite extensive.[38] It is not unusual for the licensing
process to be time-consuming or for permitting authorities to request extra-
regulatory information or impose unique operating requirements. In some
instances, legislatures and agencies have undertaken efforts to streamline
licensing procedures,[39] although the process remains challenging for many
applicants despite such efforts.

Enforcement penalties for violations vary widely, with the following
being typically within the scope of an agency's authority: fines tied to the
severity of the environmental harm; publication of the violation; restitution
for environmental damage; permit revocation, suspension, or denial; partial
or total shutdown of facilities; seizure of goods and property; administrative
arrest; and incarceration.[40] Overall, the scope and scale of penalty provisions
are increasing. In 1998, Brazil enacted a landmark environmental crimes law
with schedules of offenses and sanctions, including fines of up to 50 million
reais and prison terms up to five years.[41] A 2008 implementing regulation
provides guidelines for the application of sanctions and procedural protections for alleged violators.[42] In contrast, Colombia's environmental criminal
law establishes a presumption of guilt for acts alleged to cause environmental harm, making it one of the most procedurally stringent in the world.[43]

Enforcement of environmental laws in Latin America is trending upward.
Pressed by local citizen groups and non-governmental organizations (NGOs)
to deal with environmental challenges, agencies have begun to employ a
range of once-dormant enforcement provisions.[44] Enforcement staff numbers
and budgets have generally increased at environmental agencies, in some

cases dramatically.[45] Although not always perceived as consistent, enforcement efforts are often high profile, widely reported in the press, and intended to set examples through high penalty assessments and criminal convictions.[46]

VI. The Role of Administrative and Judicial Tribunals

Historically, the role of the judiciary, whether administrative, civil, or criminal, in Latin American environmental matters has been limited.[47] This may be attributable to several factors, including deficiencies in standing and procedural rights; objective environmental standards; judicial capacity; and efficient and ethical processing of claims.[48] Administrative complaint systems were limited and private actions could only be brought under general civil code provisions, which typically required demonstration of a specific, individual, personal injury for standing.[49] The damages potentially allowed for individual cases were low, often tied to minimum wage compensation,[50] and most Latin American legal systems lacked a mechanism for aggregate litigation (e.g., class actions),[51] providing little incentive for private lawyers to invest in individual cases. Together, these factors served as significant impediments to private actions for environmental harms.

That landscape has evolved significantly in recent decades, and the pace of change has been accelerating. Many environmental laws provide for citizen complaint mechanisms to governments.[52] While these provisions do not typically allow damages to be paid to private parties, they may trigger scrutiny and can lead to enforcement action.[53] Citizen groups have also begun to make aggressive use of other legal mechanisms to bring environmental claims, such as *amparo* actions that provide a cause of action to redress constitutional harms.[54] Moreover, in a development that may create a sea change in Latin American environmental jurisprudence, some form of class action or "collective action" is now recognized in several jurisdictions.[55] Accordingly, many of the long-standing barriers to private enforcement of environmental harm are being removed.

The region has begun to embrace the international trend of dedicated environmental tribunals, which can be expected to enhance the role of the judiciary and administrative tribunals in environmental matters.[56] For example, Costa Rica has an active environmental administrative tribunal[57] and Chile recently enacted a national environmental court.[58] Regional tribunals to address cross-border and multijurisdictional issues, environmental issues, and provide alternate means for pursuing environmental claims, such as the Latin American Water Tribunal, may also see expanded dockets and jurisdictions over time.[59]

VII. Influences of International Environmental Law and Free Trade Agreements

International environmental law plays a significant role in the development of the domestic laws of many Latin American countries.[60] Most Latin American countries are parties to most major multilateral environmental agreements, including the Basel Convention on the Control of Transboundary Movements of Hazardous Wastes and Their Disposal,[61] the United Nations Framework Convention on Climate Change,[62] the Convention on International Trade in Endangered Species of Wild Fauna and Flora,[63] the Montreal Protocol on Substances That Deplete the Ozone Layer,[64] and the Rio Declaration on Environment and Development.[65]

International environmental law often shapes domestic environmental policies or becomes the basis for domestic environmental standards. For example, Mexico and Brazil have adopted climate change laws that provide for greenhouse gas emissions reduction targets and are likely drivers of energy efficiency programs.[66] The hazardous waste standards in many countries are heavily influenced by, and in some cases adopted directly from, the Basel Convention waste classification system.[67] Although comprehensive regulation of chemicals in the region is scant, most countries have implemented the Montreal Protocol[68] and the Stockholm[69] and Rotterdam[70] conventions.

The influence of free trade agreements on domestic environmental laws in Latin America is pronounced. A number of free trade agreements, particularly those executed with the United States, demand some level of harmonization of legal provisions or minimum environmental standards among the trade partners.[71] They have also required that the domestic laws of signatory countries have in place transparency protections, citizen complaint mechanisms, or other procedural protections for environmental harms, or, in the case of the North American Free Trade Agreement (NAFTA), created an international citizen complaint mechanism.[72] Regional free trade agreements also play an increasingly important role in setting environmental policies,[73] typically through establishing model regulations and technical standards that must be adopted directly by all member countries.[74]

VIII.   Influence of Non-Governmental Organizations and Development Organizations

The role and influence of NGOs in the development of regional environmental law and policy has increased significantly in the past decade. Together with the rise of the Internet and influence of social media, international NGOs have established high-profile environmental campaigns and have become significant players in local environmental policy debates.[75] Local NGOs also have been successful in advancing domestic environmental agendas and bringing first-impression environmental lawsuits.[76]

To a limited extent, development assistance from the European Union has played a role in shaping environmental law in Latin America, particularly with respect to product stewardship laws governing electric and electronics equipment.[77] Although the laws of the United States also inform environmental laws in Latin America, many countries in the region have a history of looking to the European Union for regulatory models, a practice that is facilitated by cultural and linguistic affinities[78] and by the interagency relationships built through direct outreach from European countries. As the region readies for what it hopes will be large-scale investment in carbon sequestration and other greenhouse gas emissions-reducing projects through the Kyoto Protocol's Clean Development Mechanism, the influence of foreign development agencies can be expected to continue.

IX. Key Areas of Regulation
A. Environmental Impact Assessments

In contrast to the United States, environmental impact assessments (EIAs) are widely used in Latin America as the basis for environmental permitting.[79] EIAs are typically required for a wide range of projects, including water infrastructure and treatment projects; highway and railway construction; cable and satellite installation; pipelines; oil and gas extraction and refining; chemical manufacturing; electrical plant construction; mining; cement manufacturing; paper milling; sugar processing; hazardous waste and radioactive treatment and disposal; industrial activities in forested, wetland, and coastal zones; and development of industrial parks, airports, and tourism facilities.[80]

The standards for EIAs in most Latin American countries differ from those in the United States, where the process is designed to ensure that government agencies consider the effects of their own actions and allows for an abbreviated process if no significant impact is identified. Instead, Latin American EIA requirements typically entail a comprehensive report on all of the environmental aspects of the proposed project.[81] As such, the technical requirements for Latin American EIAs can be extensive and often include both analysis of potentially applicable regulations during construction and operations and planning for the long-term future of the affected area beyond the life of the project.[82] In some countries, the project proponent is required to hire only specially licensed environmental consultants to conduct the EIA,[83] and those consultants may have ongoing liability for any defects in the quality of their reports—which in turn may provide incentives for a highly conservative analysis of potential impacts. EIAs are usually subject to review and approval by multiple agencies, and in some cases the public at large and certain segments of society (e.g., indigenous tribes, environmental groups, and industries that may be affected by the project) may have a guaranteed opportunity to participate in the process.[84]

B. Water Quality and Quantity

Several Latin American constitutions have enshrined access to water (or to clean water) as a basic human right.[85] Water quality and availability have profound practical implications for public health and the daily functioning of society, which are keenly felt in Latin America due to the limited capacity of the water delivery infrastructure in much of the region. Such scarcity may be counterintuitive as, in the global context, Latin America is the region richest in fresh water. However, the overall abundance may be deceptive as much of the water is concentrated geographically and/or seasonally, little of the flow is collected for human use, and very little of the collected water is effectively treated for potability. Outside Argentina, Chile, and Uruguay, water supplies in the region are generally considered unsafe to drink unless filtered, as waterborne ailments are ubiquitous.

Latin American countries generally regulate industrial wastewater, in most cases adopting contaminant threshold tables from U.S. Environmental Protection Agency regulations or the World Health Organization.[86] Where applicable, these effluent standards are typically incorporated by reference into a facility's environmental operating permit. In the more developed countries, such as Brazil, facilities are required to treat wastewater prior to discharge and conduct routine monitoring of receiving water bodies, reporting the data to the environmental licensing agency.[87]

In addition to regulation of water quality, industrial facilities in Latin America face restrictions on water use.[88] In much of Brazil, for example, new facilities and those renewing permits must obtain concessions for a limited allocation of water,[89] then pay fees for water capture, consumption, and discharge.[90] In Brazil and several other Latin American countries, authority over water resources is now divided by hydrographic basins rather than political boundaries, and it is the basin authorities that set water allocation policies and use fees.[91]

C.   Air Quality

Across the region, air quality issues reach acute proportions in many of the major cities, particularly those situated in air-trapping basins such as Bogotá, Caracas, Mexico City, Santiago, and the greater São Paulo conurbation.[92] The municipal authorities of several cities have sought to curb their smog problems by enacting mobile source restrictions, such as rotating bans on cars based on license plate numbers and replacing diesel-fueled buses with electric vehicles.[93] Brazil has experimented with policy incentives and alternative fuel mandates to reduce the fossil fuel consumption of its automobile fleets—these efforts began on a large scale in the 1970s when the country's military dictatorship initiated a conversion to ethanol-only cars, and have continued with renewable fuel mixture requirements for gasoline and diesel, and emissions standards for vehicles.[94]

Most Latin American countries regulate stationary source emissions through concentration limits, and in some cases require control equipment and stack monitoring, all of which are imposed through environmental licensing.[95] Lists of regulated pollutants typically include sulfur dioxide, nitrogen oxides, carbon monoxide, ozone, size classes of particulate matter, and in some cases lead, mercury, and volatile organic compounds.[96] Some of the more developed countries have federal rules that set ambient air quality standards,[97] although effective implementation is constrained by the lack of enforcement programs or formal incentives to motivate local agencies to meet the standards. In some countries, including Mexico and Brazil, agencies have recently instituted air quality monitoring programs as an initial step toward implementation of standards, in some cases providing real-time air quality updates for particular locations in major urban areas.[98] In 2012, the Brazilian state of São Paulo instituted a complex set of emissions regulations that resemble the U.S. Clean Air Act's Nonattainment New Source Review program, possibly marking the beginning of a regional trend toward more robust stationary source regulation.[99]

D. Waste and Product Stewardship

Waste management throughout most of Latin America has historically been hampered by weak infrastructure: inadequate collection services and limited landfill capacity. Informal open-air landfills are common and urban sanitation is generally far below the standards of more developed countries.[100] Beginning in 2003, with Mexico's General Law for the Prevention and Integral Management of Wastes,[101] most of the major Latin American countries have enacted some form of framework waste legislation, and the succeeding years have been marked with various stages of implementing regulations. Prominent among the recurring elements of these laws are mandatory planning for municipal solid waste management; heightened standards and special rules for the management of hazardous wastes; and extended producer responsibility for end-of-life products.[102]

The emerging set of hazardous waste rules typically encompasses such issues as: generator requirements (e.g., registration, reporting, storage, and manifesting); complex waste classification standards based on listed categories and characteristics; special qualifications and administrative requirements for hazardous waste managers and transporters; and restrictions on final disposition through disposal in sealed landfills.[103] Certain countries, most notably Argentina, impose stringent restrictions on domestic movements of hazardous wastes across internal boundaries,[104] which may pose significant challenges to management of industrial wastes. All Latin American nations are Parties to the Basel Convention on the Control of Transboundary Movements of Hazardous Wastes and Their Disposal, which limits options for management solutions that entail export of covered wastes.[105] Several countries have adopted some form of the Basel Convention's waste classification, including its annexes, as the basis for their own domestic waste classification systems.[106]

Most of the recently enacted waste laws designate certain categories of products at their end of life as "special management wastes" subject to product stewardship obligations.[107] In such cases, product manufacturers and importers are required to provide end-of-life collection (a.k.a. product "take-back") and "environmentally adequate" disposition, which typically refers to the pollution prevention hierarchy, prioritizing reuse, recycling, and any other recovery over disposal. In Brazil, these obligations are denoted as "reverse logistics," implying a mirror-image of product distribution channels that expand the obligations to include retailers and distributors.[108] Products subject to these obligations in most countries include tires, batteries, pesticide and lubricant containers, electronics, and mercury-containing lamps; some jurisdictions include additional products and packaging.[109]

E.   Contaminated Sites and Liability

Along with the historical absence of comprehensive waste laws, most Latin American countries traditionally failed to address the most persistent impacts of unregulated disposal: widespread contamination of soils and groundwater with toxic substances. Recently, however, several countries have begun to tackle this issue, although the approaches vary and there is as yet no single regional model for contaminated site legislation and the imposition of legal liability to cover the significant costs of cleanup.[110] Consequently, this area of environmental law remains dynamic and a source of great uncertainty for companies that presently own industrial properties or are connected, either directly or through acquisitions, to past industrial activity in Latin America.

Although lacking legislation that specifically provides for contaminated site liability, many Latin American countries have espoused a generic "polluter pays" principle either in their constitutions or in their general environmental or waste laws.[111] In many cases, this principle alone has been sufficient to impose responsibility for the cleanup of chemical spills and other releases to soils. However, such an approach is not always practical because of the difficulty in many cases of identifying "the polluter" responsible for a particular site. Argentina has sought to address this problem, in part, by requiring those who undertake activities that risk harming the environment to hold dedicated insurance policies or other financial guarantees against potential contamination.[112] Another approach is found in Mexico's General Waste Law, which prohibits the transfer of contaminated properties without express authorization, effectively placing the burden of remediation on current owners.[113]

In an emerging trend, several countries are establishing liability regimes tailored to their residual legacies, beginning with inventories of contaminated sites.[114] Argentina and Peru have focused on certain sectors in which soil contamination is readily identifiable and problematic: in particular, abandoned mines and areas of concentrated industrial activity such as Argentina's Matanza-Riachuelo river basin.[115] The Brazilian state of São Paulo, a regional leader on several environmental issues, has enacted a law modeled on the U.S. Superfund statute, with a dedicated fund (by its Portuguese acronym, FEPRAC) to enable the state to remediate orphan or multiparty sites, then sue the responsible party(ies) for reimbursement.[116] The 2013 FEPRAC regulations require soil sampling at former industrial sites prior to issuance of environmental operating permits, as a mechanism to identify contaminated areas and subject them to mandatory remediation.[117]

F.   Natural Resources

Various subregions within Latin America are disproportionately rich in valuable natural resources, particularly mineral and biological resources, and several of its economies have historically been dominated by exploitation of these resources. Argentina, Brazil, Chile, Colombia, and Peru are global leaders in mineral production, particularly metals such as copper, iron, nickel, and tin.[118] Peru and Chile are, respectively, the second- and ninth-largest harvesters of marine fish in the world.[119] Despite significant deforestation, Brazil remains second only to Russia in total forest cover,[120] and has by far the largest share of tropical forest.[121] Looking beyond tropical forests, the wide array of natural habitats in South America makes it the most biodiverse continent: for example, while comprising only 12 percent of the world's land area, South America is home to 33 percent of known bird species.[122] Inspired by the 1992 Convention of Biological Diversity, some countries have sought to regulate access to the genetic resources within their borders, valued economically as a warehouse of uncataloged natural substances, many of which are expected to hold great potential for development as pharmaceuticals.[123]

In countries that have significant natural resource sectors, the laws written to regulate the extractive industries include environmental provisions that may anticipate the development of generally applicable environmental laws. As a precursor to its modern environmental laws, Brazil's 1965 Forest Code instituted an ambitious regulatory framework intended to protect all forms of native vegetation on public and private property throughout Brazil,[124] with its schedules of violations and penalties forming the apparent inspiration and basis for the progressive Environmental Crimes Law of 1998.[125] Additional examples can be found in the mining laws enacted in Argentina and Peru to address historical contamination of soils and watercourses by mine "tailings" (i.e., large volumes of leftover extracted material that often contain high concentrations of toxic elements), which provide the model and precedent for more universal contaminated site laws.[126]

G.   Energy and Climate

The energy sector in Latin America is robust and rapidly expanding to become a source of economic growth and stability. Brazil, Mexico, and Venezuela are each significant producers of petroleum, with the huge "presalt" reserves first announced in 2007 beneath the offshore waters of Brazil being among the global industry's largest discoveries in recent decades.[127] The region is also developing an increasingly diverse portfolio of renewable energy sources, including biofuels, hydroelectric, wind, and solar power. The prime example is Brazil, which has positioned itself as a global biofuel leader,[128] with large-scale production of ethanol from sugar cane since the 1970s, augmented by recent investments in biodiesel derived primarily from soybeans.[129] Brazil's electrical grid relies heavily on large hydroelectric projects,[130] including several at various stages of construction in the Amazon

Basin,[131] a source of significant controversy due to the effects on forests and indigenous inhabitants. Energy efficiency initiatives are spreading across Latin America, with several countries recently imposing energy performance labeling requirements for a wide range of products.[132] Uruguay has taken an especially comprehensive approach to alternative energy sources, mandating that an increasing share of its electricity be derived from wind and seeking to eliminate fossil-fuel-fired power plants from its national grid.[133]

Climate change policies in Latin America are influenced by both broad public acceptance of climate change as a real, human-caused, threatening phenomenon,[134] and self-interested contemplation of the potential for external funding of development projects under the Kyoto Protocol's Clean Development Mechanism or similar carbon emission offset programs.[135] In the international sphere, Brazil has prominently advocated for the advancement of multilateral agreements to reduce greenhouse gas emissions.[136] Domestically, both Brazil's federal government and several states have enacted climate change policy laws intended to stabilize or reduce greenhouse gas emissions,[137] although it remains unclear whether these governments will actually attempt to impose the extensive cuts in fossil fuel consumption that appear necessary to achieve the laws' objectives.

H.   Chemicals

No Latin American country has yet enacted comprehensive chemicals regulation, but some have shown signs of attention to the issue, perhaps most significantly in Mexico, which has advanced an initial chemicals inventory, the first of its kind in the region.[138] The legislatures of both Argentina and Brazil have recently considered bills that would restrict the content of certain substances in electronic products, generally following the contours of the EU Directive on the Restriction of Hazardous Substances (RoHS).[139] In light of this and other expressions of affinity for European environmental policy, it would not be surprising to see one or more of the major Latin American countries to adopt the EU's Registration, Evaluation, Authorization, and Restriction of Chemicals (REACH) Regulation in some form. Most Latin American countries are parties to the major international conventions that regulate certain classes of chemicals, such as the Stockholm Convention on Persistent Organic Pollutants,[140] the Montreal Protocol for Ozone-Depleting Substances,[141] and the Rotterdam Convention on Prior Informed Consent.[142]

In the related area of chemical hazard communications, Brazil and Uruguay have each adopted the Globally Harmonized System of Classification and Labeling of Chemicals (GHS), with Brazil's initially voluntary technical standard becoming fully mandatory in 2015,[143] and Uruguay's mandatory regulations under a phased implementation from 2009 to 2017.[144] Mexico adopted a GHS technical standard in 2011; it is voluntary but can be used to satisfy certain workplace safety requirements.[145]

As several Latin American countries have sizeable agricultural sectors and abundant insects, pesticides and related product classes such as fertilizers and inoculants are widely used and subject to robust regulatory regimes.[146] In recent years Brazil has become reportedly the world's largest market for pesticides,[147] and has taken steps to ameliorate their impact, banning several substances[148] and attaining the world's highest recovery rate of used pesticide containers.[149] Like most other countries in the region, Brazil requires registration of pesticides, supported by submissions of health and safety data.[150]

I.   Genetically Modified Organisms

Due to the prevalence of agriculture in their economies, many Latin American countries have significant markets for genetically modified crops. However, as in Europe, public attitudes toward genetically modified organisms (GMOs) tend to be skeptical. The regulation of GMOs in Latin America therefore balances the embrace of practical agricultural solutions against a general anxiety about the unknown potential impacts of biotechnology.[151] For example, Brazilian agribusiness has converted to GMOs for the bulk of its export crops, but for domestic consumption food products that contain 1 percent or more GMO derivatives must be prominently labeled as transgenic.[152] Several other countries have acted to restrict the import and use of GMOs. The Andean nations have been especially active in restricting GMO uses, such as Peru's ten-year moratorium[153] and indefinite bans in Bolivia and Ecuador.[154] In some cases, biosafety restrictions on GMO use are incorporated into the biodiversity laws that protect naturally occurring genetic resources.[155] A notable exception is Mexico, where corn has a special social significance, and GMO cultivars of corn are heavily regulated.[156] All major Latin American countries are signatories of the Cartagena Biosafety Protocol,[157] and some have adopted the terms of this agreement into their domestic laws.[158]

X.   Conclusion

Latin American environmental law is evolving rapidly, presenting a dynamic field of endeavor for international practitioners and diverse challenges to the regulated community. The consciousness of the populace is heightened, and legislators and regulators are acting on the concerns of their constituents. Where it was once accepted local practice to disregard environmental issues, agencies, courts, and the public are reacting to the legacies of that inattention, with legal consequences that can be unpredictable. The general trend is toward higher degrees of regulation and enforcement, and as the legal communities and agencies across the region gain experience, greater consistency in the application of environmental laws is likely to result, but that transition is far from over.

Notes

1. *See generally* David R. Boyd, The Environmental Rights Revolution: A Global Study of Constitutions, Human Rights, and the Environment 126–47 (2012); David R. Boyd, *The Constitutional Right to a Healthy Environment*, Environment (July–Aug. 2012) (stating that 16 of 18 constitutions in Latin America include a constitutional right to a healthy environment), http://www.environmentmagazine.org/Archives/Back%20Issues/2012/July-August%202012/constitutional-rights-full.html; *see, e.g.,* Constitución de la Nación Argentina arts. 41, 66–69; Constitución Política del Ecuador 2008, arts. 71–74; Constitución Política de los Estados Unidos Mexicanos arts. 1, 4, 26, 27; Constitución Política de Peru arts. 66–69); Constitución Política de la República de Chile art. 19(8); Constituição da República Federativa do Brasil de 1988 art. 225.

2. By way of example, Article 41 of the Argentine Constitution grants individual rights to a healthy environment, *see supra* note 1; the Peruvian Constitution does not make such a guarantee and only requires the government to promote sustainable use of natural resources and conservation of biological diversity, *see supra* note 1; while Bolivia has led the region and perhaps the world by adopting constitutional rights to protect "Mother Earth" (*madre tierra*) in 2009, *see infra* note 3.

3. Constitución Política del Estado Plurinacional de Bolivia art. 34 ("Cualquier persona, a título individual o en representación de una colectividad, esta facultada para ejercitar las acciones legales en defensa del derecho al medio ambiente, sin perjuicio de la obligación de las instituciones políticas de actuar de oficio frente a los atentados contra el medio ambiente."); Ley No. 300, Ley Marco de la Madre Tierra y Desarrollo Integral para Vivir Bien, G.O. 15.10.2012 (Bolivia).

4. Mexico, Argentina, and Brazil are examples of federalist systems whereby the states (Mexico and Brazil) or provinces (Argentina) have significant jurisdiction over environmental matters and can adopt restrictions that are more stringent than the national standards. *See* Constitución Política de los Estados Unidos Méxicanos art. 115; Constitución de la Nación Argentina arts. 1, 5, 41; Constituição da República Federativa do Brasil de 1988 arts. 23 ("É competência comum da União, dos Estados, do Distrito Federal e dos Municípios: . . . VI—proteger o meio ambiente e combater a poluição em qualquer de suas formas; VII—preservar as florestas, a fauna e a flora. . . ."), 24 ("Compete à União, aos Estados e ao Distrito Federal legislar concorrentemente sobre: . . . VI—florestas, caça, pesca, fauna, conservação da natureza, defesa do solo e dos recursos naturais, proteção do meio ambiente e controle da poluição. . . .").

5. In general, an *amparo* provision grants to any citizen the right to sue the government for any alleged constitutional violation (loosely analogous to the Anglo-American habeas corpus action, but with broader scope). *See, e.g.,* Constitución Política de los Estados Unidos Méxicanos arts. 103, 107; Ley de Amparo, Reglamentaria de los Artículos 103 y 107 de la Constitución Política de los Estados Unidos Mexicanos, D.O.F. 10.01.1936 (Mexico); *see also* Constitución de la Nación Argentina art. 43; Constitución de Colombia 1991 art. 86; Constitución Política de Ecuador 2008 art. 95; Constitución Política de Costa Rica 1994 art. 48.

6. *See* Boyd, The Environmental Rights Revolution, *supra* note 1, at 126–47; Fronteras Comunes, Manual de acciones colectivas y amparo para lograr la justicia ambiental (2012), http://www.fronterascomunes.org.mx/portal/images/pdf/acciones colectivas.pdf.

7. Constitución Política de los Estados Unidos Méxicanos art. 27; Constitución Política de Ecuador 2008 art. 332.

8. *See, e.g.*, WWF & DEG, Assessing Water Risk: A Practical Approach for Financial Institutions 9–10 (2011); *Sin Aqua Non: Water Shortages Are a Growing Problem, but Not for the Reasons Most People Think*, Economist (Apr. 8, 2009), http://www.economist.com/node/13447271; J. Luis Gausch et al., Public-Private Infrastructure Advisory Auth., World Bank, Renegotiation of Concession Contracts in Latin America (Apr. 2003); Philippe Marin, Public-Private Partnerships for Urban Water Utilities: A Review of Experiences in Developing Countries (Feb. 2009).

9. Mexico is included in the North America section of this volume, not the Central and South America section, and so its chapter precedes this one.

10. Ley General para la Prevención y Gestión Integral de los Residuos, D.O.F. 08.08.2003 (Mexico).

11. Reglamento de la Ley General para la Prevención y Gestión Integral de los Residuos, D.O.F. 30.11.2006 (Mexico).

12. Norma Oficial Mexicana NOM-052-SEMARNAT-2005, Que establece las características, el procedimiento de identificación, clasificación y los listados de los residuos peligrosos, D.O.F. 23.06.2006 (Mexico).

13. Norma Oficial Mexicana NOM-055-SEMARNAT-2003, Que establece los requisitos que deben reunir los sitios que se destinarán para un confinamiento controlado de residuos peligrosos previamente estabilizados, D.O.F. 03.11.2004 (Mexico).

14. Norma Oficial Mexicana NOM-138-SEMARNAT/SS-2003, Límites máximos permisibles de hidrocarburos en suelos y las especificaciones para su caracterización y remediación, D.O.F. 29.03.2005 (Mexico).

15. *E.g.*, Ley General del Equilibrio Ecológico y la Protección al Ambiente, D.O.F. 28.01.1988 (Mexico); Ley No. 99 de 1993, Por la cual se crea el Ministerio del Medio Ambiente, D.O. 22.12.1993 (Colombia); Lei No. 6938, de 31 de agosto de 1981, Dispõe sobre a Política Nacional do Meio Ambiente, seus fins e mecanismos de formulação e aplicação, D.O.U. 02.09.1981 (Brazil); Ley No. 25675, Ley General del Ambiente, B.O. 28.11.2002 (Argentina); Ley No. 19300, de 1 de marzo de 1994, sobre bases generales del medio ambiente, D.O. 09.03.1994, (Chile).

16. For example, Colombia's Renewable Natural Resources Code, Decreto No. 2811 de 1974, Código de Recursos Naturales Renovables, D.O. 18.12.1974, which remains in effect, was one of the first to be adopted in the region.

17. Lei No. 12.305 de 2 de agosto de 2010, Institui a Política Nacional de Resíduos Sólidos, D.O.U. 03.08.2010, (Brazil).

18. *See, e.g.*, Decisão de Diretoria No. 103/2007/C/E, de 22 de junho de 2007, Dispõe sobre o procedimento para gerenciamento de áreas contaminadas, D.O.E. 27.06.2007 (São Paulo State, Brazil); Decisão de Diretoria No. 195/2005/E, de 23 de novembro de 2005, Dispõe sobre a aprovação dos Valores Orientadores para Solos e Águas Subterrâneas no Estado de São Paulo, D.O.E. 03.12.2005 (São Paulo State, Brazil).

19. National legislative websites in the region that enable monitoring of bills include Mexican Chamber of Deputies, http://www.diputados.gob.mx/inicio.htm; Argentine Chamber of Deputies, http://www.diputados.gov.ar; Brazilian Chamber of Deputies, http://www2.camara.leg.br/; Chilean Chamber of Deputies, http://www.camara.cl.

20. Associao Brasiliera de Normas Técnicas, Conheça a ABNT, http://www.abnt.org.br/m3.asp?cod_pagina=929 (last visited June 4, 2013). Chile's Instituto Nacional de Normalización is similarly constituted. Instituto Nacional de Normalización, Quiénes somos, http://www.inn.cl/inn/portada/index.php (last visited June 4, 2013).

21. Instituto Nacional de Defensa de la Competencia y de la Protección de la Propiedad Intelectual, Sobre el INDECOPI, http://www.indecopi.gob.pe/0/modulos/JER/JER_Interna.aspx?ARE=0&PFL=0&JER=600 (last visited June 4, 2013).

22. In Mexico, Normas Oficiales Mexicanas (NOMs; http://www.economia-noms
.gob.mx) issued by agencies such as SEMARNAT are automatically binding. Ley Federal
sobre Metrología y Normalización art. 3(XI)), D.O.F. 01.07.1992.

23. In Mexico, Normas Mexicanas (NMXs; http://www.economia-nmx.gob.mx) are
officially non-binding standards. Ley Federal sobre Metrología y Normalización art. 3(X)).

24. *E.g.*, Norma Técnica Peruana NTP 900.064.012, que establece, en términos generales, las medidas que deben ser adoptadas para el manejo ambientalmente adecuado de
los RAEE en las diferentes etapas del manejo de los mismos (designating each of its
annexes as either "informative" or "normative") (Peru).

25. Formerly known as the American Society for Testing and Materials. ASTM Int'l,
About ASTM, http://www.astm.org/ABOUT/aboutASTM.html (last visited June 4, 2013).

26. For example, in Mexico, environmental authority was formerly granted to the
Secretaría de Desarollo Social (SEDESOL; the Secretary of Social Development). For several years, Colombia's environmental authority was a subdivision of the Ministerio del
Ambiente, Vivienda and Desarollo Territorial (MAVDT), an umbrella agency that includes
housing and development. In 2011, MAVDT was dissolved and the environmental authority reconstituted as the Ministerio de Ambiente y Desarollo Sostenible (MinAmbiente;
http://www.minambiente.gov.co).

27. In 2006, the Argentine federal environmental agency, the Secretaria de Ambiente
y Desarrollo Sustentable (SAyDS; http://www.ambiente.gov.ar), became an executive-
level agency.

28. Brazil's Ministerio do Meio Ambiente (MMA; http://www.mma.gov.br) was
established in 1985.

29. Chile's Ministerio del Medio Ambiente (MMA; http://www.mma.gob.cl) was
established as a cabinet-level agency in 2010.

30. Mexico's Secretaría de Medio Ambiente y Recursos Naturales (SEMARNAT;
http://www.semarnat.gob.mx) was established in 2000.

31. For example, Mexican environmental law is enforced through the Procuradaria
Federal de Protección del MedioAmbiente (PROFEPA; http://www.profepa.gob.mx).
Brazilian environmental laws are enforced largely through public prosecutors. *See, e.g.,*
LESLEY K. MCALLISTER, MAKING LAW MATTER: ENVIRONMENTAL PROTECTION AND LEGAL
INSTITUTIONS IN BRAZIL (2008).

32. For example, Sao Paulo State's environmental agency, CETESB, has well-developed
site contamination standards that became the model for federal standards. *See supra* note
18; *cf.* Resolução CONAMA No. 420, de 28 de dezembro de 2009, Dispõe sobre critérios e
valores orientadores de qualidade do solo quanto à presença de substâncias químicas e
estabelece diretrizes para o gerenciamento ambiental de áreas contaminadas por essas
substâncias em decorrência de atividades antrópicas, D.O.U. 30.12.2009 (Brazil). The
Province of Buenos Aires adopted a progressive electric and electronics waste law, ahead
of its federal government. Ley Provincia de Buenos Aires No. 14321, Gestión Sustentable
de Residuos de Aparatos Eléctricos y Electrónicos, B.O. 15.12.2011.

33. Mexico regulates toxic substances under its General Health Law, Ley General de
Salud, D.O.F. 07.02.1984, and its Secretariat of Health houses its federal toxic substances
agency, Comisión Federal para la Protección contra Riesgos Sanitarios (COFEPRIS;
http://www.cofepris.gob.mx). Costa Rica also regulates toxic substances and products
through its Ministry of Health. Decreto Ejecutivo No. 24099-S, del 22 de diciembre de
1994, Reglamento Registro y Control Sustancias Tóxicas y Productos Tóxicos y Peligrosos,
La Gaceta 21.03.1995 (Costa Rica).

34. In Peru, the agency with jurisdiction over the registration and control of pesticides
is the Servicio Nacional de Sanidad Agraria (SENASA; http://www.senasa.gob.pe), a

subsecretary of the Ministry of Agriculture; in Ecuador, pesticides and fertilizers are regulated by the Agencia Ecadoriana de Asegurimento de la Calidad del Agro (AGROCALIDAD; http://www.agrocalidad.gob.ec.

35. In Brazil, for example, the Agência Nacional de Transportes Terrestres (ANTT) administers the country's principal dangerous goods transport regulation, ANTT Resolução No. 420, de 12 de fevereiro de 2004, Aprova as Instruções Complementares ao Regulamento do Transporte Terrestre de Produtos Perigosos, D.O.U. 31.05.2004.

36. *See, e.g.*, Ley No. 99 de 1993, Por la cual se crea el Ministerio del Medio Ambiente, D.O. 22.12.1993, art. 49 (requiring environmental licensing of any activity that could cause deterioration of natural resources or the environment) (Colombia); Ley de Aguas Nacionales, D.O.F. 01.12.1992, art. 20 (requiring a concession for use of or discharge into national waters) (Mexico).

37. Some of these registries are publicly available through electronic portals on environmental agency websites, for example, http://www.sea.gob.cl/contenido/centro-de-documentacion (Chilean environmental impact decisions); http://vital.anla.gov.co/ventanillasilpa (Colombia integrated public database); http://tramites.semarnat.gob.mx/ (Mexican waste management plans).

38. For example, Colombia has developed comprehensive manuals for applications for environmental impact studies. *E.g.*, Manual de Evaluacion de Estudios Ambientales: Criterios y Procedimientos (Alberto Federico Mouthon et al. eds., Ministerio del Medio Ambiente 2002).

39. For example, to streamline media-specific environmental permits, Mexico has developed a streamlined "single environmental license" (*licencia ambiental unica*, LAU). *See* SEMARNAT, Trámite: Licencia Ambiental Única, http://tramites.semarnat.gob.mx/index.php/atmosfera/autorizaciones-para-la-operacion/5-semarnat-05-002-licencia-ambiental-unica (last visited June 4, 2013). The State of São Paulo has undertaken a series of reforms to its licensing process to reduce requirements for low-impact projects. *See, e.g.*, Resolução SMA-056 de 10 de junho de 2010, Altera procedimentos para o licenciamento das atividades que especifica (streamlining licensing procedures for specified projects deemed to have low environmental impact) D.O.E. 11.06.2010 (São Paulo State, Brazil).

40. *See, e.g.*, Ley General del Equilibrio Ecológico y la Protección al Ambiente, D.O.F. 28.01.1988, arts. 171–172 (Mexico); Ley No. 1333 de 1999, Por la cual se establece el procedimiento sancionatorio ambiental, D.O. 21.07.2009 (Colombia); Ley No. 19300, de 1 de marzo de 1994, sobre bases generales del medio ambiente, D.O. 09.03.1994, arts. 51–55 (Chile).

41. Lei No. 9605, de 12 de fevereiro de 1999, Dispõe sobre as sanções penais e administrativas derivadas de condutas e atividades lesivas ao meio ambiente, D.O.U. 03.02.1998, art. 54 § 2 (maximum prison term of five years for causing pollution that results or can result in harm to human health, death of animals, or significant destruction of flora) & art. 75 (maximum fine of R$50 million for violations of environmental laws) (Brazil).

42. Decreto No. 6514, de 22 de julho de 2008, Dispõe sobre as infrações e sanções administrativas ao meio ambiente, estabelece o processo administrativo federal para apuração destas infrações, D.O.U. 23.07.2008 (Brazil).

43. Ley No. 1333 de 1999 art. 5(1) (Colombia).

44. For example, in Latin America's version of Love Canal, the highly contaminated Matanza-Riachuelo River Basin, Argentine environmental authorities have ordered the closure of 239 facilities as part of a global remediation plan. *See* Press Release, ACUMAR, ACUMAR Cumple con el Control Industrial en la Cuenca, Feb. 26, 2013, http://www.acumar.gov.ar/novedades/866/acumar-cumple-con-el-control-industrial-en-la-cuenca (last visited June 4, 2013).

45. Brazil, for example, has responded to the challenges of enforcement in the Amazon Basin with the creation of the Environmental Military Police, a force that numbers in the thousands. *See generally* Polícia Militar Ambiental do Brasil, http://www.pmambiental brasil.org.br/ (last visited June 4, 2013). This force was originally authorized under legislation intended to create an Environmental National Guard. Decreto No. 6515, de 22 de julho de 2008, Institui, no âmbito dos Ministérios do Meio Ambiente e da Justiça, os Programas de Segurança Ambiental denominados Guarda Ambiental Nacional e Corpo de Guarda-Parques, D.O.U. 23.07.2008 (Brazil)).

46. Perhaps the most notorious of recent government actions in the region is the lengthy and controversial case against Chevron by the government of Ecuador resulting in a judgment of more than $18.9 billion. Victor Gómez, *Ecuador Court Upholds $18 Billion Ruling against Chevron*, REUTERS, Jan. 30, 2012, http://www.reuters.com/article /2012/01/04/us-ecuador-chevron-idUSTRE8021VS20120104 (last visited June 4, 2013). Other recently reported examples include the following: Michael Kepp, *Brazil Cracks Down on Illegal Deforestation, Issues $11.9 Million in Fines since February*, ENVTL. L. REP. (BNA), Mar. 27, 2013; Michael Kepp, *Brazilian Agency Fines Steelmaker $17.6M for Contamination Linked to Health Problems*, ENVTL. L. REP. (BNA), Apr. 10, 2013; Alexandra Ulmer & Euan Rocha, *Chile Court Suspends Goldcorp $3.9 Billion El Morro Project*, REUTERS, Apr. 30, 2012, http://www.reuters.com/article/2012/04/30/us-goldcorp-idUSBRE83T0CL20120430 (last visited June 4, 2013).

47. *See, e.g.*, INECE, *Summary of Plenary Session No. 7: The Evolving Role of the Judiciary in Environment Compliance and Enforcement*, Sixth International Conference on Environmental Compliance and Enforcement (Apr. 15–19, 2002), http://www.inece.org/conf /proceedings2/54-Plenary%20Session%207ALT.pdf. *See also* UNEP, *Aportes y sugerencias de los jueces participantes de la region de America Latina y el Caribe*, World Symposium of Judges (Aug. 18–20, 2002) (Spanish only), *available at* http://www.pnuma.org/deramb /AportacionesLACSimposioMudialjueces.pdf.

48. UNEP, JUDICIAL HANDBOOK ON ENVIRONMENTAL LAW (2005), http://www.unep .org/envrionmentalgovernance/Portals/8/documents/JUDICIAL_HBOOK_ENV_LAW .pdf.

49. *See, e.g.*, THE ROLE OF THE JUDICIARY IN ENVIRONMENTAL GOVERNANCE: COMPARATIVE PERSPECTIVES 263 (Louis J. Kotze & Alexander R. Paterson eds., 2009) (observing that the judiciary in Brazil has "in the past been strongly attached to the tradition of protecting individual rights," and arguing that the judiciary could expand its role in environmental justice in Brazil by broadening standing, among other things).

50. For example, in a 2002 decision, Colombia's Constitutional Court struck down a provision of the Penal Code that limited punitive damages in criminal cases to 1,000 times the minimum monthly salary, citing among its reasons the fact that environmental harms may not be subject to direct calculation and such a limit impeded fair compensation in such cases. *See* Sentencia No. C-916/02, Camilo Andrés Baracaldo Cárdenas, Demanda de inconstitucionalidad contra el artículo 97 de la Ley 599 de 2000, "[p]or la cual se expide el Código Penal," at ¶ 8.3.1 (Corte Constitucional, Oct. 29, 2002) (Colombia).

51. For example, Mexico recently provided for class action law suits: constitutional amendments were adopted in 2010 and legislation to implement those reforms was enacted in 2011. *See* Decreto por el que se reforman y adicionan el Código Federal de Procedimientos Civiles, el Código Civil Federal, la Ley Federal de Competencia Económica, la Ley Federal de Proteccion al Consumidor, la Ley Orgánica del Poder Judicial de la Federación, la Ley General del Equilibrio Ecológico y la Protección al Ambiente

y la Ley de Protección y Defensa al Usuario de Servicios Financieros, D.O.F. 30.08.2011 (Mexico).

52. *See, e.g.,* Ley General del Equilibrio Ecológico y la Protección al Ambiente, D.O.F. 28.01.1988, arts. 199–204 (Mexico); Ley No. 7554, Ley Orgánica del Ambiente, La Gaceta 13.11.1995, art. 107 (Costa Rica).

53. The leading example of a citizen suit leading to enforcement scrutiny may be the case of *Mendoza, Beatriz Silvia y otros c/ Estado Nacional y otros s/ daños y perjuicios derivados de la contaminación ambiental del Río Matanza Riachuelo,* Sentencia No. M.1569.XL (Corte Suprema de Justicia de la Nación, July 8, 2008), in which the Argentine Supreme Court ordered the governments of the nation, the Province of Buenos Aires and the Autonomous City of Buenos Aires to enforce the environmental laws, leading to the closure of hundreds of industrial facilities and the creation of a new regulatory regime in the highly polluted Matanza-Riachuelo River Basin.

54. *See* BOYD, THE ENVIRONMENTAL RIGHTS REVOLUTION, *supra* note 1, at 126–47.

55. *See, e.g., supra* note 52; Ley No. 472 de 1998, por la cual se desarrolla el artículo 88 de la Constitución Política de Colombia en relación con el ejercicio de las acciones populares y de grupo y se dictan otras disposiciones (Colombia); Lei No. 7347, de 24 de julho de 1985, Disciplina a ação civil pública de responsabilidade por danos causados ao meio-ambiente, ao consumidor, a bens e direitos de valor artístico, estético, histórico, turístico e paisagístico, D.O.U. 25.07.1985 (Brazil).

56. *See, e.g.,* GEORGE & CATHERINE PRING, GREENING JUSTICE: CREATING AND IMPROVING ENVIRONMENTAL COURTS AND TRIBUNALS, app. 1 (2009), *available at* http://www .accessinitiative.org/resource/greening-justice (last visited June 4, 2013) (listing specialized environmental courts and tribunals in Bolivia, Brazil, Chile, and Costa Rica).

57. Costa Rica's Tribunal Ambiental Administrativo (http://www.tribunalambiental .org) is housed within its Ministerio del Ambiente, Energia y Telecomunicaciones.

58. *See* Ley No. 20600, de 28 de junio de 2012, crea los Tribunales Ambientales, D.O. 28.06.2012 (Chile).

59. According to its website, the Latin American Water Tribunal has heard 58 cases and provided 250 consultations since its founding. Tribunal Latinoamericano del Agua, Audiencias, http://tragua.com/audiencias (last visited June 4, 2013).

60. *See, e.g.,* Maura Mullen de Bolivar. *A Comparison of Protecting the Environmental Interests of Latinamerican Indigenous Communities from Transnational Corporations under International Human Rights and Environmental Law,* 8 J. TRANSNAT'L L. & POL'Y 105 (Fall 1998).

61. Basel Convention on the Control of Transboundary Movements of Hazardous Wastes and Their Disposal, Mar. 22, 1989, 28 I.L.M. 657. All Central and South American countries are parties. Basel Convention Parties and Signatories, http://www.basel.int /Countries/StatusofRatifications/PartiesSignatories/tabid/1290/Default.aspx (last visited Feb. 22, 2013).

62. United Nations Framework Convention on Climate Change, May 9, 1992, 1771 U.N.T.S. 107. All Central and South American countries are parties. UNFCCC, List of Non-Annex I Parties, http://unfccc.int/parties_and_observers/parties/non_annex_i /items/2833.php (last visited Feb. 22, 2013).

63. Convention on International Trade in Endangered Species of Wild Fauna and Flora (CITES), Mar. 3, 1973, 993 U.N.T.S. 243. All Central and South American countries are parties. CITES, Member Countries, http://www.cites.org/eng/disc/parties/alphabet .php (last visited Feb. 22, 2013).

64. Montreal Protocol on Substances That Deplete the Ozone Layer, Sept. 16, 1987, 26 I.L.M. 1550. All Central and South American countries are parties. UNEP, Ozone Secretariat,

Status of Ratification for the Montreal Protocol and the Vienna Convention, http://ozone
.unep.org/new_site/en/treaty_ratification_status.php (last visited Feb. 22, 2013).

65. Rio Declaration on Environment and Development, June 14, 1992, 31 ILM 874
(1992). All Central and South American countries are parties. CITES, Member Countries,
http://www.cites.org/eng/disc/parties/alphabet.php (last visited Feb. 22, 2013).

66. Ley General de Cambio Climático, D.O.F. 06.06.2012, arts. 2.1, 33.II (Mexico); Lei
No. 12187, de 29 de dezembro de 2009, Institui a Política Nacional sobre Mudança do
Clima, D.O.U. de 30.12.2009 (Brazil).

67. *See, e.g.*, Ley No. 24051, Régimen Aplicable a la Generación, Manipulación,
Transporte, Tratamiento y Disposición Final de Residuos Peligrosos, B.O. 17.01.1992,
annexes I, II (Argentina); Decreto Supremo No. 148, de 12 de junio de 2003, Aprueba
Reglamento Sanitario sobre Manejo de Residuos Peligrosos, D.O. 16.06.2004, arts. 17, 90
(Chile); Decreto No. 4741 de 2005, Por el cual se reglamenta parcialmente la prevención y
el manejo de los residuos o desechos peligrosos generados en el marco de la gestión integral, D.O. 30.12.2005, annexes I–III (Colombia).

68. *See supra* note 66.

69. Stockholm Convention on Persistent Organic Pollutants, May 22, 2001, 40 I.L.M.
532. All Central and South American countries are parties. Stockholm Convention, Status
of Ratifications, http://chm.pops.int/Countries/StatusofRatifications/tabid/252/Default
.aspx (last visited Feb. 22, 2013).

70. Rotterdam Convention on the Prior Informed Consent Procedure for Certain
Hazardous Chemicals and Pesticides in International Trade, Sept. 10, 1998, 38 I.L.M. 1. All
Central and South American countries are parties. Rotterdam Convention, Status of Ratifi-
cations, http://www.pic.int/Countries/Statusofratifications/tabid/1072/language/en-US
/Default.aspx (last visited Feb. 22, 2013).

71. *See, e.g.*, North American Free Trade Agreement art. 104, Dec. 17, 1992, 32 I.L.M.
289.

72. Notable is the creation of the Commission on Environmental Cooperation under
the NAFTA environmental side agreement, North American Agreement on Environmental Cooperation, Sept. 14, 1993, 32 I.L.M. 1480. *See also* United States—Peru Trade Promotion Agreement art. 18.4, Apr. 12, 2006, http://www.ustr.gov/trade-agreements/free
-trade-agreements/peru-tpa/final-text, (providing for a commitment to enable citizens to
petition the authorities to investigate alleged violations of environmental laws).

73. *E.g.*, Andean Subregional Integration Agreement (Cartagena Agreement), May
26, 1969, 8 I.L.M. 910 (1969) (creating the Andean Community); Treaty of Asunción, Mar.
26 1991, 30 I.L.M. 1041 (1991) (creating the Common Market of the South, or
MERCOSUR).

74. *E.g.*, Decisión No. 436, Norma Andina para el Registro y Control de Plaguicidas
Químicos de Uso Agrícola, Nonagesimocuarto Período Extraordinario de Sesiones de la
Comisión, 11 de junio de 1998, Lima, Peru; MERCOSUR/GMC/RES No. 6/98—Procedimiento Uniforme de Control del Transporte de Mercancías Peligrosas y Cronograma
para el Cumplimiento de las Exigencias del Acuerdo sobre Transporte de Mercancías Peligrosas en el MERCOSUR, Grupo Mercado Común XXIX, 8 de mayo de 1998, Buenos
Aires, Argentina.

75. For example, Greenpeace International has a significant presence in Latin America, with active campaigns in Argentina, Chile, Brazil, and Mexico.

76. For example, the Border Environmental Justice Campaign (a collaboration
between the U.S.-based Environmental Health Coalition and Mexican Colectivo Chil-
pancingo Pro Justicia Ambiental) initiated a suit that led to the cleanup of the Metales y
Derivados site in Tijuana. Local NGO effort was instrumental to shutting down the plant

in 1994 and orchestrating a community-driven cleanup in 2008. *See* Stephen Siciliano, *Mexico Provides Final Funding for Cleanup of Abandoned Lead Smelting Site in Tijuana,* ENVTL. L. REP. (BNA), Aug. 22, 2007. In the Matanza-Riachuelo River Basin case in Argentina (*see supra* note 55), local NGOs and the National Ombudsman filed a prior suit that laid the groundwork for the eventual success of the Mendoza suit. *See* Kristi Innvær Staveland-Sæter, *Litigating the Right to a Healthy Environment: Assessing the Policy Impact of "The Mendoza Case,"* CHR. MICHELSEN INST. (CMI Report R 2011:6), http://www.cmi.no /publications/file/4258-litigating-the-right-to-a-healthy-environment.pdf. Four NGOs later declared their role as third parties in the Mendoza case in 2006, after the case was accepted by the Supreme Court of the Nation. *See* Fundación Ambiente y Recursos Naturales, The Matanza-Riachuelo River Basin Case Summary (July 8, 2008), http:// www.farn.org.ar/archives/10827. Locally prominent NGOs dedicated to environmental law include Centro Méxicano de Derecho Ambiental (Mexican Center for Environmental Law; http://www.cemda.org); Derecho, Ambiente y Recursos Naturales (Rights, Environment and Natural Resources (Peru); http://www.dar.org.pe/inicio.htm); Centro Ecuatoriano de Derecho Ambiental (Ecuadorian Center for Environmental Law; http:// www.ceda.org.ec).

77. For example, Swiss government grants provided the initial funding for the Plataforma Regional de Residuos Electrónicos en Latinoamérica y el Caribe (RELAC, an NGO dedicated to electronics product stewardship in Latin America; http://www.residuoselec tronicos.net). Working with environmental regulators throughout the region, RELAC has developed model electronics legislation based on EU models. Most of its e-waste initiatives have been conducted under the auspices of the Basel Convention on the Control of Transboundary Movements of Hazardous Wastes and Their Disposal. As part of their commitment to implementing the Convention, the Swiss State Secretariat for Economic Affairs (SECO) and the Swiss Federal Laboratories for Materials Testing and Research (EMPA) launched programs in 2007 and 2009, respectively, to develop e-waste management systems in Peru and Colombia. Swiss Fed. Dep't of Economic Affairs, Trade Promotion, A Swiss Contribution to the Implementation of the Basel Convention, http://www .basel.int/Portals/4/Basel%20Convention/docs/convention/XX%20Anniversary /Press%20kit/Swiss%20Project%20leaflet.pdf (last visited June 5, 2013). Additionally, the Basel Convention's Partnership for Action on Computing Equipment (PACE), whose operations are supported primarily by the Swiss government, has held several workshops on e-waste management strategies in Latin America. *See, e.g.,* INTI, Centro Regional Sudamericano Convenio de Basilea, http://crsbasilea.inti.gov.ar/gale.htm (last visited June 5, 2013); Sistema de la Integración Centroamericana, Centro Regional Convenio de Basilea para Centroamérica y México, Taller Centroamericano para la Gestión Ambientalmente Responsable de Residuos Eléctricos y Electrónicos, Feb. 28, 2013, http://www.sica .int/busqueda/Noticias.aspx?IDItem=76510&IDCat=3&IdEnt=889&Idm=1&IdmStyle=1. As early as 2006, the United Kingdom, in partnership with the United States and Canada, worked to establish a regional strategy for the environmentally sound management of used lead acid batteries in Central America, Colombia, Venezuela, and the Caribbean. Basel Convention, Revised regional strategy for the ESM of Used Acid Batteries in Central America, Colombia, Venezuela and the Caribbean island states (phase II), http:// www.basel.int/DNNAdmin/AllNews/tabid/2290/ctl/ArticleView/mid/7518/article Id/220/Revised-regional-strategy-for-the-ESM-of-Used-Acid-Batteries-in-Central-America -Colombia-Venezuela-and-the-Caribbean-island-states-phase-II.aspx (last visited June 5, 2013).

78. In particular, the fact that EU legislation is always provided in Spanish and Portuguese makes it readily available to be adopted by Latin American governments.

79. *See, e.g.*, Ley General del Equilibrio Ecológico y la Protección al Ambiente, D.O.F. 28.01.1988, art. 28 (Mexico); Ley No. 19300, de 1 de marzo de 1994, sobre Bases Generales del Medio Ambiente, D.O. 09.03.1994, art. 8. (Chile); Ley No. 25675, Ley General del Ambiente, B.O. 28.11.2002, arts. 8, 11–13 (Argentina); Ley No. 7554, Ley Orgánica del Ambiente, La Gaceta 13.11.1995, arts. 17–24 (Costa Rica); SEMARNAT, Guía para la Presentación de la Manifestación de Impacto Ambiental del Sector "Residuos Peligrosos," http://sinat.semarnat.gob.mx/dgiraDocs/documentos/dgo/estudios/2003/10DU2003ID006.html (last visited May 29, 2013) ("En México, [EIA] se aplica desde hace más de 20 años y durante este tiempo el procedimiento ha permanecido vigente como el principal instrumento preventivo para la gestión de proyectos o actividades productivas.").

80. *See, e.g.*, Reglamento de la Ley General del Equilibrio Ecológico y la Protección al Ambiente en Materia de Evaluación del Impacto Ambiental, D.O.F. 26.05.2012, art. 5 (Mexico); Resolução CONAMA No. 1, de 23 de janeiro de 1986, Dispõe sobre Critérios Básicos e Diretrizes Gerais para a Avaliação de Impacto Ambiental, D.O.U. 17.02.1986, art. 2 (Brazil); Ley No. 19300 art. 10 (Chile); Ley Provincia de Buenos Aires No. 11723, del Medio Ambiente, B.O. 02.12.1995, art. 10, annex II; Decreto Ejecutivo No. 31849-MINAE -S-MOPT-MAG-MEIC, Reglamento General sobre los Procedimientos de Evaluación de Impacto Ambiental (EIA), annex I, La Gaceta 24.05.2004 (Costa Rica).

81. *See, e.g.*, Resolução CONAMA No. 1, de 23 de janeiro de 1986, art. 6 (requiring that EIAs include full characterization of the physical, biological, and socio-economic environment) (Brazil); Ley No. 19300 art. 11 (Chile).

82. *See, e.g.*, Reglamento de la Ley General del Equilibrio Ecológico y la Protección al Ambiente en Materia de Evaluación del Impacto Ambiental, D.O.F. 26.05.2012, art. 12(7), 13(7) (requiring "environmental predictions and, where appropriate, evaluation of alternatives") (Mexico); Resolução CONAMA No. 1, de 23 de janeiro de 1986, art. 6 (requiring that EIAs include analysis of all direct, indirect, immediate, medium-term, long-term, temporary and permanent environmental impacts of the proposed project) (Brazil); Ley No. 19300 art. 12 (Chile).

83. *E.g.*, Decreto Ejecutivo No. 31849-MINAE-SALUD-MOPT-MAG-MEIC art. 31 (requiring environmental permit applicants to use only licensed and registered consultants to conduct and be responsible for EIAs) (Costa Rica).

84. *E.g.*, Resolução CONAMA No. 237, de 19 de dezembro de 1997, Dispõe sobre a revisão e complementação dos procedimentos e critérios utilizados para o licenciamento ambiental, D.O.U. 22.12.1997, art. 3 (requiring publication of EIAs to guarantee public participation in environmental licensing) (Brazil); Reglamento de la Ley General del Equilibrio Ecológico y la Protección al Ambiente en Materia de Evaluación del Impacto Ambiental art. 4(IV) ("Compete a la Secretaría: . . . Llevar a cabo el proceso de consulta pública que en su caso se requiera durante el procedimiento de evaluación de impacto ambiental.") (Mexico); Ley Provincia de Buenos Aires No. 11723 art. 2(c) (stating that all inhabitants of the Province of Buenos Aires have a right to be involved in processes designed to protect the environment and natural resources).

85. *E.g.*, Constitución Política de Colombia 1991 art. 366 ("El bienestar general y el mejoramiento de la calidad de vida de la población son finalidades sociales del Estado. Será objetivo fundamental de su actividad la solución de las necesidades insatisfechas de salud, de educación, de saneamiento ambiental y de agua potable."); Constitución Política de Ecuador art. 12 ("El derecho humano al agua es fundamental e irrenunciable. El agua constituye patrimonio nacional estratégico de uso público, inalienable, imprescriptible, inembargable y esencial para la vida."); Constitución Política de los Estados Unidos Mexicanos art. 4 ("Toda persona tiene derecho al acceso, disposición y saneamiento de agua para consumo personal y doméstico en forma suficiente, salubre, aceptable y asequible.").

86. *E.g.*, Resolução CONAMA No. 430, de 13 de maio de 2011, Dispõe sobre as condições e padrões de lançamento de efluentes, D.O.U. 16.05.2011, art. 16 (Brazil); Decreto con Fuerza de Ley No. 725, de 11 de diciembre de 1967, Código Sanitario, D.O. 31.01.1968, art. 73 (Chile); Decreto Ejecutivo No. 33601-MINAE-S, Reglamento de Vertido y Reuso de Aguas Residuales, La Gaceta 19.03.2007, arts. 4–5 (Costa Rica).

87. *E.g.*, Resolução CONAMA No. 430, de 13 de maio de 2011, art. 3 (Brazil); Ley de Aguas Nacionales, D.O.F. 01.12.1992, art. 29(XVI) (requiring concession holders to present a biannual water quality report using data from a laboratory certified by the Mexican Institute of Water Technology) (Mexico).

88. In largely arid Chile, for example, the Water Code states that water rights include the responsibility to use water in a way that will not harm others using the same water sources, with respect to quality, quantity, substance, and opportunities for use, among other things. Decreto con Fuerza de Ley No. 1122, de 13 de agosto de 1981, Código de Aguas, D.O. 29.10.1981, art. 14 (Chile). The Water Code also states that the Water Authority is required to consider a "minimal ecological flow" when granting permits for new and ongoing industrial activities. *Id.* art. 129.

89. *E.g.*, Lei No. 9433, de 8 de janeiro de 1997, Institui a Política Nacional de Recursos Hídricos, cria o Sistema Nacional de Gerenciamento de Recursos Hídricos, D.O.U. 09.01.1987, art. 12 (establishing the types of water uses for which a public concession is required) (Brazil).

90. *E.g.*, Conselho Nacional de Recursos Hídricos Resolução No. 108, de 13 de abril de 2010, D.O.U. 27.05.2010 (approving Rio São Francisco Hydrographic Basin Committee Deliberação nº 40, de 31 de outubro de 2008, imposing separate fees for water captured from, or discharged into, the Rio São Francisco or its tributaries) (Brazil).

91. *See, e.g.*, Lei No. 9433, de 8 de janeiro de 1997, arts. 37–39 (establishing "Comitês de Bacia Hidrográfica") (Brazil); Ley de Aguas Nacionales art. 12 bis (establishing "Organismos de Cuenca") (Mexico).

92. *See, e.g.*, Secretaría del Medio Ambiente del Gobierno del Distrito Federal, Programa para mejorar la calidad del aire de la Zona Metropolitana del Valle de México 2011–2020 (PROAIRE 2011–2020), Map 1.3.1, "Distribución espacial de la concentración de ozono en la ZMVM, 2005," Map 1.2.1. "Distribución de la concentración de PM10 en las cinco zonas identificadas, con base en valores promedio anuales para 2005," http://www .sma.df.gob.mx/proaire2011_2020/index.php (last visited May 29, 2013).

93. In the early 1980s, for example, Mexico began instituting a series of policies aimed at improving air quality. Air quality criteria were published in the Diario Oficial for the first time in 1982, and an automatic air pollution monitoring network was launched in the Distrito Federal in 1986. In 1986 and 1987, respectively, the government launched "21 Actions to Reduce Air Contamination" and "100 Necessary Measures." These programs marked the beginning of the phasing-out of high-sulfur fuels, reduction of lead in gasoline, and rotating bans on cars, which was initiated in 1988 with the No Car Day program. PROAIRE 2011–2020, 113 (Mexico). San José recently reinstituted a rotating license plate ban for the central part of the city in late 2012. *See* Decreto Ejecutivo No. 37370-MOPT, Restricción Vehicular mediante el Esquema Hora/Placa en el Centro de San José, La Gaceta 26.10.2012 (Costa Rica).

94. *See, e.g.*, Pedro G. Seraphim, *Brazil's Ethanol-Enhanced History*, Ethanol Producer Mag., Aug. 10, 2009, http://www.ethanolproducer.com/articles/5906/brazil%27 s-ethanol-enhanced-history. Brazil has established vehicle emission standards through a series of laws and regulations, principally Lei 8723, de 28 de outubro de 1993, Dispõe sobre a redução de emissão de poluentes por veículos automotores, D.O.U. 29.10.1993; Resolução CONAMA No. 18, de 18 de maio de 1986, Dispõe sobre a criação do Programa de Controle de Poluição do Ar por Veículos Automotores—PROCONVE, D.O.U.

17.06.1986; and Resolução CONAMA No. 418, de 25 de novembro de 2009, Dispõe sobre critérios para a elaboração de Planos de Controle de Poluição Veicular—PCPV, D.O.U. 26.11.2009.

95. *E.g.*, Resolução CONAMA No. 436, de 22 de dezembro de 2011, Estabelece os limites máximos de emissão de poluentes atmosféricos para fontes fixas instaladas ou com pedido de licença de instalação anteriores a 02 de janeiro de 2007, D.O.U. 26.12.2011, anexo XIV (providing procedures for stationary source air emissions monitoring and reporting to licensing authorities) (Brazil); Resolução CONAMA No. 382, de 26 de dezembro de 2006, Estabelece os limites máximos de emissão de poluentes atmosféricos para fontes fixas, D.O.U. de 02.01.2007, art. 7 (establishing that stationary source emissions limits will be imposed through the issuance or renewal of environmental licenses) (Brazil); Reglamento de la Ley General del Equilibrio Ecológico y la Protección al Ambiente en Materia de Prevención y Control de la Contaminación de la Atmósfera, D.O.F. 25.11.1988, art. 17 (requiring stationary sources of air pollution subject to federal jurisdiction as outlined in the Environment Law to monitor and report emissions) (Mexico).

96. *E.g.*, Resolução CONAMA No. 436, de 22 de dezembro de 2011 (establishing stationary source air emissions standards for sulfur oxides, nitrogen oxides, carbon monoxide, particulate matter, lead, fluorides, and ammonia) (Brazil); Ministerio de Ambiente, Vivienda y Desarrollo Territorial Resolución No. 601 de 2006, D.O. 04.04.2006 (establishing maximum concentrations for "criteria air pollutants": particulate matter sulfur dioxide, nitrogen dioxide, carbon monoxide, and ozone) (Colombia); Decreto 30221-S Reglamento sobre Inmisión de Contaminantes Atmosféricos, La Gaceta 21.03.2002, art. 5 (establishing maximum concentrations for air pollutants, including but not limited to sulfur dioxide, nitrogen dioxide, carbon monoxide, ozone, lead, and hydrogen sulfide) (Costa Rica); Norma Oficial Mexicana NOM-043-SEMARNAT-1993, que establece los niveles máximos permisibles de emisión a la atmósfera de partículas sólidas provenientes de fuentes fijas, D.O.F. 23.04.2003 (establishing stationary source air emissions standards for particulate matter) (Mexico).

97. *E.g.*, Resolução CONAMA No. 3, de 22 de agosto de 1990, Dispõe sobre Padrões de Qualidade do Ar, Previstos no PRONAR [i.e., Programa Nacional de Controle da Qualidade do Ar], D.O.U. 22.08.1990 (establishing air quality standards for sulfur dioxide, nitrogen dioxide, carbon monoxide, ozone, total particulate matter, inhalable particles, and smoke) (Brazil); Ministerio de Ambiente, Vivienda y Desarrollo Territorial Resolución No. 601 de 2006 (establishing maximum concentrations for "criteria air pollutants": particulate matter sulfur dioxide, nitrogen dioxide, carbon monoxide, and ozone) (Colombia).

98. In Brazil, São Paulo's state environmental agency, CETESB, has established an interactive air quality monitoring program, QUALAR, which imports live data from a network of monitoring stations, making them available for public queries in real time. *See* CETESB, Qualidade do Ar, http://www.cetesb.sp.gov.br/ar/qualidade-do-ar/32-qualar (last visited May 29, 2013); Press Release, CETESB, QUALAR—um Novo Sistema de Informações que Facilita as Consultas sobre Qualidade do Ar, Sept. 22, 2009, http://www.cetesb.sp.gov.br/noticentro/2009/09/22_ar.pdf (last visited May 29, 2013). Mexico City has established a similar program, SIMAT. Secretaría del Medio Ambiente del Gobierno del Distrito Federal, Sistema de Monitoreo Atmosférico de la Ciudad de México, SIMAT, http://www.calidadaire.df.gob.mx/calidadaire/index.php (last visited May 29, 2013). Costa Rica has established a national monitoring network and publishes air quality measurements from stations in three cities—San José, Heredia, and Belén—in the major metropolitan area of the capital. *See* Decreto 30221-S—Reglamento sobre Inmisión de Contaminantes Atmosféricos (Costa Rica). Chile is also in the process of drafting policies

to improve air quality in major metropolitan areas that would include a network of monitoring stations. *See* Ministerio del Medio Ambiente, Gobierno de Chile, Eje Transversal: Regulación Ambiental, http://www.mma.gob.cl/1304/w3-propertyvalue-16237.html (last visited May 29, 2013).

99. *See* CONSEMA Deliberação No. 25, de 13 de junho de 2012, Manifesta-se favorável à minuta de decreto que estabelece novos padrões de qualidade do ar (São Paulo State, Brazil).

100. *See, e.g.,* Emilio Godoy, *The Waste Mountain Engulfing Mexico City,* GUARDIAN (Jan. 9, 2012), http://www.guardian.co.uk/environment/2012/jan/09/waste-mountain -mexico-city.

101. Ley General para la Prevención y Gestión Integral de los Residuos, D.O. 10.08.2003 (Mexico).

102. *See, e.g.,* Lei No. 12.305 de 2 de agosto de 2010, Institui a Política Nacional de Resíduos Sólidos, D.O.U. 03.08.2010, arts. 33–34 (Brazil).

103. Laws that contain provisions that span the gamut of requirements listed here include the following: Ley No. 24051, Régimen Aplicable a la Generación, Manipulación, Transporte, Tratamiento y Disposición Final de Residuos Peligrosos, B.O. 17.01.1992 (Argentina); Decreto Supremo No. 148, de 12 de junio de 2003, Aprueba Reglamento Sanitario sobre Manejo de Residuos Peligrosos, D.O. 16.06.2004 (Chile); Decreto No. 4741 de 2005, Por el cual se reglamenta parcialmente la prevención y el manejo de los residuos o desechos peligrosos generados en el marco de la gestión integral, D.O. 30.12.2005 (Colombia).

104. *See* Secretaría de Ambiente y Desarollo Sustentable de la Nación, Tabla de Restricciones de Ingreso Jurisdiccionales en Materia de Residuos Peligrosos, http://www .ambiente.gov.ar/archivos/web/URP/File/Promociones_Prohibiciones2_julio06.pdf (last visited May 29, 2013) (listing Argentine provincial laws prohibiting or restricting entry of hazardous wastes).

105. *See supra* note 62.

106. *E.g.,* Ley Nacional No. 24051, annexes I, II (Argentina); Decreto Supremo No. 148, de 12 de junio de 2003, arts. 17, 90 (Chile); Decreto No. 4741 de 2005, annexes I-III (Colombia).

107. *E.g.,* Ley General para la Prevención y Gestión Integral de los Residuos art. 19 (Mexico); Ley No. 8839, Ley para la Gestión Integral de Residuos, La Gaceta 13.07.2010, arts. 41–42 (Costa Rica).

108. *See* Lei No. 12.305 de 2 de agosto de 2010, arts. 33–34 (Brazil).

109. *E.g., id.* art. 33 (listing categories of products and packaging subject to reverse logistics requirements). The principal implementing authority, the Reverse Logistics Orientation Committee, is authorized to expand the set of covered products and packaging, and has initiated reverse logistics requirements for "packaging in general" and pharmaceuticals. *See* Ministerio do Meio Ambiente, Comitê Orientador Logística Reversa, http:// www.mma.gov.br/cidades-sustentaveis/residuos-solidos/instrumentos-da-politica -de-residuos/comite-orientador-logistica-reversa (last visited May 29, 2013) (describing the development of reverse logistics programs and listing working groups assigned to certain categories of products and packaging).

110. While there is no regional model, several countries have enacted laws governing the remediation of contaminated sites. *See, e.g.,* Decreto No. 94, de 15 de mayo de 1995, Reglamento que fija el procedimiento y etapas para establecer planes de prevención y de descontaminación, D.O. 26.10.1995 (Chile); Ley Provincia de Buenos Aires No. 14343, Ley de Pasivos Ambientales, B.O. 23.01.2012 (regulating the identification of responsible parties); Lei No. 13577, de 8 de julho de 2009, Dispõe sobre diretrizes e procedimentos para

a proteção da qualidade do solo e gerenciamento de áreas contaminadas, D.O.E. 09.07.2009 (establishing standards and procedures for soil quality and management of contaminated sites) (São Paulo State, Brazil).

111. *E.g.,* Ley General para la Prevención y Gestión Integral de los Residuos art. 2(IV) ("Corresponde a quien genere residuos, la asunción de los costos derivados del manejo integral de los mismos y, en su caso, de la reparación de los daños.") (Mexico); Ley No. 19300, de 1 de marzo de 1994, sobre Bases Generales del Medio Ambiente, D.O. 09.03.1994, art. 3 ("Sin perjuicio de las sanciones que señale la ley, todo el que culposa o dolosamente cause daño al medio ambiente, estará obligado a repararlo materialmente, a su costo, si ello fuere posible, e indemnizarlo en conformidad a la ley.") (Chile); Ley No. 8839 art. 45 ("Los generadores de residuos de cualquier tipo y los gestores tienen la responsabilidad de manejarlos en forma tal que no contaminen los suelos, los subsuelos, el agua, el aire y los ecosistemas.") (Costa Rica); Ley No. 24051 arts. 47–48 (providing for the liability of hazardous waste generators and managers for harms caused by their wastes, regardless of measures taken to transfer or avoid such liability) (Argentina).

112. Ley No. 25675 art. 22 ("Toda persona física o jurídica, pública o privada, que realice actividades riesgosas para el ambiente, los ecosistemas y sus elementos constitutivos, deberá contratar un seguro de cobertura con entidad suficiente para garantizar el financiamiento de la recomposición del daño que en su tipo pudiere producir; asimismo, según el caso y las posibilidades, podrá integrar un fondo de restauración ambiental que posibilite la instrumentación de acciones de reparación.") (Argentina). Brazil and Costa Rica have adopted insurance or financial guarantee requirements for those who manage or dispose of wastes. Lei No. 12.305 de 2 de agosto de 2010, art. 40 ("No licenciamento ambiental de empreendimentos ou atividades que operem com residues perigosos, o órgão licenciador do Sisnama pode exigir a contratação de seguro de responsabilidade civil por danos causados ao meio ambiente ou à saúde pública.") (Brazil); Ley No. 8839 art. 45 ("[L]as instalaciones de disposición final de residuos deberán contar con garantías financieras para [. . .] de ser necesario, realizar la remediación del sitio si los niveles de contaminación en él representan un riesgo para la salud o el ambiente.") (Costa Rica).

113. Ley General para la Prevención y Gestión Integral de los Residuos art. 71 (Mexico).

114. Mexico, Peru, and the Brazilian states of São Paulo and Minas Gerais have all undertaken contaminated site inventories in the past five to ten years.

115. Both Argentina and Peru have instituted nationwide programs for the remediation of abandoned mine sites. Ley 24.585, de Protección Ambiental (Código de Minería), 24.11.1995, art. 18 (assigning liability for rehabilitation of contaminated mine sites) (Argentina); Ley 28271, Ley que Regula los Pasivos Ambientales de la Actividad Minera, D.O. 02.07.2004 (establishing a framework to inventory and assign liability for contaminated mine sites) (Peru); *see also* Ley 29134, Ley que Regula los Pasivos Ambientales del Subsector Hidrocarburos, D.O. 17.11.2007 (establishing a framework to inventory and assign liability for contaminated petroleum development sites) (Peru). Argentina is also home to the most notorious contaminated zone in Latin America, the Matanza-Riachuelo Basin. *See supra* note 44. In 2006, Law No. 26168 created the Matanza-Riachuelo Basin Authority (ACUMAR) to be the principal environmental authority of the contaminated zone. Ley No. 26168, Créase la Autoridad de Cuenca Matanza Riachuelo como ente de derecho público interjurisdiccional en el ámbito de la Secretaría de Ambiente y Desarrollo Sustentable de la Jefatura de Gabinete de Ministros, B.O. 05.12.2006. ACUMAR has forced facilities to take various corrective measures, including remediation of soils and groundwater, by requiring companies to submit Industrial Reconversion Plans (Programas de Reconversión Industrial) that address remediation, and to obtain environmental

insurance (and thus to take the steps necessary to become insurable), and ordering the closure of noncompliant facilities. *See* Resolución ACUMAR No. 278, B.O. 21.09.2010, annex II art. 7 (enumerating the required elements of Industrial Reconversion Plans) (Argentina); Resolución ACUMAR No. 372, B.O. 01.10.2010, arts. 1–3 (requiring facilities to present environmental insurance policies, per Ley No. 25675, de 6 de noviembre de 2002, Politica Ambiental Nacional, B.O. 27.11.2002, art. 22, as a condition of approval of an Industrial Reconversion Plan) (Argentina).

116. Lei No. 13577, de 8 de julho de 2009, arts. 30–37 (authorizing the Fundo Estadual para Prevenção e Remediação de Áreas Contaminadas—FEPRAC) & art. 32 (reimbursement provision) (São Paulo State, Brazil). In contrast, Costa Rica's 2010 General Waste Law provides for the government—the Ministry of Health, in conjunction with the relevant municipal authority and any other authorities—to manage any acute risks to human health and the environment, in cases in which the polluter cannot be identified. Ley No. 8839 art. 46.

117. Decreto No. 59263, de 5 de junho de 2013, Regulamenta a Lei No. 13.577, de 09 de julho de 2009 que dispõe sobre diretrizes e procedimentos para a proteção da qualidade do solo e gerenciamento de áreas contaminadas, art. 97 ("O licenciamento de empreendimentos em áreas que anteriormente abrigaram atividades com potencial de contaminação, ou suspeitas de estarem contaminadas, deverá ser precedido de estudo de passivo ambiental, submetidos previamente ao órgão ambiental competente.") D.D.E. 06.06.2013 (São Paulo State, Brazil).

118. For example, in 2010, Latin America produced 45 percent of the world's copper, 16 percent of the world's iron ore, 15 percent of the world's nickel, and 26 percent of the world's tin. Susan Wacaster et al., The Mineral Industries of Latin America and Canada, in U.S. Geological Survey 2010 Minerals Yearbook: Latin America and Canada, tbl.4 (July 2012), http://minerals.usgs.gov/minerals/pubs/country/2010/myb3 -sum-2010-latin-canada.pdf.

119. FAO, Global Capture Production Statistics Updated to 2011 Data, tbl. 2 (2013), ftp://ftp.fao.org/FI/news/GlobalCaptureProductionStatistics2011.pdf.

120. *See, e.g.,* Guardian Env't Datablog, Total Forest Coverage by Country (Sept. 2, 2009), http://www.guardian.co.uk/environment/datablog/2009/sep/02/total-forest-area -by-country (last visited May 29, 2013) (indicating that Brazil had approximately 478,000 hectares of forest, surpassed only by Russia, with approximately 809,000 hectares).

121. Brazil's tropical forest extent is approximately four times greater than that of the next country, the Democratic Republic of the Congo. Mongabay.com, Largest Area of Tropical Forest, by Country, http://rainforests.mongabay.com/deforestation_forest.html (last visited May 29, 2013) (indicating that Brazil had approximately 478,000 hectares of tropical forest, while the Democratic Republic of the Congo had approximately 134,000 hectares).

122. Approximately 3,300 bird species are known from South America; approximately 10,000 globally. *See* Avibase—Bird Checklists of the World: South America, http:// avibase.bsc-eoc.org/checklist.jsp?region=sam. For comparison, the next most biodiverse continent, Africa, has about half the diversity in proportion to its size: 25.8 percent of the world's bird species and 20 percent of the land area.

123. *E.g.,* Ley No. 28216, de Protección al Acceso a la Diversidad Biológica Peruana y los Conocimientos Colectivos de los Pueblos Indígenas, D.O. 07.04.2004 (Peru); Proyecto de Decreto XX del XX de 2011, por el cual se reglamenta el acceso a los recursos genéticos, sus productos derivados y el componente intangible asociado y la distribución justa y equitativa de beneficios derivados de su utilización y se dictan otras disposiciones (Colombia), http://www.minambiente.gov.co/documentos/DocumentosBiodiversidad/proyectos _norma/proyectos/2012/250412_proy_dec_recursos_geneticos.pdf.

124. Lei No. 4771, de 15 de setembro de 1965, Código Florestal, D.O.U. 16.09.1965, *superseded by* Lei 12651 de 25 de maio de 2012, Dispõe sobre a proteção da vegetação nativa, D.O.U. 28.05.2012 (Brazil).

125. Lei No. 9605, de 12 de fevereiro de 1999, Dispõe sobre as sanções penais e administrativas derivadas de condutas e atividades lesivas ao meio ambiente, D.O.U. 03.02.1998 (Brazil).

126. Ley 24.585, de Protección Ambiental (Codigo de Minería), B.O. 24.11.1995, art. 18 (assigning liability for rehabilitation of contaminated mine sites) (Argentina); Decreto Supremo No. 016-93-EM, Reglamento para la Protección Ambiental en la Actividad Minera-Metalurgica, D.O. 02.06.1993 (requiring environmental impact studies and setting environmental management standards for mining operations) (Peru); Ley No. 28271, Ley que Regula los Pasivos Ambientales de la Actividad Minera, D.O. 02.07.2004 (establishing a framework to inventory and assign liability for contaminated mine sites) (Peru).

127. *See, e.g.,* Joel Parshall, *Presalt Propels Brazil into Oil's Front Ranks,* J. Petroleum Tech. (Apr. 2010), http://www.spe.org/jpt/print/archives/2010/04/13Brazil.pdf.

128. As of 2011, Brazil accounted for 23 percent of global biofuel production (438,000 of the 1,897,000 world total barrels per day), second only to the United States. U.S. Energy Info. Admin., International Energy Statistics, http://www.eia.gov/ies (last visited May 29, 2013).

129. Brazil formally launched its large-scale biodiesel program in 2005 with the enactment of Lei 11097, de 13 de janeiro de 2005, sobre a Introdução do Biodiesel na Matriz Energética Brasileira, D.O.U. 15.01.2005. While certain tropical plants such as palm oil, jatropha have been touted for higher potential per-acre yields, Brazil continues to rely on soybeans as the predominant feedstock for producing biodiesel. USDA Foreign Agric. Serv., Brazil Biofuels Annual Report § 4.2 (Aug. 12, 2012), http://gain.fas.usda.gov /Recent%20GAIN%20Publications/Biofuels%20Annual_Sao%20Paulo%20ATO_Brazil _8-21-2012.pdf (last visited May 29, 2013).

130. Ministerio de Minas e Energia, Secretaria de Planejamento e Desenvolvimento Energético, Plano Decenal de Expansão de Energia 2020, at 59, tbl.42 (indicating that at the end of 2009 Brazil derived 71.7 percent of its electricity from hydroelectric projects) (2011) (Brazil), *available at* http://www.cogen.com.br/paper/2011/PDE_2020.pdf.

131. *Id.* at 69, tbls. 48–49 (listing 30 hydroelectric projects, including ten Amazonian dams, expected to begin operating between 2016 and 2020).

132. *E.g.,* Ley para el Aprovechamiento Sustentable de la Energía, D.O.F. 28.11.2008, art. 23 ("Los equipos y aparatos que requieran del suministro de energía para su funcionamiento y que cumplan con los criterios que se señalen en el Reglamento, deberán incluir de forma clara y visible información sobre su consumo energético") (Mexico); Ley No. 18957, Uso Eficiente de la Energía en el Territorio Nacional, D.O. 16.10.2009, art. 12 ("Sólo podrá comercializarse en el país el equipamiento que utilice energía para su funcionamiento que incluya información normalizada de aplicación nacional referente al consumo y desempeño energético mediante etiquetas o sellos de eficiencia energética.") (Uruguay); Decreto No. 298 de 2005, Aprueba Reglamento para la Certificación de Productos Electricos y Combustibles, D.O. 01.02.2006, art. 2 (Chile).

133. *See, e.g.,* Ministerio de Industria, Energía y Minería Decreto No. 309/011, de 24 de agosto de 2011, art. 1 (providing for 150 megawatts of electrical power to be contracted to wind generators, and for contracting an additional 150 megawatts from wind generators by 2015) (Uruguay); BusinessGreen.com, Uruguay Set to Become World Leader in Wind Power, Jan. 7, 2013, http://www.businessgreen.com/bg/news/2234025/uruguay -set-to-become-world-leader-in-wind-power ("Uruguay has set its sights on becoming one of the world's leading wind power producers as part of plans to produce 90 percent of its electricity from renewable sources by 2015.").

134. *See, e.g.*, Ley General de Cambio Climático, D.O.F. 06.06.2012, arts. 1–2 (Mexico).

135. As of 2014, for example, Brazil was ranked third in the world for number of projects registered under the Clean Development Mechanism, and Mexico was ranked fifth. *See* United Nations Framework Convention on Climate Change Secretariat, Distribution of Registered Projects by Host Party (May 2014), *available at* http://cdm.unfccc.int /Statistics/Public/files/201405/proj_reg_byHost.pdf.

136. *See, e.g.*, Tom Phillips, *Brazil Pledges Deep Emission Cuts in "Political Gesture" to Rich Nations*, GUARDIAN, Nov. 10, 2009, http://www.guardian.co.uk/environment/2009 /nov/10/brazil-emissions (stating that, in preparation for the December 2009 United Nations Climate Change Conference in Copenhagen, the Brazilian government pledged to cut greenhouse gas emissions "as a 'political gesture' aimed at pressing rich nations into agreeing to large cuts in carbon").

137. *See* Lei No. 12187, de 29 de dezembro de 2009, Institui a Política Nacional sobre Mudança do Clima, D.O.U. 29.12.2009 (Brazil); Lei No. 13798 de 9 de novembro de 2009, Política Estadual de Mudancas Climaticas, D.O.E. 10.11.2009 (São Paulo State, Brazil); Lei Ordinária Estadual No. 3135, 5 de junho de 2007, Institui a política Estadual sobre Mudanças Climáticas, Conservação Ambiental e Desenvolvimento Sustentável do Amazonas, D.O.E. 05.06.2007 (Amazonas State, Brazil); Lei No. 13594, de 30 de dezembro de 2010, Institui a Política Gaúcha sobre Mudanças Climáticas, D.O.E. 31.12.2010 (Rio Grande do Sul State, Brazil).

138. *E.g.*, Secretaría del Medio Ambiente y Recursos Naturales, Instituto Nacional de Ecología y Cambio Climático, Inventario Nacional de Sustancias Químicas: Base 2009, http://www2.ine.gob.mx/publicaciones/consultaPublicacion.html?id_pub=684   (Mexico's pilot inventory of industrial chemicals) (Mexico). Costa Rica has a registration system for hazardous chemicals, requiring the chemicals to be registered with the Ministry of Health before being manufactured, imported, stored, distributed, supplied, sold, used, or transported. *See* Decreto Ejecutivo No. 28113-S, Reglamento para el Registro de Productos Peligrosos, La Gaceta 06.10.1999 (Costa Rica).

139. Argentina Senate Bill No. 3532/2008, for example, incorporated both WEEE and RoHS concepts, whereby producers and importers would have been required to design covered devices so that the six RoHS substances and other contaminants were reduced or eliminated. Proyecto de Ley del Senado No. 3532/2008 art. 16; *cf.* Projeto de Lei do Senado 173/2009, Estabelece prazo para que computadores, components de computadores e equipamentos de informática em geral, comercializados no Brasil, atendam a requisites ambientais e de eficiência energetic (would impose RoHS restrictions on computers and other information technology equipment) (Brazil).

140. *See supra* note 69.

141. *See supra* note 64.

142. *See supra* note 70.

143. ABNT NBR 14725:2013 (adopting GHS standards for terminology, classification, labeling, and safety data sheets on a voluntary basis, becoming mandatory for pure substances on February 3, 2013, and for mixtures on June 1, 2015) (Brazil).

144. Decreto No. 307/009, G.O. 03.07.2009, (adopting GHS labeling standards) (Uruguay); Decreto No. 346/011, G.O. 13.10.2011, art. 2 (extending the implementation of GHS labeling provisions for pure substances until Dec. 31, 2012, and for mixtures until Dec. 31, 2017) (Uruguay).

145. Norma Mexicana NMX-R-019-SCFI-2011: Sistema armonizado de clasificación y comunicación de peligros de los productos químicos, D.O.F. 03.06.2011 (Mexico).

146. *See, e.g.*, Resolución No. 1178 del Servicio Agrícola y Ganadero, D.O. 28.08.1984 (providing for the registry of pesticides for agricultural use) (Chile); Ley No. 73, Ley para Formulación, Fabricación, Importación, Comercialización y Empleo de Plaguicidas y

Productos Afines de Uso Agrícola, R.O. 22.05.1990, art. 9 (same) (Ecuador); Decreto No. 1843 de 1991, D.O. 22.07.1991, arts. 141–145 (setting forth the requirements for an application to register a pesticide product) (Colombia).

147. *See, e.g.*, Paula Pacheco, *Brasil Lidera Uso Mundial de Agrotóxicos*, Estadão do São Paulo, Aug. 7, 2009, http://www.estadao.com.br/noticias/impresso,brasil-lidera-uso-mundial-de-agrotoxicos,414820,0.htm (citing a study by the Kleffmann Group that found that the Brazilian pesticide market, valued at $US7.1 billion, was the world's largest, exceeding the US$6.6 billion United States pesticide market).

148. ANVISA, Gerencia Geral de Toxicologia, Programa de Análise de Resíduos de Agrotóxicos em Alimentos (PARA): Relatório de Atividades de 2010, at 7 (Dec. 2011), http://portal.anvisa.gov.br/wps/wcm/connect/b380fe004965d38ab6abf74ed75891ae/Relat%C3%B3rio+PARA+2010+-+Vers%C3%A3o+Final.pdf?MOD=AJPERES (reporting that ANVISA's program to reevaluate the use of pesticides in Brazil, begun in 2002, had resulted in bans on nine active ingredients and restrictions on seven more).

149. In 2012, Brazil reported a recovery rate of 94 percent of the pesticide packaging discarded nationwide. Press Release, Brasil.gov.br, Brasil É Líder em Reciclagem de Embalagens de Agrotóxicos (Mar. 25, 2013), http://www.brasil.gov.br/noticias/arquivos/2013/03/25/brasil-e-lider-em-reciclagem-de-embalagens-de-agrotoxicos (last visited May 29, 2013).

150. *See* Decreto 4704, de 4 de janeiro de 2002, Regulamenta a Lei no 7.802, de 11 de julho de 1989, que dispõe sobre a pesquisa, a experimentação, a produção, a embalagem e rotulagem, o transporte, o armazenamento, a comercialização, a propaganda comercial, a utilização, a importação, a exportação, o destino final dos resíduos e embalagens, o registro, a classificação, o controle, a inspeção e a fiscalização de agrotóxicos, seus componentes e afins, D.O.U. 08.01.2002, art. 10 (setting forth the data submission requirements for applications to register a pesticide product) (Brazil).

151. Mexico's biosafety law, for example, emphasizes the need for gradual, limited releases of GMOs into the environment and includes a substantial risk assessment component. Ley de Bioseguridad de Organismos Genéticamente Modificados, D.O.F. 18.03.2005, art. 9(III-IX) (Mexico).

152. Decreto No. 4680, de 24 de abril de 2003, Regulamenta o direito à informação, assegurado pela Lei no 8.078, de 11 de setembro de 1990, quanto aos alimentos e ingredientes alimentares destinados ao consumo humano ou animal que contenham ou sejam produzidos a partir de organismos geneticamente modificados, D.O.U. 25.04.2003, art. 2 (Brazil).

153. Ley No. 29811, Ley que Establece la Moratoria al Ingreso y Producción de Organismos Vivos Modificados al Territorio Nacional por um Periódo de 10 Años, D.O. 09.12.2011, art. 1 (Peru). Note, however, that while Ley No. 29811 states its purpose as a GMO moratorium, it provides significant exceptions for research, pharamaceuticals, and food, so the scope of the moratorium is significantly narrower than the law's caption suggests. *See id.* art. 3.

154. *See* Ley No. 300, Ley Marco de la Madre Tierra y Desarrollo Integral para Vivir Bien art. 23(7)–(9) (mandating the elimination of genetically modified crops), G.O. 15.10.2012 (Bolivia); Constitución Política de Ecuador 2008 art. 401 (declaring Ecuador to be free of transgenic seeds and plants, but allowing for limited exceptions in the national interest). In Venezuela, while GMO use is formally allowed subject to regulation, *see infra* note 120, there has reportedly been a government policy effectively prohibiting all uses of GMOs. Rubén Arachín, VoltaireNet.org, Venezuela Prohibe la Agricultura Transgénica, May 11, 2004, http://www.voltairenet.org/article120873.html (last visited May 29, 2013).

155. *E.g.*, Ley de Gestión de la Diversidad Biológica, G.O. 01.12.2008, arts. 50–55 (regulating the use of GMOs) (Venezuela).

156. *See, e.g.*, ADRIANA OTERO, USDA FOREIGN AGRIC. SERV., GLOBAL AGRIC. INFO. NETWORK, MEXICO: CENTERS OF ORIGIN FOR CORN PUBLISHED IN THE FEDERAL REGISTER 2 (2012), http://gain.fas.usda.gov/Recent%20GAIN%20Publications/Centers%20of%20Origin%20 for%20Corn%20Published%20in%20Federal%20Register_Mexico_Mexico_11-7-2012.pdf ("On November 2, 2012, the Secretariat of Agriculture (SAGARPA) and the Secretariat of Environment (SEMARNAT) published in Mexico's Federal Register an Agreement to Determine the Centers of Origin and Centers of Genetic Diversity of Corn in Mexico. [. . .] this agreement is part of the legal process required by Mexico's Biosafety Law and includes a map delineating the areas in seven northern states of Mexico where the use of GM corn seeds will be forbidden. In addition, the law requires very strict requirements with storage and movement of GM corn grains through the areas delineated as centers of origin.").

157. Parties to the Protocol and signature and ratification of the Supplementary Protocol, Convention on Biological Diversity, http://bch.cbd.int/protocol/parties/ (last visited May 29, 2013).

158. *E.g.*, Ley No. 740 de 2002, por medio de la cual se aprueba el "Protocolo de Cartagena sobre Seguridad de la Biotecnología del Convenio sobre la Diversidad Biológica," D.O. 29.05.2002 (Colombia); Decreto No. 5705, de 16 de fevereiro de 2006, Promulga o Protocolo de Cartagena sobre Biossegurança da Convenção sobre Diversidade Biológica, D.O.U. 17.02.2006 (Brazil).

CHAPTER 21

Argentina

ANGELES MURGIER AND GUILLERMO MALM GREEN

I. Introduction

Argentina is a federal, institutional democracy, with a constitution based on that of the United States. As a federal republic, Argentina is composed of provinces and one autonomous city, the City of Buenos Aires, where the federal government has its offices. Provinces retain all powers that have not been delegated to the federal government in conformity with the constitution.[1]

The Argentine Constitution, as amended in 1994, recognizes the right to a healthy, balanced environment; the principle of sustainable development; the "polluter pays" principle, whereby environmental damage generates the obligation to "restore"; the right to information; and a ban on the entry into the country of hazardous waste.[2]

Because the power to protect the environment basically falls within the police power, according to the federal structure of the constitution, such power is vested in the provinces, and only by delegation, in the federal government. Nevertheless, the federal government is vested with the power to legislate the minimum standards to be met throughout the country.[3] As a result, local laws enacted by the provinces and applicable in their own jurisdiction coexist with federal laws that apply to the whole country.

Regarding agencies with environmental jurisdiction, the national environmental agency is the Secretariat of Environment and Sustainable Development (Secretaría de Ambiente y Desarrollo Sustentable, SAyDS). SAyDS is subordinate to the Office of the Chief of Staff to the Argentine President.[4] Other national agencies that regulate environmental issues are the Secretariat of Energy (Secretaría de Energía) regarding fuel storage conditions and the Secretariat of Planning for the Prevention of Drug Addiction and Fight against Drug Trafficking (Secretaría de Programación para la Prevención de la Drogadicción y la Lucha contra el Narcotráfico, SEDRONAR) concerning chemical substances.

At the provincial level, the 23 provinces have environmental agencies (mainly at the ministerial or secretariat level).[5] And the City of Buenos Aires created its own environmental protection agency in January 2008 (Agencia de Protección Ambiental). In the Province of Buenos Aires—where the vast majority of the industrial activity is conducted in the country—the Provincial Sustainable Development Agency (Organismo Provincial para el Desarrollo Sostenible, OPDS) plays a very important role in environmental regulation and permitting.

In December 2006, the Argentine Congress created the Matanza-Riachuelo Basin Authority[6] (Autoridad de Cuenca Matanza-Riachuelo, ACUMAR), which is subordinate to the SAyDS. ACUMAR was created in the context of an especially large, extensive environmental contamination case heard by the Supreme Court of Justice (known as the *Riachuelo* case),[7] as an interjurisdictional agency with preemptive jurisdiction[8] over the river basin area of the City and the Province of Buenos Aires. Since its creation, ACUMAR has been very active in regulating standards, implementing reconversion activities in the basin, and enforcing environmental regulations.

II. Air and Climate Change
A. Air Pollution Control

At the federal level, the Air Pollution Law[9] applies to all sources, both stationary and mobile, capable of causing air pollution subject to federal jurisdiction and in all provinces applying it.[10] In actual practice, this law has been scarcely applied.

Pursuant to the provisions of the Transit Law,[11] the SAyDS is the authority with jurisdiction over the emission of gaseous pollutants, noises, and radiation originating from motor vehicles. The SAyDS has approved and adopted technical criteria and gaseous pollutant limits established by certain European Union (EU) directives.[12]

At the provincial level, many jurisdictions regulate stationary source emissions through concentration limits[13] and the granting of air permits. In general, local regulations do not establish differentiated standards based on type of activities and/or fuel used. Instead, regulations set forth standards applicable to all industrial facilities operating within a specific jurisdiction.

In the Province of Buenos Aires, gaseous emissions regulations[14] apply to all generators located in the provincial territory that emit gaseous effluents into the atmosphere. Such generators must request from OPDS an air permit to do so (*permiso de descarga de efluentes gaseosos a la atmósfera*). A generator's emissions must meet the values set in the regulations. Regulations stipulate how the effluent evacuation ducts must be designed and the places where samples are taken. Furthermore, they establish that it is compulsory for all industrial facilities to keep a book, certified by OPDS, recording emergencies or irregularities at the industrial plant. Notice of any foreseeable situation, representing an environmental risk, must be previously served upon OPDS. Those industrial plants that emit hazardous substances containing elements described in the Province of Buenos Aires' law on hazardous/

special waste must draw up control programs, keep a special record book, and measure the quality of gaseous emissions. The penalties for violating these rules are fines and preventive closure if there is sufficient evidence of a health risk.

B.   Climate Change and Ozone-Depleting Substances

Argentina is a party to the United Nations Framework Convention on Climate Change (UNFCCC),[15] the Kyoto Protocol to the UNFCCC,[16] the Vienna Convention for the Protection of the Ozone Layer[17] and the Montreal Protocol on Substances That Deplete the Ozone Layer (Montreal Protocol).[18]

The Argentine Office of the Clean Development Mechanism (Oficina Argentina del Mecanismo para un Desarrollo Limpio, OAMDL) was created under the SAyDS to implement more efficient actions related to the UNFCCC in support of activities to be developed by means of the mechanisms contemplated for such purpose by the Kyoto Protocol. In 2004, the SAyDS approved the rules of procedure for the national evaluation of projects submitted before OAMDL. The letter of final approval of the project is issued by the SAyDS.

In 2005, Argentina created the Argentine Carbon Fund (Fondo Argentino del Carbono) for the purpose of facilitating and fostering the development of projects under the Clean Development Mechanism, which was created under the Kyoto Protocol. The SAyDS is the enforcement authority for any activity related to the operation, management, and administration of the FAC.

Regarding substances that deplete the ozone layer, the Ozone Program Office (Oficina Programa Ozono), reporting to the SAyDS, was created in 1996. Argentina has established a system of licenses for the import and export of controlled substances, including the recovered, recycled, and regenerated substances listed in Annexes A, B, C, and E to the Montreal Protocol. According to this system, some substances that deplete the ozone layer are subject to an import quota. In order to obtain the relevant license, importers must apply for the grant of a quota and, in addition, be registered with the Registry of Importers and Exporters of Substances That Deplete the Ozone Layer (Registro de Importadores y Exportadores de Sustancias que Agotan la Capa de Ozono)[19] subordinate to the SAyDS since 2004. The SAyDS grants the import quotas (in order to establish the maximum quantities that may be imported by new or potential importers, the SAyDS takes into account the quantities allowed to importers with a historical record).

Late in 2004, the National Halon Bank, a subagency within the National Institute of Industrial Technology (Instituto Nacional de Tecnología Industrial, INTI),[20] was created by means of a joint resolution of the SAyDS and the Secretariat of Industry, Trade and Small and Medium Businesses.[21] This resolution provides that users reconverting their facilities to replace the use of halons must have such halons removed from the site by an operator of the National Halon Bank selected from the list of operators authorized by INTI (the resolution also sets forth the requirements to qualify as an operator).

Halon users whose facilities have been reconverted and whose quality has been approved and certified by INTI (and become part of the National Halon Bank) are eligible for the Certificate of Halon Removal issued by INTI.

III.   Water

In January 2003, the National Congress passed Law No. 25,688 regulating the minimum environmental protection standards for preservation, development, and rational utilization of water. Pursuant to the law, the term "water" includes water that makes up the aggregate streams and bodies of water, either natural or artificial, surface or subsoil, as well as that held in aquifers and underground rivers, together with atmospheric water. Additionally, some activities are deemed as "utilization of waters" by the law, such as the taking and diversion of surface waters, the dumping of substances into surface waters, the discharge of substances into coastal and underground waters, and the change of the physical, chemical, or biological characteristics of water. The law provides that a permit must be previously obtained to carry on such activities. It also stipulates that the SAyDS is vested with powers to establish the maximum pollution levels pursuant to the various uses of water, the environmental guidelines and standards concerning water quality, and to draw up and update the national plan for the preservation, development, and rational use of water. However, such maximum pollution levels have not been set by the SAyDS and the law has not been regulated.[22]

At the national level, the SAyDS has been vested with police power over industrial water contamination as stipulated in National Decree Nos. 776/92 and 674/89. These regulations are applicable to facilities located in the City of Buenos Aires and some districts of the Province of Buenos Aires (according to different criteria of territorial location and use of the sewer system currently operated by Aguas y Saneamientos Argentinos S.A., AySA). The regulations require entities to (1) obtain authorization to discharge waste matter into a receiving waterbody, (2) comply with all discharge quality standards,[23] and (3) submit an annual affidavit.

In general terms, the provinces control both water intake (from surface or underground sources) and liquid effluents discharges (from a quantity and quality standpoint). Water intake and liquid effluent discharge permits are generally granted by the local agencies, and mandatory liquid effluents standards[24] are ordinarily regulated differently depending on the different receiving waterbodies (e.g., sewer system, surface bodies of water, soil absorption, open ocean).

In the Province of Buenos Aires, the law on protection of water supply sources, watercourses, and water receiving bodies and the atmosphere[25] and its regulatory decree[26] prohibits the discharge of solid, gaseous, and liquid substances into the air or the water that may harm the public health or the environment. The law establishes that no industrial establishment may be licensed or authorized to start its activities—not even on a provisional basis—without first obtaining the relevant permit and the approval of the facilities for the supply of water and of the respective industrial waste effluents.

The regulatory decree establishes the minimum conditions to be met by liquid effluents discharged into the sewage system and into water sources or courses (temperature, pH, presence of floating substances, etc.). These regulations also establish that unauthorized discharges are prohibited and result in the imposition of penalties. In addition, the decree provides that, in the case of inspections, the owner is bound to make available certain information regarding the intermittent or continuous nature of the discharges, outflow time of the most polluting effluents, and volumes.

In the Province of Buenos Aires, the agency in charge of water issues is the Water Authority (Autoridad del Agua, ADA). Resolution No. 389/98, issued by the former General Administration of Waterworks (Administración General de Obras Sanitarias, AGOSBA), approved the quality standards of discharges of waste and industrial liquid effluents into different receiving bodies of the Province of Buenos Aires. The resolution contains two annexes. Annex I is a list of types of industries the effluents of which cannot be disposed of into absorbing wells. Annex II is a table containing the quality standards for maximum permissible discharges depending on whether effluents are discharged into (1) the sewer system, (2) storm pipes or surface bodies of water, (3) soils for absorption, or (4) open ocean. ADA Resolution No. 336/03 replaced the table included in Annex II to Resolution AGOSBA No. 389/98, changing the values of certain parameters (e.g., total nitrogen, organic nitrogen, chemical oxygen demand for discharges into the sea, total hydrocarbons).

The Province of Buenos Aires Water Code[27] authorizes the ADA, inter alia, to "regulate, supervise and control the activities and works relative to the study, collection, use, preservation and elimination of water." By means of Resolution No. 289/08 the ADA has established the prerequisites to be fulfilled to apply for permits for water treatment works and drinking water distribution works, and the collection, treatment, and discharge of effluents (liquid effluent discharge permit).

Under Resolution No. 162/07, the ADA approved the penalty system procedure for infringements of Law 5,965 and its regulatory decree as well as the methodology to assess the fines to be imposed on those discharging liquid effluents likely to harm the environment. ADA Resolution No. 162/07 specifies the grounds for revocation of liquid effluent discharge authorizations, which may be either temporary or final. It sets forth both general and specific causes for revocation of such authorizations. The basis for revocation of a liquid effluent discharge authorization arises when "due to its seriousness, [the discharge] poses a risk for the health of the population and/or the water resource." Specific causes of revocation encompass water resource risk, either directly or indirectly affecting the population, inexistence of effluent treatment facilities, and quantities in excess of the authorized volume. The resolution governs the submission of adjustment plans and remediation plans. Lastly, it provides for the methods to assess the fines to be imposed by the ADA.

In September 2007, ACUMAR approved mandatory liquid effluents standards based on those established by the ADA.[28]

In September 2013 the Executive Branch of the Province of Buenos Aires issued Decree No. 429/2013, which regulates certain sections of the Provincial Water Code, governing the water use fee, new water uses, and a tax on products with a water content of 50 percent or above.

IV.   Handling, Treatment, Transportation, and Disposal of Hazardous Materials

A.   Controlled Chemical Substances

Federal regulations on chemical substances[29] govern the activities of persons who "produce, manufacture, prepare, import or export authorized chemical substances or products that, due to their characteristics or components, may be illegally derived to serve as base for or be used in the manufacture of narcotic drugs."

Controlled chemical substances are those included in the lists approved by the regulations. The main obligations established by these regulations are to (1) register annually with a registry kept by SEDRONAR; (2) keep a complete, true, and updated inventory of each substance; (3) file on a quarterly basis an affidavit with the registry reporting any movements of chemicals, to report the specific place where the books are kept; (4) report to SEDRONAR any irregular or excessive losses or disappearances of substances or any transactions whenever there are reasonable grounds to consider that such substances could be used for illegal purposes; (5) contract with persons licensed by SEDRONAR; and (6) include in all commercial documents the number of registration with the registry and to seal off and label the packages (stating name of product, the degree of purity expressed as a percentage, unit of measure, number of registration with the registry, and the name or corporate name of the packer or repacker). The relevant regulations authorize SEDRONAR to impose penalties such as warnings, fines, and the cancellation or suspension of the registrations already made in case of violation of the aforementioned obligations.

B.   Hazardous Waste

At the federal level, vehicular transportation of hazardous materials is governed by the Transit Law, its Regulatory Decree No. 779/95, and supplementary provisions. According to current regulations, each hazardous good belongs to a specific class, according to the classification prepared by the United Nations for the transportation of hazardous substances. These regulations are applicable throughout Argentine territory and provide obligations to be fulfilled by cargo carriers and shippers (including, inter alia, having the necessary equipment for emergency situations; training the personnel involved; for shippers, providing the carrier with all the information about the hazardous product being transported, the risks related thereto, the safety measures to be taken during transportation, and the precautions to be taken in emergency circumstances; delivering to the carrier the goods duly labeled and packed for transportation; and, at all times, respecting the regulations in force). According to these regulations, the transportation of hazardous waste may only be made using vehicles and equipment whose technical characteristics and state of repair provide the safety that such goods require. The regulations also establish the minimum precautions to be taken to prevent accidents or reduce the effects of an accident or emergency.

Regulations issued by the SE[30] regulate the storage of fuels in underground and aboveground storage tanks, and establish certain requirements that must be complied with throughout the country, including registrations, external safety, technical and environmental auditing services, records, and so on. These regulations also stipulate the process that must be followed in case of leakages or spills. They basically provide for the obligation to report leakages or spills of more than 100 liters to the SE and to the environmental authority of the relevant jurisdiction within 24 hours after they come to the attention of the operator, and stipulate short- and long-term actions to be implemented once the existence of the leakage is confirmed (including the obligation to submit a pollution assessment plan and, if applicable, a corrective action plan, before the environmental authority of the relevant jurisdiction).

V. Waste and Site Remediation
A. Waste

Section 41 of the Argentine Constitution, as amended in 1994, bans the entry of hazardous waste into the country. This constitutional provision was adopted by many of Argentina's provinces in their specific constitutions or laws.[31] The Province of Buenos Aires has relaxed this prohibition while regulating the procedure and requirements for obtaining permits for treatment and/or final disposal of "toxic" waste generated outside its jurisdiction.[32]

In April 1991, Argentina approved the Basel Convention on the Control of Transboundary Movements of Hazardous Wastes and Their Disposal.[33]

In 1992, federal regulations addressed imports of nonhazardous waste destined for use as industrial supplies in the production processes of different sectors.[34] In 2002, the SAyDS established procedures and formalities for obtaining authorization for the import of nonhazardous waste as well as verification, consolidation, and control procedures to be followed prior to the export of hazardous waste.[35] Although not specifically stipulated in these regulations, several years ago the Unit of Cross-Border Waste Movements[36] developed a manual of procedures applicable to the export of nonhazardous waste.

The federal Hazardous Waste Law No. 24,051 (Ley de Residuos Peligrosos, LRP) was passed in January 1992 and implementing regulations were promulgated in Decree No. 831 in May 1993. The LRP is a benchmark in Argentine environmental legislation. Provincial jurisdictions have enacted their own regulations on hazardous waste based on the LRP and some provinces have adhered to the administrative provisions of the LRP[37] (LRP general provisions regarding civil and criminal liability apply throughout the country).

The LRP is applicable to the generation, handling, transportation, treatment, and final disposal of hazardous waste that is generated or located in places subject to national jurisdiction, or even if it is located in a province, when there is an intention to relocate the waste in question outside that province.

LRP defines the term "hazardous waste" as "any waste that may damage directly or indirectly living beings or contaminate soil, water, air or the environment in general." Specifically, hazardous wastes described in appendixes to LRP are considered particularly hazardous.

To control hazardous waste management, the LRP created the National Registry of Generators and Operators of Hazardous Waste (Registro Nacional de Generadores y Operadores de Residuos Peligrosos), with which all those who generate, transport, treat, and dispose of hazardous waste are required to register.

The LRP and its regulatory decree also stipulate that the generation, transportation, and final disposal of hazardous waste shall be registered in a document known as a manifest. The contents of this manifest are expressly regulated. It must include the nature and amount of waste generated, their origin, and their transfer from the generator to the carrier and from the carrier to the treatment plant or to final disposal, as well as treatment and removal processes to which they were subjected and any other operation performed in their regard.

Administrative penalties imposed because of violations of the LRP range from fines to the cancellation and suspension of enrollment in the registry. For a second offense, the penalties increase and, when incurred by legal entities or corporations, management officials are personally and severally responsible.

Federal Law No. 25,612, regulating the minimum environmental protection standards for industrial waste and waste generated by service activities (*Ley de presupuestos mínimos de protección ambiental sobre la gestión integral de residuos de origen industrial y de actividades de servicio*, LRI), was passed in 2002 and covers all industrial waste, hazardous or not. Although not fully implemented in this regard, the LRI governs throughout the Argentine territory the obligations resulting from the generation, storage, transport, treatment, and final disposal of industrial waste. By enacting this law, the National Congress attempted to replace and repeal the LRP. The national executive branch, upon promulgating the LRI, however, vetoed section 60 thereof that provided for the repeal of the LRP. At present both laws continue to coexist.

In general terms, the LRI imposes on local authorities the duty to identify the generators of waste matter and the obligation to keep registers in which the generators, carriers, and operators of such industrial waste and services must be recorded. In turn, the generators of industrial waste and waste generated by activities involved in the rendering of services must periodically submit a sworn statement informing the authorities about the nature of the waste generated and the processes by which it was produced. Similarly, it is mandatory for them to use a manifest to document any transfer thereof.

The administrative penalties imposed for violation of LRI range from fines to suspension and cancellation of record in the registries. In the case of a second offense, the penalties become more burdensome. Executive officers of infringing corporations are jointly and severally liable.

In the Province of Buenos Aires, Provincial Law No. 11,720, its Regulatory Decree No. 806/97 (as amended) and supplementary provisions govern the generation, handling, storage, transportation, treatment, and final disposal of special (hazardous) waste. Largely based on the LRP, these instruments establish that the origin, transfer of waste by the generator to the carrier and by the carrier to the storage, treatment, or disposal plant as well as the treatment and final disposal processes must be documented in a manifest, the contents of which are expressly regulated. Generators must obtain a hazardous waste generation certificate, file annual affidavits, pay a fee, keep a book to record all aspects of special waste management, adequately manage hazardous waste with authorized providers (treatment facilities and carriers), and adequately store hazardous waste in their facilities.[38] In case of infringement, warnings, closure of the facility and fines may be imposed by OPDS.

B.   Site Remediation

Regarding remediation of contaminated sites, at the federal level, in June 2006, the SAyDS created a program for environmental management of contaminated sites. The general purposes of the program are to (1) identify, systematize, describe, and quantify degradation processes caused by contamination and (2) define prevention, control, and restoration strategies for contaminated sites. In actual practice, this program has been scarcely applied.

At a provincial level, the Province of Buenos Aires was the first jurisdiction to regulate the remediation of contaminated sites. In January 2012, it enacted Law No. 14,343 to regulate the identification of environmental liabilities and the obligation to restore contaminated sites.[39] Law No. 14,343 places the responsibility to restore contaminated sites and assume liability on the parties who caused the damage or, if the person causing the contamination cannot be found, the owners of the property.[40] It also stipulates that any impaired environment constituting a contaminated site shall be restored to meet minimum environmental and public health conditions. The statute also provides that any person or official who learns about the existence of an environmental liability must report such liability to the enforcement authority.

The law similarly establishes that in case of final discontinuation or transfer of activities, the owner must file a closing audit. Owners must restore the site if the audit reveals "significant damage to the environment." The owner will be released from such obligation only if the enforcement authority unequivocally establishes that the affected environment has been restored to an appropriate environmental condition. Law No. 14,343 also establishes the minimum requirements concerning the content of these closing audits.

Law No. 14,343 provides a penalty system imposing certain penalties, such as warnings, fines, closure of the facility (final or temporary, total or partial), and deregistration from registries in the case of contaminated sites. The law establishes that the enforcement authority may order preventive closure, either totally or partially, of a contaminated facility or site in those cases where "the situation is so serious that it is advisable to do so."[41]

VI.   Emergency Response

See section IV, *supra*.

VII.   Natural Resource Management and Protection

Argentina has many laws regulating natural resource management and protection. Because a detailed description of these laws would exceed the scope of the chapter, this section provides a summary of the main regulations on forest resources management and protection and mineral extraction.

A.   Forest Resources

The national policy on management of forest resources is vested in two different agencies. Native forests are under the jurisdiction of the Forests Bureau, a subagency within the SAyDS, while forest plantations are under the jurisdiction of the Forestry Bureau, a subagency within the Secretariat of Agriculture, Livestock, Fishing and Food (Secretaría de Agricultura, Ganadería, Pesca y Alimentos, SAGPyA).[42]

1.   Native Forests

In December 2007, the National Congress passed Law No. 26,331 on minimum environmental protection guidelines intended to enrich, restore, preserve, utilize, and sustainably manage the native forests of Argentina and the environmental services they provide to society. In 2009, the Argentine executive branch issued implementing regulations.[43]

The law (1) created the National Program for the Protection of Native Forests;[44] (2) mandates that each jurisdiction conduct a Territorial Organization of Native Forests existing within their territory, establishing different preservation categories in terms of the environmental value of different units of native forests and the environmental services provided by them; (3) requires obtaining prior authorization from the enforcement authorities having jurisdiction in the relevant territory for all native forest clearing activities or sustainable management activities; (4) established three conservation categories with respect to native forests;[45] (5) established that any request for authorization to perform forest clearing activities shall be mandatorily subject to an environmental impact assessment (EIA), as well as requests for authorization regarding sustainable utilization whenever said activities "may potentially cause substantial environmental impact";[46] and (6) created the National Fund for the Enrichment and Preservation of Native Forests.[47]

In April 2009, the SAyDS issued Resolution No. 256/09 creating the Experimental Program for Management and Preservation of Native Forests. Under this program, the SAyDS grants, through the local enforcement authorities, non-reimbursable financial contributions to native forest owners who submit plans for sustainable management of such forests.[48]

All provinces except Buenos Aires have passed laws and regulations on native forests.[49]

2. Forest Plantations

In 1999 Argentina passed Law No. 25,080 on Investments for Cultivated Forests, fostering the establishment of forests through economic subsidies and tax benefits. Such subsidies and benefits were extended in 2008 by Law No. 26,432. The enforcement authority for this regime is the SAGPyA. It also encourages the development of new industrial forest projects (integration of forest plantations and industries) and the expansion of existing ones, as long as the quantity of lumber offered increases through the establishment of new forested areas. These projects require an environmental impact study and the adoption of appropriate measures to ensure the maximum protection of forests. The enforcement authority establishes which measures are appropriate and revise them annually in conjunction with the SAyDS, taking into account those lands that, due to their natural conditions, location, and characteristics, are capable of being forested in the manner provided in the Territorial Organization of Native Forests, as established by Law No. 26,331 for the purpose of ensuring the rational use of resources.

B. Mineral Extraction

The provisions related to environmental protection applicable to mining were established in 1995 by Law No. 24,585, as Title 13 of the Mining Code, as amended by Decree No. 456/97.

Section 233 of the Mining Code establishes that "[m]iners may freely exploit their mining concessions, without being subject to rules other than those pertaining to their safety, police and environmental protection. The protection of the environment and the preservation of the natural and cultural heritage in the mining activity field shall be subject to the provisions of

Part Two of this Title and to those laid down in due time as per Section 41 of the National Constitution."

By virtue of section 18 of Law No. 24,585, currently section 263 of the Mining Code, any person causing actual or residual damage to the environment shall mitigate, rehabilitate, restore, or repair it, as appropriate.

As regards environmental management instruments, the Mining Code establishes that those performing mining activities must submit to the (provincial) enforcement authority, prior to commencing any activity specified in the Mining Code, an environmental impact report. Likewise, said Mining Code provides for an EIA procedure, which may conclude with its approval through the issuance by the competent provincial authority of an environmental impact statement for each project or actual implementation stage. The environmental impact statement must be renewed at least every two years.

Each of the mining phases (i.e., prospection, exploration, and exploitation) must be evaluated through the submission of an environmental impact report. The minimum content of the environmental impact report for each stage is established by law. Once the project is environmentally approved, the provincial Mining Authorities monitor the fulfillment of the environmental conditions, commitments, and requirements arising from the environmental impact report and the environmental impact statement.

Persons engaged in the mining business that comply with environmental protection provisions may apply for an environmental quality certificate to the enforcement authority.

Noncompliance with the environmental protection provisions applicable to mining activities, unless it is punishable under criminal law, may result in the imposition of the following penalties: (1) warning, (2) fines, (3) suspension of the environmental quality certificate for the pertinent products, (4) remediation of the environmental damage, (5) provisional suspension of the mining activities (the suspension is progressive and, if three serious violations are committed, operations at the mining facilities may be permanently suspended), and (6) disqualification from acting.

VIII. Natural Resource Damages

See section XII(A), *infra*.

IX. Protected Species

In 1981 the Argentine Congress passed the National Law on Fauna Preservation No. 22,421, which declared the wild fauna temporarily or permanently inhabiting the Argentine territory to be of public interest, as well as their protection, preservation, propagation, repopulation, and rational exploitation. Such law also provides that all inhabitants of the country have a duty to protect wildlife. The government promulgated implementing regulations in 1981 and the SAyDS has enacted various resolutions regulating the export of fauna samples for scientific purposes;[50] the commercialization of wild fauna and the procedure for obtaining the export, import, reexport, and hunting trophy certificates; the exceptions to the prohibition to import wild fauna species and subspecies products;[51] and update of applicable fines.

As regards biodiversity, in 1994 the Argentine Congress passed Law No. 24,375 approving the Convention on Biological Diversity (CBD). The Biodiversity Preservation Task Force (a subentity within the National Environmental Regulations and Biodiversity Preservation Office of the SAyDS) is in charge of granting export, import, or reexport certificates for living specimens, products, subproducts, and derivatives of wild fauna,[52] and authorizations to access, export, or import genetic resources.[53]

The National Parks Administration (Administración de Parques Nacionales, APN), a decentralized agency under the purview of the Argentine Secretariat of Tourism, manages and ensures the preservation of biological and cultural diversity of certain protected areas under its jurisdiction through what is known as the National Protected Areas System (Sistema Nacional de Áreas Protegidas, SNAP). The APN manages the SNAP, one of the fundamental tools for the preservation of the biological diversity, the natural and cultural heritage, and the outstanding landscape features of the country.

The APN safeguards national parks, marine parks, natural reserves, strictly managed nature reserves, educational reserves, and natural monuments. In March 2003, the SNAP was created pursuant to an agreement between the SAyDS, the APN, and the Federal Environmental Council.[54]

The SNAP was aimed at integrating all terrestrial and aquatic, continental, or coastal and marine ecosystem zones, with defined boundaries and under some type of legal protection. It applies to all such areas under federal or provincial protection that are voluntarily registered in the SNAP.[55]

Argentina has also created what is known as the Protected Areas Task Force, which is in charge of implementing actions under the UNESCO Man and the Biosphere Program (MaB). The MaB Program Coordination Unit is also under the purview of the SAyDS. The National Network of Biosphere Reserves lists 13 biosphere reserves within the Argentine territory.[56] The first one was created in San Juan in 1980 and the most recent one in 2007 in the Province of Buenos Aires.

Also within the scope of the Undersecretariat of Environmental Planning and Policy of the SAyDS is an Aquatic Resource Task Force. Argentina has 21 Convention on Wetlands of International Importance Especially as Waterfowl Habitat (Ramsar Convention) sites, which in the aggregate comprise 5,382,281 hectares.[57] Argentina approved the Ramsar Convention in 1991, through the enactment of Law No. 23,919 (which became effective in September 1992, after the instrument of ratification was deposited).[58]

See section XI, *infra*, on those treaties and conventions that Argentina has ratified, which include the Ramsar Convention, Convention on International Trade in Endangered Species of Wild Fauna and Flora (CITES), and the CBD.

X. Environmental Review and Decision Making

At the national level, Law No. 25,675 on general environmental protection standards for the adequate and sustainable management of the environment, known as the Environmental Framework Law (Ley General del Ambiente, LGA), provides that any work or activity that, within the Argentine territory, may degrade the environment or any of its components, or significantly impair the quality of life of the population, shall be subject to an EIA procedure before any operations commence.[59] The LGA further establishes that the procedure shall begin with the submission of an affidavit stating whether the work or activities will affect the environment. Then an environmental impact study must be submitted by the project proponent. Thereafter, the authorities will make an assessment, and issue an environmental impact statement either accepting or rejecting the studies filed.[60]

There are federal rules that provide for mandatory EIAs for specific activities (namely exploration, exploitation, and transport of hydrocarbons, hazardous waste treatment and disposal facilities, public investment projects, and mining projects),[61] and provincial regulations on EIAs procedures. Provinces that have passed laws and regulations on EIAs include Buenos Aires (see *infra*), Catamarca, Chubut, Córdoba, Corrientes, Entre Ríos, Jujuy, La Pampa, La Rioja, Mendoza, Misiones, Neuquén, Río Negro, Salta, San Juan, San Luis, Santa Cruz, Santa Fe, Santiago del Estero, Tucumán, and the Autonomous City of Buenos Aires.[62] In some jurisdictions, the entity filing the project is required to hire only specially licensed environmental consultants to conduct the EIA.[63]

In the Province of Buenos Aires, Law No. 11,723 on the protection, preservation, improvement, and restoration of natural resources and the environment contains general guidelines concerning environmental protection and restoration. This law contains a specific chapter on EIAs stipulating that all projects causing or capable of causing any negative impact on the environment within the province and/or its natural resources shall obtain an environmental impact statement issued by the provincial or municipal environmental authority. The law makes a distinction between proposed works or activities submitted to the process of EIA by the provincial environmental authority[64] and those submitted by the municipal environmental authority.[65]

Industrial Settlement No. Law 11,459 governs all industrial facilities located in the Province of Buenos Aires. In order to conduct business, industrial premises must obtain the relevant Environmental Fitness Certificate (EFC) contemplated in this law. All industrial facilities are classified into three categories depending on their level of environmental complexity (*nivel de complejidad ambiental*, NCA). The NCA is determined by application of a polynomial formula taking into account, inter alia, the business of the facility, the type of effluents it discharges, and the nature of the risks generated (fire, explosion, chemical risk, noises, and risks posed by pressure vessels). Once the NCA is determined by the provincial environmental agency, the facility is requested to file before the provincial environmental agency (for what are known as category III facilities) or municipal authority (for what are known as categories I and II facilities) the following documents and reports: (1) a note requesting issuance of the EFC (containing background information on the company), (2) an EIA report, (3) liquid and gaseous effluent discharge permits, (4) documentation evidencing solid and semisolid waste management, and (5) documentation on pressure vessels. The EFC is valid for two years. An application for renewal must be filed within one month following expiration of the previous EFC, together with an environmental audit report and a statement confirming that there have been no changes in the conditions reported at the time the EFC was issued.

XI. Transboundary Pollution
A. International Transboundary Pollution Case Involving Argentina

One well-known recent international transboundary pollution case related to the conflict with Uruguay regarding the construction of two industrial paper mills in Fray Bentos, across the River Uruguay from the Argentinean city of Gualeguaychú. Argentina essentially claimed that Uruguay breached its obligations under the Statute of the River Uruguay, a 1975 treaty signed by Argentina and Uruguay, including "the obligation to take all necessary measures to preserve the aquatic environment and prevent pollution and the obligation to protect biodiversity and fisheries, including the obligation to prepare a full, objective study on environmental impact."[66] The case, known as *Pulp Mills on the River Uruguay (Argentina v. Uruguay)*, was decided in April 2010 by the International Court of Justice, with a final adverse judgment for Argentina.[67]

B. Treaties and Conventions

Argentina has ratified many environmental treaties and conventions. The following are the most relevant to the topics covered in this chapter.

- Convention on the Prevention of Marine Pollution by Dumping of Wastes and Other Matters (Law No. 21,947)
- CITES (Law No. 22,344)
- Vienna Convention on the Protection of the Ozone Layer (Law No. 23,724)
- Montreal Protocol on Substances That Deplete the Ozone Layer and amendments (Laws No. 23,778, 24,040, 24,167, 24,418, 25,389, and 26,106)
- Ramsar Convention (Laws No. 23,919 and 25,335)
- Basel Convention on the Control of Transboundary Movements of Hazardous Wastes and Their Disposal and amendment (Laws No. 23,922 and 26,664)

- United Nations Convention to Combat Desertification (Law No. 24,071)
- UNFCCC (Law No. 24,295)
- CBD (Law No. 24,375)
- Rotterdam Convention on the Prior Informed Consent Procedure for Certain Hazardous Chemicals and Pesticides in International Trade (Law No. 25,278)
- Kyoto Protocol (Law No. 25,438)
- Stockholm Convention on Persistent Organic Pollutants (Law No. 26,011)

XII. Civil and Criminal Enforcement and Penalties
A. Civil Liability, Strict Liability System

Argentina has enacted several laws establishing a stringent strict liability system that applies throughout the country:

1. The LRP governs the generation, handling, transportation, and treatment of hazardous waste and establishes a cradle-to-grave waste tracking system. Its general provisions regarding civil and criminal liability apply throughout the country.
2. The LRI regulates all kinds of industrial waste, and sets the minimum environmental protection standards to be met throughout the country. This rule applies to all industrial waste, whether hazardous or not.
3. Both the LRP and LRI establish a special system of responsibility for damages caused by hazardous and industrial waste, as explained above.
   a. They set forth a iuris tantum (i.e., rebuttable) presumption that all hazardous and industrial waste is considered dangerous, and as a result, warrants strict liability.
   b. These laws stipulate that the generator is responsible for damages caused by the waste produced, as owner thereof. This liability continues even after its delivery to the transporter or to the treatment or waste disposal plant. Accordingly, the LRP and the LRI establish that in neither case can liability be avoided by asserting that ownership of hazardous/industrial waste has been transferred to third parties or voluntarily relinquished.
   c. They establish that the owner or custodian of hazardous/industrial waste is liable for all damages caused and is not released from liability even after showing the negligence of a third party when the damage could have been prevented by exercising the due care required in view of the circumstances.
4. The law on general environmental protection standards for the adequate and sustainable management of the environment, known as the Environmental Framework Law (Ley General del Ambiente, LGA)

deals with, among other issues, environmental damage having a collective impact. The LGA establishes that the responsible party shall be liable for restoration of the environment to its prior condition, or if technically infeasible, then it shall be liable for substitute compensation for damages. The LGA also establishes that if two or more persons are involved in causing collective environmental damage—or if it is not possible to accurately ascertain to which extent each party has been liable for the damage—all of them shall be considered jointly and severally liable for remedying such damage. That said, parties may seek contribution from the parties involved. For this purpose, the acting judge may determine the degree of liability of each party. The LGA establishes that in case of "environmental damage with a collective impact," the exemption from liability will only take place in case

a. the damage takes place due to the exclusive negligence of the victim or of an independent third party, and

b. all measures intended to prevent the damage were taken, and there was no concurrent negligence.

The LGA also provides that if the damage has been caused by a corporation, liability shall extend to its authorities and professionals, to the extent of their respective involvement.

B.   Criminal Liability

As a general principle, a legal entity may not be held criminally liable pursuant to the Argentine criminal system. Argentine legislation exclusively contemplates the liability of the individuals who govern the company (provided that they have taken part in the unlawful act). The behavior punished by criminal law may be either willful or negligent. The main applicable criminal rules on environmental issues are set forth in the criminal code and in the LRP.

C.   Environmental Insurance

The LGA was passed in 2002, and, inter alia, requires that persons "engaged in activities that may endanger the environment, the ecosystems and their elements . . . obtain insurance with adequate coverage to ensure the funding of restoration activities intended to repair any damages caused" (section 22 of the LGA).

As a consequence of the *Riachuelo* case and media and political pressure, early in 2007 the SAyDS started enacting regulations on environmental insurance. In general terms, SAyDS regulations provide criteria to determine whether an activity is "hazardous to the environment" (and therefore, subject to the obligation to obtain insurance), contain basic guidelines for the contractual conditions to be met by insurance policies, and fix the sufficient minimum insurable amounts.

From August 2008 to September 2012, the only option approved by the authorities and available in the market was insurance bonds. Insurance bonds are intended to eliminate the risks of default in payment and, as a result, guarantee government authorities that entities will fulfill their obligation to restore environmental damage by adding a second debtor, in this case, the insurance company. There were only a few companies authorized by the Argentine Superintendent of Insurance (Superintendencia de Seguros de la Nación, SSN) and the SAyDS to provide the coverage that, according to the enforcement authorities, complied with the specific requirements of the LGA, in the form of insurance bonds. This triggered significant controversy, and local industrial chambers have unsuccessfully challenged its application before administrative authorities.

There were no insurance companies authorized by the SSN and the SAyDS capable of offering environmental liability insurance. Self-insurance was not regulated (and has not been regulated yet).

In September 2012, through the decree containing implementing regulations for the LGA, the Argentine president established that, to comply with section 22 of the LGA, two types of insurance may be purchased: (1) bond insurance against environmental damage with a collective impact and (2) liability insurance against environmental damage with a collective impact. Inter alia, the decree orders the SSN to prepare insurance plans to provide coverage in compliance with section 22 of the LGA. Such plans shall be governed only by the general and uniform conditions laid down by the SSN.

In late October 2012, through Resolution No. 37,160, the SSN approved (1) the general conditions of the mandatory bond insurance against environmental damage with a collective impact; (2) the general conditions of the mandatory liability insurance against environmental damage with a collective impact; and (3) the specific conditions for the mandatory types of insurance specified in (1) and (2).

The effects of Decree No. 1638/12 and Resolution SSN 37,160 were suspended by a judicial order issued in December 2012.[68] The practical effect of this judicial rulings is that, at present, the requirement to take out environmental insurance as provided in section 22 of the LGA may be fulfilled by taking out the bond insurance policy that was originally developed by an insurance company and approved by the SSN in August 2008.

Even though regulations on environmental insurance do not contemplate penalties, different agencies[69] and the courts (in case of judicial claims) may request that entities provide evidence that they have purchased environmental insurance.

Notes

1. Section 121 of the Constitución Nacional (National Constitution) establishes: "The provinces reserve to themselves all the powers not delegated to the Federal Government by this Constitution, as well as those powers expressly reserved to themselves by special pacts at the time of their incorporation." Pursuant to section 126 of the Argentine Constitution, the provinces are not authorized to exercise the powers delegated to the nation. Among other acts, the provinces are not permitted to enact civil, commercial, criminal, and mining codes.

2. Constitución Nacional § 41.

3. Starting in July 2002, the Argentine Congress passed laws on minimum environmental protection standards on the following matters: (1) industrial waste management (and waste generated by service activities); (2) polychlorinated biphenyls; (3) general environmental protection standards for the adequate and sustainable management of the environment, known as the environmental framework law (Ley General del Ambiente, LGA), (4) water, (5) free and public access right to environmental information, management of household waste of residential, urban, commercial, medical care, health, industrial or institutional origin; (6) sustainable use and management of native forests; (7) control of burning activities; and (8) protection of glacial and periglacial zones.

4. The current structure and goals of the SAyDS are regulated by Decrees No. 1919/2006, 135/2011 and Resolution No. 58/2007 issued by the Office of the Chief of Staff to the Argentine President.

5. The Argentine provinces are Buenos Aires, Catamarca, Chaco, Chubut, Córdoba, Corrientes, Entre Ríos, Formosa, Jujuy, La Pampa, La Rioja, Mendoza, Misiones, Neuquén, Río Negro, Salta, San Juan, San Luis, Santa Cruz, Santa Fe, Santiago del Estero, Tierra del Fuego, Antártida e Islas del Atlántico Sur, and Tucumán. Argentina also has one autonomous city, the Autonomous City of Buenos Aires.

6. Law No. 26,168, passed on Dec. 5, 2006.

7. This case deals with a complaint brought by Beatriz Silvia Mendoza and other plaintiffs (including non-governmental organizations) against the National Government (National Executive Branch), the Province of Buenos Aires, the Government of the City of Buenos Aires, and more than 40 companies that carry out their industrial activities around the Matanza-Riachuelo basin. The plaintiffs claimed compensation to restore the environmental conditions of the polluted Matanza-Riachuelo river. This major case and the Argentine conflict with Uruguay over the construction of two paper mills in Fray Bentos (on the Uruguayan side of the River Uruguay) placed the environmental issues in the spotlight of Argentine politics and media.

8. The scope and extent of ACUMAR's preemptive jurisdiction has been debated extensively, particularly as concerns its territorial jurisdiction over areas of the City of Buenos Aires and other municipalities of the basin extending beyond the geographic limits of the basin.

9. Law No. 20,284.

10. The Provinces of Chaco, La Pampa, Jujuy, and Mendoza, among others, adopted to the law.

11. Law No. 24,449, Decree No. 779/95, and supplementary regulations.

12. The technical criteria and gaseous pollutants limits established by European Directive 2005/55/CE of Sept. 28, 2005, for heavy-duty motor vehicles and the technical criteria and pollutant limits denominated as Euro 5-a in Commission (EC) Regulation No. 692/2008 dated July 18, 2008, for light duty vehicles have been adopted.

13. Including the Provinces of Buenos Aires, Córdoba, Mendoza, and Santa Fe.

14. Mainly Law No. 5965, Decree No. 3395/96, and Resolution No. 242/97.

15. Law No. 24,295 dated Jan. 11, 1994.

16. Law No. 25,438 dated July 19, 2011.

17. Law No. 23,724 dated Oct. 23, 1999.

18. Law No. 23,778 dated June 1, 1990.

19. Law No. 24,040, Decree No. 1609, and supplementary regulations (including SAyDS Resolution No. 953/2004).

20. The INTI is a subagency within the Secretariat of Industry, Trade and Small and Medium Businesses of the Ministry of Economy and Production.

21. Joint Resolutions Nos. 349/2004 and 954/2004 of the Secretariat of Industry, Trade and SMBs and the SAyDS, respectively.

22. In 2007, the Argentine Ombudsman issued a resolution recommending to the Chief of Staff to the Argentine President that implementing regulations for several laws, including this law, the Industrial Waste Law and the LGA (Resolution No. 39/2007), be promulgated.

23. Resolution OSN 79179/90.

24. Including the Provinces of Buenos Aires, Catamarca, Chubut, Corrientes, Mendoza, Misiones, Neuquén, San Luis, Santa Fe, Santiago del Estero, and Tucumán.

25. Law No. 5965 (*Ley de protección a las fuentes de provisión y a los cursos y cuerpos receptores de agua y a la atmósfera*).

26. Decree No. 2009/60 (as amended by Decree No. 3970/90).

27. Approved by Law No. 12,257 (Código de Aguas de la Provincia de Buenos Aires).

28. ACUMAR Resolution No. 1/2010 (as amended) approved the same standards established by ADA Resolution No. 336/2003, except for the standards applicable to ten-minute settleable solids, sulfurs, free chlorine, fecal coliforms, phenolic substances, nickel, cadmium, mercury, selenium, and lead. ACUMAR did not create standards for sulfates and total organic carbon.

29. Chiefly Law No. 23,737, Decree No. 1095/96, and Law No. 26,045.

30. Chiefly Resolutions No. 419/93, 404/94, 1102/04, and 785/05.

31. Provinces of Buenos Aires, Catamarca, Chubut, La Rioja, Neuquén, San Juan, Santa Cruz, Tierra del Fuego, and others.

32. Basically, the operators (and not the generators as stipulated by the prior resolution of 2005 on this matter) have the obligation to submit an affidavit as well as qualitative, quantitative, and toxicological chemical analyses of the waste matter to OPDS. Once the documentation is revised, OPDS will either grant or deny the permit requested by the operator.

33. Law No. 23,922.

34. Decree No. 181 and Resolution No. 946/1992.

35. Resolutions No. 946 and 896.

36. Since 1997, the SAyDS has had a Unit of Cross-border Waste Movements in charge of managing the cross-border movements of hazardous and nonhazardous waste.

37. Provinces that adopted the LRP include Catamarca, Cordoba, Corrientes, Chubut, Entre Ríos, Formosa, Jujuy, La Pampa, La Rioja, Mendoza, Misiones, San Juan, San Luis, Santiago del Estero, and Tucumán.

38. Regulations provide for technical requirements to be complied with by facilities where special waste is stored, establishing certain conditions to be met at the area where said waste is to be stored (waterproof floor, leakage collection and retaining systems, protection against fires, etc.) and establishing in detail the conditions under which storage is to be performed (covered area, distribution in groups according to waste type, containers labeling, etc.).

39. The Legislature of the Province of Buenos Aires has gone beyond other jurisdictions and even the Argentine Congress and passed several environmental laws (such as the law on electronic waste and equipment and this law on environmental liabilities).

40. Law No. 14,343 sets forth the following definitions:

1. *Environmental Liability:* Set of environmental damages, in terms of contamination of water, soil, air, deterioration of natural resources and ecosystems, caused by any type of public or private activity, during its regular operation or due to unforeseen events throughout its history,

which creates a permanent and/or potential risk to the population's health, the surrounding ecosystem and the property, and which has been abandoned by the responsible person. (The law also provides that a liability may be found both within the facility itself or in plots of land adjacent thereto, whether public or private.)

2. *Contaminated Sites:* Any site, the physical, chemical, or biologic characteristics of which have been negatively altered by the presence of contaminating substances of human origin, in concentrations that, based on the current or expected use of the site and its surrounding areas, entail a risk to human health and/or the environment.

3. *Restoration:* Remediation, sanitation, and other activities aimed at establishing safety measures, in order to prevent damages to the population at large.

4. *Remediation:* Task or set of tasks to be carried out at a contaminated site, intended to reduce the concentrations of contaminants, to return the site to acceptable risk levels, in furtherance of the protection of human health and integrity of ecosystems.

5. *Sanitation:* The restoration of a healthy condition at a site.

41. Although not a model of clarity, Law No. 14,343 also establishes that "when environmental damage has been produced or may be produced, the party liable therefor shall, without delay and without the need of any requirement or prior administrative procedure, take any preliminary action as may be necessary to remediate, restore or replace the natural resources immediately, notwithstanding any additional criteria established for the same purpose by the enforcement authority." Moreover, the law provides that within 24 hours of a contamination incident, the responsible party must report to the enforcement authority any urgent measures adopted and propose, for the authority's approval, any actions to remediate damage caused.

42. Global Forest Resources Assessment 2010, Argentina Country Report http://www.fao.org/forestry/fra/67090/en/arg/.

43. Many social organizations requested first the approval of this law and then the issuance of its regulatory provisions. This is a case that reveals the role and influence of non-governmental organizations in the development of environmental law and policy.

44. The main goals of the National Program for the Protection of Native Forests are to (1) promote the sustainable management of native forests having medium and low preservation values by establishing sustainable management criteria and indicators tailored to each area and jurisdiction; (2) foster the creation and maintenance of sufficient and functional forest reserves; (3) promote plans for the reforestation and ecological restoration of depleted native forests; (4) keep updated information on the surface area covered by native forests and their preservation condition; (5) provide enforcement authorities from different jurisdictions with the technical capabilities to prepare, monitor, supervise, and evaluate the Plans for Sustainable Management of Native Forests existing on their territory; and (6) promote the application of preservation, restoration, utilization, and organization measures as appropriate.

45. The following is a summary of the various applicable categories. Category I (red): very high conservation value areas, which are not to be changed (areas that should exist as a forest in perpetuity, even though such areas may be inhabited by indigenous communities and be the subject matter of scientific research). Category II (yellow): medium conservation value areas, which may be managed but which, in the opinion of the jurisdictional enforcement authority, may have a high conservation value through the implementation of restoration activities, and which may be subjected to the following

uses: sustainable utilization, tourism, collection, and scientific research. Category III (green): low conservation value areas, which may be altered in whole or in part. The law prohibits the clearing of native forests falling within categories I and II and aboveground burning of waste derived from forest clearing. The law also provides that any person (whether individuals or private or government-owned legal entities) requesting authorization to perform activities related to forest clearing or sustainable utilization of native forests within categories II and III shall subject their activities to "plans for utilization of changes in the use of soil" and "plans for sustainable management of native forests," respectively. Project proponents must draft such plans in accordance with regulations established as applicable to each region and area by the enforcement authorities having jurisdiction in the relevant territory.

46. "Substantial environmental impact" means significant adverse effects on the number and quality of renewable natural resources, relocation of human communities, location near populations, protected resources and areas capable of being affected, substantial alteration of the landscape and touristic value of a given area, and alteration of monuments and other sites that are of, inter alia, anthropological, archaeological, or historical value.

47. Pursuant to the law, a fund has been created to provide compensation to jurisdictions preserving native forests (due to the environmental services provided by them). The law further provides that each jurisdiction shall allocate 70 percent of those funds received to compensate landowners and the remaining 30 percent to the development and maintenance of a network of monitoring and native forests information systems, and to the implementation of technical assistance and financial aid systems aimed at promoting sustainability of nonsustainable activities from small-sized producers.

48. According to the SAyDS, since 2009 the Argentine federal government has made three types of contributions to the provinces for the protection of forests and sustainable forest management: (1) the National Fund for the Enrichment and Preservation of Native Forests (contemplated in Law No. 26,331); (2) the Experimental Program of Management and Preservation of Native Forests (SAyDS Resolution No. 256/09); and (3) the Territorial Organization of Native Forests (section 6 of Law No. 26,331). *See* http://www.ambiente .gov.ar/default.asp?IdArticulo=10019.

49. Catamarca (Law No. 5311 and Decree No. 1663/11); Chaco (Law No. 6409, Decree No. 932/10 and Disposition 534/12); Chubut (Law XVII N° 92, Decrees No. 91/09 and 639/12 and Resolution No. 13/2012); Córdoba (Law No. 9814 and Decree No. 2342/10); Corrientes (Law No. 5974 and Decree No. 1439/09); Entre Ríos (Law No. 8967); Formosa (Law No. 1552); Jujuy (Law No. 5676, Decree No. 2187, and Resolution No. 081/09); La Pampa (Law No. 2624, Decree No. 1026/12, and Disposition 231/12); La Rioja (Laws No. 9188, 6259, and 6260); Mendoza (Law No. 8195); Misiones (Law XVI No. 105 and Decree No. 374/12); Neuquén (Law No. 2780 and Decrees No. 1837/12 and 1078/09); Río Negro (Law No. 4552 and Resolution No. 02/12); Salta (Laws No. 7543 and 2785/09); San Juan (Laws No. 8174 and 8227); San Luis (Law IX-0697/09 and Decree No. 3220/11); Santa Cruz (Law No. 3142 and Resolution No. 470/09); Santa Fe (Law No. 12,366 and Decree No. 42/09); Santiago del Estero (Laws No. 6942 and 6841, Decrees No. 1830/08 and 1162/08, and Resolutions No. 1740/08, 514/09, 1020/09, and 1220/11); Tierra del Fuego (Law and Resolution No. 339/09); and Tucumán (Law No. 8304).

50. Resolution No. 620/98.

51. Resolution No. 437/06.

52. Resolution No. 1766/05.

53. Resolution No. 226/2010.

54. *See* http://www.ambiente.gov.ar/default.asp?IdArticulo=2895.

55. *See id.*

56. *See* http://www.ambiente.gov.ar/?IdArticulo=1492.

57. *See* http://www.ambiente.gov.ar/default.asp?IdArticulo=1832.

58. *See also* Law No. 25,335 (Nov. 2000) (amendments).

59. LGA § 11.

60. LGA § 12. Section 13 of the LGA establishes that environmental impact studies shall contain, at a minimum, a detailed description of the proposed work or activity to be carried out, the identification of its consequences for the environment, and the proposed actions to mitigate any negative effects.

61. Laws No. 24,354, 24,585, and LRP and Resolutions No. 105/92 and 186/95 of the Secretariat of Energy.

62. Catamarca (Resolution No. 146/2005 for the mining sector); Chubut (Law No. 4032/94, Decree No. 144/2009 and supplementary regulations); Córdoba (Law No. 2131/2000); Corrientes (Law No. 5067 and Decree No. 2858/2012); Entre Ríos (Decrees No. 4977/2009 and 3237/2010); Jujuy (Law No. 5063 and Decree No. 5980/2006); La Pampa (Decree No. 298/2006); La Rioja (Law No. 8355/2008); Mendoza (Laws No. 5961 and 6649/1999, Decree No. 810/2013 and supplementary regulations); Misiones (Law No. 35); Neuquén (Law No. 2267 and Decree No. 2656/99); Río Negro (Law No. 3266/1999 and supplementary regulations); Salta (Law No. 7070, Decree No. 1587/2003, and Resolution No. 998/2012); San Juan (Law No. 6571 and supplementary regulations); San Luis (Decree No. 4504/2011); Santa Cruz (Law No. 2658); Santa Fe (Decree No. 101/2003); Santiago del Estero (Law No. 6321/1996); Tucumán (Decree No. 2204/1991 and supplementary regulations); and the Autonomous City of Buenos Aires (Law No. 123, Decrees No. 13527/2002 and 222/2012, and supplementary regulations).

63. Province of Buenos Aires, La Pampa, La Rioja, Misiones, Salta, San Luis, and the Autonomous City of Buenos Aires, among others.

64. Section I of Annex II to Law No. 11,723 contains a list of projected works or activities subject to the environmental impact assessment procedure by the provincial environmental authority, namely (1) generation and transmission of hydroelectric, nuclear, and thermal power; (2) management of urban and suburban sewage; (3) settlement of industrial estates and complexes; (4) installation of third-category industrial facilities under section 15 of Law No. 11,459; (5) exploration and exploitation of hydrocarbons and minerals; (6) construction of oil pipelines, gas pipelines, aqueducts, and any other conduit of power or substances; (7) water piping and treatment; (8) construction of reservoirs and dams; (9) construction of highways, routes, railways, airports, and ports; (10) forest utilization of natural and implanted forests; and (11) hazardous waste treatment and final disposal plants.

65. Proposed works or activities submitted to the EIA procedure by the municipal environmental authority listed in section I to Annex II are the following: (1) except for those listed in item I, each municipality shall determine which activities and works are capable of causing any alteration in the environment and/or its elements within their jurisdictions, and which will be subject to an EIA; (2) irrespective of the above, the following projects shall be subject to a municipal EIA: (a) settlement of new neighborhoods or expansion of existing neighborhoods; (b) settlement of tourist and sports facilities, camps, and seaside resorts; (c) conventional and garden cemeteries; (d) building maintenance works, opening of streets, and road remodeling works; and (e) installation of first- and second-category industrial facilities under the provisions of Law No. 11,459.

66. *See* Press Release, Int'l Court of Just., Argentina Institutes Proceedings against Uruguay and Requests the Court to Indicate Provisional Measures (May 4, 2006), http://www .icj-cij.org/docket/index.php?pr=1010&code=au&p1=3&p2=3& p3 =6&case=135&k=88.

67. Pulp Mills on the River Uruguay (*Argentina v. Uruguay*), Judgment, I.C.J. Reports 2010, at 14, *available at* http://www.icj-cij.org/docket/files/135/15877.pdf.

68. This suspension was ordered by the judge of the Federal First Instance Court hearing Administrative Litigation Matters (and subsequently upheld by a Panel of the Court of Appeals in Administrative Litigation Matters) in a case initiated by a local

non-governmental organization (Fundación Medio Ambiente). The ruling essentially put in place a precautionary measure requested by the plaintiff and ordered the suspension of the effects of Decree No. 1638/12 and Resolution SSN 37.160 "until a final judgment is rendered or until there is a change in the circumstances that originated it."

69. Jurisdictions such as the Province of Buenos Aires and the City of Buenos Aires have issued regulations requiring entities to provide evidence of having purchased environmental insurance before they may obtain and/or renew environmental permits. ACUMAR has created a Registry of Environmental Insurance Policies.

CHAPTER 22

Brazil

LUIZ FERNANDO HENRY SANT'ANNA AND MARISE HOSOMI SPITZECK

I. Overview and Structure

The National Environmental System, known by its Portuguese acronym, SIS-NAMA, is a network of governmental entities charged with implementing Brazilian environmental policy. SISNAMA was established by the 1981 National Environmental Policy Act, and impacts environmental policy at the federal, regional, and local levels. Its main constituent entities are (1) the Ministry of the Environment (Ministério do Meio Ambiente, MMA), the central entity; (2) the National Environmental Council (Conselho Nacional do Meio Ambiente, CONAMA), which sets pollution standards and licensing requirements; (3) the Federal Environmental Agency (IBAMA), the executive entity in charge of law enforcement; and (4) these entities' regional and local counterparts.

The judicial branch is charged with reviewing executive branch administrative acts having an environmental impact as well as the constitutionality of environmental laws and regulations. Environmental matters and related civil and criminal claims may be subject to federal or state jurisdiction. Federal courts have jurisdiction over matters involving the federal government as a party (and its respective departments and/or agencies) and issues related to interest or property owned by the federal government (such as federal parks, federal rivers, or federal protected areas). All other matters are subject to state court jurisdiction. Both federal and state court decisions may be reviewed by two higher courts: the Superior Court of Justice (STJ) and/or the Brazilian Supreme Court (STF). Some state court systems include a special chamber for environmental matters, such as the court of appeals in the state of São Paulo.

Brazil is a civil law jurisdiction. Therefore, when judging environmental cases, courts emphasize application of codes and statutes rather than previous judicial decisions. That said, Brazilian courts tend to follow judicial precedent. Judgments also tend to take a while to be rendered, and can take more than a decade to reach a final decision. Such delays result principally from a lack of clarity in legal texts and a lack of technical and economic capacity among judicial experts (*peritos*).[1]

Standing in environmental cases is available to personally injured plaintiffs and, in cases involving environmental damage impacting the public interest, to district attorneys and non-governmental organizations (NGOs). Finally, authority to legislate on environmental matters is concurrent among the federal, regional, and local legislative bodies. The federal legislative branch, composed of the House of Representatives and the Senate, has the power to enact general rules that will be either enforced as enacted or supplemented by the states. Municipalities may legislate concerning issues of local interest but may not displace existing federal or state laws. CONAMA is charged with setting environmental standards. Its regional and local counterparts have the authority to set specific standards, provided that such supplementary standards are not less restrictive than those set by CONAMA.

II.   Air and Climate Change
A.   Air Pollution

Air pollution is one of the main environmental problems in Brazil, especially in urban, highly populated areas. This is due to vehicular and industrial emissions as well as, in agricultural areas, the practice of burning native vegetation to prepare soil for crops or cattle grazing. Brazil has adopted a command-and-control approach to air pollution control. Federal and state governments set and enforce air quality standards and emission standards for stationary and mobile sources.

On the federal level, the National Environmental Policy Act[2] establishes the authority of CONAMA to set pollution standards. On the state level, such authority is exercised by CONAMA's counterparts, which may not establish standards that are less restrictive than federal ones. The principle federal regulations that apply to air pollution control are CONAMA Resolutions No. 05/1989 and 03/1990. The former creates a National Program for Air Quality Control (PRONAR). The latter establishes air quality standards which control the emission of certain air pollutants (particulate matter, smoke, inhalable particles, SO_2, CO, O_3, and NO_2).

For stationary sources, the main federal regulations are CONAMA Resolutions No. 382/2006 and 436/2011. The former caps air emissions according to the type of pollutant and source, for stationary sources installed after January 2, 2007. The latter does the same for stationary sources installed before January 2, 2007. For mobile sources, the main statute to keep in mind is Federal Law No. 8,723/1993, which caps emissions of certain air pollutants (such as CO, HC^3, NO_x, and CHO^4). Equally important are CONAMA Resolutions No. 18/1986 and 418/2009. The former creates the federal Program for Automobiles Air Pollution Control (PROCONVE). The latter regulation establishes the basis for the state and local programs for the control and reduction of air emissions by vehicles.

At the state level, the São Paulo State "air basins" program is noteworthy. Considering that São Paulo is the most industrialized state in Brazil, air pollution related to stationary sources is of great concern. In this context, State Decrees No. 48,523/2004, 50,753/06, and 52,469/07 have created Air Quality Control Regions (air basins) and established conditions for the continued operation or installation of new stationary sources in areas classified as saturated or near-saturated ones.

B. Climate Change

Brazil is a party to the principle international treaties directly or indirectly related to climate change, such as the United Nations Framework Convention on Climate Change (UNFCCC), the Vienna Convention for the Protection of the Ozone Layer, and the Montreal Protocol on Substances That Deplete the Ozone Layer.[5] All of these treaties have been incorporated into Brazil's domestic legal system through statutes and regulations. The main greenhouse gas (GHG) emission sources and, therefore, main areas for potential emission reduction in Brazil are deforestation, which results from agroforestry exploitation, and the transportation matrix in urban areas, which relies heavily on petroleum-fueled vehicles.

Of special interest is Federal Law No. 12,187/2009, which establishes Brazil's National Climate Change Policy (PNMC). Following the UNFCCC guidelines for attribution of responsibility among state parties, the PNMC establishes a national voluntary commitment to reduce the nation's GHG emissions between 36.1 percent and 38.9 percent by 2020.[6] At the state level, the Amazonas Climate and Conservation Law, No. 3135/2007, first addressed the subject.[7] This statute established guidelines for the development of government incentives and market instruments to foster conservation. Measures include the grant of a Forest Allowance, which functions as payment for environmental services flowing from forest conservation on private property, as well as tax and licensing benefits for deforestation-related emission reduction and clean energy-related emission reduction projects.[8]

III. Water

The Brazilian Constitution establishes the basis for distribution of authority over waters between the federal government and the states. Lakes, rivers, and other watercourses that are on federal lands, that cross more than one state, or that serve as or cross international borders are under federal jurisdiction, as is the territorial sea.[9] States retain authority over all other waters, including superficial or underground waters.[10]

Laws and regulations concerning water issues are abundant. The authorities of which the practitioner needs primarily to be aware are (1) the 1934 Water Code (Federal Decree No. 24,643/1934), and (2) the 1997 National Water Policy (Federal Law No. 9,433/1997). The former was the first law to regulate public and private uses of water. The latter governs water use based on the concept of water as a limited natural resource of public domain, with an economic value. Under the 1934 Water Code, management is decentralized and shared by public authorities, users, and communities. The more recent 1997 National Water Policy law was the first law to regulate public and private uses of water.

In 2000, Brazil created the Federal Water Agency (Agência Nacional de Águas, ANA) to modernize water management (Federal Law No. 9,984/2000). The agency is under the Ministry of the Environment and has regulation and enforcement powers over water management. In practice, the ANA's principle functions are to control the public and private use of waters for irrigation, power generation and sanitation, among others, through the issuance of water grants and the charging of water use fees. The ANA's state counterparts have the same functions. In addition, the National Water Policy introduced the concept of Water Basin Committees as the unit for water management issues. These committees discuss and arbitrate water use conflicts and are composed of stakeholder representatives. Finally, a specific National Policy on Ocean Resources was created in 2005 (Federal Decree No. 5,377/2005) in order to guide the exploration and development of living, mineral, and energy resources of oceanic waters and the continental shelf.

IV.   Handling, Treatment, Transportation, and Disposal of Hazardous Materials

The purchase, storage, use, and final disposal of chemicals and other hazardous substances in Brazil is subject to governmental authorizations, due to environmental and national security issues.

On the environmental side, Brazil is a party to the main international treaties on the subject, such as the Stockholm Convention on Persistent Organic Pollutants (Stockholm Convention) and the Basel Convention on the Control of Transboundary Movements of Hazardous Wastes and Their Disposal (Basel Convention).[11] All of these treaties have been adopted and implemented via domestic laws and regulations.

Federal Decree No. 5,472/2005, for example, establishes that the Stockholm Convention "shall be implemented and complied with [in Brazil] as a whole."[12] Different initiatives have been adopted for this purpose, such as the creation of the National Commission on Chemical Safety (NCCS). The NCCS is a multistakeholder forum that defines the national plan for implementation of certain aspects of the Stockholm Convention. In particular, the NCCS works to improve systems designed to control activities related to the use of chemicals, and define a National Plan for the Prevention, Preparation, and Rapid Response to Environmental Emergencies with Dangerous Chemicals.

These high-level initiatives are implemented at the local level through specific environmental license and authorization requirements as to those activities that use or generate chemical and hazardous substances, whether as raw material, product, or waste.

Finally, on the national security side, Federal Law No. 10,357/2001 and Federal Decree No. 3,665/2000 establish the list of substances used in the production of narcotics and explosives and, therefore, are subject to control by the Ministry of Justice (through the Federal Police) and/or by the Ministry of Defense (through the Army).

V.   Waste and Site Remediation

The National Solid Waste Policy Act (Federal Law No. 12,305/2010; PNRS) was enacted in August 2010 to compile the existing but scattered guidelines for regulation of the handling, treatment, and final disposal of hazardous waste. The law also served to establish new guidelines for certain types of nonhazardous waste. Its main innovation is the legal recognition of shared liability for the life cycle of products as a basic principle of waste management policy. Based on this principle, the PNRS establishes obligations on not only public sector waste managers, but also on consumers, retailers, wholesalers, manufacturers, and importers. For certain products considered to have a high potential to pollute (e.g., pesticide packaging, batteries, tires, lubricating oils, fluorescent lamps, and electronic products), the PNRS establishes a separate management system that is independent of public sanitation services.

For hazardous waste, the PNRS and the existing regulation adopts a "cradle to grave" approach. Generation, handling, transportation, treatment, and disposal of hazardous waste are limited to licensed facilities.

With regards to contamination, the regulatory scheme comprises both preventive and correctional aspects. The preventive aspects are based on the establishment of quality criteria and limits on the presence of contaminant substances on soil and waters. The correctional aspects are based on the polluter's liability for remediation of the relevant environmental damages and/ or indemnification of affected third parties.

The state of São Paulo was the first in Brazil to regulate remediation of contaminated areas. At first, management of contaminated areas was subject to administrative rules established by the state environmental agency (CETESB), chiefly the Board of Directors Decision No. 103/2007, which approved CETESB's Manual for Management of Contaminated Areas. This manual is still used as a benchmark for other states in Brazil. Later, in 2009, such administrative rules were almost entirely subsumed into a state law (State Law No. 13,577/2009), which established procedures for identifying and mapping of contaminated areas and implementing mechanisms for remediation purposes. According to this law, not only the agent that caused the contamination but also the owner, tenant, holder of effective title, and/ or whoever benefited economically from the contaminated area may be held liable for the investigation and remediation thereof.

Finally, at the federal level, management of contaminated areas is regulated by Resolution CONAMA No. 420/2009, which is not as comprehensive as São Paulo state's State Law No. 13,577/2009.

VI.   Emergency Response

The National Environmental Policy (Federal Law No. 6,938/1981) establishes the legal duty of entrepreneurs to restore, minimize impacts of, or bring to a halt environmental damages flowing from their activities.

In this context, further laws and regulations have been enacted in order to detail the obligation to develop and keep an emergency plan for certain activities that may involve accidents with a high potential to pollute.

One example is the individual emergency plan for accidents involving oil pollution in federal waters, created and regulated by Federal Law No. 9,966/2000 and CONAMA Resolution No. 398/2008. The plan is a set of measures that determine and establish the responsibilities of each sector involved. These measures also determine those actions that must be taken immediately after an accident occurs, and define the adequate material and human resources to prevent, control, and curb water pollution (Article 2, XIX). According to the CONAMA Resolution, ports, ports' installations, terminals, platforms, support installations, as well as land drills, refineries, marines, nautical clubs, and similar installations must present Individual Emergency Plans.

A second and last example is the plan for barrier safety, applicable to hydropower plants. Given the massive generation and use of hydropower in Brazil, accidents that may occur involving river barriers are of concern. Therefore, Federal Law No. 12,234/2010 created the National Barriers' Safety Policy, aimed at fostering a culture of safety and risk management.[13] This law establishes the obligation to present a safety plan that may include emergency measures, as per the licensing environmental agency's criterion, as a condition for the installation of a river barrier.

VII.   Natural Resource Management and Protection

Historically, Brazilian environmental laws and regulations have been enacted to address specific issues. As a consequence, the first basic environmental statutes in Brazil have been scattered and related to the exploitation of specific natural resources, such as water (1934 Water Code—Federal Decree No. 24,643/1934), forests (1965 Forest Code—Federal Law No. 4,771/1965, currently superseded by Federal Law No. 12,651/2012), and minerals (1967 Mining Code—Federal Decree Law No. 227/1967).

Integration came later, with the National Environmental Policy Act (Federal Law No. 6,938/1981), which listed the atmosphere, interior waters (superficial and groundwater), estuaries, territorial sea, soils, elements of the biosphere, fauna, and flora as environmental resources to be protected thereby. It also established guidelines for the protection, and required a license prior to exploitation of these resources.

In addition, the Environmental Crimes Law (Federal Law No. 9,605/1998) and its regulation (Federal Decree No. 6,514/2008) define acts related to such resources that are to be considered as environmental crimes and/or administrative violations, resulting in the imposition of penalties.

In Brazil, major conflicts arise out of economic activities that demand intense use of natural resources. Examples are hydropower generation, upon damming of rivers, flooding of forest areas for installation of water reservoirs, and occupation of indigenous lands; and cattle ranching, soybean farming, and illegal logging, upon deforestation of large areas. Industry-related issues are mostly related to soil and groundwater contamination, air pollution, waste generation, and postconsumption liability.

In Brazil natural resource management is related to land management. Land management regulation in Brazil is relatively comprehensive when compared to other natural resources. Regulation covers rural and urban lands, as well as forest and otherwise protected lands. Regulation of rural land started in 1964 with the Land Statute (Federal Law No. 4,504/1964) and focused on land reform and implementation of an agricultural policy.

Management of urban land is regulated by Federal Law No. 6,766/1979. This statute establishes general rules for the distribution of land in urban areas, which is subject to additional local zoning laws and regulations.

The Forest Code, originally passed in 1965, underwent a substantial reform in 2012 with the enactment of Federal Law No. 12,561/2012. This reform was controversial due to challenges posed by the polarized interests of preservationists and rural producers.[14] The Forest Code protects areas of environmental interest on private property, such as zones known as "legal reserve" and "permanent protection areas" (APP). The legal reserve is an area located on a rural property preserved for the conservation of native flora and fauna and/or sustainable use of natural resources. Depending on the location of the property, the legal reserve may correspond to 20 to 80 percent of the total area of the property. APPs, for their part, are areas to be protected due to specific environmental functions (e.g., river margins, hilltops, and mangroves). As a general rule, development of APPs is forbidden, except in cases of public interest, social interest, or demonstrated low environmental impact. Any such use is subject to prior licensing.

In 2006, Brazil passed an innovative statute adopting a new approach to public forest exploitation. Federal Law No. 11,284/2006 regulates the management of public forests for sustainable production, and allows for exploitation of natural resources by private parties under a concessionary regime. Finally, Federal Law No. 9,985/2000 establishes the National Conservation Units System. Under this law, conservation units are created for areas with significant natural characteristics. A special administrative regime applies in such areas defining those restrictions that apply to each category of conservation unit. Permissible development in those areas depends on the applicable conservation unit category and the respective uses permitted by law and by that category's managing plan. Specific authorization from the authority in charge of the protection unit is required.[15]

VIII.   Natural Resource Damages

As with natural resources, governmental policy relies heavily on enforcement and sanctioning rather than on prevention. In case of damages, in addition to civil liability for remediation of the environment and indemnification of affected third parties, the entity or individual causing the damage may also be subject to criminal and administrative sanctions. If damages took place in the above-mentioned protected areas, any such accident may be subject to enhanced penalties.

IX.   Protected Species

The Federal Constitution attributes to the federal government and the states authority to legislate over environmental matters, including fauna and flora, and also a duty to protect the environment.[16]

Brazil is a party to international conventions on fauna and flora protection, such as the U.N. Convention on Biological Diversity (adopted via Federal Decrees No. 2/1994 and 2,519/1998), and the U.N. Convention on International Trade in Endangered Species of Wild Fauna and Flora (CITES)[17] (Federal Decrees No. 54/1975 and 92,446/1986).

To implement its treaty commitments, Brazil has established a National Biodiversity Policy (Federal Decree No. 4,339/2002).[18] As to flora, the Ministry of the Environment's Normative Instruction 06/2008 establishes a special protection regime for endangered plant species. As to fauna, the Ministry of the Environment Normative Instruction 03/2003 defines the list and establishes the basis of a special protection regime for endangered animal species. In addition, Federal Law No. 5,197/1967 establishes a protection regime for wild fauna in general, whether endangered or not.

In 1998, a technical committee was created to discuss and update Federal Law No. 5,197/1967, but with no relevant practical results thus far. The introduction of the concept of critical habitat as a specific tool for protection of endangered fauna and flora has been the subject of much discussion. However, little has been regulated. Nevertheless, in São Paulo, State Decree No. 56,031/2010—which lists endangered species in the state—defines critical habitat and establishes special procedures for the licensing of activities to be developed in critical habitat areas.

X.   Environmental Review and Decision Making

The National Environmental Policy Act (Federal Law No. 6,938/1981) requires entities or individuals to obtain a license prior to undertaking potentially polluting activities. Usually, the licensing process involves three consecutive phases. Each corresponds to the issuance of a different license: (1) a preliminary license, which approves the activity location and project, attests to the project's environmental feasibility, and establishes the basic and conditional requisites to be met during the next implementation phases; (2) an installation license, which authorizes the activity subject to specifications in the approved plans, programs, and projects, including environmental control measures and all other conditional requirements; and (3) an operation license, which authorizes the operation of the project, after verification of effective compliance with the conditions set forth in the prior licenses.

The operator must submit an application for review by the competent environmental agency, and supply all documents and information needed for the agency to make a determination. Required documentation typically includes technical and environmental impact studies.

Usually, the decision-making process is concentrated on the assessment by the agencies' technical experts. Depending on the expected environmental impacts, the process may include public hearings.[19]

Finally, a common problem faced by operators seeking an environmental license is the issue of authority to license among federal, state, and local agencies. The 1988 Federal Constitution established that the matter should be regulated by a specific law, which was enacted only in 2011 (Federal Law No. 140/2011). This law is expected to increase the level of predictability for entities or individuals engaging in potentially polluting activities by reducing challenges to the validity of the relevant licenses. In addition, courts have recently taken a stand on the matter, establishing limits on the ability of various agencies to participate in the licensing process.[20]

XI. Transboundary Pollution

Brazil is a party to the main international treaties on transboundary pollution, such as the Basel Convention. Based on the Basel Convention, Federal Decree No. 875/1993, regulated by CONAMA Resolution No. 452/2012, establishes procedures to control waste import. It forbids the import of hazardous waste (Class I), domestic waste or the product of its incineration, and used tires, and establishes that the import of authorized waste requires a license previously issued by the IBAMA or its state and local counterparts.

XII. Civil and Criminal Enforcement and Penalties

The Brazilian Federal Constitution (Article 225) and the National Environmental Policy Act (Federal Law No. 6,938/1981, Article 14) establish that anyone who causes environmental damage may be subject to three different and independent levels of environmental liability; civil, administrative, and criminal. These three levels of liability are different and independent. One act may trigger environmental liability at each one of the three levels and, as a consequence, application of three different sanctions. In addition, absence of liability at one of these levels does not necessarily exempt the offender from liability at the other levels.

In general, the federal, state, and municipal levels of government (the latter in cases of local and specific interest) are empowered to enforce their own regulations regarding environmental protection and natural resource use at the national or regional, state, and local levels, respectively.

A. Environmental Civil Liability

Environmental civil liability results from an action or omission by the offender that results in environmental damage of any type, and is characterized as strict liability.

Such liability results in the civil penalty of remedying and indemnifying the damage caused to the environment and/or affected third parties.

In order for strict liability to attach, the government need only show that an act or omission resulted in damage to the environment, irrespective of fault (negligence, misconduct, or recklessness) by the defendant. Accordingly, environmental civil liability is ascribed, in principle, to the offender who caused the environmental damage.

In Brazil, joint and several liability may also be imposed where more than one party is deemed responsible for environmental damage, and it is not possible to apportion or estimate individual contributions for those damages (Brazilian Civil Code, Article 942).

Another law of interest is Federal Law No. 7,347/1985. This statute created the "public civil action" in Brazil. Similar to class actions in the United States, this law grants standing to the district attorney and to NGOs to file lawsuits aimed at environmental protection.

In Brazil, as a general rule, the district attorney brings lawsuits against those who caused but do not voluntarily remediate environmental damages. In specific cases where the entity or individual causing the damage does not take action to remediate it, the authorities could bring lawsuits against those who benefited from the polluting activity.

B. Environmental Criminal Liability

Criminal environmental liability is provided by Federal Law No. 9,605/1998. Pursuant to its Article 2, the following individuals may be found guilty of committing environmental crimes: corporate officers, top managers, members of the board and technical body, auditors, managers, representatives, and delegates. Others who have cooperated in any way with individuals committing certain infractions may also be found guilty. The legal entity, such as the corporation itself, may also be punished, according to Article 3 of said Law. The penalties set forth are partial or total suspension of activities, temporary shutdown of the establishment or discontinuance of work or activity, preclusion from entering into contracts with the government or from receiving governmental subsidies, and community service (e.g., financing environmental programs and projects, performance of recovery works in degraded areas, maintenance of public areas, and contribution to public environmental or cultural entities).

For criminal liability to be ascribed, the government must demonstrate causation. Individuals or companies shall only be held liable if it is proved that they directly or indirectly caused the damage at issue. In other words, strict liability is not recognized as the basis for an enforcement action under Brazilian criminal law.

Two main articles that are of particular concern for entrepreneurs in Brazil are

> Art. 54—To cause pollution of any nature at such levels that result or may result in damage to the human health, or that cause the death of animals or the significant destruction of the flora. [...]. Penalty—imprisonment of one to five years.

and

> Art. 60. To build, renovate, expand, install or operate, in any part of the Brazilian territory, potentially polluting establishments, works or services, without the applicable environmental licenses or in non-compliance with the applicable laws and regulations. Penalty: imprisonment of one to six months and/or monetary fine.

Notes

1. *Peritos* are those in charge of investigating and producing evidence of environmental damage and demonstrating a chain of causation.
2. Federal Law No. 6,938/1981.
3. Hydrocarbons.
4. Aldehydes.
5. *See* http://unfccc.int/key_documents/the_convention/items/2853.php (UNFCCC text) (last visited March 15, 2013); http://ozone.unep.org/new_site/en/Treaties/treaties_decisions-hb.php?nav_id=2081 (Vienna Convention for the Protection of the Ozone Layer) (last visited March 15, 2013); http://unfccc.int/key_documents/kyoto_protocol/items/6445.php (Kyoto Protocol text) (last visited March 15, 2013).
6. PNMC art. 12. Some have criticized Brazil's voluntary targets as well as those of other UNFCCC non-Annex I parties, that is, states with no binding emission reduction targets before 2012, for not being an effective tool for actually curbing emissions. Capacity-building has been identified as a need for developing and implementing effective GHG reduction measures.
7. *See* http://www.idesam.org.br/projetos/iniciativa/documentos%20relacionados/Relatorio%20final%20IA.pdf (last visited March 15, 2013).
8. The latter two types of projects concern the Kyoto Protocol-related mechanism for reducing of emissions from deforestation and degradation (REDD or REDD+) and clean development mechanism (CDM), respectively. REDD+ is designed to help create new, low-carbon economic development patterns in the forested areas of developing countries, while simultaneously reducing the cost of emission reductions for entities in developed countries with international or domestic emission reduction obligations. The first discussions concerning REDD+ in Brazil concentrated on preserving indigenous territories pending domain regularization in the State of Acre, in the Amazonian rainforest.

The initiative provides for the regularization of indigenous lands, upon the signature of long-term agreements to assure sustainable exploitation of standing forested areas, as opposed to other economic activities, such as mining or cattle ranching. The discussions face political and technical resistance from certain stakeholders, including some indigenous representatives, who argue that such arrangements interfere with traditional communities' autonomy, without changing historical emission patterns in developed nations.

9. Brazilian Constitution arts. 20.3, 20.4, 20.6, http://www.senado.gov.br/legislacao /const/ (Portuguese text) (last visited March 15, 2013) and http://www.wipo.int/wipolex /en/details.jsp?id=8755 (English translation).

10. Brazilian Constitution art. 26.1, http://www.senado.gov.br/legislacao/const/ (Portuguese text) (last visited March 15, 2013).

11. *See* http://chm.pops.int/Home/tabid/2121/mctl/ViewDetails/EventModID/870 /EventID/331/xmid/6921/Default.aspx; ,http://www.basel.int/.

12. Federal Decree 5,472/2005 art. 1st.

13. *See* art. 3, VII.

14. J. Tollefson, *A Light in the Forest*, FOREIGN AFFAIRS (Mar./Apr. 2013).

15. For certain endangered national biomes, specific state regulations aimed at use and conservation have been issued, as is the case of the Atlantic Rainforest in São Paulo (State Law No. 11,428/2006).

16. *See* art. 24, VI (flora and fauna) & art. 225, § 1, VII (duty to protect the environment).

17. http://www.cites.org.

18. The implementation of this policy faces practical constraints due to the lack of governmental capacity. The government, for example, lacks the ability properly to implement its commitments vis-à-vis authorizations to perform genetic research and access genetic resources while ensuring that traditional communities also benefit from such exploitation.

19. Some have criticized this process due to the agencies' lack of structure and personnel, the great discretionary powers conferred to the agencies, and the limitation to effective public participation.

20. In a recent decision, for example, the Regional Federal Court exempted the Federal Environmental Agency (IBAMA) from issuing a requested technical opinion on a licensing case under state authority (Writ of Mandamus No. 102893-RN, June 12, 2012).

CHAPTER 23

Chile

IVÁN POKLEPOVIC

I. Introduction: Chile's Institutional Framework

The primary regulations governing the protection of the environment in Chile are the Chilean Constitution and Law No. 19,300, the General Environmental Law (1994) (Ley de Bases del Medio Ambiente, LBMA).

The constitution guarantees all people the right to live in a pollution-free environment and provides to all people a cause of action to protect that right when it is affected by an illegal act or omission attributable to a specific authority or person.[1] In addition, the constitution provides that the Chilean government has the duty to safeguard this right and preserve the natural environment.

The LBMA is the chief legal statute governing the Chilean environmental legal framework. It regulates the right to live in a pollution-free environment, the protection of the environment, the preservation of nature, and the conservation of the nation's environmental heritage. The LBMA incorporates environmental management instruments to protect the environment such as strategic environmental assessment,[2] the environmental impact assessment system (*sistema de evaluación de impacto ambiental*, SEIA),[3] emission standards,[4] primary and secondary quality standards,[5] latent or saturated zone declaration,[6] and prevention and decontamination plans.[7]

More recently, Law No. 20,417, dated January 26, 2010, modified the LBMA and redesigned this framework. The new institutions created included (1) the Ministry of the Environment, charged with the design and implementation of policies, plans, norms, and programs on environmental issues; (2) the Environmental Assessment Service, charged with administering the SEIA; and (3) the Superintendence of the Environment, in charge of enforcing environmental management instruments, such as (a) environmental approval resolutions for projects subject to the environmental impact assessment requirement; (b) measures of prevention and decontamination plans; (c) quality and emission standards; (d) management plans under the LBMA; and (e) other standards and environmental instruments not under the control and oversight of other agencies of the government.[8]

In addition to the agencies described above, there are several other public agencies with environmental powers charged with the protection of specific environmental components, such as the National Forest Corporation (Corporación Nacional Forestal, CONAF),[9] the Agricultural and Livestock Service (Servicio Agrícola y Ganadero, SAG),[10] the National Fishing Service (Servicio Nacional de Pesca y Acuicultura, SERNAPESCA),[11] the National Water Authority (Dirección General de Aguas, DGA),[12] the National Mining and Geology Service (Servicio Nacional de Geología y Minería, SERNAGEOMIN),[13] and the Health Authority (Secretaría Regional Ministerial (SEREMI) de Salud), among others. These agencies are responsible for enforcing environmental laws and instruments not under the control of the Superintendence of the Environment.

II. Air and Climate Change
A. Air Pollution Control

Air pollution control is a significant challenge in Chile because of the interests involved and the health issues surrounding air policy. The major challenge concerning air quality is concentrated in the Metropolitan Region of Santiago, a region with significant air pollution issues, and where more than a third of the population lives. Like Santiago, other southern cities and boroughs, such as Temuco and Padre Las Casas, also face serious air quality problems due to the use of firewood as a source of energy.[14] In addition, the mining and energy industries have also contributed to air pollution due to poor air emissions management.

The government has a duty to enact norms to regulate the presence of pollutants in the environment to prevent them from becoming a risk for the preservation of nature, the conservation of the nation's environmental heritage, and the people's health and quality of life. In order to face air quality challenges, Chile has an array of environmental instruments designed to reach an equilibrium that allows development while preventing air pollution. Among these instruments are air quality standards, air emission standards, and prevention and decontamination plans.

For example, to protect human health, Chile has enacted primary air quality standards for air pollutants such as particulate matter (PM_{10} and $PM_{2.5}$), lead, ozone, sulfur dioxide, nitrogen dioxide, and carbon monoxide. Additionally, a secondary air quality standard for sulfur dioxide came into force in 2010.[15]

The government has also promulgated several air emission standards for both stationary and mobile sources. For stationary sources, Decree No. 4 of 1992, Ministry of the Presidency, regulates the emission of particulate matter in the Metropolitan Region of Santiago by establishing an emission compensation system. Decree No. 165 of 1999, of the same ministry, addresses arsenic emitted into the air. More recently, an emission standard for thermoelectric power plants[16] and an emission standard of particulate matter for wood-burning devices[17] came into force in 2012. In the case of mobile sources, the standards establish specific emission limitations for motor vehicles, including motorcycles, and prohibit them from operating if their emissions exceed those limits.[18]

Decontamination and prevention plans must be put into action when air quality standards are exceeded or likely to be exceeded.[19] These plans contain a schedule and objectives designed to guide the action of the authorities in charge of enforcing them in order to reduce air pollutants.[20]

Currently, the localities of Maria Elena–Pedro de Valdivia, Temuco–Padre Las Casas, Tocopilla, the central valley of the Sixth Region of Chile, and the Metropolitan Region of Santiago have decontamination plans in force. Additional zones affected by the mining industry requiring decontamination plans include the areas surrounding the Paipote, Chuquicamata, Potrerillos, and Caletones smelters, and the industrial complex of Ventanas in the Valparaiso Region.[21]

Notwithstanding the above, Chile has promulgated administrative regulations to address its air quality issues. Thus, Decree No. 3557 of 1980, Ministry of Agriculture, empowers the president to order the suspension of activities and companies that release smoke, dust, or gases into the air that affect the health of inhabitants, alter the conditions of soil, or harm the health, life, integrity, or development of animals or vegetation.[22]

There is no law regulating odors in Chile. The main regulations are administrative, such as Decree No. 144 of 1961, Ministry of Health, which establishes regulations to avoid atmospheric releases or pollutants of any kind, and Supreme Decree No. 37, of 2013, of the Ministry of the Environment, which establishes an emission standard for unpleasant odors associated with the manufacture of sulfated pulp.

With respect to noise, Decree No. 129 of 2003, Ministry of Transportation, creates the noise emission standard for urban and rural public transportation buses. Supreme Decree No. 38, of 2011, of the Ministry of the Environment, that entered in forced on June, 2014. In addition, Chilean legislation includes regulations to prevent workers from being exposed to noise at worksites.[23]

Likewise, to deal with light pollution, the government enacted a light emission standard to protect the environmental and astronomical quality of night skies in the Antofagasta Region, the Atacama Region, and the Coquimbo Region.[24]

B. Climate Change

In the global context, Chile is not a major source of greenhouse gas emissions (GHGs). Chile is only responsible for approximately 0.2 percent of total global annual emissions. That said, the country's overall emissions are on the rise mainly due to transportation and energy generation.[25] There are no laws or regulations governing climate change in Chile. Conversely, on the international plane, Chile ratified the United Nations Framework Convention on

Climate Change (UNFCCC) in 1994 and the Kyoto Protocol in 2002.[26] Both instruments offer Chile the opportunity to confront the problem of climate change synergistically with sector development agendas to address local needs such as (1) strengthening the National Environmental Policy by reducing local pollutants and other negative environmental externalities and implementing measures to reduce GHGs and adapt to climate change; (2) fostering sustainable development and reducing poverty through the transfer of technologies that mitigate GHGs and improve the ability to adapt to anticipated impacts of climate change; and (3) increasing participation in the global carbon market through the Kyoto Protocol's Clean Development Mechanism (CDM).

In order to fulfill its climate change commitments, in 1996 the government created the National Steering Committee on Global Change as an advisory panel on these issues. Its primary task was to formulate Strategic Guidelines for Climate Change for Chile, which served to focus national efforts leading up to the National Climate Change Strategy and the National Action Plan. The Strategic Guidelines reiterate the commitments established under the UNFCCC, promote the use of CDM, and propose a fund to promote scientific and technical research for climate change in Chile.

In compliance with UNFCCC's common obligations, Chile approved in January 2006 the National Climate Change Strategy. Chile developed this strategy through its Climate Change Action Plan.[27] This action plan establishes a framework for all activities aimed at evaluating the impact of, and vulnerability and adaptation to climate change and mitigating GHG emissions.[28]

In addition, there are programs and policies currently in force to deal with climate change in the following areas: energy efficiency (initiative developed by the Economic Development Agency (Corporación de Fomento, CORFO)); renewable energy (initiatives by the National Energy Commission and CORFO); sustainable transportation; forestry, agriculture, and livestock practices (initiatives supported by the Ministry of Agriculture and the private sector); urban pollution control (pollution control plans) and land use planning, especially in urban areas.

Lastly, Chile has been actively engaged in promoting and implementing projects under the Kyoto Protocol's CDM.[29] So far, there are approximately 106 Chilean projects registered at the CDM's Executive Board registry, most of them concerning renewable energy.[30]

III.   Water
A.   Inland Waters

Despite the relatively high quality of most of the water bodies in Chile, water quality remains poor in some lakes, rivers, and coastal waters due to urban and industrial releases of untreated liquid waste, heavy metals released as the result of mining activities in northern Chile, and materials used in aquaculture and rural agricultural activities (e.g., irrigation, use of pesticides).

The Chilean Water and Sanitary Codes and their implementing regulations address water pollution.[31] The Sanitary Code forbids the discharge of wastewater and mining and industrial waste into rivers or lakes or into any other source or water body used for drinking water, irrigation, or recreation without treatment.[32] The Health Authority can order the immediate suspension of discharges and require the installation of adequate treatment systems to avoid water pollution.[33] Similarly, Decree No. 594 of 1999, Ministry of Health, prohibits discharges of any radioactive, corrosive, poisonous, infectious, flammable, explosive, or otherwise hazardous substance into public sewers[34] and any discharge of industrial liquid waste into groundwater, drainage channels, aqueducts, rivers, streams, lagoons, lakes, ravines, dams, or other water bodies without being subject to prior treatment.[35]

The Water Code forbids the dumping of substances, waste, litter, and similar objects into channels that alter water quality. Municipalities must enforce penalties for violations detected, and require the cleaning up of channels obstructed by waste, litter, and other objects dumped into them.[36]

Moreover, when the National Water Authority grants water rights in rivers, it must preserve the natural environment by establishing a minimum flow that must be maintained in the river.[37] The National Water Authority may order an immediate halt of works executed in natural waterways without the corresponding authorization.[38]

Likewise, the LBMA establishes water quality standards.[39] Decree No. 143 of 2009, Ministry of the Presidency, regulates the primary quality standard for surface waters suitable for recreational activities with direct contact. Its purpose is to protect the water quality of surface inland waters to safeguard human health. Secondary water quality standards have also been enacted to protect specific bodies of waters such as Llanquihue Lake[40] and the Serrano River Basin.[41]

Along with these water quality standards, Chilean law also includes emission standards to regulate pollutants associated with the discharge of liquid industrial waste into the sewage system,[42] marine and inland waters,[43] and underground waters.[44] The Superintendence of the Environment is charged with enforcing these emission standards regulations.[45]

B. Marine Waters

Regarding marine waters, Title IX of Decree No. 2,222 of 1978, Ministry of National Defense, referred to as the Navigation Law, addresses pollution of marine waters subject to national jurisdiction. It forbids discharging ballast, rubble, or waste, spilling oil or residues, mining tailings waters, and other harmful matters that cause or may cause harm to national waters, ports, rivers, and lakes.[46] The Maritime Authority (Dirección General del Territorio Marítimo y de Marina Mercante, DIRECTEMAR) must enforce this prohibition and must inspect, apply, and enforce all national and international regulations regarding the preservation of the marine environment.[47] The Maritime Authority must implement preventive measures in the case of water pollution due to oil or other harmful substance spills to avoid the degradation of marine flora and fauna or damage to coastal zones.[48]

The other relevant regulation for ocean waters is Decree No. 1 of 1992, Ministry of National Defense, which aims to control aquatic pollution. This decree provides the same prohibitions set forth in the Navigation Law and grants to the Maritime Authority the powers to address pollution in national waters. It applies fines in the case of noncompliance with the rules on prohibition of pollution and preservation of national marine waters.[49] This regulation forbids the introduction or discharge into national waters of matters, energy, or harmful substances coming from facilities or activities without prior treatment.[50] The facilities and activities that introduce or discharge any such matters, energy, or harmful substances must provide to the Maritime Authority, prior to the operation, certain background information on the installation of the removal system.[51] However, in some cases, the Maritime Authority may authorize the introduction or discharge into national waters of matters, energy, or harmful substances that do not cause harm to the waters, flora, or fauna. In such instances, the Maritime Authority will indicate the place and manner of proceeding.[52]

In addition, Decree No. 144 of 2009, Ministry of the Presidency, adopted the primary quality standard for marine and coastal waters suitable for recreational activities. Its purpose is to protect the water quality of marine and coastal waters to safeguard human health.

IV.   Handling, Treatment, Transportation, and Disposal of Hazardous Materials

Chile currently has a National Policy of Chemical Safety and a Plan of Action. The purpose of the action plan is to reduce the risks associated with the handling and management of chemical substances in all stages of their life cycle, including import, export, production, use, transport, storage, and disposal, with the aim to protect the environment and human health.[53] In that regard, Chile is party to the 2001 Stockholm Convention on Persistent Organic Pollutants[54] and the Rotterdam Convention of 1998 on prior informed consent applicable to pesticides and hazardous chemicals subject to international trade.[55]

Chilean regulations regarding hazardous substances and materials are composed of numerous decrees and resolutions governing the registration, labeling, packaging, advertising, distribution, storage, monitoring, disposal, transportation, and handling of chemicals, and the trade in toxic and hazardous chemicals.[56]

These regulations also impose restrictions and prohibitions on the use and management of certain substances linked to the agricultural sector (e.g., pesticides). Chilean environmental law contains a comprehensive regime regulating the manufacture, distribution, and use of pesticides.[57]

In addition, Decree No. 78 of 2009, Ministry of Health, regulates the storage of hazardous substances and provides the safety conditions that storage facilities must comply with. According to this decree, hazardous substances or products are those that could pose a risk to the health, safety, or well-being of human beings and animals. They are listed in certain Chilean official regulations.[58]

The transport of hazardous substances is governed by Decree No. 298 of 1995, Ministry of Transportation, which regulates the transport of hazardous loads in streets and roads.

The government has also published regulations governing the production, refining, transport, storage, distribution, and supply of liquid fuels.[59]

Finally, according to the LBMA, the regular production, storage, transport, disposal, or reuse of toxic, explosive, radioactive, flammable, corrosive, and reactive substances must go through an environmental assessment through the SEIA.[60]

The Health Authority is the main authority charged with enforcing regulations regarding chemical and hazardous substances.[61]

V. Waste and Site Remediation

In Chile regulations exist governing the use of liquid, solid, and hazardous waste. The waste can be categorized as domestic or industrial. The concept of waste is legally defined in Decree No. 148 of 2003, Ministry of Health,[62] as a "substance, element or object that the generator gets rid of, plans to get rid of or is obligated to get rid of."[63]

In addition to domestic or industrial waste, there are types of waste associated with specific activities that are to be treated independently (e.g., medical waste).[64] In parallel to this distinction, waste can be considered hazardous or nonhazardous.

A. Liquid Waste

The Sanitary Code is the primary statute governing liquid industrial or domestic waste management.[65] According to the Sanitary Code, the Health Authority must approve projects relating to the construction, repair, modification, and enlargement of any public or private work intended for the removal, treatment, or final disposal of sewage, wastewater, and mining and industrial waste. The Health Authority must also grant authorization to operate the facility.[66]

The Health Authority also oversees the operation of plants that treat water for human use, wastewater treatment plants, and industrial and mining waste treatment plants.[67] The Health Authority must enforce the applicable regulations and impose sanctions in the case of violations.[68]

In relation to the collection and disposal of sewage or wastewater, the Superintendence of Sanitary Services (Superintendencia de Servicios Sanitarios, SISS) is charged with performing inspections to providers of such services, enforcing the applicable regulations and controlling the industrial liquid waste standards linked to sanitary services providers.[69]

The Superintendence of the Environment is charged with enforcing and controlling the industrial liquid waste standards and laws not linked to sanitary service providers.[70]

Companies must have a sanitary authorization issued by the Health Authority to accumulate, treat, or dispose of industrial liquid waste inside or outside of the industrial premises.[71]

B. Solid Waste

Chile has an Integral Management Policy for Solid Waste dated 2005,[72] but it does not have a general law on waste. Nor does it have specific laws integrally addressing the management of different types of solid waste.

The Sanitary Code is the chief statute governing solid industrial and domestic waste management. Under the Sanitary Code, municipalities must collect, transport, and eliminate wastes and rubbish deposited or produced in urban routes.[73] Furthermore, the Health Authority must approve projects relating to the construction, repair, modification, and enlargement of any solid waste treatment plant[74] and also grant authorization to install an operation for accumulating, selecting, upgrading, trading, or disposing of wastes of any kind.[75]

Decree No. 594 of 1999, Ministry of Health, regulates the accumulation, treatment, and disposal of industrial solid waste inside or outside of industrial premises. All of these activities require an appropriate authorization from the Health Authority.[76] The waste-generating company must submit to the Health Authority a statement about the quantity and quality of the industrial waste generated before treating or disposing of the waste inside or outside of the industrial premises, with all hazardous waste clearly marked.[77]

In addition, there are specific regulations regarding sanitary and safety conditions for sanitary landfills[78] and management of sludge generated from sewage treatment plants.[79]

C. Hazardous Waste

The chief regulation concerning hazardous waste is Decree No. 148 of 2003, Ministry of Health. This decree establishes certain sanitary regulations concerning hazardous waste management. Waste is regarded as hazardous when it presents one of the following characteristics: severe toxicity, chronic toxicity, intrinsic toxicity, flammability, reactivity, and corrosivity.[80]

These regulations govern the entire process of hazardous waste management from its generation to final disposal (i.e., "cradle to grave" management).[81] The storage and transport of hazardous waste and the disposal site must be authorized by the Health Authority.

Lastly, under the LBMA, environmental sanitation projects such as water or solid waste treatment plants, sanitary landfills, and the treatment and disposal of industrial waste systems, must undergo environmental assessment through the SEIA.[82]

The Health Authority may issue sanitary restoration orders requiring responsible parties to remove any waste or refuse deposited on the land and dispose of it properly.[83]

VI.   Emergency Response

Chile has enacted a regime for emergency response to oil or waste releases or spills at sea. However, it lacks a similar scheme for releases of hazardous or chemical substances on land.

The Navigation Law, Decree No. 1 of 1992, Ministry of National Defense, Regulations for Control of Aquatic Pollution and several international treaties regulating the prevention of releases of oil or waste into marine waters impose obligations on the Maritime Authority to take action in the case of marine pollution due to oil spills or releases of other noxious or hazardous substances.[84] The regulations prohibit the discharge of hazardous substances, chemicals, oil, or other kind of waste into coastal waters.[85] The Maritime Authority implements preventive measures in the case of water pollution due to spills of oil or other harmful substances to avoid the destruction of marine flora and fauna or damage to coastal zones.[86] For the discharge of some type of waste, a previous permit is required from the Maritime Authority.[87]

In addition to any fine imposed under the Navigation Law, ship owners, masters, and owners of land-based installations that cause pollution of national waters must pay the cost of cleanup for any release or oil spill.[88]

Regarding releases of hazardous substances, oil, or chemicals on land, the Health Authority may order sanitary measures when a risk for human health is involved.[89]

VII.   Natural Resource Management and Protection

The main statutes governing natural resource management in Chile are (1) Decree No. 430 of 1991, Ministry of Economy, referred to as the Fishing and Aquaculture Law; (2) Law No. 20,283 of 2008, Ministry of Agriculture (Native Forest Law); (3) Decree No. 701 of 1974, Ministry of Agriculture, on Forest Promotion; and (4) the Water Code.

A.   Marine Areas

The Fishing and Aquaculture Law applies to fishing and aquaculture activities carried out in terrestrial and ocean waters under national jurisdiction.[90] It regulates the conservation, sustainable use, and management of hydrobiological resources[91] through different instruments such as management plans,[92] marine parks, marine reserves,[93] fishing management for vulnerable marine ecosystems[94] and management and exploitation areas.[95]

A corresponding authorization granted by the Fishing Subsecretary (Subsecretaría de Pesca) is required to engage in fishing activities.[96]

Fishing is governed by three key agencies: (1) the Fishing Subsecretary, charged with the policy and the regulatory framework for the internal management of the sector and international cooperation;[97] (2) SERNAPESCA, charged with the management and application of fishing and aquaculture laws and regulations; and (3) the Fishing Promotion Institute (Instituto de Fomento Pesquero, IFOP), charged with the promotion and support of the sustainable development of the fishing sector.[98]

The Fishing and Aquaculture Law forbids trawling in zones reserved for small-scale fishing, with the exception of fishing of hydro-biological resources that only can be fished using this system.[99] A concession from the Ministry of National Defense is required before engaging in aquaculture.[100] Concessionaires are obligated to maintain clean operations in designated aquaculture zones.[101] Aquaculture and fishing are not allowed in lakes, rivers, and maritime zones belonging to the National System of Protected Wild Areas (Sistema Nacional de Áreas Silvestres Protegidas del Estado, SNASPE).[102]

B.   Forests

The government also is responsible for managing Chile's great forest richness. The resource is essential not only for its environmental, ecological, and social value (e.g., protection of biodiversity, carbon capture, scenic beauty, erosion prevention, and water capture) but also for the development of the Chilean forest industry. The regulation of forests requires the balancing of two perspectives: on one hand, the conservation of the resource and, on the other hand, its use and exploitation.

According to CONAF, forests cover 16 million hectares in Chile, which represents 21.5 percent of the national territory. Of this total, approximately 13,700,000 hectares are native forests while 2,700,000 hectares are forest plantations constituted mostly by *pino radiata* and *eucalipto*.[103] Forestry activity is the second most important economic activity in the country after the mining industry. Within the forestry sector, the most important activity is the production of cellulose, paper, and products derived from paper.

Native forests are regulated by the Native Forest Law. The specific objectives of this law are the protection, recovery, and improvement of Chile's native forests to assure their sustainability and environmental policy.[104] The Native Forest Law establishes forest classification according to the objectives of the management distinguishing among the "native forest of preservation," "native forest of conservation and protection" and "native forest of multiple use."[105] Depending on the type of forest involved, specific policies and management measures may vary. The Native Forest Law specifically regulates the management plans applicable to native forests,[106] contains regulations on forest protection[107] and incentives for the investigation, conservation, recovery, and sustainable management of native forest,[108] and sanctions for non-compliance.[109] In addition, for the protection of glaciers, the Native Forest Law forbids the cutting, destruction, removal of, or damage to native trees and bushes located less than 500 meters from a glacier.[110]

Decree No. 701 of 1974, Ministry of Agriculture, regulates forestry activities in soils that are suitable for forestry, and in degraded soils. It also establishes incentives for reforestation.[111] Decree No. 701 also regulates the use of forest management plans[112] establishing sanctions in case of noncompliance.[113] It also establishes an incentive system for reforestation and tax exemptions for areas containing certain types of plantations, native forests, and protected forests.[114]

In addition, the LBMA provides that forest development or exploitation projects in fragile soils or lands covered by native forests must undergo environmental review through the SEIA.[115]

C.   Mining

Chile is known as a mining country due to the plentiful mining resources within its borders, as well as for the importance of mining to the country's economic development.[116] However, while mining generates certain development benefits, it also adversely affects the environment (e.g., by producing water and soil pollution, air emissions, and waste, inter alia), communities, and other economic activities such as agriculture.

Among the laws and administrative regulations that address environmental aspects of mining, the Mining Code[117] establishes governmental control over all mines and regulates mining rights. These rights are the right to explore for and exploit minerals and the right to obtain mining concessions to engage in these activities.[118] In order to carry out mining in zones declared national parks, national reserves, or natural monuments, a permit from the Intendant (main regional authority) is required. For mining works in guano deposit areas, and sites of historical or scientific interest, a permit from the president is required.[119] In accordance with the Mining Code, the mining concessionaire must compensate the owner of the surface land for all damage caused.[120]

Currently, the closing of mining sites in Chile is regulated by the Mining Safety Regulations.[121] In accordance with these regulations, every mining company must file a shutdown plan for approval by SERNAGEOMIN, along with its exploitation plan. This plan must contain measures to be implemented during the operation of the project with the purpose of preventing, mitigating, and/or controlling the risks and adverse effects that could arise or continue to take place once the operation of a mining site has ceased. In order to update the requirements and contents of the plans, Law No. 20,551 of 2011, Ministry of Mining, was recently approved and entered into force on November 11, 2012. The main purpose of this law is to regulate mine closing plans to ensure the stability and protection of the environment and people when a particular mining activity is shut down and ensure compliance with the plan.[122] SERNAGEOMIN is the authority in charge of approving and overseeing compliance with the measures contained in such plans.[123]

In addition, the LBMA provides that the execution of mining development projects—including coal, oil and gas, and industrial extraction of sand, gravel, rocks, and clay—must undergo environmental review through the SEIA.[124]

VIII.   Natural Resource Damages

With regard to natural resource damages, the LBMA addresses the issue of liability for environmental harm. The LBMA establishes an "environmental cause of action," the purpose of which is to bring about the restoration of the harmed environment.[125] Anyone who negligently or intentionally causes environmental damage will be liable pursuant to the LBMA and required to restore the environment.[126]

The LBMA defines harm to the environment as "all significant loss, diminution or detriment inflicted on the environment or one or more of its components."[127] The concept of harm to the environment, in turn, implies an action affecting the "environment," defined as "the global system constituted by natural and artificial elements of a physical, chemical and biological nature, socio-cultural and its interactions, in permanent modification by natural or human action and that conditions the existence and development of life in its multiple manifestations."[128] "Restoration" is "the act of repairing the environment or one or more of its components to an equivalent quality they had before the caused harm, or in case of not being feasible, reestablishing their basic properties."[129]

The LBMA expressly specifies who has standing to sue for environmental damage: (1) the physical and legal persons, private or public, who have suffered the damage or injury, that is, the entity injured or individual who has been personally affected; (2) the municipalities where the injury occurred; and (3) the government of Chile, represented by the State Defense Council.[130] The law excludes private plaintiffs unless they have directly suffered the injury.[131]

LBMA establishes that an environmental action as well as any civil action derived from environmental damage seeking economic compensation must be brought within five years from the evident manifestation of the harm.[132]

IX.   Protected Species

Chile possesses a great variety of environments and ecosystems and within them a high proportion of endemic species unique in the world. The loss and fragmentation of habitats due to deforestation and land use changes, along with overexploitation, are the main threats to biological diversity in Chile.

Chile has numerous policies intended to protect biodiversity, such as the National Strategy for Biodiversity, dated 2003, a Plan of Action to implement this National Strategy (2004–2015), the National Policy on Protected Areas (2005), and a National Strategy for the conservation and sustainable use of wetlands in Chile.[133]

In addition to the U.N. Convention on Biological Diversity (CBD)[134] with respect to species conservation, Chile is party to the Convention on International Trade of Endangered Species of Wild Fauna and Flora (CITES)[135] the main objective of which is to ensure that the international trade of wild animals and flora does not threaten the existence of those species. It accomplishes this objective by prohibiting and regulating the international trade of such species under certain circumstances. Regarding the protection of species, the LBMA requires the Ministry of Environment to ensure that state environmental agencies design and keep an updated inventory of wild species of vegetation, algae, fungi, and animals and enforce regulations regarding their cutting, capture, hunting, trade, and transport with the purpose of adopting actions and measures aimed at conserving biodiversity and preserving these species.[136]

Separately, the Hunting Law[137] establishes "hunting prohibition areas" where the president can temporarily forbid the hunting or capture of species when catastrophic situations affecting wild fauna or producing environmental damage take place.[138] In addition, the Hunting Law prohibits the hunting or capture of wild fauna classified as endangered species and the hunting or capture of species in areas classified as virgin regions, national parks, national reserves, natural monuments, natural sanctuaries, hunting prohibition areas, urban zones, train lines, airports, public roads, and sites of scientific interest. Exceptions to such prohibitions under the Hunting Law may be granted by SAG in certain circumstances.[139]

Decree No. 29 of 2011, Ministry of the Environment, establishes the process of classifying wild species of flora and fauna into different conservation categories set forth in Article 37 of the LBMA.[140] In conformity with these classifications, the Ministry of Environment must approve recovery, conservation, and management plans for these species.[141]

Moreover, the Native Forest Law prohibits cutting, eliminating, destroying, or removing certain species of native vegetation.[142] CONAF may grant authorization to intervene or alter the habitat of native species, provided that such acts do not threaten the viability of the species, are necessary, and are for the purpose of performing scientific investigations, health-related goals, or other works or activities considered to be in the national interest (e.g., road construction, the exercise of concessions or mining, or easements for gas, ducts, or electric services).[143] In any event, when authorization by CONAF is granted, a preservation management plan is required to carry out these activities.[144]

Chile has enacted numerous decrees aimed at the protection of specific tree and bush species by regulating their exploitation and prohibiting their felling (e.g., the *alerce* and the *araucaria* tree species).[145]

Regarding cetaceans, Law No. 20,293 of 2008, Ministry of Economy, forbids the killing, hunting, capture, harassing, possessing, transporting, unloading, producing, or performing of any process of transformation as well as the trade or storage of any cetacean species that live in or cross maritime zones of national jurisdiction.[146] This statute establishes incarceration as a sanction for the killing, hunting, or capturing of any cetacean species.[147]

There is also a variety of networks of protected areas in Chile,[148] the best known of which is the SNASPE,[149] with approximately 100 units of protected areas. The SNASPE covers an area comprising more than 14.5 million hectares and is administered by CONAF. The SNASPE, together with other types of protected areas, including nature sanctuaries, Ramsar sites, and marine parks and reserves, among others, represent approximately 20.7 percent of the continental territory and 4 percent of the Chilean territorial sea.[150]

Despite not having enacted a general law on protected areas and biodiversity,[151] various regulations are relevant to the conservation of ecosystems because they create categories of protection. For example, the Convention for the Protection of Flora, Fauna, and Natural Scenic Beauties of American Countries (Washington Convention),[152] to which Chile is a party, regulates four protection categories: (1) national parks, (2) national reserves, (3) natural monuments, and (4) virgin zone regions.[153] Similarly, Law No. 17.288 of 1970, Ministry of Education, regulates natural sanctuaries.[154] Moreover, Decree No. 238 of 2004, Ministry of Economy, regulates marine parks and reserves, and the Convention on Wetlands of International Importance (Ramsar Convention),[155] to which Chile is also a party, regulates the conservation and rational use of wetlands and their resources.

In addition, under the LBMA, the Chilean government must administer the SNASPE, which includes marine parks and reserves, with the goal of protecting biodiversity, safeguarding nature, and conserving the nation's environmental heritage.[156] The national government must also promote the creation of privately owned protected wild areas.[157]

Finally, the LBMA provides that any works, programs, or activities in national parks, national reserves, natural monuments, virgin zone regions, natural sanctuaries, marine parks, marine reserves, and other areas subject to official protection must undergo environmental review through the SEIA.[158]

X.   Environmental Review and Decision Making

Industrial activities in Chile must comply with environmental legislation, including the LBMA, which defines the projects that should be submitted to the SEIA.[159]

Projects or activities that undergo environmental analysis pursuant to the SEIA will obtain their environmental permits as part of the same environmental assessment procedure. However, other permits needed for certain projects will be granted once an environmental qualification resolution (Resolución de Calificación Ambiental, RCA) is issued by the Environmental Assessment Service (Servicio de Evaluación Ambiental, SEA).

The SEIA is administered by the SEA, which is the agency in charge of approving such projects.[160] The SEA manages the environmental permitting process of SEIA and coordinates it with those governmental agencies with obligations in the environmental field to obtain the authorizations required to conduct the project or activity.

A project may need to undergo either an environmental impact study (estudio de impacto ambiental, EIA) or an environmental impact statement (declaración de impacto ambiental, DIA).[161] These reports are prepared by the project proponent (usually by means of environmental consultants) and then filed with SEA for its review and approval. The potential environmental impact of the project will determine whether an EIA or DIA is required.[162]

To ensure that the community is kept apprised, the owner of the project must publish, within ten days of submission, an abstract of the EIA in the Official Gazette and in a national or regional newspaper, as appropriate.[163] The community has the right to comment on the project.[164]

During the assessment period, copies of the EIA or DIA are distributed to the public entities with environmental regulatory authority over any portion of the project or activity to ensure compliance with all relevant regulations and comment on the measures proposed in the EIA or DIA. A consolidated report requesting any necessary clarifications, amendments, or additions (*informe consolidado de solicitud de aclaraciones, rectificaciones, o ampliaciones*, ICSARA) is then returned to the project owner. When the project owner has responded to all ICSARAs, the SEA calls for a meeting of the members of the Assessment Commission,[165] which decides whether to approve or reject a project. If the project is approved, the RCA is issued and the project may move forward.

XI. Transboundary Pollution

Notwithstanding the fact that Chile shares borders and natural resources with Argentina, Peru, and Bolivia, Chile has entered into agreements only with Argentina to address the shared use of natural resources, in particular water and mining resources.[166] The Protocol on Shared Water Resources stipulates the sustainable use of the shared resources, and imposes on both states the duty not to cause damage to the shared water resources when used by entities in either country.[167] However, this protocol does not determine liability, require restoration, or establish a mechanism for resolving transboundary resource disputes.

Chile has followed the principles of a nation's sovereignty over natural resources and the obligation not to allow activities within Chile to damage natural resources found in other countries, as well as the principle of international cooperation established in the U.N. Convention on Human Environment of 1972 (Stockholm Convention) and the U.N. Convention on Environment and Development of 1992 (Rio Convention).[168]

In addition, Chile is a party to several other treaties related to transboundary pollution, such as the Basel Convention on the Transboundary Movements of Hazardous Waste and Their Disposal,[169] the Civil Liability Convention on Oil Pollution Damage,[170] and the Vienna Convention for the Ozone Layer Protection,[171] among others.

XII. Civil and Criminal Enforcement and Penalties

The Superintendence of the Environment is the agency charged with enforcing RCAs for projects subject to SEIA and evaluating prevention and decontamination plans, quality and emission standards, and management plans under the LBMA.[172] The other administrative agencies carrying out environmental enforcement activities retain their powers in matters that are not the responsibility of the Superintendence of the Environment.

A law governing the activities of the Superintendence of the Environment—the Superintendence of Environment Organic Law—classifies environmental violations as mild, serious, and very serious, and the sanctions can take the form of (1) a written reprimand; (2) a penalty of 1,000 to 10,000 annual tax units (*unidades tributarias anuales*, UTA) (in 2014, one UTA was roughly equivalent to Chilean $506,136, or approximately US$920); (3) temporary or permanent closure; or (4) revocation of the environmental qualification resolution.[173]

This statute also provides a single sanctioning procedure, with the Superintendence as the jurisdictional entity, and establishes two rules of compatibility with the other administrative agencies. First, no agency may commence a proceeding if one has already been started by the Superintendence, unless the Superintendence lacks jurisdiction.[174] Second, no one can be punished twice based on the same facts and legal bases.[175]

The Superintendence has a nondelegable ability to impose sanctions. The law also empowers the Superintendence to order interim measures during the sanctioning procedure, such as (1) corrective, safety, or control measures to prevent continuation of the risk or damage; (2) sealing devices or equipment; (3) temporary closure of facilities; (4) temporary suspension of the RCA; or (5) ordering monitoring programs and analyses.[176]

Finally, the law establishes that at the time a sanction is imposed, if the violator has caused environmental damage, the Superintendence shall require a restoration plan. Significant penalties can be imposed if such a plan is not implemented. The plan must be assessed by the SEA and approved by the Superintendence. After a restoration plan is adopted and during its execution, further work on the project that could result in environmental damage is suspended. If the violator who caused environmental damage successfully implements the approved restoration plan, no legal action for environmental damage may be brought.[177]

The Superintendence's enforcement powers were established effective December 28, 2012, the same day the Environmental Tribunal began to operate.[178] The Environmental Tribunal was created by the Law No. 20,600, dated June 2012. The Environmental Tribunal must review environmental damage lawsuits and claims against the Superintendence's decisions, among other environmental controversies.[179]

Notes

1. Constitución Política de la República de Chile arts. 19(8), 20.

2. Law No. 19,300 art. 2(i *bis*) defines strategic environmental assessment as a process designed to incorporate the environmental considerations into general regulatory plans and policies impacting the environment or sustainability.

3. Law No. 19,300 art. 2(j) defines environmental impact assessment as a process through which the Environmental Assessment Service verifies the environmental impact of a project or activity complies with the regulations in force.

4. The emission standards establish the maximum allowed quantity for a pollutant measured in the effluent of the emitting source.

5. The primary quality standards establish values of concentrations and maximum or minimum periods permissible of pollutants whose presence or lack in the environment may pose a risk for life or people's health, whereas the secondary quality standards establish the values of concentrations and maximum or minimum periods permissible of pollutants whose presence or lack in the environment may pose a risk for the protection or conservation of the environment or the preservation of nature.

6. The latent zone declaration takes place when the measurement of concentration of pollutants in air, water, or soil is situated between 80 percent and 100 percent of the value of the respective environmental quality standard, while a saturated zone declaration takes place when one or more environmental quality standards are exceeded.

7. The prevention plan is designed to prevent environmental quality standards from being exceeded in a latent zone, whereas the decontamination plan is aimed at returning covering the levels indicated in the quality standards in a saturated zone.

8. Law No. 20,417 art. 2 created the Superintendence of the Environment and established its organic law.

9. Corporación Nacional Forestal, http://www.conaf.cl/.

10. Servicio Agrícola y Ganadero, http://www.sag.cl/.

11. Servicio Nacional de Pesca y Acuicultura, http://www.sernapesca.cl.

12. Dirección General de Aguas, http://www.dga.cl.

13. Servicio Nacional de Geología y Minería, http://www.sernageomin.cl/.

14. The massive use of firewood for heating in central and southern Chile generates air pollution problems in many cities.

15. Decree No. 22 of 2009, Ministry of the Presidency.

16. Decree No. 13 of 2011, Ministry of the Environment.

17. Decree No. 39 of 2011, Ministry of the Environment.

18. The Ministry of Transportation has enacted several decrees regulating emissions coming from light, medium, and heavy motor vehicles and motorcycles such as Decree No. 211 of 1991, Decree No. 54 of 1994, Decree No. 55 of 1994, and Decree No. 104 of 2000.

19. The Ministry of the Environment establishes these plans following the procedure regulated in Decree No. 39 of 2012, Ministry of the Environment.

20. The decontamination and prevention plans must include (1) the relationship between total emission levels and levels of pollutants to be regulated; (2) the expected deadline to meet the emission reduction; (3) the parties responsible for compliance; (4) the enforcing authorities; (5) the environmental management instruments that will be used to meet the objectives; (6) the emission reduction proportion per regulated activities; (7) estimates of economic and social costs; and (8) proposal, when possible, of emission compensation mechanisms.

21. All these decontamination plans are available at http://portalsnifa.sma.gob.cl/PlanesPrevencion.aspx.

22. Decree No. 3,557 of 1980, Ministry of Agriculture, art. 11.

23. Decree No. 594 of 1999, Ministry of Health, tit. V, para. III.

24. Decree No. Supreme Decree No. 43, of 2012, of the Ministry of the Environment.

25. Gobierno de Chile, Ministerio del Medio Ambiente, Segunda Comunicación Oficial sobre Cambio Climático (Second Official Report on Climate Change), http://www.mma.gob.cl/1304/articles-50880_docomunicadoCambioClimatico.pdf.

26. The UNFCCC was enacted in Chile by Decree No. 123 of 1995, Ministry of Foreign Affairs, and the Kyoto Protocol was enacted by Decree No. 349 of 2004, of the same Ministry.

27. Gobierno de Chile, Ministerio del Medio Ambiente, National Climate Change Action Plan 2008–2012, http://www.mma.gob.cl/1304/articles-49744_Plan_02.pdf.

28. *Id.*

29. Gobierno de Chile, Ministerio del Medio Ambiente, Clean Development Mechanism, http://www.mma.gob.cl/1304/w3-article-45012.html.

30. The projects registered at the CDM's registry are available at http://cdm.unfccc.int/Projects/projsearch.html.

31. The Sanitary Code was approved by virtue of Decree No. 725 of 1967, Ministry of Health, while the Water Code was approved by Decree No. 1122 of 1981, Ministry of Justice.

32. Sanitary Code art. 73.

33. *Id.*

34. Decree No. 594 of 1999, Ministry of Health, art. 16.

35. *Id.* art. 17.

36. Water Code art. 92.

37. Water Code art. 129 *bis* 1.

38. Water Code art. 129 *bis* 2.

39. Law No. 19,300 arts. 32, 33.

40. Decree No. 122 of 2009, Ministry of the Presidency.

41. Decree No. 75 of 2009, Ministry of the Presidency.

42. Decree No. 609 of 1998, Ministry of Public Works.

43. Decree No. 90 of 2000, Ministry of the Presidency.

44. Decree No. 46 of 2002, Ministry of the Presidency.

45. Law of the Superintendence of the Environment art. 2.

46. Navigation Law art. 142.

47. *Id.*

48. *Id.*

49. Decree No. 1 of 1992, Ministry of National Defense, art. 159.

50. *Id.* art. 136.

51. *Id.* art. 139.

52. *Id.* arts. 108, 140.

53. The National Policy and its Action Plan are available at http://www.sinia.cl/1292/article-44404_politicaNacSegQuimica.pdf.

54. Chile ratified the Stockholm Convention in 2004 and enacted it by virtue of Decree No. 38 of 2005, Ministry of Foreign Affairs.

55. Chile ratified the Rotterdam Convention in 2004 and enacted it through Decree No. 37 of 2005, Ministry of Foreign Affairs.

56. For example, Decree No. 656 of 2000, Ministry of Health, prohibits the production, import, distribution, sale, and use of asbestos and any material or product that contains it.

57. Decree No. 3557 of 1980, Ministry of Agriculture, empowers SAG to enforce the regulations on manufacture, import, use, distribution, sale, and application of pesticides.

58. Decree No. 78 of 2009, Ministry of Health, art. 2.

59. Decree No. 160 of 2009, Ministry of Economy.

60. Law No. 19,300 art. 10(ñ).

61. Sanitary Code art. 9.

62. This Decree approves the Sanitary Regulations on Hazardous Waste Management.

63. Decree No. 148 of 2003 art. 3.

64. Decree No. 6 of 2009, Ministry of Health, governs the management of waste generated in hospitals and health centers.

65. Sanitary Code, Book III, tit. II, para. I.

66. Sanitary Code art. 71.

67. Sanitary Code art. 72.

68. *Id.*

69. Law No. 18,902 of 1989 art. 2.

70. Law of the Superintendence of the Environment art. 3(n).

71. Decree No. 594 of 1999, Ministry of Health, art. 18.

72. This policy is available at http://www.sinia.cl/1292/articles-26270_pol-rsd.pdf.

73. Sanitary Code art. 11.

74. Sanitary Code art. 79.

75. Sanitary Code art. 80.

76. Decree No. 594 of 1999 art. 18.

77. Decree No. 594 of 1999 art. 20.

78. Decree No. 189 of 2005, Ministry of Health.

79. Decree No. 4 of 2009, Ministry of Presidency.

80. Decree No. 148 of 2003, Ministry of Health, arts. 10, 11.

81. Decree No. 148 of 2003, Ministry of Health, art. 1.

82. Law No. 19,300 art. 10(o).

83. Sanitary Code art. 178.

84. Navigation Law art. 142; Decree No. 1 of 1992, Ministry of National Defense, arts. 16, 82.

85. Decree No. 1 of 1992, Ministry of National Defense, art. 2.

86. *Id.* art. 8.

87. *Id.* arts. 108, 140.

88. *Id.* art. 166.

89. Sanitary Code art. 178.

90. Fishing and Aquaculture Law art. 1.

91. Fishing and Aquaculture Law art. 2 (36) defines hydrobiological resource as a living organism that has water as the normal or more frequent environment of life and that is susceptible to being used by humans.

92. Fishing and Aquaculture Law, tit. II, para. III.

93. The marine parks and reserves are regulated by Decree No. 238 of 2004, Ministry of Economy.

94. Fishing and Aquaculture Law art. 6 A.

95. The management and exploitation areas are regulated by Decree No. 355 of 1995, Ministry of Economy.

96. Fishing and Aquaculture Law art. 2 (10).

97. Subsecretaria de Pesca, http://www.subpesca.cl.

98. Instituto de Fomento Pesquero, http://www.ifop.cl.

99. Fishing and Aquaculture Law art. 49.

100. Fishing and Aquaculture Law art. 67. According to Fishing and Aquaculture Law art. 2(3), aquaculture is the human activity of producing hydrobiological resources.

101. Fishing and Aquaculture Law art. 74 and Decree No. 320 of 2001, Ministry of Economy, Environmental Regulations for Aquaculture.

102. Fishing and Aquaculture Law art. 158.

103. Corporación Nacional Forestal, http://www.conaf.cl. Forest plantations are those forests created through plantations of the same species or combined with others, carried out by man.

104. Native Forest Law art. 1.

105. *Id.* art. 2 (4) (5) (6).

106. *Id.*, tit. II.

107. *Id.*, tit. III.

108. *Id.*, tits. IV, VI.

109. *Id.*, tit. VII.

110. *Id.* art. 17.

111. Decree No. 701 of 1974, Ministry of Agriculture, art. 1.

112. *Id.*, tit. II.

113. *Id.*, tit. IV.

114. *Id.*, tit. III.

115. Law No. 19,300 art. 10(m).

116. Chile is the largest copper producer in the world.

117. Law No. 18,248 of 1983, Ministry of Mining.

118. Mining Code art. 14 & tits. II, V.

119. *Id.* art. 17.

120. *Id.* art. 122.

121. Decree No. 132 of 2002, Ministry of Mining.

122. Law No. 20,551 of 2011, Ministry of Mining, art. 2.

123. *Id.* art. 5.

124. Law No. 19,300 art. 10(i).

125. *Id.* art. 53.

126. *Id.* art. 51; Civil Code arts. 2314, 2329.

127. Law No. 19,300 art. 2(e).

128. *Id.* art. 2(ll).

129. *Id.* art. 2(s).

130. The State Defense Council is a public service, under the supervision of the President of Chile and independent of the Ministries, whose main purpose is the judicial defense of the state's interests (Article 2, Organic Law of the State Defense Council).

131. Law No. 19,300 art. 54.

132. According to Law No. 19,300 art. 63, "evident manifestation of the environmental damage" refers to the discovery of the damage itself (i.e., the contamination on the premises) as opposed to the manifestation or discovery of a consequence of contamination (like a disease), which may become manifest or apparent perhaps ten or more years after the date when the actual contamination occurred.

133. Ministerio del Medio Ambiente, http://www.mma.cl.

134. Chile ratified the Biodiversity Convention on September 9, 1994, through Decree No. 1,963 of 1994, Ministry of Foreign Affairs.

135. Chile ratified the CITES Convention on September 16, 1974, through Decree No. 141 of 1975, Ministry of Foreign Affairs.

136. Law No. 19,300 art. 38.

137. Law No. 19,473 of 1996, Ministry of Agriculture.

138. Hunting Law art. 4.

139. *Id.* arts. 3, 7.

140. The conservation categories used to classify plants, algae, fungi, and wild animals are those recommended by the IUCN (International Union for Conservation of Nature) and correspond to: extinct; extinct in wild status; in critical danger; in danger; vulnerable; almost threatened; minor concern; and unknown data.

141. Law No. 19,300 art. 37.

142. Specifically, vegetation species classified according to Article 37 of Law No. 19,300.

143. *Id.*

144. *Id.*

145. Decree No. 490 of 1976, Ministry of Agriculture, declared the *alerce* as natural monument, and Decree No. 43 of 1990, Ministry of Agriculture, declared the *araucaria araucana* as natural monument.

146. Chile possesses an important diversity of cetaceans, with 43 described species, which represents almost 50 percent of the species known worldwide.

147. Law No. 20,293 of 2008, Ministry of Economy, art. 2; Fishing and Aquaculture Law art. 135 *bis.*

148. As from the National Policy on Protected Areas dated 2005 and the new environmental institutional framework that created the Ministry of the Environment in 2010, the regulations of protected areas are moving from a diffuse network of protected areas to a National System of Protected Areas in which the terrestrial, marine, coastal, and public and private protected areas can be integrally managed.

149. The protection categories that form part of SNASPE are national parks, national reserves, and natural monuments.

150. The Legal Situation of the Current Protected Areas in Chile (La Situación Jurídica de las Actuales Áreas Protegidas en Chile), http://www.proyectogefareasprotegidas.cl /wp-content/uploads/2012/05/La_Situacion_Juridica.pdf.

151. Currently a bill of law that creates the Biodiversity and Protected Areas Service and a National System of Protected Wild Areas is being discussed in Congress.

152. The Washington Convention was ratified by Chile on October 4, 1967, through Decree No. 531 of 1967, Ministry of Foreign Affairs.

153. Washington Convention art. 1.

154. Law No. 17,288 of 1970, Ministry of Education, art. 31.

155. Chile ratified the Ramsar Convention in 1980 and enacted it through Decree No. 771 of 1981, Ministry of Foreign Affairs.

156. The administration and supervision of this system correspond to the Biodiversity and Protected Areas Service, whose creation through a bill of law is currently under discussion in Congress.

157. Law No. 19,300 art. 35.

158. *Id.* art. 10(p).

159. *Id.* art. 10.

160. *Id.* art. 8.

161. *Id.* art. 9.

162. *Id.* art. 11.

163. *Id.* art. 28.

164. *Id.* art. 29.

165. The Assessment Commission is the entity within the SEA that must approve or reject the projects submitted to the SEIA.

166. Chile and Argentina signed an Environmental Treaty and a Protocol on Shared Water Resources on August 2, 1991.

167. Protocol on Shared Water Resources arts. 1, 5.

168. U.N. Convention on Human Environment of 1972 (Stockholm Convention) and UN Convention on Environment and Development of 1992 (Rio Convention).

169. Chile ratified the Basel Convention in 1992 and enacted it through Decree No. 685 of 1992, Ministry of Foreign Affairs.

170. The Civil Liability Convention was ratified by Chile in 1977 and enacted through Decree No. 475 of 1977, Ministry of Foreign Affairs.

171. The Vienna Convention was ratified in 1985 and enacted through Decree No. 719 of 1990, Ministry of Foreign Affairs.

172. Superintendence of Environment Organic Law art. 2.
173. *Id.* art. 38.
174. *Id.* art. 59.
175. *Id.* art. 60.
176. *Id.* art. 48.
177. *Id.* art. 43.
178. Law No. 20.417 of 2010 art. 9 transitory.
179. Law No. 20,600 of 2012, Ministry of the Environment, art. 17.

CHAPTER 24

Colombia

EDUARDO DEL VALLE MORA

I. Introduction to Foundations of the Colombian Environmental Legal System

A. Basic Environmental Law: The Current Trend

Colombia's environmental laws are found in the nation's constitution, laws, and regulations. The country has been more heavily regulating the environment, natural resources, landscape, and human health, and some aspects of its regulatory system stem from international free trade agreements with other countries. This trend appears to be continuing and suggests that environmental laws in Colombia will continue to be based on both domestic and international sources.

Colombia's national constitution has been named the "Green Constitution." In fact, out of its 380 sections, 49 of them directly relate to the protection of natural resources and the environment.[1] Moreover, the constitution declares that Colombian citizens have the constitutional right to a clean and healthy environment. For that reason, the country has modified its regulations several times over the past few decades.[2] Even though most of the current environmental regulations have been issued in the last 15 years, Colombia was one of the first countries in South America to issue a comprehensive environmental and natural resources code, the 1974 Environmental and Natural Resources Code (Environmental Code). This code established the rules with which public and private actors must comply when exploiting Colombia's renewable resources.[3] Then, after the 1992 Rio Declaration on Environment and Development,[4] Colombia enacted Law 99 of 1993, which established the national institutional framework for the management of natural nonrenewable resources and the protection of the environment. Through this statute, the country created the National Environmental System (SINA) articulating the relationship between the different environmental agencies in Colombia and assigning duties to those agencies.[5]

Moreover recently, consistent with the trend internationally, Colombia has substantially regulated the use of its natural resources, the landscape, the environment, and the protection of human health. Colombia's regulations attempt to follow international environmental standards as well as international trade law. For instance, under Colombian environmental laws, environmental public policies must take into account available scientific information, be science based, and may not result in the imposition of an arbitrary or discriminatory ban on trade. That said, environmental agencies may apply the "precautionary principle" whenever there is any threat of serious or irreversible damage that could be caused by a specific activity. Thus, environmental authorities may impose any measure to prevent irreversible damage to the environment and natural resources even in the absence of absolute scientific certainty about the environmental impact of a given activity.

As part of an international trend, Colombia has recently entered into free trade agreements (FTAs) with countries including the United States, Canada, and the European Community. Under these FTAs, Colombia cannot waive or derogate from its environmental laws in a manner that weakens or reduces the protections afforded in those laws in a manner affecting trade or investment.[6] In addition, in the FTAs, Colombia has agreed to (1) maintain appropriate procedures for assessing the environmental impacts and risks of certain projects and activities defined by the government;[7] (2) conserve, protect, and improve the environment for the well-being of present and future generations;[8] (3) ensure the conservation and sustainable use of biological diversity and the preservation of traditional knowledge;[9] (4) guarantee the development of, compliance with, and enforcement of environmental laws;[10] (5) ensure transparency and public participation on environmental matters;[11] and (6) cooperate on the advancement of environmental issues.[12]

One notable example of these FTAs is the Colombia–United States of America free trade agreement,[13] which recognizes that each country is sovereign, has the right to establish its own levels of domestic environmental protection and environmental development priorities, and accordingly has the right to adopt or modify its environmental laws and policies.[14] The FTA reaffirms that each country shall strive to ensure that its laws and policies provide for and encourage high levels of environmental protection and continue to improve its respective level of environmental protection.[15]

Colombia also agreed to implement voluntary actions to protect or enhance the environment and natural resources, such as (1) partnerships involving businesses, local communities, non-governmental organizations, government agencies, or scientific institutions;[16] (2) voluntary guidelines for environmental performance;[17] and (3) voluntary sharing of information and expertise among authorities, interested parties, and the public concerning methods for achieving high levels of environmental protection, voluntary environmental auditing and reporting, ways to use resources more efficiently or reduce environmental impacts, environmental monitoring, and collection of baseline data.[18] In addition, Colombia agreed to create incentives to encourage conservation, restoration, sustainable use, and protection of natural resources and the environment, such as public recognition of facilities or enterprises that are superior environmental performers, or other instruments to help achieve environmental goals.[19]

B. Permitting: General Overview

The Environmental Code regulates the use of different kinds of natural resources by requiring that parties obtain permits and licenses before undertaking various activities involving natural resources and the environment. Different regulations apply to management of different resources.[20] The environmental code regulates the following natural resources: (1) the atmosphere and the national airspace; (2) water (in any of its natural states); (3) land, soil, and subsoil; (4) flora; (5) fauna; (6) primary sources of renewable energy sources; (7) topographic slopes with potential energy; (8) geothermal resources; (9) biological resources of marine water, soil, and subsoil; and (10) landscapes.[21]

Depending on the kind of project or activity, the Environmental Code requires a party wishing to develop or use natural resources to obtain a specific environmental license, authorization, concession, or permission, and also imposes requirements to comply with certain environmental standards.[22] An environmental license is defined in the code as the authorization granted by an environmental authority for the development of a project or activity requiring the applicant to take certain actions for the prevention, mitigation, restoration, compensation, and management of the environmental effects of the authorized work, project, or activity.[23] The license includes all required environmental permits, concessions, and authorizations.[24] The following kinds of projects require an environmental license: mining exploitation, oil and gas exploitation, construction and operation of railroads, construction and operation of airports, construction and operation of riverine and marine ports, and construction and operation of power plants, among other projects.[25]

Depending on the proposed activity, there may be environmental concessions, permits, and authorizations that are required.[26] As a general overview, the following nonexhaustive list describes the most common types of environmental permits required by law: (1) permits for the occupation of riverbeds; (2) wastewater discharge permits; (3) underground water concessions; (4) surface water concessions; (5) protected species take permits; (6) authorization for forestry projects, including logging; (7) atmospheric emissions permits; (8) water exploration permits; and (9) exploration of underground water permits.[27]

C. Key Environmental Actors

1. *National Level*

a. Colombian National Congress

The Colombian National Congress debates and adopts the main national public policies, including environmental policies.[28] The Congress dictates the general framework applicable to the protection of the natural resources and environment. According to the laws issued by the Congress, the national government, through the Ministry of Environment and Sustainable Development, regulates the protection of the environment and natural resources. Moreover, the National Congress is the entity charged with ratifying international treaties signed by the national government.[29]

b.   Ministry of Environment and Sustainable Development

The Ministry of Environment and Sustainable Development was created in 1993 after the 1992 United Nations Conference on Environment and Development, also known as the Earth Summit.[30] The ministry is in charge of the protection of the environment and management of natural resources, and for this purpose, it has the duty to establish the essential policies and regulations for the recovery, conservation, protection, use, management, and non-exploitation of renewable resources.[31] In short, the ministry is the lead environmental agency and is the entity of the national government that implements the country's environmental laws.[32]

c.   National Environmental License Agency (ANLA)

ANLA is responsible for the evaluation and granting of environmental licenses for large-scale projects or activities in Colombia.[33] Thus, ANLA grants licenses for, inter alia, large-scale mining projects, all oil and gas exploitation projects, construction and operation of national roads, production or importation of pesticides, and the construction and operation of international airports, riverine and marine ports, and 100 megawatt-plus power plants. ANLA also ensures compliance with environmental licenses, access to participation in environmental proceedings, analyzes and assesses information provided by environmental licensees, and provides support for the development and issuance of new regulations.[34] ANLA may also carry out administrative investigations when there is a breach of environmental obligations or when environmental damage occurs

2.   Local Environmental Authorities

There are many different local environmental authorities. The most relevant are the Autonomous Environmental Corporations (CAR), the Sustainable Development Corporations (CDS), and the Urban Environmental Authorities (AUU).[35] These authorities have the power to issue environmental licenses, permits, authorizations, and concessions within their respective jurisdiction. They may also issue specific regulations applicable to their jurisdictions, which, however, must not conflict with national policy or establish regulation that is less stringent than the national one.[36]

3.   Other Entities Related to the Protection of the Environment and Natural Resources

While the above-mentioned agencies are the most important ones, other agencies charged with protecting the environment and renewable resources exist, such as the General Prosecutor's Office (Fiscalia General de la Nación), Attorney General's Office (Ministerio Público), Environmental Police Department (Unidad Ambiental de la Policía), local environmental offices of the municipalities and departments (Secretarías de Planeación Ambiental y Urbana de Entes Territoriales), the Alexander von Humboldt and Sinchi Institutes, the Marine and Coastal Investigation Institute (Instituto de Investigaciones Marinas y Costeras, INVEMAR), the Inspector General's Office (Contraloría General de la República), National Planning Department (Departamento Nacional de Planeación), and the Hydrological, Meteorological, and Environmental Assessment Institute (Instituto de Hidrología, Metereología y Estudios Ambientales, IDEAM), among others.

II. Air and Climate Change
A. Air as a Natural Resource

Air is regulated as a natural resource in Colombia under the Environmental Code.[37] The code regulates noise levels for projects as well as emissions.[38] Emissions are regulated differently under the code depending on whether the emission at issue is dispersed or concentrated.[39]

The most common means of regulating air emissions is through the use of permits, which are required for certain activities under Decree 948 of 1995 and related regulations. The following are a few examples of projects requiring emission permits: (1) discharge of gases by industrial and commercial businesses; (2) open pit mining; (3) burning of solid and liquid wastes; (4) storage, transport, load, and upload of goods that may generate atmospheric emissions in ports; (5) burning of fuel and exploitation of oil and gas; (6) storage and refinery of hydrocarbons; (7) operation of thermal energy plants; and (8) operation of nuclear reactors.[40]

Even when projects are not required to obtain atmospheric emission permits, certain activities give rise to an obligation to comply with national and (in some cases stricter) local engineering standards and protocols for the construction and operation of chimneys and ducts.[41]

In addition, all emissions must comply with national and local standards, which establish the minimum physical and chemical conditions that must be satisfied when an entity is emitting gases into the atmosphere.[42]

B. Climate Change: Clean Development Mechanism Projects

Colombia ratified the Kyoto Protocol to the United Nations Framework Convention on Climate Change (UNFCCC)[43] through Law 164 of 1995. The country is an Annex B country, meaning that Colombia is not obliged to reduce its greenhouse gas (GHG) emissions, unlike countries listed in Annex A, and may host clean development mechanism (CDM) projects.

The Ministry of Environment and Sustainable Development has implemented a national strategy for the implementation of CDM projects in the country.[44] This strategy has helped Colombia to increase its participation in the international certified emission reductions market.

As a result, according to the statistics provided by the Ministry of Environment and Sustainable Development, Colombia currently hosts 154 CDM projects. Twenty-nine of these projects have already been registered with the UNFCCC Secretariat; ten have already issued certified emission reductions (CERs); and 66 have been approved by the government and are waiting to be registered with the UNFCCC Secretariat. These projects have a potential annual reduction of 20,935,440 tons GHG emissions, and a total of US$91,230,000 has been produced by the sale of the CERs in Colombia. The CDM projects are located in different sectors, with 26.62 percent of them in the energy sector, 11.04 percent in the forestry sector, 39.61 percent in the industrial sector, 14.29 percent in the waste sector, and 8.44 percent in the transportation sector.[45]

These CDM projects result in many benefits for the country, leading to greater environmental protection, conservation of Colombia's biodiversity, positioning the country as a "green country," job growth, importation and transfer of technology, reduction of GHG emissions, and the restructuring of industry.

In addition, the Chamber of Commerce of Bogotá is working on the implementation of a financial and stock platform through which voluntary carbon credits will be able to be negotiated. The Chamber of Commerce is expecting to launch this project and initiate its operation in 2015.

III. Water
A. Law Concerning the Rational Use of Energy and Water

Colombia has issued two important laws to promote the rational use of energy and water. Under Law 373 of 1997, Colombia created a national program establishing different methods to reuse water and reduce waste. It also establishes levels of water consumption and creates special incentives for those who implement programs seeking to conserve water.[46] Similarly, Law 697 of 2001 established incentives to those who import or produce wind power instruments, biogas generators, and solar panels in an effort to encourage the efficient use of energy by developing alternative and clean technologies.[47]

B. Water (Inland) as a Natural Resource

The use of water in Colombia is strictly regulated through the use of water concessions and water discharge permits. A water concession authorizes a party to take and use water and, under Decree 1541 of 1978, must be obtained before a party uses any water. Water concessions are typically required for, inter alia, irrigation, forestry, industrial use, nuclear energy generation, geothermal energy generation, mining exploitation, oil and gas exploitation, hydroelectric power generation, transportation of minerals or toxic substances, and fishing.[48]

A water discharge permit, on the other hand, allows a party to discharge wastewater into rivers, aquifers, creeks, soil, or sewer systems. According to Decree 3930 of 2010, any activity that generates a waste discharge into an aquifer or sewer system will require a discharge permit.[49] For both water concessions and water discharge permits, if it is necessary to build any infrastructure within 30 meters of a river, a special environmental permit is also required.[50]

IV. Handling, Treatment, Transportation, and Disposal of Hazardous Materials

Hazardous materials are defined as substance that due to their "corrosive, reactive, explosive, flammable, infectious and radioactive characteristics may entail risk or damage to human health and the environment." In this regard, Colombia signed the 1989 Basel Convention on the Control of Transboundary Movements of Hazardous Wastes and Their Disposal and the Montreal Protocol on Substances That Deplete the Ozone Layer.[51] This is another example on how Colombia has introduced into its regulatory system certain standards found in environmental agreements.[52]

Decree 4741 of 2005 sets forth requirements applicable to any person who generates hazardous wastes, making the generator responsible for the hazardous wastes until they are used as raw materials in an industrial process or eliminated. Generators must (1) create an integral management plan for the hazardous wastes generated by a project; (2) draft an integral management plan for all hazardous wastes to reduce contamination; (3) identify the hazardous characteristics of the wastes produced; (4) guarantee that the packing, bottling, and labeling of the wastes is duly performed in accordance with the applicable regulation; (5) comply with transportation norms (Decree 1609 of 2002); (6) register the company in the Registry of Generators of Hazardous Wastes; (7) update on a yearly basis the information of the Registry of Generators of Hazardous Wastes; (8) ensure that the personnel in charge of the management of the hazardous wastes in the facilities of the company are adequately trained, informed of the risks posed, and supplied with appropriate equipment; (9) draft and keep current a contingency plan to address any accident or eventuality and ensuring personnel are prepared to implement it; (10) maintain storage certificates, and documentation concerning proper use, treatment, and final disposition, for up to five years; and (11) contract services for the storage, proper use, recuperation, treatment, and/or final disposition of wastes.[53]

V. Waste and Site Remediation

Pursuant to the Environmental Code, neither individuals, companies, nor the government may deposit contaminants in the soil, subsoil, groundwater, or surface water or in any place that may negatively affect the environment, natural resources, landscape, or human health.[54] Therefore, based on the current applicable environmental regulation, any of these individuals or entities that do so will be obligated to undertake all necessary measures to clean up the site and remediate any negative environmental impact that their actions may have caused.[55] If not, they will be subject to an environmental sanction proceeding. In addition to an order requiring immediate remediation, such a proceeding can result in the imposition of sanctions.[56]

Furthermore, when an environmental license is required, the government must approve a proposed rehabilitation and restoration plans for use after the project development is complete (e.g., the abandonment of a mine, the closure of a drilling well). Thus, as part of the environmental license, the licensee must undertake all necessary measures to reduce and mitigate the impacts that would be generated by the construction and operation of a specific project or activity.[57]

While Colombian authorities have discussed the possibility of creating a fund to finance the remediation of orphan waste sites, such proposal has not been adopted yet. As a result, while a fund exists for the restoration of the environment in cases involving natural catastrophes, Colombia currently does not have a fund for the restoration and remediation of abandoned and contaminated sites analogous to the United States' Comprehensive Environmental Response, Compensation, and Liability Act, commonly known as Superfund. Based on international trends, Colombia may create a similar fund in the near future. Such fund would help Colombia mitigate the negative impacts caused by activities such as illegal mining, drug plantations, deforestation, and inadequate treatment and disposal of hazardous wastes.

Finally, Decree 2981 of 2013 regulates the management, treatment, transport, and disposal of solid wastes. Solid waste is defined as any object, substance, or solid material from any domestic, commercial, industrial, or service activity that is abandoned, rejected or delivered by the generator and may potentially be used as material for a new product or good or be finally disposed. As a general rule, the liability and responsibility of the generator is cut off once the solid waste is transferred to the transporter. Similarly, the transporter's liability generally is cut off after the waste is transferred to the individual or company that is responsible for its disposal.[58]

VI.   Emergency Response

Colombia is a signatory to the International Convention on Civil Liability for Oil Pollution Damage (Convention).[59] The convention became into force in Colombia on June 24th, 1990. However, on January 25, 2005, the Colombian government denounced the treaty along with the 1976 protocol thereto.[60] Thus, the convention is not currently in force in Colombia.

That said, in the event of an oil spill on Colombian territory or within Colombian waters, the responsible party is obligated to undertake all necessary measures to mitigate any negative impacts on the environment caused by the spill. The responsible party also must report the spill to the government.[61] Oil transport companies must additionally maintain a contingency plan to be implemented in the event of an oil spill. As mentioned, *supra*, in section V, responsible parties are required not only to undertake all necessary measures to mitigate the impacts at the time a spill occurs, but also restore the environment and the affected natural resources. Therefore, a person or company that is involved in an oil spill and does not restore the environment will be subject to a proceeding that may result in the imposition of sanctions as well as the immediate obligation to remediate the damage. In addition, the government is authorized to impose preventive measures in the case of an oil spill.[62]

VII.   Natural Resource Management and Protection

In Colombia, a project proponent wishing to undertake any activity potentially causing a substantial impact on natural resources or the environment or significantly alter the existing landscape must first obtain an environmental license. This obligation applies to mining projects, hydrocarbon exploitation, the construction of international airports, construction of dams, and others.

Additionally, projects may also require authorizations, concessions, and permits for activities involving the use of natural resources that may have an environmental impact but do not require an environmental license. These types of instruments are classified depending on the type of natural resource, such as the following:

- In some cases gaseous emissions may require an emissions permit identifying the type of project to be developed, the permitted emissions, and quality and quantity thereof;
- Regarding water resources, there are four different types of permits:
  1. Concessions, which grant the right of using and taking water from rivers and wells.
  2. Discharge waste permits, which grant the right to discharge waste into the water.
  3. Special permits for the use of riverbeds.
  4. Special authorizations for the subsoil exploration of wells and underground water.
- The management, treatment, and final disposition of hazardous wastes is subject to a special regulation. There are also rules applicable to the collection and environmental management of computer waste.
- External visual signage is subject to registration in the competent municipality before being installed.
- The extraction of forest products requires a permit.

A.   Citizen Participation

Pursuant to sections 69 and 70 of Law 99 of 1993, there are various ways for the public to participate in the government's decision-making process. Any person may intervene in administrative procedures regarding the granting, modification, or cancellation of environmental licenses, permits, authorizations, or concessions or environmental sanctions proceedings resulting from the violation of environmental regulations.[63] In such cases, individuals recognized as "intervening parties" are permitted to file petitions for reconsideration challenging resolutions granting any environmental license, permit, concession, or authorization.[64] In addition, individuals have the right of access to environmental information. As a result, anyone may visit the offices of environmental agencies and review the content of environmental dockets with the exception of confidential governmental or business information.[65]

In those cases in which the project, activity, or work will be executed within certain indigenous or Afro-Colombian territories, it will be necessary to develop a consultation process with these communities prior to obtaining an environmental permit. The project must also ensure that the indigenous or Afro-Colombia communities obtain the benefits derived from activities occurring within their territories and receive a proportional indemnification whenever damages may result.[66] The Ministry of Interior is the authority in charge of leading the prior consultation proceeding.

B.   Protected Areas

The national parks system is defined as a set of areas with exceptional value for the national natural patrimony. These areas are protected due to their natural, cultural, and historical characteristics. There are different kinds of areas within this system, including (1) National Natural Parks, (2) Natural Reserves, (3) Unique Natural Areas, (4) Fauna Sanctuaries, and (5) Flora Sanctuaries, among others.[67] In these protected areas, permitted activities are limited to those involving preservation, investigation, education, recreation, cultural activities, recovery, and control. High-impact activities such as mining and oil and gas projects cannot be undertaken in these protected areas.[68]

Local environmental authorities (Corporación Autónoma Regional) may also declare protected areas, such as regional parks and regional Forest Reserve Areas, within their jurisdiction.[69] Environmental regulations also authorize the establishment of so-called Civil Society Natural Reserves, by which private properties are protected with the purpose of preserving the environment and the natural resources. These properties are managed jointly with nonprofit environmental organizations.[70] Finally, the Colombian government may also declare private properties as protected areas.[71]

VIII.   Natural Resource Damages

As a general rule, a party that is responsible for causing environmental damage must undertake all necessary measures in order to restore the environment, natural resources, landscape, and human health. In addition, an environmental authority may initiate an environmental sanction proceeding against the person causing the environmental damage.[72]

IX.   Protected Species

Colombia is a party to various international instruments that protect threatened flora and fauna, such as the Convention on International Trade in Endangered Species of Wild Fauna and Flora (CITES),[73] which was ratified via Law 17 of 1981; the Convention on Biological Diversity, ratified through Law 165 of 1994; and the Convention on Wetlands of International Importance,[74] ratified through Law 357 of 1997.

Additionally, as per the Colombian Constitution, particularly sections 8, 79, and 80, the government is obliged to protect the integrity and diversity of the environment, preserve areas of special ecological interest, promote education to achieve these goals, and plan the management and use of the natural resources to promote their sustainable development, preservation, restoration, or substitution.

Decree 2811 of 1974 contains a special chapter on flora and fauna establishing measures that must be taken to preserve and protect certain species that—due to their biological, genetic, esthetic, socioeconomic value, or cultural interest—must endure.

Similarly, through Resolution 584 of 2002, the Ministry of Environment and Sustainable Development have thoroughly regulated activities related to wild flora and fauna and other species declared as threatened in the national territory and that were included in the annex of said resolution.

Finally, the most important regulation concerning fauna and flora is contained in the Environmental Code and the 1992 Convention on Biological Diversity (CBD). In particular the unlawful commerce, transportation, exploitation, and other activities related to endangered species may result in the imposition of fines and even, in some circumstances, prison time. Separately, the 2000 Cartagena Protocol on Biotechnology Security to the CBD also affects wildlife through the regulation of trade in genetically modified organisms (GMOs).

X.   Environmental Review and Decision Making

As mentioned in section I.B, depending on the project or activity, an environmental license will be required. A responsible party's license will include all required authorizations and concessions.[75]

Project proponents desiring a permit must also submit to the government an environmental impact analysis (EIA) identifying the impacts that the project or activity will have and the corrective measures that will be undertaken to compensate, prevent, restore, and mitigate the impacts on the environment.[76] Depending on the kind of permit that is required, the government will define which studies, reports, and documents must be submitted with the application.[77] The EIA must include not only biological information, but also information on the economic and social characteristics of the project area. Thus, social measures also must be included in the EIA.[78] Once the government receives the formal permit request along with its EIA and other

required additional information (e.g., certification that first nation or indigenous communities or archeological sites are not present in the project area),
a procedure begins whereby the government requests any required additional information and verifies the conditions of the proposed site.[79] After a
certain administrative procedure (Decree 2820 of 2010) is completed, the government will decide whether to grant the environmental license and the
terms of any such license. Pursuant to the applicable regulation, the applicant can file a petition for reconsideration challenging the resolution approving or rejecting an environmental license. By filing this petition, the applicant
may request the revocation, modification, or clarification of the administrative decision.[80]

Environmental authorities may also visit project sites to determine
whether a company or individual is complying with applicable environmental regulations and environmental permits (if applicable).[81]

XI.   Transboundary Pollution

Pursuant to the Colombian National Constitution and Law 1252 of 2008, the
import onto Colombian territory of nuclear, dangerous, and hazardous waste
is strictly prohibited.[82]

XII.   Civil and Criminal Enforcement and Penalties

Given that foreign investment in Colombia has significantly increased during the last ten years and Colombia has entered into FTAs with a number of
countries, it is necessary to describe the environmental liability regime in
Colombia.[83] This section will provide a broad overview of the issues confronting companies when authorities initiate an investigation and sanctioning procedures for a violation of environmental regulations or to remedy
environmental damage. In addition, in light of the current level of funding
of Colombian projects by international banks, it is necessary to offer a general overview of lenders' potential environmental liabilities.

Pursuant to Colombian environmental regulations, particularly Law 1333
of 2009, the types of liability resulting from effects to the environment, natural resources, human health, and landscape may be placed into four categories: (1) administrative, (2) extracontractual civil (tort), (3) contractual civil,
and (4) criminal liability.[84] Liability as to government officials may include
disciplinary and monetary sanctions.[85] In addition, any individual may file a
complaint based on a constitutional cause of action to protect the environment and natural resources.

A.   Administrative Liability

An individual or holder of an environmental license, permit, concession, or
authorization must comply with the provisions set forth in his permit, as well
as with applicable environmental regulations. If any entity or person violates

its environmental obligations, environmental authorities may initiate an administrative procedure to determine the responsibility of the alleged infringer.

When a person or entity is found responsible, the government may take various actions pursuant in Law 1333 of 2009 to ensure compliance with the environmental laws. For example, the government may impose sanctions, penalties, or fines for (1) noncompliance with the conditions set out in the environmental laws, licenses, permits, or authorizations or (2) any other violation of environmental regulations, including the commencement of an activity without having obtained any required environmental license, permit, or authorization.

The government may impose one or more of the following measures:[86] (1) written admonition; (2) confiscation of all items used to commit the infraction; or (3) suspension of work or activity order when they may cause damage to the environment, natural resources, the landscape, or human health. Likewise, the government may impose one or more of the following sanctions:[87] (1) daily fines up to the equivalent of approximately US$1,500,000; (2) revocation of environmental licenses, permits, or authorizations; (3) demolition of the relevant civil works, with the violating or noncomplying party bearing the expense of demolition; (4) an order requiring restoration of the fauna and flora species taken without complying applicable environmental law; and (g) community service. Additionally, the individual found liable will be listed in the National Environmental Offenders List.

B.   Criminal Liability

Environmental permits may also be enforced under Colombia's criminal code. If an individual or holder of an environmental license, permit, concession, or authorization causes severe damage to natural resources as described in the criminal code, or affects human health or natural resources, a criminal proceeding may be initiated. If the individual is found responsible, he or she will be subject to the penalties described in the criminal code. Such penalties include imprisonment from 48 to 108 months, and fines that range as high as the equivalent of approximately US$4,500,000).[88]

Under Colombian law, only individuals are subject to criminal liability. In that regard, the directors of the company that holds an environmental license, permit, concession, or authorization may be personally liable, if found to have been directly responsible for the criminal offense.

In addition to proceedings concerning environmental permits, the criminal code contemplates other criminal offenses, such as (1) illegal use of natural resources;[89] violation of international borders for the illegal use and exploitation of natural resources;[90] illicit use of GMOs, microorganisms, and organisms;[91] hazardous waste pollution;[92] pollution resulting from the illegal exploitation of minerals, gas, and oil;[93] illegal experiments with biologic agents or biochemical agents;[94] illegal fishing;[95] illegal hunting;[96] illegal occupancy of protected areas;[97] and illegal exploitation of minerals and other materials.[98]

C.   Civil Liability

General principles of liability are applicable to anyone who causes environmental damage. Under the principles of Colombian civil liability, civil liability may be contractual or extracontractual liability (tort law). Contractual liability may be found where parties entered into an agreement and where the claim is based on a breach of the agreement by one party due to the fact that the breaching party did not comply with environmental regulations or caused environmental harm. On the other hand, unlike contractual liability, extracontractual liability refers to a damage or injury committed upon a person or property regardless of whether a contract exists between the two parties.

Below we refer to general principles of extracontractual liability, because this is the most common type of liability arising from damages caused to the environment and natural resources.

Pursuant to the Colombian Civil Code, a person committing a wrong that has caused damage to a person is bound to pay the indemnification, regardless of the penalties imposed by the law.[99] The elements of extracontractual liability are

1.   Conduct: the conduct can be either an act or omission.
2.   Fault: fault is misconduct by the offender, which would not be carried out by a reasonable person in the same situation as the offender. Fault is a global concept involving fraud or the intention to cause damage and negligence.
3.   Damage: damage is understood as a material or personal loss or detriment.
4.   A nexus between the negligent/faulty conduct and the damage: the nexus is the direct link between a cause (conduct) and an effect (damage) in the sense that, but for the conduct, the effect would not have occurred.

Civil liability also applies to governmental authorities. Thus, the national and local governments are responsible if they cause damages to the environment. Public officers can be held liable for the same reasons.[100]

In addition to the foregoing, company directors holding environmental licenses may also be civilly and administratively liable where the liability was caused by intentional or gross negligence, or an act or omission of its directors.[101] In practice, director liability is found in the following way. Once the civil liability of the company holding an environmental license, permit, concession, or authorization has been determined or an environmental administrative sanction imposed, the person affected by the damage may initiate a civil procedure against the company's directors whose intentional or gross negligence acts or omissions caused the liability, to obtain the reimbursement for the damages suffered.[102]

D. Class Actions (Constitutional Action)

If any person or holder—individual or company—of a license, permit, concession, or authorization violates environmental regulations and/or obligations arising from the environmental license granted to it, that entity may be subjected to what is called a "popular action." The government or any third party may file a class action to protect collective rights and interests, such as environmental rights (i.e., the right to a healthy environment, equitable use of natural resources, or natural resources preservation).[103] Class actions may be brought to (1) prevent contingent damage; (2) mitigate threats of damage; or (3) bring an end to infringements of collective rights and interests.[104] Under Colombian law, no statute of limitations applies to extinguish the availability of class actions.[105] Class actions may also be brought against any other individual or company that, without having a license, permit, concession, or authorization, violates its obligations under applicable environmental regulations.[106]

E. Group or Constitutional Actions (Acciones De Grupo)

Group actions, in contrast to class actions, are focused on obtaining a remedy to a particular harm. Thus, group actions may be filed by a group of at least 25 persons damaged by the same environmental harm (e.g., contamination of a river affecting the crops of different peasants), notwithstanding the filing of any potential class action to protect a general interest.[107] Group actions may be filed against the permittee or against anyone who has violated environmental regulations.

Group actions seek to protect collective rights, most typically the right to enjoy a clean and healthy environment, and seek indemnification for damages. Group actions may be filed in cases where there are actions or omissions by individuals or authorities that have violated or threatened the collective rights and interests.[108]

For relief in group actions, courts will require the offender to remedy damages caused to the environment, natural resources, the landscape, or human health; and to indemnify any person that suffered damages or losses due to the offender's actions or omissions.[109]

F. Special Case Study: Lender's Environmental Liability

In light of the fact that international investment in Colombia has increased in recent years, a special section is devoted to the laws imposing potential environmental liability upon lenders. Even though Colombia has not yet regulated the potential environmental liability of lenders, such liability exists where the lender becomes the project owner or acquires direct influence in the decision-making process, as discussed below.

To the best of our knowledge, so far there has not been a Colombian case imposing environmental liability on any person or company that is not the direct perpetrator of the conduct. Particularly, it is not know of any lender that has been found responsible for its debtor's actions or omissions. However, according to the international trend that attempts to transfer a debtor's environmental liabilities to its lenders, it is necessary to review this potential scenario. Thus, to cover all the possible scenarios and future developments of lenders' liability in Colombia, it is crucial to clarify the situations in which a lender might be found liable.

Lender liability depends on the actions of the lender. Lenders may simply provide resources, without exerting any power or influence over its debtors' decisions; alternately, lenders can sometimes exercise different kinds of decision-making authority over a debtor's project. Depending on a lender's participation, it may be held responsible for environmental liabilities. With this purpose, here are some hypothetical cases.

Hypothetical No. 1: The lender is directly involved in the action or omission causing damage.

The first hypothetical involves a lender actively participating in a project, including during its preparation, implementation, and physical performance. A lender who actively participates in a project may have also materially participated in the action or the omission that produces the damage or the violation of the environmental regulations. In that case, it will be held liable under Colombian environmental and civil statutes. Liability is not based on the fact that the lender funded the project, but rather on the fact that the lender is deemed to be the offender itself.

Hypothetical No. 2: The lender made the decision causing the environmental infraction but did not execute it physically or materially; that is, that action is performed by someone else that received an instruction or guideline from the lender.

This hypothetical arises where lenders direct debtors to undertake actions that in turn give rise to liability, but do not perform the action themselves. In this case, courts will likely apply the extracontractual liability regime described in the Colombian Civil Code. Under principles of extracontractual liability, a person is deemed liable for the actions or omissions performed by those under its care.

In this situation, the extent of involvement of the lender, and particularly, whether the lender directs or controls the borrower who commits the violation, is particularly relevant. If the lender simply provides resources and does not have power over the decisions that produced the damage, the likelihood of that liability would arise is relatively low. On the other hand, if the lender actually directs the borrower to perform a unlawful act, government authorities may include the lender in administrative or civil proceedings as a responsible party. If the decision or level of involvement in the decision-making process is substantial, a lender may be targeted as a potentially responsible party.

If the lender is found liable, it may, in turn, initiate a proceeding against the borrower who performed the harmful conduct, to obtain indemnification for the sanctions imposed on him.

As discussed above, so far this type of potential liability for a lender has not been applied. Nevertheless, it is important for a lender to know that, depending on its level of participation on a project, it may be held liable pursuant to the general rules of extracontractual liability.

Hypothetical No. 3: The lender knew the borrower performed the conduct (action or omission) contrary to environmental regulations, did not try to prevent the situation from occurring, and continued to provide funds to the borrower.

In this third example, a lender is aware of the noncompliance of the borrower, does nothing to prevent it, and continues to provide funds. As in the situation described above, the degree of involvement of the lender in the project is crucial. If the lender has control over the administration of the project and decision making on environmental matters or policies, it may be considered liable.[110]

As it was previously stated, the environmental liability in this situation would have to be assessed on a case-by-case basis in order to analyze if there was an actual relationship of dependence between the borrower, who is directly responsible, and the lender.

Hypothetical No. 4: The lender knew the borrower committed an environmental infraction but conducted himself diligently to try to prevent the harm.

In the fourth hypothetical, the lender is aware of environmental damages, but tries to prevent those damages from occurring. This scenario assumes some level of direction or control by the lender. Here, the Colombian Civil Code will exclude from liability the person that has control or direction over the perpetrator, so long as that person acted with due diligence given its position.

To avoid liability, the lender would have to demonstrate that it conducted the activity with the diligence required, and that despite its best efforts, it could not prevent the environmental infringement. If the lender can establish its diligence, the lender will not be held liable.

Hypothetical No. 5: The lender is deemed to be part of the management of the borrower that committed the environmental infraction.

Pursuant to the Colombian Code of Commerce, an "administrator" of a company consists of its legal representative, its liquidator, its director with legal representation of the branch (*factor*), the members of the board of directors, and those that, according to the bylaws of the company, perform such obligations.[111] A company can also be an administrator of another company.[112] Under the Code of Commerce, the administrators of a company are jointly liable for the damages caused with willful misconduct or negligence to the company, to the partners of the company or to third parties.[113] Consequently, if a company commits an environmental infringement and the lender is deemed to be an administrator, and is shown to have acted with willful misconduct or negligence, it will be deemed liable. If the administrator is a company, its legal representative will be held liable as well.

Hypothetical No. 6: The lender is deemed to be the controlling company of the borrower committing the environmental infringement.

According to the Colombian Code of Commerce, a company is subordinate or controlled by another when its decision-making power is subjected to the will of another person or company.[114] This control may be exercised directly or through a subordinate of the controlling company.

This provision is relevant in the sense that if the subordinated company becomes insolvent, the controlling party is presumed to be liable, on a secondary basis, for the obligations of the controlled company.

Therefore, if the lender is deemed to be a company and the subordinate, in this case the borrower, does not have sufficient resources to cover an obligation caused from an environmental violation, the lender may be held responsible.

Notes

1. Colombian Constitutional Court. Constitutional Rule C-595 of 2010. Justice Jorge Iván Palacio. Constitutional Rule C-126 of 1998. Justice Alejandro Martínez Caballero. Constitutional Rule C-750 of 2008. Justice Clara Inés Vargas Hernández.

2. CONSTITUCIÓN POLÍTICA DE COLOMBIA § 79.

3. Decree 2811 of 1974 § 1.

4. *See* http://www.un.org/documents/ga/conf151/aconf15126-1annex1.htm (last visited Sept. 16, 2013).

5. Law 99, 1993.

6. Colombia–EEUU Free Trade Agreement, ch. 18, § 18.03(2); Colombia–Canada Free Trade Agreement, ch. 17, §§ 17.01, 17.02; Colombia–Canada Agreement on Environment § 2.

7. Colombia–EEUU Free Trade Agreement, ch. 18, § 18.03(2); Colombia–Canada Free Trade Agreement, ch. 17, §§ 17.01, 17.02; Colombia–Canada Agreement on Environment § 2.

8. *E.g.,* Colombia–Canada Free Trade Agreement § 17.03(a) & § 3.

9. *E.g., id.* § 17.03(c) & § 5.

10. *E.g., id.* § 17.03(d) & § 3.

11. *E.g., id.* § 17.03(e) & § 4.

12. *E.g., id.* § 17.03(f) & § 7.

13. The Colombia–United States Free Trade Agreement is enforceable as of May 15, 2012.

14. Colombia–EEUU Free Trade Agreement, ch. 18, § 18.01, Levels of Protection.

15. *Id.*

16. *Id.* § 18.05(1)(a), Mechanisms to Enhance Environmental Performance.

17. *Id.* § 18.05(1)(b).

18. *Id.* § 18.05(1)(c).

19. *Id.* § (2).

20. Decree 2811 of 1974; Law 23 of 1973.

21. Decree 2811 of 1974 § 3.

22. Decree 2811 of 1974 §§ 1–3; Law 23 of 1973.

23. Decree 2820 of 2010 § 1; Law 99 of 1993 § 53.

24. Decree 2820 of 2010 § 3; Law 99 of 1993 § 53.

25. Decree 2820 of 2010 §§ 8, 9.

26. Decree 2811 of 2010; Decree 2820 of 2010; Decree 948 of 1995; Colombian National Government Decree 3930 of 2010; Law 9 of 1979. Other decrees and laws also establish the different kinds of environmental permits, licenses, authorizations, and concessions.

27. Decree 2811 of 2010; Decree 2820 of 2010; Decree 948 of 1995; Colombian National Government Decree 3930 of 2010; Law 9 of 1979. Other decrees and laws also establish the different kinds of environmental permits, licenses, authorizations, and concessions.

28. Constitución Política de Colombia § 150

29. *Id.* § 150.

30. Law 99 of 1993 § 2.

31. *Id.* § 5.

32. *Id.*

33. Law 1444 of 2011 § 18(d), (e), (f); Decree 3573 of 2011.

34. Law 1444 of 2011 § 18(d), (e), (f); Decree 3573 of 2011.

35. Law 99 of 1993 § 4, & Chapter VI (§§ 23–41).

36. *Id.* § 63, Principles.

37. Decree 948 of 1995; Resolution 909 of 2008; Resolution 760 of 2010; Resolution 2153 of 2010; Resolution 591 of 2012.

38. Decree 948 of 1995 §§ 3, 14.

39. *Id.* §§ 1, 96.

40. *Id.* § 73.

41. *Id.*; Resolution 909 of 2008; Resolution 760 of 2010; Resolution 2153 of 2010; Resolution 591 of 2012.

42. Decree 948 of 1995; Resolution 909 of 2008.

43. *See* http://www.unfccc.org.

44. Ministry of Environment and Sustainable Development report, http://www.minambiente.gov.co//contenido/contenido.aspx?catID=829&conID=3046 (last visited June 24, 2013).

45. *Id.*

46. Law 373 of 1997 §§ 4, 5, 6, 8.

47. Law 697 of 2001 §§ 2–6.

48. Decree 1541 of 1978 § 36.

49. Decree 3930 of 2010 § 40.

50. Decree 1541 of 1978 § 93.

51. *See* http://www.basel.int/TheConvention/Overview/TextoftheConvention/tabid/1275/Default.aspx; http://ozone.unep.org/new_site/en/montreal_protocol.php (last visited Sept. 16, 2013).

52. Law 253 of 1996; Law 1252 of 2008; Decree 4741 of 2005.

53. Law 253 of 1996; Law 1252 of 2008; Decree 4741 of 2005; Decree 1609 of 2002.

54. Decree 2811 of 1974; Law 99 of 1993.

55. Law 1333 of 2009.

56. *Id.*

57. Decree 2820 of 2010.

58. Decree 2987 of 2013.

59. *See* http://www.imo.org/About/Conventions/ListOfConventions/Pages/International-Convention-on-Civil-Liability-for-Oil-Pollution-Damage-(CLC).aspx (last visited June 24, 2013).

60. *See* http://www.imo.org/blast/blastDataHelper.asp?data_id=12124&filename=30.pdf (last visited Sept. 16, 2013); http://www.imo.org/blast/blastDataHelper.asp?data_id=12123 &filename=6.pdf (last visited Sept. 16, 2013).

61. The same obligation to report will occur in case a polluted site is found.

62. Law 1333 of 2009.

63. Law 99 of 1993 §§ 69, 70.

64. Law 99 of 1993 § 69.

65. Law 99 of 1993 § 70.

66. Constitución Política de Colombia § 330; Law 21 of 1991 (International Labor Organization Convention No. 169).

67. Decree 2811 of 1974 §§ 328, 329.

68. Law 1450 of 2011 § 202.

69. Decree 2811 of 1974 § 331.

70. Law 99 of 1993 § 109.

71. Decree 2811 of 1974 § 329; Law 99 of 1993 § 110.

72. Law 1333 of 2009.

73. *See* http://www.cites.org.

74. *See* http://www.ramsar.org.

75. Law 99 of 1993; Decree 2820 of 2010. A number of different kinds of environmental permits may be required for a given project. See section I.B, *supra.*

76. *Id.*

77. Law 99 of 1993; Decree 2820 of 2010.

78. *Id.*

79. *Id.*

80. *Id.*

81. Decree 2811 of 2010; Decree 2820 of 2010.

82. Law 1252 of 2008.

83. For instance, according to the Colombian Central Bank Report (2011), foreign investment increased in the mining industry from US$627M in 2003 to US$4,708M in 2011, and in the oil and gas industry from US$277M in 2003 to US$9,445M in 2011.

84. Law 1333 of 2009 § 21.

85. Law 734 of 2002; Law 1333 of 2009; Law 610 of 2000.

86. Law 1333 of 2009 tit. III.

87. Law 1333 of 2009 § 40.

88. Crim. Law 599 of 2000 modified by Law 1453 of 2011 § 331.

89. *Id.* § 328.

90. *Id.* § 329.

91. *Id.* § 330.

92. *Id.* § 332A.

93. *Id.* § 333.

94. *Id.* § 334.

95. *Id.* § 335.

96. *Id.* § 336.

97. *Id.* § 337.

98. *Id.* § 338.

99. Civil Code § 2341.

100. Law 23 of 1973 § 16.

101. Law 1333 of 2009 §§ 1, 3, 5.

102. *Id.*

103. Law 472 of 1998 §§ 4, 5.

104. *Id.* § 25.

105. *Id.* § 11.

106. *Id.* § 9.

107. *Id.* § 4.

108. *Id.* § 46.

109. *Id.* § 46.

110. Civil Code § 2347.

111. Law 222 of 1995 § 22.

112. *Id.* § 25.

113. Commerce Code § 200.

114. Law 222 of 1995 § 26.

CHAPTER 25

Costa Rica

JOSE PABLO SANCHEZ

I. Introduction

Costa Rica's legal regime encompasses a broad array of environmental laws, from Article 50 of the Political Constitution, which includes the right to a healthy environment, to the most recently approved Wildlife Conservation Law, enacted via national referendum. The country has enacted laws and bylaws and has ratified most international environmental agreements, including Chapter 17 of the Central American Free Trade Agreement. In this agreement, Costa Rica assumed the responsibility to effectively enforce its environmental laws, and enact laws in those areas where compliance and enforcement may be weak. Costa Rica is well known for some of the richest marine and land biodiversity hot spots. However, the country faces major limitations in environmental enforcement, such as the lack of efficient mechanisms for monitoring and controlling due to limited economic resources. Major challenges, like government officials who lack sufficient knowledge about environmental laws and procedural rights, result in impacts to wildlife, the destruction of forests, and water and air pollution. This chapter discusses the country's environmental legal framework. It provides an overview of national efforts in conservation, as well as compliance and enforcement mechanisms that the country has put in place since the 1970s. These efforts include the creation of the national parks system and the establishment of a goal to become carbon neutral by 2021.

A. Foundation of the Costa Rican Environmental Legal System

1. Environmental Law Framework

Costa Rica Political Constitution, Article 50, establishes the right of every citizen to a healthy and ecologically balanced environment. A constitutional reform enacted in 1994 strengthened citizens' ability to bring an *amparo* action before the Constitutional Chamber.[1] This resolution established "legitimacy to claim the constitutional right to a healthy environment," which is referred to as "diffuse interest" (*intereses difusos*). After this resolution, the Constitutional Chamber has handled a range of cases concerning the acts of public and private entities as well as individuals for alleged violations of this constitutional right. These matters have tended to focus largely on solid waste pollution and logging.

The national constitution reform was a major achievement. That said, some additional changes were made as a result of the 1992 United Nations Conference on Environment and Development. In the more than 20 years since, the country has experienced two waves of environmental law legislation. The first wave, in the mid-1990s, included the promulgation of the Organic Environmental Law, the Biodiversity Law, the Hazardous Waste Regulation, and the Wildlife Conservation Law, as well as specific statutes concerning environmental assessment and a wastewater pollution tax. In 2010, a second wave occurred, driven mostly by the Ministry of Health, which is the entity responsible for waste management. This second wave resulted in the enactment of a set of new laws and amendments to previous waste regulations. During this second wave, the promulgation of Costa Rican Integral Waste Management Law, Electronic Waste Regulation, and Solid Waste Regulation marked a new decade of regulations.

2. *Organic Environmental Law*

The starting point in Costa Rica environmental law framework is the Organic Environmental Law. Enacted in 1995, it contains a chapter concerning public participation, and creates regional environmental councils with the authority to undertake analysis, discussion, and control of the environmental aspects of activities and projects. The law creates a duty to perform an environmental impact study and to develop national policies on territorial planning, protected areas management, and wetlands. This law also creates a Technical Secretariat, which evaluates and approves environmental impact assessment studies. Additionally, the Organic Environmental Law includes provisions for sanctions and creates the Administrative Environmental Tribunal (AET) with the ability to consider and adjudicate claims. The AET is discussed further in section XII.B.

B.   Key Regulatory Environmental Actors

1.   *Ministry of Environment, Energy, and Telecommunications (MINAET)*

The Organic Environment Law created the National Environmental Council[2] to advise the president on environmental matters. This council comprises the National Planning Minister, Health Minister, Agriculture Minister, Education Minister, and Science and Technology Minister. One important function of this council is to promote environmental policies as well as legal reforms. Moreover, the head of this council is MINAET, which has the main responsibilities for natural resources conservation, including air, water, and soil. One of the major responsibilities of the ministry is the management of terrestrial and marine natural resources, through the National Conservation Areas System.

The Organic Environmental Law also created the National System of Protected Areas, which divided the country into 11 major conservation areas. Each of these conservation areas is placed within different categories, such as

- national parks
- biological reserves
- forest reserves
- protected zones
- natural monuments
- national wildlife refuges
- wetlands

2. *Ministry of Health*

The Ministry of Health has a major role in environmental and health pollution prevention and enforcement in country.[3] It authorizes activities related to waste management and the transboundary movement of hazardous wastes. The ministry's starting point in this area is the Basel Convention on the Control of Transboundary Movements of Hazardous Wastes and Their Disposal. The Ministry of Health, through its department of human environment, coordinates the implementation of waste management plans and serves as the chair for various committees, including the Electronic Waste Management Committee. For 2013, the ministry, working with the private sector, has drafted a special waste management regulation and regulations dealing with soil restoration and hazardous waste. Finally, this entity is also in charge of supervising landfills within Costa Rica and the approval of new recycling and treatment plants.

3. *Ministry of Agriculture*

The Costa Rican Ministry of Agriculture also plays a major role in control and enforcement of pesticide usage, phytosanitary controls, and all policies for agriculture and cattle related to climate change controls. One of the agency's key projects since 2005 has been the development of alternatives to the pesticide bromide methyl, especially for its use on melon and flowers plantations. This ministry is responsible for the approval of all imports and management of pesticides.

4. *Local Governments*

Municipalities also play an important role in the day-to-day process of waste and natural resources management. The Integral Waste Management Law, Municipal Code, and the Organic Environmental Law all created specific duties for local governments. The Costa Rican territory is divided into 81 local governments with autonomy and legal capacity for waste management, urban planning, and the provision of water to local communities.[4] In 2010, Costa Rica enacted the Integrated Waste Management Law. Article 8 provides municipal entities with the capacity to create waste management plans, promote the creation of environmental management units, and promote cooperation agreements with private entities for adequate waste management. Additionally, based on the General Health Law Articles 278–284, the ministry is the authority responsible for classifying, authorizing, and supervising the management of landfills.[5]

II.   Air and Climate Change

In Costa Rica, MINAET is the institution responsible for regulating air pollution. Several regulations exist concerning air pollution control, especially for automobiles.[6] However, one of the most important regulations today is the Regulation on Emissions Controls from Cement Kiln Sources.[7] This regulation contains specific measures for allowing the use of biomass sources for energy production. One important aspect of this regulation is the authorization through adequate protocols for the elimination of hazardous wastes in cement kilns.

As for climate change, since 1997, the country has operated the sale of carbon credits through a national fund. The program has been providing payments for reforestation, forest conservation, and sustainable forest management activities. In this process, emissions trading carbon credits come primarily from two sources: first, from converting degraded agricultural and abandoned pasture lands into forests; and second, from reducing deforestation. The National Forestry Law defines payment for environmental services as those providing economic, sociocultural, and ecological services. Besides this law, the Biodiversity Law created the Water Tax Use Decree. This decree recognizes the services that forests provide and permitted private owners to receive a financial incentive for the conservation of forest, water, aesthetic, and biological services. Based on this program, Costa Rica has set for itself the national goal of becoming carbon neutral by 2021. This challenge has prompted the launch of a national emissions trading scheme with a domestic market of emissions trading. Using international standards such as International Standards Organization 14064 and 14065, the National Technical Institute of Standards has launched a national standard that aims to include private companies and public companies in the national market and to set up mechanisms for verification of emissions reductions and compensation.

III.   Water

A.   Water Law

The Costa Rican Water Law was passed in 1942 by Congress. It establishes that all sources of water are in the public domain. This law establishes that rivers, lakes, beaches, islands, and other waterbodies are national property. Accordingly, anyone intending to use water for human, commercial, or industrial use must request a concession from the government.[8]

B. Wastewater Tariff Regulation

The Wastewater Tariff Regulation[9] governs the tariff to be paid by anyone engaged in dumping polluted waters into any water source. This tariff is based on the polluter pays principle. As such, the tariff regulation must be paid by any person or company whose wastewater is introduced into rivers or other water sources. Specifically, this decree calculates the amount to be paid according to the quality and quantity of polluted water to be mixed with clean water.[10]

IV. Handling, Treatment, Transportation, and Disposal of Hazardous Materials

Enacted in 2010, the Integrated Waste Management Law attempts to promote the pricing of wastes and the use of wastes for energy production whenever possible. One chapter of this regulation sets forth new responsibilities for municipalities, specifically the development of waste management plans, and the promotion of public institutions' green procurement purchasing. Article 29 promotes the establishment by public institutions of green procurement processes that incentivize the purchase of low-carbon products, and also reinforces the principle of producer responsibility. The law promotes the import of ordinary wastes for valorization if available technologies exist and a set of new rules for transboundary movement of hazardous wastes. Finally, the last chapter creates specific sanctions with major penalties and promotes the creation of new regulations for ordinary, special, and hazardous wastes.

A few months before the Integrated Waste Management Law was enacted, the Ministry of Health—with support from academic institutions, the private sector, and non-governmental organizations (NGOs)—drafted the Regulation for Electronic Waste Management. This regulation promotes the principle of extended producer responsibility. It requires importers, producers, traders, and distributors to develop e-waste management plans. One important aspect of this regulation is the creation of the National Committee on Electronic Wastes. The committee has promulgated technical guidelines for adequate management of electronics at the end of their useful lives. Finally, as mentioned above, in 2013 the Ministry of Health drafted a special waste management regulation. It aims to regulate certain wastes that could pose significant risks to human health and the environment if not properly managed. The regulation establishes specific measures requiring the creation of management plans for such wastes.

V. Waste and Site Remediation

On June 19, 2013, the Ministry of Health with the Ministry of Environment promulgated a site remediation regulation for contaminated land. It creates specific sanctions, but more importantly, the heavy metal and other pollutant thresholds beyond which particular sites must undergo remediation. This regulation establishes specific responsibilities for generators and land owners for waste site pollution.

VI.   Emergency Response

Costa Rica has not enacted an emergency response statute or regulations per se. That said, any response to an accident or spill must be based on a private entity's contingency plan, which the entity is required to have in place prior to obtaining a sanitary and commercial permit.

VII.   Natural Resource Management and Protection
A.   Protected Areas

As noted above, the Organic Environmental Law created different categories of protected areas. One area, however—marine protected areas—was excluded. The Organic Environmental Law defines in a separate chapter marine resources and includes wetlands within this category. The country has more than 350 wetland sites covering around 350,000 hectares (7 percent of the country). The law adopted a definition of wetlands, and declared wetlands as in the public interest and multiple use.[11] Separately, a particular situation exists with respect to mangroves.[12] Since 2005, Costa Rica has promoted marine conservation and wetlands protection to an even greater extent. For example, Cocos Island National Park, which is a World Heritage Site, expanded its conservation limitations. Finally, Costa Rica has been well recognized for creation of its national parks since the 1970s, when Corcovado and Braulio Carrillo National Park were created. But the country has not stopped with national parks: forested areas, wildlife refuges, archeological sites, and volcanoes buffer areas are also well protected by law, permitting the country to offset its greenhouse gas emissions. These measures make it possible for Costa Rica to make progress toward its goal of becoming carbon neutral by 2021.

B.   Forestry Law

In 1996, the Forestry Law,[13] in the wake of the Organic Environmental Law, established the government's obligation to preserve and manage forestry resources. Given the public interest assigned to forest resources, this law prohibited logging and limited the use of forests on private property. As a result, every logging activity requires authorization from the government. The Forestry Law was followed two years later by the Biodiversity Law.[14] The latter created the National System for Natural Areas Conservation (NSNAC). The NSNAC brought together different authorities and functions such as wildlife protection, water resources, conservation, and the protection of forests. The 1995 Forestry Law included several sanctions, including sanctions for logging and unauthorized use of rivers, lakes, and wetlands protection zones. Perhaps more importantly, the law established the National Forestry Fund. This fund is used to create a payment system for the environmental services provided by water, forest, and scenic views. Since its creation, the fund has encouraged private owners throughout the country to consolidate their properties and receive payments for conservation and avoid forest degradation and deforestation.

VIII. Natural Resource Damages

In cases of environmental damages, private parties must pay for the environmental harm to the government "as reparation or restitution" under the Costa Rican Civil Code.

IX. Protected Species

The Wildlife Conservation Law sets out new rules prohibiting sport hunting and fishing, and increases the penalties for hunting and removing plants without a license. Under this statute, the government may grant licenses for investigation and export of species for research purposes. Interestingly, the law contains specific sanctions for land contamination and water contamination. The law fills gaps existing in the 1942 Water Law, discussed above. Whereas the seven-decades-old Water Law has not been updated, and some penalties are less than 600 colones (US$1), the Wildlife Law creates criminal sanctions with two months to three years in prison for water pollution and land contamination.

X. Environmental Review and Decision Making

A. Environmental Impact Assessment

According to Costa Rica Organic Environmental Law, Article 17, "human activities that may alter or destroy environmental elements or generate wastes, toxic or hazardous materials will require an Environmental Impact Assessment (EIA) approved by Costa Rica National Technical Secretariat." This approval is required before an entity initiates any activity or project. Laws and regulations indicate which activities or projects require an EIA. First, an entity must engage in an initial environmental assessment. At this stage, the evaluation office will determine the specific instrument the developer must utilize. Specifically, at this stage a project is placed into one of four categories:

Category A. Potentially High Impact
Category B. Moderated Potentially High Impact
Category B1. Moderated High Potential Environmental Impact
Category B2. Low

B. Sanitary Operation Permits

Once projects are approved by the National Environmental Technical Secretariat, project proposers must request a sanitary permit from the Ministry of Health. This permit is classified in accordance with the associated risk levels. Some activities with medium or high risk, such as hazardous waste management, are characterized as requiring a class A sanitary operation permit.[15]

XI. Transboundary Pollution

The Environment Organic Law establishes the duty to produce an EIA and cooperate with neighboring states if any project may harm the sovereign rights of that country. That said, Costa Rica's EIA regulation does not provide any specific requirement that entities undertake transboundary EIA.

XII.   Civil and Criminal Enforcement and Penalties
A.   General Penalties Available

In Costa Rica, the criminal code establishes that directors and officers assume personal liability for environmental wrongdoing jointly and severally. In other words, one or several individuals can be separately or jointly responsible for actions or omissions.

Costa Rica law prescribes three types of liabilities for a breach of environmental laws: administrative liability, criminal liability, and strict liability. Administrative liability by a breach of a permit can lead to the suspension of the permit and thus the closure of a project or industrial operation. If found to have violated environmental statutes or regulations, private parties can also be subject to fines and prison sentences under certain criminal aspects of Costa Rican environmental law.

Under the strict liability standard, an individual who holds shares in a company can be held liable for breaches of environmental law committed by the company. It is also possible that parent companies can in some instances be sued in a national court for pollution caused by a foreign subsidiary.

B.   Enforcement of Environmental Laws through the Supreme Court

Environmental enforcement can be brought before the Constitutional Chamber of the Supreme Court, the AET, or the environmental prosecutor. The Constitutional Chamber reviews all cases when Article 50 of the Costa Rica Political Constitution is allegedly violated by a private or public entity. Because the Constitutional Chamber tends to render its judgments more quickly than many other judicial entities, most citizens submit *amparo*[16] actions before this chamber. The subject matter of cases can vary from an alleged omission by a public entity to a private violation of environmental rights. The chamber can, in most cases, request that the defendant undertake preliminary measures on the basis of the precautionary principle. This principle is applied in order to avoid any possible further environmental damage.[17]

As mentioned above, the Organic Environmental Law created an AET[18] with capacities to seek and receive claims in all Costa Rican territory. Specifically, the AET receives claims for any violation of environmental laws and regulations. The AET also can initiate its own actions concerning the alleged violation of Costa Rica environmental laws. One of the most important aspects of this AET is the capacity to order that compensation be paid for environmental damage.[19]

Notes

1. Constitutional Chamber Resolution No. 2233-93.
2. Organic Environmental Law, No. 7554, Oct. 4, 1995, art. 77.
3. The Ministry of Agriculture also plays an important role in environmental matters, especially on pesticides imports and environmental pollution. *See, e.g.,* Ministry of Agriculture Organic Law art. 48.
4. Municipal Code of Costa Rica, Law 7794.
5. Decree No. 27378-S, Regulation on Sanitary Landfills.
6. Regulation on Atmospheric Emissions, No. 17334-S; *see also* Regulation for Cement Kilns No. 12421-MINAET-MINSA.
7. Decree No. 30222-S-MINAE.
8. Water Law, No. 276 art. 2.
9. Regulation No. 31176-MINAE.
10. *Id.* at arts. 4 and 5.
11. Organic Environmental Law art. 41.
12. *See* Maritime Terrestrial Zone Law (placing mangroves within the public domain).
13. Law 7575, Forestry Law.
14. Law 7788, Apr. 30, 1998 (Biodiversity Law).
15. Several additional permits that are necessary are location and wastewater permits. Location permits are granted by the Ministry of Health in accordance with occupational health and sanitation regulations. This permit is specially requested for industrial activities that may not be in accordance with land regulation plans. The country is organized in the great metropolitan area in commercial, industrial, residential, and agricultural lands. Based on this organization the Ministry of Health must grant the permit if the industrial activity is carried out in accordance with land planning.

Separately, the Biodiversity Law allows bioprospecting permits for research such as pharmaceutical and genetic plant research. The statute created a Commission for Management of Biodiversity. This commission receives, reviews, and approves bioprospection permits, and ensures that they are allow for prior informed consent of affected communities.
16. *See* A. Thomas, *Shared Knowledge, Shared Jurisprudence: Learning to Speak Environmental Law Creole,* Tul. Envtl. L. Rev. (2005).
17. The *Linda Vista* case is an example of one landmark environmental case undertaken by the Constitutional Chamber. Costa Rica Constitutional Chamber, Resolution No. 3705-93. The *Linda Vista* matter is particularly important in Costa Rica jurisprudence because the Constitutional Chamber had determined for many years that technical aspects of environmental impact assessments were not a constitutional matter. The chamber in this case highlights the importance of governmental duties, especially in the environmental impact assessment process.
18. Organic Environmental Law art. 103.
19. *Id.* art. 111.

CHAPTER 26

European Union Overview:
The Shift of Power in the European
Union and Its Consequences
for Energy and the Environment

NOAH M. SACHS*

I. Introduction

Since the 1980s, the European Union (EU) has expanded its role in environmental lawmaking considerably. It has expanded its role internally, as the principal driver of environmental policy making in Europe, and also externally, as an influential player in international environmental negotiations. The growing role of the EU in environmental policy has meant that Brussels frequently sets environmental standards for the member states. As a result, a clear trend has emerged in which EU environmental law has become more uniform, and the autonomy of the member states over environmental policy has decreased. Member states still retain flexibility, however, in the implementation and enforcement of environmental law and in the adoption of policies not covered by EU rules.[1]

EU institutions have evolved considerably since the 1980s, moving beyond traditional areas of concern, such as trade harmonization, to new areas of competence, such as energy efficiency policy, product regulation, climate change mitigation, toxic chemical regulation, and environmental liability. Along with this growing breadth of competence, the membership of the EU has also expanded. Since it was founded in 1957, the EU has grown from six member states to 28 member states. The enlargement in 2004, with ten new countries joining 15 existing member states, was the largest single expansion of the EU, followed by two more member states in 2007 and Croatia in 2013. The EU now has a population of over 500 million, and with a

*The author would like to thank Dr. Bettina Enderle of Allen & Overy LLP in Frankfurt for many helpful suggestions on drafts of this chapter and Eric Wallace for invaluable research assistance.

2011 GDP of $17.6 trillion, the EU comprises about one-fifth of the global economy.[2] As a result of its geographic scope, economic power, and legislative and regulatory authority, the EU is now a major player in international environmental law.

This chapter reviews several recent trends in EU environmental law. It does not attempt to summarize every piece of EU environmental legislation. Instead, this chapter focuses on institutional changes in EU governance and major new developments in EU environmental policy in the last decade.

II.   Centralization of Decision Making

In the past three decades, there has been a major shift in control over environmental lawmaking in Europe: a shift from the member states to EU institutions, including the Council, the Parliament, and the Commission (especially the Directorate-General for Environment, the Directorate-General for Energy, and the new Directorate-General for Climate Action). The roles and responsibilities of each of these institutions are described in greater detail in chapter 27, The European Union. Here, I discuss both the causes and the effects of policy centralization.

A.   Causes of Policy Centralization

One cause of the centralization of decision making is that the member states, through various treaty amendments, have conferred greater authority on EU institutions to act in the environmental realm. The Single European Act (1986)[3] contained key environmental provisions, including the principle that the environment should be considered in all Community legislation, and the Treaties of Maastricht (1992) and Amsterdam (1997) made sustainable development one of the Community's central objectives.[4]

Treaty amendments over the past three decades have also conferred more power on the Parliament. This trend culminated in the Treaty of Lisbon (2009), through which the Parliament became, for most matters, a co-equal decision maker with the Council in the ordinary legislative procedure of the EU.[5] The Parliament has been an important forum for consumer and environmental interests in Europe. The European Green Party and pro-environment Members of Parliament from other parties have taken a leading role in promoting environmental legislation, and the Parliament's rising power and authority have helped to support the increasing scope of EU environmental law making.[6]

Policy centralization is also the result of the transboundary nature of environmental problems in Europe. Climate policy and water quality are two notable examples of the need for centralized lawmaking at a supranational level. Chemical regulation is another example. European chemical manufacturers produce for both a European and an international market, and a patchwork of national legislation would be less effective than EU legislation at ensuring both public safety and continued growth in the chemical industry. The EU has also taken the lead on legislation aimed at reducing the environmental impacts of products. Because of the traditional role of the EU in ensuring harmonized standards and minimizing barriers to cross-border trade, the EU has enacted standards for product safety, environmental impacts, and recycling, rather than leaving those issues to the member states.[7]

The European Court of Justice (ECJ)—the final arbiter of treaty provisions governing environment, trade, and enforcement—has played an important role in fostering environmental policy uniformity and centralization. The ECJ has frequently ruled against member states when they fail to implement EU environmental law properly,[8] and it has rejected national legislation that contravenes EU environmental law.[9] The ECJ has also considerably extended rights for private litigants in environmental law. For example, in a 2011 case involving a German power plant project, the ECJ interpreted the EU's Environmental Impact Assessment Directive to provide environmental non-governmental organizations (NGOs) with a broader right to challenge national decisions in a judicial hearing than had been provided by German procedures.[10]

The centralization of environmental policy in the EU is often in tension with the principle of subsidiarity, a core principle of EU law contained in Article 5(3) of the Treaty on European Union.[11] The subsidiarity principle holds that action should be taken at the EU level only where the objectives of the legislation cannot be met through member state action. While some environmental policy areas clearly justify action from Brussels, some recent EU environmental legislation appears contrary to the subsidiarity principle. For example, the 2004 Environmental Liability Directive established EU-wide rules for remediation and compensation for environmental damage.[12] Most environmental damage occurs, however, within the boundaries of a single member state, and transboundary environmental damage is just a small fraction of the overall scope of environmental damages to which the directive applies.

B. Effects of Policy Centralization

As a result of the centralization of policy making in Brussels, environmental policy throughout Europe has become more uniform. Each member state is obliged to approximate European Union law—that is, to ensure that its national laws, rules, and procedures are sufficient to carry out the mandates of EU law. The most important component of approximation is transposition: the obligation of each member state to ensure that EU rules, regulations, and procedures are fully incorporated into its national legal system.[13] In environmental law, the transposition process ensures that the overall framework for addressing an environmental problem, set in Brussels, becomes reflected in national legislation in each member state (with some variation due to national circumstances).

Moreover, when the EU legislates in the environmental field through regulation, rather than directives, the regulation has direct effect and is immediately binding on individuals and firms without further action from member states.[14] Although the EU has enacted only about 10 percent of all environmental legislation through regulation,[15] it has relied on regulation to address some of the most important environmental problems. For example, legislation on animal and fish conservation[16] as well as the Registration, Evaluation, Authorization, and Restriction of Chemicals (REACH) legislation for chemical testing and safety,[17] were enacted as regulations, with direct effect and uniform applicability across the EU.

The centralization of environmental policy making in Brussels has had international ripple effects, and the EU's internal environmental lawmaking has become increasingly influential as a global model. With EU institutions setting environmental policy for the world's largest economy, other nations are increasingly looking to Europe for policy models for their own domestic legislation. Moreover, multinational firms wishing to sell in the European marketplace must design their products to comply with EU product standards and other EU legislation. EU legislation consequently has extraterritorial effects and shapes product design decisions globally. The "regulatory turbulence" from the EU's internal legislation has made the EU a de facto international regulator of product safety and environmental impacts.[18] For example, many Asian countries that are large electronics exporters have adopted bans on certain toxic substances in electronics that closely mimic a ban on six toxic substances in electronics that the EU enacted in 2003.[19]

The policy centralization and increased breadth of lawmaking in the EU has led to an active debate about whether global environmental leadership has switched—from the United States, which was the dominant global environmental player in the 1970s, to the European Union. This debate is often framed as a question of whether the two jurisdictions have "traded places" or "flip-flopped" in their global leadership role in the environmental field.[20] Defining international "leadership" in the environmental field is difficult, however, given that leadership is a highly subjective concept open to a wide variety of interpretations. Making cross-national comparisons about environmental stringency or levels of precaution is also conceptually difficult, given that stringency is a function not just of the law itself, but also of enforcement mechanisms and the severity of underlying environmental problems. It may not be possible to generalize by identifying one "leader" jurisdiction across all areas of risk regulation.

In the area of climate change, however, it is clear the EU has been a very active policymaker and is a global leader in the field. The EU is committed to ambitious goals for greenhouse gas (GHG) reduction, and it has enacted substantial legislation to achieve those goals.

III.   EU Climate and Energy Policy
A.   The Emissions Trading System

The centerpiece of EU climate policy is its Emissions Trading System (ETS), enacted by directive in 2003 and launched in 2005.[21] The ETS is a cap-and-trade system originally designed to help achieve the EU goal under the Kyoto Protocol of an 8 percent reduction in GHG emissions below 1990 levels by 2008–2012.[22] Under the ETS, emissions allowances are distributed to major emitting firms, and the firms are free to buy and sell allowances on the open market. The number of allowances distributed each year is capped, and the cap in 2020 will be 21 percent lower than in 2005.[23]

The ETS initially ran into substantial criticism due to volatility in allowance prices. For example, in April 2006, the spot price of allowances declined 54 percent in a single week when it was revealed that the Commission had overallocated allowances based on inflated estimates (submitted by member states) of industry emissions. Following that initial stumble, the EU has gradually shifted to an auction system for allowances, in which allowances are distributed by the Commission itself rather than by member states. The ETS is now entering its third phase, which will last through 2020, and according to the Commission, at least half of the available allowances in 2013 were auctioned.[24]

There is substantial debate over whether the ETS is responsible for emissions reductions in Europe or whether those reductions have occurred because of the European economic crisis. Carbon dioxide emissions in 27 member states of the EU have declined 9.5 percent since 2005.[25] The global economic slowdown that began in 2008 is certainly responsible for part of this emissions decline. The economic crisis has resulted in reduced demand for allowances in Europe, and the spot price for ETS allowances has consequently remained low—below 13 euros for most of the past two years.[26] Allowances were trading around eight euros at the end of 2012, far below the prices initially envisioned for the program,[27] and they hit a record low of 2.81 euros in late January 2013.[28] These low prices, easily absorbed in the balance sheets of fossil-fuel-dependent firms, have substantially undercut the effectiveness of the ETS. Critics charge that the ETS has done little to spur a green economy and low-carbon technology in Europe, and there are increasing calls to "re-establish scarcity" in the allowance market through tightening emissions caps.[29] Despite the unexpectedly low prices for allowances, the EU deserves credit both for its ambitious goals and for demonstrating that a cap-and-trade system for greenhouse gas emissions is workable across 28 nations with diverse economies.

The ETS is just one component of a larger suite of legislation codifying the EU's so-called 20-20-20 targets.[30] Under a 2009 legislative package, the EU committed to achieve, by 2020, a 20 percent reduction in GHG emissions below 1990 levels, a 20 percent reduction in energy use below a projected business-as-usual baseline, and a 20 percent share of its energy mix from renewable sources.[31] Some member states have set their own climate goals. In 2008, for example, the United Kingdom enacted legislation to achieve an 80 percent reduction in emissions below its 1990 baseline by 2050.[32]

B. Other Energy and Climate-Related Legislation

The ETS is the most complex component of EU climate change policy, but it represents only one piece of the EU's overall climate and energy strategy. The ETS applies to about 11,000 major industrial sources of emissions,[33] but it does little to address household and individual energy consumption or transportation-related GHG emissions. The EU has enacted more than a dozen pieces of legislation designed to curb emissions and meet its 2020 targets. The legislation addresses a few principal sectors:

1. Transportation

In response to a 36 percent increase in EU GHG emissions from the transportation sector between 1990 and 2007, the EU implemented several policies targeting transportation emissions.[34] These include carbon dioxide emissions limits for new cars,[35] GHG intensity targets for transportation fuels,[36] rolling resistance limits and labeling requirements for tires, and a tire pressure monitor mandate for new vehicles.[37] To reduce aviation emissions, the EU brought airlines within the ETS in 2008.[38] That decision prompted international outcry because of its impacts on global trade. In November 2012, the Commission froze for one year the portion of that legislation that applies to flights originating outside of Europe, due to intense opposition from the United States, China, and India.[39] In April 2014, the Council and Parliament extended the non-applicability of the ETS through the end of 2016 for flights originating outside Europe.[40]

2. Eco-Design Directive

The 2009 Eco-Design Directive was enacted to increase the energy efficiency of products that use, generate, transfer, or measure energy.[41] The directive applies both to products that consume energy, such as boilers, computers, televisions, and transformers, and to products that indirectly impact energy consumption, such as windows, insulation, and shower heads.[42] The directive is implemented through "implementing measures" that set minimum energy performance standards for particular product classes. Between 2008 and 2012, the Commission enacted implementing measures for 13 different product classes,[43] and the Commission estimates that performance standards promulgated under the Eco-Design Directive could reduce European electricity consumption by more than 12 percent from 2009 levels by 2020.[44]

3. Effort-Sharing Decision

The Effort-Sharing Decision establishes binding GHG emission reduction targets for each member state through 2020.[45] The targets range from a 20 percent decrease below 2005 levels for Ireland and Luxembourg to a 20 percent increase for the poorest member state, Bulgaria.[46] The Effort-Sharing Decision focuses on emissions from transportation, buildings, agriculture, and waste,[47] sectors not covered by the ETS. The ultimate goal of the Effort-Sharing Decision is an EU-wide reduction in emissions from sectors not covered by the ETS of 10 percent below 2005 levels by 2020.[48]

4. Energy Efficiency

In October 2012, the EU enacted the Energy Efficiency Directive, outlining legally binding measures to increase energy efficiency in member states.[49] The directive aims to drive energy efficiency improvements in electric utilities, households, and commercial and transportation sectors.[50] For example, under the directive, member states must require energy distributors to achieve energy savings of 1.5 percent per year,[51] and each member state is required to renovate 3 percent of government buildings each year to comply with minimum energy performance standards.[52]

5.   *Energy Performance of Buildings Directive*

The EU's Energy Performance of Buildings Directive[53] requires member states to set minimum energy performance requirements for new and existing buildings. Additionally, member states must certify building energy performance and ensure regular inspections of boilers and air conditioning systems.[54] By 2021, all new buildings in the EU must be "nearly zero-energy buildings."[55]

6.   *Carbon Capture and Sequestration (CCS)*

In 2009, the EU enacted a directive establishing a framework for the geological storage of carbon dioxide (CO_2).[56] The directive outlines a broad program for the underground storage of CO_2 emissions. It contains requirements governing site exploration, site selection, storage, permitting, financial security in the event of leakage, monitoring, and reporting. The directive also requires that, if certain conditions are met, new combustion plants with an output of 300 MW or more must be capable of being fitted with carbon capture technology.[57] For example, such plants must set aside suitable land on the site for the necessary carbon capture and compression equipment.[58] Member states are beginning to implement the directive to both promote and regulate CCS.[59]

7.   *Adaptation*

The EU has included adaptation considerations in many of its decisions related to environmental law.[60] For example, the EU's Floods Directive[61] directly addressed climate change adaptation, requiring member states to undertake risk assessments for floods that specifically consider the effects of climate change on precipitation and water levels.[62] Additionally, by 2015, member states must prepare flood hazard maps and flood management plans, which member states must review every six years, "taking into account the likely impact of climate change."[63] Eight member states, mainly in northwest Europe, have adopted their own national climate adaptation plans as well.[64]

IV.   Changes in the EU Energy Mix

In the past two decades, the EU has seen substantial changes in its energy mix. The long-term trend between 1995 and 2010 was a shift away from coal and an increase in renewable energy and natural gas. These changes were driven by underlying economic trends, such as the declining price of natural gas, and by government policy (such as the ETS and national feed-in tariffs). Recently, however, coal consumption has increased in Europe, and dozens of coal-fired power plants are under construction or in planning stages.

The EU's overall energy mix in 2010 was 13 percent nuclear, 16 percent coal, 10 percent renewables, 25 percent natural gas, and 35 percent oil.[65] Compared to the energy mix in 1995, the EU relied five percentage points more on renewables and about six percentage points less on coal.[66] The expansion of renewable energy between 1995 and 2010 was driven by expansions in solar capacity in Italy, Spain, and Germany and by dramatic expansions in wind power in Germany, Scandinavia, France, and the United Kingdom. Notably, European nations have some of the lowest per capita energy use among industrialized nations—sparked by dense land use patterns, efficiency investments, and comparatively high gas taxes.

The change in the energy mix has been most dramatic in Germany. In 2011, after the Fukushima nuclear accident in Japan, Germany committed to the complete phase-out of all nuclear power, at a time when Germany was relying on nuclear power for 22 percent of its electricity needs.[67] Through a generous feed-in tariff program that supports renewables, Germany now obtains more than 20 percent of its electricity from renewables and has committed to raise that share to 35 percent by 2020.[68]

Although Germany is aggressively shifting toward renewable energy, one unintended impact of the phase-out of nuclear power in Germany is an increase in coal consumption. More than 20 new coal-fired power plants, with a total output of 10 gigawatts, are being planned or are already under construction in Germany (natural-gas-fired plants are being constructed as well).[69] Some of these coal-fired plants may be delayed or abandoned due to litigation, however. In Europe as a whole, coal consumption has increased since 2010, due in part to cheap coal exports from the United States, where natural gas has been replacing coal in the energy mix.[70] The increase in carbon emissions from the shift toward coal combustion will make it more difficult for the EU to achieve its long-term climate mitigation goals.

V.   Toxic Chemicals Regulation

In addition to energy and climate legislation, the EU is also exerting greater centralized control in the area of toxic chemical regulation. The EU's core legislation is the 2006 REACH regulation.[71] REACH establishes a precautionary toxicity review system for existing and new chemicals produced or imported into Europe.[72] At over 800 pages, with thousands of pages of guidance documents, REACH is the largest environmental law ever enacted in the EU.

REACH replaced over 40 prior directives and regulations on chemical safety, and it has four main functions: (1) it increases the supply of data on chemical toxicity; (2) it decreases the informational demands on regulatory authorities; (3) it improves risk communication to the public and to commercial users of chemicals; and (4) it promotes the use of substitutes for hazardous chemicals.[73]

REACH ends prior distinctions among "existing" and "new" chemicals and imposes on industry a default burden of data production on all chemicals as a condition of manufacturing or importing chemicals in the EU. In particular, REACH requires that all substances imported or manufactured in Europe in annual quantities of one ton or greater (approximately 30,000 substances) be registered with a new European Chemicals Agency (ECHA) by 2018.[74] If a company does not submit the required chemical registration package, it will be denied access to sell that product on the €537 billion European chemical market.

In addition to expanding the supply of chemical toxicity data, REACH also shifts the burden of proving the safety of certain classes of chemicals to industry. Under REACH's authorization procedures, the burden of proof on safety is shifted to industry for the most hazardous classes of chemicals, those identified as "substances of very high concern" (sVHC) during the registration and evaluation stages of REACH. These are chemicals that can cause cancer, birth defects, or genetic mutations, as well as chemicals that are persistent or bioaccumulative in the environment.[75] Regulators may grant a time-limited authorization to continue to market an sVHC chemical if the manufacturer or importer can demonstrate that the risks to human health and the environment are "adequately controlled"; or, if this showing cannot be made,[76] the proponent must demonstrate (1) that the socioeconomic benefits exceed the risks and (2) that there are no suitable substitute chemicals or technologies.[77]

There are now 155 substances on the so-called "candidate list" for authorization.[78] These substances have been identified as sVHC chemicals and may later become subject to the authorization process. Given the long phase-in period for chemical registration (through 2018), and the slow process of identifying chemicals for authorization, REACH has recently come under fire from environmental groups for the slow pace of progress.[79]

Under REACH, chemical producers and importers must communicate to downstream users the known risks of all chemicals and recommended risk management techniques.[80] Downstream users must inform upstream suppliers of any new hazards they discover from a chemical, as well as any indication that the risk management instructions they received are inadequate.[81] REACH also provides incentives to find safer substitutes for known hazardous substances because of public disclosure of toxicity information in the registration process, the potential market risk from being identified as an sVHC chemical, and the administrative burden of the authorization process.

REACH represents an ambitious effort to develop toxicity information for the most widely used chemicals in Europe. The full impact of REACH on the chemical market, and on public health, will not be apparent for a few more years, as the registration process concludes and the authorization process commences.

VI.   Integrated Product Policy

REACH is one component of the EU's Integrated Product Policy (IPP), a broad package of policies and legislation aimed at minimizing the environmental impacts of products throughout the product life cycle. The IPP recognizes that products may adversely affect the environment in each stage (natural resource extraction, product design, manufacture, assembly, marketing, distribution, sale to the consumer, and final disposal). Therefore, the IPP deploys policy tools (economic incentives, substance bans, voluntary agreements, labeling and design requirements, etc.) for each product life-cycle stage and for each actor involved.[82]

One goal of the IPP is to incentivize customers to purchase greener products. For over two decades, the EU has authorized the flower eco-label to identify and promote environmentally friendly products in the marketplace.[83] The EU has also embraced the principle of extended producer responsibility (EPR), which makes producers responsible for the end-of-life environmental impacts of their products.[84] The theory behind EPR is that if manufacturers are held responsible for end-of-life environmental impacts, they will design products that have fewer adverse effects and that are more recyclable. The EPR principle is prominent, for example, in legislation enacted in 2000 governing end-of-life vehicles[85] and in legislation enacted in 2003 requiring that manufacturers take back discarded electronic equipment from consumers.[86]

Other legislation within the IPP includes the Eco-Design Directive, green public procurement policies, the Waste Framework Directive, and the Batteries Directive.[87] The Commission issued a report reviewing IPP implementation in 2009.[88]

VII.   Strengthening Implementation and Enforcement

Because EU law is enacted in Brussels and enforcement rests primarily with the member states, observers have noted an "implementation gap" in EU law.[89] In environmental law, member states are primarily responsible for transposing EU law into national legislation, permitting facilities and setting pollution limits for those facilities, conducting inspections, and enforcing against violators. Consequently, enforcement of EU environmental law occurs within hugely varying national conditions and national capacities. Legislation enforced strictly in one country may be enforced lackadaisically in another, creating competitive effects on industry operating in different nations. Given that EU law is often implemented by member states against a backdrop of years or even decades of national legislation affecting the same subject area, member states often view EU legislation "as an immigrant, if not an intruder" in their national legal systems.[90]

Though the Commission has no formal competence to enforce law within the member states, it may resort to the treaty's infringement procedures to challenge a member state's nonenforcement or underenforcement of EU environmental law.[91] More recently, the EU has taken additional steps to improve enforcement of environmental law. One trend has already been mentioned: Legislating through regulation rather than directives avoids the transposition process and ensures that EU law becomes directly applicable across Europe without further action from the member states (though member states are still responsible for implementation). The Commission is also increasingly relying on guidance documents to provide its own interpretation of EU regulations and directives. Although guidance documents are not legally binding, they carry persuasive weight, and they can assist member states with their implementation of EU law, helping to promote uniformity of implementation across the EU.

Another recent trend relevant to environmental enforcement is the establishment of informal networks of environmental enforcement officials among the member states. These networks promote information sharing, exchange of best practices and procedures, and resolution of issues involving transboundary environmental harm. One of the most prominent enforcement networks is CLEEN, the Chemicals Legislation European Enforcement Network. Established in 2000, CLEEN is an informal network of regulatory authorities located throughout the EU that coordinates and improves the enforcement of EU chemicals legislation, including REACH.[92] Another important network for consumer safety is RAPEX, a "rapid alert" system allowing any member state that identifies a product safety hazard to alert the Commission, which then alerts all the other member states and publishes a weekly bulletin on products with safety issues.[93] In 2010, the system was expanded to include products that posed significant risks to human health and the environment.[94]

VIII.   Conclusion

The EU has become an active environmental lawmaker over the past few decades, and there is little sign that it intends to withdraw from this role now that the legal and institutional architecture is in place to centralize lawmaking in Brussels. The EU has set ambitious goals for 2020 for climate mitigation, and it will be a tremendous challenge to achieve those goals at a reasonable cost. If the EU can succeed in reducing its GHG emissions far below 1990 levels by 2020, it will offer an important model for reducing emissions in advanced industrialized countries through sustained policy intervention.

Notes

1. For more information on enforcement of environmental law in the EU, see chapter 27 in this volume, The European Union.

2. *See* European Comm'n, Eurostat, http://epp.eurostat.ec.europa.eu/portal /page/portal/eurostat/home/ (last visited Sept. 4, 2012); Int'l Monetary Fund, World Economic Outlook Database (Apr. 2012), http://www.imf.org/external/pubs/ft/weo/2012

/01/weodata/index.aspx; *see also* Matej Hruska, *EU Population Tops 500 Million*, BLOOM-BERG BUSINESSWEEK (July 29, 2010), http://www.businessweek.com/globalbiz/content/jul2010/gb20100729_623637.htm.

3. Single European Act, Feb. 17, 1986, 1987 O.J. (L 169) 1.

4. Treaty of Amsterdam Amending the Treaty on European Union, the Treaties Establishing the European Communities and Certain Related Acts, Oct. 2, 1997, 1997 O.J. (C 340) 1, 7, 24–25; Treaty on European Union art. 130 r, Feb. 8, 1992, 1992 O.J (C 191) 1, 36–37.

5. Treaty of Lisbon Amending the Treaty on European Union and the Treaty Establishing the European Communities, Dec. 13, 2007, 2007 O.J. (C306) 1, 16–17.

6. *See* ELIZABETH BOMBERG, GREEN PARTIES AND POLITICS IN THE EUROPEAN UNION (1998); Gail McElroy & Kenneth Benoit, *Party Groups and Policy Positions in the European Parliament*, 13 PARTY POL. 5, 6, 13–14 (2007).

7. Nicolas de Sadeleer, *Principle of Subsidiarity and the EU Environmental Policy*, 9.1 J. EUR. ENVTL. & PLAN. L. 61, 64–65 (2012) (explaining that disparate approaches to environmental protection could lead some states to enact regulations that restrict trade).

8. *See generally* EUROPEAN COMM'N, NATURE AND ENVIRONMENTAL CASES, RULINGS OF THE EUROPEAN COURT OF JUSTICE 47–112 (2006), http://ec.europa.eu/environment/nature/info/pubs/docs/others/ecj_rulings_en.pdf.

9. For example, in Case C-412/85, Comm'n v. Germany, 1987 E.C.R. 3503, the ECJ declared a provision of German law incompatible with an EU directive on wild bird habitats (today codified in Council Directive 2009/147/EC, 2010 O.J. (L 20) 7, on the conservation of wild birds). The German law had stated that ordinary agricultural and forestry activities did not constitute a significant disturbance of natural habitat, and the ECJ held that the law improperly derogated from the clear language of the directive.

10. Case C-115/09, Bund für Umwelt und Naturschutz Deutschland, Landesverband Nordrhein Westfalen eV v. Bezirksregierung Arnsberg, 2011 E.C.R. I-03673; *see also* Slovak Brown Bears Case, Case C-240/09, Lesoochranárske zoskupenie VLK v. Ministerstvo životného prostredia Slovenskej republiky, 2011 E.C.R. I-01255.

11. *See* Consolidated Version of the Treaty on the Functioning of the European Union art. 15, Mar. 30, 2010, 2010 O.J. (C 83) 1, 18 [hereinafter TFEU] ("[I]n areas which do not fall within its exclusive competence, the Union shall act only if and in so far as the objectives of the proposed action cannot be sufficiently achieved by the Member States, either at central level or at regional and local level, but can rather, by reason of the scale or effects of the proposed action, be better achieved at Union level.").

12. Council Directive 2004/35/CE of the European Parliament and of the Council of 21 April 2004 on Environmental Liability with Regard to the Prevention and Remedying of Environmental Damage, 2004 O.J. (L143) 56. For an argument against the Environmental Liability Directive on subsidiarity grounds, see Kristel de Smedt, *Is Harmonization of Environmental Liability Rules Needed in an Enlarged European Union?*, 13 REV. EUR. CMTY. & INT'L ENVTL. L. 164, 166 (2004) (arguing that any centralized regulation of environmental liability "should be limited and targeted to . . . transboundary externalities").

13. *See* JAN H. JANS & HANS H.B. VEDDER, EUROPEAN ENVIRONMENTAL LAW 127 (3d ed. 2008).

14. *See* Consolidated Version of the Treaty on the Functioning of the European Union art. 288, Mar. 30, 2010, 2010 O.J. (C 83) 171–72 (stating that a regulation "shall be binding in its entirety and directly applicable in all Member States"); *see also* JANS & VEDDER, *supra* note 13, at 149 (discussing direct application of environmental regulations).

15. EUROPEAN COMM'N, GUIDE TO THE APPROXIMATION OF ENVIRONMENTAL LEGISLATION § 3.3 (2012), http://ec.europa.eu/environment/archives/guide/part1.htm.

16. *See, e.g.,* Council Regulation 2371/2002 of 20 December 2002 on the Conservation and Sustainable Exploitation of Fisheries Resources Under the Common Fisheries Policy, 2002 O.J. (L 358) 59 (EC); Council Regulation 338/97 of 9 December 1996 on the Protection of Species of Wild Fauna and Flora by Regulating Trade Therein, 1997 O.J. (L 61) 1 (EC).

17. Regulation 1907/2006 of the European Parliament and of the Council of 18 December 2006 Concerning the Registration, Evaluation, Authorisation and Restriction of Chemicals (REACH), 2006 O.J. (L396) 1 (EC).

18. *See, e.g.,* Noah M. Sachs, *Jumping the Pond: Transnational Law and the Future of Chemical Regulation,* 62 VAND. L. REV. 1817, 1845 (2009) (describing "regulatory turbulence"); *see also* Anu Bradford, *The Brussels Effect,* 107 Nw. U. L. REV. 1 (2012).

19. Directive 2002/95 of the European Parliament and of the Council of 27 January 2003 on the Restriction of the Use of Certain Hazardous Substances in Electrical and Electronic Equipment, 2003 O.J. (L 37) 19, replaced by Directive 2011/65 of the European Parliament and of the Council of 8 June 2011 on the Restriction of the Use of Certain Hazardous Substances in Electrical and Electronic Equipment, 2011 O.J. (L 174) 88. For an analysis of similar legislation in China, see Chris Muller & Henry Yu, *China RoHS: How the Changing Regulatory Landscape is Affecting Process Equipment Reliability,* 100 LECTURE NOTES IN ELECTRICAL ENGINEERING 57 (2011) (comparing the China RoHS directive to the EU RoHS directive).

20. The "trading places" argument is closely associated with Professor David Vogel at the University of California, Berkeley. *See* R. Daniel Kelemen & David Vogel, *Trading Places: The Role of the United States and the European Union in International Environmental Politics,* 43 COMP. POL. STUD. 427 (2010); David Vogel, *The Hare and the Tortoise Revisited: The New Politics of Consumer and Environmental Regulation in Europe,* 33 BRIT. J. POL. SCI. 557, 557–62 (2003). For a contrary view, arguing that there has been no shift in leadership and that levels of precaution in the two jurisdictions are roughly equivalent, see JONATHAN B. WEINER ET AL., THE REALITY OF PRECAUTION: COMPARING RISK REGULATION IN THE UNITED STATES AND EUROPE (2010); James K. Hammitt et al., *Precautionary Regulation in Europe and the United States: A Quantitative Comparison,* 25 RISK ANALYSIS 1215, 1215–16 (2005).

21. Directive 2003/87/EC of the European Parliament and the Council of 13 October 2003 Establishing a Scheme for Greenhouse Gas Emission Allowance Trading within the Community, 2003 O.J. (L 275) 32.

22. Kyoto Protocol to the Framework Convention on Climate Change, *opened for signature* Mar. 16, 1998, 37 I.L.M. 22 (1998).

23. Recital 14 of Directive 2009/29 of the European Parliament and the Council of 23 April 2009 amending Directive 2003/87 so as to Improve and Extend the Greenhouse Gas Emission Allowance Trading Scheme of the Community, 2009 O.J. (L 140) 63 (EC); *see also* European Comm'n, Climate Action: Emissions Trading System, http://ec.europa.eu /clima/policies/ets/index_en.htm (last visited Nov. 27, 2012).

24. European Comm'n, Climate Action: Auctioning, http://ec.europa.eu/clima /policies/ets/cap/auctioning/index_en.htm (last visited Sept. 12, 2013).

25. EUROPEAN COMM'N JOINT RESEARCH CTR., TRENDS IN GLOBAL CO2 Emissions 28 (2012) [hereinafter TRENDS IN GLOBAL CO2 Emissions].

26. BLUENEXT, STATISTICS, HISTORICAL TRANSACTIONS (Nov. 29, 2012), http://www .bluenext.eu/statistics/downloads.php.

27. *Id.*

28. Pilita Clark & Javier Blas, *EU Carbon Prices Crash to Record Low,* FIN. TIMES (Jan. 24, 2013), http://www.ft.com/cms/s/0/77764dda-6645-11e2-b967-00144feab49a.html#ax zz2eiEjTIq6.

29. *See, e.g.*, Selina Williams & Alessandro Torello, *As Carbon Prices Sink, Unease Rises*, WALL ST. J. (Apr. 5, 2012), http://online.wsj.com/article/SB10001424052702304072004577323890893009020.html.

30. Council Directive 2003/87, 2003 OJ (L 275) 32 (EC), as amended by Council Directive 2009/29, 2009 OJ (L 140) 63.

31. *Id.*

32. Climate Change Act, 2008, c. 27, § 1 (U.K.).

33. European Comm'n, Climate Action: Emissions Trading System, http://ec.europa.eu/clima/policies/ets/index_en.htm (last visited Nov. 27, 2012).

34. European Comm'n, Climate Action: Reducing Emissions from Transport, http://ec.europa.eu/clima/policies/transport/index_en.htm (last visited Sept. 12, 2013).

35. *See* Commission Regulation 443/2009 of the European Parliament and of the Council of 23 April 2009 Setting Emissions Performance Standards for New Passenger Cars, 2009 O.J. (L140) 1. Under the Cars Regulation, the fleet average to be achieved by all new cars is 130 grams of CO_2 per kilometer (g/km) by 2015 and 95g/km by 2020. *Id.* at 2.

36. Council Directive 2009/30, 2009 O.J. (L 140) 88 (EC).

37. *See* Commission Regulation 458/2011, 2011 O.J. (L 124) 11 (EU).

38. Directive 2008/101, of the European Parliament and of the Council of 19 November 2008 amending Directive 2003/87 so as to Include Aviation Activities in the Scheme for Greenhouse Gas Emission Allowance Trading Within the Community, 2009 O.J. (L 8) 3 (EC).

39. *Proposal for a Decision of the European Parliament and the Council Derogating Temporarily from Directive 2003/87/EC Establishing a Scheme for Greenhouse Gas Emission Allowance Trading within the Community*, COM (2012) 697 final (Nov. 20 2012); Fiona Harvey, *EU Freezes Airlines Carbon Emissions Law*, GUARDIAN (Nov. 12, 2012), http://www.theguardian.com/environment/2012/nov/12/eu-airline-emissions-law.

40. http://eur-lex.europa.eu/legal-content/EN/TXT/PDF/?uri=CELEX:32014R0421&from=EN.

41. Directive 2009/125 of the European Parliament and of the Council of 21 October 2009 Establishing a Framework for the Setting of Ecodesign Requirements for Energy-Related Products, 2009 O.J. (L 285) 10 (EC).

42. European Comm'n, Enterprise and Industry: Sustainable and Responsible Business: Ecodesign, http://ec.europa.eu/enterprise/policies/sustainable-business/ecodesign/index_en.htm (last visited Sept. 12, 2013).

43. European Comm'n, Enterprise and Industry: Sustainable and Responsible Business: Implementing Measures, http://ec.europa.eu/enterprise/policies/sustainable-business/documents/eco-design/legislation/implementing-measures/index_en.htm (last visited Sept. 12, 2013).

44. EUROPEAN COMM'N, ECODESIGN YOUR FUTURE 4, http://ec.europa.eu/enterprise/policies/sustainable-business/ecodesign/files/brochure_ecodesign_en.pdf.

45. Decision 406/2009 of the Parliament and the Council of 23 April 2009 on the Effort of Member States to Reduce Their Greenhouse Gas Emissions to Meet the Community's Greenhouse Gas Emission Reduction Commitments up to 2020, 2009 O.J. (L 140) 136 (EC).

46. *Id.* Annex II.

47. European Comm'n, Climate Action: Effort Sharing Decision, http://ec.europa.eu/clima/policies/effort/index_en.htm (last visited Nov. 30, 2012).

48. *Id.*

49. Directive 2012/27 of the European Parliament and of the Council of 25 October 2012 on Energy Efficiency, 2012 O.J. (L 315) 1 (EU).

50. European Comm'n, Energy: Energy Efficiency Directive, http://ec.europa.eu /energy/efficiency/eed/eed_en.htm (last visited Sept. 12, 2013).

51. Directive 2012/27, *supra* note 48, art. 7.

52. *Id.* art. 5.

53. Directive 2010/31 of the European Parliament and of the Council of 19 May 2010 on the Energy Performance of Buildings, 2010 O.J. (L 153) 13 (EU).

54. *Id.* arts. 14–15.

55. *Id.* art. 9.

56. Directive 2009/31 of the European Parliament and of the Council of 23 April 2009 on the Geological Storage of Carbon Dioxide, 2009 O.J. (L 140) 114, 119 (EC).

57. *Id.*

58. *Id.*

59. *See, e.g.*, Bettina Enderle, *The New Act on CCS, A "Special Mining Law" for a Controversial Bridging Technology*, 6 WORLD OF MINING 358 (2012) (describing German experience with CCS).

60. European Comm'n, Climate Action: Adaptation to Climate Change, http:// ec.europa.eu/clima/sites/change/what_is_eu_doing/marine_en.htm (last visited Sept. 14, 2012).

61. Directive 2007/60 of the Parliament and the Council on the Assessment and Management of Flood Risks, 2007 O.J. (L 288) 27 (EC).

62. *Id.* art. 4.

63. *Id.* art. 14.

64. *See* European Comm'n, Climate Action: Adaptation to Climate Change, http:// ec.europa.eu/clima/policies/adaptation/documentation_en.htm (last visited Sept. 13, 2013).

65. EUROPEAN COMM'N, EU ENERGY IN FIGURES: STATISTICAL POCKETBOOK 16 (2012), http://ec.europa.eu/energy/observatory/statistics/statistics_en.htm (providing 2010 data as the most recent available).

66. *Id.*

67. Aaron Wiener, *German Activists Do a Slow Burn: Environmentalists are Unhappy with How the Nation's Nuclear Phaseout is Going*, L.A. TIMES, Apr. 20, 2012, at A3.

68. Damian Carrington, *Germany's Renewable Energy Revolution Leaves UK in the Shade*, GUARDIAN (May 30, 2012), http://www.theguardian.com/environment/2012 /may/30/germany-renewable-energy-revolution.

69. TRENDS IN GLOBAL CO2 emissions, *supra* note 25, at 21.

70. Stanley Reed, *Volatility of Renewables Pushes Europe Back toward Dependence on Coal*, N.Y. TIMES (Oct. 31, 2012), http://www.nytimes.com/2012/11/01/business/energy -environment/01iht-green01.html?_r=0.

71. Regulation 1907/2006 of the European Parliament and of the Council of 18 December 2006 Concerning the Registration, Evaluation, Authorisation and Restriction of Chemicals (REACH), 2006 O.J. (L 396) 1 (EC).

72. *See* JANS & VEDDER, *supra* note 13, at 396–98 (overview of REACH provisions).

73. *See* Sachs, *supra* note 18, at 1834.

74. *See* REACH tit. II (Registration of Substances); *id.* art. 20 (Duties of the European Chemicals Agency).

75. *See id.* art. 57 (identifying substances subject to authorization).

76. REACH presumes that risks cannot be adequately controlled for persistent and bioaccumulative chemicals and for chemicals that do not have a known safe threshold below which a lack of adverse effects can be documented. *Id.* art. 60(3).

77. *Id.* art. 60(4).

78. *See* European Chems. Agency, Candidate List of Substances of Very High Concern for Authorisation, http://echa.europa.eu/candidate-list-table (last visited June 25, 2014).

79. *See European Commission Lags on Green Goals*, 35 Int'l Env't Rep. (BNA) 681, 681 (Jul 18, 2012).

80. REACH arts. 31 & 32.

81. REACH art. 37.

82. European Comm'n, Environment: Integrated Product Policy, http://ec.europa.eu/environment/ipp/ (last visited Sept. 13, 2013).

83. Regulation 66/2010 of the European Parliament and of the Council of 25 November 2009 on the EU Ecolabel, 2010 O.J. (L 27) 1 (EC); Regulation 1980/2000 of the European Parliament and of the Council of 17 July 2000 on a Revised Community Ecolabel Award Scheme, 2000 O.J. (L 237) 1 (EC), repealing Regulation 880/92, 1992 O.J. (L 99) 1.

84. For a discussion of extended producer responsibility and its implementation, see Noah Sachs, *Planning the Funeral at the Birth: Extended Producer Responsibility in the European Union and the United States*, 30 Harv. Envtl. L. Rev. 51, 53 (2006).

85. Directive 2000/53 of the European Parliament and of the Council of 18 September 2000 on End-of Life Vehicles, 2000 O.J (L 269) 34 (EC).

86. Directive 2002/96 of the European Parliament and of the Council of 27 January 2003 on Waste Electrical and Electronic Equipment, 2003 O.J. (L 37) 24 (EC), replaced by Directive 2012/19 of the European Parliament and of the Council of 4 July 2012 on Waste Electrical and Electronic Equipment, 2012 O.J. (L 197) 38 (EU).

87. Council Directive 2002/96, 2003 O.J. (L 37) at 26–28.

88. *Report from the Commission to the Council, the European Parliament, the European Economic and Social Committee and the Committee of the Regions on the State of Implementation of Integrated Product Policy* 1–3, COM (2009) 693 final (Dec. 21, 2009).

89. *See* James J. Friedberg, *Views of Donana: Fragmentation and Environmental Policy in Spain*, 3 Colum. J. Eur. L. 1, 18 (1997); *see also* Luke W. Goodrich, *Implementing Environmental Law in the European Union: Lessons from the Bathing Water Directive*, 16 Geo. Int'l Envtl. L. Rev. 301, 307 (2004).

90. Ludwig Kramer, EC Environmental Law 423 (6th ed. 2007).

91. *See* Jans & Vedder, *supra* note 13, at 157–64; *see also* TFEU, *supra* note 11, art. 258.

92. *See* European Enforcement Network, Chemical Legislation European Enforcement Network, http://www.cleen-europe.eu/about-cleen/overview/ (last visited Sept. 13, 2013).

93. *See* European Comm'n, Rapid Alert System for Non-Food Products Posing a Serious Risk, http://ec.europa.eu/consumers/safety/rapex/index_en.htm (last visited Sept. 13, 2013).

94. *Id.*

CHAPTER 27

The European Union

GLORY FRANCKE

I. Introduction

European environmental protection laws resonate globally for their operational impact and trend-setting influence. The European Union's (EU) flagship chemical legislation, dubbed the "REACH regulation,"[1] provides a good example. Compliance with the REACH regulation requires input from the global supply chain, highlighting the international relevance of EU environmental law. At the same time, important trading partners, including China, Japan, and Korea, continue to adopt legislation inspired in part by REACH's data registration requirements, which illustrates the "copy-cat" potential of EU environmental law and policy.

Given the global implications of such environmental protection laws and the EU's authority to legislate in these matters, it is increasingly helpful for environmental lawyers and compliance professionals to understand the players, principles, and processes that shape these laws and policies. To that end, this chapter addresses EU environmental law writ large, beginning with legal sources and key principles and followed by an introduction to the EU institutions and processes that create EU environmental law. The middle section of this chapter briefly addresses implementation of EU environmental law while the final section focuses on enforcement and the challenges confronting parties seeking access to justice in EU environmental matters.

This chapter does not address substantive EU environmental laws. See the EU country-specific chapters of this book for such information.

II. Sources and Key Principles of EU Environmental Law

The sources and key principles of EU environmental law derive from three types of EU laws: primary, secondary, and supplementary. Primary EU law is "constitutional" law. It defines the structure of the EU political system, the relationship of the various organs to the whole and the boundaries of EU lawmaking power. The EU constitution is not a comprehensive legal document. Instead, it spreads across (1) the "EU Treaties," (2) the laws produced by the EU institutions, and (3) the supplementary law of the EU.

The term "EU Treaties" covers the founding treaties that established the EU,[2] the treaties amending the EU,[3] the protocols annexed to those treaties, the additional treaties that change specific sections of the founding treaties,[4] and the accession treaties whereby new countries joined the EU.[5] Amended and updated over time, the Treaty on the EU (TEU) and the Lisbon Treaty, formally known as the Treaty on the Functioning of the EU (TFEU), together form "the Treaties" that govern today's EU. These entered into force on December 1, 2009.

Secondary EU law is composed of regulations, directives, decisions, recommendations, and opinions that constitute either "legislative acts" or "nonlegislative acts" depending upon the procedure for adoption.[6] The European Commission (the Commission) proposes and the European Parliament and the Council of Ministers adopt legislative acts. The Commission alone proposes and adopts nonlegislative acts. In other words, adoption procedure is the only difference between legislative and nonlegislative acts. For practical purposes, they are equally binding legislation.

There are important differences between an EU regulation and a directive. A regulation, such as the REACH regulation, is a law addressed to all member states, natural, and legal persons. A regulation is binding across the EU and member state implementation of the obligations is not required. Regulations confer rights and impose obligations directly on citizens just as a national law would. Member states regulate administrative sanctions (such as fines) in their national laws, since the EU does not have jurisdiction in this respect. Conversely, member states are the sole addressees of environmental directives, which do not, as a rule, confer rights or impose obligations on natural or legal persons. Such rights and obligations flow only from member state transposition of the directive,[7] that is, adoption of national legislation or, under certain preconditions, administrative measures[8] to implement the directive.

A directive sets out binding legal goals and objectives to varying degrees of detail. Sometimes these goals will be nearly aspirational. For example, the EU Packaging and Packaging Waste Directive requires member states to ensure that all packaging placed on the market is "designed, produced and commercialized in such a way as to permit its reuse or recovery, including recycling, and to minimize its impact to the environment" upon disposal.[9] As this requirement alone is too vague to be enforceable, member states must set precise levels and standards related to the reusability and recoverability of such packaging. Meanwhile, other provisions of environmental directives are so specific that member states retain little to no room for maneuver. For example, the Batteries Directive specifies the precise levels of heavy metals permitted in batteries placed on the EU market, and member states may not "impede, prohibit, or restrict the placing on the market" of batteries and accumulators that meet the requirements of the Battery Directive.[10]

EU decisions are binding on addressees while recommendations and opinions have no binding force but are nonetheless important. For example, in October 2011, the Commission published its recommendation for the definition of "nanomaterial" for regulatory purposes.[11] The recommendations are not legally binding but they are widely used in practice, which tends to result in similar administrative practices across the EU. Incorporation of the nanomaterial definition into sector- or product-specific legislation (such as REACH) will also make the Commission's recommendation legally enforceable.

EU regulations and directives delegate a great deal of authority to the Commission to adopt the previously mentioned nonlegislative measures. The Lisbon Treaty created two categories of such measures: implementing acts[12] and delegated acts.[13] Distinguishing between the two is the difficult subject of much academic speculation.[14] Suffice to say, what is important to understand is that these nonlegislative EU acts—regardless of which category—are not just "little rules"; rather, such nonlegislative measures constitute the overwhelming bulk of EU law. Indeed, 97 percent of all EU measures adopted between 2004 and 2009 were nonlegislative acts.[15]

Supplementary EU law includes international law, general principles of law, and the "judge-made law" developed through the case law of the Court of Justice of the European Union (the ECJ), the EU's highest legal instance. In regards to international law, the EU's obligations under the Aarhus Convention on Access to Information, Public Participation in Decision-Making, and Access to Justice in Environmental Matters (the Aarhus Convention) are of particular importance to EU environmental law.[16]

A. The United Nations Aarhus Convention in the EU and Why It Matters

The Aarhus Convention and the EU Aarhus Legislation,[17] which implements the convention into EU law, create broad and powerful rights for private parties (natural and legal persons as well as associations) in matters related to the environment. In particular, EU, national, and local authorities must provide, protect, and enforce:

- the right to environmental information,
- the right to public participation in environmental decision making, and
- the right to access to justice in environmental matters.[18]

There is a growing body of case law clarifying the status of these Aarhus provisions in EU environmental law. Fundamentally, case law established that the Aarhus Convention forms an integral part of the EU legal order.[19] The General Court recently took that a step further and affirmed that the Aarhus Convention takes precedence over the Aarhus Regulation.[20]

The case involved the scope of a relatively new legal instrument dubbed the Request for Internal Review (RIR) procedure. In 2008, the Commission refused an RIR request made by the applicants, two environmental nongovernmental organizations (NGOs). The Commission defended this decision by pointing to the text of the Aarhus Regulation,[21] which limited the acts subject to an RIR to those of "individual" scope, which excluded the NGOs. The General Court dismissed the Commission's argument, noting that the Aarhus Convention itself contained no such limitation. Therefore, the "individual scope" provision of the Aarhus Regulation was out of line with the convention and illegal.[22]

The General Court's ruling indicates that for environmental matters, the decision-making procedures of the European institutions and standing and judicial review rules of the EU courts must meet the standards of the Aarhus Convention. This is a crucial point that could have important ramifications in areas such as the Commission's adoption of implementing and delegated acts and the EU courts' interpretation of the EU's standing provisions. Indeed, the President of the Commission, José Manuel Barroso, deemed the potential consequences of the judgment "very far-reaching."[23] The Commission, joined by the European Parliament and the EU Council of Ministers, is appealing the decision, a fact underscoring the importance of this matter.[24]

B.   Key Principles of EU Law

Core principles of EU law determine the power and use of EU legislative authority. Foremost is the principle of conferral, which determines the EU's legislative mandate. According to this principle, the EU can only legislate within areas with a "legal basis," that is, policy area explicitly set out in the TFEU, and then only according to the procedures, conditions, and objectives set out therein.

The legal basis for a legislative act is important because different legal bases provide for varying degrees of EU authority. Some legal bases, such as competition, customs, and international trade, give the EU the exclusive right to take action.[25] In other areas, such as the environment, energy, and climate change, member states share authority with the EU in a lopsided manner: Member states retain their individual power to legislate, but only to the extent that the EU has not already done so.[26] An example of this relationship is the notification of consumer products containing nanomaterials. Currently, Germany, France, Belgium, and Denmark are in various stages of considering or implementing independent nanomaterial notification requirements. Creation of an EU-wide system, for example, an explicit inclusion in the REACH regulation, would require these countries to align their national approaches with the EU-wide requirements.

The primary objective of a law determines its legal basis. Several laws that appear to aim at environmental protection, such as the Framework Directive on Eco-design of Energy-Related Products,[27] exist primarily to level the playing field of the EU internal market. As such, they are based on internal market provisions within the TFEU.[28] EU legislation aimed instead at fulfilling one of the treaty's general environmental protection objectives, such as Directive 2008/50/EC on Ambient Air Quality and Cleaner Air for Europe, have environmental protection for their legal basis.[29]

The conferral of legislative power triggers two critical principles that regulate the use of this power. First, all proposed EU law must be justified according to the requirements of the subsidiarity principle, which provides that EU action is justified only where member state action alone cannot sufficiently achieve the legislative objective.[30] Environmental protection laws and harmonization standards will nearly always pass the subsidiarity test due to the cross-border aspects of issues such as air and water pollution, biodiversity protection, and climate change.[31] The second principle, the principle of proportionality, dictates that a measure must be "necessary" and "appropriate" in order to achieve the objectives set out in the Treaties.[32] The principle limits action—at the EU *and* the national level—to the minimum necessary and dictates that EU legislation should allow the maximum degree of member state autonomy. This explains the frequent use of minimum standards in environmental protections laws, which allow member states to impose stricter requirements.[33] In sum, because member states retain more autonomy through directives, directives are preferable to regulations, even though implementation can yield widely varied results across the EU.

C. Principles of EU Environmental Law

In addition to the general principles discussed above, Article 191 second paragraph of the TFEU requires EU environmental law and policies to adhere to several environment-specific principles:

- the precautionary principle,
- the prevention principle (preventive action should be taken when possible),
- the source principle (environmental damage should be rectified at its source), and
- the polluter pays principle.

The EU's use of the precautionary principle is particularly notable as it provides lawmakers a large blanket of justification to cover environmental measures.[34] Case law allows that decision makers' use of the precautionary principle is justified if (1) a potentially negative health consequence of a substance is identified (it may not be hypothetical) and (2) a comprehensive risk assessment based on the most reliable scientific data and international research is completed.[35] Importantly, the precautionary principle justifies EU action even if such scientific evidence is lacking or inconclusive provided that the decision-making process fulfilled these procedural requirements.[36]

III. The Creators of EU Environmental Law: The EU Institutions

The EU Treaties created and empowered seven supranational EU bodies referred to as institutions: the European Parliament; European Council; the Council of the European Union (hereinafter referred to as the Council of

Ministers or the Council); European Commission; Court of Justice of the European Union; European Central Bank (ECB), and the Court of Auditors.

Of these, the Court of Justice of the European Union constitutes the judicial branch while the European Commission (representing the interests of the EU), the Council of Ministers (representing member states' interests), and the European Parliament (representing EU citizens' interests) form the "Institutional Triangle" that promulgates EU legislative and nonlegislative acts.

A.   The EU Judicial Institution

The EU judicial institution oversees the work of the decision-making institutions and clarifies the parameters of EU authority. It comprises the Court of Justice of the European Union (ECJ), the General Court (formerly known as the Court of First Instance), and the European Civil Service Tribunal. The ECJ is the highest instance, outranking national supreme courts and issuing judgments affecting individuals, member states, and the EU institutions. Its jurisdiction primarily covers failure of a member state or EU body to fulfill treaty obligations; judicial review of laws passed by EU bodies; and preliminary rulings on cases on the interpretation of EU law or implemented EU law respectively handed up by national courts.

Eight advocates general (AG) assist the ECJ's 27 judges (one from each member state) by issuing independent, impartial legal opinions prior to the judges' deliberations. The AG's opinion generally deals with the legal issues more comprehensively and systematically than a court judgment, which is more strictly limited to the particular matters at hand. Although only advisory, the AG's opinion is nonetheless influential and aides lawyers and practitioners seeking to interpret and better understand not only the judgments of the ECJ but the relevant EU law in general.

The General Court is an independent court working in parallel alongside the ECJ. Its primary role is to hear all actions brought by individuals, companies, and some organizations in addition to cases related to competition law.

B.   The Legislative Institutions

1.   Council of Ministers

Together with the European Parliament, the Council of Ministers (the Council) approves and adopts EU secondary legislative acts. It is composed of member state ministers; senior national politicians responsible for national policy areas. These ministers meet in ten different policy "configurations" or councils.[37] Accordingly, Ministers of the Environment come together in the Environment Council to decide on EU environmental issues while Ministers of Agriculture convene in the Agriculture and Fisheries Council. It is important to understand that these ministers are "moonlighting" in their council roles. Most fly into Brussels for a day or two of meetings (frequency varies depending on configurations) and then return to their full-time day jobs as high-level national politicians.

Given these circumstances, the Council's efficient promulgation of EU law and policy would be nearly impossible without an iceberg of support from the so-called Council "preparatory bodies." Forming the iceberg's tip are the Brussels-based member state permanent representations, or "Perm. Reps."[38] Member state ambassadors, assisted by a deputy, lead each Perm. Rep. and in most cases, a third ambassador is responsible for EU foreign policy issues. These ambassadors meet to decide sensitive matters such as external relations and economic and financial affairs in the second section of the Committee of Permanent Representatives Section II (Coreper II), while the deputy ambassadors meet in the Committee of Permanent Representatives Section I (Coreper I) which is responsible for issues including the environment and the internal market. Technically, Coreper I and II cannot make substantive decisions.[39] In practice, however, 85 percent of Council decisions are adopted without discussion based on Coreper's recommendations.[40]

Similarly, Coreper does not actively develop many of its own recommendations; instead, Coreper is advised by the 160 working parties and senior committees that form the base of the Council's legislative iceberg. These committees, composed of national civil servants and diplomats, review and amend technical proposals and hash out compromises.[41] The Environment working party is particularly prolific. It meets about three days a week and addresses a broad range of issues including air pollution, chemicals, waste, resource efficiency, natural resources, biodiversity, and the marine environment.[42]

The leadership of the Council introduces another EU idiosyncrasy—the six-month rotating presidency. Every six months a new EU member state chairs all Council meetings, sets the agenda and overall work program, and acts as facilitator within the Council and between the Council and other institutions.[43]

2. The European Parliament

The European Parliament with its 750-plus members (MEPs) constitutes the only directly elected EU institution. EU citizens, who vote according to national lists, elect the MEPs to five-year terms. For example, a Swedish citizen residing in Sweden votes for candidates on the list for a Swedish party. Once elected, the MEPs join forces in European political groups.

Most legislation is discussed and shaped in Parliament's policy committees, of which the Environment, Public Health, and Food Safety Committee (ENVI Committee) is active and influential. It considers draft legislative proposals related to environmental protection and agrees on amendments that are subsequently put to a vote in the Parliament's plenary session.

The Parliament, historically the least powerful of the three EU institutions, has grown in power through the treaty revisions. With the TFEU, the

Parliament finally assumed the role of co-legislator on equal footing to the Council in most policy areas. The Parliament also plays a significant role in the EU budget negotiations and has a veto right for most international agreements, including enlargement, through the consent procedure whereby the European Parliament cannot formally suggest any amendments, but it can approve or reject a text as a whole.

3.   The European Commission

The word "Commission" covers two different concepts. First, it refers to the College of Commissioners, a body of 27 commissioners (one for each member state), each appointed by the president of the European Commission and approved by a majority of the European Parliament. This body sets the agenda and formally approves draft legislative proposals. Second, the word "Commission" refers to some 40,000 civil servants staffing over 40 different divisions of the Commission, called directorates-general (DG).

The DGs are separated according to policy areas. DG Environment, DG Energy, DG Climate Action, DG Trade, and DG Enterprise are particularly important for European environmental law and policy. The principle of collective responsibility, introduced in Article 1 of the Rules of Procedure of the Commission, requires these DGs to work together to coordinate the preparation and implementation of the College of Commissioners' decisions.[44] In reality, however, the different objectives and legislative powers of the DGs often result in conflicting positions. For example, DG Environment's precautionary approach toward environmental protection often appears at odds with DG Enterprise's mandate to strengthen the EU's industrial base and DG Trade's mandate to avoid unnecessary trade restrictions. Moreover, as DGs are concerned with different aspects of the same issue, varied degrees of apparent coordination may yield parallel and overlapping regulations on a single subject.

IV.   How EU Environmental Law Is Created
A.   Adoption of Legislative Acts

The EU decision-making and judicial institutions interact within complex machinery that often confuses the initiated and is even more puzzling to an outsider. One of the most unusual aspects is the fact that only the Commission can introduce an EU legislative proposal. Such work begins in a specific policy unit of a DG that will "own" the matter going forward. Under Article 249 TFEU the Commission adopts its own rules of procedure, which are, for the most part, very general and do not dictate the preparatory work a DG must undertake. Consequently, procedures vary. However, as part of an ongoing "better regulation" strategy the Commission encourages certain common steps set out in a plethora of guidelines, reports, and discussion papers, all grouped into 13 thematic areas on the Commission's website.[45]

The first step in preparing a legislative proposal is often to produce a policy-setting "roadmap." This will generally involve a public consultation, which although expected is not legally required. Public consultations are web-based and input is generally limited to fixed multiple-choice responses with limited space for additional comment. As an example, DG Climate Action opened an online public consultation in mid-January 2012 on "including maritime transport emissions in the EU's greenhouse gas reduction commitment."[46] In order to fulfill the consultation's objective of gathering information on the shape of a possible Commission proposal, the consultation asked "yes," "no," or "partially agree" questions and allowed substantiation with a maximum of 1000 characters. Given the often early, vague, and limited nature of European public consultations, they have been criticized as more of a "tick-the-box" exercise in good governance than a tool for meaningful public participation.

Following completion of the public consultation, the relevant DG typically conducts an impact assessment, meant to prepare evidence for political decision makers. There are no binding procedural rules dictating when or precisely how to conduct an impact assessment. Instead, the Commission's Impact Assessment Guidelines explain, "[I]n general, impact assessments are necessary for the most important Commission initiatives and those which will have the most far-reaching impacts."[47] The guidelines also indicate that an impact assessment culminates with submission of a report to the Commission's Impact Assessment Board for consideration. This Board does not have the legal power to return unsatisfactory work. Instead, it opines on the quality of the report and may recommend further work. The legal status of the European impact assessment is unclear.[48] Does internal Commission policy, in the form of the Impact Assessment Guidelines, create a legal requirement to conduct an impact assessment? Can a stakeholder challenge a proposal on the grounds of an inadequate, or missing, impact assessment? Only the EU courts can answer these questions, but according to the guidelines, impact assessment "supports and does not replace decision-making—the adoption of a policy proposal is always a political decision that is made only by the College" (the 27 members of the College of Commissioners).[49]

After, or in conjunction with, the impact assessment and public consultation, the DG drafts a legislative proposal. Importantly, the DG proposes the need for executive measures (implementing or delegated acts) to delegate back to itself. In other words, when the Commission DG drafts legislation for the approval of the Parliament and the Council, it will also propose the scope of its own executive powers such as mandate and duration.

Once complete, the impact assessment report and proposal enter "Inter-Service Consultation," an internal Commission process, taking days or months to conclude, during which concerned DGs can comment on the proposal and raise objections. This aspect of Commission decision making requires consensus. If the DGs do not reach agreement, the issue is elevated to the commissioners' cabinets (individual support staff). The cabinets attempt to prepare an agreement for subsequent adoption by the College of

Commissioners through a tacit approval process. As a result, the commissioners themselves debate only controversial proposals. Once adopted, the Official Journal of the European Communities publishes the draft proposal and an EU legislative proposal is born.

It is important to understand that the Commission considers everything up to this point to be confidential decision-making business, that is, private. However, the EU's obligations under the Aarhus Convention together with general EU access to document rules and cases such as T-166/05 *Borax Europe Ltd v. Commission*, in which the lower court annulled a Commission decision refusing access to documents and sound recordings, provide legal arguments and jurisprudence to the contrary.[50] Stakeholders are entitled to the internal documents that support Commission decision making, particularly in relation to environmental matters.

Once a draft proposal leaves the Commission, more transparent lawmaking occurs, generally under the ordinary legislative procedure. Simply put, the Commission simultaneously presents a legislative proposal to the Parliament and the Council. Parliament evaluates the proposal, approves it "as is" or with amendments, and forwards this position to the Council. If the Council approves the Parliament's proposed text, that text is adopted and becomes EU law in a "First Reading Agreement." If not, then a legislative "ping-pong" match ensues leading to eventual agreement on a text or the failure of the measure.

B.   Adoption of "Nonlegislative" Acts: Comitology before and after Lisbon

Prior to the Lisbon Treaty, the EU version of U.S. federal rulemaking occurred through a procedure collectively described by the term "comitology." Although the Lisbon Treaty "reformed" comitology, the term and the procedure remain widely used, and comitology remains a central concept in EU environmental decision making. Comitology describes the Commission's work with hundreds of committees of national civil servants to reach a qualified majority agreement on EU rules. Once agreed upon by the committee, the Council or Parliament can oppose the proposal on extremely limited grounds.

In contrast to the public participation and access to document rights mandated by the Aarhus Convention, the Commission considers comitology committee meetings private, and the names of the national experts are generally not publicly available. In some processes, interested stakeholders may be permitted to attend all or a part of these meetings. However, this is not a right but rather a privilege, and the decision is subject to the discretion of the Commission civil servants in charge of the comitology exercise. Meeting minutes are confidential although a heavily sanitized version may be available upon request. Eventually the sanitized public version is published; however; such minutes can appear anywhere from a few weeks to months after a meeting, which, coupled with the heavy redacting, render their helpfulness limited. The Commission does not generally conduct an impact assessment for the delegated or implementing acts it adopts. There-fore, effective advocacy on rulemaking at the EU level requires significant amounts of detective work, patience, and a good network of contacts within the institutions.

The Treaty of Lisbon replaced the comitology procedures with the afore-mentioned nameless regime whereby the objectives, content, scope, and duration of the delegation of power are written into each piece of legislation adopted by the Parliament and the Council on a case-by-case basis. The new system is not simple. As previously mentioned, distinguishing between del-egating and implementing acts is difficult,[51] and the new regulation govern-ing the adoption of implementing acts is complex, riddled with exceptions and even exceptions to exceptions.[52]

Several stakeholders, especially the Parliament, have nonetheless praised this new system because it introduces the possibility to write greater control over the Commission into each new piece of legislation. Warnings from vet-eran EU observers offset this optimism, however, with the argument that the Lisbon Treaty made matters worse in terms of transparency. The system is more confusing than ever and shifted even more power to the Commission. They argue that the Parliament and the Council do not have the technical expertise or resources to monitor how the Commission delegates power back to itself in every draft legislative proposal.

V. Implementation of EU Environmental Law

The term "implementation" refers to complying with the obligations imposed by EU law. The European law scholars Jans and Vedder divide this process into four phases.[53] The first phase of implementation involves member state "transposition" of directives into national law (regulations do not need to be transposed). Next is "operationalization" of the regulation or directive whereby the administrative and procedural framework is set in place to establish the authorities and procedures for enforcement. "Application" of the regulation or national rules implementing a directive constitutes the third phase. Finally, monitoring and ensuring compliance with the regula-tions or national laws implementing the directives occurs with the "enforce-ment" phase. See the country-specific chapters for detailed information on the first three phases of implementation of EU law.

According to the Commission, overall member state implementation of EU environmental law is insufficient and costly and requires improvement.[54] This is evidenced by the high number of infringement issues (e.g., a claimant alleges that an EU directive was not duly implemented affecting the subject matter of the court proceedings) brought by citizens or NGOs before national courts or raised in alternative fora, for example, by way of petitions before national parliaments or the EU Parliament. Recent estimates place the direct costs (impacts on human health and the environment) of the failure to imple-ment current legislation at €50 billion per year.[55] Further, fragmented imple-mentation of environmental standards, obligations, and liabilities yields an uneven economic playing field harming the EU's common market. The various solutions for improving member state implementation of EU environmental legislation include improving the EU's procurement and evaluation of information on member state implementation status; "compliance promotion" to identify potential national implementation problems already in the drafting stage of EU legislation;[56] and upfront analysis of member states' environmental situations in order to facilitate the subsequent transposition phase.

VI.   Enforcement of EU Environmental Law

The Commission, national legal systems, and the EU courts enforce EU environmental law. As "guardian of the Treaties," the Commission is tasked with ensuring that member states establish the legal and administrative framework necessary to properly apply and enforce EU environmental law.[57] If a member state fails to fulfill these obligations, the Treaties give the Commission the legal tool of "infringement proceedings" whereby the Commission refers the matter to the European Court of Justice.[58]

If the court finds that a member state has failed to meet its treaty obligations, it must take the measures needed to conform. The Commission can ask the court to impose a lump-sum fine or a penalty if a member state still fails to comply.[59] For example, in April 2012, the Commission asked the court to impose financial penalties ranging from €15,000 to €67,000 per day on Bulgaria, Hungary, Poland, and Slovakia for failure to comply with EU waste legislation.[60]

Despite the threat of Commission infringement proceedings, member states often miss implementation deadlines.[61] Even member states such as Germany, which might be considered "model students" in other areas, regularly miss implementation deadlines. This may be because it takes an average of six years from the time the Commission notifies the defaulting member state until the judgment of the ECJ.[62] Moreover, although individuals could sue the member state for damages incurred because of failure to transpose EU environmental law, practical hurdles including restrictive standing rules, difficulties in establishing a causal link, and excessive costs render the risk of such actions low.[63]

A.   Enforcement by National Courts

Private applicants can challenge national measures implementing EU environmental laws through national courts, which must provide sufficient remedies to ensure effective legal protection in all fields covered by EU law.[64] Under the principle of procedural autonomy, these courts do so according to their national procedural rules.[65] Such rules vary widely with differences in time limits for appeal, standing requirements, access to legal aid, intensity of judicial review, court and other legal costs, and length of proceedings.[66] In general, EU law requires only that national procedural rules governing an EU law are as favorable as those covering an equivalent dispute (principle of equivalence) and that the rules do not make it excessively difficult for an applicant to rely on the rights conferred by EU law (principle of effectiveness).

In the field of the environment, however, recent case law relying on the Aarhus Convention and Legislation sets an important new locus standi standard. In the *Slovak Bears* case, the ECJ ruled on whether Article 9(3) of the Aarhus Convention provided a Slovakian environmental NGO the standing necessary to challenge a decision regarding protection for a species of brown bear.[67] According to Article 9(3) of the Aarhus Convention:

> [E]ach Party shall ensure that, where they meet the criteria, if any, laid down in its national law, members of the public have access to administrative or judicial procedures to challenge acts and omissions by private persons and public authorities which contravene provisions of its national law relating to the environment.

According to the ECJ, national procedural laws must be interpreted "to the fullest extent possible" to allow private parties an "Aarhus" level of access to justice as set out in Article 9(3) of the Aarhus Convention.[68] Following the court's judgment, the Supreme Court of the Slovak Republic reversed its previous case law, quashed the decision of the Ministry of the Environment to refuse the NGO standing, and remitted the case to the ministry.

Once standing is established, national courts generally apply EU environmental law in one of three ways: by invoking the direct effect of EU environmental law, by interpreting national requirements in accordance with the relevant EU law, or through the doctrine of state liability for infringements of EU environmental law.[69]

According to case law, a provision of EU law has direct effect if it is "unconditional and sufficiently precise" to allow its application by national courts acting within their judicial power.[70] Environmental product standard directives like the aforementioned Batteries Directive,[71] which establish precise and detailed compliance conditions, are directly effective.[72] If a provision of EU law does not have direct effect, the national courts are nonetheless obliged to interpret national law in conformity with EU environmental law.

B.   EU Courts

Private applicants can challenge EU environmental laws before EU courts by referral from a national court or directly before the General Court. The latter route has traditionally been fraught with challenge due to restrictive standing requirements. The TFEU contains the following rules dictating who can bring an action for annulment:

> Any natural or legal person may, under the conditions laid down in the first and second paragraphs, institute proceedings against an act addressed to that person or which is of direct and individual concern to them, *and against a regulatory act which is of direct concern to them and does not entail implementing measures.*[73]

Here it is helpful to recall that the TFEU entered into force at the end of 2009. The first phrase of this paragraph, however, repeats the language of the previous treaty, and establishes that an applicant has standing if the act was "addressed to that person" or "of direct and individual concern."

The *Plaumann*[74] rule established the ECJ criterion for "individual concern," which is extremely restrictive, particularly in regards to environmental matters. According to *Plaumann*, an applicant must show that the contested act affects his situation in a manner so distinct from every other possible claimant, that he could have been the addressee of the act:

> [A]n applicant shows "individual concern," "by reason of certain attributes which are peculiar to it [the applicant] or by reason of circumstances in which it [the applicant] is differentiated from all other persons and by virtue of those factors distinguishes it individually just as in the case of the person addressed."[75]

Applicants rarely suffer an environmental impact uniquely; consequently, the *Plaumann* case law has nearly sealed off the courts from private/individual challengers of environmental measures.

The *Greenpeace* case[76] illustrates this effect of *Plaumann*. Three NGOs and 16 individual citizens asked the CFI (now the General Court) to annul the European Commission's decision to fund the construction of two power stations on the Canary Islands without conducting an environmental impact assessment.[77] In regards to standing, the applicants argued that the *Plaumann* case law did not apply in environmental matters and urged the CFI to admit the challenge on "the existence of harm suffered or to be suffered."[78]

The CFI did not agree and applied the *Plaumann* test. Despite the fact that some of the applicants were fishermen and farmers whose activities would be affected by the power stations, the CFI held that this did not distinguish them from "all the people who live or pursue an activity in the areas concerned" and that Greenpeace could not have standing if the members it claimed to represent lacked standing.[79] The ECJ confirmed the CFI's rulings on appeal.

Greenpeace was decided according to the "old" standing requirements. Since then the second phrase of Article 263 paragraph 4 of the Treaty of Lisbon removed the word "individual" and consequently the *Plaumann* requirement. According to Judge Koen Lenaerts, President of Chamber at the ECJ and Professor of European Union Law at KU Leuven, the new language shows the intent to open access to EU courts for private parties, particularly when it is difficult to find a national measure that enables challenge through national courts.[80]

Given this change, the terms "direct concern" and "regulatory act" take on critical importance for an applicant hoping to annul an EU environmental decision. In regards to "direct concern," the court continues to interpret direct concern such that the measure contested:

must directly affect the legal situation of the individual and leave no discretion to the addressees of that measure who are entrusted with the task of implementing it, such implementation being purely automatic and resulting from Community rules without the application of other intermediate rules.[81]

The treaty does not define the term regulatory acts and heated debate surrounded the question of whether such acts include legislative acts.[82] Two judgments delivered by the General Court in autumn 2011 clarify the meaning of regulatory acts.[83] The applicants in *Inuit Tapiriit Kanatami* (a group of companies, associations, and natural persons) challenged the legality of an EU regulation on trade in seal products.[84] The European Parliament and the Council responded with the assertion that the contested regulation was not a "regulatory act" in the meaning of Article 263(4) TFEU. The court supported this assertion, stating that such regulatory acts are "all acts of general application apart from legislative acts."[85] Consequently, those acts adopted by the ordinary legislative procedure (or in rare cases, by special legislative procedure), are not regulatory acts.[86] Given the aforementioned fact that the majority of EU environmental laws and policies are not legislative acts, this should mean that the majority of EU environmental acts come within the scope of the regulatory act, and are subject to review.

Such incremental relaxation of the EU's standing requirements will move the EU closer to compliance with its Aarhus obligations. Currently, the Aarhus Convention Compliance Committee deems the jurisprudence established by the European Court of Justice under the "old" standing rules as "too strict to meet the criteria of the Convention."[87] Noting the removal by the Lisbon Treaty of the word "individual" from the EU standing provisions, the committee expressed the hope that the European courts would establish a "new direction" for their jurisprudence by interpreting the standing provisions in a manner compliant with the Aarhus Convention.

Overall, the combination of changes in the Lisbon Treaty and compliance with the Aarhus Convention may well prove the tipping point that makes EU courts more accessible to those who wish to challenge EU environmental decision making.

Notes

1. Regulation (EC) No 1907/2006 of the European Parliament and of the Council of 18 December 2006 concerning the Registration, Evaluation, Authorisation and Restriction of Chemicals (REACH), establishing a European Chemicals Agency, amending Directive 1999/45/EC and repealing Council Regulation (EEC) No 793/93 and Commission Regulation (EC) No 1488/94 as well as Council Directive 76/769/EEC and Commission Directives 91/155/EEC, 93/67/EEC, 93/105/EC and 2000/21/EC, O.J. L 396, 30.12.2006, as amended.

2. The Treaty of Paris (18 April 1951); the Treaties of Rome (Euratom Treaty and the Treaty establishing the European Economic Community) (25 March 1957); the Maastricht Treaty on European Union (7 February 1992).

3. The Single European Act (17 and 28 February 1986); the Treaty of Amsterdam (2 October 1997); the Treaty of Nice (26 February 2001); the Treaty of Lisbon (13 December 2007) entered into force on 1 December 2009.

4. Treaty on the merger of the executive institutions (8 April 1965); Treaty amending certain budgetary provisions of the Community treaties (22 April 1970); Treaty of Brussels amending certain financial provisions of the Community treaties and establishing a Court of Auditors (22 July 1975); "Act" on the election of members of the European Parliament by direct universal suffrage (20 September 1976).

5. United Kingdom, Ireland, Denmark, and Norway (22 January 1972); Greece (28 May 1979); Spain and Portugal (12 June 1985); Austria, Finland, Norway, and Sweden (24 June 1994); the Czech Republic, Cyprus, Estonia, Hungary, Latvia, Lithuania, Malta, Poland, Slovakia, and Slovenia (16 April 2003); Romania and Bulgaria (25 April 2005).

6. TFEU art. 288; legislative acts are adopted by ordinary or special legislative procedure while "non-legislative acts" are generally executive measures adopted by the Commission.

7. A directive can be directly applied if (1) a member state did not correctly implement it within the given period, (2) the directive is unconditional (i.e., application is not subject to conditions and does not require further acts of member states or the EU) and (3) the directive is sufficiently precise. *Cf., e.g.,* Case 126/82, D. J. Smit Transp. B.V. v. Commissie Grensoverschrijdend Beroepsgoederenvervoer [1983], European Court of Justice, 25/1/1983. Efficient enforcement of EU law in member states requires *effêt utile.* Generally, a directive applies directly only vis-à-vis the noncompliant member state and not vis-à-vis its citizens.

8. The ECJ does not always require a directive to be implemented formally and verbatim in a parliamentary law or an ordinance. Yet individuals must be in a position to know with certainty their rights and obligations arising from the directive. For example, in a case where an EU directive on air quality limit values was implemented by Germany in a technical norm (classifying as general administrative provision without binding character) the ECJ held that the implementation did not comply with primary law. (Case C-361/88, Comm'n of the European Cmtys. v. Fed. Republic of Germany [1991], European Court of Justice, 30/5/1991 (TA-Luft Case).

9. European Parliament and Council Directive 94/62/EC of 20 December 1994 on packaging and packaging waste (Packaging and Packaging Waste Directive), O.J. L 365, 31.12.1994, at 10–23, as amended. Annex II by way of Article 9 Packaging and Packaging Waste Directive.

10. Directive 2006/66/EC of the European Parliament and of the Council of 6 September 2006 on batteries and accumulators and waste batteries and accumulators and repealing Directive 91/157/EEC (the "Batteries Directive") O.J. L 266, 26.9.2006, at 1–14 art. 6, as amended.

11. Commission Recommendation of 18 October 2011 on the definition of nanomaterial Text with EEA relevance (2011/696/EU) O.J. L 275, 20.10.2011, at 38–40.

12. TFEU art. 291.

13. TFEU art. 290.

14. Paul P. Craig, *Delegated Acts, Implementing Acts and the New Comitology Regulation,* 36 European L. Rev. 671, 674–77 (Oct. 2011) (Oxford Legal Studies Research Paper No. 58/2011), *available at* http://ssrn.com/abstract=1959987; M. Kaeding & A. Hardacre, *The Execution of Delegated Powers after Lisbon. A Timely Analysis of the Regulatory Procedure with Scrutiny and Its Lessons for Delegated Acts* (EUI Working Paper, RCAS 2010/85, 2010), *available at* http://cadmus.eui.eu/bitstream/handle/1814/14956/RSCAS_2010_85.pdf; K.

Lenaerts & M. Desomer, *Towards a Hierarchy of Legal Acts in the European Union? Simplification of Legal Instruments and Procedures,* 11(6) EUROPEAN L.J. 744–65 (Nov. 2005).

15. During the sixth EU legislature under Barroso I (2004–2009), 454 EU legislative acts were adopted compared with 14,522 nonlegislative acts, *see* Gijs Jan Brandsma & Jens Blom-Hansen *The Post-Lisbon Battle Over Comitology: Another Round of the Politics of Structural Change* 1 (European Univ. Inst. Working Paper SPS 2011.02, 2011), *available at* http://cadmus.eui.eu/bitstream/handle/1814/18440/SPS_2011_03.pdf?sequence=1; Kaeding & Hardacre, *supra* note 14, at 1.

16. Convention on Access to Information, Public Participation in Decision-Making and Access to Justice in Environmental Matters done at Aarhus, Denmark on 25 June 1998, *available at* http://www.unece.org/fileadmin/DAM/env/pp/documents/cep43e.pdf.

17. The EU implements the Aarhus Convention into the EU legal order primarily through two pieces of legislation: (1) Regulation (EC) No. 1367/2006 of the European Parliament and of the Council of 6 September 2006 on the application of the provisions of the Aarhus Convention on Access to Information, Public Participation in Decision-making and Access to Justice in Environmental Matters to Community Institutions and Bodies, O.J. L 264, 25.9.2006, at 13, and (2) Directive 2003/4/EC of the European Parliament and of the Council of 28 January 2003 on public access to environmental information and repealing Council Directive 90/313/EEC, O.J. L 41, 14.2.2003, at 26.

18. Aarhus Convention art. 2(4).

19. Case C-240/09, Lesoochranárske zoskupenie VLK v. Ministerstvo životného prostredia Slovenskej republiky, 8/3/11, para. 30; 2005/370/EC; *see also* Council Decision of 17 February 2005 on the conclusion, on behalf of the European Community, of the Convention on access to information, public participation in decision-making and access to justice in environmental matters.

20. Case T-338/08, Stichting Natuur en Milieu and Pesticide Action Network Europe v. European Comm'n, European Court of Justice, 6/14/12; 116 DEN A-3, 6/18/12.

21. *Id.* para. 4.

22. *Id.* paras. 76, 83. Interestingly, the European Court of Justice held a similar German provision to be null and void that limited environmental NGOs' action rights to such environmental provisions that conferred rights to individuals, that is, granted action rights to neighbors of a project or citizens (Case C-115/09, Bund für Umwelt und Naturschutz Deutschland, Landesverband Nordrhein Westfalen eV (BUND) v. Bezirksregierung Arnsberg, intervening party: Trianel Kohlekraftwerk Lünen GmbH & Co. KG (Trianelcase), 11/5/11). The famous case ultimately led to the suspension of a preliminary permit for a power plant that had already been erected, because of noncompliance with European nature protection laws (which had not been challengeable before the ECJ's ruling). It has opened, at least in Germany, an entirely new playing field to the environmental NGOs being now able to invoke noncompliance of permits with "objective" environmental regulations (i.e., regulations that do not confer any rights to natural persons).

23. Minutes of the 2011th meeting of the Commission held in Brussels (Berlaymont) on Wednesday 18 July 2012 (morning) (PV (2012) 2011 final), at 11.

24. Commission Decision of 18.7.2012 on the submission of an appeal before the Court of Justice (C(2012) 5069 final).

25. TFEU art. 3.

26. TFEU art. 4.

27. Directive 2009/125/EC of the European Parliament and of the Council of 21 October 2009 establishing a framework for the setting of ecodesign requirements for energy-related products, O.J. L 285, 31.10.2009, at 10–35.

28. TFEU art. 114, which replaced EC art. 95 and EEC 100a.

29. Article 191 TFEU contains the EU's environmental objectives while Article 192 TFEU serves as the actual legal basis for EU environmental protection laws.

30. TEU art. 5.

31. JAN H. JANS & HANS H.B. VEDDER, EUROPEAN ENVIRONMENTAL LAW: AFTER LISBON 17 (4th ed. 2012).

32. TEU art. 5(4).

33. See Council Resolution on the drafting, implementation, and enforcement of Community environmental law; O.J. 1997 C 321/1.

34. MARIA LEE, EU ENVIRONMENTAL LAW: CHALLENGES, CHANGE AND DECISION-MAKING 97. (2005)

35. Case C-33/08, Comm'n v. France [2010] para. 92; Case C-343/09, Afton Chemical, Judgment of 08 July 2010; Case C-77/09, Gowan Comércio Internacional e Serviços [2010]. See also the discussion in JANS & VEDDER, supra note 31, at 41–43.

36. Case C-77/09, Gowan Comércio Internacional e Serviços [2010] para. 76.

37. The council configurations are General Affairs; Foreign Affairs; Economic and Financial Affairs; Justice and Home Affairs (JHA); Employment, Social Policy, Health, and Consumer Affairs; Competitiveness (internal market, industry, research, and space); Transport, Telecommunications, and Energy; Agriculture and Fisheries; Environment; Education, Youth, Culture, and Sport. For more on this work of the Council Configurations, see http://www.consilium.europa.eu/council/council-configurations?lang=en (last visited Nov. 9, 2012).

38. For a list of Permanent Representations, see http://europa.eu/whoiswho/public/index.cfm?fuseaction=idea.hierarchy&nodeid=3780 (last visited Nov. 22, 2012).

39. P. Craig, Institutions, Power and Institutional Balance, in THE EVOLUTION OF EU LAW 45 (Paul Craig & Grainne de Burca eds., 2011); see also J. Lewis, The Methods of Community in EU Decision-Making and Administrative Rivalry in the Council's Infrastructure, 7 J. EUROPEAN PUB. POL'Y 26 (2000).

40. F. HAYES-RENSHAW & H. WALLACE, THE COUNCIL OF MINISTERS 77 (2d ed. 2006).

41. C. EGENHOFER ET AL., THE EVER-CHANGING UNION: AN INTRODUCTION TO THE HISTORY, INSTITUTIONS, AND DECISION-MAKING PROCESSES OF THE EUROPEAN UNION 26 (2d rev'd ed. 2011).

42. Id.

43. See Council Decision of 1 January 2007 determining the order in which the office of President of the Council shall be held (2007/5/EC, Euratom), available at http://eur-lex.europa.eu/LexUriServ/LexUriServ.do?uri=OJ:L:2007:001:0011:0012:EN:PDF.

44. Rules of Procedure of the Commission (C(2000)3614) O.J. L 308, 8.12.2000, at 26.

45. http://ec.europa.eu/governance/better_regulation/key_docs_en.htm#_br.

46. DG Climate Action Policy Unit B.3, Public Consultation—Including maritime transport emissions in the EU's greenhouse gas reduction commitment, open from 19 January 2012 to 12 April 2012.

47. European Comm'n, Impact Assessment Guidelines, 15 January 2009 (SEC(2009)92) § 1.4.

48. Alberto Alemanno, The Better Regulation Initiative at the Judicial Gate: A Trojan Horse within the Commission's Walls or the Way Forward?, EUROPEAN L.J. (2009), available at http://ssrn.com/abstract=1297170.

49. EUROPEAN COMM'N, IMPACT ASSESSMENT GUIDELINES § 1.1 (SEC(2009)92).

50. Case T-166/05, Borax v. Comm'n [2009] E.C.R. II-00028.

51. Craig, supra note 14, at 674–77; Kaeding & Hardacre, supra note 14; Lenaerts & Desomer, supra note 14, at 744–65.

52. Regulation 182/2011 laying down the rules and general principles concerning mechanisms for control by Member States of the Commission's exercise of implementing powers (2011) O.J. L55/13.

53. JANS & VEDDER, *supra* note 31, at 139.

54. Communication from the Commission to the European Parliament, the Council, the European Economic and Social Committee and the Committee of the Regions: Improving the delivery of benefits from EU environment measures: building confidence through better knowledge and responsiveness, (COM(2012) 95 final).

55. *Id.* at 1.

56. *Id.* at 6.

57. Koen Lenaerts & José A. Gutiérrez-Fons, *The General System of EU Environmental Law Enforcement*, 30(1) Y.B. EUROPEAN L. 3, 3–4 (2011).

58. TFEU art. 258.

59. TFEU art. 260.

60. European Comm'n, Press Release, Environment: Commission Asks Court to Impose Financial Penalties on Four Member States, Urges Belgium to Comply with EU Waste Legislation (Apr. 26, 2012), http://europa.eu/rapid/press-release_IP-12-422_en .htm?locale=en.

61. P. WENNERÅS, THE ENFORCEMENT OF EC ENVIRONMENTAL LAW 252 (2007).

62. M. HEDEMANN-ROBINSON, ENFORCEMENT OF EUROPEAN UNION ENVIRONMENTAL LAW: LEGAL ISSUES AND CHALLENGES 6–7 (2007).

63. Lenaerts & Gutiérrez-Fons, *supra* note 57, at 4.

64. TEU art. 19(1).

65. Case 45/76, Comet [1076] E.C.R. 2043; Case 33/76, Rewe [1976] E.C.R. 1989; Case 265/78, Ferwerda [1980] E.C.R. 617.

66. JANS & VEDDER, *supra* note 31, at 229–30.

67. Case C-240/09, Lesoochranárske zoskupenie VLK v. Ministerstvo životného prostredia Slovenskej republiky, E.C.R. 2011 Page I-01255.

68. *Id.* para. 50.

69. JANS & VEDDER, *supra* note 31, at 228.

70. Case C-236/92, Comitato do coordinamento per la difesa della Cava v. Regione Lombardia [1994] E.C.R. I-485; Case C-115/09, Trianel Kohlekraftwek LüJudgment of 12 May 2011; see also the discussion in JANS & VEDDER, *supra* note 31, at 183–210.

71. Directive 2006/66 on batteries and accumulators and waste batteries and accumulators, O.J. 2006 L 266/I.

72. JANS & VEDDER, *supra* note 31, at 189.

73. TFEU art. 263(4) (emphasis added).

74. Case 25/62, Plaumann v. Comm'n [1963] E.C.R. 95, para. 107.

75. *Id.*

76. Case T-585/93, Stichting Greenpeace Council v. Comm'n [1995] E.C.R. II-2205; Case C-321/95P Stichting Greenpeace Council v. Comm'n [1998] E.C.R. I-1651.

77. Council Directive 85/337/EEC of 27 June 1985 on the assessment of the effects of certain public and private projects on the environment, O.J. L175/40.

78. Case T-585/93, Stichting Greenpeace Council v. Comm'n [1995] E.C.R. II-2205 para. 51.

79. *Id.* para. 64.

80. Lenaerts & Gutiérrez-Fons, *supra* note 57, at 18.

81. Case T-262/10, Microban Int'l and Microban (Europe) v. Comm'n [2011] E.C.R. II-0000 [para 27]; Case C-386/96P Societe Louis Dreyfus & Cie v. Comm'n [1998] E.C.R. I-2309 [43].

82. *See, e.g.*, Advocate General Kokott's opinion of January 17, 2013 on Case C-583/11P, Inuit Tapiriit Kanatami v. Parliament & Council.

83. Case T-18/10, Inuit Tapiriit Kanatami v. European Parliament & Council [2011] E.C.R. II-0000; Case T 262/10, Microban Int'l and Microban (Europe) v. Comm'n [2011] E.C.R. II-0000.

84. Regulation (EC) No 1007/2009 of the European Parliament and of the Council of 16 September 2009 on trade in seal products, O.J. L 286, 31.10.2009, at 36–39.

85. Case T-18/10, Inuit Tapiriit Kanatami v. European Parliament & Council [2011] E.C.R. II-0000, para. 56.

86. *Cf.* TFEU art. 289.

87. Findings and Recommendations of the Compliance Committee with Regards to Communication ACCC/C/2008/32 (pt. 1) Concerning Compliance by the European Union, adopted on April 14, 2011.

CHAPTER 28

France

DAVID DESFORGES

I. Institutional Framework
A. Constitutional Charter of the Environment and Statutory Affirmation of Principles

In 2005, France adopted the 2004 Charter of the Environment affirming "one's right to live in a balanced and healthy environment."[1] As a consequence of the "constitutionalization" of environmental protection, French laws must abide by principles affirmed by the Charter. Most French environmental laws are transposed from norms established at the European Union (EU) level. For its part, the French Environmental Code establishes the following key environmental principles:[2] (1) precautionary principle, (2) preventive action and corrective action at the source principle, (3) polluter pays principle, (4) the freedom of access to environmental information principle, and (5) the public participation principle (in environmental decision making). These constitute guiding principles for the enactment of specific environmental legislation and must be complied with by subordinate regulatory and administrative acts (i.e., decrees, ministerial orders, individual permits). The Environmental Code further adopts five sustainable development objectives:[3] (1) the fight against global warming; (2) the preservation of biodiversity, open spaces, and resources; (3) social cohesion and solidarity among territories and generations; (4) the self-development of all human beings; and (5) the promotion of development patterns based on responsible production and consumption models.

B. Role and Impact of EU Legislation on the Formation of Domestic Environmental Law

With the establishment of environmental protection by the 1992 Treaty on European Union in Maastricht, the Netherlands, as an objective of paramount importance,[4] EU legislation in the area of environmental protection is now abundant. EU legislation is not always automatically applicable in EU

521

member states (with the notable exception of European Community regulations); the obligation of member states is to transpose EU directives into domestic law to ensure the proper domestic enforcement of EC obligations through the adoption of complementary legislation or regulations.

C.   Domestic Sources of Environmental Law

The Environmental Code represents a continuous effort to organize, compile, codify, and update with new laws and regulations about 200 years of environmental law.[5] The Environmental Code is therefore regularly updated as environmental laws and regulations are being modified to accommodate EU environmental law obligations. Some decrees and ministerial orders remain uncodified and "survive" under their original headings. Additionally, the Environmental Code is not the only source of provisions regarding environmental protection. Numerous other environment-related provisions are to be found, for example, in the Public Health, Planning, Labor, Rural, and Forestry Codes. It is therefore always advisable not to limit inquiries to the Environmental Code alone.

D.   Parliament and Government Prerogatives

The Parliament votes on proposed statutes relating to the protection of the environment. In most instances, such laws actually transpose EU directive objectives, arguably limiting the latitude that French lawmakers enjoy. The government promulgates regulations supplementing such laws and generally transposing the more technical aspects of the directives or, where relevant and necessary, independently of any EU requirement.[6] In some circumstances, based on a desire to increase efficiency, the government may request from the Parliament the authorization to legislate through ordinances (*ordonnances*), which constitute substantive statutory provisions enacted by the government.[7] In recent times, this procedure has often been used to enact environmental legislation.[8]

E.   Permitting Procedures

Despite decentralization (a move initiated in the early 1980s to transfer prerogatives and decision making from the national government to the regional departments and regions (*départements* and *régions*)),[9] France remains centralized. Unsurprisingly, environmental protection powers therefore remain essentially vested with the national government. As a consequence thereof, permitting is essentially a prerogative of the national government. The authority issuing operating permits for activities is generally the Préfet (i.e., the representative of the national government in each *département*). Several exceptions do apply, however. For example, military installations operate under permits issued by the Minister of Defense[10] while nuclear installations operate under permits issued by the minister in charge of the nuclear industry. Pipeline permits are issued either by the minister in charge of such infrastructure or by the Préfet, depending on the status, nature, and geography of the pipeline in question.[11]

Depending on the status of activities involved, the permitting process may include a public inquiry,[12] which is often the case for activities subject to authorization. These will also require the completion and submission of a comprehensive environmental impact assessment (EIA).[13] Indeed, EIAs are necessary for any project, undertakings, public or private, which, due to their nature, size, or location, are likely to carry significant adverse environmental or health impacts. Regulatory provisions establish that some projects must automatically undergo an EIA while others are analyzed on a case-by-case basis and meet applicable thresholds before an EIA requirement applies. When a given project involves several undertakings carried out simultaneously, each of them is subject to the EIA requirement, and an assessment of the entire program must be performed by the project proponent. Finally, the significance of EIAs in the permitting procedure is illustrated by their status in the context of judicial review of administrative decisions before administrative courts. In summary proceedings challenging administrative decisions requiring an EIA, in the absence of an EIA, the court must enjoin the decision.[14]

A less cumbersome permitting avenue—the "déclaration" procedure—generally does not require a public inquiry. Conversely, when a given permit involves environmental or public health protection issues, or the marketing of products or substances, it falls under the responsibility of several ministers (the Ministers of Ecology, Sustainable Development and Energy,[15] Agriculture, and Health, for the most part). The issuance of such permits often involves the filing of no less burdensome applications (with risk assessments, for example) and often requires the prior advisory opinion of agencies or of ad hoc bodies.

F. Local Authorities' Residual Permitting Prerogatives

Local authorities enjoy residual permitting authority concerning environmental protection. Building permits (involving construction that may have an environmental impact) are governed by the Planning Code and are issued by mayors (subject to some exceptions concerning, for example, energy-related facilities, which are issued by national government authorities). Similarly, permits relating to commercial advertising (signage, billboards, etc.) are also a prerogative of mayors, subject to a comprehensive and complex legislative and regulatory framework now codified in the Environmental Code.[16]

II. Air and Climate Change
A. Air Pollution Control
1. Stationary Industrial Activities

Air emissions from stationary activities qualifying as industrial installations warranting an environmental permit (*Installations Classées pour la Protection de l'Environnement*, ICPE) must obtain an operating permit issued to the operator of any such installation. *See infra* Section X. A variety of compounds are regulated (e.g., dust, CO_2, SO_x, NO_x, volatile organic compounds).[17] Specific limit values may also apply to certain activities.[18] Depending on the potential severity of adverse effects and the sensitivity of the surrounding environment, operators of such installations are subject to strict monitoring and reporting requirements.

2. *Mobile Sources*

Air emissions from motor vehicles are governed by the Road Code.[19] Levels enforced in France are taken from EU emission standards, which define the acceptable limits for exhaust emissions of new vehicles sold in EU member states.[20] Currently, emissions of NO_x, total hydrocarbon (THC), nonmethane hydrocarbons (NMHC), carbon monoxide, and particulate matter (PM) are regulated for most vehicle categories except seagoing ships and aircraft.

B.   Climate Change

France implements the Kyoto Protocol to the U.N. Framework Convention on Climate Change (UNFCCC) and EU directive objectives[21] relating to greenhouse gas (GHG) emissions. As a result, certain CO_2 emitting installations and now aircraft operators are accountable for their CO_2 emissions.[22] The system is based on the annual allocation of CO_2 allowances to operators. Each allowance represents one metric ton of CO_2, or of any other GHG included at Annex II of EU Directive 2003/87/EC having the equivalent warming potential. Thus far, allocations have been made yearly based on historical emissions.[23] The system accounts for (1) new entrants (through existence of a reserve), (2) emission increases and decreases, and (3) partial or full site closures.[24] At the beginning of each year (February 15 at the latest), operators of stationary installations are obliged to declare their emissions during the previous year and surrender an equivalent number of allowances (April 30 at the latest).[25] Operators may trade excess allowances. In the case of a failure to surrender the necessary quantity of allowances, the operator must purchase the balance on the market, surrender them, and additionally pay a €100 fine per allowance. Thus far, allowances have been allocated free of charge to operators. A fraction thereof will be auctioned from 2013 to 2020.

III.   Water
A.   General Framework

Water law is complex and combines provisions from the Environmental Code, the Public Health Code (e.g., buffer zones for drinking water, or mineral water quality), and the Local Governments Code. The latter governs, inter alia, the obligations of municipalities with respect to water treatment, distribution, and drainage. Uses of water in industrial activities are essentially governed by the Environmental Code. As a general rule, operators must limit to the extent feasible their uses of water.[26] For certain activities, the quantity of waters used may not exceed certain levels.[27] The operation of open-loop cooling circuits, for example, is also prohibited.[28] The water permit regime mirrors that of registered installations and operates on the basis of a categorization of activities subject to prior declaration or to authorization depending on their magnitude and impact on water resources.[29] All such activities are enumerated in a list (*nomenclature*).[30] Activities subject to authorization entail a more cumbersome permitting procedure involving the completion of an EIA and public inquiry.[31] The competent authority is the Préfet.[32] Due to the sensitivity of water resources, those responsible for accidents likely to affect water resources, operators and landowners are under the duty to report incidents and accidents.[33] Violations of these norms can lead to relatively harsh punishments.[34]

B. Water Extraction

Water extraction is subject to the above regime. Depending on the type of water extraction and source, applicable criteria include yearly volumes that may be extracted, hourly flow rates. These criteria also take into consideration the geographic nature of the relevant watershed basin.[35]

C. Wastewater Treatment

Wastewater treatment is a standard requirement. The segregation of wastewater networks between sanitary, runoff, and process waters is also a standard requirement. The degree of treatment required will depend on the quantity and nature of effluents discharged and on the discharge milieu. Where wastewaters are discharged into the public sewer network, the treatment required will essentially consist of pretreatment to a level that meets certain pollution thresholds acceptable to the local network treatment capabilities. In these circumstances, the operator will have to secure the municipality's approval for its discharges of wastewater or to enter into a contract with the local network and treatment operator where such prerogatives have been transferred by the municipality to a public or private third-party entity.[36] Where the discharge is to the natural milieu, applicable limit values will, by definition, be more stringent and will be set out in the site's operating permit.

D. Water Discharges

Applicable criteria vary in accordance with the activity generating wastewater and the sensitivity of the particular waters to which the discharge takes place. General thresholds apply.[37] Regulations governing some activities carry their own thresholds also.[38] The parameters taken into consideration vary (e.g., temperature, pH, BOD$_5$, COD, TSS, heavy metals, hydrocarbons). Particularly when confronted with water discharge issues, the Préfet may increase the applicable thresholds where the sensitivity of the local environment warrants such an approach.

IV. Handling, Treatment, Transportation, and Disposal of Hazardous Materials

A. Radioactive Substances

The preparation, transformation, manufacturing, packaging, conditioning, and storage of radioactive substances (as sealed sources or not) constitute specific types of ICPE activities.[39] These activities are subject to the ICPE regime due to the radioactive nature of the activity in question. Depending on the radioactivity at issue, a particular, activity will either be regulated under the ICPE or the nuclear installations regime.

B. Asbestos Containing Materials

Subject to very limited exceptions, since 1997 the use, sale, and import of asbestos containing materials (ACMs) has been banned in France.[40] The current regulatory framework addresses ACMs present in buildings and related obligations[41] as well as occupational health and safety in relation to asbestos exposure.[42] When in place prior to the ban, the presence of ACMs in buildings per se is not prohibited. However, building owners are under a duty to survey buildings for the presence of ACMs and carry out either regular surveys, removal, or confinement operations, depending on the state of degradation of the materials. Building owners must compile documents relating to the presence of ACMs (so-called asbestos technical file) and provide it to workers present in the building as well as to potential building purchasers.

C. Chemical Substances and Products

The self-applicable provisions of the European Community regulation concerning the registration, evaluation, authorization, and restriction of chemicals (REACH)[43] are de facto incorporated into the French legal regime governing the control of chemical products.[44] The regime has nevertheless been amended to include REACH-specific sanctions. This regime is essentially twofold. On the one hand, it addresses the control of chemical substances. On the other, the regime addresses the marketing of biocide products such as pesticides. Pursuant to REACH's chemical substances and products regime, manufacturers, importers, and downstream users are as a preliminary matter required to collect data relating to human health or environmental risks that such substances or products may pose.[45] Such data must be forwarded to relevant authorities upon request so that such authorities may regulate such substances and products accordingly.[46]

Second, provisions applicable to biocides apply to active substances and to mixtures containing one or more active substances. Biocides may not be placed in the market or used in the absence of an administrative authorization. The authorization is granted for ten years[47] by the Minister of the Ministry of Ecology, Sustainable Development and Energy (*Ministère de l'Écologie, du Développement durable et de l'Énergie*, MEDDE).[48] Administrative and criminal sanctions complement this very technical scheme.[49] Separately, numerous provisions addressing occupational risks related to chemical substances and products are to be found in the Labor Code.[50]

D. Nanomaterials

The regulation of manufacturing and use of nanomaterials in France remains surprisingly nonintrusive at this juncture. It is reported that nanomaterials are customarily used in over 2,000 products already on the marketplace. Declaration to the government of the manufacture, import, and distribution of nanomaterials, alone or contained in products, is now mandatory on an annual basis.[51] The declaration threshold is 100 grams.[52] The declaration must include details regarding the nature of the material, uses of such materials, and the identities of professional users.[53] Where so indicated by applicable regulations, information provided will be held confidential. If the materials are used in a research and development setting with no marketing of the product, the declarant may limit the information to his identity and the sector of activity concerned.[54]

E. Genetically Modified Organisms

The legal regime governing genetically modified organisms (GMOs) closely regulates the confined use of GMOs and the voluntary dissemination of GMOs whether with the intent to market them or not.[55] The marketing of GMOs requires a preliminary administrative authorization.[56] Where, subsequently, the relevant authority has reason to believe that the use of a GMO entails risk to human health or the environment based on information gathered after the issuance of the authorization, such authority may

- limit or prohibit, temporarily, the use of such GMO on French territory;
- in the case of a severe risk, suspend or permanently prohibit the marketing of such a GMO and inform the public thereof.[57]

V.   Waste and Site Remediation
A.   Definition of Waste, Categorization of Waste, and Governing Principles

Waste is defined as any object, and more generally any movable property, that the holder discards, intends to discard, or has an obligation to discard.[58]

Waste is further categorized according to a certain EU classification system.[59] Regulations set out dangerous waste criteria and classify waste under 20 categories (and multiple subcategories) based on their origin. Waste must be managed in accordance with certain principles (e.g., prevention at the source, sorting, recycling), taking into consideration the right of affected communities to information regarding the impact of the management of waste on the environment and human health.[60] The Environmental Code now provides the long-awaited criteria distinguishing waste from secondary materials[61] and to consider when, upon completion of certain operations, waste no longer qualifies as waste.[62]

B.   Obligations of Waste Producers and Waste Holders

Waste producers and waste holders are liable for the disposal of waste according to the waste management principles set out in the Environmental Code.[63] Such disposal may be carried out by such persons or entrusted to third parties to whom liability for disposal is then transferred. In both cases, waste disposal must be carried in duly permitted installations. In all cases, the traceability of waste must be secured through the filling out of waste consignment notes. Although waste may be contractually transferred to a third party, such transfer does not exonerate the original producer or holder from liability should the waste not be adequately disposed of or abandoned. Where waste has been abandoned or illegally treated, the relevant administrative authority may request the original producer or holder to take responsibility for such waste and appropriately dispose of it.[64]

C.   "Extended" Producer Liability in Relation to Waste

Due to the quantities of waste that certain products generate, the producers of certain categories of products are now required to set up and finance collective or individual waste recovery schemes.[65] This is commonly referred to as the "extended producer liability" regime. This applies, for example, to spent lubricants, packaging, batteries and accumulators, waste tires, end-of-life vehicles, electric and electronic equipment, print publications, textile products, and shoes.[66] For certain products, the regime also imposes certain mandatory materials recycling targets and includes so-called "eco-conception" obligations.

D.   Regulation of Waste Storage or Waste Recycling Facilities

Waste storage and waste treatment facilities, including all operations, from sorting and transit to recycling and disposal, qualify as ICPE installations.[67] As such, these installations must be permitted. Waste storage installations in particular require the posting of a financial bond (*garanties financières*) by the operator, which must cover site monitoring operations, emergency intervention in case of an accident, and postclosure remediation.[68] This regime carries a significant range of potential criminal sanctions.[69]

E. Soil and Groundwater Remediation Issues

1. Remediation Obligations

Soil and groundwater remediation obligations are essentially dealt with in the framework of the ICPE regime. Remediation obligations can accrue at any time during the operation of a site where contamination likely to affect interests protected under the Environmental Code has occurred.[70] Remediation is, furthermore, an obligation at the time of the closure of an activity or of a site.[71] Remediation does not consist of restoring the site to its original condition. Rather, it is limited to the prevention of hazards and must take into consideration the future intended use of the site. Part of the calculus are the applicable requirements of enforceable zoning documents, and the use of land in the vicinity of the site. Remediation entails for the operator the following duties: (1) ensuring the safety of the site (by removal of waste and hazardous materials, prevention of fire and explosions, etc.); (2) carrying out soil and groundwater assessments and undertaking subsurface measures (ventilation, water extraction and treatment, excavation, on-site or off-site soil treatment, etc.) where necessary;[72] and (3) ensuring postremediation monitoring.

French law does not establish mandatory remediation levels. Remediation values eventually enforced against operators are risk-based and site specific. Scientific and health and safety literature is relied upon in setting out the applicable levels for a particular site and situation.

2. Allocation of Liabilities over Time and Applicable Law

Controlling case law provides that operators remain liable to remediate a given site for as long as waste and residue generated by their activities remains likely to impact the environment.[73] Where a number of operators have been involved at a site over time, remediation obligations attach to the last operator of the activities being terminated or of the activities under way at the time remediation was ordered.[74] Remediation is required for contamination traceable to an operator's activity or to activity continued from a predecessor operator.[75] The law applicable is that in force at the time remediation is identified and ordered. It does not matter that the provisions relied upon were not in force at the time the contamination actually occurred.[76] Where a 30-year period has lapsed from the time administrative authorities were aware of or notified of a site closure or the termination of an activity, relevant authorities will be precluded from enforcing remediation prerogatives against the last operator of such activities.[77]

3. Limitations to the Contractual Management of Liabilities

Although the financial burden of remediation may be contracted away in the context of an asset or share deal, the operator may not shift his liability vis-à-vis relevant authorities to a third party unless such third party files a declaration or applies for an authorization to be substituted for the current operator as the new title operator of the site. The sale of the land does not shift the liability for remediation to the land purchaser. The liability for remediation attaches to the last operator.

4. Risks of Landowner Liability

Except in particular circumstances, the risks of a landowner assuming liability are limited. Controlling case law indicates that pursuant to the ICPE regime, remediation may not be enforced by competent authorities against landowners in their sole landowner capacity.[78] Pursuant to waste law, contaminated, nonexcavated soils no longer qualify as waste, thereby preventing mayors from enforcing waste removal obligations against landowners.[79]

Finally, a new polluted soil remediation regime aims at filling the gaps where no solvent or otherwise attainable operator is reachable under the ICPE regime, or where no landowner can legally be forced to remediate soil contamination.[80] It is too early to determine, however, precisely how this regime will be enforced.

VI.   Emergency Response
A.   Operational Measures

The activities referred to above require responsible parties to prepare emergency response procedures and report all accidents. Most notable are provisions governing so-called internal operations plans (*plans d'opérations internes*, POI) and specific intervention plans (*plans particuliers d'intervention*, PPI), which apply essentially to sites designated under an EU directive known as the Seveso Directive.[81] POIs are mandatory for Seveso installations and may be imposed by the Préfet to installations subject to authorization.[82] The plans define organizational measures, intervention methods, and means to be implemented by the operator to protect employees, populations, and the environment in case of accident or incident. These are defined with local fire safety services (*service départemental d'incendie et de secours*, SDIS) and must be tested and updated at least every three years.

For their part, PPIs are established on the basis of accident scenarios identified in risk assessments pertaining to Seveso sites, such as underground gas or chemicals storage installations.[83] These plans are intended to supplement POIs where the consequences of an accident are likely to result in off-site impacts. These must also be tested jointly with safety and emergency services and updated at least every three years.

B.   Urban Planning Measures

In order to delineate technological hazards and to implement necessary prevention measures, the national government further establishes technological hazards prevention plans (*plans de prévention des risques technologiques*, PPRT) in areas where Seveso installations are located. These plans identify risk exposure radiuses and take into account the intensity of technological risks identified in risk assessments.[84] Within identified radiuses, such plans allow the restriction of land use activities to institute relinquishment or expropriation rights and to impose any relevant risk prevention measures.[85]

VII.   Natural Resource Management and Protection
A.   Quarries

Quarries are a specific category of ICPE installation, and are further governed by several ad hoc principles.[86] Quarries are permitted for fewer than 30 years (or 15 years where prior land clearing is necessary).[87] Renewal for equivalent periods is possible. In addition to the duration of the exploitation, the quarry permit sets out the maximum tonnage extracted, as well as remediation conditions.[88] Remediation issues are key to the operation of quarries. Failure by an operator to comply with such remediation provisions may subsequently preclude the issuance of new quarry permit to that operator.[89] Quarry operators must post a financial bond to account for hazards related to such activities. The amount of the bond is based on the magnitude of the associated hazards, and must cover the cost of postclosure remediation (i.e., monitoring of waste storage installations, emergency intervention, and measures to be implemented in case of an accident).[90]

B.   Mines

Minerals and substances listed in the Mining Code and qualifying as "mining substances" are governed by the Mining Code.[91] By operation of the law, mining substances are not the property of landowners but rather the government's. The exploration and exploitation of such substances requires permits issued by the national government. Moreover, permits issued pursuant to the Mining Code are not enforceable in the absence of a valid statement of consent by the relevant surface landowners.[92] Such statements can include research permits,[93] exploitation permits, and concessions for the mining of substances or the underground storage of gas.[94] In addition to these permits, prior to commencing any mining operation, a project proponent must obtain certain administrative authorizations[95] and post a financial bond for the operation of mining waste storage installations.[96]

As a general rule, mining operators must comply with environmental protection principles and preserve protected environmental interests.[97] Failure on the part of the operator to comply with mining law obligations or with mining permit prescriptions may result in the suspension, withdrawal, or curtailment of the scope of a permit, as well as criminal prosecution.[98] In its current version, the Mining Code results from a recent codification of series of provisions adopted since 1956 for the most part. The current debate on the exploration and exploitation of shale gas in France is likely to bring about significant changes to this code in a near future.

C. Forestry

With 16.3 million hectares—approximately 40 million acres—and 10 percent of Europe's forest cover, the protection and management of forests is governed by the Forestry Code.[99] The Forestry Code promotes the sustainable management of wooded areas and aims to ensure the satisfaction of wooden resource needs.[100] To achieve these objectives, the code provides for forest fire prevention measures[101] as well as for the protection of certain species and landscapes.[102] Tree felling[103] and clearing[104] are fairly strictly regulated under the Forestry Code. Recent provisions establish the possibility of an eco-certification to be awarded to sustainably managed forests.[105] A decree is yet to be adopted and should lay out the conditions on the basis of which products manufactured out of wood originating from such forests shall also benefit from such eco-certification.

VIII.   Natural Resource Damages
A.   Transposition of Directive 2004/35/EC

The Law of August 1, 2008, transposed into domestic law Directive 2004/35/EC of April 21, 2004, on environmental liability with regard to the prevention and remedying of environmental damage.[106] The law places on operators the duty to prevent and remedy damages to the environment even where the operator did not act negligently and was not at fault.[107] In case of an imminent risk of damage, the operator must take all necessary precautions to prevent the damage or limit its effects. Where the threat persists, or where the damage has occurred, competent administrative authorities must be informed without delay while the operator takes all necessary measures at its sole expense.

Where damage has occurred, the authorities evaluate its nature and consequences and may require the operator to undertake its own evaluation. Remediation measures aim to restore natural resources and their associated ecological services and eliminate any severe risk to human health.[108] Where several operators are involved, administrative authorities allocate costs among them.[109]

B.   Recent Judicial and Legislative Developments

Recent case law recognizes (albeit in an ambiguous manner) the notion of "pure ecological prejudice," thus opening the path to the indemnification of ecological prejudice even in the absence of harm to one's image, reputation, or economic interests.[110]

On May 16, 2013, the French Senate unanimously adopted a draft modification of the civil code. The draft would establish that "any person causing damage to the environment shall be under the duty to remedy such damage"[111] and "the remediation of environmental damage shall be preferably carried out in nature. Where remediation in nature shall not be possible, remediation shall take the form of financial compensation paid to the national government or to any organization designated by the national government and shall be allocated, as provided for by decree, to the protection of the environment."[112] This proposal, however, has not yet been adopted by the National Assembly on these terms and therefore has not yet become law.

IX. Protected Species

Multiple provisions provide for the protection of wildlife. Most of these provisions are now codified in the Environmental Code.

A. Habitats and Birds

The EU Birds Directive[113] and Habitats Directives[114] have been transposed into French law, which now secures the legal existence of the network of EU protected areas known as Natura 2000 sites.[115] Two categories of sites have been defined:

- marine or terrestrial special conservation zones (*zones spéciales de conservation*), which include threatened natural habitats or habitats harboring rare fauna or flora, species that are vulnerable or threatened with extinction, or species that are worthy of special consideration due to the specificity of their habitat or the impact of their exploitation on their conservation status;[116]
- marine or terrestrial special protection zones (*zones de protection spéciale*), which include either sites specifically relevant to the survival or reproduction of wild birds with a special focus on sites serving as reproduction, molting, or hibernation areas for migratory birds.[117]

The administrative designation of such zones takes into consideration local and regional economic, social, and cultural requirements.

A Natura 2000 impact assessment (*évaluation des incidences*) must be carried out prior to any project likely to bring about any impact on such zones.[118] Where a likely impact is ascertained, projects can only be approved if (1) it is shown that the project is squarely in the public interest and (2) proposed compensatory measures are implemented to uphold the overall coherence of the Natura 2000 network.[119]

B. Hunting and Freshwater Fishing

Hunting and freshwater fishing regulations are also part of France's wildlife protection regime. Hunting practices must allow for the renewal of species,[120] a requirement that translates into strict regulation of hunting seasons and methods.[121] Limited quantities of specimens may seasonally be hunted.[122] Freshwater fishing is equally regulated for the preservation of fishery resources. Specific habitat and watercourse maintenance requirements apply to beneficiaries of fishing rights.[123] Approved fishermen associations (*associations agréées de pêche et de protection du milieu aquatique*) enjoy extended monitoring prerogatives.[124] Severe criminal sanctions complement the fishing regime regarding spills of any substance destroying or impairing the resource or destroying its reproductive or feeding habitats.[125]

X.   Environmental Review and Decision Making

A.   Permitting of Industrial and Commercial Activities Likely to Impact the Environment

1.   Installations Registered for the Purpose of Environmental Protection

Most industrial and commercial activities are governed by the ICPE regime.[126] The ICPE regime categorizes activities based on their nuisance potential either in the ordinary course of their operation, or due to the likelihood of an incident or accident.[127] These are enumerated in a list.[128] The ICPE regime sets out a three-tier system. Activities are subject to either a declaration, registration, or authorization procedure based on their potentially adverse environmental effects.[129] The more potentially adverse, the more likely an activity is to be subject to authorization. These three regimes may alternatively apply to the same type of activity. Such activity will in that case be subject to the regime corresponding to its magnitude (computed in terms of storage capacity, electrical output, tonnage of materials treated, etc.). This categorization now combines with that derived from Directive 2010/75/EC of November 24, 2010, on industrial emissions, which for certain existing installations may carry significant operating permit reviews and updates in order to ensure these apply the best available techniques.[130] In practice, an ICPE site generally consists of an aggregation of activities, the site as a whole being subject to the most demanding applicable regime. The regime is inclusive insofar as permits issued thereunder regulate all environmentally relevant aspects of the operation of a given site (air emissions, waste, water consumption and discharges, noise, vibrations, etc.). Decrees and ministerial orders govern all such aspects and serve as a basis for individual prescriptions. On a case-by-case basis, Préfets may strengthen applicable regulatory provisions, provided the sensitivity of the natural and/or human environment warrants it. The Préfet may not, however, weaken such provisions.

ICPE permits (for activities subject to authorization) require in-depth site-adapted EIAs, the legal regime for which was recently amended to conform to EU requirements. ICPE permits also take into consideration the technical and financial capabilities of operators.[131] Furthermore, ICPE permits contain no built-in expiration date except for activities entailing certain uses of the soil (e.g., landfills, quarries) or for temporary activities. Permits become void if not implemented within three years of their issuance or where the activity remains idle for more than two consecutive years.[132] In the course of the operation of their sites, operators must comply with new regulations as they become enforceable with deferred enforcement dates applying to existing installations.[133] For certain categories of installations, operators are also required to post a financial bond computed on the basis of an appraisal of accident or incident remediation and emergency measures costs.[134] Activities concerned include Seveso (ultrahazardous) sites, waste storage sites, quarries, wind farms, and a selection of other threshold-based hazardous activities.[135] Such financial bonds must ensure the availability of funds to the government should the operator be insolvent at the time a damaging event requiring rapid action occurs. Such financial bonds are never intended to cover harm to third parties. Operators are required to notify incidents and accidents.[136] Operators are also required to notify environmental authorities of the permanent termination of activities (complete or partial site closure).[137]

2. Geological CO_2 Storage Installations

Works carried out for the identification of geological formations fit for CO_2 capture and storage are governed by the Mining Code and require the issuance of an exclusive research permit.[138]

Where undertaken for climate change abatement purposes, the operation of such sites is governed by the Environmental Code and requires a permit issued pursuant to the ICPE procedure, subject to some adaptations.[139] The operator must further put in place financial guarantees governing not only the monitoring and preservation of the safety of the site in case of an accident, but also the restitution of CO_2 allowances in case of leakage.[140]

Where an entity wishes to store CO_2 for industrial purposes, such CO_2 storage sites are additionally governed by the Mining Code.[141] In this case, the examination of the permit application is subject to the applicant being the beneficiary or having applied for a geological CO_2 storage concession, per the Mining Code.[142] In each of the above cases, the operation of such CO_2 storages sites must as a general rule comply with the environmental protection provisions of both the Environmental and Mining Codes.[143]

3. Nuclear Facilities

Nuclear facilities (*Installations nucléaires de base*, INB) encompass a wide variety of activities including operation of nuclear reactors and particle accelerators, and nuclear fuel preparation, enrichment, manufacturing, and operation of fuel storage facilities.[144] Equipment and installations necessary to the operation of such facilities are also regulated by the INB regulatory regime. Nuclear installations are overseen and inspected by the Nuclear Safety Authority (*Autorité de sûreté nucleaire*, ASN).[145] The ASN also acts as an advisory body to the national government in matters of nuclear safety and has regulatory power to issue technical regulations designed to complement decrees and ministerial orders related to nuclear matters.[146] Permits for the operation of nuclear installations are issued by the minister in charge of nuclear installations (in general, the Minister of Industry) with a prior public inquiry and an advisory opinion of the ASN.[147] Nuclear permits are issued with due consideration of the petitioner/operator's technical and financial capabilities to safely operate the installations and bear the costs of dismantling the installations and remediating any damages caused.[148] Changes in the operator, modifications of the perimeter of the installations, and significant modifications of the installations require the issuance of a new permit. Moreover, significant modifications require a new public inquiry.[149] Failure on the part of the operator to comply with applicable provisions may result in nuclear permits being suspended.[150] Considering the risks presented by such activities, the regime governing nuclear installations also includes criminal sanctions[151] and liability.[152] Finally, nuclear installation operators are specifically required to establish plans for projected site closure, future site dismantling, and maintenance and monitoring costs, as well as costs related to managing spent nuclear fuel and radioactive waste.[153]

B.   Interactions between Environmental Permits and Other Permitting Regimes

1.   General Provisions Governing the Protection of the Environment

Permits issued for activities likely to affect the environment are subordinate to statutory or regulatory provisions governing the protection of the environment.[154] As a consequence, the obligations and prohibitions deriving from general provisions enacted for environmental protection will be taken into consideration in the examination of applications for permits and, eventually, in the permits themselves. Permits ordinarily reiterate generally applicable principles, refer to such principles by incorporation, and contain site-specific or activity-specific provisions. Authorities will decline to issue a permit, however, where no provisions are likely to effectively prevent environmental hazards.[155]

2.   ICPE Permits and Building Permits

The applicant for an ICPE permit must establish proof of his having also applied for a building permit where his project involves construction requiring a building permit.[156] Where a building permit has been applied for, it may be issued but construction may not begin before the public inquiry administered for permitting of the industrial operations is complete, or before the issuance of the registration of the activity.[157] Except in specific circumstances and for specific constructions, building permits are ordinarily granted by mayors and not by Préfet, thereby making the above articulation between procedures all the more necessary.

3.   ICPE Permits and Water Permits

ICPE permits and water permits (i.e., permits governing activities impacting water resources such as water abstraction wells and discharges into surface water courses[158]) may be issued separately. However, prescriptions applicable to ICPE installations must factor in the requirements of water resources protection provisions.[159] In practical terms, also, where relating to the same project, the applications for both the ICPE and water permits are submitted to the same public inquiry. This is so that the public may have a comprehensive picture of the consequences and impact of the project on the environment as a whole. Consequently, the Préfet issues the ICPE permit and water permit jointly in the same instrument.

4. ICPE Permits and Clearing Permits

Forest clearing (*défrichement*) may be necessary to establish an industrial site, quarry, or mine. Clearing permits are governed by the Forest Code.[160] As a general principle, where a project subject to an administrative authorization also requires a clearing permit, the clearing permit must be issued prior to that authorization, except for projects subject to the ICPE regime (ICPE installations, quarries, geological CO_2 storage sites) where no such precedence is required.[161]

XI. Transboundary Pollution

As a signatory of the February 25, 1991, Espoo Convention on Environmental Impact Assessment in a Transboundary Context, France addresses transboundary pollution in a preventive way. Indeed, this convention sets out the obligations of parties to assess the environmental impact of certain activities at the early stage of planning. In particular, it lays down the general obligation for states to notify and consult each other on all major projects under consideration that are likely to have a significant adverse environmental impact that transcends boundaries. As a consequence, the Environmental Code requires the French government to submit to adjacent member states or Espoo Convention parties (automatically, as well as at such states' request) the documentation (including EIAs) relating to projects the implementation of which is likely to affect such member states.[162] The same is true for draft plans and of documents the implementation of which are likely to have transboundary effects.[163] To make the above practicable for such states, the Environmental Code further provides that of the public inquiry must be communicated to them while the nontechnical summary of the projects' EIAs must be translated in that state's language.[164] Upon completion of the procedure, the administrative decision taken is forwarded to that state's governmental authorities.

Other international instruments may come into play concerning prevention. The Basel Convention of March 22, 1989, on the control of transboundary movements of hazardous wastes and their disposal institutes as a matter of principle the control of transboundary movements to prevent pollution.[165] Finally, as a consequence of Directive 2004/35/EC of April 21, 2004, on environmental liability, the Environmental Code provides for mandatory notification of environmental damage or likelihood of the same affecting neighboring EU member states to secure joint remediation undertakings where necessary.[166]

As far as remedies for transboundary pollution damage are concerned, Regulation (EC) 864/2007 of July 11, 2007, on the law applicable to noncontractual obligations (Rome II) essentially governs the matter. In environmental matters, this regulation affords to plaintiffs the choice of opting either for the law of the country in which the damage occurs (Article 4.1) or the possibility of seeking compensation on the basis of the law of the country in which the event giving rise to the damage occurred (Article 7).

XII.   Civil and Criminal Enforcement and Penalties

A.   Judicial Review of Permits by Administrative Courts

Because environmental permits involve administrative decisions, an operator or third party can challenge them before administrative courts, which unlike in the United States form part of the judiciary in France.[167] Operators are afforded two months to challenge permit decisions from the date of notification.[168] Third parties (e.g., environmental protection associations, local governments, private individuals) are afforded one year from the date of publication of the decision.[169]

As a general rule, a judicial review action does not automatically stay the execution of the decision challenged, except in limited circumstances.[170] Rather, the decision remains enforceable and binding pending the court's decision. Administrative courts in France enjoy wide-ranging powers and can either annul the decision (in which case it is presumed to have never existed and forces the operator to apply anew) or amend it (in which case court-reformed provisions are substituted for the offending provisions and become enforceable either immediately or within the time frame established by the court).

B.   Civil Liability

Permits are always issued subject to third parties' rights.[171] This means that regardless of the operator's compliance with the terms of his permit, third parties may file a challenge seeking indemnification for harm caused by the operator's activity undertaken under the permit. Plaintiffs may base their challenge on a tort, negligence, or "exceptional" nuisance (private nuisance) theory.

If a plaintiff proceeds on the basis of a tort theory, he must demonstrate (1) the existence of a tort on the part of the operator, (2) actual and personal prejudice, and (3) causation.[172] Noncompliance by the operator with a permit will be used as evidence of the existence of a wrongful act. Noncompliance by an operator with an administrative circular applicable to her activity is also deemed to evidence a wrongful act on the part of the operator.[173] Courts further recognize and indemnify a variety of prejudices (physical, moral, loss of enjoyment, loss of property value, etc.). Prejudice must further be certain and determinable. Where uncertain, a prejudice will in certain circumstances be compensable where the plaintiff is prejudiced by the loss of the probability of occurrence of a favorable event where such probability appears significant. In France, indemnification does not include treble or punitive damages. The burden of proof is borne by the plaintiff.

Negligence-based actions can also be problematic for operators. The civil code affords plaintiffs the possibility of seeking indemnification in the absence of a tort or private nuisance.[174] Operators have been found to have acted negligently in matters involving noise or air emissions generated by installations under their custody. In such cases, causation is demonstrated where "things," for example, vibrations, wastewater, or atmospheric pollutants, have caused damage to another.

Finally, plaintiffs may, in the absence of a tortious act or act of negligence, seek indemnification on a private nuisance basis (*trouble anormal de voisinage*). The legal basis for this ground resides in civil code provisions relating to the enjoyment of one's property.[175] Actions may be instituted on this basis where an activity results in "exceptional" nuisances that the plaintiff should not in fairness have to bear. Case law on point therefore only compensates "exceptional" nuisances and that part of the prejudice traceable to such a nuisance. In this context, nonexceptional nuisances are not compensable because the purpose of environmental protection provisions is not to prevent the occurrence of all nuisances or to reach a "zero nuisance" level, but rather to achieve a balance between the protection of the environment and an acceptable degree of unavoidable nuisances. Moreover, defenses to exceptional nuisance actions nevertheless exist. For example, an action to abate an exceptional nuisance is barred to a plaintiff that came to a nuisance.[176]

C. Environmental Protection Associations' Prerogatives

Environmental protection associations are frequent stakeholders in indemnification actions or judicial review proceedings. Standing for an environmental organization in a compensation action is typically demonstrated if the organization can demonstrate harm to the environmental interests that it seeks to preserve according to its bylaws. It is also common for environmental associations to seek indemnification and join in criminal proceedings instituted in matters involving violations of environmental laws where they claim the alleged criminal act prejudiced them.[177]

Furthermore, the Environmental Code establishes a standing presumption to government-approved environmental protection associations (*associations agréées*) to seek judicial review of decisions directly affecting their interests (provided also their approval predates the date of the challenged decision).[178] For other environmental protection associations, administrative courts tend to be more restrictive when considering standing questions (in particular with respect to associations with nationwide, broadly defined interests challenging decisions with a merely local impact).

D.   Administrative Sanctions

All of the permitting regimes discussed herein permit the government, in the case of a violation by a permit holder (whether general or permit-specific), to impose administrative sanctions. Noncompliance must be officially recorded by way of detailed, authenticated account (*procès-verbal*) and by designated law enforcement officers and inspectors. Sanctions are preceded by administrative injunctions (*mises en demeure*) affording operators time to comply with applicable regulations. For minor instances of noncompliance, competent inspection authorities often warn operators, urging them to comply before issuing an injunction. Where an injunction is not complied with, competent authorities may resort to administrative sanctions. Environmental law essentially replicates the same pattern of sanctions, which include

- the mandatory deposit with the Public Treasury of an amount corresponding to the cost of the measures to be carried out by the noncompliant operator (such amount will be returned once required measures are taken);[179]
- the execution of the necessary works by the authorities at the operator's expense;[180]
- the suspension of the permit;[181]
- a fine of up to €15,000 and a daily penalty of up to €1,500 commencing on the decision notification date.[182]

For products, where the responsible entity fails to comply with an injunction,[183] sanctions imposed may include, inter alia: the payment of a fine and of daily fixed-penalties,[184] restrictions to the import, manufacture, or marketing of products,[185] the mandatory return of imported products,[186] or the elimination of such products as waste.[187]

E.   Criminal Enforcement

Violations of applicable environmental protection provisions carry criminal prosecution and sentences. Such violations qualify either as petty offenses (*contraventions*) or as misdemeanors (*délits*). The court charged with adjudicating petty offenses is the police tribunal (*tribunal de police*). Sanctions are essentially limited to what are known as third-, fourth-, and fifth-class fines (*peines d'amende prévues pour les contraventions des 3ème, 4ème, et 5ème classes*).[188]

The court charged with adjudicating misdemeanors is known in French as the *tribunal correctionnel*. The *tribunal correctionnel*'s procedures do not afford parties the right to trial by jury. Sentences include imprisonment and/or fines. Violations of water laws or of ICPE laws, for example, entail imprisonment sentences ranging from six months to two years and fines ranging from €12,000 to €300,000 (for individuals). Legal entities may also be prosecuted.[189] Where found guilty, fine amounts faced by legal entities may be increased fivefold[190] and other sanctions be substituted for prison sentences (e.g., prohibition to bid on public contracts, forced site closure, etc.).[191] Where necessary, criminal courts can also order remediation in addition to the relief discussed above.[192]

Notes

1. *See* Constitutional Law n° 2005-205 of March 1, 2005, Charter of the Environment art. 1.

2. Environmental Code (*Code de l'environnement*) art. L. 110-1 II 1° to 5° as amended by Law n° 2012-1460 of December 27, 2012.

3. *Id.* art. L. 110-1 IV.

4. Treaty on European Union arts. 3.3, 2.2 d, and 2.2 f; *see also* Treaty on the Functioning of the European Union arts. 4, 11, and 190 to 193.

5. The Environmental Code includes a statutory section (*Partie législative*) and a regulatory section (*Partie réglementaire*). Statutory provisions are referred to as L. and regulatory provisions as R. or D.

6. Such regulations are enacted in the form of Decrees (*décrets*) or of Ministerial Orders (*arrêtés ministériels*).

7. French Constitution art. 38.

8. *See, e.g.,* Ordinance (*Ordonnance*) n° 2012-827 of June 28, 2012, on the EU GHG allowance trading scheme for the 2013–2020 period.

9. Metropolitan France is subdivided in 22 régions and 96 départements.

10. Environmental Code arts. L. 517-1, L. 517-2 and R. 517-1 *et seq.*

11. *Id.* art. R. 555-4.

12. *Id.* arts. L. 123-1 to L. 123-19 and arts. R. 123-1 to R. 123-46.

13. *Id.* arts. L. 122-1 to L. 122-12 and arts. R. 122-1 to R. 122-24.

14. *Id.* art. L. 122-2.

15. Ministère de l'Écologie, du Développement durable et de l'Énergie.

16. Environmental Code arts. L. 581-1 to L. 581-45 and arts. R. 581-1 to R. 581-88 (formerly law n° 79-1150 of December 29, 1979, and Decree n° 80-923 of November 21, 1980, as amended).

17. *See, e.g.,* Ministerial Order of February 2, 1998, on the emissions and effluents of ICPE installations subject to authorization as amended arts. 26 to 29.

18. *Id.* art. 30.

19. Road Code (*Code de la route*) arts. L. 311-1, L. 318-1 to L. 318-3 and arts. R. 318-1 to R. 318-10; *see also* Environmental Code arts. L. 224-4 and L. 224-5.

20. Directive 2007/715/EC of the European Parliament and of the Council of 20 June 2007 on type approval of motor vehicles with respect to emissions from light passenger and commercial vehicles (Euro 5 and Euro 6) and on access to vehicle repair and maintenance information.

21. Directive 2003/87/EC of the European Parliament and of the Council of 13 October 2003 establishing a scheme for greenhouse gas emission allowance trading within the Community and amending Council Directive 96/61/EC as notably amended by Directive 2008/101/EC of the European Parliament and of the Council of 19 November 2008.

22. Environmental Code arts. L. 229-5 to L. 229-19; *see id.* art. R. 229-5 III for the list of activities concerned. The extension of the scheme to aircraft operators is currently on hold.

23. *Id.* art. R. 229-7.

24. *Id.* arts. R. 229-9 to R. 229-16.

25. *Id.* arts. R. 229-20 and R. 229-21; *see also id.* R. 229-37-7 and R. 229-37-8 (for aircraft operators).

26. *Id.* arts. L. 211-1 *et seq.; see also, e.g.,* Ministerial Order of February 2, 1998, as amended art. 14.

27. Ministerial Order of June 30, 2006, governing surface treatment activities subject to item n° 2565 of the ICPE categorization of activities, art. 21, imposing a limit of 8 m³/sq. meter of material treated.

28. Ministerial Order of February 2, 1998, as amended, art. 14.

29. Environmental Code arts. L. 214-1 *et seq.* and arts. R. 214-1 *et seq.*

30. *Id.* art. L. 214-2.

31. *Id.* art. L. 214-4.

32. *Id.* art. R. 214-12.

33. *Id.* art. L. 211-5.

34. *Id.* arts. L. 216-3 to L. 216-13.

35. *Id.* art. R. 214-1, *Nomenclature,* tit. I, items 1.1.1.0 to 1.3.1.0.

36. Public Health Code (*Code de la santé publique*) art. L. 1331-10.

37. Ministerial Order of February 2, 1998, as amended, arts. 31 and 32.

38. *Id.* art. 33; *see also* other ministerial orders governing specific activities.

39. *See Nomenclature ICPE,* Environmental Code art. R.511-9, 17xx categories.

40. *See* Decree n° 96-1133 of December 24, 1996, relating to the prohibition of asbestos. *See also, e.g.,* WTO case No. 135, ruling adopted on April 5, 2001 (Canada's challenge to France import ban on asbestos and asbestos-containing products was rejected reinforcing the view that the WTO Agreements support members' ability to protect human health and safety at the level of protection they deem appropriate).

41. *See* Public Health Code arts. L. 1334-12-1 to L. 1334-17 and arts. R. 1334-14 to R. 1334-29-7.

42. Labor Code arts. 4412-94 to R. 4412-148.

43. Regulation (EC) No 1907/2006 of the European Parliament and of the Council of 18 December 2006 concerning the Registration, Evaluation, Authorization, and Restriction of Chemicals (REACH), establishing a European Chemicals Agency, amending Directive 1999/45/EC and repealing Council Regulation (EEC) No 793/93 and Commission Regulation (EC) No 1488/94 as well as Council Directive 76/769/EEC and Commission Directives 91/155/EEC, 93/67/EEC, 93/105/EC, and 2000/21/EC.

44. Environmental Code arts. L. 521-1 to L. 521-24 (on chemical substances) and arts. R. 521-1 to R. 521-68; *see also id.* arts. L. 522-1 to L. 522-19 and arts. R. 522-1 to R. 522-47(on biocides); *see also id.* arts. R. 523-1 to R. 523-11 (provisions applicable to both chemicals substances and products and to biocides).

45. *Id.* art. L. 521-5.

46. *Id.* art. L. 521-6.

47. *Id.* arts. L. 522-4 and L. 522-5.

48. *Id.* art. R. 522-14.

49. *Id.* arts. L. 521-17 to L. 521-24 and arts. R. 521-2-14 to R. 521-2-; *see also id.* arts. L. 522-15 to L. 522-16.

50. Labor Code arts. L. 4411-1 to L. 4412-1 and arts. R. 4411-1 to R. 4412-160.

51. *Id.* art. L. 523-1.

52. *Id.* arts. R. 523-12 *et seq.*

53. Ministerial Order of August 6, 2012, relating to the contents and lay-out of the yearly nano-materials declaration, Annex.

54. Environmental Code art. R. 523-14.

55. *Id.* arts. L. 531-1 to L. 533-9 and arts. R. 532-1 to R. 536-11.

56. *Id.* art. L. 533-5.

57. *Id.* art. L. 533-8.

58. *Id.* art. L. 541-1-1.

59. *Id.* arts. R. 541-7 and R. 541-8—Annexes I and II.

60. *Id.* arts. L. 125-1 and L. 541-1.

61. *Id.* art. L. 514-4-2.

62. *Id.* art. L. 514-4-3 and arts. D. 541-12-4 to D. 541-12-15.

63. *Id.* art. L. 541-2-1.

64. *Id.* art. L. 541-3.

65. *Id.* arts. L. 541-9 to L. 541-10-8.

66. *Id.* arts. R. 543-3 to R. 543-270.

67. *Nomenclature ICPE,* Environmental Code art. R.; 511-9, 27xx categories.

68. Environmental Code art. R. 516-2 IV 1°.

69. *Id.* arts. L. 541-44 to L. 541-48 and arts. R. 541-76 to R. 541-85.

70. *Id.* art. L. 512-20.

71. *Id.* art. L. 512-6-1 (for sites subject to authorization), art. L. 512-7-6 (for sites subject to registration), and art. L. 512-12-1 (for sites subject to declaration).

72. *Id.* arts. R. 512-39-1 to R. 512-39-6 (for sites subject to authorization), arts. R. 512 -46-25 to R. 512-46-29 (for sites subject to registration), and arts. R. 512-66-1 to R. 512-66-2 (for sites subject to declaration).

73. Conseil d'Etat, Mar. 24, 1978, *société La Quinoléine et ses dérivés,* n° 01291.

74. Conseil d'Etat, Mar. 20, 1991, *SARL Rodanet,* n°83776.

75. Conseil d'Etat, Apr. 11, 1986, *société Pechiney Ugine-Kuhlman,* n° 62234.

76. Conseil d'Etat, Jan. 10, 2005, *société Sofiservice,* n° 252307.

77. Conseil d'Etat, July 1, 2005, *société Alusuisse-Lonza-France,* n° 247976.

78. Conseil d'Etat, Feb. 21, 1997, *SCI Les Peupliers,* n° 160250.

79. Environmental Code art. L. 541-4-1.

80. *Id.* art. L. 556-1.

81. *Id.* art. L. 515-8. The EU website, http://ec.europa.eu/environment/seveso/ (last visited Sept. 3, 2013), explains that "In Europe, the Seveso accident in 1976 prompted the adoption of legislation aimed at the prevention and control of such accidents. The resulting [EU] 'Seveso' directive now applies to around 10,000 industrial establishments where dangerous substances are used or stored in large quantities, mainly in the chemicals, petrochemicals, storage, and metal refining sectors. The Seveso Directive obliges EU Member States to ensure that operators have a policy in place to prevent major accidents. Operators handling dangerous substances above certain thresholds must regularly inform the public likely to be affected by an accident, providing safety reports, a safety management system, and an internal emergency plan. Member States must ensure that emergency plans are in place for the surrounding areas and that mitigation actions are planned. There is a tiered approach to the level of controls: the larger the quantities of dangerous substances present within an establishment, the stricter the rules ('upper-tier' establishments have bigger quantities than 'lower-tier' establishments and are therefore subject to tighter control)."

82. Environmental Code art. R. 512-29; *see also* Administrative circular letter of January 12, 2011 (BOME n° 11/2011).

83. Law n° 2004-811 of August 13, 2004, on the modernization of civil safety (art. 15) now codified in the Domestic Safety Code (*Code de la sécurité intérieure*), art. L. 741-6; *see also* Decree n° 2005-1158 of September 13, 2005.

84. Environmental Code arts. L. 515-15 *et seq.* and arts. R. 515-39 to R. 515-50.

85. *Id.* art. L. 515-16; *see also* Administrative circular letter of May 10, 2010 (BOME n° 12/2010).

86. Environmental Code arts. L. 515-1 to L. 515-6; *see also* Mining Code arts. L. 100-2 and L. 311-1 to 311-3.

87. Environmental Code art. L. 515-1.

88. *Id.* art. R. 512-35.

89. *Id.* art. L. 515-4.

90. *Id.* art. R. 516-2 IV 2°; *see also* Ministerial order of February 9, 2004, relating to the amount of financial bond required for the remediation of quarries.

91. Mining Code art. L. 111-1.

92. *Id.* art. L. 153-1 *et seq.*

93. *Id.* arts. L. 121-1 to 126-2; *see also* Decrees n° 2006-648 and 2006-649 of June 2, 2006.

94. Mining Code arts. L. 131-1 to 136-4; *see also* Decrees n° 2006-648 and 2006-649 of June 2, 2006.

95. Mining Code art. L. 162-1.

96. *Id.* art. L. 162-2.

97. *Id.* arts. L. 161-1 and L. 161-2.

98. *Id.* arts. L. 173-1 to L. 173-7 (administrative sanctions) and arts. L. 512-1 to L. 512-12 (criminal sanctions).

99. Forestry Code (*Code forestier*).

100. *Id.* art. L. 112-2.

101. *Id.* arts. L. 131-1 to L. 136-1 and arts. D. 131-1 to R. 134-6.

102. *Id.* arts. L. 141-1 to L. 144-1 and arts. R. 141-1 to R. 143-9.

103. *Id.* arts. L. 311-1 to L. 315-2 and arts. R. 312-1 D. 315-9.

104. *Id.* arts. L. 341-1 to L. 342-1 and arts. R.341-1 to R. 341-9.

105. *Id.* art. L. 125-2.

106. Law n° 2008-757 of August 1, 2008, as codified in Environmental Code arts. L. 161-1 to L. 165-2 and arts. R 161-1 to R. 163-1.

107. Environmental Code art. L. 162-1.

108. *Id.* art. L. 162-9.

109. *Id.* art. L. 162-18.

110. Court of Appeals of Paris, Mar. 30, 2010, n° 08/02278 and Cass. Crim., Sept. 25, 2012, n° 3439.

111. Proposed Civil Code art. 1386-19 (unofficial translation).

112. Proposed Civil Code art. 1386-20 (unofficial translation).

113. Directive 79/409/EC of April 2, 1979, as amended.

114. Directive 93/43/EC of May 21, 1992, as amended.

115. Environmental Code arts. L. 414-1 to L. 414-11 and arts. R. 414-1 to D. 414-31. Natural 2000 is the center piece of EU nature & biodiversity policy, http://ec.europa.eu /environment/nature/natura2000/ (last visited Sept. 1, 2013). It is an EU-wide network of nature protection areas established under the 1992 Habitats Directive. *Id.* As of 2011, the French Natura 2000 network covered 12.55 percent of the national territory and included 1,753 "Habitats" sites and 369 "Birds" sites.

116. Environmental Code art. L. 414-1 I.

117. *Id.* art. L. 414-1 II.

118. *Id.* art. L 414-4.

119. *Id.* arts. L. 414-4 VIII and arts. R. 141-19 to R. 414-29.

120. *Id.* arts. L. 424-1 and arts. R. 424-1 to R. 424-3.

121. *Id.* arts. L. 424-2 to L. 424-7 and arts. R. 424-4 to R. 424-19.

122. *Id.* arts. L. 425-14 and arts. R. 425-18 to R. 425-20.

123. *Id.* arts. L. 432-1 to L. 432-12 and arts. R.432-1 to R. 432-18.

124. *Id.* arts. L. 434-3 *et seq.*

125. *Id.* arts. L. 432-2 and L. 432-3.

126. *Id.* arts. L. 511-1 *et seq.* (*installations classées pour la protection de l'environnement*).

127. *Id.* art. L. 511-2.

128. *Id.* art. R. 511-9. The list is referred to as the *Nomenclature ICPE.*

129. *Id.* arts. L. 512-1, L. 512-7 and L. 512-8.

130. *Id.* arts. L. 515-28 to L. 515-31 and arts. R. 515-59 to R. 515-84; *see also* Ministerial Orders of February 20, 2013, and May 2, 2013.

131. Environmental Code art. L. 512-1.

132. *Id.* art. R. 512-74.

133. *Id.* art. L. 512-5 and art. L. 512-10.

134. *Id.* arts. L. 516-1 *et seq.* and arts. R. 516-1 *et seq.*

135. *Id.* arts. R. 516-1 to R. 516-6 as amended by Decree n° 2012-633 of May 3, 2012.

136. *Id.* art. R. 512-69.

137. *See infra* section XII.

138. Environmental Code art. L. 229-30; *see also* Mining Code arts. L. 211-2 *et seq.* and L. 122-1 to L. 122-3.

139. Environmental Code arts. L. 229-32 *et seq.* and arts. L. 229-37 *et seq.*

140. *Id.* arts. L. 229-38 *f* and L. 229-39.

141. Mining Code arts. L. 211-2 *et seq.*

142. Environmental Code art. L. 229-37.

143. *Id.* art. L. 511-1 and Mining Code art. L. 161-1.

144. Environmental Code art. L. 593-2. (*Installations nucléaires de base*).

145. *Id.* arts. L. 592-1 *et seq.* and arts. L. 592-35 to L. 592-40 relating to technical investigations.

146. *Id.* arts. L. 592-19 and L. 592-25.

147. *Id.* art. L. 593-8.

148. *Id.*

149. *Id.* art. L. 593-14.

150. *Id.* art. L. 596-15 3°.

151. *Id.* arts. L. 596-24 to L. 596-31.

152. *Id.* arts. L. 597-1 to L. 597-46.

153. *Id.* arts. L. 594-1 to L. 594-13.

154. Environmental Code Book II on the protection of physical environments, Book III on natural areas, and Book IV on flora and fauna.

155. *See, e.g.,* Environmental Code art. L. 512-1 (for ICPE Permits).

156. *Id.* art. R. 512-4; *see also* Planning Code (*Code de l'urbanisme*) art. R. 431-20.

157. Environmental Code art. L. 512-2; *see also* Planning Code art. R. 425-10.

158. Environmental Code arts. L. 214-1 *et seq.* and arts. R. 214-1 *et seq.*

159. *Id.* art. L. 214-7.

160. Forest Code (*Code forestier*) arts. L. 341-1 to L. 341-11 and arts. R. 341-1 to R. 341-9.

161. *Id.* art. L. 341-7.

162. Environmental Code art. R. 122-10.

163. *Id.* art. L. 122-9.
164. *Id.* arts. L. 123-7 and art. R. 122-10 I.
165. Basel Convention, art. 2 § 3. Note also that self-applicable Regulation (EC) 1013/2006 of June 14, 2006, on shipments of waste affirms EC's commitment to enforce the Basel Convention, which it is a party to since 1994.
166. Environmental Code art. R. 162-5.
167. *See, e.g., id.* arts. L. 216-2 and L. 514-6 (for water permits and ICPE permits).
168. *Id.* art. R. 514-3-1.
169. *Id.* (except for wind farms (6 months) as per art. L. 553-4).
170. *Id.* art. L. 122-2 (in the absence of impact assessment), art. L. 123-16 (where the permitting procedure involved a negative advisory opinion of the public inquiry commissioner or commission); *see also* Administrative Justice Code art. L. 521-1 (summary proceedings, *référé*).
171. Environmental Code art. L. 514-19.
172. Civil Code (*Code civil*) art. 1382 ("Any act whatever by an individual, which causes damage to another, obliges the one by whose fault it occurred, to compensate the other.").
173. Créteil Court of First Instance, 1ˢᵗ chamber, Oct. 20, 1998, *Ass. Lozaits, Cie CIRP vs. Société Missenard Quint, cit in* JEAN PIERRE BOIVIN, LES INSTALLATIONS CLASSÉES 476 (2d ed. 2003).
174. Civil Code art. 1383 ("Each of us is liable for the damage he causes not only by his intentional act, but also by his negligent conduct or by his imprudence.").
175. Civil Code art. 544 ("Ownership is the right to enjoy and dispose of things in the most absolute manner, provided they are not used in a way prohibited by statutes or regulations.").
176. Construction and Housing Code (*Code de la construction et de l'habitation*) art. L. 112-16.
177. *Constitution de partie civile.*
178. Environmental Code arts. L. 414-1 to L. 141-3, arts. L. 142-1 to L. 142-4 and arts. R. 141-1 to R. 141-26; *see also id.* art. L. 433-2 (for fishermen and aqueous milieu protection associations).
179. *See, e.g., id.* art. L. 171-8 II 1°.
180. *See, e.g., id.* art. L. 171-8 II 2°.
181. *See, e.g., id.* art. L. 171-8 3°.
182. *Id.* art. L. 171-8 4°; *see also* Administrative Circular of July 19, 2013, on the enforcement of administrative sanctions and criminal penalties in matters involving ICPEs.
183. *See, e.g.,* Environmental Code art. L. 521-17 (for chemical products).
184. *See id.* art. L. 521-18 1° (for chemical products).
185. *Id.* 2°.
186. *Id.* 3°.
187. *Id.* 4°.
188. *See, e.g., id.* arts. R. 216-1 to R. 216-17 (for water permits); *see also, e.g., id.* arts. R. 514-4 and R. 514-5 (for operating permits) and arts. R. 521-2-14 to R. 521-2-16 (for chemical products).
189. *See, e.g., id.* art. L. 173-8.
190. Criminal Code (*Code pénal*) art. 131-38.
191. Criminal Code art. 131-39.
192. *See, e.g.,* Environmental Code art. L. 173-5.

CHAPTER 29

Germany

DR. BETTINA ENDERLE

I. Introduction: Structures and Key Environmental Actors

A. Interrelationship with European Environmental Laws and National "Domains"

There is no field of public and administrative law in Germany that has been determined and influenced by European Union (EU) law more than environmental law. More than 65 percent of the German environmental laws are based on EU prerogatives, a harmonization leaving fewer and fewer national "domains." Soil protection is one of the few subjects that has not yet been comprehensively regulated on the European level. In light of the cross-border nature of environmental pollution, the associated impacts, and the need to avoid "environmental dumping" across the EU member states (i.e., the relocation of production and industry to states with less rigid environmental laws or enforcement for reasons of cost-cutting), the widespread Europeanization of environmental law should come as no surprise.

1. Implementation of Directives and Interpretation in Line with Directives

In the EU, most legislation is enacted as directives, and is subsequently implemented as national laws at the member state level. Among the most important directives are the Industrial Emissions,[1] the Waste Framework,[2] the Water Framework,[3] the Flora-Fauna-Habitat Directive, and the directive establishing the European Emissions Trading Scheme (EU ETS). To ensure directives are timely implemented into national law and contain sufficiently precise obligations, directives are directly applicable in each EU member state (1) after the lapse of the due date of implementation, and (2) if they contain precise and enforceable obligations (*effêt utile*). For example, the European Court of Justice (ECJ) recently held that the German action rights for environmental non-governmental organizations (NGOs) were not in compliance with the

547

Environmental Impact Assessment Directive (which is based on the Aarhus Convention) and, thus, directly applicable until legislation compliant with the directive was enacted.[4]

In cases of noncompliance, the national German provisions cannot be applied, but are not automatically null and void either. To avoid conflicts with EU law, national laws must be interpreted in conformity with EU law to the greatest extent possible. This rule of construction is most relevant in the field of environmental law, which is chiefly driven by EU legislation and harmonization. Similarly, primary and secondary EU laws prevail over (noncompliant) national law including constitutional law.[5] Due to Germany's federal structure, where EU directives are implemented at both, the federal and state levels, the implementation of EU directives is often a difficult, time-consuming process, and frequently entails infringement proceedings before the ECJ.[6]

A new trend in EU legislation is to adopt regulations (instead of directives), which automatically apply in all EU member states (direct application) and only require national provisions on competent authorities, enforcement, and fines. Recent examples of important pieces of environmental legislation are the regulation concerning the Registration, Evaluation, Authorisation and Restriction of Chemicals (REACH)[7] and the regulations on cosmetics,[8] plant protection products,[9] cross-border shipments of waste, detergents,[10] ozone-depleting substances,[11] and emission performance standards for new light commercial vehicles.[12]

2. Impact Assessments

An important field of regulation based on EU directives is the assessment of impacts deriving from certain plans and projects. The requirements of European law set by the Environmental Impact Assessment (EIA) Directive 2011/92/EU,[13] the Strategic Environmental Assessment (SEA) Directive 2001/42/EC, and by international law, in particular the Espoo Convention,[14] have been integrated into German law mainly through the Environmental Impact Assessment Act (Gesetz über die Umweltverträglichkeitsprüfung, UVPG). Additionally, implementation has been accomplished by amendments to the Federal Mining Act (Bundesberggesetz, BBergG), the Building Code (Baugesetzbuch, BauGB), the Federal Regional Planning Act (Raumordnungsgesetz, ROG), and laws of the federal states. In Germany, the EIA is integrated into the authorization procedures for specific projects, such as industrial installations and large-scale infrastructure projects.[15] The SEA is part of the elaboration of specific public plans and programs such as the Federal Transport Infrastructure Plans for Motorways and Trunk Roads, Railways or the Federal Grid Development Plan, which are the basis for individual projects. Taking into account the particular challenges in the transboundary context, Germany has concluded bilateral agreements with neighboring countries so as to lay down the details of a transboundary EIA and ensure a smooth procedure.[16]

3. *Procedural Safeguards*

German courts are obliged to ensure the primacy of EU law when national law conflicts with it. In such cases, the courts must generally request a preliminary ruling of the ECJ (Art. 267 AEUV) to ensure a uniform interpretation and application of EU law. Where a German judge does not submit questions on the interpretation of EU law to a preliminary ruling of the ECJ, the claimant can pursue his right of access to the legal judge by way of a complaint under German constitutional law. The German Constitutional Court will then decide whether the judge arbitrarily declined to submit questions to the ECJ. As a consequence, the German Constitutional Court does generally not review the German laws and ordinances implementing EU laws in light of German constitutional law, but refers its interpretation to the ECJ as the guardian of compliance with EU law.[17]

4. *Legislation*

Environmental protection has been a governmental objective in Germany since 1994, as set forth in the German Constitution (Grundgesetz, GG), which states: "The state and its bodies are obliged to protect natural resources and animals for future generations." In the field of environmental law, the federal government enjoys so-called "concurrent" legislative power. In other words, the federal states can only enact laws as long as and as far as the federal government has not made use of its legislative powers. This mechanism has proven to be effective, in particular when implementing EU environmental legislation and in view of rapid and homogenous national lawmaking. The Grundgesetz, however, grants some explicit rights to the 16 federal states to adopt deviating legislation.[18]

Despite this general provision, the Grundgesetz does not establish a fundamental right to environmental protection. Citizens may challenge environmental impacts hazardous to human health based on their fundamental right to life and physical integrity or, in some cases, on their right to property, but may do so only where such impacts were caused by the government and its authorities or agencies, but not by other individuals. Ensuring that environmental law complies with constitutional law is addressed in permits or plan approvals where the scope of fundamental rights of neighbors or citizens is spelled out. The citizens do not, however, have a constitutional right to the adoption of specific law provisions or enforcement. Compliance with laws in rank below constitutional law is reviewed in the regular legal redress procedure before the administrative courts.

The adoption of a comprehensive and uniform German Environmental Code has been on German lawmakers' agenda for several decades. In 1999, the Federal Department for the Environment (Bundesumweltministerium, BMU) presented a draft of Part I of an Environmental Code, which failed due to the lack of constitutional power of the federal government (*Bund*) to enact laws for the management of water resources, nature, and landscape. After a reform of the federal legal system that took place in 2006, the Bund finally had the power to adopt an Environmental Code, but the draft presented in 2008 was ultimately not supported by a majority. When the legislative period ended in 2009, the draft lapsed due to discontinuity,[19] and a new attempt to tackle the problem has not yet been undertaken since then.

5. Administration

a. Federal Level

i. Federal Department for the Environment (BMU) and Related Agencies

The BMU was established in 1986[20] and is responsible for the environmental policy of the federal government. It consists of six directorates-general[21] and, for historical reasons, has offices in Bonn and Berlin. There are three federal agencies operating under the auspices of the BMU:

- The Federal Environment Agency (Umweltbundesamt, UBA)
- The Federal Agency for Nature Conservation (Bundesamt für Naturschutz, BfN)
- The Federal Office for Radiation Protection (Bundesamt für Strahlenschutz, BfS).

ii. Other Agencies

The Emissions Trading Agency (Deutsche Emissionshandelsstelle, DEHSt) is a division of the UBA and is entrusted with implementing the market instruments of the Kyoto Protocol to the U.N. Framework Convention on Climate Change,[22] the requirements of the EU ETS, and related German legislation.

Additional federal departments and agencies dealing with environmental issues include the Agency for Occupational Health and Safety and Occupational Medicine (Bundesanstalt für Arbeitsschutz und Arbeitsmedizin, BAuA). The BAuA conducts research and development in the field of safety and health at work, promotes the transfer of knowledge into practice, advises policymakers (e.g., under REACH), and performs sovereign functions concerning hazardous substances, product safety legislation, and the health data archive. It operates under the auspices of the Federal Department for Labor and Social Affairs.[23]

The Federal Institute for Materials Research and Testing (Bundesanstalt für Materialforschung und Prüfung, BAM) undertakes research in key areas of safety engineering and testing methods, for example, for eco-design requirements for energy-related products.[24] It further issues notifications in the rank of technical rules (see *infra* section I.B) on testing and product safety requirements, for example, for food-contact materials.

iii. Network Agency

The Network Agency (Bundesnetzagentur, BNetzA) is a federal authority under the German Federal Department of Economics and Technology.[25] The central tasks of the Network Agency in the field of energy are to ensure compliance with the Energy Act (Energiewirtschaftsgesetz, EnWG), liberalize and deregulate the energy market through nondiscriminatory access and efficient use-of-system charges, and secure efficient operation of energy supply networks. The Network Agency also plays a role in the expansion of the German supergrids intended to transport electricity from the northerly regions of Germany (especially from offshore wind parks) to the more southerly regions, where the majority of energy-intensive industry is situated.

The BNetzA also ensures compliance with product regulations, such as electromagnetic compatibility, labeling requirements, and the health and safety issues of products. It has the power to order product recalls or sales bans and is therefore a particularly important agency for U.S. companies marketing their products in Germany and the EU.

b. State Level

Each of the 16 German states has a State Department for the Environment. These departments are supplemented by state agencies, such as, e.g., the Hessian Agency for the Environment and Geology (Hessisches Landesamt für Umwelt und Geologie, HLUG) in the State of Hesse. This agency is a technical and scientific authority that cooperates with several universities and is charged with environmental monitoring.

Because the federal states are responsible for enforcing most of the environmental laws, each has higher and lower environmental protection authorities in place. The higher authorities are usually responsible for issuing permits for industrial installations, approving plans for infrastructure projects and water management, or ensuring environmental protection in a region.

The lower environmental protection authorities are based on the district or municipal level and are concerned with more local issues, e.g., among other things, the designation of protected landscape areas (*Landschaftsschutzgebiete*) and the protection of biotopes. They also grant permits under nature protection legislation as required for the mining of gravel and sand.

B. Technical Rules and Guidelines

The superior administrative authority, as a rule, enacts technical rules and guidelines having the aim of guaranteeing a uniform application of the relevant legislation. The technical rules and guidelines usually interpret laws, provide guidance on how to structure discretionary decisions, and concern organizational issues. In the field of environmental law, technical rules and guidelines apply, for example, in environmental impact assessments,[26] species protection laws,[27] and air quality controls (Technische Anleitung zur Reinhaltung der Luft, TA Luft).[28] The technical rules and guidelines are in principle only binding on administrative bodies, and can therefore be subject to judicial review.[29]

Yet, as an exemption, the technical rules and guidelines have indirect external effects (*mittelbare Außenwirkung*) and as such are binding on the courts, provided they fulfill certain conditions. The technical rules must have been adopted (1) based on a comprehensive procedure involving scientific and technical expertise and (2) after performing a stakeholder consultation, while (3) such procedure is provided for in the law and (4) the rules are up to date. This applies for instance to certain air emission values for industrial installations.[30]

II.   Air and Climate Change
A.   The Federal Emissions Control Act and Supplemental Regulations

For certain facilities, a permit under the Federal Emissions Control Act (Bundes-Immissionsschutzgesetz, BImSchG) is required.[31] The BImSchG is supplemented by 39 ordinances[32] and the technical instructions on air quality control (the TA Luft controls, *supra* section I.B) and on noise (TA Lärm). The German emission control law sets out certain requirements for the erection, operation, and decommissioning of facilities, such as limit values for the emission of hazardous substances and noise, restrictions concerning the use of certain substances, safety precautions to prevent accidents, and the appointment of emission control and accident officers, as well as monitoring and reporting requirements. It also contains requirements for a site-related regulation of air emissions (*Lufreinhalteplanung*) and noise (*Lärmminderungsplanung*).

The procedure for obtaining a permit under the Federal Emissions Control Act is usually very extensive and involves the public. After a permit has been granted, the competent authority may issue orders addressed to the operator to enforce compliance with certain obligations, including those requiring precautions to prevent hazardous effects on the environment. The operator's obligations are partly defined by reference to the current state-of-the-art technology, meaning the competent authority may demand existing facilities be modernized.

The permit under the Federal Emissions Control Act consolidates all relevant permits. This means that instead of several procedures resulting in several permits, only the emissions permit procedure is carried out.[33] Neighboring entities cannot seek any legal redress under German civil law once the permit has become final. Neighbors are compelled to participate in the permit procedure and bring forward their objections prior to the permit's issuance.

The German emissions control rules are increasingly impacted by European legislation. Directive 2010/75/EC on Industrial Emissions (IED) contains provisions of a more prescriptive nature than has been the case compared to earlier legislation. It provides for a stricter EU-wide application of the "best available techniques" as basis for the permit conditions and strengthens the permit updating obligations of the member states.[34] In Germany, approximately 9,000 installations fall under the scope of the IED. The provisions have recently been implemented into German law by amend-ments to the Federal Emissions Control Act, the Water Management Act, and other environmental laws.

B.   The Major Accidents Ordinance (Seveso Ordinance)

The Major Accidents Ordinance implements the Seveso II Directive[35] and sets forth requirements for installations where the tonnage thresholds for certain particularly hazardous substances are surpassed (such as distances between "Seveso" installations and residential areas). The operators must implement measures to prevent incidents and, in case an incident that fulfills defined criteria occurs, to report it to the authorities. Parts of the safety report required under the Major Accidents Ordinance have to be presented in the permit procedure under the BImSchG. Distance requirements under the Seveso Ordinance resulted in a suspension of permit for a power plant built too close to a residential area.

C.   The Act on the Trading of Emissions Allowances for Greenhouse Gases (GHGs)

Nearly 2,000 installations in Germany (out of a total of more than 15,000 installations EU-wide) are subject to the EU ETS.[36] Under the EU ETS, plant operators, which are entitled to emit CO_2 emissions in accordance with the permits issued under EU member states' respective emissions control laws, are required to hold an equivalent number of allowances. One allowance confers the right to emit the equivalent of one metric ton of CO_2 during a specified allocation period. The total amount of allowances cannot exceed the emissions cap, limiting total emissions of the relevant overall plant oper-ators to that level.[37]

In Germany, emissions trading is governed by the Act on the Trading of Emission Allowances for Greenhouse Gases (Treibhausgas-Emissionshan-delsgesetz, TEHG) and the Allocation Ordinance 2020 (Zuteilungsverord-nung 2020, ZuV 2020). The German Emissions Trading Agency (Deutsche Emissionshandelsstelle, DEHSt) is the competent authority in Germany for managing the allocation and issuance of emission allowances, revising emis-sions reports, and administering the German part of the EU Emissions Trad-ing Registry. It also administers the project-based mechanisms known as Joint Implementation and the Clean Development Mechanism. In January 2013, the third trading period started with substantial design changes. First, instead of national caps, there is a single EU-wide cap declining annually by the linear factor of 1.74 percent.[38] Second, the trading period was extended from five to eight years. Third, the amount of auctioned allowances was sig-nificantly increased from 20 percent auctioning in 2013 for the industrial sec-tor to 70 percent by 2020.

Sectors such as refineries, aluminum, steel, paper, and chemical production, are exempted from auctioning. Installations in these sectors receive 100 percent of the benchmarked emissions allowances for free because of the risk of these industries leaving Europe for cost reasons (so-called "carbon leakage").[39] In the first eight years of EU ETS, the member states had some leeway in establishing their own rules for the free allocation of emissions allowances. However, because of the EU-wide harmonized rules, there is no need for national allocation (plans or laws) anymore.

For the auctioning in the third trading period, the member states and the European Commission selected the European Energy Exchange AG (EEX) in Leipzig, Germany, as the common, EU-wide platform to auction emission allowances on behalf of the member states.[40] Germany, Poland, and the United Kingdom opted out of this common platform and established their own auction platforms. In Germany, the EEX is at the same time Germany's own auction platform.

With the nuclear phase-out in Germany starting in 2017, and Germany's subsequent reliance on coal-fired power plants to satisfy its energy needs, an increase of GHG emissions, and in particular CO_2, is expected. After a decrease in 2011 attributable to the mild winter, in 2012 and 2013 GHG emissions increased by ca. 1.2 percent each year. Still, the expanding use of renewable energy sources limited the increase, and the Federal Environment Agency, predicts that because increased CO_2 emissions from coal power generation will be offset with CO_2 emissions reductions elsewhere due to the EU ETS, the German nuclear phase-out will not lead to an increase of total GHG emissions.

D. Carbon Reduction (via Carbon Capture and Storage)

While the European Commission sees carbon capture and storage technology (CCS) as a very promising technology to combat climate change, Germany passed, after a long and controversial debate, in 2012 a federal act on the demonstration and application of technologies for the capture, transport, and permanent storage of carbon dioxide (Kohlendioxid-Speicherungsgesetz, KSpG; CCS Act). However, public resistance in Germany, the model country in matters of climate change policy, against underground storage remains strong. Correspondingly, the material scope of the CCS Act is limited. Also, the states can designate areas in which CO_2 storage is permissible and where it is not. Thus, the future of CCS in Germany is to a great extent in the hands of state-level politics.

Moreover, far-reaching transparency provisions and action rights for private parties and environmental NGOs have been introduced, a result of the extensive debate on the risks of CCS, which will, in addition, lead to resistance against CCS projects in Germany. The CCS Act may also be relevant for the construction of CO_2 transport pipelines and CO_2 storage in the seabed (which are excluded from the German states' opt-out clause).[41]

III. Water

A. The Structure of German Water Law

German water laws do not only protect water as such but also regulate the uses of water for different purposes. The prime goal of the laws is "economic management of natural waters depending on their quantity and quality."[42] German water law is fragmented and consists of different but overlapping levels of regulation. It is one of the most complex legal areas of German environmental law.

With the recent reform of the federal system, the legislative competences of the federal government and the federal states have been reallocated. The federal government now can adopt comprehensive legislation based on its legislative powers[43] with some deviation powers to the states. With regard to regulations on substances hazardous to water and installations, however, no such deviations are possible because they are core parts of water legislation. To address any issue under water law, an assessment of the legislation at the federal and state level and of their interplay is required.

B. Internal and Coastal Waters

The protection and resource management of internal and coastal waters is governed by European, federal, and state legislation. The EC Water Framework Directive[44] constitutes a framework for measures in the field of water policy, which was implemented into German law by amendments to the German Water Management Act and other as well as by adopting specific regulations.

C. Federal and State Law

The main federal legislation is the Water Management Act (Wasserhaushaltsgesetz, WHG) of March 1, 2010, requiring the sustainable management of water bodies. All uses of water, such as withdrawal or discharge, require a permit under the WHG. The decision whether to grant such a permit is generally at the discretion of the administrative body. Under the WHG, strict liability is established for adverse effects on the quality of surface water, coastal water, and groundwater caused by any direct release or spill of substances, for example, those originating from plants manufacturing, processing, storing, discharging, or transporting such substances.[45]

The states' water laws supplement and detail the WHG. Most states have already adopted their own water laws or enacted new water laws. In some states, a fee, the "water cent" (*Wasserpfennig*), is charged for the abstraction of ground or surface water.

To implement the EU Water Framework Directive, requirements for the establishment of programs of measures and management plans were included in the WHG. For all ten river basin districts (*Flussgebietseinheiten*) relevant to Germany, such management plans and programs of measures were established by December 22, 2009. These include reduction measures to limit the induction of phosphates, pesticides, and nitrogen into rivers. The states implement the programs of measures in cooperation with national authorities and the authorities of neighboring countries.

The European Commission brought a lawsuit against Germany in the ECJ on May 31, 2012, based on a dissenting opinion concerning the application of the Water Framework Directive's[46] principle of cost recovery for "water services" (*Wasserdienstleistungen*).[47] While Germany applies the principle of cost recovery for water services only to the supply of drinking water and the disposal and treatment of wastewater, the European Commission's interpretation is much more far-reaching, and includes activities such as water abstraction for the cooling of industrial plants. The decision of the ECJ is still pending.

D. Sewage Regulations

The Sewage Act (Abwasserabgabengesetz, AbwAG) requires that an effluent charge be paid for direct discharges of wastewater into a water body. The rate depends on the quantity and the noxiousness of the discharge.

E. Supplementing Regulations

Currently, every state has its own regulations concerning substances hazardous to water. A unifying regulation on the federal level replacing state regulations, however, has been in preparation for a while but still not been adopted.

As regards the protection of groundwater, a federal regulation is in place.[48] Directive 2008/105/EC of 16 December 2008 regarding environmental quality standards in the field of water policy (EQS Directive) was implemented by the Regulation on Surface Waters (Oberflächengewässerverordnung, OGewV) of July 20, 2011. In Germany, it is debated whether the requirements of the Water Framework Directive and the EQS Directive and their impacts on mercury discharges mean that coal-fired power plants would have to cease operation by 2028 and whether the construction of new plants may be prohibited.[49]

F. Provisions Applying to Marine Waters

The Marine Strategy Framework Directive (MSFD)[50] aims at the protection of marine ecosystems. It provides legal instruments to determine the current environmental status and to achieve or maintain the good environmental status of European marine areas. It was implemented into German law mainly by amendments to the German Water Management Act and the Federal Nature Protection Act. The new provisions of the WHG apply to marine waters, defined as coastal waters, the German exclusive economic zone, and the waters overlying the continental shelf. Like the EU Habitats and the

Birds Directive, which protect habitats and species, the MSFD aims to protect ecosystems with a holistic protection approach. The German authorities have prepared the required reports assessing the current environmental status of German marine waters, determined what "good environmental status" for the North Sea and the Baltic Sea means, and identified the targets necessary for reaching a good environmental status by 2020. According to the reports, the current environmental status of the North Sea and the Baltic Sea cannot be regarded as "good." In order to achieve the targets set by the MSFD, the German federal and state authorities cooperate closely.[51]

As user conflicts between sectors such as shipping, fishing, wind energy parks, oceanographic research, and offshore oil and gas exploration continue to grow, they must be balanced with the objectives of environmental protection. To solve these conflicts, and ensure balance with environmental goals, marine spatial planning has become a focus of regulators. The EU has, in order to ensure coherent planning of maritime activities at sea within European waters, recently proposed a directive establishing a framework for marine spatial planning and integrated coastal management.[52] In Germany, some maritime spatial plans based on the Federal Spatial Planning Act (Raumiordnungsgesetz, ROG) have already taken effect to separate conflicting uses such as shipping lanes, offshore windparks, protected habitats, and fishing.[53]

IV. Handling, Treatment, Transportation, and Disposal of Hazardous Material

A. REACH

Most of the chemical industry in the EU is located in Germany.[54] The European Commission has long been bothered by the general lack of knowledge about the properties and uses of chemicals. In order to address this concern, the German chemical industry voluntarily committed to generate information on chemicals in 1997.[55] Despite having followed through on this commitment, the Commission determined that mandatory legislation was required for all substances.[56] Consequently, Regulation (EC) No. 1907/2006, the Registration, Evaluation, Authorisation and Restriction of Chemicals (REACH), went into force on June 1, 2007, and has significantly affected many German companies.

REACH introduced a comprehensive system for the manufacture, evaluation, and labeling of chemicals, affecting primarily manufacturers and importers, but also other actors in the supply chain. Before REACH, generation of information was required for "new" substances only. This provision excluded all substances deemed to be on the market as of September 18, 1981, which are also known as "existing substances."[57]

One of the main purposes of REACH is the protection of human health and the environment, including the reduction of the extent of animal testing. REACH intends to achieve this objective by generating information on substances and their uses. Manufacturers and importers working with quantities over one ton per year are obliged to register with the European Chemicals Agency (ECHA). While this "no data, no market" principle was more stringent before REACH because parties were required to notify the ECHA when 10 kg or more of a substance were manufactured or imported, the obligation was restricted to "new" substances. As REACH requires registration of all substances, it was necessary to prioritize the registration obligation for the most relevant substances. On the one hand, specifically hazardous substances were made subject to (early) registration. On the other hand, the threshold was increased.[58] ECHA registration allows the agency to identify hazards associated with the chemical directly and dangers arising from specific uses of the chemical. Depending on the outcome, ECHA will require measures be taken to protect human health and the environment. These measures include authorization and restriction. When substances of very high concern (SVHC) are at issue, ECHA will mandate authorization of the sale and use of the chemicals.[59] When non-SVHC chemicals are at issue, certain conditions may have to be met—called "restriction" under REACH—prior to their manufacture, sale, or use. REACH lists the substances subject to authorization and restriction in its annexes.[60]

There is overlap between REACH and other legislation.[61] Generally, REACH applies to workplace and environmental legislation. For instance, REACH obligates manufacturers and importers to carry out risk assessments related to their substances and to suggest risk management measures. These risk assessments are required under occupational health and safety legislation also. With regard to environmental legislation, REACH applies, for example, to electrical and electronic equipment at the same time as Directive 2011/65/EU on the restriction of the use of certain hazardous substances in electrical and electronic equipment (RoHS Directive).

Though REACH applies directly in the EU member states, the member states are individually obliged to set up their own appropriate frameworks to impose effective, proportionate, and dissuasive penalties for noncompliance. Under German law, noncompliance with REACH's obligations may be punished by up to five years in prison, or, as an administrative offense, include a fine of up to €100,000.

B.   German Chemicals Act and Related Ordinances

The German Chemicals Act (Chemikaliengesetz, ChemG) provides the framework for more specific chemicals legislation and includes provisions on responsibilities, surveillance, enforcement, criminal sanctions, and administrative fines.

The Ordinance on the Prohibition of Certain Chemicals (Chemikalienverbotsverordnung, ChemVerbotsV) provides for bans and restrictions of certain chemicals. For instance, it prohibits the sale of specific chemicals, includes permit requirements for other chemicals, and provides for information and documentation obligations when certain chemicals are supplied to third parties.

Potential exposure of employees to hazardous substances requires occupational health and safety regulations, and thus, the Ordinance on Hazardous Substances (Gefahrstoffverordnung, GefStoffV) obliges employers to implement specific safety measures if their employees are or may be exposed to hazardous substances. Hazardous substances under this law are those that, due to their chemical or physical features, are highly flammable, toxic, explosive, corrosive, or carcinogenic. The employer must carry out a risk assessment, issue working orders to employees, and maintain a register of hazardous substances.

V. Waste and Site Remediation
A. Waste and Product Laws
1. Background

Waste management policy in the EU, coupled with detailed regulation, has been a success story in the entire EU. It has drastically reduced waste quantities by increasing the volumes of waste that are subject to recycling and recovery.[62] The growing number of European laws on waste management— such as the Waste Framework Directive,[63] the directive on the disposal of polychlorinated biphenyls and polychlorinated terphenyls (PCB/PCT),[64] the directive on the landfill of waste,[65] the directive on end-of-life vehicles,[66] the directive on the incineration of waste,[67] the directive on waste electrical and electronic equipment,[68] the directive on batteries and accumulators and waste batteries and accumulators,[69] and the regulation on shipments of waste[70]—progressively overlay national regulations. That said, there are considerable differences in national waste laws of the EU member states. In Germany, the waste management system, formerly operated by municipalities and counties, was gradually transferred to private companies that changed the structure of the waste management industry. Waste collection and recovery has become an economic driver and a billion dollar business.

The evolution of a closed-cycle waste management "bred" a new area of law, the so-called "product laws" promoting waste prevention and recovery. They establish "producer responsibility" for specific product groups by setting requirements for the design, use, energy efficiency, and facilitation of reuse, recycling, and disposal of certain substances. Typically certain hazardous substances are either phased out or restricted in products. Additionally, take-back systems established by the producers are required, including under the directive on packaging and packaging waste,[71] Regulation 1005/2009/EC on ozone-depleting substances,[72] and RoHS Directive.[73]

2. The Closed Substance Cycle Act and Related Ordinances

The German Closed Substance Cycle Act puts a particular focus on recycling. It spells out the five-step hierarchy of waste handling as laid down in the Waste Framework Directive: (1) prevention, (2) preparing for reuse, (3) substance recycling, (4) energy recovery or backfilling, and (5) disposal. This hierarchy is not mandatory in cases where measures on the next level result in an environmentally better result. Further, it provides for a recycling quota of 65 percent for municipal waste[74] and 70 percent for building waste.

Waste recycling and recovery is generally mandatory if it is technically feasible and economically reasonable. Waste that cannot be recycled must be disposed of in a manner not harmful to the public, meaning either by incineration in an approved installation or, after pretreatment, in a lawfully permitted and operated landfill.

As a general rule, if a company or business lawfully disposes of waste in a landfill that is lawfully operated by a third person, the company or business is not automatically released from its legal responsibility. The Federal Administrative Court also held that a previous holder of waste remains strictly liable for waste disposal until the entire process of disposal is completed.[75] However, the court was clear that the obligation is limited to the share of waste the company lawfully supplied to the contractor.[76]

As a rule, the generator or holder of waste is responsible for waste recycling or disposal. However, private household waste and wastes from other specific sources, especially industrial wastes, must instead be delivered to public waste management organizations unless certain exemptions apply.

B.   Selected Product Regulations

Ultimately, waste prevention and recycling starts with the product design. Design-related requirements are, as a result, also based on waste laws (see section V.A, *supra*) on the European level as implemented by national legislation, which often includes national characteristics and features. For example, the German Ordinance on Packaging regulates disposal and take-back obligations for B2B and B2C packaging.[77] The ordinance has substantially reduced the circulation of ecologically disadvantageous beverage cans, while various take-back systems were established for ecologically sound beverage (glass) bottles. Also, several disposal and take-back systems were set up for electrical and electronic equipment and batteries under the German Act on Electrical and Electronic Equipment and the Batteries Act.

Environmental protection is not the only reason to take back and recycle the remains of abandoned packaging and used electrical equipment. Rather, a second factor is the value of the recyclable portions and raw materials contained in these pieces of "waste." In Germany, the political aim to establish an efficient closed substance cycle economy is deemed to serve both the environment and the growing economic needs for affordable and accessible raw materials, which are indispensable for German industry. This rationale is the essence of a modern understanding of waste law and product regulations. This way of thinking ahead is illustrated by the draft name of the planned successor regulation to the Ordinance on Packaging—the Act on Valuable Resources (Wertstoffgesetz).

C. Soil

1. The Federal Soil Protection Act

The main body of law concerning soil protection in Germany is the Federal Soil Protection Act (Bundes-Bodenschutzgesetz, BBodSchG).[78] The act aims to preserve the soil functions and, if necessary, restore them. It assigns liability for hazardous soil alterations and groundwater contamination caused by soil contamination. This includes the obligation to investigate, clean up, contain, or otherwise limit contamination, or to take precautionary measures to avoid soil contamination at the liable party's expense. The Federal Soil Protection Act distinguishes between trigger and action values, each of which requires the liable party to take a different action. Trigger values are values that if exceeded, require a soil investigation to be initiated, taking into account the actual use of the soil. Such an investigation is carried out in order to assess whether or not a site is contaminated.[79] Action values are values that, if exceeded, indicate the presence of soil contamination after taking into account the current use of the soil and require further measures such as a cleanup.

2. Liability

Liability under the BBodSchG is strict and joint and several. When there is confirmed or suspected hazardous soil alteration, the polluter, the current owner of the site, the former owner (under certain preconditions),[80] the current tenant, and shareholders (in exceptional cases when the corporate veil is pierced),[81] can be liable regardless of the extent of their contribution to the contamination. The soil protection authority has discretion as to which of the parties orders are imposed on, and takes into account the "polluter pays" principle and considers the goal of efficient and fast site remediation. Often the owner is liable as the most financially sound party—the "deep pocket" principle. The administrative decision is subject to limited judicial review only, but the liable party does have the right to seek financial redress from the parties who contributed to the pollution in proportion to their contribution.

Liability may be limited in three statutory scenarios. First, the administrative body considers the permissible use of the site under planning law and the associated protection level when determining the extent of the remediation measures. Second, when contamination was caused after March 1, 1999, remediation is only required where this is proportionate, taking into consideration previous soil pollution. Third, if the property was transferred after March 1, 1999, and the former owner in good faith did not expect an adverse effect from the site's use and, under the circumstances the former owner's good faith is worthy of protection, a cleanup obligation may not exist. Apart from these three statutory exceptions, for constitutional reasons, the owner's liability is limited to the value of the site after decontamination.[82]

3. Impact of EU Laws

The European Commission's 2006 soil protection framework directive is not yet effective. It would not lead to major changes in German soil protection law. There is, however, a difference between how contaminated sites are identified. Whereas under the BBodSchG "sufficient suspicion that a harmful soil change exists" is required for action, the Proposed Soil Framework Directive ties action to "potentially soil polluting activities."[83] For the industry sectors included in the directive this may result in an increase of investigation orders or, at least, a shift in the burden of proof.

The situation for some industrial sectors has already changed due to the integration of the IED (see section II.A, *supra*) into German law. This directive provides that an operator must prepare and submit a baseline report on soil and groundwater contamination by hazardous substances to the soil protection authority. The baseline report is meant to enable a comparison with the state of an industrial property after definitive cessation of activities and is thus the basis for remediation obligations upon cessation. This new obligation will probably trigger more investigations and remediation orders by the authorities.

VI.   Emergency Response

For information concerning emergency response law in Germany, see section II.B, *supra*.

VII.   Natural Resource Management and Protection
A.   Nature and Species Protection

In the past three decades, awareness of nature protection issues has continuously grown in Germany. This is evidenced by the fact that state nature protection laws were replaced, to a large extent, with federal legislation. The Federal Nature Protection Act now includes stringent provisions aimed at a higher level of nature protection. Impacts on nature have to be assessed in most permit procedures and lead, especially for infrastructure and industrial projects, to added expense and extra delays in the planning, approval, and legal redress phases of projects.

1.   Landscape and Biotope Protection

The BNatSchG designates different categories of protected areas based on differences in objectives and the desired level of protection. Nature conservation areas (*Naturschutzgebiete*) are aimed at protecting the biotopes of certain plant and animal species. About 3.6 percent of the German territory has been designated as a nature conservation area.[84] National parks (*Nationalparks*) share most features of the nature conservation areas, but are huge areas with little human impact. Germany has currently 14 national parks with a total surface area of 1,029,496 hectares.[85] Due to the sophisticated requirements for such areas and the population density[86] in Germany, it is unlikely that further national parks will be designated. Biosphere reserves (*Biosphärenreservate*) protect large-scale areas that qualify partly as nature conservation areas and protected landscape areas (*geschützte Landschaftsschutzgebiete*). Germany has currently 16 biosphere reserves encompassing 1,846,904 hectares.[87] Protected landscape areas aim at the protection of the specific functions and features of a certain area. Their level of protection is lower than that of nature conservation areas and national parks. Some 28.5 percent of Germany is protected as landscape area.[88] Natural preserves (*Naturparks*) are large-scale areas designated for recreational purposes in a spatial plan and are constituted of nature conservation areas and protected landscape areas. Approximately 27 percent of the German territory is designated as natural preserve area.

2. *Natura 2000*

In response to the progressive loss of natural habitats and wild species, the EU adopted Directive 92/43/EEC of May 21, 1992, as frequently amended. It addresses the conservation of natural habitats and of wild fauna and flora (the Habitats or FFH Directive). Its ambitious objective is to safeguard the most threatened species and habitats in the EU and restore them to a favorable conservation status. To achieve these goals, the Habitats Directive established "Natura 2000 sites," which comprise special areas of conservation under the Habitats Directive and Special Protection Areas under Directive 2009/147/EC of November 30, 2009, on the conservation of wild birds (Birds Directive). The Natura 2000 sites form a coherent network across the EU. The BNatSchG implements the provisions of the Habitats Directive into German law.[89]

If a plan or a project is designated in the vicinity of a Natura 2000 site, the responsible authority must assess whether the plan or project alone or in combination with other plans/projects may have a significant adverse effect on the Natura 2000 sites. The project proponent must provide the authority with all information required to carry out the assessment. The assessment may comprise up to four steps:

1. *Screening:* In the screening, the likely effects of a plan or project (either alone or in combination with other plans or projects) are examined. The assessment can be based on existing data of the Natura 2000 site (e.g., from the environmental authorities) and no new data must be collected. Further, the effects of the plan or project do not have to be assessed in detail. An approximate assessment is sufficient. If the plan or project may have significant adverse effects on the conservation objective of the Natura 2000 site (which is typically the case) it must undergo step two of the assessment.

2. *Appropriate assessment:* At this stage, a detailed assessment of the effects of the plan or project on the conservation objectives of the Natura 2000 site is required (either alone or in combination with other plans or projects). The assessment must be based on current

data of the Natura 2000 site and on the best available scientific knowledge in the field.[90] Further, measures mitigating the adverse effects of the plan or project can be proposed by the project proponent and must then be taken into account as well. If the assessment results in at least the possibility that the plan or project may have significant adverse effects on the conservation objectives of the Natura 2000 site, the plan or project generally must not be approved.

3. *Derogation procedure:* The project proponent may then apply for an exemption, the so-called "derogation procedure." The exemption will be awarded if there are (a) imperative reasons of overriding public interest in favor of the project, for example, economic interests with an impact on the public, and (b) no acceptable technical or spatial alternatives that can be realized with proportionate efforts.

4. *Compensatory measures:* Ultimately, the project proponent must propose compensatory measures required to compensate for the impairments of the conservation objectives of the Natura 2000 site in order to maintain the coherence of the Natura 2000 network. This includes, for example, upgrading other Natura 2000 sites or suitable areas in the vicinity.[91]

In practice, Natura 2000 has been an effective instrument in the hands of environmental NGOs to challenge, delay, and increase costs of infrastructure, industrial, and energy projects. The plan approval for the German motorway section of Hessisch Lichtenau (a town in the middle of Germany)—connecting Polish motorways with the Benelux states via Germany and forming part of the East-Western magistrales of the Transeuropean Networks—took more than 15 years due to three court procedures mainly based on noncompliance with Natura 2000 issues, which all ended up before the Federal Administrative Supreme Court.

Due to a specific crested newt species, a tunnel was built, which raised the construction costs by several million euros. Another example is the *Trianel-case*,[92] where deficiencies of the appropriate assessment relating to air emissions and their possible impacts on a woodrush beech forest (a protected habitat under the Natura 2000 regime) resulted in the suspension of the operational permit of a power plant for several years although the plant was already completed.[93]

In addition to the Natura 2000 regime, German law requires an approval for intrusions in nature and landscape (*Eingriffe in Natur und Landschaft*). Compensatory measures for compliance with the Natura 2000 network may constitute an intrusion in nature and landscape under German law, such that another permit under the BNatSchG including additional compensation measures is generally needed. However, such a permit may be already covered by other permits already acquired for the project (e.g., under emission control law) or the plan approval decision (so-called "concentration effect") so that it is not needed.

B. Environmental Energy Law

In the last decade, the Act on Renewable Energies and related legislation, as well as the international and national laws on carbon emissions trading, have increasingly been referred to in Germany as "environmental energy law" (*Umweltenergierecht*). Such "hybrid" terminology highlights the ongoing process of expansion of environmental law principles and considerations to areas of law that were previously not regarded as "environmental law."

The most prominent examples of this are the regulations on renewable energies, in particular the Act on Renewable Energies. Yet other energy-related areas of law have been influenced by environmental laws and concerns, expanding from the fairly modern laws on the development of new energy grids to the more traditional mining laws.

1. *Renewable Energies Legislation*

The German Act on Renewable Energies (Erneuerbare-Energien-Gesetz, EEG), with its precursor legislation tracing back to 1991, is the central legal instrument used to promote renewable energies in Germany. The EEG promotes the exploitation of renewable energy sources by granting elevated (i.e., above market price) and fixed feed-in tariffs for 20 years, to be paid by the grid operators to suppliers of electricity from renewable energies[94] with different regulations in detail for the various types of renewable energy sources. The additional costs generated by this subsidy-like promotion scheme are passed on by the grid operators to the electricity end-consumers who pay an EEG levy (*EEG-Umlage*). This levy amounted to 5,277 eurocents per kWh in 2013.

This system proved to be highly successful in substantially increasing the share of renewable energies in the overall electricity production in Germany within a relatively short time frame (from 3.1 percent in 1990 to 20.5 percent in 2011). The fixed feed-in tariffs provided a reliable incentive for both industrial and financial investors planning and realizing large-scale projects (like onshore/offshore wind farms) and private households investing, for example, in roof top photovoltaic modules. In order to safeguard workplaces and domestic economic structures, the EEG and related regulations provided for substantial options to exempt industry companies from the extra costs generated by the subsidized feed-in of electricity from renewable energies.

In light of the "energy turnaround" (*Energiewende*) in Germany and the accelerated nuclear phase-out since 2011, the exploitation of renewable energies gained additional importance. At the same time, the constant rise of electricity costs has become a subject of political controversy, as these costs increasingly impact private households and other parties not eligible to benefit from an exemption. With such costs peaking in 2012 and 2013, at least a general political consensus developed that the EEG must undergo reform toward a more equal sharing of financial burdens and more market economy elements in the generation and marketing of renewable energies, for example, by way of reduction of feed-in tariffs. Whether the EEG system will be able to ensure stable electricity prices and adequately promote renewable energies at the same time, or will be entirely replaced in the long term by another system (e.g., a quota model) is difficult to predict.

In any event, the EEG, which served as a model for similar legislation in many other countries, turned out to be a perfect starting point for a change in energy supply. It did not, however, provide a viable way forward, if not amended.

Further examples of legislation on renewable energies and energy savings include the Renewable Energies Heat Act (Erneuerbare-Energien-Wärmegesetz, EEWärmeG) stipulating that owners of new buildings must obtain a portion of their heat supply with renewable energies. Also, the Energy Conservation Act (Energieeinsparungsgesetz, EnEG) and the Energy Savings Ordinance (Energieeinsparverordnung, EnEV) set forth energy-related requirements for "green" buildings as of 2009. In addition, the Act on Combined Heat and Power Generation (Kraftwärmekopplungsgesetz, KWKG) aims to ensure that industrial plants generating electricity and processing heat at the same time do not release process heat into the environment, but rather use it for either industrial purposes or for district heating (for instance, paper production using heat for drying paper). The fuel is thus utilized more efficiently in comparison to conventional production in separate installations, and generates fewer CO_2 emissions.

2.   Laws on Energy Grid Development

As a reaction to the Fukushima nuclear disaster, the German Bundestag decided on June 30, 2011, with an overwhelming majority[95] to amend the Atomic Energy Act (Atomgesetz, AtG), immediately decommissioning eight nuclear power plants, with subsequent progressive shutdowns of the remaining nine by or before December 31, 2022. Germany therefore will phase out nuclear energy much more quickly than predicted. Thus 23 percent of the German electricity generated by nuclear power plants in 2012 must be replaced by 2022.[96] To avoid supply bottlenecks, the energy transition will require constructing new, efficient, and flexible (gas fired) power plants, energy-saving policies, and a substantial promotion of renewable energies.[97] Due to the lack of electricity following the nuclear phase-out, it is necessary to develop new "smart" power grids, for example, to connect offshore wind parks in the north of Germany with the southern parts of the country, where most energy-intense industry is located. Also, the increasingly decentralized and large-scale feed-in of renewable energies requires the provision of flexible and efficient technical features. Thus, the "new age" of renewables calls for rapid realization of large new energy infrastructures that will literally change the landscape of the country and strongly impact on nature and the environment.[98]

The German Act on the Acceleration of Transmission Grid Development (Netzausbaubeschleunigungsgesetz Übertragungsnetz, NABEG), enacted in

August 2011, aims at a swift development of transmission grids by accelerating planning procedures. It exclusively applies to power lines listed in a specific act (Bundesbedarfsplangesetz, BBPlG), identifying them as necessary to ensure grid operability. Such power lines can be the highest-voltage power lines—between 220 and 380 kV—crossing national or state borders, and also high-voltage power lines with a voltage of at least 110 kV. The NABEG's scope has recently been extended to connection grids from offshore wind power plants to the onshore grid.

Essentially, the NABEG accelerates the development of transmission grids by two means: (1) increasing public acceptance by extensive public participation efforts and (2) transferring authority from the state to the federal level. As a consequence of growing public opposition against large infrastructure projects, the legislature expanded public involvement in the planning process under the NABEG.[99] For example, the NABEG requires a public conference (*Antragskonferenz*) between project proponents, public stakeholders, and recognized environmental NGOs, which must take place directly after the project proponent has submitted its application. NABEG further enhances public participation by a mandatory public hearing on objections of concerned citizens and environmental concerns raised after the publication period of the detailed project plan.

The second way NABEG works is by transferring authority from the states to the BNetzA.[100] Previously, the authorities of the German states were charged with managing the entire planning procedure. As this led to considerable delays when transmission grids crossed the territory of several states, the legislature intended, initially, to transfer the whole planning procedure under NABEG to BNetzA.[101] Due to opposition in the legislative process, the planning responsibilities under NABEG are now to be shared between BNetzA and state authorities. Yet an important part of planning has been assumed by BNetzA, as it determines the approximate position of the transmission grids in Germany, leaving a range of only about 500 to 1,000 meters to the states. The state-level authorities are charged with the "fine-tuning," that is, determining the exact position of the transmission grids in a plan approval procedure (*Planfeststellungsverfahren*). The states recently even declared that they would agree to a transfer of jurisdiction for the entire planning procedure to BNetzA. An ordinance largely transferring jurisdiction to BNetzA will probably be enacted soon.

The federal act identifying 36 grid development projects as necessary for grid operation is about to enter into force. As a result, BNetzA will determine the approximate position of the power grids under the NABEG. In Germany, both the public and experts will follow the procedure with curiosity to see whether the legislature can achieve its goal of acceleration.

3. *Mining Laws*

German mining laws,[102] which date back to the Middle Ages where mining rights were granted by way of royal prerogative, have become controversial recently. Most remarkably, the mining laws—governing an industry that strongly impacts the environment—are among the regulations that are most favorable to entrepreneurs. That said, recent legislative amendments and proposals[103] claim a "green" revision of these laws, including broadened EIA requirements, more public participation and, generally, the end of the supremacy of economic considerations over environmental and public concerns. This culminated in the heated discussion on the advantages and assumed risks related to the exploitation of unconventional gas resources by use of hydraulic fracturing techniques (fracking). The federal government issued a proposal in February 2013 to put in place restrictive permit procedures for fracking in the exploration and exploitation phases,[104] and has been perceived as inhibiting instead of encouraging the use of such technology. Against a backdrop of general European antipathy toward fracking, Germany, with its peculiar energy policies, may be foregoing a cheap, domestic energy resource too easily despite sharply increasing energy costs. This is because the use of the subsurface is one element required to accomplish the extremely costly "energy turnaround" in Germany (roughly estimated at €1 billion and, thus, similar to the costs for the reunification of Eastern and Western Germany) following the decision to phase out nuclear energy in 2011.

Currently, German mining laws are being given increased attention[105] together with the increasing exploitation of the subsurface for purposes such as underground gas storage, geothermal energy, storing technologies for renewable energies, carbon capture and storage,[106] as well as submarine cable and storage technologies in coastal waters and exclusive economic zones. For instance, Germany is among the "big five" underground gas storing nations worldwide.[107] At the heart of the ongoing reform discussion is the subject of permitting mining operations under a comprehensive review of the suitable location and general economic benefits, and the environmental and third-party impacts. This kind of weighing exercise (e.g., regional planning, cost-profit considerations, property and environmental issues) is new for mining law, where the interests of the individual entrepreneurs have historically driven the permit process.[108]

The above-mentioned examples give an idea of a development pattern that increasingly blurs the lines between environmental law and energy-related legislation. Some areas of the latter are strongly influenced by environmental law concepts, while others appear to have entirely been merged with environmental law—such as the renewable energy regulations. This process of expansion is particularly visible in Germany, with its strategic goal to become the trailblazer for a "new age" of renewables and the world's first major economy accomplishing the transition to large-scale renewable energy supply. Yet, a long-term merging of both areas of legislation will be inevitable for any economy seriously pursuing a strategy for sustainably preserving the environment and effectively combating climate change.

VIII.   Natural Resource Damages

For information concerning natural resource damage law in Germany, see section XII.A, *infra*.

IX.   Protected Species

Germany, like most countries in the EU, is densely populated. Habitats of wild animals are often repressed or collide with infrastructure and settlement zones. This constitutes a material issue for biodiversity. The Natura 2000 regime is therefore supplemented by specific regulations on the protection of species. These regulations protect wild species wherever they occur and do not relate to specific sites (in contrast to Natura 2000). Under German law, species protection is provided by a general protection regime based on national law and a special protection regime based on EU law.

The German general protection regime protects all wild species from unnecessary impairments like willful disturbances. Impairments of species and their habitat are therefore permitted under the general protection regime if the specific impairments are justified by a sound reason or an approved intrusion in nature and landscape.

The European special protection regime is generally independent from the Natura 2000 regime.[109] It covers all animals and plants belonging to specific wild species[110] irrespective of their occurrence in specific protection sites.[111] It prohibits harm to wild animal species, to disturb them during their breeding period, or to destroy their breeding places. Further, specific wild plants must not be removed from nature or destroyed.

In particular, plans and projects must generally comply with the requirements of the special species protection regime, for example, ensuring wind farms do not kill protected birds or that infrastructure projects do not cause a disturbance of breeding places. Yet the competent authority may grant a derogation of the species protection requirements if (1) there are no satisfactory alternatives, (2) the derogation is not detrimental to the maintenance of a favorable conservation status of the affected species, and (3) there are specific reasons in favor of the project—in particular imperative reasons of an overriding public interest including those of an economic nature. This exemption is based on the principle of proportionality, and comparable to stage 3 of the Natura 2000 assessment.

X.   Environmental Review and Decision Making

See material on EIA in sections I and VII, *supra*.

XI.   Transboundary Pollution

For information concerning transboundary pollution law in Germany, see, for example, sections I.A.2, *supra*, and XII, *infra*.

XII.   Civil and Criminal Enforcement and Penalties
A.   Liability

The Environmental Damage Act is the most recent piece of legislation establishing liability related to certain industrial activities. It establishes a compensation scheme for environmental damages vis-à-vis public bodies. The less recent Environmental Liability Act imposes strict civil liability for property and health damages of any party (not limited to public bodies). Finally, natural persons can become criminally liable under the federal criminal code and single environmental laws.

1.   *Environmental Damage Act*

The number of contaminated sites and a dramatically accelerated loss of biodiversity caused the EU to adopt Directive 2004/35/EC of 21 April 2004 on environmental liability with regard to the prevention and remedying of environmental damage (Environmental Liability Directive). The Environmental Liability Directive is based on the "polluter pays" principle and gives incentives to operators to adopt measures and develop practices to minimize the risks of environmental damage. The Environmental Damages Act (Umweltschadensgesetz, USchadG) implements the Environmental Liability Directive into German law. It does not go beyond the requirements of the Environmental Liability Directive. The USchadG defines environmental damage as damage to (1) habitats and species protected by the Habitats Directive or the Birds Directive (Biodiversity Damage); (2) surface waters or groundwater; or (3) the soil.

Liability for environmental damage depends on specific occupational activities listed in Annex I to the USchadG. It applies regardless of fault if a causal link can be established between the damage and the relevant Annex I activity. For occupational activities other than those listed in Annex I that caused environmental damage, environmental liability applies to biodiversity-related damages only, and the responsible party must have acted with intent or negligence. Because German regulations on soil, surface water, and groundwater contamination already provide for strict liability for damages to these natural media, the USchadG is in practice only relevant for biodiversity-related damages.

If environmental damage is imminent, the USchadG requires the liable party to take preventive measures at its own expense. When environmental damage has already occurred, the responsible party is obliged to either perform the containment and cleanup measures (which must be approved by the responsible authority) or assume those costs.

The USchadG authorizes the German States to release the liable party from liability for remediation costs if the party acted in compliance with a valid permit (permit defense) or ensured that it deployed the state of scientific and technical knowledge in its operations (state-of-the-art defense). No German state, however, has used this option so far. Under the USchadG, the operator does not have to provide financial security (such as compulsory insurance, *Deckungsvorsorge*). It appears at this time that the authorities are reluctant to apply the law in practice.

2. Environmental Liability Act

The German Environmental Liability Act (Umwelthaftungsgesetz, UmweltHG)[112] of 1990 imposes on operators the duty to implement precautionary environmental protection measures and provides redress for those who suffer damages caused by environmental effects of specific installations. The operators of such installations are obliged to compensate individuals for damages irrespective of fault except in cases of *force majeure* and when property is damaged and it occurred because of the permitted operation of an installation and the damage was negligible or acceptable considering the situation. The UmweltHG eases the burden of proof for the person who sustained damage, with assumptions of causation and rights to information. This, however, does not apply when the installation was operated in compliance with the relevant regulations.

Liability for the same environmental effect is limited to a total amount of €85 million for all fatalities, injuries, and health damages, and to a total amount of €85 million for any property damage. For some industrial plants,[113] operators are required to provide financial security (*Deckungsvorsorge*) based on a specific ordinance issued by the federal government. However, the ordinance has not been officially issued. There is therefore no current obligation to do so. The UmweltHG does not rule out any, possibly more far-reaching, liability claims under other laws, such as the Federal Soil Protection Act[114] or the Water Management Act.[115]

3. Environmental Criminal Law

Germany was one of the first countries to establish an environmental criminal law. In 1980 criminal sanctions for environmental offenses were introduced into the federal criminal code (Strafgesetzbuch, StGB).[116] As a rule, the polluter only commits a criminal offense when they act without a permit.[117] Actions punishable under the federal criminal code include water pollution, soil pollution, air pollution, noise pollution, vibration and nonionizing radiation, illegal disposal of dangerous waste, unlicensed operation of a plant, unlawful handling of radioactive substances and of other dangerous substances and goods,[118] causing a nuclear explosion, misuse of radiation and preparatory acts in this respect, releasing ionizing radiation, construction of a defective nuclear facility, causing a common danger by poisoning,[119] and damaging natural monuments.[120] There are supplementary provisions containing criminal offenses in the environmental codes, which include endangering protected species and illegally handling dangerous substances.

The German environmental criminal law does not contain a specific provision that holds government officials (*Amtsträger*) liable for not executing their duties regarding environmental protection. Government officials may, however, be held liable in three scenarios: if the official (1) wrongfully issued a permit,[121] (2) failed to revoke an unlawful permit,[122] or (3) failed to intervene in case of illegal pollution.[123] In cases (1) and (2) where government officials may have discretionary power, they are criminally liable only if the acts or omissions went beyond their discretionary power. Further, liability can be established when a government official neglects an operational duty (*Betreiberpflichten*), such as in sewage purification plants, swimming pools, hospitals, or landfill sites.[124]

B.   Legal Redress

1.   *The German Court System and the ECJ*

The German administrative and environmental court system is composed of administrative courts (Verwaltungsgericht, VG) and higher administrative courts (Oberverwaltungsgericht or Verwaltungsgerichtshof) in each of the German federal states,[125] and the Federal Administrative Court (Bundesverwaltungsgericht, BVerwG) based in Leipzig. As a general rule, cases start in the VG, but certain special projects (e.g., large combustion energy plants) begin in the higher administrative courts. Further, cases involving infrastructure projects related to certain listed railways, trunk roads, waterways, transmission grids, and magnetic levitation trains may begin in the BVerwG and cannot be appealed to any higher court.[126]

On the European level, there are two main scenarios for environmental issues to be brought before the ECJ. First, if a member state fails to comply with environmental obligations imposed by European law, it is the European Commission's responsibility to commence infringement proceedings. These may, after a procedure involving the Commission and member state, be decided by the ECJ. Second, environmental issues also may be subject to a preliminary ruling made at the request of a court of a European member state. The latter was the case in the *Trianel-ruling* where the Higher Administrative Court of North-Rhine Westphalia submitted three questions concerning action rights of NGOs in environmental law cases.[127]

2.   *Ex Officio Investigation*

In administrative procedures, the authorities are not limited to the facts and evidence and arguments provided by the parties, but rather perform investigations ex officio (*Amtsermittlungsgrundsatz*). The parties, however, can and should contribute to the investigation of the facts and circumstances and especially provide the facts and evidence they are aware of. The principle of ex officio investigation also applies to court cases.

3.   *Action Rights in Environmental Law Cases*

Individuals have rights in environmental matters based on the violation of legal provisions granting "subjective rights" (*subjektive öffentliche Rechte*).

These are legal provisions that are meant to protect the rights of a particular individual, such as neighbors affected by noise emissions of an industrial plant. The counterpart are legal provisions that serve the interest of the general public only, which applies to many provisions of environmental law. German environmental NGOs may bring suit based on violations of procedural rights and for specific environmental issues. Foreign environmental NGOs may bring suit in Germany to the extent they have been recognized under the German laws and comply with the other preconditions for legal redress and, under certain preconditions, even without such acknowledgment. The scope of legal redress for environmental NGOs in EU member states has been subject to the judicial review of the ECJ several times. With regard to Germany, the ECJ ruled that a limitation of the NGOs' action rights in environmental matters must not be limited to subjective rights, as is the case for individuals.[128] This rule has been implemented by an amendment to the German Environmental Appeals Act (Umweltrechtsbehelfsgesetz, UmwRG). Environmental NGOs now have rights based on an alleged violation of practically all environmental protection provisions.

Apart from industrial plant permits, environmental NGOs regularly challenge plan approvals for large-scale projects, often by claiming a violation of Natura 2000 provisions. Such lawsuits may result in a time-consuming new environmental studies of protected species and habitats, an amendment of the plan approval, or, in the most significant case, even in a repeal of the approval. If the court repeals the plan approval, the project cannot go forward until an amended plan approval, based on a supplementary plan approval procedure, has been issued by the authority.

Notes

1. Directive 75/2010/EC of 24 November 2010 on industrial emissions (integrated pollution prevention and control).

2. Directive 2008/98/EC of 19 November 2008 on waste and repealing certain Directives.

3. Directive 2000/60/EC of 23 October 2000 establishing a framework for Community action in the field of water policy, last amended by Directive 2009/31/EC of 23 April 2009.

4. The "Trianel"-ruling, ECJ, C -115/09, 12/05/2011 (BUND vs. Bezirksregierung Arnsberg) and the amended Environmental Appeals Act.

5. ECJ, C-6/64, 03/06/1964, 1251 (Costa/E.N.E.L.); decision of the German Constitutional Court, Bundesverfassungsgericht, BVerfGE 73/339 (374 *et seq.*) (Solange II) and 123, 267 (402) (Lisbon-Treaty).

6. Germany is composed of 16 states (*Länder*): Baden-Württemberg, Bavaria, Berlin, Brandenburg, Bremen, Hamburg, Hesse, Lower Saxony, Mecklenburg-Vorpommern, North Rhine-Westphalia, Rhineland-Palatinate, Saarland, Saxony, Saxony-Anhalt, Schleswig-Holstein, and Thuringia. Ongoing infringement procedures relate, for instance, to deficits in the assessment of impacts on Natura 2000 sites in the approval of air routes to the new airport in Berlin, deficiencies in the application of the Water Framework Directive, and, once more, in the implementation of a broad access of environmental NGOs to courts under the Environmental Appeals Act.

7. Regulation 1907/2006/EC of 18 December 2006 on the Registration, Evaluation, Authorisation and Restrictions of Chemicals (REACH), as amended.

8. Regulation 1223/2009/EC of 30 November 2009 on cosmetic products, last amended by Regulation 483/2013 of 24 May 2013.

9. Regulation 1107/2009/EC of 21 October 2009 concerning the placing of plant protection products on the market.

10. Regulation 648/2004/EC of 31 March 2004 on detergents, last amended by Regulation 259/2012/EU of 14 March 2012.

11. Regulation 1005/2009/EC of 16 September 2009 on substances that deplete the ozone layer, last amended by Regulation 744/2010/EU of 18 August 2010.

12. Regulation 510/2011/EU of 11 May 2011 setting emission performance standards for new light commercial vehicles as part of the Union's integrated approach to reduce CO_2 emissions from light-duty vehicles, last amended by Regulation 205/2012/EU of 6 January 2012.

13. Last amended by Directive 2014/52/EU of 6 April 2014.

14. Convention on Environmental Impact Assessment in a Transboundary Context (Espoo, 1991), see http://www.unece.org/env/eia/about/eia_text.html (last visited Oct. 30, 3013).

15. The plan approval procedure includes a participation of public stakeholders, a publication of the plan and in the case of a large-scale project an environmental impact assessment.

16. See, e.g., Agreement of 11 April 2006 between the Federal Republic of Germany and the Republic of Poland on the transboundary Environmental Impact Assessment.

17. The requirement for such judicial self-restraint of the German Constitutional Court is that the German fundamental rights are effectively protected vis-à-vis the EU. This corresponds to the minimum and indispensable level of protection under German constitutional law. See Solange II, supra note 5.

18. The federal states can, inter alia, deviate in nature protection law (unless the general principles, species protection, and marine nature protection would be concerned), they can further deviate from laws concerning water management, but not from regulations concerning substances and installations.

19. The discontinuity principle means that bills are considered to have failed if the Parliament did not adopt them within one legislative period.

20. The first minister of the BMU was Walter Wallmann and the third Angela Merkel (today's chancellor of Germany), both members of the conservative party. The fourth minister, Jürgen Trittin, to date the only BMU minister from the Green Party, officiated from 1998 to 2005.

21. Directorate-general N dealing with nature conservation and sustainable use; directorate-general IG responsible for environmental health, emission control, safety of installations, and transport and chemical safety; directorate-general WA dealing with water, waste, and soil; directorate-general RS responsible for nuclear safety, radiological protection, and the nuclear fuel cycle; directorate-general E dealing with the transformation of the energy system (Energiewende), climate policy, and European and international environmental policy; and directorate-general ZG dealing with strategic aspects.

22. See http://unfccc.int/kyoto_protocol/items/2830.php (last visited Oct. 30, 2013).

23. Bundesministerium für Arbeit und Soziales, BMAS.

24. Directive 2009/125/EC of 21 October 2009 establishing a framework for the setting of ecodesign requirements for energy-related products and implementing legislation last amended by Directive 2012/27/EU of 4 November 2012.

25. Bundesministerium für Wirtschaft und Technologie, BMWi.

26. Guideline for the application of the law on environmental impact assessment (Allgemeine Verwaltungsvorschrift für die Ausführung des Gesetzes über die Umweltverträglichkeitsprüfung) enacted by the federal government on 18 September 1995.

27. Guidelines on the application of species protection law (*Vollzugshinweise zum Artenschutzrecht*) enacted by the BMU on 15 September 2000.

28. The technical instruction on air quality control are guidelines issued on the basis of Federal Emissions Control Act § 48 and were enacted on 24 July 2002.

29. BVerfG, decision of 31 May 1988, register number 1 BvR 520/83, NJW 1989, 666 (667).

30. These are so-called "norm-concretising technical rules," e.g., laid down in the Technical Instruction on Air Emissions, *see* Federal Administrative Supreme Court (Bundesverwaltungsgericht, BVerwG), judgment of 20 December 1999, register number 17 C 15/98, NVwZ 2000, 440 (440)—*TA Luft-case*; BVerwG, judgment of 28 October 1998— register number 8 C 16.96 -, BVerwGE 107, 338 (341 *et seq.*)—*Sewage Ordinance-case.*

31. This applies to the establishment and the operation of installations which, on account of their nature or their operation, are particularly likely to cause harmful effects on the environment or otherwise endanger or cause considerable disadvantages or considerable nuisance to the general public or the neighborhood, as well as to the establishment and operation of stationary waste disposal plants. With the exception of the latter, installations that do not serve commercial purposes and are not used within the framework of business undertakings shall not be subject to licensing unless they are particularly likely to have harmful effects on the environment through air pollution or noise. For installations that do not need a permit other requirements exist.

32. Among other things, these ordinances relate to specific installations such as large combustion or so-called Seveso plants, the permit procedure, the emissions declaration, and certain hazardous substances.

33. This is, for example, the case as concerns building permits. There are, however, exceptions: no concentration effect applies for plan approvals, operating plans as required by mining law, decisions on the basis of atomic law and water permits.

34. B. Enderle, *The EU Industrial Emissions Directive: Implications for Environmental Permit Holders*, 14(2) ABA Envt., Energy & Res. Newsl. 18 (July 2012).

35. Directive 96/82/EC of 9 December 1996 on the control of major-accident hazards involving hazardous substances, last amended by Directive 2012/18/EU of 4 July 2012. The directive is repealed by Directive 2012/18/EU of 4 July 2012 (Seveso III) with effect from 1 June 2015.

36. Directive 2003/87/EC of 13 October 2003 establishing a scheme for greenhouse gas emission allowances trading within the Community and amending Council Directive 96/61/EC, as last amended by Regulation (EU) No. 412/2014 of 30 April 2014.

37. Europe seeks to include more and more sectors such as recently the very controversial inclusion of the aviation sector. The next area under security is the shipping sector, *see* Enderle & Erler, *Kommt der Emissionshandel für die Seeschifffahrt? (Will Shipping Become Subject to the European Emissions Trading Scheme?)*, HANSA Int'l Mar. J. 71–74 (2011).

38. It relates to the average annual total quantity of allowances issued by member states in 2008–2012.

39. The new Allocation Ordinance 2020 was enacted by the federal government on 24 August 2012 and fully transposes European requirements into German law for the third trading period.

40. Regulation 1031/2010/EU of 12 November 2010, Auctioning Regulation.

41. *See* B. Enderle, *The New Act on CCS—A "Special Mining Law" for a Bridging Technology*, World of Mining 358 (2012).

42. BVerfG, decision of 30 October 1962, register number 2 BvF 2/61, BVerfGE 15, 1–25 (15).

43. "Concurrent legislative powers," discussed in section I.A.4.

44. Directive 2000/60/EC of 23 October 2000 establishing a framework for Community action in the field of water policy last amended by Directive 2013/64/EU of 28 December 2013.

45. This does not apply if the damage has been caused by force majeure.

46. European Comm'n Press Release IP/12/536.

47. Art. 9 of the Water Framework Directive requires the member states to take account of the principle of cost recovery of water services, including environmental and resource costs and due regard to the polluter pays principle. Member states are obliged to ensure that water-pricing policies provide adequate incentives to users to use water efficiently and constitute an adequate contribution to the recovery of the costs of water services.

48. The German Regulation on the protection of groundwater of 2010 implements the Water Framework Directive as well as the Groundwater Daughter Directive 2006/118/EC.

49. For an interpretation of the relevant provisions as a strict prohibition to discharge mercury into water bodies at the latest from 2018 onwards, see Silke R. Lasowski, *Kohlekraftwerke im Lichte der EU-Wasserrahmenrichtlinie (Coal-fired power plants in the light of the EU-Water Framework Directive)*, ZUR 2013 131, 142. For the opposing opinion, see Wolfgang Durner & Nela Trillmich, *Ausstieg aus der Kohlenutzung kraft europäischen Wasserrechts (Cessation of coal utilization by virtue of European water law?)*, DVBl 2011, 517, 525.

50. Directive 2008/56/EC of 17 June 2008 establishing a framework for community action in the field of marine environmental policy (Marine Strategy Framework Directive).

51. The administrative agreement establishing the coordinating institutions entered into force on 30 March 2012 (*Verwaltungsabkommen Meeresschutz*), see http://www.landtag .ltsh.de/infothek/wahl17/umdrucke/3600/umdruck-17-3617.pdf.

52. Proposal for a Directive establishing a framework for maritime spatial planning and integrated coastal management, Brussels of 12 March 2013, COM (2013) 133 final.

53. Ordinance on Spatial Planning in the German Exclusive Economic Zone in the North Sea (AWZ Nordsee-ROV) of 2009 and Ordinance on Spatial Planning in the German Exclusive Economic Zone in the Baltic Sea (AWZ Baltic Sea-ROV) of 2009.

54. Cefic European Chem. Indus. Council, *The European Chemical Industry in Worldwide Perspective*, FACTS & FIGURES 2012, at 7. In 2011, Germany generated 29 percent of the EU chemicals sales, followed by France (15.4 percent), the Netherlands (10.3 percent), and Italy (9.7 percent). See http://www.cefic.org/Documents/FactsAndFigures/2012/Chemicals -Industry-Profile/Facts-and-Figures-2012-Chapter-Chemicals-Industry-Profile.pdf.

55. *See* http://www.bmu.de/uebrige-seiten/selbstverpflichtungen-nicht-mehr-in -kraft/.

56. European Commission, Proposal for a Regulation of the European Parliament and of the Council concerning the Registration, Evaluation, Authorisation and Restriction of Chemicals (REACH), COM(2003) 644 final.

57. Directive 67/548/EEC of 27 June 1967 on the classification, packaging, and labeling of dangerous substances as amended will be repealed as of June 2015 by Regulation (EC) No 1272/2008 by introducing the Globally Harmonised System of Classification and Labelling of Chemicals (GHS). For "existing substances" manufactured or imported in high quantities, manufacturers and importers were, as a rule, obliged only to report information while hazard assessments were carried out by the EU member states (Regulation 753/93/EEC of 23 March 1993 on the evaluation and the control of the risks of existing substances).

58. European Commission, White Paper—Strategy for a Future Chemicals Policy, COM (2001) 88 final, at 12.

59. *See* B. Enderle, *Substances in Articles*, ch. 8 *in* REACH-BEST PRACTICE GUIDE TO REGULATION (EC) No 1907/2006 (Drohmann & Townsend eds., 2013).

60. REACH Annex XV, XVII.

61. *See* B. Enderle, *Scope of REACH*, ch. 2 *in* REACH-BEST PRACTICE GUIDE TO REGULATION (EC) No 1907/2006 (Drohmann & Townsend eds., 2013).

62. In Germany 75 percent of the total waste quantity is recovered; in specific substance cycles the quota is even higher for instance in steel and paper recycling.

63. Directive 2008/98/EC of 19 November 2008 on waste and repealing certain Directives.

64. Directive 96/59/EC of 16 September 1996 on the disposal of polychlorinated biphenyls and polychlorinated terphenyls (PCB/PCT), last amended by Regulation 596/2009/EC of 18 June 2009.

65. Directive 1999/31/EC of 26 April 1999 on the landfill of wastes, last amended by Directive 2011/97/EU of 5 December 2011.

66. Directive 2000/53/EC of 18 September 2000 on end-of-life vehicles, last amended by Directive 2013/28/EU of 17 May 2013.

67. Directive 2000/76/EC of 4 December 2000 on the incineration of waste, last amended by Regulation 1137/2008/EC of 22 October 2008. The Directive is repealed by Directive 2010/75/EU of 24 November 2010 on Industrial Emissions (IED Directive) with effect from 7 January 2014.

68. Directive 2002/96/EC of 27 January 2002 on waste electrical and electronic equipment (WEEE), last amended by Directive 2008/112/EC of 16 December 2008, repealed by Directive 2012/19/EU of 4 July 2012 with effect from 15 February 2014. Directive 2012/19/EU, the WEEE recast directive, must be implemented by 14 February 2014.

69. Directive 2006/66/EC of 6 September 2006 on batteries and accumulators and waste batteries and accumulators, last amended by Directive 2013/56/EU of 20 November 2013.

70. Regulation 1013/2006/EC of 14 June 2006 on shipments of waste, last amended by Regulation 255/2013/EU of 20 March 2013.

71. Directive 94/62/EC of 20 December 1994 on packaging and packaging waste, last amended by Directive 2013/2/EU of 7 February 2013.

72. Regulation 1005/2009/EC of 16 September 2009 on substances that deplete the ozone layer, last amended by Regulation 744/2010/EU of 18 August 2010.

73. Directive 2011/65/EU of 8 June 2011 on the restriction of the use of certain hazardous substances in electrical and electronic equipment (RoHS recast), last amended by Directive 2012/51/EU of 10 October 2012.

74. As compared to the 50 percent required for paper, metal, plastic, and glass under the Waste Framework Directive.

75. BVerwG, judgment of 28 June 2007, register number 7 C 5.07, marginal note 20.

76. BVerwG, judgment of 28 June 2007, register number 7 C 5.07, marginal note 22.

77. On imports of packaging into Germany see Enderle & Rehs, *Zwischen Pflicht und Chance—Verpackungsrecht für Importprodukte (Between Duty and Opportunity—Packaging Law for Imported Products)*, ABFALLR 2012, 285 *et seq.*

78. The requirements of the Environmental Liability Directive, as they relate to soil contamination, have been implemented in the BBodschG.

79. The relevant action and trigger values are laid down in the Federal Soil Protection and Contaminated Site Ordinance (Bundes-Bodenschutz und Altlastenverordnung).

80. The former owner escapes liability if he can demonstrate that he was unaware of contamination and that he was not negligent.

81. For example, in case of intentional undercapitalisation of a company holding contaminated sites.

82. This does not apply where the owner contributed to the soil contamination or enjoys benefits from the risky use of the site (e.g., receives lease payments).

83. Proposal for a Directive establishing a framework for the protection of soil and amending Directive 2004/35/EC, COM(2006) 232 final.

84. Germany has 8,481 conservation areas. BfN, Nature Conservation Areas in Germany, http://www.bfn.de/0308_nsg.html.

85. For example, the Bavarian Forest, the Wadden Sea, and the Harz Mountains.

86. On average, 230 people per square kilometer live in Germany (U.S.: 32 people per square kilometer).

87. For example, the Rhoen, the southeast of the island of Ruegen, and the Spree Forest.

88. As of December 2009, Germany has 7,409 protected landscape areas. BfN, Protected Landscape Areas in Germany, http://www.bfn.de/0308_nsg.html.

89. In the last 20 years, Germany designated 5,266 Natura 2000 sites on its territory. These sites cover 15.4 percent of the German land area and nearly equal the area of the state of West Virginia. Further, 45 percent of the German maritime area has been designated as Natura 2000 sites, nearly equaling the area of the state of Rhode Island. In order to reach the national quota of Natura 2000 areas Germany also designated sites in urban areas, which today lead to conflicts with urban development (for instance, the Stuttgart 21 project).

90. ECJ, Judgment of 7 September 2004, Case C-127/02 (*Cockle fishing*), marginal numbers 54 and 61.

91. The compensatory measures must be implemented before the first impairments of the project actually occur. Further, the project proponent must ensure that the compensatory measures are legally safeguarded, for example by purchasing the respective land parcels.

92. *See supra* note 4.

93. *See generally* Enderle & Thaysen, *Geht in NRW das Licht aus? (Do they turn off the light in North-Rhine Westfalia?)*, UPR 2012, 173.

94. These include onshore and offshore wind energy, biomass, biogas, geothermal energy, photovoltaic, and hydro power.

95. 513 of the 600 parliamentarians present voted in favour, 79 voted against and 8 abstained.

96. *See* http://www.bmu.de/themen/klima-energie/energiewende/fragen-und-ant worten/kernenergie/#c5.

97. *See also supra* section V.A.

98. B. Enderle, Is the Grass Greener? Hot Topics in European Environmental Law: Whose lawn is greener?—Germany's struggle with the EU Commission over environmental and climate change strategies, 41st Annual Conference on Environmental Law, Salt Lake City, Utah, American Bar Association, Mar. 22–24, 2012.

99. Printing matters of the German Parliament (Deutscher Bundestag) No. 17/6073, at 19.

100. Bundesnetzagentur, Federal Network Agency (see *supra* section I.A.5.a.iii).

101. *See* §§ 18 *et seq.* in printing matters of the German Parliament No. 17/6073, at 25.

102. *E.g.*, the Federal German Mining Act (Bundesberggesetz) of 13 August 1980, Federal Law Gazette (BGBl.) No. I 1980, 1310 as amended, and additional laws and ordinances on the federal and state level.

103. *Cf.* printing matters of the German Parliament No. 17/8133 of 14 December 2011; No. 17/9560 of 9 May 2012; No. 17/9034 of 21 March 2012.

104. See the website of the German Federal Ministry for the Environment on the most recent draft legislation: http://www.bmu.de/service/publikationen/downloads/details /artikel/regelungsvorschlaege-bmubmwi-zum-thema-fracking/?tx_ttnews%5Bback Pid%5D=2378.

105. And play a more and more important role in M&A transactions, B. Enderle, *Types and Transfer of German Mining Rights—"Rediscovered" Legal Instruments for New Energies and Modern Corporate Practice*, WORLD OF MINING 2012, at 110 *et seq.*; Enderle & Rehs, *Die Übertragung bergrechtlicher Rechtspositionen—Praxisprobleme beim Betrieb unterirdischer Gasspeicheranlagen (The Transfer of Mining Rights—Legal Issues in the Operation of Underground Gas Storages)*, NVwZ 6/2012, at 338 *et seq.*

106. Enderle, *supra* note 41.

107. On the legal framework see Enderle & Rehs, *Altes Recht für neue Energien—Das Bergrecht als rechtlicher Rahmen für "moderne" Energieinfrastruktur (Old Law for New Energies—Mining Laws as a Legal Framework for "Modern" Energy Infrastructure)*, EMW 2012/1, at 78 *et seq.*

108. Enderle, *supra* note 41.

109. BVerwG, judgment of 9 July 2008, register number 9 A 14.07 (Bad Oeynhausen), marginal note 57.

110. This includes (1) all natural occurring bird species, (2) species listed in Annex IV of the Habitats Directive, and (3) species listed in the German Federal Ordinance on Species Protection (Bundesartenschutzverordnung).

111. BVerwG, judgment of 9 July 2008, register number 9 A 14.07 (Bad Oeynhausen), marginal note 58.

112. Claims for damages caused to individual objects can also be based on civil liability rules contained, for example, in the Civil Code, the Federal Water Management Act, the Federal Mining Act, or the Federal Nuclear Energy Act.

113. This applies to plants mentioned in Annex of the UmweltHG, encompassing, for example, plants requiring a safety analysis as provided for in the Major Accidents Ordinance.

114. Bundesbodenschutzgesetz section V.C. (Soil).

115. Wasserhaushaltsgesetz ch. III. (Water).

116. 18th Federal Criminal Code Amendment (18. Strafrechtsänderungsgesetz) dated 28 March 1980, Federal Law Gazette (BGBl) I, at 373, put into force on 1 July 1980. Germany implemented Directive 2008/99/EC on the protection of the environment through criminal law into German law. Only minor amendments were necessary as the German criminal law did already fulfil most of the requirements of the directive.

117. Federal Criminal Code § 330 lit. a) contains an exception to this rule by sanctioning serious endangerment through emission of poisonous substances.

118. Federal Criminal Code ch. 29, "Offences against the environment." In aggravated cases of an environmental offence as laid down in chapter 29, the penalty constitutes imprisonment from six months to ten years.

119. The offenses relating to nuclear energy, radiation, and poisoning are laid down in chapter 28 of the Federal Criminal Code, "Offences causing a common danger."

120. Federal Criminal Code § 304.

121. In this case the government officials can be criminally liable as accessory or indirect perpetrator, *see* MICHAEL KLOEPFER & HANS-PETER VIERHAUS, UMWELTSTRAFRECHT (ENVIRONMENTAL CRIMINAL LAW) 43–44 (2d ed. 2002).

122. Higher Civil Court of Frankfurt, NJW 1987, 2753 (2756–57).

123. *Id.* at 2757.

124. Federal Supreme Court (Bundesgerichtshof, BGH), NJW 1992, 3247 (3249).

125. The states of Berlin and Brandenburg have a joint Higher Administrative Court located in Berlin.

126. Parties to such a court proceeding may still file a claim with the BVerfG. This claim, however, can be based on constitutional law only, for example, the claim can only be based on the misinterpretation of emission control regulations in case this misinterpretation affected the constitutional rights of the claimant.

127. See *infra* section XII, on action rights in environmental law cases.

128. The "Trianel"-ruling, ECJ, C -115/09, 12/05/2011 (BUND vs. Bezirksregierung Arnsberg) was only one in a series of decisions broadening environmental NGO's action rights across Europe.

CHAPTER 30

United Kingdom

OWEN LOMAS, DOUGLAS BRYDEN, AND CARL BOEUF

I. Introduction

This chapter provides a high-level overview of environment law in the United Kingdom (U.K.) and looks at key practical issues including environmental permitting, protection of land and water resources, nature conservation, environmental impact assessment, and waste and hazardous materials management. It also briefly discusses laws to control and respond to the effects of climate change.

U.K. environmental law has a long history, with the first formal attempts to control the polluting effects of the industrial revolution dating back to the 19th century. Common law torts such as nuisance have also provided an indirect route to environmental protection for a similar period. The current scope of U.K. environmental law is very broad and has expanded rapidly since the early 1990s, largely as a result of legislative and policy developments at the European Union (EU) level. Consequently, this is a heavily regulated area, with detailed, complex, and often overlapping regimes. Additionally, while health and safety and planning matters are generally regulated separately from environmental matters, there are a number of areas of common ground.

The U.K. government departments with primary responsibility for developing environmental policy and law are the Department for Environment, Food and Rural Affairs (Defra) and the Department of Energy and Climate Change (DECC). Additionally, the Department for Business, Innovation and Skills (BIS) takes the lead with respect to product-related environmental regulation. The Environment Agency (EA) is the regulator with primary responsibility for environmental law enforcement, although local authorities also carry out these functions for some (generally lower risk) activities.

The first part of this chapter, as for the other jurisdiction-specific chapters in this book, sets out U.K. environmental law in terms of the environmental media and activities to which it applies (air, water, land, waste management, etc.). However, it should be noted that the Environmental Permitting (England and Wales) Regulations 2010 (as amended) (EPR), which provide the regulatory framework concerning the control of environmentally impacting activities in England and Wales, provide for a single integrated environmental permit that seeks to regulate the permit holder's material environmental impacts across all environmental media and activities. Equivalent regimes exist in Scotland[1] and Northern Ireland.[2]

It should also be noted that the EU is increasingly moving toward a holistic "life cycle" approach to the environmental regulation of products (including packaging)—seeking to limit the environmental impacts of such products at each stage from design to disposal. For example, regimes such as the EU's Registration, Evaluation, Authorisation and Restriction of Chemicals (REACH) regulation[3] and recast Directive on the Restriction of the Use of Certain Hazardous Substances in Electrical and Electronic Equipment (RoHS)[4] restrict the use of certain substances in the manufacture of specified product types. Other laws govern issues such as the environmental impacts and energy efficiency of products prior to disposal. Additionally, EU-derived "producer responsibility" regimes exist, which require producers to take financial responsibility for the environmental impact of the products that they place on the market when those products become waste. In the U.K., there are separate EU-derived producer responsibility regimes with respect to waste packaging,[5] Electrical and Electronic Equipment (WEEE),[6] batteries[7] and motor vehicles,[8] for example.

It should finally be noted that there is some variation between the environmental laws of England, Scotland, Wales, and Northern Ireland. This chapter primarily deals with the laws of England and Wales, unless otherwise specified.

II. Air and Climate Change
A. Air Pollution Control

Emissions to air are primarily regulated through permits under the EPR. Such permits govern most gaseous emissions other than carbon dioxide. Carbon dioxide is regulated separately via greenhouse gas (GHG) emissions permits, which are discussed below. EPR permits contain emission limit values and other conditions based on the application of best available techniques (BAT).[9] Emissions must be monitored and reported against the emission limit values. Operating a regulated facility without a permit or breaching a permit condition is a criminal offense.[10] Conviction for the most serious offenses under the EPR may lead to an unlimited fine and imprisonment for up to five years.[11]

Additionally, enforcement of air pollution standards may also be undertaken by local authorities under the Environment Act 1995, which requires those authorities to review and assess compliance with the U.K. Air Quality Strategy (which consolidates European and international air pollution standards) in their area. If the standards are not being met, local authorities may designate air quality management areas and implement remedial action plans.

B. Climate Change

1. *EU-Derived Climate Change Legislation*

The EU's Emissions Trading Scheme (EU ETS)[12] is one of the measures introduced to help the EU meet its GHG emissions reduction target under the Kyoto Protocol. It is a cap-and-trade system that obliges participating installations to purchase allowances equal to their carbon dioxide emissions each year (one allowance represents one metric ton of carbon dioxide equivalent). Failure to surrender the requisite number of allowances at the end of a compliance year can lead to a fine for each metric ton of carbon dioxide. In addition, the operator must make up the shortfall in allowances during the next calendar year.

The EU ETS is presently in its third phase, which commenced on January 1, 2013, and runs until December 31, 2020. The key U.K. legislation implementing the EU ETS is the Greenhouse Gas Emissions Trading Scheme Regulations 2012.

Operators of U.K. installations that fall within the EU ETS must obtain a GHG emissions permit.[13] Installations required to participate in the scheme include those conducting energy activities, production and processing of ferrous metals (such as steel), mineral industries, and pulp and paper manufacture.

From the start of 2012, airline operators were required to participate in the scheme with respect to emissions from most commercial flights to or from EU airports. The perceived extraterritoriality of the EU ETS was challenged by the Air Transport Association of America in the U.K. and EU courts. The European Court of Justice held in December 2011 that the inclusion of international aviation emissions in the EU ETS was lawful. Following international pressure (including the passing of laws in the U.S. and China prohibiting national airlines from complying with the EU ETS), the EU decided in April 2013 to temporarily defer enforcement against aircraft operators in respect of international flights for 2012, pending progress within the International Civil Aviation Organisation (ICAO) general assembly. The EU's position remains that, in the event that a global market-based mechanism to reduce international aviation emissions is not reached within the ICAO, aircraft operators will be expected to surrender sufficient allowances in accordance with the EU ETS. Of note, at the time of writing, the ICAO has recently announced plans to develop, by 2016, a global market-based mechanism for international aviation emissions from 2020. The EU has responded by welcoming the plans and announcing that, in coordination with the EU member states, it will assess the ICAO decision in more detail before deciding on its next steps with respect to the EU ETS.

2. *U.K. Climate Change Legislation*

The U.K. has a legally binding target to reduce its GHG emissions by 80 percent below the 1990 baseline by 2050.[14] The following schemes are fundamental to the government's strategy for achieving this.

3. Carbon Reduction Commitment Energy Efficiency Scheme (CRC)

The CRC[15] is a mandatory scheme aimed at improving energy efficiency and cutting carbon emissions in medium to large public and private sector organizations. Special rules apply to emissions already covered by the EU ETS[16] or Climate Change Agreements (see below) to reduce double accounting. Organizations (including groups of companies) qualify as a CRC participant based on their half-hourly electricity usage. Participants must monitor their energy use and purchase allowances for each metric ton of carbon dioxide they emit. The CRC Energy Efficiency Scheme Order 2013, which came into force on May 20, 2013, simplifies this complex scheme. Key changes included in the 2013 order include a simplification of the qualification rules, a reduction in the number of fuels covered, more structured sales of allowances, and, importantly for corporate transactions, simplified rules for large acquisitions and disposals, and greater flexibility for disaggregation. The government will review the effectiveness of the CRC (again) in 2016. This review is expected to consider whether the CRC remains the appropriate policy to meet industrial energy efficiency and carbon reduction objectives, and is also expected to consider alternative approaches that could achieve the same objectives.

4. The Climate Change Levy (CCL)

CCL[17] is a tax on the supply of specified energy products (including electricity, natural gas, liquid petroleum gas, coal, lignite, and coke) for use by industry, commerce, and the public sector. The aim of the CCL is to encourage businesses to become more energy efficient and reduce their GHG emissions, consequently electricity generated from renewable energy sources is exempt. Climate Change Agreements (CCA) provide a voluntary mechanism for energy-intensive businesses to receive a significant discount from the CCL in return for agreement holders meeting energy efficiency targets. Until April 1, 2013, fuels used in the production of electricity (for example, gas or coal) were exempt from CCL. However, since that date, such fuels have been subject to "carbon price support rates of CCL" in line with the U.K.'s carbon price floor.

5. Renewables Obligation

The Renewables Obligation Order 2009 (as amended) requires electricity suppliers to source an increasing proportion of their electricity from eligible renewable sources each year. Suppliers must either demonstrate compliance to the authority, Ofgem,[18] by submitting renewable obligation certificates (ROCs) obtained from eligible renewable energy generators or pay a "buy-out price" to cover the shortfall.

6. Renewable Transport Fuel Obligations

The Renewable Transport Fuel Obligations Order 2007 requires certain suppliers of fossil fuels to ensure that a percentage of the fuel that they supply each year is a renewable transport fuel (RTF) such as bioethanol or biodiesel. Compliance is demonstrated by accumulating sufficient RTF certificates from the Renewable Fuels Agency to cover the obligation. RTF certificates can be traded and if a supplier does not meet its obligation for a compliance period, it may either buy RTF certificates from the market or pay a "buy-out price" to cover the shortfall.

7. *Feed-in Tariffs (FITS)*

FITs, which came into force on April 1, 2010, under powers derived from the Energy Act 2008, are financial incentives encouraging deployment of small-scale (less than 5MW), low-carbon electricity generation in the U.K. and are complementary to ROCs. The scheme is implemented by a combination of statutory instruments and modifications to the Standard Licence Conditions of Electricity Supply Licences.[19] Under this scheme, operators of qualifying installations are guaranteed a specified tariff for each kilowatt hour they generate. In addition, operators may opt either to receive a fixed export tariff or to sell their electricity on the open market. As with other European jurisdictions, the U.K.'s FITs are the subject of ongoing government review.

8. *Mandatory GHG Reporting*

U.K. companies are under a variety of mandatory reporting requirements, the majority of which are contained in the Companies Act 2006 (as amended). The Companies Act 2006 (Strategic Report and Directors' Report) Regulations 2013 has recently brought about two significant changes to mandatory reporting requirements for financial years ending on or after 30 September 2013. First, all companies (other than exempt companies) must produce a stand-alone "strategic report" in addition to the standard directors' report. This requirement is, in the main, a structural change, as opposed to a change to the substantive requirements: previously, companies were obliged to prepare a "business review" within the directors' report. Strategic reports must include an analysis of the company's business using key performance indicators. In addition, quoted companies must include information about the impact of the company's business on the environment and social, community, and human rights issues. Second, quoted companies must, for the first time, report on the annual amount of GHG emissions for which the company is responsible, including from the combustion of fuel and the operation of any facility. The government will, following a review of the first two years of GHG emissions reporting, take a further decision in 2016 on whether to extend the reporting requirement to large companies.

9. *Renewable Heat Incentive (RHI)*

The RHI, billed by the U.K. government as the world's first long-term financial support program for renewable heat, pays participants that generate and use renewable energy to heat their buildings. The aim of the RHI is to encourage the supply of low-carbon heat. The RHI launched for the nondomestic sector in November 2011 and opened to the domestic sector in spring 2014. Eligible technologies include solar thermal, ground source heat pumps, onsite biogas combustion, and deep geothermal. Support rates vary depending on the technology installed.

III.   Water

The body of EU and U.K. law governing water use and quality is extensive. In the interests of space, therefore, this chapter will deal predominantly with the laws governing inland and coastal water pollution and water abstraction. Water and groundwater discharges are permitted via the EPR. It is a criminal offense to cause or knowingly permit any polluting matter to enter controlled waters except and to the extent authorized by an EPR permit.[20] In addition to its numerous powers available pursuant to the EPR, where water pollution has occurred, or is likely to occur, the EA may require the polluter to take steps to clean up or prevent the pollution by issuing a works notice under section 161A of the Water Resources Act 1991 (WRA). The contaminated land regime and the Environmental Damage (Prevention and Remediation) Regulations 2009 (EDR) are also relevant (see section V for a more detailed discussion of these regimes).

The WRA governs water abstraction and impounding activities[21] and it is a criminal offense to abstract water without a license (subject to certain exemptions).[22] Discharges to public sewers are governed by the Water Industry Act 1991, which requires occupiers of trade premises to obtain a trade effluent consent from the relevant sewerage undertaker.[23] Failure to obtain such a consent is a violation of that statute.[24]

In terms of offshore activities, a marine license under the Marine and Coastal Access Act 2009 is required for many activities involving the deposit or removal of a structure or object below the mean high water springs mark or in any tidal river to the extent of the tidal influence.[25] Noncompliance may constitute an offense.[26]

IV.   Handling, Treatment, Transportation, and Disposal of Chemicals and Hazardous Materials

In addition to the more specific regimes outlined below, there is an extensive body of health and safety law that governs activities in the workplace and beyond. The primary legislation is the Health and Safety at Work etc. Act 1974 (HASAWA), which sets out the general duties that employers owe to employees and members of the public, and employees have to themselves and to each other. HASAWA is then supplemented by extensive regulation, approved codes of practice, and guidance. For example, the Control of Substances Hazardous to Health Regulations 2002 (as amended) (COSHH) require employers to carry out suitable and sufficient assessments of the risk to their workforce, contractors, visitors, and customers from each hazardous substance in the workplace, and to prevent or adequately control those risks.[27] Failure to comply with these obligations, as with obligations under health and safety regulations more generally, may result in criminal liabilities.[28]

EU Directive 96/82/EC on the control of major accident hazards involving dangerous substances (Seveso II Directive) is intended to prevent major accidents caused by dangerous substances and to limit their consequences.[29] The land use planning provisions of the Seveso II Directive are implemented in the U.K. via the Planning (Hazardous Substances) Act 1990 and Planning (Hazardous Substances) Regulations 1992. Under these provisions, operators of sites storing or using certain specified hazardous substances at or above certain controlled quantities require consent from the Hazardous Substances Authority (usually the local planning authority). The operational requirements of the Seveso II Directive are implemented via the Control of Major Accident Hazards Regulations 1999 (COMAH). The COMAH regulations impose a general duty on operators to prevent accidents and mitigate their effect on human health and the environment.[30]

The EU's Classification, Labeling and Packaging of Substances and Mixtures (CLP) Regulation (No 1272/2008) implements across the EU the globally harmonized system on the classification and labeling of chemicals. CLP also places obligations on chemical suppliers. Failure to comply with these obligations may result in criminal liability.[31] The U.K. is currently in a transitional phase between the Chemicals (Hazard Information and Packaging for Supply) Regulations 2009 (CHIP) and the CLP Regulation. The transitional period ran to December 1, 2010, for substances, and continues until June 1, 2015, for mixtures (preparations).

The EU REACH regulation[32] governs the registration, evaluation, authorization, and restriction[33] of chemicals in the EU. It came into force on June 1, 2007, and replaced a number of European directives and regulations with a single system.[34] REACH applies to chemical substances, preparations, and articles that are manufactured in or imported into the EU in quantities of one metric ton or more per year. Manufacturers, importers, distributors, and professional users that market or use chemicals (on their own, in mixtures, and in some cases in products) covered by REACH must ensure, where necessary, that those chemicals are registered with the European Chemicals Agency (ECHA). Registration requires the provision of information on the environmental and human health properties of the chemical substance and an assessment to ensure that the risks arising from its use are properly managed. Some substances that are deemed particularly harmful to human health or the environment require authorization for use or are banned outright. REACH also places specific notification, communication, and other obligations on producers, manufacturers, and importers. Failure to comply with these obligations may result in criminal liability.[35]

The Restriction of the Use of Certain Hazardous Substances in Electrical and Electronic Equipment Regulations 2012 (RoHS Regulations) implement

Directive 2011/65/EU on the restriction of the use of certain hazardous substances in electrical and electronic equipment (recast) (recast RoHS Directive). The recast RoHS Directive[36] seeks to reduce the risks posed by hazardous substances in electrical and electronic equipment (EEE) to health and the environment and extends the categories of EEE subject to restrictions under the original RoHS Directive[37] (subject to transitional provisions and certain exemptions). It is closely related to the WEEE Directive,[38] which requires producers to take financial responsibility for the environmental impact of the EEE that they place on the market, specifically when those products become waste. The RoHS Regulations ban the placing in the EU market of new EEE containing lead, cadmium, mercury, hexavalent chromium, polybrominated biphenyl, and polybrominated diphenyl ether flame retardants in amounts in excess of defined maximum concentration values. Failure to comply with these obligations may result in criminal liability. In addition, under the RoHS Regulations, manufacturers who have reason to believe that EEE that they have placed on the market is not in conformity with the requirements of the RoHS Regulations have an obligation to take corrective measures to bring that EEE into conformity, including, where appropriate to withdraw it or recall it, and to immediately inform the competent national authorities of the noncompliance.

The Control of Asbestos Regulations 2012 (CAR) impose a positive duty on duty holders (including owners, landlords, tenants, and management companies who control premises) to manage the risks from existing asbestos in nondomestic premises.[39] Failure to comply with these obligations may result in criminal liability. Additionally, employees who suffer illnesses caused by the inhalation of asbestos fibers in the course of their employment may also bring personal injury claims against past or current employers. Damages in respect of a successful claim may be a material liability. In a landmark decision in 2012, the court of appeal found a parent company directly liable in negligence for its failure to protect an employee of its subsidiary from the risks of asbestos. This judgment highlights that, in certain circumstances, parent companies, by way of their superior knowledge of the nature and management of health and safety risks, may assume a duty of care for a subsidiary's employees. The importation, supply, and use of all forms of asbestos is prohibited under REACH (subject to certain exemptions).[40]

In addition, certain categories of products (for example, toys, cosmetics, and food-contact materials) are subject to a range of specific regulatory restrictions concerning the types and concentrations of substances they may contain.

V.   Waste and Site Remediation
A.   Site Remediation

Part IIA of the Environmental Protection Act 1990 (EPA) sets out the U.K.'s statutory contaminated land regime (as well as the U.K.'s statutory nuisance and overarching waste regimes). It provides a risk-based approach to the identification and remediation of land where contamination poses an unacceptable risk to human health or the environment (including controlled waters). The regime is jointly regulated by local authorities and the EA (or in Scotland, the Scottish Environmental Protection Agency (SEPA)). That said, local authorities will, in the first instance, take the lead role.

Under the regime, local authorities are required to inspect their areas of responsibility to identify any land that should be classified as contaminated and, once identified, specify how it should be remediated. Revised statutory guidance to assist English local authorities in carrying out this function entered into force in April 2012.[41] The starting point under the new guidance is that land should not be identified as contaminated unless there is good reason to consider otherwise.

Once land has been identified as being contaminated, the local authority (or EA, in the case of "special sites") must then consider what, if anything, is to be done by way of remediation to reduce the associated risks to acceptable levels. In reaching its decision, the regulator must take into account what is reasonable, taking into account the likely costs involved and the seriousness of the harm. If the regulator considers that action is required, it will serve a remediation notice. Failure to comply with a remediation notice without reasonable excuse is a criminal offense.[42]

The regime places primary liability on those who caused or knowingly permitted the presence or continued presence of the substances concerned. If no such persons are found, liability may, in very limited circumstances, attach to the current owner or occupier of the site. It should be noted, however, that owners and occupiers may be subject to liability in their capacity as "knowing permitters" of the presence or continued presence of the substances that have led to actual or threatened contamination, depending on the factual circumstances. This means that a knowing permitter can in some circumstances be found liable for substances in the ground before 1990 (when the contaminated land regime entered into force) and/or before they took over operations at the site.

It is important to note that if contamination is caused by an activity that is regulated by a permit under the EPR, the contaminated land regime will not apply and this will instead be a breach under the EPR. Additionally, at the end of the term of an EPR permit, the operator will be required to return the site to a satisfactory state (at least to the state it was in before operations began). These conditions are potentially more stringent than those under the contaminated land regime whereby remediation is only required where necessary to reduce the risks associated with the presence of substances to acceptable levels. There is also considerable overlap between the contaminated land regime and the WRA.

Additionally, the EDR,[43] which transpose the EU's Environmental Liability Directive into U.K. law, are also relevant. The EDR establish a regime for the prevention and remediation of certain specified types of environmental damage (serious damage to surface or groundwater, land contamination resulting in significant risk to human health, and serious damage to certain protected habitats, species, or sites). However, the EDR are of more limited application than the contaminated land regime because they apply only in respect of damage that has occurred since the regulations entered into force in 2009. For certain more heavily regulated industrial activities liability under EDR is strict but, for all other activities that cause or threaten environmental damage, liability is fault-based.

Under the EDR, if an operator's activities threaten to cause (or have caused) environmental damage, the operator must take all practicable steps to prevent that damage (or further damage) from occurring and, unless the threat has been eliminated, inform the appropriate authority.

The EDR give the competent authorities (generally the EA or local authority) powers to serve prevention and remediation notices. Remediation requirements are broad and may include primary remediation to restore the damage; complementary remediation to compensate where primary remediation does not fully restore the damage; and compensatory remediation for the loss of natural resources while the damage is restored. In some circumstances, the authorities may carry out work themselves and recover the costs of doing so from the relevant operator.

In addition, the U.K.'s detailed planning regime is relevant—if a planning application is made to develop a contaminated land site, the planning authority may impose conditions to the effect that remediation must be carried out predevelopment. This is the most common route to contaminated land cleanup in the U.K.

There are also U.K. laws protecting amenity values and landscapes. Sites may be designated as national parks or areas of outstanding natural beauty (AONB) under the National Parks and Access to the Countryside Act 1949 and Countryside and Rights of Way Act 2000, for example. National parks are areas protected because of their beautiful countryside, wildlife, and cultural heritage. AONBs are areas of high scenic quality that have statutory protection from development in order to conserve and enhance their natural beauty.

B.   Waste

Waste legislation in England and Wales is extensive. The definition of "waste" is that provided in the EU Waste Framework Directive[44] (WFD). The WFD defines waste to include any substance or object that the holder discards, intends to discard, or is required to discard. However, difficulties with the definition often arise, and in August 2012 the U.K. government published new guidance on the legal definition of waste and its application.[45]

The EPA imposes a general statutory duty of care on all those who produce, import, carry, hold, treat, or dispose of "controlled waste" (commercial, industrial, or household waste) to take all reasonable steps to ensure that waste is managed properly.[46] Additionally, an EPR[47] permit is required for most waste operations involving the treatment, disposal, recovery, or transfer of controlled waste (subject to certain exemptions for some low risk waste-handling operations).

Additional requirements apply in relation to hazardous waste under the Hazardous Waste (England and Wales) Regulations 2005. These include requirements to notify the EA of premises where hazardous waste is produced and to keep records. The List of Wastes (England) Regulations 2005 set out wastes that are to be considered hazardous.

The 2008 revision to the WFD, which sets requirements for the collection, transport, recovery, and disposal of waste, have been implemented in England and Wales through the Waste (England and Wales) Regulations 2011 (WR). The WR require businesses to apply the waste management hierarchy, which ranks waste management options according to what is best for the environment, namely: prevention; reuse; recycling; other recovery; and disposal, when transferring waste and to include a declaration of compliance on their waste transfer note or consignment note. The regulations also require businesses collecting, transporting, or receiving waste paper, metal, plastic, or glass to ensure separate collection from January 1, 2015.

Additionally, as noted in the introduction to this chapter, the EU is increasingly moving toward a holistic "life cycle" approach to the environmental regulation of products (including packaging). This approach seeks to limit the environmental impacts of such products at each stage from design through disposal. With respect to waste, EU-derived "producer responsibility" regimes exist, which require producers to take financial responsibility for the environmental impact of the products that they place on the market, specifically when those products become waste. They seek to reduce the amount of such waste going to landfills by encouraging separate collection and subsequent treatment, reuse, recovery, recycling, and environmentally sound disposal. In the U.K., there are separate EU-derived producer responsibility regimes with respect to waste: (1) packaging, (2) EEE, (3) batteries, and (4) end-of-life (scrap) motor vehicles. More information on the U.K.'s waste packaging EEE regimes is provided below.

The U.K.'s packaging waste regime was introduced in 1997[48] to implement the EU's packaging waste directive.[49] It places a legal obligation on "producers" making or using packaging (raw materials manufacturers, converters, packer/fillers, and sellers) to ensure that a proportion of the packaging they place on the market is recovered and recycled. Annual packaging recycling and recovery targets apply to different packaging materials (e.g., paper/card, aluminum, and glass). Producers demonstrate compliance by either (1) joining an approved compliance scheme, which will take on the producer's packaging waste obligations, calculate its packaging waste obligation (based on the volume of packaging it handles), and purchase Packaging Waste Recovery Notes (PRNs) on its behalf; or (2) calculating their own packaging waste obligation and purchasing sufficient PRNs to offset this.

The original WEEE Directive[50] was transposed into U.K. law by the Waste Electrical and Electronic Equipment Regulations 2006 (as amended). It covered a wide range of products intended for household and/or commercial use that are dependent on electrical currents or electromagnetic fields to work properly. Obligations were imposed on "producers" (manu-facturers, rebranders, or importers) of ten categories of new EEE to regis-ter with an approved producer compliance scheme (which will collect, treat, and recycle the producer's WEEE on its behalf). Additional obliga-tions fell on retailers of EEE. The WEEE Directive was recently recast, and in particular, the WEEE Directive 2012 extends the scope of WEEE to all EEE covered from August 2018 and imposes new higher recovery targets on member states. The recast directive also introduces a new collection obligation on certain retailers of EEE to collect very small household WEEE free of charge.

VI.   Emergency Response

As already noted, the EPR[51] provide the main U.K. regulatory framework concerning the permitting of environmentally impacting activities (including waste management, pollution prevention and control, water discharges, groundwater authorizations, and radioactive substances). Modern EPR per-mits require facilities to have written accident management plans in place. If an accident or incident causes damage to the environment, or risks doing so, operators must immediately implement the accident management plan, report the accident to the EA without delay, and take action to minimize the environmental consequences.

It is a criminal offense under EPR to operate a regulated facility without a permit, cause or knowingly permit a water discharge activity or ground-water activity without a permit, or fail to comply with a permit or an enforce-ment related notice. However, the EPR provide a defense where it can be shown that the breach resulted from acts taken in an emergency in order to avoid danger to human health, and that the defendant took all reasonably practicable steps to minimize pollution and provided a description of the events to the EA as soon as reasonably practicable.

Alongside the EPR, the EDR[52] apply in cases of serious environmental damage to surface water, groundwater, land, sites of scientific interest, pro-tected species, and natural håbitats. For further information on the EDR, see section V, above.

Additionally, as noted in section IV above, COMAH[53] applies to the man-ufacture, storage, or use of hazardous substances (such as chlorine, liquefied petroleum gas, and explosives) above a specified quantity and operators must obtain consent to carry out such activities. COMAH aims to prevent and limit the environmental and human health consequences of major acci-dents arising from these regulated activities. The regulations impose a gen-eral duty on operators to take all measures necessary to prevent such accidents and mitigate their effect on human health and the environment.

In addition to the more specific regimes outlined above, environmental obligations and liability for accidents and emergency situations may, depend-ing on the circumstances, arise under more general environmental law and health and safety law.

VII. Natural Resource Management and Protection

U.K. laws with respect to natural resources management and protection are voluminous and a detailed discussion of them is beyond the scope of this chapter. Instead, we focus on some of the key regimes relating to minerals extraction and forestry management.

A. Mineral Extraction

Most forms of development in the U.K., including mineral[54] extraction and related activities, require planning permission before development can take place. The majority of land use planning decisions are made at a local level by local planning authorities in accordance with local plans.[55] A local authority with responsibility for mineral planning, including deciding planning applications, is called a Mineral Planning Authority (MPA). The Department for Communities and Local Government (DCLG) has responsibility for the operation of the system in England.[56]

Development proposals will be screened by MPAs to identify whether an environmental impact assessment is required.[57] Even if an environmental impact assessment is not required, environmental and health impacts (including in relation to dust, off-site noise, and traffic, for example) may be addressed through the conditions of planning permission. Conditions may also be imposed in respect of site restoration and aftercare once operations have ceased. MPAs are responsible for ensuring operators comply with these conditions.

Mineral extraction and related activities generally also require an EPR permit before operations can begin. COMAH may also be relevant, as will a wide range of other operational health and safety laws. Additional licenses, permits, permissions, and/or authorizations may be required before exploration, extraction, and exploitation can commence; this will be dependent upon the type of mineral or natural resource being exploited and its location and method of extraction.

B. Forestry Management

Approximately one-third of U.K. woodland is publicly owned, the majority of it managed by the Forestry Commission and, in Northern Ireland, the Forest Service. The remaining two-thirds is privately owned. Of note, at around 13 percent, the U.K.'s forest cover is among the lowest of any country in Europe.[58]

In terms of the applicable legislative regime, the Forestry Act 1967 (FA) places general duties on the Forestry Commission to promote the interests of forestry, the development of afforestation, and the production and supply of timber and other forest products in Great Britain.[59] The FA also gives the Forestry Commission powers to regulate tree felling (a felling license will be required in certain circumstances). Alongside the FA, the Plant Health Act 1967 empowers the Forestry Commission to make orders to prevent the introduction and spread of timber pests and diseases. Planning laws and the environmental impact assessment (EIA) regulations may also be relevant where development is proposed on a woodland site. Operational health and safety legislation will also be relevant for most commercial forestry activities.

In addition, the EU Timber Regulation[60] prohibits, from March 2013, the placing on the EU market for the first time of illegally harvested timber and related timber products. The Timber Regulation also requires that EU traders who place timber products on the EU market for the first time exercise due diligence to minimize the risk of placing illegally harvested timber and related timber products on the EU market. Additionally, to facilitate the traceability of timber products, traders are obliged to keep records of what timber products have been bought, and from whom, and where applicable, to whom they were sold.

The United Kingdom Forestry Standard (UKFS) is the Forestry Commission's reference standard for sustainable forest management in the U.K. The UKFS and supporting guidelines, which apply to all U.K. forests and woodlands, set out the approach of the U.K. governments to sustainable forest management. Meeting the requirements of the UKFS helps forest and woodland owners, managers, and others to demonstrate that forestry operations and activities are both legal and sustainable. Separate from the UKFS, a number of voluntary national and international assurance schemes provide independent assurance that timber and products bearing their labels, and the forests from which that timber and products are derived, have been responsibly managed.[61]

VIII.   Natural Resource Damages

In addition to potential liability under the contaminated land regime, EPR and WRA (discussed above), in cases of serious environmental damage that has occurred since the EDR[62] entered into force in 2009, operators may be liable for remediation under those regulations. This could include undertaking primary remediation to restore the damage, complementary remediation to compensate where primary remediation does not fully restore the damage, and compensatory remediation for the loss of natural resources while the damage is restored.

Further protection may also be available via the EPA's statutory nuisance regime.[63] Statutory nuisance provides a cost-effective remedy for dealing with problems causing unacceptable risk to human health or harm to amenity. Under this regime (in contrast to traditional private nuisance), the affected party does not need to have property rights impacted by the nuisance in order to bring proceedings. The regulatory authority may serve an abatement notice on the party causing the nuisance or the affected party can apply to the magistrates' court for a nuisance order requiring that it be abated or prevented. The magistrates' court can also make a compensation order to compensate any person who has suffered personal injury, damage, or loss as a result of the statutory nuisance offense. The compensation order must not exceed £5,000 and the amount is taken into account in calculating any damages award in civil nuisance or negligence proceedings. The complainant may also be entitled to its reasonable costs in bringing the proceedings.

If the affected party has property rights that are impacted by nuisance it may be able to bring proceedings in private nuisance. Remedies for private nuisance include damages and/or injunctive relief. Compensation is for the interference with the claimant's property rights, rather than any personal injury. The complainant may also be entitled to its reasonable costs in bringing the proceedings.

Public nuisance may also be relevant where an act that endangers the life, health, property, morals, or comfort of the public or obstructs the public in the exercise or enjoyment of rights common to all and the statutory nuisance regime is not applicable. Public nuisance allows the claimant to recover damages for personal injury, as well as damage to property rights (although the affected party does not need to have property rights impacted by the nuisance in order to bring proceedings). The complainant may also be entitled to its reasonable costs in bringing the proceedings.

IX. Protected Species

In addition to the general protection offered under the EPA, the EPR,[64] and planning regimes, there are numerous laws protecting flora and fauna in the U.K. Some are species-specific (such as those protecting badgers), while others have more general application, such as the EDR.[65] The EU Natura 2000 program, which implements the Habitats[66] and Birds[67] Directives at EU level, has resulted in the designations of Special Areas of Conservation (habitat specific) and Special Protection Areas (bird specific) in the U.K. Most Natura 2000 sites in the U.K. are also protected as Sites of Special Scientific Interest (SSSI) under the Wildlife and Countryside Act 1981 (as amended).

The Habitats and Birds Directives are transposed into U.K. law through the Conservation of Habitats and Species Regulations 2010. The directives are also implemented offshore (beyond 12 nautical miles) by virtue of the Offshore Marine Conservation (Natural Habitats, &c.) Regulations 2007 (as amended). They protect flora and fauna by requiring plans or projects in the designated areas to undergo an appropriate assessment for any adverse effects. In practice this obligation is discharged through the EIA process.

Flora, fauna, and habitats protected under both the Natura 2000 and SSSI regimes are afforded specific protection under the EDR.[68] As noted above, in cases of serious environmental damage to protected areas, operators may be liable for remediation, including undertaking primary remediation to restore the damage, complementary remediation to compensate where primary remediation does not fully restore the damage, and compensatory remediation for the loss of natural resources while the damage is restored.

In addition to national nature reserves, the national conservation agencies are responsible for enforcing the rules that protect other protected sites, such as SSSIs. Activity that is adverse to the flora and fauna protected by an SSSI may be prohibited or strictly regulated pursuant to the Wildlife and Countryside Act 1981 (as amended).

Additionally, in order to protect native biodiversity more generally, there are controls to prevent the spread of certain nonnative species of plants and animals. For example, Japanese knotweed is one of the most common and problematic nonnative species in the U.K. and, where present on a site, the owner or occupier is under a duty to prevent its escape onto adjoining land.[69]

X. Environmental Review and Decision Making
A. Environmental Review

Environmental assessment in England is largely governed by the Town and Country Planning (Environmental Impact Assessment) Regulations 2011 (EIAR), which implement the EU's Environmental Impact Assessment Directive. There are separate, parallel regimes that apply to projects falling outside the Town and Country Planning regime, such as those that apply to projects affecting marine areas and harbor works. Under the EIAR, an environmental assessment must be undertaken for certain development proposals specified in schedules 1 and 2 of the EIAR before planning permission is granted. For schedule 1 projects (those deemed to have a significant environmental impact, such as oil refineries, power stations, and motorways) an EIA is mandatory. For schedule 2 projects (such as certain industrial, agricultural, and mining activities), an EIA is necessary only when significant environmental effects are likely to occur due to factors such as their nature, size, or location. It is important to note that an EIA is not a license for development. Rather, it is merely a procedural requirement of the development consent process, albeit an important one). Operators may need to apply separately for operational EPR[70] permits. In October 2012, the European Commission adopted a proposal for a significant amendment to the EIA Directive. The proposed amendment has only recently commenced the European legislative process and it is unclear when, and in what form, any amendment may enter into force.

The strategic environmental assessment (SEA) of plans and projects is governed in England by the Environmental Assessment of Plans and Programmes Regulations 2004. These regulations implement the EU's Strategic Environmental Assessment Directive. The SEA is intended to increase the consideration of environmental issues during decision making related to strategic documents such as plans, programs, and strategies. The SEA identifies the significant environmental effects that are likely to result from the implementation of the plan or alternative approaches to the plan.

B. Environmental Permitting

The EPR[71] implement the Industrial Emissions Directive (IED)[72] into law in England and Wales (different provisions apply in Scotland and Northern

Ireland). The IED consolidated and replaced seven previous EU directives on pollution from industrial installations (including the IPPC Directive[73]) and was required to be implemented by the member states by 7 January 2013.[74] At the time of writing, there is a complex transitional phase from the provisions of the old regime to that of the IED. Transitional provisions for existing installations include key milestones at January 7, 2014 (for installations previously covered by the IPPC Directive), July 7, 2015 (for regulated installations not previously covered by IPPC and not qualifying as large combustion plants), and January 1, 2016 (for large combustions plants). However, the new rules apply to all new installations on or after January 8, 2013.

The EPR provide a single permitting framework integrating waste management licensing, pollution prevention and control, water discharge consenting, groundwater authorizations, and radioactive substances regulation.

Under the EPR, permits are required for a wide range of business and commercial activities, from energy production through to intensive pig and poultry farming. Depending on the activities undertaken at the regulated facility, the EPR permit will include specific conditions with respect to issues such as

- raw material and energy use
- how the site operates and the technology used
- emissions to air, water, and land
- how any waste produced is managed
- accident prevention

Operators are also obliged to operate their facilities using BAT, that is, the most cost-effective way, or ways, to prevent or minimize negative environmental impacts.

C. Decision Making

In England and Wales, the EA currently[75] has primary responsibility for environmental law enforcement and awarding of EPR[76] permits (local equivalents exist in Scotland and Northern Ireland). There is also a degree of overlap with other regulators such as local authorities and the Health and Safety Executive (HSE). Local authorities are responsible for the lower-tier facilities under the EPR and also have primary responsibility for the contaminated land regime. They are also responsible for local development control and air quality management.

The HSE is primarily responsible for health and safety law enforcement, but it also regulates COMAH sites and has responsibility for REACH and nuclear matters. The National Measurement Office Enforcement Authority is responsible for enforcement of RoHS and regulations on batteries and accumulators,[77] energy-related products,[78] and energy labeling.[79] Natural England, Scottish National Heritage, and the Countryside Council for Wales[80] have responsibility for biodiversity, species and habitats conservation, and general nature conservation.

Additionally, the Marine Management Organisation has responsibility for U.K. marine licensing and conservation (among other things).

The EA has adopted an enforcement and prosecution policy and supporting guidance to help it decide when and what type of enforcement action is necessary.[81] The HSE has a similar enforcement policy.[82] These documents set out the factors that will be taken into account when making enforcement decisions. The regulator will examine incidents on a case-by-case basis and use sanctions in a manner that is appropriate to the offense. If an operator is not complying with the law the EA will generally provide advice and guidance to help it do so. Where appropriate, the EA will agree to solutions and timescales for making any improvements with the operator. However, for significant, persistent, and/or recurring breaches, enforcement action is likely. Enforcement action (specifically the imposition of a sanction) can normally be appealed either through the criminal court process or as a result of specific appeal provisions. Once all other appeal avenues have been exhausted, the lawfulness of administrative decisions may in certain circumstances be challenged by judicial review.

XI.   Transboundary Pollution

Transboundary air pollution has been an issue of U.K. and international concern over the last 40 years, especially since the identification of the problems caused by acid rain in the 1970s. More recently identified transboundary air pollution problems include eutrophication and ground-level ozone. In addition to the large body of EU law applicable to transboundary pollution that has been implemented by the U.K., some of the key international environmental treaties to which the U.K. is a direct party include

- Gothenburg Protocol to Abate Acidification, Eutrophication and Ground-level Ozone (1998)
- Aarhus Protocol on Persistent Organic Pollutants (POPs) (1998)
- Kyoto Protocol to the United Nations Framework Convention on Climate Change (1997)
- Geneva Protocol concerning the Control of Emissions of Volatile Organic Compounds or their Transboundary Fluxes (1991)
- Montreal Protocol on Substances That Deplete the Ozone Layer (1987)
- Basel Convention on the Control of Transboundary Movements of Hazardous Wastes and Their Disposal (1989)
- Convention on Long-range Transboundary Air Pollution (1979)

Additionally, the U.K.'s Climate Change Act 2008 introduced a long-term, legally binding framework to help tackle the dangers of climate change. For example, the Act introduced a legally binding target of at least an 80 percent cut in GHG emissions against a 1990 baseline by 2050, to be achieved through action in the U.K. and abroad.

XII. Civil and Criminal Enforcement and Penalties
A. Civil Action

Civil claims may be brought for nuisance (including statutory, private, and public nuisance), trespass, or breach of statutory duty. The usual remedy is injunction, although the courts also have discretion to grant damages where this is considered more appropriate. The question of which remedies are available to those affected, and the defenses or grounds of appeal available to an operator who finds itself on the receiving end of proceedings, will be a question of the individual facts and circumstances in each case.

An action for statutory nuisance under the EPA[83] can be brought by a local authority or a person affected by that nuisance. Where a statutory nuisance has been determined, local authorities must serve an abatement notice on the person responsible for the nuisance (or, where they cannot be found, the owner or occupier of the premises). Local authorities have a general duty to investigate complaints of statutory nuisance from people living in their areas[84] and, where satisfied that a statutory nuisance exists or is likely to occur, serve an abatement notice.[85] If a local authority fails to investigate, a person aggrieved by the statutory nuisance can apply to the magistrates' court to make an order abating the nuisance.[86] Failure to comply with an abatement notice or order is an offense.[87]

An action in private nuisance may be brought by a person who (generally) has an exclusive right to possession of land where an unlawful interference with that person's use and enjoyment of that land has occurred. In 2012, the court of appeal considered the relationship between EPR[88] permit compliance and private nuisance.[89] In doing so, the court confirmed that it is not a defense to nuisance proceedings to show that the activities giving rise to the nuisance were carried out in accordance with an EPR permit. In addition, in 2014, the Supreme Court ruled on a landmark case concerning the relationship between common law nuisance and the U.K.'s statutory planning regime. In particular, the Supreme Court concluded that planning permission should not deprive a property owner of the right to object to what could otherwise be a nuisance.

Public nuisance provides a private right of action where an unlawful act or omission endangers or interferes with the lives, comfort, property, or common rights of the public. In some circumstances a public nuisance may also be a criminal offense.

Additionally, contractual claims may follow a breach of environmental law if it is also a breach of an environmental warranty or it triggers an indemnity.

B. Enforcement and Penalty Provisions of Environmental Statutes

Generally, breach of environmental law will be a criminal offense and material incidents will be investigated accordingly. The authorities have wide powers under specific environmental statutes, such as the EPA, to obtain information, enter and search premises, conduct sampling, and interview persons in the course of their investigations. Refusal to cooperate is a criminal offense. Interviews must be held under caution and interviewees must be permitted to have legal representation if answers are to be used against them in court. They also have powers to take steps to abate or control an emergency situation. On completion of the investigation the authorities will consider what, if any, enforcement action is necessary.

The EA and local equivalents in Scotland and Northern Ireland have a wide range of civil and criminal enforcement powers and sanctions available to them, including

- enforcement notices and works notices (to prevent or remedy a contravention);
- prohibition notices (where there is an imminent risk of serious environmental damage);
- suspension or revocation of EPR[90] permits and licenses;
- variation of EPR permit conditions;
- injunctions;
- carrying out remedial works (the regulator will seek to recover the full costs incurred from the responsible party);
- criminal sanctions; and
- civil sanctions (for certain offenses).

Civil sanctions, including financial penalties, may be imposed as an alternative to criminal prosecution for certain less serious offenses. There are six types of civil sanctions, including compliance notices (requiring action to ensure compliance); restoration notices (to restore harm caused by noncompliance); stop notices; and fixed and variable monetary penalties.[91] Additionally, where available for a particular breach, the offender may propose an enforcement undertaking to the EA setting out how it proposes to put the matter right. If accepted by the EA, the enforcement undertaking becomes a legally binding voluntary agreement. Criminal sanctions include fines and, in extreme cases, the imprisonment of individuals if the offense was committed with their consent or connivance, or was attributable to their neglect.

When deciding on appropriate sanctions, the courts can consider a number of aggravating or mitigating factors, including the economic value of the damage, the previous convictions and culpability of the defendant, and his or her behavior before and after the incident. The defendant may also have to pay a contribution toward the prosecution's costs (and even the costs of investigating the incident in question) and compensation to anyone who directly suffered from the offense.

In most cases, breach of environmental law will be a strict liability offense (there is no need for the regulator to establish fault). However, some environmental regimes do include statutory defenses. For example, under EPR,[92] it is a defense to show that the breach resulted from acts taken in an emergency in order to avoid danger to human health and that the defendant took all reasonably practicable steps to minimize pollution and provided particulars of the acts to the EA as soon as reasonably practicable.

There are no statutory indemnities or "safe harbor" provisions under U.K. law. Indemnities are contractual remedies that, as a matter of public policy, will generally be unenforceable against criminal liabilities. The statutory limitation period (six years for contract claims and 12 years for claims in respect of deeds) runs from the time the loss is suffered, and not from the time of the event causing the loss.

In certain circumstances a defendant may have a statutory right to claim for contribution from another person where they are jointly or otherwise liable for the same debt or damage.

Enforcement action (specifically the imposition of a sanction) can normally be appealed either through the criminal court process or as a result of specific appeal provisions. Rights of appeal are subject to time limits and to specified grounds, although these will often be fairly broad. In the majority of cases, an appeal is made to the secretary of state, who has the power to appoint an appropriate person to hear the appeal.

Once all other appeal avenues have been exhausted, the lawfulness of administrative decisions may in certain circumstances be challenged by judicial review. The main grounds of judicial review are that the decision maker has acted outside the scope of its statutory powers, that the decision was made using an unfair procedure, or that the decision was an unreasonable one. However, it is important to note that judicial review is a challenge to the way in which a decision has been made, rather than the rights and wrongs of the conclusion reached.

Notes

1. Pollution Prevention and Control (Scotland) Regulations 2012.

2. The Pollution Prevention and Control Regulations (Northern Ireland) 2003 and Pollution Prevention and Control (Industrial Emissions) Regulations (NI) 2012.

3. Regulation (EC) No 1907/2006 of the European Parliament and of the Council of 18 December 2006 concerning the Registration, Evaluation, Authorisation, and Restriction of Chemicals (REACH) (as amended).

4. Directive 2011/65/EU of the European Parliament and of the Council on the restriction of the use of certain hazardous substances in electrical and electronic equipment.

5. Producer Responsibility Obligations (Packaging Waste) Regulations 2007 (as amended).

6. Waste Electrical and Electronic Equipment Regulations 2013 (as amended), which implement Directive 2012/19/EU on waste electrical and electronic equipment (WEEE) (recast)).

7. Waste Batteries and Accumulators Regulations 2009.

8. End-of-Life Vehicles (Producer Responsibility) Regulations 2005 (as amended).

9. BAT represents the most effective techniques to achieve a high level of environmental protection, taking into account the costs and benefits of doing so. It includes both the technology used and the way an installation is built, operated, and maintained.

10. Environmental Permitting (England and Wales) Regulations 2010 (as amended), Regulation 38.

11. Environmental Permitting (England and Wales) Regulations 2010 (as amended), Regulation 39.

12. Established by Directive 2003/87/EC establishing a scheme for GHG emission allowance trading within the Community (as amended).

13. Greenhouse Gas Emissions Trading System Regulations 2012, Regulation 9.

14. Climate Change Act 2008, pt. 1, ss 1.

15. Established by the CRC Energy Efficiency Scheme Order 2010 (as amended).

16. Established by Directive 2003/87/EC establishing a scheme for GHG emission allowance trading within the Community (as amended).

17. Established by the Climate Change Levy (General) Regulations 2001 (as amended).

18. *See* https://www.ofgem.gov.uk.

19. FITs were first established by the Feed-in Tariffs (Specified Maximum Capacity and Functions) Order 2010, now revoked and replaced by the Feed-in Tariffs Order 2012.

20. Environmental Permitting (England and Wales) Regulations 2010 (as amended), Regulation 38.

21. This is an area for planned future reform.

22. Water Resources Act 1991 § 24.

23. Water Industry Act 1991 § 118(1).

24. *Id.* § 118(5).

25. Marine and Coastal Access Act 2009 § 65.

26. *Id.* § 85.

27. Control of Substances Hazardous to Health Regulations 2002 (as amended), Regulation 6.

28. HSAWA § 33(1).

29. Note that Directive 2012/18/EU on the control of major-accident hazards involving dangerous substances, amending and subsequently repealing Council Directive 96/82/EC (Seveso III Directive) entered into force on 13 August 2012. Member states are required to implement the Seveso III Directive into national law by 1 June 2015 (art. 31).

30. Control of Major Accident Hazards Regulations 1999, Regulation 4.

31. Chemicals (Hazard Information and Packaging for Supply) Regulations 2009, Regulation 14.

32. Regulation (EC) No 1907/2006 concerning the Registration, Evaluation, Authorisation and Restriction of Chemicals (REACH), establishing a European Chemicals Agency, amending Directive 1999/45/EC and repealing Council Regulation (EEC) No 793/93 and Commission Regulation (EC) No 1488/94 as well as Council Directive 76/769/EEC and Commission Directives 91/155/EEC, 93/67/EEC, 93/105/EC and 2000/21/EC.

33. For example, the manufacture, importation, or use of certain substances may be restricted or banned. The restricted substances are listed in Annex XVII to the REACH Regulation.

34. *Id.*

35. REACH Enforcement Regulations 2008, pt. 5.

36. Directive 2011/65/EU on the restriction of the use of certain hazardous substances in electrical and electronic equipment (recast).

37. Directive 2002/95/EC on the Restriction of the Use of Certain Hazardous Substances in Electrical and Electronic Equipment.

38. Directive 2012/19/EU on waste electrical and electronic equipment (WEEE) (recast).

39. Control of Asbestos Regulations 2012, Regulation 4.

40. REACH (Registration, Evaluation, Authorisation and Restriction of Chemicals) Regulations 2006, ANNEX XVII.

41. Environmental Protection Act 1990: pt. 2A Contaminated Land Statutory Guidance, Defra, Apr. 2012.

42. Environmental Protection Act 1990 § 78M.

43. The Environmental Damage (Prevention and Remediation) Regulations 2009.

44. Directive 2008/98/EC on waste and repealing certain Directives.

45. Guidance on the legal definition of waste and its application, Defra, Aug. 2012.

46. Environmental Protection Act 1990 § 34.

47. Environmental Permitting (England and Wales) Regulations 2010 (as amended).

48. The Producer Responsibility Obligations (Packaging Waste) Regulations 2007 (as amended) cover recycling and recovery, while the Packaging (Essential Requirements) Regulations 2003 (as amended) cover single market and optimisation aspects of the packaging waste directive.

49. Directive 94/62/EC of 20 December 1994 on packaging and packaging waste (as amended by Directives 2004/12/EC and 2005/20/EC).

50. Directive 2002/96/EC on waste electrical and electronic equipment (WEEE).

51. Environmental Permitting (England and Wales) Regulations 2010 (as amended).

52. Environmental Damage (Prevention and Remediation) Regulations 2009.

53. Control of Major Accident Hazards Regulations 1999.

54. Minerals are defined in the Town and Country Planning Act 1990 as including all substances of a kind ordinarily worked for removal by underground or surface working, except that it does not include peat cut for purposes other than sale. Industrial minerals (including china clay, ball clay, clay, shale, limestone, chalk, dolomite, silica sand, gypsum, potash, salt, barites, calcite, lead, zinc, other metals, slate, talc, iron ore) are widely distributed in England and occur in all regions with the exception of London (*see, e.g.*, British Geological Survey, Industrial Minerals, Issues for Planning, 2004). Additionally, the U.K. has reserves of coal, oil, and gas, including unconventional hydrocarbons such as shale gas (although shale gas has yet to be extensively commercially developed).

55. Of note, there is a presumption in favor of sustainable development that is the basis for every local plan and every planning decision—National Planning Policy Framework, DCLG, Mar. 2012. Local planning authorities must consult the EA before they grant planning permission for certain types of development.

56. In Wales and Scotland, control resides with the Welsh government and the Scottish government respectively.

57. Mining and extraction operations generally fall within Schedule 2 of Directive 85/337/EEC on the assessment of the effects of certain public and private projects on the environment (the EIA Directive). The directive is primarily implemented in the U.K. by the Town and Country Planning (Environmental Impact Assessment) (England and Wales) Regulations 1999 (as amended). An EIA is required when a development is likely to have significant effects on the environment by virtue of factors such as its nature, size, or location.

58. *See* U.K. Forestry Standard, The Governments' Approach to Sustainable Forest Management (3d ed. 2011).

59. Note that Natural Resources Wales takes over the functions previously carried out by Forestry Commission Wales from 1 April 2013.

60. Regulation (EU) No 995/2010 of the European Parliament and of the Council of 20 October 2010 laying down the obligations of operators who place timber and timber products on the market.

61. For example, the Forest Stewardship Council (FSC) and PEFC (Programme for the Endorsement of Forest Certification).

62. Environmental Damage (Prevention and Remediation) Regulations 2009.

63. EPA 1990 pt. III (§§ 79–82).

64. Environmental Permitting (England and Wales) Regulations 2010 (as amended).

65. Environmental Damage (Prevention and Remediation) Regulations 2009.

66. Directive 92/43/EEC of 21 May 1992 on the conservation of natural habitats and of wild fauna and flora.

67. Directive 2009/147/EC of 30 November 2009 on the conservation of wild birds.

68. Environmental Damage (Prevention and Remediation) Regulations 2009.

69. Wildlife and Countryside Act 1981 as amended.

70. Environmental Permitting (England and Wales) Regulations 2010 (as amended).

71. Environmental Permitting (England and Wales) Regulations 2010 (as amended).

72. Directive 2010/75/EU on industrial emissions (integrated pollution prevention and control) (Recast)).

73. Directive 2008/1/EC of the European Parliament and of the Council of 15 January 2008 concerning integrated pollution prevention and control (Codified version).

74. Of note, this deadline was missed slightly for England and Wales, with amendments to the EPR being made on 20 February 2013.

75. As of April 1, 2013, a new regulatory body called Natural Resources Wales (NRW) will replace the Environment Agency Wales, the Countryside Council for Wales, and the Forestry Commission Wales.

76. Environmental Permitting (England and Wales) Regulations 2010 (as amended).

77. Batteries and Accumulators (Placing on the Market) Regulations 2008 (as amended).

78. The Ecodesign for Energy-Related Products Regulations 2010 (as amended).

79. The Energy Information Regulations 2011.

80. *See supra* note 76.

81. Enforcement and Sanctions Statement, EA, 4 January 2011; Enforcement and sanctions—Guidance, EA, 4 January 2011; Offence Response Options (ORO), EA, June 1, 2012.

82. Enforcement Policy Statement, HSE, Feb. 2009.

83. Environmental Protection Act 1990.

84. *Id.* § 79.

85. *Id.* § 80.

86. *Id.* § 82.

87. *Id.* §§ 80 and 82.

88. Environmental Permitting (England and Wales) Regulations 2010 (as amended).

89. Barr v. Biffa Waste Servs. Ltd [2012] EWCA Civ 312.

90. Environmental Permitting (England and Wales) Regulations 2010 (as amended).

91. Regulatory Enforcement and Sanctions Act 2008.

92. Environmental Permitting (England and Wales) Regulations 2010 (as amended).

CHAPTER 31

Italy

ANTONELLA CAPRIA, EDWARD RUGGERI, AND FRANCESCA LIBERA FALCO

I. Introduction

In Italy, the fundamental rights and the organization of the national government's powers are enshrined in the constitution, which entered into force in 1948.[1] However, the protection of the environment was given explicit constitutional relevance only in 2001.[2]

In the environment sector, as a general rule, the national government is charged with adopting general and technical legislation, while the regional governments, such as that of Tuscany, are empowered to adopt the regulations within their devolved competencies and planning activities. On the other hand, municipalities are primarily responsible for the protection and management of the environment, and the provincial governments retain monitoring and supervision powers.[3]

Although the above-mentioned allocation of responsibilities may seem quite clear-cut, over the years the environment has been the center stage of a "tug of war," mainly between the central and regional governments. In practice, at first, the responsibilities and powers relating to the environment were centralized (1980s); subsequently they were partially devolved to the regional governments (1990s).[4] Currently, following the amendment of the constitution in 2001, the national government has regained its primacy, with particular regard to the legislative powers. In particular, the national government retains exclusive legislative powers for the protection of the environment and the nation's cultural heritage. Regional governments may not impose a lower level of environmental protection than that provided by the national government in Rome.[5]

At the national level, the first step toward the centralization of functions occurred with the creation of the Environment Ministry in 1986.[6] The ministry, through its various departments,[7] is entrusted with carrying out the national government's functions concerning environmental protection.[8] Finally, the Environment Ministry supervises and promotes coordination between the various levels of environmental governance, both at the national and European Union (EU) level. The Environment Ministry obtains technical and scientific support from the Institute for Environmental Protection and Research (*Istituto Superiore per la Ricerca e la Protezione Ambientale*, ISPRA), which is subject to its direction and control.[9] It is also useful to note that, in general, the national government may step in for the regional, provincial and municipal authorities in case of a breach of EU legislation or danger to public safety, or when unity of the legal system or protection of the essential levels of the services concerning civil and social rights so require.[10]

On the other hand, the regions have wide planning and monitoring responsibilities within their territories, coupled, in some cases, with authorization powers. In particular, the regions are entrusted with legislative powers in order to increase the value of cultural heritage and the environment, without impacting to the national government's ability to determine relevant fundamental principles.[11] Moreover, the regions may enact statutes necessary to implement and/or integrate national legislation. The regional and provincial environmental protection agencies (*agenzie regionali e provinciali per la protezione dell'ambiente*, ARPA and APPA) are the competent authorities for technical, scientific, and monitoring activities.[12] ARPA and APPA are subject to the direction and control of ISPRA.

Municipalities, pursuant to the constitution,[13] are responsible for all the administrative functions concerning the actual management of the environment, except when uniformity requires conferral of these functions to the provinces, regions, or the national government, on the basis of the principles of subsidiarity, differentiation, and suitability.[14] As mentioned above, the Supreme Constitutional Court has been instrumental in upholding environmental protection, even before its formal inclusion in the constitution. The other judiciary bodies that are competent for environmental matters are mainly the regional administrative tribunals (*tribunali amministrativi regionali*, TAR) and the Council of State (*Consiglio di Stato* (Rome)). The former entered into function, in every region, in 1974, and handle claims against governmental actions having a regional scope.[15] Their rulings can be appealed to the Council of State. The Council of State also has advisory duties both concerning specific inquiries from the public administration and those arising during the legislative process. Over the years, the TAR and the Council of State have had the complex task of interpreting national and regional laws in accordance with the constitution and the EU legal framework, including judgments of the European Court of Justice (notably, the definition of waste).

Finally, with regard to the national environmental regulatory framework, practitioners should know that the majority of the relevant provisions are located in Decree No. 152 of April 3, 2006 (Environmental Code). The Environmental Code regulates, inter alia, air emissions, environmental impact assessment, strategic environmental assessment, soil and water protection from pollution and management of the water resources, integrated pollution prevention and control (IPPC), waste management, cleanup and remediation procedures, and environmental damage. On the other hand, the Environmental

Code does not cover certain areas that are subject to specific legislation, such as parks, habitat, protected species, emergency response, incinerators, and emissions trading.

II. Air and Climate Change
A. Air Pollution

At the national level, air pollution was first addressed in 1966. However, the relevant legislation only established a series of general prescriptions, without fixing air emissions threshold limit values. From the early 1980s, European Community legislation drew attention to air quality and its tight links with human health. Thus, in 1988,[16] the Italian Parliament finally established pollution concentration thresholds and outlined a structured set of legal requirements, paving the way for more detailed legislation. This detailed legislation is currently set forth in the Environmental Code.

In general, practitioners should be aware that the provisions concerning air pollution[17] apply to installations and activities that actually generate emissions into the atmosphere. They also outline the relevant threshold limit values, prescriptions, sampling methods, and the criteria for assessing the measured values when compared with those set by the Environment Code. On the other hand, these provisions are not applicable to other installations and activities, chiefly those generating de minimis emissions (such as research and analysis laboratories and pilot plants).[18] The Environmental Code provides a graduated authorization system depending on the significance of air emissions. First, plants generating air emissions exceeding certain thresholds must be authorized by the competent region or the delegated province or municipality. The competent authority is obliged to issue the authorization within 150 days from receipt of the application.[19] This authorization lasts 15 years and may contain specific prescriptions for the start-up and temporary and permanent shutdown of facilities. Otherwise, the emission limit values established by the law are solely applicable to the normal operation of the plant. Moreover, the operator is obliged to communicate all modifications of the plant to the competent authority. If the modification is not "substantial,"[20] the competent authority proceeds to update, if necessary, the air emissions authorization. If the competent authority does not respond within 60 days from receipt of the mentioned communication, the operator may carry out the communicated modification. In any event, the competent authority retains the right to act thereafter. However, if the modification is considered "substantial,"[21] the operator must apply for a new authorization, covering, depending on the impact of the modification itself, the single installation or the entire plant. On the other hand, emissions from plants and activities entailing nonsignificant impacts on the atmosphere[22] are subject to a simplified authorization procedure.[23] Finally, the Environmental Code envisages a variety of sanctions for any breach of its air pollution control provisions.[24]

B.   Climate Change and Emissions Trading

Legislative Decree 216/2006 implemented the EU CO_2 emission trading system (EU ETS) established by Directives 2003/87/EC, 2004/101/EC, and 2009/29/EC. This legislation establishes a cap-and-trade system of greenhouse gas (GHG) emission quotas. The latter are allocated to companies through specific permits. Such permits are then traded in order to meet the demand of those companies that exceed the cap for their productive activities. Quotas may be exchanged directly between two parties or through stock exchanges all over Europe. Italy established an exchange platform in 2007 managed by the company entrusted with the national electricity market administration (GME). At the governmental level, the National Committee for the Implementation of Directive 2003/87/EC—within the Environment Ministry—has been established as the competent national authority (National Committee). The National Committee is mainly entrusted with drafting the National Allocation Plan (NAP).[25] The NAP outlines the total number of emissions quotas to be allocated. Moreover, the National Committee's other responsibilities include issuing CO_2 emission permits and imposing sanctions.[26] With regard to emission permits, as from entry into force of Legislative Decree 216/2006, plants with activities falling within its scope of application (e.g., refineries, plants producing glass, ceramic, paper) cannot operate without the National Committee's authorization. An Italian registry, based on the United Kingdom's GRETA[27] software, managed by ISPRA, has been established to support the exchange market concerning the issuance, holding, transfer, and cancellation of allowances.

III.   Water
A.   Regulatory Framework

At the national level, Directive 2000/60/EC of the European Parliament and of the European Council, which establishes a framework for EC action in the field of water policy, has been implemented by Part III of the Environmental Code.[28] In a nutshell, the Environmental Code (1) divides the national territory into eight river basins; (2) institutes the District River Basin Authority; (3) establishes the District River Basin Plan; and (4) establishes the River Basin Management Plan as an extension of the District River Basin Plan. These basin plans[29] create a general framework for sectoral activities and seek to ensure the conservation and protection of soils and the wise use of water resources in a given area. Accordingly, basin plans include water protection plans, aimed at ensuring the respect of a high standard of water protection and the achievement of the quality goals set forth by the Environmental Code.

B.   Water Discharges

The protection of water resources from pollution is addressed in section II, part III of the Environmental Code. In particular, Article 73 lists the aims, which include, among other things, the prevention and reduction of water pollution and the restoration of contaminated waters. A powerful tool for achieving a high level of protection is the regulation and control of wastewater discharges,[30] which are classified by the Environmental Code on the basis of their origin: domestic, industrial, or urban. Urban wastewaters are a mixture of domestic and industrial wastewaters originating from an urban area and discharged into sewers. Moreover, discharges into the soil, the subsoil, or aquifers are forbidden, with limited exceptions. Consequently, the Environmental Code generally only envisages waters discharges into the sewers or superficial waters,[31] in compliance with the threshold limit values listed in Annex V of the Environmental Code or those fixed by the regions. However, as a general rule, an authorization from the province or a separate authority established at regional level is always required.[32] The authorization is issued to the discharger within 90 days from receipt of the application,[33] and lasts four years, except if the activities are subject to an IPPC permit.[34] The Environmental Code establishes administrative and criminal sanctions and orders that may be imposed by the competent authority for noncompliance with the provisions concerning water discharges.[35]

IV. Handling, Treatment, Transportation, and Disposal of Hazardous Materials

A. Introduction

At the national level, the applicable provisions on chemical and hazardous substances stem directly from EU legislation. In particular, Regulation 1907/2006 (REACH) established a comprehensive set of rules concerning the registration, evaluation, authorization, and restriction of chemical substances. REACH has been complemented by Regulation 1272/2008 (CLP Regulation), which aligned the EU to the U.N. GHS system (Globally Harmonized System of classification and labeling of chemicals), introducing specific prescriptions regarding classification, packaging, and labeling with regard to hazardous substances. Specific exemptions are provided regarding medicinal and radioactive substances. Transport and waste management of hazardous substances are not addressed by these regulations.

In the past, Italy implemented Directive 67/548/CE (now repealed and substituted by the REACH and the CLP Regulation through Legislative Decrees No. 52/1997[36] and No. 65/2003[37]). Although the decree's provisions have been replaced by the current EU regulations, the provisions concerning classification, labeling, and packaging remain applicable through June 1, 2015.

B. Competent Authorities

The Health Ministry[38] is the competent body responsible for performing the tasks allotted under REACH in Italy. The Health Ministry has established a

Technical Coordination Committee to coordinate the administrative activities and organize inspections to monitor compliance with the chemicals legislation. Inspections are then carried out by the national and local entities listed in the State/Regions Agreement of October 29, 2009.[39] Technical issues of REACH are addressed by the National Center for Chemical Substances (CSC), established within the Institute for Health (*Istituto Superiore di Sanità*, ISS). In addition, ISPRA is entrusted with working and liaising with the CSC, contributes to national training, prepares and manages informational activities, and cooperates with the Health Ministry with regard to monitoring activities.

Pursuant to Legislative Decrees No. 52/1997 and No. 65/2003, the Health Ministry and the ISS have also been identified as the competent authorities with regard to the classification, packaging, and labeling of hazardous substances.

C. REACH Regulatory Framework

REACH established a system based on the registration of any new substance in a special database run by the European Chemicals Agency (ECHA). The production and commercialization of the most hazardous substances are subject to a specific authorization procedure carried out by ECHA and the EU Commission. In addition, restrictions are set forth regarding those substances considered particularly dangerous. Pursuant to Article 126 of REACH, in 2009 Italy established the relevant sanctions for breaches of REACH.[40]

D. CLP Regulatory Framework

Under the CLP Regulation, manufacturers, importers and downstream users must themselves classify substances or preparations in accordance with three main hazard classes: (1) physical and chemical hazard; (2) toxicological hazard (i.e., causing harmful effects on humans); and (3) eco-toxicological hazard (i.e., when the substance entails a risk for the environment). If the substance is subject to registration and is classified as hazardous, notification duties to ECHA are envisaged. With regard to labeling prescriptions, Articles 20, 21, and 22 of Legislative Decree No. 52/1997, Articles 9 and 10 of Legislative Decree No. 65/2003, and Title III of CLP Regulation establish that a substance or preparation classified as hazardous must bear a label including product's identifiers, hazard pictograms, and specific signal words and phrases describing the nature of the hazards and providing for precautionary measures. As to packaging, Article 19 of Legislative Decree No. 52/1997, Article 8 of Legislative Decree No. 65/2003, and Article 35 of the CLP Regulation outline the requirements concerning their design, construction, and ingredients.

Finally, both Legislative Decree No. 52/1997 and Legislative Decree No. 65/2003 establish criminal sanctions for any breach.[41]

V. Waste and Site Remediation

A. Waste

1. *Scope of Authority*

At the national level, the general waste regulatory framework is set forth by the Environmental Code, which implemented the EU's Directive 2008/98/EC (Waste Directive) in Italy. Currently "waste" is defined as "any substance or object that the holder discards or intends or is required to discard."[42] "By-products" and excavated soil are excluded from the scope of application of the waste rules and regulations, provided certain conditions are met.[43]

2. *Responsibilities and Administrative Procedures*

Waste management responsibilities are allocated between the central government (general coordination and orientation), and the regional and local authorities (local planning, authorization, and monitoring). Italian waste regulation is based on the hierarchy established by the waste directive. This hierarchy identifies prevention as the first goal in waste management, followed by reuse, recycle, recovery and, lastly, disposal. It is pursued through the application of the "polluter pays" principle, which encourages reduction of waste production and is aimed at ensuring its effective management. Moreover, the Environmental Code establishes that, as a general rule, the producer or the holder of waste is liable and responsible for the entire chain of waste management, from collection to treatment and disposal (i.e., "cradle to grave" approach).[44]

The Environmental Code explicitly prohibits unlawful management and disposal of waste on or beneath the ground or into surface or underground waters, as well as the mixing of hazardous and nonhazardous waste or different categories of hazardous waste. In this latter regard, the producer of waste is responsible for classifying and characterizing waste in accordance with the European Waste Catalog, on the basis of a double dichotomy: waste can be hazardous or nonhazardous[45] and can be classified as urban or special waste on the basis of its origin.[46]

Several obligations are established for all companies and individuals involved in waste management. First, producers, collectors, transporters, dealers, brokers, and whoever undertakes disposal and recovery activities must file documentation indicating the quantity and classification of the processed waste.[47] Furthermore, the producer, transporters, and disposal/recovery plants must file a waste identification transport form. Moreover, producers of waste and whomever collects, treats, transports, or disposes of waste must submit to the Register of Environmental Operators[48] an annual environmental declaration on the origin, classification, and description of the waste produced (*Modello Unico di Dichiarazione*, MUD).[49] Also, whoever is involved in collecting, transporting, or brokering wastes, or is engaged in cleanup activities, must become a member of the National Registry of Environmental Managers.[50] Finally, the Environmental Code establishes a heavy set of administrative and criminal sanctions for breaches of waste management rules and regulations.[51]

B.   Site Remediation

1.   *Division of Authority*

In Italy, the government first imposed rules and regulations concerning remediation in 1997.[52] These provisions implemented the EU "polluter pays" principle, and required the responsible party to restore contaminated sites, regardless of when the contamination occurred.[53] Subsequently, Directive 2004/35/EC drew further attention to liability in the field of prevention and remediation of environmental damage and finally laid the foundations for the legislation in force today. Part IV of the Environmental Code currently outlines a comprehensive site remediation regulatory framework.

2.   *Procedure*

The responsibility for carrying out administrative procedures concerning remediation of contaminated sites mainly lies with the regional governments or the delegated local authorities. However, the Environment Ministry retains the exclusive obligation to clean up certain contaminated sites known as sites of national interest (SIN), which are characterized by the particular gravity and scope of the contamination.[54]

As to the procedure, in case an event occurs that could potentially cause contamination, the polluter must implement the necessary preventive measures and immediately inform the competent authorities.[55] In addition, in case of sudden contamination events, the polluter must carry out emergency safety measures (MISE).[56] Subsequently, the polluter must carry out a preliminary analysis and ascertain whether certain contamination threshold values (CSC)[57] have been exceeded. If so, the responsible party must inform the competent authorities and file a characterization plan for approval.[58] On the basis of the results of the characterization, the polluter must carry out a site-specific risk analysis to determine the relevant risk threshold values (CSR) for the area.[59] If the CSRs are exceeded, the polluter must file with the competent authority an executive remediation project. Once approved, such projects authorize the polluter to carry out the remediation.[60] If the government cannot identify the polluter, or the polluter does not undertake the necessary cleanup activities, and no responsible party voluntarily undertakes any remediation,[61] the cleanup procedure may be carried out by the competent authority.[62] Should this occur, expenses related to any such activities in effect create a transferable property lien (*onere reale*) on the site.

Three additional issues bear mentioning. First, the expenses borne by the competent authority are also aided by a special real estate privilege (*privilegio speciale immobiliare*), which may impact any rights acquired by a party as to the contaminated site.[63] Second, criminal sanctions are fixed by the Environmental

Code for breaches of the provisions governing remediation of contaminated sites.[64] Finally, in order to ensure an effective and comprehensive cleanup, a responsible party may enter into a voluntary agreement with the competent authority determining the timing, financing, and substantive aspects of the measures to be implemented.[65]

C.   Innocent Landowners

In accordance with the polluter pays principle, on its face the Environmental Code does not impose a legal obligation on innocent landowners to undertake remediation. That said, however, upon discovery of a potential spill, the innocent landowner must immediately notify the authorities and, in addition, carry out all necessary preventive actions.[66] Moreover, the mentioned property lien and the special real estate privilege can be used against the innocent landowner if the competent authority demonstrates that (1) the responsible party cannot be identified, or is insolvent; or, more generally, (2) the government is otherwise unable to seek redress from the responsible party. In any event, the government may request that innocent landowners reimburse any expenses incurred for remediation activities up to the postremediation fair market value of the property. At that point, the innocent landowner seeks redress from the responsible party (if the responsible party can be identified) for the expenses incurred, and potentially, additional.[67]

All of the above notwithstanding, while not the majority view, some recent court decisions[68] have imposed an obligation on innocent landowners to remediate a contaminated site, without expressly limiting liability to the property's fair market value. Such courts have reasoned that, under the polluter pays principle, the effects of pollution cannot be borne by the Italian citizenry as a whole.[69] However, the Plenary Assembly of the Council of State recently confirmed that innocent landowner cannot be obliged to carry out the site remediation.[70]

D.   Liability Transfer

The extent to which Italian law transfers liabilities for contaminated sites depends on whether the transaction at issue is a simple asset/business branch transfer or a merger/demerger or acquisition of shares. The former would typically involve the transfer of physical property or rights having a monetary value. In this case, the former industrial owner would be held responsible for contamination occurring before the transfer and must carry out the emergency safety measures, remediation of the site. On the other hand, for the latter, all liabilities are transferred to the new or the incorporating company, which will be held liable for cleanup activities.[71] In case of a demerger, the company's liabilities must be clearly allocated.[72] If the liabilities have not been so allocated, the beneficiary companies bear these liabilities in proportion to the corporate assets they obtained as a consequence of the demerger. Finally, also in the event of acquisition of shares, the purchaser acquires the rights and obligations of the company. Consequently, as a rule, the purchaser would negotiate the insertion of clauses in the acquisition deed aimed at governing the financial aspects of potential future remediation issues. However, these clauses are only effective between the parties and would not impact any remediation obligations.

VI.   Emergency Response
A.   Scope

Italy has implemented Council Directive 96/82/EC on the control of major-accident hazards involving dangerous substances (and subsequent amendments) through Legislative Decree No. 334/1999 (Seveso Decree).[73] In particular, the Seveso Decree, in accordance with the directive, applies to all establishments where dangerous substances are present in quantities equal to or in excess of the quantities listed in Annex I. In general, the Seveso Decree establishes a different set of obligations and controls depending on the quantities of dangerous substances at issue.

B.   Obligations of the Operator

In general, operators must take all necessary measures to prevent major accidents and minimize their consequences to humans and the environment.[74] One set of obligations pertains to establishments listed in Annex A (e.g., chemicals, refineries), maintaining a level of dangerous substances less than the thresholds set forth in Annex I. In such instances, the operator must also (1) identify applicable major accidents hazards by completing a safety report[75] and (2) adopt adequate safety measures and provide information, training, and equipment to on-site workers.[76] A second set of obligations pertains to establishments maintaining a level of dangerous substances equal to or more than those listed in Annex I. In such instances, the operator must, inter alia, (1) outline a major-accident prevention policy, together with implementation of a safety management system; (2) notify the competent authorities of the start of the building activities at least 180 days in advance;[77] (3) file with the competent authorities information on the major-accident risk to be communicated to the public and the workers; and (4) file with the competent authorities the information necessary to draft emergency plans. Such emergency plans outline, inter alia, the arrangements for providing early warning of any incidents. Finally, on top of the previously mentioned obligations, in the case of establishments holding a level of dangerous substances equal to or more than of those listed in Annex I, parts 1 and 2, column 3, the operator must also, prior to start of the activities, file a safety report with the authorities. The safety report must demonstrate that adequate safety precautions and reliability have been incorporated into the design, construction, operation, and maintenance of a given establishment and that the internal emergency plans have been put into place. A version of the safety report[78] must be sent to the regional government. The regional government, in turn, makes it available to the public. Finally, the Seveso Decree establishes both criminal and administrative sanctions for any breach.[79]

C. Modifications to Establishments

In the event of a significant modification to an establishment, such as the shutdown of an industrial plant, a significant increase in the production of hazardous substances, the change of the operator, as well as other modifications that could have significant repercussions on major-accident hazards, the operator must promptly update the notification information. In this latter regard, Ministerial Decree of August 9, 2000, lists the modifications that could have significant repercussions on the preexisting level of risk. In this case the operator, besides updating the safety report and the prevention policy on major-accident hazards, must also inform the Environment Ministry of the modifications.

VII. Natural Resource Management and Protection
A. Landscape

Natural resource protection has been traditionally included in the general protection of cultural heritage, pursuant to Article 9 of the Italian Constitution, which establishes that "the Republic promotes cultural, scientific, and technical development. The Republic preserves the landscape and the National artistic and historical heritage." To this end, the Cultural Heritage and Landscape Code (Legislative Decree No. 42/2004)[80] unifies the previous rules and regulations governing the matter and implements the principles enshrined in the European Landscape Convention. Part III of the Cultural Heritage and Landscape Code, which establishes a protection scheme for landscape heritage, defines "landscape" as the material and visible representation of the national identity, whose characteristics are the result of the action and interaction of natural and/or human factors. On one hand, the landscape heritage includes some areas directly identified by the code.[81] On the other hand, special regional Commissions can issue a "declaration of considerable public interest" in order to enable some immovable properties to benefit from the landscape protection scheme.[82]

B. Natural Protected Areas

Law No. 394/1991[83] outlines the fundamental principles for the creation and management of natural protected areas to ensure and promote the conservation of the Italian natural heritage and increase its value. In this regard, natural heritage is defined as the "physical, geological, geomorphological, and biological formations with a relevant environmental and natural value." This statute establishes four different categories of protected natural areas: (1) national parks, (2) natural reserves, (3) marine protected areas, and (4) regional parks. The first three areas are identified by the Permanent Steering Committee[84] and included in a specific list published in the Official Journal by means of a ministerial decree. Regional parks, on the other hand, are created by the regional governments, in cooperation with all the local authorities.

National parks are defined as terrestrial, marine, fluvial, or lake areas with intact or partially intact ecosystems of a particular national or international interest with regard to their natural, scientific, aesthetic, cultural, and educational qualities. A park management body, under the coordination of the Environment Ministry, adopts the park regulation governing the activities allowed in the park's territory. In accordance with the aim of conservation and promotion of the natural area, some handicraft, agricultural, or pastoral activities may be allowed as well as scientific and biological research. On the other hand, Law No. 349/1991 expressly forbids some activities such as hunting, picking local vegetation, waste dumping, and interfering with the existing natural equilibrium. Any development within the park's boundaries must be authorized by the park management body, which can also issue some specific protective measures.

For their part, natural reserves are created to preserve one or more species of the local fauna and flora or an ecosystem with a particular biodiversity. The Environment Ministry identifies the main characteristics of the area and imposes restrictions. In particular, restricted access to the reserve must be provided. The park management body enacts a reserve's plan, which defines those activities that are permitted, in accordance with guidance issued by the Environment Ministry. Law No. 349/1991 envisages that the regulation of national parks also applies to marine protected areas with some further specific provisions. In particular, motor sailing, fishing, and altering the water biological characteristics is forbidden and the management of the marine area is entrusted to the Marine Defense Service, with the help of the relevant port authorities. Regional laws instituting regional parks create the relevant managing bodies and establish preservation measures.[85] In addition, Law No. 349/1991 forbids hunting in these areas, with the exception of selective hunting authorized where an ecological imbalance has arisen.

Monitoring of national parks and reserves is entrusted to the Environment Ministry and the Rangers Corp. On the other hand, the monitoring of regional parks is carried out by the regional governments.

VIII.   Natural Resource Damages
A.   Definition of Environmental Damage

In Italy, the first rules and regulations concerning environmental damage were introduced in 1986.[86] In particular, any willful or negligent breach of the applicable law resulting in deleterious effects to the environment gave rise to the obligation to pay damages. After the entry into force of Directive 2004/35/EC, the current applicable environmental damage regulatory framework is outlined in Part VI of the Environmental Code. Environmental damage is defined as any significant and measurable effect, direct or indirect, on the soil, species, or natural habitats as well as internal, coastal, and territorial waters.[87]

B.   Remedying Environmental Damage

The Environment Ministry retains exclusive authority to present environmental damage claims before civil and criminal courts.[88] Alternatively, the ministry may adopt reasonable ordinances covering such damages.[89]

In particular, any illegal or fraudulent action (or omission) causing environmental damage gives rise to an obligation by the responsible party to restore the damaged natural resources to the baseline condition. On the other hand, strict liability applies if the damage has been caused by certain activities—listed in Annex V of the Environmental Code—deemed particularly dangerous vis-à-vis the environment.[90] The provision of strict liability—applicable to damages caused after 2006[91]—was incorporated into the Environmental Code in August 2013, following the EU infringement proceeding n. 2007/4679. This proceeding was initiated against Italy for having failed to correctly implement Directive 2004/35/CE.[92]

If direct restoration is not possible, the polluter must undertake compensatory remediation measures, as defined by Directive 2004/35/EC. However, if neither restoration nor the adoption of compensatory remediation measures is carried out, or if the measures taken by the responsible party differ from the public authorities' prescriptions, the Environment Ministry may request that the polluter pay the assessed costs of the necessary remediation activity to be carried out by the public authorities. The rules and regulations concerning environmental damage are not applicable, inter alia, to damages originating from incidents occurring more than 30 years ago.

IX. Protected Species

Besides the natural protected areas described above in section VI, the conservation of biological diversity is further pursued by means of the European Directives 92/43/EC (Habitats Directive) and 2009/147/EC (Birds Directive).[93] These instruments created the network Natura 2000, aimed at preserving ecosystems and natural habitats[94] through a comprehensive approach taking into consideration large biogeographical areas in Europe.[95] The Habitats Directive requires each EU member state to identify the areas of its territory whose conservation deemed to represent a European priority (Sites of Community Importance (SCI)), insofar as they significantly contribute to maintaining and preserving those natural habitats and species listed in the Annexes of the Directive. Italy has implemented the Habitats Directive through Presidential Decree No. 357/1997,[96] which sets forth the procedure for identifying the SCI. Once the SCI are identified, they are included in a specific list by the European Commission and then designated Special Areas of Conservation (SAC) by the Ministry of Environment in coordination with the relevant regional government. The regions are entrusted with the preservation of these areas through the implementation of protective measures, such as specific plans and regulations. Moreover, Article 5 of Presidential Decree No. 357/1997 provides a further protection scheme for SCIs and SACs. In fact, any territorial plan, urban plan, or project to be developed in one of these sites must be assessed by the competent region[97] with regard to their possible effects on the protected environment (so-called incidence or VINCA procedure[98]). If the region deems that the project entails a negative effect on the protected site, the project cannot be implemented. Exceptions are provided for reasons of overriding public interest, or human health and public safety considerations.

The Italian Parliament has also implemented the EU Birds Directive, by way of an amendment to Law 157/1992[99] concerning wildlife. This law now establishes the creation of Special Protection Areas (SPA) in order to protect certain avifauna migration corridors. So far, 609 SPAs have been identified in Italy. In addition, Article 6 of Presidential Decree No. 357/1997 extends the above-mentioned VINCA procedure to these areas.

X. Environmental Review and Decision Making
A. Environmental Impact Assessment
1. Scope and Procedure

At the national level, Italy has implemented the European Council Directives 85/337/EEC of June 27, 1985, and 2011/92/EU of the European Parliament and the Council of December 13, 2011, through the Environmental Code.[100] In line with EU requirements, in Italy, before the competent authority permits the realization of a project having significant effects on the environment due to its nature, size, or location, the project proponent must conduct an environmental impact assessment (EIA). To this end, the EIA identifies, describes, and assesses the direct and indirect effects of a project on (1) human beings, flora, and fauna; (2) soil, water, air, climate, and the landscape; and (3) material assets and the cultural heritage. From a procedural point of view, the EIA comprises, among other things, screening and monitoring. An EIA is required for projects having a considerable and negative impact on the environment and the cultural heritage. Certain categories of projects are singled out for attention in Annexes II and III to part 2 of the Environmental Code (e.g., gas pipelines, regasification terminals, chemical plants). An EIA is also required for (1) any change or extension of a covered project, where such a change or extension in itself meets the thresholds, if any, set out in Annexes II and III; and (2) any other change or extension of the project that may have significant adverse effects on the environment. The Environmental Code establishes that the competent authorities are the Environment Ministry or the regional authority, depending on the project's characteristics. In general, the term within which the EIA procedure must conclude itself ranges from 150 to 330 days.[101]

If the project has not been subject to this EIA procedure, or if the scope of work differs substantially from the final approved project, the competent authority may suspend the project and can require demolition and site recovery. On the other hand, no administrative or criminal sanctions are explicitly established for a breach of the EIA provisions.

2. Screening and Monitoring

The EIA screening procedure consists of an evaluation carried out to ascertain whether modifications of approved projects or certain other projects may have a significant adverse effect on the environment and consequently must be subject to a full EIA.[102] If the variation of the authorized project could entail considerable adverse effects on the environment, the proponent must file the preliminary project and a preliminary environmental survey. This procedure must be completed within 90 days.[103] The screening procedure may result in an EIA procedure requirement, or a decision that an EIA is not required. Even if excluded from the EIA procedure, the responsible government authority may prescribe certain conditions to ensure that the project does not adversely impact the environment.

The EIA decision must contain all the necessary specifications for planning, environmental impact mitigation, and monitoring. If the monitoring and control activities highlight further different adverse environmental impacts compared to those assessed in the EIA decision, the competent authority may modify the decision and establish further conditions. Furthermore, the competent authority may order the suspension of the project or authorized activities until corrective measures are established.

B. Integrated Pollution Prevention and Control (IPPC)

Without prejudice to the EIA provisions, the proponent must also obtain all necessary authorizations concerning air emissions, waste management, water discharge, and so on in order to lawfully carry out the activity.

In this regard, Directive 2010/75/EC sets forth the IPPC permitting procedure, implemented in Italy by the Environmental Code as amended by Decree 46/2014. The aim of IPPC provisions is to prevent or, where that is not practicable, to reduce emissions in the air, water, and land from some industrial activities, in order to achieve a high level of protection of the environment. Therefore, the industrial activities listed in Annex VIII of the Environmental Code must obtain an IPPC permit from the Environment Ministry or the regional authority, depending on the project's characteristics. The IPPC permit replaces air emission, waste, and water discharge authorizations as well as the special permit to dispose of machineries containing PCB/PCT.[104]

In case of noncompliance with the prescriptions of the IPPC permit, the competent authority, depending on the seriousness of the breach, may issue a formal warning, suspend the operations or revoke the IPPC permit and shut down the installation. These sanctions apply without prejudice to criminal and administrative sanctions that are otherwise envisaged by the Environmental Code.[105]

XI. Transboundary Pollution

Since the 1960s, European governments have endeavored to limit transboundary pollution as much as possible. In this regard, air pollution was the issue addressed first, following the observation of the acid rain effects in northern Europe. Combustion processes and industrial activities pollute the atmosphere with substances like nitrogen oxides, sulfur dioxide, and heavy metals, which are then transferred by the rain to the ground and water after traveling very long distances. As a consequence, vegetation, soil, and surface and underground waters are adversely affected by these pollutants in different countries from where the pollution source is located.

In 1979, the members of the UNECE (United Nations Economic Commission for Europe), including Italy, signed the Geneva Convention on Long-range Transboundary Air Pollution, which addressed the problem through international scientific collaboration and policy negotiation.

Air emissions are the most likely to have transboundary effects but other environmental issues may also have a transnational nature and a global scope. The Lisbon Treaty of the European Union acknowledges the need to tackle these issues through a coordinated supranational policy-making. Consequently, EU law harmonized member states' law with regard to many different pollution sources including air emissions but also the management of chemicals, waste, water policy, and industrial accidents.

In addition to EU environmental law, Italy is bound by many international and regional agreements regarding, for example, the issue of climate change, the protection of the ozone layer, and marine pollution. These agreements include

- POP Stockholm Convention on Persistent Organic Pollutants (2001)
- Helsinki Convention on the Transboundary Effects of Industrial Accidents (1992)
- UNFCCC Framework Convention on Climate Change (1992) and Kyoto Protocol (1997)
- Vienna Convention for the Protection of the Ozone layer (1985) and Montreal Protocol
- Espoo Convention on Environmental Impact Assessment (1991)
- Alpine Convention (1991)
- Convention on the Conservation of Antarctic Marine Living Resources (1980)
- Basel Convention on hazardous waste (1989)
- International Convention on Civil Liability for Oil Pollution Damage (1969) and Protocol
- International Convention on Civil Liability for Bunker Oil pollution damage (2001)

XII.   Civil and Criminal Enforcement and Penalties

The environmental requirements set forth by the legislation outlined in the previous paragraphs are enforced through orders of the public authority or administrative pecuniary penalties, civil remedies, and criminal sanctions.

A.   Administrative Sanctions

The authorities that can issue orders to enforce the environmental regulation are the local entities (municipalities and provinces), the regions, and the Ministry of Environment. In case of breach of a permit, the competent authority may issue a formal warning and order to eliminate the irregularity within a certain period. In addition, it can simultaneously order to suspend the activities. Finally, if the breaches have not been eliminated or there are repeated violations endangering public health and the environment, the authority may revoke the permit and stop the activity. In case of risk of environmental damage, the authority may also order the responsible subject to prevent the risk or carry out remedial works.

The competent authority can also impose pecuniary sanctions established by the environmental regulations such as the Environmental Code. According to Law No. 689/1981[106] when a monitoring body (e.g., police forces, public health agencies) ascertains an infringement, the competent authority must notify the applicability of the sanction to the responsible subject and make him aware of his right to file documents or defend himself in a hearing. Subsequently, the administrative authority[107] may order the payment of the sanction through issuance of a deed that can be challenged before the administrative tribunals.

B. Civil Remedies

Private and public entities (including environmental associations) affected by a conduct in breach of the environmental regulations may bring a civil claim before the civil tribunals to avert a nuisance or a danger, enjoin the restoration to the baseline condition, or to obtain compensation for damage.

The Italian civil code grants the right to obtain compensation to whoever has been affected by damages due to an infringement of laws and regulations, including environmental provisions. If the damage originates from a dangerous activity, strict liability of the responsible subject is established. This claim for compensation for noncontractual damages is subject to the statute of limitations (i.e., five years from the occurrence of the damage). The claimant may also request the restoration of the baseline condition, if possible. The Environmental Code also establishes a particular civil claim for the compensation of environmental damage that can only be brought by the Ministry of Environment (see section VII.B).

Without prejudice to the claim for compensation and restoration, the civil code outlines a series of actions aimed at protecting ownership and possession of an immovable property. The owner can bring a claim against whoever causes nuisances to his property in exceedance of the normal tolerability threshold (noise, air emissions, etc.), by requesting the tribunal to stop the noxious conduct. This claim is not subject to any statute of limitation. On the other hand, specific actions can be brought before the civil tribunal also by the holder of immovable property (i.e., not the owner) in order to stop a nuisance or prevent a possible damage or danger to the property. These claims lapse in one year from the nuisance or the event entailing a possible damage or danger.

C. Criminal Sanctions

Breach of environmental laws and regulations may also constitute a criminal offense. The Environmental Code establishes criminal sanctions for the breach of some of its provisions, including those regarding waste management, site remediation, IPPC, and air emissions.

In addition, also the Italian criminal code sanctions some environmental crimes, such as environmental disaster and emissions of hazardous gas and other hazardous substances.

Criminal penalties are applied by the judicial authority (criminal courts) in accordance with the Italian Code of Criminal Procedure. They may entail the payment of a fine and/or a term of imprisonment, depending on the seriousness of the crime and the misconduct of the responsible person. In general, criminal liability only pertains to natural persons. However, Law 231/2001 introduced the principle of administrative responsibility of companies for crimes committed for their benefit or by their representatives, including environmental crimes. In case the judicial authority ascertains a crime, the company would be subject to an administrative pecuniary sanction.

Notes

1. Italy is a civil law jurisdiction.

2. Constitutional Law No. 3, of October 18, 2001. Prior to 2001, the Italian Constitution only contemplated landscape protection. On the other hand, the protection of the environment as a fundamental principle within the Italian legal system was asserted by the Supreme Italian Constitutional Court, with a series of judgments dating back to 1986. *See, e.g.,* Supreme Constitutional Court, Judgment No. 151/1986; No. 210/1987; No. 641/1987; No. 1029/1988; No. 1031/1988; No. 67/1992; No. 318/1994.

3. The regions (*regioni*) of Italy are the first-level administrative divisions of the state. There are 20 regions. Each region (except for the Aosta Valley) is divided into provinces. A province (*provincia*) is an administrative division of intermediate level between a municipality (*comune*) and a region.

4. *See, e.g.,* Legislative Decree No. 112/1998.

5. Const. art. 117; *see also* Judgments No. 367 and 368 of 2007 and No. 244 of October 31, 2012, of the Supreme Constitutional Court.

6. Law No. 349 of July 8, 1986; *see also* Legislative Decree No. 287, of December 6, 2002.

7. Presidential Decree No. 140 of August 3, 2009.

8. Inter alia, the Ministry's functions include (1) the creation and conservation of natural protected areas as well as the preservation of biodiversity; (2) waste management; (3) cleanup and remediation procedures; (4) management and preservation of the soil and water resources; (5) pollution and industrial risks (Integrated Pollution Prevention and Control (IPPC), environmental impact assessment, emergency response, etc.).

9. Law No. 61 (Jan. 21, 1994); Ministerial Decree No. 123 (May 21, 2010).

10. Const. art. 120.

11. *Id.* art. 117.

12. Law No. 61 (Jan. 21, 1994).

13. Const. art. 118.

14. Both the provincial and municipal governments are also responsible for administrative functions specifically assigned to them by the regional or national governments (*see, e.g.,* Law No. 142 (June 8, 1990), and the Environmental Code). Typically, when this occurs, the provincial governments are generally entrusted with powers relating to, for

example, air emission and water discharge permits, while municipalities retain a significant role in cleanup and remediation procedures.

15. On the other hand, the deeds of the administrative authorities with a transregional scope are within the purview of the Regional Administrative Tribunal of the Lazio Region (Rome).

16. Presidential Decree No. 203 of May 24, 1988.

17. Environmental Code arts. 267 *et seq.*

18. Other cases of industrial plants and activities that are exempted from the applicability of the air emissions discipline comprise those used for national defense purposes, mineral oil storage plants (including liquefied natural gas), and activities producing emissions originating from vents used to ensure health and safety in workplaces.

19. This term, however, is not mandatory. In any event, the applicant may initiate an administrative challenge. Provided that the application is grounded, the competent administrative tribunal would typically order the authority to issue the air emissions authorization.

20. "Substantial" is defined as a modification resulting in an increase or a qualitative or quantitative variation of the emissions, or altering the conveyance thereof.

21. The criteria establishing whether a modification is substantial or not vary from region to region.

22. Such activities are listed in part II of Annex IV to part 5 of the Environmental Code.

23. Furthermore, the Environmental Code establishes specific prescriptions and limit values for large combustion plants, in accordance with EU Directive 2001/80/EC. Finally, the Environmental Code also indicates the permitted combustible substances in industrial plants, civil thermal systems, and maritime applications, together with the relevant conditions.

24. In particular, some sanctions may be directly applied by the competent authority, while others are of criminal and administrative nature. As to the first category, if the authorizations' prescriptions are breached, the competent authority may issue a warning and require the operator to comply with the prescriptions within a fixed term. Moreover, if the breach entails a danger to health or to the environment, the competent authority may also order suspension of the activities/shutdown of the plant or revoke the authorization itself. On top of the abovementioned ordinance powers, in general the exercise of a plant without or in breach of the authorization or the applicable law is punishable with a term of imprisonment up to two years and/or a fine up to €1,032. Finally, if the operator also exceeds the air quality threshold limit values established by the applicable law, he will be liable to a term of imprisonment up to one year.

25. The NAP is issued every five years and must be approved by the Environment Ministry and the Ministry for Economic Development.

26. In general, whoever operates a plant without the necessary permit for greenhouse gas emissions is punished with a fine up to €250,000. An additional €100 is due for every ton of CO_2 emitted without the authorization in the relevant period. Moreover, failure to request an authorization within 30 days of the violation assessment can lead to the suspension of the plant's activity. Legislative Decree No. 216/2006 also establishes other fines in case the operator does not provide the National Committee with the necessary information relating to the assignment of quotas or updates of the authorization.

27. GRETA is the United Kingdom's greenhouse gas registry for emission trading arrangements.

28. The Environmental Code covers discharges into coastal waters. The statute does not explicitly address marine waters. However, Laws No. 979/1982 and No. 394/1991

identify protected marine areas, characterized by significant natural qualities. They also establish several particular restrictions guaranteeing a high level of protection. In addition, Italy is a party to the main international covenants dealing with marine pollution such as the U.N. Convention on the Law of the Sea (UNCLOS) 1982 and the Convention on the Prevention of Marine Pollution by Dumping of Wastes and Other Matter. Moreover, through the incorporation into the Italian legal system of the International Convention for the Prevention of Pollution from Ships (MARPOL), the MARPOL Protocol of 1978, the 1969 International Convention on Civil Liability for Oil Pollution Damage (1969 CLC), and the 1971 International Convention on the Establishment of an International Fund for Compensation for Oil Pollution Damage (1971 Fund Convention), the Italian legislator established a detailed discipline aimed at preventing marine pollution from ships.

29. Notwithstanding the apparently clear provisions of the Environmental Code, the District River Basin Authorities have still not been created. Accordingly, the previously identified Basin Authorities continue to operate, without a defined set of functions and responsibilities. The Environmental Code has also centralized the decision-making process of the District Basin Authorities through involvement of various ministries. This represents a marked shift from the structure of the former Basin Authorities, which has generated problems in coordination between central and regional levels of environmental governance. Although the requirements of the WFD have, for the most part, formally been implemented in Italian legislation, the practical enactment of the measures has not yet been fully carried out, mainly due to conflicting institutional interests and legislative fragmentation (*see* M. Alberton & E. Domorenok, *Water Management and Protection in Italy*, *in* 1 F. PALERMO ET AL., STUDIES IN TERRITORIAL AND CULTURAL DIVERSITY GOVERNANCE (2012). As a result, Italy is currently facing an EU infringement procedure for noncompliance with the WFD (EU Commission Procedure No. 2007/4680), in addition to those already commenced in the past.

30. Water discharge is defined as "any introduction [of effluent] carried out by means of a stable and uninterrupted collection system from the production process to superficial waters, soil, subsoil or the public sewer, regardless of its pollutant nature, also subject to prior purification treatment."

31. Superficial waters include lakes, artificial basins, rivers, canals, torrents, and coastal waters.

32. One general exception from the authorization requirement is the discharge of domestic wastewaters into sewers. In any event, such water discharges must comply with the threshold value limits established by the competent authority.

33. This term, however, is not mandatory.

34. The application for renewal of the water discharge authorization must be filed at least a year before the expiry thereof. Provided that the renewal application is timely, pending renewal the water discharge may be temporarily continued in compliance with the former authorization. However, if the water discharge contains hazardous substances, a renewal must be granted explicitly within six months from the expiry date. If the renewal is not issued within the six-month period, the discharge must cease immediately.

35. In general, administrative sanctions are established for exceedance of the threshold value limits for nondangerous substances (up to €30,000). On the other hand, criminal sanctions are established for whomever discharges industrial wastewaters without an authorization (imprisonment from two months up to two years or a fine from €1,500 up to €10,000). These sanctions are increased if dangerous substances are discharged. In this latter case, together with the following, administrative sanctions also apply to the corporate entity. Moreover, whomever discharges dangerous substances without complying with the prescriptions of the authorization or those imposed by the competent authority

is liable to a term of imprisonment up to two years. Furthermore, if also the threshold limits for dangerous substances are exceeded, the responsible person is liable, depending on the substances involved, to a term of imprisonment up to three years and a fine up to €120,000. Other criminal sanctions are envisaged if the holder of the discharge permit prevents the authorities from accessing the plant, or if discharges from ships or airplanes contain substances restricted by the relevant international conventions. Finally, it is important to note that in cases of a breach of the authorization—on top of the abovementioned sanctions—the competent authority, depending on the gravity of the breach, may issue a warning, or suspend or revoke the authorization.

36. Legislative Decree No. 52 (Feb. 3, 1997).

37. Legislative Decree No. 65 (Mar. 14, 2003).

38. Ministerial Decree 22 Nov. 2007; art. 5 *bis* of Law No. 46 (Apr. 6, 2007).

39. These entities are the state police, military force, Institute for Prevention and Safety in Workplaces (ISPELS), Offices for Maritime, Air, and Frontier Safety (USMAF), Inspection Division of the Ministry of Health, ARPA, and other bodies identified by the regional legislation.

40. Legislative Decree No. 133 (Sept. 14, 2009). In particular, administrative sanctions up to €150,000 are levied for the breach of obligations regarding registration, informational duties, testing, compliance with European Chemical Agency (ECHA) opinions, and the authorization's proscriptions. On the other hand, criminal sanctions exist for placing on the market or using a hazardous substance without the necessary authorization, regardless of the restrictions imposed.

41. In particular, Article 36 of Legislative Decree No. 52/1997 establishes a criminal sanction ranging from €5,000 up to €30,000 for whoever sells hazardous substance without complying with the relevant classification, packaging, or labeling provisions. Moreover, Article 18 of Legislative Decree No. 65/2003 punishes with a term of imprisonment up to six months whoever places on the market a dangerous mixture in violation of the relevant classification, packaging, or labeling provisions.

42. Environmental Code art. 183, para. 1, lett. a). This definition has radically modified the previous one, insofar as it has eliminated the so called "objective criteria." Such criteria previously classified an object or a substance as waste if it was also listed in Annex A of the Environmental Code. The rationale underlying the abovementioned amendment to the definition of waste is the need to comply with European Court of Justice (ECJ) case law, which established that the concept of waste and of the term "discard" cannot be interpreted restrictively and must be determined in light of all the circumstances (*e.g.*, Case C-129/96, para. 26; Case C-1/03, para. 42; Case C-195/05, para. 34; and Case C-252/05, para. 24; Joined Cases C-418/97 and C-419/97, paras. 36 to 40; Case C-194/05, para. 41). On the contrary, the Italian Parliament has often tried to typify the various cases by introducing presumptions aimed at excluding certain materials from the definition of waste, in contrast with the EU approach. Moreover, in the past, Parliament has also tried to define the term "discard" to limit it to the activities involving "recovery" or "disposal" of waste, thus excluding abandonment.

43. Italian legislation governing packaging, waste packaging, and waste originating from electric and electronic equipment with specific prescriptions differs slightly from the EU's general waste rules and regulations. Packaging and waste packaging are governed by part VI of the Environmental Code, implementing Directive 94/62/EC. Waste electric and electronic equipment is addressed by Legislative Decree No. 151/2005, implementing Directive 2002/95/EC and subsequent modifications.

44. This means that the producer/holder of waste is obliged to ascertain whether all the subjects involved in the chain of custody (transporters, disposal plant, etc.) are duly authorized. If not, the producer/holder will be held liable for aiding and abetting the unlawful management of the waste.

45. Hazardous wastes are identified on the basis of Annex I to part IV of the Environmental Code, which lists the possible causes of hazard as flammability, toxicity, carcinogenicity, infectivity, and so on.

46. According to article 184 of the Environmental Code, urban wastes are mainly identified in domestic waste and waste produced in connection with the maintenance of urban areas. Special wastes include wastes originating from industrial and commercial activities, construction works, sanitary activities, and so on. Nonhazardous special waste can be assimilated to urban waste according to the criteria set forth by the relevant municipalities and article 198, paragraph 2(e) of the Environmental Code.

47. *Registro di carico e scarico*, in accordance with the indications set forth in Ministerial Decree No. 148 of April 1, 1998, and Ministerial Circular of August 4, 1998.

48. This register is established within each local Chamber of Commerce throughout Italy.

49. Law No. 70 (Jan. 25, 1994).

50. Furthermore, in 2009 the Italian Parliament issued rules and regulations establishing that waste managers must carry out these obligations by uploading the relevant information on a web-based waste traceability system (SISTRI). Specific administrative and criminal sanctions are provided for the breaches of the SISTRI regulation. The new system entered into operation in October 2013. However, the related set of sanctions will be applicable as from January 1, 2015.

51. Pursuant to Article 258 of the Environmental Code, breaches of communication duties or errors in the keeping of the unloading and uploading register and the waste transport identification form lead to an administrative fine, which varies depending on whether the waste is hazardous (up to €93,000). Each omission or error in registers or forms constitutes a single violation conduct. On the other hand, criminal sanctions are generally also coupled with administrative fines applicable to the corporate entity. In particular, whoever manages waste without the prescribed authorization is liable to a term of imprisonment from three months up to one year or, alternatively, a fine up to €26,000. If hazardous waste is concerned, the responsible person is punished with a term of imprisonment ranging from six months up to two years, together with the abovementioned fine. These sanctions are also applicable to whoever dumps or abandons waste or introduces it into superficial or underground waters, or mixes hazardous and nonhazardous wastes. Higher sanctions are applicable to whoever manages a nonauthorized landfill (Environmental Code art. 256). For waste managers obliged to enrill to SISTRI, as from January 1st, 2015, the above-mentioned sanctions related to the paper-based waste traceability system are replaced by those established by SISTRI regulation.

52. Legislative Decree No. 22 art. 17 (Feb. 5, 1997); Ministerial Decree No. 471 (Oct. 25, 1999).

53. Case law clarified that it was not a case of a retroactive enforcement of the law. On the contrary, the applicability of Legislative Decree No. 22/1997 and Ministerial Decree No. 471/1999 was based on the fact that contamination is a "permanent event" that persists until removal of its causes. In other words, the contamination event was considered ongoing when applying the newly introduced set of rules. Consequently, no retroactive enforcement was established and no cleanup obligation was deemed applicable to contamination for which the responsible party no longer existed in 1997.

54. There are currently approximately 50 SINs in Italy, which have been identified through several Ministerial Decrees. *See* Decrees Nos. 426/1998, 468/2001, 179/2002, and 266/2005.

55. *See* Environmental Code arts. 242 *et seq.* Judicial authority has established that the polluter is strictly liable with regard to the obligation to carry out all the necessary measures of reinstatement. In fact, his intent to pollute or negligence is not taken into

account when applying the relevant obligations. On the other hand, a causality nexus must always be proved. With regard to industrial contaminated sites, the ECJ issued Judgment C-378/08 establishing that the competent authority may presume the causality nexus on the basis of evidence such as the vicinity of the subject's plants to the contaminated area and the correlation between the contaminants and the substances used in the industrial cycle.

56. MISE are defined by article 240 of the Environmental Code as the immediate or short-term actions to be implemented in case a sudden contamination event occurs. They are meant to restrain the diffusion of the sources of contamination, prevent their contact with the environmental matrices, and remove them, in view of possible further cleanup or restoration procedures.

57. CSCs are listed in Annex 5, part IV of the Environmental Code.

58. Characterization plans must comply with the requirements included in Annex 2, part IV of the Environmental Code.

59. The criteria that must be applied in order to carry out the risk analysis are defined by Annex 1, part IV of the Environmental Code. The majority of jurisprudence considers this risk-analysis based procedure as not compliant with Directive 2004/35/EC. The latter requires the government to take into account the various aspects of the environmental damage to determine the correct remediation measures. In fact, the abovementioned risk-analysis does not seem to consider the risk of sole environmental damage but rather limits its focus to the risks to human health.

60. The possible remediation activities are described in Annex 3, part IV of the Environmental Code.

61. The majority view is that an interested subject who voluntarily commences the cleanup must then complete it.

62. Environmental Code art. 250.

63. *Id.* art. 253.

64. Pursuant to the Environmental Code, whoever causes the contamination of the soil, subsoil, superficial waters, or groundwater is punished with a term of imprisonment up to one year or a fine up to €26,000 if he does not carry out a cleanup of the site, in accordance with the approved project. This sanction is increased if the pollution involves hazardous substances. In this regard, courts have stated that, as a general rule, this sanction cannot be applied to the "innocent" landowner insofar as it only addresses the actual polluter of the site. On the other hand, other courts have clarified that the landowner could be found guilty for aiding and abetting the polluter's violation should he fail to carry out sound prevention measures once he became aware of a risk of contamination leading to a deleterious effect on the environment. Moreover, failure to notify the competent authorities of the contamination is sanctioned with a term of imprisonment up to one year or a fine of up to €26,000. In this regard, it is worth noting that recent case law has excluded application of the mentioned sanction to the innocent landowner who failed to communicate the contamination to the competent authorities. The abovementioned violations may also result in administrative sanctions for the corporate entity. In addition, other higher criminal sanctions are envisaged for whomever attempts to cause or causes an environmental disaster.

65. With regard to SINs, Ministerial Decree No. 208/2008 establishes that the agreements regarding cleanup implementation may also include a settlement agreement covering the financial aspects of the remediation activity and environmental damages.

66. Environmental Code art. 245.

67. *Id.* art. 253.

68. TAR Lazio, Roma, No. 2263/2011; TAR Piemonte, Torino, No. 136/2011; TAR Sicilia, Catania, No. 2117/2012.

69. *But see* Council of State, No. 3885 of June 16, 2009; Council of State, No. 4561 of July 15, 2010; TAR Milan, No. 408 of April 7, 2010.

70. Council of State, Plenary Assembly, No. 21 of September 25, 2013.

71. Article 2504 *bis* states, "[T]he company originating from the merger or the incorporating company acquires the rights and obligations of the companies which partake in the merger, carrying on all their relationships, even procedural, prior to the merger." *See also* Council of State, No. 6055 of December 5, 2008.

72. *See* Italian Civil Code art. 2506 *bis*.

73. Legislative Decree No. 334 of August 17, 1999. Note that EU member states must implement Directive 2012/18/EU of the European Parliament and of the Council of 4 July 2012 on the control of major-accident hazards involving dangerous substances, amending and subsequently repealing Council Directive 96/82/EC, before May 31, 2015.

74. Legislative Decree No. 334/1999 art. 5.

75. *See* Legislative Decree No. 81 of April 9, 2008 (safety report concerning health and safety at the workplace).

76. *See* Ministerial Decree of March 16, 1998.

77. Environment Ministry, Region, Province, Municipality, Prefect, Regional Technical Committee, Provincial Fire Brigade Headquarters, and ARPA.

78. This is an obligation of the operator.

79. Article 27 of Legislative Decree No. 334/1999 establishes a heavy set of criminal and administrative sanctions. In addition, the competent authority may also order the shutdown of the establishment in cases of reiterated noncompliance with the relevant prescriptions. With regard to the criminal sanctions, the operator who does not file the notification concerning the commencement of the activities or the safety report within the established term may be subject to a term of imprisonment up to one year. Moreover, except when it does not constitute a more serious crime, if a major accident occurs due to noncompliance with the competent authorities' proscriptions, the operator may be subject to a term of imprisonment up to three years. Other administrative sanctions are established if, among other things, the operator does not implement the internal safety plan (up to €92,000).

80. Legislative Decree No. 42 (of January 22, 2004).

81. Namely, coastal areas, territories bordering on lakes, some kinds of superficial waters, mountains, glaciers, forests and woods, volcanoes, wetlands of international importance pursuant to the Convention on Wetlands of International Importance (Ramsar Convention), and areas of archaeological interest.

82. Such assets include buildings or gardens of particular aesthetic or historical interest, old town centers, and panoramic views.

83. Law No. 394 (Dec. 6, 1991).

84. The Permanent Steering Committee is a public body constituted under the Presidency of the Council of Ministers and composed of the representatives of the central government, regions, and autonomous provinces. Its task is to facilitate cooperation over the different policy levels.

85. Article 30 of Law No. 394/1991 establishes a term of imprisonment up to one year, together with an administrative sanction, for breaches of protection measures and relevant restrictions with regard to national parks, reserves, marine areas, and regional parks. The same sanction is established for building works in a national park without the relevant authorization. In addition, the violation of the specific protection measures implemented by the managing bodies of the protected areas is punished with a pecuniary sanction up to €1,000.

86. Law No. 349/1986 art. 18.

87. Environmental Code art. 300.

88. *Id.* art. 311.

89. *Id.* art. 313.

90. Annex V of the Environmental Code includes, inter alia, the activities subject to IPPC provisions, waste management operations, the production, use, treatment, or storage of dangerous substances as defined in article 2 of EU Directive 67/548/CEE, and the transport of dangerous goods.

91. From April 3, 2006, the date of entry into force of the Environmental Code.

92. *See* art. 25, Law no. 97 of August 6, 2013.

93. This directive replaced previous Birds Directive 79/409/EC and integrated it with subsequent modifications.

94. Natural habitats are defined by article 2 of Presidential Decree No. 357/1997 as the "terrestrial or aquatic areas distinguished by geographic, abiotic and biotic features, whether entirely natural or semi-natural."

95. In particular, the Habitats Directive identifies the following nine European biogeographical areas with homogeneous ecologic characteristics: Steppic, Pannonian, Black Sea, Boreal, Continental, Atlantic, Alpine, Macaronesian, and Mediterranean areas.

96. Presidential Decree No. 357/1997.

97. Such functions could also be undertaken by the Ministry of Environment, in a matter involving territorial planning of national importance.

98. The proponent must file with the relevant region a survey including a detailed description of the project together with an analysis of the effects with the targeted protected site. If the project is also subject to the EIA procedure, the assessment concerning the project's implications on the site is issued within the EIA. Modalities and timing of the procedure are set forth by the competent region. However, in case the regional legislation does not regulate the matter, Presidential Decree No. 357/1997 establishes that the assessment must be issued within 60 days from receipt of the application. Documental integration can be requested once and in this case additional 60 days are envisaged for completion of the assessment. In addition, European methodological guidelines for the VINCA procedure have been issued by the European Commission in the document titled "Assessment of plans and projects significantly affecting Natura 2000 sites. Methodological guidance on the provisions of Article 6(3) and (4) of the Habitats Directive 92/43/EEC."

99. *See* Law No. 157 of February 11, 1992.

100. *See* Environmental Code arts. 4 *et seq.*

101. However, these terms are not mandatory and may vary (and also increase) depending, inter alia, on the participation and the complexity of the inquiry. The final EIA decision contains the conditions for building, operations, and decommissioning, as well as malfunctioning. In case the competent authority exceeds the relevant terms, the project proponent may challenge the authority's inaction in front of the competent administrative court to obtain a judicial order obliging the competent authority to conclude the EIA procedure.

102. The Environmental Code defines a substantial modification as a change or extension of the project's characteristics and functioning that, in the opinion of the competent authorities, causes significant adverse effects on the environment. *See* Environmental Code art. 5, lett. 1 *bis.* The competent authorities have wide discretion in determining whether a modification is substantial. On the other hand, the applicable legislation, also including the EU provisions, does not flesh out the scope/meaning of what is to be considered a "substantial" modification. Annex V of the Environmental Code lists some general selection criteria that must be (cumulatively) taken into account for screening purposes, such as the characteristics of the project, location, and potential impact. Moreover, the majority of case law has generally clarified that an EIA assessment is not required if the modifications to an approved project do not outline a markedly different

project and are in any case carried out to comply with the authorities' proscriptions in order to mitigate the project's environmental impact.

103. This term, however, is not mandatory.

104. The IPPC permit procedure lasts 150–180 days from receipt of the application. The IPPC permit must contain emission limit values for polluting substances that may be discharged by the installation into the environment in significant quantities. In particular, the emission limit values shall be based on the best available techniques and may not be less restrictive than those established by the applicable legislation. In addition, the IPPC permit must contain all necessary measures to ensure soil and water protection and for waste management; appropriate requirements concerning the periodic monitoring of soil (at least every 10 years) and groundwater (at least every 5 years) in relation to relevant hazardous substances; monitoring requirements for the emissions that specify the manner and frequency of the measurements and reporting duties; measures concerning conditions different from normal operation (start-up and halt of the installation, malfunctioning, shutdown); and prescriptions for industrial risks (if applicable). The competent authority periodically reconsiders the IPPC permit at its discretion, confirming or updating the relevant prescriptions, as from the granting of the permit. In some cases, the authority reconsiders the IPPC permit, also following requests by other governmental entities. Among other cases, the authority reconsiders the IPPC if (1) the pollution originating from the installation is such that a review or application of new emission limit values is necessary, (2) the best available techniques have undergone substantial modifications, (3) safety reasons require application of other techniques, and (4) new EU legislation or national statutes require a reconsideration of the permit. On top of the discretionary periodic reconsideration, the renewal of the IPPC permit takes place (1) within 4 years of publication on the EU Official Journal of relevant decisions on BAT; (2) in general, after 10 years as from the granting of the permit; (3) after 16 years if the plant is registered in the EMAS system of eco-management; and (4) after 12 years if the plant is certified under standard UNI EN ISO 14001.

105. In this regard, in general, sanctions established by sectorial provisions (e.g., emissions, waste) are not applicable to installations subject to an IPPC permit. The Environmental Code provides criminal sanctions for whoever operates a plant without an IPPC permit or violates the permit prescriptions. In this case, the sanctions are tailored on the specific breach occurred. If hazardous substances are involved, the sanctions are increased. In addition, please note that all modifications must be communicated to the competent authority. If necessary, the government will update the IPPC permit, or, if the modification is deemed substantial, require the operator within 60 days to file a new IPPC application. Criminal sanctions are also provided for whoever substantially modifies an installation without the relevant permit.

106. Law No. 689 of November 24, 1981.

107. The competent administrative authority may be the Region, the Province, or the Municipality, depending on the specific provisions of the Environmental Code. Moreover, in case of violations of the regulation concerning the IPPC permit issued by the Environmental Ministry, the related administrative sanctions are applied by the competent prefect representing the central government on the Province's territory.

CHAPTER 32

The Netherlands

LEROY C. PADDOCK AND JESSICA WENTZ

I. Introduction

The Netherlands is a small and densely populated country, with 16,730,632 citizens inhabiting 33,893 sq. km of land.[1] Approximately 24 percent of the land is below sea level, protected by a system of dikes, canals, and pumping stations. Despite its geographic constraints, the Netherlands has the 17th largest economy in the world,[2] and is a leading exporter of natural gas, petroleum products, chemicals, machines, manufactured goods, and food.

A. Government Structure

The Dutch government consists of three administrative layers: the national government, 12 provinces, and hundreds of local municipalities. Although most environmental policy decisions are made at the national level, the provinces and municipalities play an important role in the implementation and enforcement of environmental laws. The provincial governments are also responsible for drawing up regional environmental plans and policies that accord with national objectives. Local authorities—including municipalities and water boards—conduct most permitting, inspection, and enforcement activities.[3]

1. Legislative Activities

The national government operates as both a constitutional monarchy and a parliamentary democracy. Legislative authority is shared between the States General, which is the Netherlands' bicameral parliament, and the executive branch, which consists of the Monarch and the Council of Ministers. Bills may be presented by the monarch or the House of Representatives, but not the Senate. The monarch, the ministers, and the House of Representatives may also propose amendments to bills. The Senate, however, may only pass or reject laws in full. Bills become valid once they are approved by both branches of the Parliament and affirmed by the monarch. In addition to this formal legislative process, there are alternative avenues for the promulgation of national regulations. For example, general administrative orders may be made by royal decree and then submitted to the Council of Ministers and the Council of State (an executive advisory body) for approval. Ministries may also promulgate administrative rules as may be necessary to fulfill their statutory duties.

2. *Executive Branch*

Within the executive branch, there are 11 ministries. The Ministry of Infrastructure and the Environment (I&M) is primarily responsible for the implementation and enforcement of national environmental policies. Other agencies that support the I&M include the Inspectorate for Transport, Public Works and Water Management (IVW), the Inspectorate for Housing, Spatial Planning and the Environment (VI), the Royal Netherlands Meteorological Institute (KNMI), the Netherlands Emissions Authority (NEA), the Netherlands Environmental Assessment Agency (PBL), and Rijkswaterstaat (RWS), which is responsible for executing public works and water management projects.

3. *Judiciary*

The Netherlands is a civil law jurisdiction—thus all core legal principles are codified, and customary law is only applied for the purposes of interpretation. Moreover, the judiciary is not authorized to review the constitutionality of laws. Thus, the courts have very limited involvement in law and policy making, and are primarily responsible for settling specific disputes.

B. Environmental Policy: The Macro View

The Dutch government has developed an extensive environmental policy agenda, which emphasizes spatial efficiency, sustainable development, and integrated resource management. As explained in the country's Second Sustainability Outlook:

> The Netherlands has to fit all of its housing, employment and transport onto a relatively small land surface area, while maintaining the quality of the living environment and the landscape. The way to use the available space as effectively as possible is to view these functions and features as an integral whole, including the additional demands made on water management, caused by the effects of climate change.[4]

The government's commitment to environmental protection has arisen as a matter of necessity. In the 1960s, the Netherlands was one of the most polluted countries in the world, and faced what was publicly recognized as an "environmental crisis." This crisis was triggered by a number of factors, including pollution from the country's large manufacturing, chemical, and agricultural sectors; the country's location downwind and downstream from other highly industrialized countries; and the country's significant spatial constraints. During the 1970s and 1980s, the Dutch government responded to this crisis by implementing a series of traditional command and control regulations that were designed to address discrete environmental issues.

During the late 1980s, the national government substantially modified its approach to environmental management. The new approach emphasized integrated management of all environmental resources, as well as the participation of all involved stakeholders in policy-making. To facilitate this new approach, the Dutch government published a series of National Environmental Policy Plans (NEPPs), which provided a broad framework for environmental management. The NEPPs identified the country's primary environmental concerns, established environmental quality objectives, and articulated strategies for achieving these objectives.

The first NEPP was published in 1989, and subsequent NEPPs were published every four years thereafter up until the publication of NEPP-4 in 2001. Since then, Dutch environmental policy has become encapsulated by European Union (EU) regulations, and no additional NEPPs have been published. However, the overarching framework for environmental management articulated in the NEPPs is still largely intact. Some of the key features of the Netherlands' current policy are described next.

1. Integrated Environmental Management

Since NEPP-1, the Dutch government has pursued an integrated approach to pollution control and environmental management, which recognizes that concerns such as air and water quality are not discrete issues, but rather are interconnected phenomena that should be addressed through holistic policy. The integrated management approach also seeks to reconcile economic development objectives and environmental objectives by decoupling economic growth from negative environmental impacts.

In accordance with this policy, the Dutch government consolidated most of the country's environmental laws into a single statute—the 1993 Environmental Management Act (EMA)—which established a unified regulatory scheme encompassing all levels of government. The EMA contains basic requirements for permitting and reporting on environmental impacts, as well as a framework for future regulation of environmental issues. Specific provisions of the EMA are discussed in subsequent sections of this chapter, as they relate to different environmental media.

Other important laws include the Activities Decree (2007), which imposes rules on businesses to regulate their conduct with respect to the environment, and the General Act for Environmental Permitting (WABO) (2010), which creates a unified permitting regime for activities that impact the environment. The Activities Decree and WABO are discussed in more detail in section X, below.

2.   Coalition Building (Target Groups and Negotiated Agreements)

One key feature of Dutch governance is a strong emphasis on public engagement and consensus building. This is in part due to the fact that the Netherlands has a multiparty system, with approximately 12 different groups represented in the Parliament. Thus, lawmaking requires some level of cooperation and agreement between many parties with diverse interests.

Dutch policy also relies heavily on consensus building with the private sector, as reflected in the frequent use of negotiated agreements with industry in order to achieve policy objectives. In order to promote a cooperative approach to environmental management, the NEPPs identify "target groups" representing various economic sectors, and direct the central government to work closely with these groups to determine the means through which environmental objectives are fulfilled. Since the 1990s, the government has negotiated a wide variety of agreements that specify how each target group will achieve the targets set forth in the NEPPs and other policy documents. The main benefit of these agreements is that they encourage the private sector to participate in environmental decision making, which presumably leads to more cost-effective and appropriate solutions, as well as a higher likelihood of compliance. Although sometimes referred to as "voluntary" agreements, these covenants may be legally binding and enforceable in court, depending on the language used therein.

3.   Public Participation

A third key feature of Dutch environmental policy, which is closely related to the use of target groups and negotiated agreements, is an overall emphasis on public participation. Dutch policy makers encourage and explicitly rely upon reports prepared by non-governmental organizations (NGOs) when assessing environmental problems and the effectiveness of solutions. The public can also enforce its environmental rights by seeking third-party damages for permit violations, or by bringing a civil claim to enforce a negotiated agreement.

4.   Internationalization

Since 2001, Dutch policy has been largely driven by external policy objectives, including EU directives and international treaty obligations. In 2006, the Dutch Cabinet published a "Future Agenda" which set forth the government's plan for achieving goals set forth in NEPP-4, and also integrated various EU goals for environmental progress. With the publication of NEPP-4 and the Future Agenda, the Dutch government shifted its focus from a primarily domestic agenda for environmental protection to an agenda that emphasizes the importance of international cooperation and engagement. As such, the government has made it a key priority for the Netherlands to achieve compliance with EU targets, and has largely substituted international targets in place of domestic targets. The Ministry of Infrastructure and the Environment estimates that approximately 80 percent of Dutch environmental law is now derived from EU legislation.[5]

II. Air and Climate Change

Air quality is a major issue for the Netherlands, due to its geographic situation downstream from other industrial countries, as well as its own industrial activities. Climate change is also a significant concern, given that nearly one-third of the country's land is below sea level and thus susceptible to both sea level rise and extreme weather events. Since the early 2000s, Dutch policy with respect to both traditional air pollutants and greenhouse gas (GHG) emissions has been primarily driven by EU directives.

A. Air Pollution Control

By the 1970s, air pollution from sulfur dioxide (SO_2), particulates (PM), nitrogen oxides (NO_x), carbon monoxide (CO), hydrocarbons, and lead compounds had become a serious problem in the Netherlands. In 2001, the national government found that "[s]ome of these emissions have since become more or less manageable, although particulates, NO_x and smog are still problematic."[6] In light of these findings, NEPP-4 established ambitious targets for the reduction of NO_x, SO_2, PM, and volatile organic chemicals (VOC) for the year 2030.[7] The government has since backed off from those targets, and has focused instead on the attainment of EU directives, including, inter alia, the National Emissions Ceilings (NEC) Directive (2001/81/EC) and the new Air Quality Directive (2008/50/EC). This section will discuss some key sources of national law and policy through which those directives are implemented.

1. The Environmental Management Act of 2004 (Wet Milieubeheer)

Chapter 5 of the 2004 EMA authorizes the Council of Ministers—which consists of the heads of each Dutch ministry—to establish environmental quality targets with respect to any issue that is "of more than provincial concern," including any targets that are necessary to implement EU directives.[8] Such targets may constitute "limit values" (which establish mandatory targets and timetables) or "guideline values" (which should be achieved to the extent practicable).[9] The Dutch government has issued limit values and guideline values through the national decrees and guidelines discussed below.

Chapter 8 of the EMA contains permitting and reporting requirements for entities that emit threshold levels of air pollutants. For more information on permitting, and the relationship between the EMA's requirements and WABO, see section X.

2. Activities Decree

Chapter 5 of the Activities Decree establishes SO_2, NO_x, PM, and carbon monoxide limitations on industrial emissions, including emissions from large combustion plants and waste incineration. Chapter 5 also imposes certain monitoring, reporting, and operational requirements on such installations. These requirements will not enter into force until 2016 for large combustion plants for which a license was granted or approved before January 1, 2013. In the meantime, large combustion plants remain subject to the requirements in "Bees A," discussed below.

Chapters 3 and 4 of the Activities Decree specify emissions limitations and related requirements for other types of installations and activities (e.g., section 4.4 imposes PM limitations on the mechanical processing of rubber and plastics). Section 2.3 sets forth general rules on how to monitor and measure air pollution to verify compliance with emission standards, which are applicable to the activities and installations regulated under Chapters 3 and 4.

3. Decrees on Emission Limits for Combustion Plants

The original combustion plant decree came into force in 1987, and was amended in 2005 to incorporate requirements from the European Directive for Large Combustion Plants (2001/80/EC). Originally, there were two different versions of the decree—Version A (Bees A), which addressed emissions from larger plants (e.g., refineries, power stations, and large petrochemical companies), and Version B (Bees B), which addressed emissions from smaller installations. Bees B has recently been replaced with a new directive, the Medium Size Combustion Plant Emissions Requirements (BEMS).

Under these decrees, stationary sources are subject to specific emissions limits for SO_2, NO_x, and PM, as well as requirements for inspections and maintenance. Specifically, owners of covered installations must have an accredited assessor or a certified installation contractor confirm that emission limits are not being exceeded, and must have inspection and maintenance performed on a regular basis by a company certified by the Combustion Plant Inspection and Maintenance Certification Foundation (SCIOS). The capacity of the combustion plant determines the frequency of inspections.

4. Environmental Management Establishments and Licenses Decree

This decree incorporated the EU Directive on Integrated Pollution Prevention and Control (IPPC) (2008/1/EC) into Dutch law. In accordance with the IPPC Directive, "permits for industrial installations must ensure that those installations will take all appropriate preventative measures against pollution, in particular through application of the Best Available Techniques (BAT)."[10] The directive's requirements extend to existing as well as new installations.

5. Netherlands Emission Guidelines for Air (NER)

These guidelines, issued in 2004, establish specific emissions standards for various pollutants and sources. The standards contained in the NER are based on the emissions reductions achievable through application of BAT, as required by the EU Industrial Emissions Directive (2010/75/EU). The NER was drafted jointly by the provinces, municipalities, and the central government, to encourage different municipalities and provinces to include similar emissions standards in permits issued to similarly situated entities, and thus to harmonize the permitting process for air pollution sources.[11] Unlike the EMA, the NER is not a statute and not legally binding—however, the judiciary has interpreted the NER as a reference point for the reasonableness of actions undertaken by permitting authorities.

6.   *Air Quality Orders*

In 2001, the Dutch government issued an Air Quality Order that requires local and provincial authorities to provide exhaustive information about air quality impacts resulting from administrative and permitting decisions undertaken by those authorities. Specifically, the order specified that, for every task performed by an administrative body that could affect air quality concentrations, the body should provide a report that detailed how the European limit for particulate matter (PM_{10}) or nitrogen dioxide (NO_2) would not be exceeded in future years. In 2005, the order was adjusted to provide more flexibility for provincial and local authorities, but also to provide for enhanced uniformity in measurements and reporting.

7.   *National Air Quality Cooperation Programme (NSL)*

The Dutch National Air Quality Cooperation Programme entered into force in 2009, with the purpose of ensuring that the Netherlands remains within EU limits for PM_{10} and NO_2. Within this program, "local, regional and state authorities work together in ensuring the implementation of the measures set up by each administrational level."[12] The NSL specifies certain local measures that municipal and provincial governments will undertake to reduce these pollutants—e.g., (1) the establishment of "environmental zones" in ten large cities, where trucks are prohibited unless they comply with the Euro-2 standard or higher, and (2) programs to stimulate the development of clean public transport. The NSL also contains additional reporting requirements for local and regional authorities, and establishes an annual monitoring process for PM_{10} and NO_2.

8.   *So$_2$ Negotiated Agreements*

In order to implement the NEC Directive for sulfur dioxide (SO_2), the Dutch government has negotiated agreements with the energy sector and refineries, which establishes a national SO_2 emission ceiling and allocated emissions among different entities within each sector. The energy agreement specifies that the total annual SO_2 emissions from that sector shall not exceed 13.5 kt (mean value over three years), plus 1.5 kt for new plants entering operation between 2010 and 2019. The agreement with the refineries limits their SO_2 emissions to 14.5 kt from 2010 onwards.[13]

9. NO_x Emissions Trading

To reduce NO_x emissions in accordance with the NEC Directive, the Dutch government has established a NO_x trading program. The Dutch government allocates emission allowances based on the performance standard rate (PSR) for each category of installation (defined as grams of NO_x generated per unit of energy used by the facility), multiplied by the total fuel input.[14] Any establishment that has NO_x emissions that exceed the performance standard must purchase NO_x emission allowances to cover the excess. Between 2005 and 2010, the performance standard became increasingly stringent. As of 2010, the Dutch government had reduced emissions allowances for larger installations that fall under the NO_x trading system from 40 g NO_x per Giga Joule primary energy use in 2010 to 37 g/GJ in 2013.[15] As of 2012, the Dutch government is making plans to terminate the NO_x trading scheme in 2014.

B. Climate Change

As with traditional air pollutants, Dutch policy with respect to climate change is now largely driven by external directives. The Netherlands is a party to the United Nations Framework Convention on Climate Change (UNFCCC) and the Kyoto Protocol, and has implemented those obligations in cooperation with the European Community. In accordance with the EU's Burden Sharing Agreement, the Netherlands was obliged to reduce its GHG emissions by 6 percent over 1990 levels, on average for the period 2008–2012. Based on its average emissions reductions over the period from 2008 to 2011, the Netherlands was on track to meet its burden-sharing target, but only by acquiring additional emissions credits through Kyoto's flexibility mechanisms.[16]

The Netherlands also has a number of distinct obligations under the EU regime. About half of the country's GHG emissions are regulated through the EU Emissions Trading System (ETS).[17] The ETS establishes a cap-and-trade system for CO_2 emissions from power plants, oil refineries, factories, and other industrial installations, with a goal of reducing those emissions by 21 percent over 2005 levels by 2020. During the first two phases of the ETS (2005–2007, 2008–2012), the Netherlands was assigned a national emissions cap, and was responsible for determining how to allocate its allowances through the promulgation of a National Allocation Plan (NAP). As of 2013, the ETS has entered into its third phase and system for allocating emissions allowances has changed significantly. In place of the national caps, there is now a single, EU-wide cap on emissions from power stations and other fixed emissions, which will reduce by 1.74 percent each year so as to reach the 2020 target. Moreover, an increasing share of emissions allowances will be auctioned, rather than allocated freely, meaning that most installations will need to purchase an increasing proportion of their allowances through government-held auctions.

The Netherlands' remaining GHG emissions are regulated by the European Commission's "Effort-Sharing Decision." That Decision establishes binding annual emissions targets for member states for the period from 2013 to 2020, covering emissions from sectors such as transport (except aviation), buildings, agriculture, and waste. The Netherlands' emission target for 2020 is a 16 percent reduction over 2005 levels.[18]

The Netherlands is also subject to the EU Renewable Energy Directive (2009/28/EC), which aims to ensure that the EU will achieve a 20 percent share of renewable energy by 2020. Under that directive, the Netherlands' binding national target for renewable energy is 14 percent by 2020. Although the Netherlands asserts that it is currently on track to achieve the non-ETS target for 2020, it is unlikely that the country will be able to increase its renewable energy share (currently 4 percent) to 14 percent in the next eight years, based on current policies.[19]

With respect to domestic policy, the Netherlands originally adopted GHG targets that exceed those established by the EU. NEPP-4 aimed at a 50–60 percent reduction in CO_2 emissions by 2030, as compared with 1990. In 2007, the Dutch government announced a "Clean and Efficient Work Program" that established a slightly less ambitious agenda for climate change: to cut emissions of greenhouse gases by 30 percent in 2020 compared with 1990 levels; double the rate of annual energy efficiency improvement from 1 percent to 2 percent in the immediate future; and increase the share of renewable energy to 20 percent by 2020. As of 2012, however, the Dutch government has backed off from these ambitious targets, and is now focused on the attainment of EU directives. The most recent Green Deal, promulgated in 2011, did not contain a new long-term strategy for addressing climate change. Rather, the current coalition government has actually cut back a number of programs designed to reduce GHG emissions, stimulus programs for green investment, subsidies for renewable heat, and the feed-in tariff program. Some of the domestic policies that the Dutch government has implemented over the past decade are discussed below.

1. Transport

To reduce emissions from the transport sector, the Dutch government has utilized a combination of (1) mandates, such as eco-labeling and technology requirements; (2) financial tools, including a fuel tax, an airplane tax, and a motor vehicle tax, which is differentiated on the basis of emissions levels to encourage the sale of energy efficient cars; (3) informational programs; and (4) transportation planning programs.

2. Industry

For industrial sectors, the government has relied on the use of covenants to reduce energy consumption. Between 1992 and 2000, the government entered into a number of long-term agreements on energy efficiency with energy-intensive industries. Under these covenants, industries agreed to "introduce all appropriate process efficiency measures with a pay-back period of five years and to implement energy management systems."[20] Since 2000, those agreements have been replaced by a "covenant on benchmarking" for energy-intensive industries, in which they have "agreed to be among the most efficient companies in the world."[21]

3.   Building and Appliance Efficiency

With respect to building and appliance efficiency, the Dutch government has relied upon both traditional regulation and covenants. One key mechanism that the government has used to encourage efficiency is a relatively high tax on electricity consumption in households. The government also regulates the efficiency of new buildings through performance standards. The Dutch Building Decree of 1995 established minimum standards for new building performance, and Energy Labeling for appliances was introduced in 1996. As of 2010, the Dutch government's stated target was to have all new buildings be climate neutral by 2020. In order to address efficiency in existing buildings, the Dutch government has negotiated a series of agreements with key players within the housing, energy, and construction sectors. The government also provides some financial incentives for retrofits to existing buildings.

4.   Renewable Energy

In 2003, the central government introduced a feed-in tariff, which allowed Dutch producers of renewable electricity to receive a fixed price per kWh of generation, for a guaranteed period of ten years. However, this program was abolished in 2006 when the Minister for Economic Affairs determined that the Netherlands would be able to reach its previous target of 9 percent renewable electricity by 2010.[22] A new law was introduced in 2007, which resembled the 2003 FIT, and allowed renewable energy producers to get a premium that covers the wholesale energy price plus extra costs for a period of ten years. This law, *Besluit stimulering duurzame energieproductie* (SDE), entered into force in April 2009.

The Dutch government also provides a tax incentive for investments in renewable energy projects, known as the Energy Investment Deduction scheme (EIA). Under the CO_2 Reduction Plan, additional incentives are also available for projects that may reduce CO_2 emissions in general, including renewable energy projects.

III.   Water

A key feature of Dutch water policy is the integrated management of water systems and spatial planning. This accords with the country's overall environmental management strategy, as set forth in NEPP-1 and subsequent policy documents. Under this policy, water is viewed as an integrated system composed of surface and groundwater, riverbeds, banks, and so on as well as land features. Management strategies typically focus on the restoration and conservation of hydrological networks, rather than individual bodies of water.

The primary authority on water law in the Netherlands is the Water Act (2010), which reflects the integrated water management approach and establishes the primary objectives for water management. This Act is explicitly linked to the Spatial Planning Act (2006), and together, these laws provide the basis for land use and watershed management in the Netherlands. The Dutch Policy Document on Sustainable Crop Production (2004) also regulates water quality, to the extent that it sets forth policies for agricultural management practices. As with air emissions, specific requirements for water discharges from particular installations or activities are detailed in Chapters 3 and 4 of the Activities Decree.

Finally, the EU directives, including the Water Framework Directive, the Groundwater Directive, and the Drinking Water Directive, inter alia, impose external requirements on Dutch water policy. This section will first describe some of the basic requirements from the EU directives, and then will describe the domestic regulatory framework for water management in the Netherlands.

A. Water Quality Directive

The Water Quality Directive, adopted in 2000, establishes a basic model for water management in EU countries. It also identifies water quality objectives for surface waters, and requires member states to develop river basin management plans identifying how the government plans to achieve water quality objectives for each river basin within a specified time frame. The directive explicitly mandates that countries adopt adequate public participation procedures when developing those plans. Finally, the directive requires member states to charge prices for water that reflect the actual cost of extracting water (including costs associated with environmental damage as well as depleted water supply).

B. Groundwater Directive

The Groundwater Directive, adopted in 2006, requires member states to develop groundwater quality standards in accordance with specific quality criteria no later than 2008. In addition, member states must develop measures to prevent inputs of pollutants into groundwater, so as to achieve the quality standards, no later than 2015.

C. Drinking Water Directive

The Drinking Water Directive, adopted in 1998, establishes water quality standards for drinking water and requires member states to monitor drinking water so as to ensure that it meets those standards.

D.   Water Act

Adopted in 2010, the Water Act establishes the overall water management scheme in the Netherlands. The three main objectives of the Act are to (1) prevent and, where necessary, limit flooding, swamping, and water shortage; while simultaneously (2) protecting and improving the chemical and ecological status of water systems; and (3) allowing water systems to fulfill societal functions.[23] To achieve these objectives, the Act articulates specific standards, as well as procedures for setting future standards, with respect to both flood defense safety[24] and water quality management.[25]

With respect to water quality, the Act directs the provinces to establish standards for determining the "appropriate storage and conveyance capacity for regional waters."[26] However, standards for the "chemical and ecological status of water systems" are to be established by the central government, as specified by Chapter 5 of the EMA, and in accordance with environmental objectives set forth in section 4 of the Water Framework Directive.[27] The act also authorizes the Ministry of Transport, Public Works and Water Management to establish standards for "national waters and, with a view to international obligations or supraregional interests, for regional waters."[28]

Chapter 3 of the Act provides for the "organization of water management" and assigns "management and due care responsibilities." These responsibilities are divided between the "municipalities," "water authorities," the "provincial executive," and the Minister of Transport, Public Works and Water Management. Chapter 3 also authorizes water authorities of different water systems within the same river basin district to enter into water management agreements with other water authorities (or other public authorities, including municipalities).

In accordance with Chapter 4, the Minister of Transport, Public Works and Water Management must consult with other ministers in order to establish "a national water plan containing the main elements of national water policy and the associated aspects of national spatial policy." Chapter 4 also identifies the minimum elements for that plan, including required subcomponents: river basin management plans (to be drafted by provincial authorities) and local management plans. The Act specifies that these plans are to be periodically revised every six years, and permits interim revision of the plans at more frequent intervals.

Chapter 5 empowers water authorities to construct and/or manage the development of "water management structures," and establishes the procedures that must be followed when constructing, relocating, or reinforcing such structures. Chapter 5 also contains special provisions regarding the pollution of the bed and shore of surface water bodies, and mandates that the appropriate water authority take measures, without delay, to mitigate any such pollution. Under this chapter, water authorities are authorized to order persons with title to land containing pollution, or whose activities have caused pollution, to investigate such pollution in a specified manner, and to take temporary safety measures to mitigate water quality impacts.

Chapter 6 of the Water Act creates requirements for private individuals. It prohibits the "introduction of substances into a body of surface water" and the sea, as well as discharges "into a treatment plant with the aid of a structure other than a public sewer," unless the discharging entity has been granted a permit by the water board (regional waters) or the minister (national waters), or an administrative order has expressly granted permission for such discharge.[29] However, the chapter carves out an exception for: "discharges as a consequence of the use of fertilizer on agricultural land in forelands and areas outside the dikes in the course of normal agricultural activities, insofar as rules have been laid down on this subject pursuant to the Fertilizer Act."[30]

Chapter 6 also prohibits extraction of groundwater or recharge of water without a permit in several contexts: (1) for industrial purposes, if the quantity of water to be extracted exceeds 150,000 m^3 per year; (2) for the public drinking water supply; and (3) for geothermal energy storage.[31] The water authorities retain discretion to prohibit additional acts, including discharges and withdrawals under circumstances not specified in the Act.[32] The Minister of Transport, Public Works and Water Management may also establish additional rules, via administrative order, with respect to discharges and withdrawals.

Section 2 of Chapter 6 contains additional provisions with respect to water permits, including requirements for where permits should be submitted,[33] as well as guidance to water authorities regarding decisions to grant, amend, or revoke permits for discharges and withdrawals.[34] For example, the permitting authority must revoke any permit that has not been used for three consecutive years, or if it would be incompatible with other requirements in the Act.[35] This section expressly incorporates international law, stating that permits must be revoked "in the event a treaty or a decision by an international organization that is binding for the Netherlands or a legal provision implementing such a treaty or decision so compels."[36] Section 2 also specifies the types of conditions and restrictions that may be placed upon permits for discharges and withdrawals; for example, a permitting authority may require "removal, compensation or limitation of adverse effects for the water system of the activity permitted or the discontinuation of such activity."[37] The Minister of Transport, Public Works and Water Management retains authority to establish additional permitting rules via administrative order.[38] Section 3 of Chapter 6 also sets forth some restrictions with respect to permits for recharge of water, specifying that such permits "shall be granted only where there is no danger of pollution of groundwater," and that such danger should be evaluated pursuant to the rules laid down in section 12 of the EMA.[39]

Finally, Chapter 6 requires that any person whose act or omission causes the pollution or impairment of a bed or shore of a body of surface water must (1) report that pollution or impairment to the proper water authority, and (2) "take any measures that may reasonably be required ... to prevent such pollution or impairment ... or to limit and eliminate as far as possible such pollution or impairment and the direct consequences thereof."[40]

Chapter 7 of the Act authorizes the imposition of taxes for water pollution and extractions. It mandates that a "pollution tax shall be imposed on discharges into a body of surface water under State management."[41] In addition, water boards may impose a pollution tax on discharges into a body of surface water that is under the management of that water board,[42] and the provincial executive may impose a "groundwater tax" on extraction of groundwater to defray costs incurred by the province with respect to maintaining and monitoring the quality/quantity of groundwater reservoirs.[43]

Water pollution taxes may be imposed on residential users, commercial users, persons responsible for managing public sewers and water treatment plants, and any person who is responsible for a particular discharge.[44] However, certain discharges are exempt from taxation, including discharges via a wastewater sewer, discharges of substances from a treatment plant by a water authority into a body of surface water under that water authority's management, and discharges of substances originating from a treatment plant other than by the water authority, provided the discharge occurs into a body of surface water under that authority's management and the amount of pollutants or hazardous substances has not increased.[45]

Chapter 8 discusses enforcement issues. It designates water authorities as the primary enforcers of both regulations set forth under Chapters 5 and 6,[46] and also authorizes permitting authorities to revoke a water permit for failure to comply with permit terms or the provision of incorrect data.[47] Chapter 9 sets forth some procedures for legal review of administrative decisions made under the Act.[48]

The Act also address surface water allocation, specifying that "[t]he priority of social and ecological needs that shall determine the distribution of available surface water in the event or threat of a water shortage shall be laid down by administrative order."[49]

E. Spatial Planning Act

The Spatial Planning Act, promulgated in 2006, creates a regulatory framework for land use planning at the national, regional, and municipal levels. The Act provides for coordination between land use planners and water authorities, so as to ensure that land use plans include provisions to ensure that water resources will be adequately protected and conserved.

IV. Handling, Treatment, Transportation, and Disposal of Hazardous Materials

Since 2000, Dutch policy regarding the handling, treatment, and disposal of chemicals and hazardous materials is predominantly driven by international standards, including the EU REACH regulation on the registration, evaluation, authorization, and restriction of chemicals and the Classification, Labeling, and Packaging (CLP) regulation. The EMA establishes domestic rules with respect to the handling and disposal of hazardous wastes, which are elaborated upon in the National Waste Management Plan (NWMP). The Activities Decree imposes specific requirements on particular activities and installations. This section briefly describes the EU directives and other international sources of law which govern the Netherlands' hazardous waste policy, and will then examine the domestic mechanisms through which these external directives are implemented.

A. REACH Regulations

The REACH regulations, which were phased into Dutch law between 2007 and 2008, specify how businesses should address the issue of working with dangerous chemical substances. Under the regulations, industry bears the burden of proof to collect or generate data necessary to ensure the safe use of chemicals. Such data is made publicly available through a central database held at the European Chemicals Agency. REACH also provides rules for the phasing out and substitution of particularly dangerous chemicals. The requirements of REACH have been expressly incorporated into all relevant permits since 2008.

REACH regulations are designed to manage chemical substances throughout their life-cycles, imposing restrictions on manufacturers and downstream users, as well as importers and distributors. Thus, REACH contains rules regarding (1) preregistration of chemicals and exchange of information; (2) registration of substances; (3) evaluation by the relevant authorities; and (4) authorization by the relevant authorities. Because of its focus on preventing public health or environmental harms, REACH regulations are generally stricter on upstream users—manufacturers and importers—who are required to collect data on chemical substances before they can be introduced to the EU market. Downstream users and distributors are obliged to communicate information on use and exposure to risks, and to take actions in implementing risk reduction measures.

B. Classification, Labeling and Packaging (CLP) Regulation

The CLP Regulation, promulgated in 2009, complements REACH by imposing uniform classification criteria and labeling rules on chemical substances and mixtures. The CLP regulations are drawn from internationally agreed standards, as articulated in the U.N.'s Globally Harmonized System of Classification and Labeling of Chemicals (GHS)—the goal being to facilitate trade while also providing greater protection for human health and the environment. Under CLP, industry is responsible for identifying the hazardous substances and mixtures before they are placed in the market, and classifying them in accordance with regulatory specifications. Industry must also ensure that such substances comply with the labeling and packaging standards contained in CLP.

C. Seveso III Directive

The Seveso III Directive, adopted in 2012, aims to reduce the risk of major accidents by establishing requirements for the storage and processing of hazardous substances, safety management systems, emergency planning, and land use planning. The directive requires member states to ensure that operators have adequate contingency plans to prevent major accidents, and to ensure that the public is adequately informed and protected when accidents do occur.[50] The Netherlands has already adopted the predecessors to this directive—Seveso I and II—and will have to phase in the amended rules from the Seveso III Directive by June 1, 2015.

D. Electronic Waste Directives

The Netherlands is also subject to requirements under the Restriction of Hazardous Substances (RoHS) Directive and the Waste Electrical and Electronic Equipment Directive (WEEE). The WEEE Directive (2002/96/EC) sets collection, recycling, and recovery targets for electrical goods in order to address the problem of toxic e-waste. The RoHS Directive (2002/95/EC) restricts the use of six hazardous materials in the manufacture of electronic and electrical equipment.

E. International Agreements

The Netherlands is also a party to several international agreements that regulate chemicals and hazardous waste, including the Rotterdam Convention (which requires the Dutch government to implement a prior informed consent (PIC) procedure for hazardous chemicals), the Stockholm Convention on Persistent Organic Pollutants (which requires a ban on the production of certain pesticides), and the Helsinki Convention on the Transboundary Effects of Industrial Accidents (which obliges the Netherlands to adopt measures that reduce the risk of accidents with potential transboundary effects, and to consult with and notify other countries that may be affected by such accidents).

F. Domestic Policy

As noted above, Dutch policy on this issue is now driven by external directives, and the EMA and the NWMP are the primary sources of domestic implementing law. The Council of Hazardous Waste, an independent advisory body established in 2004, plays a key role in the development of domestic policy. The council's primary function is to "advise on policy and legislation on technical and organizational measures to prevent disasters arising from the production, storage and use of hazardous substances."[51]

G. Environmental Management Act

The EMA stipulates that the Ministry for Infrastructure and Environment should prepare, every six years, a "national waste management plan that regulates municipal waste collection, disposal of discarded equipment such as refrigerators and TVs, and permits for hazardous waste shipment."[52] The EMA also specifies that any private parties who discharge environmentally harmful materials are required to obtain permits that stipulate limits for the discharge of such harmful substances. In addition, many private companies—including those involved in metal processing or chemical production—are required to publish an annual report on their activities.[53] These reports must comply with requirements specified in the EU Pollutant Release and Transfer Register (PRTR).

Chapter 9 of the EMA contains the bulk of requirements for "substances, preparations and other products," including hazardous substances. It contains specific provisions relating to new substance notification, labeling, and packaging requirements, and reporting requirements. Chapter 10 addresses "waste substances" and contains provisions regarding the waste management plans, discussed above, for prevention and recovery of waste. Title 10.6 specifically addresses the management of industrial and hazardous wastes, including rules and guidelines for future rules relating to the collection, transport, and receipt of hazardous wastes, as well as shipment within, into, and from the European Community.

H.   Strict Liability (Civil Code)

Article 6:175 of the Dutch Civil Code imposes strict liability on persons who knowingly produce, handle, transport, store, dispose, or are otherwise in possession of hazardous substances, for any damage caused by such substances. Article 6:175 applies to any substance with "such characteristics that it causes a special danger of a serious nature for persons or property," including any substance that is "explosive, oxidising, inflammable, light inflammable, heavily inflammable, poisonous or very poisonous according to the criteria and methods as set under Article 9.2.3.1, third paragraph of the Environmental Management Act."[54] If these substances enter the control of a "keeper who makes it his business to store such substances," including carriers and other shipping agents, then liability transfers to the keeper.[55]

I.   National Waste Management Plan

The NWMP establishes the general policy for waste management in the Netherlands. It covers all wastes to which the EMA applies, including hazardous wastes. Pursuant to the EMA, the Ministry for Infrastructure and Environment is obliged to review this plan and revise it every six years. The NWMP sets standards for both public and private actors. It establishes specific permitting requirements for activities involving hazardous wastes, and integrates EU directives into national law. It also contains provisions recording the proposed import, export, and transshipment of waste, which accord with the EU Waste Shipments Regulation. Certain wastes do not fall within the scope of the NWMP, because they are regulated under other programs. This includes radioactive waste, which is regulated under the Nuclear Energy Act and the Policy Document on Radioactive Waste.

V.   Waste and Site Remediation

The Netherlands has adopted a "waste management hierarchy" as its official policy, wherein the hierarchy of managements practices are defined as (1) avoid, (2) minimize, (3) recycle, (4) treat, (5) dispose.[56] Although the government has made some investments in avoiding, minimizing, and recycling waste under this policy, about 80 percent of infrastructural investments have been made in incineration and landfilling.[57] Generally speaking, the proportion of waste disposed in landfills has decreased, while incineration has significantly increased—leading to some conflict with the country's air pollution and climate goals.

Dutch waste management is also regulated by EU directives, though to a lesser extent than hazardous materials management. The NWMP, discussed next, implements several directives, including the Landfill Directive 99/31, Landfill Decision 33/03, and Incineration Directive 76/00. Dutch businesses are also subject to the requirements of the Waste Shipment Regulation (1013/2006). This regulation sets forth basic procedures for waste shipments, prohibits the shipment of certain wastes, and establishes notification and disclosure requirements for the shipment of other wastes.

The primary sources of domestic law relating to waste management are the 2004 Environmental Management Act (EMA) and the National Waste Management Plan (NWMP). The Netherlands also implements its waste management policy through its National Waste Management Partnership with the private sector.

The EMA establishes specific requirements licensing requirements for establishments where "waste substances are recovered or disposed."[58] Such licenses must contain at least two obligations: (1) an obligation for the establishment to record the quantity, nature, and origin of waste substances that are recovered or dispose of at the establishment, as well as any other substances that are used, consumed, or generated during recovery or disposal; and (2) an obligation to keep this recorded data for at least five years.[59]

As noted in section IV, the NWMP establishes the general policy for waste management in the Netherlands. For example, the NWMP establishes "national objectives for the separate collection of waste and general principles for the use of instruments such as licensing and enforcement."[60] The NWMP also clarifies the Netherlands' position on international agreements and negotiations related to waste management. The primary agency responsible for implementing the NWMP is the EVOA Waste Management Department.

The scope of the NWMP extends to all waste that is covered under the EMA, including hazardous wastes. The NWMP does not apply to specific types of wastes that are regulated under alternative regimes, including radioactive waste, sewage sludge, manure surpluses, dry rendering waste, and communal wastewater.

In addition to the overarching national policy, the NWMP contains 34 sector plans, which provide additional detail on specific waste management policies, including rules for licensing, imports and exports, and waste monitoring, as they relate to particular economic sectors in the Netherlands.

A. National Waste Management Partnership

Founded in 2008, this public-private partnership represents the entire waste management chain as well as the Dutch government. The objective of the partnership is to promote cooperation between companies, government, and the public, in order to improve sustainability of waste management practices in EU, and also to identify business opportunities in waste management—e.g., opportunities to export best practices and technologies to international markets.[61]

B. Local Legal Duties

Provinces and municipalities are primarily responsible for the licensing of waste treatment facilities (including both incinerators and landfills), and enforcement of national laws and specific permit requirements. The provinces are also responsible for maintaining landfills and protecting against environmental impacts into the future. To facilitate this, the provinces are authorized to charge a levy for wastes. Municipalities are responsible for collecting household waste in their respective jurisdictions—this includes all wastes arising from private households, with the exception of wastewater and car wrecks. Municipalities are required to collect organic household waste separately. Municipalities may also enact local rules relating to the disposal of household waste—e.g., which components have to be kept separate, and the frequency of waste collection.

C. Brownfields Redevelopment

Due to the Netherlands' spatial constraints and significant manufacturing and chemical sectors, the redevelopment of brownfields is an important issue for the country. The Soil Protection Act (2006) is the primary authority on remediation requirements. It establishes the procedures and time frame for cleaning up sites based on the level of contamination (serious, urgent, and nonurgent), and authorizes provincial and local governments to issue cleanup orders for contaminated sites. Chapter 3 of the Activities Decree also contains applicable requirements—for example, section 3.1 (Wastewater Management) sets forth additional rules for investigations and remediations under the Soil Protection Act.

In accordance with the "polluter pays" principle, the individual or organization that causes pollution is generally held liable for the costs of cleaning up that pollution.[62] However, Dutch law also holds subsequent owners liable for site contamination, and thus it is important for prospective owners to conduct due diligence before acquiring a brownfields site.[63] For additional information about the imposition of strict liability upon owners and operators of contaminated sites, see section IV and section XII.

The Dutch government has implemented several policies in order to stimulate the development of brownfields. The Soil Protection Act offers some flexibility for developers by allowing remediation to be carried out in phases,[64] and allowing for partial remediation.[65] The central government also administers a redevelopment program, which provides support for the cleanup and subsequent development of priority sites. The provinces and municipalities play a key role in identifying and directing resources to those sites:

> Using a three-tiered assessment system developed at the national level, local governments prioritize sites based upon threats to human health and the environment. National funds are directed to those sites suffering from "serious contamination" and in "urgent need" of remediation. Cleanup proceeds according to a "function-oriented" or risk-based corrective action program, where remediation efforts are tied to future land use. Prospective land uses are classified into four categories established by the national government—residential and recreational green areas, non-recreational green areas, built-up and paved areas, and agriculture and nature.[66]

The central government also provides support for private sector remediation efforts through a cost-sharing program that covers up to 60 percent of remediation costs.[67] In addition, Dutch law authorizes the use of contaminated soil in construction projects, "provided the introduced soil does not have higher levels of contamination than the soil to which it is added."[68]

VI.   Emergency Response

The Ministry of Infrastructure and the Environment is the primary agency responsible for responding to most environmental emergencies, including oil spills as well as discharges of other hazardous and noxious substances. The Netherlands Coast Guard is the primary authority for marine pollution responses.

The Netherlands' emergency response measures are largely guided by the Seveso III Directive, discussed in the previous section. In addition, the Dutch government has promulgated a National Contingency Plan for Oil Spills, and is currently working on a revised national contingency plan for emergencies caused by other hazardous and noxious substances, as an extension to the Oil Contingency Plan. Currently, the Netherlands primarily relies upon the same agencies and procedures for responding to hazardous and noxious substances that it uses to respond to oil spills.[69]

The 2006 Revised National Contingency Plan for Oil Spills identifies which agency has jurisdiction over which spills, allocates responsibility for responding to oil spills between private and public actors, and establishes specific emergency response procedures, such as reporting requirements for companies. Under the plan, the Ministry of Infrastructure and Environment is primarily responsible for oil pollution response (operating through the Rijkwswaterstaat (RWS) and Provinciale Waterstaat), the municipalities are responsible for spills in municipal waterways, port authorities are responsible for spills in municipal ports of Rotterdam and Amsterdam, and the Netherlands Coast Guard is responsible for coordinating responses to marine incidents.[70]

The Netherlands has also implemented the Dutch System for Coordinated Regional Incident Control to address national disasters, including environmental emergencies. This system is a "national arrangement on the up scaling of disaster control for professional rescue services (police force, fire department, ambulance services, etc.), regionally organized in one of the nation's 25 Security regions."[71]

VII.   Natural Resource Management and Protection

Some of the Netherlands' most valuable resources include its arable land, fisheries, oil and gas reserves, and other minerals. The Dutch government manages these resources through a variety of issue-specific legislation. The EMA also contains some provisions that contribute to natural resource protection, including requirements for environmental impact assessments and licensing rules. These procedural requirements are discussed in section X.

A.   Soil

The Soil Protection Act, promulgated in 1987 and revised in 2008, contains restrictions on activities that could possibly damage or pollute soil, such as construction or the discharge of substances. The Act gives authority to provincial governments to establish specific policies for soil protection, and to impose cleanup requirements or cleaning costs on entities that are responsible for pollution to soil or groundwater.

B.   Fisheries

The Fisheries Act (1963) establishes the basic framework for regulation of marine and inland fisheries. The Regulation on Aquaculture (1993) contains more specific requirements for the farming, processing, and trade of fish and other aquaculture products. The central government works closely with the private sector to establish national quotas for various fish species.

C.   Natural Gas, Petroleum, and Other Minerals

The Mining Act (2003) establishes basic rules concerning the exploration and production of mineral resources in the Netherlands. The resources covered by the Act include natural gas and petroleum. The Act contains specific licensing requirements, as well as rules to ensure that mining operations are carried out in a safe manner. It also regulates the financing of covered activities. The Act also establishes a Mining Council, which is the primary entity responsible for advising the minister on the sufficiency of policies put in place under the Act.

The Dutch government has also entered into a covenant with the private sector, the purpose of which is to stimulate hydrocarbon exploration and production and to enable CO_2 storage projects on the Dutch continental shelf.

The covenant sets forth a procedure to encourage new and renewed exploration, production, and storage activities in areas for which mining permits have already been granted. The procedure is applied based on the voluntary cooperation of companies in the oil and gas industry.

D.   Biodiversity and Habitat Resources

The Nature Conservation Act (1998) establishes the basic framework for the protection of land and biodiversity resources. The substantive provisions of this Act are discussed in section IX.

E.   Raw Materials

The Dutch government uses supply chain certificates in order to encourage the use of sustainably produced raw materials, and reduce the overall ecological footprint of the Netherlands.[72] These certificates indicate that products have been made in compliance with sustainability criteria developed by the government in cooperation with NGOs. The Dutch government has not yet set any quantitative targets for the market share of sustainable production for most raw materials, with the exception of certified wood (target is 50 percent of market share) and coffee (25 percent of market share).[73]

VIII.   Natural Resource Damages

Efficient land management is an especially important issue for the Netherlands, due to the country's spatial constraints. In order to maximize the productivity of land while minimizing environmental impacts, the Dutch government has implemented a series of policies to encourage sustainable practices with respect to land use planning and development, transportation systems, the preservation of historic and natural landscapes, and agricultural management.

A.   Land Use Planning and Development

The National Spatial Strategy (2004) established specific goals for land use planning, emphasizing the importance of urban densification. The objective of the densification strategy is to protect the surrounding landscape, limit the use of private cars, and promote thriving urban areas with highly functional public transport systems.[74] The Spatial Planning Act (2006) sets forth the regulatory framework for development and land use decisions. The Act requires the national government, provinces and municipalities to adopt "structure schemes" which identify the main elements of spatial policy for their respective jurisdictions, proposed developments in the area, and how the municipal council intends to provide for the realization of that development within the context of its spatial policy goals.[75] The municipal governments must also adopt separate land use plans "in which the intended uses of the land included in the plan are designated in the interests of effective spatial planning and rules are laid down regarding those intended uses."[76] The Act also contains a number of additional provisions that establish the scope of municipal authority for the creation and implementation of land use plans, as well as decisions about proposed developments.

Following the introduction of the Rural Areas Investment Budget in 2007, the provincial governments now share greater responsibility for achieving central government targets for land management activities. For example, the provinces are now primarily responsible for implementing national landscape objectives, primarily via the "area-based planning processes" in which the national government, provinces, and municipalities "work together on the development and implementation of plans" for specific areas.[77]

B.   Transportation and Accessibility

The Dutch Planning Vision for Infrastructure and Landscape complements the Netherlands' spatial planning goals. Under this policy, the national government directly invests in transit infrastructure, and also uses financial incentives such as pricing policies to encourage private actors to take responsibility for transportation and land use decisions that will improve the connectivity between services, work locations, and residences.

C.   Historic and Natural Landscape Management

To protect areas with high cultural-historical, natural, and landscape value, the Ministry of Agriculture, Nature and Food Quality, in cooperation with the former Ministry of Housing, Spatial Planning and Environment, designated 20 "unique or characteristic regions" as National Landscapes.[78] The National Landscapes occupy approximately 800,000 hectares, about three-quarters of which is countryside.[79] National Landscapes do not have the same degree of protection as the National Reserves and Natura 2000 areas, which are discussed in section IX. The goal in National Landscapes is to ensure that "greater care and attention [are] given to the preservation, management and strengthening of the landscape and its natural, cultural-historic and recreational values" while still providing some scope for spatial development in the future.[80] The government achieves this through land use restrictions, and also through financial contributions for the management of the landscape.

The Dutch government has also established National Buffer Zones, which "protect rural zones between the cities of the Randstad, to keep a green zone around these cities and conserve the landscape."[81] The primary objective of these zones is to prevent cities from coalescing, in order to protect recreational, aesthetic, and ecological value in the areas surrounding cities. Building is only permitted in such zones if it contributes to recreational or other values.[82]

D. Agricultural Management

The Dutch government has also implemented specific policies in order to reduce the environmental impacts of agricultural activities, particularly impacts to water quality. The Dutch Policy Document on Sustainable Crop Production (2004) establishes an overarching framework for agricultural management. In addition, the Dutch government has implemented specific Policy Agendas for Sustainable Livestock and Sustainable Food Systems. The government has also entered into cooperative agreements with farmers under its Programmatic Approach to Nitrogen, the goal being to encourage area-specific coordination around nitrogen-sensitive ecosystems, particularly in Natura 2000 areas.[83]

E. Natural Resource Damages (NRD)

As for NRD provisions of the Netherlands' environmental regime, see the material in section XII(2), *infra*, regarding the Environmental Management Act, which incorporates the EU Environmental Liability Directive into Dutch law and is the primary law governing NRD.

IX. Protected Species

The Netherlands protects endangered species, key habitat, and biodiversity through a combination of domestic legislation and active involvement in regional and international protection programs. Some of the key sources of international, regional, and domestic wildlife law are discussed below.

A. International Treaties

The Netherlands has ratified a number of international agreements on wildlife protection, including the Convention on Biological Diversity (CBD) and the Convention on the International Trade of Endangered Species (CITES). In accordance with its obligations under CITES, the Netherlands has restricted the import, export, and domestic trade of any endangered species. In accordance with the CBD, the Netherlands has prepared a National Biodiversity Policy Programme (2008–2011), which establishes the country's specific biodiversity objectives and details how current policy initiatives will achieve those objectives.

B. Wild Birds and Habitats Directives

These two directives establish obligations for the preservation of wild birds and for natural habitat, respectively. In accordance with these directives, all member states are obliged to establish protected areas for birds (Special Protection Areas) as well as other endangered species (Special Areas of Conservation). The habitat protection requirements under both directives have been incorporated into the "Natura 2000" program, an EU conservation initiative developed under the Habitats Directive, under which member states have agreed to create an EU-wide network of ecologically protected areas. Each member state is responsible for designated Natura 2000 areas on the basis of guidelines promulgated under the directives. Natura 2000 areas do not necessarily have to be strict conservation areas wherein all human activities are prohibited—rather, they may include land that is privately owned and partially developed. Participation in the Natura 2000 program also satisfies obligations under the CBD.

C. Nature Conservation Act (1998)

This Act establishes a regulatory regime for the protection of "nature areas," focusing primarily on habitat and landscape conservation and restoration.[84] The Act designates some nature areas of outstanding national or international importance as domestic nature reserves and Natura 2000 areas, respectively.[85] The areas protected under the act are considered part of a "National Ecological Network." The goal of establishing this network is to set aside large tracks of land so as to create an unbroken network of functioning ecosystems.[86]

The Act also establishes what activities are allowed or prohibited in the protected areas, and establishes permitting requirement for certain activities, such as camping or construction. Finally, the Act establishes a duty of care for entities that manage or otherwise conduct activities in protected areas.[87]

D. Flora and Fauna Act (2002)

This Act establishes protection regimes for certain plant and animal species regardless of whether they occur in nature reserves.[88] The Act generally prohibits actions that "might reasonably be assumed to cause damage to species or their immediate environment are essentially prohibited."[89] For example, the Act prohibits anyone from killing, catching, or disturbing protected animals, and from removing protected plants. The Act also contains provisions relating to the designation of protected habitats for endangered species, the management of species that may cause damage to the human environment (e.g., disrupting agriculture), and restrictions on trade and hunting.

X. Environmental Review and Decision Making

The Ministry of Infrastructure and the Environment (I&M) is the agency responsible for reviewing environmental policies and establishing standards for permitting and other decision-making activities. The Netherlands Environmental Assessment Agency (PBL) also plays a key role in reviewing the country's environmental policies, in order to determine whether those policies achieve their stated objectives. Municipal government authorities are typically responsible for issuing and enforcing permits, although the EMA also recognizes several instances where provincial or national government agents are the "competent authorities" for permitting and enforcement purposes.

A.   Activities Decree

The Activities Decree (2007) establishes basic rules for companies that may have an impact on the environment, including (1) general environmental rules relating to all activities (e.g., a general duty of care, requirements relating to discharges into air and water, etc.),[90] (2) substantive rules for specific types of activities,[91] and (3) procedural rules relating to permits and reporting.[92] The substantive rules in the Activities Decree include quantified target requirements (which indicate the maximum allowable environmental impact of an activity) along with suggestions for "recognized measures" for achieving those targets, as well as compulsory measures that specific companies must undertake.[93]

With respect to permitting and reporting requirements, the Activities Decree classifies companies into one of three categories depending on their level of impact. Companies with no or negligible impact on the environment (category A) must comply with the general rules set forth in the decree, but need not submit an environmental management notification or apply for environmental permits. Companies that have moderate environmental impacts (category B) must notify the municipal authority of their activities, and must submit an environmental management notification. Such companies may also need to apply for a permit depending on the nature of their activities—e.g., if they construct a new facility—but they are not automatically required to obtain a permit under the Activities Decree. Companies that have extensive environmental impacts (category C) must acquire a permit from the municipal or provincial authorities, and in exceptional cases, from the minister of Infrastructure and the Environment or the minister of Economic Affairs.[94]

B.   Permitting

In 2010, the General Act for Environmental Permitting (WABO) entered into force. WABO consolidates preexisting permitting requirements for the construction, modification, and operation of installations with environmental impacts. As described by the Dutch government, WABO streamlines the permitting process such that there is "one permit, one procedure and one set of submittal requirements followed by one legal remedies procedure and enforcement by one authority."[95] Thus, all environmental permits, building permits, demolition permits, and the like are now consolidated in an all-in-one permit for physical aspects.[96] One key exception to this is water permits, which are still required for discharges and extractions, as well as certain other activities that may impact water quality or quantity.[97]

Under WABO, permit applications may be submitted to an online portal 24 hours a day.[98] WABO also creates a flexible process wherein permit applicants may apply in advance for a single permit that covers all anticipated activities, or may submit multiple permit applications for incremental activities as a project proceeds.

WABO does not establish any new or amended criteria for examining applications, nor does it alter the level of protection afforded by prior legislation.[99] Rather, the substantive permitting rules set forth in the EMA are still in place (to the extent that they do not conflict with WABO's amended permit procedures). The EMA requires private parties to obtain permits for the construction, modification, or operation of installations that may have an adverse impact on the environment.[100] It also specifies that an environmental impact assessment is required before a permit can be issued for an activity with significant environmental impacts. The specific types of installations that are subject to these requirements are defined in the Environmental Protection Installments and Permits Decree.

The EMA also establishes guidelines for the evaluation of permit applications and the conditions that may be placed upon permits. The municipal governments are generally authorized to approve and reject permit applications, but the Ministerial Council retains the authority to vest permitting authority in the central or provincial governments, if such action is deemed "necessary in view of the nature and extent of the effects which the establishments designated therein may have on the environment, or with a view to the efficient protection of the environment or where it is deemed to be in the general interest."[101] The Minister of Economic Affairs also retains some authority over permitting with respect to mines, underground waste storage, or where permits raise national security concerns.[102]

Finally, the EMA imposes obligations related to the reporting, record keeping, and monitoring of environmental impacts, which are incorporated into environmental permits. For example, qualifying establishments (e.g., large industrial operations) are required to prepare an annual environmental report (MJV) on waste, air emissions (including greenhouse gases), and water discharges. Businesses completing an MJV must also submit an electronic PRTR report for the European Pollutant Release Transfer Register.

C. Environmental Policy Review

The Netherlands Environmental Assessment Agency (PBL) is responsible for reviewing the Netherlands' environmental policies in order to determine whether such policies are making adequate progress toward key environmental objectives. PBL seeks to "improv[e] the quality of political and administrative decision-making by conducting outlook studies, analyses and evaluations in which an integrated approach is considered paramount."[103] PBL is an independent advisory agency, and thus has autonomy in defining its research questions and methodologies.

XI.   Transboundary Pollution

The Netherlands has long been concerned about transboundary pollution, as it is situated downstream from other major industrial economies. In order to address this problem, Dutch policy has emphasized the importance of international cooperation—the idea being that the government can best address transboundary pollution by meeting all EU targets, actively participating in EU negotiations, and assisting other countries with reducing air pollution. For example, NEPP-4 explicitly endorses a "twin-track policy" to reduce national emissions as much as possible while actively engaging other EU member states to encourage reductions in line with the Gothenburg Protocol and to advocate for more stringent EU targets in the future.

The Gothenberg Protocol, part of the Convention on Long-Range Transboundary Air Pollution, aims to reduce acidification, eutrophication, and ground-level ozone, by requiring significant reductions in the emissions of sulfur, NO_x, VOCs, and ammonia. Under the protocol, the Netherlands must comply with tight limit values and best available techniques requirements for specific emission sources such as combustion plants. In addition to these obligations, the Netherlands has also implemented a trading scheme for NO_x emissions, as well as a range of policies to reduce SO_2 from the transport and electricity sectors. For additional information, see section II.

In addition, the EMA establishes procedural requirements that the government and private entities must undertake with respect to activities that may have transboundary impacts, and requires the preparation of an environmental impact statement for such activities.[104]

XII.   Civil and Criminal Enforcement and Penalties

As noted in section X, municipal governments are typically responsible for issuing and enforcing permit requirements, and are thus the primary enforcers of environmental regulations in the Netherlands. Depending on the scale and nature of the activity, the "competent authority" for permitting and enforcement purposes may be the provincial government. Enforcement actions typically begin as administrative proceedings, but may subsequently become criminal investigations, depending on the nature of the violation. Since the 1990s, the judiciary has also played an increasingly important role in the enforcement of environmental laws and permits, as well as negotiated agreements between the government and the private sector.[105] The Netherlands is a civil law country, so most legal principles are codified and the application of customary rules is limited.

A.   Permit Violations

Entities that violate permit requirements or undertake an activity without an obligatory permit may be subject to either administrative or criminal sanctions. The General Administrative Law Act lists four types of administrative sanctions that can be applied to both legal and natural persons: (1) administrative orders, designed to reverse the effects of the offense and/or prevent further violations; (2) administrative coercion, which allows the enforcing authority to implement any outstanding permit or legal obligations and recover costs from the violating entity; (3) administrative penalties (fines), intended to punish the violating entity; and (4) revocation of the permit.[106]

Criminal sanctions may also be available for certain offenses that "endanger" the environment, particularly those that fall within the scope of the 1997 Economic Offenses Act. One example would be operating a polluting facility without the required permit.[107] Under the Economic Offenses Act, there are two categories of crimes and offenses: Category 1 "crimes" are punishable with up to six years in prison, community service, and a maximum fine of €76,000; Category 1 "offenses" are punishable with one year in prison, community service, or a maximum fine of €19,000; Category 2 "crimes" are punishable with two years in prison or a maximum fine of €19,000; Category 2 "offenses" are punishable with six months in prison or a maximum fine of €19,000.[108]

B. Liability for Environmental Damage

The EU Environmental Liability Directive (2004/35/EC) creates a common framework for liability arising from damage to animals, plants, habitats, water resources, and other natural resources. In accordance with the directive, entities engaged in dangerous or potentially dangerous activities (as listed in Annex III to the directive) may be subject to strict liability for environmental damage. For all other activities, there must be some showing of fault in order to hold the owner or operator liable. The directive also contains guidelines for how the costs of preventing and remedying damage may be allocated to owners and operators, and authorizes the imposition of joint and several liability.

The Environmental Liability Directive has been primarily implemented through revisions to the EMA, which imposes strict liability for environmental damage caused by Annex III activities, and fault-based liability for other activities.[109] Like the directive, the EMA does not create retroactive liability for past actions. It does, however, authorize the Dutch government to impose strict liability in circumstances other than those covered by the directive.

The directive also permits member states to recognize two defenses to strict liability: where an operator demonstrates either that damage was caused by an "authorized emission" or that the emission occurred despite the use of state-of-the-art techniques. Under the EMA, these defenses may only be used to mitigate a cost recovery action for remedial actions undertaken by a competent authority, and cannot be used to shield liability more broadly. Thus, these defenses are unavailable to an operator who takes remedial action.[110]

Chapter 17 of the EMA contains special provisions for environmental damage caused by industrial facilities. In particular, Article 17.1 requires operators to take immediate remedial action in the event of an "exceptional incident" that causes or threatens adverse environmental effects. Such action includes "all measures which may reasonably be expected of it in order to prevent the consequences of the incident, limit them as far as possible to reverse them."

The Dutch Civil Code also contains provisions that impose liability in the context of special risk. Specifically, Article 6:175 specifies that any person who uses a substance "in the course of his professional practice or business," and who knows that the substance has "such characteristics that it causes a special danger of a serious nature for persons or property," will be held liable when that potential danger is realized. Article 6:175 also contains additional provisions about how to allocate liability when multiple entities are involved. For example, "If the substance is under control of a keeper who makes it his business to store such substances, then the liability from the first paragraph rests on him."[111] Article 6:182 imposes joint and several liability on cooperators, regardless of whether they are acting jointly.

C.   Negotiated Agreements

Depending on their language, negotiated agreements may be considered binding contracts, and thus may be enforceable in civil court. Third parties who qualify as "interested parties" may bring a civil suit to enforce these agreements when the government fails to act.[112]

D.   Standing

Prior to 2005, Dutch law provided relatively broad standing for parties challenging environmental and land use decisions. However, on July 1, 2005, the "Actio Popularis" for environmental claims was abolished by national legislation, and in order for a party to have standing they must now establish that they are an "interested party"—in other words, that the party "may be exposed to the actual consequences of the decision."[113] Under the revised standard, NGOs typically have broader standing than private parties, since they can represent general interests.[114] However, NGOs may not have standing with respect to a particular matter if their interests are too broad or general.[115]

Notes

1. U.S. Cent. Intelligence Agency (CIA), The World Factbook: Netherlands, https://www.cia.gov/library/publications/the-world-factbook/geos/nl.html (last visited Nov. 28, 2012).

2. As measured by 2011 GDP.

3. Jan Teekens & Pieter-Jan Van Zanten, *Towards More Effective and Efficient Environmental Supervision—Trends and Developments in the EU and the Netherlands* 489, Ninth International Conference on Environmental Compliance and Enforcement (2011).

4. NETHERLANDS ENVTL. ASSESSMENT AGENCY (PBL), SECOND SUSTAINABILITY OUT-LOOK: THE PHYSICAL LIVING ENVIRONMENT IN THE NETHERLANDS 9 (2010).

5. Dutch Ministry of Infrastructure & Envt. (I&M), Roles and Responsibilities of the Ministry, http://english.verkeerenwaterstaat.nl/english/topics/the-environment/roles_and _responsibilities_of_the_ministry (last visited Nov. 28, 2012).

6. DUTCH MINISTRY OF HOUS., SPATIAL PLANNING, & THE ENVIRONMENT (VROM), WHERE THERE'S A WILL, THERE'S A WORLD: WORKING ON SUSTAINABILITY, SUMMARY OF THE 4TH NATIONAL ENVIRONMENTAL POLICY PLAN (2002).

7. Specifically, the 2030 targets set forth in NEPP-4 included (as compared with 1990 levels): 40–60 percent reduction in CO_2; 80–90 percent reduction in NO_x; 80–90 percent reduction in SO_2; 75–90 percent reduction in VOC; 85–95 percent reduction in particulates.

8. Dutch Environmental Management Act (EMA) § 5.1.

9. *Id.*

10. I&M, Best Available Techniques (BAT).http://www.infomil.nl/english/subjects /best-available (last visited Nov. 28, 2012).

11. DUTCH MINISTRY OF INFRASTRUCTURE & ENVT. (I&M), NETHERLANDS EMISSIONS GUIDELINES FOR AIR, http://rwsenvironment.eu/subjects/air/netherlands-emission/ (last visited Nov. 28, 2012).

12. I&M, AIR QUALITY, http://rwsenvironment.eu/subjects/air/air-quality/ (last visited Nov. 28, 2012).

13. European Env't Agency (EEA), The European Environment—State and Outlook 2010, Country Assessments: Netherlands (Nov. 26, 2010), http://www.eea.europa.eu /soer/countries/nl/soertopic_view?topic=air%20pollution.

14. Int'l Energy Agency (IEA) Clean Coal Ctr., Emissions Standards Database: Netherlands, http://www.iea-coal.org.uk/site/2010/database-section/emission-standards (last visited Nov. 29, 2012).

15. EEA, *supra* note 13.

16. European Assessment Agency, *Greenhouse Gas Emission Trends and Projections in Europe 2012—Tracking Progress Towards Kyoto and 2020 Targets* (EEA Report No. 6/2012, Oct. 24, 2012), http://www.eea.europa.eu/publications/ghg-trends-and-projections-2012.

17. NETHERLANDS ENVTL. ASSESSMENT AGENCY (PBL), ASSESSMENT OF THE HUMAN ENVIRONMENT (2012).

18. Decision No. 406/2009/EC of the European Parliament and of the Council of 23 April 2009 on the effort of member states to reduce their greenhouse gas emissions to meet the Community's greenhouse gas emission reduction commitments up to 2020 (2009).

19. PBL, *supra* note 17, at 21.

20. ENERGY RESEARCH CTR. OF THE NETHERLANDS (ECN), ENERGY EFFICIENCY POLICIES AND MEASURES IN THE NETHERLANDS 42 (2012).

21. *Id.*

22. EUROPEAN RENEWABLE ENERGY COUNCIL (EREC), RENEWABLE ENERGY POLICY REVIEW: THE NETHERLANDS (2009).

23. Water Act § 2.1.

24. *Id.* §§ 2.2–2.7.

25. *Id.* §§ 2.8–2.11.

26. *Id.* § 2.8.

27. *Id.* § 2.10.

28. *Id.* § 2.11.

29. *Id.* §§ 6.2, 6.3.

30. *Id.* § 6.2.

31. *Id.* § 6.4.

32. *Id.* § 6.5.

33. *Id.* § 6.15.

34. *Id.* §§ 6.16, 6.21, 6.16.

35. *Id.* § 6.22.

36. *Id.*

37. *Id.* § 6.20.

38. *Id.* § 6.14.

39. *Id.* § 6.26.

40. *Id.* § 6.8.

41. *Id.* § 7.2.

42. *Id.*

43. *Id.* § 7.7.

44. *Id.* § 7.2.

45. *Id.* § 7.8.

46. *Id.* § 8.1.

47. *Id.* § 8.4.

48. *Id.* § 9.1–9.5.

49. *Id.* § 2.9.

50. European Comm'n, Chemical Accidents (Seveso III)—Prevention, Preparedness and Response, http://ec.europa.eu/environment/seveso/index.htm (last visited Nov. 29, 2012).

51. Gov't of the Netherlands Official Website, Organization: Other Authorities, http://www.government.nl/ministries/ienm/organisation/other-authorities (last visited Nov. 29, 2012).

52. Gov't of the Netherlands Official Website, Environmental Management Act, http://www.government.nl/issues/environment/roles-and-responsibilities-of-central -government/environmental-management-act (last visited Nov 29, 2012).

53. *Id.*

54. Dutch Civil Code § 6:175.

55. *Id.* § 6:175(2).

56. Maarten Wolsink, *Contested Environmental Policy Infrastructure: Socio-political Acceptance of Renewable Energy Water and Waste Facilities*, 30 Envtl. Impact Assessment Review 302, 308 (2010).

57. *Id.* at 309.

58. EMA § 8.14.

59. *Id.*

60. Dutch Ministry of Economic Affairs, National Waste Management Plan, http://www.agentschapnl.nl/en/programmas-regelingen/national-waste-management-plan (last visited Nov. 29, 2012).

61. Netherlands Waste Mgmt. P'ship (NWMP), Netherlands Waste Management Partnership: Teamwork in the Waste Chain (2012).

62. Dutch Ministry of Hous., Spatial Planning & Envt., Into Dutch Soils 13 (2010).

63. *Id.* at 47.

64. Soil Protection Act § 38(3).

65. *Id.* § 40.

66. Int'l Econ. Dev. Council (IEDC), International Brownfields Development (2005), http://www.iedconline.org/Downloads/International_Brownfields_Summary.pdf.

67. *Id.*

68. *Id.*

69. Int'l Tanker Owners Pollution Federation (ITOPF), Country Profiles, a Summary of Spill Response Arrangements and Resources Worldwide: Netherlands (2011), http://www.itopf.com/_assets/country/netherla.pdf.

70. *Id.*

71. Teekens & Van Zanten, *supra* note 3, at 489.

72. PBL, *supra* note 17, at 22.

73. *Id.*

74. Kersten Nabielek, *The Compact City: Planning Strategies, Recent Developments and Future Prospects in the Netherlands* 2, AESOP 26th Annual Congress (2012).

75. Spatial Planning Act § 2.

76. *Id.* § 3.1.

77. PBL, Nature Balance 8 (2009).

78. Ministry of Agric., Nature & Food Quality, Nature Conservation in the Netherlands 10 (2005).

79. *Id.*

80. *Id.*

81. PBL, Nature Balance, *supra* note 77, at 6.

82. *Id.* at 18.

83. PBL, Assessment of Human Environment, *supra* note 17, at 40.

84. Ministry of Agric., Nature & Food Quality, *supra* note 78, at 13.

85. *Id.*

86. PBL, Halting biodiversity loss in the Netherlands: Evaluation of Progress 5 (2010).

87. Ministry of Agric., Nature & Food Quality (2005), *supra* note 78, at 13.

88. *Id.*

89. *Id.*

90. Activities Decree, ch. 2.

91. *Id.* ch. 3–6.

92. *Id.* ch. 1, § 1.2.

93. Ministry of Infrastructure & Env't, Activities Decree: Purpose Regulations, Approved and Mandatory Measures, http://www.infomil.nl/onderwerpen/integrale /activiteitenbesluit/activiteitenbesluit/doelvoorschriften (last visited Jan. 18, 2013).

94. Dutch Point of Single Contact (Answers for Business), All-in-One Permit for Physical Aspects, http://www.answersforbusiness.nl/regulation/notification-environmental -management (last visited Feb. 4, 2013); *see also* Activities Decree § 1.2.

95. Ministry of Infrastructure & Env't, All-in-one Permit for Physical Aspects (2010).

96. General Act for Environmental Permitting (WABO) art. 2.

97. Dutch Point of Single Contact (Answers for Business), Water Permit, http:// www.answersforbusiness.nl/regulation/water-permit (last visited Feb. 4, 2013).

98. Ministry of Infrastructure & Env't, supra note 95.

99. *Id.*

100. EMA § 8.

101. *Id.* § 8.2.

102. *Id.*

103. PBL, About PBL, http://www.pbl.nl/en/aboutpbl (last visited Nov. 29, 2012).

104. EMA § 7.8.

105. Magali Delmas & Ann Terlaak, *Regulatory Commitment to Negotiated Agreements: Evidence from the United States, Germany, The Netherlands, and France*, 4 J. Comparative Pol'y Analysis: Research & Practice 5, 18 (2002).

106. Milieu Ltd., *Overview of Provisions on Penalties Related to Legislation on Industrial Installations in the Member States* 434–35 (Report prepared for the European Comm'n, Jan. 2011).

107. Michael Faure & Katarina Svatikova, *Criminal or Administrative Law to Protect the Environment? Evidence from Western Europe*, 24 J. Envtl. Law 253 (2012).

108. Milieu Ltd., *supra* note 106, at 435.

109. EMA §§ 17.6–17.18, 18.2g.

110. Int'l Law Office, Dutch Implementation of the EU Environmental Liability Directive (Mar. 23, 2009), http://www.internationallawoffice.com/newsletters/Detail.aspx?g=dc6086b1-1a75-4b7a-83ab-cacca75f1797&redir=1.

111. Dutch Civil Code § 6:175(2).

112. Delmas & Terlaak, *supra* note 105, at 18.

113. Ass'n of the Councils of State and Supreme Administrative Jurisdictions of the EU, *Answers to Questionnaire on Behalf of the Council of the State of Netherlands* 4, part of a seminar on access to justice and organization of jurisdictions in environmental litigation: national specificities and influences of European Union Law (2012).

114. *Id.*

115. Decision of 1 October 2009 (case no. 200801150/1).

CHAPTER 33

Spain

HÉCTOR RODRÍGUEZ MOLNAR

I. Overview and Political Structure
A. Spain and Its Political Subdivisions

In Spain, the duty to protect the environment is vested in the various levels of government.[1] Taking into account the territorial (regional) organization of the Spanish state established by the Constitution of 1978, one can distinguish between the central government, the 17 regional governments (autonomous regions), and the local (municipal) authorities as well as the two autonomous cities of Ceuta and Melilla, located on the north coast of Africa.

The adequate operation of the legislative allocation of authority in Spain as a civil law country (see below) depends mainly on the coordination between the central government and the autonomous regions, which is sometimes far from being efficient. Moreover, the state is the sole responsible representative before the European Union (EU) at the international level on environmental matters. As a result, even in the case of authority that pertains to the autonomous regions, it is the central government that is eventually responsible before the EU for the autonomous regions' action (or lack of action). This is a source of various conflicts.

B. The Central Government and Autonomous Regions: Scope of Authority

Pursuant to Articles 148 and 149 of the Constitution, the central government is vested with the authority to enforce the nation's basic legislation on environmental protection. The autonomous regions, however, retain the authority to enact additional and/or more stringent regulations and to take action to enforce national environmental legislation at the regional level.

This allocation of authority was established by the different statutes of autonomy (corresponding to the 17 autonomous regions), which were all enacted between 1979 and 1983. These statutes define different levels of legislative and/or enforcement authority. While some statutes (among others,

Cataluña, Madrid, and País Vasco) specifically acknowledge the authority of their regional governments to enact additional protective regulations, other statutes (as, among others, Asturias, Cantabria, and Aragón) restrict the environmental role of the communities to the enforcement of the central government legislation within their respective territories. The different approaches adopted by the different regions stemmed basically from the economic strength of each region and the human resources and knowledge available in each of them.

The autonomous regions created regional environmental agencies and/or inspection agents vested with delegated control and inspection authority, while the distribution of responsibilities on environmental matters also includes a large degree of authority that is vested in and exercised only by large municipalities.

As a result of the above political allocation of environmental authority, the practitioner facing a project in Spain should always compare the particular details of the regional regulations of interest with the contents of the general national framework to identify those aspects that are critical to his/her business and may be more stringently controlled or regulated at the regional level. The environmental agencies of the different regions normally have specific departments dealing with all the areas relevant to the granting of Integrated Pollution Prevention and Control (IPPC) permits.

These comments are valid for almost all the subject matters discussed in this chapter.

C.   Municipal Authority

The legislation on the local entities regime (Law 7/1985 on the Regime of Local Entities—Ley de Bases de Régimen Local—as repeatedly amended[2]) provides for different levels of municipal authority on environmental matters based upon the number of inhabitants. In general, only cities with more than 50,000 inhabitants are responsible for assuring full environmental protection. Under existing rules, all municipalities are bound to provide for street cleaning, the supply of drinking water, sewage, control of foodstuffs and beverages, and collection of household waste. Municipalities with populations in excess of 5,000 inhabitants must also provide for the selective collection of waste. The autonomous regions have reached agreements with the different municipalities within their jurisdictions to delegate some of the above-mentioned obligations.

D.   Environmental Litigation

In connection with transboundary civil liability of a European scope, the jurisdictional aspects are dealt with in the Convention on Civil Liability for Damage Resulting from Activities Dangerous to the Environment (Lugano, June 21, 1993) (Lugano Convention). The Lugano Convention is based on the "polluter pays" principle and provides that actions for compensation may be brought under the convention by a party with a legitimate interest in the subject matter of the lawsuit before the courts of the place where (1) the damage was suffered, (2) the dangerous activity was conducted, or (3) the defendant has his usual place of residence.

At the national level, environmental protection rules can be found in the criminal code, the civil code, and administrative legislation, setting forth their own jurisdictional principles. See section XII, *infra*. In general, litigation is based on the principle that jurisdiction is vested in the courts and tribunals of the place where damage was caused. These would normally be the courts of the domicile of the defendant, but this is largely contingent upon the nature of the damage caused, as the principle of the "place where damage occurred" must be assessed in light of the rules governing the international protection of the environment. However, particular jurisdictional rules may exist.

The practitioner must be aware of the existence of one particular court in Spain: the Water Court of Valencia, Spain, which is a sophisticated court system with historical roots, adjudicating disputes between the members of the regional Community of Water Users (Comunidad de Regantes) and having its own procedural rules. The participation of an expert local counsel is mandatory. The sections of this chapter deal with the constitutional and legal allocation of authority between the central and regional governments in each of the subject matter areas to be reviewed.

II. Air and Climate Change

Spain is bound by a number of international treaties and conventions, such as the U.N. Framework Convention on Climate Change (UNFCCC) and the Montreal Protocol on Substances That Deplete the Ozone Layer. Likewise, the EU has implemented a number of rules, such as Directive EC/84/360 on atmospheric pollution from industrial facilities and Directive EC/2008/50 of May 21 on air quality.

At the central government level, the key rule on protection against atmospheric contamination is Law 34/2007 of November 15 on Air Quality and Protection of the Atmosphere,[3] which was subsequently implemented through Royal Decree 100/2011[4] and Royal Decree 102/2011,[5] of January 28, both intended to implement EU directives into Spanish law and reflect the new scenario resulting from the existence of Spain's 17 autonomous regions.

However, perhaps because of the extremely complicated nature of the environmental issues raised by air contamination (including, but not limited to, transboundary pollution), only a few regions have implemented regional legislation on this subject matter.[6]

In connection with the allocation of authority on air pollution, the central government is responsible for the monitoring of air quality and for establishing maximum emission levels. In turn, the autonomous regions are vested with material constitutional authority, such as (1) developing and implementing national legislation at the regional level, including the authority to approve additional and/or more stringent regulations; (2) implementing rules on noxious, disturbing, or harmful activities; (3) issuing statements declaring "contaminated atmosphere areas"; and (4) exercising authority in the energy field, such as issuing authorizations to facilities or activities involving renewable energies, industrial cogeneration, and others.

A.   Air Pollution Control

At the international level, Spain has ratified various protocols developed within the framework of the Convention on Long-Range Transboundary Air Pollution (Geneva, 1979).[7] In particular, the protocol on the reduction of acidification, eutrophication, and tropospheric ozone, adopted in Gothenburg, Sweden, on November 30, 1999, identifying limit values for emissions of sulfur dioxide (SO_2) and nitrogen oxides (NO_X).[8] At the European level, the EU enacted Directive EC/2001/80 of October 23 on the limitation of emissions of certain pollutants from large combustion plants into the air.[9]

The contaminants that Spain is bound to control are SO_2, to protect health and ecosystems; nitrogen dioxide (NO_2, to protect health); NO_X, to protect vegetation; suspended particulate matter of less than 10 micrometers (μm) (PM_{10}) and of less than 2.5 μm ($PM_{2.5}$); iron (Pb); benzene (C_6H_6); carbon monoxide (CO); ozone (O^3, for the protection of health and vegetation); arsenic (As); cadmium (Cd); nickel (Ni); and benzoapirene (B(a)P).

At the central government level, the key regulation is Royal Decree 430/2004, dated March 12,[10] which transposes Directive EC/2001/80/ as recently amended by Royal Decree 687/2011, of May 13.[11] Material importance is given to the National Plan for the Reduction of Emissions from Large Combustion Facilities (LCF), approved by means of Ministerial Order PRE/77/2008, of January 17.[12]

Royal Decree 430/2004 of March 12 was implemented by different orders and resolutions.[13] At the international level, note the UNFCCC, the scope of which was defined by the Kyoto Protocol to the UNFCCC of 1997[14] providing for the reduction of emissions of greenhouse gases (GHGs) from 2008 to 2012. Other key regulations exist.[15] Air emission permits are granted at national level pursuant to Law 16/2002 on Integrated Pollution Prevention and Control.[16]

B.   Air Quality

The current legal framework provides that the autonomous regions and municipalities, where applicable, are responsible within their jurisdiction for collecting data and assessing the concentrations of regulated contaminants, and preparing plans intended to improve the quality of air where the limit or other objective values are exceeded in a given area of human concentration.[17] In turn, the Ministry of Agriculture, Food and Environment (MOGRAMA) is responsible for relaying to the European Commission the data and information required by EU regulations.[18]

The Spanish Council of Ministers approved, on November 4, 2011, the National Plan for the Control of Air Quality[19] providing for general reduction goals for PM_{10}, NO_2, and ozone precursors through a series of procedures and measures described in Annex II thereof.

Spain has developed an Inventory of Emission of Contaminants into the Atmosphere with a view to assessing and updating—on a yearly basis—the levels of anthropogenic emissions and absorption levels of those GHGs governed by the Kyoto Protocol and of other contaminants falling under the scope of the 1979 Convention on Long-Range Transboundary Air Pollution, all in accordance with current international rules and criteria pursuant to EU guidelines.[20]

C. Climate Change

The Spanish Climate Change Office[21] (OECC) was created by Royal Decree 376/2001 of April 6[22] as a body reporting to the Directorate General for Environmental Assessment and Quality of the former Ministry of the Environment. The OECC is responsible for developing a national policy on climate change in furtherance of international and EU regulations on the subject and for proposing legislation and developing efficient administrative and planning instruments allowing Spain to implement climate change policies. Immediately under the authority of the OECC is the National Climate Council, entrusted with such specific tasks and instructed to assess the impact and strategies and to limit the effects of GHG emissions.[23]

The actions of the OECC are "activity focused" and developed in a number of specific sectors, of which the most important are

1. Energy: aiming at substituting coal and implementing other measures intended to increase the efficiency in power generation;
2. Industry: by increasing energy efficiency through programs intended to achieve a 25 percent reduction in CO_2 emissions, providing for the replacement of old processes and installations with more efficient technologies, and reducing the escape of, recovering, and recycling fluorocarbons; and
3. Transportation: reduction of the energy efficiency of light vehicles to achieve reductions ranging from 10 to 25 percent in emissions, controlling cooling material emissions—for an extra 10 percent reduction—and, to the extent possible, the application of fiscal pressure on the use of certain fuels.

Perhaps the most significant official action in this area was the creation of the Carbon Fund for a Sustainable Economy (known as FES-CO2 and created by Article 91 of Law 2/2011 of March 4, as amended).[24] This instrument of climatic financing was implemented by Royal Decree 1494/2011, of October 24.[25] It provided that the activity of the FES-CO2 fund shall concentrate on acquiring emission rights in what are known as "diffuse sectors" (not subject to the European emissions trading regime) related to low carbon projects known as Climate Projects. The acquisitions shall be to the benefit of such clean activities or technologies by contributing to the reduction of emissions within the Spanish national territory.[26]

III. Water

In a country like Spain, where some 50 percent of the national territory is affected by significant degrees of erosion and deforestation and recurring drought periods, the water regime is critical. The three main aspects to highlight are (1) the public nature of water resources, (2) the importance of hydrological planning, and (3) the important role of basin authorities. First, as to the public nature of water resources, in Spain all waters (surface, coastal, and underground alike) are a part of what is known as the "public hydraulic domain." Private users are entitled to use but not own the waters or wells except for those enjoying very old rights coming from the days when underground waters pertained to the owner of the land where they were allegedly located. Accordingly, the use of water is subject to the granting of different authorizations and concessions (water use, discharge permits, etc.) under Legislative Royal Decree 1/2001, of July 20. That decree approved the Restatement of the Water Law.

Second, planning is the main water instrument applied in the different basins. It is carried out by means of hydrological plans approved for each basin under the umbrella authority of the framework National Hydrological Plan. In spite of its critical importance, the plan has been subject to continuous criticism. Material delays in the implementation of the plan result from disputes over the extent of the solidarity principles applicable to the shared use of water, particularly in times of drought.

Third, basin authorities (*organismos de cuenca*) play an important role. Basin authorities are the public entities charged with preparing and managing the hydrological plans at national level. Among other responsibilities, Article 80 of the Water Law provides that each basin authority must keep a water registry, including all water concessions granted and transfers thereof. These are public registers documenting the existence and characteristics of each concession.

The practitioner should be aware that almost all regional authorities have varying degrees of administrative authority on water matters.

A.   Reception of the Water Framework
Directive and Jurisdiction

The status and quality of water bodies is the main concern of the Water Framework Directive. This directive sets forth the EU's water action program, which came into effect on December 22, 2000.[27] The directive was transposed into Spanish domestic legislation by means of Article 129 of Law 62/2003 of December 30 on Fiscal, Administrative and Social Measures,[28] introducing an amendment to the Restatement of the main Law 1/2001 of July 20 (Water Law).[29]

Pursuant to Article 149.1.22 of the Spanish Constitution, the central government has exclusive jurisdiction to legislate and grant concessions on the use of waters flowing through more than one autonomous region. While the autonomous regions are responsible in matters expressly mentioned in their respective statutes of autonomy, the enactment of Organic Law 9/1992, of December 23[30] (setting forth the principles to transfer legislative authority to the autonomous regions) caused this authority to become quite homogeneous in a number of regions. Judgment 227/1988 of the Constitutional Court of November 29 set forth the criteria for interpreting the allocation of authority as to inland water management.

B. The Hydraulic Public Domain, Hydrological Planning, and Water Basins

Under the name of "hydrographic confederations," the national basin authorities exercise their regulating powers on all basins containing water running through more than one autonomous region, known as intercommunity basins.[31] With regard to intracommunity basins, that is, those basins with waters flowing within only one region, such as the Canary and Balearic Islands, but also some continental regions, different water plans have been approved.[32]

In addition to the above-mentioned Water Law, the other key regulation is Royal Decree 9/2008, of January 11,[33] amending Royal Decree 849/1986 of April 11,[34] which approved the implementing regulations to the legislation on the Hydraulic Public Domain.[35] These regulations have been repeatedly amended and currently make up a complex web of regulations.

The main administrative instrument to implement the national water policy is the National Hydrological Plan. It aims to achieve sustainable water use and provide for the environmental recovery of the public domain affected by the inappropriate use and lack of water. It does not address any particular use of water but is intended to balance the distribution of water resources and limit the damaging impact of illegal subsurface water. The current plan, approved in 2011 (as amended), encountered a great deal of opposition (namely in Aragón and Cataluña). Its application has thus far been uneven.[36]

C. Permits and Concessions

Pursuant to the Restatement of the Water Law approved by Legislative Royal Decree 1/2001 of July 20,[37] the use of surface or subsurface waters for industrial or agricultural uses by individuals or legal entities is subject to the granting of a concession by the competent hydrographic confederation. Depending on the nature of the concession and the amount of water required pursuant to the application, the permit may be subject to the prior preparation of technical reports and will be subject to the payment of a concession fee to be determined on a case-by-case basis. The granting of a concession does not affect an entity's obligation to secure any other permit or license that may be required at the regional or municipal level.[38]

In turn, the granting of discharge permits falls under the authority of the relevant autonomous regions. Such permits are normally a part of the permits granted pursuant to the IPPC regulations.

D.   Surface and Underground Water

Traditionally, the management of surface water and the quality thereof was based on the identified uses of a given water body. The implementation of the Water Directive, however, adopted a more eco-systemic approach. In Spain, the availability of water is heavily dependent upon the status and levels of the many water reservoirs scattered around the country. As a result, in addition to the control of river flows and the quality of their waters, the legal regime is heavily focused on assuring the availability of quality water in such reservoirs.

The key aspects of interest with regard to continental (surface and underground) waters are those relevant to preventing contamination of drinking water and unauthorized discharges. Companies are required to undertake a number of activities aimed at achieving such goals. First, they are subject to prohibitions with regard to activities that physically, chemically, or biologically alter naturally occurring waters. Second, entities must apply for and secure relevant discharge permits and pay approved discharge fees, while respecting at all times the characteristics of the discharges and the discharge limits shown on the permits. To these effects they must accomplish water samplings and treatments and undergo the number of periodical inspections established by responsible environmental agencies.

Annex I of the Regulations on the Hydraulic Public Domain (Royal Decree 849/1986 of April 11, as amended[39]) lists those forbidden substances that must never be present in discharges. Other regulations provide for the required samplings and testing methods and equipment to monitor water quality.

Throughout the country, the autonomous regions have established and operate, either directly or through outsourcing (concessions), water treatment plants with capacities in accordance with the quality and volume of the waters to be treated. Water use in coastal regions normally requires more intense treatment due to the higher salt or chemical content than inland (surface and underground) waters.

E.   Coastal and Marine Waters: Management and Protection

Spanish coasts are approximately 8,000 kilometers long and extend through 25 provinces and 428 municipalities. One-third of the Spanish population lives in coastal areas, which receive three out of every four tourists that visit the country every year. This results in substantial environmental impacts. Some coastal communities grow by a factor of four in the summer, with the associated ecosystem stress. In Cataluña, for example, areas located within 15–20 km from the coast host natural riches that coexist with touristic or economic activities such as fishing, agriculture, maritime communication, leisure, and others, providing for permanent sources of contamination.

Regarding the protection of marine waters, the central government is responsible for, among other matters, (1) water management and protection; (2) discharges from ships or airplanes (following the constitutional authority vested in the central government to approve environmental protection legislation); (3) the regeneration of beaches; (4) the granting of permits for access to and work on coastal areas; and (5) ports of general interest. In turn, Article 114 of the Law on Coasts[40] provides that the autonomous regions are responsible for (1) coastal urban planning, (2) other ports, (3) discharges into the sea, and (4) any other specific authority that may be expressly provided for in the corresponding statutes of autonomy.

The autonomous regions have the authority necessary to enforce international agreements and conventions in all matters falling under their specific scope of authority.[41] Municipal authorities have limited degrees of authority with respect to coastal areas under their jurisdiction, which vary significantly from region to region.

The general impact of discharges into the ocean is conditioned by different factors.[42] Discharges from land to sea require specific permits, as the most significant contamination of maritime coastal waters stems from land sources. Spain is a party to numerous multilateral conventions on maritime contamination.[43] A number of domestic regulations have been enacted in furtherance of Spain's obligations under such conventions, such as Royal Decree 1381/2002 of December 20 on Port Facilities for the Reception of Waste from Ships and Cargo Downloads.[44] At the national level, the Law on Coasts regulates direct discharges of solids and liquids into coastal ocean waters. Indirect discharges are governed by Legislative Royal Decree 1/2001 of July 20, approving the Restatement of the Law on Waters.[45]

IV. Handling, Treatment, Transportation, and Disposal of Hazardous Materials

European legislation on the handling, treatment, transportation, and disposal of hazardous materials stems from Regulation EC/1907/2006, the Regulation on the Registration, Evaluation and Authorisation of Chemicals (REACH)[46] as amended. REACH came into effect on June 1, 2007, and was intended to improve the protection of human health and the environment against the risks presented by the manufacture, marketing, and use of chemical substances and compounds present in daily life. To meet the requirements of REACH, companies must identify and manage risks associated with the substances that they manufacture and market within the EU. Companies must (1) furnish their customers or users guidance as to the ways in which the substances they manufacture and market within the EU must be used in a safe manner; and (2) report to the interested parties any and all information concerning the relevant risks.

A.   Application of REACH in Spain

REACH was implemented in Spain by means of Law 8/2010 of March 31[47] and Royal Decree 1802/2008 of November 3,[48] updating the regime on the Notification of New Substances and the Classification, Packaging and Labeling of Dangerous Substances that was first approved in Spain by former Royal Decree 363/1995, of March 10.

Law 8/2010 requires the administrative authority to survey, inspect, and ensure compliance with REACH. It also requires the autonomous regions to implement and enforce REACH. As an exception, in cases of upmost urgency, the central government shall itself promote, coordinate, or take any measure necessary to assure compliance with both Law 8/2010 and Royal Decree 1802/2008.

B.   Chemical Marketing, Transportation, Storage, and In-Plant Handling

The EU Regulations on the Marketing and Use of Certain Dangerous Substances and Preparations (namely, Regulation EC/1907/2006 of the European Parliament and Council of December 18,[49] which repealed Directive EC/76/769), was received into Spanish domestic law by Royal Decree 1406/1989 of November 10 on the Marketing and Use of Certain Dangerous Substances and Compound Preparations,[50] as repeatedly amended to implement updated rules to control the national and international trade of dangerous chemicals.

Transportation has been extensively regulated through different Royal Decrees dealing with transportation of dangerous substances by rail (Royal Decree 412/2001 of April 2[51]), road, or navigable waters (Royal Decree 551/2006, of May 5, regulating transportation within the Spanish territory[52]). All products must be accompanied by certain mandatory transportation forms. Transportation companies must prepare and file with the Regional Authorities Annual Reports summarizing their yearly activities.[53]

Other national rules govern the Storage of Chemical Products to avoid accidents, leaks, and so on. The key rule is Royal Decree 379/2001 of April 6, approving the Regulations on the Storage of Chemical Products and their seven additional technical instructions (*instrucciones técnicas complementarias*, ITCs): (1) MIE APQ-1 (storage of flammable and combustible liquids); (2) MIE APQ-2 (storage of ethylene oxide); (3) MIE APQ-3 (storage of chlorine); (4) MIE APQ-4 (storage of ammonia); (5) MIE APQ-5 (storage of compressed gases, both liquid and dissolved under pressure); (6) MIE APQ-6 (storage of corrosive liquids); and (7) MIE APQ-7 (storage of toxic liquids).[54] These ITCs provide for additional safety measures including, but not limited to, antitheft devices, spills containment, and detection of leaks in underground tanks or containers.

Significantly, the operator of a facility where chemicals are stored must file with the responsible body of the relevant autonomous region, every five years, a certification issued by a duly registered certification entity demonstrating that the facilities continue to meet all the requirements of the applicable ITC and a copy of a civil liability insurance policy for a minimum initial amount of €601,012.10 per damaging event or accident, which amount must be updated on a yearly basis.

In the event that a facility stores two or more products subject to different ITCs, the above referenced certification must demonstrate that the facility applies the protective measures foreseen in the most stringent one.

C. Biocides and Persistent Organic Pollutants

Pesticides are classified in Spain in accordance with their intended uses, as follows:

- Pesticides for use in agriculture, also known as phytosanitary products. The key regulation is Royal Decree 3349/1983 of November 30, as amended by Royal Decree 162/1991, approving the Technical Health Rules Governing the Manufacture, Marketing and Sale of Pesticides,[55] subsequently modified by Regulation EC 1107/2009. This Royal Decree sets forth the basis for assessing the maximum level of debris (waste) admissible in pesticides to prevent intoxications and limit the risks associated with their direct and indirect uses in furtherance of the principles set forth in European Parliament and Council Regulation EC/396/2005 on the matter.
- Pesticides for use in cattle breeding and nonagricultural uses, known as biocides. In connection with the control of biocides, the EU approved Parliament and Council Directive EC/8/98, of February 16, establishing (1) controls with regard to the approval and marketing of biocides in member states, (2) the mutual recognition of authorizations within the boundaries of the EU, and (3) a list of active substances that can be used in the manufacture of biocides. This directive was implemented via Royal Decree 1054/2002 of October 11,[56] governing the procedures applicable to the prior official assessment necessary to secure authorization to register and sell biocides. The administrative procedures for applying for the necessary authorizations are found in different orders (e.g., Order of August 4/1993—Annex I, as amended) setting forth the requirements for each application.
- For miscellaneous uses such as disinfection, control of insects or pests and personal hygiene for environmental or domestic uses.

Regarding persistent organic pollutants, Spain is a party to the Stockholm Convention of May 22, 2001, which was implemented at European level by Regulation EC/850/2004. In furtherance of the requirements of the regulation, the Spanish government approved, on February 2, 2007, the National Plan on Persistent Organic Pollutants (Plan Nacional de Contaminantes Orgánicos Persistentes).

D. Export/Import of Hazardous Chemicals

Regulation EC/689/2008, on the Exportation and Importation of Hazardous Chemical Products, implements within the EU the Rotterdam Convention on the Prior Informed Consent Procedure for Certain Hazardous Chemicals and Pesticides in International Trade, with a view to protecting human health and the environment.[57] The convention applies to pesticides and industrial chemicals and requires the express approval (i.e., prior informed consent) of the importing country in connection with products listed in Annex III thereof. Both the convention and the regulation foresee the appointment of one or more national designated authorities (NDAs) to undertake the administrative burdens arising from the convention.[58] The EU Commission is the common authority for the EU and works jointly with the NDAs of the different member states.

The most recent development on this subject is the approval of European Parliament and Council Regulation EU/649/2012, which updates the contents of Regulation EC/689/2008. It introduces changes in the "express consent" procedures to facilitate exportation in cases where no reply is received from the importing country. This regulation came into effect on July 25, 2012, and became applicable on March 1, 2014, when Regulation EC/689/2008 shall be repealed. In the interim, MOGRAMA has approved different procedures to provide notice of the exportation of dangerous chemicals within the scope of application of Regulation EC/689/2008.[59]

V. Waste and Site Remediation
A. Inventories of Contaminated Sites

The central government is responsible for enacting the basic waste legislation that must subsequently be implemented by the different autonomous regions, either at the same or higher level of protection.[60] While the responsibility for enforcement is vested primarily in the regions, the central government retains the authority to take whatever steps it may consider necessary to guarantee the nationwide application of waste legislation. As such, the central government produces periodic national waste plans and issues rules on the transborder movement of waste, as a part of its constitutional authority on international relations and trade.

Within the framework of their general obligations on environmental issues, the municipalities are responsible for the collection and disposal of urban solid (household) waste and are entitled to issue ordinances or waste management plans to organize and control the relevant collection and disposal services. The National Integrated Waste Plan for 2008–2015 foresees different goals in connection with the reduction and/or recycling of waste and procedures related to the remediation of contaminated soil.

The key legal instruments are Law 22/2011 of July 27 on Waste and Contaminated Land,[61] and Royal Decree 9/2005 of January 14 with regard to the procedures to identify contaminated parcels of land.[62] Under Law 22/2011, the autonomous regions are instructed to identify and declare the existence of contaminated land and implement the mandatory actions to remediate the land in the way and within the time periods that the regions shall determine.[63]

The autonomous regions must prepare, update, and report to the central government their regional contaminated land inventories, allowing the government to prepare the corresponding national inventory.

The regions must assure that the inventory is kept up to date as to the levels of contamination, the remediation activities undertaken, and the declaration of decontamination for each property. In line with the principles of Law 26/2007 of October 23 on Environmental Liability,[64] remediation/decontamination must be undertaken by the individual(s) or entity(ies) that caused the contamination (if several, in a joint and several manner) or, in the absence of action by the referred persons, by the owners and holders (operators) of the same in that order.[65]

Royal Decree 9/2005, dated January 14, approved both the list of potentially contaminating activities and the criteria and standards that the authorities will have to apply to declare that a given piece of land is contaminated. This Royal Decree, while formally still in effect, may be repealed upon the enactment of the future implementing regulations to the new Waste Law 22/2011. It is still useful, however, to the extent that it defines "contaminated soil" as "any soil . . . having its physical, chemical, or biological characteristics negatively altered by the presence of dangerous components of human origin in concentrations implying a risk for human health or the environment and . . . that has been declared as contaminated by means of an express resolution."

The existence of contamination is determined pursuant to specific criteria and standards identified as "generic reference levels" (*niveles genéricos de referencia*). "Contamination" is defined as "the presence in the land of a contaminating substance in a concentration not involving risks for human health or the ecosystems beyond the acceptable maximum levels, as calculated pursuant to the criteria described in Annex VII."

Law 22/2011 does not apply to (1) wastewaters; (2) animal by-products not intended to be incinerated, landfilled, or used for biogas or compost encompassed by European Parliament and Council Regulation 1069/2009 of October 21; (3) dead animals; and (4) waste from exploration, treatment, and storage of mineral resources or open pit mines, which are governed by their own specific legislation.

B.   Waste Flows

Spanish waste legislation is based on the idea of addressing the problems and particular features of each specific waste "flow." At present, the concept of "waste flow" includes all aspects of the handling, storage, and disposal of the different kinds of waste other than household waste. There are many subclassifications such as construction waste, mining waste, electric and electronic waste, and others that are briefly described next.

C. Manufacturers' Extended Liability

Manufacturers of products that may become waste at the end of their life cycle are obliged to prevent and manage the recycling or disposal processes either individually or jointly, by enforcing integrated management systems (*sistemas integrados de gestión*, SIG). The law sets forth the scope of this extended liability of producers by establishing a myriad of obligations (still to be implemented in detail) regarding the design, production, and management of products and their waste, and applicable either individually (through their own management systems established individually by each producer or manufacturer) or through the existing or new SIGs, a number of which already exist.[66] The existing SIGs will have to adjust to the requirements of the Waste and Contaminated Land Law 22/2011.

D. Polychlorinated Biphenyls (PCBs)

At present, the use of PCBs in new equipment is forbidden, but PCBs are still contained in many pieces of equipment and tools having a long useful life. Spain has a national inventory of PCBs that was prepared by MOGRAMA by merging the information produced by the different autonomous regions. The key regulation is still the old Royal Decree 1378/1999 of August 27, as amended by Royal Decree 228/2006 dated February 24,[67] setting forth measures to eliminate and manage PCBs, polychlorinated terphenyls (PCTs), and equipment that contain them. Under the Royal Decree, owners of PCBs (whatever their regulated form) must deliver them to an authorized waste handling agent (*gestor autorizado*) and justify the contents thereof. Handling agents were bound to provide for decontamination or elimination of the PCBs before January 1, 2011.

In addition, certain equipment containing PCBs or PCTs had to be declared to the relevant autonomous regions for purposes of inventory (Annex I of the Royal Decree) by September 2000 at the latest. These pieces of equipment must be at all times properly marked and labeled for purposes of adequate identification. Inventory obligations affect equipment with PCB contents in excess of five cubic decimeters or with a PCB volume between one and five cubic decimeters.

Certain pieces of equipment, such as transformers with high concentrations of PCBs, are subject to specific obligations, while this Royal Decree also provides for storage and fire fighting requirements. Breaches subject to the penalties are found in Law 10/1998 on Waste (now repealed by Law 22/2011, see *supra*).

E. Electric and Electronic Waste

The amount of electric and electronic waste increases every day and is subject to EU control through European Parliament and Council Directive 2002/96/EC of 27 January 2003 on waste from electrical and electronic equipment (WEEE). WEEE was implemented in Spain by Royal Decree

208/2005 of February 25 on Electric and Electronic Waste,[68] encompassing 10 different kinds of electric and electronic waste and including, but not limited to, large and small household appliances, computer and telecommunications equipment, consumer electronic products, illumination equipment, and electric or electronic tools. It does not apply to products that are embodied or are a part of other products not encompassed by its provisions or to military products for national defense.

A number of obligations apply from as early as the design phase of the equipment. The main goal is to reduce the presence of dangerous substances normally used in the manufacturing process. Transition periods apply, as authorized by the directive. Particular emphasis is placed on products from households, as these are the main source of electric and electronic waste.[69] In case manufacturers elect not to implement such management procedures themselves, they will have to deliver the waste to authorized waste handling agents or participate in SIGs organized by the industry.[70]

WEEE defines the "equipment" to which the regulation applies[71] and describes (Article 3) the prevention measures that manufacturers must implement to assure a quality design of the products. In addition, it sets forth the obligation of producers to furnish the authorized waste handling agents—at their request—with the information necessary to properly dispose of the products.

Consumers and users have a parallel obligation to return the products to the manufacturers or distributors at the end of their useful lives, provided the consumers bear no cost in doing so. Upon the purchase of a new product, the dealer must take delivery of waste products and assure that they are properly channeled into the recycling/waste flow cycle. Producers of equipment must implement the procedures necessary to pick the delivered products up from dealers or other receiving points.

Producers are responsible for the adequate management of their waste. Manufacturers electing to organize their own collection and treatment systems must bear all the costs associated to the legal requirements, by withdrawing the waste delivered by users at the transitory receiving/delivery points.

Municipalities having more than 5,000 registered inhabitants have significant obligations in connection with the handling and treatment of equipment waste from households. For municipalities of fewer than 5,000 registered inhabitants, Royal Decree 208/2005 leaves to the autonomous regions the task of regulating the obligations applicable at regional level. Products containing one or more dangerous substances must be decontaminated as required by Royal Decree 208/2005 prior to any treatment or other action. In particular, it requires the mandatory use of the best available techniques through certified management systems that the regions must implement within their boundaries. Any cross-border transfer of equipment waste must be in accordance with the provisions in Council Regulation EC/259/93 on the Surveillance and Control of Waste Transfers within, at the entry, and exit of the EU.

Annex IV of the Royal Decree 208/2005 lists the technical requirements applicable to the facilities devoted to receiving and treating electric and electronic equipment[72] and the recycling goals to be met.[73] Electric and electronic equipment must be properly marked in order to allow for the identification of the manufacturer and confirm the date on which the products were placed in the market. The authorities must be timely and accurately informed (on a yearly basis) of the changes in the integrated systems to be implemented pursuant to the Royal Decree 208/2005. The information and documentation to be provided must be certified by an external auditor.

F. Industrial Oils

Law 22/2011 of July 28 on Waste and Contaminated Land defines used oils as "all industrial or lubricating oils that are no longer used as originally intended, such as oils from combustion motors, gear boxes, turbines, and hydraulic equipment." Used oils from motor vehicles usually originate in repair shops, gas stations, and other similar locations. Other kinds of used oils come from miscellaneous industrial uses, such as the lubrication of machinery during maintenance processes. While the damaging impact of oil spills can be felt on land and waters alike, impact to water bodies is particularly problematic for Spain, where water is a scarce and critical element. The density of oil prevents oxygen from reaching water, thus altering its biological balance, while the presence of toxic oil components can enter the human food chain through fish species. Used oils must be collected and treated and managed by authorized waste handling agents. The key regulation is Royal Decree 679/2006, of June 2, as amended,[74] governing the Management of Used Industrial Oils.

Manufacturers of industrial oils are obliged to meet their legal obligations in proportion to the amount of new oil that they place on the market, based upon a coefficient of waste generation per liter of new oil so marketed. The former Ministry of the Environment (now MAGRAMA) "may" approve such "coefficients" in cooperation with the autonomous regions, based upon the best available data, while manufacturers must ensure proper financing of the resulting costs.

The regulations apply to industrial oils placed in the national market and either manufactured in Spain or purchased in another EU member state; waste from oil generated in the Spanish territory; and used industrial oils imported or coming from other EU member states. Importers, purchasers, or recipients will be responsible for the adequate management of all these products. These regulations *do not* apply to used oils containing PCBs or PCTs or those taken from equipment containing such PCBs or PCTs. The management of used oils laced with or containing PCBs or PCTs is governed by Royal Decree 1378/1999, of August 27 (see section V.C, *supra*).[75] Plans for avoiding damaging environmental impacts must be prepared and updated every four years.

Regeneration and other forms of recycling and energy value adding are priorities, in this order. The regulations set forth the recovery and value-adding targets to be met by the manufacturers of industrial oils.[76] Used oils intended to be abandoned will be treated as toxic waste. The enforcement of violations of these recycling obligations is uneven in the different regions. Of particular interest are the provisions devoted to the raising of finance required by the implementation of selective collection systems: the manufacturers contribute funding in proportion to the amount of industrial oil they release into the national market. No additional financing would be available from the regions when used oils are used for energy-added-value purposes, including alternatives involving the use of used oil as fuel or in incineration processes.

Liabilities are assessed on the owners or managers of facilities producing or handling used oils. Obligations include the need to properly store used oils (no mixings allowed; regeneration of some oils possible) and to deliver them to authorized handling agents.[77]

Finally, Law 16/2002 of July 1 on Integrated Pollution Prevention and Control provides that "installations for value-adding activities with a processing capacity of ten tons per day or more, including the management of used oils or the elimination thereof by means other than landfilling, must secure an Integrated Environmental Permit."[78]

G.   Sludges and the National Sludge Register

Wastewater treatment stations (WWTS) are the main source of waste sludges and, as such waste producers, they must ensure the correct management thereof. Management can be undertaken by the WWTS directly or by delivering the sludges to authorized waste handling agents as provided for in Law 22/2011 of July 28 on Waste and Contaminated Land. At present, the general guidelines that the WWTS must follow and the goals they must achieve are included in the current National Integrated Waste Plan for the period 2008–2015.[79]

Sludges from urban wastewater treatment plants are governed by the general waste legislation, except that their use as fertilizers is specifically governed by (1) Royal Decree 1310/1990 of October 29,[80] setting forth a series of controls that the autonomous regions must put into operation when following up the use of sludges in agricultural activities—this Royal Decree created the National Sludges Register (NSR); (2) an Order of October 26, 1993,[81] on the use of sludges from WWTPs in agriculture; and (3) Royal Decree 824/2005 of July 8 on Fertilizers,[82] as amended, with particular reference to the use of sludges from WWTS.

H.   Vehicles at the End of their Useful Life; Used Tires

Vehicles discarded by their owners or possessors become waste and must be delivered to an authorized management center to receive a certificate witnessing that the vehicle has been scrapped.

This kind of waste is governed by Royal Decree 1383/2002 on Management of Vehicles at the End of their Useful Life,[83] which obliges manufactures

(Article 3) to take some preventive measures in manufacturing their vehicles, such as reducing the use of dangerous substances, using recyclable materials, and designing and manufacturing vehicles in a manner that will facilitate their final disassembling and/or decontamination processes. This Royal Decree applies to motor vehicles having (1) at least four wheels for the transportation of people and having a maximum of eight (8) seats, driver included; (2) at least four wheels for the transportation of merchandise and with a maximum mass of 3.5 tons; or (3) three symmetrical wheels and internal combustion with horsepower not exceeding 50 cm^3 and manufactured not to exceed a speed of 45 kilometers per hour.[84]

This Royal Decree applies to manufacturers as well as importers, dealers, distributors, insurance companies, repair shops, authorized decontamination centers, and companies carrying out value-adding operations or disposal operations. The main economic players have created the Spanish Association for the Environmental Management of Out of Use Vehicles (SIGRAUTO), aimed at assuring a correct disposal of the vehicles.[85]

Similarly, separate regulations govern the disposal of used tires. The EU Landfill Directive prohibited the landfilling of whole tires as of July 1, 2003, in all EU member states and the landfilling of even shredded tires as of July 1, 2006. Spain produces some 200,000 tons of used tires, namely in repair shops where tires are changed and in authorized management centers for end-of-life vehicles.

The main regulation is Royal Decree 1619/2005 of December 30 on the Management of Used Tires.[86] Royal Decree 1619/2005 encompasses all tires placed on the market, except tires for use in bicycles and tires with a diameter in excess of 1400 millimeters, and provides that tire manufacturers (and importers) must finance the management of used tires. Two integrated management systems currently exist.

The regulations define a number of concepts, such as the "producer" of tires, as opposed to the "generator" of this kind of waste. "Producer" is defined as the individual or legal entity either manufacturing, importing, or acquiring tires in other EU member states, while the generator is the legal person—other than the owner or end user—generating this type of waste.

Producers are bound to (1) implement prevention plans aimed at minimizing the production of waste, (2) take back worn-out tires, and (3) ensure the adequate financing of the collection and disposal systems. These activities can be organized individually or collectively, through the operation of the selective collection systems authorized by the relevant autonomous regions. It is worth mentioning that the systems foreseen in this Royal Decree would not differ substantially from other collection systems (e.g., for glass) currently in place pursuant to the Waste Law, while bearing in mind the particular features of this kind of waste. Contributions to the operation of the systems shall be made in proportion to the number of tires marketed by each manufacturer in any given year.[87]

Prevention plans must be implemented to identify procedures to extend the useful life of tires, their recycling, and other means to add value to the waste. Plans to be prepared by importers or entrepreneurs purchasing tires in other EU member states can—in addition to applying the entrepreneur's own criteria—describe prevention actions implemented by the corresponding manufacturers. Prevention plans prepared under the selective collection systems must identify the producers supporting the relevant systems and ensure that the entity handling the systems actually supports the plans, without prejudice to the ultimate liability that this Royal Decree places on producers. In turn, producers are also ultimately responsible for the achievement of the goals laid out in the National Plan for Used Tires 2001–2006. This Royal Decree also discusses handling activities (*actividades de gestión*). The operation of a handling system would only require prior notice to the autonomous region concerned, while value-adding and elimination activities are subject to authorization pursuant to chapter II of the Waste Law.

This Royal Decree also governs storage activities by setting forth the technical requirements applicable with regard to access issues, fire prevention, and other specific features of storage facilities.

Such technical requirements are set forth in an annex to this Royal Decree and are in addition to those already established with regard to the recycling and/or disposal of parts of end-of-life vehicles. Storage in facilities provided by generators cannot exceed a year and will be limited to a maximum of 30 tons. In turn, storage in facilities operated by handling agents is subject to specific rules. Storage of waste intended to be eliminated cannot exceed six months or 30 tons, while storage of waste intended to be subject to value-adding activities cannot exceed one year and the maximum authorized storage capacity must not exceed half of the annual authorized treatment capacity.

Royal Decree 1619/2005 specifically bans landfilling of used tires, mostly because of their high volumes in landfills, but also because of their flammability, which makes extinguishing rubber fires extremely difficult.

Some tires can be recycled. Those that cannot be recycled are used as fuel in cement plants, thermal centrals, and so on. Rubber dust is used in industry and public works to be incorporated into highway construction and in the manufacturing of hard pavements.

The National Integrated Waste Plan for 2008–2015 lays out different targets for 2015 as to the reduction of tire uses (by 8 percent), value adding (98 percent), and recycling (up to a maximum of 55 percent according to the different uses).

I. Medical Waste and Biowaste

Medical waste is waste generated in hospitals, clinics, health centers, labs, and other health care or research units. Depending on their ability to implement national regulations, certain autonomous regions also regulate waste produced in drug rehabilitation treatment centers and funeral homes. As a whole, some 12 out of the 17 existing autonomous regions have specific regulations on medical waste resulting in differences in the classifications and product nomenclatures between regions. This matter cannot be dealt with in a uniform manner but must be focused with a strictly regional approach before any action is taken.[88]

VI. Emergency Response

Preventing or mitigating labor risks requires careful planning and project design. In Spain, the obligations in this regard stem from two pieces of legislation: (1) what is known as the Workers' Statute, approved by Legislative Royal Decree 1/1995,[89] Article 4.2.d of which highlights the right of workers to their physical safety and to being subject to (and being bound to observe) a consistent entrepreneurial safety and hygiene policy, and (2) Law 31/1995 of November 8 on Labor Risk Prevention.[90] Claims based on the violation of Risk Prevention and Control regulations are normally handled by the social courts of the domicile of the company concerned.

A. In-Plant Safety

1. Risk Prevention Services and Emergency Preparedness

Regulation of risk prevention is structured pursuant to Royal Decree 39/1997 of January 17, enacted in furtherance of the mandate of Law 31/1995 of November 8 (see above) directing the Spanish government to implement rules on the procedures necessary to evaluate labor risks and the ways in which the prevention services would be organized, operated, and controlled. Likewise, Law 31/1995 requires that the government establish the training requirements for those individuals entrusted with risk prevention, in line with Directive 89/391/EC.

This legislation focuses on the ways to complete an initial assessment of labor risks within the company and to ensure adequate risk prevention in the light of the structure and operating features of the relevant facilities and the level of risk of their activities. Depending upon such evaluation, prevention can be organized internally or by resorting to external sources;[91] in the latter case, the entities or organizations carrying out said prevention activities would have to meet the qualification requirements described in this Royal Decree and be properly registered as such.[92]

In turn, entrepreneurs establishing their own internal prevention measures must put in place the necessary auditing resources to control the status of prevention activities.

This Royal Decree approves different levels of preventive training (basic, intermediate, and high), with different requirements applicable to each level. Companies must establish their own written emergency plans to handle accidents occurring in-plant. The law makes a distinction between large and smaller facilities.

A key regulation is Royal Decree 1254/1999, of July 16,[93] as amended, approving steps to control risks inherent in serious accidents caused by or involving dangerous substances and applying to facilities (establishments) using or containing dangerous substances in amounts equal to or in excess of those specified in column 2 of parts 1 and 2 of Annex I thereto.

This Royal Decree does not apply to facilities not meeting the quantities or thresholds of dangerous substances established by this decree or to facilities or activities that are subject to specific regulations, such as military facilities or areas, nuclear energy activities, waste landfills, mining activities, or transportation and temporary storage (for transportation purposes) of dangerous goods.

This Royal Decree is intended not only to prevent accidents that may be caused by dangerous substances but also to avoid or restrict the consequences that may result from such accidents for individuals, assets, and the environment by avoiding possible follow-on effects.[94]

Finally, facilities handling dangerous substances listed in Annex I in amounts in excess of certain listed limits must also prepare (and file before the activity in the facility begins) a safety report (*informe de seguridad*) intended to confirm to the authorities that the company has prepared and put into operation an effective risk prevention policy and has identified and evaluated existing risks and the possibilities that a domino effect may occur between buildings of the same facility. Such assessment involves the preparation of an internal emergency plan and demands that the facility provides the information necessary for the authorities to safely evaluate applications for the granting of additional permits to other facilities that may wish to have located in the vicinity.

The adequate preparation of said internal plans would allow the civil protection authorities to operate promptly and efficiently in the event of an accident that may impact on the population.[95] A safety report must be presented before construction or operation of the facility starts. The timing for the filing must be confirmed with the regional authorities.

The internal emergency plan and safety report must be updated as follows: in a general manner, every five years; at any time when the facility introduces changes that may alter the level of risk; and upon the occurrence of new technical safety developments. Facilities that do not meet the thresholds set forth by the Royal Decree must comply with the general labor risk prevention regulations applicable to the relevant activity.

2. *General In-Plant Safety Rules; Self-Protection Rules*

In-plant safety is an extremely broad area and a comprehensive discussion exceeds the scope of this kind of work. Spanish legislation on in-plant safety deals with an array of matters related to workers' protection and safety, such as minimum health and safety conditions at the workplace, minimum health and safety requirements applicable to the use of personal protective equipment, in-plant sign posting, and notification of work accidents. Other matters dealt with on this subject include regulations governing the handling of work loads, the use of safety belts and harnesses, the operation of tower cranes, self-propelled mobile cranes, and so on.[96]

3. Chemical Safety

European Council Directive EC/98/24, on the Protection of Health and Safety of Workers against Chemical Risks at Work approved the minimum provisions to be applied in connection with protection against chemical hazards at work. This directive was supplemented by European Commission Directive EC/2000/39 of June 8, setting forth a first list of maximum exposure limits that EU member states had to incorporate into their respective national laws. Both directives were incorporated into Spanish law by Royal Decree 374/2001 of June 6, on the matter, as amended,[97] which introduced in the new Royal Decree the maximum exposure limits that had been previously applied by the Spanish National Institute of Health and Safety at Work.

The provisions of this Royal Decree apply without prejudice to the continuing application of other key regulations such as:

- provisions on radiological protection of workers exposed to chemical agents;
- any other more stringent provisions set forth in Royal Decree 665/1997 of May 12 on Protection of Workers against Risks related to the Exposure to Carcinogens at Work,[98] and
- any other (more stringent or specific) provisions in effect with regard to the transportation of dangerous goods by road.

The regulations list a number of chemicals (and activities involving the handling of said chemicals) that cannot be produced, manufactured, or used in a work environment. The banned products are listed and identified by their EINECS (European Inventory of Existing Commercial Chemical Substances) and CAS (Chemical Abstracts Service) numbers.

The safe in-plant handling of chemical products is linked to the legal requirements applicable to the classification, packaging, and labeling of dangerous compounds, approved by Royal Decree 255/2003 of February 28.[99] Many of the products encompassed by these provisions are bound to apply the labeling requirements provided for in the prior Royal Decree 363/1995 of March 10 on the Labeling of Dangerous Substances.[100] The latter provided for specific labeling requirements for each chemical substance foreseen in the Royal Decree.

4. Fire Safety

National provisions exist on the matter, and the autonomous regions are entitled to adjust and/or expand their scope at regional level, thus making it mandatory for the practitioner to carry out preliminary research of regional laws and regulations in order to obtain a clear understanding of the applicable framework. Such national provisions are included in Royal Decree 2267/2004, of December 3.[101] This Royal Decree is divided in different chapters describing (1) the scope of application of the Royal Decree (summarized above); (2) the requirements of the construction and service features of facilities subject to the Royal Decree; (3) the procedures and requirements for periodical inspections; (4) the actions to be undertaken in case of fire emergency (see above comments); (5) the specific safety requirements; and (6) violations and penalties.

Technical Instruction MIE APQ-1 of the Regulations on the Storage of Chemical Products approved by Royal Decree 379/2001 of April 6 (see section IV, *supra*) and the regulations on oil storage and facilities approved by Royal Decree 2085/1994 of October 20 are both fully applicable to the effect of complying with the fire safety requirements foreseen in the national Royal Decree.

The requirements applicable to fire-fighting equipment and systems as well as to the activities of installation and maintenance agents thereof are foreseen in the Regulations on Fire Protection Devices and Installations approved by Royal Decree 1942/1993 of November 5[102] and a Ministerial Order of April 16, 1998.[103]

5.   *Evacuation Measures and Signs; Drills*

The matter has been dealt with in part when discussing the actions to be taken in case of serious accidents (emergency preparedness as per section VI.A.1, *supra*) and the sign posting requirements applicable to industrial facilities (as per section VI.A.2, discussed previously). All signs must be clear and visible during the different emergency situations. The civil protection regulations approved by Royal Decree 1196/2003, of September 19,[104] provide that all company emergency plans must provide for drills to take place from time to time.[105]

B.   National Network of Health & Safety

The Spanish Network of Health & Safety (RedSST) is a network of Spanish suppliers of health and safety information over the Internet. The information is structured in a manner similar to other similar European networks coordinated by the European Agency for Health at Work. The network is managed by the Spanish National Institute for Health and Safety at Work.[106] This agency is charged by Law 31/1995 on Labor Risk Prevention with the task of assuring safe transmission of health and safety information to all interested parties at the national level.

C.   Nuclear Emergency Plan

Nuclear emergencies are governed by Royal Decree 1546/2004, of June 25, as amended, which approved the Basic Plan for Nuclear Emergencies.[107] In Spain, nuclear emergency planning is structured on two different levels. On the one hand, the plan establishes actions to be taken at plant level, pursuant to the Internal Emergency Plans required and governed by Royal Decree 1836/1999, dated December 3 in connection with the safety aspects of nuclear and radioactive installations.[108] On the other hand, the external aspects of nuclear emergencies are dealt with in accordance with the specific civil protection regulations applicable to the subject matter.

The Basic Nuclear Emergency Plan (PLABEN) is the guideline to be followed in connection with the norms and criteria to produce and implement civil protection nuclear emergency plans.

VII.   Natural Resources Management and Protection
A.   Environmental Liability Regime

The Spanish regime concerning natural resource management and protection is based on Law 26/2007 of October 23 on Environmental Civil Liability,[109] which incorporated into Spanish domestic law the contents of European Parliament and Council Directive EC/2004/35, of April 21. This law implemented a system of strict and unlimited environmental liability focused on the "damage prevention" and "polluter pays" principles that apply to a number of activities listed in Annex III of the law. These include, but are not limited to, water discharges, waste management, manufacturing of dangerous substances and compounds, and transportation of dangerous goods. The law includes a detailed breakdown of minor, serious, and very serious violations that are subject to sliding-scale penalties.

B.   Protection of Natural Heritage and Biodiversity; Natura 2000 Network

Spain has one of the highest levels of biodiversity in the EU. This is due, inter alia, to its location, geological diversity, and the existence of significant island areas. The key regulation on the matter is Law 42/2007 of December 13 on Natural Wealth and Biodiversity,[110] focusing on two main principles: support for essential ecological processes and systems, and respect for the uniqueness and beauty of natural ecosystems and landscapes. The law provides for different legal instruments aimed at organizing and encouraging a more thoroughgoing knowledge of the natural heritage and biodiversity, such as the National Heritage Inventory, the Strategic Plan for Natural Wealth and Biodiversity, and the Guidelines for the Organization of Natural Resources.

C.   Wetland Protection

In furtherance of the commitments acquired under the Ramsar Convention, as updated,[111] the Directorate General for Biodiversity (administrative authority in charge of managing the Ramsar Convention in Spain) fostered the preparation of the Strategic Plan for the Preservation and Rational Use of Wetlands, intended to integrate all separate existing policies on the matter. The document acknowledges the loss of wetlands suffered worldwide with regard to surface and environmental quality. It also acknowledges that Spain has seen a similar trend to that prevailing worldwide and estimates that some 60 percent of the Spanish wetlands have disappeared in the last 40 years.[112]

D. Protection against Forest Fires

The governmental authority responsible for preventing forest fires is the Directorate General for Rural Development and Forest Policy of the Ministry of Agriculture, Food and Environment. This agency is charged with coordinating all national activities related to fighting forest fires. However, the regional governments shoulder the bulk of the responsibility for fighting forest fires. The regional governments must provide the physical and human resources for controlling forest fires within their boundaries. The activities can be split into fire prevention, coordination, and fire-fighting programs and activities, mostly developed at the regional level. Legislative developments can be traced back to the Order of April 2, 1993, whereby the Council of Ministers approved the Basic Civil Protection Emergency Guidelines against Forest Fires.[113] These guidelines were subsequently developed by chapter III (arts. 43 et seq.) of Law 43/2003 of November 23, (Forestry Law) as amended.[114]

E. Fight against Desertification

A substantial portion of the Spanish territory is affected by a significant degree of erosion and deforestation. In fact, more than two-thirds of the country is subject to an arid, semi-arid, or dry subhumid climate. The combination of unfavorable and recurring circumstances such as droughts, forest fires, and overexploitation of aquifers has led to the current situation.

As a party to the U.N. Convention to Combat Deforestation (UNCCD), Spain has approved the required National Action Plan against deforestation.[115] Actions to be taken pursuant to the UNCCD also involve other agencies within the Spanish central government, such as the Ministry of Foreign Affairs and Cooperation, the High Council of Scientific Research (CSIC), and the Spanish Agency for International Cooperation and Development (AECID) of the Ministry of Economy and Competitiveness.

One of the significant instruments in the fight against deforestation is the Project to Combat Deforestation in the Mediterranean Basin (LUCDEME), implemented by the Directorate General for Rural Development and Forestry Policy of the Ministry of Agriculture, Food and Environment.

VIII. Natural Resources Damages

Spain is politically organized at three levels: the central government, the autonomous regions, and the local entities (i.e., municipalities). Legislative powers are separated by areas and authority is mostly split between the central and regional levels.[116] And while the central government has no legislative authority in matters of land zoning and housing, it does have legislative power in connection with land governance, planning, and management.

The authority to legislate on land zoning and housing and to enforce the relevant regulations thus lies exclusively with the autonomous regions, even though almost all the planning instruments implemented by the different regions recognize a common origin: the Land Law of 1956.[117] Land planning acts as a framework that is almost always limited by the structure of the specific regional general urban plans that have been approved through the years and that resulted in the development of specific regional development plans. The current decentralization of authority in the area of urban development should allow the adaptation to the legislative developments to the different cultures, climates, and territories of government in Spain. The process, however, has so far been neither easy nor homogeneous.

IX.   Protected Species
A.   Legal Framework

Spain is also committed to protecting its natural heritage and biodiversity in connection with the conservation of endemic wild species. The main legal provision is Law 42/2007, of December 13.[118] It sets forth the principle that "the Autonomous regions shall take the steps necessary to guarantee the preservation of biodiversity . . . ; in particular, with regard to the preservation of habitats and approving protection regimes for those wild species that will so require" (Article 52). Such species must be included in the Roster of Wild Species Subject to Special Protection (Listado de Especies Silvestres en Régimen de Protección Especial) and in the Spanish Catalog of Endangered Species (Catálogo Español de Especies Amenazadas) published by the Ministry of Agriculture, Food and Environment.

B.   The CITES Regime in Spain: The Spanish Inventory of Endangered Species

The Convention on International Trade in Endangered Species of Wild Fauna and Flora (CITES) is a multilateral convention intended to apply uniform rules to prevent the international trade of endangered species of wild fauna and flora from resulting in their extirpation. At present, CITES is applied nearly worldwide and offers varying degrees of protection to some 30,000 species of animals and plants. Some of the species are vulnerable but still not in danger of extinction, even though the name of the convention would lead one to believe that only "endangered" species are protected.

Spain has taken a number of steps to implement the convention, including but not limited to the recently approved Royal Decree 139/2011 of February 4,[119], which led to the development of the Roster of Wild Species under Special Protection and the Spanish Inventory of Endangered Species, which identified those species that are vulnerable and those that are in danger of extinction.

In turn, Decision EC/77/585 allowed the European Economic Community—an entity that has since then been subsumed into the EU—to join the Convention for the Protection of the Mediterranean against Pollution, known as the Barcelona Convention. The convention was followed by the implementation of different additional protocols,[120] including, but not limited to, the Protocol on Specially Protected Areas and Biological Diversity.[121]

C. Ministerial Guidelines

With a view to implementing the protection principles of Law 42/2007, the central government has approved technical guidelines for the application of the law. These include principles and approved methods for capturing certain predator species and bird (Fringillidae family) species, such as the goldfinch, the blackbird, and other songbird species, and for feeding carrion-eating (necrophagous) species.

X. Environmental Review and Decision Making
A. Environmental Impact Assessment

As with all other subject matter areas described in this chapter, the central government has authority to enact basic legislation applicable nationwide concerning environmental impact assessment (EIA), while the autonomous regions have legislative powers and enforcement authority, depending upon the contents of their respective statutes of autonomy. Some regions have established obligations in addition to those found in national legislation. Others restricted themselves to enforcing national legislation within their boundaries. The current legal framework on the matter is based on Legislative Royal Decree 1/2008 of January 11 (LRD),[122] which approved a restatement of the existing previous legislation on the matter, dating back to 2006. This legislation spelled out which activities must be subject to an EIA procedure, and which simply require environmental studies.[123]

A favorable review will result in the granting of what is known as an integrated environmental permit (IEP), as described in section X.B, *infra*.

B. Integrated Pollution Prevention and Control Regime and Permits

Law 16/2002 of July 1 (the IPPC Law) incorporated into domestic law the contents of Directive EC/96/61 on Integrated Pollution Prevention and Control. It governs the construction, assembly, exploitation, or transfer of all public or privately owned industrial plants undertaking activities listed in any of the industrial categories and subcategories included in an annex to the law. The law repealed a number of prior legal provisions, including former regulations governing the procedures to secure the different kinds of the then-existing permits.

The procedure selected by Spain to receive the directive was to create a new administrative document, the IEP, which merges all the different environmental permits that the activity would need, thus resulting in a single and unified permit. IEPs must be issued by the responsible environmental agencies of the regions where the facilities are located. The process requires joint and concerted action, including the issuing of binding reports, of all agencies involved in the granting of the different specific permits required by those facilities listed in the referred annex.[124]

The IPPC Law has been implemented by Royal Decree 509/2007, of April 20, as amended,[125] and Royal Decree 508/2007, also of April 20,[126] governing the contents of both the information on emission levels and the IEPs. More recently, Directive EU/2010/75 on Industrial Emissions merged the contents of seven previous directives on the matter. Most likely, the directive will be received into Spanish law by means of a forthcoming law that at the time of this writing is subject to public comments, and a future Royal Decree implementing the statute.

XI.   Transboundary Pollution

Transboundary contamination is often identified with air pollution. But even though cross-border air contamination is the most common type of such pollution, transboundary pollution can also derive from common rivers or shared lakes, or the migration of underground water contamination or toxic waste. That said, acid rain (in the short term) and global warming are the most important cross-border contamination issues facing Spain. In particular, acid rain is responsible for altering the chemical makeup of the air and soil, degrading forestry ecosystems, and altering minerals such as stone.

The Geneva Convention on Long Distance Cross Border Contamination, signed in Geneva in 1979, came into effect for the EU in 1981 (Decision EC/81/462/ of June 11) and was ratified by Spain in June 1982. The convention sets forth a framework of intergovernmental cooperation to protect human health and the environment from transboundary air pollution. To combat such effects, the parties commit to restrict, prevent, and reduce stepwise the emission of air contaminants, thus preventing the side effect of cross-border contamination.[127]

At the domestic level, IEPs issued pursuant to the IPPC Law must include the specific actions that the permit holder must take to mitigate transboundary contamination risks.

XII.   Civil and Criminal Enforcement and Penalties
A.   Administrative, Civil, and Criminal Liability and Penalties

The protection of the environment in Spain finds support in Article 45 of the Constitution of 1978, which states:

1. All persons have the right to enjoy an environment that is adequate for their personal development, as well as the duty to preserve it.
2. Public authorities shall ensure the rational use of natural resources, with a view to protecting and improving the quality of life as well as to protecting and restoring the environment, based upon the essential requirement of collective solidarity.
3. Whomsoever shall violate the provisions of the above paragraph [Art. 45(2)] shall be subject to criminal or, as appropriate, administrative penalties, as well as the obligation to remedy the damage caused, as established by the law.

Paragraph 3 of this article thus opens the door to the possibility of levying administrative fines, bringing civil claims, and pursuing criminal penalties for environmental violations.

B. Principles of Criminal Liability

Environmental crimes are relatively new in Spanish legal history. The oldest criminal provisions date back to periods prior to the coming into effect of the 1978 Spanish Constitution.[128]

Organic Law 10/1995 of November 23 approved the new wording of Article 325 of the Criminal Code, which developed the concept of an "ecological offense." This concept was first introduced in 1983 as a new set of provisions within Spain's legal system.[129]

The most recent development in Spanish criminal law is the principle that criminal provisions of the Spanish legal system also apply to legal entities. This put an end to the application of the Latin criterion that companies could not be charged with criminal culpability (Latin: *societas delinquere non potest*). Article 327 of the Criminal Code describes the principles of liability applicable when the offenses are committed by or through legal entities, setting forth penalties that are higher than those that are applicable to individuals.

Enforcement is quite uneven in the different regions, but recent history of court cases does register an increasing number of judgments ordering the imprisonment of administrators or managers of mercantile companies.

C. Environmental Protection in the Civil Code

The environmental protection provisions found in the Spanish Constitution have also given rise to provisions on civil liability for damages (Article 1.902 of the Civil Code). According to this provision, anyone causing damage to others due to fault or negligence is obliged to repair the damage so caused.

This general principle of noncontractual liability has been developed by Spanish courts in a number of different ways. An in-depth exploration of the details of Spanish court cases on this subject is unfortunately beyond the scope of this chapter. However, the practitioner must be aware that the traditional principles of civil liability have been materially impacted by the approval of Law 26/2007 of October 23 on Environmental Civil Liability,[130] which incorporated into Spanish law the contents of Parliament and Council Directive EC/2004/35, of April 21 (discussed in more detail in section VII.A, *supra*).

Notes

1. The Ministry of Agriculture, Food and Environment (MOGRAMA) is the main source of administrative information at the national level on many of the subjects discussed in this chapter. English versions of legislation are rarely available (for example, the regulations on Contaminated Land can be found in English in a link at http://www.magrama .gob.es/es/calidad-y-evaluacion-ambiental/temas/suelos-contaminados).

2. *See* http://www.boe.es/buscar/act.php?id=BOE-A-1985-5392.

3. *See* http://www.boe.es/buscar/doc.php?id=BOE-A-2007-19744.

4. *See* http://www.boe.es/buscar/doc.php?id=BOE-A-2011-1643.

5. *See* http://www.boe.es/buscar/doc.php?id=BOE-A-2011-1645.

6. *See* section II.B, *infra,* on the allocation of authority on air quality control.

7. *See* http://www.boe.es/buscar/doc.php?id=BOE-A-1983-7293.

8. *See* http://www.boe.es/buscar/doc.php?id=BOE-A-2005-5834. Sulfur dioxide (SO_2) is produced when, for example, power plants burn coal and heavy oil. Nitrogen oxides (NO_X) is produced, for example, from combustion of fossil fuels in the transportation and industrial sectors.

9. This directive will be repealed as of January 1, 2016, by Directive EU/2010/75 of November 24, 2010, on industrial emissions (integrated pollution prevention and control), which shall regulate such facilities (chapter III of Directive EU/2010/75) and will set forth emission limit values (Annex V of the same EU directive).

10. There is no official English version of the regulations discussed in this chapter. *See* http://www.boe.es/buscar/doc.php?id=BOE-A-2004-5117.

11. *See* http://www.boe.es/buscar/doc.php?id=BOE-A-2011-9139.

12. *See* http://www.boe.es/buscar/doc.php?id=BOE-A-2008-1467. LCFs are defined as either (1) a single combustion facility with a nominal thermal power equal to or exceeding 50 MWts or (2) different facilities, operating together and having a combined nominal thermal power equal to or exceeding 50 megawatts.

13. Namely, (1) Order ITC/1389/2008, of May 19, regulating procedures for (a) limiting emissions of SO_2, NO_X, and particles, (b) controlling the accuracy of measuring devices, and (c) dealing with the management and spreading of information concerning such emission; and (2) Resolution of 8 July 2009, of the State Secretariat for Energy, regulating certain aspects relative to the implementation of the Order referred to in subparagraph (i) and Ministerial Order PRE/3539/2008, of November 28, 2008.

14. *See* http://www.boe.es/buscar/doc.php?id=BOE-A-2005-1967. Concerning the Kyoto Protocol to the UNFCCC, see http://unfccc.int/kyoto_protocol/items/2830.php (last visited Nov. 2, 2013).

15. In particular, one could mention Law 40/2010 of December 29, on Geological Storage of Carbon Dioxide receiving into Spanish domestic legislation the contents of Directive EC/2009/31 on the Geological Storage of CO2 for installations that exceed 300 MW of nominal power; Royal Decree 1370/2006 of November 24 approving the National Plan for the Allocation of GHG Emission Rights for the period 2008–2012; and Law 13/2010 of July 5, amending Organic Law 1/2005 of 9 March, supplementing the greenhouse gas emission allowance trading scheme to include aviation activities.

16. *See* http://www.boe.es/buscar/doc.php?id=BOE-A-2002-12995. At the time of preparing this chapter, MOGRAMA was reviewing a draft Royal Decree intended to enforce the implementing regulations to Law 16/2002 on Integrated Pollution Prevention and Control.

17. *See* also section I.C, *supra.*

18. For information on MAGRAMA, see http://www.magrama.gob.es/en/ (last visited Nov. 2, 2013).

19. *See* http://www.magrama.gob.es/es/calidad-y-evaluacion-ambiental/temas /atmosfera-y-calidad-del-aire/ (document PNMCA_tcm7-181205.pdf).

20. Noise and light pollution are also regulated in Spain. Noise is perhaps one of the main "noticeable but administratively neglected" environmental pollution factors. Noise levels in large Spanish urban areas quite often exceed the maximum legal limits. The key regulation is Law 37/2003, of November 17, as amended (see http://www.boe.es/buscar

/act.php?id=BOE-A-2003-20976), which incorporated into Spanish Law the contents of Parliament and Council Directive EC/2002/49 of June 25, on the Assessment and Management of Environmental Noise, see http://eur-lex.europa.eu/LexUriServ/LexUriServ .do?uri=OJ:L:2002:189:0012:0025:EN:PDF, as implemented in Spain by Royal Decree 1513/2005, of December 16, as amended, see http://www.boe.es/buscar/act.php?id =BOE-A-2005-20792.

In general, Law 37/2003 legislates beyond the limits of this directive, regulating also events of natural noise having an environmental impact.

In turn, the Spanish Basic Information System on Noise Contamination (SICA) created by the above-mentioned Royal Decree 1513/2005 includes the databases necessary to organize existing information on noise contamination. (SICA allows one to look for, identify, and download the "acoustic plans" established by the Spanish government in furtherance of the requirements of Directive EC/2002/49 (see link above) as well as data on the different action plans produced in furtherance of the requirements of Law 37/2003 of November 17. SICA can be consulted at http://sicaweb.cedex.es/).

Light pollution is only minimally regulated by the Fourth Additional Provision of Law 37/2003. The Fourth Additional Provision provides that the government must foster the prevention and reduction of light pollution. In furtherance of this legal mandate, Royal Decree 1890/2008 of November 14, see http://www.boe.es/buscar/doc.php?id=BOE -A-2008-18634, approved regulations applicable to outdoor lighting installations. Royal Decree 1890/2008 was subsequently implemented by "Additional Technical Instructions" EA-01 and EA-07, which set out technical principles intended to foster energy savings and limit night glare or light contamination. These rules are subject to further regional implementation. (Law 34/2007 authorizes the autonomous regions to develop their own legislation on the matter. Several regions such as Cataluña, Andalusia, Cantabria, and Extremadura, among others, have approved their own regional light contamination standards and adopted corrective measures valid within their respective regions).

21. Spain has seen little individual legislative activity in this area. Spain is mostly following European initiatives. Regarding the Climate Change Office (Oficina Española de Cambio Climático, OECC), see ww.magrama.gob.es/es/cambio-climatico/temas /organismos-e-instituciones-implicados-en-la-lucha-contra-el-cambio-climatico-a-nivel -nacional/oficina-espanola-en-cambio-climatico/default.aspx (last visited Nov. 2, 2013).

22. *See* http://www.boe.es/buscar/doc.php?id=BOE-A-2001-6924.

23. Concerning the National Climate Counsel, see http://www.magrama.gob.es /es/cambio-climatico/temas/organismos-e-instituciones-implicados-en-la-lucha-contra -el-cambio-climatico-a-nivel-nacional/el-consejo-nacional-del-clima/ (last visited Nov. 2, 2013).

24. *See* http://www.boe.es/buscar/act.php?id=BOE-A-2011-4117.

25. *See* http://www.boe.es/buscar/act.php?id=BOE-A-2011-17631.

26. Article 7 of the referred Royal Decree 1491/2011 describes the (relatively complex) requirements to implement such acquisitions.

27. At the time this chapter was being finalized, the European Commission delivered its Water Blueprint, an action plan to protect water resources throughout Europe. With this strategy, the EC would like to ensure that citizens, the economy, and the environment are able to take advantage of good quality water to meet their needs. The Water Blueprint is made up by a set of tools that member states can implement to improve the management of water in different river basins, which are based on the innovation on certain water agreements released in May of 2012.

28. *See* http://www.boe.es/buscar/act.php?id=BOE-A-2003-23936.

29. *See* http://www.boe.es/buscar/act.php?id=BOE-A-2001-14276.

30. *See* http://www.boe.es/buscar/doc.php?id=BOE-A-1992-28426.

31. There are nine Water Basin Authorities, regulating the use of the water flows of the key rivers: Miño-Sil, Cantabric, Duero, Tajo, Guadiana, Guadalquivir, Segura, Júcar, and Ebro.

32. Intracommunity Plans were approved for the areas of Galicia Costa (Royal Decree 1332/2012 of September 14); Tinto, Odiel & Piedras (Royal Decree 1329/2012 of September 14), Guadalete—Barbate (Royal Decree 1330/2012; and Cuencas Mediterráneas Andaluzas (Royal Decree 1331/2012). Back in 2011, the river plan for the Catalonian region was approved by means of Royal Decree 1219/2011, of September 5, while the Hydrological Plan for the Balearic Islands has been in place since 2001 (Royal Decree 378/2001).

33. *See* http://www.boe.es/buscar/doc.php?id=BOE-A-2008-755.

34. *See* http://www.boe.es/buscar/doc.php?id=BOE-A-1986-10638.

35. In accordance with the Water Law, the Hydraulic Public Domain is made up of, but not limited to, the beds of natural continuous or discontinuous currents and the beds of lakes, lagoons, and surface reservoirs existing on public beds. Only rainwater flows that start and end within private properties can be privately owned.

36. *See* http://www.boe.es/buscar/act.php?id=BOE-A-2001-13042. The socialist government subsequently approved the A.G.U.A. Program (Actions for Management and Use of Water) that intends to foster the use of desalination plants and put an end to past water transfers from the Ebro River to neighboring regions in need of water. This new program raised objections from the coastal autonomous regions. The program is being applied in part on the Mediterranean coast and is planned to be extended to the rest of the territory, political changes and economic outlook permitting.

37. *See* http://www.boe.es/buscar/act.php?id=BOE-A-2001-14276.

38. Main Regulations are Articles 59 to 80 of the Restatement of the Water Law approved by Legislative Royal Decree 1/2001 of July 20, and the above-mentioned Royal Decree 849/1986 of April 11 (several articles thereof).

39. *See* http://www.boe.es/buscar/act.php?id=BOE-A-1986-10638.

40. *See* http://www.boe.es/buscar/act.php?id=BOE-A-1988-18762.

41. Constitutional Court Judgment 149/1991.

42. Impact of discharges is conditioned by three main factors: first, the area where the discharges take place, affecting more severely those urban or heavily populated areas as well as those with more fragile ecosystems, where aspects such as the time required by maritime live species to reproduce are of the essence. The second factor is the hydrometeorological pattern of the affected areas, such as the levels of high/low tides, strength of currents, and prevailing winds. The third and final factor is the mix of the discharged contaminants and the duration and intensity of the discharges.

43. Describing these conventions in detail is beyond the scope of this work. However, for one example, see International Convention on the Prevention of Marine Pollution by Dumping of Wastes and Other Matter 1972, (known as MARPOL), as amended, governing the deliberate disposal at sea of wastes or other matter from vessels, aircraft, and platforms. It does not regulate discharges from land-based sources such as pipes and outfalls, wastes incidental to normal operation of vessels, or placement of materials for purposes other than mere disposal, providing such disposal is not contrary to aims of the Convention.

44. *See* http://www.boe.es/buscar/act.php?id=BOE-A-2002-24910.

45. *See* http://www.boe.es/buscar/act.php?id=BOE-A-2001-14276. The Law on Coasts has placed significant restrictions on the private ownership of coastal areas that are a part of the public domain, where unrestricted private property still remains only because of the survival of very old grants. Among the main restrictions, it is worth mentioning the existence of a 100-meter protective easement (*servidumbre de protección*) from

the line of high tides, preventing the neighboring properties from constructing or carrying out within such limits certain activities such as the dumping of solid waste or construction debris and the discharge of nontreated wastewaters. Law on Coasts art. 25.1.b. Other possible easements include transit and sea access restrictions.

46. *See* http://eur-lex.europa.eu/LexUriServ/LexUriServ.do?uri=OJ:L:2006:396:0001:0849:EN:PDF.

47. For the text in force at the time of writing this chapter, see http://www.boe.es/buscar/act.php?id=BOE-A-2010-5293.

48. *See* http://www.boe.es/buscar/doc.php?id=BOE-A-2008-17630.

49. *See* original text at http://eur-lex.europa.eu/.

50. *See* http://www.boe.es/buscar/doc.php?id=BOE-A-1989-27466.

51. *See* http://www.boe.es/buscar/act.php?id=BOE-A-2001-8796.

52. *See* http://www.boe.es/buscar/doc.php?id=BOE-A-2006-8348.

53. Order FOM/2924/2006 of September 19, regulating the minimum contents of the annual report for the transportation of dangerous goods by road, rail, or navigable waters. *See* http://www.boe.es/buscar/doc.php?id=BOE-A-2006-16784.

54. *See* http://www.boe.es/buscar/doc.php?id=BOE-A-2001-8971.

55. *See* http://www.boe.es/buscar/act.php?id=BOE-A-1984-1791.

56. *See* http://www.boe.es/buscar/act.php?id=BOE-A-2002-19923.

57. *See* http://www.pic.int (last visited Nov. 2, 2013).

58. In Spain, as of January 1, 2009, the sole appointed NDA is the Directorate General of Quality, Assessment and Natural Environment (Dirección General de Calidad y Evaluación Ambiental y Medio Natural) while all administrative tasks have been delegated to the Under-Directorate General for Air Quality and Industrial Environment (Subdirección General de Calidad del Aire y Medio Ambiente Industrial).

59. Such procedures set forth that the exporter must (1) verify that the chemical to be imported is actually listed in Annex I of the Regulation; and (2) ask the ministry for a user name and password to access the Internet EDEXIM program that has been implemented to allow the exporter companies to process their applications. Companies wishing to export hazardous chemicals to Spain must serve a similar notification upon the Under-Directorate General for Air Quality and Industrial Environment to Buzon-ExporImporPQP@magrama.es and attach the Material Safety Data Card for the relevant product drafted in accordance with Article 31 and Annex II of the REACH Regulation EC/1907/2006, as amended by Regulation EU/ 453/2010.

60. *See* Spanish Constitution art. 149.1.23.

61. *See* http://www.boe.es/buscar/act.php?id=BOE-A-2011-13046.

62. *See* http://www.boe.es/buscar/doc.php?id=BOE-A-2005-895.

63. As a result of such determination, the existence of contamination in the property shall be registered at the Land Register by way of a marginal note on the property's sheet, and all building and/or in rem and/or other relevant rights shall be suspended if and when the exercise of such rights shall prove to be incompatible with the remediation and recovery measures that the regional governments may decide to apply. The suspension shall last until the land is declared to be free from contamination.

64. *See* http://www.boe.es/buscar/act.php?id=BOE-A-2007-18475.

65. Decontamination procedures can be agreed upon by means of agreements executed between the responsible parties and the corresponding region pursuant to the principles set forth in Law 30/2007 of October 30 on Public Contracts. While costs shall always be borne by the obligated parties, they may benefit from public economic incentives, *id.* art. 36(4).

66. SGIs exist for pharmaceutical products, certain packaging materials, electric and electronic waste, batteries, and others.

67. *See* http://www.boe.es/buscar/act.php?id=BOE-A-1999-18193.

68. *See* http://www.boe.es/buscar/act.php?id=BOE-A-2005-3242.

69. End users will be entitled to return the products, at no cost, to their distributors or local agencies that will be bound to receive them on a temporary basis, subject to further reception, disposal, or recycling by their respective producers (see *infra*). Similar procedures may apply to equipment used in professional activities.

70. The implementation procedures foreseen by the Royal Decree mandate that as of August 13, 2005, manufacturers and/or producers must pick up equipment waste—at no cost—from the transitory receiving (deposit) points established by the distributors or local retail points. The Royal Decree also allows for the possibility that manufacturers or producers may agree to finance the costs of equipment products placed in the market before said date, also distinguishing between household and professional equipment.

71. This is defined by Article 2 as "equipment working on electric currents or electromagnetic fields intended for use at nominal tensions not exceeding 1.000V in case of alternating current and 1.500V in case of direct (continuous) current as well as the equipment necessary to generate, transmit and measure such currents and fields." In turn, "Waste from Electric and Electronic Equipment" is defined as "electric and electronic equipment, their components, consumables and subassemblies from households and professional environments, as of the moment they become waste."

72. Said requirements are described separately for facilities storing electric and electronic equipment (requiring sufficient nonpermeable surfaces, spill protections, decanters, cleaning systems, etc.) or treating them (requiring availability of weights, storage areas for disassembled parts, adequate containers for items such as batteries, PCB- or PCT-containing condensers, etc).

73. At present, the following goals must be met: (1) An average of four kg per inhabitant/year of household waste must be collected; (2) 80 percent by weight of each category of large appliances and vending machines must receive added value; (3) 75 percent by weight of components, materials, and substances shall be reused and recycled; (4) 75 percent by weight of each category of computer, electronics (end user products), and telecommunications equipment must receive added value; (5) 65 percent by weight of each category of components, materials, and substances shall be reused and recycled; (6) 70 percent by weight of each category of small appliances, illumination equipment, electric and electronic tools, toys, and sports equipment as well as surveillance and control instruments must receive added value; and (7) fifty per cent (50%) by weight of their components, materials, and substances shall be reused and recycled.

The percentage of reuse and recycling of components, materials, and substances from gas discharge lamps must be at least 80 percent of their weight. Note that the expression "average weight" used in the directive is not reproduced in the Royal Decree.

74. These substances must nevertheless be managed as provided for in Royal Decree 679/2006. The foregoing notwithstanding, Royal Decree 679/2006 shall apply to oils with concentrations of PCBs under 55 parts per million that may be obtained from PCB decontamination processes. *See* http://www.boe.es/buscar/act.php?id=BOE-A-2006-9832.

75. Some of the key features of the regime include the following: (1) industrial oils must be manufactured in such a way that they minimize the amounts of dangerous or contaminating substances and facilitate the correct management of waste derived from their use; (2) manufacturers of industrial oils are bound to assure proper management of used oils and to meet the costs of the necessary operations; (3) management practices shall respect the legislation applicable to packaging materials and dangerous waste (packages containing used oil shall be subject to selective collection and shall not be mixed with other waste); (4) labels on packages of industrial waste placed on the market must

show the following phrase: "The ecological management of used oils generated by the use of this oil is governed by Royal Decree 679/2006, of June 2, on the management of used industrial oils, providing that the owner of this kind of waste must deliver it to the manufacturer or to an Agent authorized to handle it or to an Integrated Management System authorized for this kind of waste." These same labels must identify the kind of collection system involved through a logo allowing the identification of the person responsible for the correct management thereof.

76. Present targets are (1) recovery of at least 95 percent of used oils; (2) value adding of 100 percent of used oils recovered; and (3) regeneration of some 65 percent of used oils recovered. The National Plan for the Management of Waste 2008–2015 did provide for an update on these percentages in 2009, but so far, such update has not taken place, while the plan observes that a number of deficiencies still exist in the development and achievement of the main targets of this particular Royal Decree.

77. Annex II of the Royal Decree approved the official form of the Follow Up and Control Document (Documento de Control y Seguimiento) for Used Oils. This Annex has been updated by an Order of June 13, 1990.

78. For text of Law 16/2002 (IPPC Law), see http://www.boe.es/buscar/doc.php?id=BOE-A-2002-12995.

79. *See* http://www.boe.es/boe/dias/2009/02/26/pdfs/BOE-A-2009-3243.pdf. The basic goals set forth in the National Integrated Waste Plan include, but are not limited to the following: (1) quality goals: (a) to improve the information system and the control over agricultural activities while monitoring the adequate use of sludges in agriculture, and (b) apply the national waste management techniques to sludge management, that is, by guaranteeing storage capacity therefore, assuring that management practices minimize energy consumption, avoiding long distance transportation and minimizing landfilling; and (2) quantitative goals (use in agricultural land, 67 percent; incineration, 18 percent; landfilling, 12 percent; correct environmental management of ashes from incineration, 100 percent).

80. *See* http://www.boe.es/buscar/doc.php?id=BOE-A-1990-26490. According to the information made available by the NSR, some 80 percent of the total sludges are used in agriculture. Landfilling has been reduced to a current 8 percent (exceeding the target) and incineration is becoming more and more important, now reaching some 4 percent of the total but still far from the target. Nonagricultural uses are negligible.

81. *See* http://www.boe.es/buscar/doc.php?id=BOE-A-1993-26572.

82. *See* http://www.boe.es/buscar/act.php?id=BOE-A-2005-12378.

83. *See* http://www.boe.es/buscar/act.php?id=BOE-A-2003-92.

84. Historic or collectors' vehicles either still in operation, in museums, or disassembled are not encompassed by this Royal Decree.

85. *See* http://www.sigrauto.com/. Annex I of the Royal Decree sets forth the basic technical requirements to be complied with—and standards to be met by—entities or facilities willing to handle end-of-life vehicles.

86. *See* http://www.boe.es/buscar/act.php?id=BOE-A-2006-41.

87. The system requires the filing with the responsible agencies of the autonomous regions (before May 1 each year for producers not participating in a selective collection system and before March 1 each year for producers participating in such systems), of yearly reports on the activities carried out in the preceding year. Handling agents must file similar reports on their activities before March 1 of each year.

88. The following is a general classification of the kinds of waste that can be found or produced at Spanish health centers: (1) household (urban solid) waste; (2) certain kinds of biosanitary waste, similar to urban solid waste, that do not entail infection risks associ-

ated with the activity of the health centers (e.g., bandages, gauzes, gloves) and can thus be managed together with urban solid waste; (3) corpses and human remains (which are to be handled in accordance with specific mortuary health regulations; (4) biosanitary waste (including different kinds of waste to be handled consistent with their associated degrees of infection risk; this waste is normally regarded to include cutting or stabbing products, regardless of their level of infection risk); (5) chemical waste involving waste of different kinds that becomes chemically contaminated such as waste bearing cancer, mutagenic, cytostatic, or reproductive risks; and (6) radioactive waste.

These last four categories must be managed as toxic and hazardous waste pursuant to Law 22/2011 on Waste and Contaminated Land (see, discussed previously). This means that they have to be segregated at the health center concerned by depositing them in specific standardized containers that must be opaque, resistant to humidity and piercing, and free from combustion or toxic emission sources; they are to be delivered to a handling agent (*gestor de residuos*) authorized by and registered at the relevant autonomous region and then disposed of or recycled in accordance with the nature of the waste.

89. As amended. *See* http://www.boe.es/buscar/act.php?id=BOE-A-1995-7730.

90. *See* http://www.boe.es/buscar/act.php?id=BOE-A-1995-24292. Restatement including amendments by Law 54/2003, of December 12 and the Regulations on prevention Services approved by Royal Decree 39/1997, of January 16 and Royal Decree 604/2006 of May 19.

91. Companies with more than 500 employees cannot outsource the prevention services and are required to staff and train personnel exclusively in connection with these obligations.

92. *See* Order TIN/2504/2010 of November 20, http://www.boe.es/buscar/act .php?id=BOE-A-2010-14843, on the requirements for the implementation of external prevention services and the authorization of companies to act as such.

93. *See* http://www.boe.es/buscar/act.php?id=BOE-A-1999-15798.

94. Among the different definitions that can be found in this Royal Decree, one could highlight the definition of "serious accident," defined as any incident, either in the form of escape, spill, fire, or explosion (1) derived from a noncontrolled (chemical) process occurred during the operation of any facility, (2) which may imply a serious risk for individuals, assets, and the environment, and (3) which involves one or more "dangerous substances." Dangerous substances are any individual substance, mix, or preparations thereof either in the form of raw materials, products, by-products, wastes, or intermediate products as well as, in general, any substance that (1) is toxic, flammable, combustible, or explosive; (2) may react in a violent manner in contact with water; or (3) may release toxic gases. Facilities falling under the scope of this Royal Decree are also required to produce company-specific risk prevention plans (Article 7) and submit them to the regional authorities.

95. Discussing the current Civil Protection Guidelines (see http://www.boe.es/buscar /doc.php?id=BOE-A-2003-18682) would exceed the limits of this chapter. That said, legislation exists setting forth the need to assure coordination between facilities and the civil protection authorities to achieve a concerted and efficient action in case of accidents.

96. The main rules on the matter refer to minimum health and safety conditions at the workplace applicable to the different kinds of activities pursuant to Royal Decree 486/1997, of April 14, as amended, that received into Spanish law the requirements of EU Directive 89/654/EC on the matter, and minimum health and safety requirements applicable to the use of personal protective equipment, pursuant to Royal Decree 1215/1997 of July 18 as amended by Royal Decree 2177/2004, dated November 12, to include specific provisions on the use of equipment for work at heights, specifically with regard to scaffoldings and portable ladders. This Royal Decree incorporated into Spanish law the con-

tents of Directive EC/89/655, of November 30, as amended by Directive EC/95/63, of December 5, establishing the Minimum Health and Safety Requirements for the use of Work Equipment. In Plant Sign Posting, governed by Royal Decree 485/1997 of April 14, received into Spanish law the contents of Directive EC/92/58 and governs all safety signs at all kinds of workplaces. Employers must comply with all the requirements described in the Seven Annexes of the Royal Decree on Signs, Oral Expressions, Manual and Visual Signs, etc. Notification of Work Accidents, governed by Order of December 16, 1987, approves different official reporting forms. Different Annexes (amended by Order TAS/2926/2002) include the instructions, codes, and additional information to be provided with regard to the kind of work accident, substances, or equipment involved, circumstances surrounding the accident, and others. In addition, this Order approved the electronic programs and applications necessary to report work accidents in electronic format, through the Electronic Work Accident Declaration System (Delta), which can be accessed through https://www.delta.mtas.es. (Site safety issues may make third-party access difficult). Other matters dealt with on this subject include regulations governing the handling of work loads, the use of safety belts and harnesses, the operation of tower cranes, self-propelled mobile cranes, and the like.

97. *See* http://www.boe.es/buscar/act.php?id=BOE-A-2001-8436.

98. *See* http://www.boe.es/buscar/act.php?id=BOE-A-1997-11145.

99. *See* http://www.boe.es/buscar/act.php?id=BOE-A-2003-4376.

100. *See* http://www.boe.es/buscar/doc.php?id=BOE-A-1995-13535.

101. *See* http://www.boe.es/buscar/act.php?id=BOE-A-2004-21216. The regulations approved by the Royal Decree under review apply to (1) new industrial establishments (facilities), that is, establishments authorized to alter the coming into effect of the Royal Decree; and (2) existing establishments that are relocated, modified, or devoted to a different activity. As an exception, the provisions in chapter IV (actions in°case of fire) apply directly to any and all establishments existing at the effective date of the Royal Decree. The scope of application of the Royal Decree also impacts on facilities that increase their useful surfaces or are subject to subsequently increased risk levels. The autonomous regions can request, if they would so deem advisable, that the contents of the Royal Decree are applied to other sectors and fire areas or, even, to the whole of the facility concerned.

102. *See* http://www.boe.es/buscar/act.php?id=BOE-A-1993-29581.

103. *See* http://www.boe.es/buscar/doc.php?id=BOE-A-1998-9961. Following an initial inspection of the facilities (prior to start up), periodic inspections must take place at intervals of five, three, or two years depending upon the levels of risk of the relevant facilities identified pursuant to the risk criteria set forth in Annex I, while Annex II includes the construction requirements applicable in the light of the risk levels so identified. Finally, Annex III features the requirements of the specific firefighting equipment and installations to be installed.

104. *See* http://www.boe.es/buscar/doc.php?id=BOE-A-2003-18682.

105. Concerning civil protection emergency plans with regard to accidents involving dangerous substance, see section VI.A, *supra*.

106. *See* http://www.insht.es/portal/site/Insht/.

107. *See* http://www.boe.es/buscar/act.php?id=BOE-A-2004-13061. The Basic Plan for Nuclear Emergencies furthered the principles set forth in Royal Decree 1196/2003, of September 19 (see section VI.A.4, *supra*) approving the Basic Rules on Civil Protection, which set forth rules governing civil protection actions to prevent major accidents caused by dangerous substances.

108. *See* http://www.boe.es/buscar/act.php?id=BOE-A-1999-24924.

109. *See* http://www.boe.es/buscar/act.php?id=BOE-A-2007-18475. The law was implemented in part by Royal Decree 2090/2008 of December 22, as amended, providing that all operators of activities capable of causing environmental damage are bound to take the steps conducive to prevent such damage or, when damage has been caused, to restore the affected environment to the status prior to the damage.

110. *See* http://www.boe.es/buscar/act.php?id=BOE-A-2007-21490. With regard to the preservation of natural habitats and spaces, the Law includes provisions on Protected Marine Waters and the European Natura 2000 Network (see next). Regarding the conservation of wild biodiversity, the law created an Inventory of Specifically Protected and Endangered Species and a Catalog of Exotic Invasive Species. The law also created the Fund for Natural Heritage and Biodiversity, a financing instrument aimed at assuring the achievement of national targets and regulating the different bodies in charge of implementing national policies on the sustainable use of the existing heritage and biodiversity. In line with the mandate of the Habitats Directive EC/92/43, Spain has provided for the list of significant European habitats submitted by the autonomous regions (currently updated at November 2011) to MOGRAMA for transmission to the European Commission. The way in which the information has been produced has changed through the years, thus requiring an effort to make the information homogeneous.

111. Ramsar Strategic Plan for 2009–2015. Spain adhered to the Ramsar Convention by Instrument of March 18, 1982. *See* http://www.boe.es/buscar/doc.php?id=BOE-A-1982-21179.

112. The second part of the document (the really practical part) includes ten main targets to be reached by pulling together minor specific targets involving specific concrete actions at local or regional levels. The government implemented such targets by approving the Spanish Wetlands Inventory, through Royal Decree 435/2004 of March 12. Pursuant to this Royal Decree, the ministry is bound to prepare and update the inventory on the basis of the information that the autonomous regions must provide from time to time. The inventory is public and can be consulted in the database kept and managed by the Inventory Office through a specific request addressed to the Department of Wetlands Conservation and Inventory of the Directorate General for Environmental Quality and Assessment of the Natural Environment.

113. *See* http://www.boe.es/buscar/doc.php?id=BOE-A-1993-9779.

114. *See* http://www.boe.es/buscar/act.php?id=BOE-A-2003-21339.

115. Key aspects of the plan can be consulted at MOGRAMA, http://www.magrama .gob.es/es/biodiversidad/temas/desertificacion-y-restauracion-forestal/ (in Spanish).

116. *See* section I, *supra,* on the features of the allocation of political authority in Spain.

117. Currently, Legislative Royal Decree 2/2008 of June 20, see http://www.boe.es /buscar/doc.php?id=BOE-A-2008-10792, which approved the Restatement of the Land Law 8/2007.

118. *See* http://www.boe.es/buscar/act.php?id=BOE-A-2007-21490. In general, the law prohibits killing, damaging, disturbing, or intentionally threatening wild animals not subject to other regulations (i.e., those dealing with hunting, agriculture, or river or sea fishing), regardless of the manner and moment of their biological cycles, thus applying the principle that "all species are protected but some can be exploited." For the rest of species (namely vegetal species such as flora in general and fungus) there is a general prohibition against collecting, cutting, mutilating, tearing, marketing, or intentionally destroying wild species listed in the Roster of Wild Species under Special Protection (Law 42/2007 arts. 52–56).

119. *See* http://www.boe.es/buscar/act.php?id=BOE-A-2011-3582.

120. Approved by means of Decisions EC/81/420,EC/83/101/ and EC/84/132. The Annexes to this protocol include lists setting forth (1) common criteria that the parties to the Convention have to apply to select the coastal and sea areas requiring protection under the Convention; (2) a breakdown (Annex II) of vulnerable or endangered species; and (3) a list of species subject to regulated exploitation. Annex II of the Protocol was last updated in Spain by Ministerial Order AAA/75/2012 of January 12.

121. *See* http://ec.europa.eu/world/agreements/prepareCreateTreatiesWorkspace /treatiesGeneralData.do?step=0&redirect=true&treatyId=598.

122. *See* http://www.boe.es/buscar/act.php?id=BOE-A-2008-1405.

123. Following Council Directive EC/85/337/CEE on the assessment of the environmental impact of certain public projects, as restated by Parliament and Council Directive EU/2011/92/ of December 13, 2011. The legislative Royal Decree referred to in the subchapter approved a list of activities that must necessarily undergo an environmental impact assessment process as a condition precedent to their receiving the necessary permits. In general, the regulations follow the EU guidelines and foresee the existence of two kinds of projects and activities, depending upon whether such projects and activities mandatorily require an environmental impact assessment (private or public projects or activities listed in Annex I to the legislative Royal Decree—i.e., Mining, Infrastructures, Hydraulic and Water Management Projects, textile industry, and others) or whether the need to have an environmental impact assessment is left to the decision of the corresponding autonomous region (for activities listed in Annex II) a distinction that must be based upon certain threshold criteria specifically set forth in Annex III to the legislative Royal Decree. The regulations provide for detailed procedures that (1) start with a permit application to the corresponding Environmental Agency, supported by an environmental impact study prepared by the applicant; (2) are subject to public review; (3) require the prior opinion of the different environmental bodies concerned; and (4) end up with the issuing by the relevant agency of the autonomous region of an environmental impact statement.

124. Annex I lists miscellaneous significant activities and large facilities such as combustion installations, oil and gas refineries, facilities devoted to the production and processing of metals, chemical industries, waste management plants, and others. Installations or parts of installations that are used for research, development, and testing of new products and processes and that are not listed in Annex I are not encompassed by the Law and continue to be governed by their respective individual regulations.

Each IEP sets forth the emission restrictions, discharge limits, and other technical measures and conditions that the facilities must respect. Said limits and conditions will be set by taking into account miscellaneous factors such as the information to be provided by the owner or operator, the technical features of the installations, the technology to be used thereat, the potential migration of eventual contamination, the obligations Spain may have assumed under EU legislation, and other legal provisions applicable to the activity or facility concerned. (Annex 4 of the Law).

125. *See* http://www.boe.es/buscar/act.php?id=BOE-A-2007-8352.

126. *See* http://www.boe.es/buscar/act.php?id=BOE-A-2007-8351.

127. The convention was followed by different additional protocols; namely, the Protocol to Abate Acidification, Eutrophication and Ground-level Ozone signed at Gotteborg (Sweden) in 1999 and effective since 2005. The EU adhered to the Protocol in 2003 (Decision EC/2003/507) and Spain ratified it also in April 2005. This protocol sets forth the maximum allowable levels for the emission of the four contaminants that cause acidification, eutrophication, and ground-level ozone, that is, sulfur dioxide, nitrogen oxides, VOCs, and ammonia. On other legal instruments, see mention of the Stockholm Convention on

VOCs in section IV.C, *supra,* and Spain's obligations under the Kyoto Protocol in section II.A, *supra.*

128. For example, see Article 84 of Law dated April 29th 1964 on the use of nuclear energy, making it a criminal offense to put at risk the life, health, or property of persons (even in the absence of explosion) through the release of nuclear energy.

129. The provisions in Articles 325 through 331 of the Criminal Code set forth (1) penalties ranging from two to five years of imprisonment; (2) fines of up to a maximum of 24 months, and (3) disqualification for the practice of a profession or craft for a maximum of up to three years in case of unlawful actions or omissions that may cause emissions, spills, radiations, vibrations, injections, or damage to land, the atmosphere, the underground soil, or waters (also when effects are felt cross-border) that may seriously "affect the balance of natural systems."

130. *See* http://www.boe.es/buscar/act.php?id=BOE-A-2007-18475.

CHAPTER 34

Ukraine

ARMEN KHACHATURYAN AND OLEH FURMANCHUK

I. Air and Climate Change
A. Air Pollution Control

Under the Law on Protection of the Environment, dated June 25, 1991, as amended (Environmental Law), and the Law on Protection of Ambient Air, dated October 16, 1992, as amended (Air Protection Law), companies operating in Ukraine may emit polluting substances into the atmosphere via stationary sources only if they obtain a special air pollution permit listing approved limits for each permitted substance and pay an ecological tax.[1]

Air pollution permits are issued for a term of at least seven years by the Ministry of the Ecology and Natural Resources of Ukraine (Ministry of the Environment) or a relevant local government administration, depending on the degree of negative environmental impact involved. In each case, before issuance of such permits, the issuing authority must receive the consent of the relevant office of the State Sanitary-and-Epidemiological Service of Ukraine.[2]

To receive an air pollution permit, an applicant must submit to the issuing authority an application, together with the documents evidencing the anticipated amounts of polluting substances emitted into the atmosphere, and must publish in the local press an announcement on the intent to receive an air pollution permit. The public announcement must contain specific contact information for the local government administration, which is required to collect comments from public organizations and individuals and forward them to the issuing authority (the Ministry of the Environment or a relevant department of the local government administration). The issuing authority has 30 days from the application date to decide whether to issue the air pollution permit. The issued permit indicates the maximum amounts of each polluting substance that may be emitted into the atmosphere. Such limits may not exceed the pollution limits established by the Ministry of the Environment.[3]

B.   Climate Change

Ukraine has been a party to the United Nations Framework Convention on Climate Change (UNFCCC) since 1996[4] and the Kyoto Protocol to the UNFCCC since 2004.[5] Since 2008, the State Environmental Investment Agency of Ukraine has been the authority primarily charged with the implementation of policy regarding climate change, fulfillment of the UNFCCC and Kyoto Protocol, and the trade of emission units.[6] Other authorities in this area include the Ministry of the Environment, the Ministry of Foreign Affairs, and the Ministry of Economic Development and Trade.[7]

International trade in greenhouse gas emissions and air pollution accounting are generally subject to tight regulation, while a legal regime encouraging further reduction of such emissions is not yet properly established. The regulatory mechanism includes the National Electronic Register of Anthropogenic Emissions and Greenhouse Gas Absorption, the National Center of Accounting of Greenhouse Gas Emissions, the procedure for approval of ecological (i.e., "green") investments projects, public procurement mechanism for such investments, sale and purchase of emission quotas, and so on.[8]

II.   Water

A.   General Framework of Water Use

Under the Environmental Law and the Water Code of Ukraine, dated June 6, 1995, as amended (Water Code), companies may extract and use water, and discharge polluting substances into water, only upon receipt of a special water use permit listing certain approved quantities and payment of an ecological tax.[9]

Water use permits concerning use of national water bodies are issued by the local government administrations, while water use permits concerning use of local water bodies are issued by regional local councils upon consent of the local government administrations. A water use permit may be issued for a short term (up to three years) or for a long term (up to 25 years).[10]

To receive the water use permit, an applicant must submit to the issuing authority an application together with documentation of the requested water consumption quantity. The documentation must be preapproved by a number of state offices depending on the targeted water source (open water, subsurface water, recreational waterbodies, etc.). The local government administrations and regional coucils have 30 calendar days from the application date to decide whether to issue the water use permit to the applicant. The issued water use permit indicates the maximum volume of water intake, water use, and amount of each polluting substance that may be discharged into a water source.[11] Copies of the water use permit must be submitted to the territorial bodies of the State Sanitary-and-Epidemiological Service of Ukraine and the State Agency of Water Resources of Ukraine.[12]

Companies may also receive water from the local water supply company and discharge sewage water into the sewage system without obtaining a water use permit, provided that the terms and conditions of such discharge are agreed upon with the water supply company in a written agreement. Such an agreement includes an annex with a description of the water source, water use, and discharge limits not exceeding the water use limits established for the water supply company in its own water use permit.[13]

B. Marine Waters

With the extensive coastline of the Black Sea and Azov Sea, Ukraine is a party to the following international conventions:

- International Convention Relating to Intervention on the High Seas in Cases of Oil Pollution Casualties, 1969 (ratified December 17, 1993)[14]
- Convention on the Prevention of Marine Pollution by Dumping of Wastes and Other Matter (London Convention), 1972 (ratified December 24, 1975)[15] International Convention for the Prevention of Pollution from Ships, 1973, and Protocol thereto, 1978 (ratified September 21, 1993)[16]
- United Nations Convention on the Law of the Sea, 1982 (ratified February 4, 1994)[17]
- Black Sea Biodiversity and Landscape Conservation Protocol (ratified February 22, 2007)[18]
- International Convention on Civil Liability for Oil Pollution Damage, 1992 (ratified July 4, 2002)[19]

A number of domestic statutes transform rules of international law into Ukrainian domestic law. Upon ratification, international treaties become a part of, and supersede, if they conflict with, domestic laws.[20]

The Water Code of Ukraine, the principal statute regulating the use of water resources, contains only a few articles specifically addressing protection of marine waters. The Water Code provides, inter alia, for a general prohibition on the discharge of waste or polluting substances of a chemical, radioactive, or other origin from vessels, various platforms, and other maritime structures into marine waters.[21]

The marine water protection regime is established with a higher degree of specificity in the Rules on Protection of Internal Sea Waters and Territorial Waters of Ukraine against Pollution and Littering, approved by the Cabinet of Ministers of Ukraine on February 29, 1996. The rules establish certain exemptions from the prohibition on discharge of polluting substances into marine waters and additionally regulate pollution of oceanic waters by onshore structures. For example, wastewater discharge from vessels is permitted if a vessel located in the ocean or ports first purifies the wastewater in compliance with requirements of the International Convention for the Prevention of Pollution from Ships, 1973, or if there are not more than 10 persons on board a vessel.[22]

III.   Handling, Treatment, Transportation, and Disposal of Hazardous Materials

Under Ukrainian environmental law, a company must receive a toxic waste permit for the production, storage, transportation, usage, and utilization of poisonous and biotechnological products.[23] The toxic waste permit is issued by the Ministry of the Environment upon the consent of Ministries of Health, Internal Affairs, Infrastructure, the State Service of Mining Supervision and Industrial Safety of Ukraine, and the State Sanitary-and-Epidemiological Service of Ukraine.[24] The list of such poisonous and biotechnological products is approved by the Cabinet of Ministers of Ukraine.[25] The Ministry of the Environment has 60 days from the application date to decide whether to issue the toxic waste permit.[26]

Under Ukrainian environmental law, companies processing or storing radioactive waste must receive a special license from the State Inspection of Nuclear Regulation of Ukraine.[27] Producers of radioactive waste are required to dispose of such waste at sites owned by specialized enterprises.[28] The State Agency on Administration of the Exclusion Zone (established around the Chernobyl nuclear power station after the 1986 nuclear accident resulted in an extensive nuclear spill) maintains a State Register of Radioactive Waste containing information on the production, specification, transportation, and storage of radioactive waste collected from its producers on a quarterly basis.[29] The State Agency on Administration of the Exclusion Zone also maintains a State Register of Depots and Sites for Temporary Storage of Radioactive Waste based on information reported by owners of designated storage sites.[30] International transportation of radioactive waste in Ukraine may be conducted with a permit of the State Inspection of Nuclear Regulation of Ukraine and the State Service of Export Control of Ukraine (except for transit transportation of radioactive waste).[31]

Export or import of dangerous waste is carried out on the basis of specific terms. On July 1, 1999, Ukraine acceded to the Basel Convention on the Control of Transboundary Movements of Hazardous Wastes and Their Disposal, 1989 (Basel Convention).[32] The nation's laws were accordingly adapted to ensure that Ukraine could carry out its international obligations. Waste is considered to be dangerous waste based on what is known as the Yellow Waste List and Green Waste List, approved by the Cabinet of Ministers of Ukraine.[33] Export, import, and transit of dangerous waste require a special dangerous waste transportation permit from the Ministry of the Environment.[34] An exporter must notify the Ministry of the Environment at least 70 days before the expected transportation date. The Ministry of the Environment issues its permit to the exporter, which requires compliance with certain mandatory requirements.[35] The dangerous waste transportation permit for import or transit of dangerous waste is issued within 70 or 60 days, respectively, of the application date.[36] Importation into Ukraine of dangerous waste for storage or burial is prohibited.[37]

IV. Waste and Site Remediation

Under Ukrainian environmental law, industrial, domestic, and other waste must be stored at special sites. A company may store such waste at its own site or may transfer it to another company under a contract.[38] A company producing waste in its operational activities must receive a special waste permit with specified limits of allowed waste production and storage (unless the waste produced is below a certain amount) and must pay a respective ecological tax.[39]

A. Waste Permit

Waste permits are issued for three years by relevant local government administrations.[40] Applications for waste permits must be submitted before April 1 (by companies storing but not producing waste) or June 1 (by companies producing and storing waste on their land) of the year immediately preceding the year for which the waste permit is sought. Each application should include a number of supporting documents.[41] By July 1 of each year, the relevant issuing authority must either issue the waste permit to the applicant for the next calendar year, or provide a reasoned explanation for its rejection and establish a new deadline for a revised application.[42] Waste permits are effective from the date of approval of the waste limits.[43]

In addition to the waste permit, an owner of the site designated for storage of waste must obtain a waste site certificate.[44] The waste site certificates are drafted by the site owners and approved by local government administrations and regional offices of the State Sanitary-and-Epidemiological Service of Ukraine.[45] A local government administration reviews each waste site certificate annually based on verifications and reports submitted by the waste site certificate holder.[46] Local government administrations maintain waste site registers on all sites for which waste site certificates are issued.[47]

Waste producers that exceed certain production levels and owners of waste recycling or utilizing equipment with a capacity of at least 100 tons per year are required to prepare registration cards containing various information concerning the waste and recycling technology used.[48] The registration cards must be approved by the local government administrations upon the consent of the regional offices of the State Sanitary-and-Epidemiological Service of Ukraine and are subject to annual review.[49]

B. Waste Limits

Waste limits are issued to all waste owners (i.e., those who have ownership right to a unit of waste—waste producers and owners of waste recycling or utilizing equipment that receive waste from its producers), except (1) those who are engaged in the collection and storage of secondary raw materials pursuant to their statutory documents; and (2) those waste owners that are not associated with waste producers exceeding certain production levels or owners of waste recycling or utilizing equipment with a capacity of at least

100 tons per year. Waste owners under category (2) annually submit declarations on waste to local government administrations.[50] By February 1 of each year, local government administrations determine the list of companies that need to obtain waste limits for the next year. By March 1, these companies will receive a notice from the local government administrations requiring them to prepare a draft report of required limits on waste production and storage. A company must submit the draft report of required limits on waste production and storage together with its application for the waste permit.[51] Based on the issued waste permit, a company prepares a final version of the draft report of required limits on waste production and storage and submits it to the local government administration by September 1.[52] The local government administration approves the waste limits for a three-year term and notifies the applicant of its decision by October 1.[53] On April 26, 2014, amendments were made to the Law of Ukraine "On Waste" that completely excluded references to waste limits. However, the relevant by-laws regulating waste limit procedures described above have not been amended or abolished yet. For this reason, the legal regulation of waste treatment is still in the process of development in Ukraine.

V.   Emergency Response

Ukrainian law includes the notion of an "ecological emergency," meaning an emergency resulting from negative effects to the environment within a certain territory and requiring application of emergency measures by the government. Negative environmental effects include the loss, deterioration, or destruction of natural systems and resources as a result of excessive environmental pollution, natural disasters, or other factors damaging the environment and impacting human economic activities.[54] The affected territorial area may be declared an area of ecological emergency by the president at the suggestion of the Council of National Security and Defense of Ukraine or the Cabinet of Ministers of Ukraine.

The declaration of an ecological emergency may lead to limitations on certain activities, such as the construction and functioning of projects causing an increased environmental threat; the application of hazardous substances (chemical, radioactive, toxic, biological, etc.); crop protection agents that may damage the environment; the functioning of health resorts; and the conduct of any other activities representing an increased environmental threat to people, plants, and animals.[55] If the ecological emergency requires urgent and wide-scale emergency response, the president may involve the Ukrainian armed forces and various paramilitary units.[56]

VI.   Natural Resource Management and Protection

Under Ukrainian environmental law, the use of natural resources is classified as either "general use" (the use of natural resources by individuals for personal needs, for which no permit or fee payment is required) and "special use" (the use of natural resources by individuals and companies for commercial or other purposes, for which a permit and fee payment is required). A company can exploit natural resources for its activities only for special, not general use. It must therefore pay a "special use" fee and obtain a special use permit.[57] A special use permit may be issued by the Ministry of the Environment or other governmental agency depending on the specific natural resource (in the case of national natural resources), or by local councils, with the consent of the local government administration (in the case of local natural resources).[58]

Under the Environmental Law, national natural resources include the following:

- territorial and internal marine waters;
- natural resources located in the continental shelf and exclusive economic zone (EEZ);
- the atmosphere;
- underground water;
- surface waters located or used within more than one region;
- forest resources of national significance;
- natural resources within recreational areas of national significance;
- wild animals in their natural habitat within the territory of Ukraine, its continental shelf, and the EEZ, and other fauna covered by the Law of Ukraine "On the Animal World," dated December 13, 2001, that are owned by the national government, and the fauna that have, as provided by applicable legislation, been acquired to become communal or private property and declared to be of national value; and
- mineral resources, except those that are widely available.

All other natural resources are deemed local national resources.[59]

A. Special Use Permits

Under the current environmental registration system, a company is required to apply for a special use permit if it intends to use any natural resources in its production or other business activities. An application must be approved by one or more specialized governmental agencies, depending on the specific resource for which the permit is sought. The authorized agency must decide whether to issue a special use permit within one month of the application date.[60]

B. Special Use Limits

The Ministry of the Environment and local government administrations establish special use limits for holders of special use permits, except for special use limits concerning underground resources. The Ukrainian Cabinet of Ministers establishes the latter.[61] Such special use limits are based on the aggregate amount of natural resources that may be used in Ukraine during a given period of time. Local government administrations set the aggregate limits with respect to local natural resources;[62] the Ministry of the Environment sets them with respect to national natural resources.[63]

C. Special Use Payments

Any company holding a special use permit is required to pay a special use fee in the amount established by the Decrees of the Cabinet of Ministers of Ukraine or the Tax Code of Ukraine, dated December 2, 2010.[64] The special use fees are established by the Cabinet of Ministers of Ukraine for the following natural resources:

- *Wild animals:* Standard rates per animal range from the equivalent of US$0.01 to the equivalent of US$300, depending on the species; rates increase by a factor of five for usage in excess of special use limits.[65]
- *Fish and other aquatic fauna:* Standard rates per ton range from the equivalent of US$0.07 to the equivalent of US$56, depending on the species.[66]

Liability for violations of natural resources protection rules is outlined *infra* in section XI, Civil and Criminal Enforcement and Penalties.

VII. Natural Resource Damages

Ukrainian environmental law provides for various procedures for calculating and quantifying damages to the environment. [67] The calculation is used by the respective officials of the Ministry of the Environment and courts to evaluate the extent of the violator's civil and administrative liability. It may also be used by the public prosecutor's offices and courts to evaluate the gravity of the investigated ecological crime and resulting liability. The Environmental Law provides for full compensation for damages sustained by the environment[68] as a result of the following activities: (1) pollution and littering of land resources;[69] (2) pollution of water bodies, including subsurface and open water, and unauthorized use of water resources;[70] (3) pollution of the environment during the transport of hazardous substances and waste;[71] (4) human-induced and natural emergencies;[72] (5) unauthorized emissions of pollutants into the atmosphere;[73] (6) harm to certain fauna and flora;[74] and (7) other activities.[75]

Certain clarifications on damage compensation were provided by the High Commercial Court of Ukraine in 2001. The court explained that the damages must be calculated pursuant to the procedures effective at the time the environmental violation occurred. If the time of the violation cannot be identified, the procedures effective at the time the violation was detected are applied. If appropriate, the court may request that an expert calculate the amount of damages.[76]

VIII. Protected Species

Specifically protected endangered species (including animals, plants, fungi, algae, and nonpathogenic microorganisms) are formally registered in what is known as the Red Book of Ukraine, maintained by the Ministry of the Environment.[77]

The species in the Red Book are afforded special treatment to ensure their protection and reproduction, including

- *Protection measures:* The establishment of a special protection regime for rare and imperiled species of plants and animals, prohibition or restriction of their use for commercial and military purposes; prioritized establishment of natural reserves and other similar sites with a special focus on Red Book species' occupied habitat and migration routes of protected animals; establishment of centers for preservation of genetic resources of protected species; and breeding (cultivation) of protected species in special artificial conditions (zoological parks, farms, botanical gardens, dendrological parks, etc.).
- *Reproduction measures:* Assistance in recruitment of rare and imperiled animal and plant species; breeding (cultivation) of the species in artificial conditions; and so on. Rare and vanishing animals are bred if they cannot be preserved in their natural conditions. Permits on breeding of Red Book animals are issued by the Ministry of the Environment.[78]

The information included in the Red Book is subject to public disclosure (also through mass media). Public disclosure is limited to the extent that publication of its range and location may reduce the species' protection and negatively impact reproduction. The Cabinet of Ministers officially publishes the Red Book at least once every ten years.[79]

Research institutions, state and non-governmental organizations, and individuals may submit proposals to include animal and plant species in the Red Book. Such proposals are analyzed and systematized by the National Commission for the Red Book of Ukraine. The Ministry of the Environment adopts the decision on inclusion of animal and plant species into the Red Book based on the recommendations of the National Commission for the Red Book of Ukraine.[80]

The animals and plants that are not included in the Red Book but that have special research or other value may be included in lists of animals or plants that require special protection. The Ministry of the Environment is responsible for compiling the special protection lists with regard to animals, and local regional councils are responsible for forming the special protection lists with regard to plants located within their respective territories. The same governmental authorities approve procedures for the protection of plants and animals included in the special protection lists.[81]

IX. Environmental Review and Decision Making

Under Ukrainian environmental law, certain commercial and industrial projects that may affect the environment are subject to mandatory governmental ecological analysis.[82] Analyses conducted by non-governmental organizations, private companies, and individuals are nonbinding, but may be taken into account during the governmental ecological analysis and public decision making.[83]

The ecological analysis is conducted by the Ministry of the Environment (regarding projects requiring approval of the Cabinet of Ministers of Ukraine) and the local government administrations in connection with

- investment programs and feasibility studies;
- production plans with respect to new equipment, materials, or technology;
- general zoning and city development plans;
- drafts of laws and other regulatory documents governing business activity that may affect the environment;
- design documents on any plant, object, or site the temporary closing of which is hazardous to the environment; and
- documents on genetically modified organisms that are created for use in an open circuit system.[84]

An ecological analysis is mandatory when the business activities or specific objects represent a significant hazard to the environment. The official Cabinet of Ministers' list of such activities and projects includes, inter alia, nuclear energy, industrial and domestic waste treatment, the oil and gas industry, the chemical industry, metallurgy, and cattle breeding.[85]

Application documents for an ecological analysis must be approved by the Ministry of Health of Ukraine, the State Service of Mining Supervision and Industrial Safety of Ukraine, and the Fire Protection Department of the State Emergency Service of Ukraine prior to their submission to the authority responsible for the ecological analysis.[86] The latter must complete the ecological analysis within 120 days from the application date.[87] The ecological analysis is valid for three years.[88]

An applicant is responsible for costs and expenses related to the ecological analysis. This fee ranges from 0.2 to 3.5 percent of the cost of preparing the project documentation.[89]

Positive conclusions of the ecological analysis trigger financing and implementation of the relevant projects and programs. Negative conclusions of the ecological analysis result in the interested party's obligation to amend and resubmit the necessary documents for a subsequent ecological analysis.[90]

X.   Transboundary Pollution

Ukraine has taken part in international processes concerning the prevention and mitigation of transboundary pollution. For example, a number of international instruments dealing with the protection of marine water resources were ratified by Ukraine (see section II, *supra*, Water). Also, as noted previously, on July 1, 1999, Ukraine ratified the Basel Convention.[91]

Ukraine is also a party to

- the Convention on Long-Range Transboundary Air Pollution, 1979 (ratified on May 13, 1980)[92] and several protocols thereto:[93] the Protocol on Long-Term Financing of the Cooperative Programme for Monitoring and Evaluation of the Long-Range Transmission of Air Pollutants

in Europe (ratified on August 30, 1985); Protocol on the Reduction of Sulphur Emissions or their Transboundary Fluxes by at least 30 per cent, 1985 (ratified on October 2, 1986); Protocol Concerning the Control of Emissions of Nitrogen Oxides or their Transboundary Fluxes, 1988 (ratified on July 24, 1989)
- the Convention on Environmental Impact Assessment in a Transboundary Context, 1991 (ratified on March 19, 1999)
- the Convention on the Protection and Use of Transboundary Watercourses and International Lakes, 1992 (ratified on October 8, 1999) and Protocol on Water and Health, 1999 (ratified on September 26, 2003)

Upon ratification, these international treaties became a part of Ukrainian domestic law.[94] Separately, Ukraine transposed certain provisions of the treaties into domestic laws and regulations (see also sections II and III, *supra*), for example, National Action Plan on Environmental Protection for 2011–2015, dated 2011 (which provides, inter alia, for creation of a monitoring station for long-range transboundary air pollution, correction of the methodology for creating an inventory of sources and amounts of emissions, etc.),[95] and the Methodological Recommendations on Practical Application of Convention on Environmental Impact Assessment in a Transboundary Context, dated 2012.[96]

XI. Civil and Criminal Enforcement and Penalties

Civil liability of companies and individuals for ecological violations is based on the damage sustained by the environment as a result of unlawful behavior.[97] As noted in section VII, *supra*, Ukrainian environmental law establishes various procedures for the calculation of damage to land, water resources, the air, and other resources. The damage calculated pursuant to the established procedures is subject to judicial remedies unless paid by the violator voluntarily in response to the demand of the State Ecological Inspectorate of Ukraine.[98]

Criminal liability of individuals for environmental crimes is established by a separate section of the criminal code of Ukraine.[99] Environmental crimes include improper performance of an ecological analysis;[100] violation of ecological rules during project design and construction;[101] nonperformance of requirements related to the elimination of pollution;[102] nondisclosure of information on environmental pollution;[103] pollution of the land, inland waters, ocean, and air, and damage to plant and animal biodiversity;[104] and illegal game hunting.[105] The criminal code distinguishes culpability for "endangering" human life, health, and environmental safety and "other severe consequences" for a violation related to the environment. The Supreme Court has clarified that endangering human life, health, or environmental safety should be understood as the possibility of death or infection of a least one person, a decrease in life expectancy, effects to children's health, or similar events. Severe consequences resulting in stricter liability should be understood as mass death or epidemic disease, material deterioration of the environment,

mass extinction of plant and animal biodiversity, impossibility of environmental remediation, genetic mutations, and so on.[106] The following range of
criminal penalties exists under the criminal code for environmental crimes: a
fine of up to UAH 13,600 (approx. US$1,150), arrest for up to six months,
restriction of freedom (a more lenient penalty than imprisonment) for up to
five years, imprisonment for up to 12 years, restriction of the right to occupy
certain environment-related positions or engage in certain environment-
related activities for up to three years, or confiscation of hunting weapons or
extracting appliances with hunted (extracted) animals, fish, forest, or mineral
resources.[107]

Environmental violations by individuals not qualifying as environmental
crimes can still give rise to administrative liability in the form of fines, as
provided by the Code on Administrative Offenses of Ukraine. The fines are
imposed by governmental environmental inspectors.[108] The amounts of
administrative fines are smaller than criminal fines and range from UAH 17
(approx. US$1.4) to UAH 10,200 (approx. US$860).[109]

Enforcement of environmental laws is performed by a number of governmental authorities, including courts of general jurisdiction and public
prosecution offices specializing in the protection of the environment.[110] One
of the most important enforcement authorities is the Ecological Inspectorate (including its regional offices). It has broad authority regarding ecological monitoring and securing compliance in such spheres as radiological
safety, protection of land, water resources, air quality, forestry, rare plant
and animal species, utilization of electrochemical power sources, and waste
treatment.[111]

Notes

1. The Law of Ukraine "On Protection of Environment" of June 25, 1991, No. 1264-XII,
art. 3; the Law of Ukraine "On Protection of Ambient Air" of October 16, 1992, No. 2707-XII,
arts. 10–11; the Tax Code of Ukraine of December 2, 2010, No. 2755-VI, § VIII.

2. The Law of Ukraine "On Protection of Ambient Air" of October 16, 1992, No.
2707-XII, art. 11; Procedure of Performance and Payment for Works Related to Issuance of
Permits to Emission of Polluting Substances into the Ambient Air via Stationary Sources,
and Maintenance of Records of Enterprises, Establishments, Organizations, and Private
Entrepreneurs that Received Such Permits—approved by the Decree of the Cabinet of
Ministers of Ukraine of March 13, 2002, No. 302, para. 3.

3. *Id.* paras. 2, 5–8; Normative Standards of Allowable Emissions of Polluting Substances via Stationary Sources—approved by the Order of the Ministry of the Environment of Ukraine of June 27, 2006, No. 309.

4. The Law of Ukraine "On Ratification of the United Nations Framework Convention on Climate Change" of October 29, 1996, No. 435/96-BP.

5. The Law of Ukraine "On Ratification of the Kyoto Protocol to the United Nations
Framework Convention on Climate Change" of February 4, 2004, No. 1430-IV.

6. Decree of the Cabinet of Ministers of Ukraine "On Securing of Implementation
of International Obligations of Ukraine Pursuant to the United Nations Framework Convention on Climate Change and the Kyoto Protocol thereto" of April 17, 2008, No. 392,
para. 1.

7. Procedure of Participation of Central Bodies of Executive Power in the Activities of International Organizations to which Ukraine is a Member—approved by the Decree of the Cabinet of Ministers of Ukraine of September 13, 2002, No. 1371.

8. Regulation on the National Electronic Register of Anthropogenic Emissions and Greenhouse Gas Absorption—approved by the Decree of the Cabinet of Ministers of Ukraine of May 28, 2008, No. 504; the Procedure of Review, Approval, and Implementation of Projects of Ecological (Green) Special-Purpose Investments and Proposals on Implementation of Actions Related to Such Projects and to Performance of Obligations of the Parties to the Kyoto Protocol to the United Nations Framework Convention on Climate Change—approved by the Decree of the Cabinet of Ministers of Ukraine of February 22, 2008, No. 221; Procedure of Public Procurement Tender on Acquisition of Goods, Works, and Services in the Context of Implementation of Projects of Ecological (Green) Special-Purpose Investments and Proposals on Implementation of Actions Related to Such Projects and to Performance of Obligations of the Parties to the Kyoto Protocol to the United Nations Framework Convention on Climate Change for Money Received from Sale of Greenhouse Gas Emission Quotas—approved by the Decree of the Cabinet of Ministers of Ukraine of 16 July 2012, No. 672.

9. The Law of Ukraine "On Protection of Environment" of June 25, 1991, No. 1264-XII, art. 3; the Water Code of Ukraine of June 6, 1995, No. 213/95-BP, art. 49; the Tax Code of Ukraine of December 2, 2010, No. 2755-VI, § VIII.

10. Procedure of Approval and Issuance of Permits for Special-Purpose Water Use—approved by the Decree of the Cabinet of Ministers of Ukraine of March 13, 2002, No. 321, paras. 2, 6.

11. *Id.* paras. 3–5; the Water Code of Ukraine of June 6, 1995, No. 213/95-BP, art. 49.

12. *Id.* para. 8.

13. Rules of Collection of Companies Waste Water into Communal and Local Sewage Systems at Urban Settlements of Ukraine—Approved by the Order of the State Committee of Construction, Architecture, and Residential Policy of Ukraine of February 19, 2002, No. 37, § 6; Letter of the Ministry of the Environment of Ukraine "On Provision of Clarification" of March 15, 2011, No. 5515/16/10-11-MП.

14. Decree of the Verkhovna Rada of Ukraine "On Ukraine's Participation in International Convention Relating to Intervention on the High Seas in Cases of Oil Pollution Casualties, 1969" of December 17, 1993, No. 3734-XII.

15. Decree of the Presidium of the Verkhovna Rada of Ukrainian SSR "On Ratification of Convention on the Prevention of Marine Pollution by Dumping of Wastes and Other Matter" of December 24, 1975, No. 519-IX.

16. Decree of the Cabinet of Ministers of Ukraine "On Ukraine's Accession to International Convention for the Prevention of Pollution from Ships, 1973, amendments of 1984, 1985, 1987, 1990, and 1992, and Protocol of 1978 thereto" of September 21, 1993, No. 771.

17. Decree of the Verkhovna Rada of Ukraine "On Ratification of Convention on the Protection of the Black Sea against Pollution" of February 4, 1994, No. 3939-XII.

18. The Law of Ukraine "On Ratification of Black Sea Biodiversity and Landscape Conservation Protocol to Convention on the Protection of the Black Sea against Pollution" of February 22, 2007, No. 685-V.

19. The Law of Ukraine "On Ukraine's Accession to International Convention on Civil Liability for Oil Pollution Damage" of July 4, 2002, No. 44-IV.

20. The Law of Ukraine "On International Treaties of Ukraine" of June 29, 2004, No. 1906-IV, art. 19.

21. The Water Code of Ukraine of June 6, 1995, No. 213/95-BP, art. 102.

22. Rules on Protection of Internal Sea Waters and Territorial Waters of Ukraine against Pollution and Littering—approved by the Decree of the Cabinet of Ministers of Ukraine of February 29, 1996, No. 269, para. 5.

23. Procedure of Obtainment of Permit for Production, Storage, Transportation, Use, Burial, Removal and Utilization of Poisonous Substances, Including Biotechnological Products and Other Biological Agents—approved by the Decree of the Cabinet of Ministers of Ukraine of June 20, 1995, No. 440, para. 2.

24. *Id.* para. 3.

25. List of Poisonous Substances Including Biotechnological Products and Other Biological Agents, which Production, Storage, Transportation, Use, Burial, Removal and Utilization Is Performed Subject to Availability of the Permit—Annex to Procedure of Obtainment of Permit for Production, Storage, Transportation, Use, Burial, Removal and Utilization of Poisonous Substances, Including Biotechnological Products and Other Biological Agents—approved by the Decree of the Cabinet of Ministers of Ukraine of June 20, 1995, No. 440.

26. Procedure of Obtainment of Permit for Production, Storage, Transportation, Use, Burial, Removal and Utilization of Poisonous Substances, Including Biotechnological Products and Other Biological Agents—approved by the Decree of the Cabinet of Ministers of Ukraine of June 20, 1995, No. 440, para. 4.

27. The Law of Ukraine "On Treatment of Radioactive Waste" of June 30, 1995, No. 255/95-BP art. 9.

28. *Id.* art. 17.

29. Regulation on State Register of Radioactive Waste—approved by the Decree of the Cabinet of Ministers of Ukraine of April 29, 1996, No. 480, paras. 2, 4.

30. Regulation on State Register of Depots and Sites for Temporary Storage of Radioactive Waste—approved by the Decree of the Cabinet of Ministers of Ukraine of April 29, 1996, No. 480, paras. 3, 5.

31. Regulation on Procedure of Transportation of Radioactive Materials at the Territory of Ukraine—approved by the Decree of the Cabinet of Ministers of Ukraine of October 15, 2004, No. 1373, para. 9.

32. The Law of Ukraine "On Ukraine's Accession to Basel Convention on the Control of Transboundary Movements of Hazardous Wastes and their Disposal" of July 1, 1999, No. 803-XIV.

33. Green Waste List and Yellow Waste List—approved by the Decree of the Cabinet of Ministers of Ukraine of July 13, 2000, No. 1120.

34. Regulation on Control over Transboundary Transportation of Dangerous Waste and its Utilization/Removal—approved by the Decree of the Cabinet of Ministers of Ukraine of July 13, 2000, No. 1120, paras. 12–13, 16.

35. *Id.* paras. 7, 12–13.

36. *Id.* paras. 19, 28.

37. *Id.* para. 16.

38. The Law of Ukraine "On Waste" of March 5, 1998, No. 187/98-BP, art. 33; Procedure of Drafting, Approval and Revision of Limits to Waste Production and Storage—approved by the Decree of the Cabinet of Ministers of Ukraine of August 3, 1998, No. 1218.

39. The Law of Ukraine "On Protection of Environment" of June 25, 1991, art. 3; the Law of Ukraine "On Waste" of March 5, 1998, No. 187/98-BP, art. 17, 20; the Tax Code of Ukraine of December 2, 2010, No. 2755-VI, § VIII.

40. The Law of Ukraine "On Waste" of March 5, 1998, No. 187/98-BP, art. 20.

41. Procedure of Drafting, Approval and Revision of Limits to Waste Production and Storage—approved by the Decree of the Cabinet of Ministers of Ukraine of August 3, 1998, No. 1218, para. 12.

42. *Id.* para. 13.

43. *Id.* para. 15.

44. Procedure of Register Keeping for Waste Removal Sites—approved by the Decree of the Cabinet of Ministers of Ukraine of August 3, 1998, No. 1216, para. 5.

45. *Id.* paras. 12–14.

46. *Id.* para. 19.

47. *Id.* paras. 4, 8–10.

48. Procedure of Register Keeping for Objects of Production, Processing and Utilization of Waste—approved by the Decree of the Cabinet of Ministers of Ukraine of August 31, 1998, No. 1360, paras. 8–9.

49. *Id.* paras. 11, 15.

50. Procedure of Drafting, Approval and Revision of Limits to Waste Production and Storage—approved by the Decree of the Cabinet of Ministers of Ukraine of August 3, 1998, No. 1218, para. 8.

51. *Id.* paras. 10–12.

52. *Id.* para. 14.

53. *Id.* para. 18.

54. The Law of Ukraine "On the Zone of Ecological Emergency" of July 13, 2000, No. 1908-III, art. 1.

55. *Id.* art. 12.

56. *Id.* art. 10; the Law of Ukraine "On State of Emergency" of March 16, 2000, No. 1550-III, arts. 16–17.

57. The Law of Ukraine "On Protection of Environment" of June 25, 1991, No. 1264-XII, art. 38.

58. Regulation on Procedure of Issuance of Permits to Special-Purpose Use of Natural Resources—approved by the Decree of the Cabinet of Ministers of Ukraine of August 10, 1992, No. 459, para. 4.

59. The Law of Ukraine "On Protection of Environment" of June 25, 1991, No. 1264-XII, art. 39.

60. Regulation on Procedure of Issuance of Permits to Special-Purpose Use of Natural Resources—approved by the Decree of the Cabinet of Ministers of Ukraine of August 10, 1992, No. 459, paras. 3–6.

61. Regulation on Procedure of Setting Limits on Use of Natural Resources of National Importance—approved by the Decree of the Cabinet of Ministers of Ukraine of August 10, 1992, No. 459, para. 3.

62. The Law of Ukraine "On Natural Reserve Fund of Ukraine" of June 16, 1992, No. 2456-XII, art. 9-1.

63. Regulation on Procedure of Setting Limits on Use of Natural Resources of National Importance—approved by the Decree of the Cabinet of Ministers of Ukraine of August 10, 1992, No. 459, paras. 7–9.

64. The Tax Code of Ukraine of December 2, 2010, No. 2755-VI, §§ XVI-XVII.

65. Decree of the Cabinet of Ministers of Ukraine "On Approval of Provisional Procedure of Payment for Special-Purpose Use of Wild Animals" of January 25, 1996, No. 123.

66. Procedure of Payment of Duty for Special-Purpose Use of Fishery and Other Water Live Resources—approved by the Decree of the Cabinet of Ministers of Ukraine of April 6, 1998, No. 449.

67. Land use is also subject to regulation by Ukrainian law. The Land Code of Ukraine, dated October 25, 2001, as amended, is the primary legal act regulating land relations (including land management) in Ukraine. Pursuant to the Land Code all land is divided into the following categories: (1) agricultural lands; (2) lands of residential and public

development; (3) lands of natural reserves and other environmental purpose; (4) lands of health-improving purpose; (5) lands of recreational purpose; (6) land of historic and cultural purpose; (7) lands of forest management purpose; (8) lands of water fund; (9) lands of industry, transport, communication, energy sector, military defense, and other purpose. Each land category is managed within a special legal framework.

The lands are assigned to a certain category by decisions of state authorities and local councils pursuant to their respective competence. Violation of procedure for establishment and change of the land designated purpose (land category) may result in (1) invalidation of decisions of state authorities and local councils on transfer of land plots to individuals and legal entities; (2) invalidation of agreements on land plots; (3) refusal of state registration of land plots or invalidation of such registration; (4) prosecution of persons and individuals responsible for violation of the procedure for establishment and change of the land designated purpose (land category).

Land management deals with land plots as special civil law objects. To become a civil law object a land plot must be identified, that is, information on its size, boundaries, and owner (or authorized user) must be included into the State Land Cadaster (unified database of land plots within the boundaries of Ukraine with information on their designated purpose, restriction on their use, their quantitative and qualitative characteristics, etc.). Registration of a land plot in the State Land Cadaster results in assigning of a cadaster number to the land plot.

68. The Law of Ukraine "On Protection of Environment" of June 25, 1991, No. 1264-XII, art. 69.

69. Methodology of Calculation of Damages Amount Resulting from Pollution and Littering of Land Resources Conditioned by Violations of Environmental Law—approved by the Order of the Ministry of the Environment of Ukraine of October 27, 1997, No. 171.

70. Methodology of Calculation of Compensation for Damage Sustained by the State as a Result of Violation of Laws on Protection and Rational Use of Water Resources—approved by the Order of the Ministry of the Environment of Ukraine of July 20, 2009, No. 389.

71. Provisional Methodology for Calculation of Anticipatory Damages Resulting from Transportation of Hazardous Substances and Waste—approved by the Order of the Ministry of Ecology and Natural Resources of Ukraine of May 15, 2001, No. 181.

72. Methodology of Estimation of Damages Resulting from Emergencies of Technogenic and Natural Character—approved by the Decree of the Cabinet of Ministers of Ukraine of February 15, 2002, No. 175.

73. Methodology of Calculation of Compensation for Damage Sustained by the State as a Result of Limit-Exceeding Emissions of Polluting Substances into Ambient Air—approved by the Order of the Ministry of the Environment of Ukraine of December 10, 2008, No. 639.

74. Methodology of Calculation of Damages Sustained by the Fishing Industries as a Result of Violation of Laws on Environmental Protection—approved by the Order of the Ministry of the Environmental Protection and Nuclear Safety of Ukraine of May 18, 1995, No. 36; Methodology of Calculation of Damages Sustained by the Fishing Industries as a Result of Violation of Rules of Fishing Industry and Protection of Water Live Resources—approved by the Order of the Ministry of Agrarian Policy of Ukraine, the Order of the Ministry of the Environment of Ukraine of July 12, 2004, No. 248/273; Decree of the Cabinet of Ministers of Ukraine "On the Amount of Compensation for Illegal Taking, Destruction, or Damage of Animal and Plant Species Recorded into the Red Book of Ukraine, and also for Destruction or Deterioration of their Environmental Conditions" of November 7, 2012, No. 1030; Decree of the Cabinet of Ministers of Ukraine "On

Approval of Tariffs for Calculation of Compensation for Damage Resulting from Illegal Taking (Gathering) or Destruction of Valuable Species of Water Bioresources" of November 21, 2011, No. 1209.

75. Decree of the Cabinet of Ministers of Ukraine "On Approval of Tariffs for Calculation of Compensation for Damage Resulting from Violation of Laws on Natural Reserve Fund" of July 24, 2013, No. 541.

76. Clarification of the High Commercial Court of Ukraine "On Certain Practical Issues Related to Litigation Involving Laws on Protection of the Environment" of June 27, 2001, No. 02-5/744, para. 1.2.

77. The Law of Ukraine "On the Red Book of Ukraine" of February 7, 2002, No. 3055-III, arts. 4, 15; Procedure of State Registration of Rare Animal and Plant Species and those Species that are under the Threat of Extinction, which are Recorded into the Red Book of Ukraine—approved by the Order of the Ministry of Ecology and Natural Resources of Ukraine of October 9, 2012, No. 486, para. 5.

78. The Law of Ukraine "On the Red Book of Ukraine" of February 7, 2002, No. 3055-III, art. 11.

79. *Id.* art. 12.

80. *Id.* art. 14.

81. The Law of Ukraine "On Animal World" of December 13, 2001, No. 2894-III, art. 44; the Law of Ukraine "On Plant World" of April 9, 1999, No. 591-XIV, art. 30.

82. The Law of Ukraine "On Protection of Environment" of June 25, 1991, No. 1264-XII, § VI; the Law of Ukraine "On Ecological Analysis" of February 9, 1995, No. 45/95-BP, art. 12.

83. The Law of Ukraine "On Ecological Analysis" of February 9, 1995, No. 45/95-BP, arts. 12, 16.

84. *Id.* art. 14.

85. *Id.* art. 13; List of Activities and Objects that Represent a Serious Hazard to the Environment—approved by the Decree of the Cabinet of Ministers of Ukraine of August 28, 2013, No. 808.

86. The Law of Ukraine "On Ecological Analysis" of February 9, 1995, No. 45/95-BP, art. 15; Procedure of Transfer of Documents to State Ecological Analysis—approved by the Decree of the Cabinet of Ministers of Ukraine of October 31, 1995, No. 870, para. 11.

87. The Law of Ukraine "On Ecological Analysis" of February 9, 1995, No. 45/95-BP, art. 38.

88. *Id.* art. 40.

89. Normative Standards of Expenses to State Ecological Analysis—approved by the Decree of the Cabinet of Ministers of Ukraine of June 13, 1996, No. 644.

90. The Law of Ukraine "On Ecological Analysis" of February 9, 1995, No. 45/95-BP, art. 39.

91. The Law of Ukraine "On Ukraine's Accession to Basel Convention on the Control of Transboundary Movements of Hazardous Wastes and their Disposal" of July 1, 1999, No. 803-XIV.

92. Decree of the Presidium of the Verkhovna Rada of Ukrainian SSR "On Ratification of Convention on Long-Range Transboundary Air Pollution" of May 13, 1980, No. 231-X.

93. In this paragraph the information on the dates of Ukraine's ratification (acceptance, accession) of the international instruments is taken from the convention's site, http://www.unece.org/.

94. The Law of Ukraine "On International Treaties of Ukraine" of June 29, 2004, No. 1906-IV, art. 19.

95. Order of the Cabinet of Ministers of Ukraine "On Approval of National Action Plan on Environmental Protection for 2011–2015" of May 25, 2011, No. 577-p.

96. Order of the Ministry of Ecology and Natural Resources "On Methodological Recommendations on Practical Application of Convention on Environmental Impact Assessment in a Transboundary Context" of February 15, 2012, No. 59.

97. The Law of Ukraine "On Protection of Environment" of June 25, 1991, No. 1264-XII, art. 69.

98. Regulation on the State Ecological Inspectorate of Ukraine—approved by the Decree of the President of Ukraine of April 13, 2011, No. 454/2011, para. 6(12).

99. The Criminal Code of Ukraine of April 5, 2001, No. 2341-III, § VIII.

100. *Id.* art. 236.

101. *Id.* arts. 236, 253.

102. *Id.* art. 237.

103. *Id.* art. 238.

104. *Id.* arts. 240–243, 245–247, 249–251.

105. *Id.* art. 248.

106. Decree of the Plenum of the Supreme Court of Ukraine "On Court Practice in Cases Related to Environmental Crimes and Other Environmental Violations" of December 10, 2004, No. 17, paras. 5–7.

107. The Criminal Code of Ukraine of April 5, 2001, No. 2341-III, § VIII.

108. The Code of Ukraine on Administrative Offensives of December 7, 1984, No. 8073-X, art. 242-1.

109. *Id.* arts. 57, 66.

110. The Law of Ukraine "On Protection of Environment" of June 25, 1991, No. 1264-XII, arts. 37, 67; the Law of Ukraine "On Judicial System and Status of Judges" of July 7, 2010, No. 2453-VI, art. 17.

111. Regulation on the State Ecological Inspectorate of Ukraine—approved by the Decree of the President of Ukraine of April 13, 2011, No. 454/2011, para. 4.

CHAPTER 35

Russian Federation

IRINA O. KRASNOVA

I. Introduction

Environmental law in Russia was created in the context of a federal system
of government. Environmental legislation under Article 72 of the Constitution of the Russian Federation falls within the concurrent competence of the
Federation and the 85 separate Russian federal regions. In practice, this
means that both the Federation and the federal regional governments have
the authority to legislate in the environmental arena.[1] Federal-level environmental legislation is currently the primary source of the nation's environmental laws.[2] However, some statutes delegate the fulfillment of certain
powers to the regional governments. This is the case, for example, for the
Russian Water and Forest Codes, the statute concerning ecological expertise,
and others.

Structurally, many of the federal laws impose a framework. In such
cases, the statute's mandates are further developed via executive orders
adopted by the Federation government and Federation ministries. The State
Duma frequently amends texts of laws, sometimes substantially changing
the initial rules.[3]

II. Air and Climate Change
A. Federal Law on Air Protection

The federal law "On Air Protection," adopted in 1999, establishes the legislative framework for addressing air pollution.[4] The law is focused primarily
on air protection requirements, air quality standards, and emission limitations. It provides for two types of air quality standards: environmental standards (for areas outside of inhabited areas) and health standards (for human
settlements and industrial regions). These standards are to be adopted by the
Ministry of Natural Resources and Ecology and the Ministry of Health,
respectively. Currently, only health-based standards have been adopted. The
air regulations cover over 4,000 substances and compounds.

The law states that the regulators of stationary sources of air pollution must develop pollutant emission limitations at a level not exceeding established air quality standards. These regulations are then approved by the Federal Agency for Nature Use Supervision (Rosprirodnadzor). Emissions are allowed after obtaining a permit issued by Rosprirodnadzor, valid for five years. Operators of stationary sources that are not able to comply with pollutant emission limitations are allowed to emit above those limitations in accordance with temporary emission limitations, provided that the operator submits a plan for emission reductions. Vehicles and other mobile sources must also comply with air pollutant limitations established on for specific vehicle types or models. Other emission control measures include government registration of pollutants and other potentially harmful substances, the certification of fuels, and air monitoring requirements that establish sanitary zones around certain pollution sources.

B.   Climate Change

Although in Russia climate change is recognized as a serious environmental problem, legislation remains in the incipient stages of development. Certain goals and principles are proclaimed in the Climate Doctrine of the Federation, approved by the president in December 2009.[5] The federal law "On Energy Saving and Improvement of Energy Efficiency" of November 2009[6] seeks to reduce emissions of greenhouse gases (GHGs) by establishing special requirements for industry to reduce consumption and save energy. For example, certain entities must provide data on energy efficiency and maintain "energy passports"—internal energy consumption registers. Certain building efficiency requirements also apply. At present, the statute does not require entities to reduce their GHG emissions.

III.   Water
A.   Water Code

All aspects of water regulation, including the discharge of wastewater and other impacts, are regulated by the Water Code of June 2006.[7] All water belongs to the government of the Federation and is available to individuals for general uses such as bathing or drinking water. Generally, no private ownership of water is allowed, except for artificial ponds within private land lots. Waters may be used by individuals or entities for economic purposes listed in the Water Code via either a contract for water use (use of aquatic areas, hydroelectric production, intake for economic activities) or a decision to grant a right to use water for purposes such as discharges of wastewater or construction of stationary facilities. This process, including the ability to conclude contracts and adopt decisions, is delegated to the regional governments. However, regulatory powers, such as the establishment of overall water quality standards, are reserved to the central government. Wastewater discharge limitations are subject to approval by Rosprirodnadzor. Rosprirodnadzor issues permits to each discharge source for a five-year term. Additionally,

Basin Councils are currently being set up for each of the nation's 20 water basin districts. These councils will serve to ensure a comprehensive approach to water use regulation and protection.

B. Federal Law on Protection of the Lake Baikal

Lake Baikal, located in southeastern Siberia, is designated as a United Nations Educational, Scientific and Cultural Organization (UNESCO) World Heritage Site.[8] It is of unique significance to the country because it is the country's largest source of clean fresh water, and also provides important natural habitat. A special protection regime for the lake itself and adjacent land areas was established in the 1999 federal statute "On Protection of Lake Baikal."[9] The law provides for the zoning of the lake and adjacent land areas. It states that economic activities may be carried out only after obtaining a favorable review of the proposed activities by a designated ecological expert. Certain types of activities, such as forestry, mineral development, and certain kinds of industrial production, are prohibited. The taking of endemic species is also restricted.

C. Federal Law on Inland Marine Waters, Territorial Sea, and Contiguous Zone

Specific rules for the use and protection of marine waters conforming with relevant international agreements—such as the U.N. Convention on the Law of the Sea—are established by the federal law "On Inland Marine Waters, Territorial Sea and Contiguous Zone," enacted in 1998.[10] This law regulates shipping issues, including shipping along the Northeast Passage in the Arctic region, a historically important transportation route. The law also covers marine scientific research. Protection of the marine environment is ensured by special environmental quality standards, and the requirement that a positive review by an ecological expert must be obtained for all economic activities within marine waters. Quality standards also require monitoring studies, and prohibit the disposal of wastes and other harmful substances in the ocean.

IV. Handling, Treatment, Transportation, and Disposal of Hazardous Materials

A. Federal Law on Environmental Protection

Pursuant to Article 47 of the federal law "On Environmental Protection," enacted in 2002 (Environmental Protection Law),[11] production and handling of potentially dangerous chemical substances is allowed only after toxicological and sanitary tests demonstrate conformity with environmental standards, the adoption of handling rules, and governmental registration of the substances at issue. These requirements are established in relation to pesticides and agrochemicals under the 1997 federal law "On the Safe Handling of Pesticides and Agrochemicals."[12] This law is implemented by the Ministry of Agriculture, and establishes a State Catalog of any pesticides and agrochemicals allowed within the territory of the Federation.

B.   Environmental Protection against Biological Impact

The Agency for the Protection of Consumer's Rights, which, since June 2012, directly reports to the Federation government, manages the movement and production of invasive plants and wild organisms in the country.[13] The Environmental Protection Law requires a favorable review by an environmental expert, development of measures to prevent the uncontrolled reproduction of invasive organisms, and a government permit. The 1996 federal law "On State Regulation of Genetically Modified Organisms (GMO) Handling"[14] requires that products made with genetically modified organisms obtain a certificate or an approved declaration of product conformity to the established standards.

C.   Handling of Radioactive Materials and Substances

Article 47 of the Environmental Protection Law establishes that radioactive materials may only be managed after completion of applicable toxicological and health-related tests, the adoption of certain handling rules, and registration with the federal government.

Under the 1995 federal law "On Nuclear Energy,"[15] handling of radioactive materials for the production of energy is subject to special norms and rules, including the Safety Rules for Storage and Transportation of Radioactive Fuels at Nuclear Energy Objects adopted by the federal agency for Ecological, Technological and Nuclear Supervision (Rostechnadzor). Rostechnadzor requires a company wishing to transport hazardous materials to first demonstrate that it is capable of safely storing and transporting such materials.

V.   Waste and Site Remediation

The general framework for handling all solid wastes, including radioactive wastes, is established by Article 51 of the Environmental Protection Law. This law prohibits the discharge of solid and radioactive wastes into water bodies, the subsoil, and onto land. It also prohibits disposal of such wastes in areas adjacent to human settlements or ecologically valuable ecosystems (e.g., specially protected areas and spawning grounds), the burial of dangerous wastes and radioactive wastes within the watersheds of underground water deposits, the importation of dangerous wastes for their burial or treatment, and the importation of radioactive wastes for storage, except under certain limited exceptions.

A.   Federal Law on Industrial and Municipal Wastes

Under the federal law "On Industrial and Municipal Wastes," enacted in 1998,[16] the production, collection, storage, use, treatment, transportation, and disposal of solid wastes are subject to special handling rules. Industrial wastes are first classified on a scale of 1–5 according to their dangerousness (1 designates extremely dangerous material, while 5 designates nondangerous material).

Activities connected with the handling of dangerous wastes classed 1–4 require a license. Landfills may be operated with a government permit; upon closure, operators must rehabilitate the affected lands and arrange for temporary monitoring of environmental impacts of wastes on groundwater and other environmental amenities. Handling of municipal wastes falls within the purview of local governments.

B.   Federal Law on Handling of Radioactive Wastes

The full cycle of handling of radioactive wastes from their production to burial in radioactive disposal sites, including their importation, is regulated by the federal law "On Handling of Radioactive Wastes," enacted in 2011.[17] The statute provides for classification of radioactive wastes based on different criteria. Different rules for the temporary storage, disposal, transportation, treatment, and location of radioactive disposal sites exist for each. The law states that wastes containing radioactive materials and radioactive wastes produced before enactment of the statute shall be exclusively owned by the federal government and managed by what is referred to as the "National Operator." By its Order No. 384-r dated March 20, 2012, the federal government appointed the Federal State Unitary Facility as the National Operator for Handling of Radioactive Wastes.[18]

Each entity in possession of radioactive wastes should maintain documentation containing information about the content and volume of wastes, their operators, and so on. Those involved in the transport, treatment, or storage of such wastes must have a permit to do so. Radioactive wastes must be disposed of in special disposal sites to ensure their security. The federal law "On Special Ecological Programs on Rehabilitation of Radioactively Polluted Areas," dated July 10, 2001,[19] was adopted to allow for importation of certain radioactive "wastes" that are not enumerated wastes. It overcomes the strict prohibition against the importation of radioactive wastes for storage and burial within the Federation. Under the law, radioactive components of nuclear reactors that are no longer used for extraction of radioactive materials may be imported as long as anything left over is exported back to the originating country.

The Chernobyl nuclear accident of 1986 and other more recent problems related to radioactive pollution have necessitated remediation in some areas. The federal law "On Special Ecological Programs on Rehabilitation of Radioactively Polluted Areas" allows for the import of devices designed for the temporary technological storage and treatment of radioactive materials. Under Article 4, finances received for these activities according to foreign trade contracts are channeled to a special account of the budgetary fund of competent public authorities, including the Ministries of Defense, Health, and Industry and Trade. Out of the amounts received, 75 percent are set aside to cover the expenses connected with fulfillment of special programs for rehabilitation of radioactively polluted areas. Several programs now are being implemented.

VI.   Emergency Response
A.   Federal Laws on Industrial Security

The federal law "On Industrial Security of Dangerous Production Facilities," dated July 21, 1997,[20] establishes that dangerous industrial facilities are subject to registration and licensing. Licenses are issued for five years after review of an application showing a declaration on industrial security, a positive decision of industrial expertise, a permit to use relevant technical devices, and insurance against civil liability for damage to health and property. Such facilities may be operated provided that they have an emergency plan, a contract with professional rescue teams for cases of industrial accidents, warning system, and material, technical, medicinal, and financial funds sufficient to respond to industrial accidents. The responsible public authority is Rostechnadzor.

Similar requirements are established for hydrotechnical constructions by the federal law "On Security of Hydrotechnical Constructions," dated July 21, 1997,[21] including their registration, licensing, and submission of security declarations. The responsible authority is the Federal Agency for Water Resources.

B.   Federal Law on the Protection of the Population and Territories against Natural and Man-Made Emergencies

Preparedness and response actions to be taken by public authorities or rescue teams during emergency situations are established in the federal law "On Protection of the Population and Territories against Natural and Man-Made Emergencies," of December 21, 1994.[22] The law classifies emergencies into several types, and allocates responsibilities between various levels of government. It also regulates the procedure for declaring emergency zones and outlines the regime applicable to their management.

VII.   Natural Resource Management and Protection
A.   Forest Code

Under the Forest Code of December 2006,[23] forested areas and designated as forested lands are owned by the federal government and may be used for various economic commercial purposes with a leasing contract. Other purposes, such as religious activities, are allowed on a free, temporary basis. Individuals have free access to such lands for activities such as collecting berries, resting, or walking. Tree cutting by individuals for personal use may only be done with a sales contract. Leasing contracts indicate the age, amount of, and type of timber that may be cut. The amount of timber to be harvested is set according to the amount established for each forest unit by the regional governments. Users are obliged to protect forests against fires and pests and to reforest affected areas. Commercial users are obliged to submit forest development plans as a leasing condition. All administrative powers are delegated to the regional governments.

B. Federal Law on Minerals

Under the federal law "On Minerals," first enacted in 1992 and amended in 1995,[24] use of subsoil for geological surveys, minerals extraction, or the collection of mineral, paleontological, and archeological artifacts requires a temporary or permanent license issued by the Federal Subsoil Agency. All subsoil—the area under the land surface within the territory of the Federation—belongs to the federal government. Minerals extracted according to license conditions typically belong to licensees; however, certain mineral deposits important for the defense and security of the country may be included on a special list of deposits with federal significance. The government may refuse to allow individual entities the right to exploit these mineral deposits if they are the subject of foreign investments. Specific rules for the development of gold, precious metals, other valuable minerals deposits, and deposits within the continental shelf are established by the federal laws "On Precious Metals and Previous Stones," of March 26, 1998,[25] and "On the Continental Shelf," dated November 30, 1995.[26]

C. Specially Protected Areas

Ecosystems with an ecological, esthetic, cultural, recreational, or other noneconomic value and land areas with valuable natural objects may be declared as specially protected. Pursuant to the federal law "On Specially Protected Areas," dated March 14, 1995,[27] such areas are designated as (1) natural reserves (all economic activities are prohibited); (2) national parks (recreational and commercial activities are allowed); (3) natural monuments; (4) resorts and others. Separate regulations apply to each category. They may be set up both by the Federation (federal protected areas), regional governments (regional protected areas) and local authorities. The area is owned by the respective entity. There is no provision allowing for privately protected areas. Individual government offices managing particular federal protected areas reporting to the Ministry of Natural Resources and Ecology manage the areas, and may arrange for scientific research, education, or special ecological protection measures.

VIII. Natural Resource Damages

Regarding provisions of Russian environmental law concerning compensation for natural resource damages,[28] see sections X and XII, *infra*.

IX. Protected Species
A. Federal Law on Wildlife

A framework for rules on wildlife use and protection, including genetic resources, biological diversity, and habitats of wild animals, are provided for in the federal law "On Wildlife," dated April 24, 1995.[29] The statute declares that all wildlife within the territory of the Federation is owned by the public. Ownership may be transferred to interested persons only for a designated purpose—fishing, hunting, reproduction of animals, or wildlife conservation— by a government permit. Rare and endangered species listed in the International Union for the Conservation of Nature's Red List of Threatened Species inhabiting the Federation or of the federal regions are subject to special protection. Provisions protect the habitats of endangered species through restrictions and prohibition of commercial activities that may threaten the population of wildlife or through specially protected areas.

B.   Federal Law on Fishing

According to the federal law "On Fishing and Conservation of Aquatic Bioresources," adopted on December 20, 2004,[30] fishing is classified into categories including commercial, coastal, scientific, educational, fish reproduction, and sports fishing. All aquatic resources within the territory of the Federation are owned by the federal government and may be exploited only by permit. Using scientific research, the Federal Fisheries Agency determines the yearly catch allotment for each water basin and separately for fishing over the continental shelf and in the nation's exclusive economic zone (EEZ). Quotas are then divided into shares and sold at auctions or established in contracts. Fishing vessels must obtain a permit for the right to fish in a certain area.

C.   Federal Law on Hunting

The federal law "On Hunting and Preservation of Hunting Resources," adopted on July 24, 2009,[31] regulates wildlife hunting. Hunting is allowed within designated hunting areas. Such areas are generally for general public use, except where granted exclusively to an individual or organization. The right to exclusive hunting areas is granted to entities or individuals upon a hunting contract and is valid from 20 to 49 years. Hunting is allowed within established hunting seasons by hunters holding a gun license (to be obtained from the police department). All hunting permit decisions are delegated to the regional governments. Similar to fishing, hunting is classified into types. The Ministry of Agriculture is empowered to establish hunting limits for each species. The hunting limit is established on the basis of scientifically determined norms. Each hunting entity organizes hunting within exclusive hunting areas and grants hunting permits using the hunting quotas determined for them.

X.   Public Access to Environmental Information and Judicial Review in Environmental Matters
A.   Federal Law on the Hydrometeorological Service

Under Article 42 of the Constitution of the Russian Federation, and Article 11 of the Environmental Protection Law, individuals have the right to obtain information about the state of the Russian environment. The federal law "On Hydrometeorological Service," dated August 19, 1997,[32] provides that individuals may obtain this information free of charge upon request from the Federal Agency for Hydrometeorology and Monitoring of the Environment. It also states that information about the state of the environment will cover data on pollution and other qualitative characteristics of the environment obtained through monitoring. Other types of environmental or natural resources information is also accessible from other governmental agencies and according to special rules.

B. Judicial Review of Actions and Decisions

Under the general rule established by the Law of the Russian Federation "On Judicial Review of Actions and Decisions That Infringe on the Rights and Freedoms of Citizens," dated April 27, 1993,[33] both individual and regulatory acts by public authorities that infringe individual rights and freedoms, including refusal of public authorities to provide environmental information, may be challenged by citizens or organizations to a higher level within the agency involved or, alternatively, in court.

C. Procedural Laws

The administrative procedure for the review of complaints is outlined in the federal law "On the Procedure for the Consideration of Citizens' Applications," dated May 2, 2006.[34] Under the law, citizens may petition public authorities with proposals, complaints, and statements and receive responses within 30 days. Procedures for judicial review are generally established by the Code on Civil Procedure dated November 14, 2002,[35] for claims involving individuals and public bodies, all claims seeking compensation for environmental damage, or claims seeking the suspension of activities violating environmental rules; and the Code on Arbitration Procedure dated July 24, 2002 (economic claims of juridical persons).[36] According to the Regulation of the Plenum of the Federation Supreme Courts "On Judicial Review of the Legislation on Liability for Environmental and Natural Resources Violations," dated October 18, 2012, courts of general jurisdiction shall be the venue for challenges involving compensation for environmental damage.[37]

Under Article 42 of the Constitution of the Russian Federation and Article 11 of the Environmental Protection Law, individuals have the right to compensation if damage is caused to their health or property by an unlawful activity. Damages are compensated in full, either voluntarily by the violator or following a judicial decision. The same rule extends to damages to nature by pollution and other negative impacts. However, it should be noted that because almost all natural objects are federally owned (i.e., waters, forests, subsoil, wildlife), compensation for general civil infractions or criminal offenses of an environmental variety is paid to the federal government, except in cases involving special private ownership or use. Compensation for damage inflicted to regions by destruction of regionally owned natural resources (there are not many of the same) is distributed to the affected region government.

XI.   Environmental Review and Decision Making

A.   Federal Law on Ecological Expertise

Under the federal law "On Ecological Expertise," dated November 23, 1995,[38] activities subject to the government ecological opinion requirement include development within specially protected areas and activities on the continental shelf and in the EEZ. The official ecological expertise designation is bestowed by an independent commission consisting of experts. All designations are subject to the approval of the head of Rosprirodnazor. Individuals responsible for a project must first submit documents on the project, including results of an environmental impact assessment (EIA) to be fulfilled according to Ministerial Order No. 372, dated May 16, 2000, "On Regulations on Environmental Impact Assessment."[39]

B.   Urban Development Code

All construction projects, except for those covered by the federal law "On Ecological Expertise," are subject to the government ecological expertise requirement. These activities are regulated by the regional governments under the Urban Development Code, dated December 29, 2004.[40] Article 49 of the code requires that all construction projects ensure compliance with environmental and other relevant laws. Operators of projects submit EIA materials to obtain an expert opinion.

C.   Pollution Permits and Charges

Emissions of pollutants into the air, discharges into water, and operation of landfills require a government permit pursuant to the federal laws "On Air Protection," the Water Code, and the statute "On Industrial and Municipal Wastes," mentioned above. Assuming emissions and discharges conform to emission and discharge limitations, permits are issued by the Federal Agency for Natural Resources Use (under the Ministry of Natural Resources and Ecology) for a period of five years.

Pollution is subject to a charge calculated pursuant to the Government Order dated August 28, 1992, "On Approval of the Procedure for Determining the Charges and its Amounts for the Pollution of the Environment, Disposal of Wastes, Other Types of Harmful Impacts."[41] Charges are calculated on the basis of the "Basic Charge Rates for the Emission of Pollutants into the Air by the Stationary and Mobile Sources of Pollution, Discharges of Wastewater into Surface and Underground Water Bodies, Disposal of Industrial and Municipal Wastes," dated June 12, 2003.[42]

XII.   Civil and Criminal Enforcement

A.   Administrative Enforcement and Penalty Provisions of the Code on Administrative Liability

Noncompliance with environmental requirements is punishable by administrative fines imposed by inspectorates according to the Code on Administrative

Violations, dated December 12, 2001.[43] The majority of administrative offenses with penalties are listed in chapter 8, Administrative Offenses Relating to Environmental Protection and Use of Natural Resources. They cover noncompliance with waste-handling rules, ecological expertise/opinion requirements, concealing environment-related data, and violation of land, subsoil, forest, and water protection rules, among other things. Other offenses are included in chapter 9, Administrative Offenses in Industry, Building and Energy; chapter 5, Administrative Offenses Infringing on the Public Rights; and others. In addition, courts may order facilities to suspend their operations and other activities for 90 days.

B. Criminal Enforcement and Penalty Provisions of the Criminal Code

Criminal penalties can be meted out for more serious offenses. Criminal penalties for environmental offenses are provided for by chapter 26, Environmental Crimes, of the Criminal Code of June 13, 1996.[44] The degree of risk of prosecution depends on the damage inflicted. On October 18, 2012, the Plenum of the Supreme Court of the Russian Federation adopted a regulation titled "On Enforcement of the Legislation about Liability for Environmental Offenses."[45] It explains the enforcement of certain articles of the criminal code and interprets the terms "significant damage," "other grave consequences," "damage to health," "crime with the use of an official post," and other important terms. Article 358 provides for criminal liability for the significant destruction of plant life and wildlife, poisoning of water, air, and other acts that may cause an ecological catastrophe. That said, criminal liability is applied in only rare and extreme cases.

C. Compensation of Environmental Damage Provisions of the Environmental Laws and the Civil Code

A violator must fully compensate damages to human health, property, or the environment caused by an environmental offense. General rules are established in chapter 59 (part 2) "Responsibilities Arising from Damage" of the Civil Code dated January 26, 1996.[46] Damage is compensated either by rehabilitation of the affected environment, treating polluted water bodies or lands, restoration of an affected animal population, or financial compensation, calculated using special methodologies. The rates have been established by governmental orders in relation to damage to forests and wildlife.

Strict liability is provided for violations in the context of higher-risk activities (nuclear power plants, other dangerous industrial facilities). In some cases, damage is compensated using insurance funds. Nuclear facilities and dangerous industrial facilities are obliged to insure the risk of their civil liability for the damage to health and property. Damage to the environment, if not insured, comes from the responsible party's own funds. After judicial review, in cases concerning environmental damage, courts may also suspend or close the operation of a facility.

Notes

1. *See* Organisation for Economic Co-operation and Development, Environmental Law and Policy in Russia: The Implementation Challenge 26 (2006), http://www.oecd.org/env/outreach/38118149.pdf.

2. Texts of laws and executive decrees are officially published in the Collected Legislation of the RF. They are also available from different legal databases, like Consultant Plus, that are accessible in Russian free on weekends at http://www.consultantplus.ru.

3. The Federal Assembly is the legislature of the Russian Federation. It consists of the State Duma—the lower house—and the Federation Council—the upper house. Both houses are located in Moscow.

4. Collected Legislation of the RF. 1999. No. 18. Art. 2222.

5. Collected Legislation. 2009. No. 51. Art. 6305; *see also* http://archive.kremlin.ru/eng/text/docs/2009/12/223509.shtml (last visited Sept. 13, 2013).

6. Collected Legislation. 2009. No. 48. Art. 5711.

7. Collected Legislation. 2006. No. 23. Art. 2381.

8. The lake is so designated under the UNESCO Convention on Cultural and Natural Heritage (World Heritage Convention); *see also infra* chapter 12, Protected Species, regarding the World Heritage Convention.

9. Collected Legislation. 1999. No. 18. Art. 2220.

10. Collected Legislation. 1998. No. 31. Art. 3833.

11. Collected Legislation. 2002. No. 2. Art. 133.

12. Collected Legislation. 1997. No. 29. Art. 3510.

13. Governmental Regulation "On Amending Certain Governmental Regulations due to the Change in Functioning of Agency for Protection of Consumers' Rights" No. 612 (June 19, 2012), Collected Legislation. 2012. No. 27. Art. 3729.

14. Collected Legislation. 1996. No. 28. Art. 3348.

15. Collected Legislation. 1995. No. 48. Art. 4552.

16. Collected Legislation. 1998. No. 26. Art. 3009.

17. Collected Legislation. 2011. No. 29. Art. 4281.

18. National Operator for Handling of Radioactive Wastes, http://www.norao.ru (last visited Sept. 13, 2013).

19. Collected Legislation. 2001. No. 29. Art. 2947.

20. Collected Legislation. 1997. No. 30. Art. 3588.

21. Collected Legislation. 1997. No. 30. Art. 3589.

22. Collected Legislation. 1994. No. 35. Art. 3648.

23. Collected Legislation. 2006. No. 50. Art. 5278.

24. Collected Legislation. 1995. No. 10. Art. 823.

25. Collected Legislation. 1998. No. 13. Art. 1463.

26. Collected Legislation. 1995. No. 49. Art. 4694.

27. Collected Legislation. 1995. No. 12. Art. 1024.

28. Land use is a related area covered by Russian law. All land-related issues are regulated by the Land Code, adopted on October 25, 2001. Collected Legislation. 2001. No. 44. Art. 4147. This law covers ownership and use rights, land granting procedures, termination of rights, and taking of lands both for public policy purposes. It also determines specific features for seven categories of lands recognized as such depending on their use designation. The categories include agricultural, human settlement, industrial, specially protected areas, water-covered, forested-covered, and reserved lands. Chapter 2 of the law states that lands shall be used to ensure the preservation of ecological systems, conservation of lands as a material basis for agriculture and forestry, and land area for human activities. It also outlines land protection measures that include obligations of

owners and users of land plots to improve the state of the soil, increase its fertility, and rehabilitate lands after being impacted by mining activities or after the closure of a facility.

As to urban areas, territorial planning rules, including construction requirements within human settlements, are provided by the Urban Code adopted on December 29, 2004. Collected Legislation. 2005. No. 1 (pt. 1). Art. 16. The law states that urban areas shall be divided into territorial zones by certain settlement plans. The regime of each zone, including the list of permitted uses, is established by urban development regulations.

In agricultural areas, before the 1990s many farms were collective. These farms were regulated separately from other types of property. Land law reform legalized by several presidential orders and other regulatory acts abolished all collective farms and required farmers to divide their lands into shares between members of former collective farms. Under the federal law "On Deals with Agricultural Lands" dated July 24, 2002, agricultural lands may not belong to foreign persons and may be used by them only by way of lease. Collected Legislation. 2002. No. 30. Art. 3018. Separately, under the federal law "On State Regulation of Ensuring Soil Fertility of Agricultural Lands" dated July 16, 1998, owners and users of lands are obliged to grow agricultural products in a way that ensures the preservation and reproduction of soil fertility. Farmers must also inform public authorities about pesticides and agrochemicals used in their growing process.

29. Collected Legislation. 1995. No. 17. Art. 1462.
30. Collected Legislation. 2004. No. 52 (pt. 1). Art. 5270.
31. Collected Legislation. 2009. No. 30. Art. 3735.
32. Collected Legislation. 1998. No. 30. Art. 3609.
33. Collected Legislation. 1993. No. 19. Art. 685.
34. Collected Legislation. 2006. No. 19. Art. 2060.
35. Collected Legislation. 2002. No. 46. Art. 4532.
36. Collected Legislation. 2002. No. 30. Art. 3012.
37. Bulletin of the Supreme Court of the Russian Federation, No. 12 (December 2012).
38. Collected Legislation. 1995. No. 48. Art. 4556.
39. Bulletin of Executive Orders. No. 31. 31.07.2000.
40. Collected Legislation. 2005. No. 1 (pt. 1). Art. 16.
41. Acts of the President of the RF and the Government of the RF. 1992. No. 10. Art. 726.
42. Collected Legislation. 2003. No. 25. Art. 2528.
43. Collected Legislation. 2002. No. 1 (pt. 1). Art. 1.
44. Collected Legislation. 1996. No. 25. Art. 2954.
45. Published in the *Rossiyskaya Gazeta*. No. 251. 31.10.2012.
46. Collected Legislation. 1996. No. 5. Art. 410.

CHAPTER 36

East and South Asia Overview

ROGER MARTELLA AND J. BRETT GROSKO

Since the 1960s, a number of South and East Asian nations have experienced tremendous and rapid economic growth. This has been especially true in China, with the opening of the economy by reforms led by Deng Xiaoping in 1978, and in India with the economic reforms begun in 1991 under the guidance of then finance minister Manmohan Singh. Rapid growth also was experienced in Japan during the 1960 to late 1980s postwar economic miracle, South Korea since the early 1960s with the adoption of an outward-looking economic strategy, and Vietnam since the government undertook reforms in the mid-1980s that brought about a shift to a socialist-oriented market economy.

This rapid economic growth in Asia has lifted millions of people out of poverty. But, during this same time, there is perhaps no area of the world where rapid economic growth has come with greater environmental consequences. China, for example, is one of the world's largest industrial economies and consumers of energy, but also now the world's leading emitter of greenhouse gases. Separately, Japan relied on nuclear power as a key component in its economic rise to offset a lack of domestic energy resources. The 2011 Fukishima disaster, however, led Japan as well as other countries to reevaluate the use of nuclear power.

Despite rising environmental concerns, there is little sign that multinational companies will halt their reliance on Asia as a critical component of global supply chains, commerce, and customers. Companies from this region increasingly are looking abroad both for natural resources and trading partners. Against this backdrop, all nations appear to be doing more to address the international criticism of lax environmental regimes. Questions remain, however, regarding the efficacy of both the laws that have been enacted and the mechanisms, resources, and attitudes toward implementation and enforcement.

The following chapters aim to demonstrate what the laws look like "on the books" in China, India, Japan, South Korea, and Vietnam. That said, the actual enforcement and implementation of the laws is a more complicated question that varies not only nation by nation, but within each province, prefecture, or state as well. Consultation with local experts on how they are being implemented at the national and provincial levels will be key in assessing an environmental law question.

CHAPTER 37

China

TAD FERRIS AND STEVE WOLFSON*

I. Introduction

China's ongoing environmental crisis is a familiar story to those who follow the headlines around the world, including in China: small particulate pollution in Beijing and other cities has soared well above the levels considered safe, at times forcing grounding of airplane flights, and causing widespread outcry; some Chinese citizens lack access to safe drinking water, while a number of cities lack municipal wastewater treatment; and the country leads the world in total greenhouse gas emissions, giving rise to air pollution emissions estimated to contribute to air quality violations as far away as the United States.

Although China's economic growth rates have been impressive for years, outside observers, the Chinese public, and the government have recently and more broadly come to recognize the high costs of the environmental crisis to the health of the population and economy overall. This recognition is perhaps no surprise, as studies and media reports of the crisis reflect an alarming environmental situation. For instance, the World Bank estimates that the combined costs of pollution, including the effects on crops, forests, and public health, are more than 3.5 percent of GDP.[1] Air pollution in China reportedly kills more than one million people annually.[2]

Pollution has led to growing calls for action inside China. Hu Jintao, the former secretary general, indicated at the 18th Communist Party Congress in November 2012 that China is facing "tightening resource constraints, rampant pollution, and worsening environmental degradation."[3] Concomitantly, the State Council, the highest administrative body in China's executive branch, described China's environmental situation as extremely grim despite positive progress, and highlighted the fact that China, in just a 20-year

---

*The views expressed are those of the authors and do not necessarily represent those of their organizations or any other entity. The authors wish to thank Brett Grosko for his assistance in drafting sections III and V–IX. The authors also wish to thank Weiwei Luo for her assistance with the discussion of the Marine Environmental Protection Law.

period, is grappling with industrialization problems Western countries experienced during a span of over 100 years. Nevertheless, despite these problems, China is making significant progress in establishing institutions, laws, and discrete directives to address environmental issues.

In 1979, China enacted the cornerstone Environmental Protection Law (EPL),[4] (amended in 1989, and recently in 2014), and today has more than 20 statutes addressing topics from air pollution and climate change to forestry and fisheries, resulting in a patchwork of authority for environmental protection. The Ministry of Environmental Protection (MEP), a cabinet-level ministry in the executive branch, has authority to issue regulations to address environmental pollution, as well as prepare or comment on proposals for national pollution-focused legislation. The MEP has a Beijing headquarters office and allied research institutes, as well as six regional supervision centers (RSCs).[5] As a general matter, under the Chinese environmental legal regime, new projects in China must comply with environmental impact reporting requirements and also incorporate pollution control measures at the design, construction, and operational stages (the "Three Simultaneous" policy).

On the legislative side, the National People's Congress (NPC), the highest legislative body in China, has authority to enact national legislation and oversee implementation of laws. The State Council, an administrative body of the NPC, has authority to review legislative proposals prior to referral to the NPC, promulgate regulations, issue decisions and orders, and oversee the work of ministries. The State Council's Office of Legislative Affairs prepares annual and five-year legislative drafting plans, which provide important cues as to what legislative changes the NPC is likely to consider.[6]

This chapter provides a brief overview of China's environmental and natural resources law regime and touches on some of the challenges that China faces in the field of environmental regulation. Given the scope of the present volume, the discussion in this chapter of specific statutes and regulations has necessarily been sharply abbreviated. Chinese cultural and legal systems differ from those of the United States in ways that result in some topics being framed differently in practice than in the subheadings below, which are utilized for consistency with the other chapters of this volume.

II.   Air and Climate Change

The principal legal measure governing the control of air pollution from mobile and stationary sources is the 1987 Air Pollution Prevention and Control Law (APPCL),[7] amended in 1995 and again in 2000. Under the APPCL, vehicles and vessels are prohibited from emitting pollution in amounts exceeding prescribed standards.[8] Stationary sources of air pollution must register with the local environmental protection bureaus (EPBs) and submit an emission report.[9]

The APPCL provides that enterprises in areas that exceed ambient standards, known as "control" areas, must obtain emissions permits. Implementation of the regulatory permitting system, however, has been limited: many emitters lack permits, and the permits that do exist sometimes lack important details such as monitoring requirements.[10] Despite these limitations, there has nevertheless been progress in reducing emissions of sulfur dioxide (SO_2). This has been accomplished in part through administrative controls, including (1) closing outdated plants; (2) using a "Total SO_2 Reduction Letter of Responsibility" to allocate emissions reductions among provincial governments, municipal authorities, and major electric power companies; (3) implementing price premiums for electricity generated by coal plants with scrubbers; (4) creating a draft Desulfurization Operation and Management Plan to tighten implementation of scrubber use and installation of automatic emissions monitoring equipment; and (5) increasing the levy for SO_2 emissions.[11]

Violators of the APPCL are subject to administrative sanctions, civil liability, or criminal penalties.[12] Current administrative sanctions range between 200 and 500,000 renminbi (RMB), depending on the type of violation and other considerations.[13] Examples of administrative sanctions available under the APPCL include fines, temporary closing for treatment, or permanent termination of an operation depending on the gravity of the offense.[14]

Other policies that have contributed to the control of emissions and improved energy efficiency include providing funding to reward enterprises that can demonstrate significant energy savings; using demand-side management to incentivize large-scale energy efficiency investments; implementing increasingly stringent building energy codes and stricter vehicle fuel efficiency standards; and enhancing accountability by increasing consideration of pollution control and energy efficiency when evaluating government officials' performance. Additional examples include power plant standards that tighten controls on soot, SO_2, nitrogen oxide (NO_2), and mercury emissions from power plants, and a new Guiding Opinion providing for increased air pollution control coordination across jurisdictions.[15]

Now that some of the initial air pollution reductions have been achieved, achieving the latest targets—such as an 8 percent reduction in SO_2 emissions and 10 percent reduction in NO_2 emissions—may require increased reliance on legal and market measures, like permitting and emissions trading.[16]

In 2013, China announced ten measures designed to improve air quality and respond to the dense smog observed in Beijing and other major Chinese cities in recent years, including a mandate that heavy polluters such as coal-fired power plants and metal smelters release detailed environmental information to the public.[17] China's State Council is reportedly working on additional measures to combat air pollution.[18]

The National Development and Reform Commission (NDRC) mandated carbon-trading pilot programs in Beijing, Shanghai, Tianjin, Chongqing, and Shenzhen, and the provinces of Guangdong and Hubei in 2011. This initiative is part of an effort to rapidly establish regional carbon-trading pilot programs to be followed by a national program. The trading pilot programs may encounter challenges establishing reliable emission monitoring, verification, and inventories, and legal provisions to govern data collection, emissions rights/permits, trading rules, and enforcement. The pilot programs signal a period of experimentation—sometimes described in China as "crossing the river by feeling the stones" (摸着石头过河)—as a test of whether carbon trading has yet become an effective policy tool in the context of the Chinese environmental regulatory system.[19]

III.   Water

The key statutes pertaining to freshwater and marine water pollution control are the Water Pollution Control Law of 1984 (PCWP), most recently amended in 2008, and the 1982 Marine Environmental Protection Law (MEPL).[20]

The PCWP and its implementing regulations govern water pollution control for surface water and groundwater pollution.[21] Discharge without a permit is prohibited and discharges are required to be reported to local EPBs. National water quality control and effluent standards are found in regulatory measures such as the Discharge Standards for particular industry operations (separate standards for specific industries, such as the ammonia or woolen textiles industry), the Marine Water Quality Standard, the Groundwater Quality Standard, the Water Quality Standards for Fisheries, the Agricultural Irrigation Water Quality Standards, and the Surface Water Environmental Quality Standards.

The 2008 amendments to the PCWP increased the severity of available administrative sanctions to a range of 500 to 1 million RMB or 20 percent to 30 percent of the direct losses incurred due to violation of the PCWP, improved government supervision, and implemented emergency measures for water pollution emergencies.[22] The 2008 amendments also increased the scope of acts deemed illegal by the PCWP[23] and strengthened regulation of water pollutant discharges.[24]

The MEPL focuses on pollution into marine waters and governs pollution associated with coastal construction projects, offshore oil exploration, land-based projects, and the shipping industry.[25] It also covers solid waste dumping at sea.[26] The 1999 amendments added provisions providing for the comprehensive control of pollution amounts into certain marine areas, emergency response requirements in the event of a disaster, civil damages for oil spills, maritime oil pollution insurance requirements, and liability for civil damages for losses.[27] The MEPL requires the installation of waste disposal facilities at ports and oil terminals to treat and dispose of hazardous wastes, for example, oily residues.[28] Mobile and stationary oil production platforms may not dispose of oily waste at sea.[29] The MEPL also prohibits sewage discharge within designated marine sanctuaries, aquaculture facilities, and certain scenic areas.[30]

IV.   Handling, Treatment, Transportation, and Disposal of Hazardous Materials

Several observations concerning key trends that are shaping chemical substance regulation in China today may be made. First, international laws and policy "influence" Chinese chemicals regulatory authorities. The chemical laws, policies, and associated regulatory approaches outside China influence law and policymakers within China. This influence is akin to "inspiration" and, where necessary, these imported policies are adjusted to meet China's particular needs.[31] In the chemicals regulatory area, examples of this influence are numerous. For instance, Chinese chemical regulatory authorities are clearly aware of and in many cases have considered the European Community Regulation on Registration, Evaluation and Authorisation of Chemicals (REACH),[32] but China's chemical law activities since development of the REACH have not included the development of a comprehensive Chinese equivalent.[33] Additionally, it is noteworthy that the U.S. Toxic Substances Control Act's low-volume exemptions were key considerations in China's development of rules governing registration or notification of low volumes of substances under the Regulations on Environmental Management of New Chemical Substances. China did not completely adopt a low-volume exemption, but instead, opted for a simplified procedure for registration of certain low volumes of new chemical substances imported or manufactured in China, and a notification procedure for certain low volumes of new chemical substances imported or manufactured for specified scientific purposes.[34]

Second, over the past several years the Chinese government has become increasingly sensitive to the environmental and social effects of the manufacturing boom in China. For example, China recognizes the environmental problems arising from the manufacturing of products for export, which leave China with environmental burdens but not consumer benefits. In response to this situation, some resistance within the government to providing exemptions within regulatory programs has been on the rise. For instance, exemptions for operations in duty-free (e.g., foreign trade) zones were removed in the 2010 amendments to the Regulations on Environmental Management of New Chemical Substances.

Third, multiple authorities in China regulate chemicals. In China, the aforementioned situation wherein multiple agencies engage in environmental regulation is echoed in the chemicals management area. There is no comprehensive coordinating body or overall lead for all chemical programs, which can foster national, predictable, comprehensive, and meaningful regulatory programs for chemicals. For example, when different ministries are responsible for implementation of different aspects of the same regulatory program or for regulation of the same chemical under different programs, each ministry may differ in interpretation of important chemical regulatory issues such as exemptions or volume thresholds.

Examples of authorities with chemical regulatory responsibility include

- Administration for Quality Supervision, Inspection and Quarantine (with key responsibilities such as chemical import conformity inspection and chemical waste import control)
- General Administration of Customs (with key responsibilities such as chemical import and inspection, and restricted chemical control at ports of entry)
- Ministry of Commerce (with key responsibilities such as chemical precursors, chemical import, and sale/operations controls, other controlled chemicals)
- Ministry of Environmental Protection (responsibilities such as "new" chemicals, "toxic" chemicals, chemical waste, and "dangerous" chemicals)
- National Health and Family Planning Commission (formerly Ministry of Health) (with key responsibilities such as pharmaceuticals, precursors, and doping agents)
- Ministry of Industry and Information Technology (with key responsibilities such as general chemical industry oversight and control, particular controlled/sensitive chemical category requirements, materials restrictions, and chemical issues arising within the information technology sector)
- Ministry of Public Security (with key responsibilities such as "hypertoxic" chemical regulation and chemical fire safety)
- State Administration of Sports (with key responsibilities such as implementing China's antidoping substance controls)
- State Administration of Work Safety (with key responsibilities such as "dangerous" chemicals, chemical occupational safety, and chemical hazard communication and labeling)
- China Food and Drug Administration (with key responsibilities such as pharmaceuticals and pharmaceutical precursor controls)

Fourth, newly issued laws and chemical accidents increase the likelihood of enforcement or investigation. One should not assume that the chemical suppliers or other companies one deals with in China are compliant with China's new chemical laws. Chinese chemical regulatory authorities may lack resources to undertake enforcement and related investigation campaigns. Political pressure to increase enforcement in the chemicals area can increase when chemical laws are newly issued, and can also arise when serious chemical accidents are discovered or reported. Thus, enforcement actions aimed at chemical registration requirements, for instance, are frequently initiated as a result of government investigations of a company after safety or environmental accidents at the company. When investigators are at a particular company site, they often investigate the company's general compliance surrounding the accident in question, including whether the chemicals released were properly managed and registered. It is also increasingly common for enforcement to involve one or more of the following: warnings, fines, orders to cure noncompliance by specific dates, permit revocations, operation suspension orders, operation shut down orders, chemical registration prohibitions, and even criminal sanctions, media announcements, or inclusion of the violator's name on government "blacklists."

Fifth, certain chemical tests must be conducted in China using Chinese test subjects. Chinese authorities contend that only eco-toxicological tests conducted in China using Chinese test subjects can accurately reflect the eco-toxicological affects that the chemicals would have in China. This belief is reflected in the testing requirements under the 2010 amendments to the Regulations on Environmental Management of New Chemical Substances. China may consider a country's proposal to allow labs in the requesting country to conduct these eco-toxicological tests or other tests if the country provides similar rights to Chinese labs in the form of an accreditation or mutual recognition program (i.e., full reciprocity). This reciprocity is often politically difficult to realize. The OECD has approached China concerning the OECD Council Acts on the Mutual Acceptance of Data (MAD), but as yet this issue is unresolved.[35]

Sixth, chemical information protection obligations or requests in the context of information disclosure programs present challenges for authorities and the regulated community. China has moved aggressively to provide greater access to information that the government develops or collects. The Chinese authorities involved in chemical regulatory programs, such as the Ministry of Environment, have issued laws, reports, and policy documents clarifying their procedures and requirements related to environmental information access. These law and policy documents include the Ministry of Environmental Protection Government Information Disclosure Report issued and effective March 23, 2012, and the Circular on Further Strengthening Disclosure of Environmental Protection Information, issued and effective October 30, 2012. A complicating challenge associated with implementation of these information disclosure policies and laws is the Chinese authorities' need to concurrently develop programs to strictly protect confidential information and programs to disclose program and policy/law information (i.e., information transparency programs).

We have observed that meeting the concurrent aims of protecting and disclosing information can be challenging for authorities that are not accustomed to information disclosure as a matter of course.[36] In the chemicals area in particular, officials' continued lack of familiarity with balancing confidentiality and disclosure policies has contributed, in part, to a tendency to sometimes limit the scope of information that is afforded official confidentiality protections on chemical registration forms, while on other occasions officials may decline to release information subject to release under the law.[37] We delve deeper into trends in information access and disclosure, *infra*.

Article 20 of the EPL requires the government to prevent soil pollution and ensure the proper use of chemical fertilizers, pesticides, and plant growth hormones.[38] Separately, the Regulations Concerning Pesticide Registration regulate the manufacture, sale, use, and import of pesticides.[39] All new pesticides must be registered and manufacturers must provide information including information on potentially harmful impacts to human health and the environment.[40]

V.   Waste and Site Remediation

Under China's Law on the Prevention and Control of Environmental Pollution by Solid Wastes (1995), as amended in 2004 and 2013, significant solid waste discharges are subject to an order requiring cleanup within a specified time.[41] Illegal discharges may also be subject to administrative penalties and criminal punishment.[42] Additionally, in 1990, pursuant to the MEPL, the State Council promulgated Regulations of the PRC to Prevent Land-Originating Pollutants from Damaging the Marine Environment. These regulations prohibit any unauthorized storage, dumping, or disposal of solid waste on beaches.[43]

Third, in the product sale and associated postconsumer waste management areas, China has enacted regulations that draw, in some respects, on the EU's directives on the Restriction of Hazardous Substances (RoHS) and Waste Electrical and Electronic Equipment (WEEE).[44] These regulations impose obligations upon those who sell certain types of products in China. These obligations vary from the use of specific labels and other product-content disclosures to payment into a government fund, which supports the proper disposal of certain discarded products.

VI.   Emergency Response

Under the WPCL, among other obligations, entities must report serious water pollution incidents within 48 hours. Environmental authorities may invoke emergency enforcement measures, including the requirement that all discharges be reduced or halted completely.[45] The MEPL addresses reporting of oil spills.[46]

VII.   Natural Resource Management and Protection

The Chinese statutes governing natural resource management and protection include the Land Management, Forestry, Grasslands and Mineral Resources laws. [47] The 1986 Land Management Law (amended in 1988, 1998, and 2004) and 1998 implementing regulations require governments at various levels to implement policies concerning the rational use of land, land use planning, improvement of land management and development practices, and protection of natural resources.[48] Accordingly, under Chinese law, project proponents must apply for permission from local governments to develop undeveloped, government-owned areas, including riverbanks and beaches.[49]

Under the Forestry Law (enacted in 1984 and amended in 1998), the government is empowered to issue forest ownership or right to use certificates to individual entities.[50] As part of this process, the government may impose restrictions or controls on the felling of trees based on applicable state or local land use plans.[51] Certain forests are designated for silvicultural activities or protected for ecological reasons and are managed according to those designations.[52] The Grassland Law (enacted in 1985 and amended in 2002, 2009, and 2013) forbids the destruction of grassland areas[53] and requires any individual adversely affecting grassland areas to restore the grassland to its original condition.[54] The Mineral Resource Law (enacted in 1986 and amended in 1996) requires a permit prior to mineral exploration and exploitation.[55] Prior to issuing a permit, the government must take into account the project's location, scope, design, technologies, and environmental measures to be employed.[56] The Fisheries Law (enacted in 1986 and amended in 2000 and 2004) similarly provides for fishing permits.[57]

VIII. Natural Resource Damages

China's environmental law does not contain specific provisions for recovery of natural resource damages as that concept has been developed under, for example, the United States' environmental law regime. A related concept of ecological compensation has been more prominent in China to date.[58]

IX. Protected Species

Legal authorities relevant to species protection include the Protection of Wildlife Law (1988, amended in 2004); the Regulations on the Administration of the Import and Export of Endangered Wild Animals and Plants (2006); and the 1983 Administrative Order Concerning Strict Protection of Precious and Endangered Wildlife.[59] These authorities prohibit and control hunting and other activities affecting species considered to be in danger of extinction.[60]

X. Environmental Review, and Decision Making

Before the start of any construction project, the Environmental Impact Assessment Law (2002) requires that the entity conduct an environmental impact assessment (EIA). The extent of documentation and associated approval procedures vary depending on the extent of the impact and other factors.

Effective implementation of the EIA law has sometimes been hampered by limited public involvement, the practice of allowing companies that failed to complete an EIA prior to construction to do makeup assessment after the fact, limited public disclosure, and low penalties. Faced with frequent public protest over environmental impacts from projects across China, MEP has moved to strengthen public participation in construction project assessments.[61] For example, the Interim Measures on Public Participation for Environmental Impact Assessment sets out the methodology for seeking public opinion during EIA approval, defines the content of impact assessment documents and the parts that are subject to public disclosure, and provides that "openness, equality, extensiveness, and convenience" serve as key principles for public participation.[62] The Interim Measures do not extensively detail the protections provided for private sector confidential information, however. For instance, the very fact that a particular project is being planned for construction may be considered confidential where company competitors are concerned. The Interim Measures do essentially specify, however, that projects carried out under laws that stipulate it is necessary to maintain confidentiality may not be subject to certain public information disclosures.[63]

Additional reforms include guidance on disclosure provided by MEP's Circular on Further Strengthening Disclosure of Environmental Protection

Information, issued and effective October 30, 2012. This Circular provides details on the specific environmental information subject to disclosure, including information on industrial environmental protection investigations, construction project EIAs, approval processes, standards, conditions, and details concerning solid waste importation and hazardous waste operation licenses. The Circular also clarifies that air quality monitoring data and the names of enterprises discharging pollutants in violation of the law will be disclosed to the public.[64]

The "Three Simultaneous" policy is also relevant to entities operating in China. Under Article 26 of the EPL, the project proponent must design, build, and commission all pollution prevention and control installations at a development project simultaneously with the design, construction, and operation phases of the project.[65] In other words, during the design phase, the design of all pollution prevention and control installations must be submitted to the relevant authority for approval before construction begins.[66] During construction, mitigation measures must be implemented to prevent and control pollution caused by the construction.[67] Finally, the pollution prevention and control measures must be put into operation simultaneously with the start of operations.[68]

Parallel to these requirements, Chinese authorities have made a measure of progress in terms of increasing requirements for environmental information disclosure. In 2007, the State Council issued the Regulations on Disclosure of Government Information.[69] Government information is defined under the regulations as any information produced or acquired by government agencies in performing their respective functions and recorded and stored in certain formats. The regulations also broadly describe procedures for disclosure of such information and exceptions to the disclosure requirements. For instance, the scope of information subject to disclosure is described as information that is related to vital interests of private parties, that requires broad participation and public knowledge, and that describes the structures, functions, or procedures of agencies. The regulations indicate that an agency should publish information by means of public announcements, websites, news conferences, newspapers, and broadcasting and television. In addition, the regulations provide that a private person may request in writing that the government agencies at or above the county level release certain information.

Generally speaking, information constituting state secrets or information that might undermine social stability would not be included in the disclosure requirements.[70] In practice, decisions as to whether to disclose environmental information can turn on concern over possible public unrest arising from such disclosures. For example, if information on lead exposure levels arising from soil, air, or other contamination might stir angry protests, such information might be withheld from release.

The implementation of public input requirements applicable to EIAs, like the Regulations on Disclosure of Government Information, has thus far been uneven. The annual China Pollution Information Transparency Index showed increasing disclosure by some cities while some others still provided almost no environmental information. The report suggests that most cities still lag in disclosing EIA information, providing records of environmental violations, and releasing emissions data.[71]

Another development that illustrates the trend toward greater public participation in environmental decision making is increasing stakeholder activism with respect to environmental law violations. Chinese environmental laws now routinely include general provisions referencing the right of stakeholders, including members of the public at large and organizations, to report or file charges against those that pollute or damage the environment.[72] While these general provisions do not detail how these rights will be protected, and are devoid of what many would call "whistleblower" protections, citizens in China are becoming more active in engaging government and/or private sector enterprises about perceived violations of environmental law. For example, the 2008 amendments to the Water Pollution Prevention and Control Law and other recent and pending legal reforms recognize a public interest cause of actions against polluters.[73]

The relevance of these participation provisions is increasing when one considers the growth in numbers of environmental non-governmental organizations (NGOs) in China, the goals of which are to encourage community participation and activism in environmental projects. Some of these organizations are also active in efforts to monitor environmental law compliance or raise awareness of environmental law issues. Over the past two decades, the numbers of such NGOs working in China has grown from a handful to thousands.[74] The Center for Legal Assistance to Pollution Victims, led by Professor Wang Canfa, operates a hotline that fields environmental complaints and brings lawsuits seeking compensation for environmental harms.[75] The Institute of Public and Environmental Affairs, led by Goldman Environmental Prize winner Ma Jun, publicizes information on certain environmental law violators.[76]

XI. Transboundary Pollution

China emits more greenhouse gases than any other country. Moreover, air pollution generated in China travels across the Pacific Ocean and reportedly impacts the air quality of several western states in the United States.[77] Other Asian countries have expressed concern that air pollution originating in China impacts their air pollution. China participates in numerous multilateral environmental treaty regimes, including the U.N. Framework Convention on Climate Change, the Kyoto Protocol, the Basel Convention on Transboundary Movements of Hazardous Waste, the Rotterdam Convention on Prior Informed Consent Procedure for Certain Hazardous Chemicals and Pesticides in International Trade, the Stockholm Convention on Persistent Organic Pollutants, the Montreal Protocol on Substances That Deplete the Ozone Layer, the Convention on Biological Diversity, and the Convention on International Trade in Endangered Species. In addition, cooperation on regional issues such as international transport of air pollution is addressed in fora such as the Tripartite Environmental Ministers Meeting among Japan, China, and the Republic of Korea.[78]

XII.   Civil and Criminal Enforcement and Penalties

While the MEP headquarters office has overall responsibility for environmental law and policy, the duties of China's RSCs, mentioned *supra*, include certain oversight of local governments, including local EPBs, to prevent administrative inaction, corruption, or dereliction of duty in the process of environmental management. Because the RSCs have developed only in the last few years, it remains unclear whether they will have sufficiently trained staff, robust oversight mechanisms, or necessary legal authority to effectively carry out their duties. These duties include

- supervising the implementation of national environmental policies, laws, regulations, and standards in the region within the RSC jurisdiction;
- investigating major environmental pollution and ecological damage incidents and coordinating and settling major environmental disputes in transprovincial areas and river basins;
- assisting with supervision of emergency responses to and management of major environmental accidents;
- inspecting, or joining inspection of, environmental law enforcement matters;
- supervising the implementation of the "Three Simultaneous" policy (a key part of China's construction project and EIA system involving the requirement that environmental protection facilities be designed, constructed, and put into operation at the same time as the associated construction project); and
- managing complaints related to environmental pollution within the RSC jurisdiction.[79]

While MEP has broad jurisdiction over pollution issues, numerous other government agencies have authority over various topics relevant to environmental protection. For instance, the NDRC claims primary dominion over climate change, energy, carbon-trading pilot projects, and economic development issues. The NDRC also implements a system used by the Chinese government to evaluate the performance of government officials around the country. Because this system has recently placed significant emphasis on meeting pollution control and energy conservation targets, it can have an important impact on environmental policy implementation. Examples of other government agencies that exercise primary authority over various environmental issues include the Customs Administration (covering issues such as entry inspections involving wastes), the Ministry of Commerce (covering issues such as used-product processing, chemicals management, and tire and electronics recycling), the Ministry of Industry and Information Technology (covering general industrial management and electronic-product substance restrictions and recycling), the Ministry of Construction (covering landfill construction), and the Ministry of Finance (covering recycling fees).

At the subnational level, provincial and local EPBs are engaged in much of China's environmental law implementation and enforcement. The environmental law implementation effectiveness of local and provincial-level EPBs varies widely. Some such institutions have limited technical or legal capacity hampering their ability to adequately address complex or even routine environmental compliance issues without significant external support. Others possess more robust capacity and are far more effectual in their activities. An acknowledged and common challenge for these local-level EPBs is that they are involved in decision making that is sometimes driven more by local economic interests than by environmental protection objectives. Additionally, MEP's limited oversight authority compounds this problem. Although MEP's RSCs have certain oversight responsibilities for the EPBs, it is not yet clear whether they will positively affect this situation.

The practice of environmental law in China is complicated by limited local environmental law implementation and enforcement. It is further complicated by often unclear and sometimes overlapping authority for some subjects and the difficulty of obtaining consistent, written interpretations of ambiguous laws and associated measures. Furthermore, despite significant and laudable developments since 1979, China's current system of environmental law is still being supplemented to address key inadequacies. Specifically, recent analyses by Chinese and international experts have identified gaps in China's legal authority to regulate, in its implementing mechanisms and oversight, and in its enforcement apparatus. Chinese government authorities recognize the need for reform, evidenced by legislative priorities related to amendment of the framework Environmental Protection Law and the Air Pollution Prevention and Control Law. Moreover, China's State Council observed in 2005 that "it is not uncommon that environmental laws are not fully observed or strictly enforced."[80] This observation holds true today, despite recent efforts to address these issues by beginning to strengthen coordination across jurisdictions.

Furthermore, systemic issues, such as local government interference in judicial proceedings, can substantially hamper impartial decision making. China's judges have limited or no training on complex issues such as causation and environmental risks, and government investment in these skills has not been extensive, although there is a recent, marked focus on this situation that may result in significant capacity building. Historically speaking, "law" in China has sometimes appeared to reflect a raw exercise of the power by the state, rather than a system of peaceful resolution of private differences. Specialized legal institutions, such as a legal bar and courts, are not longstanding institutions in China, but rather twentieth-century developments. As a result, these institutions have not yet fully developed, nor have they yet attained independence. There appears to be improvement on the horizon as China's top leaders increasingly cite the importance of law and the need to move away from "rule by man" toward "rule by law," and worsening environmental pollution increases pressure for political action, but only time will tell how these aspirations lead to true reform in China.[81]

XIII. Conclusion

China's environmental crisis stems in large part from legal and institutional development issues that will require significant time to address in order to realize a more effective environmental governance regime. These issues include

- limited access to environmental information;
- uneven public participation in, and judicial review of, environmental decisions;
- the need for additional compliance and implementation guidance associated with numerous environmental regulatory programs;
- limited meaningful coordination among national agencies with responsibility for environmental regulatory responsibilities, and between the national MEP and provincial EPBs responsible for many environmental law implementation and enforcement tasks;
- continued use of government targets and associated political pressures to achieve environmental regulatory aims, without yet fully developing the associated governance regime needed to ensure meaningful and uniform compliance;
- constraints associated with the still-developing legal system, such as local government interference in judicial proceedings.

Effective environmental governance regimes are transparent and participatory, with multiple entry points for a wide range of stakeholders to play a role in ensuring accountability. The "Air-pocalypse" air quality crisis that made headlines in early 2013 has sharpened interest in strengthening legal and policy tools for control of air pollution, enhancing momentum that builds upon a wave of very laudable legal and institutional reforms to strengthen environmental governance over recent years. Recent developments noted in this brief overview include

- elevation of MEP to ministry status;
- creation of six MEP RSCs that might be able to foster closer coordination between MEP and provincial-level implementing bodies (albeit with limited staff and authority);
- deployment of administrative tools resulting in substantial progress in reducing emissions of air pollutants such as SO_2;
- increasing efforts toward developing and enhancing regulatory and market mechanisms for reducing pollution;
- establishment of reliable emission monitoring, verification, and inventories, and legal provisions to govern data collection, emissions rights/permits, trading rules, and enforcement;
- sensitivity to the environmental and social effects of items manufactured in China;
- development of extensive new (although sometimes unclear or overlapping) initiatives to regulate chemicals and products;
- improvement of access to environmental information, albeit with uneven implementation across jurisdictions;

- movement toward strengthened public participation, including in assessment of environmental impacts and in providing for a public interest cause of actions against polluters;
- continued receptivity of law and policymakers to international (or foreign) environmental best practices and lessons in the environmental governance area; and
- growth in activity by environmental NGOs and other stakeholders in China focused on monitoring environmental law compliance and other governance-strengthening activities.

Only time will tell whether these and other changes will result in sufficient reform of China's environmental governance to yield a marked improvement in protection of the environment and human health.

Notes

1. THE WORLD BANK, COST OF POLLUTION IN CHINA: ECONOMIC ESTIMATES OF PHYSICAL DAMAGES (2007). Regarding China's environmental performance, *see generally* China Environmental Performance Index, http://envirocenter.yale.edu/chinaepi (last visited Jan. 24, 2014).

2. E. Wong, *Air Pollution Linked to 1.2 Million Premature Deaths in China*, N.Y. TIMES, Apr. 1, 2013, http://www.nytimes.com/2013/04/02/world/asia/air-pollution-linked-to -1-2-million-deaths-in-china.html?_r=0 (last visited Apr. 7, 2013); *see also Beijingers Call for Clean Air Act*, CHINA DAILY, Jan. 29, 2013, http://www.chinadaily.com.cn/china/2013 -01/29/content_16185385.htm.

3. *See* Hu Jin Tao, 18th Speech (full text), Nov. 8, 2012, § 8, *available at* http://www .boxun.com/news/gb/china/2012/11/201211081409.shtml#.USP9mjK9Kc0 (last visited Mar. 28, 2013).

4. Environmental Protection Law, enacted for trial implementation Sept. 13, 1979, as amended Dec. 26, 1989, and amended April 24, 2014. Note that the 2014 amendment of the Environmental Protection Law was announced after the completion of this article. Hence, these and other subsequent changes in law have not been incorporated into this chapter. Nonetheless, readers should keep the 2014 Environmental Protection Law amendments in mind when reviewing this chapter, because those changes may significantly affect interpretation and application of Chinese environmental laws in a number of areas. Notable provisions in the 2014 Environmental Protection Law include the following:

- Suspension of approvals in non-attainment areas: Environmental departments shall suspend EIA approvals for new construction projects that will increase total emissions of key pollutants in a region that fails to fulfill the emission control quota or achieve the assigned environmental quality targets (Article 44).
- Public disclosure: Key pollution emission units shall publicly disclose their main pollutants "and receive public supervision" (Article 55).
- Environmental Public Interest Litigation: Social organizations may file litigation for activities that pollute and harm public interest (Article 58).
- Daily Fines: Government departments can impose continuous fines calculated on a daily basis against polluters refusing to take corrective actions ordered for illegal discharges (local regulation can broaden coverage) (Article 59).

5. Other organizations under MEP include the Nanjing Institute of Environmental Sciences, China Research Academy of Environmental Science, South China Institute of Environmental Sciences, China Society for Environmental Sciences, and the China Association of the Environmental Protection Industry.

6. *See generally* R. Ferris & H. Zhang, *Environmental Law in the People's Republic of China: An Overview Describing Challenges and Providing Insights for Good Governance, in* CHINA'S ENVIRONMENT AND THE CHALLENGE OF SUSTAINABLE DEVELOPMENT 69–80 (Kristen A. Day ed., 2005).

7. For English translations of the APPCL and other Chinese environmental statutes, see http://english.sepa.gov.cn/Policies_Regulations/laws/ (last visited Jan. 24, 2014). *See also* D. Zhang & S. Dong, *Environmental Law of the People's Republic of China, in* COMPARATIVE ENVIRONMENTAL LAW 15-8-15-11 (N. Robinson ed., 2011); C. MCELWEE, CHINESE ENVIRONMENTAL LAW (2010).

8. Zhang & Dong, *supra* note 7, at 15-8-15-11.

9. *Id.* In July 2013, China's cabinet adopted ten measures designed to improve air quality and respond to the dense smog that was observed in Beijing and other major Chinese cities in recent years, including a mandate that heavy polluters such as coal-fired power plants and metal smelters release detailed environmental information to the public. K. Bradsher, *China Sets New Rules Aimed at Curbing Air Pollution*, N.Y. TIMES, June 15, 2013.

10. P. Hoff & M. Wegman, *An Analysis of Environmental Regulation of the Steel Industry in China* (Sept. 26, 2008, draft) (on file with authors).

11. U.S.–China Joint Economic Research Group, *U.S.–China Joint Economic Study: Economic Analysis of Energy Savings and Pollution Abatement Policies for the Electric Power Sectors of China and the United States, Summary for Policymakers* (Dec. 2007) (Joint Economic Study).

12. Zhang & Dong, *supra* note 7, at 15-12-15-13.

13. *See* APPCL ch. VI; *see also* W. Canfa, *The Rapid Development of Environmental Protection Law, in* CHINA'S JOURNEY TOWARD THE RULE OF LAW: LEGAL REFORM 1978–2008, at 529 (C. Dingjian ed., 2010).

14. *Id.* Note that in February 2013, the MEP published a circular establishing a number of emission standards for particular industries and regions that MEP has formulated since 2010. Scott Daniel Silverman et al., *China Issues New Environmental Insurance Requirements and Limits on Emissions*, BAKER & MCKENZIE, Apr. 2013, http://www.bakermckenzie.com/ALChinaEnvironmentalInsuranceApr13/.

15. State Council of Regional Cooperation on Control of Air Pollution—Guiding Opinion No. 33 (May 2010); *see* Barbara Finamore, *Taming the Dragon Heads . . .* , ENVTL. L. REP. 11,446–47.

16. *See* http://www.epa.gov/ogc/china/air%20pollution.pdf; China Clean Air Policy Briefings No. 1 (Clean Air Alliance of China trans., Apr. 2013), http://www.epa.gov/ogc/china/air%20pollution.pdf.

17. K. Bradsher, *China Sets New Rules Aimed at Curbing Air Pollution*, N.Y. TIMES, June 15, 2013. A recent study found that southern Chinese citizens on average have lived at least five years longer than their northern counterparts in recent decades due to the health effects of pollution from use of coal in the north. E. Wong, *Pollution Leads to Drop in Life Span in Northern China, Research Finds*, N.Y. TIMES, July 8, 2013, at A6.

18. *See Toxic Smog Threatens Millions of Chinese Lives*, TELEGRAPH, Feb. 18, 2014, http://www.telegraph.co.uk/news/worldnews/asia/china/10646593/Toxic-smog-threatens-millions-of-Chinese-lives.html.

19. GUOYI HAN ET AL., CHINA'S CARBON EMISSION TRADING: AN OVERVIEW OF CURRENT DEVELOPMENT (Stockholm Env't Inst., 2012); Y.C. Chang & N. Wang, *Environmental Regulations and Emissions Trading in China*, 38(7) ENERGY POLICY 3356–64 (2010); Bo Kong & Carla Freeman, *Making Sense of Carbon Market Development in China*, 194 CARBON & CLIMATE L. REV. (Dec. 2013); Ranping Song & Hongpeng Lei, *Emissions Trading in China:*

First Reports from the Field, World Res. Inst. China FAQs (Jan. 23, 2014), http://www
.chinafaqs.org/blog-posts/emissions-trading-china-first-reports-field#sthash.dndzl7rj
.dpuf. *See also* International Emissions Trading Association and Environmental Defense
Fund: A Case Study Guide to Emissions Trading, http://www.ieta.org/assets/EDFCase
StudyMarch2014/china%20ets%20case%20study%20march%202014.pdf.

20. For English translations of the EPL, PCWP, MCEP, and other Chinese environmental statutes, see http://english.sepa.gov.cn/Policies_Regulations/laws/ (last visited
Jan. 24, 2014); *see also* EPA–China Envtl. Law Initiative, Legal Resources, http://www
.epa.gov/ogc/china/legal_resources.htm#statutes (last visited Jan. 24, 2014).

21. For a comparison of water pollution control under Chinese law and U.S. law, see
Dawn Winalski, *Cleaner Water in China? The Implications of the Amendments to China's Law
on the Prevention and Control of Water Pollution,* 24(1) J. Envtl. L. & Litig. 181 (2009), *available at* https://law.uoregon.edu/org/jell/docs/232/Winalski.pdf.

22. Canfa, *supra* note 13, at 529; *see also* W. Golding, *Amended Water Law in China
Holds Promise of Enhancing Enforcement by Establishing National Standards and Personal
Accountability,* ABA SEER Int'l Envtl. Law Newsl. (2010). Other authorities relevant to
water pollution control include (1) Rules for Implementation of the People's Republic of
China on the Prevention and Control of Water Pollution, (2) Regulations Regarding Technology Policies for Pollution and Control of Water Pollution, (3) Interim Management of
the Water Pollution Discharge Permit Regime, (4) Regulations on the Management of
Effluent Fees (2003), and (5) Pollution Control Regulations for Protected Zones for Drinking Water Zones. *See* Canfa, *supra* note 13, at 503–04.

23. Canfa, *supra* note 13, at 504.

24. Jingyun Li & Jinjing Liu, *Quest for Clean Water: China's Newly Amended Water Pollution Control Law,* Woodrow Wilson Center China Environment Forum (Jan. 2009),
http://www.wilsoncenter.org/publication/quest-for-clean-water-chinas-newly-amended
-water-pollution-control-law.

25. *See* Marine Environmental Protection Law, amended by the Standing Comm.
People's Cong. Dec. 28, 2013, and effective the same date, art. 2.

26. *See id.* ch. 7.

27. *See id.* chs. 2–5.

28. *See id.* chs. 4–5.

29. *See id.* art. 52.

30. *See id.* art. 30.

31. *See, e.g.,* China Policies and Actions on Climate Change (2011), http://www.gov
.cn/jrzg/2011-11/22/content_2000047.htm (underscoring particular considerations applicable to China's characteristics that influence China's climate change policy, in the discussion of common but differentiated responsibilities) (last visited Mar. 28, 2013); *see also*
Ministry of Human Resources & Social Security, Discussion on Extension of Retirement
Age According to the China Situation, http://news.cnfol.com/121025/101,1592,13512393,00
.shtml (last visited Mar. 28, 2013).

32. EC 1907/2006.

33. *See* R. Ferris, *REACH's Impact in the Rest of the World: China, in* The European
Union REACH Regulation for Chemicals Law and Practice (L. Bergkamp ed., October 2013).

34. *See* Guidelines for New Chemicals Notification, issued Sept. 16, 2010, under the
Regulations on Environmental Management of New Chemical Substances, issued Sept.
12, 2003, as amended Jan. 19, 2010, with the effective date of Oct. 15, 2010.

35. These Acts and related documents provide that safety data developed in one
Organisation for Economic Co-operation and Development (OECD) member country will
be accepted for use by the relevant registration authorities in assessing the chemical or
product in another OECD country (i.e., the data does not have to be generated a second

time for the purposes of safety assessment). There are non-OECD member country adherents to the Council Acts associated with MAD in the assessment of chemicals (for instance, Israel). However, China, a non-OECD member, has not committed to the Council Acts. *See generally* http://www.oecd.org/env/ehs/mutualacceptanceofdatamad.htm (last visited Mar. 28, 2013).

36. *See, e.g.,* Ministry of Environmental Protection Government Information Disclosure Report, issued and effective Mar. 23, 2012 (calling for strengthening of operational guidance on environmental information disclosure, in-depth research, organizational communication, training, and other activities aimed at improving organizational ability and levels of environmental information disclosure).

37. Guidelines for New Chemicals Notification issued Sept. 16, 2010, under the Regulations on Environmental Management of New Chemical Substances issued Sept. 12, 2003, as amended Jan. 19, 2010, with the effective date of Oct. 15, 2010, pt. III (Application Form and Instructions for New Chemical Substance Conventional Registration).

38. Zhang & Dong, *supra* note 7, at 15-16.

39. *Id.*

40. *Id.*

41. Prevention and Control of Environmental Pollution by Solid Wastes Law.

42. *Id.*

43. *Id.* In December 2009, the MEP published a provisional set of Rules on Environmental Management of the Soil of Contaminated Sites and related guidelines and specifications on investigation, assessment, remediation, and monitoring of contaminated sites. *See* Inga Caldwell & Xinyu Wang, *A Hidden Problem: China's Contaminated Site Soil Pollution Crisis* (AID/Vermont Law School U.S.–China Partnership for Environmental Law, Aug. 5, 2011) http://www.vermontlaw.edu/Documents/China%20Program/CaldwellWangPaper3.pdf.

44. SQUIRE SANDERS, CHINA UPDATE (2009), http://www.squiresanders.com/files/Publication/ed692a0e-eb1e-4f11-a782-4131ad6232b7/Presentation/PublicationAttachment/d29f61f9-902c-4ac4-8820-416c003408ca/China_Update_June_2009.pdf (last visited Jan. 24, 2014); *see also* chapter 49, Germany, in this volume.

45. Zhang & Dong, *supra* note 7, at 15-14.

46. *Id.* at 15-15.

47. *Id.* For English translations of these statutes, see http://english.sepa.gov.cn/Policies_Regulations/laws/ (last visited Jan. 24, 2014); *see also* EPA–China Envtl. Law Initiative, Legal Resources, http://www.epa.gov/ogc/china/legal_resources.htm#statutes (last visited Jan. 24, 2014). Water shortages are one natural resource issue with which China has had to contend. S. Mufson, *As Economy Booms, China Faces Major Water Shortage*, WASH. POST., Mar. 16, 2010, http://www.washingtonpost.com/wp-dyn/content/article/2010/03/15/AR2010031503564.html.

47. Zhang & Dong, *supra* note 7, at 15-19. *See also* Grassland Law of the People's Republic of China, as amended, adopted by the Standing Comm. Nat'l People's Cong. Dec. 28, 2002, and effective Mar. 1, 2003.

48. Zhang & Dong, *supra* note 7, at 15-19.

49. *Id.*

50. *Id.* at 15-20.

51. *Id.*

52. *Id.*

53. *Id.*

54. *Id.*

55. *Id.* at 15-19.

56. *Id.* at 15-20.

57. *Id.* at 15-21. The Water Law regulates water use and impacts power-generating and other projects that rely on water resources. *Id.*

58. *See, e.g.,* World Bank, Promoting Market-oriented Ecological Compensation Mechanisms: Payment for Ecosystem Services in China (Dec. 2007), http://www.caep.org.cn/english/paper/Policy-Note-of-Payment-for-Ecological-Service-in-China-EN-FINAL.pdf.

59. Zhang & Dong, *supra* note 7, at 15-19.

59. *Id.*

60. Canfa, *supra* note 13, at 507.

61. The term "public participation" can refer to public expression of protest, even if not necessarily clearly protected in environmental laws. However, for the purposes of this section, we focus on participation encouraged or protected in China's environmental laws, or participation in the environmental lawmaking process.

62. *See* Interim Measures on Public Participation for Environmental Impact Assessment, issued by the Ministry of Environmental Protection Feb. 14, 2006, and effective Mar. 18, 2006. The term "interim" in the title of this law does not necessarily mean that the measures were issued for only a specific period of time. "Interim" tends to be used in the titles of laws that are "new" in the China legal experience, and therefore subject to revision if the circumstances warrant.

63. *See id.* art. 5.

64. *See* Circular on Further Strengthening Disclosure of Environmental Protection Information, issued and effective Oct. 30, 2012, *available at* http://www.mep.gov.cn/gkml/hbb/bgt/201210/t20121031_240771.htm (last visited Mar. 28, 2013).

65. *Id.*

66. *Id.*

67. *Id.*

68. *Id.*

69. Regulations on Disclosure of Government Information, promulgated by the State Council Apr. 5, 2007, and effective May 1, 2008.

70. *See, e.g., id.* art. 14.

71. *See* B. Finamore, *Step Forward for Environmental Transparency in China,* Energy Collective, Apr. 1, 2013, http://theenergycollective.com/barbarafinamore/204071/environmental-transparency-china (last visited Apr. 8, 2013); Inst. of Pub. & Envtl. Affairs & Nat. Res. Def. Council, Open Environmental Information: Taking Stock (2011) http://www.ipe.org.cn/Upload/Report-PITI-2011-EN.pdf (annual China pollution information and transparency index).

72. *See, e.g.,* Circular Economy Promotion Law, enacted by the Standing Comm. Nat'l People's Cong. Aug. 29, 2008, and effective Jan. 1, 2009, art. 10, which provides:

> Citizens have the right to report activities that waste resources or are destructive to the environment, and have the right to information regarding the government's promotion of the circular economy, and to submit opinions and recommendations.

73. Article 85 of the 2008 amendments to the Water Pollution Control Law provides as follows:

> The party whose rights and interests are damaged by a water pollution accident is entitled to ask the party discharging pollutants to eliminate the damage and make compensation for their losses.
>
> If the damage is caused by force majeure, the party discharging pollutants bears no liability for compensation, unless it is otherwise prescribed by law.
>
> If the damage is caused by the victim on purpose, the party discharging pollutants bears no liability for compensation.
>
> If the damage is caused by the gross negligence of the victim, the liability for compensation of the party discharging pollutants may be mitigated.

> If the damage is caused by a third party, the party discharging pollutants has the right to, after making compensation according to law, recover the compensation from the third party.

For a similar provision of arguably broader applicability, see Article 55 of the revised Civil Procedure Law (providing that relevant organs and organizations prescribed by law may initiate lawsuit at competent courts against conducts jeopardizing the public interests, such as causing environment pollution or damaging the interests of a large number of consumers). Also relevant is a similar provision being considered in the pending amendments to the framework Environmental Protection Law, although possible limitations on standing to initiate such lawsuits might limit its impact. *See generally China Environment Forum Hosts Event on Environmental Public Interest Law,* Woodrow Wilson Center China Environment Forum (Nov. 12, 2012), http://www.wilsoncenter.org/article/event -environmental-public-interest-law-china.

74. In 1999, the International Fund for China's Environment convened what was widely recognized as the first U.S.-China Environmental NGO forum. At that event, the majority of participants were from Western (non-Chinese) NGOs, and the Chinese NGOs numbered in the tens. At present, however, including university/academic groups, such organizations in China number in the thousands, and hundreds may be represented at the annual NGO forum, which continues to this day. *See generally* http://www.ifce.org.

75. *See generally* http://www.clapv.org/english_lvshi/.

76. *See generally* http://www.ipe.org.cn/en/.

77. E. Wong, *China Exports Pollution to U.S., Study Finds,* N.Y. TIMES, Jan. 20, 2014, http://www.nytimes.com/2014/01/21/world/asia/china-also-exports-pollution-to -western-us-study-finds.html?_r=0. The same report notes that a significant portion of the emissions transported to the United States are related to production of goods exported from China to the United States; *see also* J. Kim, *A China Environmental Health Project Fact Sheet: Transboundary Air Pollution—Will China Choke On Its Success?* (Feb. 2, 2007), http:// www.wilsoncenter.org/sites/default/files/transboundary_feb2.pdf.

78. *See* http://www.env.go.jp/earth/coop/coop/english/dialogue/temm.html (last visited Feb. 15, 2014).

79. *See generally* RSCs issued by the administrative and personnel division of the Ministry of Environmental Protection, Oct. 30, 2008:

> http://www.mep.gov.cn/gkml/zzjg/qt/200910/t20091023_180890.htm
> http://www.mep.gov.cn/gkml/zzjg/qt/200910/t20091023_180886.htm
> http://www.mep.gov.cn/gkml/zzjg/qt/200910/t20091023_180887.htm
> http://www.mep.gov.cn/gkml/zzjg/qt/200910/t20091023_180888.htm
> http://www.mep.gov.cn/gkml/zzjg/qt/200910/t20091023_180889.htm
> http://www.mep.gov.cn/gkml/zzjg/qt/200910/t20091023_180890.htm

80. Decision on Implementation of Scientific Development and Strengthening on Environmental Protection (State Council, Dec. 3, 2005), *available at* http://english.mep .gov.cn/Policies_Regulations/policies/Frameworkp1/200712/t20071227_115531.htm (last visited July 22, 2014).

81. See P. McCubbin, *China and Climate Change: Domestic Environmental Needs, Differentiated International Responsibilities, and Rule of Law Weaknesses,* ENVTL. & ENERGY L. & POL'Y J. (2008); A. Wang, *The Role of Law in Environmental Protection in China: Recent Developments,* 8 VT. J. OF ENVT'L L. 203 (2006–2007); J. Dellapenna, *A Few Words on Law and the Environment in China,* 24 TEMP. J. SCI. TECH. & ENVT'L L. 367 (2005), J. Liu, *Overview of the Chinese Legal System,* 41 ENVT'L L. REP. 10885, 10887 (2011).

CHAPTER 38

India

KRISHNA VIJAY SINGH AND SHEPHALI MEHRA BIRDI

I. Introduction

A. Constitution of India and Environment Protection

The Indian Constitution recognizes the significant role of environment and natural resources in the well-being of the nation and the need for preserving and protecting the same along with all of its vital components. The constitution entrusts the state as well as Indian citizens with a duty to protect and improve the natural environment. Article 51A(g) casts a duty on every citizen to "protect and improve the natural environment including forests, lakes, rivers and wild life, and to have compassion for living creatures."[1] Similarly, the Directive Principles of the State Policy (Directive Principles) under Article 48A provides that the "State shall endeavor to protect and improve the environment and to safeguard the forests and wildlife of the country."[2]

The constitution also guarantees to all persons a fundamental right to life. Article 21 states that "no person shall be deprived of his life or personal liberty except according to the procedure established by law."[3] In a number of cases, the Indian Supreme Court and various high courts have expanded the scope of the right to life to include the right to a clean and pollution-free environment. In *Subhash Kumar v. State of Bihar*,[4] the court observed that the "right to live is a fundamental right under Article 21 of the Constitution and it includes the right of enjoyment of pollution-free water and air for full enjoyment of life."[5] In another important case, *Damodhar Rao v. S.O.M.C. Hyderabad*,[6] the Andhra Pradesh High Court observed:

> [I]t would be reasonable to hold that the enjoyment of life and its attainment and fulfillment guaranteed by Article 21 of the Constitution embraces the protection and preservation of nature's gifts without which life cannot be enjoyed. There can be no reason why practice of violent extinguishment of life alone should be regarded as violative of Article 21 of the Constitution. The slow poisoning by the polluted atmosphere caused by environmental pollution and spoilation should also be regarded as amounting to violation of Article 21 of the Constitution.[7]

In the context of India, it is important to understand the legislative competence of the central government, or "Union,"[8] and the various states on environment and its various components. The Union has been exclusively empowered to legislate on subjects such as fishing and fisheries beyond territorial waters, regulation and development of interstate rivers and river valleys, and regulation of mines and mineral development. Conversely, the states have been vested with the power to legislate on land use, inland fisheries, and water (water supply, irrigation and canals, drainage and embankment, water storage). On certain vital subjects, such as forests, wildlife, animals, and birds, both the Union as well as the states have been empowered to legislate.

In addition, certain important environmental legislation has been enacted at the Union level based on Article 253 of the Constitution,[9] which empowers the Parliament to make laws implementing India's international obligations, as well as any decision made at an international conference, association, or other body. Such legislative competence is also supported by entry 13 of the "Union List,"[10] which covers "participation in international conferences, associations and other bodies and implementing of decisions made thereat."[11] Using its powers under Article 253, read with entry 13, the Parliament has enacted several significant statutes for giving effect to its international law and treaty obligations, such as the Environment Protection Act, 1986 (enacted pursuant to the United Nations Conference on the Human Environment in 1972, also known as Stockholm Conference) and the Biological Diversity Act, 2002 (enacted to fulfill India's obligations under the U.N. Convention on Biological Diversity (1992)).

Thus, the constitutional provisions on environment are backed by a comprehensive and an extremely varied legal framework comprising a plethora of laws, rules, and notifications. Laws regulating exploitation of natural resources and ecosystems, such as forests, forest resources, and wild animals and birds, have been in existence since the preindependence era.[12] Postindependence (i.e., post-1947), these laws have evolved to address changing government policies, international regime, and environmental, social, and economic parameters. The other set of laws, including those regulating harmful pollutants, chemicals, wastes, dangerous goods, climate change, and energy efficiency have come into existence mainly to cater to the demands of modern industry at the national as well as the global level. India also has an array of marine laws, which, inter alia, regulate safety and conservation of ports, pollution from ships, shipbreaking industry, and oil spills.

On the enforcement aspect, it is important to understand that in India, several government ministries and departments are responsible for implementation of different laws having a bearing on environment. At the national level, there is the Ministry of Environment & Forests[13] (MoEF), which is responsible for planning, promoting, coordinating, and overseeing the implementation of India's environmental and forestry laws, policies, and program. However, certain environmental issues entail involvement of other government ministries as well. For example, while the rules regulating hazardous chemicals are enforced by the MoEF, transportation of such chemicals by road, air, or water is governed by the respective ministries responsible for transportation, such as the Ministries of Road Transport and Highways[14] and Shipping,[15] among others. Similarly, water pollution is regulated by the MoEF, while the Ministry of Water Resources is charged with the overall management of water resources, and irrigation.[16] The Ministry of New and Renewable Energy[17] is in charge of research and development in new, clean, and renewable sources of energy, such as solar energy, wind energy, hydropower, and energy generated from biomass.

B.   Environment Protection Act, 1986: The Umbrella Legislation on Environmental Protection

The enactment of the Environment (Protection) Act, 1986 (EPA) is considered as the defining moment in India's environmental policy and regulatory regime. Prior to passage of the EPA, there were multiple laws in India regulating different environmental constituents, that is, forests,[18] wildlife,[19] fisheries,[20] water,[21] and air pollution,[22] but no single general law laying down the broad framework for environment protection and improvement. The EPA was enacted to give effect to the decisions taken at the 1972 Stockholm Conference. The Bhopal gas tragedy[23] is also believed to have triggered the enactment of the EPA. The EPA provides an overall framework for various aspects of environmental protection and management, including water, air, land, and the interrelationship between the natural environment, land, plants and human beings, other living creatures, and microorganisms.

The EPA vests the central government, through the MoEF, with certain vital functions and powers, such as coordinating the actions of state governments; laying down standards for the quality of the environment; restricting the setting up of industries, operations, or processes in ecologically sensitive areas; establishing environmental laboratories; collecting and analyzing samples of air, water, soil, or any other substances from an industrial establishment; examining manufacturing processes, materials, and substances; and initiating penal action against industries engaged in unlawful activities. The EPA also creates a mechanism for the compulsory reporting of environment pollution by industry and recovery of costs of reclamation from such polluting industry.

The umbrella framework offered by the EPA has been used creatively by the central government to establish standards for discharges of environmental pollutants from industries and to frame rules and regulations on waste management, the management of chemicals, environment impact assessment, and regulation of developmental activities in coastal stretches and ecological sensitive areas. These rules and regulations will be discussed in a subsequent part of this chapter.

The government has also promulgated the Environment (Protection) Rules, 1986 (EPR) pursuant to the EPA. These rules lay down the standards for emission or discharge of environmental pollutants from more than 100 industries, operations, and processes. These rules prescribe the factors to be taken into consideration by the central government while prohibiting or restricting the location of industries or for prohibiting or restricting the handling of hazardous substances.

The EPA also empowers the central government to constitute specialized authorities and agencies for the discharge of various powers and functions of the central government under the EPA. Under the EPA's enabling provision, the Union has, over the years, established subject-specific authorities, such as the Water Quality Assessment Authority, National Coastal Zone Management Authority, Aquaculture Authority, and Central Empowered Committee, among others.

II.   Air and Climate Change
A.   Air (Prevention and Control of Pollution) Act, 1981

The Air (Prevention and Control of Pollution) Act, 1981 (Air Act)[24] was, like the EPA, enacted to implement the decisions taken at the Stockholm Conference. The Air Act, which provides for prevention, control, and abetment of air pollution, came into force in 1987. The Central Pollution Control Board (CPCB) and State Pollution Control Boards (SPCBs) created under the Water Act have been entrusted with the task of enforcement of the Air Act. Similar to the Water Act, the Air Act also regulates establishment of industries and operations in air pollution control areas and emission of air pollutants therefrom. Prior approval of the concerned SPCB or Pollution Control Committees (PCCs), as the case may be, in the form of consent to establish or operate, is required to be obtained for establishment and continued operation of an industry in an air pollution control area.

B.   Climate Change and Energy Efficiency

India is a party to the United Nations Framework Convention on Climate Change (UNFCCC).[25] Being a developing country, it does not contain any binding greenhouse gas (GHG) mitigation commitments; however, India has undertaken numerous response measures that are contributing to the objectives of the UNFCCC. These measures have essentially been targeted at enhancing the capacity of renewable energy installations, improving air quality in major cities, and increasing afforestation. Other similar measures have been implemented by committing additional resources and realigning new investments, thus putting economic development on a climate-friendly path.

1.   Clean Development Mechanism in India

The central government has constituted the National Clean Development Mechanism (CDM) Authority for the purpose of protecting and improving the quality of the environment, consistent with the Kyoto Protocol to the UNFCCC.[26] The National CDM Authority evaluates and approves the CDM projects in India. The evaluation process includes an assessment of the probability of eventual successful implementation of the project and the extent to which projects meet the sustainable development objectives.

2. *National Action Plan on Climate Change*

In June 2008, the Prime Minister's Office released the National Action Plan on Climate Change (NAPCC), highlighting eight priority national missions: (1) mission on enhanced energy efficiency;[27] (2) mission on sustainable habitat;[28] (3) mission on sustainable agriculture;[29] (4) Green India mission;[30] (5) water mission;[31] (6) national solar mission;[32] (7) national mission for sustaining the Himalayan ecosystem;[33] and (8) national mission on strategic knowledge for climate change.[34] The concerned government ministries and departments have already framed comprehensive mission documents on these subjects.

Under these missions, the central government has taken significant initiatives with a view to combating climate change. For instance, India has announced a clean energy levy on coal, at the rate of 50 rupees (Rs) (approximately US$1) per ton. This levy will apply to both domestically produced and imported coal. This money will in turn be deposited into a National Clean Energy Fund that will be used to fund research, innovative projects in clean energy technologies, and an environmental remediation program. Similarly, the National Mission on Energy Efficiency sets out a mechanism for specific energy consumption targets in large energy-consuming industries and a system for the trade of energy-savings certificates.

Another important initiative is the national mission for sustaining the Himalayan ecosystem (NMSHE).[35] The mission recognizes that the Himalayan ecosystem is fragile and diverse and is vital to the ecological security of the Indian landmass. It provides forest cover, feeding perennial rivers that are the source of drinking water, irrigation, and hydropower, and conserves biodiversity, providing a rich base for high-value agriculture and spectacular landscapes for sustainable tourism. As per this mission, the Himalayan ecosystem has the potential to affect the lives of more than 51 million people who practice hill agriculture and remain vulnerable. The primary objective of the mission is to develop, in a time-bound manner, sustainable national capacity to continuously assess the health status of the Himalayan ecosystem and to enable policy bodies in their policy-formulation functions and assist states in the Indian Himalayan Region with implementation of actions for sustainable development. This would call for suitable learning systems for balancing changes in ecosystems with responsible human actions.[36]

III. Water

The Water (Prevention and Control of Pollution) Act, 1974 (Water Act) was the first legislation designed to prevent and control a specific form of pollution—water pollution—by regulating the establishment of industries and discharge of trade and sewage effluents therefrom into water bodies or on land.

The most significant contribution of the Water Act has been the establishment of the CPCB at the national level and the SPCBs and PCCs at the state and Union territory level, respectively, for the implementation of pollution control laws.

The Water Act mandates obtaining prior consent from the SPCB or PCC, as the case may be, for the establishment or operation of an industrial operation or a process that is likely to discharge effluents into a water body or on land. Such consent is required for bringing into use any new or altered outlet for the discharge of sewage. Specifically, prior to the establishment of an industry or operation, obtaining the "consent to establish" such industry or operation must be obtained from the relevant governmental authority. Thereafter, consent to operate the industry is required from time to time, during the entire lifespan of the industrial project.

The SPCBs and PCCs, while granting the above-mentioned consent orders, stipulate the standards for discharge of certain effluents from the relevant industrial project, including their maximum permissible quantity and the measures to be taken for treatment prior to the discharge of effluents.

The Water Act and rules promulgated thereunder establish a comprehensive framework for the abatement and prevention of pollution by authorizing SPCBs and PCCs to inspect industries and collect and analyze samples of effluents discharged therefrom. The authorities have also been empowered to take punitive action against polluting industries.[37]

IV.   Handling, Treatment, Transportation, and Disposal of Hazardous Materials

The EPA empowers the central government to regulate the handling and management of hazardous substances and dangerous goods. Accordingly, the central government has framed various rules for regulating hazardous chemicals and hazardous wastes, including electronic waste (e-waste), batteries, hazardous microorganisms, genetically engineered organisms, and ozone-depleting substances.

A.   Hazardous Chemicals

As the name suggests, the Manufacture, Storage, and Import of Hazardous Chemical Rules, 1989 (MSIHC Rules)[38] have been promulgated to regulate the usage, storage, transportation, and import of hazardous chemicals in India, primarily in industrial operations. The MSIHC Rules seek to prevent and mitigate the effects of accidents that may occur while handling hazardous chemicals in bulk. The occupiers of facilities engaged in the handling and use of such chemicals require prior authorization under the MSIHC Rules. These facilities are also required to prepare safety reports and on-site emergency plans and to conduct safety audits and mock drills from time to time. The measures for packaging and labeling of hazardous chemicals are also stipulated under the MSIHC Rules.

B.   Waste Management

The central government has framed separate rules under the EPA for use and management of various classes of wastes, such as hazardous wastes, biomedical wastes, plastic wastes, and municipal solid wastes. These rules cover an array of stakeholders, such as industries, hospitals and healthcare facilities, municipal bodies, regulatory bodies, and households.

1.   *The Hazardous Wastes (Management, Handling and Transboundary Movement) Rules, 2008*

The Hazardous Wastes (Management, Handling and Transboundary Movement) Rules, 2008 were formulated under the EPA for the purpose of regulating the generation, storage, transportation, recycling, treatment, import, or export of hazardous wastes. These rules seek to ensure that hazardous wastes are handled in an environmentally sound manner and that wastes are channeled to appropriate and authorized treatment and disposal facilities. Handling, reprocessing, and recycling of hazardous wastes require prior authorization from the concerned SPCB or PCC.

The Hazardous Wastes Rules incorporate India's obligations under the Basel Convention on the Control of Transboundary Movement of Hazardous Wastes and Their Disposal,[39] specifically the requirements concerning "prior informed consent" of the countries concerned in the transboundary trade of hazardous wastes. Import of hazardous wastes into India is permitted only for the purpose of recycling, reuse, and reprocessing. The Hazardous Wastes Rules prohibit import of wastes for dumping and disposal in India.

2.   *The Municipal Solid Wastes (Management and Handling) Rules, 2000*

The Municipal Solid Wastes (Management and Handling) Rules, 2000 (MSW Rules) provide a framework for the collection, segregation, processing, and disposal of solid wastes in municipal areas. The municipal authorities are responsible for enforcement of the MSW Rules. The MSW Rules have facilitated establishment and development of infrastructure for treatment and disposal of municipal wastes, such as landfills, incineration, and composting sites.

3.   *Bio-Medical Waste (Management and Handling) Rules, 1998*

The Bio-Medical Waste Rules seek to regulate biomedical waste generated by hospitals, clinics, dispensaries, laboratories, blood banks, and other health care institutions.[40] Under the Bio-Medical Waste Rules, all healthcare institutions providing services to 1,000 or more patients every year require authorization for the generation, collection, storage, transportation, treatment, disposal, or handling of biomedical wastes. Detailed guidelines for the segregation, labeling, and packaging of biomedical wastes have been established to ensure that they do not mix with other wastes or biomedical wastes of some other category.

4. E-Waste (Management and Handling) Rules, 2011 (E-Waste Rules)

The E-Waste Rules[41] are relatively recent[42] rules framed under the EPA and have a great bearing on the electronics and information technology (IT) industry in India. The E-Waste Rules have been drafted based on the principles of extended producer responsibility and product life-recycle management. Accordingly, the E-Waste Rules contain provisions for restrictions on the use of hazardous substances (RoHS) and mandatory take-back of end-of-life electronic products by producers. The E-Waste Rules mandate compulsory registration of manufacturers, importers, and assemblers/dismantlers of e-waste and require the consumers and bulk consumers of regulated electronic products to channel their e-waste to authorized and registered collection or recycling facilities. Currently, the E-Waste Rules are only applicable to limited industries, including consumer electronics, IT, and telecom equipment.

C. Other Dangerous Goods and Substances

In addition to the above, other dangerous goods and substances are also regulated under Indian environmental regulations. The Ozone-Depleting Substances (Regulation and Control) Rules, 2000[43] discharge India's obligations under the Montreal Protocol on Substances That Deplete the Ozone Layer (Montreal Protocol),[44] thereby regulating the production, use, and international trade in such substances. Import or export of ozone-depleting substances to countries that are not signatories to the Montreal Protocol is prohibited under the Ozone-Depleting Substances Rules.

The Manufacture, Use, Import, Export, and Storage of Hazardous Micro-Organisms/Genetically Engineered Organisms or Cells Rules, 1989[45] aim to protect the environment and health in connection with the application of gene technology and microorganisms. These rules are extremely significant for industries and institutions engaged in research into genetically modified organisms, such as pharmaceuticals, seeds, and food stuffs, and their production, import, sale, or use in India.

There also exist regulations on batteries, although they are limited in their scope and application. India's battery-specific legal authority is the Batteries (Management and Handling) Rules, 2001,[46] which only regulates lead-acid batteries. The Battery Rules set out the responsibilities of manufacturers, importers, assemblers, and reconditioners. These entities are required to ensure that used batteries are collected back against new batteries sold. As regards other types of batteries, their transportation is governed by the Central Motor Vehicles Rules, 1989.[47] They are also covered under the Ecomark

Scheme,[48] which aims at incentivizing manufacturers and importers to reduce adverse environmental impact of products.

V.   Waste and Site Remediation

Regarding Indian law on waste management, see section IV, *supra*.

As regards site remediation, though India does not have any specific legislation providing for compulsory remediation of a contaminated or polluted site, the mandate for the same can be found in certain environmental statutes and environmental principles applied by the higher judiciary while handling pollution matters, such as the polluter pays principle and the absolute liability principle.[49]

The EPA provides for remedial measures to be taken by the pollution control boards in case of discharge of environmental pollutants in excess of the permissible standards and recovery of the cost of cleanup and remediation from the polluter. The Hazardous Waste Rules also hold the occupier, transporter, importer, or operator of a facility liable for damage caused to the environment or a third party due to improper handling or disposal of hazardous waste. In such cases, SPCB may impose penalties for violation of any provision of the said rules.

Further, the MoEF, while granting the environment impact assessment clearance or forest clearance for mining or other large construction projects, may stipulate certain conditions for environmental remediation and restoration, including afforestation.

In addition to the above statutory provisions, the higher courts in India have been applying the universally accepted environmental principles, such as the principles of absolute liability and polluter pays to recover the cost of environmental damage, which can then be applied for remediation and restoration of environment and natural resources. For example, the Supreme Court applied the polluter pays principle in *Indian Council for Enviro-Legal v. Union of India*,[50] wherein a polluting industry involved in use of harmful chemicals was required to compensate for the removal of sludge in and around their manufacturing plant. Similarly, the courts have also applied the absolute liability principle and have held the polluting entity or person absolutely liable for the damage done to the environment and third parties[51] to ensure that the polluter pays for the entire cost of the environmental restoration.

However, the Indian law lacks a holistic and nuanced approach toward such environmental remediation and restoration. While the cost of remediation may be recovered from the polluter, the manner in which the amount so collected should be applied toward remediation or which agency or authority should be responsible for restoration are not adequately addressed.

VI.   Emergency Response

Regarding Indian law on emergency response as to chemical spills, see section IV, *supra*. In addition, there also exist the Chemical Accidents (Emergency

Planning, Preparedness and Response) Rules, 1996 framed under the EPA. These rules provide for establishment of crisis groups at four levels: central, state, district, and local. These crisis groups are responsible for handling a chemical accident, including pre- and post-accident challenges. A major chemical accident means an occurrence, including any major emission, fire, or explosion involving one or more hazardous chemicals and resulting from uncontrolled developments in the course of industrial activity or transportation or arising due to natural events likely to cause substantial loss of life and property including adverse effects on the environment.

India also has an elaborate regime dealing with oil pollution, spills, and their impact on marine environment. The Territorial Waters, Continental Shelf, Exclusive Economic Zone and Other Maritime Zones Act, 1976 establishes the national government's sovereign right to preserve and protect the marine environment and to prevent and control marine pollution on the continental shelf and within the exclusive economic zone of India. Oil pollution in marine areas (over which India exercises control) is specifically governed under the Merchant Shipping Act, 1958, which incorporates the provisions of the International Convention on Civil Liability for Oil Pollution Damage, 1992. Under the Merchant Shipping Act, the owner of the ship is liable for any pollution damage caused by oil escaping or being discharged from the ship. The Merchant Shipping Act also provides for a limitation of liability with respect to an incident or occurrence by constitution of a limitation fund as per the directions of the concerned High Court. The owner of the ship that carries 2,000 tons or more oil in bulk as cargo is required to maintain insurance or other financial security as prescribed under the Merchant Shipping Act.

The Merchant Shipping Act also incorporates the provisions of the International Convention on the Establishment of an International Fund for Compensation for Oil Pollution Damage, 1992 and provides for contribution to the fund and the application of the fund toward compensation for pollution damage. The government has framed the Merchant Shipping (International Fund for Compensation for Oil Pollution Damage) Rules, 2008 to set out the modalities of the fund. The Merchant Shipping Act and the rules framed thereunder[52] also sets out the provisions for prevention and containment of oil pollution of the sea.

VII.   Natural Resource Management and Protection
A.   Forests

Perhaps the broadest and oldest element of India's natural resources regulatory regime is its framework on forests. Both the Union as well as state governments have the authority to legislate on forests. The Indian Forest Act, 1927 (IFA)[53] is the most important legislation on forestry and aims at consolidating the law relating to forests, transit of forest produce, and the duty leviable on timber and other forest products. The IFA provides an umbrella framework that can be adopted and modified by a state; alternatively, the state may enact its own forest law in accordance with the IFA. The IFA provides for classification of forest or waste lands, being the property of the central government or on which the central government has proprietary rights, in three different categories: (1) reserve forest, (2) protected forest, and (3) village forest. As the name suggests, reserve forest is the most regulated category. All human or commercial activities, such as the collection of minor forest products, grazing, mining, and industry, are strictly regulated. The designation of any forest or waste land as a reserve, protected, or village forest follows an elaborate process of inquiry into and settlement of forests rights of individuals and communities over the forest land. Once settled, such rights are clearly recorded in forests settlement records. The settlement process is a long and cumbersome process. In the case of many forests, settlement has not yet been completed.

The IFA controls and regulates collection and transit of timber and other forest products from notified forests areas. Most states have formulated specific rules on the transit of forest products.

In addition to the IFA, the central government has also enacted the Forest (Conservation) Act, 1980 (FCA),[54] which is extremely significant in terms of commercial and industrial activities involving the use of forests and forest lands. The FCA prohibits dereservation of forests or the use or alteration of forest lands for nonforestry purposes without obtaining prior approval of the MoEF. Cultivation of coffee, spices, rubber, palms, oil-bearing plants, and medicinal plants qualify as nonforest purposes. The FCA also provides for the creation of an advisory committee to advise the central government on various matters covered under the FCA. The Forest (Conservation) Rules, 2003[55]—promulgated under the FCA—establish the procedure for the submission of applications by the user entities desiring to use forestlands for nonforestry purposes.

The central government has also enacted the Scheduled Tribes and Other Traditional Forest Dwellers (Recognition of Forest Rights) Act, 2006 (Forest Rights Act)[56] to secure the forest rights of traditional forest dwellers. These rights include individual tenurial and access rights, as well as community rights over forest resources. These rights can also be categorized as land rights, access rights, usage rights, ownership rights, and management and control rights. The Forests Rights Act has added another dimension to the forest clearance process laid down under the FCA. Any industrial or commercial activity on a forest or forest land may be taken up only after settlement of forest rights in terms of the Forest Rights Act. Further, the prior consent of the local community body—known as the Gram Sabha—is also required for undertaking such activities.

B. Coastal Ecology

In 2011, the MoEF issued the revised Coastal Regulation Zone (CRZ) Notification, 2011,[57] which superseded the previously established CRZ Notification,

1991. Around the same time, the MoEF also issued the Island Protection Zone Notification, 2011 (IPZ Notification),[58] designating the islands of Andaman and Nicobar and the Lakshadweep and their coastal stretches as island protection zones. The CRZ Notification 2011 aims to reconcile three important objectives: (1) preservation of coastal ecology; (2) protection of livelihoods of traditional fisherfolk communities; and (3) promotion of economic activities that are required to be located in coastal regions.

The term "coastal regulation zone" has been defined to include the water area up to 12 nautical miles into the ocean and the entire water area of a tidal water body, such as creek, river, or estuary. It also includes the land area from the high-tide line to 500 meters on the landward side, as well as the land area from the high-tide line to 100 meters or the width of the creek, whichever is less, on the landward side along tidally influenced water bodies connected to the ocean.

The objective of the CRZ Notification is to check growth of human and industrial activities within the ecologically fragile CRZ areas, such as the manufacture, handling, storage, or disposal of hazardous substances; the set-up and expansion of fish processing units, including warehousing; and the dumping of municipal waste for the purposes of land filling. The CRZ is divided into four categories, depending on its geomorphology and existing features of settlement: (1) CRZ-I (ecologically sensitive); (2) CRZ-II (built-up area); (3) CRZ-III (rural area); and (4) CRZ-IV (water areas up to the territorial waters and the tidally influenced water bodies). The CRZ Notification 2011 also contains detailed guidelines on development of beach resorts and hotels in the designated areas of CRZ-III for temporary occupation by tourists and visitors, with prior approval of the MoEF.

VIII.   Natural Resource Damages

Regarding Indian law on natural resource damages, see section V, *supra*, and section IX (for provisions concerning environment impact assessments).

IX.   Protected Species

The Wildlife (Protection) Act, 1972 (WLPA)[59] governs protection and preservation of wildlife and their natural habitat. The WLPA lists the protected species of wild animals and birds, and restricts and/or prohibits hunting of such wild animals. Similarly, the WLPA contains a list of specified plants, with a view to protect them from destruction, uprooting, or damage.

The WLPA further provides for four different categories of protected areas: national parks, sanctuaries, community reserves, and conservation reserves. The WLPA includes detailed provisions on declaration of areas as any of the protected categories, the activities restricted and prohibited in such areas, and protection of wildlife and their natural habitat therein. The WLPA also regulates possession, acquisition, transfer or trade, and commerce in wild animals, trophies, and animal articles.

Biodiversity per se also receives protection. The Biological Diversity Act, 2002[60] was enacted for laying down a framework for conservation of biological diversity, sustainable use of its components and fair and equitable sharing of the benefits arising out of the use of biological resources and knowledge. The Biological Diversity Act was enacted to give effect to the decisions taken at the Convention on Biological Diversity, signed at Rio de Janeiro in 1992.[61] The Biological Diversity Act, inter alia, sets forth the framework for commercial utilization of biological resources and the use of traditional knowledge on biodiversity. The statute also imposes restrictions on commercial utilization of biological resources by foreign nationals and entities as well as Indian entities having any non-Indian participation in their share capital or management. With respect to intellectual property rights, the restrictions imposed by the act are aimed at ensuring that the benefits of the research, including traditional knowledge, and the benefits from commercial utilization based on such research or based on traditional knowledge are shared with local communities. Further, it seeks to provide measures for minimizing environmental impact of collection activities or generally for conservation of biodiversity.

X. Transboundary Pollution

Regarding Indian law on transboundary pollution, see section IV, *supra*.

XI. Environmental Review and Decision Making
A. Siting and Permitting

Over the years, India's environmental laws have evolved to address the concerns raised by growing industrialization and its intersection with the environment and natural resources. Environmental regulations play a significant role in the growth and development of industry in an environmentally sustainable manner. The objective of such laws is not to restrain industry, but to check and preempt its harmful effects on the environment, health, and safety.

Environmental laws may come into play as early as the stage of site identification for the industry. Siting of industries—especially polluting industries in ecologically sensitive areas, such as forests, wildlife sanctuaries, national parks, and coastal areas—is strictly regulated under specific statutes. In the case of certain specified polluting industries, mining, and large-scale building and construction projects, it is mandatory to conduct a prior environment impact assessment to assess and preempt the potential adverse impact of such activity on the environment. The environmental laws continue to regulate industrial activities during their entire life span. The day-to-day management and operation of industries and their various aspects, such as procurement and use of chemicals and other dangerous goods, generation of waste, and discharge of effluents, emissions, and sewage from the industry, as well as the disaster preparedness of a hazardous industry and its liability in case of a mishap, are regulated under the environmental law regime. The environmental laws assume great relevance for industries primarily based on natural resources, such as wood-based industries, hydro-power projects, mining, and research on gene technology, hazardous microorganisms, and biological resources.

In recent years, the central government has made certain attempts to incorporate the principles of product stewardship and extended producer's liability in laws and policies, thereby making manufacturers responsible for environmentally sound disposal and recycling of end-of-life and defective products. The government has also been promoting cleaner technologies and manufacturing processes and minimizing the use of harmful substances in products.

B.   Environmental Impact Assessment

In India, the concept of environment impact assessments (EIAs) came into existence around 1978; however, at that time, it was restricted to river valley projects. It was not until 1994 that the concept of EIA was formalized by issuance of a notification under the EPA, which was subsequently superseded by Environment Impact Assessment Notification, 2006 (EIA Notification).[62]

This EIA Notification mandates obtaining prior environmental clearance for setting up new projects relating to certain specified industries or processes. Such clearance is also required for the expansion or modernization of these specified processes or operations. The EIA seeks to assess and address the environmental as well as social impact of the industry. The EIA Notification applies to projects or processes such as mining, river valley projects, thermal power plants, cement plants, airports, building and construction projects, and special economic zones, which require prior environmental clearance.

Under the EIA Notification, all projects and activities are broadly categorized into two categories—Category A and Category B—based on the extent of potential impacts on human health and on natural and man-made resources. All projects included under Category A, including expansion and modernization of existing projects, or activities and change in product mix, require prior environmental clearance from the MoEF. Similarly, the projects or activities covered under Category B require prior environmental clearance from the state or Union territory Environment Impact Assessment Authority, which bases its decision on the recommendations of a state or Union territory-level Expert Appraisal Committee.

The EIA Notification provides a detailed procedure for obtaining environmental clearance, such as screening, scoping, public consultation, and appraisal. The EIA Notification also provides additional guidance on the postclearance monitoring process.

XII.   Civil and Criminal Enforcement and Penalties
A.   Enforcement of Environmental Statutes

Almost all major environmental statutes in India, including the IFA, FCA, EPA, and WLPA, treat the violation of law or noncompliance as a criminal offense. An offense against the environment and natural resources is considered an offense against the state, which in India is a trustee of all natural resources.[63]

The penal provisions under the environmental regulatory regime are duly backed by the provisions of the Indian Penal Code, 1860 (IPC) and Criminal Procedure Code, 1973 (CrPC). The IPC contains several provisions relating to offenses affecting the public health and safety and fouling of water bodies or making atmosphere noxious to health, which are punishable under the relevant provisions of the IPC. Similarly, section 133 of the CrPC empowers a district magistrate or a subdivisional magistrate to deal with matters relating to the construction of a building, or disposal of any explosive or flammable substance, or causing the unlawful obstruction of rivers or channels. In a number of cases, the courts have taken action under the above-mentioned statutes to deal with issues concerning environmental degradation.[64] For example, the Madhya Pradesh High Court—taking note of the provisions of section 133 of the Code of Criminal Procedure on a petition having been filed by the residents of Ratlam Municipality, who were tormented by stench and stink caused by open drains—issued appropriate directions to the municipal bodies to take remedial action. In *Ratlam Municipality v. Vardhi Chand*,[65] this decision of the Madhya Pradesh High Court was upheld by the Apex Court.

The environmental statutes in India also provide for civil liabilities. The enforcement agencies are authorized to issue show-cause notices or improvement notices to industries and individuals engaged in unlawful activities. In the case of noncompliance with pollution laws, the enforcement agencies may also resort to actions such as temporary suspension of utility services, such as electricity or water connection to the industrial entity with a view to compel the entity to take corrective and remedial steps before any stringent criminal action is taken.

B. National Green Tribunal Act, 2010

India has recently enacted the National Green Tribunal Act, 2010 to provide for the establishment of a National Green Tribunal for the effective and expeditious disposal of cases relating to environmental protection and the conservation of forests and other natural resources.[66]

The National Green Tribunal has jurisdiction over all civil cases that involve a substantial question relating to the environment, including enforcement of any legal right relating to environment, as well as cases in which an environment-related question arises out of the implementation of certain specified enactments like the EPA, Biological Diversity Act, and FCA.

C. Public Interest Litigation

The scope of environmental statutes in India has been significantly widened by the activism of the upper echelons of India's judiciary, which through various judgments has relaxed the rules of locus standi[67] and proof of injury.[68] This has resulted in the advent of public interest litigation. The above judicial activism is strongly rooted in Articles 32 and 226 of the Constitution of India, which provides the Supreme Court and the High Courts, respectively, powers to issue writs and directions for protection of fundamental rights.

Public interest litigation on environmental matters has culminated in significant development and streamlining of the regulatory framework, strengthening the interpretation and enforcement of such provisions for protection and improvement of environment, and development and adoption of certain important environmental principles, such as the precautionary principle,[69] polluter pays principle,[70] absolute liability principle,[71] and sustainable development.[72]

Notes

1. Constitution of India art. 51A(g), *available at* http://lawmin.nic.in/olwing/coi/coi-english/Const.Pock%202Pg.Rom8Fsss%288%29.pdf, at 1.

2. Constitution of India art. 48A, *available at* http://lawmin.nic.in/olwing/coi/coi-english/Const.Pock%202Pg.Rom8Fsss%287%29.pdf, at 3.

3. Constitution of India art. 21, *available at* http://lawmin.nic.in/olwing/coi/coi-english/Const.Pock%202Pg.Rom8Fsss%286%29.pdf, at 5.

4. (1991) 1 S.C.C. 598.

5. (1991) 1 S.C.C. 598.

6. Damodhar Rao v. S.O.M.C. Hyderabad, A.I.R. 1987 AP 171.

7. *Id.* [para. 24].

8. The "Union Parliament" refers to the supreme legislative body in the country having the power to legislate for the whole or any part of the territory of India. The Union Parliament comprises the president and the two houses, the Lok Sabha (House of the People) and Rajya Sabha (Council of States).

9. Article 253 states that "Notwithstanding anything in the foregoing provisions of this Chapter, Parliament has power to make any law for the whole or any part of the territory of India for implementing any treaty, agreement or convention with any other country or countries or any decision made at any international conference, association or other body."

10. Schedule VI to the Constitution of India.

11. Entry 13, List I (Union List), Seventh Schedule to the Constitution of India.

12. This covers the time period prior to August 15, 1947, when the nation was under British rule.

13. *See* http://envfor.nic.in/.

14. *See* http://morth.nic.in/.

15. *See* http://shipping.nic.in/.

16. *See* http://wrmin.nic.in/.

17. *See* http://www.mnre.gov.in/.

18. Indian Forests Act, 1927.

19. Wildlife Protection Act, 1972.

20. Indian Fisheries Act, 1897.

21. Water (Prevention and Control of Pollution) Act, 1974.

22. Air (Prevention and Control of Pollution) Act, 1981.

23. The Bhopal gas disaster is considered the world's worst industrial disaster. It caused an unprecedented death toll. It occurred on the night of December 2–3, 1984, at

the Union Carbide India Limited pesticide plant in Bhopal, which was the Indian subsidiary of Union Carbide Corporation, USA. This tragedy occurred due to leakage of methyl isocynate and other chemicals from the plant. The Indian Council of Medical Research (ICMR) estimated that out of a total population of Bhopal of 832,904, nearly 63 percent suffered from inhalational toxicity. It was estimated that approximately 2,000 people who were exposed to the lethal gas died in the first 72 hours and a large proportion of the survivors suffered acute multisystem morbidities—eyes and lungs being the main target organs. It is also estimated that a large proportion of the population that survived this tragedy developed morbidity of varying degrees over the subsequent 30 years.

24. Air (Prevention and Control of Pollution) Act, 1981, (Act 14 of 1981), *available at* http://www.moef.nic.in/legis/air/air1.html.

25. *See* http://unfccc.int/2860.php.

26. The Kyoto Protocol to the United Nations Framework Convention on Climate Change was adopted on December 11, 1997, in Kyoto, Japan, and entered into force on February 16, 2005. The protocol sets binding obligations on industrialized countries to reduce emissions of greenhouse gases. At the 2012 Doha, Qatar, climate talks, parties to the Kyoto Protocol agreed to a second commitment period of emissions reductions from January 1, 2013, to December 31, 2020, which takes the form of an amendment to the Protocol. For more information, refer to http://unfccc.int/kyoto_protocol/items/3145.php.

27. *See* http://www.beeindia.in/schemes/schemes.php?id=8.

28. *See* http://urbanindia.nic.in/programme/uwss/NMSH.pdf.

29. *See* http://agricoop.nic.in/Climatechange/ccr/National%20Mission%20For%20Sustainable%20Agriculture-DRAFT-Sept-2010.pdf.

30. *See* http://www.naeb.nic.in/documents/GIM_Brochure_26March.pdf.

31. *See* http://wrmin.nic.in.

32. *See* http://www.mnre.gov.in/solar-mission/mission-document-3.

33. *See* Mission Document of the National Mission for Sustaining the Himalayan Ecosystem, *available at* http://www.dst.gov.in/scientific-programme/NMSHE_June_2010.pdf.

34. *See* http://www.dst.gov.in/scientific-programme/NMSKCC_July_2010.pdf.

35. *See* Mission Document, *supra* note 33.

36. *See* http://www.dst.gov.in/scientific-programme/NMSHE_June_2010.pdf.

37. India also has enacted rules governing noise pollution. The Noise Pollution (Regulation and Control) Rules have been framed under the EPA to regulate and control noise producing and generating sources. The Noise Pollution Rules prescribe the ambient air quality standards with respect to noise for different areas or zones, including industrial, commercial, residential, and silence zones. These rules also regulate and restrict the use of loudspeakers and public address systems. Noise Pollution (Regulation and Control) Rules, 2000, S. O. No. 123 (E) dated Feb. 14, 2000, *available at* http://moef.nic.in/downloads/public-information/noise-pollution-rules-en.pdf.

38. Manufacture, Storage and Import of Hazardous Chemical Rules, 1989, S. O. No. 966 (E) dated Nov. 27, 1989, *available at* http://www.moef.nic.in/legis/hsm/hsm2.html.

39. The Basel Convention on the Control of Transboundary Movements of Hazardous Wastes and Their Disposal was adopted in 1989, in response to a public outcry following the discovery of deposits of toxic wastes imported from certain developing countries. The overarching objective of the convention is to protect human health and the environment against the adverse effects of hazardous wastes. *See* http://www.basel.int/Home/tabid/2202/mctl/ViewDetails/EventModID/8051/EventID/330/xmid/8052/Default.aspx. The text of the Basel Convention is at http://www.basel.int/Portals/4/Basel%20Convention/docs/text/BaselConventionText-e.pdf.

40. Bio-Medical Waste (Management and Handling) Rules, 1998, S. O. No. 630 (E) dated July 20, 1998, *available at* http://envfor.nic.in/legis/hsm/biomed.html.

41. E-waste (Management and Handling) Rules, 2011S. O. No. 1035 (E) dated May 12, 2011, *available at* http://envfor.nic.in/downloads/rules-and-regulations/1035e_eng.pdf.

42. The MoEF notified the E-Waste Rules under the EPA in May 2011; however, the said rules came into effect only on May 1, 2012.

43. Ozone Depleting Substances (Regulation and Control) Rules, 2000, [S O. No. 670 (E)] dated July 19, 2000, *available at* http://www.moef.nic.in/legis/ods/odsrcr.html.

44. The Montreal Protocol on Substances That Deplete the Ozone Layer was designed to reduce the production and consumption of ozone-depleting substances in order to reduce their abundance in the atmosphere, and thereby protect the Earth's fragile ozone layer. The original protocol was signed on September 16, 1987 and entered into force on January 1, 1989. *See* http://ozone.unep.org/new_site/en/montreal_protocol.php.

45. Manufacture, Use, Import, Export and Storage of Hazardous Micro-Organisms Genetically Engineered Organisms or Cells Rules, 1989, G.S.R. 1037 (E) dated Dec. 5, 1989, *available at* http://www.moef.nic.in/legis/hsm/hsm3.html.

46. Batteries (Management and Handling) Rules, 2001, S. O. No. 432(E) dated May 16, 2001, *available at* http://www.envfor.nic.in/legis/hsm/leadbat.html.

47. Central Motor Vehicles Rules, 1989 [G.S.R. 590 (E), dated June 2, 1989], *available at* http://www.tn.gov.in/sta/cmvr1989.pdf. The Central Motor Vehicles Rules regulate batteries fluid (alkali), batteries wet (filled with acid), batteries wet (filled with alkali), batteries wet (nonspillable), batteries containing sodium or cells containing sodium, batteries dry (containing solid potassium hydroxide).

48. The Eco-mark scheme was issued in 1991 to provide accreditation and labeling for household and other consumer products that meet certain environmental criteria along with quality requirements for that product. The eco-mark identifies environment-friendly products that are made, used, or disposed of in a way that significantly reduces the harm the products would otherwise cause the environment. For more information, refer to http://www.cpcb.nic.in/scheme_eco.php.

49. Absolute liability and strict liability are similar in some ways. The principle of strict liability is based on the premise that if a person brings on his lands and collects and keeps there anything likely to do mischief if it escapes, he must keep it at his peril, and, if he does not do so, he is prima facie answerable for all the damage that is the natural consequence of its escape. However, such a person can be excused by showing that the escape was not owing to any act or omission on his part or was the consequence of vis major, or an act of god. The underlying rationale for absolute liability is the same as for strict liability; however, the principle of absolute liability does not provide any exemptions from liability for no fault or for an act of god. The Supreme Court of India conceived the absolute liability principle in the famous case of *M.C. Metha v. Union of India,* also known as the Oleum gas leakage case [(1987) 1 S.C.C. 395], by enlarging the scope of strict liability principle. The components of absolute liability may be identified as follows:

1. It applies to an enterprise that is engaged in inherently dangerous or hazardous activity;
2. The duty of care is absolute;
3. The exception to the strict liability developed in *Ryland v. Fletcher* is not applicable;
4. The larger and the greater the industry, the greater the compensation payable should be.

50. Indian Council for Enviro-Legal v. Union of India, A.I.R. 1996 S.C.W. 1069.

51. M.C. Mehta v. Union of India (1987 A.I.R. 1086, 1987 S.C.R. (1) 819).

52. The Merchant Shipping (Prevention of Pollution by Oil from Ships) Rules, 2010.

53. Indian Forest Act, 1927 (Act 16 of 1927), *available at* http://envfor.nic.in/legis/forest/forest4.html.

54. Forest (Conservation) Act, 1980, [Act 69 of 1980], *available at* http://www.moef.nic.in/legis/forest/forest2.html.

55. Forest (Conservation) Rules, 2003, [G.S.R. 23 (E) dated Jan. 10, 2003], *available at* http://www.envfor.nic.in/legis/forest/gsr23%28e%29.pdf.

56. Scheduled Tribes and Other Traditional Forest Dwellers (Recognition of Forest Rights) Act, 2006 [Act 2 of 2007], *available at* http://tribal.nic.in/writereaddata/mainlinkFile/File1033.pdf.

57. Coastal Regulation Zone Notification, 2011, Notification dated Jan. 6, 2011, *available at* http://moef.nic.in/assets/so19e.pdf/.

58. Island Protection Zone Notification, 2011, [S.O.20 (E) dated Jan. 6, 2011, *available at* http://lakshadweep.nic.in/documents/SnT_Notice/Annexures/Annexure_4.pdf.

59. Wildlife (Protection) Act, 1972, [Act 53 of 1972], *available at* http://www.moef.nic.in/legis/wildlife/wildlife1c1.html.

60. Biological Diversity Act, 2002, [Act 18 of 2003], *available at* http://www.moef.nic.in/divisions/csurv/nba_act.htm.

61. Gov't of India, Ministry of Envt. & Forests, Biodiversity, http://moef.nic.in/division/biodiversity (last visited Jan. 28, 2013).

62. Environment Impact Assessment Notification, 2006, [S.O. 1533 (E), Sept. 14, 2006], *available at* http://envfor.nic.in/legis/eia/so1533.pdf.

63. *See* M.C. Mehta v. Kamal Nath (1997) 1 S.C.C. 388 and MI Builders Pvt. Ltd. v. Radhey Shyam Sahu, A.I.R. 1996 S.C. 2468, upholding the public trust doctrine.

64. *See* A.I.R. 1980 S.C. 1622.

65. *See id.*

66. National Green Tribunal Act, 2010 (Act 19 of 2010), *available at* http://envfor.nic.in/downloads/public-information/NGT-fin.pdf.

67. Mumbai Kamgar Sabha v. Abdulbhai, A.I.R. 1976 S.C. 1455; Fertilizer Corp. Kamgar Union v. Union of India, A.I.R. 1981 S.C. 344.

68. Bangalore Med. Trust v. B.S. Muddappa, (1991) 4 S.C.C. 54.

69. Vellore Citizens Welfare Forum v. UOI, A.I.R. 1996 S.C. 2718, Narmada Bachao Andolan v. UOI, A.I.R. 2000 S.C. 375.

70. Vellore Citizens Welfare Forum v. UOI, A.I.R. 1996 S.C. 2718.

71. *See* M.C. Mehta v. UOI, A.I.R. 1987 S.C. 1086; Narmada Bacho Andolan v. UOI, A.I.R. 2000 S.C. 375.

72. *See* M.C. Mehta v. UOI, A.I.R. 1997 S.C. 734, and State of Himachal Pradesh v. Ganesh Wood Products, A.I.R. 1996 S.C. 149.

CHAPTER 39

Japan

HANA HEINEKEN AND JUTA WADA*

I. The Japanese Environmental Law Framework

From the postwar period of the 1950s to the era of rapid growth in the mid-1960s, Japan's serious problems with pollution provided the impetus for the development of key environmental statutes. The most notable cases included (1) the first Minamata disease incident, caused by mercury poisoning in the Minamata Bay of Kumamoto Prefecture; (2) the second Minamata disease incident, caused by mercury poisoning in the Agano River of Niigata Prefecture; (3) the Yokkaichi Asthma incident, caused by sulfur oxide pollution in Yokkaichi city of Mie Prefecture; and (4) the Itai-itai disease incident, caused by cadmium poisoning in Toyama Prefecture. The Basic Environmental Law for Environmental Pollution Control (1967) was established in order to systemically and comprehensively confront these problems.

In the 1980s and 1990s, other problems emerged having to do with quality of life and the urban environment, the protection of nature, hazardous waste management, and global environmental issues such as climate change and marine pollution. The need to address these issues prompted the enactment of the Basic Environmental Law (1993).[1]

A. The Basic Environmental Law

The Basic Environmental Law is the foundation of Japanese environmental policy. Its ultimate purpose is "to ensure healthy and cultured living for both present and future generations of the nation as well as to contribute to the welfare of mankind."[2] It is based on the following principles: "enjoyment and future success of environmental blessings,"[3] "creation of a society ensuring sustainable development with reduced environmental load,"[4] and "active promotion of global environmental conservation through international cooperation."[5]

---

*The authors would like to recognize and thank the following individuals for contributing to the writing of this chapter: Takaaki Kagohashi, Masato Yoshida, Shiho Masumoto, Satoshi Kojima, Natsumi Kimura, Natsuki Taira, Akihito Kubota, Takashi Mori, Yukiji Okazaki, Ayako Ichino, Akihiro Shima, and Sayaka Gohara.

In order to achieve the above goal and principles, the government is required to establish a Basic Environmental Plan as a roadmap for comprehensive and systematic environmental policy[6] and Environmental Quality Standards consisting of numeric targets.[7] Moreover, as a means to achieve the Basic Environmental Plan and Environmental Quality Standards, the Basic Environmental Law stipulates, inter alia, the promotion of environmental impact assessments;[8] the introduction of economic measures;[9] the promotion of use of recycled resources and other materials, products, and services that contribute to the reduction of environmental impacts;[10] education and learning on environmental conservation;[11] and the provision of information.[12]

Although the Basic Environmental Law is an important law that serves as a guideline for Japanese environmental policies, it does not clearly stipulate the right to enjoy a healthy environment, and includes many aspirational goals that lack legally enforceable standards.

B.   Key Environmental Actors

The code of conduct in the environmental sector is largely established by specific environmental laws enacted by the Japanese legislature, the National Diet. However, the majority of laws in Japan are based in large part on bills prepared by the administrative branch (the Cabinet Office and various government ministries and agencies), and results in an administrative branch with considerable influence over Japanese environmental law.

The laws typically stipulate the respective competent authorities, and each governmental ministry or agency decides on the necessary administrative orders or regulations (ordinances) based on the law, and implements the relevant provisions. The Ministry of Environment (MoE) is responsible for global environmental protection, pollution prevention, nature conservation and maintenance, and other planning for environmental protection.[13] The MoE, however, does not have sole jurisdiction over all environmental laws. Other ministries such as the Ministry of Agriculture, Forestry and Fisheries (MAFF);[14] the Ministry of Economy Trade and Industry (METI); and the Ministry for Land, Infrastructure and Transport, and Tourism (MLIT) may also have jurisdiction.

Government ordinances, ministerial ordinances, and notices are important in the implementation of environmental law. Ordinances are administrative orders or regulations promulgated by the Cabinet Office (government) or by particular government ministries or agencies (ministerial). Provided that there exists a legal mandate, such ordinances have the force of law. Separately, notices are explanations given from a higher-level administrative agency to a lower-level agency, providing guidance on the interpretation of ordinances. Notices are not binding on citizens. That said, in practice they serve as an important guide, due to the fact that lower-level administrative offices must abide by them[15] and the judiciary tends not to provide an effective check on the administrative branch, as explained below. Licensing and other approval systems are also important mechanisms for environmental regulation, and are used most extensively in property development (e.g., in changes to the land character).[16]

Local governments play an important role in implementation by adopting individualized regulations and administering the law. For example, under the Water Pollution Control Law (1970), the national government, namely the MoE, decides the national environmental standards and effluent standards.[17] Local governments, while ensuring that such standards are upheld, can enact stricter emission standards than those of the national government[18] as well as regulate additional pollutant substances not subject to national government regulation.[19]

Among non-state actors, businesses wield significant influence on lawmaking and implementation, while the role of environmental non-governmental organizations (NGOs) is limited. One of the key corporate actors is the Japan Business Federation (Nippon Keidanren), which consists of over 1,200 notable corporations. As a group representing the interests of large corporations, it sends people to various governmental councils, and exercises a substantial influence on legislative and administrative processes. Within Nippon Keidanren, policy committees dealing with environmental issues include committees on (1) environment and safety, (2) nature conservation, and (3) energy and resources.

Numerous environmental NGOs are active in Japan and engage in activities such as educating ordinary citizens. Some environmental NGO members serve on governmental councils. However, in such councils, the number of members representing the interests of the for-profit sector tends to be greater than the number of members representing NGOs.

II. Air and Climate Change
A. Air Pollution Control

The Air Pollution Control Law (1968)[20] aims to provide protection for people's health from air pollution, preserve the living environment, and protect those victimized by air pollution by demanding liability for damages from responsible emitters.[21] Under this law, emission standards are established by type and scale of the facility and by type of pollutant for air pollutant particles that are emitted from stationary sources (factories and business sites). This includes soot, volatile organic compounds, or fine particulate matter. This statute enforces compliance with its emissions standards by permitting the government to issue an improvement order to an emitter whose continued emissions pose a risk of violation, or an order of suspension or modification of plans to those facilities at risk of violation. The law also authorizes site inspections, notification for the establishment of facilities that emit soot or other pollutants, and a requirement that emitters measure the concentration of their pollutants. Where there is a violation of these regulations, penalties may apply.

Mobile sources are subject to the Law Concerning Special Measures for Total Emission Reduction of Nitrogen Oxides from Automobiles in Specified

Areas (1992)[22] (NO$_x$-PM Law). This law was established with the aim of (1) controlling the emission of nitrogen oxides and other air pollutants from automobiles; (2) clarifying the responsibilities of the national and regional governments, businesses, and ordinary citizens; and (3) with respect to specific areas where pollution is significant, securing environmental standards on air pollution resulting from nitrogen dioxide and suspended particulate matter.

While nitrogen oxide and other emissions from stationary sources have decreased as a result of laws such as the Air Pollution Control Law, nitrogen oxide and other emissions from mobile sources, particularly automobiles, have not decreased and are fairly high in the areas around large cities. The NO$_x$-PM Law, therefore, is vital in that it requires certain operators beyond a given size to draft, submit, and report to the prefectural governor their implementation plans for reducing automobile emissions of nitrogen oxide. It also empowers the prefectural governor to provide guidance and advice, or recommendations and orders on necessary measures. For some automobiles, a permissible limit is established for automobile nitrogen oxide emissions. This is intended to encourage a switch from diesel-powered to gasoline-powered cars. Areas with a high concentration of automobile traffic such as Tokyo, Osaka, and Nagoya are the main targets.

The Law Concerning Special Measures against Dioxins (1999)[23] (Dioxin Law) aims to protect human health by preventing and eliminating environmental pollution from dioxins. Earnest efforts to address dioxin began in 1997, with a focus on waste incinerators, but after a serious incident of vegetable dioxin contamination in the city of Tokorozawa, Saitama Prefecture, efforts expanded to residential and other daily use areas.

The established emissions controls on dioxins apply to waste incineration facilities and other specific facilities. Under the Dioxin Law, the basic standard for dioxin policy is total daily intake, and the environmental standards for dioxin pollution of the air, water, and soil are established on this basis. This law requires notification for construction of new facilities, which is subject to orders for plan modification, and also prescribes improvement orders against operators at risk of violating the emission and total emission control standards. Where such requirements are violated, penalties may be assessed. Prefectures are empowered to impose stricter standards than the national law.

Lastly, the Pollution-Related Health Damage Compensation Law (1973) was enacted to provide victims swift and fair protection and secure their health by providing restitution for health damages caused by significant air or water pollution, pollution-related health welfare programs, and activities to prevent health damages caused by air pollution. The system for pollution-related health damage compensation is funded by a charge on all domestic entities that can potentially cause air pollution. Under this system, public institutions certify pollution-related disease through a simple procedure, and provide relief to victims in a swift and reliable manner. Besides the actual expense of medical fees, compensation also takes into account lost profits and consolation.

The law divides victims by location into two categories: Category 1 Areas, in which significant air pollution occurs over a considerable range, giving rise to nonspecific diseases (e.g., chronic bronchitis and bronchial asthma), and Category 2 Areas, in which significant air or water pollution takes place over a considerable range, causing specific diseases (i.e., a pollution-related disease with a specific substance the causal relationship of which to the disease is clear). The Minamata and Itai-itai disease events fall into the latter category. In Category 1 areas, in order to provide expedited relief, individual certification of a causal relationship is not necessary for compensation, and the prefectural governor may give authorization if confirmed that the individual lived or worked in the designated area over a certain period.

B.   Climate Change

The Law Concerning the Promotion of Measures to Cope with Global Warming (1998)[24] was established as a framework to address climate change. It requires the national government, local governments, businesses, and citizens to work together to ensure that Japan meets its commitments under the Kyoto Protocol to the U.N. Framework Convention on Climate Change (UNFCCC), adopted at the Third Conference of Parties to the UNFCCC, to reduce greenhouse gas (GHG) emissions to 6 percent below 1990 levels.

Concretely, the national government is required to draw up a Kyoto Protocol Target Achievement Plan and National Government Action Plan, and local governments are required to decide on policies to mitigate GHG emissions. Under this law, businesses emitting large quantities of GHGs are required to calculate their emissions and report that data to the government, while the government is obligated to record, tally, and publish such data to the general public.

The Act on Special Measures Concerning the Procurement of Renewable Energy by Operators of Electric Utilities (2011) (Feed-in Tariff Law) was established to set up a feed-in-tariff system for renewable energy. It took effect on July 1, 2012, and requires electric utility operators to purchase electricity that is generated from a renewable source (solar, wind, hydro, geothermal, biomass) at a fixed price over a specific period. The cost of purchasing the renewable energy is ultimately borne by the consumer and businesses.

Based on this system, the supplier of renewable energy is guaranteed steady high revenue for a certain duration. In Germany and Spain, which have already introduced this system, the popular use of renewable energy spread rapidly. In Japan, it is expected to serve as the trigger for popularizing renewable energy.

The Law Concerning the Rational Use of Energy (1979)[25] (Energy Conservation Law) aims to ensure the effective use of fuel sources and the rational use of energy. It addresses the mechanism to rationalize energy use in factories and plants as well as energy standards for automobiles and home electronics.

Concretely, factories and plants of a certain scale are required to report to the government the creation of an energy efficiency plan and the amount of decrease in energy consumption. Where the rationalization of energy use is noticeably inadequate, they may be subject to publication, orders, or penalties. Moreover, owners of buildings that are over a certain size are required to notify the administrative agency of anything related to energy efficiency measures before new construction or extension and structural alteration of a building.

With respect to home electronics, the Law takes the most energy-efficient product as the standard, and sets the regulation value on that basis. Where performance does not meet this standard, the government is authorized to provide recommendations, issue orders, publicize, or assess penalties as necessary.

In Japan, existing carbon credit trading schemes include Japan's Voluntary Emissions Trading Scheme (2005) introduced by the MoE; an Experimental Introduction of an Integrated Domestic Market for Emissions Trading (2008); and a city-wide Emissions Trading System (2008) (Tokyo ETS), established by reform of an environmental protection ordinance of the Tokyo Metropolitan Government.

Most notable among these is the Tokyo ETS, which was introduced along with the obligation to reduce total GHG emissions. Plants that annually use energy equivalent to more than 1,500 kiloliters of oil are required to comply with the emissions reduction obligations; violations can result in advice and publication. Target businesses must ensure that they are reducing emissions on their own, or fulfilling the requirement through the emissions trading system or credit system. The Tokyo ETS system differs from the other two mentioned above in that all relevant plants must comply with the emissions reduction requirement.

III.   Water

The Water Pollution Control Law (1970) (WPCL)[26] aims to regulate effluents such as discharges of water into public water bodies and penetration into groundwater from specified factories at which a specified facility has been installed. Moreover, for water pollution discharged by factories and establishments, it aims to provide protection to victims where harm to human health occurs.

Effluent standards are established in order to prevent pollution of water quality. For water bodies where compliance with effluent standards are recognized as insufficient to prevent water pollution (for example, Tokyo Bay or the Inland Sea of Japan), total pollutant load control systems are established. Moreover, under this law, local governments may by ordinance impose stricter effluent standards or increase the types of items or factories subject to the law. Those who violate the effluent standard can be subject to penalties.

The WPCL is the core environmental law in Japan for preventing ocean pollution. Government ordinances or ministerial ordinances provide specific emissions standards, as well as technology standards for ships. These ordinances require the use of equipment to ensure the control of oil, hazardous liquid, and waste discharges into the ocean.

IV. Handling, Treatment, Transportation, and Disposal of Hazardous Materials

The Law Concerning the Evaluation of Chemical Substances and Regulation of Their Manufacture, etc. (1973)[27] (Chemical Substances Control Law) was established in response to environmental pollution problems caused by polychlorinated biphenyls (PCBs), and has been revised several times thereafter. The Chemical Substances Control Law requires businesses to provide notification prior to the manufacture or import of new chemical substances. Before such substances enter the consumer market, the national government must inspect its environmental persistence and safety. Various controls such as a permitting system apply depending on the nature of the chemical substance and how it is handled.

The Waste Management and Public Cleansing Law (1970)[28] establishes the definition of waste, who is responsible for disposal, and the standards for waste management methods, waste management facilities, and waste management services. It aims to conserve the environment and improve public sanitation by restraining the discharge of waste and managing it appropriately.

Under the statute, industrial and general waste are subject to different treatment. Businesses discharging the waste are responsible for managing industrial waste, while the local government is responsible for managing general waste. It also sets permitting standards for entities engaged in managing industrial waste or building industrial waste management facilities. In the application process for permission to build a waste management facility, businesses are required to conduct an assessment. In addition, where businesses are contracted with a third party to transport or dispose of the industrial waste, the law requires the use of a manifest system[29] to track the flow of the waste until its final disposal.

Japan has also enacted legislation to implement its obligations under the Basel Convention on the Control of the Transboundary Movements of Hazardous Waste and Their Disposal (1989) (Basel Convention). The Law for the Control of Export, Import and Others of Specified Hazardous Wastes and Other Wastes (1992)[30] establishes a prior approval system for the import or export of specific hazardous wastes and other wastes. Where such provisions are violated, the person engaged in the import or export may be issued an administrative order.

After 1995, Japan adopted various specific laws to promote recycling of packages, home appliances, and cars. These specific laws shifted the responsibility formerly held by the local government to collect and manage the waste to the manufacturer, to take back or remanufacture the waste.

In 2000, in parallel with the establishment of the Law Promoting a Sound Material-Cycle Society, the Law for the Promotion of Effective Utilization of Resources[31] was passed. In addition to strengthening Japan's specific law on recycling, it also introduced measures for reuse and reduction. In the same year, specific laws were also established for construction materials and food recycling.

Lastly, the Law on Confirmation, etc. of Release Amounts of Specific Chemical Substances in the Environment and Promotion of Improvements to the Management Thereof (1999)[32] (PRTR Law) aims to prevent chemical substances from hindering environmental conservation by understanding the amount of hazardous chemical substances discharged into the environment, and thereby promoting voluntary improvements in management of chemical substances by businesses that handle chemical substances.

Chemical substances covered by this statute include those with properties that could be harmful to human health or the ecosystem, and they are divided into two classes depending, in part, on the amount present in the environment. For the most part, Class 1 chemical substances are subject to the law. Moreover, when a business that uses designated chemical substances transfers or provides to another business a designated chemical substance that includes both Class 1 and 2 chemical substances, it is required to submit to that business information on the properties and handling of the chemical substance. This information is incorporated into what are known as material safety data sheets.

V. Waste and Site Remediation

The Basic Act for Establishing a Sound Material-Cycle Society (2000) (Waste Law)[33] is the primary law regulating the waste and recycling sectors. It was enacted following the Basic Environmental Law, and sets forth the fundamental approach to waste management and recycling.

The Waste Law defines a sound material-cycle society as one where waste generation is restrained, recycled materials are used appropriately, materials that cannot be reused or recycled are disposed of appropriately, the consumption of natural resources is limited, and the burden on the environment is reduced as much as possible. Furthermore, this law establishes the fundamental principles for a sound material-cycle society, and the responsibilities of the national government, local governments, businesses, and citizens.

The Law Concerning the Promotion of Procurement of Eco-Friendly Goods and Services by the State and Other Entities (2000)[34] (Green Purchasing Law) was passed as a more specific law in the wake of the Waste Law. The Green Purchasing Law requires the national government and other public entities to take the lead in promoting the use of eco-friendly goods (goods and services that contribute to reducing the impact on the environment). It also promotes the dissemination of appropriate information on eco-friendly goods. It thereby seeks to shift demand and promote sustainable development patterns. Under the Green Purchasing Law, the national government is required to decide on a basic policy and to draft and implement a procurement policy in conformity with that basic policy. Local governments are required to make an effort to draft a procurement policy and use eco-friendly goods, and the private sector is encouraged to make similar efforts whenever possible.

In terms of waste site remediation, in 2002, the Soil Contamination Countermeasures Law[35] was established to prevent human health impacts caused by the neglect of soil contamination at work sites where hazardous substances are handled. The law requires that the landowner report the results of its inspection of soil contamination by specified hazardous substances to the prefectural governor for (1) land used as a site for a plant or workplace for an abolished specified facility using hazardous substances; (2) land at risk of soil contamination, where changes are made to its character; and (3) land recognized by the prefectural governor as at risk of causing harm to human health as a result of soil contamination. Land that is designated by this law is entered into the Designated Area Register.[36] As a general rule, that register is made public.[37]

Under this statute, where it is determined that the soil contamination in a designated area poses a risk of causing harm to human health, the landowner or polluter is ordered to remove the contamination. Furthermore, changes to the character of such land are restricted.

VI. Emergency Response
A. Nuclear Power Incidents

In 1999, the critical accident of the JCO Uranium fuel processing plant in Ibaraki Prefecture, Tokai village, led to a discussion on the need to strengthen nuclear power disaster prevention. The Law on Special Measures Concerning Nuclear Emergency Preparedness (1999)[38] was enacted shortly thereafter. This law authorizes the prime minister to exercise emergency powers upon the declaration of a nuclear power emergency situation, in order to be able to take direct command over not only the national government but also local governments and nuclear power businesses. Such a declaration also enables the prime minister to take measures to prevent the effects of any disaster from becoming more widespread and order evacuations.

The Act on Compensation for Nuclear Damage (1961)[39] was established to provide relief to victims of nuclear damage caused by the operation of a nuclear reactor, including power generation, nuclear fuel production, and reprocessing. Entities owning and operating nuclear power facilities must obtain liability insurance. The maximum compensation from the insurance is 120 billion yen per business. Where damages exceed this limit, and the nuclear power business cannot pay the full amount of the compensation with its own funds, the national government covers the shortfall. Other than the responsible party, which bears indemnification liability, no person shoulders any responsibility. This concept is known as channeled liability. Businesses that supplied equipment to the responsible nuclear power business are exempt from responsibility for compensating victims.

As a result of the earthquake and nuclear disaster of March 2011, described next, a new Nuclear Regulation Authority (NRA) was formed as an affiliate of the MoE under Article 3(2) of the National Government Organization Law, a so-called Article 3 Commission. It has considerable independence from the Cabinet Office. The NRA consists of a chair and four members appointed by the prime minister following approval by both houses of legislature. Individuals who are employers or employees of nuclear power businesses are not permitted to sit on the NRA.

On March 11, 2011, at 130km offshore of Miyagi Prefecture, the Great East Japan Earthquake occurred at a magnitude of 9.0. Approximately one hour later, the Tokyo Electric Power Company (TEPCO) Fukushima Number 1 Nuclear Power Plant was hit by a tsunami of 14 to 15 meters high and completely lost power. The nuclear reactor could not be cooled and two reactors experienced meltdowns. This led to hydrogen being released in large quantities and eventually to a hydrogen explosion, which in turn resulted in a severe nuclear accident.[40] An estimated 160,000 people fled from Fukushima Prefecture. According to the Reconstruction Agency, 58,608 people were still taking refuge outside of the prefecture as of November 1, 2012. Based on Article 18 of the Act on Compensation for Nuclear Damage, a Dispute Reconciliation Committee for Nuclear Damage Compensation was established, under which a Center for Resolving Disputes over Nuclear Damage Compensation was created. Mediation of a settlement has, however, met resistance from the electric power industries, and has not proceeded as expected. As of August 23, 2013, over two years after the accident, 601,000 cases out of 1,968,000 filed had been settled.[41]

B.   Oil Spills

The Law relating to the Prevention of Marine Pollution and Maritime Disaster (1970) was established to regulate the discharge of oil from ships. It was later amended to ensure the effectiveness of measures to clean up discharged oil and put in place provisions to prevent maritime disasters. The law is frequently revised to be consistent with the situation of domestic ocean pollution and international efforts to prevent ocean pollution.

The Law for Reparation and Compensation of Damage by Oil Pollution (1975) (Oil Pollution Statute) was established to implement domestically the International Convention on the Establishment of an International Fund for Compensation for Oil Pollution Damage (1971) (Oil Pollution Damages Convention). This statute provides for the indemnification for damages suffered by individuals and in some cases liability for vessel owners, where oil pollution occurs.

The Oil Pollution Damages Convention addresses accidents by tankers. Owing to the frequency of shipwrecks by nontanker vessels, the Oil Pollution Statute was revised in 2004 to also regulate liability for damages and indemnity contracts for the discharge of bunker fuel from nontanker ships. Moreover, based on this law, ocean-going vessels are required to hold protection and indemnity insurance, and uninsured ships are prevented from entering Japanese ports.

VII.   Natural Resource Management and Protection

Japan has enacted a number of laws governing natural resource management and protection.[42] The Natural Parks Law (1957) was established to protect places of natural scenic beauty and promote their utilization. These objectives were expanded to include contribution to the conservation and sustainable use of biodiversity.[43] Outstanding landscapes are designated as a national park, a quasi-national park, or a prefectural natural park. In Japan, these natural parks take up a total of 5,430,000 hectares, 14.3 percent of the total land area in Japan (as of June 1, 2012).

National and local government-owned lands as well as privately owned lands are considered for the designation as natural parks. This differs from public parks in countries such as the United States or Canada, where the state gains the right to own or use the designated land and manage it accordingly. Because in Japan the national and prefectural government can designate privately owned land without owning it, it is possible to designate a wider area of land as a natural park. However, this also makes it more difficult to impose significant restraints on human activities in such areas. Under the law, zoning is done according to the need for protecting the natural environment. For areas with a greater need for protection, stronger controls on activities are put in place, thereby protecting the natural environment.

Because the aim of the Natural Parks Law is to protect outstanding landscapes, it can exclude natural areas that are critical from the perspective of nature conservation or science even if they are not valued for their scenery. Moreover, this law tends to increase the use of the land, which can lead to environmental destruction as a result of promoting industrial activities. As such, a key concern is to achieve the balance between environmental protection and industrial activity.

Similar to the Natural Parks Law, the Nature Conservation Law (1972) (NCL) was established to designate areas, and by controlling activities within those areas, conserving the environment. However, unlike the Natural Parks Law, the NCL aims to conserve only those areas that embody significant wilderness values, or areas exhibiting natural features that are rare, critical, vulnerable, and difficult to reproduce, and of high scientific value. Because the NCL's aim differs from that of the Natural Parks Law, an area designated as a natural park cannot also be protected under this law.

Based on the character of the area and the necessity for nature conservation, the land is designated as either "Wildlife Conservation Area," "Nature Conservation Area," or "Prefectural Nature Conservation Area." The NCL controls activities within those areas. In Wildlife Conservation Areas, because the aim is to conserve the wild state of the environments that remain uninfluenced by human activity, the NCL provides strict protection by restricting access to the land. The land area designated as any one of these three conservation areas totals 104,500 hectares (as of March 31, 2011).

Japan's forested area is estimated at roughly 25,100,000 hectares and constitutes two-thirds of the total land area (as of March 31, 2011). Of this, over 40 percent is planted forest. The Forest Law (1951) was established to increase sustainable cultivation of plantations and production of timber. Subsequently, the Basic Forestry Law (1964) was enacted to improve forest management for timber production, and was later amended by the Basic Forest and Forestry Law (2001). The latter statute shifted the primary objective of the law to environmental protection. To prevent environmentally damaging development of forests or deterioration of forests, the Ministry of Agriculture, Forestry and Fisheries (MAFF) and the prefectural governors are charged with drafting individual forestry plans and manage forests systematically and comprehensively based on that plan. The plans are to be drafted with a long-term perspective: the national plan is based on a 15-year term, while the prefectural plan is based on a 10-year term.

Additionally, where the forest's ecosystem services—such as conservation of watersheds, prevention of soil erosion, defense against fires, preservation of public health, and protection of scenic beauty—are in particular demand, the MAFF or the prefectural governor can designate such areas as protected forest. Logging and development activities are controlled in these areas. The area of protected forest is 12,023,000 hectares (as of March 31, 2011), and constitutes roughly 48 percent of the current forested area.

The above-mentioned Green Purchasing Law encourages ministries and public agencies to procure eco-friendly goods, including legally produced forestry products. Since amendment of the Basic Policy on Promoting Green Purchasing in April 2006, the government is required to purchase legally harvested wood and wood products and favor sustainably produced wood products.[44] Specific standards for procurement are outlined in the Guidelines for Verification on Legality and Sustainability of Wood and Wood Products (2006), which is administered by the Forestry Agency. The standards contained in the guidelines are particularly relevant because Japan is a significant importer of tropical timber products. However, the guidelines have been criticized for their limited scope of application, the lack of a due diligence requirement, and overall weak enforcement.[45]

Japanese natural resource law also touches on the protection of wetlands. Japan ratified the Ramsar Convention on Wetlands in 1980. In 2010, 37 of its wetlands had been registered with the Ramsar Secretariat in Gland, Switzerland. In terms of domestic legislation, Japan lacks a statute designed specifically to preserve wetlands. The protection afforded thus far is limited to the designation of a protected area under the Wildlife Protection and Hunting Management Law, mentioned next. As such, the protection of wetlands is limited, and the loss of wetlands as a result, inter alia, of land reclamation development is problematic.

Recently, the following case has increased recognition of the important place of wetlands in ecosystems and awareness of the need to protect them.

In 1997, the government initiated land reclamation activities in Isahaya Bay, enclosing roughly 3,500 hectares of tidal flats with floodgates, and damaging the ecosystem in the tidal land. The damage extended beyond Isahaya Bay to the nearby Ariake Sea, recurrent harmful algal bloom, or "red tide," occurred and resulted in significant problems. These included impacts on seaweed cultivation and decreases in the volume of the seafood caught. Accordingly, fishermen living in the area and others filed a lawsuit to stop the reclamation activities of Isahaya Bay and to demand the opening of the floodgates. In 2010, the Fukuoka High Court recognized the causal relationship between the closing of the floodgates and the damage to the fishing activities, and issued a landmark decision requiring the floodgates to remain open for five years to allow for the investigation of the effects of the reclamation activities on the environment.[46]

VIII. Natural Resource Damages

The restoration of natural resources is addressed under several different laws including the Law for the Promotion of Nature Restoration (2002)[47] and the Law for the Conservation of Endangered Species of Wild Fauna and Flora (1992) (CSWFF).[48] The Law for the Promotion of Nature Restoration aims to preserve biodiversity by promoting the participation of and cooperation with the local community, based upon scientific knowledge and the principle of adaptive management. Pursuant to the Law for the Promotion of Nature Restoration, in 2002 the government formulated a basic policy for promoting nature restoration, which included a requirement to devise an overall plan for nature restoration.

Under the CSWFF, the minister of environment is required to draft a national guideline for the conservation of endangered species of wild fauna and flora, including programs to rehabilitate natural habitats and maintain viable populations by, for example, promoting breeding.[49] The provision applies specifically to species that are designated as national endangered species. Further details on this statute are explained in section IX, below.

IX. Protected Species

The Game Law of 1895, the Wildlife Protection and Hunting Law (1918), and a 2002 amendment to the latter establish requirements for the protection of wildlife and biodiversity in Japan. "Wildlife" is defined as including all bird and mammal species that inhabit Japan. Prefectural governors create wildlife protection project plans in conformity with basic guidelines issued by the minister of environment. They are also authorized to adopt measures to carry out their respective plans. The national government provides advice and other assistance so that activities conducted by the prefectural governor can effectively and efficiently be implemented.

The above-mentioned statutes provide controls on the taking of wildlife and bird eggs; breeding and selling; protection and maintenance of habitat based on the designation of wildlife protected areas; and operation of a hunting regulatory system. As a general rule, the taking, collection, and harming of wildlife and bird eggs is prohibited, but may be permitted under certain circumstances and under specified conditions. Certain wildlife and bird eggs specified by order of the MoE generally may not be sold, imported, or exported.

Additionally, the minister of environment or the prefectural governor has the authority to designate areas as Wildlife Protection Areas, Special Wildlife Protection Areas, or Designated Areas for Special Protection if deemed necessary for the protection of wildlife.

In 1992, following Japan's ratification of the Convention on International Trade in Endangered Species of Wild Fauna and Flora (CITES) and the Convention on Biological Diversity (CBD), the government enacted the above-mentioned CSWFF.[50] It aims to preserve a sound natural environment by protecting particular species of wild fauna and flora at risk of extinction domestically and abroad. The statute seeks to protect foreign endangered species designated as "international endangered species" through CITES and the Convention for Protection of Migratory Birds; "national endangered species" as designated from the endangered species listed in the MoE's Red Data Book; and "temporarily designated endangered species" as designated by the MoE, due to the urgent need to provide protection.

In addition, the CSWFF prohibits the hunting, taking, killing, or injuring of national endangered species and temporarily designated endangered species. It is generally prohibited to receive, transfer, or exhibit with the objective of selling or distributing any species included in any of these three categories. The minister of economy, trade, and industry and the minister of environment may require illegally imported endangered species to be returned to the country of export or origin. Moreover, where the minister of environment deems it necessary for the protection of national endangered species, she may designate "habitat protection areas" or conduct protection propagation programs by drawing up plans for such programs.

Fishery activities are principally governed by the Fisheries Law (1949, as revised in 1962). Its aim is the exploitation of fisheries, and not the protection of the environment. Protection for marine life is provided principally by the Act on the Protection of Fishery Resources (1951) as revised in 2007 (PFR) and by the Act on Preservation and Control of Living Marine Resources (1996) (PCLMR). The PFR seeks to protect and cultivate fishery resources, and prohibits or restricts the gathering of aquatic animals and plants (1) using harmful substances, or (2) in protected waters where they spawn, breed, or produce seeds. For its part, the PCLMR seeks to protect living marine resources and promote the fishing industry as well as stability in the supply of marine products. For the allowable catch per amount of fishing effort expended (i.e., labor), the PCLMR stipulates that each prefectural government will decide on guidelines and plans for the protection and management of the resources based on the basic plan drawn up by the national government.

One example of the application of the foregoing authorities occurs in the whaling context. Following the adoption by the International Whaling Commission (IWC) in 1982 of a moratorium on commercial whaling, Japanese commercial whaling in the Antarctic Ocean as well as commercial whaling of minke and sperm whales in the Pacific Ocean halted in 1986 and 1988, respectively. At present, Japan is conducting scientific whaling falling under IWC jurisdiction as well as coastal whaling operations, namely small-scale whaling (including dolphins) that occurs without IWC jurisdiction. However, its activities have been criticized by various governments and NGOs,[51] and its scientific whaling in the Antarctic Ocean has, at times, given rise to disputes with antiwhaling groups. Japan aims to revive the commercial whaling industry on the basis that whales are an important source of food and, like other biotic resources, should be sustainably used based on the best scientific facts; and that there should be a mutual understanding of the eating habits and food culture of respective regions that have developed over time in Japan.

X. Environmental Review and Decision Making

Disclosure of environmental information is encouraged under Article 27 of the Basic Environmental Law. This provision requires the national government to only endeavor to disclose environmental information. For this reason, in order to obtain environmental information, one must demand information using the Information Disclosure Law (1999) or information disclosure ordinances established by each prefecture. Japanese courts, however, are reluctant to require disclosure of some businesses' environmental information that is in the government's possession.[52]

Environmental impact assessments (EIAs) are required under the Environmental Impact Assessment Law (1997)[53] (EIA Law) and may also be required by local government ordinance or the Basic Law on Biodiversity.[54] The EIA Law requires the project proponent to survey and assess the likely impact of the proposed project on the environment. Projects are categorized, based on their scale, into either Class 1 projects that require EIAs or Class 2 projects that may require an EIA. The procedures stipulated in the law include (1) determination of whether the project necessitates an assessment, in the case of Class 2 projects;[55] (2) determination of how the proponent will conduct the assessment;[56] (3) carrying out of the assessment;[57] (4) preparation and disclosure of the Draft EIA;[58] (5) preparation of the EIA by the proponent;[59] and (6) disclosure of the final EIA.[60]

A Class 1 project is defined as "a large-scale project that is designated by government ordinance as likely to have a serious impact on the environment"[61] and must involve (1) road and dam construction, railways, airports, power generating structures, waste disposal sites, reclamation projects, land readjustment projects, new urban residential area development, industrial park development, new urban infrastructure development, distribution business center development, or other projects designated by government ordinance as having an environmental impact over a broad area and requiring an EIA to the same degree as the above projects; and (2) a government action, such as a license or subsidy. Class 2 projects are smaller in scale, but must meet the same criteria as above and be subject to the determination of the permitting/licensing authority on whether to require an EIA. The latter determination is made after any comments are received from the relevant prefectural government.

If a project proponent violates the EIA procedures, it raises a yet undetermined issue as to whether the validity of contracts between private persons may be affected. Moreover, when a proponent violates the EIA procedures, it raises the question of whether it affects the legality or validity of the administrative authority's license or other approval. In this case, the license or other approval is illegal if no EIA was conducted. However, the legal effect is less clear when the EIA was conducted but inadequate.[62]

XI.   Transboundary Pollution

Japan is a party to various international conventions addressing transboundary pollution. These include MARPOL and its Protocol of 1997, the London Dumping Convention 1972 and its Protocol of 1996, the Stockholm Convention on Persistent Organic Pollutants 2001, the Rotterdam Convention on the Prior Informed Consent Procedure for Certain Hazardous Chemicals and Pesticides in International Trade 1998, and Basel Convention on the Control of Transboundary Movements of Hazardous Wastes and Their Disposal 1992. However, Japan is not a party to the Convention on Long-Range Transboundary Air Pollution 1979 nor the Espoo Convention.

XII.   Civil and Criminal Enforcement and Penalties
A.   Government Enforcement authority

The government has, in addition to the authority to enforce by administrative means, the authority to collect information and undertake criminal enforcement. With respect to the collection of information, mechanisms under individual laws demand various notifications. Other notable mechanisms include the requirement to provide notification of the amount of emissions of Class 1 Designated Chemical Substances under the PRTR Law,[63] and the calculation and reporting of GHG emissions under the Law Concerning the Promotion of Measures to Cope with Global Warming.[64] Moreover, under the Air Pollution Control Law[65] or the Water Pollution Control Law,[66] the government can require polluting facilities to report on emissions and can inspect the facility.

Additionally, the requirement to conduct EIAs under the EIA Law[67] and the Waste Management and Public Cleansing Law[68] provide the government with the authority to collect information on activities that have environmental impacts.

Criminal enforcement is exercised through the use of measures such as imprisonment, with or without hard labor, detention, fines, and petty fines. Administrative penalties also include correctional fines.

B.   Civil Liability

Strict liability exists under the Air Pollution Control Law[69] and the Water Pollution Control Law,[70] where the polluter is held strictly liable for health damages caused by specified hazardous substances. The aim is to provide relief for pollution-related harm. Other examples of strict liability are found with respect to soil contamination in warranties against defects[71] and landowner claims against the polluter for the cost of removal of the soil contamination.[72]

Where several businesses jointly cause a pollution incident, each business is jointly and severally liable for the total resulting damages if it satisfies the requirements of Article 719 of the Civil Law Code. In Japan, lender liability does not exist in the area of environmental law, nor are punitive damages recognized by law or by court decision.

C.   The Role of the Environmental Dispute Coordination Commission

With respect to pollution as defined under Article 2(3) of the Basic Environmental Law, where the harm is significant, resolution can be sought through conciliation, mediation, arbitration, or judgment by the Environmental Dispute Coordination Commission. The commission has the authority to judge the liability of the party and the amount of damages, as well as the causal relationship between the harm and an entity's conduct. A judgment as to the latter is not legally binding, but a judgment on damages is deemed final if the defendant does not appeal within 30 days of the judgment.[73] Moreover, the commission can examine evidence and conduct fact-finding.[74]

D.   Citizen Suits and Class Actions

In Japan, citizen suits do not exist. Moreover, in environmental law, group lawsuits are neither recognized as a mechanism nor as legal precedent, and there are no class actions.

E.   Standing

The role of courts is limited by its own narrow definition of standing. For example, in the case of a lawsuit demanding the cancellation of an illegal administrative action, standing is limited to the persons who could benefit under the law by their demand for cancellation of the action.[75] The courts have narrowly interpreted the concept such that only those directly affected by the administrative action have standing.[76] On the other hand, there are cases where the court has interpreted standing fairly liberally.[77]

In terms of administrative suits, the courts tend to give the administrative branch wide discretion in interpreting the law, and unless an egregious error occurred, administrative actions are not judged to be illegal.[78] When coupled with the narrow definition of standing, courts' general deference to administrative branch action shows that the courts do not serve as an effective check on the actions by the administrative branch and allow the administrative offices charged with implementation of environmental law to play a largely unfettered role.

XIII.   General Observations

While this chapter has examined various Japanese environmental laws separately, several common features can be observed.

First, in most cases where conduct is likely to have an impact on the environment, businesses are required to notify the national or local government and obtain a license or other approval. Where such approval is not obtained, the entity will be subject to both direct measures, such as administrative orders or penalties, and indirect measures such as administrative guidance. Administrative guidance entails the government asking the entity to voluntarily modify its conduct. While such guidance lacks force, if not complied with, the entity will in practice no longer be able to receive the government's support, and there are instances where business operations have been delayed as a result.

Second, disclosure is a key means of enforcement. The government will often seek to persuade regulated entities to improve environmental performance by disclosing the business's environmental information, or by forcing a business to disclose information about its environmental performance. This method is used in the Dioxin and PRTR laws. Even where the disclosed information is quantitative and thus neutral, depending on the content of the information, market and popular evaluation of a business can induce a change in behavior.

Third, subsidies or tax measures for environmental protection are often used as economic inducements. For example, in the area of renewable energy, subsidies have been used to advance environmental policy, while taxes have been levied on certain environmentally harmful activities, such as cars and the use of fossil fuels.[79]

Lastly, environmental dispute resolution through the courts can often be difficult. Once an environmental or pollution incident occurs, it is typical for the victim to file a claim against the business for an injunction based on personal rights, or for damages based on responsibility for the illegal act under civil law. In addition, where an administrative action is challenged due to its illegality, the law recognizes an action for its revocation. However, as mentioned above, it is very difficult for citizens to seek protection of the environment through the courts due to (1) the narrow definition of standing; (2) the absence of citizen suits, group actions, or class actions; and (3) the considerable discretion afforded to the government by the courts.

As shown by this analysis, environmental laws are well developed in Japan, but it is important to keep these features in mind as one addresses legal issues concerning the environment.

Notes

1. Law No. 91 of 1993, *available at* http://www.env.go.jp/en/laws/policy/basic/index.html (last visited Nov. 24, 2012).
2. Basic Environmental Law art. 1.
3. *Id.* art. 3.
4. *Id.* art. 4.
5. *Id.* art. 5.
6. *Id.* art. 15.
7. *Id.* art. 16.
8. *Id.* art. 20.
9. *Id.* art. 22.
10. *Id.* art. 24.
11. *Id.* art. 25.
12. *Id.* art. 27.
13. Act for Establishment of the Ministry of the Environment art. 3.
14. As an example of forestry laws, the MAFF has the authority to decide the national forestry plan in consultation with the environment minister in this process. Forest Law art. 4.
15. National Government Organization Act art. 14.2.
16. *See, e.g.,* the development permitting system under the City Planning Law art.29.
17. Basic Environmental Law art. 16; Water Pollution Control Law art. 3.
18. Water Pollution Control Law art. 3.
19. *Id.* art. 29.
20. Law No. 97 of 1968, *available at* http://www.env.go.jp/en/laws/air/air/alch.html#ch2 (last visited Nov. 24, 2012).
21. Discussion of natural resource damage law is contained in sections II and III of this chapter.
22. Law No. 70 of 1992, *available at* http://www.env.go.jp/en/laws/air/amobile.html (last visited Feb. 1, 2013).
23. Law No. 105 of 1999, *available at* https://www.env.go.jp/en/laws/chemi/dioxin.pdf (last visited Feb. 1, 2013).
24. Law No. 117 of 1998, *available at* http://www.env.go.jp/en/laws/global/warming.html (last visited Feb. 1, 2013).
25. Law No. 49 of 1979, *available at* http://www.eccj.or.jp/law/revised/10aug2005.pdf (last visited Feb. 1, 2013).
26. Law No. 138 of 1970, *available at* http://www.env.go.jp/en/laws/water/wlaw/index.html (last visited Nov. 24, 2012).
27. Law No. 117 of 1973, *available at* http://www.meti.go.jp/english/policy/mono_info_service/kagaku/chemical_substances/downloadfiles/cChemicalControl.pdf (last visited Feb. 1, 2013).
28. Law No. 137 of 1970, *available at* http://www.env.go.jp/en/laws/recycle/01.pdf (last visited Feb. 1, 2013).

29. *Id.* art. 12-3.

30. Law No. 108 of 1992, *available at* http://www.env.go.jp/en/laws/recycle/13.pdf (last visited Feb. 1, 2013).

31. Law No. 48 of 1991, *available at* http://www.meti.go.jp/english/information /data/cReEffectLe.pdf (last visited Feb. 1, 2013).

32. Law No. 86 of 1999, *available at* http://www.meti.go.jp/policy/chemical _management/english/files/actPRTR.pdf (last visited Dec. 5, 2012).

33. Law No. 110 of 2000, *available at* http://www.env.go.jp/en/laws/recycle/12.pdf (last visited Feb. 1, 2013).

34. Law No. 100 of 2000, *available at* http://www.env.go.jp/en/laws/policy/green /index.html (last visited Nov. 24, 2012).

35. Law No. 53 of 2002, *available at* http://www.env.go.jp/en/laws/water/sccact .pdf (last visited Feb. 1, 2013).

36. *Id.* art. 6(1).

37. *Id.* art. 6(2).

38. Law No. 156 of 1999, *available at* http://www.nsr.go.jp/archive/nisa/english /resources/legislativeframework/files/EmergencyPreparedness.pdf (last visited Feb. 1, 2013).

39. Law No. 147 of 161, *available at* http://www.oecd-nea.org/law/legislation /japan-docs/Japan-Nuclear-Damage-Compensation-Act.pdf (last visited Feb. 1, 2013).

40. The incident was a Level 7 nuclear accident on the International Atomic Energy Agency's International Nuclear and Radiological Event Scale.

41. *See* http://www.tepco.co.jp/comp/jisseki/index-j.html (last visited Aug. 31, 2013).

42. Japanese law also enables certain government entities to protect landscapes. The Landscapes Act (2004) is intended to promote the preservation and formation of good landscapes. Law No. 110 of 2004, *available at* http://www.mlit.go.jp/crd/townscape/keikan /pdf/landscapeact.pdf (last visited Feb. 1, 2013). In order to do so, it provides planning authority to landscape administration entities (prefecture; city designated by ordinance; core city; and cities, towns, and village that have the consent of the prefectural governor). The concept of a "good landscape" is not clear, and based on the environmental, historical, and cultural background, that landscape can differ by area. Therefore, it is necessary that each area agree on which "good landscape" should be protected. In the planning process, the law requires public hearings and explanatory briefings to ensure that resident opinions are taken into account. Moreover, in the drafting of a landscape plan, the law allows residents to make proposals on drafting and revising the plan (art. 11). Under this law, if construction within a landscape plan area does not abide by the restrictions stipulated in the landscape plan, the head of the landscape administration entity can issue a recommendation of change (art. 16(3)). If the building design and color do not conform to the landscape plan, a coercive measure in the form of a modification order can be issued, though it is limited to the building's form and design (art. 17(1)).

43. *Id.* art. 1.

44. *See, e.g.,* http://www.goho-wood.jp/world/outline/policy.html.

45. *See, e.g.,* FEDERICO LOPEZ-CASERO & HENRY SCHEYVENS, INST. FOR GLOBAL ENVTL. STRATEGIES (IGES), PUBLIC PROCUREMENT POLICIES FOR LEGAL AND SUSTAINABLE TIMBER (Mar. 2008), *available at* http://enviroscope.iges.or.jp/modules/envirolib/upload/1051 /attach/policybrief007_e.pdf (last visited Feb. 1, 2013).

46. Decision of the Fukuoka High Court, December 6, 2010.

47. Law No. 148 of 2002, *available at* http://www.env.go.jp/en/laws/nature/law _pnr.pdf.

48. Law No. 75 of 1992, *available at* http://www.biodic.go.jp/english/biolaw/syu _e/index.html (last visited Feb. 1, 2013).

49. *Id.* arts. 6, 45–48.

50. Law No. 75 of 1992, *available at* http://www.biodic.go.jp/english/biolaw/syu _e/index.html (last visited Feb. 1, 2013).

51. *See, e.g.*, Case concerning Whaling in the Antarctic (Australia v. Japan), ICJ No. 2012/34 [decision pending]; GREENPEACE, "SCIENTIFIC" WHALING—A SEA CHANGE (Dec. 2012), http://www.greenpeace.org/international/PageFiles/476082/Scientific%20Whaling %20Sea%20Change.pdf.

52. *See, e.g.*, Decision by the Supreme Court, Second Petty Bench, Oct. 14, 2011 (holding that under Article 11 of the Law concerning the Rational Use of Energy (prior to revision by Law No. 93 of 2005), information on the amount of fuel and electricity used in each industrial unit that is described in the regular reports submitted by the manufacturing businesses to the director of the Bureau of Economy, Trade and Industry, falls under information that need not be disclosed as stipulated under Article 5.2 (b) of the Information Disclosure Law, *available at* http://www.courts.go.jp/search/jhsp0030?hanreiid=8168 8&hanreiKbn=02.

53. Law No. 81 of 1997, *available at* http://www.env.go.jp/en/laws/policy/assess /index.html (last visited Nov. 24, 2012).

54. Law No. 58 of 2008, art. 25, *available at* http://faolex.fao.org/docs/texts/jap 100101.doc.

55. *Id.* art. 4 (Screening).

56. *Id.* art. 5 (Scoping).

57. *Id.* arts. 11–13)

58. *Id.* arts. 14–20.

59. *Id.* art. 21.

60. *Id.* arts. 23–25, 27.

61. *Id.* art. 2(2).

62. *See, e.g.*, Decision by the Yokohama District Court, Sept. 5, 2007, Local Government Case No. 303, p. 51 (judgment on the binding nature of environmental impact assessment ordinances).

63. Law No. 86 of 1999 art. 5.

64. Law No. 117 of 1998 art. 21-2.

65. Law No. 97 of 1968 art. 26.

66. Law No. 138 of 1970 art. 22.

67. Law No. 81 of 1997 art. 3.

68. Law No. 137 of 1970 art. 15.

69. Law No. 97 of 1968 art. 25.

70. Law No. 138 of 1970 art. 19.

71. Civil Law Code art. 570.

72. Law No. 53 of 2002 art. 8(1).

73. Law Concerning Settlement of Environmental Pollution Disputes art. 42-20.

74. *Id.* arts. 42-16, 42-18, 42-33.

75. Administrative Case Litigation Law art. 9.

76. *See* Decision of the Supreme Court, March 14, 1978, vol. 32, No. 2, p. 211.

77. *See, e.g.*, Decision of the Supreme Court, Dec. 7, 2005, vol. 59, No. 10, p. 2645 (requesting cancellation of project approval based on the City Planning Law).

78. *See, e.g.*, Decision of the Supreme Court, Nov. 2, 2006, vol. 60, No. 9, p. 3249.

79. In October 2012, the Japanese government approved a carbon tax, which will be phased in gradually.

CHAPTER 40

South Korea

KYOUNG YEON KIM, YONG HEE YOON, SEUNG MIN LEE,
JUNG PYO SEO, AND DUK GUEN YUN

I. Overview and Structure

There are various environmental laws and regulations under South Korean
legal system.[1] The Basic Act on Environmental Policy (BAEP) sets out the
fundamental environmental policy goals, such as preventing pollution and
managing natural resources for sustainable use and enjoyment. In addition,
while the BAEP is treated as a starting point, other environmental laws and
regulations have also been enacted and are enforced in areas such as air and
water pollution abatement and waste management.

The most important regulatory authority for environmental matters is
the Ministry of Environment (MOE) (including its regional offices). The MOE
plays a key role in legislating and enforcing national environmental laws.
Each local government (city or provincial government) also plays an important role because they can

- enact their own local environmental regulations providing for more
  stringent local environmental standards;
- grant permits for (or accept filings of reports for), installation of certain environmental facilities; and
- enforce environmental laws, based on statutory delegation of power
  from the MOE.

In relation to measures to counter climate change, the MOE works closely
with the Ministry of Knowledge Economy (MKE). In addition, the Ministry of
Land, Transport and Maritime Affairs (MLTM) is the chief government agency
involved in environmental zoning matters. Lastly, the police and prosecutor's
office are in charge of criminal sanctions for environmental offenses.

II.   Air and Climate Change
A.   Air Pollution Control

In order to regulate gaseous pollutant emissions and to improve air quality, the Clean Air Conservation Act (CACA) has been enacted and is in effect.[2] Also, Special Act on Seoul Metropolitan Air Quality Improvement (Special Act) has been enacted and enforced to regulate air pollution, particularly in the vicinity of Greater Seoul Metropolitan Area.[3]

B.   Climate Change

In the past, however, the CACA lacked specific regulations; it merely established foundational policies for the reduction of greenhouse gas emissions. The Special Act also failed to regulate greenhouse gas emissions and only regulated pollutants such as NO_2, SO_2, dust, and so on.[4] Therefore, the national government faced a certain degree of difficulty when confronted with regulating greenhouse gas (GHG) emissions under the CACA and Special Act. In response, to address climate change due to GHG emissions, the Korean government enacted a comprehensive statute, the Framework Act on Low-Carbon Green Growth Act (Low-Carbon Act) in 2010.

The Low-Carbon Act establishes the government's obligation to establish basic plans for appropriate measures to address climate change[5] and the basis for a GHG emission allowance trading regime.[6]

In addition, in May 2012, the Act regarding Allocation and Trading of Greenhouse Gas Emissions Allowance (Allocation Act), which allocates and establishes a trading system for GHG emission allowances, was enacted. The Allocation Act took effect in November 2012. According to the Allocation Act, from 2015 to 2017, the government will allocate a certain amount of GHG emission allowances based on an entity's past emissions, free of charge. Entities would then be free to trade (i.e., purchase and sell for money) their emission allowances among themselves. In a second phase, from 2018 to 2020, 3 percent of entire allowances will be allocated for a fee, with the balance being granted free of charge. In a third phase starting in 2021, the MOE intends to increase the percentage of allowances that will be sold for a fee to 10 percent or more.[7] Also, if an entity emits more GHG emissions than its allowances permit, the entity is assessed a penalty amounting to three times their market price.[8]

III.   Water

South Korea's laws and regulations with respect to water quality are categorized into many areas according to the source of the wastewater, such as municipal wastewater, industrial wastewater, and wastewater from livestock operations. Among these laws and regulations, the Water Quality and Ecosystem Conservation Act (Water Act) provides the framework for Korea's water pollution control system.

The most noteworthy of the Water Act's implementing regulation is the Quantity Regulation of Water Quality Pollutants (Quantity Regulation), which has been enforced more restrictively since 2004. The Quantity Regulation acknowledges the limitations of the previous regulatory approach, which only attempted to control the concentration of pollutants, and not the overall quantity of pollutants. The Quantity Regulation therefore set a water quality standard, and within that standard established a cap on the quantity of the point source contaminants allowed in particular areas. In this way, the Quantity Regulation adopts a watershed/drainage area management scheme that attempts to both preserve water quality and allow for development.

Pursuant to the Quantity Regulation, the plant operator (discharger) for whom the MOE minister or the head of the local government has established a cap on the quantity of its point source, is obligated to install and operate monitoring devices that measure and record the amount of discharge in its point source. If the plant operator exceeds the allocated cap, the MOE minister or the head of the local government may order the operator to install pollution prevention devices or to undertake other measures deemed necessary. However, if the operator fails to comply with such orders, the minister or the head of the local government may temporarily enjoin the plant's operations or even permanently shut it down. Even then, the plant operator must pay additional fees based on amount discharged in excess of the allocated cap.

With respect to marine pollution, the Marine Pollution Prevention Act was adopted in 1973 to implement marine pollution-related provisions from the Convention on the Prevention of Marine Pollution by Dumping of Waste and Other Matter.[9] On January 19, 2012, Korea replaced the foregoing statute with the Marine Environment Management Act. The latter remains the fundamental law in effect for the purpose of preventing degradation and pollution of the marine environment.

The Marine Environment Management Act applies, inter alia, to the discharge of oil, noxious liquid substances, or harmful substances in packaged form taking place in areas such as Korea's territorial sea, exclusive economic zone, environmental management sea area, and submarine mining area.[10] When any such discharge takes place, the law imposes sanctions to compensate the government for damages to the water resource, in accordance with the 'polluter pays' principle. With respect to the discharges taking place in the aforementioned areas, the Marine Environment Management Act applies in lieu of the Wastes Control Act, the domestic law that generally regulates discharge of wastes.

IV. Handling, Treatment, Transportation, and Disposal of Hazardous Materials

Toxic chemicals are currently handled under the Toxic Chemicals Control Act (Toxic Act). Under the Toxic Act, any person who wishes to produce or import a new chemical substance must first obtain a toxicity evaluation from the MOE.[11] Additionally, the MOE, in accordance with the Toxic Act, makes a quantitative assessment of chemical substances produced from companies larger than a predetermined size.[12] The MOE encourages companies to reduce emissions, publish emissions test results, and limits or prohibits the production, import, and sale of substances deemed to be toxic.

The bill for the Act on the Registration and Evaluation of Chemicals (Korea REACH) and a bill to amend the Toxic Act and rename it the Chemicals Control Act were passed by the National Assembly in April 2013 and May 2013, respectively. As a result, the Korea REACH and the Chemicals Control Act will replace the current Toxic Act starting January 1, 2015. According to Korea REACH, manufacturers, importers, and distributors of new chemical substances or of existing substances of more than one ton per annum will have to register those substances prior to their production or importation and annually report their uses and quantities. The MOE minister will assess and evaluate the hazardous nature of the registered chemical substances and may dispose of or confiscate products containing toxic chemicals that do not comply with certain standards.

The Chemicals Control Act regulates the management of toxic chemicals and requires any person intending to install and/or operate facilities handling toxic chemicals to prepare and submit an environmental impact statement (EIS) to the MOE minister for review. A person who engages in the production, distribution, preservation, storage, delivery, or use of toxic chemicals must also obtain approval from the MOE minister.

V.   Water and Site Remediation

The Wastes Control Act defines "wastes" as materials such as trash, emissions, and waste fuels that are no longer necessary by households or business entities.[13] The act sets forth different regulations for household wastes and commercial wastes. For example, any person generating commercial wastes must report the type and amount of such waste to a local government pursuant to a set of regulations established for each type of waste. In the event that such wastes are not managed pursuant to these regulations, the MOE or a local government agency retains the right to impose appropriate measures on such person or the relevant waste management company.

Any person desiring to enter into the waste management business, including waste collection, transportation, and disposal, must obtain a permit for each business from the local mayor or the governor.[14]

However, pursuant to the recent Supreme Court case[15] rendered on May 26, 2011, contaminated soils do not qualify as waste. There, the court provided three reasons in support of its holding: (1) earth and sand that constitute soil at its natural state are not designated as "wastes" under the Waste Control Act; (2) soil cannot be designated as a waste under "contaminated soil" in and of itself; rather, soil is a mixture of substances merely subject to contamination by other contaminants; and (3) contaminated soil, while subject to purification according to an established procedure, cannot be subject to disposal or discarding. Accordingly, the Supreme Court held that contaminated soils regulated as wastes under the Waste Control Act in excess of the legal threshold do not fall under the purview of the Waste Control Act. Given the Supreme Court's position, in the event that wastes designated under the Waste Control Act are disposed of in the soil, such contaminated soil may need to be managed through a contaminated soil purification process pursuant to the Soil Environment Conservation Act.[16]

VI. Emergency Response

Currently there are no comprehensive legal authorities regulating emergency measures in the case of environment pollution in the Republic of Korea. However, pursuant to the Toxic Chemicals Controls Act, emergency measures must be taken in the event of an actual or likely accident occurring in the process of managing dangerous chemicals in excess of a certain quantity.[17] Further, any person managing toxic chemicals must report to the local government, the environmental local government office, the police department, or the regional Office of the Ministry of Employment and Labor where the risk of an accident posed by such toxic chemicals arises that may be harmful to the environment or human health.[18] The office receiving such a report must report to the MOE regarding the cause and the effect of such accident. Upon receiving such report, the MOE must conduct research on the effects of such accident on the environment and human health and impose any postmanagement measures deemed necessary.

VII. Natural Resource Management and Protection

The Mining Industry Act acts as the general legal authority concerning the management and protection of Korean natural resources. The minerals regulated by the Mining Industry Act include almost all minerals, such as gold, silver, platinum, zinc, tin, mercury, and iron, and rare earth resources. To acquire a mining right for exploration and extraction of such minerals, a license must be obtained from the Minister of Knowledge Economy. When granting a license on a mining right, the minister of knowledge economy retains wide discretion to impose certain restrictions if compelled by public policy considerations, such as effective development of the mining industry. For instance, granting mining rights to a foreigner is limited to certain circumstances, such as when there is a treaty requiring Korean government to do so, or when Korean nationals are granted a reciprocal mining right with the same set of conditions in the project proponent's country.

In addition, the Aggregate Extraction Act governs aggregate extraction activities. An environmental impact assessment may be required under Environmental Impact Assessment Act for extraction of rocks, sand, gravel, or hard minerals in specific areas.[19]

VIII.   Natural Resource Damages

The Soil Environment Conservation Act is the legal authority for preserving and managing soil in Korea. This statute seeks to prevent soil pollution by managing facilities subject to soil pollution control and locating contaminated soil through soil pollution inspection regularly conducted by a special agency on the land and surrounding area of such facilities. With respect to other areas, contaminated soils are located by regular inspection, soil pollution inspection, or soil in-depth examination by the MOE, the local mayor, or the governor. Such contaminated soils are then categorized into Level 1 (Concern Criteria) and Level 2 (Response Criteria), and regulated accordingly. Further, the Supreme Court held that a person who acquired land on which facilities subject to the control of soil contamination are built should be considered as a "person causing soil contamination" under Article 10-3, section 1 of the Soil Environment Conservation Act except when the person is bona fide and without faults.[20]

Similarly, the Natural Environment Conservation Act acts as the foundational legal authority on preserving natural resources. This statute regulates the prevention of damage to the natural environment, protection of ecosystems and natural scenery, preservation of biodiversity, and the management of natural resources. Additionally, the Natural Parks, Protection of Wild Fauna and Flora, Baekdudaegan Protection, and Wetlands Conservation Acts, and the Special Act on Ecosystem Preservation in Island Areas including Dokdo Island, seek to preserve the natural environment.

IX.   Protected Species

The Wildlife Protection and Management Act,[21] Cultural Properties Protection Law, and the Fisheries Act were enacted to protect endangered wildlife, natural monuments, and marine life, respectively.

Endangered species are categorized under the Wildlife Protection and Management Act into two levels of vulnerability: Class I and Class II. Around 220 species are currently classified as endangered.[22] Capturing, gathering, processing, distributing, storing, exporting, importing, and removing or bringing in any of these species is prohibited by law.

X.   Environmental Review and Decision Making

Environmental laws set various environmental standards. The Framework Act on Environmental Policy sets regional environmental standards, the CACA sets emissions allowance standards, the Water Quality and Ecosystem Conservation Act sets water waste quality standards, and the Soil Environment Conservation Act establishes soil pollution concerns and solutions. These standards are used to determine legal levels of pollution and the severity of environmental damage. They are also the basis for various regulatory systems (e.g., air pollution alerts and waste facility installations).

As outlined above in section VII, South Korean law also imposes an obligation to conduct EISs for some types of projects, including urban development projects, industrial complex and tourism complex development projects, energy, water and mountain development projects, port, road, railway, and airport construction projects, sports facilities and waste disposal facilities installation projects, and defense and military facilities installation projects.

XI.   Transboundary Pollution

The Republic of Korea's primary example of a cross-border pollution dispute is the yellow dust dispute between the ROK and China. Yellow dust occurs when dust originating from the dry desert regions of northwest China and Mongolia is suspended in the air by the wind and carried eastward toward the ROK. Yellow dust is known to cause various health problems including respiratory illness and inflammation of the eyes. It is also a cause of an increase in product defects in the semiconductor and electronic devices industry. The discovery of disulfuric acid gas and nitrogen oxide (both which are known to cause acid rain) in yellow dust has heightened the severity of the problem.

In response to the yellow dust issue, the ROK government has cooperated with the Chinese government to create a joint Korean-Chinese yellow dust surveillance and observation system in China, which includes an observation center and tower. The ROK government has also supported assembly systems in western China.

However, the Chinese government has not altered its environmental laws to prevent damage from yellow dust, nor timely acted to prevent such incidences. Meanwhile, international law indicates that because the damage arises from Chinese territory, China should bear the burden of preventing yellow dust.

XII.   Civil and Criminal Enforcement and Penalties

There are various remedies and injunctions available for environmental damage in the ROK, including civil remedies based on a tort liability,[23] relief for ownership or possessory rights impaired by nuisances caused by third parties,[24] and products liability.[25] In such cases, whether a particular act is unlawful is determined based on whether the level of environmental damage is generally within a range that can be tolerated in a communal society.

Criminal environmental offenses are generally prosecuted under the environmental laws.[26] Nevertheless, the Act on Special Measures for the Control of Environmental Offenses enumerated a specific list of certain anti-environmental activities. Under the act, those anti-environmental activities are subject to enhanced punishment and the existing environmental laws where the activities were subject to lesser charges are displaced and do not apply to the activities. For example, under the existing environment laws, a person who committed those anti-environmental activities would not be criminally charged in a case involving negligence or gross negligence. However, under the act, the activities can be criminally punishable either by imprisonment or fine, even in cases where the violation occurred as a result of negligence or gross negligence. In addition, most environmental laws contain joint liability provisions, according to which an employer who fails to exercise an appropriate level of caution or supervision may be vicariously liable and have to pay the fine for the polluting acts committed by his or her employees.

Notes

1. South Korea is alternatively referred to in this chapter as Korea, the Republic of Korea, or ROK.

2. *See* http://www.moleg.go.kr/english/korLawEng?pstSeq=47541&brdSeq=33 (last visited Sept. 2, 2013). Under the act, the minister of environment must ensure that a network of pollution-measuring devices are installed, and measure at all times the degree of air pollution in Korea and the Special Metropolitan City. Regional and city leaders must do the same for their jurisdictions and report to the minister. If air pollution exceeds certain atmospheric standards as prescribed in Article 12 of the Framework Act on Environmental Policy, an air pollution warning to an affected area may be issued. Ad hoc measures to reduce air pollution in affected areas may be taken by local authorities. Mobile and stationary sources are covered in chapters III and IV, respectively.

3. In one case, plaintiffs who lived or worked in the Seoul metropolitan area who claimed damage from respiratory diseases for which they had been diagnosed or treated filed suit against car manufacturers and sellers. The plaintiffs argued that the damage to their health was caused by air pollution. The Seoul district court found that there was no direct evidence to conclude that such diseases were caused by vehicle exhaust, nor did it find evidence of a nexus between the vehicle exhaust and respiratory diseases in light of documents and studies submitted by the plaintiffs. The court also found that because vehicles do not constitute a main cause of fine dust and carbon dioxide in the air, the causal connection between vehicle exhaust and respiratory diseases also could not be established. *See* Seoul Central District Court, Case No. 2007Gahap16309 (Feb. 3, 2010).

4. Special Act on Seoul Metropolitan Air Quality Improvement art. 8 § 1.

5. Framework Act on Low Carbon Green Growth Act art. 40.

6. *Id.* art 46.

7. Enforcement Decree of the Act regarding Allocation and Trading of Greenhouse Gas Emissions Allowance art. 13 §§ 2, 3.

8. Act regarding Allocation and Trading of Greenhouse Gas Emissions Allowance art. 34.

9. Convention on the Prevention of Marine Pollution by Dumping of Waste and Other Matter, 11 I.L.M. 1294 (1973).

10. *See* http://www.moleg.go.kr/english/korLawEng;jsessionid=scEhXaZQzH1Vo wU57qoCop3h3pz7Y3rinxT42enJx1AdYmOi2QPzEhtXkoGcv4iD.moleg_a1_servlet _engine2?pstSeq=52755&brdSeq=33 (last visited July 9, 2014).

11. Toxic Chemicals Control Act art. 10.

12. *See* http://ncis.nier.go.kr/ncis/Index (last visited Sept. 2, 2013).

13. *See* http://eng.me.go.kr/eng/web/board/read.do?pagerOffset=0&maxPageItems =10&maxIndexPages=10&searchKey=titleOrContent&searchValue=Control&menuId=28&or

gCd=&boardId=13&boardMasterId=529&boardCategoryId=&decorator= (last visited July 9, 2014).

14. South Korea is divided into eight provinces, one special autonomous province, six metropolitan cities, and one special city. Governors are elected for these provincial-level governments every four years.

15. Case No. 2008do2907.

16. *See* http://www.moleg.go.kr/english/korLawEng?pstSeq=47550 (last visited July 9, 2014).

17. Toxic Chemicals Control Act art. 40, § 1.

18. *Id.* § 2.

19. *See* http://www.moleg.go.kr/english/korLawEng?pstSeq=47539 (last visited July 9, 2014).

20. *See* Supreme Court Decision No. 2009Du12778 (December 24, 2009).

21. *See* http://elaw.klri.re.kr/eng_mobile/viewer.do?hseq=24747&type=part&key =37 (last visited July 9, 2014).

22. *Id.*

23. Civil Code art. 750.

24. *See* Civil Code arts. 205, 206, 214, 217.

25. *See* Product Liability Act.

26. *E.g.,* the Clean Air Conservation Act, Water Quality and Ecosystem Conservation Act, Soil Environment Act, Toxic Chemicals Control Act, Sewerage Act, Wastes Control Act, Agrochemicals Control Act.

CHAPTER 41

Vietnam

YEE CHUNG SECK AND ANDREW FITANIDES

I. Introduction

Vietnam spans more than a thousand miles from north to south but is just over 30 miles wide at its narrowest point. The tropical south and monsoonal north are low and flat deltas rising to the hilly and mountainous terrain of the central highlands, northwest, and far north. Vietnam is one of the world's most densely populated countries with an estimated population of over 90 million.[1] Although Vietnam is officially one of the world's four remaining communist countries, the "Doi Moi" economic reforms that began in 1986 have moved Vietnam a long way toward the government's goal of creating a "socialist-oriented market economy."[2] Reforms have led to the rapid growth of the economy, industry, population, and urban centers—resulting in serious environmental problems that Vietnam has yet to fully address.[3] Although Vietnam has begun to develop a comprehensive legal framework to protect the environment, enforcement is often decentralized, inconsistent, and nontransparent, creating important concerns for businesses, while doing little to improve Vietnam's environment.

II. Overview and Structure

Vietnam is a civil code jurisdiction based on communist legal theory and French civil law.[4] The national government is composed of the National Assembly, the executive, and the judiciary. The National Assembly has the power to amend the constitution, to promulgate codes, laws, and resolutions, and to ratify treaties. The National Assembly also empowers the Standing Committee of the National Assembly to stipulate resolutions and ordinances according to programs it has approved.

The executive[5] has the power to issue legal documents, usually in the form of decrees, and resolutions, to provide further guidance on the implementation of laws and ordinances or on matters not covered by existing laws or ordinances (for example, sanctions for administrative violations). As head of the government, the prime minister is empowered to issue decisions and directives to enforce laws, ordinances, and treaties. Government ministries and ministerial agencies, in coordination with political and social organizations, provide further guidance on the implementation of laws in the form of circulars, directives, joint resolutions, and joint circulars.

The judiciary plays a limited role. The Board of Judges of the Supreme People's Court issues resolutions and the Head of the Supreme People's Procuracy issues decisions, directives, and circulars interpreting laws, particularly with regard to violations of law and the settlement of disputes.

In addition to the above bodies, the president[6] has the power to issue orders and decisions to enforce laws, ordinances, and those treaties outside the jurisdiction of the National Assembly.

Before 1986, Vietnam had little environmental policy or law. The Constitution of Vietnam (1992) states that the nation's land, forests, wildlife, water, and natural resources belong to the Vietnamese people and are to be managed by the government and the specific groups it may appoint.[7] In 1994, Vietnam introduced the Law on Environmental Protection, the first comprehensive law to prevent and remediate damage to Vietnam's environment. Current environmental law and policy are based primarily on the Law on Environmental Protection (2005) (LEP)[8] and provisions of the Law on Land (2003),[9] the Law on Forestry Protection (2004),[10] the Law on Minerals (2010),[11] the Law on Biodiversity (2008),[12] Law on Water Resources (1998),[13] and other related laws, decrees, and circulars. Vietnam is party to several international environmental treaties, including the Kyoto Protocol (1998) and the United Nations Framework Convention on Climate Change (1994) (UNFCCC). Despite the comprehensive scope of Vietnam's environmental laws, in practice environmental policy is crippled by weak, inconsistent, and often arbitrary enforcement.[14] Furthermore, sanctions have yet to be promulgated for the violation of many environmental laws. In 2002, the Ministry of Natural Resources and Environment (MONRE) was established to manage Vietnam's natural resources and environment. The National Environment Administration of MONRE helps to manage national environmental protection activities throughout Vietnam. At the provincial level, various Departments of Natural Resources and Environment (DONRE) manage environmental policy for provinces and for the five cities under central government administration.[15] In 2007 the Environmental Police Agency was established, consisting of 120 policemen in 30 provinces and cities,[16] to conduct inspections and administer sanctions for environmental violations.

III.   Air and Climate Change
A.   Air Pollution Control

Vietnam's overall air quality ranks in the bottom 10 countries in the world.[17] Environmental experts predict that it will continue to deteriorate before it improves.[18] In a number of urban air pollution "hot spots," pollution from industry and vehicles have caused the air quality to fall below Vietnamese national air quality standards.[19] Enforcement of air quality and vehicle emission standards is hampered by a lack of monitoring equipment and the use of outdated monitoring technology.[20] However, Vietnam lacks a comprehensive legal framework to control or even monitor air quality.[21]

Vietnam's major cities and industrial zones suffer from severe air pollution caused by vehicles and industrial emissions. According to a senior official of MONRE, approximately 70–80 percent of air pollution in urban areas is caused by vehicle emissions.[22] Pollution from Ho Chi Minh City's estimated five million motorbikes and more than a half a million automobiles make it one of the worst 10 cities in the world in terms of air quality.[23]

The basis for Vietnam's air pollution control regime is found at Article 7(6) of the LEP, which prohibits "[e]mitting smoke, dust or gases with toxic substances or odour into the air; dispensing radiation, radioactivity and ionized substances at levels in excess of permitted environmental standards."[24] The relevant air quality standards are called for in Article 10[25] of the LEP and are detailed in regulations promulgated under Circular No. 16.[26] Article 97(2)(a) of the LEP calls for the periodic testing of air quality. However, monitoring of air quality is hampered by a lack of resources and is generally ineffective.[27]

The Ministry of Transportation drafts plans for vehicle emissions standards, in coordination with the Ministry of Science, Technology and Environment (MOSTE), for approval by the government. Although they are generally not enforced, vehicle emission standards are implemented by the Vietnam Register under the Ministry of Transportation. Since 2007, Vietnamese emissions standards have conformed to the European Union's Euro 2 standards.[28] In 2011, the government issued its roadmap for improving vehicle emissions standards for new vehicles with standards augmented to the EU's Euro 4 level by January 2017, Euro 5 by 2022 for vehicles, and Euro 3 for motorcycles by 2017. There will be no standards for the current fleet of vehicles.[29]

B.   Climate Change

Vietnam's diverse and often fragile ecosystems and its lengthy coastline make it particularly vulnerable to the effects of climate change. A one meter rise in sea levels would flood an estimated 10 percent of the country, affecting millions of Vietnamese and threatening the national economy.[30] In recognition of this danger, Vietnam has participated in international climate negotiations, ratified the UNFCCC and the Kyoto Protocol (2002), and attended the 2012 Doha Climate Change Conference. Vietnam is classified by the UNFCCC as a developing country that is especially vulnerable to the adverse impacts of climate change.[31] The UNFCCC seeks to encourage activities that address the needs of such vulnerable countries.[32] In 2010, Vietnam also endorsed the nonbinding Copenhagen Accord.[33] The government has assigned MONRE to serve as the National Focal Point for the implement of its obligations under the UNFCCC and Kyoto Protocol.[34]

Vietnam's national policy on climate change is represented mainly by its National Communications under the UNFCCC[35] and Vietnam's National

Target Program (2007)(NTP).[36] The NTP outlines an overall climate change strategy, with long-term goals for adaptation and mitigation, the basis for action planning in all sectors and localities, and support for research and awareness campaigns.[37] In 2008, Decision No. 158[38] was promulgated to implement the NTP to bring Vietnam's climate change policy into better alignment with international standards. The strategic objectives of the NTP are to assess the effects of climate change in Vietnam, promote more sustainable development, and prepare for the transition to a lower carbon footprint economy.[39] As such, the NTP's targets for 2010 and 2015 focus on assessment and capacity building and do not establish concrete commitments to reduce emissions of greenhouse gases (GHGs).[40]

IV. Water

Vietnam's freshwater resources are badly polluted with industrial emissions and raw sewage, particularly in downstream and urban areas. According to MONRE, an estimated 80 percent of diseases in Vietnam are caused by contaminated water sources.[41] The worst affected areas are Hanoi and the Dong Nai and Nhue-Day river basins, which have experienced rapid industrial growth and urbanization. In 2012, the National Assembly enacted a new Law on Water Resources[42] to replace the 1998 Law on Water Resources.[43] The 2012 Law on Water Resources defines "water resources" broadly to encompass all surface, ground, rain, and seawater within the territory of Vietnam.[44] Its broad scope provides for the management, protection, and exploitation of water resources and the prevention, control, and remediation of harmful effects caused by water pollution.[45] The Law on Water Resources requires MONRE to conduct a survey of Vietnam's water resources and to create a master plan for the prime minister's approval.[46] The approved MONRE master plans are then to be used by ministries, ministerial-level agencies, and provincial People's Committees to create their own plans for water resources.[47] The provincial People's Committees have broad authority and responsibility to protect and manage water resources within their jurisdictions and may be assisted by district and provincial People's Committees.[48] The provincial People's Committees are charged with controlling and mitigating pollution of water resources in areas under their management and must report incidents of pollution to MONRE.[49]

Organizations or individuals wishing to discharge wastewater must obtain a license from MONRE or the provincial People's Committee.[50] The Law on Water Resources requires investors whose projects will use water resources or discharge wastewater, to coordinate with local government entities, consult with representatives of affected communities, and include this community feedback in the dossiers they submit to the competent state agencies for approval of their investment project.[51] Additionally, investors must publicize their plans for the exploitation of water resources, or the discharge of wastewater, before they may implement these projects.[52]

Article 9 of the Law on Water Resources prohibits, among other things, the pollution of water resources by the discharge of solid, liquid, or gas waste, the taking of sand and gravel from fresh water resources, and the building of water exploitation facilities in contravention of the water resource master plans.[53] Organizations whose activities are likely to cause water source pollution must create plans, and have the necessary means, to remediate any water pollution they may cause.[54] Hospitals, cemeteries, landfills, and hazardous chemical producing or processing facilities may not be built in areas defined as "water source protection corridors."[55] Whether an establishment's wastewater discharge constitutes pollution or serious pollution is determined by Decree No. 04.[56] Decree No. 04 provides industry-specific environmental parameters for wastewater, which, if exceeded, may constitute pollution or severe pollution.[57]

V. Handling, Treatment, Transportation, and Disposal of Hazardous Materials

General provisions for hazardous waste management are contained in chapter VIII of the LEP, which defines hazardous waste as "waste with toxic, radioactive, inflammable, explosive, infectious, poisonous and other hazardous characteristics."[58] The LEP creates record keeping and permitting requirements and code numbers for the management of hazardous wastes.[59] It also establishes requirements for the sorting, collection, transportation, and treatment of hazardous waste and promulgates broad requirements for those who treat, bury, and collect hazardous waste.[60] Article 74 of the LEP requires that hazardous waste treatment organizations must prepare environmental impact assessment reports, comply with related government hazardous waste plans, register all wastes to be treated and technologies used, be located a safe distance from residential and conservation areas and water sources, create plans for accident response, undergo inspection prior to operation, and ensure the safety of workers.

Guidance for the implementation of the hazardous waste provisions of the LEP are contained in Circular No. 12.[61] Circular No. 12 mandates that hazardous waste producers must register with the provincial-level DONRE and use licensed transporters and disposal services. It also outlines the registration and licensing processes for these organizations. Circular No. 12 also lists categories of hazardous waste and gives specifications for bags, equipment, containers, storage areas, transportation and treatment equipment, and treatment systems used by businesses that handle hazardous waste.

VI. Waste and Site Remediation

The collection, recycling, and disposal of nonhazardous solid waste is addressed by Articles 66–69 of the LEP. At the end of 2009, Decision No. 2149[62] promulgated a national strategy for solid waste management with phased objectives through the year 2050, including specific targets for increased recycling of household, industrial, and hazardous wastes; reduction of the creation of solid waste; and increases in government fees to finance the creation of a modern waste collection and recycling system for Vietnam.[63]

General provisions for the identification and remediation of contaminated land are contained in the LEP.[64] More detailed guidance on sanctions is given by Decree No. 117[65] following the concept of "polluter pays."[66] When a violator can be identified, the maximum fine that can be imposed is 500 million VND (approximately US$25,000). Other sanctions provided by Decree No. 117 include the revocation of a violator's right to use Environmental Standard Satisfaction Certificates[67] and the compulsory remediation of environmental damage at the violator's expense. Land or water is legally defined as polluted if the levels of one or more pollutants exceeds environmental quality standards.[68] The provincial People's Committees, in coordination with MONRE, are responsible for investigating and identifying contaminated areas where pollution covers more than one province.[69] In instances where contamination spans multiple provinces, the prime minister may direct the implementation of remediation efforts.[70] If the polluter cannot be identified, or if contamination is the result of natural causes, the responsibility for cleanup rests with the government of Vietnam.[71] The responsible government authority has unfettered discretion to determine relative responsibility, and the proportional cost for the cleanup, for all involved parties.[72]

VII.   Emergency Response

Vietnamese law does not have specific laws for the emergency response to serious environmental contamination analogous to the emergency response provisions of the United States' Oil Pollution Act (OPA).[73] However, the LEP stipulates that the response to serious environmental incidents shall comply with the provisions of particular law concerning a state of emergency.[74]

VIII.   Natural Resources Management and Protection

The protection and management of Vietnam's natural resources is primarily governed by the LEP, the Fisheries Law (2003),[75] the Law on Forest Protection and Development, the Law on Minerals, and their implementing decrees and circulars. In practice, the management of natural resources in Vietnam is highly decentralized, leading to the uncertain and inconsistent application of environmental laws in different areas of the country.[76]

The Fisheries Law calls for the rational exploitation of Vietnam's rich fishery resources according to the national master plan for fisheries development.[77] The Fisheries Law specifically prohibits the use of explosives, poisons, and electricity in fishing.[78] The Fisheries Law also requires that new aquiculture facilities obtain approval from the Ministry of Fisheries and that all aquaculture farms avoid using drugs, additives, and chemicals that are prohibited for aquaculture, feed productions, fish processing, and preservation. The law defines permitting requirements for fishing vessels larger than one-half ton and makes it illegal to dump untreated wastewater from aquaculture businesses. Significantly, however, the law sets no catch limits or other stock-preservation policies. Under Article 58 of the Fisheries Law, violators are liable for administrative or criminal sanctions. Specific sanctions for violations of the Fisheries Law are given in Decree No. 31[79] in the form of fines, compensation payments, and the confiscation of equipment and evidence.

The forests of Vietnam have over time been significantly damaged by decades of war and an ever-increasing demand for agricultural land. From 1990 to 2008, reforestation efforts succeeded in raising the percentage of Vietnam's lands that are forested from a low of 27 percent to over 38 percent.[80] However, illegal logging and illegal wood imports[81] continue to be a serious problem. The Law on Forest Protection and Development grants the government broad powers to manage and protect forest resources, to approve their exploitation through permitting and leasing, and to establish forest recovery and reforestation methods.

The Law on Forest Protection is implemented by the Ministry of Agriculture and Rural Development, which sets annual exploitation limits for natural forests below the annual limits set by the prime minister and is responsible for developing and implementing sanctions for the violation of the forestry laws.[82] Timber companies must obtain approval for a sustainable exploitation plan from a particular provincial-level Department of Agriculture and Rural Development. Foreign organizations and individuals may lease forest land from the government for logging.[83] Circular No. 99[84] provides technical guidance for the management and exploitation of commercial forest plantations. Circular No. 56,[85] which replaced Circular No. 99, outlines methods for forest regeneration and contains technical definitions of poor forest health. Administrative sanctions for forest management, protection, and forest products are provided by Decree No. 159[86] and Decree No. 99.[87] Despite these sanctions, the Forest Protection Department records approximately 50,000–60,000 forest crimes per year.[88]

The Law on Minerals defines a national strategy for mining exploitation and provides for the auctioning of mineral rights.[89] It also provides for the issuance of mineral rights and for the assessment of mineral right fees.[90] The government sets and collects mineral rights fees based on a number of factors, including the value, established reserves, and quality of minerals or the category or group of minerals and mining conditions.[91] Implementing Decree No. 15[92] provides guidance and implementation of some articles of the Law on Minerals, making MONRE responsible for monitoring for environmental contamination by toxic minerals and for reporting the same to the provincial-level People's Committee.[93] The latter has overall responsibility for the management of mining pollution.

Mining licenses granted by the MONRE set exploitation limits in agreement with total exploitation limits set by the prime minister.[94] The current Law on Minerals includes a number of changes from the prior 1996 law including changes to licensing requirements and new financial requirements for investors seeking to obtain mineral licenses. Mineral processing licenses are also no longer required, and prospecting may be conducted without a license with the written consent from the local People's Committee. However, to help ensure the participation of potential investors, an entity must contribute owner's equity capital of not less than 50 percent of the total investment capital for an exploration project (30 percent for a mining project).[95]

IX.   Natural Resources Damage

Vietnamese law does not have specific laws governing natural resource damages to remedy environmental contamination analogous to those provisions of United States law, such as OPA, that do.[96]

X.   Protected Species

Vietnam is one of the most biologically diverse countries in the world and has been the focus of a number of international conservation efforts. Forest fires, illegal animal trade, and rapid economic development threaten biodiversity in the country.[97] The principal legal instruments addressing biodiversity conservation are the LEP, the Law on Biodiversity, and Decree No. 32.[98] Vietnam is also a party to the Convention on the International Trade in Endangered Species of Wild Fauna and Flora (1994), the Convention on Biological Diversity (1994), and the Ramsar Convention on Wetlands (1989).

The LEP regulates the time and manner of hunting and fishing and prohibits the exploitation of animals listed as "rare."[99] The Law on Biodiversity assigns MONRE general responsibility for the management and protection of Vietnam's biodiversity—with the assistance of relevant ministries for activities under their management, and with the cooperation of People's Committees at all levels.[100] The Law on Biodiversity also calls for a "national master plan on biodiversity conservation"[101] for the assessment and management of biodiversity.[102] The Law on Biodiversity categorizes conservation areas and applicable land use restrictions designed to protect biodiversity.[103] It also outlines the process for requesting amendments of the list of endangered, precious, and rare species and government priorities for species protection.[104] Furthermore, it addresses the creation and management of biodiversity conservation facilities, the control of invasive species, the management of genetic resources and information pertaining to genetic resources, the management of risks caused by genetically modified organisms, the international cooperation in biological diversity, and the mechanisms and resources to help preserve biological diversity and sustainable development and stipulates that damages for violations of the Law on Biodiversity shall be paid to the government.[105] Specific sanctions for violations of the Law on Biodiversity are given in Decree No. 99[106] in the form of fines, compensation payments, and the confiscation of equipment and evidence. Decree No. 32[107] creates two categories of protected species, found in two separate annexes.

The exploitation of species listed in Appendix II is restricted (legal within defined limits), but prohibited in all circumstances for species listed in Appendix I.

Despite the above measures, illegal wildlife trade remains a serious problem in Vietnam.[108] Much of the demand for illegal wildlife products comes from outside of Vietnam. International conservation groups fear that the number of cross-border trafficking connections to Vietnam has increased in recent years.[109] The Environmental Police Agency estimate that approximately 90 percent of wildlife trafficking cases are not detected.[110] Additionally, Vietnamese actions against traffickers are often based on information obtained from abroad.[111]

XI. Environmental Review and Decision Making

Vietnam's environmental review process is detailed in Decree No. 29,[112] which requires predevelopment assessments and commitments. Depending on the nature, scale, and environmental impact level of a proposed project, an investor must prepare either a strategic environment assessment report (SEA), environmental impact assessment (EIA), or an environment protection commitment (EPC).[113] An SEA is required for any large-scale national-level project, for example, a project under the direction of the National Assembly, the executive branch, or the prime minister.[114] SEAs are drafted by a committee formed by the MONRE or a ministry if the project was created by a government ministry.[115] SEA reports must describe the project, its objectives, and environmental impact, and propose methods and measures to assess and remediate any environmental impact.[116]

EIA reports are required for large national-level projects, or those affecting environmentally sensitive areas such as conservation zones or water sources.[117] The content of an EIA is generally similar to that of an SEA, but also contains opinions from local-level People's Committees and community groups and cost estimates for needed environmental protections measures.[118] Review and approval for EIA reports is similar to that for SEA reports.[119] An EPC is required for any project that does not require an SEA or EIA report.[120]

XII. Transboundary Pollution

In 2002, Vietnam became a party to the Association of Southeast Asian Nations (ASEAN) Agreement on Transboundary Haze Pollution. The agreement, which came into effect in 2003, was created in response to the environmental crisis caused by the unchecked burning of croplands and forests in Sumatra in the 1990s that caused severe pollution in Singapore and Malaysia. Under the agreement, Vietnam committed to cooperate in developing and implementing measures to prevent, monitor, and mitigate transboundary haze pollution by controlling sources of land and forest fires; developing monitoring and assessment measures and early warning systems; exchanging information and technology; and providing assistance to other signatory states.[121] At the second meeting of the Ministerial Committee on Transboundary Haze Pollution, the Deputy Director General of the Vietnamese Directorate of Forestry pledged to increase forest coverage in Vietnam to 45 percent in the near future to help combat transboundary haze pollution.[122]

Vietnam has also, with the governments of Laos, Thailand, and Cambodia, worked to improve regional water quality through the Mekong River Commission, which was created by the 1995 Agreement on the Cooperation for the Sustainable Development of the Mekong River Basin with Laos, Thailand, and Cambodia.[123] Vietnam's commitments under the treaty include protecting the environment, natural resources, and ecological balance of the Mekong River Basin from pollution or harmful effects resulting from future development plans and uses of water from the river.[124]

XIII.   Civil and Criminal Enforcement Penalties

Vietnamese law provides both administrative and criminal sanctions for the violations of environmental laws. Administrative sanctions are generally provided in the implementing decrees for specific environmental laws. However, there has been a substantial delay between the issuance of new Vietnamese environmental laws and the promulgation of sanctions through decrees. For example, the Law on Water Resources was in effect for seven years before Decree No. 34[125] established sanctions for administrative violations of the law in 2005. Decree No. 179/2013/ND-CP[126] specifies administrative sanctions for violations of Article 49[127] of the LEP and other legal instruments including the violations of environmental contamination standards, environmental review procedures, environmental pollution controls, natural resource laws, hazardous and nonhazardous waste laws, and the nonpayment of environmental protection fees. Decree No. 179, administrative fines for a single violation may not exceed VND 2 billion (approximately US$94,160). In addition to fines, environmental violations may result in compelled remediation measures, the confiscation of equipment or assets, the revocation of business licenses, and other measures.[128]

Serious environmental violations may also carry criminal liability under the Penal Code of Vietnam.[129] Chapter XVII of the Penal Code lists criminal environmental offenses including causing pollution, importing noncompliant technologies or materials, spreading epidemics, destroying aquatic or forest resources, violating protected species regulations, and violating the wildlife protection regimes for conservation areas. Under Article 182 of the Penal Code, a person who is responsible for the discharge into the air, water, or land of pollutants or radiation in excess of the national standards for "serious" level pollution or causes other serious consequences may be fined up to VND 500 million (approximately US$25,000) and imprisoned for up to five years. Decree No. 72[130] provides for the prevention and combating of environmental crimes and environment-related violations. Decree No. 72 grants the specialized agencies charged with environmental crime prevention and enforcement wide powers to monitor and investigate suspected environmental crimes, stop violations, and seize assets related to violations. These specialized enforcement agencies are created by the Ministry of Public Security, provincial-level departments of security and district-level subdepartments of security.[131]

Overall, Vietnam's environment is seriously threatened by rapid industrial and population grown and increased urbanization. In 2005, Vietnam ranked at the bottom of the ten ASEAN countries in terms of its ability to protect its environment, and was ranked 98 out of 117 developing countries.[132] In 2012, Vietnam was singled out by the World Wildlife Fund as the country with the worst record for regulating the illegal trade in wildlife.[133] Although Vietnam has introduced a number of laws to help protect the environment, vague provisions, an overreliance on provincial authorities, weak sanctions, limited technical expertise, and insufficient funding have limited their effectiveness. The LEP has also been widely criticized for being "too vague" to be effective and has resulted in few prosecutions.[134] Many provisions of the LEP and other environmental laws make the local Peoples' Committees and the DONREs responsible for detecting and prosecuting violations. This reliance on local enforcement taxes the limited technical expertise of regional authorities and produces inconsistent results between jurisdictions that contribute to business uncertainty and discourage investment.

The enforcement of Vietnamese environmental law has also been hampered by a weak sanctions regime. In many instances, sanctions have never been issued, are promulgated years after a law has been enacted, or are not severe enough to deter violations of the law. There are currently too few environmental officers with the necessary technical expertise to investigate and prosecute environmental violations, and their efforts have received inadequate funding. As a result, local regulatory authorities often do not enforce the requirements for full EIA reports, meaning that corporate pollution in some areas is still virtually unregulated.[135]

Notes

1. CIA World Fact Book, Vietnam, https://www.cia.gov/library/publications/the -world-factbook/geos/vm.html.

2. Swiss Econ. Coop. & Dev., Vietnam Country Strategy 2013–2016, at 6 (2012), *available at* http://www.seco-cooperation.admin.ch/laender/05148/05150/index.html?lang =en&download=NHzLpZeg7t,lnp6I0NTU042l2Z6ln1ad1IZn4Z2qZpnO2Yuq2Z6gpJCDeH 59g2ym162epYbg2c_JjKbNoKSn6A—.

3. Vietnam ranks 136th in the world in overall environmental quality ranks according to Yale University's Environmental Performance Index, http://epi.yale.edu/epi /country-profile/viet-nam.

4. A continuing European influence is evidenced by the fact that new environmental laws and regulations are frequently modeled on the laws of the European Union or its member states. *See, e.g.,* Circular No. 30/2011/TT-BCT Stipulating Temporarily the Permissible Content Limitation of Some Toxic Chemicals in the Electronic, Electrical Products, issued on August 10, 2011, which is based on Restriction of the Use of Certain Hazardous Substances in Electrical and Electronic Equipment Regulations 2008, which

implements the provisions of the European Parliament and Council Directive No. 2002/95/EC on the Restrictions of the use of Certain Hazardous Substances in Electrical and Electronic Equipment, as amended.

5. Constitution of Socialist Republic of Vietnam, NA, art. 94 (2013). The government consists of the prime minister, deputy prime ministers, ministers, and other members.

6. *Id.* art. 86.

7. INT'L UNION FOR CONSERVATION OF NATURE, PREPARING REDD IN VIET NAM, LAO PDR AND CAMBODIA 36 (2010), *available at* http://www.iucn.org/dbtw-wpd /edocs/2010-082.pdf.

8. Law No. 52/2005/QH11, NA (Nov. 29, 2005) (on Environmental Protection).

9. Law No. 45/2013/QH13, NA (Dec. 25, 2013). The Law on Land (2013) prescribes the powers and responsibilities of the state; the regime of land management and use; and the rights and obligations of land users.

10. Law No. 29/2004/QH11 (Dec. 3, 2004) (on Forest Protection and Development).

11. Law No. 60/2010/QH12, NA (Nov. 17, 2010).

12. Law No. 20/2008/QH12, NA (Nov. 28, 2008) (on Biodiversity Conservation and Sustainable Development).

13. Law No. 08/1998/QH10 (May 20, 1998) (on Water Resources).

14. INT'L UNION FOR CONSERVATION OF NATURE, STRENGTHENING VOICES FOR BETTER CHOICES 13 (2010), *available at* http://www.iucn.org/dbtw-wpd/edocs/Rep-2010-010.pdf.

15. The five centrally administered cities are Hanoi, Ho Chi Minh City, Can Tho, Da Nang, and Hai Phong.

16. CSR Asia, Environmental Police Introduced in Vietnam (2007), http://www.csr -asia.com/index.php?id=9381.

17. Yale Univ., Environmental Performance Index, http://epi.yale.edu/epi/country -profile/viet-nam (Vietnam is ranked 170th in air quality—among the ten countries with the worst overall air quality).

18. *Vietnam Air Pollution Among the Worst in the World*, TUOITRE NEWS, May 2, 2012, http://tuoitrenews.vn/features/482/vietnam-air-pollution-among-the-worst-in-the-world.

19. PLANNING & DEV. COLLABORATIVE INT'L, ENVIRONMENTAL COMPLIANCE AND ENFORCEMENT IN VIETNAM 7 (2005), *available at* http://www.aecen.org/sites/default /files/VN_Assessment.pdf.

20. *Ha Noi's Air Quality Declines*, VIETNAM.NET BRIDGE (2012), http://english.vietnam net.vn/en/environment/18251/hanoi-s-air-quality-declines.html.

21. *Id.*

22. MONRE, *HCM City in Top 10 for World's Most Air Polluted Cities* (Nov. 5, 2012), http://vea.gov.vn/en/EnvirStatus/StateOfEnvironmentNews/Pages/HCM-City-in-top -10-for-world's-most-air-polluted-cities.aspx.

23. *Id.*

24. *Supra* note 8, art. 7(6).

25. *Id.* art. 10.

26. Circular No. 16/2009/TT-BTNMT, PM (Oct. 7, 2009), provides the following national technical regulations; QCVN 06: National technical regulation on hazardous substances in ambient air; QCVN 05: outlines the National technical regulation on ambient air quality. Circular No.25/2009/TT-BTNMT, PM (Nov. 16, 2009), provides the following national technical regulations; QCVN 19: National technology on Industrial emission of Inorganic substances and dusts; QCVN 20: National technology on Industrial emission of Organic substances; QCVN 21: National Technical Regulation on Emission of Chemical

Fertilizer Manufacturing Industry; QCVN 22: National Technical Regulation on Emission of Thermal Power industry; and QCVN 23: National Technical Regulation on Emission of Cement Manufacturing Industry.

27. MONRE, *Taking Steps to Curb Air Pollution* (Oct. 20, 2010), *available at* http://vea .gov.vn/en/EnvirStatus/StateOfEnvironmentNews/Pages/TakingStepsToCurbAirPollu- tion.aspx. For example, as of October 2010, Vietnam had only 21 air quality surveillance stations, making it difficult to control dust pollution.

28. Circular No. 31/2009/TT-BGTVT, NA (Nov. 20, 2009) (Providing the National Technical Regulation on Emissions of Gaseous Pollutants from Assembly-manufactured Automobiles and New Imported Automobiles).

29. Decision No. 49/2011/QD-TTg, PM (Sept. 1, 2011).

30. Swiss Econ. Coop. & Dev., *supra* note 2, at 8.

31. United Nations Framework Convention on Climate Change, List of Non-Annex I Parties to the Convention (2012), http://unfccc.int/parties_and_observers/parties/non _annex_i/items/2833.php.

32. United Nations Framework Convention on Climate Change, Parties & Observers (2012), http://unfccc.int/parties_and_observers/items/2704.php.

33. Norton Rose Group, Asia Pacific Climate Change Series: Vietnam (2011), http://www.nortonrose.com/files/asia-pacific-climate-change-policy-series-viet- nam-52314.pdf.

34. V. T. Nguyen & T. Tran, Vietnam Inst. of Meteorology, Hydrology and Envi- ronment, Climate Change Adaptation Policies and Actions in Vietnam 1(2011), *avail- able at* http://jsps-th.org/wp-jsps/wp-content/uploads/2011/02/23.-Vietnam_adaptation _Pol_Act.pdf.

35. United Nations Framework Convention on Climate Change (Apr. 21, 1994).

36. Decision No. 158/2008/QD-TTg, MNRE (Dec. 2, 2008) (on Approval of National Target Program to Respond to Climate Change).

37. *Id.*

38. Decision No. 158 was replaced in part by Decision No. 43/QD-TTg regarding the establishment of National Committee on Air Climate Change.

39. *Supra* note 36, art. 1.

40. REDD Countries, National Target Programme to Respond to Climate Change (2011), http://theredddesk.org/countries/plans/national-target-programme-respond-climate -change.

41. *Water Related Diseases Rampant in Vietnam*, Thanh Hien News, Mar. 29, 2010, http://www.thanhniennews.com/2010/pages/20100329120426.aspx.

42. Law No. 17/2012/QH13 (Jun. 21, 2012).

43. Law No. 8/1998//QH10, NA (May. 20, 1998).

44. *Supra* note 42, art. 2(1).

45. *Id.* art. 1(1).

46. *Id.* art. 10(1)–(3).

47. *Id.* art. 10(3).

48. *Id.* art. 32.

49. *Id.* art. 27.

50. *Id.* art. 73.

51. *Id.* art. 6(1).

52. *Id.* art. 6(1)(b).

53. *Id.* art. 9(1)–(10).

54. *Id.* art. 27.

55. *Id.* art. 26. Water resource protection corridors are broadly defined under Article 31 of the Law on Water Resources to include most bodies of water that are used for water as well as conservation areas.

56. Decree No. 04/2012/TT-BTNMT, MONRE (May 8, 2012) (on Specifying Criteria to Determine the Facility Causing Environmental Pollution, Severe Environmental Pollution).

57. *Id.* annexes 1–25.

58. *Supra* note 8, ch. I, art. 3(10).

59. *Id.* ch. VIII, § 2, arts. 70–80.

60. *Id.* ch. VIII, § 2, arts. 71–73.

61. Circular No. 12/2011/TT-BTNMT (April 11, 2011) (Providing the Management of Hazardous Waste).

62. Decision No. 2149/QD-TTg, PM (Dec. 17, 2009) (Approving the National Strategy for Integrated Management of Solid Waste up to 2025).

63. *Id.* art. 1.

64. *Supra* note 8, ch. IX, § 2, arts. 92–93.

65. Decree No. 117/2009/ND-CP, PM (Dec. 31, 2009) (on the Handling of Law Violations in the Domain of Environmental Protection) replaced by Decree No. 179/2013/ND-CP, PM (Nov. 14, 2013).

66. *Supra* note 8, ch. IX, art. 93; Decree No. 179/2013/ND-CP (2013).

67. An Environmental Standard Satisfaction Certificate can be applied for at the MONRE or DONRE. Its purpose is to prevent the negative impacts on the environment caused by production and service activities.

68. *Supra* note 8, ch. IX, § 2, art. 92.

69. *Id.* ch. IX, § 2, art. 93(2)(b).

70. *Id.* ch. IX, § 2, art. 93(5).

71. *Id.* ch. IX, § 2, art. 93(4).

72. *Id.* ch. IX, § 2, art. 93(3).

73. Decree No. 179/2013/ND-CP does provide for administrative sanctions, for other environmental violations, oil spills, and so on.

74. *Supra* note 8 ch. IX, art. 90(3).

75. Law No. 17/2003/QH11, NA (Nov. 26, 2003).

76. INT'L UNION FOR CONSERVATION OF NATURE, *supra* note 7, at 40.

77. *Supra* note 75, art. 5(3).

78. *Id.* art. 6(6).

79. Decree No. 103/2013/ND-CP (Sep. 12, 2013) (regulating administrative penalties in aquaculture sector).

80. INT'L UNION FOR CONSERVATION OF NATURE, *supra* note 7, at 40.

81. E.F. Lambin & P. Meyfroidt, *Forest Transition in Vietnam and Displacement of Deforestation Abroad,* 106(38) PROC. NAT'L ACAD. SCI. 16,139 (2009), *available at* http://www .pnas.org/content/106/38/16139.full.

82. *See, e.g.,* Decision No. 34/2011/QD-TTg (Jun. 24, 2011), amending and supplementing a number of articles of the regulation on forest management promulgated together with the Prime Minister's Decision No. 1867/2006/QD-TTg (Aug. 14, 2006).

83. *Supra* note 9, art. 56(1)(e).

84. Circular No. 99/2006/TT-BNN was partly amended by Circular No. 57/2007/ TT-BNN (Jun. 13, 2007) and Circular No. 25/2011/TT-BNNPTNT (Apr. 6, 2011) and Circular No. 23/2013/TT-BNNPTNT (May 4, 2013).

85. Circular No. 56/2012/TT-BNNPTNT (Nov. 6, 2012) replaced by Circular No. 23/2013/TT-BNNPTNT (May 4, 2013).

86. Decree No. 159/2007/ND-CP, PM (Oct. 30, 2007) (on Sanctioning Administrative Violations in the Domain of Forest Management, Forest Protection and Forest Product Management) replaced by Decree No. 157/2013/ND-CP (Nov. 11, 2013).

87. Decree No. 99/2009/ND-CP, PM (Nov. 2, 2009) (on Settlement of Administrative Violations in Forest Management, Forest Protection and Management of Forest Product) replaced by Decree No. 157/2013/ND-CP (Nov. 11, 2013).

88. INT'L UNION FOR CONSERVATION OF NATURE, *supra* note 7, at 40.

89. *Supra* note 11, art. 40(2a).

90. *Id.* art. 42.

91. *Id.* art. 77(2).

92. Decree No. 15/2012/ND-CP, PM (Mar. 9, 2012) (detailing a number of Articles on Mineral Law).

93. *Id.* art. 6.2.

94. *Id.*

95. MAYER-BROWN JSM, VIETNAM'S 2010 MINERAL LAW 1 (2011), http://www.mayer brown.com/publications/vietnams-2010-mineral-law-03-14-2011/.

96. The Law on Land requires that zoning and land use regulations must provide for the protection of the environment. (*Supra* note 9, art. 35(4)). However, Vietnamese land use planning focuses primarily on economic development with little attention being given to environmental protection. For example, Decision No. 1353 creates 15 economic zones in coastal areas, where Vietnam's fragile ecosystems are most threatened. Decision No. 1353/QD-TTg, PM (Sept. 23, 2008) (Approving the Project Master Plan on Development of Coastal Economic Zones of Vietnam up to Year 2020. The Decision's key objectives are to form dynamic economic zones with diverse industries that will promote development, in particular for poorer coastal areas, and to help attract investment capital (especially foreign investment). *Id.* art. 1(1b).

97. PLANNING & DEV. COLLABORATIVE INT'L, *supra* note 19, at 7.

98. Decree No. 32/2006/ND-CP, PM (Mar. 30, 2006) (on Management of Endangered, Precious, and Rare Species of Wild Plants and Animals) supplemented by 160/2013/ND-CP (Nov. 12, 2013).

99. *Supra* note 12, art. 5.

100. *Id.* art. 6.

101. *Id.* art. 8.

102. *Id.*

103. *Id.* arts. 16–33.

104. *Id.* arts. 37–41.

105. *Id.* at chs. II–VII.

106. *Supra* note 87.

107. *Supra* note 101.

108. *4,500 Tons of Wildlife Smuggled through Vietnam Annually*, VIETNAM.NET BRIDGE, DEC. 23, 2010, http://english.vietnamnet.vn/fms/society/2818/society-in-brief-23-12.html.

109. *Throw Book at Wildlife Trader: Conservationists*, TALK VIETNAM, Oct. 25, 2012, http://talkvietnam.com/2012/10/throw-book-at-wildlife-trader-conservationists/.

110. *Wildlife Smugglers Are Becoming More Cunning: Environmental Police*, TALK VIETNAM, APR. 5, 2012, http://talkvietnam.com/2012/04/wildlife-smugglers-are-becoming -more-cunning-environmental-police/.

111. *Id.*

112. Decree No. 29/2011/ND-CP, MNRE (Apr. 18, 2011) (Providing Strategic Environmental Assessment and Environmental Protection Commitment) supplemented by Decree No. 35/2014/ND-CP (Apr. 29, 2014).

113. *Id.*

114. *Id.* art. 14(1).

115. *Id.* art. 15(1).

116. *Id.* art. 16.

117. *Id.* art. 18.

118. *Id.* art. 20.

119. *Id.* arts. 21–22.

120. *Id.* art. 24.

121. Univ. of Oslo, ASEAN Agreement on Transboundary Haze Pollution, http:// www.jus.uio.no/english/services/library/treaties/06/6-03/asean_transboundary_pollution .xml.

122. *ASEAN Environment Ministers Meet in Bangkok*, Talk Vietnam, Sept. 28, 2012, http://talkvietnam.com/2012/09/asean-environment-ministers-meet-in-bangkok.

123. Agreement on the Cooperation for the Sustainable Development of the Mekong River Basin (1995), http://www.kellnielsen.dk/mekong/agreem.htm.

124. *Supra* note 124.

125. Decree No. 34/2005/ND-CP, NA (Mar. 17, 2005) (on the Handling of Law Violations in the Domain of Water Resources) replaced by Decree No. 142/2013/ND-CP (Oct. 24, 2013) (on the Handling of Law Violations in the Domain of Water Resources and Minerals).

126. Decree No. 179/2013/ND-CP (2009).

127. Article 49 refers to the sanctions handed to polluting production, business, and service establishments.

128. *Supra* note 12, art. 3(2)(a)–(b).

129. Penal Code No. 15/1999/QH10, NA (Dec. 21, 1999), as amended by Law No. 37/2009/QH12, NA (Jun. 19, 2009) (on Amending and Supplementing a Number of Articles of the Penal Code).

130. Decree No. 72/2010/ND-CP, PM (Jul. 8, 2010) (Providing for Prevention and Combat of Environmental Crimes and Other Environment-related Violations).

131. *Id.* art. 7.

132. *Supra* note 102, art. 6.

133. *Countries Fail to Protect Endangered Species from Illegal Trade*, WWF, July 23, 2012, http://www.wwf.org.au/?4700/Countries-fail-to-protect-endangered-species-from -illegal-trade.

134. *Vietnam's Environment Protection Law Never Enforced*, CleanBiz Asia, Oct. 4, 2011, http://www.cleanbiz.asia/news/vietnams-environment-protection-law-never-enforced.

135. *Id.*

CHAPTER 42

Israel

TZVI LEVINSON AND GIL DROR

I. Overview
A. Introduction

The Israeli environmental law regime bears notable similarities to the body of environmental law in other countries; this is due in part to Israel's common law influences as well as its avid participation in the growing internationalization of environmental law through multinational conventions and more informal global principles. The result is a substantial civil, administrative, and criminal code making up the relatively new field of environmental law in Israel. To understand the practicalities of environmental compliance in Israel, one must first understand the unique aspects of Israel's legal structure as they apply to environmental legislation and enforcement.

B. Structure of Israel's Environmental Legal System

There are a plethora of authorities that govern legal issues in the environmental arena in Israel. Among these are the Ministries of Environmental Protection; Health, Energy, and Water; and the Interior. In addition to these national authorities, local authorities also have control and legislative powers over environmental issues. Finally, various courts adjudicate issues arising from environmental disputes.

C. Ministry of Environmental Protection

The Ministry of Environmental Protection is charged with the primary responsibility for implementing and enforcing environmental laws on a national scale.

In practice, however, the ministry's powers are neither absolute nor exclusive and there is overlap between the authority of the Ministry of Environmental Protection and other agencies. Each of these ministries has mandates that touch upon environmental issues and each is enabled by law to

827

implement restrictions and enforce the laws under their scope. All agencies have the power to promulgate regulations, based on their enabling laws. Among these agencies, no single agency has clear supremacy over another. That said, there is discussion about increasing the relative influence of the Ministry of Environmental Protection. Practitioners should take care to consider the reach of each of the authorities having environmental responsibilities and seek to comply with each of their compliance processes.

D.   Ministry of Health

The Ministry of Health is given power over issues affecting public health, an area that is directly related to environmental protection. It controls the licensing of manufacturers in certain industries, such as the food industry, as well as the quality of drinking water. It also has the power over certain waste issues, including municipal, industrial, and agricultural wastewater, its treatment, and reuse.

E.   Ministry of Energy and Water

The Ministry of Energy and Water is particularly relevant to environmental regulation by virtue of its control over pollution created as a by-product of energy production, for example, greenhouse gases (GHGs), and a subagency within the Ministry of Energy and Water, the Water Authority. Quotas for water consumption (e.g., from industry, agriculture, etc.) must be approved by the Water Authority.

F.   The Ministry of the Interior

The Ministry of the Interior has authority over business licensing (which may carry environmental conditions) and supervises local authorities, which may pass their own local environmental bylaws. It is also one of the ministries responsible for controlling water and wastewater corporations. Under the Water and Sewage Corporation Law, these corporations have recently been "semi-privatized" from local authorities and become instead local corporations.

G.   The Court System

No one court in Israel handles all environmental issues. The issues, depending on their nature and the nature of their progression through the system, may end up in any number of courts, including courts of special jurisdiction set up to control limited areas of environmental adjudication.

1.   Administrative Courts

There is a tendency to process most environmental administrative issues, such as appeals on the denial of a permit, through administrative courts.

This tendency is by no means exclusive. If a dispute arises with the decision of an administrative agency or ministry that controls the issue, e.g., over the granting of a toxics permit, the case goes directly to the Supreme Court. This is vital because despite the limited route through the court system, the Supreme Court will not hear witnesses or consider arguments challenging findings of fact after they are established by the administrative agency or ministry.

2. District Courts

The six district courts in Israel have jurisdiction over criminal and civil issues. Criminal and civil cases originating in the trial courts may be appealed through the district courts. Civil cases where the matter in dispute is over 2.5 million Israeli new shekels (NIS) may be initiated in the district court or if certain environmental legislation stipulates that district court has direct authority over it. Parts of the administrative court system are under the district courts. For instance, judges from the district courts are appointed to serve for a term on the administrative courts while they are still sitting as district court judges.

3. Water Tribunal and Maritime Court

The Water Tribunal and the Maritime Court are parts of the district court in Haifa and have jurisdiction over certain water and maritime issues in Israel. This jurisdiction includes appeals on decisions of the Water Authority, for example, water quota denial, requests to clean up polluted sources of water and certain appeals regarding marine pollution from vessels. These courts are not, however, authorized to deal with all water and maritime issues. A few of the judges from the Haifa District Court are appointed to serve also on the Water Tribunal and Maritime Court.

4. Transportation Courts

Transportation courts are on the same level as trial courts. Their special jurisdiction over transportation includes issues of air pollution from vehicles.

5. Trial Courts

Almost all cases arising from a criminal violation of environmental laws are under the jurisdiction of the 30 trial courts, which are located in the various parts of Israel. A ruling from one of these courts is not binding upon another. The existing legal division in which the adjudication of environmental issues is split between different fora is not optimal and necessitates particular caution. For example, a petition on the matter of a cancellation of a toxics permit will be heard by the Supreme Court, but a petition for the cancellation of an order for the disposal of toxics will be heard by the trial court. The reality is that the case law of the Supreme Court on environmental issues is sparse and occasionally nonexistent. In almost any factual situation presented to the court on environmental issues it is almost impossible to know what the result will be based on existing case law, and the handling of the file and the evaluation of the likelihood of success at all its stages depends on the skill and experience of the attorney dealing with the matter.

H.   Environmental Legislative Process

There are three legislative instruments of primary importance to environmental law in Israel: laws, regulations, and bylaws.

1.   Laws

When we speak of laws in Israel, we refer to laws passed by the Knesset, Israel's parliament. Laws are passed in the Knesset through a three reading process roughly similar to that of other legislatures based on the British parliamentary model. The Knesset is a unicameral legislature.

2.   Regulations

Environmental laws passed by the Knesset will indicate the ministries and/ or agencies charged with implementing and enforcing it, including the power to promulgate regulations. Sometimes the law entrusts these powers to only one ministry/agency, such as in the case of the Hazardous Substances Law, placed under the authority of the Ministry of Environmental Protection. At other times, multiple agencies are given authority. The Water Law, for instance, provides several ministries with the power to promulgate implementing regulations: the Ministries of Health, Environmental Protection, and others.

3.   Bylaws

Bylaws are forms of legislation passed by regional authority or municipalities. Most bylaws must be sent to the Ministry of the Interior to receive approval. The ministry may deny approval; however, in practice, this rarely takes place. All the same, most of the environmental norms in Israel are not found in legislation, but rather in the specific provisions found in the permits and the licenses issued in accordance with the applicable legislative framework, for example, the conditions in a toxics permit under the Hazardous Substances Law, or the conditions in an emission permit under the Clear Air Law. Here our concern is not with legislation that is not specific and that applies to the general public, but rather with a permit or a license given to a plant or to a specific body, and to the extent that it was legally issued, it is binding exclusively upon that plant or body.

Another body of legal norms of importance in the area of environment relates to the national, district, and local outline plans that are issued pursuant to the Planning and Building Law. The articles of these plans include numerous provisions relating to environmental matters and in practice they tend to be ignored, despite their importance.

II. Air and Climate Change
A. The Clean Air Law

Israel's recent Clean Air Law[1] is a prime example of the influence of global developments on Israel legal landscape. It is based on international environmental principles (like the precautionary principle and sustainability) and on legislation in modern countries and has ambitious goals and methods as to the control and reduction of air pollution (such as the prevention greenhouse gas (GHG) emissions) as well as the overall improvement of air quality.

It requires the establishment of a national plan for pollution, under the authority of the Ministry for Environmental Protection. The ministry is tasked with establishing maximum air quality standards on the basis of "updated scientific and technological knowledge."[2] These values (like protecting nature and biodiversity) are to be based upon the international conventions to which Israel is a party.[3]

The law establishes various requirements in order to obtain an emission permit. The Clean Air Regulations[4] set forth the application process for permits. Guidance issued by the ministry specifies the form and content and sets out the documents that must be attached. All applications and decisions are made available for public scrutiny.[5]

This legislation has interconnectivity with other environmental permits like building permits and business licenses.[6] Once granted, the permit is valid for 7 years, unless the minister chooses at her discretion to grant a conditional permit.[7] Renewal must be applied for 1 year before expiry.[8] The emissions source that is the subject of the permit cannot undergo substantial change in operation without approval from the ministry.[9] Practitioners should be aware that in case of ownership transfer, the permit expires unless an approval was issued by the minister, prior to the closing of the transaction. Local authorities are also given a role under this law in preventing air pollution by means of certain bylaws.[10]

A motor vehicle shall not be registered and a license shall not be granted to it or renewed by any licensing authority or by a person it authorized to do so, unless it meets the provisions prescribed under this law.[11]

B. The Energy Sources Law and Climate Change

The Energy Sources Law[12] and its implementing regulations mandate energy efficiency and require industries, inter alia, to submit energy reduction plans and appoint internal energy supervisors.

This law is a classic example of the tension in Israel in environmental matters between progressive legislation and feeble or delayed implementation and enforcement. A broader perspective of the law and its goals indicates that this is a law that already in 1989 came to provide a response to the issue of climate change by way of primary legislation and dozens of regulations issued pursuant to it.

The regulations mandate the undertaking of an exploitation test in those installations that are high in energy consumption, such as water pumping installations (Mekorot—the largest water company in Israel, is the largest single consumer of electricity in Israel), steam boilers, electric motors, and so on. The regulations also regulate energy exploitation in the domestic sector, by way of provisions that mandate the use of energy-saving technology in areas such as air conditioning and lighting.

As stated above, this legislation was not implemented for many years and was largely ignored. Notwithstanding the criminal liability imposed both on corporations and their managers (section 9 of the law) to date there has been almost no enforcement of this criminal tool. Just recently a governmental offer was published, inviting private lawyers to submit applications for appointments by the attorney general to serve as criminal prosecutors for the enforcement of the law (this practice of the authorization of lawyers by the attorney general for purpose of filing indictments is recognized in the Israeli criminal legislation and has been used for many years in the enforcement of environmental laws such as the Water Law, the Hazardous Substances Law and Air Pollution Law, and others). Israel's governmental initiative has occurred, inter alia, in light of its international undertakings in the climate change arena. These include Israel's decision to join the Organisation for Economic Co-operation and Development (OECD) and declarations made by Israel in international fora regarding the objective of limiting the damage from GHGs (Israel is classified in the Kyoto Protocol to the U.N. Framework Convention on Climate Change as a developing state; therefore, while it has undertaken to lodge reports after conducting emissions inventories, it is not required to comply with concrete reduction objectives). Accordingly, one can anticipate that criminal enforcement in this realm will increase, as will the financial investments that entities will need to dedicate in terms of in manpower and technology for the purpose of ensuring compliance with the law. The minister charged (section 1) with implementation is the minister of energy and water (until recently this office was known as the National Infrastructures Ministry and before that the Ministry of Energy; the frequent changes in the name of the ministry are the result of political motivations and from the fact that subject matter areas have been moved from one ministry to another in accordance with changing political coalitions). This is another example of the existing division in Israel in environmental issues between different ministers, such as the minister for environmental protection and the ministers of health, energy and water, interior, and others. This division is for the most part without any logical basis and in many cases results in the significantly detrimental effects to environmental governance and the lack of a holistic treatment of environmental issues.

III.   Water

A.   Water Law

The Water Law[13] establishes the framework for the control and protection of Israel's water resources. It establishes that all water sources in Israel are public property and that every person is entitled to use water as long as such use does not cause pollution or deplete the water resource. The law has been amended several times (1971, 1990, etc.) to include prohibitions against direct or indirect water pollution, regardless of the state of the water beforehand. The minister of the environment is authorized to protect water quality and to prevent water pollution and to promulgate regulations accordingly.

Separately, under the Public Health Ordinance, the Ministry of Health is responsible for the quality of drinking water. The authority to regulate the use of water in the Water Law was given to a special authority—the Water Authority (formerly known as the Water Commission). The authority carries out water policy; it allocates water for different uses and regulates its supply, grants the licenses and permits required for the activities regulated in the Water Law; and regulates the activities of those who are likely to cause water pollution. Even though the Water Law grants the Water Authority numerous enforcement powers with respect to the prevention of water pollution, in practice it barely makes use of its powers, and most of the criminal enforcement in the matter of water pollution is done by the Ministry of Environmental Protection. Challenges to decisions of the Water Authority are lodged primarily in the Water Tribunal in Haifa.

B.   Prevention of Marine Pollution

The Prevention of Marine Pollution Law[14] controls dumping of waste at sea. Israeli legislation adopted the amended Convention on the Prevention of Marine Pollution by Dumping of Wastes and Other Matter[15] and the provisions of Annex V of the International Convention for the Prevention of Pollution from Ships (MARPOL"[16]). This law prohibits the dumping of any waste from vessels or aircraft into the ocean except if done pursuant to a permit.

In addition, the law provides that any loading of waste on vessels or aircraft for the purpose of dumping them into the sea may only be done by permit, and that the owner or the captain of a vessel or aircraft will not permit the dumping of waste into the sea unless convinced that it was done in accordance with a permit.

The Prevention of Marine Pollution from Land-Based Sources Law,[17] which entered into force in 1990, deals with the major land-based sources of marine pollution. To allow it to implement certain changes to the Barcelona Convention[18] for the Protection of the Mediterranean Sea against Pollution and its Protocol for the Protection of the Mediterranean Sea against Pollution from Land-Based Sources and Activities, Israel amended this law in June 2005. The law prevents the discharge of waste from land-based sources into the sea, directly or indirectly, except with a permit.

In 2011 Israel also created a financial levy to discourage pollution discharges into the ocean via The Prevention of Sea Pollution from Land-Based Sources Regulations. These regulations determine the sum of the levy on entities that discharge pollution into the sea under a permit. The aim of these regulations is to inculcate an awareness of the external costs generated by the discharge of sewage into the sea.

C.   Treatment of Sewage

The treatment and discharge of sewage in Israeli environmental law is regulated primarily pursuant to regulations under the Water Law, the Public Health Ordinance, the Licensing of Businesses Law, and the Water Corporations Law.

1.   Two Examples of Regulations Concerning the Prevention of Water Pollution

First, the Water Regulations for Gasoline Stations[19] establish guidelines and standards for the construction of a fueling station and the use of tanks (such as protections against corrosion, the installation of fuel separators, and use of tanks within a secondary container). The regulations also establish obligations concerning the undertaking of tank tightness tests once every five years for underground tanks, and monthly monitoring of piezometers. In the event that there is a reasonable suspicion of a gasoline leak of an amount in excess of one cubic meter, the operator must immediately stop the use of the tank, and report the leak to the Supervisor of the Environment, and act in accordance with the instructions of the Ministry of Environmental Protection.

Second, the Prevention of Water Pollution from Metals and Other Pollutants Regulations[20] regulate sewage discharged from plants in general, and specifically plants for metal coating. They prohibit diluting sewage with water or increasing the consumption of water in the production line with the goal of reducing the concentration of the pollutants in the sewage. There is an obligation to separate the discharges, and also to install a pretreatment facility before discharging the sewage. They also specify maximum permitted concentrations that can be discharged into the sewage system.

2.   Effluent Quality Standards and Rules for Sewage Treatment

These regulations were enacted pursuant to the Public Health Ordinance to (1) protect public health; (2) prevent pollution of water sources from sewage and effluents, to facilitate the recovery of effluents as a water source; and (3) protect the environment, including ecological systems and biological diversity, soil and agricultural crops.[21]

The producer of the sewage is defined as a local authority or a plant, and may be a large or small producer of sewage. It provides that the producer of sewage will treat the sewage and will prevent the discharge of the sewage into the sewage system if its quality prevents the STP from treating it in accordance with the standards prescribed. An operator who holds a business license, or a person who owns, possesses, or supervises an STP must treat the sewage in accordance with the maximum standards prescribed. These norms are determined in accordance with the size of the STP and its geographical location. An exceptions committee consisting of the supervisor of the environment (a representative of the Ministry of Environmental Protection), the supervisor of health (representative of the Ministry of Health) and the director of the Water Authority, is authorized to grant exceptions or to be more stringent in the determination of the standards prescribed by the regulations.

3. *Industrial Sewage Discharged into Sewage System Regulations*

These rules were published[22] pursuant to the Water and Sewerage Corporations Law. They established the organizational and legal framework for the establishment and operation of water corporations in Israel. These rules grant extensive and new enforcement powers to the water corporations in the area of supervision of the quality of industrial sewage discharged into the sewage system, and define what constitutes prohibited sewage. The rules provide that prohibited sewage will not be discharged into the sewage system. Certain exceptional sewage may only be discharged after a written approval. The rules also establish a substantial sewage tariff for the discharge of prohibited or exceptional sewage.

IV.   Handling, Treatment, Transportation, and Disposal of Chemicals
A.   Hazardous Substances Law

The Hazardous Substances Law[23] provides that a hazardous substance is either a toxic as specified in the first schedule or a harmful chemical, as specified in the second schedule. These schedules allow for the categorization irrespective of whether the substances have been mixed with other substances. The law provides that no person may manage toxics unless he holds a toxics permit from the Supervisor of the Environment. Managing is defined as including production, import, packaging, commerce, transfer, storage, possession, and use. The hazardous substances regulations for classification and exemption[24] stipulate the threshold quantities and the concentrations below which managing hazardous substances does not require a toxics permit. The duration of the permit's validity will be determined in accordance with Criteria for Determining Validity Period of Permits.[25]

The authority of the Supervisor of the Environment under the Hazardous Substances Law is broad: she is authorized to grant toxics permits subject to special conditions that must be complied with before the permit is granted, and may add or remove conditions to protect the environment or public health, and she may even cancel a toxics permit at any time for the same reasons.

The Hazardous Substances Law also provides that the party in possession of hazardous waste may be subject to a levy to prevent or reduce the accumulation of hazardous waste and encourage recycling or restoring the waste. The rate of the levy is determined based on the type or the quantity of hazardous waste, the intended place of disposal, the manner of disposal, the degree of risk to human health and to the environment, and the existence of applicable alternatives for treatment of the hazardous waste.

In 2008 amendment to the Hazardous Substances Law determined that an administrative financial sanction can be imposed on a person who violates the law for the sum of NIS 54,000 for individuals and NIS 867,070 for a corporation the sales of which exceed NIS 500 million. In 1994, the Hazardous Substances Regulations for the Import and Export of Hazardous Substances Waste[26] was enacted, which implemented the provisions of the Basel Convention on the Control of Transboundary Movements of Hazardous Wastes and Their Disposal (Basel Convention).[27] The amendment of the regulations in 2008 stated that a person shall not export or import hazardous waste, except in accordance with a permit certificate issued by the Supervisor of the Environment, and only after it is shown to the satisfaction of the Supervisor that certain conditions have been fulfilled.

1.   Licensing of Businesses Regulations

Additional legislation dealing with the regulation of the use of hazardous waste appears in the Licensing of Businesses Regulations. According to the Licensing of Businesses Regulations (Disposal of Hazardous Substances Waste) of 1990,[28] the owner of a plant must dispose of all waste from hazardous substances as soon as possible and no later than six months from the time of its generation. Such disposal must take place at the neutralization and treatment of hazardous wastes plant in Neot Hovav after having been packed and transported in accordance with the law and subject to the supervisors' guidelines.

2.   Land-Based Conveyance of Hazardous Substances

Under the Transportation Services Law[29] a person may not provide transportation services, by himself or by another unless he possesses a transporter's license. Transportation service is defined as the transportation of cargo in a commercial vehicle, and a commercial vehicle is defined as a vehicle the total weight of which is over 10,000 kilograms. With respect to the transportation of hazardous substances, transportation in a commercial vehicle of any weight requires a transporter's license. The law established the Supervisor's authority from the Ministry of Transport to grant a license, to set additional conditions, to change or add to the conditions of the license, or to cancel it. The Transportation Services Regulations provide that a person shall not transport, nor permit any other person to transport hazardous substances, unless the shipment was done in accordance with a cargo deed or a cargo certificate for hazardous substances.

It bears note that in order to convey hazardous substances by land by way of vehicles there is a requirement for additional permits and licenses: a business license in accordance the Licensing of Businesses Law;[30] a toxics permit in accordance with the Hazardous Substances Law; in the event that the substance being conveyed is an explosive substance, in accordance with the Explosive Substances Regulations for trade, transfer, production, storage and use.[31] In the event that gas is conveyed—a license under the Gas Law for the safety and licensing[32] is required.

V. Waste and Site Remediation
A. Maintenance of Cleanliness Law

The Maintenance of Cleanliness Law[33] established a prohibition on littering the public domain and dumping waste, building debris, or vehicle scrap in the public domain, or from the public domain into the private domain. The law defines waste to include food remnants, papers, bottles, boxes, packages of any sort and refuse of any kind, as well as anything else likely to cause uncleanness or untidiness, with the exception of building debris and vehicle scrap. Judicial authority has held that the definition of waste is broad, and can also include the discharging of sewage or emissions into the air.

According to the Maintenance of Cleanliness Law, the minister for environmental protection or person authorized by him has the authority, prior to the submission of an indictment, to issue a maintenance of cleanliness order.

B. Collection and Disposal of Waste for Recycling Law

The Collection and Disposal of Waste for Recycling Law[34] imposes obligations on local authorities. The law determines that local authority are obligated to allocate, in their own jurisdictions, sites for the establishment of recycling centers and to install, recycling installations and designated containers. Similarly, it provided that local authorities must establish bylaws for arrangements for the collection and disposal of waste for recycling.

C. Processing of Packaging Law

Israel is a small country. The many uses of land lead to a reduction in the available space for landfills, to the point that a total lack of space is anticipated in the near future. To this are added environmental dangers posed by the waste landfill sites. This led the Knesset in 2011 to pass the Packaging Law,[35] the objective of which is the reduction of the use of packaging, reduction of the use of hazardous materials in packaging and the application of the principle of extended producer responsibility and the imposition of extended obligations on producers of packaging and on the importers of packaging, to carry out accredited recycling.[36] The purpose of the law is to create financing for arrangements for the separation of packaging from the flow of general waste as well as its collection, for the purpose of recycling or return. The goal is to by 2020 prohibit landfilling of packaging at waste disposal sites.[37]

According to the Packaging Law, accredited recycling may be carried out in two ways: the first, which is the default procedure, is by means of a contract with a recycling corporation. The deadline for entering into such a contract was July 2011.

A producer or importer who is not interested in contracting with a recycling corporation must submit an application to the Ministry of Environmental Protection for an exemption from the duty to contract.[38] The application must provide a justification and demonstrate the ability to collect and carry out accredited recycling of product packaging that the applicant manufactures or imports.

The Packaging Law imposes criminal liability on corporate officers, including the directors.[39] Liability extends to the duty to supervise and to take all necessary steps to comply with the law. The law also has administrative ramifications, such as the possibility of imposing an administrative financial sanction against the corporation or a personal sanction against a corporate officer.[40]

D. Environmental Treatment of Electronic Equipment and Batteries

Similar to the European Union's Waste Electrical and Electronic (WEEE) Directive, Israeli law requires that entities arrange for the collection and treatment of electronic equipment, batteries, and the like.[41] It does so to encourage the recycling and reduction of the amount of such waste, prevent their burial, and reduce the environmental and health hazards resulting from such waste by imposing extended producer's responsibility on manufacturers and importers. The law establishes an obligation on the manufacturer and importer of electrical and electronic equipment to recycle 20 percent of such waste beginning in 2015 and 45 percent of such waste by 2020.

E. Hazardous Waste Site Cleanup

To date, Israel has not enacted a specific statute concerning site remediation akin to the U.S. Comprehensive Environmental Response, Compensation, and Liability Act.

VI. Emergency Response

According to the Businesses Regulations (Hazardous Plants) of 1993,[42] the owner of a hazardous plant must adopt all measures necessary for handling hazardous substances in his plant in accordance with the best accepted technology and subject to the manufacturer's instructions. This includes having adopted measures to prevent and managing incidents. As such, the owner of a hazardous waste plant shall not handle nor allow the handling of hazardous substances in his plant area except by skilled manpower that has undergone appropriate training.

VII.   Natural Resource Management and Protection
A.   Streams and Springs Authority Law

The Streams and Springs Authority Law[43] empowers the minister of environmental protection to establish a stream authority for a particular stream or part thereof, for a spring, or for any other water source.[44] In accordance with section 3, the function of a stream authority is primarily to plan and to carry out activities related to regulation of the flow of water in the stream, with a view to maintaining a suitable water level throughout the year; removal of sewage hazards that involve pollution or vary the flow of water.

To date, only three stream authorities have been set up in Israel—the Yarkon Stream Authority in 1988, the Kishon Stream Authority in 1994, and the Beer-Sheva Stream Authority in 2011. The boundaries of the stream authorities that were set up are limited in the extreme—20 meters from the riverbank in the case of the Yarkon River Authority and 25 meters from the riverbank in the case of the Kishon River Authority. There are several river administrations (Bssor River, Hadera River) that operate with funding and on the initiative of the Jewish National Fund. These administrations, which have no legal powers, should not be confused with the stream authorities, which have statutory powers, including the power to promulgate regulations.

There are some regions in which the Drainage Authority, which was established by virtue of the Draining and Flood Protection Law,[45] was granted the powers of a stream authority by the minister of environmental protection.

In relation to all activity taking place close to the river, it is therefore recommended to check whether a stream or drainage authority exists, and if so, to check what the scope of its authority is and how it is implemented.

B.   National Parks, Nature Reserves, National Sites, and Memorial Sites Law

This law is another example of the existing fragmentation between the various government offices in the environmental arena. The law authorizes the minister of the interior to declare a certain area to be a nature reserve and national park or a memorial site.[46] The law establishes a statutory corporation called the Nature and Parks Authority, the function of which is to plan, set up, and to maintain these sites. The authority oversees and enforces the provisions of the law to prevent building, hunting, and commerce in protected natural areas. The fines that courts are authorized to impose by virtue of the law in criminal proceedings initiated by the authority are considered to be low (thousands and tens of thousands of NIS) and, unfortunately, do not have a sufficiently deterrent effect.

C. Protection of the Coastal Environment Law

The objectives of the Protection of the Coastal Environment Law[47] are to (1) protect the coastal environment and the seawater and related natural resources, (2) remediate and to preserve them as a natural resource of unique value, (3) reduce and prevent harm to them, and (4) establish principles and provisions for the administration, development, and sustainable use of the shoreline. The law prohibits actions that are detrimental to the shoreline, and permits use of the shore only if the use shall benefit the population at large and there is no other economically viable or environmentally preferable alternative. An act in contravention of the law constitutes a criminal offense and can also serve as the grounds for an environmental representative action. If one wants to carry out building or developmental activity close to the shoreline of the Mediterranean or the Red Sea or the Sea of Galilee (this is how section 2 of the law defines the coastal zone), it is advisable to check whether such activity is not prohibited.

VIII.   Natural Resource Damages

In Israel a number of statutes enable the government to seek to restore natural resources, the function of which has been harmed by pollution, including the (1) National Parks, Nature Reserves, National Sites Statute (prohibition of damaging protected nature values) of 1983; (2) National Parks, Nature Reserves, National Sites and Monuments Announcement (Protected Nature Values) Law, 2005; (3) Botanical Gardens Law of 2006; (4) Prohibition of Driving a Vehicle on the Beach Law of 1997; (5) Planning and Construction Law (Amendment No. 89) of 2008; and (6) Protection of Wildlife Law.[48]

IX.   Protected Species
A.   Wildlife Protection

Today, the existing Wildlife Protection Law, which was enacted in the 1950s, affords protection of wildlife or preservation of protected populations in their breeding grounds. The Ministry of Agriculture initiated an amendment to the Wildlife Protection Law with a view to improving and strengthening the means of protection of wildlife in Israel, and regulating their trade and possession, by setting constraints designed to protect wildlife. The new amended law states that all wildlife will be "protected wildlife" except for a small number of "harmful" species. This in effect puts an end to all recreational hunting, which today takes place by means of hunting licenses.

B.   Protection of Animals

The Animal Welfare (Protection of Animals) Law[49] prohibits specific acts toward animals and prescribes imprisonment and fines for such prohibited behavior. Awareness of the subject of animals has risen dramatically in recent years, as has the criminal enforcement of the Ministry of Environmental Protection, which is responsible for implementation of the law, in animal cruelty cases.

C.   Biological Diversity

There is evidence of the first signs of legislation to preserve biodiversity in Israeli environmental law. Thus, for example, the Clean Air Law[50] states that its purpose is to protect human life, health, quality of life, and the environment, including natural resources, ecological systems, and biodiversity. In April 2010, the Public Health Regulations were published, which regulate the standard for wastewater for the purpose of directing it to agricultural irrigation or to streams. These regulations similarly establish the preservation of ecosystems and biodiversity as a goal. At the same time, in the absence of explicit legislation with punishments sufficient to deterrent prohibited acts, it appears that the law in this area will be insufficient to significantly curb harm to biodiversity.

X.   Transboundary Pollution

Israeli environmental law concerns itself with cross-border pollution primarily in two contexts. The first is in the context of marine pollution. Regarding marine pollution, the Marine and Oil Pollution Regulations[51] implement MARPOL[52] 1973/1978. MARPOL prohibits the discharge of oil, ballast water, or bilge water into the ocean. Similarly, the commencement of the Compensation for Oil Pollution Damage[53] relates to pollution caused to one of the following: (1) coastal waters; (2) the Israeli exclusive economic zone (EEZ) (defined as the area of the Mediterranean Sea beyond Israeli coastal waters, up to a distance that is not more than 200 nautical miles from the low tide point on the beach); (3) pollution damage caused in the waters of a party to the International Convention on Civil Liability for Oil Pollution Damage (CLC)[54] for an incident occurring in its sovereign territory, including within the territorial waters of that state or in its EEZ, and in the absence of a declared EEZ, a zone regarding which it made declaration, in accordance with section 2 of the CLC. In the Regulations for Compensation for Oil Pollution Damage (Responsibility) (Participatory Impost in the International Fund) 2007,[55] a duty is imposed on the conveyors of oil to pay a participatory tax based on the amount of oil transferred by sea.

The second context for the operation of transboundary pollution is hazardous waste transfer between states. The 1994 Hazardous Substances

Regulations,[56] as amended in 2008, implement the Basel Convention, as stipulated in chapter IV.

XI. Environmental Review and Decision Making
A. Licensing of Businesses Law

Inter alia, the Licensing of Businesses Law was designed to secure the following objectives: (1) proper environmental quality, and the prevention of nuisances and hazards; (2) prevention of risk of animal disease, and prevention of pollution of water sources by pesticides, fertilizers, and pharmaceuticals; and (3) public health, including proper sanitary conditions.

The Licensing of Businesses Law states that a person will not engage in certain business unless he has a business license, a temporary permit, or a summary permit. The Licensing of Businesses (General Provisions) Regulations,[57] establishes which businesses require a license.

According to the statute, the license issuer can at any time add to, change, or cancel additional conditions for the business license. The addition of conditions is subject to the rules of administrative law, the laws of natural justice, and the right of the applicant to be given a justification for any decision.

In view of the decision of an interministerial committee that decided to reform the procedure for licensing businesses in the State of Israel to reduce bureaucracy and the administrative obstacles, the Licensing of Businesses Law was amended[58] and the Licensing of Businesses (General Provisions) Regulations were amended in November 2011.

The Licensing of Businesses Law states that violation of the provisions of the law can lead to a criminal sanction of a fine or 18 months in prison. Moreover, the license issuer may, prior to filing the indictment, issue an administrative order to close the business down for 30 days, and to extend the order for an additional 30 days. An administrative decision taken by virtue of the Licensing of Businesses Law can be challenged in the Court for Administrative Affairs, whereas an administrative closure order can be challenged in the trial court.

B. Planning and Building Law

The Planning and Building Law[59] establishes those institutions that approve construction in Israel, their powers, and their mode of operation.

The law regulates the activity of the Committee for National Infrastructures, which deals with the preparation of national infrastructure plans. National plans are prepared, which address, inter alia: (1) designation of the land and its use, while preserving the agricultural designation of suitable lands; (2) industrial regions and areas for quarries; (3) the network of main roads, rail tracks, national supply lines, ports, arteries for the national supply of water, dams, collection lakes, energy stations, the electricity grid, airports and the aerial access routes to them, including delineation of the territories in which restrictions will apply for the sake of aerial safety; (4) recreational lands, forestry and land preservation; (5) the preservation of antiquities, holy places, scenic values, and areas that will remain in their natural state; (6) places for enterprises and for public purposes that are of national importance.

According to the Planning and Building regulations on the obligations and content of environmental impact assessment,[60] one who submits an application for a construction plan on one of the following matters must, after receiving operational guidelines, submit an environmental impact assessment:

1. an energy plant, except for a photovoltaic installation whose area does not exceed 750,000 square meters, an airport, a port, a marina, a refinery, a hazardous waste disposal site, land reclamation from the ocean or a lake (a project proponent for one of these types of projects must draft a local plan, a partial regional outline plan for a defined area, or a partial national outline plan for a defined area);

2. any project that has a significant impact on the environment and that relates to one or more of the following matters, or that would take place in one of the following regions:
   a. industrial regions; electricity line of high voltage or super-high voltage; very active land-based transportation centers; places for mass meetings; centers for the production, storage, or transportation of polluting or dangerous materials; mining or quarrying sites;
   b. an area of high environmental sensitivity due to the nature of the local natural resources or scenery;
   c. an area exposed to environmental obstacles that are likely to frustrate the execution of the plan or to have a significant impact on the activity proposed;

3. a project having a significant impact on the environment.

The survey must also include an environmental opinion that examines the types of impact of a planned project on the environment, including the impact on the unique conditions of the environment in which the project would be implemented.

XII. Civil Administrative and Criminal Enforcement and Penalties

A. Criminal Punishment

Israeli environmental law includes provision for penal sanctions. Most environmental laws impose strict liability. Most of the laws provide for imposition of the punishments of imprisonment and fines. For example, in the Clean Air Act, the maximum punishment for an individual is two years' imprisonment and a maximum fine of NIS 600,000, and for a corporation, a maximum fine of NIS 1,200,000. In the event that aggravating circumstances are present, the maximum punishment for an individual is 3 years imprisonment, and doubles the maximum fine for the corporation. In 1996, the Supreme Court commented in a judgment that the time has come to raise the level of punishment for environmental offenses. Since then, there has been a clear judicial trend toward increasing the fines that are imposed by the courts.

B.   Liability of an Officer in a Corporation

Under Israeli environmental laws, corporate officers have a duty to oversee and to take all necessary measures to prevent the commission of offenses under these laws by the corporation or by an employee of the corporation, as relevant.

An officer is usually defined as an active manager in the corporation, a partner (excluding limited partners), or another employee who is responsible on behalf of the corporation for the area in which the offense was committed. In recent years, however, laws have been enacted (such as the Clean Air Law) that also include directors as officers.

With respect to the liability of an officer, the environmental laws invoke a legal presumption whereby if an offense has been committed by a corporation, or by one of its employees, the presumption is that the officeholder in a corporation, as relevant, was in violation of his duty unless he proves that he took all necessary measures to fulfill his duty.

The officer will have a defense if he can prove that the offense was committed without his knowledge, and that he took the necessary steps to prevent the offending conduct from occurring.

C.   Administrative Fines

In many environmental laws in Israel, financial administrative sanctions may be imposed on a corporation and on corporate officers. Thus, for example, under the Clean Air Law, a financial sanction of up to NIS 400,000 may be imposed on an individual, and up to NIS 800,000 on a corporation. In the Hazardous Substances Law, the amount of the financial sanction is determined according to the annual profits of the business.

Separately, an administrative sanction does not prevent the filing of a separate indictment by the government. However, in the event of a conviction, the financial sanction that has been paid will be deducted from the punishment.

D.   The Polluter Pays Law

In 2008, the government published the Environmental Protection Polluter Pays Law.[61] This law is a comprehensive update of Israeli environmental law. In certain cases it updates out of date mandatory provisions. The main provisions of the law are as follows:

- increase in the penal sanctions: Updates to the punishments in a number of laws, providing up to three years' imprisonment (thus, for example, related to offenses under the Water Law, the Maintenance of Cleanliness Law, the Hazardous Substances Law, and others).
- significant increase in economic penal sanctions: A doubling of the basic fines in most of the environmental laws. In addition, the law authorizes the court to impose fines, in addition to the basic fines, in the amount of the profit, benefit, or savings to the offender (whichever is highest).
- increased efficiency to the criminal process: most of the environmental offenses will involve strict liability that does not require proof of mens rea in order to secure a conviction.
- a mechanism for administrative sanctions (financial sanctions) in addition to the criminal process: the administrative sanctions are a rapid and efficient way for the government to impose high financial costs on polluters, in parallel to the criminal proceedings (in this law, financial sanctions are imposed in proportion to the size of the corporation: sanctions as high as NIS 2.4 million, with the addition of 1/20 of the amount of this sanction for each day that the violation continues. An administrative sanction is imposed by the administrative authority without any legal process. An individual who does not agree to the sanction can file an administrative petition, but the filing of the petition does not stay the payment. In an administrative petition, as opposed to a criminal process, the burden of proof lies with the petitioner (the polluter), and the process is rapid and quick. This mechanism has already been implemented in the Clean Air Law, as well as the Hazardous Substances Law, the Prevention of Pollution of the Sea law, and others.
- Payment of a tax—even one who pollutes by virtue of a license must pay. This obligation has made its way, for example, into the Maintenance of the Coastal Environment Law, whereby even a person who harms the environment by virtue of a license will be required to pay a levy for the damage he causes. The objective is to motivate corporations to switch to clean technologies and reduce their pollution levels, even when these are within permitted bounds.
- The local authorities are permitted to fix environmental hazards at the expense of the polluters and to collect from the polluters double the expenses (for example, by virtue of the Water Law, the Prevention of Pollution Law, the Hazardous Substances Law, and others).

E. Environmental Enforcement by Local Authorities

The main objective of the Environmental Enforcement by Local Authorities Law[62] is to grant local authorities the power to enforce legislation in the area of the quality of life and of the environment of its residents. It affects 18 environmental laws. The law states that a large local authority or town association, the main concern of which is the preservation of the quality of the environment, will act within their area of jurisdiction to enforce the environmental laws in accordance with the provisions of the law, whereas a small local authority is permitted to act within its area of jurisdiction to enforce the environmental laws—whether all or part—in accordance with the provisions of the law.

To enable implementation, it was determined that the head of a local authority is empowered to authorize, from among the workers of the local authority, inspectors with powers according to the law—some of them or all of them.

F.   Class Actions Law

The purpose of the Class Actions Law[63] is to establish uniform rules for submitting and conducting class actions, to improve the protection of rights, and to promote the

1. right of access to the courts, including for sectors of the population for whom it is difficult to turn to the court as individuals;
2. enforcement of the law and deterrence in the face of violations;
3. suitable remedies for those harmed by the violation of the law;
4. efficient, fair, and exhaustive court proceedings.

The Second Appendix to this law states the grounds for serving a complaint and subsequently requesting class action approval. Section 6 of the same appendix states that an action in connection with an environmental hazard constitutes grounds for submitting a class action.

Notes

1. The Clean Air Law of 2008, OJ 2174.
2. Ch. 3, art. 2.
3. *Id.*
4. The Clean Air Regulations (Emission Permits) of 2010, OJ 6904.
5. Ch. 4, art. 2(21)(2).
6. Ch. 4, art. 2(24)(a).
7. Arts. 25(a); 22(a).
8. Art. 25(a).
9. Art. 27.
10. Ch. 3, art 3.
11. Ch. 5, 37(a).
12. The Energy Sources Law of 1989, OJ 1296.
13. Water Law of 1959, OJ 288.
14. The Prevention of Sea Pollution (Dumping of Waste) Law of 1983, OJ 1084.
15. http://www.imo.org/About/Conventions/ListOfConventions/Pages/Convention-on-the-Prevention-of-Marine-Pollution-by-Dumping-of-Wastes-and-Other-Matter.aspx.
16. http://www.imo.org/About/Conventions/ListOfConventions/Pages/International-Convention-for-the-Prevention-of-Pollution-from-Ships-(MARPOL).aspx.

17. The Prevention of Sea Pollution from Land-Based Sources Law of 1988, OJ 1256.

18. *See* http://www.unepmap.org/index.php?module=content2&catid=001001004.

19. Water Regulations (Prevention of Water Pollution) (Gasoline Stations) of 1997, OJ 5849.

20. Water Regulations (Prevention of Water Pollution) (Metals and Other Pollutants) 2000, OJ 6064.

21. Public Health Regulations (Effluent Quality Standards and Rules for Sewage Treatment) 2010, OJ 6886.

22. Rules of Water and Sewerage Corporations (Industrial Sewage Discharged into Sewage System), 2014, OJ 7387.

23. Hazardous Substances Law of 1993, OJ 1408.

24. Hazardous Substances (Classification and Exemption) Regulations of 1996, OJ 5762.

25. Hazardous Substances Regulations (Criteria for Determining Validity Period of Permits), 2003, OJ 6243.

26. Hazardous Substances Regulations (Import and Export of Hazardous Substances Waste) of 1994, OJ 5612.

27. *See* http://www.basel.int/Portals/4/Basel%20Convention/docs/text/BaselConventionText-e.pdf.

28. Licensing of Businesses Regulations (Disposal of Hazardous Substances Waste) of 1990, OJ 5298.

29. Transportation Services Law of 1997, OJ 1636.

30. Licensing of Businesses Law of 1968, OJ 537.

31. Explosive Substances Regulations (Trade, Transfer, Production, Storage and Use), 1994, OJ 5576.

32. Gas Law (Safety and Licensing) of 1989, OJ 1286.

33. Maintenance of Cleanliness Law 1984, OJ 1118.

34. Collection and Disposal of Waste for Recycling Law of 1993, OJ 1422.

35. Processing of Packaging Law of 2011, OJ 2275.

36. *Id.* § 6.

37. *Id.* § 27.

38. *Id.* § 9(5).

39. *Id.* § 32(3).

40. *Id.* § 34.

41. Environmental Treatment of Electronic Equipment and Batteries Law, 2012, OJ 2372.

42. Businesses Regulations (Hazardous Plants) of 1993, OJ 5539.

43. Streams and Springs Authority Law of 1965, OJ 457.

44. *Id.* § 2.

45. Draining and Flood Protection Law, 1957, OJ 236.

46. National Parks, Nature Reserves, National Sites and Memorial Sites Law of 1998, OJ 1666.

47. Protection of the Coastal Environment Law of 2004, OJ 1958.

48. *See* National Parks, Nature Reserves, National Sites (prohibition of damaging protected nature values) of 1983, OJ 4535; National Parks, Nature Reserves, National Sites and Monuments Announcement (Protected Nature Values), 2005, OJ 6369; Botanical Gardens Law of 2006, OJ 2051; Prohibition of Driving a Vehicle on the Beach Law of 1997, OJ 1615; Planning and Construction Law (Amendment No. 89) of 2008, OJ 2190; Protection of Wildlife Law, 1955, OJ 170.

49. The Animal Welfare (Protection of Animals) Law of 1994, OJ 1447.

50. *See supra* note 3.

51. Marine and Oil Pollution (Execution of the Convention) Regulations of 1987, OJ 5006.

52. *See* http://www.mar.ist.utl.pt/mventura/Projecto-Navios-I/IMO-Conventions%20(copies)/MARPOL.pdf.

53. The Compensation for Oil Pollution Damage (Responsibility) Law, 2004, OJ 1923.

54. http://www.transportrecht.org/dokumente/HaftungsUe_engl.pdf.

55. Oil Pollution Damage (Responsibility) (Participatory Impost in the International Fund) of 2007, OJ 6569.

56. *See supra* note 26.

57. The Business Licensing (Businesses Requiring a License) Order of 2013, OJ 7229.

58. Licensing of Businesses Law (Amendment no. 27) of 2010, OJ 2262.

59. Planning and Building Law of 1965, OJ 467.

60. Planning and Building (Environmental Impact Assessment) Regulations of 2003, OJ 6246.

61. The Polluter Pays Law of 2008, OJ 2181.

62. Local Authorities (Environmental Enforcement by Powers of Inspectors) Law, 2008, OJ 2155.

63. Class Actions Law of 2006, OJ 2054.

CHAPTER 43

Turkey

NILÜFER ORAL AND BAŞAK BAŞOĞLU

I. Introduction

Connecting the Asian and European continents, Turkey is located in an environmentally strategic position between Asia, Eurasia, Europe, and Africa and serves as a vital migratory route for millions of birds each year. It is a peninsula surrounded by three seas: the Black Sea in the north, the Mediterranean in the south, and the Sea of Marmara in the west. It is the only country in the region with coasts on both the Black Sea and Mediterranean Sea. The Black Sea is connected to the Mediterranean Sea by the narrow Turkish Straits, which comprise the Strait of Istanbul and the Strait of Çanakkale. The topography of Turkey is a rich mosaic of marine, dune, forest, mountain, and steppes ecosystems. The total territory is 777.971 km², of which 8,333 km² lies along the coast. In 2012 the total population of Turkey was approximately 73 million.[1]

Turkey is encircled by a number of important mountain ranges that form part of the Alpine-Himalayan chain. The main mountain ranges are the Northern Anatolian mountains along the Black Sea coast in the northeast (3,932 m); the Toros Mountains range along the southern Mediterranean coast (3,068 m); and the Eastern Anatolian range, which contains the highest mountain in Turkey, Mount Ağri (Ararat) measuring 5,165 meters.[2] The central Anatolian plateau is encircled by the Köroğlu Mountains in the west. In contrast to the mountainous areas, central Anatolia is made of semi-arid steppes. Over 40 percent of Turkish territory is made up of steppes.[3]

Turkey also has many wetlands. Of the total 250 wetlands, 58 are classified as "internationally important," 18 are classified as "Class A,"[4] and 13 have been listed under the Convention on Wetlands of International Importance (Ramsar Convention).[5] The Ramsar wetlands are the Göksu Delta,[6] Burdur Lake,[7] Seyfe Lake, Kuş Lake,[8] Sultan Marshes,[9] Kizilirmak Delta, Akyatan Lagoon,[10] Lake Ulubat,[11] Gediz Delta,[12] Meke Lake,[13] Yumurtalık Lagoon,[14] Kızören Pitch,[15] and Kuyucuk Lake.[16]

In addition, Turkey has some 200 natural lakes (totaling 906,000 hectares). The largest is the Van Lake in eastern Turkey, followed by Tuz (Salt)

Lake (128,000 hectares). Turkey also has 72 lagoons, of which two located along the Mediterranean coastal area, Köyceğiz and Bafa, account for 60 percent of the total lagoon area in Turkey.[17]

The principal rivers in Turkey include the Kizilirmak, Yeşilirimak, Çoruh, and Sakarya, which flow into the Black Sea; the Susurluk, Biga, Gönen Aksu, Köprüçay, Manavgat, Göksu, Ceyhan, and Seyhan, which flow into the Mediterranean Sea; the Kücük Menderes, Büyük Menderes, and Gediz, which flow into the Aegean Sea; and the famous Firat (Euphrates) and Dicle (Tigris), which flow into the Persian Gulf.

Turkey is one of the richest countries in terms of biological diversity. Of the 12,000 plant species found in Europe, over 9,000 are found in Turkey. Furthermore, of these approximately 3,000 are endemic to Turkey.[18] Turkey is also considered to be one of the world's most important centers for genetic resources with an estimated 18,000 animal species recorded thus far. Turkey has 39 biogeographic regions. It is also an important route between Africa and Europe for millions of migratory birds each year. However, only 0.7 percent of the country is protected under IUCN categories I–V.[19]

II.   Institutional Structure

The Turkish Republic was established on October 29, 1923, a date that is celebrated each year as national Independence Day. Turkey is a secular democratic state based on the parliamentary system of governance. The constitution provides for separation of powers among the executive, legislative, and judiciary branches. The current constitution was adopted in 1982.[20] The head of state is the president, who is elected by the 550-member Turkish National Grand Assembly.[21] The prime minister is the head of the government and serves for a term of five years. The legislative and primary governing body is the Grand Assembly, whose responsibilities include the adoption, amendment, and repeal of laws; overseeing the ministers and the Council of Ministers; and publishing the laws it passes.[22] In 2004 Turkey became a candidate country to the European Union.[23]

The Turkish legal system is based on the continental European code model. Most of Turkish laws were directly adapted from European codes, such as the Italian criminal code, the Swiss civil code, and the German Business Code. The judiciary is composed of the lower first instance courts, the appellate courts, and a Constitutional Court. Except for the Constitutional Court, the courts are divided into civil, criminal, administrative, and military courts. The administrative court system consists of the Council of State, an appellate court, and various administrative courts of first instance. The Council of State reviews decisions of the lower administrative courts, hears cases of original jurisdiction concerning administrative disputes, and, upon request, provides opinions on draft legislation submitted by the prime minister and the Council of Ministers. Environmental disputes also fall within the jurisdiction of the administrative courts.

III. Development of Environmental Law in Turkey

Parallel to international developments, Turkish environmental law began to take shape during the 1970s. First, an office responsible for the environment was created attached to the office of the prime minister; later, the office became the undersecretariat for environmental affairs. The growing importance of the environment was reflected in the 1982 Turkish Constitution, which expressly recognized the right to a healthy and balanced environment.[24] This was followed with the promulgation of the first environmental protection law, in 1983.[25] Environmental Law of 1983 was amended substantially in 2006 (Amended Environmental Law). However, it was not until 1991 that a separate Ministry of the Environment was created. In 2003 the Ministry of the Environment and the Ministry of Forestry were merged into the Ministry of Environment and Forestry (MoEF). However, in 2011 the MoEF was divided into two new Ministries: the Ministry of the Environment and Urbanization (MoEU), and the Ministry of Forestry and Water.[26] Accordingly, the duties of the MoEF have been delegated to the MoEU. In addition, a number of other ministries and governmental agencies have responsibilities relating to environmental matters. These are the Ministry of Agriculture and Rural Affairs;[27] the Ministry of Natural Resources and Cultural Heritage; the Ministry of Transport, Maritime Affairs and Communications;[28] the Naval Coastal Safety (Coast Guard); the General Directorate for Water Resources;[29] the State Planning Organization; and the Environmental Commission of the Turkish Grand National Assembly. However, the MoEU is the main executive body responsible for protected areas designated under the Law on Protection of Natural and Cultural Assets.[30]

IV. Air and Climate Change
A. Air Pollution Control

Until recently, the primary national measure for controlling air pollution was the 1986 Regulation for the Protection of Air Quality.[31] However, Environmental Law, as amended in 2006, expressly included addendum 6 for the development of clean energy to protect air quality and prevent air pollution. Other related legal instruments that have since been adopted include the Regulations for the Control of Industrial Air Pollution,[32] Regulations for Air Pollution from Climate Warming,[33] Regulations for the Control of Motor Vehicle Emissions,[34] and the Regulations on Measures against the emission of gaseous and particulate pollutants from internal combustion engines to be installed in non-road mobile machinery.[35]

B. Climate Change

The level of CO_2 emissions in Turkey has increased significantly since 1990, although it remains below the average emission per capita of OECD countries. Greenhouse gas (GHG) emissions between 1990 and 2007 increased from 170 million tons of CO_2 to 372 million tons of CO_2 in 2007.[36] Most emissions are from transport, low-quality domestic heating fuel (coal), and industry. In 2004 nearly 77 percent of the total CO_2 emissions came from the energy sector, 28 percent from industry, 17 percent from transportation, and 15 percent from other energy-related fuel consumption. Turkey imports approximately 72 percent of its energy needs. In 2004, energy demands were met primarily with oil (37 percent), natural gas (23 percent), hard coal (16 percent), lignite (11 percent), biomass (6 percent), hydro (5 percent), and other renewables (2 percent). According to Turkey's UNFCCC First National Report, 12.3 percent of its total primary energy supply comes from renewable energy sources.[37] However, most of this comes from biomass (mostly wood) and hydropower (dams). Nevertheless, Turkey has a very strong potential for alternative and non-CO_2 resources such as wind, solar, and geothermal.

Nuclear energy has also been included in Turkey's portfolio of energy resources. The current administration has given nuclear power priority for meeting Turkey's growing energy needs and plans on building three nuclear power plants with a total capacity of 4,500 MWe by 2015. They will be located on the coasts of the Mediterranean and Black Seas.

Turkey signed the 1992 U.N. Framework Convention on Climate Control (UNFCCC) on May 24, 2004,[38] only after lengthy negotiations to have its name deleted from Annex II and adopted a resolution that "invited Parties to recognize the special circumstances of Turkey."[39] However, the meaning of "special circumstances" was not clarified. Turkey is currently listed in Annex I of the UNFCCC. In 2009 Turkey ratified the Kyoto Protocol.[40] However, Turkey does not have a quantified emission reduction limit or commitment under Annex B of the Kyoto Protocol. In 2010, by consensus the Parties at the 16th Conference of the Parties (COP 16) held in Cancun formally recognized the special circumstances of Turkey as an Annex I party in a situation different from that of other parties included in Annex I to the convention.[41] In 2012 the UNFCCC Conference of the Parties adopted a decision that aims to facilitate support to Turkey for financial, technological, technical, and capacity building and assist Turkey in implementing its national climate change strategies and action plans and developing low-emission development strategies or plans.[42]

Domestically, the State Planning Organization incorporated climate change for the first time into the eighth five-year development program for the period 2001– 2005.[43] Climate change has also adopted on the ninth five-year development program for the period 2007–2013 that "in the framework of the conditions of Turkey, and with the participation of the relevant parties, a National Action Plan that sets forth the policies and measures for reducing greenhouse gas emissions will be prepared. Thus, responsibilities concerning the U.N. Framework Convention on Climate Change will be fulfilled."[44]

Turkey is also a party to the UNECE Convention on Long-Range Transboundary Air Pollution (1979);[45] the Protocol to the Convention on Long-

Range Transboundary Air Pollution;[46] the Convention for the Protection of the Ozone Layer (1985);[47] and the Montreal Protocol on Substances That Deplete the Ozone Layer (1987).[48]

Turkey has a significant potential for generating emission reductions from land use, land change, and forestry measures (LULUCF) if Turkey's forest and land degradation meets the post-2012 requirements for LULUCF-generated project credits; it is not clear how much of Turkey's current deforestation would meet the current criteria adopted for "reforestation" and "afforestation" projects under Dec. 11/COP 7 of the Marrakesh Accords. As it stands, over 50 percent of Turkey's 52.4 million acres of forest is classified as either degraded or unproductive.[49] Ninety-nine percent of Turkey's forest is state-owned, of which 81 percent is used for commercial purposes. Agricultural land occupies 35 percent of Turkey's total land (66.7 million acres). In 2004 only 44.5 million acres was under cultivation. Agriculture, which represented 24 percent of the total GDP in 1980, decreased to 12 percent by 2005. Turkey's unsustainable agricultural practices, based on small farming dependent on fossil fuels and poor irrigation practices, had resulted in 50 percent energy waste. According to the Ministry of Environment and Urbanization, as a result of afforestation activities the total forest area in Turkey has increased from 20.2 million hectares in 1973 to 21.6 million hectares in 2012.

V.   Water

Many of Turkey's major rivers and lakes are at high risk from pollution and nonsustainable water use. For example, the Konya Basin, Turkey's largest river basin and one of the most important of 200 in the world, covering 500 million km^2 area with a population of approximately three million, provides 40 percent of Turkey's freshwater supplies. The Konya Basin encompasses 11 smaller wetlands. It is extremely important for its high degree of biological diversity, and is the site for 11 important bird areas, eight important plant areas, and several important plant species listed under CITES[50] and Berne.[51] In the past 40 years, as a result of poor agricultural practices and water policies, Turkey's 1,300,000 hectares of wetland has lost its ecological and economic functions.[52]

During the past 40 years the average amount of useable freshwater per capita in Turkey decreased from 4,000 m^3 to 1,519 m^3, placing Turkey in the category of water-scarce countries. Water resource management in Turkey is divided among 14 different responsible authorities and numerous laws, regulations, and other secondary legislation. Water is approaching soil erosion as a critical environmental problem for Turkey. The Ninth National Development Plan noted that at the present rate of population growth and water use, in 20 years Turkey would have an estimated population of 87 million people and an average per capita amount of freshwater of approximately 1,000 m^3— bringing Turkey into the category of water-poor countries.[53]

Turkey is considered to be one of the richest countries for wetlands in Europe, with a total of approximately 1,851,000 hectares, including artificial lakes.[54] Since 1997 Turkey has been a party to the Ramsar Convention.[55] Despite having nine of its wetlands listed as wetlands of importance, nearly 50 percent have disappeared, including the Sultan Marshes, which was recognized as a wetland of importance for Turkey, Europe, and the Middle East. The primary reasons for the loss of wetlands started in the 1950s with the enactment of the Law on the Drying Up of Wetlands and Use of the Land Reclaimed.[56] This law remains in force in contradiction to the Environmental Law, as amended in 2006, requiring protection of wetlands and Turkey's commitments under the Ramsar Convention.

Turkey is a peninsula surrounded by three seas: the Black Sea, the Sea of Marmara (an inland sea), and the Mediterranean Sea. Furthermore, the Black Sea and the Aegean Sea are connected by the narrow and environmentally sensitive Turkish Straits. One of the important issues to dominate the last decade has been the increase in transport of hazardous cargoes through the Turkish Straits, mostly as a direct result of oil and gas development in the neighboring Caspian basin.[57] In the decade between 1996 and 2006 the volume of oil and oil products transported through the Turkish Straits increased from 60 million tons annually (mta) to nearly 150 mta. Furthermore, the number of transporting dangerous substances rose from a total of 4,937 in 2000 to nearly 10,000 in 2006.[58] During the past 50 years over 500 accidents have taken place in the Turkish Straits including several serious tanker accidents. The collision between the MT *Independenta* and the MV *Shipbroker* in 1979 has been ranked in the top 12 oil spills.[59]

Turkey's marine environment is also under pressure from land-based point and diffuse source pollution such as nutrient input, pesticides, chemicals, untreated sewage and wastewater, industrial output, dumping, and aquaculture. One of the important problems is the lack of adequate wastewater treatment facilities and hazardous substance treatment facilities.

Fishing is an important economic activity for Turkey. Reported catches place Turkey in the leading position among Black Sea and Mediterranean Sea countries.[60] Important commercial fish for Turkey include anchovy (particularly from the Black Sea), grey mullet, Atlantic horse mackerel, and Atlantic bonito. However, total fish stock and the number of commercial fish species has decreased over the years as a result of overfishing, poor fishing methods, pollution, and introduction of invasive species. The Black Sea, for example, as a result of nutrient input from the Danube River and the introduction of alien species, saw the number of commercial fish species decrease from 26 to six.[61] The introduction of the jellyfish *Mnemiopsis leidyi* precipitated a critical collapse of the Black Sea anchovy stock.[62] The decline in fish stock made aquaculture economically profitable. In 2002 aquaculture and mariculture accounted for 13.6 percent of marine and freshwater catches.[63] Unfortunately, fish farms were inadequately regulated and established in some of the most sensitive coastal areas, particularly along the Mediterranean coast.

The prohibition of marine pollution falls within the general ambit of Article 8 of the Environmental Law, as amended in 2006, and specifically Article 29 of the 1998 Turkish Straits Regulations.[64] The Environmental Law, as amended in 2006, imposed strict administrative penalties for vessel-source pollution. Specifically, the illegal discharge of oil, oil products, sludge, slop, bilge water, refined products, and similar material is subject to administrative fines in accordance with the tonnage of the vessel and the type of vessel.[65] Tankers are subject to higher fines than other vessels. The illegal discharge of dirty ballast water and solid waste is subject to a slightly lower fine scale.[66] However, the illegal discharge of hazardous waste is subject to a fine tenfold of these.[67] If the violating vessel cleans the pollution by its own means, however, the fine will be reduced to one-third of its original amount.[68] A vessel that is unable either to pay these fines immediately or to provide an acceptable security will be detained at the nearest port.[69]

Article 20 Environmental Law, as amended in 2006, also includes provisions applicable to Turkish flagged vessels that violate the similar laws of a foreign coastal state. Accordingly, if the foreign coastal state chooses not to impose its own law and notifies the Turkish administration of such violations the penalties provided under Article 20 will be imposed.

The Turkish Straits Regulations were adopted in 1994 in response to the growing threat of increased tanker transport and were amended in 1998.[70] The regulations specifically include a provision requiring all ships to take preventive measures against pollution during passage through the Straits.[71] Furthermore, the regulations adopted strict reporting requirements for nuclear-powered ships and transporting nuclear cargo or waste, or other hazardous or dangerous substances.[72]

Turkey is party to a number of international and regional agreements related to the protection of the marine environment.[73] These include MARPOL 73/78.[74] Turkey is also a party to regional agreements including the Convention for the Protection of the Mediterranean Sea against Pollution (Barcelona Convention) as amended in 1995;[75] Protocol for the Prevention of the Mediterranean Sea by Dumping from Ships and Aircraft, as amended in 1996;[76] Protocol Concerning Cooperation in Combating Pollution of the Mediterranean Sea by Oil and Other Harmful Substances in Cases of Emergency;[77] Protocol Concerning Cooperation in Combating Pollution of the Mediterranean Sea from Ships and, in Cases of Emergency, Combating Pollution of the Mediterranean Sea;[78] Protocol for the Protection of the Mediterranean Sea from Land-based Sources, as amended in 1996;[79] Protocol to the Barcelona Convention Concerning Specially Protected Areas of the Mediterranean Sea;[80] Protocol to the Barcelona Convention Concerning Specially Protected Areas and Biological Diversity of the Mediterranean Sea;[81] Convention on the Protection of the Black Sea against Pollution (Bucharest Convention) and its related protocols; [82] the Convention on the Transboundary Transport of Hazardous Substances (Basel Convention);[83] the 1992 Civil Liability Convention;[84] the 1992 FUND Convention;[85] and the 1990 Oil Pollution and Response Convention. [86] However, Turkey is still not a party to either the 1972 London Dumping Convention[87] or its 1996 Protocol.[88]

Subsequent to Turkey's ratification of CLC, FUND, and OPRC Conventions, in 2005 Turkey adopted the "Law on Emergency Response and

Compensation for Damages in the Case of Pollution of the Marine Environment by Oil and Other Harmful Substances" (Emergency Response Law)[89] and the implementing regulation.[90] Although the primary responsibility for implementation of the Emergency Response Law rests with the MoEU, additional responsibilities have been allocated to the Undersecretariat for Maritime Affairs and the Turkish Coast Guard.

Other related domestic legislation for protection of the marine environment include the 1988 Regulations for Water Pollution Control,[91] Regulations on Water Products,[92] the Regulations on Ship Waste,[93] and Regulations on Procedures for the Proof and Assessment of Penalties against Ships and Marine Vessels. [94]

VI.   Handling, Treatment, Transportation, and Disposal of Hazardous Materials

Hazardous chemicals are defined under Article 2 of Law 2872 on the Environment. Accordingly, hazardous chemicals are defined as all chemicals and materials that contaminate the ecological balance and nature of the human, animals, and organisms by its physical, chemical, and/or biological adverse effects. The liability for production, trade, storage, and utilization of hazardous chemicals is regulated under Article 13 of Law 2872 on the Environment. Accordingly, strict liability has been foreseen for these activities and the people engaged in these activities shall be jointly liable for environmental damages. The most important feature of this article is that liability insurance and authorization from the ministry are required for activities engaged with hazardous waste and chemicals.

Moreover, parallel to the European Union *acquis*, Chemical Inventory and Control Regulation;[95] Regulation on Authoring and Distribution of Safety Data Sheets for Hazardous Substances and Preparations;[96] Regulation on Classification, Labeling and Packaging of Dangerous Substances and Preparations;[97] and Regulation on Restrictions for the Manufacture, Marketing and Use of Some Chemicals[98] have been issued.[99] Accordingly, activities related to hazardous chemicals and materials are subject to environmental permit in accordance with Chemical Inventory and Control Regulation; toxic chemical products are also subject to environmental permit in accordance with Regulation on Authoring and Distribution of Safety Data Sheets for Hazardous Substances and Preparations.

VII.   Waste and Site Remediation

Environmental Law, as amended in 2006, identifies four main types of waste: wastewater, solid waste, domestic waste, and hazardous waste. The disposal of waste and hazardous substances is regulated by Article 11 of the Environmental Law and related directives and regulations. Article 11 specifically prohibits the issuing of construction, operational, and use license for construction activities without a plan of how the waste will be disposed in accordance with the law and actual disposal of the waste accordingly. The same article also specifies that wastewater treatment plants and activities are subject to the control, supervision, and authorization of the Greater Municipalities Law; in nonmunicipal areas, they are subject to the state governor; in designated tourist areas, the Ministry of Tourism and Culture; and in industrial free zones, the designated zone administration. The municipalities are responsible for establishing or facilitating the establishment of domestic waste disposal facilities.

Article 13 of the Environmental Law, as amended in 2006, provides that the ministry, after taking into account the views of the relevant ministries, shall adopt directives for the identification, production, import, labeling, packaging, classification, storage, assessment of risks, and transport of hazardous waste. Moreover, Article 13 prohibits the import of hazardous waste. The Article also imposes joint and several liability on the parties who produce, sell, store, use, and collect dangerous chemicals; and collect, transport, store, recycle, reuse, and dispose of hazardous waste. For this reason, such parties are obligated to have third-party liability insurance and must show proof of such insurance to the ministry as a condition before engaging in such activities. Related directives adopted by the MoEU for waste disposal include regulations for the disposal and control of oily wastewater,[100] regulations for the disposal and control of packaging and packaging waste,[101] regulations on the disposal and control of used accumulators,[102] the amendment to the regulations on the control of hazardous chemicals and products,[103] regulations on urban wastewater treatment,[104] regulations for the control of medical waste,[105] regulations on soil pollution control,[106] and regulations for the control of pollution water and surroundings from hazardous substances.[107]

VIII.   Natural Resource Management and Protection

In 2011[108] Turkey had a total of 40 registered national parks (848,119 hectares), 31 nature protected areas (63,694 hectares), 18 nature parks (81,231 hectares), 80 wildlife protected areas (1,201,212 hectares), and 15 specially protected areas, of which nine are coastal. These include specially protected areas (SPA) for the endangered Mediterranean monk seal (*Monachus monachus*) and the Caretta turtle nesting areas.[109] All of these SPAs are also primary locations for tourism where there has been a great deal of resort and summer home developments. These SPAs are under the administration of the MoEU Agency for Specially Protected Areas.

As one of the earliest areas of human habitation, the Anatolian peninsula is rich in archeology with a total of 3,029 archeological sites and 115 historical sites. Turkey is also a party to the Convention for the Protection of the World Cultural and Natural Heritage (World Heritage).[110] Eleven historical cultural sites have been included in the World Heritage List: Göreme National Park and the Rock Sites of Cappadocia, Great Mosque and Hospital of Divriği, historic areas of Istanbul, Hattusha: the Hittite Capital, Nemrut Dağ, Hierapolis-Pamukkale, Xanthos-Letoon, City of Safranbolu, archaeological site of Troy, Selimiye Mosque and its Social Complex, and the neolithic site of Çatalhöyük.

There are two agencies responsible for natural resource management and protection: Undersecretariat of Protection of Natural Assets of MoEU and General Directorate of Natural Conservation and Natural Parks of Ministry of Forestry and Water. However, it should be noted that the draft code of Protection of Nature and Biological Diversity aims to unify the management of natural resources.

IX.   Natural Resource Damages

Soil erosion is considered to be Turkey's primary environmental threat. According to the MoF, 59 percent of agricultural areas, 64 percent of meadows, and 54 percent of forests in Turkey are threatened by erosion.[111] Turkey has approximately 20 million hectares of land categorized as forestland, comprising approximately 26 percent of the country's total surface area. However, despite the strict constitutional protection of forests, much of this area has been lost. Deforestation occurred mostly during the period between 1955 and 1997, when 55 percent of forest fell to deforestation activities.[112] As a result there is only 0.31 hectares of forest land per capita compared to 1.3 million hectares in the United States, 7.2 million hectares in Australia, and 18.7 million hectares in Canada.[113] Approximately 98 percent of forest land in Turkey is state property. The reasons for deforestation include poor regulations, fire, poor forestry practices, and conversion to agricultural and urban uses.

X.   Protected Species

As previously stated, Turkey is one of the richest countries in terms of biological diversity. However, only 0.7 percent of the country is protected under IUCN categories I–V.[114] Turkey is also considered to be one of the world's most important centers for genetic resources with an estimated 18,000 animal species recorded thus far. Turkey has 39 biogeographic regions. It is also an important route between Africa and Europe for millions of migratory birds each year. In addition, there are 40 registered national parks (848,119 hectares), 31 nature protected areas (63,694 hectares), 18 nature parks (81,231 hectares), 80 wildlife protected areas (1,201,212 hectares), and 15 specially protected areas, of which nine are coastal. The species in these areas are protected, which include the endangered Mediterranean monk seals and the Caretta turtles. Also there is a special breeding station for the Northern Bald Ibis in Birecik, established in 1989 under the directory of General Directorate of Natural Parks and Nature Preserve.

Turkey has been a party to both the Convention on Biological Diversity and Convention on International Trade in Endangered Species of Wild Fauna and Flora since 1996.

XI. Environmental Review and Decision Making

Although Turkey has not yet become a party to the Aarhus Convention on Access to Information, Public Participation in Decision-Making and Access to Justice in Environmental Matters,[115] in 2003 Turkey adopted the Law on the Right of Access to Information.[116] The law recognizes that everyone has a right to information and, subject to certain exceptions such as national security, imposes the obligation on state and state agencies to provide information in a speedy manner to the public when requested.[117] Furthermore, the EIA requirements, as provided by the new EIA Regulation,[118] include public participation, particularly of those who would most directly be affected, during the assessment of the proposed project by the MoEU Commission.[119] Furthermore, Article 30 of Environmental Law, as amended in 2006, also recognizes the right of the public to obtain information regarding polluting activities and to demand the cessation of the activity. However, Article 30 provides an exception for the release of information that could result in harming rare species or habitats can be refused.

XII. Transboundary Pollution

Turkey is party to a number of international and regional agreements regarding the transboundary pollution; including UNECE Convention on Long-Range Transboundary Air Pollution (1979);[120] the Protocol to the Convention on Long-Range Transboundary Air Pollution;[121] the Convention for the Protection of the Ozone Layer (1985);[122] and the Montreal Protocol on Substances That Deplete the Ozone Layer (1987),[123] MARPOL 73/78.[124] Turkey is also a party to regional agreements including the Convention for the Protection of the Mediterranean Sea against Pollution (Barcelona Convention) as amended in 1995;[125] Protocol for the Prevention of the Mediterranean Sea by Dumping from Ships and Aircraft, as amended in 1996;[126] Protocol Concerning Cooperation in Combating Pollution of the Mediterranean Sea by Oil and Other Harmful Substances in Cases of Emergency;[127] Protocol Concerning Cooperation in Combating Pollution of the Mediterranean Sea from Ships and, in Cases of Emergency, Combating Pollution of the Mediterranean Sea;[128] Protocol for the Protection of the Mediterranean Sea from Land-based Sources, as amended in 1996;[129] Protocol to the Barcelona Convention Concerning Specially Protected Areas of the Mediterranean Sea;[130] Protocol to the Barcelona Convention Concerning Specially Protected Areas and Biological Diversity of the Mediterranean Sea;[131] Convention on the Protection of the Black Sea against Pollution (Bucharest Convention) and its related protocols;[132] the Convention on the Transboundary Transport of Hazardous Substances (Basel Convention);[133] the 1992 Civil Liability Convention;[134] the 1992 FUND Convention;[135] and the 1990 Oil Pollution and Response Convention.[136]

XIII.   Civil and Criminal Enforcement and Penalties

The Turkish Criminal Code, as adopted in 2004, included new provisions creating environmental crimes.[137] Accordingly, environmental crimes are divided as direct and indirect crimes. Direct environmental crimes are regulated in Articles 181–184 of the Turkish Criminal Code. According to Article 181, paragraph (1), the intentional introduction of waste in violation of regulations into the air, water, or soil is subject to a jail sentence of six months to two years, and fines. If the effects have the characteristic of being long-lasting, the penalties are to be doubled.[138] If the act is based on negligence the penalty is two months to two years.[139] There is no provision doubling the penalty in cases of potentially long-lasting effects. In case of intentional waste disposal, if the polluting waste material carries the potential to produce health hazards the treatment of which is difficult, or could affect the reproductive cycle of humans or animals, or could modify the natural makeup of animals or plants, the penalty can be no less than five years. Noticeably absent, however, is a maximum jail term. If the act is based on negligence the penalty is a minimum of one year and a maximum of five years jail sentence.[140] Furthermore, the illegal import of waste is subject to a potential maximum jail sentence of three years.[141] Noise pollution that can harm human health[142] and landscape pollution, based on violation of construction laws and regulations,[143] are also subject to criminal penalties.

Indirect environmental crimes are regulated under the Environmental Crimes section of the Turkish Criminal Code, but provisions are related to the protection of the environment and human health. Homicide through environmental pollution is defined as intentionally[144] and negligently;[145] risking others' life, health, or property by causing explosion by release of atomic energy;[146] storage or delivery of hazardous substances without permission;[147] mixing toxic substances to drinking water or food or causes decaying of any other consumption goods used as beverage and foodstuff;[148] or trading of decayed or transformed food or drugs.[149]

Turkish environmental law, as amended in 2002, abolished the funds that were established for the prevention of pollution. On the other hand, Turkish environmental law, as amended in 2006, provides for the collection of environmental contributions from specific investments in order to support the prevention of pollution.[150] In addition, in order to encourage pollution-prevention activities such as establishing waste treatment centers the Environmental Law, as amended in 2006, provides for the adoption of economic incentives.[151] Moreover, Article 28 of Environmental Law foresees a strict civil liability regime applicable to persons and entities that pollute the environment. Thus, the parties who pollute the environment and cause environmental damage will be held responsible for environmental pollution and degradation regardless of the existence of any misconduct. Moreover, the new Turkish Code of Obligation[152] has introduced a strict liability regime for dangerous activities.[153] Accordingly, the owner or manager of an enterprise that engages in dangerous activities will be liable for the damages caused by such activities. Furthermore, under the same law, even if enterprises are permitted by law to engage in dangerous activities, persons who suffer from any resulting damages have the right to demand compensation for their losses.

Notes

1. Türkiye İstatistik Kurumu (National Statistics Institute), http://www.tuik.gov.tr.
2. Mount Ağrı was declared a national park on 1 November 2004.
3. *Id.* 4.
4. E. ÖZHAN, PAP/RAC: COASTAL AREA MANAGEMENT IN TURKEY, PRIORITY ACTIONS PROGRAMME REGIONAL ACTIVITY CENTRE 7 (2005).
5. Convention on Wetlands of International Importance (Ramsar Convention), *Official Gazette* No. 21937, 17 May 1994.
6. Listed on 13 July 1994.
7. Listed on 13 July 1994.
8. Listed on 13 July 1994.
9. Listed on 15 April 1998.
10. Listed on 15 April 1998.
11. Listed on 15 April 1998.
12. Listed on 15 April 1998.
13. Listed on 21 June 2005.
14. Listed on 21 June 2005.
15. Listed on 2 May 2006.
16. Listed on 2 April 2009.
17. *See supra* note 3.
18. Dünya'da ve Türkiye'de Biyolojik Çeşitliligi Koruma Türkiye Bilimler Akademesi Raporları, No. 13, 2006. (Protection of Biological Diversity in Turkey and the World, Turkish Scientific Academy Reports, No. 13, 2006.)
19. IUCN, GUIDELINES FOR PROTECTED AREA MANAGEMENT CATEGORIES.
20. Amended in 2001.
21. Turkish Republic Constitution art. 75.
22. *Id.* art. 87.
23. Turkey was formally accepted as a candidate country for accession in 1999. See http://ec.europa.eu/enlargement/countries/detailed-country-information/turkey/index_en.htm.
24. Turkish Republic Constitution art. 56.
25. Law No. 2872, *Official Gazette* No. 19132, 11 August 1983.
26. Orman ve Su İşleri Bakanlığının kurulması ile bazı kanun ve kanun hükmünde kararnamelerde değişiklik yapılması; 6/4/2011 tarihli ve 6223 sayılı Kanunun verdiği yetkiye dayanılarak, Bakanlar Kurulu'nca 29/6/2011 tarihinde kararlaştırılmıştır. (On the establishment of the Ministry of Forestry and Su as decided by the Council of Ministers on 29/6/2011 based upon the authority granted under Law No. 6223 dated 6/4/2011.)
27. Includes the Directorate General for Rural Affairs.
28. Legislative Decree numbered 655 on the Organization and the Duties of the Ministry of Transport, Maritime Affairs and Communications (*Official Gazette* No. 28,102, 1 November 2011).
29. Under the auspices of the Ministry for Natural Resources and Energy.
30. *Official Gazette* No. 18,113, 23 July 1983.
31. *Official Gazette* No. 19,269, 2 November 1986.
32. *Official Gazette* No. 25,606, 7 October 2004 as amended *Official Gazette* No. 26,236, 22 July 2006.

33. *Official Gazette* No. 25,699, 31 January 2005.

34. *Official Gazette* No. 25,869, 8 July 2005.

35. *Official Gazette* No. 24,984, 5 January 2003.

36. MINISTRY OF ENV'T & URBANIZATION, REPUBLIC OF TURKEY CLIMATE CHANGE STRATEGY 2010–2020, at 9 (2012). *See also* REPUBLIC OF TURKEY, FIRST NATIONAL COMMUNICATION ON CLIMATE CHANGE (2007), *available at* http://unfccc.int/essential_background /library/items/3599.php?rec=j&priref=5834&suchen=n.

37. REPUBLIC OF TURKEY, FIRST NATIONAL COMMUNICATIONON CLIMATE CHANGE (2007), *supra* note 36.

38. *Official Gazette* No. 25,320, 18 December 2003.

39. UNFCCC Dec. 26/CP.6 (Marrakech, 2001).

40. Law No. 5836 dated 5 February 2009. *Official Gazette* No. 27,227, 13 May 2009. The ratification instrument was submitted to the UN Secretariat General on May 28, 2009, and Turkey officially became a party to the Protocol on August 26, 2009.

41. UNFCCC Dec. 1/CP.16, para. 141 (Cancun 2010).

42. UNFCCC Dec. 1/CP 18 (Doha 2012).

43. FIRST NATIONAL COMMUNICATION ON CLIMATE CHANGE, *supra* note 35.

44. Ninth Five-Year Development Program (2007–2013), para. 461, *available at* http:// pbk.tbmm.gov.tr/dokumanlar/kalkinma-plani-9-genel-kurul.pdf.

45. *Official Gazette* No. 17,796, 23 March 1983.

46. *Official Gazette* No. 18,820, 23 July 1985.

47. *Official Gazette* No. 22,155, 28 December 1994.

48. As amended in 1987, *Official Gazette* No. 22,155, 28 December 1994; *Official Gazette* No. 22,419, 29 September 1995; *Official Gazette* No. 25,131, 7 June 2003; *Official Gazette* No. 25,141, 17 June 2003.

49. National Communication, *supra* note 36, 55.

50. The Convention on International Trade in Endangered Species of Fauna and Flora (1973).

51. The Berne Convention on the Conservation of European Wildlife and Their Natural Habitats (1979).

52. Türkiye'deki Ramsar Alanlari Değerlendirme Raporu WWF-Türkiye (2008) (Assessment of Wetlands in Turkey, WWF-Turkey) http://www.wwf.org.tr/pdf/WWF _Turkiye_Ramsar_Alanlari_Degerlendirme_Raporu.pdf.

53. The Environment, Special Experts Report, Ninth Development Plan (2007–2013) State Planning Organization, *available at* http://plan9.dpt.gov.tr/oik22_cevre/cevre.pdf.

54. *See supra* note 3.

55. Convention on Wetlands of International Importance (RAMSAR), *Official Gazette* No. 21,937, 15 March 1994.

56. Law No. 5516, adopted 18 January 1950, *Official Gazette* No. 7413, 23 January 1950.

57. Nilufer Oral, *Oil and Water: Caspian Oil and Transportation Challenges Facing the Turkish Straits, in* CURRENT MARINE ENVIRONMENTAL ISSUES AND THE INTERNATIONAL TRIBUNAL FOR THE LAW OF THE SEA 329–64 (Myron H. Nordquist & John Norton Moore eds., 2001).

58. Statistics provided by the Turkish Undersecretariat for Maritime Affairs.

59. The International Tanker Owner Pollution Federation Ltd., Major Oil Spills, http://www.itopf.com/information%2Dservices/data%2Dand%2Dstatistics/statistics /index.html#major.

60. *Supra* note 3, at 9. *See also* Ertug Duzgunes & Naciye Erdogan, *Fisheries Management in the Black Sea Countries,* 8 TURK. J. FISH. & AQUATIC SCI. 181–92 (2008).

61. Black Sea Environmental Programme, The Black Sea Transboundary Diagnostic Analysis (1997), 22 June 1996.

62. *Id.*

63. *See supra* note 3.

64. Turkish Straits Maritime Traffic Regulations, Decision No. 98/11860, *Official Gazette* No. 23,515, 6 November 1998.

65. *Id.* art. 20(i) as amended by the Decree No. 28171 dated 12 January 2012 increasing fine amounts.

66. *Id.*

67. *Id.* art. 20.

68. *Id.*

69. *Id.*

70. *Supra* note 64.

71. *Id.* art. 29.

72. *Id.* art. 26.

73. Turkey is not a party to the 1982 United Nations Convention on the Law of the Sea, adopted 10 Nov. 1982 1833 U.N.T.S. 3, entered into force 16 Nov. 1994.

74. *Official Gazette* No. 20,558, 24 June 1998.

75. *Official Gazette* No. 17,368, 12 June 1981; *Official Gazette* No.24,854, 22 August 2002.

76. *Id.*

77. *Official Gazette* No. 17,368, 12 June 1981.

78. *Official Gazette* No. 25,113, 20 May 2003.

79. *Official Gazette* No. 19,404, 18 March 1987 as amended by *Official Gazette* No. 24,854, 22 August 2002.

80. *Official Gazette* No. 19,968, 12 October 1988.

81. *Official Gazette* No. 24,854, 22 August 2002.

82. *Official Gazette* No. 21,788, 14 December 1993.

83. Law No. 3957, Official Gazette No. 21,935, 15 May 1994.

84. Law No. 4507, *Official Gazette* No. 23,948, 29 January 2001.

85. Law No. 4658, *Official Gazette* No. 24,397, 9 May 2001.

86. Law No. 4882, *Official Gazette* No. 25,233, 18 September 2003.

87. The Convention on the Prevention of Marine Pollution by Dumping Wastes and other Matters, 1972 Nov. 1972, 1046 U.N.T.S. 120, entered into force 30 August 1975.

88. 1996 Protocol to the 1972 London on the Prevention of Marine Pollution by the Dumping of Wastes and Other Matter, 7 Nov. 1996, *reprinted in* 36 ILM 1 (1997), entered into force 24 March 2006.

89. Law No. 5312, *Official Gazette* No. 25,752, 11 March 2005.

90. *Official Gazette* No. 26,326, 21 October 2006.

91. *Official Gazette* No. 19,919, 3 September 1988, as amended in 1998, 1999, 2000, and 2002.

92. *Official Gazette* No. 22,223, 10 March 1995.

93. *Official Gazette* No. 25,682, 11 December 2004.

94. *Official Gazette* No. 19,623, 3 November 1987.

95. *Official Gazette* No. 27,092, 26 December 2008.

96. *Official Gazette* No. 27,092, 26 December 2008.

97. *Official Gazette* No. 27,092, 26 December 2008.

98. *Official Gazette* No. 27,092, 26 December 2008.

99. *Official Gazette* No. 27,092, 26 December 2008.

100. *Official Gazette* No. 25,353, 21 January 2004.

101. *Official Gazette* No. 25,538, 30 July 2004.

102. *Official Gazette* No. 25,744, 3 March 2005.

103. *Official Gazette* No. 25,730, 17 February 2005.

104. *Official Gazette* No. 26,047, 8 January 2006.

105. *Official Gazette* No. 25,883, 22 July 2005.

106. *Official Gazette* No. 25,831, 31 May 2005.

107. *Official Gazette* No. 26,005, 26 November 2005.

108. According to the statistics published by General Directorate of National Conservation and National Parks, http://www.milliparklar.gov.tr/Anasayfa/istatistik.aspx?sflang=tr.

109. The nine specially protected areas are Fethiye/Göcek, Köyceğiz/Dalyan, Gökova Bay, Göksu Delta, Kekova, Patara, Belek, Datca Peninsula, and Foça. ÖZHAN, *supra* note 3, at 8.

110. Convention for the Protection of the World Cultural and Natural Heritage, 16 Nov. 1972, 11 ILM 1358 (1972); Turkey became a party in 1983. *Official Gazette* No. 17,959, 14 February 1983.

111. Turkish Ministry of Forestry and Water, Draft Action Plan for Combating Erosion 2013-2017, http://www.cem.gov.tr/erozyon/Files/yayinlarimiz/EROZYON%20EYLEM.pdf.

112. NECMETTIN CEPEL, ORMAN EROZYONU (2007).

113. *Id.*

114. IUCN, *supra* note 18.

115. Done at Aarhus, Denmark, on 25 June 1998, 2161 U.N.T.S. 447, entered into force 30 October 2001.

116. Law No. 4982 *Official Gazette* No. 25,269, 24 October 2003.

117. *Id.* art. 4.

118. Regulation on Environment Impact Assessment, *Official Gazette* No. 26,939, 17 July 2008.

119. Arts. 9 and 10.

120. *Official Gazette* No. 17,796, 23 March 1983.

121. *Official Gazette* No. 18,820, 23 July 1985.

122. *Official Gazette* No. 22,155, 28 December 1994.

123. As amended in 1987, *Official Gazette* No. 22,155, 28 December 1994; *Official Gazette* No. 22,419, 29 September 1995; *Official Gazette* No. 25,131, 7 June 2003; *Official Gazette* No. 25,141, 17 June 2003.

124. *Official Gazette* No. 20,558, 24 June 1998.

125. *Official Gazette* No. 17,368, 12 June 1981; *Official Gazette* No. 24,854, 22 August 2002.

126. *Official Gazette* No. 17,368, 12 June 1981; *Official Gazette* No. 24,854, 22 August 2002.

127. *Official Gazette* No. 17,368, 12 June 1981.

128. *Official Gazette* No. 25,113, 20 May 2003.

129. *Official Gazette* No. 19,404, 18 March 1987, as amended by *Official Gazette* No. 24,854, 22 August 2002.

130. *Official Gazette* No. 19,968, 12 October 1988.

131. *Official Gazette* No. 24,854, 22 August 2002.

132. *Official Gazette* No. 21,788, 14 December 1993.

133. Law No. 3957, *Official Gazette* No. 21,935, 15 May 1994.

134. Law No. 4507, *Official Gazette* No. 23,948, 29 January 2001.

135. Law No. 4658, *Official Gazette* No. 24,397, 9 May 2001.

136. Law No. 4882, *Official Gazette* No. 25,233, 18 September 2003.

137. Law No. 5237, *Official Gazette* No. 25,611, 12 October 2004.

138. *Id.* art. 181(3).

139. *Id.* art. 182 (1).

140. *Id.* art. 182 (2).

141. *Id.* art. 181 (2).

142. *Id.* art. 183. The penalty range is two months to two years.

143. *Id.* art. 184 (1)–(5). The penalty range is one year to five years.

144. Turkish Criminal Code art. 81.

145. *Id.* art. 85.

146. Arts. 172–173.

147. *Id.* art. 174.

148. *Id.* art. 185.

149. *Id.* art. 186.

150. Environmental Law Arts. 17–19.

151. *Id.* art. 29.

152. Law No. 6098, *Official Gazette* No. 27,836, 4 February 2011, entered into force 1 July 2012.

153. *Id.* art. 71.

CHAPTER 44

Nigeria

TONBOFA EVA ASHIMI, TOLULOPE ABIMBOLA MOSELI, AND FRANCIS ETIVIEYA

I. Introduction

Environmental law in Nigeria has evolved in the context of the government's significant role in the exploration and development of oil and gas resources. These oil and development projects damaged the environment and exposed its people to pollution, ultimately leading the Nigerian federal and state governments[1] to pass laws to prevent and reduce pollution. Despite these efforts, the incidence of environmental pollution continues to rise, with the worst cases occurring in the oil producing areas—where oil can still commonly be seen floating on water surfaces, and gas flaring remains a common practice. This chapter identifies the primary Nigerian environmental laws that have emerged in this context, but acknowledges that the failure to enforce laws remains a serious barrier to the amelioration of Nigeria's environmental problems.

II. Air and Climate Change
A. Air Pollution Control

The National Environmental Standards and Regulations Enforcement Agency Act, 2007 (NESREA Act),[2] under sections 20 and 21, deals with air quality and atmospheric pollution. Section 20(1) provides that the National Environmental Standards and Regulations Enforcement Agency may make regulations setting specifications to protect and enhance the quality of Nigeria's air resources, so as to promote the public health or welfare and the natural development and productive capacity of the nation's human, animal, marine, or plant life. To achieve these objectives, the agency is required to observe or carry out the following:

- maintain essential air quality standards;
- control the concentration of substances in the air;
- formulate the most appropriate means to prevent and combat atmospheric pollution;

867

- control of pollution originating from energy sources, such as aircraft, factories, and other self-propelled vehicles;
- formulate applicable standards of emission from new mobile or stationary sources; and
- use appropriate means to reduce emissions to permissible level.

The agency has promulgated the National Environmental (Control of Vehicular Emission from Petrol and Diesel Engine) Regulations, 2011, which makes violation of the regulations an offense. Any offender will, upon conviction, be liable for a fine not exceeding Nigerian naira (₦) 200,000 or one year's imprisonment; in the case of a corporate entity, the liability is ₦2 million. Additional fines of ₦20,000 for individuals and ₦50,000 for corporations are imposed respectively for each day the offense continues.

The government has also enacted the Associated Gas Re-injection Act 1979 and Associated Gas Re-injection (Continuation of Flaring of Gas) 1985, aimed at regulating gas flaring in the oil and gas industry as a result of oil exploration and exploitation. Under these laws, gas flaring is generally prohibited, except with the consent of the minister of the agency. The minister's consent will only be granted where an applicant has demonstrated a willingness to adhere to conditions set as part of the agency's approval.

B. Climate Change

1. *The Kyoto Protocol*

The major feature of the Kyoto Protocol to the U.N. Framework Convention on Climate Change (UNFCCC) is that it sets binding targets for 37 industrialized countries and the European Community for reducing greenhouse gas (GHG) emissions, and permits those countries to purchase Certificates of Emission Reduction from Clean Development Mechanism (CDM) projects hosted in developing nations. Such projects can lead to GHG reductions and can then be counted as part of those countries' efforts to reduce their emissions. The Nigerian Department of Climate Change and the Special Climate Change Unit under the Federal Ministry of Environment are currently responsible for ensuring Nigeria's implementation of the Kyoto Protocol. Nigeria operates six CDM projects registered by the UNFCCC Secretariat in Bonn, Germany.[3]

The federal government, pursuant to the UNFCCC, approved the National Policy on Climate Change and Response Strategy (NPCC-RS) on September 12, 2012. The policy includes objectives related to climate change mitigation, adaptation, climate science and technology, public awareness, private sector participation, and strengthening national institutions and mechanisms.

Nigeria is also developing a Strategic Framework for Voluntary Nationally Appropriate Mitigation Action (NAMA) as a step toward meeting national obligations under the UNFCCC. The NAMA strategic framework will allow Nigeria to develop long-term measures and programs supporting a low-carbon, climate-resilient, progrowth, and gender-sensitive sustainable development pathway. In addition to specific climate change-related policies, Nigeria has several environmental and sectoral policies and plans in place where climate change adaptation policies could apply. For example, the National Policy on Environment supports "the prevention and management of natural disasters such as floods, drought, and desertification." And one of the objectives of Nigeria's Agricultural Policy is to "protect agricultural land resources from drought, desert encroachment, soil erosion, and floods." Other examples include Nigeria's Drought Preparedness Plan, National Policy on Erosion and Flood Control, National Water Policy, National Forest Policy, and National Health Policy.[4]

There are a number of federal government agencies currently involved in climate change adaptation issues, including the Nigerian Meteorological Agency (NIMET), National Emergency Management Authority (NEMA), and the National Planning Commission (NPC). The House of Representative of the Nigerian Federal Legislature in June 2012 passed a bill into law establishing the Climate Change Commission. The bill is as of this writing before the House of Senate.[5] The Climate Change Commission is to be charged with advising the government on climate change policies, promoting technological progress promoting climate change research, and coordinating all other entities involved in climate change.[6]

III.   Water
A.   Water Resources Act

To protect against flooding, among other water related problems, the Water Resources Act[7] promotes the optimum planning, development, and use of Nigeria's water resources and other related matters. The act vests the right to use and control all surface and groundwater and any watercourse, riverbed, and banks affecting more than one state in the federal government. The act provides for the coordination of activities that are likely to influence the quality, quantity, distribution, use, and management of water. It also ensures the application of appropriate standards and techniques for the investigation, use, control, protection, management, and administration of water resources and facilitation of technical assistance and rehabilitation for water supplies. The minister in the federal executive arm of government charged with water resource management is to implement the act.

While the minister of water resources administers the Water Resource Act, to ensure the proper use of the nation's waters, regulations made under NESREA are made by the minister of environment. Those regulations seek to prevent pollution of water sources. From the date of enactment, the diversion, storage, pumping, or use on a commercial scale of any water or the construction, maintenance, operation, or repair of any bore-hole or any hydraulic works shall be carried out pursuant to a license issued by the minister of water resources. The minister of water resources is also empowered under section 13 of the NESREA Act to impose a fee for a license concerning the industrial use of water.

B. Marine Pollution

1. *Maritime and Safety Agency Act*

The Nigerian Maritime and Safety Agency Act (NIMASA Act)[8] establishes the Nigerian Maritime and Safety Agency (NIMASA) and empowers it to ensure maritime safety and control marine pollution, among other functions. NIMASA may make regulations related to the dumping of ships and shore-generated waste and removal of wrecks that are a threat to the marine environment. In making such regulations, NIMASA is to consider international conventions to which Nigeria is a party. Ships carrying harmful substances can only do so in compliance with the NIMASA Act and must carry a manifest listing the harmful substances carried and establishing that the substances are well secured. NIMASA regulates the terms and conditions under which the harmful substances must be stored and the procedure for washing leaks overboard. A breach of the NIMASA Act constitutes an offense and the offender will be liable for a fine or imprisonment upon conviction.[9]

NIMASA established a department under it called Marine Environmental Management. This department oversees the implementation of all relevant International Maritime Organization (IMO) conventions by not only drafting a framework for their implementation but also formulating national guidelines to ensure compliance. The department also monitors Nigerian territorial waters through aerial surveillance and routine patrol; monitors oil cargo tank and washing exercises of tankers to ensure compliance with Annex 1, Reg. 13 and 13A of the International Convention for the Prevention of Pollution from Ships (MARPOL)[10] and other environmental standards; conducts inspection of antipollution equipment onboard vessels; and ensures that all marine environment-related projects are conducted consistent with best management practices.

2. *The 1977 Convention on the Prevention of Marine Pollution by Dumping of Waste and Other Matters*

This convention is an agreement to control marine pollution by dumping and to encourage regional agreements to supplement the convention. It covers the deliberate disposal at sea of wastes or other matter from vessels, aircraft, and platforms. It does not cover discharges from land-based sources, such as pipes and outfalls, wastes generated incidentally to the normal operation of vessels, or placement of materials for purposes other than mere disposal, provided that such disposal is not contrary to aims of the convention.

IV. Handling, Treatment, Transportation, and Disposal of Hazardous Materials

A. Harmful Waste Act

The Harmful Waste Act[11] prohibits the carrying, depositing, transporting, importing, selling, or buying of harmful waste on or into the territory and territorial waters of Nigeria[12] and provides for punishment, including life imprisonment, for offenders. Harmful wastes under the Harmful Waste Act refer to any injurious, poisonous, toxic, or noxious substance. The term includes nuclear waste emitting any radioactive substance if the waste is in such a quantity, whether with any other consignment of the same or of different substance, that it subjects any person to the risk of death, fatal injury, or incurable impairment of physical or mental health. The fact that the harmful waste is placed in a container does not by itself excuse the exposure of the public to any risk that might be expected to arise from the harmful waste.

The minister charged with the responsibility of works and housing in the federal executive arm of government is responsible for enforcing the provisions of this act.

B. The Bamako Convention, 1991

The Bamako Convention on the Ban of the Import into Africa and the Control of Transboundary Movement and Management of Hazardous Wastes within Africa (Bamako Convention)[13] was entered into by African nations to prohibit the import of any hazardous (including radioactive) waste. The convention was negotiated by 12 nations of the Organization of African Unity at Bamako, Mali, in January 1991, and came into force in 1998. The need for the Bamako Convention arose from the failure of the Basel Convention on the Control of Transboundary Movements of Hazardous Wastes and Their Disposal (Basel Convention)[14] to prohibit trade of hazardous waste to less developed countries (LDCs), and from the realization that many developed nations were exporting toxic wastes to Africa. This impression was strengthened by several prominent cases. One important case, which occurred in 1987, concerned the importation into Nigeria of 18,000 barrels (2,900 m^3) of hazardous waste from the Italian companies Ecomar and Jelly Wax. These entities had agreed to pay a local farmer named Sunday Nana $100 per month for storage. The barrels, found in storage in the port of Lagos, contained toxic waste including polychlorinated biphenyls, and their eventual shipment back to Italy led to protests closing three Italian ports.

Steps being taken by the Nigerian government to secure the implementation of the Bamako Convention in Nigeria include the passage of the Electronic Waste Bill, which is at the time of this writing being considered by the Nigerian Parliament. This bill, when passed into law, would ban the importation and illegal trafficking of electronic and electrical waste from developed countries to Nigeria. Separately, the agency is currently coordinating the national implementation of the Toxic Waste Dump Watch Programme, which monitors and prevents illegal dumping of hazardous wastes in Nigeria.

V.   Waste and Site Remediation

Under the Petroleum Act,[15] regulations have been promulgated requiring the government to monitor, control, and regulate the exploration of oil in Nigeria. The Petroleum (Drilling and Production) Regulations, by Regulation 25, which was established based on section 9 of the Petroleum Act, requires licensees to adopt all practical measures, including installation of up-to-date equipment, to prevent the pollution of inland waters, rivers, watercourses, the territorial waters of Nigeria, or the high seas by oil, mud, or other fluid or substances that might contaminate the water, banks, or shoreline, or that might cause harm or destruction to freshwater or marine life. Where any such pollution occurs or has occurred, responsible parties shall take prompt steps to control and, if possible, stop the pollution.

Also under Regulation 41, a licensee is obligated to drain all waste oil, brine, and sludge or refuse from all vessels, boreholes, and wells into proper receptacles constructed in compliance with safety regulations for proper disposal.

In respect of the nonoil sectors, the agency, as empowered by the NES-REA Act, has promulgated regulations to monitor, control, and regulate waste management and effluent discharge. The National Environmental (Sanitation and Waste Control) Regulations, 2009 are one example of such regulations. These regulations require all owners or occupiers of premises to provide waste receptacles for storage of waste. The regulations also require owners or persons who control waste-generating facilities to reduce, reuse, and recycle waste to minimize pollution. The facility owner is required to adopt cleaner production principles to conserve raw materials and energy; segregate wastes at the source; undertake resource recovery, recycling, and reuse; and ensure safe disposal. A licensed waste manager is obligated to collect the waste at a designated point and at a scheduled time.

Also, effluent discharges from housing estates, hotels, commercial facilities, waste management facilities, hospitals, abattoirs, and livestock farms are not to be discharged into public drains or natural environments without a permit from the agency. The regulations also prohibit throwing or causing any liquid, solid, or gaseous substance that may cause pollution to flow into or near water bodies. Under Regulation 71, various offenses are established, punishable by imprisonment—upon conviction—for a period ranging from six months to two years, and fines ranging from ₦20,000 to ₦500,000.

VI.   Emergency Response
A.   National Oil Spill Detection Response Agency Act

The National Oil Spill Detection Response Agency Act[16] establishes the National Oil Spill Detection and Response Agency (NOSDRA), which is charged with detecting and responding to all oil spills in Nigeria and ensure compliance with all existing environmental legislation in the petroleum sector. The NOSDRA receives reports of oil spills and—in collaboration with other agencies—assesses the extent of damage to the environment. NOSDRA advises the federal and state governments on possible effects of spills on human health and ensures that appropriate remedial action is taken for the restoration of the environment. NOSDRA also mediates between affected communities and the responsible party.

VII. Natural Resource Management and Protection
A. The Constitution of the Federal Republic of Nigeria

The Nigerian Constitution[17] makes it the responsibility of the Nigerian government to ensure the protection of the environment. Although the federal and state governments share authority to make these laws, under the constitution, regulation of certain activities, such as construction, meteorology, mines and minerals, oil and gas, nuclear energy, and their environmental effects is exclusively reserved to the federal government. Because these activities reserved for the federal government constitute the major sources of environmental pollution, existing environmental laws are primarily those enacted by the federal government.

B. Petroleum Act

The Petroleum Act sets certain standards for the exploration of petroleum from the territorial waters and continental shelf of Nigeria. The act vests the control and supervision of the operations of exploration of petroleum in the federal government, which owns all petroleum resources. Any person desiring to explore or prospect for petroleum or seeking an oil-mining lease to search for, capture, transport, and dispose of petroleum is required to apply for licenses from the minister of petroleum.

Also, no refinery shall be constructed or operated in Nigeria without a license granted by the minister. No person shall import, store, sell, or distribute any petroleum products in Nigeria without a license granted by the minister.[18] That said, storage, sale, or distribution of not more than 500 liters of kerosene and such other categories of petroleum products as may be exempted by the minister do not require a license. Similarly, no license is required for storage of petroleum products undertaken not for the purpose of importation, sale, or distribution of petroleum products.

However, anyone undertaking any of those activities requiring a license without obtaining the requisite license shall be liable on conviction to imprisonment for two years or a fine (as may be fixed by the court) and forfeiture of the petroleum concerned. Petroleum under the act means mineral oil (or any related hydrocarbon) or natural gas as it exists in its natural state in strata. It does not include coal or bituminous shales or other stratified deposits from which oil can be extracted by destructive distillation.

The Department of Petroleum Resources (DPR) is the organ responsible for supervising all petroleum industry operations and enforcing safety and environmental regulations and standards according to international standards. The DPR reviews license applications from operators in the oil and gas sector and makes recommendations to the petroleum minister. The DPR inspects operations and projects sites used by oil and gas operators to ensure compliance with relevant laws.

VIII.   Natural Resource Damages
A.   Oil in Navigable Waters

The objective of the Oil in Navigable Waters Act[19] is to take action to prevent pollution of the Nigerian coast and territorial waters by oil discharged from ships. The act implements the provisions of the International Convention for the Prevention of Pollution of the Sea by Oil, 1954.[20]

Where any oil or mixture containing oil is discharged into the sea within the seaward limits of the territorial waters of Nigeria or all other waters (including inland waters) within the seaward limits of the waters and are navigable by seagoing ships, from any vessel, the owner or master of the vessel shall be guilty of an offense.[21] Where the discharge is from a place on land, the occupier of that place shall also be guilty of an offense. Where the discharge is from an apparatus used for transferring oil from or to a vessel, the person in charge of the apparatus shall be guilty of an offense under the act and subject to prosecution by the attorney general of the Federation.

B.   MARPOL

MARPOL[22] applies to all ships, except tankers of under 150 tons gross tonnage and other ships of under 500 tons gross tonnage, registered in the territory of, or having the nationality of, a party. Naval ships and ships engaged in whaling are also excepted by Article 2 of MARPOL. The convention's objective is to take action to prevent marine pollution by oil discharged from ships. The Nigerian Legislature has passed an act to make this convention applicable and enforceable in Nigeria.[23]

IX.   Protected Species
A.   The 1973 Convention on International Trade in Endangered Species of Wild Fauna and Flora (CITES)

CITES aims at ensuring that international trade in specimens of wild animals and plants does not threaten their survival in the wild, and it accords varying degrees of protection to more than 33,000 species of animals and plants. Nigeria has ratified this convention to take full advantage of its status as a party. To protect flora and fauna in Nigeria consistent with CITES, laws have been passed to control excessive exploitation of the nation's terrestrial biodiversity, especially its wild fauna, preserve wild animal populations, protect endangered species, and designate national parks. To facilitate its application and enforcement in Nigeria, the Nigerian Legislature has passed the Endangered Species (Control of International Trade and Traffic) Act, which provides for the conservation and management of wildlife and the protection of endangered species. Under the act, the trade in species specified in the first schedule as provided in section 1(1) is absolutely prohibited. However, the minister charged with responsibility for wildlife can grant permits to individuals to trade in species specified in the second schedule, provided that certain conditions are met.

X. Environmental Review and Decision Making
A. Ministries of Environment

The federal and state governments in Nigeria have a Ministry for the Environment headed by a minister and a commissioner respectively. The Ministries for Environment generally issue guidelines, standards, rules, and regulations to ensure protection of the environment.

B. NESREA

The NESREA Act[24] establishes the NESREA, which is charged with enforcing all environmental laws, guidelines, policies, standards, and regulations in Nigeria, except in the oil and gas sector. The NESREA is also charged with enforcing compliance with the provisions of international agreements, protocols, conventions, and treaties on the environment.

The NESREA has powers to:

- prohibit processes and use of equipment or technology that undermine environmental quality;
- make proposals for the approval of the minister of environment on atmospheric protection, air quality, ozone-depleting substances, noise control, effluent limitations, water quality, waste management and environmental sanitation, erosion and flood control, coastal zone management, dams and reservoirs, watershed management, deforestation and bush burning, control of hazardous substances and removal control methods, and other forms of pollution and sanitation;
- inspect, enter, and search with a warrant issued by a court any premises—including any land, vehicle, tent, vessel, floating craft (except maritime tankers, barges, or floating production storage offload and oil and gas facilities or any inland water)—for the purpose of conducting inspections, searching, and taking samples for analysis reasonably believed to be used for activities or the storage of goods that contravene environmental standards or legislation.

The NESREA has issued a large number of media- and industry-specific regulations.[25] The NESREA conducts situation investigation and assessment before it licenses the operation of certain activities affecting the environment. It monitors compliance and, where there is contravention, may seize an offending article or even arrest the perpetrators of the offensive activities. To effectively do these, the NESREA has set up a working mechanism by establishing a zonal office in each of the six geo-political zones in the country and functional offices in 17 states. There also exists the Federal-State Regulatory Dialogue on compliance monitoring and enforcement, which provides a forum for participants from the various regulatory agencies to share experiences.

An important initiative of the NESREA is the Toxic Waste Dump program.[26] The main objective of this program is to halt the flow of hazardous wastes into Nigeria, enforce federal regulations to reduce the dumping of wastes, and respond to calls and alerts concerning suspected dumping at sea.

Separately, the NESREA conducts registration for importers of waste electrical and electronic equipment to control the type of electrical and electronic equipment being imported into the country. The NESREA also works to increase networking and collaboration with other entities. For instance, Nigeria is a member of Seaport Environmental Security Network and the International Network for Environmental Compliance and Enforcement (INECE). These memberships have yielded positive results and assisted in the prevention of toxic substance dumping in Nigeria.

C.   Environmental Impact Assessment Act[27]

All private and public organizations must obtain approval from the NESREA[28] on the environmental impact of any proposed activity before commencing the activity. The NESREA invites government agencies, members of the public, experts in any relevant discipline, and interested groups to comment on the environmental impact assessment (EIA) and will not take its decision until the designated period for comments has lapsed.[29] NESREA must provide a written basis for its decision, which should include its reasoning and means to prevent or mitigate damage to the environment. Where the NESREA believes the proposed project will not cause significant adverse environmental effects, or that the effects can be mitigated, the NESREA may exercise any power or perform any duty to facilitate performance of the project and ensure that mitigation measures are implemented. The NESREA shall refuse to permit the activity to move forward where it believes that the activity will cause significant adverse environmental effects that cannot be mitigated.[30]

XI.   Transboundary Pollution

A.   The 1981 Convention for Co-operation in the Protection and Development of the Marine and Coastal Environment of the West and Central African Region (Abidjan Convention)

The Abidjan Convention[31] seeks to ensure the protection and development of the marine and coastal environment of the West and Central African regions. It provides an important framework through which national policy makers and resource managers of the parties to the convention can implement national control measures to effectuate its goals. The Abidjan Convention is expected to play a leading role in guiding and sustaining environmental action for the protection and development of the coastal and marine areas through concerted efforts and activities to which party governments and their citizenry can positively respond to facilitate in the complex challenges of the management processes of coastal areas.

The convention calls for regular meetings of the parties once every two years and extraordinary meetings at any other time deemed necessary, upon the request of the Organization of African Unity or at the request of any party, supported by at least three other parties. The parties shall at such meetings review the convention's implementation and its related protocols and in particular review the state of pollution in the marine and coastal environment of the West and Central African regions. Nigeria is a party and has taken steps to ratify it and make it enforceable.

B.   The Basel Convention

The Basel Convention[32] is an international treaty designed to reduce the movements of hazardous waste between nations, and specifically to prevent transfer of hazardous waste from developed to LDCs. It does not, however, address the movement of radioactive waste. It is also intended to minimize the amount and toxicity of wastes generated, to ensure their environmentally sound management as closely as possible to the source of generation, and to assist LDCs in environmentally sound management of the hazardous and other wastes they generate. Nigeria ratified the convention in March 1991.

XII.   Civil and Criminal Enforcement and Penalties
A.   International Convention on Civil Liability for Oil Pollution Damages

The International Convention on Civil Liability for Oil Pollution Damages[33] (Civil Liability Convention) was adopted to ensure that adequate compensation is available to persons who suffer oil pollution damage resulting from maritime casualties involving oil-carrying ships.[34] The convention places the liability for such damage on the owner of the ship from which the polluting oil escaped or was discharged. It establishes strict liability for discharges, with several exceptions described in Regulation 11. These are (1) the discharge is necessary for the purpose of securing the safety of a ship or saving life at sea; (2) the discharge results from damage to a ship or its equipment, provided that all reasonable precautions have been taken after the occurrence of the damage or discovery of the discharge for the purpose of preventing or minimizing the discharge, and the owner or the master has not acted intentionally or recklessly to cause damage with knowledge that damage would likely occur; or (3) the discharge is being used for the purpose of combating specific pollution incidents to minimize the damage from pollution (this latter exception is, however, subject to the approval of the government in whose jurisdiction the discharge is contemplated to occur). Thus, where pollution results solely from the fault or negligent act of the owner or master, he is liable. The convention requires ships covered by it to maintain insurance or other financial security in sums equivalent to the owner's total liability for one incident. This convention has been ratified and adopted as part of the Nigerian laws on environmental protection. NIMASA is the governmental agency charged with the responsibility for preventing marine pollution in Nigeria as well as implementing the provisions of this and related conventions.

B.   International Convention on the Establishment of an International Fund for Compensation for Oil Pollution Damages

The International Convention on the Establishment of an International Fund for Compensation for Oil Pollution Damages[35] establishes an international fund to provide compensation for pollution damage to the extent that the protection afforded by the Civil Liability Convention is insufficient.[36] The compensation would be available for the dual purpose of, on the one hand, relieving the ship owner of the financial burden of paying compensation to persons who suffer oil pollution damage resulting from maritime casualties involving oil-carrying ships and, on the other hand, providing additional compensation to the victims of pollution damage in cases where compensation under the Civil Liability Convention was either inadequate or unobtainable. The convention was ratified by the International Convention on the Establishment of an International Fund for Compensation for Oil Pollution Damage 1971 as amended (Ratification and Enforcement) Act.[37] NIMASA is the department charged with ensuring and preventing marine pollution in Nigeria, and implementing this convention.

C.   Judicial Enforcement

There are cases decided by the Nigerian judiciary that have enforced the various environmental laws in the country. Some of these decisions involve environmental torts founded upon the civil law actions of negligence, nuisance, trespass, and damages. They are usually instituted by private individuals seeking damages for unreasonable interference with the use of their environment and their enjoyment of public rights. The plaintiff must have the right to commence the action by showing that he possesses sufficient interest in the action. The Supreme Court of Nigeria clarified all issues on the right to sue in environmental actions in the case of *Adediran v. Interland Transport Limited*,[38] where the appellants as residents of a particular area instituted the action for nuisance due to noise, vibration, dust, and obstruction of the roads in the area. The Supreme Court of Nigeria held that in light of section 6(6)(2) of the 1979 Constitution of the Federal Republic of Nigeria,[39] a private person can commence an action for public nuisance without the consent of the attorney general and without joining him as a party where the plaintiff proves that he has suffered injury above that of the public. A victim of environmental pollution can also seek an injunction. He can do this by filling a writ of summons, but he must have a valid cause of action. Some of the causes of actions include negligence, nuisance, damages, and injunction. In *Shell Petroleum Development Co. of Nigeria Limited v. Chief Otoko*,[40] the plaintiffs sued the defendant for negligence arising from a crude oil spill resulting in injurious effects to their river and creeks. The court entered judgment in their favor.

With respect to pollution to communally owned land, surrounding waters, and air, the affected communities and not individuals are permitted to sue for pollution. An individual can only sue if he proves he has also suffered a private injury and he can claim only for his personal loss. For example, in the case of *Chijuka v. Maduwesi*,[41] the plaintiffs brought suit seeking, inter alia, a declaration that the first defendant's action of building a hotel in a strictly residential area, if permitted, would amount to a violation of the environmental and planning laws. The plaintiffs alleged that the hotel's construction would cause grave damage for which no sufficient or adequate remedy would be available. The court, in answering the question as to who has the responsibility to prevent a public nuisance, emphasized that a nuisance—whether public or private—is an injury conferring on affected individuals a right of action. Even where the injury is an injury to the public, it may also constitute injury to the individual. The individual, however, must establish that an injury exists before he is granted a right of action against.

In *Gbamre v. S.P.D.C. Nigeria Ltd*,[42] the plaintiff sued on behalf of himself and the people of the Iwherekan Community, requesting the Federal High Court, Benin Division, to declare that gas flaring is illegal and harmful to their health and the environment, and therefore constitutes a violation of their right to life as guaranteed by the 1999 Constitution of the Federal Republic of Nigeria and reinforced by the African Charter on Human and Peoples' Rights (African Charter).[43] In his judgment, Justice V.C Nwokorie held in favor of the applicants, finding that the continuing flaring of gas is a violation of the rights provided by the constitution and the African Charter. The judgment has been lauded in several local and international quarters and to date stands as one of the most far-reaching decisions given by a Nigerian court on issues relating to the environment. Despite Nigeria's wealth in natural gas deposits, oil extraction remains more prevalent, and this is one of the few cases involving pollution by natural gas.[44] With the Nigerian government's intention to increase Nigeria's natural gas supply, however, gas drilling has increased and there are more instances of environmental pollution arising from natural gas drilling, with a few communities suing operators for damages arising from pollution by escape of natural gas.[45]

Judicial decisions establishing liability have at times been vulnerable to what is arguably a reluctance on the part of multinational corporations to accept initial Nigeria court rulings, and a tendency to engage in protracted litigation through the appellate levels. Nigerian claimants have turned to foreign courts in countries where these multinationals have head offices to obtain redress. For example, in a recent Dutch court decision against Shell Petroleum Development Company of Nigeria Limited (SPDC) the court held SPDC, a subsidiary of the Royal Dutch Shell plc, liable for damages to Niger River delta farmers from Ogoni land in Nigeria for failure to protect against sabotage in its operations. This case will encourage other claimants to seek redress abroad.

D. Enforcement by Regulators

The NESREA actively guards environmental standards by imposing fines and shutting down businesses for environmental infractions.[46] However, the process or procedures by which the NESREA resolves claims against companies that it has identified as violating its environmental standards is not clear. The extent to which companies ultimately pay the fines that the NESREA imposes, and whether the NESREA subsequently tends to accept lesser sums or absolves the targeted companies from paying the sums demanded, is also less than clear. It does appear that the NESREA's enforcement discretion is not insulated from the influence of other political entities. For instance, when the NESREA shut down stations owned by certain telecommunication companies and imposed huge fines on these companies to be paid before their stations could be reopened, the National Communications Commission, Federal Ministry of Environment, and the Senate brokered a settlement between the NESREA and the communication operators.[47]

Another regulator active in enforcing environmental infractions in the Nigerian maritime sector is NIMASA. NIMASA has taken action against companies and individuals involved in illegal refinery operations and oil operators whose drilling has polluted surrounding waters.[48]

In the oil and gas sector, generally, the environmental regulators—DPR and NOSDRA—work closely with operators in this sector in dealing with environmental infractions. Where fines are imposed, such fines are usually negligible, as the maximum fines permitted in the enabling laws are negligible.[49] Since its enabling laws do not allow it to impose heavy fines, NOSDRA recently recommended to the National Assembly and the president that Chevron Nigeria Limited be fined the sum of US$3 billion for pollution arising from a gas explosion from gas wells operated by Chevron.[50]

State governments also have organs that actively enforce environmental regulations and provide for environmental protection. The Lagos State government, for example, is a pacesetter in dealing with environmental issues. It has developed its climate change policies and is taking steps to mitigate environmental problems like floods. Except for matters dealing exclusively with minerals and petroleum, federal and state governments may enact legislation dealing with most environmental matters. State governments have enacted several laws that regulate the environment in areas under their respective jurisdiction.

XIII.   Conclusion

It is clear that the paucity of pollution prevention laws is not the reason why Nigeria still suffers from significant rates of pollution arising from industrial activities such as oil, natural gas exploration, telecommunication masts, building materials, and private power generation. To the contrary, lax enforcement tends to be the more predominant underlying cause. Competition among environmental pollution regulators has also negatively impacted enforcement efforts.[51] Where these regulators collaborate on enforcement, their acts will more effectively deter operators from ignoring environmental laws.

Nigeria is developing industrially, and the federal government wants more natural gas and electricity produced to meet industrial and residential demands. Furthermore, the various states are working toward building future cities, with increased commercial activities, better transportation systems, and more industry. As the Nigerian government seeks to encourage Nigeria along the path to becoming a developed nation, it would do well to ensure all sectors include pollution control as a significant component of their development plans.

Notes

1. Nigeria operates a federal system of government where power is shared amongst the federal, state, and local governments. Nigeria also operates a presidential system of government that encourages separation of power amongst the executive, legislative, and judicial branches. The federal government, led by the president and its ministers, comprises the federal executive. The National Assembly, made up of the House of Representative and Senate, comprise the Legislature at the federal level. Each state executive comprises its executive governor and commissioners, and the State Legislature is the House of Assembly.

2. The National Environmental Standards and Regulations Enforcement Agency was formerly known as the Nigerian Environmental Protection Agency.

3. *See* Michael Simere, *How Nigeria Can Earn N86b yearly from CDM*, DAILY INDEP., July 2012, http://dailyindependentnig.com/2012/07/how-nigeria-can-earn-n86b-yearly -from-cdm/. There are more CDM projects to be hosted by Nigeria awaiting registration.

4. National Adaptation Strategy and Plan of Action on Climate Change for Nigeria (NASPA-CCN) December 2011, prepared by the BRNCC Project in partnership with the Federal Ministry of Environment, *available at* http://nigeriaclimatechange.org/docs /naspaAug2012.pdf (last visited November 3, 2012).

5. In 2010, both the House of Representative and Senate, which comprise the National Assembly at the federal government of Nigeria, passed the Climate Change Commission Bill into law and sent the law to the president for assent as the Nigerian Constitution requires. The president, at that time, did not assent to the bill before 30 days lapsed, as required by Section 58(4) of the 1999 Constitution. The National Assembly, in compliance with Section 58(5) of the 1999 Constitution, has recommenced the process of passing the bill into law. If both Houses pass the bill into law by two-thirds majority, the assent of the president shall not be required.

6. *See* http://www.nassnig.org/nass/legislation.php?pageNum_bill=28&totalRows _ bill=636 (last visited Nov. 3, 2012).

7. Cap. W2 LFN 2004.

8. Cap. 17 LFN 2007.

9. The authors are not aware of any regulations made by NIMASA relating to environmental pollution. The NIMASA DG has notified the public of some regulations which it shall soon release and complains that its lack of prosecution powers restricts its enforcement abilities. *See* http://www.compassnewspaper.org/index.php/special-desk/maritime/5862 -nimasa-enacts-fresh-regulations (last visited Nov. 12, 2012).

10. *See* http://www.imo.org/About/Conventions/ListOfConventions/Pages/Inter national-Convention-for-the-Prevention-of-Pollution-from-Ships-(MARPOL).aspx (last visited Sept. 16, 2013).

11. Nigeria Harmful Waste (Special Criminal Provisions etc.) Act Cap. H1 LFN 2004.

12. This includes Nigeria's territorial waters, contiguous zone, and inland waterways.

13. *See* http://www.africa-union.org/root/au/Documents/Treaties/Text/hazardous wastes.pdf (last visited Sept. 16, 2013).

14. *See* http://www.basel.int (last visited Sept. 16, 2013).

15. Petroleum Act Cap. P10 LFN 2004. There is currently a petroleum bill before the National Assembly to amend the Petroleum Act in a manner that is expected to result in more petroleum benefits to Nigeria.

16. National Oil Spill Detection and Response Agency (Establishment Act) Cap. N157 LFN 2004.There is currently a bill to amend this act before the Nigerian House of Senate. This bill seeks to impose stiffer penalties on oil and gas operators for oil spillages. It is difficult to determine how long it will take for this bill to be passed into law or if the current National Assembly will pass it before its tenure lapses.

17. Constitution § 20. The Constitution has been amended three times by the Legislature of the Federal Republic of Nigeria: (First Alteration) Act, 2010 Act No.1, (Second Alteration) Act, 2010 Act No. 2, and (Third Alteration) Act, 2010 Act No.3.

18. Petroleum Act § 4.

19. Act Cap. O6 LFN 2004.

20. *See* http://www.ecolex.org/ecolex/ledge/view/RecordDetails?id=TRE-000135 &index=treaties (last visited Sept. 16, 2013).

21. Oil in Navigable Waters Act § 3.

22. 1973 and 1978 Protocol (Ratification and Enforcement) Act Cap. I28 LFN 2004.

23. Via the International Convention for the Prevention from Ships1973 and 1978 Protocol (Ratification and Enforcement) Act Cap. I28 LFN 2004.

24. National Environmental Standards and Regulations Enforcement Agency Establishment Act Cap. N. 25 2007.

25. These regulations address the following subject matters: wetland, riverbanks, and lakeshores; watershed, mountainous, hilly, and catchment area; sanitation and waste control; permitting and licensing system; access to genetic resources and benefit sharing; mining and processing of coal, ores, and industrial minerals; ozone layer protection; food beverages and tobacco sector; textile, wearing apparel, leather, and footwear industry; noise standards and control; chemicals, pharmaceuticals, soap, and detergent manufacturing industry; soil erosion and flood control; standards for telecommunication and broadcast facilities; desertification control and drought mitigation; base metals, iron, and steel manufacturing/recycling industries sector; control of bush, forest fire, and open burning; protection of endangered species in international trade; domestic and industrial plastic, rubber, and foam sector; coastal and marine area protection; construction sector; control of vehicular emissions from petrol and diesel engines; nonmetallic minerals manufacturing industries sector; and surface and groundwater quality control.

26. The National Toxic Dump Watch Programme has been reactivated with a committee consisting of the Nigerian Navy, Nigerian Custom Service, Nigeria Ports Authority, State Security Service, National Intelligence Agency, Defence Intelligence Agency, Nigeria Police, Nigerian Maritime Administration, and Safety Agency and NESREA.

27. Cap. E11 LFN 2004.

28. Established by the Federal Environmental Protection Act Cap. F10 LFN 2004, which has been repealed by Section 36 of the Nigerian Environmental Standards and Regulation Agency Act 2007. The NESREA is the agency responsible for enforcing the Environmental Impact Assessment Act.

29. *See* Environemtal Impact Assessment Act § 7.

30. There is growing awareness of the importance of environmental impact assessments amongst Civil Society Organisations and project host communities.

31. Convention for Cooperation in the Protection and Development of the Marine and Coastal Environment of the West and Central African Region.

32. Basel Convention on the Control of Transboundary Movements of Hazardous Wastes and Their Disposal, Mar. 22, 1989, 28 I.L.M. 657.

33. (Ratification and Enforcement) Act Cap. I29N LFN 2004.

34. *See* http://www.imo.org/About/Conventions/ListOfConventions/Pages/International-Convention-on-Civil-Liability-for-Oil-Pollution-Damage-(CLC).aspx (last visited Sept. 19, 2013). The Convention was amended in 1992 and entered into force on May 30, 1996.

35. 1971 amended (Ratification and Enforcement) Act Cap I30 LFN 2004. For the text of the convention, see http://www.imo.org/About/Conventions/ListOfConventions/Pages/International-Convention-on-the-Establishment-of-an-International-Fund-for-Compensation-for-Oil-Pollution-Damage-(FUND).aspx (last visited Sept. 16, 2013).

36. The old regime was amended in 1992.

37. Cap. I30 LFN 2004.

38. [1992] 9 NWLR (pt. 214), 155.

39. Now section 6(6)(b) of the 1999 Constitution of the Federal Republic of Nigeria.

40. [1990] 6 NWLR (pt. 159) 693.

41. [2011] 16 NWLR pt. 1272 at 181.

42. Suit No. FHC/CS/B/152/2005.

43. See http://www.achpr.org/instruments/achpr/ (last visited Sept. 16, 2013).

44. The country, through the Department of Petroleum Resources, set December 2012 as an initial date to attain zero percent gas flaring in the oil and gas sector, but due mainly to lack of infrastructure about 24 percent of its 7.8 cubic feet of gas well production is still flared. Nigeria is ranked by OPEC as the second-largest gas-flaring country in the world.

45. Suit No: FHC/L/CS/1033/12, Fabby Young v. Chevron Nigeria Ltd. & Anor; where the plaintiffs in both suits have sued Chevron Nigeria Limited for damages arising from a gas explosion that occurred on the Chevron operated Funiwa 1a gas well on the North Apoi Fields in Bayelsa State, Nigeria.

46. *See* Mustapha Salihu, *NESREA Shuts Four Tanneries in Kano,* Punch, Oct. 25, 2012, http://www.punchng.com/business/business-economy/nesrea-shuts-four-tanneries-in-kano/; *NESREA Unseals Julius Berger's Corporate Headquarters,* Punch, July 12, 2012, http://www.punchng.com/news/nesrea-unseals-julius-bergers-corporateheadquarters/.

47. *See* http://www.vanguardngr.com/2012/08 (last visited Aug. 27, 2012).

48. *See* Godwin Oritse, *Bonga Spill: Agbakoba Leads NIMASA's Legal Team against Shell,* Vanguard, Feb. 20, 2012, http://www.vanguardngr.com/2012/02/bonga-spill-agbakoba-leads-nimasas-legal-team-against-shell/; Nigerian Mar. Admin. & Safety Agency, http://www.nimasa.gov.ng/pub.php (last visited Nov. 8, 2012).

49. The House of Senate is currently reading a bill to amend the NOSDRA Act to increase the fines the NOSDRA can impose on oil and gas operators.

50. *See* http://www.punchng.com/business/business-economy/rig-explosion-nosdra -recommends-n465bn-fine-for-chevron/ (last visited Nov. 8, 2012). The National Assembly and the president have to approve this recommendation. The fine to be paid is currently being negotiated by Chevron and the Nigerian government.

51. *See Rig Explosion: NOSDRA Recommends N465bn Fine for Chevron,* PUNCH, Aug. 15, 2012, http://www.vanguardngr.com/2012/11/ministry-dpr-nimasa-others-disagree -over-environment-regulation/.

CHAPTER 45

Australia

JOHN TABERNER

I. Introduction to the Australian Environmental Legal System

In Australia, environmental law is a diverse field. The chief reason for this is Australia's federal system of government. Under the Australian Constitution, the Federal Parliament has a limited (but overriding) legislative authority and the state parliaments are constrained principally by the scope of federal legislation in force from time to time. The "environment" is not listed in the Australian Constitution as a power on which the Federal Parliament may legislate. As a result, the demarcation of legislative authority in the field of environmental law in Australia between the federal and state parliaments is complex.

The demarcation of environmental legislative authority is clearest in relation to environmental legislation operating outside Australia or in respect of the Australian territories. The Australian Federal Parliament has a plenary power to legislate for a territory[1] and to make laws with respect to matters and things geographically outside Australia.[2] There are two principal limitations on this power, namely, the limitations resulting from

1. The limited grants of territorial self-government effected by the Northern Territory (Self-Government) Act 1978 (Cth), the Norfolk Island Act 1979 (Cth), and the Australian Capital Territory (Self-Government) Act (Cth); and

2. The "offshore settlement" effected with the Australian States by the Seas and Submerged Lands Act 1973 (Cth), the Coastal Waters (State Powers) Act 1980 (Cth), the Coastal Waters (State Title) Act 1980 (Cth), the Coastal Waters (Northern Territory Powers) Act 1980 (Cth), the Coastal Waters (Northern Territory Title) Act 1980 (Cth), and the Fisheries Management Act 1991 (Cth).

The demarcation of legislative authority is less clear in relation to federal environmental legislation operating within the states and territories. In the absence of an explicit power over the environment, federal capacity to enact such environmental legislation is only derivative, arising indirectly in other express or implied federal powers in the Australian Constitution. Sections 51(i), 51(xx), and 51(xxix) of the Australian Constitution[3] are the commonly used sources of indirect power over the environment,[4] and each of these sources has peculiar capacities and limitations,[5] and is subject to express limitations in the Australian Constitution.[6]

Despite the complex distribution of legislative power, environmental laws are familiar in Australia. The common law of Australia contains rudimentary forms of environmental control. The tort actions in nuisance and trespass are of ancient origin. The tort action in negligence is more recent. Other forms of environmental control available at common law include those effectuated by means of contract, by restrictive covenants over land, and by easement. However, the most important environmental controls in Australia arise by way of legislation. Three broad categories of environmental legislation are now discernible in each Australian jurisdiction:

1. Legislation concerned in general with land use and environmental impact assessment;
2. Legislation concerned in general with environmental protection, including pollution control and regulation of the use of environmentally hazardous substances; and
3. Legislation concerned with the conservation of natural and cultural resources.

A fourth category of legislation has been recently added: in July 2012, comprehensive federal carbon pricing legislation came into effect. Although some environmental legislation was enacted prior to 1970 in state legislatures[7] and in the federal legislature,[8] environmental legislation has been enacted in Australia only since 1970. Since then, all Australian states have enacted environmental legislation in most categories described above, and the Australian Federal Parliament has enacted legislation in all of them. A substantial bulk of legislation has developed.

II.   Air and Climate Change
A.   Air Pollution Control

Except as regards carbon emissions, Australian legislation controlling air pollution has emerged only at the state and territory level. All states and territories have, and have had for some time, a wide range of environment protection legislation covering, inter alia, air pollution control. The principal legislation in each state is

- Protection of the Environment Operations Act 1997 (NSW) (POEO Act)
- Environment Protection Act 1970 (Victoria state (VIC))
- Environmental Protection Act 1994 (Queensland state (QLD))
- Environmental Protection Act 1986 (Western Australia state (WA))

- Environment Protection Act 1997 (Australian Capital Territory—the area surrounding the federal capital, Canberra (ACT))
- Environmental Management and Pollution Controls Act 1994 (Tasmania state (TAS))
- Environment Protection Act 1993 (South Australia state (SA))
- Environmental Assessment Act 1992 (Northern Territory (NT))

Some or all of the provisions in the state and territory acts are enforceable by third parties. For example, under the POEO Act, any person may bring proceedings in the New South Wales (NSW) land and environment court for an order to remedy or restrain a breach of the POEO Act or the regulations, regardless of whether there is any environmental harm. Environmental protection legislation is also enforced by the relevant environment protection authority in each state or territory.

B. Carbon Pricing Legislation

The Clean Energy Act 2011 (Cth) and a suite of 18 related acts (2011 Carbon Legislation)[9] came into operation on July 1, 2012. The Clean Energy Act is administered by a Clean Energy Regulator established under the Clean Energy Regulator Act 2011 (Cth) (Regulator). The Clean Energy Act operates in two distinct phases: a fixed charge phase for FY2012–13, FY2013–14, and FY2014–15; and a flexible charge phase from FY2015–16 and onwards. There are (as yet unenacted) proposals to start the flexible phase one year earlier. If, in either the fixed charge phase or the flexible charge phase, a liable entity has a unit shortfall, a charge is imposed on the unit shortfall. Unit shortfall is calculated by reference to the number of eligible emissions units (EEUs) surrendered by the liable entity for the relevant fiscal year. EEUs are

- carbon units issued by the Regulator under the Clean Energy Act;
- domestic credits—eligible Australian carbon credit units (as defined in Carbon Credits (Carbon Farming Initiative) Act 2011 (Cth)); and
- international units—eligible international emissions units (as defined in Australian National Registry of Emissions Units Act 2011 (Cth)).

Carbon units, eligible Australian carbon credit units, and eligible international emissions unit are all "financial products" for the purposes of the Corporations Act 2001 (Cth).[10] In the fixed charge phase, eligible international emissions units cannot be surrendered, but up to 5 percent of liability (or 100 percent of liability in the case of a landfill facility) for a relevant FY can be met using eligible Australian carbon credit units. In the flexible charge phase,

- there is no limit on the number of eligible Australian carbon credit units that may be surrendered; and
- subject to any regulations prohibiting the surrender of specified eligible international emissions units up to 50 percent of liability can be offset using eligible international emissions units during the first five years of the flexible phase after which time there is no limit on the number of international credits that may be used.

In the flexible charge phase, up to 5 percent of liability for a relevant FY can be met by "borrowing" carbon units of the next vintage year.

From July 1, 2012, the price of carbon units issued under the Clean Energy Act will be fixed for three financial years: the fixed charge in FY2012–13 has been $23 per metric ton of carbon dioxide equivalent (CO_2e), and will rise by approximately 5 percent in each of the two subsequent years. In the first three years of the flexible charge phase, there will be no price floor for carbon units issued at auction under the Clean Energy Act—$15 in FY2015–16, $16 in FY2016–17, and $17.05 in FY2017–18. But this is subject to any reserves that the minister may set. In the first three years of the flexible charge phase, there will be a price ceiling for FY2015–16 to FY2017–18. But this is only if regulations are in place for that purpose. The aim is to publish such regulations by May 31, 2014. Such regulations cannot be made after July 1, 2015. If such regulations are made, the price ceiling in FY2015–16 will increase by 7.625 percent in each of FY2016–17 and FY2017–18.

In the flexible charge phase, the total number of carbon units issued under the Clean Energy Act for any particular year will align with the carbon pollution cap number for that year. Regulations specifying the pollution cap numbers for the first five flexible charge years (FY2015–16 to FY2019–20) are tabled no later than May 31, 2014. The five years of pollution caps will be extended by a year every year so that five years of pollution caps are always known. Table 1 illustrates the timeline.

Table 1

Deadline	Pollution Cap Announced for Fiscal Year(s)
May 31, 2014	FY2015–16, FY2016–17, FY2017–18, FY2018–19 and FY2019–20
June 30, 2016	FY2020–21
June 30, 2017	FY2021–22

Pollution caps will continue to be set annually.

If no cap number is set by regulation, a default cap number is set: for FY2015–16, the total covered emissions for FY2012–13 less 38 million; and in subsequent financial years, the cap number of the previous year less 12 million. The default caps follow a trajectory consistent with Australia's unconditional target of reducing national emissions to 5 percent below 2000 levels by 2020.

1. Liable Entities

There are four species of liable entity under the 2011 Carbon Legislation. In short, the 2011 Carbon Legislation applies to

1. Entities with operational control (as defined in the National Greenhouse and Energy Reporting Act 2011 (Cth) (NGER Act) of certain types of facilities (as defined in the NGER Act), subject to special provisions for liability transfer certificates and designated joint ventures;[11]

2. Entities that supply natural gas, subject to special provisions about obligation transfer numbers;
3. From July 1, 2013, onwards, the following entities:
    a. entities that import liquefied petroleum gas (LPG) or liquefied natural gas (LNG) for consumption in Australia, subject to special provisions about obligation transfer numbers;
    b. entities that manufacture or produce LPG or LNG in Australia, subject to special provisions about obligation transfer numbers;
    c. entities that resupply imported, manufactured or produced LPG or LNG and that quote an obligation transfer number; and
4. From July 1, 2013, onwards, entities that
    a. acquire, manufacture, or import certain fuels regulated under the Fuel Tax Act 2006; and
    b. are designated opt-in persons under an opt-in scheme to be set up in regulations under the Clean Energy Act.

2. *"Operational Control" of "Facility"*

The entity with operational control of the facility is the liable entity for the facility.[12] An entity has "operational control" of a facility if, in short, it has authority to introduce and implement operating, health and safety, or environmental policies for the facility.[13] Where more than one entity has this authority, it is the entity that has the greatest authority to introduce and implement operating and environmental policies for the facility that will be taken to have "operational control."[14] A "facility" means "an activity, or a series of activities (including ancillary activities)"[15] that "involve greenhouse gas emissions, the production of energy or the consumption of energy"[16] and "form a single undertaking or enterprise."[17]

3. *Liability "Threshold"*

Only certain types of facility attract liability under the Clean Energy Act. The facility must either "pass the threshold test": the facility must (with exceptions relating to landfills) emit annual covered emissions in excess of 25,000 metric tons a year[18] or be a large gas-consuming facility.[19] "Covered emissions" means[20] scope 1 emissions—direct atmospheric emissions[21]—of greenhouse gases.[22]

There are important exclusions from "covered emissions."[23]

4. *Liability Transfer*

While a liability transfer certificate (LTC) is in force in relation to a facility, the entity with "operational control" is taken not to have operational control of the facility[24] and instead the holder of the LTC is the liable entity.[25] There are two types of LTC: a member of the corporate group of the entity with "operational control" can apply for an LTC to transfer liability to it[26]—an intragroup LTC; and a person that is outside the corporate group of the entity with "operational control" and that has "financial control"[27] over the facility can apply for an LTC to transfer liability to it[28]—a financial control LTC.

5. "Natural Gas Liability"

Certain types of supply of natural gas attract the operation of the Clean Energy Act.[29] There must be a supply of natural gas to another person; a withdrawal of the supplied natural gas from a natural gas pipeline; and a withdrawal in Australia.

Supply means "supply (including re-supply) by way of sale, exchange or gift"[30] and (subject to regulations) occurs when the gas is physically delivered.[31] Natural gas, natural gas supply pipeline, and withdrawal are all defined by regulations:[32] the supplier of natural gas is liable *unless* the recipient quotes an obligation transfer number (OTN) in relation to the supply,[33] in which case the recipient is a liable entity.[34] OTNs must be quoted in some circumstances and may be quoted in others.

6. LPG and LNG Liability

From July 1, 2013, onwards,[35] a person who imports LPG or LNG for nontransport-related consumption within Australia[36] is a liable entity in relation to the importation.[37] However, if importer "supplies" the LPG or LNG to another person (recipient) and if the recipient quotes an OTN in relation to the importation, the recipient is a liable entity in relation to the importation.[38] Similarly, from July 1, 2013, onwards,[39] a person who manufactures or produces LPG or LNG in Australia for nontransport-related consumption[40] is a liable entity in relation to the manufacture or production.[41] However, if the manufacturer or producer "supplies" the LPG or LNG to another person (recipient) and if the recipient quotes an OTN in relation to the manufacture or production, the recipient is a liable entity in relation to the manufacture or production.[42]

7. Obligation Transfer

From July 1, 2013, onwards,[43] the recipient of a supply of LPG or LNG either must or may quote an OTN, depending on whether conditions in the regulations to the Clean Energy Act are met.[44] Advance notice of OTN quotation is required.[45] OTNs are not transferable.[46]

8. "Opt-in" Liability

From July 1, 2013, onwards,[47] a designated opt-in person is a liable entity.[48] A "designated opt-in person" is a person who acquires, manufactures, or imports certain types of fuel[49] in the circumstances specified in the Clean Energy Act. The mechanism for "opt-in" will be created under regulations to be in place by December 15, 2012.[50]

III. Water

A. Environment Protection (Sea Dumping) Act 1981 (Cth)

Legislation controlling water pollution is characteristically state and territory legislation, not federal legislation, and the principal legislation is listed in II(A), discussed previously.

At the federal level, the Environment Protection (Sea Dumping) Act 1981 (Cth) (the Sea Dumping Act) came into effect on March 6, 1984. It was enacted in response to Australia's international obligations under the Convention on the Prevention of Marine Pollution by the Dumping of Wastes and Other Matter (now known as the London Protocol). The London Protocol aims to protect and preserve the marine environment from all sources of pollution and to prevent, reduce, and eliminate pollution by controlling the dumping of wastes and other materials at sea. Under the Sea Dumping Act, the Commonwealth aims to minimize pollution threats by

- prohibiting ocean disposal of waste considered too harmful to be released in the marine environment; and
- regulating permitted waste disposal to ensure environmental impacts are minimized.

The Sea Dumping Act is administered by the Department of Sustainability, Environment, Water, Population and Communities (SEWPAC).

The Sea Dumping Act primarily applies to disposal of human-made structures such as vessels, aircraft, and platforms in Australian waters. It is also applicable to all Australian vessels and aircrafts in any part of the sea. The United Nations Convention on the Law of the Sea (UNCLOS) generally allows coastal states to apply licensing regulations to all territorial waters, Australia's exclusive economic zone (prescribed by the UNCLOS), and the continental shelf.

Permits are required for all sea dumping operations, such as dredging, creation of artificial reefs, dumping of vessels, platforms and other man-made structures, and burials at sea. However, the Waste Assessment Guidelines, developed to provide guidance to parties to the convention, clarify that permits should not be given if there are feasible alternatives such as reusing, recycling, or other forms of treatment.

Some sea dumping projects may require approval under both the Environment Protection and Biodiversity Conservation Act 1999 (Cth) (EPBC Act) and the Sea Dumping Act, and if so, the projects can be assessed concurrently under both acts.

SEWPAC aims to ensure compliance with the conditions of permitted activities through

- analysis of information reported as a condition of permits and approvals;
- audits;
- patrols and investigations; and
- a department-wide compliance and enforcement policy.

The Act does not apply to operational discharges from ships, such as sewage and galley scraps. The Australian Maritime Safety Authority regulates these discharges under separate legislation.

IV. Handling, Treatment, Transportation, and Disposal of Hazardous Material
A. Hazardous Waste (Regulation of Exports and Imports) Act 1989 (Cth)

The Hazardous Waste (Regulation of Exports and Imports) Act 1989 (Cth) commenced on July 17, 1990. The act was developed to enable Australia to comply with specific obligations under the Basel Convention on the Control of the Transboundary Movements of Hazardous Wastes and Their Disposal (Basel Convention), a convention set up to control the international movements of hazardous wastes. The main purpose of the Hazardous Waste Act is to regulate the export and import of hazardous waste to ensure that hazardous waste is disposed of safely so that human beings and the environment, both within and outside Australia, are protected from the harmful effects of the waste.[51] The Hazardous Waste Act requires that a permit be obtained before hazardous waste is exported from Australia or imported into Australia. It does not affect movements of hazardous waste within Australia.

Only hazardous wastes are covered by the Hazardous Waste Act. A number of factors need to be considered before deciding whether a material is or is not a hazardous waste under the act. These factors include

- whether the material is destined for a final disposal operation;
- whether the material is destined for a recovery operation;
- how and why the material is produced;
- whether the material has economic value;
- whether a recovery operation is necessary;
- whether the material is suitable for its originally intended use; and
- whether the material is destined for direct reuse or alternative uses.

The Basel Convention defines wastes as "substances or objects that are disposed of or are intended to be disposed of or are required to be disposed of by the provisions of national law."[52] Under the convention, "disposal" means any operation specified in Annex IV to the convention.[53] Adopting the Basel Convention definition, the Hazardous Waste Act defines waste as a substance or object that

- is proposed to be disposed of; or
- is disposed of; or
- is required by a law of the Commonwealth, a state, or a territory to be disposed of.[54]

The following wastes that are subject to transboundary movement are "hazardous wastes" for the purposes of the Basel Convention:

- wastes that belong to any category contained in Annex I of the Basel Convention, unless they do not possess any of the characteristics contained in Annex III; and
- wastes that are not covered under paragraph (a) but are defined as, or are considered to be, hazardous wastes by the domestic legislation of the party of export, import, or transit.[55]

For the purposes of the Hazardous Waste Act, "hazardous waste" means:

- waste prescribed by the regulations, where the waste has any of the characteristics mentioned in Annex III to the Basel Convention; or
- wastes covered by paragraph 1(a) of Article 1 of the Basel Convention; or
- household waste;[56] or
- residues arising from the incineration of household waste;
- but does not include wastes covered by paragraph 4 of Article 1 of the Basel Convention.[57]

Both the Basel Convention and the Hazardous Waste Act define "disposal" as any operation specified in Annex IV to the convention.[58] Final disposal of waste involves operations such as incineration or landfill. The Australian government has banned exports of waste for final disposal except in exceptional circumstances.[59] Recovery includes recycling or reclamation of waste materials and also includes recovery of energy from waste (except by direct incineration). These shipments are permitted provided certain conditions are met.[60] Waste shipments may only take place between countries that are parties to the Basel Convention,[61] except where a specific arrangement exists with a non-party under Article 11 of the Basel Convention. There are various types of permits that can be obtained to export or import waste. The type of permit required depends on the type, origin, and destination of the waste.

V. Waste and Site Remediation
A. Federal Role

Australia does not have a federal statute similar to the United States' Comprehensive Environmental Response, Compensation, and Liability Act (CERCLA), commonly known as "Superfund." However, the state and territory legislation outlined in section II.A above contains extensive provisions relating to liability for contaminated land. Measures established by the National Environment Protection Council (NEPC)[62] help establish a nationally consistent approach to liability for and assessment of land contamination. The National Environment Protection (Assessment of Site Contamination) Measure (Site Contamination NEPM) was finalized by the NEPC on December 10, 1999. The Site Contamination NEPM aims to establish a nationally consistent approach to the assessment of site contamination and, where site contamination has occurred, to protect human health and the environment. Contamination is defined to mean "the condition of land or water where any chemical substance or waste has been added at above background level and represents, or potentially represents, an adverse health or environmental impact." All Australian states and territories have introduced legislation giving effect to the Site Contamination NEPM.

B.   Product Stewardship Act 2011 (Cth)

On August 8, 2011, the Product Stewardship Act 2011 (Cth) (PS Act) came into effect. The PS Act creates a national scheme of "product stewardship," which the PS Act describes as "an approach to reducing the environmental and other impacts of products by encouraging or requiring manufacturers, importers, distributors and other persons to take responsibility for those products."

The PS Act provides a framework for three kinds of product stewardship:

1. *Voluntary product stewardship:* This involves accrediting voluntary arrangements designed to further the objects of the PS Act in relation to products, and authorizing the use of product stewardship logos in connection with such arrangements.

2. *Coregulatory product stewardship:* This involves requiring some manufacturers, importers, distributors, and users of products (called liable parties), who have been specified in the regulations, to be members of coregulatory arrangements approved by the minister. These arrangements must have outcomes, specified in the regulations that are designed to further the objects of the PS Act. Administrators of approved coregulatory arrangements are required to take all reasonable steps to ensure those outcomes are achieved in accordance with the regulations.

3. *Mandatory product stewardship:* This involves the making of regulations to require some persons to take, or not to take, specified action in relation to products.

Before regulations are made specifying liable parties for a class of products under the coregulatory product stewardship scheme, or requiring action to be taken in relation to products under the mandatory product stewardship scheme, the minister must be satisfied that the product stewardship criteria are met. The product stewardship criteria are satisfied in relation to a class of products if the products in the class are in a national market and if, in addition, at least one of the following applies in relation to the products in the class:

- the products contain hazardous substances;
- there is the potential to significantly increase the conservation of materials used in the products, or the recovery of resources (including materials and energy) from waste from the products;
- there is the potential to significantly reduce the impact that the products have on the environment, or that substances in the products have on the environment, or on the health or safety of human beings.

To date, one stewardship scheme has been put in place under the act: on November 8, 2011, a coregulatory stewardship scheme for televisions and computers was put in place by the Product Stewardship (Televisions and Computers) Regulations 2011.

VI. Emergency Response

Federal emergency response legislation exists in respect of Australia's territorial seas. The principal legislation is the Protection of the Sea (Prevention of Pollution from Ships) Act 1983 (Cth). Also, the state and territory legislation outlined in section II.A, *supra*, contains extensive provisions relating to emergency response.

VII. Natural Resource Management and Protection
A. Environmental Protection and Biodiversity Conservation Act 1999 (Cth)

The EPBC Act is the primary piece of federal environmental legislation, which regulates the impact of activities on matters of national environmental significance. It implements international obligations, such as those under the Convention on Biological Diversity and the Convention on the Conservation of Migratory Species of Wild Animals. The provisions of the EPBC Act govern the declaration and management of various types of protected area managed by the Commonwealth. The minister can prepare a bioregional plan for a region that is within a Commonwealth area.[63] A bioregion is an area comprising a whole ecosystem or several connected ecosystems that may be geographically separated from each other. If a bioregional plan is endorsed under the EPBC Act subsequent actions taken in accordance with the plan can be exempted from separate or individual approval processes. Interconnected mechanisms for promoting and conserving biodiversity under the EPBC Act include

- identification of biodiversity;[64]
- listing of threatened species;[65]
- listing of threatened ecological communities;[66]
- creating a register of critical habitat (habitat that is critical to the survival of a listed threatened species or ecological community) and prohibitions on taking any action on Commonwealth land knowing that it will significantly damage the habitat;[67]
- listing of migratory species;[68]
- listing of marine species;[69]
- authorizations or exemptions for otherwise prohibited actions, for example, if the action may make some contribution to the conservation of a species;[70]
- identifying key threatening processes and then preparing threat abatement plans for such processes (if required);[71]

- recovery plans providing for the research and management actions necessary to stop decline and support recovery of listed threatened species and ecological communities;[72]
- wildlife conservation plans;[73]
- regulating import and export of plants and animals (wildlife) and products derived from wildlife;
- conservation orders made by the minister prohibiting, restricting, or requiring specified activities in Commonwealth areas;[74] and
- establishing reserves as protected areas and formulating management plans for these areas;[75]

Protected areas include reserves, which can be proclaimed over any area of land or sea that is[76]

- an area owned by the Commonwealth;
- an area leased by the Commonwealth;
- an area that is a Commonwealth marine area; and
- an area outside Australia that Australia has international obligations to protect.

These reserves must fall under one of the following categories:[77]

- a strict nature reserve;
- a wilderness area;
- a national park;
- a natural monument;
- a habitat-species management area;
- a protected landscape-seascape; and
- a managed resource protected area.

"Conservation zones" are also provided for by the act, which have the purpose of protection of biodiversity, other natural features, and heritage in Commonwealth areas while they are being assessed for inclusion in a Commonwealth reserve.[78] The EPBC Regulations prescribe activities in conservation zones, which are much the same as the controls applicable to Commonwealth reserves (however, prior usage rights are generally protected). Each protected area is managed in accordance with management principles and sometimes management plans. Such principles include

- community participation;
- effective and adaptive management;
- precautionary principle;
- minimum impact;
- ecologically sustainable use (underlying the requirement that ecological processes should be maintained);
- transparency of decision making; and
- joint management with Aboriginal people.[79]

B. Antarctic Acts

Australian has adopted legislation that implements its international obligations in relation to Antarctica.

1. *Australian Antarctic Territory Act 1954 (the Antarctic Territory Act)*

The Australian Antarctic Territory (AAT) encompasses over 5,800,000km^2 of eastern Antarctica, making it the largest claimed area on the continent. The Antarctic Territory Act established a comprehensive legal regime for the AAT whereby Commonwealth laws expressly apply to the AAT.

2. *Antarctic Treaty Act 1960 (the Treaty Act)*

The Treaty Act gives effect to the Antarctic Treaty, which was signed in Washington in 1959 by 12 nations. The Antarctic Treaty stipulates that Antarctica should be used exclusively for peaceful purposes and guarantees freedom to conduct scientific research.

3. *Antarctic Treaty (Environment Protection) Act 1980 (the Environment Protection Act)*

The Environment Protection Act gives effect to the Protocol on Environmental Protection to the Antarctic Treaty (Madrid Protocol), setting out environmental protection obligations for all activities in the Antarctic Treaty area. Under this act, the minister may declare certain species of native mammals, birds, or plants to be specially protected if they are specified in the Madrid Protocol.[80] It is an offense to injure or interfere with any native mammal, invertebrate, bird, or plant, or to introduce nonindigenous wildlife without a permit, or in breach of the terms of a permit.[81] To gain a permit, an environmental impact assessment must also be carried out. Permits will not be issued for activities that adversely modify, to a significant extent, the habitat or population of a native species of flora or fauna. Enforcement mechanisms include penalties and/or imprisonment for noncompliance, and inspectors with powers of arrest and seizure.

4. *Antarctic Marine Living Resources Conservation Act 1981 (the Conservation Act)*

The Conservation Act implements the Convention on the Conservation of Antarctic Marine Living Resources. It regulates harvesting of all living organisms found in the marine environment within the convention area, research into such organisms, and fishing for recreational purposes. Permits are required for such activities, unless authorized under another Commonwealth Act. In deciding whether to grant a permit, conservation of Antarctic marine living resources must be considered, particularly factors such as population size, ecological balance, and avoiding significant impacts on the marine system.

Finally, the EPBC Act also applies to activities undertaken on the AAT.

C. Great Barrier Reef Marine Parks Acts

The Great Barrier Reef Marine Park Act 1975 (Cth) (GBRMPA) was enacted as a result of investigation into the resource and conservation aspects of management of the Great Barrier Reef, prompted by the possibility of oil drilling on the reef coupled with the national and international significance of the area. The area of the reef, as a world heritage property, would ordinarily fall under the EPBC Act, however approval for action under the EPBC Act is not required if taken in accordance with the GBRMPA.[82] The authority responsible for administering the GBRMPA and the management of the park is the Great Barrier Reef Marine Park Authority. Activities are controlled by zoning plans, except those for the recovery of minerals, which are prohibited (except for scientific purposes).[83] In developing zoning plans, the Great Barrier Reef Marine Park Authority must outline its environmental, economic, and social objectives, and the environmental, economic, and social values of the area.[84] The authority must also have regard to other criteria specified in the GBRMPA, relevant state legislation, and the EPBC Act.

The authority can prepare management plans for particular areas, species, and ecological communities within the park, having regard to world heritage values and the precautionary principle, and in accordance with zoning plans, for example, zoning as scientific research, preservation, and special management areas. It is an offense to enter or use zones other than for a permitted purpose.[85] It is also an offense to intentionally or negligently discharge waste without permission except in accordance with certain conditions.[86]

The Great Barrier Reef Marine Park Regulations 1983 (Cth) govern requirements for permits to carry out activities that are prohibited under a zoning plan, such as fishing. Environmental management charges may be imposed under the Great Barrier Reef Marine Park (Environmental Management Charge—Excise) Act 1993 (Cth) and the Great Barrier Reef Marine Park (Environmental Management Charge—General) Act 1993 (Cth). Injunctions can be obtained by the Great Barrier Reef Marine Park Authority or any person whose interests have been, are, or would be affected by contravening conduct. Where there are reasonable grounds for suspecting an offense has been committed, the minister has extensive powers to prevent, mitigate, or repair damage and remove structures, and recover costs if a person is convicted.[87]

D. State and Territorial Statutes

The vast majority of land acquired for parks and reserves in the states and territories is Crown land, either recommended by the relevant minister or declared by legislation to be national parks. The objects of reservation are much the same in all states and territories:

- the protection of flora and fauna and natural features;
- the provision of recreational facilities; and
- for educational, scientific, and research purposes.

The administrative structure is also similar whereby the legislation is administered by a director within a national parks and wildlife service or similar authority. Regulations that assist with the carrying out of the functions of the authority within reserves are enforced by authorized officers, such as rangers. Each state and territory allows for land to be reserved for a wide variety of purposes, such as the creation of national parks, state conservation areas, and nature reserves.[88]

VIII.   Natural Resource Damages

There is no legislation in Australia, at either Commonwealth or state or territorial level, that is specifically addressed to the recovery of money by relevant administrative bodies to restore or replace injured natural resources. However, there is legislation in the Australian states and territories concerning land contamination allowing limited recovery of the costs of remediation of the relevant contamination.

IX.   Protected Species

In addition to the legal provisions discussed above, each state and territory in Australia has legislation that allows listing of endangered or threatened species. The criteria used for listing at state and national levels can differ, so species and ecological communities can be listed under both state and national legislation, or under only one of these. Some states have incorporated biodiversity provisions within national parks and wildlife legislation, others also introduced special legislation.[89] For example, in NSW, the Office of Environment and Heritage (OEH) is responsible for protecting and conserving biodiversity in NSW. Each state and territory has an equivalent department regulating and enforcing conservation legislation.[90]

X.   Transboundary Pollution

Australia shares no land boundary with any other country, a fact that may have led to a relatively low priority having been placed on enacting legislation specifically addressing transboundary pollution. It is not, for example, a party to the Convention on Long-Range Transboundary Air Pollution[91] or the Convention on Environmental Impact Assessments in a Transboundary Context.[92] That said, Australia is a party to the Basel Convention. Section IV.A, *supra*, describes the Australian legislation relevant to its implementation.

XI.   Environmental Review and Decision Making

A.   Environmental Protection and Biodiversity Conservation Act 1999 (Cth)

The broad objects of the EPBC Act are to protect aspects of the environment that are of national environmental significance and to promote biodiversity and ecologically sustainable development. The EPBC Act carries out these objects by providing that certain actions that have, will have, or are likely to have a significant impact on the environment are prohibited unless the minister gives approval or decides that approval is not required. There are significant penalties, including civil and criminal charges, for taking such an action without approval. Also, the act has broad "third party" enforcement provisions enabling proceedings in federal courts to remedy or restrain threatened or actual breaches of the act. There are 13 sets of circumstances in which the taking of "action" is prohibited without approval. These circumstances arise where the action

1.   concerns a declared world heritage property; a national heritage place; a wetlands of international importance; a threatened species; a threatened ecological community; a migratory species; or a Commonwealth Heritage place that is outside the Australian jurisdiction; or
2.   is a nuclear action; an action within Commonwealth marine area; fishing in coastal waters; a prescribed action; an action on Commonwealth land; or an action by the Commonwealth or a Commonwealth agency in or affecting the Australian jurisdiction.

An action that has, or is likely to have, a significant impact on any one or more of the matters in (1), or an action in (2) that has, or is likely to have, a significant impact in the environment, is a "controlled action" and is prohibited without approval. If the proponent of a project feels that the project may be a "controlled action," it must be referred to the minister. The minister will advertise the project for public comment and, taking into account any public comments, will determine whether the proposed action is likely to have a significant impact on the environment. When assessing a proposed action, the minister considers all documentation provided by the applicant, the results of assessments of the impact, community input, and the principles of ecologically sustainable development. There are five methods of assessment and the processes for assessment are different for each. These assessment methods are

- accredited assessment (bilateral agreement)
- assessment on referral information
- assessment on preliminary documentation
- assessment by environmental impact statement or public environment report
- assessment by public enquiry

The minister may approve the action, approve the action subject to conditions, or refuse to approve the action. Bilateral agreements exist between the state and the Commonwealth governments to prevent duplication of assessment. Under a bilateral agreement, the Commonwealth delegates to the states and territories the responsibility for conducting the environmental assessment. If a proposed action is covered by bilateral agreement, then it will be assessed and approved by the state or territory in accordance with an agreed management plan. No further approval is required from the minister under the EPBC Act.

B. State Legislation

All Australian states and territories have their own land use and environmental impact assessment (EIA) legislation. EIA requirements have been developed most often in environmental planning[93] or environment protection[94] legislation, although separate legislation dealing exclusively with EIAs exists in the Northern Territory[95] and Victoria.[96]

XII. Civil and Criminal Enforcement and Penalties

In addition to the material provided supra, practitioners should note the following. Traditionally in common law jurisdictions such as Australia, a litigant seeking to enforce environmental law has to show a "special interest" over and above other members of the public in order to establish standing. Federal and state environmental legislation is now alike in typically (but not always) altering this common law position as regards the subject matter of particular legislation. The most expansive statutory changes to the traditional rules for standing are in NSW, where "any person" may bring civil or criminal enforcement proceedings in a specialist land and environment court that carries the same status as the NSW Supreme Court.[97] NSW legislation also gives rights of appeal on the merits to certain categories of person.[98] Certain other state and federal legislation creates similar rights.

Notes

1. Australian Constitution s 122. *Australian Nat'l Airways Pty Ltd. v. Commonwealth* (1945) 71 CLR 29, at 62. See *Teori Tau v Commonwealth* (1969) 119 CLR 564, at 570: "The grant of legislative power by section 122 is plenary in quality and unlimited and unqualified in point of subject matter." Approved: *Northern Land Council v Commonwealth* (1986) 161 CLR 1, at 6. The power to legislate for a territory includes power to regulate extra-Territorial activities affecting the territory: see *Attorney-General (WA) v Australian Nat'l Airlines Comm'n* (1976) 138 CLR 492, at 512–15 and 531, and (for example) *Canberra Water Supply (Googong Dam) Act 1974* (Cth). The Territories currently under the control of the Australian Federal Parliament include the Ashmore and Cartier Islands, the Australian Antarctic Territory, the Australian Capital Territory, Christmas Island, the Cocos (Keeling) Islands, the Coral Sea Islands, Heard and McDonald Islands, Norfolk Island, and the Northern Territory.

2. Australian Constitution s 51(xxix): *Polyukhovich v Commonwealth* (1991) 172 CLR 501, at 528, 602, 632, 696, 714. *See* Barwick CJ in *Commonwealth v New South Wales* (1975) 135 CLR 337, at 360: "The power extends . . . to any affair which in its nature is external to the continent of Australia and the island of Tasmania subject always to the Constitution as a whole. For this purpose, the continent of Australia and the island of Tasmania are . . . bounded by the low-water mark on the coasts." It appears, but it has not yet been the subject of judicial consideration, that the power to legislate with respect to matters and things geographically outside Australia includes power to legislate with respect to matters and things affecting matters and things geographically outside Australia and that, accordingly, the Australian Federal Parliament could legislate to protect Australia's coastal waters by regulating the land-based emission of pollutants into rivers and estuaries.

3. "The Parliament shall . . . have power to make laws with respect to . . . (i) Trade and commerce with other countries and among the States; . . . (xx) Foreign corporations and trading or financial corporations formed within the limits of the Commonwealth . . . (xxix) External affairs."

4. The Australian Federal Parliament also has power, under section 96 of the Australian Constitution, to grant financial assistance to the states "on such terms and conditions as the Parliament thinks fit," and this includes terms and conditions that amount in substance to an exercise of power not within section 51 of the Australian Constitution (*see Victoria v Commonwealth* (1926) 38 CLR 399, at 406). Section 96 of the Australian Constitution has been used at various times to support, for example, legislation providing financial assistance in areas relating to national water resource management, soil conservation, air quality monitoring, and urban and regional development. The expansive use made of a similar power by the U.S. Congress in, for example, the Clean Water Act, 38 U.S.C. § 1251, and the Clean Air Act, 42 U.S.C. § 7401, has not yet been attempted by the Australian Federal Parliament. The Australian Federal Parliament's power, under section 51(ii) of the Australian Constitution, "to make laws with respect to . . . (ii) Taxation" also founds the creation by legislation of tax credits and penalties relating to the control of pollution. For example, on 24 December 1992, the Taxation Laws Amendment Act (No. 5) 1992 (Cth) came into effect, section 25 of which amends the Income Tax Assessment Act 1936 (Cth) to allow immediate tax deductions for expenditure incurred on or after 19 August 1992 on pollution control and waste management.

5. The concept of "trade and commerce" in section 51(i) of the Australian Constitution (*see W. & A. McArthur Ltd. v Queensland* (1920) 28 CLR 530, at 547) has so far been construed not to include manufacturing: *Grannall v Marrickville Margarine Pty Ltd.* (1955) 93 CLR 55, at 72.

Section 51(xx) of the Australian Constitution offers an expansive federal legislative power over the environment. Section 51(xx) allows regulation of the activities of trading corporations "formed" (that, is, "in existence") within the limits of the Commonwealth: *see New South Wales v Commonwealth* (1990) 169 CLR 482, at 498. *Commonwealth v Tasmania* (1983) 158 CLR 1 establishes that the concept of "trading corporation" is wide (see pages 155–57, 179–80, 239–40, and 292–93) and that any act by a trading corporation "for the purpose of trading" will come within Commonwealth power even if that act was "not of a trading nature" (see pages 199 and 240–41). As well, there were indications by individual judges in the case that laws regulating any activities of a trading corporation (see pages 269–72) or any law regulating trading corporations (see pages 149 and 179) will come within Commonwealth power.

Section 51(xxix) of the Australian Constitution possibly offers the widest potential for general federal environmental legislation. Section 51(xxix) is not limited to matters geographically external to Australia and may be widely used to make laws operating solely within Australia. The breadth of section 51(xxix) in this latter respect was first recognized by the High Court in *Roche v Kronheimer* (1921) 29 CLR 329, in which it was said, at 338–39, that "it is difficult to see what limits (if any) can be placed on the power to legislate as to external affairs. There are none expressed." Recently, *Commonwealth v Tasmania* (1983) 158 CLR 1 held that intraterritorial federal environmental legislation, relying on appropriate international conventions or agreements, is valid (see pages 123–24, 170, 218–19, and 258–59), and the High Court affirmed this view in *Richardson v Forestry Comm'n* (1988) 164 CLR 261, at 295–96 and in *Queensland v Commonwealth* (1989) 167 CLR 232, at 241–42. The courts will not be concerned with the particular means by which legislation implements the international convention or agreement, provided that the legislation is "capable of being reasonably considered to be appropriate and adapted to giving effect to" the convention or agreement (*see Richardson v Forestry Comm'n* (1988) 164 CLR 261, at 303), and the courts will support legislation "calculated to discharge not only Australia's known obligations but also Australia's reasonably apprehended obligations" (*see Richardson v Forestry Comm'n* (1988) 164 CLR 261, at 295, 300, 327–28, and 336). Matters of "international concern," even if not the subject of international conventions or agreements, may also found valid Commonwealth legislation: *see Koowarta v Bjelke-Petersen* (1982) 153 CLR 168, 220, 234, 242, 258. However, it is unclear when a matter is sufficiently of international concern.

6. State and federal environmental legislation will offend section 92 of the Australian Constitution, and will be invalid to the extent that, in substance, it discriminates against the interstate trade and commerce of a particular state or states: *see Castlemaine Tooheys Ltd v S. Australia* (1990) 169 CLR 436; J.G. Taberner & D. Lee, *Section 92 and the Environment*, 65 ALJR 266 (1991). Federal environmental legislation must, by virtue of section 51(xxxi) of the Australian Constitution, compensate on "just terms" if the legislation amounts to an acquisition of property: *see Commonwealth v Tasmania* (1983) 158 CLR 1, at 145, 181–82, 247, 289–90; *Minister for Arts Heritage and Environment v Peko-Wallsend Ltd* (1987) 75 ALR 218.

7. In 1961, the New South Wales parliament enacted the Clean Air Act. State mining legislation contains long-standing provisions allowing for matters such as "sludge abatement" that may be fairly described as "environmental." They also grant discretionary powers to the governor or the minister to declare areas out of bounds to miners and other persons, and these powers may well be used for environmental purposes. Recent mining legislation is more specifically or exclusively devoted to the subject of environmental control. For example, Part 11 of the Mining Act 1992 (NSW) is specifically devoted to "protection of environment."

8. Immediately after the Second World War, the federal government offered the states financial incentives to improve their land use laws by virtue of the Commonwealth and State Housing Agreement Act 1945: *see* clauses 3 and 4 of the Schedule to the *Commonwealth and State Housing Agreement Act 1945*. In 1953, the Atomic Energy Act 1953 (Cth) envisaged (in section 38) the making of regulations for the safe working, storage, and transportation of radioactive substances and enabled the minister (in section 55) to declare areas of land or water "restricted" for reasons of human and environmental safety as well as national security. In 1967 the Petroleum (Submerged Lands) Act 1967 (Cth) concerned itself (in section 97) with the safety of persons and the protection of the environment from substandard oil field practices, and contained (in section 57) prohibitions on "interference with other rights" including fishing and the conservation of the resources of the sea and the seabed. In April and May 1968, the Australian Senate resolved to establish Joint Select Committees on air and water pollution. The Committees reported in June

and September 1969. The senators who constituted these Joint Committees agreed unanimously upon the need for the Federal Parliament to take the lead in the field of environmental law: *see* Commonwealth Parliamentary Debates 71 H of R 1217-30. In November 1970, during a campaign toward a Federal Senate election, the then federal government announced a decision to set up within the prime minister's department an Office of the Environment, to approach the states regarding the formation of a national advisory council to coordinate federal and state action in the field of pollution control. The office was established in December 1970 but the office and the proposal for a national advisory council were abandoned in February 1971 because the two major states were unwilling to take part. In April 1971, the Federal Ministry was expanded by the addition of a Department of Aboriginal Affairs, Arts and the Environment within which department the Office of Environment was relocated.

9. The 18 related acts are Clean Energy (Charges-Customs) Act 2011; Clean Energy (Charges-Excise) Act 2011; Clean Energy (Consequential Amendments) Act 2011; Clean Energy (Customs Tariff Amendment) Act 2011; Clean Energy (Excise Tariff Legislation Amendment) Act 2011; Clean Energy (Fuel Tax Legislation Amendment) Act 2011; Clean Energy (Household Assistance Amendments) Act 2011; Clean Energy (Income Tax Rates Amendments) Act 2011; Clean Energy (International Unit Surrender Charge) Act 2011; Clean Energy Regulator Act 2011; Clean Energy (Tax Laws Amendments) Act 2011; Clean Energy (Unit Issue Charge—Auctions) Act 2011; Clean Energy (Unit Issue Charge—Fixed Charge) Act 2011; Clean Energy (Unit Shortfall Charge—General) Act 2011; Climate Change Authority Act 2011; Ozone Protection and Synthetic Greenhouse Gas (Import Levy) Amendment Act 2011; Ozone Protection and Synthetic Greenhouse Gas (Manufacture Levy) Amendment Act 2011; Steel Transformation Plan Act 2011.

10. *Corporations Act 2001* (Cth) ss 764A(kaa), (ka), (kb).

11. A "joint venture" for this purpose is "an unincorporated enterprise carried on by 2 or more persons in common otherwise than in partnership": *Clean Energy Act 2011* (Cth) s 5.

12. *Clean Energy Act 2011* (Cth) ss 20(3), 23(3).

13. *National Greenhouse and Energy Reporting Act 2007* (Cth) s 11(1)(a).

14. *Id.* s 11A.

15. *Id.* s 9(1).

16. *Id.*

17. *Id.* s 9(1)(a).

18. *Clean Energy Act 2011* (Cth) ss 20(1)(b)(i) and 20(4)–(5), 21(1)(d)(i) and 21(4)–(5), 22(1)(b)(i) and 22(4)–(5).

19. *Id.* ss 20(b)(1)(ii), 21(d)(1)(ii), 22(1)(b)(ii). A large gas-consuming facility means a facility in which, in FY2010–11 or a subsequent fiscal year, the combustion of natural gas results in covered emissions in excess of 25,000 metric tons (or another amount in regulations) or more: *id.* s 55A.

20. *Id.* s 30.

21. *See id.* s 5; *National Greenhouse and Energy Reporting Act 2007* (Cth) ss 7, 10; *National Greenhouse and Energy Reporting Regulations 2008* (Cth) cl. 2.23.

22. CO_2, methane, nitrous oxide, sulfur hexafluoride, prescribed hydrofluorocarbons, prescribed perfluorocarbons, and "prescribed gas": *Clean Energy Act 2011* (Cth) s 5.

23. *Id.* s 30(2).

24. *Id.* ss 20(7), 23(7).

25. *Id.* ss 22(3), 25(3).

26. *Id.* s 83.

27. *See id.* s 92. An entity has "financial control" over a facility if, in short, the entity with "operational control" operates the facility on behalf of that entity (and other entities) or if the entity controls the trading or financial relationships of the operator.

28. *Id.* s 87.

29. *Id.* ss 33(1)(a), 35(1)(a).

30. *Id.* s 5. A "sale" involves a transfer of ownership in exchange for monetary consideration: *see Sun World v Registrar Plant Variety Rights* (1997) 75 FLR 528, at 540. An "exchange" (or barter) involves a transfer of ownership in exchange for other goods or services. A "gift" involves a transfer of ownership for no consideration: *see Leary v Fed. Comm'r of Taxation* (1980) 32 ALR 221, at 237. Accordingly, there is no "supply" where, for example, gas is supplied to an electricity producer for combustion by the producer, the gas supplier retains title to the gas supplied and, in consideration of the gas supply, the electricity producer agrees to deliver to the gas supplier electricity produced from combustion of the gas. Similarly, there is no "supply" where gas is supplied to a gas transporter for transportation, the gas supplier retains title to the gas supplied and, in consideration of the gas supply, the gas transporter agrees to transport the gas.

31. *Clean Energy Act 2011* (Cth) s 6.

32. *Id.* s 5.

33. *Id.* s 33(1)(e).

34. *Id.* s 35(3)(b).

35. *Id.* s 36B(1)(c).

36. *Id.* s 36B(1)(b).

37. *Id.* s 36B(2)(b).

38. *Id.* s 36D(2)(b).

39. *Id.* s 36C(1)(c).

40. *Id.* s 36C(1)(e).

41. *Id.* s 36C(2)(b).

42. *Id.* s 36D(2)(b).

43. *Id.* ss 58AA(1)(b), 58AB(1)(b).

44. *Id.* ss 58AA(1)(c), 58AB(1)(c). No regulations are yet in place.

45. *Id.* ss 55B(2), 57(2), 58(2), 58AA(2), 58AB(2).

46. *Id.* s 44.

47. *Id.* s 92A(7).

48. *Id.* s 92A(1).

49. *Id.* s 92A(1)(a)(i).

50. *Id.* s 92A(6).

51. *Hazardous Waste Act* s 3.

52. *Basel Convention* art. 2.1.

53. *Id.* art. 2.4.

54. *Hazardous Waste Act* s 4.

55. *Basel Convention* art. 1.1.

56. *Hazardous Waste Act* s 4 defines "household waste" as waste collected from households, but does not include waste specified in the regulations.

57. Article 1.4 provides that wastes that derive from the normal operations of a ship, the discharge of which is covered by another international instrument, are excluded from the scope of this Convention.

58. *Hazardous Waste Act* s 4; *Basel Convention* art. 2.4.

59. *Hazardous Waste Act* s 18A(1).

60. *Id.* s 18B(2).

61. A list of parties to the Basel Convention can be found at http://www.basel.int /ratif/ratif.html. Australia accepted the Convention on 5 February 1992 but has not ratified it.

62. *See National Environment Protection Council Act 1994* (Cth) s 9(1).

63. *Environment Protection and Biodiversity Conservation Act 1999* (Cth) s 176.

64. *Id.* s 171.
65. *Id.* s 178.
66. *Id.* s 181.
67. *Id.* s 207A.
68. *Id.* s 209.
69. *Id.* s 248.
70. *Id.* ss 200–207, 303A, 19.
71. *Id.* s 270B.
72. *Id.* s 206A.
73. *Id.* s 285.
74. *Id.* ss 474, 464.
75. *Id.* s 344.
76. *Id.* s 344(1).
77. *Id.* s 347.
78. *Id.* ss 390C, 390D, 390J.
79. Practitioners should also be familiar with the Native Title Act 1993 (Cth). In June 1992, the High Court of Australia delivered its judgment in what is now known as the *Mabo* case. *Mabo v Queensland* (1992) 175 CLR 1. Until this decision, the Australian legal system did not recognize that Australia's indigenous inhabitants had any rights or interests in relation to land or waters. Native title, as now recognized, is composed of rights and interests over land held by Aboriginal or Torres Strait Islander people who have a connection with that land by reason of their traditional customs and laws. The nature of these rights and interests vary depending on those traditional customs and laws.

Following the High Court's decision in the *Mabo* case, the Native Title Act 1993 (Cth) (the Commonwealth NTA) was enacted. It has been amended on several occasions since its enactment, most significantly on 30 September 1998 by the Native Title Amendment Act 1998 (Cth), in response to the High Court's decision in the *Wik* case. *Wik Peoples v Queensland* (1996) 187 CLR 1. The Commonwealth NTA operates against the backdrop of the Racial Discrimination Act 1975 (Cth) (RDA). The RDA provides that it is unlawful for a person to do any act that discriminates against another person on the basis of race, color, descent, or national or ethnic origin. The Commonwealth NTA applies to "acts" that "affect" native title. Under the Commonwealth NTA s 227, an act "affects" native title if it extinguishes native title rights and interests or is wholly or partly inconsistent with their continued existence, enjoyment, or exercise.

An "act" is very broadly defined under the Commonwealth NTA. It encompasses (but is not limited to) proposals for land use, and existing land uses, including infrastructure uses. An "act" may be done by the Crown in any of its capacities or by any other person. There are three main types of "acts":

1. "Past" acts (acts done after 31 October 1975 and before the commencement of the Commonwealth NTA on 1 January 1994)—the Commonwealth NTA states that past acts "attributable to the Commonwealth" are valid, and are taken always to have been valid;
2. "Intermediate period" acts (certain acts done after 1 January 1994 but before the judgment of the High Court in the *Wik* Case on 23 December 1996)—the Commonwealth NTA states that intermediate acts "attributable to the Commonwealth" are valid, and are taken always to have been valid; and
3. "Future" acts (acts done after 1 January 1994).

Essentially, future acts will only be valid if the process by which they are done conforms with the procedural requirements contained in the Commonwealth NTA. The following general rules apply: a future act will be valid if the parties to indigenous land use agreements (ILUAs) under section 24EB of the Commonwealth NTA consent to the act; also, a future act will be valid to the extent covered by any of the sections listed in sections 24AA(4)(a) to (k) of the Commonwealth NTA.

A "right to negotiate" procedure applies in relation to certain future acts. These include acts that create or vary a right to mine. If the right to negotiate applies to the doing of an act then, before the act is done, the government must give notice of the act to certain parties, including the registered native title claimants and any registered native title body corporate. The government, and other negotiation parties, must negotiate in good faith with a view to obtaining the agreement of the native title parties to the doing of the act, with or without conditions. If no agreement is reached within a specified period of time following notification, then any party may seek a determination by an arbitral body (generally the National Native Title Tribunal) as to whether the act may proceed.

The Commonwealth NTA establishes a scheme for compensation for extinguishment or impairment of native title rights and interests by future acts. An act "affects" native title if it extinguishes the native title rights and interests or if it is otherwise wholly or partly inconsistent with their continued existence, enjoyment, or exercise. The Commonwealth NTA establishes a regime for the making of "native title determinations." A native title determination is a court decision that native title does or does not exist in a particular area of land or waters. Claimants can lodge applications with the Federal Court of Australia. The court can also make a determination about whether compensation should be paid in a compensation application. The Commonwealth NTA established the National Native Title Tribunal (NNTT) to help mediate native title claims and determine whether native title exists. Most native title claimant applications are made with the aim of gaining formal recognition of native title through a determination. The determination process is often long and difficult.

80. *Antarctic Treaty (Environment Protection) Act 1980* (Cth) s 7C.

81. *Id.* s 19.

82. *Environment Protection and Biodiversity Conservation Act 1999* (Cth) s 43; *Great Barrier Reef Marine Park Act 1975* (Cth) s 39.

83. *Great Barrier Reef Marine Park Act 1975* (Cth) s 38.

84. *Id.* ss 34, 35.

85. *Id.* ss 38A–38D.

86. *Id.* s 38J.

87. *Id.* ss 61A–61C.

88. *National Parks and Wildlife Act 1974 (NSW); Nature Conservation Act (ACT); Nature Conservation Act 1992 (QLD); Territory Parks and Wildlife Conservation Act 1976 (NT); National Parks and Wildlife Act 1972 (SA); Nature Conservation Act 2002 (Tas); National Parks Act 1975 (Vic); Land Administration Act 1997 (WA).*

89. For example, the *Threatened Species Conservation Act 1995* (NSW).

90. Department of Sustainability and Environment (VIC), Department of Environment and Resource Management (QLD), Department of Environment and Conservation (WA), Environment and Sustainable Development Directorate (ACT), Department of Environment, Water and Natural Resources (SA), Department of Primary Industries, Parks, Water and Environment (TAS), and Department of Land Resource Management (NT).

91. *See* http://www.unece.org/env/lrtap/ (last visited Sept. 16, 2013).

92. *See* http://www.unece.org/env/eia/ (last visited Sept. 16, 2013).

93. *Planning and Development Act 2007 (ACT); Environmental Planning and Assessment Act 1979 (NSW); Sustainable Planning Act 2009 (QLD); State Development and Public Works Organisation Act 1971 (QLD); Development Act 1993 (SA).*

94. *Environment Protection and Biodiversity Conservation Act 1999 (Cth); Environmental Protection Act 1994 (QLD); Environmental Protection Act 1986 (WA); Environmental Management and Pollution Control Act 1994 (Tas).*

95. *Environmental Assessment Act 1982* (NT).

96. *Environmental Effects Act 1978* (Vic).

97. For example, the South Australian Environment, Resources and Development Court and the Queensland Planning Environment Court is composed of district court judges, and environmental criminal offenses in Victoria are heard by magistrates' courts.

98. *Environmental Planning and Assessment Act 1979* (NSW) ss 4 ("objector"), 98; *Threatened Species Conservation Act 1995* (NSW) s 106 ("person who has made written submissions").

CHAPTER 46

New Zealand

ROBERT MAKGILL*

I. Overview and Structure

New Zealand (Aotearoa) is an archipelago located in the Southern Pacific Ocean southeast of Australia. The two main islands are the North Island (Te Ika a Maui) and the South Island (Pounamu). These islands are over 1,600 km in length,[1] and characterized by an extraordinarily varied landscape. New Zealand's total land area is 268,670 square kilometers (km),[2] making it about the size of the state of Colorado.[3] Its coastline measures 18,000 km[4] and its territorial waters encompass 16.3 million hectares.[5] The country's exclusive economic zone (EEZ) is the fourth largest in the world, with an area about 15 times that of its land mass (or 5.7 percent of the world's EEZ).[6] Close proximity to the coastline and a vast ocean jurisdiction means that the coastal environment plays an important role in New Zealand's culture and economy, while a relatively small population (4,451,052)[7] means that exports of natural resources account for a large proportion of gross domestic product.[8] New Zealand's principal industries are agriculture, horticulture, fishing, forestry, and mining, which make up about half of the country's exports.[9] Major sources of environmental pressure include agriculture, transport, tourism, and energy production and consumption.[10]

New Zealand is a Westminster-styled parliamentary democracy.[11] The Crown[12] is the foundation of the executive, legislative, and judicial branches of government.[13] The Crown does not, however, participate in the legislative process save for granting assent to bills passed by Parliament to be enacted into law. The political party (or coalition) with an elected majority of seats in Parliament forms the government. The government is controlled by a prime minister and his/her cabinet. The cabinet is responsible for deciding key government policy and actions. New Zealand's reliance on natural resources means that the management of natural resources is a principal focus of environmental policy (irrespective of which political party controls the government at a given moment).[14]

*The author would like to thank Susann Kerstan, an intern at the New Zealand Center for Environmental Law, Auckland University, for her assistance in writing this chapter.

909

New Zealand's legal system finds its roots in the English common law tradition. Subsequently, it does not have a written constitution and is formed by two main sources of law: statutory law (or legislation) made by Parliament and common law developed by judges through decisions of courts. Environmental law in New Zealand is principally administered through public law,[15] and is therefore composed of a comprehensive set of statutes that codify environmental rights and duties. The country's environmental common law is composed of the decisions of its judiciary and the judiciary of other commonwealth courts where relevant (especially that of the United Kingdom, Australia, and Canada). Although common law is typically thought of as precedent formed in the absence of statute, it is important to note that most of New Zealand's existing environmental precedent is founded on the interpretation and application of environmental statutes. As environmental law has an administrative tradition in New Zealand, public statutes do not always satisfactorily address issues of private liability (i.e., liability to private parties as opposed to the Crown,[16] which acts on behalf of the public). This means that parties must resort to common law remedies for environmental damage where statutes fail to remedy or mitigate the private cost of an act causing environmental harm.[17]

A.   Principal Environmental Statutes

The Resource Management Act 1991 (RMA) is the principal overarching statute for managing natural and physical resources. It is important to note that this excludes the allocation of minerals and hydrocarbons (i.e., gas and oil), and all fishing activities (including protection of areas from fishing activities). However, the RMA does address the *effects* of mining activities and of facilities and infrastructure associated with fishing.[18] Enacted before the Rio Earth Summit, the government drew on the Brundtland Report's[19] treatment of sustainable development to shape the purpose of the RMA. The fact that the RMA introduced the concept of sustainability into domestic legislation facilitated New Zealand's rapid signing of Agenda 21,[20] and the subsequent ratification of two international environmental agreements and the U.N. Convention on the Law of the Sea (UNCLOS), which includes extensive environmental provisions.[21]

Sustainable development is defined under the Brundtland Report as "development that meets the needs of the present without compromising the ability of future generations to meet their own needs."[22] The concept of "needs" under the report pays particular attention to the needs of the poor, to which the report suggests overriding priority should be given.[23] To this extent, sustainable development "implies a concern for social equity," and can be said to seek to redress imbalances in resource allocation.[24] In context, the purpose of section 5 under the RMA is deliberately based on sustainable *management* rather than sustainable *development*. It does not seek to regulate social equity. It does not seek to redistribute wealth, and it does not seek to *equitably* allocate rights to development. It is effectively a form of development control and regulation. Accordingly, the Environment Court observed in *Marlborough Ridge Ltd v Marlborough District Council* that

> We question whether it is the role of this Court to make judgements about social, economic or cultural wellbeing (as opposed to creating circumstances which enable that wellbeing to be created by people and communities) . . . Our role as we perceive it under s5 is to enable people to provide for that wellbeing. In other words, the scheme is to provide the 'environment' or conditions in which people can provide for their wellbeing.[25]

The RMA was conceived as a framework for integrating and rationalizing environmental management generally. To those ends it repealed or modified 59 statutes and modified 50 regulations. These acts often provided similar administrative powers and functions to authorities that had quite separate responsibilities in relation to the management of the same natural and physical resources. Past environmental regulation had proceeded on an ad hoc basis whereby different aspects of development had been controlled in isolation. The Honorable Simon Upton, minister for environment, in his third reading of the bill that was ultimately enacted, stated:

> The current law allows—indeed encourages—almost limitless intervention for a host of environmental and socio economic reasons. That has resulted in a plethora of rules and other ad hoc interventions that are intended to achieve multiple and often conflicting objectives. In many instances they achieve few clear objectives, but they impose enormous costs on development of any kind.
>
> In addition there was a multiplicity of legislative acts and control authorities relevant to any proposal. The duplications, overlaps, delays, and costs resulted in the call for an integrated and streamlined statute with a clear purpose and focus.[26]

Accordingly, the architects of the RMA sought to replace the existing legislation with a single statute, which provided for the integrated reform of regulatory environmental powers.[27] To a large extent, the act is the child of the neoliberal ideology that swept across New Zealand in the 1980s. It focuses on the effects of activities rather than the activities themselves. Rather than have central government direct where and what type of development should take place, it relies on the market to efficiently decide the most appropriate uses of resources. Using economic terminology, the intent of the act is to encourage the internalization of externalities. Consistent with this neoliberal approach, the purpose of the RMA is intended to *enable* activities that promote people's well-being while creating an obligation to deal with the adverse effects of those activities on the environment. A person's use of their land can only be restricted if it breaches the requirements set out in the RMA or contravenes a rule in a regional or district plan, in which case a resource consent is required. This approach is often referred to as the "enabling purpose" of the RMA.[28]

Nevertheless, the enabling purpose of the RMA must be balanced with environmental considerations. Accordingly, the sustainable management purpose is only achieved if the social, economic, and cultural well-being generated by an activity is acceptable in terms of the scale and significance of its adverse effects on the environment. This effectively requires an assessment of environmental effects (AEE)[29] to be carried out for all activities, and the RMA provides clear guidance on the aspects that must be included in such assessments. All decision making under the RMA is subsidiary to and must achieve the purpose of sustainable management.[30]

Part II of the RMA supports section 5 by providing guiding principles and therefore lists "matters of national importance"[31] and "other matters."[32] Furthermore, section 8 mirrors another specialty of New Zealand's legal system: the coexistence of the Crown in New Zealand and Maori as the indigenous people, where the Treaty of Waitangi (Te Tiriti o Waitangi) signed in 1840 guides the relationship between the aforementioned as treaty partners. The principles of the constitutional document, like good faith, partnership, and active protection, aim to protect a living Maori culture as well as conferring the right to govern to the Crown in the interest of all inhabitants. Against this backdrop, section 8 requires all persons exercising functions and powers under the act to take into account the principles of the treaty.[33]

The RMA, with sustainable management at its core, is the centerpiece of New Zealand's system of environmental legislation for land and sea out to the 12 nautical mile (nm) territorial sea boundary. Its implementation of the principle of sustainability and integrated management means that over 20 years since its enactment, it is still regarded as one of the most progressive environmental statutes in the world.[34] Although the RMA has broad application, it is supplemented by a number of other key environmental statutes, including the Exclusive Economic Zone and Continental Shelf (Environmental Effects) Act 2012 (EEZ Act), the Marine and Coastal Area (Takutai Moana) Act 2011 (MCAA), the Climate Change Response Act 2002 (CCRA), and the Hazardous Substances and New Organisms Act 1996 (HSNO). These acts are discussed in more detail later in this chapter.

B.   Institutions and Governance Structures

The principal government department responsible for the general management, protection, and preservation of the environment is the Ministry of Environment (MfE).[35] The department was established under the Environment Act in 1986. Its current responsibilities include administration of the RMA, EEZ Act, HSNO Act, Climate Change Response Act, and Environmental Protection Authority Act 2011 (EPA Act). MfE's primary function is to advise the environment minister on all aspects of environmental administration, including such things as policy, significant impacts of proposals, and ways to ensure effective public participation in decision making.[36] Additionally, it provides the government, its departments, and other public authorities with advice on numerous matters such as the effect of other legislation and procedures for environmental impact assessments. To fulfill its consultative role, it obtains information and conducts and supervises research. Another aspect of the ministry's work consists of the provision and distribution of information and services to stimulate environmental policies like effective public participation in planning. Furthermore, it has primary responsibility for ongoing reforms and amendments to the RMA, and other environmental legislation. It also has powers to prepare national policy statements (NPS),[37] recommend preparation of national environmental standards (NES),[38] and direct local authorities to carry our reviews of their environmental planning documents that have been prepared under the RMA.[39]

The Environmental Protection Authority (EPA) was established as a new stand-alone entity by the EPA Act in May 2011. The EPA is intended to strengthen national environmental regulatory functions previously spread across a number of ministries (government departments). MfE will continue to lead the development of national policy, whereas the EPA will effectively become the national regulator responsible for administration of legislation and related operational matters. The EPA's main functions include processing proposals of national significance under the RMA, administering and regulating activities in the EEZ and continental shelf under the EEZ Act, performing regulatory functions under the HSNO Act, and administering the Emissions Trading Scheme and Registry under the Climate Change Response Act. The EPA functions as an advisor to the environment minister on issues arising out of its duties under the EPA Act and other environmental legislation. The EPA is also required, at the request of the minister, "to contribute to and co-operate with international forums and carry out international obligations related to its functions under an environmental Act."[40]

Whereas the central government is responsible for issuing national guidelines to direct the formulation of regional and district plans, local government (regional councils and territorial authorities) are where the proverbial rubber meets the road under the RMA. Regional and district plans make provision for, among other things, objectives, policies, and rules concerning activities that are not otherwise permitted as of right under the RMA. The primary function of regional councils[41] is the integrated management of natural and physical resources.[42] They are obliged at all times to have one regional policy statement that provides an overview of regional resource management issues, and policies and methods for achieving integrated management of the region's natural and physical resources.[43] Although only regional coastal plans are compulsory, in practice regional councils will have a number of regional plans in place to provide rules for giving effect to matters over which regional councils have responsibility.[44] Territorial authorities (district and city councils) have responsibility for the integrated management of land use, development, and protection.[45] Every territorial authority is required to have a district plan in order to carry out these functions. District plans must give effect to regional policy statements and plans.[46] In addition to the aforementioned policy and planning functions, regional councils and territorial authorities are also responsible for processing consent applications for activities that are not permitted, monitoring of compliance, and enforcement for noncompliance.

C. Role of the Courts

The Judicature Act 1908 and the District Courts Act 1947 define the area of jurisdiction for each court within New Zealand's hierarchical court system.[47] The Supreme Court is at the top of the hierarchy, followed in descending order by the Court of Appeal, the High Court, and the district courts. This system of inferior and superior courts allows the right of appeal to a higher court. According to the common law tradition, a decision of a higher court is binding on lower courts. This follows the rule of precedent, where similar cases are generally decided in the same way, and which is intended to ensure consistency and certainty in juridical decision making. A unique feature of the New Zealand judiciary is the Environment Court.[48] Its status is equivalent to that of a district court in New Zealand, or comparatively an intermediary between U.S. federal district courts and a U.S. circuit court of appeals.

Formerly called the Planning Tribunal, and established under the Resource Management Amendment Act 1996, the Environment Court has jurisdiction over a number of environmental statutes.[49] The bulk of cases that are appealed to the Environment Court arise out of public law litigation under the RMA. For example, the court hears appeals relating to the content of regional and district policy statements and plans, public works, resource and subdivisions consent applications, and abatement notices and enforcement orders. The Environment Court hears matters on a de novo basis, which means that fresh evidence may be given and new factual material examined. An Environment Court judge generally sits with two commissioners who are experts in the field of environmental management or engineering. Experts providing evidence on behalf of litigant parties have a duty to provide any opinions objectively and impartially. Experts are expected to caucus prior to a hearing in order to narrow the factual matters under dispute. The court may also appoint its own experts where there is insufficient evidence before it on a certain matter. As a result, the court has the ability to make sophisticated decisions often in the face of complex scientific data. Appeals of Environment Court decisions may only be taken on points of law. In effect, the Environment Court is the last opportunity to challenge questions of fact.

II. Air and Climate Change
A. Air Pollution Control

The purpose of RMA under section 5 is "to promote the sustainable management of natural and physical resources." Natural and physical resources are defined under section 2 of the act to include air. Section 5(2)(3) requires that adverse effects of activities on the environment (e.g., air) must be remedied, mitigated, or avoided. Accordingly, section 15 creates a presumption that no contaminants[50] may be discharged into the air unless the discharge is expressly allowed under a particular NES, regional plan, or resource consent. The NES for air quality came into force under the RMA in 2004.[51] These nationally applied regulations are reviewed regularly, and were last amended in 2011. The NES prohibits discharges into the air of unacceptable levels of dioxins and other toxics, carbon monoxide, fine particulate matter, nitrogen dioxide, sulfur dioxide, and ozone. Moreover, they establish design standards for newly installed wood burners in urban areas and the collection and destruction of gas from large landfills.[52]

Direct responsibility for managing air quality is assumed by regional councils under the RMA. Regional plans, as a matter of practice, address air quality issues specific to each region. A resource consent must be sought from the regional council for discharge activities that are not permitted under the regional plan, but which are not prohibited by the NES on air quality. In considering an application for consent, the regional council must consider the actual and potential effects of allowing the discharge. Many regional plans are premised on the requirement that a discharge to air should not be "noxious, offensive or objectionable."[53] The phrase has not been specifically addressed in the context of cases involving discharges to air. However, in *Watercare Services Ltd v Minhinnick* the Court of Appeal emphasized the objective nature of the test, observing that

> The bona fide assertion of the person seeking an . . . order that the matter in question is offensive or objectionable is not enough. There must be some external standard against which that assertion can be measured.[54]

B. Climate Change

New Zealand ratified the United Nations Framework Convention on Climate Change (UNFCCC) in 1993 and the Kyoto Protocol in December 2002. Under the Protocol, New Zealand committed to reduce its greenhouse gas emissions to 1990 levels during the first commitment period between 2008 and 2012. However, New Zealand announced its decision at the Doha Climate Change Conference in November 2012 not to sign on for a second commitment period between 2012 and 2020. The incumbent government decided that New Zealand would take its next commitment under the UNFCCC, aligning its climate change efforts with developed and developing countries, which collectively are responsible for 85 percent of global emissions. This includes the United States, Japan, China, India, Canada, Brazil, Russia, and many other major economies.[55] New Zealand seeks to address its obligations under the UNFCCC through the Climate Change Response Act. This act makes provision for, among other things, an emissions trading scheme (ETS) designed to price emissions throughout the economy. New Zealand's ETS is based on a cap-and-trade model. However, there are no caps on emissions within individual sectors or even within New Zealand.[56] The lack of a cap, prolonged entry dates, and the period of extended free emissions has brought into question the effectiveness of New Zealand's ETS.[57]

III. Water

Natural and physical resources are defined under section 2 of the RMA to include water. Water is, in turn, defined as meaning "water in all its physical forms whether flowing or not and whether over or under the ground" including "fresh water, coastal water, and geothermal water." Water is recognized in the RMA not just as a natural and physical resource but also as a resource of particular importance to Maori and, in some contexts, as a resource of national importance. The preservation of the natural character of the coastal environment, wetlands, lakes, rivers, and their margins, and the protection of them from inappropriate subdivision, use, and development are all matters of national importance under section 6 of the RMA.[58] The primary basis for the management and control of water are sections 14 and 15 of the RMA. These sections generally provide that no person may take, use, dam, or divert any water unless that activity is expressly allowed by a rule in a regional plan or a resource consent,[59] and that no person may discharge any contaminant into water, or into land in circumstances that may result in it entering water unless the discharge is permitted under a regional plan or a resource consent.[60]

Hydroelectric generation followed by irrigation are by far the largest users of fresh water in New Zealand. Hydro is considered to be a nonconsumptive use because the water reenters the river system downstream. Irrigation is considered to be a consumptive use because the water does not reenter a water body.[61] Regional councils have the power to establish rules in regional plans to allocate the taking and use of water under the RMA. Generally, regional plans allocate water by establishing minimum flows and the maximum amount of water that can be taken from the water body.[62] Allocation between competing applications for the same resource is determined by the first-in, first-served rule, as established in the Court of Appeal's decision in *Fleetwing Farms Ltd v Marlborough District Council*.[63] Historically New Zealand's abundant supply of fresh water was thought to be inexhaustible. However, the country's reliance on fresh water for electricity generation, and agricultural and horticultural demands, mean that New Zealand's fresh water resources continue to be placed under greater demand. Competition for fresh water is fierce and claims to property rights in respect of water has consequently been the subject of much litigation, with the leading case being the High Court's decision in *Aoraki Water Trust v Meridian Energy Limited*.[64]

The RMA has jurisdiction over land (including seabed and foreshore), air, and water out to the 12 nm boundary of the territorial sea. Central government is responsible for national coastal policy through the New Zealand Coastal Policy Statement (NZCPS). This NPS sets out national guidelines that all agencies must consider when making decisions about planning or coastal development. Regional policy statements and plans (including coastal plans) must give effect to the NZCPS.[65] Regional coastal plans promote the sustainable management of the coastal marine area (i.e., that area between the line of mean high water at spring tide and the outer boundary of the territorial sea) and the coastal environment. Regional plans covering land and water areas landward of the coastal plan are optional. However, in practice, regional councils generally seek to implement regional plans concerning a region's other natural resources (i.e., those in addition to the coastal marine area). Some regional councils go further and combine their regional coastal plan with landward regional plans to create an integrated coastal management plan.[66]

There is a presumption under the RMA against activities taking place in the area between mean high water springs and the 12 nm limit (i.e., the coastal marine area). At the time the RMA was passed it was assumed that this area was public domain administered by the Crown. The owners were considered to be the public.[67] As a consequence, if one member of the public wishes to acquire space or carry out activities that would affect other members of the public, they are not able to do so unless the rules in a plan allow them to, or they have obtained what is known as a "resource consent" to do so. This is seen as inherently precautionary and restrictive in comparison to the enabling terrestrial regime. Accordingly, the RMA specifies that use and development must not occur in the coastal marine area (e.g., the erection of a structure that is fixed in, on, under, or over the foreshore or seabed) unless expressly allowed by a rule in a regional coastal plan or resource consent. If a person does wish to carry out an activity that is not expressly allowed by a rule in a regional coastal plan, they need to apply for resource consent to the relevant regional council. The resource consent process is carried out pursuant to the RMA and the relevant regional plan. When considering a resource consent application, the regional council must consider any actual or potential effects on the environment of allowing the activity, the NZCPS, regional policy statements, regional (land, water, and air) plans, and the coastal plan.[68]

The EEZ Act sets up an environmental management regime for New Zealand's EEZ and continental shelf. It was enacted to fill the gaps in New Zealand's existing environmental management regime beyond the 12 nm territorial sea boundary, and to give effect to New Zealand's obligations under UNCLOS to manage and protect natural resources of the EEZ.[69] The EEZ's purpose is to promote the sustainable management of the natural resources of the EEZ and continental shelf.[70] This enables integrated decision making (i.e., integrated management) in cases where there are cross-boundary proposals for development in the EEZ under the EEZ Act and the 12 nm territorial sea under the RMA.

This is consistent with an extensive body of international literature extolling the administrative virtues of providing for integrated management within legislation governing the marine and coastal environment. It is relevant in this context that the RMA is generally extolled among that body of literature as a legislative model for the implementation of "integrated management."[71] It is worth noting that there was significant debate during the passage of the EEZ Act as to whether it should, or indeed did have, a more liberally worded purpose than that set out under section 5 of the RMA. This debate was largely rendered void when it was pointed out that the initial wording chosen by legislators for the act's purpose is interpreted under international law as *sustainable development*.[72] Unsurprisingly, given the policy of successive governments to encourage a neoliberal effects-based approach to environmental management, the final act adopted sustainable management as its core purpose.

The MCAA represents the culmination of many years of debate and law reform concerning Maori customary rights to the foreshore and seabed (or coastal marine area). The debate essentially began in 2003 when the Court of Appeal in the decision of *Ngati Apa v Attorney-General* found that the Maori Land Court had jurisdiction to determine claims of customary ownership over the foreshore and seabed.[73] This decision was contrary to government policy and legislation that had been based on the understanding that Maori customary title to the foreshore and seabed had been extinguished. The government's response to the *Ngati Apa* decision was to enact the Foreshore and Seabed Act 2004 (FSA) in order to clarify the status of public access and ownership. The FSA removed the ability of Maori to seek recognition of their customary title and vested the beneficial ownership of the foreshore and seabed in the Crown, but allowed existing freehold title to remain.[74]

The purpose of the MCAA under section 10 is to protect the legitimate interests of all New Zealanders in the territorial sea (or coastal marine area)[75] while recognizing customary interests exercised by iwi, hapu, and whanau as tangata whenua (i.e., the Maori people). To these ends the MCAA under section 6 restores customary interests in the foreshore and seabed that were extinguished by the FSA and confirms that any application for the recognition of customary interests must be considered and determined as if the FSA had not been enacted. The MCAA's restoration of customary interests intersects with the RMA in three key ways. First, Maori groups do not need consent under the RMA to carry out customary use rights that would otherwise be prohibited or restricted under the RMA.[76] Second, Maori groups who hold customary title have the right to permit (or withhold permission for) activities requiring a resource consent in the area covered by the title.[77] Third, Maori groups who hold customary title also have the right to prepare a planning document setting out the objectives and policies for their customary marine title area, which are to be recognized and provided for by the relevant regional council planning documents for the territorial sea.[78]

IV.   Handling, Treatment, Transportation, and Disposal of Hazardous Materials

The HSNO Act introduced a standardized and coordinated approach to the control of hazardous substances, based on the intrinsic risk characteristic of each substance.[79] As with other pieces of environmental legislation, the HSNO Act was used to consolidate the piecemeal approach to hazardous substance control that had been in effect prior to its enactment. The HSNO Act prohibits the importation and manufacture of any hazardous substance, and the importation, development field testing, or release of any new organism unless done in accordance with an approval issued under the act.[80] New Zealand's remote and secluded geography contains a number of unique ecosystems. These ecosystems are important to New Zealanders not just because of their intrinsic value, but also because New Zealand's economic reliance on natural resources requires their protection. This helps explain why the HSNO Act was the first act to directly incorporate the precautionary principle into New Zealand's domestic legislation.[81]

The purpose of the HSNO Act is to "protect the environment . . . by preventing or managing the adverse effects of hazardous substances and new organisms."[82] The initial draft bill qualified the concept of "protection" in this statement with the words, "so as to enable the maximum national benefit." This was changed during the course of the bill's passage through Parliament due to concerns that "whatever the trade offs, the only acceptable outcome is the protection of the environment, and the health and safety of people."[83] Section 7 of the act requires that "[a]ll persons exercising functions, powers, and duties under this Act . . . shall take into account the need for caution in managing adverse effects where there is scientific and technical uncertainty about those effects." In *Bleakley v Environmental Risk Management Authority*, the High Court held that the precautionary approach only applies where there is technical and scientific uncertainty, and the approach does not extend to social or ethical uncertainty.[84] Further, in *Mothers Against Genetic Engineering Inc v Minister for the Environment*,[85] the High Court found that section 7 is not concerned with the prevention of adverse effects, but management of adverse effects that will or may occur.[86]

V. Waste and Site Remediation

Currently within New Zealand there is no comprehensive or integrated statutory framework for the management of waste and hazardous waste. Instead, it is controlled through a variety of statutes such as the Waste Minimization Act 2008 (WMA), RMA, and HSNO Act. The purpose of the WMA is to encourage waste minimization and a decrease in waste disposal to (1) protect the environment from harm and (2) provide environmental, social, and cultural benefits.[87] Every territorial authority (i.e., district or city council) is under a duty to promote effective and efficient waste management within its district. The territorial authority must adopt a waste management plan, which provides objectives, policies, and methods for collection, recycling, and disposal of waste. In particular, the territorial authority must consider methods relating to reduction, reuse, recycling, recovery, treatment, and disposal, and must ensure that the collection, transport, and disposal of waste do not become a nuisance.[88]

The RMA takes effect through NESs, regional policy statements, and regional plans. Regional plans will generally contain rules that require resource consents to be obtained for proposed landfills, prohibit the discharge of solid waste or treated hazardous waste to land, and regulate the incineration of waste. More often than not, the establishment of a landfill will ultimately result in contamination of the landfill site. Regional councils are required to undertake "the investigation of land for the purposes of identifying and monitoring contaminated land."[89] Territorial authorities are required to prevent or mitigate "the adverse effects of the development, subdivision or use of contaminated land." Many regional and territorial authorities require resource consents to be obtained for the decontamination or development of contaminated sites.[90] A regional council or territorial authority can require an owner or occupier to clean up a contaminated site where persons or entities have caused illegal discharges to occur on land or in the water, or likely adverse effects on the environment. This means that the landowners, occupiers, and polluters can all be held liable for cleanup of contaminated sites.

However, the Environment Court held in *Voullaire v Jones* that it did not have jurisdiction to impose liability for sites contaminated prior to the 1991 enactment of the RMA.[91] This means that there are a number of orphan sites for which no entity is presently liable. Although the government has investigated the problem of historically contaminated sites, legislative changes clarifying liability for the remediation of pre-1991 sites have yet to be made.[92]

VI. Emergency Response

The Civil Defense Emergency Management Act 2002 (Civil Defense Act) applies to central and local governments in the case of civil defense emergencies. The definition of "emergency" under the act is extensive and includes such things as explosions, earthquakes, and eruptions (natural disasters) to leakage or spillage of any dangerous gas or substance (human-made disasters).[93] The Civil Defense Act requires a risk management approach to be taken when dealing with hazards, and a precautionary approach in cases where there is scientific or technical uncertainty about risk.[94] The Civil Defense minister may declare a state of national emergency in respect of any part of New Zealand, and local authorities may declare local emergencies. Once a state of emergency is declared, civil defense groups have wide-ranging powers, including carrying out works, clearing roads or other public works, removing and disposing of dangerous structures or materials, and providing rescue and/or relief to endangered persons.[95] Following the major earthquake centered in Christchurch City on February 22, 2011, which caused extensive loss of life and property damage, Parliament enacted the Canterbury Earthquake Recovery Act 2011. This act is designed to facilitate rapid response and recovery. It enables the suspension or revocation of obligations under the RMA, and strategies and recovery plans prepared under the act prevail over any RMA planning document. If necessary, councils must amend their planning documents to comply with the strategy and recovery plan without the usual public consultation or notification required under the RMA.[96]

The regulatory framework governing pollution in the marine environment principally comprises the Maritime Transport Act 1994 (MTA) and the RMA. One of the MTA's primary purposes is to regulate the discharge and dumping of harmful substances into the ocean.[97] The MTA requires Maritime New Zealand[98] to prepare and implement plans and responses to protect the environment in the event of an oil spill. On-scene commanders have significant powers under the act in the event of an oil spill. Those powers include directing the actions of the master of the ship (or offshore oil installation), removing vehicles or ships impeding oil spill response, and requisitioning private property to assist oil spill response. New Zealand's worst maritime environmental disaster occurred when the MV *Rena* grounded close to Tauranga on October 10, 2011, spilling an estimated 350 tons of oil into the coastal marine area (territorial sea). Criminal prosecutions for oil spills were brought under the RMA, which establishes a strict liability regime for offenses. This meant that Crown prosecutors only needed to establish responsibility for the incident, and not intent. The master and second mate were sentenced to six months in prison and the owners were fined $300,000.[99] The maximum pecuniary penalties under the RMA are generally considered to be too light for significant pollution offenses,[100] and the fine imposed on the owners was light in the context of the maximum that might have been imposed.

In addition, New Zealand is a signatory to the Convention on Limitation of Liability for Maritime Claims 1976. Consequently, the MTA enables the owners to seek orders from the High Court to limit their total liability for all damage and loss resulting from the MV *Rena* incident based on the tonnage of the vessel (i.e., NZ $11.5 million). This is only a fraction of the Crown's cleanup costs (i.e., NZ $50 million),[101] and damages to the environment, community, and Maori. At the time of writing this chapter, the Crown had settled for half of its cleanup costs, while the issue of environmental and private damages remains unresolved. This situation led the New Zealand Law Society to comment that even though changes proposed to the MTA "enable greater recovery of loss and damages resulting from maritime disasters, it is noted that even the increased limits are likely to fall far short of the levels of actual loss and damage that may arise from such occurrences."[102]

VII. Natural Resource Management and Protection

The purpose of section 5 of the RMA is "to promote the sustainable management of natural and physical resources." Sustainable management is defined as "managing the use, development, and protection of natural and physical resources in a way ... which enables people and communities to provide for their social, economic, and cultural wellbeing."[103] Natural and physical resources are not limited to resources with actual or potential economic value. The act is concerned with the use of land, water, and air, irrespective of their economic value.[104] Regional councils promulgate policy statements for the integrated management of the region's natural and physical resources. They are also responsible for natural and physical resource use and development consent, monitoring and compliance, and enforcement. The RMA is an effects-based piece of legislation. Accordingly, regional council policies and rules tend to identify scientifically based environmental standards (i.e., performance standards) rather than proscribe what type of resource uses and development are and are not permitted in any particular location. The effects-based approach to natural resource management is considered to be one of the strengths of the RMA, as it enables resource consent decisions about use and development to be driven by scientific innovation rather than bureaucracy.[105]

The protection and/or preservation of a number of key natural and physical resources are identified as being matters of national importance. These include the coastal environment, wetlands, lakes, rivers, outstanding natural landscapes, and significant indigenous vegetation and fauna.[106] The High Court has found that the duty to "recognise and provide for" matters subject to the duty creates a significant priority for those matters. They cannot be merely an equal part of a general balancing exercise.[107] The duty requires regional councils to do something more than "have regard to" or "take into account." It is a strong phrase and requires the decision maker to take action.[108] There are two steps in the process of applying this duty. The first step involves recognizing that a matter is pertinent. The second step entails taking action to make provision for that matter.[109] Accordingly, the identification of natural and physical resources as matters of national importance creates a strong obligation for regional councils to protect and/or preserve those resources when exercising their policy and planning, resource consent, monitoring and compliance, and enforcement functions under the RMA.

VIII.   Natural Resource Damages

Although land is included within the definition of natural and physical resources under section 2 of the RMA, regional councils only have limited jurisdiction over land use.[110] Rather, territorial authorities (i.e., district and city councils) have jurisdiction within their respective districts for land use and subdivision.[111] Every territorial authority is required to have a district (or city) plan in order "to achieve integrated management of the effects of the use, development, or protection of land."[112] Consistent with the enabling purpose and neoliberal foundations of the RMA, land use as a general rule is permitted unless it contravenes a rule in a district plan. If the use does contravene a rule in a plan, it may be permitted if a resource consent is obtained.[113] District plans generally identify zones that control different types of activities and/or the effects of those activities. However, effects-based (or performance-based) rules tend to work better in the management of natural resources where environmental standards can be scientifically established, rather than in town and country planning where many decisions about land use and development have a more subjective element to them (e.g., visual amenity including things such as building form, height, and color). Nevertheless, most district plans that control land use activities (or effects) retain some form of residual discretion for the territorial authority to decide whether a land use proposal meets the sustainable management purpose of the act.[114]

IX.   Protected Species

The Department of Conservation (DoC) was established under the Conservation Act 1987 for the purposes of advocating and promoting the conservation of New Zealand's natural and historic resources. Natural resources are defined as including plants and animals of all kinds; the air, water, and soil in or on which any plant or animal lives; and systems of interacting living organisms and their environment.[115] In addition to the Conservation Act, DoC administers a number of other statutes including the Wildlife Act 1953, Reserves Act 1977, and Marine Reserves Act 1971, which all make provision for the protection of endangered species in New Zealand. DoC is responsible under these statutes for managing national parks, national reserves, conservation land, marine reserves, marine mammal sanctuaries, and wildlife reserves. The Wildlife Act establishes a protection system for wildlife, with some species absolutely protected and some partially protected. The act also makes provision for various types of wildlife refuges, sanctuaries, management reserves, and the creation of management plans. The purpose of the Reserves Act includes the preservation and survival of indigenous flora and fauna in its natural habitat, and the preservation of samples of natural ecosystems.[116] Likewise, the purpose of the Marine Reserves Act is "preserving, as marine reserves for the scientific study of marine life, areas of New Zealand that contain . . . marine life, of such distinctive quality, or so typical, or beautiful, or unique, that their continued preservation is in the national interest."[117] National parks, reserves, and other land held by the DoC accounts for roughly one-third of New Zealand's land area.[118] Their existence, together with the low population density across large areas of New Zealand, forms part of the country's cultural identity and is an important component of the country's tourism economy.

X.   Environmental Review and Decision Making

Resource consent must be sought under the RMA for natural resource use and development activities not permitted under regional plans, and land use and development activities controlled by district plans. Regional councils are the consent authorities with respect to natural resources, while district councils process land use applications. The EPA has responsibility for processing proposals that are deemed to be of national significance under the RMA, and also proposals for marine consent within New Zealand's EEZ and continental shelf under the EEZ Act. Both the RMA and the EEZ Act are effects-based statutes, which means that consent decisions are generally based upon whether the averse effects of a proposal can be sustainably managed. As a general rule of thumb, if an applicant can show that the adverse effects of a proposed activity will not be more than minor, he/she will invariably be granted consent to undertake his/her proposal. The clear incentive of the effects-based planning regime is to encourage people to internalize the cost of addressing the effects of their activity by investing in technology, designs, or procedures that will reduce adverse environmental effects to an acceptable level.[119]

This incentive is strengthened by the public participation provisions of the RMA, which provide two different paths down which an application might proceed. These are the notified and nonnotified paths. A notified application requires a public hearing, which is often costly. If an affected party gives written approval for the activity under the RMA, then the effects of the application on that party are no longer capable of being considered by the consent authority processing the application. The process of obtaining written approval from affected parties for an application often requires the applicant to offer measures that avoid, remedy, or mitigate the environmental effects of the proposed activity. This is because even if a party provides written approval for the activity, thereby excluding consideration of effects on that party, the consent authority is still required to consider the effects of the activity on the broader environment. Generally, applicants will try to make a proposal as environmentally acceptable as possible in order to obtain the agreement of potentially affected persons (e.g., through agreement on mitigation measures or environmental/financial compensation) so that an application can proceed on a nonnotified basis.[120] All applications for marine consent must be publicly notified under the EEZ Act.[121] Nevertheless, there is still some incentive for proponents to deal constructively with submitters, as the EPA retains a discretion not to hold a hearing in cases where neither the applicant nor a submitter requests a hearing.[122]

All decisions must achieve the purpose of the RMA and EEZ Act. Accordingly, in deciding whether to grant or refuse consent, the consent authority must exercise an overall discretion to decide whether the application satisfies the sustainable management purpose of the act. If the consent authority or EPA is satisfied, it can grant the application, but it may impose conditions.[123] A decision to either grant or refuse an application for resource consent may be appealed to the Environment Court on a de novo basis under the RMA.[124] A decision to grant or refuse a marine consent by the EPA under the EEZ Act may only be appealed to the High Court on questions of law.[125] It is unclear why marine consent applications cannot be appealed to the Environment Court on questions of fact. It is, however, likely that it has something to do with the present government's policy of encouraging the development of deep sea natural resources (e.g., petroleum and minerals).

Resource and marine consents will invariably contain reporting and monitoring conditions that require the consent holder to provide councils or the EPA with information concerning the operation of the consent. The information requirements that accompany consents are generally linked to the complexity of the consented activity. Accordingly, proposals that are dependent on science-based conditions will have more information requirements (e.g., adaptive management conditions)[126] than less technical consents where the effects of an activity are more clearly understood. The council or the EPA will in most instances observe information gathering by the operator to ensure its veracity. Where data is highly technical in nature, councils and the EPA will generally seek peer review and analysis from outside agencies or private sector consultancies. Consents will also contain conditions empowering councils or the EPA to require a review of the conditions and/or the cessation of operations in order to address an adverse effect, or the risk of an adverse effect on the environment, detected as a result of environmental monitoring.

XI. Transboundary Pollution

Transboundary pollution is generally understood to be pollution originating in one state and spilling over into another. Due to New Zealand's geographic isolation it does not have many domestic laws that directly seek to regulate transboundary pollution. Notwithstanding, New Zealand was involved in one of the most prominent attempts to adjudicate an international transboundary pollution dispute in 1973, when together with Australia it filed complaints with the International Court of Justice (ICJ) asking it to declare that French nuclear-weapons testing in the Pacific unlawfully threatened downwind populations with radioactive fallout. Although the ICJ proceeded to grant interim relief, France ignored the order and continued with testing.[127] As with other states, New Zealand's responsibilities and obligations for transboundary pollution derive from international law. However, those responsibilities and obligations can only be given effect in a domestic setting through legislation.

This is because Parliament's power to legislate is unfettered in New Zealand. The most recent authority on this point is *Greenpeace v Minister of Energy and Resources*, where the High Court found that "[i]f questions arise as to the extent to which New Zealand—as a State—met its international obligations that must be a matter upon which Parliament might choose to legislate. It is not a matter upon which the Court can direct Parliament."[128] The EEZ Act, for example, seeks to address New Zealand's international obligations in respect of the marine environment. Accordingly, section 11 of that act provides that it "continues or enables the implementation of New Zealand's obligations under various international conventions, including" the UNCLOS and Convention on Biological Diversity 1992. It is important to note that the wording of section 11 does not appear to directly incorporate those conventions into domestic law.[129] This means administrative decision making is dependent on the statutory expression of the obligations contained in those conventions, rather than the conventions themselves. Accordingly, it is likely that the conventions will provide an interpretational guide to decision making under the EEZ Act where international the performance of international obligations is called into question at a domestic level.

XII.   Civil and Criminal Enforcement and Penalties

In New Zealand, most enforcement and penalties for environmental offenses are provided for under statute. Regional councils and the EPA, for example, respectively have responsibility for enforcing compliance with the RMA and EEZ Act. In cases of noncompliance, regional councils and the EPA may issue abatement notices or apply to the Environment Court for an enforcement order. Abatement notices can require a person to either stop a noncomplying activity, or require a person to take positive action to remedy or mitigate an adverse effect. Enforcement orders are proceedings where a party applies for an order to the Environment Court. Technically any person can apply for an enforcement order. More often than not, however, enforcement orders will be sought by the regulator (e.g., council or EPA). Enforcement orders, like abatement notices, can both prohibit or require action to ensure compliance with the RMA or EEZ Act. In the worst cases offenders may be criminally prosecuted for breaches of either act. Offenses under the RMA and EEZ Act are strict liability. This means prosecutors do not need to show intent (i.e., mens rea) and that establishing responsibility for a breach is sufficient for a conviction under either act. Nevertheless, the Court of Appeal has held that while Parliament justifies strict liability in the public interest, "[a]bsolute criminal liability is not to be imposed where the defendant establishes reasonable lack of knowledge, or reasonable precautions, plus the taking of 'all reasonable steps to remedy any effects of the act or omission giving rise to the offence.'"[130]

Public law enforcement (i.e., abatement notices and enforcement orders) and criminal prosecution are the more traditional forms of deterrence for environmental damage in New Zealand. However, while enforcement orders and criminal sentencing can impose requirements to remedy or mitigate adverse effects on the environment, pecuniary penalties are comparatively low for offenses causing significant adverse effects when compared with other jurisdictions.[131] Furthermore, public law forms of enforcement in New Zealand are not designed to compensate individuals for private damage resulting from environmental negligence.[132] The common law remedies for environmental nuisance and negligence are the principal avenues of recourse when seeking compensation for private damages. For example, nuisance has been applied in cases where activities have been found to constitute an unreasonable interference with a landowner's right to the use and enjoyment of land, and several cases have involved plaintiffs' successfully pleading negligence in relation to pollution and damage caused by pesticide spraying.[133] Nevertheless, despite the availability of common law remedies, more often than not environmental disputes in New Zealand are determined through recourse to public and criminal law.

Notes

1. D. McKenzie, Heinemann New Zealand Atlas (1987).
2. Statistics New Zealand, Geography, http://www.stats.govt.nz/ (last visited Jan. 1, 2013).
3. *See* http://www.nationsencyclopedia.com/economies/Asia-and-the-Pacific/New -Zealand.html.
4. Ministry for Environment, Environment New Zealand 2007, at 6 (Dec. 2007).
5. H. Rennie, *Coastal Fisheries and Marine Planning in Transition, in* Environmental Planning & Management in New Zealand 216 (P.A. Memon & H. Perkins eds., 2000).
6. Ministry for Environment, Improving Regulation of Environmental Effects In New Zealand's Exclusive Economic Zone 1 (Aug. 2007).
7. Statistics New Zealand, Estimated Resident Population of New Zealand, http:// www.stats.govt.nz/ (last visited Jan. 1, 2013).
8. OECD Environmental Performance Reviews: New Zealand 1 (2007). The OECD is the Organisation for Economic Co-operation and Development. It is headquartered in Paris, France. *See* http://www.oecd.org.
9. New Zealand Treasury, New Zealand Economic and Financial Overview 2010: Industrial Structure and Principal Economic Sectors (Apr. 2010).
10. OECD, *supra* note 8.
11. The system is a series of procedures for operating a parliamentary legislature employed by Commonwealth and ex-Commonwealth nations.
12. The Crown is represented by a governor-general appointed by the monarch (Queen Elizabeth II at the time of writing this chapter) at the recommendation of the prime minister.
13. Cabinet Office, Cabinet Manual 1–2 (2008).
14. OECD, *supra* note 8.
15. As used in this chapter, "public law" means the body of law that governs relations between a state and its citizens. It addresses the structure and operation of the government, and includes constitutional, administrative, and criminal law.
16. In New Zealand, as in other Commonwealth countries, the Crown remains (at least figuratively) both the embodiment of the state and the head of executive government. Prof. Philip Joseph explains that "[t]oday it is quite appropriate to say that the Crown is *the State,* personifying its national culture, history, and continuity." Furthermore, "For the courts, the expressions the Crown and Her Majesty are symbolic of the executive authority of the State, and include references to the central executive government." P. Joseph, Constitutional and Administrative Law in New Zealand 585 (3d ed. 2007).
17. D. Bennington, *Potential Class Action Looms on Rena Horizon,* 179 N.Z. Law. 8 (2012).
18. R. Makgill & H. Rennie, *A Model for Integrated Coastal Management Legislation: A Principled Analysis of New Zealand's Resource Management Act 1991,* 27 Int'l J. Marine & Coastal L. 135, 143 (2012).
19. G. Brundtland, *Our Common Future: The World Commission on Environment and Development,* Report to General Assembly, Annex to document A/42/427.
20. Agenda 21 is a compendium of principles signed at the 1992 U.N. Conference on Environment and Development in Rio de Janerio, Brazil, that was designed to guide nations in their implementation of sustainable development.
21. The Convention on Biological Diversity 1992 (ratified 1993), the U.N. Framework Convention on Climate Change 1992 (ratified 1993) (UNFCCC), and the U.N. Convention

on the Law of the Sea (UNCLOS) (ratified 1996). It is important to note that Agenda 21 sets out nonbinding environmental principles, whereas the three conventions mentioned here are legally binding and make provision for legally binding actions to be taken. Nevertheless, New Zealand's RMA, Biosecurity Act 1993, and Local Government Act 2002 are all considered to be largely in accord with the principles of Agenda 21.

22. Brundtland, *supra* note 19, ch. 2, para. 1.

23. *Id.*

24. *Id.*, para. 3 ("[S]ustainability cannot be secured unless development policies pay attention to such considerations as changes in access to resources and in the distribution of costs and benefits. Even the narrow notion of physical sustainability *implies a concern for social equity* between generations, a concern that must logically be extended to *equity within each generation.*" (emphasis added)).

25. [1998] NZRMA 73, at 86. For policy debate concerning the purpose of the RMA see K. Grundy, *In Search of Logic: s 5 of the Resource Management Act*, N.Z. L.J. 40 (1995); Hon. S. Upton, *re s 5 of the Resource Management Act*, N.Z. L. J. 124 (1995); P. Skelton & A. Memon, *Adopting Sustainability as an Overarching Environmental Policy: A Review of Section 5 of the RMA*, Res. Mgmt. J. 1–10 (Mar. 2002); S. Upton, Helen S. Atkins & G. Willis, *Section 5 Revisited: a Critique of Skelton & Memon's Analysis*, Res. Mgmt. J. 10–22 (Nov. 2002).

26. 51b Hansard, Resource Management Bill Third Reading 3018 (July 1991).

27. K. Palmer, Local Government Law in New Zealand 567–68 (1993); K. Palmer, *Resource Management Act 1991: Integrated Resource Management and Sustainability, in* Environmental and Resource Management 95–202 (D. Nolan ed., 2011).

28. Makgill & Rennie, *supra* note 18, at 145. *See also* Hon. S. Upton, *The Stace Hammond Grace Lecture 1995: Purpose and Principle in the Resource Management Act* 8 (May 26, 1995) (unpublished, Univ. of Waikato) ("The [RMA] provides us with a framework to establish objectives with a biophysical bottom line that must not be compromised. Provided that those objectives are met, what people get up to is their own affair. As such the [RMA] provides a more liberal regime for developers. On the other hand, activities will have to be compatible with hard environmental standards.").

29. Makgill & Rennie, *supra* note 18. An AEE is often referred to in international law and other domestic jurisdictions as an environmental impact assessment (EIA).

30. *Id.*

31. RMA § 6.

32. RMA § 7.

33. K. Palmer, *Resource Management Act 1991: Treaty of Waitangi, in* Environmental and Resource Management, *supra* note 27, at 146–51; P. Majurey & C. Whata, *Maori in Environmental Law, in* Environmental and Resource Management, *supra* note 27, at 897–913; A. Tunks, *One Indigenous Vision for Sustainable Development Law?, in*, 3 Environmental Law for a Sustainable Society 97 *et seq.* (K. Bosselmann & D. Grinlinton eds., New Zealand Ctr. for Envtl. Law Monograph Series, 2002).

34. S. Gordon, *The Resource Management Act 1991: "A Biophysical Bottom Line" vs "A More Liberal Regime"; A Dichotomy?*, 6(3) Canterbury L. Rev. 499 (1997); K. Bosselmann, *New Zealand, in* The Role of the Judiciary in Environmental Governance 360 (L. Kotzé & A. Paterson eds., 2009).

35. K. Palmer, *The Sources and Institutions of Environmental Law, in* Environmental and Resource Management, *supra* note 27, at 65–68.

36. Environment Act § 31.

37. RMA §§ 45, 46.

38. RMA § 24 (b).

39. RMA §§ 25A, 25B.

40. EPA Act § 13.

41. There are 11 regional councils and 67 territorial authorities (city or district councils). Six of the territorial authorities are unitary authorities. This means they perform the functions of both regional councils and territorial authorities.

42. RMA § 30(1)(a).

43. RMA §§ 59, 60.

44. Palmer, *supra* note 33, at 193.

45. RMA § 31(1)(a).

46. RMA § 74.

47. For information on the historical development of the court system, see Bosselmann, *supra* note 34, at 374 *et seq.*; R. MULHOLLAND, INTRODUCTION TO THE NEW ZEALAND LEGAL SYSTEM 37, 77–79 (10th ed. 2001).

48. Palmer, *supra* note 35, at 53–54.

49. This includes the RMA, Historic Places Act 1993, Forests Act 1949, and Crown Minerals Act 1991.

50. "Contaminant" is broadly defined under section 2 of the RMA to include virtually any substance including heat and energy.

51. Resource Management (National Environmental Standards relating to Certain Air Pollutants, Dioxins and Other Toxicontinental Shelf) Regulations 2004.

52. B. Matheson, *Air, in* ENVIRONMENTAL AND RESOURCE MANAGEMENT, *supra* note 27, at 679.

53. *Id.* at 692.

54. [1998] 1 NZLR 294, 304.

55. *See* T. Groser, *It's Time to Move Past Kyoto Agreement*, N.Z. HERALD, Dec. 20, 2012 (climate change minister's explanation of New Zealand's position):

> When Kyoto was signed, developed countries accounted for nearly 60 per cent of global emissions. But it took a body blow right at the start. On July 25, 1997 Ted Kennedy and John Kerry (the next Secretary of State), along with 93 other Republican and Democrat senators voted the treaty down 95-0. I call that pretty decisive. Today, the countries that are prepared to do a second Kyoto commitment for the period beyond 2012 account for some 14 per cent of global emissions. In a few years time 90 per cent of emissions will be outside Kyoto. The unrelenting emphasis on "Kyoto, Kyoto, Kyoto" has sucked the political energy out of the negotiations, diverting attention from the real problem. It is time to move beyond Kyoto and find a solution that can have a real environmental impact.

56. A. Arthur-Young, *Climate Change, in* ENVIRONMENTAL AND RESOURCE MANAGEMENT, *supra* note 27, at 1054.

57. For further analysis of New Zealand's ETS see D. BULLOCK, THE NEW ZEALAND EMISSIONS TRADING SCHEME: A STEP IN THE RIGHT DIRECTION? (2009), and K. Price, L. Daniell & L. Cooper, *New Zealand Climate Change Laws, in* CLIMATE CHANGE LAW 89–99 (W. Gumley & T. Winter-Bottom eds., 2009).

58. S. Christensen, *Water, Contaminants and Discharges, in* DSL ENVIRONMENTAL HANDBOOK WM3 (S. Blakeley ed., Brookers online & looseleaf eds. 2012).

59. RMA § 14(2)(a), (3)(a). Coastal water is treated separately so that taking, use, damming, or diversion is only illegal where to do so contravenes a rule in a regional plan.

60. RMA § 15(1)(a), (b).

61. R. Makgill, *A New Start for Fresh Water: Allocation and Property Rights*, 2(1) LINCOLN PLANNING REVIEW 5, 5 (2010).

62. *Id.*

63. [1997] 3 NZLR 257.

64. [2005] 2 NZLR 268. *See* Makgill, *supra* note 61, at 8–9; F. Neil, *The Law around New Zealand's "Liquid Gold,"* 801 Lawtalk 6–7 (2012).

65. RMA §§ 62(3), 67(3)(b).

66. Makgill & Rennie, *supra* note 18, at 147–48 & 154–55.

67. The presumption of Crown ownership over the coastal marine area (or foreshore and seabed) was removed with the passage of the MCAA, which is discussed below. Although the Crown retains sovereign rights over the coastal marine area, the MCAA removes it from the Crown's beneficial ownership. This situation now is that nobody owns the coastal marine area under the MCCA, and it appears to be held in some form of public trust. For a further discussion of Crown ownership and nonownership of the coastal marine area, see R. Makgill, *Feeling Left Out at Sea? Navigating No Ownership, Customary Rights and Resource Management,* Res. Mgmt. Theory & Prac. 162, 171–83 (2012); R. Makgill, *Public Property and Private Use Rights: Exclusive Occupation of the Coastal Marine Area of New Zealand, in* 3 Water and Sustainability 87–90 (K. Bosselmann & V. Tava eds., New Zealand Ctr. for Envtl. Law Monograph Series, 2011).

68. Makgill & Rennie, *supra* note 18, at 147–48, 154–55.

69. R. Makgill, K. Dawson & N. de Wit, *The Exclusive Economic Zone and Continental Shelf (Environmental Effects) Bill,* Res. Mgmt. J. 1, 1 (Apr. 2012).

70. EEZ Act § 10(1).

71. Makgill & Rennie, *supra* note 18, at 135–65.

72. Makgill, Dawson & de Wit, *supra* note 69, at 3.

73. [2003] 3 NZLR 643.

74. Makgill, *Feeling Left Out at Sea?, supra* note 67, at 162–219; R. Makgill & K. Fraser, *The Marine and Coastal Area (Takutai Moana) Act 2011: The Commons, Customary Rights and the Marine and Coastal Area, in* DSL Environmental Handbook, supra note 58; R. Makgill & H. Rennie, *The Marine and Coastal Area Act 2011,* Res. Mgmt. J. 1–7 (Apr. 2011) l.

75. For an examination of public rights in respect of the territorial sea (or coastal marine area) see Makgill, *Public Property and Private Use Rights, supra* note 67; Makgill, *Feeling Left Out at Sea?, supra* note 67, at 117–83.

76. Makgill, *Feeling Left Out at Sea?, supra* note 67, at 189; Makgill & Fraser, MC6.02; Makgill & Rennie, *supra* note 74, at 3.

77. Makgill, *Feeling Left Out at Sea?, supra* note 67, at 190; Makgill & Fraser, MC6.03; Makgill & Rennie, *supra* note 74, at 5–6.

78. Makgill, *Feeling Left Out at Sea?, supra* note 67, at 190–93; Makgill & Fraser, MC6.03; Makgill & Rennie, *supra* note 74, at 6–7.

79. J. Gardner-Hopkins, *Hazardous Substances, in* Environmental and Resource Management, *supra* note 27, at 713.

80. *Id.* at 715.

81. *Id.* at 718.

82. HSNO Act § 4.

83. R. Boardman & M. Cave, *The Resource Management Act and the Hazardous Substances and New Organisms Legislation,* 1 1996 New Zealand Petroleum Conference Proceedings 231 (Mar. 10–13, 1996).

84. [2001] 3 NZLR 213.

85. CIV-2003-404-673.

86. Gardner-Hopkins, *supra* note 79, at 718.

87. WMA § 3.

88. K. Palmer, Local Authorities Law in New Zealand 649–52 (2012).

89. RMA § 30(1)(ca).

90. Gardner-Hopkins, *supra* note 79, at 757.

91. [1997] 4 Envtl. L. Rep. NZ 75.

92. Gardner-Hopkins, *supra* note 79, at 761–62.

93. Civil Defence Act § 4.

94. K. Palmer, *supra* note 89, at 1041–42.

95. *Id.* at 1045–46.

96. *Id.* at 1051–52.

97. At the time of writing this chapter, the government had introduced Marine Legislation Bill 2012 to the house. Part 2 of the bill transfers regulation of discharges and dumping of waste, within the EEZ and the continental shelf, from Maritime New Zealand to the Environmental Protection Authority.

98. Maritime New Zealand is a Crown entity responsible for maritime transport and safety.

99. *Mar. New Zealand v Balomaga* CRI-2011-070-7734, 25 May 2012; *Mar. New Zealand v Daina Shipping Co.* CRI-2012-070-1872, 26 October 2012.

100. New Zealand Law Society, Submission on Marine Legislation Bill 2012, paras. 36 to 39.

101. For a full discussion of Crown cleanup costs see B. Marten, *Limitation of Liability in Maritime Law and Vessel-Source Pollution: A New Zealand Perspective*, N.Z. L. Rev. 199–225 (2013).

102. New Zealand Law Society, *supra* note 100, para. 7. For additional analysis of the limitation and liability related to the MV *Rena* incident, see R. Makgill, J. Mossop & K. Scott, *Liability and Limits for the Rena Pollution Incident*, 172 NZ Law. 16–17 (2011); B. Marten, *The Rena and Liability*, N.Z. L.J. 341–44 (2011); Marten, *supra* note 102.

103. RMA § 5(2).

104. *Burnett v Tasman DC* [1995] NZRMA 280.

105. Makgill & Rennie, *supra* note 18, at 152–53.

106. RMA § 6(a), (b), (c).

107. *Bleakley v Envtl. Risk Mgmt. Auth.* [2001] 3 NZLR 213 at 235 (HC).

108. *EDS v Mangonui Cnty.* [1989] 3 NZLR 257 at 272 (CA).

109. *Haddon v Auckland Reg'l Council* [1994] 1 NZRMA 49 at 58 (PT).

110. RMA § 30(1). This includes such things as soil conservation; the investigation of land for the purposes of identifying and monitoring contaminated land; discharges of contaminants into or onto land; and the strategic integration of infrastructure with land use through objectives, policies, and methods.

111. RMA § 31(1)(a), (b).

112. RMA § 31(1)(a).

113. RMA §§ 9(1) to 9(3).

114. This is because resource consent applications are generally deemed to be controlled, discretionary, and noncomplying; decisions in respect of which all are subject to the ultimate purpose of the RMA. Prohibited is the only classification category for which resource consent may not be sought, and this category is generally only used in exception circumstances. See *Thacker v Christchurch City Council* EnvC C026/09, where the Environment Court emphasized the severity of imposing prohibited status on an activity. Prohibition must reflect relevant policies and objectives and must be the most appropriate of the options available.

115. Conservation Act § 2.

116. Reserves Act § 3(1)(a), (b).

117. Marine Reserves Act § 3(1).

118. *See* http://www.doc.govt.nz/conservation/land-and-freshwater/land/.

119. Makgill & Rennie, *supra* note 18, at 153.

120. *Id.*

121. EEZ Act § 45.

122. EEZ Act § 50.

123. Makgill & Rennie, *supra* note 18, at 157.

124. RMA § 120.

125. EEZ Act § 105.

126. Adaptive management is an example of the precautionary approach. In simple terms it enables proponents and regulators to monitor the effects of an activity and control the activity on the basis of the effects observed. Key Environment Court decisions concerning the use of adaptive management conditions include *Crest Energy Kaipara Ltd v Northland Regional* A132/2009; *Clifford Bay Marine Farms Ltd. v Marlborough District Council* C131/2003; and *Golden Bay Marine Farmers v Tasman District Council* W019/2003.

127. *Nuclear Tests* (Austl. v. Fr.), 1973 I.C.J. 99, 135. *See* T. Merrill, *Golden Rules for Transboundary Pollution*, 46 DUKE L.J. 932, 958 (1997).

128. [2012] NZHC 1422.

129. The wording of section 11 in the original EEZ Bill provided that it "must be interpreted, and all persons performing functions and duties under it must act, consistently with New Zealand's obligations under the [UNCLOS]." This wording was most likely amended to the present wording due to the complexity it would create for domestic decision-making. *See* Makgill, Dawson & de Wit, *supra* note 69, at 2.

130. *Canterbury Reg'l Council v Newman* [2002] 1 NZLR 289 para. 83.

131. New Zealand Law Society, *supra* note 101; Marten, *supra* note 102.

132. This is to be distinguished from public and criminal orders under the RMA to recover private cleanup costs in the event of an environmental incident (e.g., pollution). *See* Marten, *supra* note 102.

133. K. Kirman & C. Whata, *Environmental Litigation, in* ENVIRONMENTAL AND RESOURCE MANAGEMENT, *supra* note 27, at 1214, 1223.

CHAPTER 47

Arctic Region

PETER H. OPPENHEIMER AND BRIAN ISRAEL*

The Arctic, unlike the opposite pole,[1] is not the subject of a uniform environmental legal regime, or even a precise, internationally agreed legal definition for all purposes.[2] The most basic geographic definition of the region—comprising the area above the Arctic Circle, 66° North latitude—encompasses land territory of Canada, Denmark, Finland, Iceland,[3] Norway, Sweden, the Russian Federation, and the United States. These eight "Arctic States" are the members of the Arctic Council, the high-level intergovernmental forum for issues of common interest in the Arctic.[4] Five of the Arctic States—Canada, Denmark (via Greenland), Norway, Russia, and the United States—have coastal frontage in the Arctic Ocean,[5] and thus sovereignty, sovereign rights, and jurisdiction in maritime zones extending well into the Arctic Ocean.[6] However defined, the Arctic region comprises land territory of the Arctic States, maritime zones of Arctic Ocean coastal states, and high seas areas. Thus, while the region shares common environmental dynamics and challenges, the legal landscape is a complex latticework of international and national laws in which the applicable law is often highly location-dependent.

The Arctic environment is of paramount importance to the region's approximately four million inhabitants,[7] many of whom subsist on local fish and mammals.[8] Environmental protection imperatives are therefore balanced with the needs of Arctic inhabitants for subsistence, economic development, and maintenance of traditional ways of life. The region and its inhabitants are disproportionately affected by long-range pollution. Persistent organic pollutants (POPs) and heavy metals such as mercury carried to the Arctic from lower latitudes by air and ocean currents, as well as rivers, are found in high concentrations in Arctic fish and marine mammals, and the indigenous populations that subsist on them.[9]

The global relevance of the Arctic environment is growing as the effects of climate change on the Arctic are felt within and beyond the region. Changes in the region's environmental parameters such as ice cover "that affect the earth's energy balance and circulation of the oceans and atmosphere, may have profound impacts on regional and global climates."[10] The diminishing

---

*The views expressed are personal and do not necessarily reflect those of the U.S. government.

sea ice is rendering increasing swaths of the Arctic seasonally accessible,[11] presenting opportunities for new shipping routes and hydrocarbon resources development.[12] With these opportunities come risks, including local pollution as a result of both emerging shipping and oil and gas activities.[13]

I.   Interplay of International Law and National Laws of Arctic States

Of central importance to environmental law in the Arctic is the interplay of international law and the national laws of the Arctic States. In most instances, within the presently accessible Arctic, the applicable legal standards are found in the national laws and regulations of the Arctic States.[14] However, these national environmental laws must be consistent with applicable international law, and in fact many such national laws are enacted pursuant to, or in implementation of, international law. What follows is a concise taxonomy of the international law most relevant to the practice of environmental law in the Arctic region—with particular attention given to emerging activities in the Arctic, such as offshore oil and gas development and shipping—and important actors to watch in the development of law and policy applicable to these activities.

A.   Who Regulates Which Areas of the Arctic Marine Environment

Although the jurisdiction of the Arctic States to regulate the environment within their land territory and internal waters is relatively straightforward, it becomes more complex in the marine areas of the Arctic. The law of the sea defines the rights, duties, and jurisdiction of the Arctic coastal states in the marine areas appurtenant to their coastlines. The applicable legal framework is the United Nations Convention on the Law of the Sea (UNCLOS), to which four of the five Arctic Ocean coastal states are party, and much of which the fifth state—the United States—recognizes as customary international law.[15] As relevant here, UNCLOS (1) governs where and how Arctic Ocean coastal states may prescribe and enforce national environmental laws, and (2) defines the rights of Arctic Ocean coastal states to explore, exploit, manage, and conserve natural resources in the water column and on the sea floor and its subsoil in various parts of the Arctic.

1.   Jurisdiction to Prescribe and Enforce National Environmental Laws

The jurisdiction of the Arctic Ocean coastal states, acting in that capacity, to prescribe and enforce environmental laws against foreign vessels extends, in varying degrees, as far as 200 nautical miles from shore. UNCLOS divides ocean and coastal waters into zones to which the regulatory authority of coastal states corresponds; in general, this authority is most robust in the waters closest to land.[16] The sovereignty of a coastal state extends throughout its territorial sea—a belt of water up to 12 nautical miles from shore—subject to the right of innocent passage of foreign vessels and other applicable rules of international law.[17] Arctic Ocean coastal states thus have authority to regulate activities to protect the marine environment within their territorial sea that is similar to their authority to regulate activities to protect the environment on land.[18] Canada, Norway, the Russian Federation, and the United States have delineated 12 nautical mile territorial seas; Denmark has delineated a three nautical mile territorial sea around Greenland.[19]

While the sovereignty of Arctic Ocean coastal states does not extend beyond the territorial sea, they enjoy certain sovereign rights and jurisdiction to prescribe and enforce environmental laws up to the seaward limit of their exclusive economic zones (EEZs)—up to 200 nautical miles from shore.[20] Beyond the territorial sea, Arctic Ocean coastal states' jurisdiction to prescribe and enforce environmental laws is generally more limited than in the territorial sea. For example, coastal state regulation of pollution from foreign-flagged vessels typically must conform and give effect to "generally accepted international rules and standards," in particular those established through the International Maritime Organization (IMO).[21] The authority of Arctic Ocean coastal states to enforce their marine pollution laws with respect to pollution within the EEZ is also more limited than in the territorial sea.[22] Of special importance for the Arctic region is UNCLOS Article 234 on ice-covered areas, which provides:

> Coastal States have the right to adopt and enforce non-discriminatory laws and regulations for the prevention, reduction, and control of marine pollution from vessels in ice-covered areas within the limits of the exclusive economic zone, where particularly severe climactic conditions and the presence of ice covering such areas for most of the year create obstructions or exceptional hazards to navigation, and pollution of the marine environment could cause major harm to or irreversible disturbance of the ecological balance. Such laws and regulations shall have due regard to navigation and the protection and preservation of the marine environment based on the best available scientific evidence.

At the time of this writing, Canada and the Russian Federation had enacted laws, purportedly pursuant to Article 234, regulating vessel traffic in certain Arctic waters under their respective jurisdiction. These national regulations highlight unresolved interpretive questions concerning the scope and content of Article 234 (e.g., the meaning of "ice-covered areas),[23] and brought to the surface disputes about the consistency of these laws with UNCLOS; in particular, the mandate in Article 234 that "[s]uch laws and regulations have due regard for navigation."[24] As seasonal shipping and other vessel traffic is expected to increase as the Arctic sea ice diminishes, the interpretation and application of Article 234 will be an important issue to watch.

2. *Rights to Exploit, Manage, and Conserve Arctic Ocean Resources*

Beyond the specific jurisdiction to prescribe and enforce laws for the protection and preservation of the marine environment,[25] international law accords

Arctic Ocean coastal states sovereign rights for the purpose of exploring, exploiting, managing and conserving natural resources—whether living or nonliving—in the water column and on the seabed and its subsoil within their respective EEZs.[26] Accordingly, the five coastal states manage the living marine resources in the portions of the Arctic Ocean within their EEZs—up to 200 nautical miles from shore—through national laws and regulations.[27]

The rights of Arctic Ocean coastal states in the seabed and its subsoil— on their respective continental shelves—is of growing relevance for environmental law in the Arctic. Diminishing sea ice, strong demand for hydrocarbon resources and estimates placing large amounts of the Earth's hydrocarbon resources in the Arctic, all foreshadow a substantial increase in oil and gas exploration in the Arctic region.[28] Each Arctic Ocean coastal state exercises "sovereign rights for the purpose of" exploring or exploiting the natural resources of its respective continental shelf.[29] These rights "are exclusive in the sense that if the coastal State does not explore the continental shelf or exploit its natural resources, no one may undertake these activities without the express consent of the coastal State."[30] These continental shelf rights extend throughout the breadth of the EEZ, and potentially well beyond 200 nautical miles, depending on the geomorphology of the continental margin concerned.[31] At the time of this writing, Norway was the only Arctic Ocean coastal state to have completed the process for obtaining formal international recognition of the outer limits of its continental shelf in the Arctic Ocean through the process established by UNCLOS; Denmark, Russia, Canada, and the United States are in various stages of determining the outer limits of their continental shelves or awaiting the recommendations of the Commission on the Limits of the Continental Shelf (CLCS).[32]

It is foreseeable that some or all of the Arctic Ocean coastal states will be recognized as having extended continental shelves that extend well beyond 200 nautical miles under the Arctic Ocean. For example, the geomorphology of the continental margin appurtenant to the north coast of the U.S. state of Alaska suggests that it extends more than 600 nautical miles into the Arctic Ocean. The practical implication is that control over the exploitation—or conservation of— the natural resources, both living and nonliving, of much of the seabed and subsoil of the Arctic Ocean lies with the five Arctic Ocean coastal states. While the rights of a coastal state with respect to its continental shelf exist ipso facto, ab initio, and thus do not depend on the CLCS process set forth in UNCLOS,[33] the process through which the Arctic Ocean coastal states delineate the outer limits of their respective continental shelves in the Arctic over the coming years should add clarity and certainty as to which of them controls offshore oil and gas exploration and exploitation in which parts of the Arctic Ocean.

B.   Regional and Global Instruments Relevant to the Arctic Environment

Many national laws relevant to the Arctic environment are enacted in implementation of regional and global agreements. For example, through the 1973

Agreement on the Conservation of Polar Bears, the Arctic Ocean coastal states undertook to "enact and enforce such legislation and other means as may be necessary for the purpose of giving effect" to the conservation framework established by the Agreement.[34] The regional and global environmental instruments surveyed in this chapter facilitate some commonality in approaches of Arctic States to shared environmental challenges and marine mammal populations.

No international environmental instrument applies to "the Arctic," as such; unlike the Antarctic Treaty area, no such general-purpose legal definition exists. The handful of regional environmental agreements among the Arctic States specify a geographic scope of application for their own purposes, generally in relation to the territory and areas under the jurisdiction of the parties. For example, the scope of the 2013 Agreement on Cooperation on Marine Oil Pollution Preparedness and Response in the Arctic is defined in relation to marine areas over which a party exercises sovereignty, sovereign rights, or jurisdiction under international law above a southern limit.[35] The bulk of international agreements relevant to the Arctic environment are not Arctic-specific, but global in scope. Global agreements such as the International Convention for the Prevention of Pollution from Ships (MARPOL) and the Convention on the Prevention of Marine Pollution by Dumping of Wastes and Other Matter (London Convention) address pollution generated by or disposed of from ships—including into the Arctic Ocean—and agreements such as the Convention on Long-Range Transboundary Air Pollution and the Stockholm Convention on Persistent Organic Pollutants (Stockholm Convention) address pollution transported from great distances, the effects of which are acutely felt in the Arctic region.

II. Important International Environmental Actors
A. Arctic Council

The Arctic Council is the focal point for international cooperation among the Arctic States to promote sustainable development and environmental protection in the Arctic. Established in 1996 as the successor to the Arctic Environmental Protection Strategy,[36] the council comprises the eight Arctic States as well as Permanent Participants, a status created to "provide for active participation and full consultation with the Arctic indigenous representatives within the Arctic Council."[37] The Arctic Council is not an international organization with separate legal personality from its members, but an intergovernmental forum facilitating cooperation among the Arctic States at all levels—from foreign ministers to staff scientists—in consultation with Permanent Participants.

The structure of the Arctic Council and the modalities of its work are set out in the 1996 Ottawa Declaration establishing the council, and elaborated in its Rules of Procedure. Decisions of the Arctic Council are by a consensus of the Arctic States.[38] The council meets biennially at the foreign minister level, with the bulk of business between ministerial meetings conducted under the direction of the Senior Arctic Officials (SAOs). The Chairmanship of the Arctic Council rotates among the Arctic States for two-year periods. In addition to the high-level policy work conducted at ministerial and SAO meetings, cutting-edge research, analysis, policy development, and cooperation in sustainable development and environmental protection are carried out in the council's six working groups: Arctic Contaminants Action Program (ACAP), Arctic Monitoring and Assessment Program (AMAP), Conservation of Arctic Flora and Fauna (CAFF), Emergency Preparedness and Response (EPPR), Protection of the Arctic Marine Environment (PAME), and the Sustainable Development Working Group (SDWG). In addition, the council occasionally establishes task forces to carry out specific projects. For example, two legally binding international agreements among the Arctic States— addressing cooperation in search and rescue[39] and oil pollution preparedness and response[40]—were negotiated in task forces established for this purpose.

Notwithstanding the two international agreements negotiated to date under the auspices of the Arctic Council, the council is not a lawmaking body; while its declarations, decisions, and recommendations may reflect political commitments, they do not have legal force. The Arctic Council is nevertheless an important actor in international environmental law and policy, in the Arctic and beyond. The pioneering science and analysis conducted by the working groups, in particular, shed light on trends, challenges, and opportunities in the Arctic environment, bringing issues such as the effects of climate change and long-range pollution on Arctic inhabitants to the attention of decision makers.

These scientific assessments inform not only policy, but also international legal instruments. For example, the AMAP Working Group routinely provides information products to conferences of the parties of global agreements on long-range pollution.[41] And the Inuit Circumpolar Conference, an Arctic Council Permanent Participant, brought issues such as elevated levels of POPs in the breast milk of women in the Arctic region, far from the pollution sources, to the attention of the intergovernmental committee negotiating what became the Stockholm Convention.[42] The scientific cooperation conducted through the Arctic Council brings to light and raises the profile of environmental challenges—such as the role of black carbon as a short-lived climate forcer—for policy makers of the Arctic States. In May 2013, Arctic Council Ministers mandated two new task forces to explore opportunities for collective action by the Arctic States to address black carbon and methane emissions and oil pollution prevention.[43] The work of the Arctic Council today may foreshadow future international agreements or other cooperative arrangements among the Arctic States.

B.   International Maritime Organization

The IMO is a specialized agency of the United Nations recognized as the international organization with primary responsibility for the safety and security of shipping and the prevention of marine pollution by ships.[44] In light of diminishing Arctic sea ice and increasing volumes of both destinational and trans-Arctic shipping,[45] the IMO's mandate accords it one of the most significant roles of any international body with respect to human activity in the region. Although shipping activities in the Arctic have increased only modestly over the last decade, continuing and projected growth and the attendant risk of vessel sinkings, groundings, and other incidents with potentially adverse environmental impacts underscore the importance of IMO's Arctic role.

Established by a convention adopted in 1948 that entered into force ten years later,[46] the IMO has 170 member states (as of June 2013) including all eight Arctic States.[47] The governing body of the IMO is the Assembly, which meets every two years. Between assembly sessions, a council consisting of 40 member governments elected by the IMO Assembly governs the organization. The IMO is supported by a secretariat of several hundred civil servants, headed by a secretary general elected by the council and approved by the Assembly. The IMO conducts most of its work through a number of committees and sub-committees that cover specific subject areas such as safety, environmental protection, ship design and equipment, and training and watchkeeping.

To carry out its overall objectives, captured in IMO's slogan of "safe, secure and efficient shipping on clean oceans,"[48] IMO member governments have adopted numerous legally binding and globally applicable conventions as well as several hundred recommendatory instruments and guidelines. Among the most important of the conventions are the International Convention for the Safety of Life at Sea (SOLAS) and MARPOL. Separately, approximately 100 states have become party to either the London Convention or its 1996 Protocol (London Protocol), for which IMO provides secretariat services. Each of these agreements is addressed in greater detail below.

III.   Regional Activities with Important Environmental Consequences
A.   Commercial Shipping

The Arctic Ocean comprises a significant portion of the Arctic region, and Arctic sea ice has been decreasing in extent and thickness for some time.[49] Diminishing Arctic sea ice provides new opportunities for offshore energy extraction, maritime transportation, and tourism. As businesses pursue these opportunities, commercial shipping activities are increasing. Regulation of these shipping activities, in particular their environmental impacts, is accomplished through an existing set of well-developed rules codified in several international instruments.

1.   Global Instruments
a.   UNCLOS

As noted in section I.A., UNCLOS establishes a widely accepted international framework governing all uses of the sea. UNCLOS contains the general obligation of states to protect and preserve the marine environment,[50] an obligation that is given content in UNCLOS part XII. With respect to commercial shipping, UNCLOS specifies that states shall address pollution of the marine environment from vessels.[51] This includes ship-generated pollution (e.g., intentional and unintentional discharges and pollution resulting from accidents) as well as dumping of wastes transported by vessels from land. UNCLOS also reflects states' obligations concerning measures to prevent and minimize the threat of maritime casualties that might cause pollution of the marine environment,[52] and measures necessary to prevent and control the introduction of aquatic nuisance species that may cause significant and harmful changes to the marine environment.[53] Generally speaking, states have acted through the IMO to set global rules and standards to implement these UNCLOS obligations.

b. SOLAS

First adopted in 1914 in response to the sinking of the RMS *Titanic*, SOLAS is considered the most important international instrument concerning the safety of commercial shipping.[54] Updated several times, the current version was adopted in 1974 and entered into force in 1980, and has been amended numerous times since. As of December 2012, 162 states are party to SOLAS, including all Arctic States.[55] The main purpose of SOLAS is to "promot[e] safety of life at sea by establishing in a common agreement uniform principles and rules directed thereto."[56] State parties must ensure that ships flying their flag comply with minimum safety standards in construction, equipment, and operation. SOLAS Annex chapter V, which addresses safety of navigation and sets forth provisions of an operational nature, includes regulations of particular interest to Arctic marine operations. These include provisions regarding navigational warnings, meteorological services, search and rescue services, hydrographic services, and ship routing and reporting systems.[57] It should not be overlooked that SOLAS's promotion of ship safety has direct and collateral environmental benefits that result from the reduced risk of spills and other environmental damage that can result from maritime casualties.

c. MARPOL

MARPOL[58] regulates prevention of pollution of the marine environment by ships from operational or accidental causes.[59] MARPOL's original purpose— "to prevent the pollution of the marine environment by the discharge of harmful substances or effluents containing such substances"[60]—was furthered in two technical annexes addressing pollution from oil and from noxious liquid substances in bulk. MARPOL has been augmented since it was adopted in 1973 by protocols and technical annexes that broaden its scope to cover harmful substances carried in package form, sewage, garbage, and air pollution from ships.[61] Several of MARPOL's technical annexes provide for the designation of particular areas of the ocean as "special areas" wherein more stringent vessel discharge requirements apply.[62] MARPOL is primarily implemented and enforced by its parties through their flag state jurisdiction, with an important role for port state control as well. All Arctic States are party to Annex I and Annex II, as required by MARPOL. MARPOL parties also can consent to be bound by Annexes III–VI. With few exceptions, all Arctic States are party to Annexes III–VI.[63] Although no MARPOL "special areas" have been designated in the Arctic Ocean, the convention's global applicability and the large number of flag states that are MARPOL parties make it indispensable in helping to limit the environmental impact of shipping activities in Arctic waters.[64]

d. London Convention/London Protocol

All Arctic States are among the 87 state parties to the London Convention,[65] which prohibits the dumping at sea of certain particularly harmful materials and limits the dumping of a range of other identified materials.[66] In 1996, London Convention parties adopted the London Protocol,[67] which entered into force in 2006.[68] The protocol, which is meant to supersede the London Convention, takes a different approach to the regulation of dumping at sea. Instead of identifying individual materials that may not be dumped, the protocol prohibits the dumping of all materials except for eight types of wastes that are listed in an annex to the protocol. All Arctic States have ratified the 1996 protocol with the exception of the United States, which signed the protocol in 2006.

e. Other IMO Conventions
i. *Anti-Fouling Convention*

The International Convention on the Control of Harmful Anti-Fouling Systems on Ships, 2001 (Anti-Fouling Convention)[69] bans the use of harmful organotins in anti-fouling paints that are used on ships to prevent marine organisms such as mollusks from attaching themselves to the hull, thereby decreasing the ship's speed and efficiency.[70] Organotins, while effective, can cause significant adverse impacts on the marine environment when they leach out or are scraped off the hull.[71] Organotins and their breakdown products have been detected in marine species and seabirds in the Arctic.[72] The Anti-Fouling Convention entered into force in 2008; all Arctic States are parties.

ii. *Ballast Water Management Convention*

The preamble of the International Convention for the Control and Management of Ships' Ballast Water and Sediments, 2004 (Ballast Water Management Convention)[73] sets forth a resolve "to prevent, minimize and ultimately eliminate the risks to the environment, human health, property and resources arising from the transfer of Harmful Aquatic Organisms and Pathogens through the control and management of ships' Ballast Water and Sediments."[74] Ballast water, which is taken up and discharged by ships in port and while underway to maintain stability and maneuverability, is one of the most significant pathways for the transfer of aquatic nuisance species.[75] Aquatic nuisance species can cause significant environmental harm, degrade aquatic resources, and make waters unfit for recreation.[76] Numerous aquatic nuisance species have been found in the Arctic and their number is expected to increase with climate change and the projected growth in human activities in the region.[77]

When it enters into force, the Ballast Water Management Convention will mandate that ships on international voyages comply with a ballast water management standard, carry a ballast water management plan, and keep records of ballast water operations.[78] Of the Arctic States, Canada, Denmark, Norway, the Russian Federation, and Sweden have ratified the Ballast Water Convention.[79]

f.   Other Relevant Documents
i.   IMO Guidelines for Ships Operating in Polar Waters, 2009

To address the unique challenges of navigation in the extreme conditions found in polar waters, IMO has developed numerous guidelines and recommendations over the last 20 years for marine operations in the Arctic and Antarctic regions. In 2009, the IMO updated and consolidated these in the Guidelines for Ships Operating in Polar Waters.[80] The objective of these recommendatory guidelines is to mitigate the additional risk to shipping and address the demands polar conditions impose on ship systems, including navigation, communications, life-saving appliances, machinery, environmental protection, and damage control.[81] The guidelines also recognize that safe operation in polar conditions demands close attention to human factors, including training and operational procedures.

Shortly after the guidelines were adopted, Denmark, Norway, and the United States proposed the creation of a legally binding Polar Code for ships operating in polar waters. The IMO agreed with the proposal and has been working since to develop such a code.[82] The Code, which in draft contains separate safety and environment chapters, is expected to be implemented through amendment of existing IMO instruments.

ii.   2009 Arctic Marine Shipping Assessment (AMSA) Report

In the Tromsø Declaration adopted at the 2009 Ministerial Meeting, Arctic Council Ministers approved the AMSA Report that had been prepared by the PAME Working Group.[83] The central focus of the AMSA Report is ships: their uses of the Arctic Ocean, their potential impacts on humans and the Arctic marine environment, and their marine infrastructure requirements.[84] Based on the findings it contains, the AMSA Report makes 17 recommendations under three broad, interrelated themes as a guide for future action by the Arctic Council, Arctic States, industry, and others. The three themes are enhancing Arctic marine safety, protecting Arctic people and the environment, and building Arctic marine infrastructure. The PAME Working Group, in collaboration and consultation with other Arctic Council working groups, Permanent Participants, observers, and Arctic States, has taken the lead in implementing many of the AMSA Report recommendations.[85]

B.   Offshore Oil and Gas Development

The Arctic contains large oil and gas reserves. While the region has witnessed extensive hydrocarbon development activity, most of that has been on land and for the most part in Russia.[86] Diminishing sea ice, among other factors, is bringing about change that is resulting in greater interest in—and activity to locate and recover—offshore oil and gas in the Arctic.[87] Energy experts believe that oil drilling in Arctic waters could produce up to one million barrels per day, equal to approximately 10 percent of domestic U.S. production.[88] The risk of oil spills associated with increasing offshore oil and gas activities presents a significant threat to the Arctic marine environment.

1.   *UNCLOS*

The Law of the Sea Convention is among the first legally binding global agreements governing pollution from seabed activities. Seabed activities under UNCLOS include oil and gas exploration and exploitation.[89] Article 208 sets forth that coastal states are to adopt laws and regulations, and take other measures as may be necessary, to prevent, reduce, and control pollution of the marine environment arising from or in connection with seabed activities subject to their jurisdiction.[90] Such laws, regulations, and measures must be no less effective than international rules, standards, and recommended practices and procedures.[91] Article 208 further provides that states, acting through competent international organizations or diplomatic conference, must establish such global and regional rules, standards, and recommended practices and procedures.[92]

Although to date no global convention has been negotiated solely directed to seabed activities, a few binding regional agreements and non-binding guidelines are relevant to the control of pollution from hydrocarbon development in the Arctic region, in addition to the OPRC Convention described next. The legally binding Agreement on Cooperation on Marine Pollution Preparedness and Response in the Arctic[93] signed by all Arctic States on May 15, 2013, aims to facilitate prompt and effective cooperative responses to marine oil spills and substantially improves procedures for combating such pollution of the Arctic marine environment. The agreement applies to oil pollution incidents that occur in or may pose a threat to any marine area over which a state whose government is a party exercises sovereignty, sovereign rights, or jurisdiction (and to a more limited extent to marine areas beyond any state's jurisdiction) consistent with international law and above a specified southern limit.[94] The Convention for the Protection of the Marine Environment of the North-East Atlantic (OSPAR Convention),[95] to which Finland, Iceland, Norway, Denmark, and Sweden are parties[96] and which includes waters commonly considered to be part of the Arctic region,[97] requires that discharges from offshore sources be subject to "strict" regulation by the competent authorities of contracting parties who must also provide for a system of monitoring and inspection to ensure compliance with such regulation.[98] The 1993 Agreement Between Denmark, Finland, Iceland, Norway and Sweden Concerning Cooperation in Measures to Deal with Pollution of the Sea by Oil or Other Harmful Substances obliges the parties to undertake to cooperate in the protection of the marine environment against pollution of the sea by oil or other harmful substances, and to respond to incidents such as oil spills and investigate the situation, provide information, assist in the production of evidence, and establish measures for abatement of the pollution.

The nonbinding Arctic Offshore Oil and Gas Guidelines,[99] most recently revised and approved by the Arctic Council in 2009,[100] define a set of recommended practices and outline strategic actions for consideration by those responsible for regulation of Arctic offshore oil and gas activities, indicate that all Arctic offshore oil and gas activities should be based on the precautionary approach as reflected in Principle 15 of the Rio Declaration, the polluter pays principle as reflected in Principle 16 of the Rio Declaration, continuous improvement, and sustainable development—and set forth recommended environmental impact assessment procedures, environmental monitoring methods, and operating practices.[101]

IMO's revised Code for the Construction and Equipment of Mobile Offshore Drilling Units,[102] adopted in 2009, contains recommendatory guidelines for mobile offshore drilling units to facilitate their international movement and operation and to promote a level of safety consistent with that required of conventional ships on international voyages.

2. OPRC Convention

Adopted within the framework of the IMO, the International Convention on Oil Pollution Preparedness, Response and Co-operation, 1990 (OPRC Convention)[103] requires parties to prepare for and respond to oil pollution incidents whether from ships, offshore units, or other sources.[104] Operators of offshore units under the jurisdiction of parties are required to have oil pollution emergency plans that must be coordinated with national systems for responding to oil pollution incidents.[105] Parties are also subject to provisions regarding the provision assistance to each other in the event of a pollution emergency.[106] All Arctic States are party to this convention.[107]

IV. The Environmental Impact of Global Phenomena and Long-Range Pollution in the Arctic
A. Long-Range Pollution

Pollution in the Arctic comes primarily from outside the region, transported by wind through the atmosphere and by water via rivers and ocean currents.[108] As a result, many regions of the Arctic are far from pristine.[109] The disproportionate impact on the Arctic of pollution transported great distances underscores the importance of effective global regimes to address long-range pollution.

1. Stockholm Convention

POPs are organic chemicals that remain intact in the environment for long periods, become widely distributed geographically, accumulate in fatty tissues of humans and wildlife, and have potentially significant adverse effects on human health and the environment. POPs have been used as pesticides and in a variety of chemical processes. Because they are capable of being transported great distances, POPs have been found in some populations of Arctic mammals and birds, including polar bears, northern fur seals, and peregrine falcons.[110] The 2001 Stockholm Convention was adopted to protect human health and the environment from POPs.[111] It entered into force in 2004 and has 178 parties, including Denmark, Finland, Iceland, Canada, the Russian Federation, Sweden, and Norway.[112] The convention requires parties to prohibit the production and use of, and restrict trade in, certain listed POPs and take measures to reduce releases of other listed POPs.[113]

2. Basel Convention on the Control of Transboundary Movements of Hazardous Wastes and Their Disposal

The Basel Convention on the Control of Transboundary Movements of Hazardous Wastes and Their Disposal, 1989,[114] regulates the international trade, transport, and disposal of hazardous waste with the overarching objective of protecting human health and the environment from the adverse effects of such wastes.[115] The convention also contains provisions regarding the reduction of hazardous waste generation, the promotion of environmentally sound management of hazardous wastes, and the treatment and disposal of such wastes as close to the point of generation as possible.[116] With the exception of the United States, all Arctic States are parties to the convention, which entered into force in 1992.[117]

3. Convention on Long-Range Transboundary Air Pollution, 1979 (LRTAP)

All Arctic States are party to the Convention on Long-Range Transboundary Air Pollution, 1979 (LRTAP),[118] a regional treaty of the Northern Hemisphere that requires parties to endeavor to limit, reduce, and prevent air pollution, including long-range transboundary air pollution.[119] Since its entry into force, LRTAP has been supplemented by eight protocols, many of which target specific pollutants, such as sulfur, nitrogen oxide, volatile organic compounds, and toxic heavy metals, and for which the membership of Arctic States varies. Implementation of LRTAP and its protocols has contributed to substantial declines of regulated pollutants in Europe and North America.[120]

4. *Global Programme of Action for the Protection of the Marine Environment from Land-Based Activities (GPA)*

Land-based pollution sources are the greatest source of marine pollution, accounting by some estimates for as much as 80 percent of all pollution of the marine environment.[121] Although UNCLOS provides that states shall prevent, reduce, and control pollution of the marine environment from land-based sources taking into account internationally agreed rules,[122] such global rules have yet to be adopted. The nonbinding GPA[123] is as far as the global community has come. The GPA was adopted in 1995 under the auspices of the United Nations Environment Programme and "aims at preventing the degradation of the marine environment from land-based activities by facilitating the realization of the duty of States to preserve and protect the marine environment."[124] At the Arctic regional level, two instruments are of relevance. The first is the nonbinding Regional Programme of Action for the Protection of the Arctic Marine Environment from Land-Based Activities (RPA-Arctic) approved by Arctic Council ministers in 1998 and subsequently updated in 2009.[125] The RPA-Arctic is intended to be a source of conceptual and practical guidance for regional and national authorities in devising and implementing action to prevent, reduce, control, and eliminate marine degradation from land-based activities. The second relevant instrument is the legally binding 1992 OSPAR Convention, addressed previously in section III.B.1. Annex I of the convention addresses land-based sources of marine pollution and requires parties to regulate point source discharges in the maritime area covered by the convention as well as releases to water or air that may affect the maritime area.[126]

5. *Minamata Convention on Mercury*

Mercury pollution is among the most pressing environmental challenges in the Arctic region. Although the Arctic is far from most anthropogenic sources of mercury, mercury is transported to the region predominantly by winds, ocean currents, and rivers, where it bioaccumulates and is biomagnified in the fish and marine mammals on which many indigenous residents rely for food.[127]

On January 19, 2013, delegates from more than 140 countries adopted the text of the Minamata Convention on Mercury. The product of three years of negotiations under the auspices of the United Nations Environment Programme, the convention provides for the reduction of mercury emissions to the air, reduction of mercury use in products and industrial processes, and supply, storage, and waste management of mercury.[128] The convention was opened for signature at a diplomatic conference in October 2013.[129] On November 6, 2013, the United States signed and deposited its Instrument of Acceptance, becoming the first state to join the Minamata Convention.[130]

B.   Climate Change and Atmosphere

Of all the world's regions, the Arctic has undergone the most dramatic changes as a result of climate change.[131] It is a region that has also witnessed the effects of stratospheric ozone depletion, with a "hole" of varying size regularly opening up in the atmosphere above the Arctic, exposing inhabitants to high doses of harmful ultraviolet radiation.[132] Climate change and ozone depletion, including the main global instruments that address them—the U.N. Framework Convention on Climate Change, the Kyoto Protocol, and the Vienna Convention on the Protection of the Ozone Layer and the Montreal Protocol on Substances that Deplete the Ozone Layer—are addressed comprehensively in chapters 5 and 49.

V. Conservation of Arctic Flora and Fauna
A. Marine and Land Mammals

The Arctic region serves as the permanent home or migratory ground for a range of marine and land mammals, including polar bears, caribou, seals, and whales.[133] In addition to fish, marine mammals and caribou are important sources of food for the region's indigenous populations.[134] Through regional and global agreements, the states concerned have established management structures to balance conservation with a sustainable subsistence harvest.

1. Polar Bears

All five of the Arctic Ocean coastal states are party to the 1973 Agreement on the Conservation of Polar Bears, through which they have committed to take "appropriate action to protect the ecosystems of which polar bears are a part,"[135] and to a moratorium on the taking of polar bears, subject to limited exceptions. Through the agreement, the parties undertake to "manage polar bear populations in accordance with sound conservation practices based on the best available scientific data,"[136] and to enact national laws and measures necessary to give effect to the agreement.[137] A distinctive feature of the 1973 agreement is its prohibition of the taking (i.e., hunting, killing, or capturing) of polar bears, except for "bona fide scientific purposes," or "by local people using traditional methods in the exercise of their traditional rights and in accordance with the laws of that Party," as well as certain other limited exceptions.[138] The skins and other by-products resulting from polar bear take in accordance with the latter exception may not be made available for commercial purposes,[139] and the use of aircraft and large motorized vehicles for polar bear take is prohibited.[140] Although the 1973 agreement allows state parties to authorize the taking of polar bears in accordance with the agreement, the national laws of some parties are more restrictive; the laws of Norway and Russia, for example, ban any taking of polar bears.[141]

In furtherance of the 1973 agreement, the United States and Russian Federation concluded the Agreement on the Conservation and Management of the Alaska-Chukotka Polar Bear Population in 2000. To coordinate the management and conservation of their shared polar bear population, the U.S.-Russia agreement provides for the establishment of the U.S.-Russia Polar

Bear Commission. In accordance with the agreement, the commission is composed of two national sections, each comprising one government representative and "a representative of its native people."[142] Among the commission's tasks are "determining on the basis of reliable scientific data, including traditional knowledge of the native people, the polar bear population's annual sustainable harvest level,"[143] "determining the annual taking limits not to exceed the sustainable harvest level,"[144] "adopting measures to restrict the take of polar bears for subsistence purposes," within the annual taking limits, including restrictions on seasons, sex, and age.[145] The United States and Russia are each entitled to harvest, in accordance with the agreement, one-half of the annual taking limit determined by the commission, although Russia has banned polar bear take since 1956.[146] The commission is additionally charged with a range of tasks involving the study and conservation of the shared polar bear population and its habitats.[147] Decisions of the commission are to be by consensus, including among the commissioners of each national section,[148] giving an important and powerful role to indigenous communities in management and conservation decisions.[149]

Polar bears are additionally listed on Appendix II of the Convention on International Trade in Endangered Species of Wild Fauna and Flora (CITES), to which 175 states, including all Arctic States, are party. The Appendix II listing of polar bears subjects international trade of polar bear specimens, including parts (e.g., skins), to strict controls.[150] At the Sixteenth CITES Conference of the Parties in March 2013, the United States again proposed "uplisting" the polar bear to Appendix I[151]—which would have imposed the strictest CITES controls on trade if adopted, including a ban on trade for primarily commercial purposes[152]—but the proposal failed to achieve the requisite two-thirds majority and was rejected.[153] The U.S. proposal attributed the threat of polar bear extinction in part to diminishing Arctic sea ice.[154]

2. *Caribou*

Caribou is the most important land mammal for the subsistence of indigenous peoples in the Arctic region.[155] To coordinate the management and conservation of the porcupine caribou herd that migrates between their borders, the United States and Canada concluded the Agreement on the Conservation of the Porcupine Caribou Herd in 1987. Through the agreement, the parties undertake, inter alia, to "take appropriate action to conserve the Porcupine Caribou Herd and its habitat,"[156] subject certain activities potentially affecting the Herd to impact assessments,[157] and to prohibit the commercial sale of meat from the Herd.[158] The agreement establishes an advisory board that may "make recommendations and provide advice on those aspects of the conservation of the Porcupine Caribou Herd and its habitat that require international co-ordination,"[159] including, inter alia, "appropriate harvest limits" for each party "taking into account the Board's review of available data, patterns of customary and traditional uses and other factors the Board deems appropriate."[160] Such recommendations are not binding on the parties.[161]

3.   Whales

The Arctic region is a permanent or seasonal home for 17 species of whales. Although there is not an international agreement on whales specific to the Arctic region, global instruments for the protection of large whales are applicable to the Arctic region. In particular, the 1946 International Convention for the Regulation of Whaling[162] sets out an international legal framework for the regulation of commercial whaling and subsistence hunting by indigenous peoples. The convention establishes an International Whaling Commission (IWC) composed of members from each of the 88 contracting governments[163] empowered to adopt regulations, on the basis of scientific findings, concerning, inter alia, specific species, seasons, waters, and methods for harvesting whales.[164] These regulations are recorded as amendments to the schedule, which forms an integral part of the convention.[165] An international moratorium on commercial whaling has been in effect since 1986.[166]

As relevant to the Arctic region, all Arctic States except Canada are party to the convention; Canadian national law prohibits commercial whaling[167] and regulates subsistence hunting by indigenous peoples[168] in Canada's internal waters, territorial sea, and EEZ.[169] Iceland has taken a reservation to the commercial whaling moratorium,[170] although state parties disagree as to the legal consequences of Iceland's reservation.[171] Norway registered an objection to the moratorium at the time the commission adopted it[172] and the moratorium is therefore not in effect for Norway.[173] The Russian Federation has also registered an objection to the moratorium decision but does not exercise it.[174]

The moratorium on commercial whaling does not apply to aboriginal subsistence whaling, practiced by indigenous peoples across the Arctic. The IWC sets stock-specific catch limits for aboriginal subsistence whaling in the Arctic region,[175] shared stocks are apportioned among neighboring states as necessary,[176] and the catch limits and other IWC regulations concerning aboriginal subsistence whaling are implemented through national laws and regulations.[177]

4.   Fur Seals

Fur seals, one of ten pinniped species in the circumpolar Arctic,[178] have been afforded protection internationally since 1911 when the Convention between the United States and Other Powers Providing for the Preservation and Protection of Fur Seals (commonly known as the North Pacific Fur Seal Convention) was signed by the United States, Great Britain (on behalf of Canada), Japan, and Russia.[179] The convention, widely considered the first international treaty to address wildlife conservation, outlawed pelagic sealing and remained in force until World War II.[180] The convention helped to arrest the sharp decline in the fur seal population due to rampant hunting. In 1957, a successor agreement to protect North Pacific fur seals was signed among the original signatories.[181] Like its 1911 predecessor, the 1957 convention prohibited pelagic sealing.[182] It was subsequently amended by a number of protocols that continued it in force until it expired by its own terms in 1984.[183]

Although Northern fur seals in the Bering Sea constitute more than a quarter of the worldwide population, numbering upwards of 650,000 animals, the loss of Arctic sea ice poses a significant threat to them.[184]

5. *Birds*

Birds that occur regularly in the Arctic comprise some 200 different species, a high proportion of which are migratory.[185] Fourteen of these 200 species are listed as threatened by the International Union for the Conservation of Nature.[186] Threats to Arctic birds include overharvesting, loss of habitat, and, potentially, oil spills. Although there is no international instrument the sole objective of which is to protect Arctic bird species, a few agreements have been negotiated that afford protection to some of them.

a.   Migratory Birds Convention of 1916

In 1916, the United States and Great Britain (on behalf of Canada) negotiated a treaty[187] to protect migratory birds "whose pilgrimages traverse international borders."[188] The United States subsequently entered into three similar treaties, the one with the Soviet Union being the most germane to the Arctic.[189] These treaties generally prohibit the taking, sale, and transportation of migratory birds, their nests, and eggs. Each of these treaties lists the birds that are protected under its terms, and each has been modified since its adoption by additional conventions and protocols, generally to enhance protection of the listed species.[190] Bird species that occur in the Arctic are among those protected by these treaties.

b.   Convention on the Conservation of Migratory Species of Wild Animals

The objective of the Convention on the Conservation of Migratory Species of Wild Animals[191] is to conserve migratory species, including birds, throughout their range.[192] Concluded under the aegis of the United Nations Environment Programme, the convention has 119 state parties as of April 1, 2013, including the Arctic States of Denmark, Finland, Norway, and Sweden.[193] Migratory species threatened with extinction—including several Arctic bird species[194]—are listed in Appendix I of the convention, and parties endeavor to protect them and to conserve or restore their habitats. Migratory species that would significantly benefit from international cooperation are listed in Appendix II, and parties that are range states for Appendix II species are encouraged to conclude global or regional agreements to protect them. In this respect, the convention serves as a framework for other legally and non-legally binding agreements negotiated to protect migratory species. Among the agreements negotiated in furtherance of the convention's objectives is the Agreement on the Conservation of Albatrosses and Petrels, discussed next.

c. Agreement on the Conservation of Albatrosses and Petrels

The Agreement on the Conservation of Albatrosses and Petrels[195] is a multilateral agreement that seeks to conserve albatrosses and petrels by coordinating international activity to mitigate known threats to their populations. The agreement currently has 13 parties, including Norway,[196] and covers 30 species of albatrosses, petrels, and shearwaters,[197] including a few species of seabirds that may occur in the Arctic.[198]

VI. Conclusion

International law is central to the practice of environmental law in the Arctic region. Although the region comprises a patchwork of land territory, maritime zones in which the Arctic States enjoy sovereign rights and jurisdiction, and high seas areas, the Arctic faces common environmental challenges, many of which originate from outside the region. Because the effects of distant pollution are so acutely felt in the Arctic, global environmental agreements—such as those addressing emissions of POPs, heavy metals, and greenhouse gases—are particularly relevant to the Arctic environment. Looking into the future, as diminishing sea ice enables Arctic shipping, tourism, and hydrocarbon activities to increase, so too will the importance of regulating local pollution. International law delineates where and how states may prescribe and enforce their national environmental laws and regulations in the Arctic. That these laws must be consistent with applicable international law—and, in fact, are often enacted pursuant to or in implementation of international law—facilitates some commonality in the approach of Arctic States to shared environmental challenges.

Notes

1. The Antarctic Treaty and its Environmental Protocol prescribe a comprehensive environmental law regime for the Antarctic Treaty Area. Antarctic Treaty, *opened for signature* Dec. 1, 1959, 12 U.S.T. 794, 40 U.N.T.S. 71; Protocol on Environmental Protection to the Antarctic Treaty, XIth Special Consultative Meeting in Madrid, *opened for signature* Oct. 4, 1991, 30 I.L.M. 1455. For detailed comparisons of the international environmental law applicable at the respective poles, see Linda Nowlan, *Arctic Legal Regime for Environmental Protection* (Int'l Union for Conservation of Nature, Environmental Policy and Law Paper No. 44, 2001), http://www.iucn.org. *See also* Timo Koivurova, *Environmental Protection in the Arctic and Antarctic: Can the Polar Regimes Learn from Each Other?*, 33 Int'l J. Legal Info. 204 (2005).

2. The national laws of Arctic States generally define "the Arctic" in relation to their land territory. *See, e.g.*, Protection of the Arctic Marine Environment (PAME) Working Group, Arctic Council, Arctic Ocean Review (AOR) Phase I Report 2009–2011, at 3–4 (2011), http://www.aor.is/images/stories/AOR_Phase_I_Report_to _Ministers_2011.pdf [hereinafter AOR Phase I Report]; 15 U.S.C. § 4111 ("As used in this

chapter, the term 'Arctic' means all United States and foreign territory north of the Arctic Circle and all United States territory north and west of the boundary formed by the Porcupine, Yukon, and Kuskokwim Rivers; all contiguous seas, including the Arctic Ocean and the Beaufort, Bering, and Chukchi Seas; and the Aleutian chain.").

3. The Arctic Circle bisects Grímsey, a small offshore island of Iceland.

4. Arctic Council, Declaration on the Establishment of the Arctic Council, Ottawa, Sept. 19, 1996, 35 I.L.M.1387, *available at* http://www.arctic-council.org/index.php/en /document-archive/category/5-declarations?download=13:ottawa-declaration [hereinafter Ottawa Declaration].

5. PAME WORKING GROUP, ARCTIC COUNCIL, ARCTIC MARINE SHIPPING ASSESSMENT 2009 REPORT 51 (2009), http://www.pame.is/amsa/amsa-2009-report [hereinafter AMSA 2009 REPORT].

6. *See* Ilulissat Declaration, May 28, 2008, 48 I.L.M. 362, *available at* http://www .oceanlaw.org/downloads/arctic/Ilulissat_Declaration.pdf.

7. *See* STEFANSSON ARCTIC INST., ARCTIC HUMAN DEVELOPMENT REPORT 27 (2004), http://www.svs.is/AHDR/index.htm. This approximate figure dates to 2004, and population figures are highly dependent on the geographic definition of the Arctic employed.

8. *See id.*

9. *See* ARCTIC COUNCIL, ARCTIC MONITORING & ASSESSMENT PROGRAMME (AMAP), ARCTIC POLLUTION ISSUES: A STATE OF THE ARCTIC ENVIRONMENT REPORT 71–110 (2007), *available at* http://amap.no/documents/index.cfm?dirsub=/Arctic%20Pollution%20Issues %20-%20A%20State%20of%20the%20Arctic%20Environment%20Report [hereinafter AMAP SOAER 97] (regarding persistent organic pollutants and heavy metals). *See also, e.g.,* Shannon Mala Bard, *Global Transport of Anthropogenic Contaminants and the Consequences for the Arctic Marine Ecosystem,* 38 MARINE POLLUTION BULL. 356 (1999).

10. ARCTIC COUNCIL & INT'L ARCTIC SCI. COMM. (IASC), ARCTIC CHANGE IMPACT ASSESSMENT 4–5 (2005), http://www.acia.uaf.edu/pages/scientific.html. For a review and synthesis of published literature on the role of Arctic sea ice in shaping global atmospheric processes, see Dagmar Budikova, *Role of Arctic Sea Ice in Global Atmospheric Circulation: A Review,* 68 GLOBAL & PLANETARY CHANGE 149 (2009), *available at* http://www .arctic.noaa.gov/future/docs/ArcticAND_Globe.pdf.

11. AMSA 2009 REPORT, *supra* note 5.

12. AMAP, Arctic Council, ARCTIC OIL AND GAS ASSESSMENT 2007 (2008), *available at* http://www.amap.no/oga/ [hereinafter AOGA].

13. AMSA 2009 REPORT, *supra* note 5; AOGA, *supra* note 12.

14. The laws and regulations of flag states and port states are also important sources of law for the Arctic, with special relevance to certain activities (e.g., shipping) and areas of the region (e.g., high seas areas).

15. *See, e.g.,* Statement by President Reagan, U.S. Oceans Policy, 83 DEP'T ST. BULL. No. 2075, at 70–71, 22 I.L.M. 464 (1983) ("[T]he convention also contains provisions with respect to traditional uses of the oceans which generally confirm existing maritime law and practice and fairly balance the interests of all states . . . (t)he United States is prepared to accept and act in accordance with the balance of interests relating to traditional uses of the ocean. . . .").

16. RESTATEMENT (THIRD) FOREIGN RELATIONS LAW § 511, cmt. a (1987).

17. United Nations Convention on the Law of the Sea, Dec. 10, 1982, 1833 U.N.T.S. 397, 21 I.L.M. 1261 [hereinafter UNCLOS], art. 2 (legal status of the territorial sea), art. 3 (breadth of territorial sea), arts. 17–19 (right of innocent passage, and meaning of innocent passage), art. 21 (coastal state laws and regulations relating to innocent passage), art. 211(4) ("Coastal States may, in the exercise of their sovereignty within their territorial sea, adopt laws and regulations for the prevention, reduction and control of marine pollution

from foreign vessels, including vessels exercising the right of innocent passage. Such laws and regulations shall, in accordance with Part II, section 3, not hamper innocent passage of foreign vessels.")

18. *See* RESTATEMENT (THIRD) FOREIGN RELATIONS LAW § 512 (1987).

19. AMSA 2009 REPORT, *supra* note 5, at 51.

20. UNCLOS, *supra* note 17, arts. 56 (rights, jurisdiction, and duties of the coastal state in the EEZ), 57 (breadth of the EEZ).

21. *Id.* art. 211(5).

22. *Id.* arts. 220(3), 220(5). Note that within the contiguous zone—up to 24 miles from shore—a coastal state may additionally "exercise the control necessary" to prevent and punish "infringement of its customs, fiscal, immigration or sanitary laws and regulations *within its territory or territorial sea*." UNCLOS, *supra* note 17, art. 33 (emphasis added).

23. AMSA 2009 REPORT, *supra* note 5, at 53.

24. *See, e.g.,* August 18, 2010, diplomatic note from the U.S. Embassy in Ottawa to the Department of Foreign Affairs and International Trade of Canada, expressing concern about the Northern Canada Vessel Traffic Services Zone Regulations (NORDREGs), *available at* http://www.state.gov/documents/organization/179287.pdf; IMO, *Report of the Maritime Safety Committee on its Eighty-Eighth Session,* ¶¶ 11.28–11.39, *available at* http://www.uscg.mil/imo/msc/docs/msc88-report.pdf.

25. UNCLOS, *supra* note 17, art. 56(1)(b).

26. *Id.* art. 56(1)(a).

27. Although not within the Arctic Ocean, Iceland has coastal frontage and an EEZ in the Norwegian Sea. Sweden and Finland have coastal frontage in the Barents Sea.

28. AOGA, *supra* note 12, at 31.

29. UNCLOS, *supra* note 17, art. 77(1). Art. 77(4) defines the "natural resources" of the continental shelf to consist of "the mineral and other non-living resources of the seabed and subsoil together with living organisms belonging to sedentary species, that is to say, organisms which, at the harvestable stage, either are immobile on or under the seabed or are unable to move except in constant physical contact with the seabed or the subsoil." *See also* 16 U.S.C. § 1811(b)(2) ("The United States claims, and will exercise in the manner provided for in this chapter, exclusive fishery management authority over . . . [a]ll continental shelf fishery resources beyond the exclusive economic zone.").

30. *Id.* art. 77(2).

31. *Id.* art. 76 (sets out the geological and morphological criteria and process for delineating the outer limits of a coastal state's continental shelf).

32. *See* http://www.un.org/depts/los/clcs_new/clcs_home.htm.

33. *Id.* art. 77(3); Territorial and Maritime Dispute (Nicar. v. Colom.), Judgment, ¶ 251 (I.C.J. Nov. 19, 2012), *available at* http://www.icj-cij.org/docket/files/124/17164.pdf.

34. Agreement on the Conservation of Polar Bears art. VI(1), Nov. 15, 1973, 27 U.S.T. 3918.

35. Agreement on Cooperation on Marine Oil Pollution Preparedness and Response in the Arctic, done 15 May 2013 at Kiruna, Sweden, *available at* http://www.state.gov/r/pa/prs/ps/2013/05/209406.htm.

36. Arctic Environmental Protection Strategy, Jan. 14, 1991, 30 I.L.M. 1642, *available at* http://www.arctic-council.org/index.php/en/document-archive/category/4-founding-documents?download=53:aeps.

37. Ottawa Declaration, *supra* note 4.

38. Arctic Council, Rules of Procedure, Provision 7, as adopted by the Arctic Council at the First Arctic Council Ministerial Meeting, Iqaluit, Canada, Sept. 17–18, 1998, *available*

at http://www.arctic-council.org/index.php/en/document-archive/category/4-founding -documents.

39. Agreement on Cooperation on Aeronautical and Maritime Search and Rescue in the Arctic, May 12, 2011, *available at* http://www.ifrc.org/docs/idrl/N813EN.pdf.

40. Agreement on Cooperation on Marine Oil Pollution Preparedness and Response in the Arctic, *supra* note 35.

41. *See* AMAP, AMAP 2011–2013 WORK PLAN, *available at* http://www.arctic-council .org/index.php/en/document-archive/category/425-main-documents-from-kiruna -ministerial-meeting?download=1942:agreement-on-cooperation-on-marine-oil-pollution -preparedness-and-response-in-the-arctic-final-formatted-version.

42. *See* Comments by Sheila Watt-Cloutier, Vice-President for Canada of the Inuit Circumpolar Conference to the International Negotiating Committee Regarding the Need for a Global Treaty on Persistent Organic Pollutants, June 29, 1998, *available at* http:// inuitcircumpolar.com/index.php?auto_slide=&ID=119&Lang=En&Parent_ID=&current _slide_num=.

43. *See* Kiruna Declaration, Kiruna, Sweden, May 15, 2013, *available at* http://www .arctic-council.org/index.php/en/document-archive/category/425-main-documents -from-kiruna-ministerial-meeting; Senior Arctic Officials Report to Ministers, Kiruna, Sweden, May 15, 2013, *available at* http://www.arctic-council.org/index.php/en/document -archive/category/425-main-documents-from-kiruna-ministerial-meeting.

44. IMO, Marine Environment, http://www.imo.org/OurWork/Environment /Pages/Default.aspx.

45. AMSA 2009 REPORT, *supra* note 5; PAME, Arctic Council, ARCTIC OCEAN REVIEW (AOR), PHASE II REPORT, (2011–2013) *available at* http://www.pame.is/images/PAME _Ministerial_2013/AOR_final_report_15_May_2013.pdf.

46. Convention on the International Maritime Organization (IMO), March 6, 1948, 289 U.N.T.S. 1520.

47. *See* IMO, Status of Conventions, http://www.imo.org/About/Conventions/Status OfConventions/Pages/Default.aspx. IMO also has three associate members: Faroes, Hong Kong, and Macao.

48. *See* IMO, Frequently Asked Questions, http://www.imo.org/about/pages/faqs .aspx.

49. AMSA 2009 REPORT, *supra* note 5, at 4. September 2012 marked the record minimum sea ice extent to date and is nearly 50 percent below the 1979–2000 average minimum. D. Perovich et al., *2012: Sea Ice*, ARCTIC REPORT CARD 2012, http://www.arctic .noaa.gov/reportcard. Sea ice extent is used to describe the state of the Arctic sea ice cover. Accurate records of extent based on satellite imagery have been kept since 1979. There are two months each year that are of particular interest: September, at the end of summer, when the ice reaches its annual minimum extent, and March, at the end of winter, when the ice is at its maximum extent.

50. UNCLOS, *supra* note 17, art. 192.

51. *Id.* arts. 210–212.

52. *Id.* arts. 194(3)(b), 211(1).

53. *Id.* art. 196(1).

54. IMO, International Convention for the Safety of Life at Sea, Nov. 1, 1974, 1184 U.N.T.S. 278, 32 U.S.T. 47, T.I.A.S. No. 9700, *available at* http://www.imo.org/About /Conventions/ListOfConventions/Pages/International-Convention-for-the-Safety-of -Life-at-Sea-(SOLAS),-1974.aspx [hereinafter SOLAS].

55. *Id.*

56. *Id.* at pmbl.

57. *Id.* at Annex ch. V, Regulations 4, 5, 7, 9–11.

58. International Convention for the Prevention of Pollution from Ships, Nov. 2, 1973, 1340 U.N.T.S. 184, 12 I.L.M. 1319, as modified by the Protocol of 1978 relating thereto, *available at* http://www.imo.org/about/conventions/listofconventions/pages /international-convention-for-the-prevention-of-pollution-from-ships-(marpol).aspx [hereinafter MARPOL].

59. *Id.*

60. *Id.* art. 1(1).

61. E.g., Protocol of 1997 to Amend the International Convention for the Prevention of Pollution from Ships, 1973, as Modified by the Protocol of 1978 Relating Thereto (adding Annex VI).

62. MARPOL, *supra* note 58. Annexes I (oil), II (noxious liquid substances in bulk), IV (sewage), and V (garbage) provide for the designation of special areas. MARPOL Annex VI (air pollution) provides for the analogous concept of an emission control area. *See* IMO, *Guidelines for the Designation of Special Areas under MARPOL 73/78*, adopted Jan. 15, 2002, IMO Resolution A.927(22), annex I. These guidelines were updated by IMO's Marine Environmental Protection Committee in 2012. *See* Report of the Marine Environmental Protection Committee on its Sixty-Third Session, approved Mar. 14, 2012, IMO MEPC 63/23/Add.1, annex 27.

63. Iceland is not a party to the 1997 Protocol (Annex VI). The U.S. is not a party to Annex IV. *See* IMO, Status of Conventions, *supra* note 47.

64. The Arctic Council's PAME Working Group is conducting a study to determine whether any high seas areas of the Arctic Ocean merit additional protection through measures that may be adopted at the IMO. PAME, PAME 2013–2015 WORK PLAN, at 7, *available at* http://www.pame.is/pame-work-plan/work-plan-2013-2015.

65. Convention on the Prevention of Marine Pollution by Dumping of Wastes and Other Matter, Dec. 29, 1972, 1046 U.N.T.S. 120, 26 U.S.T. 2403, T.I.A.S. No. 8165, *available at* http://www.imo.org/about/conventions/listofconventions/pages/convention-on-the -prevention-of-marine-pollution-by-dumping-of-wastes-and-other-matter.aspx [hereinafter London Convention].

66. *Id.* art. IV. Eighty-seven countries are party to the London Convention. *See* IMO, Status of Conventions, *supra* note 47.

67. Protocol to the Convention on the Prevention of Marine Pollution by Dumping Wastes and Other Matters, Nov. 8, 1996, 36 I.L.M. 7 (1997) [hereinafter London Protocol]. The full text of the London Protocol as amended in 2006 is available at http://www.imo .org/blast/mainframemenu.asp?topic_id=1499. *See also* IMO, London Protocol, *available at* http://www.imo.org/ourwork/environment/pollutionprevention/pages/1996-protocol -to-the-convention-on-the-prevention-of-marine-pollution-by-dumping-of-wastes-and -other-matter,-1972.aspx.

68. *See* MARPOL, *supra* note 58.

69. International Convention on the Control of Harmful Anti-Fouling Systems on Ships, Oct. 18, 2001, IMO Doc. AFS/CONF/26.

70. International Convention on Control of Harmful Anti-Fouling Systems on Ships, 2001, Oct. 5, 2001, S. Treaty Doc. No. 110-13 (2008), available at http://www.gc.noaa.gov /documents/afs-convention.pdf.

71. P. Wright & S. Walmsley, *Organotins in the Marine Environment—A Review of Work Since 2000* (Organotin Lit. Rev., WWF), http://www.ngo.grida.no/wwfneap/Publication /Submissions/CONSSO2004/WWF_IGSS_SEPT04_TBT_Annex.doc.

72. *See, e.g.,* J. A. Berge et al., *Organotins in Marine Mammals and Seabirds from Norwegian Territory,* 2004 J. ENVTL. MONITORING 108–12, available at http://www.ncbi.nlm.nih .gov/pubmed/14760453.

73. International Convention for the Control and Management of Ships' Ballast Water and Sediments, Feb. 16, 2004, IMO Doc. BWM/CONF/36, p. 425, *available at* http://www.imo.org/About/Conventions/ListOfConventions/Pages/International -Convention-for-the-Control-and-Management-of-Ships%27-Ballast-Water-and-Sediments -%28BWM%29.aspx [hereinafter Ballast Water Management Convention].

74. IMO, Adoption of the Final Act and Any Instruments, Recommendations and Resolutions Resulting from the Work of the Conference: International Convention for the Control and Management of Ships' Ballast Water and Sediments, 2004, U.N Doc. BWM /CONF/36 (Feb. 16, 2004), *available at* http://www.bsh.de/de/Meeresdaten/Umwelt schutz/Ballastwasser/Konvention_en.pdf.

75. U.S. Fed. Aquatic Nuisance Species Task Force, Ballast Water, http://anstask force.gov/ballast.php.

76. U.S. FED. AQUATIC NUISANCE SPECIES TASK FORCE, U.S. FEDERAL AQUATIC SPECIES TASK FORCE REPORT TO CONGRESS 12 (2004), http://anstaskforce.gov/Documents /ANSTF_RTC_Final.pdf.

77. *See* Arctic Council Working Group on Conservation of Arctic Flora and Fauna (CAFF), ARCTIC BIODIVERSITY TRENDS 2010: INVASIVE SPECIES (HUMAN-INDUCED) (2010), available at http://www.arcticbiodiversity.is/index.php/en/species/invasive-species -human-induced.

78. Ballast Water Management Convention, *supra* note 73.

79. The U.S. Coast Guard has issued regulations, effective June 21, 2012, that establish a ballast water discharge standard based on the Ballast Water Management Convention. Standard for Living Organisms in Ships' Ballast Water Discharged in U.S. Waters, 77 Fed. Reg. 17,254 (Mar. 23, 2012) (amending 33 C.F.R. pt. 151 and 46 C.F.R. pt. 162). All ships discharging ballast water in U.S. waters must comply with the discharge standard according to the Implementation Schedule for Approved Ballast Water Management Methods. *See also* U.S. Coast Guard, Ballast Water Management, http://www.uscg.mil /hq/cg5/cg522/cg5224/bwm.asp. The U.S. Environmental Protection Agency also regulates discharge of ballast water through its Vessel General Permit Program. *See* U.S. EPA, National Pollutant Discharge Elimination System (NPDES), Vessel General Permit, http:// cfpub.epa.gov/npdes/vessels/vgpermit.cfm.

80. IMO, Resolution A.1024(26) (Dec. 2, 2009), *available at* http://www.imo.org /blast/blastDataHelper.asp?data_id=29985&filename=A1024(26).pdf.

81. *Id.* at 4.

82. IMO, Shipping in Polar Waters, http://www.imo.org/mediacentre/hottopics /polar/Pages/default.aspx.

83. Arctic Council, Tromso Declaration, 2009, *available at* http://www.arctic-council .org/index.php/en/document-archive/category/5-declarations?download=38:tromso -declaration.

84. AMSA 2009 REPORT, *supra* note 5.

85. *See, e.g.,* ARCTIC COUNCIL, STATUS ON IMPLEMENTATION OF THE AMSA 2009 REPORT RECOMMENDATIONS, May 2011, http://www.arctic-council.org/index.php/en /document-archive/category/445-pame; PAME, PROGRESS REPORT TO SENIOR ARCTIC OFFICIALS (March 2012), *available at* http://www.arctic-council.org/index.php/en/document -archive/category/108-60-working-group-administration?download=428:doc-61e -pame-progress-report-to-saos.

86. AOR PHASE I REPORT, *supra* note 2, at 27.

87. In 2008, the U.S. Geological Survey (USGS) estimated that the area north of the Arctic Circle contained an estimated 90 billion barrels of undiscovered, technically recoverable oil, 1.670 trillion cubic feet of technically recoverable natural gas, and 44 billion barrels of technically recoverable natural gas liquids. USGS Press Release, 90 Billion Barrels of Oil and 1,670 Trillion Cubic Feet of Natural Gas Assessed in the Arctic, July 23, 2008, http://www.usgs.gov/newsroom/article.asp?ID=1980. These resources, which account for about 22 percent of the undiscovered, technically recoverable hydrocarbon resources in the world, are mostly located offshore. *See also* USGS Fact Sheet 2008–3049: Circum-Arctic Resource Appraisal: Estimates of Undiscovered Oil and Gas North of the Arctic Circle (2008), http://pubs.usgs.gov/fs/2008/3049/.

88. C. Krauss, *Shell Delays Arctic Oil Drilling Until 2013,* N.Y. TIMES, Sept. 17, 2012, at B1, *available at* http://www.nytimes.com/2012/09/18/business/global/shell-delays-arctic -oil-drilling-until-next-year.html?pagewanted=all&_r=0.

89. *See, e.g.,* UNCLOS, Letters of Transmittal and Submittal and Comments, U.S. Dep't of State Dispatch Supplement, Vol. 6, Supplement No. 1, at 21 (Feb. 1995).

90. UNCLOS, *supra* note 17, art. 208(1) & (2).

91. *Id.* art. 208(3).

92. *Id.* art. 208(5).

93. Agreement on Cooperation on Marine Oil Pollution, Preparedness and Response in the Arctic, May 15, 2013, *available at* http://www.arctic-council.org/index.php/en /document-archive/category/425-main-documents-from-kiruna-ministerial-meeting.

94. *Id.* art. 3.

95. Convention for the Protection of the Marine Environment of the North East Atlantic, Sept. 22, 1992, 32 I.L.M. 1069, *available at* http://www.ospar.org/html _documents/ospar/html/OSPAR_Convention_e_updated_text_2007.pdf [hereinafter OSPAR Convention].

96. *Id.*

97. The "Maritime area" covered by the Convention is defined in Article 1(a). Approximately 40 percent of this area is considered by its parties to be Arctic waters. *See* OSPAR Convention, *supra* note 95.

98. OSPAR Convention, *supra* note 95, at Annex III.

99. PAME WORKING GROUP, ARCTIC COUNCIL, ARCTIC OFFSHORE OIL AND GAS GUIDELINES (April 29, 2009), *available at* http://www.pame.is/offshore-oil-and-gas /77-arctic-offshore-oil-and-gas-guidelines-2009.

100. Arctic Council, Tromso Declaration, *supra* note 83. The Tromso Declaration also "urge[s] all States to apply these Guidelines throughout the Arctic as minimum standards in national regulations."

101. *See supra* note 97.

102. IMO, Assembly Resolution A.1023(26), Dec. 2, 2009, IMO document A26 /Res.1023, Jan. 18, 2010, *available at* http://www.imo.org/blast/blastDataHelper.asp?data _id=29983&filename=A1023(26).pdf.

103. International Convention on Oil Pollution Preparedness, Response and Co-Operation, Nov. 30, 1990, 1891 U.N.T.S. 51, 30 I.L.M. 733.

104. *Id.* pmbl.

105. *Id.* art. 3(2).

106. *Id.* art. 7.

107. *See* IMO, Status of Conventions by Countries, *supra* note 46.

108. AOR PHASE I REPORT, *supra* note 2, at 24.

109. AMAP SOAER 97, *supra* note 9, at 172 (regarding Pollution and Human Health).

110. AOR PHASE I REPORT, *supra* note 2, at 25.

111. Stockholm Convention on Persistent Organic Pollutants, May 22, 2001, 2256 U.N.T.S. 119.

112. UNEP, Stockholm Convention, Status of Ratifications, http://chm.pops.int /Countries/StatusofRatifications/tabid/252/Default.aspx. The United States signed the Convention in 2001 but has not ratified it.

113. Stockholm Convention on Persistent Organic Pollutants, *supra* note 91, arts. 3 & 5.

114. Basel Convention on the Control of Transboundary Movements of Hazardous Wastes and their Disposal art. 4, March. 22, 1989, 1673 U.N.T.S. 57, 28 I.L.M. 657 [hereinafter Basel Convention].

115. *Id.*

116. *Id.* art. 4(a) (Ban Amendment). The Ban Amendment was adopted in 1995. It has not yet entered into force. Seventy-three countries have ratified the Ban Amendment. Of the Arctic States, Finland, Sweden, Norway, and Denmark have ratified the Convention.

117. UNEP, Parties to the Basel Convention, http://www.basel.int/Countries/Status ofratifications/PartiesSignatories/tabid/1290/language/en-US/Default.aspx#a-note-1. The U.S. signed the Convention in 1990 but has not yet ratified it.

118. Convention on Long-Range Transboundary Air Pollution, Nov. 13, 1979, 1302 U.N.T.S. 217, 18 I.L.M. 1442 [hereinafter LRTAP]. LRTAP has 51 parties. *See* LRTAP, Status of Ratifications, at http://www.unece.org/fileadmin/DAM/env/documents/2012/air /Status_of_the_Covention.pdf.

119. *Id.* art. 2.

120. United Nations Economic Commission for Europe, ÚNECE's Convention on Long-range Transboundary Air Pollution Celebrates 30th Anniversary, http://www .unece.org/env/lrtap/30anniversary.html.

121. UN General Assembly, Oceans and the Law of the Sea, Report of the Secretary-General of 18 August 2004, A/59/62/Add.1, 29, para. 97, *available at* http://www.un.org /ga/59/documentation/list0.html.

122. UNCLOS, *supra* note 17, art. 207.

123. United Nations Environmental Programme, Global Program of Action for the Protection of the Marine Environment from Land-Based Activities, UN Doc. UNEP(OCA)/ LBA/IG.2/7 (1995), *available at* http://www.gpa.unep.org.

124. *Id.* § I(B).

125. Arctic Council, Regional Programme of Action for the Protection of the Arctic Marine Environment from Land-based Activities (April 29, 2009), *available at* http:// www.pame.is/index.php/regional-program-of-action. Arctic Council Ministers approved this Regional Programme of Action in the 2009 Tromso Declaration.

126. OSPAR Convention, *supra* note 95, at Annex I, art. 2.

127. Arctic Pollution 2011, Report of the Arctic Monitoring and Assessment Programme (AMAP), http://amap.no.

128. UNEP(DTIE)/Hg/INC.5/7—Annex to the report of the intergovernmental negotiating committee to prepare a global legally binding instrument on mercury on the work of its fifth session—Draft Minamata Convention on Mercury; U.S. EPA, Global Mercury Negotiations, http://www.epa.gov/international/toxics/mercury/mnegotiations.html.

129. *Id.*

130. http://www.state.gov/r/pa/prs/ps/2013/11/217295.htm.

131. H. Huntington & G. Weller, *An Introduction to the Arctic Climate Impact Assessment*, ch 1 *in* ARCTIC CLIMATE IMPACT ASSESSMENT (2005), *available at* http://www.acia.uaf.edu /PDFs/ACIA_Science_Chapters_Final/ACIA_Ch01_Final.pdf. The Arctic has experienced the greatest regional warming on Earth in recent decades and average annual temperatures have risen by about 2–3 degrees Celsius since the 1950s. This increase in tempera-

tures has resulted in extensive melting of glaciers, thawing of permafrost, and reduction in sea ice in the Arctic Ocean.

132. *Id.* Stratospheric ozone depletion events of up to 45 percent below normal have been recorded in the Arctic in recent years. *See also* G.L. Manney et al., *Unprecedented Arctic Ozone Loss in 2011*, 478 NATURE 469–75 (Oct. 27, 2011), *available at* http://www.nature .com/nature/journal/v478/n7370/full/nature10556.html.

133. AOR PHASE II REPORT, *supra* note 45.

134. AMAP SOAER 97, *supra* note 9, at 54.

135. *Id.* art. II.

136. *Id.*

137. *Id.* art. VI(1).

138. *Id.* art. III(1).

139. *Id.* art. III(2).

140. *Id.* art. IV.

141. United States, Proposal Three, Convention on International Trade in Endangered Species of Wild Fauna and Flora, Convention of the Parties 16, Bangkok, (Mar. 3–14, 2013), at 13, *available at* http://www.cites.org/eng/cop/16/prop/E-CoP16-Prop-03.pdf.

142. Agreement on the Conservation and Management of the Alaska-Chukotka Polar Bear Population, U.S.–Russ., Oct. 16, 2000, S. Treaty Doc. No. 107-10, arts. 8(1), 8(2) [hereinafter 2000 Agreement].

143. *Id.* art. 7(b).

144. *Id.* art. 7(c).

145. *Id.* art. 7(d).

146. United States, Proposal Three, *supra* note 141.

147. 2000 Agreement, *supra* note 142, arts. 7(e), 7(f), 7(h), 7(i), 7(j).

148. *Id.* art. 8(3); 22 U.S.C. § 1423e.

149. Although not a legally binding international agreement among governments, the 1988 Inupiat-Inuvialuit Agreement for the Management of Polar Bears of the Southern Beaufort merits attention. This user-to-user agreement between indigenous communities in the United States and Canada addresses sustainable harvest levels as well as methods for harvesting polar bears. For a detailed description of the agreement and assessment of its efficacy, see C.D. Brower et al., *The Polar Bear Management Agreement for the Southern Beaufort Sea: An Evaluation of the First Ten Years of a Unique Conservation Agreement*, 55 ARC-TIC 362, 371 (2002).

150. *See* Convention on International Trade in Endangered Species of Wild Fauna and Flora, arts. 2, 4, Mar. 3, 1973, 27 U.S.T. 1087, T.I.A.S. No. 8249, 993 U.N.T.S. 243, Envtl. L. Rep. Stat. 40,336 [hereinafter CITES].

151. United States, Proposal Three, *supra* note 141.

152. *See* CITES, *supra* note 150, arts. II, III.

153. CITES Sixteenth Meeting of the Conference of the Parties, Summary Record of the Sixth Session of Committee I, March 7, 2013, *available at* http://www.cites.org/common /cop/16/sum/E-CoP16-Com-I-Rec-06.pdf.

154. United States, Proposal Three, *supra* note 141.

155. AMAP SOAER 97, *supra* note 9, ch. 5 at 54.

156. Agreement on the Conservation of the Porcupine Caribou Herd, July 17, 1987, U.S.-Can, T.I.A.S. No. 11259, art. 3(a).

157. *Id.* art. 3(c).

158. *Id.* art. 3(f).

159. *Id.* art. 4(d).

160. *Id.* art. 4(d)(4).

161. *Id.* art. 4(e).

162. International Convention for the Regulation of Whaling with Schedule of Whaling Regulations, December 2, 1946, T.I.A.S. No. 1849 [hereinafter ICRW and ICRW Schedule].

163. As of May 2013. *See* Status of International Convention for the Regulation of Whaling, *available at* http://www.state.gov/documents/organization/191051.pdf.

164. ICRW, *supra* note 162, arts. IV, V.

165. *Id.* art. I(1).

166. *Id.* Schedule ¶ 10(e).

167. *See, e.g.,* Regulations Respecting Marine Mammals, SOR 93/56, at § 13 (prohibiting the sale, purchase, trade, or barter of edible parts of a cetacean or walrus, except by certain indigenous peoples), *available at* http://laws-lois.justice.gc.ca/PDF/SOR-93-56.pdf.

168. *See id.* §§ 4–6 (licensing) & pt. II (setting species, location, and season-specific restrictions on the taking of cetaceans).

169. *See id.* § 3(a) (defining the scope of the Marine Mammal Regulations as "fishing for marine mammals and related activities in Canada or in Canadian fisheries waters"); Fisheries Act, R.S.C., 1985, c. F-14 at § 2 (defining "Canadian fisheries waters" as "all waters in the fishing zones of Canada, all waters in the fishing zones of Canada, all waters in the territorial sea of Canada and all internal waters of Canada."); Fishing Zones of Canada (Zone 6) Order, C.R.C., c. 1549 (defining the "fishing zones of Canada" in the Arctic region as extending 200 nautical miles from baselines).

170. Iceland's October 10, 2002, instrument of adherence to the Whaling Convention and 1956 Protocol contained a reservation to paragraph 10(e) of the Schedule, which also stated certain commitments by Iceland to limit commercial whaling notwithstanding the reservation. ICRW, *supra* note 162.

171. A number of objections to Iceland's reservation by states parties to the Convention are set out in the status document, *id.* ¶¶ 40–60. New Zealand, in particular, contended that the Icelandic reservation is incompatible with the object and purpose of the Convention and thus without legal effect. *Id.* ¶ 55. Norway, by contrast, defended the legitimacy of the reservation. *Id.* ¶ 54.

172. AOR Phase II Report, *supra* note 45, at 48.

173. *See* ICRW, *supra* note 162, art. 5(3) (providing that an amendment to the Schedule shall not become effective with respect to a contracting government that objects with a specified period).

174. AOR Phase II Report, *supra* note 45, at 48.

175. ICRW Schedule, *supra* note 162, ¶ 13.

176. *See, e.g.,* February 20, 2013, arrangements between the United States and the Russian Federation, apportioning the quotas for bowhead and gray whales set by the IWC, *available at* http://www.nmfs.noaa.gov/ia/species/marine_mammals/inter_whaling/us_russia.pdf.

177. In the United States the International Convention for the Regulation of Whaling is implemented through the Whaling Convention Act, 16. U.S.C. §§ 916 *et seq.* and 50 C.F.R. pt. 230. Pursuant to 50 C.F.R. § 230.6, aboriginal subsistence whaling quotas set by the ICW are published in the Federal Register.

178. AOR Phase II Report, *supra* note 45, at 43.

179. Convention between the United States and Other Powers Providing for the Preservation and Protection of Fur Seals, done at Washington July 11, 1911, 37 Stat. 1542, *available at* http://docs.lib.noaa.gov/noaa_documents/NOS/ORR/TM_NOS_ORR/TM_NOS-ORR_17/HTML/Pribilof_html/Documents/THE_FUR_SEAL_TREATY_OF_1911.pdf.

180. NOAA, North Pacific Fur Seal Treaty of 1911, at 2, http://celebrating200years .noaa.gov/events/fursealtreaty/.

181. The Interim Convention on Conservation of North Pacific Fur Seals, done at Washington, Feb. 9, 1957. T.I.A.S. No. 3948, 8 U.S.T. 2283, *available at* http://sedac.ciesin .columbia.edu/entri/texts/acrc/1957FS.txt.html.

182. *Id.* art. III.

183. The Interim Convention required action by the parties no later than six years after it entered into force on October 14, 1957, to prevent its termination. Interim Convention art. XIII, ¶ 4. The Interim Convention's termination date was extended by the parties through amendments in 1964, 1969, 1976, and 1981. The 1981 extension was the last, and amended the Interim Convention so that it read: "[T]he Convention shall continue in force for twenty-six years [after it entered into force] and thereafter until the entry into force of a new or revised fur seal convention between the Parties, or until the expiration of one year after such period of twenty-six years, whichever may be the earlier." Protocol Amending the Interim Convention on Conservation of North Pacific Fur Seals, July 2, 1981, 32 U.S.T. 5581, art. V. Since no further action was taken to extend the termination date, the Interim Convention expired in 1984.

184. ARCTIC COUNCIL, CONSERVATION OF ARCTIC FLORA AND FAUNA WORKING GROUP, ARCTIC BIODIVERSITY ASSESSMENT: STATUS AND TRENDS IN ARCTIC BIODIVERSITY 117, 119 (2013), *available at* http://www.arcticbiodiversity.is/.

185. *Id.* at 30; AOR Phase I Report, *supra* note 2, at 17.

186. AOR Phase I Report, *supra* note 2, at 17.

187. Convention for the Protection of Migratory Birds, U.S.-Gr. Brit., Aug. 16, 1916, 39 Stat. 1702.

188. United States v. Pitrone, 115 F.3d 1, 2 (1st Cir. 1997).

189. Convention for the Conservation of Migratory Birds and Their Environment, U.S.-U.S.S.R., Nov. 19, 1976, T.I.A.S. No. 9073, 29 U.S.T. 4647.

190. In 1918, the U.S. Congress enacted the Migratory Bird Treaty Act to give effect to the terms of the U.S.-Great Britain Convention. The Act as amended authorizes the secretary of the interior to adopt regulations governing and permitting the hunting, possession, sale, and transportation of migratory birds consistent with all four migratory-bird treaties. *See* Noe v. Henderson, 373 F. Supp. 2d 939, 943 (E.D. Ark. 2005).

191. Convention on the Conservation of Migratory Species of Wild Animals, done at Bonn, 23 June 1979, 19 I.L.M. 11 (1980), *available at* http://www.cms.int/document s/index.htm.

192. *See generally* http://www.cms.int/en.

193. National Participation in the Convention on the Conservation of Migratory Species of Wild Animals and its Agreements as of 1 April 2013, *available at* http://www.cms.int /about/part_lst.htm. Denmark submitted a reservation at the time of ratification stating that the Convention does not apply to Greenland. *See* Application of CMS to Overseas Territories/Autonomous Regions of Parties, http://www.cms.int/en/document/application -cms-overseas-territoriesaut-onomous-regions-parties-and-reservations-regarding.

194. Convention on the Conservation of Migratory Species of Wild Animals, Appendices I and II, *available at* http://www.cms.int/documents/appendix/cms_app1_2 .htm#appendix_I. Birds listed on Appendix I that occur in the Arctic include *Numenius borealis, Anas formosa,* and *Eurynorhynchus pygmeus. See Arctic Biodiversity Assessment,* app. 4.1, *Breeding Bird Species in the Different Geographic Zones of the Low and High Arctic* (2013), *available at* http://abds.is/publications/doc_download/133-aba-2013-appendix-4-1; *see also* ARCTIC BIODIVERSITY ASSESSMENT: STATUS AND TRENDS IN ARCTIC BIODIVERSITY ch. 4.2.1., 144–47 (2013), http://www.caff.is/publications/doc_download/209-arctic-biodiversity

-assessment-2013-chapter-4-birds. Birds listed on Appendix II that occur in the Arctic include *Gavia arctica arctica, Gavia arctica suschkini,* and *Sterna paradisaea. Id.*

195. Agreement on the Conservation of Albatrosses and Petrels, done at Canberra, June 19, 2001, 2258 U.N.T.S. 257, *available at* http://www.acap.aq/index.php/acap-agreement [hereinafter ACAP].

196. *See* Parties to ACAP, http://www.acap.aq/index.php/resources/parties-to-acap. Canada and the United States regularly attend ACAP meetings and the United States is seeking to become a party. *See* S. Treaty Doc. No. 110-22, *available at* http://www.gc.noaa .gov/documents/treaty-doc_110-22_9.26.08.pdf.

197. *See* ACAP, Species Assessment, http://www.acap.aq/index.php/resources /acap-species2.

198. AOR Phase II Report, *supra* note 45, at 45. Other sources put the number of sea-bird species that breed in the Arctic as high as 64. *See* Arctic Ocean Biodiversity: Seabirds, http://www.arcodiv.org/SeaBirds.html.

PART IV

Global and Cross-Border Issues

CHAPTER 48

Mechanisms for Global Agreements

I. Introduction

This chapter will cover the primary instruments and vehicles through which international environmental law is developed, memorialized, and implemented. Practitioners should understand these processes in order to ensure that they have considered all relevant regimes in addressing specific questions. This procedural background will also provide important context to help facilitate an understanding of the substantive impact and legal effect of these regimes.

The chapter first discusses nonbinding "soft law" regimes, paying particular attention to the comparative advantages offered by a mechanism based on collaboration and voluntary participation. It also discusses the ways in which soft law may serve as a harbinger for hard law.

The second part of this chapter considers binding mechanisms and how they shape the field. Binding mechanisms are sundry: they may be bilateral, regional, or global, and they may take the form of agreements, frameworks, or protocols to frameworks or agreements. This section outlines the technical differences among various binding mechanisms for the practitioner. We focus in particular on the relatively exotic institutional and legal structures underpinning global multilateral environmental agreements. The remainder of the chapter is devoted to resolving questions that arise in practice, including which parties are bound by what agreements and whether a given text is binding or nonbinding.

II. Nonbinding Soft-Law Regimes

In theory, the sources of international environmental law are the same as those of general international law: international conventions, international custom, "general principles of law recognized by civilized nations," and writings of

---

*The author thanks Peter Keays and Elizabeth A. Brody for their assistance in preparing this chapter.

highly qualified jurists.[1] In practice, however, the practitioner can in most cases focus solely on conventional law—multilateral treaties, regional and bilateral treaties, and their progeny. In part this reflects the newcomer status of the field: unlike customary laws governing war or maritime trade, which have crystallized over millennia, legal norms regarding the protection of the environment, as well as the history of states' behavior in this sector, are relatively new.[2]

Nevertheless, in response to the uniquely critical challenges posed by environmental degradation, a significant body of nonbinding agreements, statements, declarations, resolutions, and recommendations has emerged in international environmental law. We will refer to these resources as "soft laws": that is, declarations, recommendations, resolutions, or guidance documents that, while negotiated among states on the international plane, are not legally binding and are discretionary in nature. The number of such texts— along with the nonbinding fora and initiatives that generate them—has grown rapidly in the past 30 years. The most prominent and foundational example is the Agenda 21 plan of action adopted at the 1992 U.N. Conference on Environment and Development (Rio Earth Summit).[3] The plan comprises a series of nonbinding chapters on key institutional and substantive topics such as transboundary air pollution, biodiversity, access to environmental information, biotechnology, and chemicals. In many of these subfields, Agenda 21 has guided substantive environmental policy-making at the international level for the past two decades.[4]

As evidenced by the impact of Agenda 21, "soft" does not mean irrelevant. Since the founding of the United Nations, international soft-law regimes governing everything from human rights to outer space have proliferated in quantity, in scope, and in influence of public and private sector behavior.[5] Soft law is particularly important in the field of international environmental law. First, soft-law regimes provide a low-resistance path for the introduction of solutions surrounding a given environmental issue, offering an opportunity for stakeholders to coalesce around concrete actions without the need to outline penalties or remedies for noncompliance. Most conventional, binding law in our field first emerged as soft-law guidance or resolutions that over time hardened into firm commitments that later were adopted as binding. Moreover, the development of soft-law mechanisms allows for the more direct and influential participation of non-state actors—including both environmental non-governmental organizations and business organizations—than is the case in treaty negotiations.[6] Soft law also influences domestic regulatory developments and frequently serves as guidance to domestic decision makers (legislators, regulators, or judges) who are faced with new or emerging environmental challenges at the domestic level that can directly affect practitioners. As discussed further next, this is particularly the case with respect to nonbinding decisions by conferences of the parties to global treaties, which serve as highly instructive interpretive guidance to flesh out the details of these broad framework agreements. For these reasons, it is important that practitioners track (and even try to influence) soft-law initiatives that can affect their clients' interests.

Two key examples of nonbinding fora that generate influential nonbinding soft law help illustrate why practitioners should pay attention to these important sources of influence. The first are United Nations Environment Program (UNEP) Governing Council decisions, which frequently evolve into negotiated treaties. (The Governing Council was replaced in 2013 with a successor body known as the United Nations.) UNEP's approach to mercury provides a good example. UNEP's attention to the issue of mercury pollution began with a Governing Council decision in 2001 calling for, inter alia, comprehensive studies of the anthropogenic sources of mercury, existing toxicity studies, and prevention and control technologies. Subsequent decisions built on those studies and led ultimately to a 2009 decision to establish an Intergovernmental Negotiating Committee. This committee was tasked with negotiating a global, legally binding instrument on mercury to be adopted in 2013.[7] Although driven by governments, each stage of this process was open to input from non-governmental stakeholders (both environmental activists and industry representatives). A practitioner seeking to influence the adoption of regulatory requirements applicable to mercury emissions and uses in any given country would therefore have done well to track and engage in these processes throughout their development. On January 19, 2013, participating states agreed to the text of the global, legally binding instrument on mercury, called the Minamata Convention on Mercury.[8] Minamata, Japan, was the site of industrial mercury dumping and subsequent widespread mercury poisoning in the mid-20th century[9] and will be the site of the diplomatic convention that formally adopts the treaty. The final text targets primary mining and emissions from coal combustion and contains restrictions on certain categories of mercury-containing products.[10] The Minamata Convention opened for signature from October 9 to 11 at a diplomatic convention in Kumamoto and Minamata, Japan.

The Strategic Approach to International Chemicals Management (SAICM) is another example of new soft-law venues that can presage the development of binding domestic or international commitments. SAICM was launched at the 2006 International Conference of Chemicals Management (ICCM). SAICM's stated objective is to "achieve the sound management of chemicals throughout their life cycle so that, by 2020, chemicals are used and produced in ways that lead to the minimization of significant adverse effects on human health and the environment."[11] SAICM, which is designed as a multistakeholder forum that is open to governments as well as civil society, is expressly intended to serve as a driver of national chemicals regulatory measures, especially in developed countries. In the absence of a formal agreement or another forum on chemicals management, however, SAICM currently serves as the primary global forum for international chemicals policy. Workshops and resolutions adopted under SAICM, including at the third ICCM in 2012, are already driving national regulatory activity on chemicals management and influencing private sector decision making with respect to, for example, disclosure of chemicals in products.[12]

Indeed, because private sector actors anticipate that soft-law decisions may drive future policy and regulatory decisions in key markets, soft-law decisions also frequently shape corporate behavior, even before hardening into binding legal obligations. Many voluntary sector-specific commitments on sustainability, such as the Equator Principles for large project finance institutions and the Electronic Industry Citizenship Coalition's Code of Conduct for electronics manufacturers, incorporate and reflect soft-law environmental and social responsibility policies adopted at the global level.[13] At the level of individual companies, soft law can also influence corporate social responsibility policies and actions, including responsible procurement. In the minerals sector, for example, U.N. General Assembly resolution 55/56, introduced in 2000, led to the development of the Kimberley Process Certification Scheme used by the diamond industry to certify the origins of diamonds from conflict-free sources.[14]

Accordingly, practitioners should give consideration to how soft-law agreements can shape their approach to legal questions, open channels for client advocacy, predict future industry guidance and codes of conduct, and guide their predictions of future binding laws and regulations. Issues related to soft law arising in practice will be addressed later in this chapter.

III.   Sources of Binding International Environmental Law

We turn next to the mechanisms for global agreements that practitioners will most readily associate with international environmental law: treaties. Treaties and related agreements take a wide variety of forms, ranging from bilateral to regional to global in scope. Any given international environmental issue, moreover, may implicate agreements at more than one level. It is therefore important for practitioners to understand the different types of agreements and how they interact.

A.   Bilateral Agreements

International environmental practitioners should first consider whether their matter is addressed by obligations found within a bilateral treaty between the affected jurisdictions. Bilateral agreements are, in brief, enforceable agreements between two states. In the environmental field, they are frequently concluded between two adjacent states in relation to either a shared natural resource (e.g., a shared watershed) or a transboundary pollution source. These agreements impose binding obligations on the parties, who in turn may impose obligations on private actors within their jurisdiction through domestic implementing laws. Notable examples include the United States–Canada Air Quality Agreement of 1991, which focused originally on measures to reduce acid rain in the shared airshed,[15] and the Boundary Waters Treaty of 1909, which established the International Joint Commission (IJC) to oversee water resource issues involving the United States and Canada.[16] A practitioner working on an infrastructure or effluent matter involving the Great Lakes or other boundary watercourses, for example, would need not only to carefully review the international obligations that each party bears under the treaty but also to understand the procedural role that the IJC plays in regulatory processes in each country.

Relevant obligations may also be found in bilateral treaties that are not, strictly speaking, environmental agreements. Recent bilateral U.S. trade promotion agreements, for instance, have frequently included provisions that impose environment-related obligations. These include obligations to effectively enforce domestic environmental laws and regulations and obligations to take measures to implement certain multilateral environmental agreements. Both mature, long-standing treaties relating to "Friendship, Commerce, and Navigation" and newer bilateral investment agreements may implicate environmental issues.

Because of the sheer number of potentially relevant bilateral agreements, it can be a challenge for practitioners to identify and locate those that may be relevant to their matters. In the United States, practitioners should start with the State Department's Treaties in Force.[17] While practitioners may observe that many of the bilateral agreements are relatively unknown or inactive, obligations under the agreement are still effective as long as the agreement remains in force and has not been superseded by subsequent agreements in force between those parties.

B. Regional Agreements

Practitioners should also be aware that environmental obligations can also be found in regional treaties. These regional agreements take a variety of forms. In some cases, regional agreements may be freestanding and independent regimes that are tailored to the unique environmental circumstances of a given region. This is the case, for example, with the regional seas agreements adopted under UNEP, such as the Convention for the Protection and Development of the Marine Environment of the Wider Caribbean Region and its protocols.[18] These regional agreements fit comfortably within the institutional architecture of ocean environmental management established under the much better-known U.N. Convention on the Law of the Sea, but their obligations are distinct from or in addition to obligations set out in the Convention itself.

In other cases, regional environmental agreements cover the same substantive terrain as global environmental agreements, but layer on additional obligations that apply only among the parties to the regional agreement. For example, the Bamako Convention,[19] adopted in 1991 under the auspices of the Organization of African Unity, amplifies and extends obligations set out in its global predecessor, the Basel Convention.[20] In still other cases, regional environmental agreements may overlap with but impose slightly different obligations than those set out in comparable global agreements. This scenario arises where the regional agreement may have preceded and served as a model for the subsequent global agreement. This is the case, for example, with the Protocol on Persistent Organic Pollutants to the Convention on

Long-Range Transboundary Air Pollution (LRTAP Protocol), which predates a global agreement that was adopted on the same topic: the Stockholm Convention on Persistent Organic Pollutants (Stockholm Convention). Although their basic structure and function is very similar, there are subtle distinctions among the obligations in each agreement as well as in the lists of chemicals that they cover.[21] While generally it is possible to reconcile the multiple obligations of each party in such circumstances, it is critical that practitioners carefully examine and unpack the overlapping obligations as well as identify which states are party to which agreements. In cases of overlapping agreements, the determination of which obligations apply is subject to the rules of treaty interpretation, primarily those set out in the Vienna Convention on the Law of Treaties (which also generally reflects customary international law in this field).[22]

In still other cases, relevant regional agreements are not environment-focused at all but instead are directed primarily at trade or investment matters. As with the bilateral agreements discussed above, however, regional trade agreements may include important environmental substantive and procedural obligations. Examples of pertinent regional trade agreements include NAFTA[23] and its cousin in the Southern Cone, MERCOSUL.[24]

C. Global Multilateral Environmental Agreements

Global multilateral environmental agreements (MEAs) are the charismatic megafauna of the international environmental law ecosystem: they attract the most attention, and they can be fascinating to watch even when they do nothing. Indeed, for many people, "international environmental law" begins and ends with the MEAs. And although their impact and influence may be overrated, the MEAs do matter to the practitioner.

We focus in this chapter on the legal and institutional structure of MEAs (their substantive provisions are addressed elsewhere.[25] A key defining feature of the MEAs is that they are purpose-built agreements aimed at particular topics with limited (rather than open-ended) mandates and scopes. Dozens of MEAs have been negotiated across the spectrum of policy clusters, including chemicals/waste (e.g., Stockholm Convention; Basel Convention); biodiversity (e.g., Convention on International Trade of Endangered Species of Wild Fauna and Flora (CITES), Convention on Biological Diversity (CBD), Cartagena Protocol); atmosphere and climate (e.g., U.N. Framework Convention on Climate Change (UNFCCC)), and oceans (U.N. Convention on the Law of the Sea). Each of these agreements—most of which have been negotiated under UNEP auspices—is legally and institutionally distinct from the others, and each has a limited, substantive mandate.

1. Conferences of the Parties

Unlike other fields of international law (e.g., trade, labor, nonproliferation, or human rights) the international environmental field does not have a global institutional architecture that serves as a platform or hub for all related activity. Instead, each agreement, once it is negotiated and enters into force, establishes its own institutional governance structure and—crucially—its own quasi-regulatory processes. The plenary body for most MEAs is known as the Conference of the Parties (COP). The COP is an organization that comprises representatives from each party and that meets periodically (annually or biannually). The MEA typically designates the COP as the primary decision making authority for the treaty, which is intended to be dynamic and evolutionary in nature. As such, the COP is given not only the power to review compliance with and implementation of the treaty but also the authority to create subsidiary bodies, consider new information, and adopt resolutions that fill the interstices of the agreements through amendments and "decisions."[26] (We turn in more detail next to the evolutionary function played by COPs and COP decision making.) In addition, the MEAs each designate a secretariat—a permanent administrative staff to facilitate and record the meetings of the COP and its subsidiary bodies.

2. Framework Agreements and Protocols

Some of these agreements are expressly designated or otherwise function as "framework" agreements: broad and relatively shallow agreements that are intended to serve largely as platforms for later and more focused negotiations, typically through the subsequent adoption of protocols. They include most notably (1) the Vienna Convention on the Protection of the Ozone Layer, which spawned the much better-known Montreal Protocol; (2) the UNFCCC, which created the Kyoto Protocol; and (3) the CBD, which has given rise to a series of targeted protocols including the Cartagena Protocol on trade in transgenic organisms and the recently concluded Nagoya Protocol on access and benefit sharing. While such protocols typically share the institutional framework (i.e., shared secretariats and, often, shared meeting events) with their progenitors,[27] the protocols are themselves unique MEAs with a separate legal standing and separate party rosters. Although in some cases it may be important as a legal matter to interpret the obligations in a protocol against the terms of the parent convention (just as a regulation must often be understood against the backdrop of the primary legislation that authorized it), there are no inherent legal distinctions between MEAs that are designated as "conventions" and those that are designated as "protocols."

3. COP Technical Work, Amendments, and Decisions

For the practitioner, the COP serves several important functions. First, the COP can set in motion intersessional activity, such as meetings of subsidiary bodies or technical experts. Wholly apart from the formal outcome of such processes, this activity is often valuable to track and observe in its own right.[28] Because such processes frequently involve the participation of key technical experts from capitals, the technical work and policy activity that takes place under the rubric of each MEA often serves as a benchmarking and training exercise for national regulators.[29] As a result, the technical processes and activities that the COP sets in motion can indirectly influence national regulatory developments. Conversely, the positions that national regulators take in these meetings can often provide practitioners with a window into the likely approach that national regulators may take in response to cutting-edge environmental issues.

Second, as a formal matter, COP decision making can lead to new legal obligations through amendments and the adoption of new protocols. Pursuant to amendments that may be adopted according to detailed procedures set out in the treaties, MEAs are frequently designed to evolve over time. The procedures vary by agreement but typically provide that amendments are adopted by supermajority decision making within the COP; those amendments typically do not enter into force until they have been ratified by a minimum threshold number of parties,[30] although recent MEAs have embraced a more expedited approach to address the problem of delay at the national ratification level. This approach flips the default result: amendments enter into force automatically after one year for all parties except those that have affirmatively provided notice of their rejection of the amendment.[31] One result is that not all amendments to an MEA are necessarily applicable to all MEA parties. It is vital for practitioners to understand the amendment processes and entry into force rules in order to understand both which obligations in an MEA have binding force and which obligations are applicable to which party.

Third, certain COP "decisions" can have impacts that, for the practitioner, are equal to or even more important than formal amendments. For example, COP decisions can take the form of guidance to the parties and the private sector about the meaning of ambiguous treaty terms. This process is now under way in the Basel Convention, for example, where the parties are negotiating the text of a guidance document that will help parties determine when used electronic equipment should be considered a "waste" that is subject to the trade disciplines set out in the agreement.[32] Even though it will not be legally binding, the decision, once adopted, will have a significant impact on the trade flows of used electronics because it will shape the approach that national regulators are likely to adopt, therefore informing the processes that shippers of such material will also adopt.

Finally, some MEAs expressly provide for the adoption of decisions that do have legally binding effect. These decisions allow for rapid evolution of legal obligations without triggering the more burdensome process for treaty amendments or national ratification decisions. This is the case, for example, with respect to decisions to list or delist species by the COP for CITES, which triggers obligations on parties to impose trade restrictions on those species,[33] and decisions to "adjust" the phase-out schedule for ozone-depleting substances under the Montreal Protocol.[34]

In many cases, the agreements provide detailed procedures that must be followed before an issue is considered ripe for adoption by the COP, either as a nonbinding decision, a binding decision, or as an amendment. These technical procedures—and the meetings and processes that they trigger—provide an important opportunity for engagement by practitioners seeking to influence the evolution of the MEAs.

4. *Tracking and Influencing*

How can practitioners track the activities at these COPs? All the major MEAs now maintain detailed websites. Researchers can track not only the documentation that is considered and adopted at each meeting (including decisions and amendments adopted, as well as official meeting "reports" that summarize the outcomes of each session), but also in many cases the proceedings of intersessional technical meetings and interim reports. Some secretariats maintain "handbooks" or compilations of decisions that are indexed and organized by topic. One useful but nonofficial resource for tracking developments, and for summarizing the background and history of key initiatives, in major international environmental fora is the Earth Negotiations Bulletin reporting service provided by the International Institute for Sustainable Development.[35]

In addition, most MEA meetings are open to direct stakeholder participation, although typically some type of accreditation is required before participation is permitted. For those seeking to influence (rather than merely track) these developments, there are two key considerations to take into account. First, most government delegations have adopted their negotiating positions on key issues well in advance of the MEA meeting itself, so it is often essential to initiate your lobbying activity in national capitals prior to the meeting you are seeking to influence. Second, it is very difficult to "parachute" into a long-standing intergovernmental process and be successful: relationships and individual and institutional credibility are important in these fora, and an effective lobbying campaign therefore typically involves sustained participation in the processes across multiple meetings (which can involve months or years of involvement).[36]

Notes

1. RESTATEMENT (THIRD) OF THE FOREIGN RELATIONS LAW OF THE UNITED STATES § 102, Reporters' Note 1 (1986).

2. *See* Table 2: Growth in the Number of International Environmental Treaties, at viii, in WILLIAM H. RODGERS, JR., ENVIRONMENTAL LAW (2d ed. 1994), *reproduced from* N. Choucri & R.C. North, *Global Accord: Imperatives for the Twenty-First Century, in* GLOBAL ACCORD: ENVIRONMENTAL CHALLENGES AND INTERNATIONAL RESPONSES 477, 493 & fig.15.1 (N. Choucri ed. 1993) (based on compilations by Haas with Sundgren and derived from UNEP's International Registry of Environmental Treaties).

3. Agenda 21, Proc. of United Nations Conference on Environment & Development, Brazil, Rio De Janerio. UN, 1992, *available at* http://sustainabledevelopment.un.org/content/documents/Agenda21.pdf.

4. *See* William Onzivu, *International Environmental Law, the Public's Health, and Domestic Environmental Governance in Developing Countries,* 21 Am. U. Int'l L. Rev. 597, 614 (2006).

5. *See* Pierre-Marie Dupuy, *Soft Law and the International Law of the Environment,* 12 Mich. J. Int'l L. 420, 421 (1990–1991).

6. *See* Duncan B. Hollis, *Why State Consent Still Matters—Non-State Actors, Treaties, and the Changing Sources of International Law,* 23 Berkeley J. Int'l L. 137, 138 (2005) (acknowledging that "international organizations, multinational corporations, nongovernmental organizations (NGOs), and even individuals . . . exercise increased influence in the creation, implementation, and enforcement of international law").

7. United Nations Environment Programme Governing Council decision 25/5 III, *available at* http://www.chem.unep.ch/mercury/GC25/GC25Report_English.pdf.

8. Press Release, United Nations Environment Programme, "Minamata" Convention Agreed by Nations: Global Mercury Agreement to Lift Health Threats from Lives of Millions Worldwide, INC5 Press Release (Jan. 19, 2013).

9. M. Harada, *Minamata Disease: Methylmercury Poisoning in Japan Caused by Environmental Pollution.* 25(1) Crit. Rev. Toxicol. 1–24 (1995), http://www.ncbi.nlm.nih.gov/pubmed/7734058?report=abstract (abstract only).

10. For detailed coverage of the negotiations, see Pia M. Kohler et al. eds., *Summary of the Fifth Session of the Intergovernmental Negotiating Committee to Prepare a Global Legally Binding Instrument on Mercury: 13–19 January, 2013,* 28(22) Earth Negotiations Bull. (2013).

11. Strategic Approach to International Chemicals Management, SAICM, http://www.saicm.org.

12. *See generally* United Nations Environment Programme (UNEP), Strategic Approach to International Chemicals Management, Progress Report on the Chemicals in Products Project, including proposed recommendations for further international cooperative action, U.N. Doc. SAICM/ICCM.3/15 (June 21, 2012).

13. The Equator Principles III, for example, references due diligence obligations as referenced by the United Nations Office of the High Commission on Human Rights (OHCHR), *Guiding Principles on Business and Human Rights: Implementing the United Nations "Protect, Respect, and Remedy" Framework,* HR/PUB/11/04 (2011). Version 4.0 of the Electronic Industry Citizenship Coalition's Code of Conduct cites as reference documents the U.N.'s Universal Declaration of Human Rights, Convention against Corruption, and Global Compact.

14. Kimberley Process Certification Scheme, Kimberley Process Authority para. 6 (Nov. 5, 2002).

15. Agreement between the Government of the United States of America and the Government of Canada on Air Quality, U.S.-Can., Mar. 13, 1991, 1991 U.S.T. LEXIS 108.

16. Treaty between the United States and Great Britain Relating to Boundary Waters, and Questions Arising between the United States and Canada, U.S.-G.B., Jan. 11, 1909, *available at* http://www.ijc.org/rel/agree/water.html#text.

17. http://www.state.gov/s/l/treaty/tif/index.htm.

18. Convention for the Protection and Development of the Marine Environment of the Wider Caribbean Region, Mar. 24, 1983, 1984 U.S.T. LEXIS 254.

19. Bamako Convention on the Ban of the Import into Africa and the Control of Transboundary Movement and Management of Hazardous Wastes within Africa, adopted in 1991 under the auspices of the Organization of African Unity.

20. Basel Convention on the Control of Transboundary Movements of Hazardous Wastes and Their Disposal, Mar. 22, 1989, 1989 U.S.T. LEXIS 240.

21. For a discussion of the differences, see REPORT FROM THE COMM. ON AGRIC. TO THE COMM. OF THE WHOLE HOUSE ON PIC AND POPs AND THE LRTAP POPs PROTOCOL IMPLEMENTATION ACT, H.R. REP. No. 109-668 (2006), *available at* http://www.gpo.gov/fdsys/pkg/CRPT-109hrpt668/html/CRPT-109hrpt668.htm.

22. *See* RESTATEMENT (THIRD) OF THE LAW OF THE FOREIGN RELATIONS OF THE UNITED STATES pt. III, Introductory Note, for a discussion of the relationship between the Vienna Convention and U.S. law.

23. North American Free Trade Agreement, Jan. 1, 1994, *available at* https://www.nafta-sec-alena.org/Default.aspx?tabid=97&language=en-US.

24. Treaty Establishing a Common Market between the Argentine Republic, the Federal Republic of Brazil, the Republic of Paraguay, and the Eastern Republic of Uruguay, Mar. 26, 1991, *available at* http://www.sice.oas.org/trade/mrcsr/mrcsrtoc.asp.

25. See chapter 49, Key Environmental Treaties and Agreements, in this volume.

26. For a detailed history on the origin and evolution of this institutional arrangement, see Robin R. Churchill & Geir Ulfstein, *Autonomous Institutional Arrangements in Multilateral Environmental Agreements: A Little-Noticed Phenomenon in International Law*, 94 AM. J. INT'L L. 623 (2000).

27. In such cases, the meetings of the Protocol parties are typically referred to as Meetings of the Parties (MOPs), and joint meetings of both bodies under the framework agreement are known as meetings of the COP/MOP.

28. "The importance of communication between scientists and decisionmakers to raise government concern, improve implementation and compliance with treaty commitments, and thereby further global environmental protection, has been noted by several authors." Dagmar Lohan, *A Framework for Assessing the Input of Scientific Information into Global Decisionmaking*, 17 COLO. J. INT'L ENVTL. L. & POL'Y 1, 25 (2006).

29. *Id.* at 36.

30. *See* Churchill & Ulfstein, *supra* note 26, at 636.

31. The Stockholm Convention, for example, adopts such an expedited procedure for adding new chemicals to the global restrictions and phase-out obligations in the agreement.

32. Eleventh Meeting of the Conference of the Parties to the Basel Convention, Geneva, Switz., May 2013, Draft technical guidelines on transboundary movements of e-waste and used electrical and electronic equipment, in particular regarding the distinction between waste and nonwaste under the Basel Convention (Dec. 22, 2012), UNEP/CHW.11/7/Add.1.

33. Article XV of CITES provides that "amendments adopted at a meeting [of the COP] shall enter into force 90 days after that meeting for all Parties except those which make a reservation in accordance with paragraph 3 of this Article." Convention on the International Trade in Endangered Species of Wild Fauna and Flora art. XV, Mar. 3, 1973, TIAS 8249.

34. Montreal Protocol on Substances That Deplete the Ozone Layer art. 2, Sept. 16, 1987, 1987 U.S.T. LEXIS 207.

35. The International Institute for Sustainable Development, http://www.iisd.org. The Earth Negotiations Bulletin is available at http://www.iisd.ca/enbvol/enb-background.htm.

36. A good resource for practitioners looking for guidance on how to engage in these settings is MICHAEL STRAUSS, HOW TO LOBBY AT INTERGOVERNMENTAL MEETINGS (2004).

CHAPTER 49

Key Environmental Law Treaties and Agreements

ANDREW LONG

I. Introduction: Global Environmental Problems

The rapid growth of international environmental law (IEL) in the last 40 years responds to an increasing scientific understanding of humanity's ability to fundamentally alter natural systems on a global scale. Just as U.S. environmental law emerged as the public came to understand the risks generated by industrial activity—such as recognition of unintended harm from widespread use of chemical products following the popularity of Rachel Carson's seminal book *Silent Spring*—IEL has grown as a result of increasing public awareness that environmental issues transcending national boundaries threaten significant harm. Early international environmental agreements tended to focus on discrete issues and national implementation, such as protection of economically valuable wildlife species. Since the hole in the ozone layer captured the public imagination in the mid-1980s, however, global collective action problems have become increasingly predominant in defining the IEL landscape. Global resource systems that once seemed to hold limitless bounty (such as the oceans) or to be beyond humanity's reach (such as the atmosphere) have become vulnerable to massive changes resulting from human activity. Such problems create grave risks for people throughout the world and require cooperative action among countries because they cannot be addressed by any one country acting alone. The basic dilemma underlying IEL today is that the nations of the world can only avoid long-term collective risk by assuming near-term restraints on their sovereign activities. The global effort to respond to climate change has come to epitomize this dilemma for many people.

This chapter provides a brief digest of major IEL agreements that have come into existence over the last 40 years. It is meant to serve as a quick digest for the practitioner of some of the most significant agreements and principles that drive the development of IEL. It begins by discussing the two most important "soft law" agreements for establishing the core principles of

977

IEL: the Declaration of the United Nations Conference on the Human Environment (Stockholm Declaration)[1] and the Rio Declaration on Environment and Development, U.N. Conference on Environment and Development (Rio Declaration).[2] From there, the chapter briefly highlights the key agreements addressing the following topics: the atmospheric commons; the ocean commons; biodiversity; and pollution. These topical areas were chosen both for their significance as a matter of environmental quality and because of the legal and/or political significance of the agreements designed to regulate them.

II. Agreements Establishing Environmental Principles
A. Stockholm Declaration

In many important respects, the 1972 Stockholm Conference on the Human Environment marks the beginning of IEL to address globally significant environmental problems. Prior to Stockholm, IEL agreements consisted almost exclusively of bilateral and regional treaties addressing a relatively narrow resource preservation issue affecting a limited geographic area, such as the Pacific Fur Seals Treaty. The international aspect of these early agreements arose from cross-border concerns rather than global collective action problems. The Stockholm Conference had the symbolic importance of gathering the nations of the world together to begin cooperation toward solving global environmental problems and created the U.N. Environment Program. But perhaps the most important outcome of the conference for the development of IEL was the Stockholm Declaration, which was the first multilateral statement of IEL principles. The principles enshrined in the Stockholm Declaration laid the foundation upon which the conceptual framework of IEL and international environmental policy has been constructed in the last 40 years.

Principle 21 of the Stockholm Declaration has arguably been the most important principle in IEL since 1972 because it sets the context within which all further development has occurred. Principle 21 provides that states have "the sovereign right to exploit their own resources pursuant to their own environmental policies, and the responsibility to ensure that activities within their jurisdiction or control do not cause damage to the environment of other States or of areas beyond the limits of national jurisdiction." This principle, which recognizes countries' sovereignty over resources within their territory, and a corresponding obligation to avoid harm to other nations and the commons (a principle against transboundary harm), was recognized as expressing customary international law by the International Court of Justice (ICJ) in its *Legality of the Threat or Use of Nuclear Weapons (New Zealand v. France)* advisory opinion.[3] In their influential treatise, Philippe Sands and Jacqueline Peel describe it as the "cornerstone of international environmental law."[4] Principle 21 establishes the essential parameters that frame negotiations to address the collective action problems at the heart of IEL—the challenge of engaging and coordinating independent sovereign states to regulate their own activities for the protection of globally significant resources lying primarily beyond their individual control.

Another important principle of the Stockholm Declaration is Principle 1, which suggests a nascent human right to a healthy environment and related obligations to future generations (often expressed as the principle of intergenerational equity). It can be understood as a precursor to the concept of sustainable development because complying with its terms requires management of natural resources in a way that supports both human development and the maintenance of those resources at a level that will support similar benefits for future generations. Further, Principle 1 may be viewed as presaging the union of human rights and environmental protection that has become increasingly prominent in national and international instruments since the Stockholm Declaration was adopted.[5]

B. Rio Declaration

Although the Stockholm Declaration serves as a foundation of IEL, the 1992 Rio Declaration may now be regarded as the most important expression of IEL principles. The 1992 U.N. Conference on the Environment and Development (UNCED) marked a shift in IEL from focus on traditional international issues in the environmental context to an effort to regulate extremely complex and inescapably global problems. A comparison of the Convention on the International Trade in Endangered Species of Wild Fauna and Flora (CITES),[6] which was opened for signature in 1973, and the Convention on Biological Diversity (CBD),[7] which was signed at UNCED, illustrates the change. CITES seeks to regulate trade—a classic subject of international law—affecting imperiled species, while the CBD seeks to promote conservation of biodiversity generally. While CITES requires specific national measures of compliance targeted to very specific activities affecting species preservation, the CBD calls for a broad range of actions at multiple scales on the leading edge of scientific understanding. These include the creation of incentives in international and national law to support species' adaptation to climate change.

The Rio Declaration also highlighted the increasing significance of developing countries in environmental negotiations, both because of their growing power to affect outcomes and because of their necessary role in addressing environmental problems. Moreover, it formalizes the recognition of the different positions of developed and developing countries in terms of their relative capacity to take action through the principle of "common but differentiated responsibilities." Like the Stockholm Declaration, the Rio Declaration can be understood as expressing the principles that have guided subsequent IEL development. These include the right to development and intergenerational equity (Principle 3), common but differentiated responsibilities (Principle 7), the precautionary principle (Principle 15), the polluter pays principle (Principle 16), and the importance of environmental impact assessment (Principle 17).

II.   Protection of the Atmospheric Commons

International efforts to regulate activities affecting the atmospheric commons epitomize the intensive attention to and growth of IEL in recent decades. Arguably, protecting the ozone layer and responding to climate change have galvanized public attention and political action on globally important environmental issues to a greater extent than any other environmental concerns. The notable successes of the Montreal Protocol on Substances That Deplete the Ozone Layer[8] sparked a new "generation" of multilateral environmental agreements (MEAs) that include much greater international institutional development and legal complexity than earlier agreements.

A.   The Ozone Regime: Vienna Convention and Montreal Protocol

The Vienna Convention for the Protection of the Ozone Layer,[9] which opened for signature in 1985 and entered into force in 1988, serves as a "framework agreement" for international regulation of ozone-depleting substances. Negotiation of the treaty received little attention at the time, although the regime that these negotiations initiated would become among the most influential and successful in IEL.

The Vienna Convention establishes an overarching obligation "to protect human health and the environment against adverse effects resulting or likely to result from human activities which modify or are likely to modify the ozone layer."[10] It promotes international cooperation related to research and observation (Article 3), information exchange relevant to the regulation of ozone-depleting substances (ODS) (Article 4), and technology transfer.[11] The Vienna Convention, however, did not establish specific legal obligations on use and production of ODS. Such obligations were agreed to during negotiation of the Montreal Protocol, which was signed in 1987 and rapidly overshadowed the Vienna Convention in legal significance.

Within months of the negotiations in Vienna, publication of scientific data confirming the existence if an "ozone hole" over Antarctica and the resulting threat of harm to public health from radiation led to strong public interest in the issue. Increasing scientific understanding of ozone depletion and corresponding public attention, as well as U.S. industry interests favoring a phase-out of the most significant ODS—chlorofluorocarbons (CFCs)—created a political environment favorable to the negotiation of a strong MEA to address ozone-depleting substances. The development and implementation of the resulting Montreal Protocol is arguably the single greatest success story in IEL. It is also among the most important agreements in IEL because of its influence on the agreements negotiated at UNCED in 1992, which produced the Rio Declaration, Agenda 21, the U.N. Framework Convention on Climate Change, and the CBD, among other agreements. The Montreal Protocol's approach to ODS also influenced thinking about policy and legal mechanisms for years after Rio, arguably shaping many aspects of the Kyoto

Protocol, for example, and encouraging lofty hopes that international law might come to address environmental problems with the same binding precision that domestic law regularly achieves.

The Montreal Protocol was opened for signature in 1987 and entered into force two years later. With 197 parties, the Montreal Protocol and the Vienna Convention became the first treaties in the history of the United Nations to receive universal ratification in 2009.[12]

The Montreal Protocol is a highly innovative agreement that establishes a "basket" approach to ODSs by assigning "depletion values" that allow consumption of all gases to be assessed by a single metric based on levels of production, imports, and exports.[13] The initial agreement froze production and adopted a relatively modest requirement for a 50 percent reduction in ODSs. It also provided for financial and technical assistance to developing countries, along with a small increase in ODS consumption and ten-year grace period that would allow them to take advantage of low-cost CFCs and plan for implementation of the phase-out.[14] In addition, the 1987 protocol established creative trade-related measures—prohibiting most trade of ODS and products containing ODS with non-parties—that effectively encouraged participation in the regime.[15]

Among the most notable aspects of the Montreal Protocol is its rapid expansion and increasing stringency. Beginning with the 1990 London Adjustments and Amendments to the Montreal Protocol, several amendments adopted by the Meeting of the Parties significantly strengthened the terms of the original agreement. In 2007, the Meeting of the Parties (MOP) reached beyond a narrow focus on ODS to accelerate the phase-out of hydrochloroflorocarbons (HCFCs) not only for ozone protection, but also because they are potent greenhouse gases.[16] Following this decision, some commentators described the Montreal Protocol as "the most successful climate treaty to date" because, along with tremendous success in reducing ozone depletion, many of the substances it regulates have a very high "global warming potential," meaning that the Montreal Protocol has likely had a greater practical impact on the mitigation of climate change than the entire climate change regime.[17]

In conjunction with amendments made to it, the Montreal Protocol establishes the following phase-out schedule:

- CFCs: 1996 (developed countries), 2010 (developing countries)
- Halons: 1994 (developed countries), 2010 (developing countries)
- Caron tetrachloride: 1996 (developed countries), 2010 (developing countries)
- Methyl chloroform: 1996 (developed countries), 2015 (developing countries)
- Hydrobromofluorocarbons: 1996 (developed countries), 1996 (developing countries)

The phase-out schedules for HCFCs and methyl bromide are more complex, including a total HCFC phase-out by 2020 for developed countries and

2040 for developing countries, as well as a total methyl bromide phase-out by 2015 for developed countries and 2005 for developing countries.[18]

Another important innovation of the Montreal Protocol is the Implementation Committee, created under Annex IV adopted at the 1995 MOP in Copenhagen. The Implementation Committee serves as a mechanism addressing noncompliance and facilitating implementation. Its involvement is triggered by a party's submission of concerns related to another party's implementation.

Although many aspects of the Montreal Protocol's success have proven difficult (perhaps impossible) to replicate, subsequent regimes have also embraced the evolving nature of the ozone regime. This is perhaps nowhere more apparent than with the other major regime addressing the atmospheric commons: the climate change regime.

B. The Climate Change Regime: The U.N. Framework Convention on Climate Change (UNFCCC) and the Kyoto Protocol

Climate change is among the most pressing issues on the international agenda and has gained a level of sustained political attention that is unprecedented in IEL. The massive and complex nature of both the impacts of climate change as well as the legal and political response needed to address or avoid them has forced policy makers and others to confront the limits of IEL. In particular, the enormous political efforts and modest on-the-ground results demonstrate that the success of the ozone regime does not necessarily mean that broad multilateral participation in negotiation of MEAs will provide the necessary catalyst to address a given global environmental problem. This lesson has become particularly salient for climate change law, where the legal structure was partially modeled on the ozone regime. Unlike ozone depletion, an effective response to climate change would likely require coordination of a broad array of policies and activities in sectors with tremendous importance to national economies and international trade, such as energy, transportation, and forestry. Thus, the climate change regime raises questions about the limits of IEL treaties as a means to address global environmental problems.

1. UNFCCC

The UNFCCC[19] was one of the most important outcomes of UNCED. Today, it continues to provide the overarching goal of the climate change regime in Article 2 (Objective):

> The ultimate objective of this Convention and any related legal instruments that the Conference of the Parties may adopt is to achieve . . . stabilization of greenhouse gas concentrations in the atmosphere at a level that would prevent dangerous anthropogenic interference with the climate system. Such a level should be achieved within a time frame

sufficient to allow ecosystems to adapt naturally to climate change, to ensure that food production is not threatened, and to enable economic development to proceed in a sustainable manner.

In addition, the UNFCCC embraces several important principles of IEL in Article 3, including

- Intergenerational equity (Article 3.1);
- Common but differentiated responsibilities (Article 3.1), which specifically provides that "developed country Parties should take the lead in combating climate change and the adverse effects thereof"; and
- the Precautionary principle, including a statement that "[w]here there are threats of serious or irreversible damage, lack of full scientific certainty should not be used as a reason for postponing such measures, taking into account" a preference for "cost-effective" policies and measures.

Further, although the UNFCCC does not include a binding greenhouse gas (GHG) emissions limitation, it does include several other commitments.[20] These commitments center around cooperation and building the necessary legal and institutional elements for addressing climate change, as well as obligations of developed country parties to support developing country parties. The UNFCCC creates a division between developed and developing countries, reflected in the annex system it establishes and upon which the Kyoto Protocol to the UNFCCC[21] builds. Although this division in the obligations serves as a clear incorporation of the "common but differentiated responsibilities" principle, its continuation has also become one of the most contentious issues related to the future of the climate change regime.

2. *Kyoto Protocol*

The Kyoto Protocol sought to employ firm requirements that would ensure developed countries begin to take measures necessary to meet the overall goals of the climate change regime. The binding "first commitment period" expired in December 2012. Negotiations in 2012 produced the Doha amendment to the Kyoto Protocol to the UNFCCC, which would establish a second commitment period for the Kyoto Protocol effective through 2020 upon its entry into force. However, a number of significant countries that participated in the first commitment period would not participate in a second commitment period even if the Doha amendment enters into force. Nonetheless, the Kyoto Protocol was a particularly important step in the development of climate change law and IEL more generally. An understanding of its provisions may prove critical to working with current and future developments in the larger climate regime.

The Kyoto Protocol centers around "quantified emission limitation and reduction commitments" adopted by the developed, or "Annex I," parties to the UNFCCC.[22] These parties agreed to specific levels of emission reductions from the level of their GHGs in a baseline year (1990 for carbon dioxide and most other gases and for most countries). The Kyoto Protocol includes four "flexibility mechanisms" that were created to reduce the burden of implementation. These four mechanisms collectively create the "cap-and-trade" approach of the Kyoto Protocol, which is modeled on the Acid Rain Program created by the 1990 amendments to the U.S. Clean Air Act. The creation of emissions trading in Article 17 allows for Annex I parties to buy carbon credits to meet their obligations even if emissions exceed commitments or to sell credits reflecting reductions beyond their obligations.[23] Article 4 permits parties to agree to meet their obligations in the aggregate, as if they were within a single "bubble."[24] The remaining two mechanisms allow Annex I parties to acquire emission credits by undertaking or sponsoring projects in other countries. The "joint implementation" mechanism of Article 6 allows projects to be undertaken within Annex I party countries, while the "clean development mechanism" (CDM) of Article 12 allows projects in non-Annex I countries (i.e., developing countries). Among other things, the CDM provides a means of reducing emissions in developing countries without imposing reduction obligations on them and may also serve as a vehicle for spreading advanced clean energy technology to developing countries. In addition, the Kyoto Protocol includes a compliance regime designed to perform both facilitation and enforcement functions. As is true of several other aspects of the climate change regime, the Kyoto Protocol's compliance mechanism was an effort to extend approaches developed in the ozone regime to the much more complex climate change context.

3.   Recent Developments

Since the Kyoto Protocol's negotiation, development in the climate change regime has occurred through the decisions of the Conference of the Parties to the UNFCCC (COP). Particularly notable recent decisions include the Bali Road Map decisions from COP-13 in 2007. The roadmap established building blocks for post-Kyoto negotiations toward a new and potentially more comprehensive treaty. It also established the Ad Hoc Working Group on Long-term Cooperative Action (AWG LCA) to lay the groundwork for future international cooperative action. However, the decisions in Bali contemplated a new agreement to be reached in 2009 at COP-15 in Copenhagen. COP-15 was a major disappointment to many, producing only the Copenhagen Accord.[25] The Cancun Agreements from COP-16 addressed several of the most important issues for developing an effective treaty in the future. These include enhanced mitigation by developed countries, promoting mitigation in developing countries, improving adaptation, and crediting emissions reductions from avoided deforestation. This last issue is the subject of significant development outside of the formal treaty framework on climate change under the commonly used title "REDD+," which stands for reduced emissions from deforestation and degradation plus reforestation.[26] This developing mechanism seeks to provide financial incentives to reduce GHG emissions from the forestry sector by providing carbon credits equivalent to the amount of such reductions.

COP-17 and COP-18 seem likely to stand as turning points in the history of the climate change regime. At COP-17 in 2011, the parties created the Ad Hoc Working Group on the Durban Platform on Enhanced Action with a mandate to enable the COP "to adopt a protocol, another legal instrument or an agreed outcome with legal force" no later than 2015 so that it may be implemented beginning in 2020.[27] At COP-16, the parties terminated the Bali Action Plan and the two working groups that had been created in 2007, thus signaling that the Durban Platform and the DPA represent the future direction of the regime for at least the next couple of years. However, important obstacles stand in the way of developing another major MEA to address climate change. Among the most significant unresolved issues are the extent to which developing countries with high GHG emissions (including the world's largest overall emitter, China) will agree to emissions limitations obligations, the participation of the United States, and funding questions related to both mitigation and adaptation. Thus, the future shape of the climate change regime remains an open question in several key respects. Given its broad importance, the uncertainty surrounding future international climate change law suggests the possibility of significant changes in the field of IEL more generally in the near future.

III.   Protection of Ocean Commons
A.   U.N. Convention on the Law of the Sea (UNCLOS)

Although not primarily an environmental agreement, UNCLOS[28] is the most important legal instrument for marine environment and resource governance. Opened for signature in 1983, UNCLOS entered into force and now includes approximately 166 parties. Despite the non-party status of the United States and others, many UNCLOS provisions reflect customary international law that is binding on all nations.[29] It addresses a wide variety of issues beyond the scope of IEL, but also provides the core principles, rights, and obligations that constitute IEL pertaining to the seas.

Perhaps the most broadly important provisions of UNCLOS are those defining national jurisdiction over the oceans. Building on preexisting practice and customary international law, UNCLOS reaffirms complete national jurisdiction over the "territorial sea," which extends 12 nautical miles from a state's coastline. Similarly broad national jurisdiction exists over the "contiguous zone" from 12 to 24 nautical miles off the coast of each state. Importantly, UNCLOS also defined national rights and responsibilities within a state's "exclusive economic zone" (EEZ), which extends to 200 nautical miles off the coastline. Each state has exclusive rights to all resources within its EEZ, as well as corresponding obligations to protect the environment and ensure conservation of resources within the EEZ.

The jurisdictional zones created by UNCLOS are perhaps the largest-scale example of using jurisdictional rights (akin to property rights) to address the classic "tragedy of the commons" problem that threatens the world's fisheries.[30] In theory, the jurisdictional zones could have reduced overfishing by creating an incentive for each state to ensure the sustainability of the fisheries within its jurisdiction. In reality, however, the solidification of jurisdictional zones in UNCLOS did not significantly reduce the problem of overfishing. Among other reasons, states' continued rights to permit fishing on the high seas prevented effective protection of fish species that moved between jurisdictional waters and the high seas.[31]

Among the most relevant provisions of UNCLOS for the protection of the marine environment are:

- Article 193, which articulates countries' sovereign right to exploit resources within their jurisdiction "in accordance with their duty to protect and preserve the marine environment";
- Article 194, which requires states to take "all measures necessary" to prevent damage to the marine environment from pollution, including protection of "rare or fragile ecosystems as well as the habitat of depleted, threatened, or endangered species"; and
- Article 196, which includes a duty to prevent harm caused by releasing alien species.

These and other environmental duties contained in UNCLOS "represent a fundamental shift in the law of the sea—away from maritime power and toward shared duties—as the basis for international relations."[32]

Along with the treaty provisions in UNCLOS, the regime governing ocean resources includes narrower, more environmentally focused agreements. The International Convention for the Prevention of Pollution from Ships (MARPOL), which was negotiated prior to UNCLOS, and international fish stock treaties, negotiated under the UNCLOS framework, represent important aspects of the UNCLOS regime by providing extensive coverage of these two critical aspects of marine environmental protection. They are also among the most specific treaties in terms of the implementation obligations imposed upon parties.[33]

B.   Marine Pollution: MARPOL

MARPOL[34] entered into force in 1983 and currently has over 130 parties. The agreements known collectively as MARPOL include an initial convention negotiated in 1973 and a subsequent protocol adopted in 1978. Together they regulate operational discharges from marine vessels. MARPOL does not address intentional marine dumping, which is covered by the 1972 London Convention. MARPOL was negotiated under the International Maritime Organization (IMO), a U.N. agency dating from the 1950s, which still serves as the MARPOL Secretariat. Along with broad coverage of pollution types and methods, MARPOL authorizes the IMO Marine Environment Protection

Committee to adopt technical regulations through amendment of the MAR-POL annexes. This has allowed an evolution in the regulatory scheme to keep pace with technological developments and led to the negotiation of annexes on disposal of garbage, wastewater, air emissions, and other more specific issues.[35] Both MARPOL and the London Convention are incorporated by reference into UNCLOS and, thus, are arguably binding on all UNCLOS parties or, perhaps, all nations as a matter of customary international law. Several regional seas now also include stricter regulation adopted pursuant to MAR-POL provisions pertaining to special areas warranting greater protection.

C.   Fish Stocks Treaty

Protection of marine fisheries has long been limited by the ability of states to fish the high seas because many fish species move from national waters to the commons of the high seas. Despite the extensive national control recognized by UNCLOS, many fisheries continued to decline because of fishing beyond the reach of national regulation. The U.N. Agreement for the Implementation of the Provisions of the United Nations Convention on the Law of the Sea of 10 December 1982 relating to the Conservation and Management of Straddling Fish Stocks and Highly Migratory Fish Stocks (Fish Stocks Treaty)[36] was negotiated and opened for signature in 1995 to address this problem. The Fish Stocks Treaty entered into force in 2001 and currently includes 81 parties. It provides the most important international law framework for regulating fish stocks that move between jurisdictional waters and the high seas. Its purpose is "to ensure the long-term conservation and sustainable use of straddling fish stocks and highly migratory fish stocks through effective implementation of the relevant provisions of [UNCLOS]."[37] Perhaps the most notable aspect of the Fish Stocks Treaty is that it sharply limits the ancient principle of freedom of the high seas by granting broad authority to regional organizations to regulate areas of the high seas that are important to the conservation of straddling stocks.

D.   Treaties Regulating the Exploitation of Ocean Species

Several treaty regimes exist to regulate exploitation of specific ocean species. These treaties reflect the international nature of these resources. Treaties of this type were among the first IEL regimes, such as the North Pacific Fur Seal Convention of 1911 regulating sealing among the United States, the United Kingdom, Russia, and Japan in the early 20th century. Although the North Pacific Fur Seal Convention is no longer operational, several other species-specific treaties remain important. Among the most significant for IEL generally is the International Convention for the Regulation of Whaling (ICRW). Another important aspect of ocean resource policy is the negotiation of regional fishery management treaties that create regional fisheries management organizations, such as the International Convention for the Conservation of Atlantic Tunas (ICCAT).

The ICRW was created in 1946, following earlier efforts to regulate the whaling industry. The ICRW creates the International Whaling Commission (IWC) as a regulatory body composed of one member drawn from each party. The IWC has authority under the ICRW to regulate whaling through a schedule setting forth the species covered and specific restrictions. In 1982, following significant public attention to whaling as an environmental and animal rights issue, the IWC adopted a complete moratorium on whaling, effective in 1986. Thus, while the ICRW was initially intended to conserve whales for the purpose of preserving the economic value of the whaling industry, it has become a focal point of broader debates on the purposes of species protection and the propriety of hunting whales, among the most sentient of nonhuman species, as an economic resource. In particular, considerable controversy surrounds Japan's continuation of whaling under an ICRW provision that allows parties to permit whaling "for the purposes of scientific research."[38]

ICCAT is a regional treaty designed to cooperatively manage tuna and several other fisheries in the Atlantic Ocean and associated seas. It was signed in 1966, entered into force in 1969, and currently has 49 contracting parties. The treaty creates the International Commission for the Conservation of Atlantic Tunas, which serves as the primary international fisheries management organization for the species regulated by ICCAT. ICCAT has been the focus of criticism for failing to prevent overfishing of species within its jurisdiction, but is not unique in this respect. Regional fisheries management organizations, on the whole, have not effectively curbed overfishing.

UNCLOS and, especially, the Fish Stocks Treaty are understood to support regional fisheries management organizations as an approach to cooperative management of ocean fisheries. In fact, the majority of regional fisheries management bodies were created after the adoption of the Fish Stocks Treaty in 1995. Thus, despite a relatively poor historical record, these organizations are expected to continue to play an important role in IEL.

IV.   Protection of Biodiversity

Current rates of biodiversity loss pose a profound threat to the continuation of current environmental conditions favorable to human well-being. The causes of biodiversity loss are extremely complex and diverse. Not surprisingly, international law concerning the protection of biodiversity is among the most complex and extensive areas of IEL. It includes several MEAs designed specifically to combat biodiversity loss (such as the CBD), a number of other international agreements that include significant provisions for biodiversity protection (such as the UNCLOS), and other instruments that affect biodiversity conservation (such as the UNFCCC).[39] Although this area of law is highly fragmented into distinct regimes with distinct areas of competence and authority, a number of important formal and informal relationships exist among the various regimes. Nonetheless, implementation of international biodiversity law remains profoundly challenging and biodiversity loss continues at dangerously high rates.

A. The CBD

The CBD serves as a framework agreement for international biodiversity law. It was opened for signature at the 1992 UNCED, entered into force in 1993, and currently has 193 parties. The United States actively participated in negotiations and signed the CBD, but has not ratified it. The CBD includes three main objectives: conservation of biodiversity; sustainable use of biodiversity's components; and equitable sharing of benefits derived from biodiversity. Negotiation of the CBD included discussion of economic issues related to use of biodiversity's components and sharing of benefits, particularly as these related to development by corporations headquartered in developed countries of pharmaceuticals and other products partially derived from biological resources located in developing countries. Thus, CBD reflects compromise on economic distribution issues as much as a global desire to preserve biodiversity.

The CBD's conservation objectives are expressed through several articles that require parties to take concrete actions, such as assessing and reporting on the biodiversity within their territories. However, most of these provisions include highly qualified language that undermines the ability to ensure that parties actually engage in measures that improve the conservation of biodiversity.

The CBD requires that parties develop national plans on the issue and integrate it into other areas of activity (Article 6). It also includes provisions that promote conservation of biodiversity by requiring, with qualification, that parties identify and monitor important components of biodiversity (Article 7), and establish protected areas (Article 8(a)).

Two protocols to the CBD have been negotiated. The Cartagena Protocol on Biosafety was adopted in 2000 and entered into force in 2003. It regulates the use and trade in genetically modified organisms, with the following objective: "to contribute to ensuring an adequate level of protection in the field of the transfer, handling and use of living modified organisms resulting from modern biotechnology that may have adverse effects on the conservation and sustainable use of biodiversity."[40] The second protocol, the Nagoya Protocol on Access to Genetic Resources and the Fair and Equitable Sharing of Benefits Arising from their Utilization, was opened for signature in 2010 and will require ratification by 50 countries to enter into force.

B. Other Biodiversity Treaties

There are a large number of treaties that regulate some aspect of biodiversity, including specialized treaties such as the ICRW.[41] Due to space constraints, only two are addressed next.

1. CITES

CITES, which opened for signature in 1973 and entered into force in 1975, is among the oldest globally applicable MEAs and stands as a sort of conceptual bridge between older wildlife-oriented law and more recent biodiversity-centered agreements. CITES has a relatively simple international institutional structure, and provides specific requirements for implementation that aim to secure enforcement of its provisions through national administrative bodies. CITES requires parties to designate a "scientific authority" and a "management authority," which are responsible for ensuring compliance with the treaty's trade restrictions and monitoring and reporting obligations. CITES employs an annex system to designate protected species. Annex I includes species that are threatened with extinction and may be harmed by trade. Trade in species (or parts of species) listed in Annex I is sharply restricted. Such trade requires that permits be issued by both the exporting and importing country's scientific authority, which must certify that the trade is not for primarily commercial purposes. Annex II and III restrictions are much less restrictive and do permit commercial trade.

CITES has been broadly ratified, with 180 parties, and has affected endangered species regulation throughout the world. Arguably, CITES exemplifies the potential and limitations of a "hard law" approach to IEL. CITES' goal—the elimination or regulation of international trade in endangered species—explains both the effectiveness of CITES in securing compliance, and the limitations of the regime for addressing the problem of biodiversity loss in all but a relatively small number of potential extinction scenarios.

2. Ramsar Convention

The only MEA to focus on a specific habitat throughout the world, the Convention on Wetlands of International Importance Especially as Waterfowl Habitat (Ramsar Convention)[42] has played a unique role in biodiversity conservation. Like CITES, Ramsar entered into force in 1975 and has received broad ratification (168 parties). It has evolved and currently serves as an implementation body for the conservation requirements of the CBD as they apply to wetlands. Ramsar is also significant in its own right, bringing broad international attention to the significance of wetlands for environmental and other values, although it has very few formally binding requirements.

VI.   Treaties to Control Pollution and Waste

A.   Stockholm Convention on Persistent Organic Pollutants

Of the many persistent organic pollutants (POPs) affecting the environment internationally, 12 chemicals known as the "dirty dozen" have generated the most policy debate.[43] The Stockholm Convention on Persistent Organic Pollutants,[44] which entered into force in 2004 and has 179 parties, regulates these and many other POPs primarily through bans and phase-out schedules, while also creating a relatively streamlined mechanism for bringing new chemicals within the ambit of the treaty. It divides POPs into three categories—pesticides, industrial chemicals, and unintended by-products (i.e., wastes)—and uses an annex system imposing varying levels of restriction on listed chemicals. The convention also creates the POPs Review Committee with authority to add chemicals to one of the treaty's three annexes of regulated chemicals (Annex A–C) according to the procedure established in Article 8 and based on a screening criteria stated in Annex D as well as, if these criteria are met, a "risk profile" as described in Annex E.

B. Basel Convention

In the absence of regulation, economic incentives exist to spur the transport of hazardous waste from developed countries to developing countries, many of which are incapable of adequately managing and safely disposing of significant quantities of hazardous materials. This reality poses major health risks to many developing country populations. In response to a rising tide of transboundary shipment of hazardous waste and resulting risks, more than 100 countries negotiated for two years to create the Basel Convention on the Control of Transboundary Movements of Hazardous Wastes and Their Disposal (Basel Convention).[45] The Basel Convention opened for signature in 1989, entered into force in 1992, and currently has 151 parties. It establishes a system of notification and consent applicable to transboundary shipment of hazardous waste among parties and requires environmentally sound management and disposal of such waste by all parties.

The scope of the waste covered by the Basel Convention is defined in Article 1 by reference to Annexes I and III, which identify streams of waste production and characteristics of hazardous substances, respectively, and Article 2, which makes the convention applicable to all waste considered hazardous waste by the exporting, transporting, or importing country.

The Basel Convention prohibits shipment of hazardous waste to Antarctica or to non-parties, but otherwise does not ban shipments to any particular destination. A 1995 Amendment known as the "Basel Ban" would prohibit all shipments of hazardous wastes from developed to less developed countries. Although the Basel Ban has not received sufficient ratifications to enter into force, the European Union and others have enacted legislation to achieve its aims.

In 1999, the fifth COP produced the Protocol on Liability and Compensation, which provides a comprehensive scheme to address liability and related issues resulting from damage caused by transboundary shipments of waste, including illegal transport. Although the protocol was the result of extensive negotiations over six years, it has not entered into force.

C. Other Pollution Regulation Treaties

Several other significant treaty regimes regulate pollution. The Rotterdam Convention on the Prior Informed Consent Procedure for Certain Hazardous Chemicals and Pesticides in International Trade,[46] for example, regulates international trade in certain hazardous pesticides and industrial chemicals by creating a mandatory prior informed consent procedure. Signed in 1998 and entered into force in 2003, it responds primarily to concerns related to hazardous chemicals importation and use in developing countries. The Rotterdam Convention operates through an annex system, with the listing of chemicals on Annex III as a trigger for a procedure that requires parties to specify whether they will continue to import the chemical. It also provides for and supports information exchange regarding a broad range of chemicals.

In January 2013, 140 nations agreed to the Minamata Convention on Mercury after four years of negotiation efforts. Although the agreement has not yet opened for signature at the time of this writing, much less begun to receive ratifications, it may prove to be a significant development for IEL. Among the most significant provisions of the agreement are a ban on import and export of certain mercury-containing products that would take effect in 2020, measures to curb the use of mercury in mining and other operations, and measures designed to reduce mercury limitations.

VII. Conclusion

The scope of IEL has come to be as broad as domestic environmental law, in many respects. The agreements highlighted in this chapter are but a sampling of the more than 200 IEL agreements adopted in the last few decades. Practitioners should be mindful that along with the broad and globally applicable treaties discussed in this chapter, a wide variety of regional and bilateral treaties regulate activities with environmental implications.

The issue areas discussed in this chapter are by no means exhaustive. Although often less formal or less successful, MEAs address many other matters of environmental concern. These include the U.N. Economic Commission for Europe Watercourses Convention addressing transboundary rivers and lakes, several agreements on tropical and other forests adopted under the U.N. Forum on Forests or the International Tropical Timber Organization, various instruments of the U.N. Food and Agricultural Organization, treaties and annexes seeking to protect and conserve Arctic and Antarctic resources, and agreements that are part of multilateral or binational free trade agreements. Moreover, a variety of trade-related agreements have direct impacts on environmental regulation or policy areas that may be environmentally sensitive.

This chapter serves as a quick digest for the practitioner seeking an overview of some of the major international environmental agreements. It has sought only to provide an overview of the field through its major treaties, including both hard law and soft law. Hopefully, this overview provides a context within which more specific questions can be understood and more targeted research may be undertaken.

Notes

1. United Nations Conference on the Human Environment, Stockholm Declaration, June 16, 1972, UN Doc. A/CONF.48/14 (1972), *reprinted in* 11 I.L.M. 1416, 1419 (1972).

2. Rio Declaration on Environment and Development, U.N. Conference on Environment and Development, UN Doc. A/CONF.151/5/Rev. 1 (1992), 31 I.L.M. 874 (1992).

3. 1996 ICJ Reports 241, para. 29.

4. Philippe Sands & Jacqueline Peel, Principles of International Environmental Law 191 (3d ed. 2012).

5. *E.g.*, Svitlana Kravchenko & John E. Bonine, Human Rights and the Environment Cases, Law, and Policy 67 (2008) (identifying the Stockholm Declaration as a precursor to protection of environmental human rights in national constitutions).

6. March 3, 1973, 12 I.L.M. 1085 (1973).

7. June 5, 1992, 31 I.L.M. 818 (1992).

8. Montreal Protocol on Substances That Deplete the Ozone Layer, Sept. 16, 1987, 26 I.L.M. 1550 (1987).

9. Vienna Convention for the Protection of the Ozone Layer, Mar. 22, 1985, 26 I.L.M. 1529 (1987).

10. Vienna Convention art. 2.

11. Vienna Convention arts. 3 & 4.

12. *See* http://ozone.unep.org/new_site/en/montreal_protocol.php.

13. Montreal Protocol art. 3.

14. Montreal Protocol arts. 5, 10, 10A.

15. See Montreal Protocol art. 4.

16. Decision XIX/6: Adjustments to the Montreal Protocol with Regard to Annex C, Group I, Substances (hydrochlorofluorocarbons), Report of the 19th Meeting of the Parties to the Montreal Protocol (2007).

17. Mario Molina et al., *Reducing Abrupt Climate Change Risk Using the Montreal Protocol and Other Regulatory Actions to Complement Cuts in CO2 Emissions*, 106 Proc. Nat'l Acad. Sci. 20,616 (2009).

18. For discussion, see, for example, David Hunter, James Salzman & Durwood Zaelke, International Environmental Law and Policy 560 (4th ed., 2010).

19. May 9, 1992, 31 I.L.M. 849.

20. UNFCCC art. 4.

21. Dec. 11, 1997, 37 I.L.M. 22.

22. Kyoto Protocol arts. 2, 3, Annex B.

23. Kyoto Protocol art. 17.

24. This approach is exemplified by the member states of the European Union.

25. UNFCCC members did not adopt the Copenhagen Accord.

26. REDD+ also has served to bring attention to other social and environmental issues related to forests. *See* chapter 22, Brazil, in this volume.

27. Decision 1/CP.17: Establishment of an Ad Hoc Working Group on the Durban Platform for Enhanced Action, FCCC/CP/2011/9/Ad.1 (2011).

28. October 10, 1982, 21 I.L.M. 1261 (1982).

29. The United States has not ratified UNCLOS primarily because of its objections to provisions related to international seabed mining (Part XI) and other issues of sovereignty. Nonetheless, the United States has long complied with most aspects of UNCLOS as customary international law.

30. *See, e.g.*, Daniel Bodansky, The Art and Craft of International Environmental Law 52 (2010) (citing UNCLOS as an example of using property rights to address problems of the commons).

31. Such fisheries have more recently become regulated by certain treaties on management of fish stocks, as discussed next.

32. Hunter, Salzman & Zaelke, supra note 18.

33. Bodansky, *supra* note 30, at 210–11.

34. Nov. 2, 1973, 12 I.L.M. 1319.

35. *See, e.g.*, David Freestone & Salman M.A. Salman, *Ocean and Freshwater Resources, in* The Oxford Handbook of International Environmental Law 346 (D. Bodansky, J. Brunee & E. Hey eds. 2007).

36. Dec. 4, 1995, 34 I.L.M. 1542.

37. UNCLOS art. 2.

38. International Convention for the Regulation of Whaling art. VIII. Two other nations continue to permit whaling but have drawn less persistent criticism for doing so because of their legal bases for doing so. Iceland withdrew from the ICRW in response to the moratorium and Norway has effectively objected to it under international law.

39. *See generally* Andrew Long, *Developing Linkages to Preserve Biodiversity*, 21 Y.B. Int'l Envtl. L. 1 (2012).

40. Cartagena Protocol, 31 I.L.M. 1257 (2000), art. 1.

41. The ICRW is arguably among the oldest multilateral environmental agreements in existence, having been negotiated in 1946. Its unique history illustrates the gradual shift in emphasis from allocation of rights to exploit living resources to protection of the whale species due to environmental concern.

42. Feb. 2, 1971, 11 I.L.M. 969.

43. Hunter, Salzman & Zaelke, supra note 18, at 928. These chemicals are (1) the pesticides aldrin, DDT, dieldrin, endrin, chlordane, mirex, toxaphone, and heptachlor; and (2) the industrial chemicals or by-products dioxins, furans, PCBs hexachlorobenzene, and toxaphene.

44. May 22, 2001, 40 I.L.M. 532 (2001).

45. Mar. 22, 1989, 28 I.L.M. 657 (1989).

46. Sept. 11, 1998, 38 I.L.M. 1 (1999).

CHAPTER 50

The Role of International Standards

ANDREW LONG

I. Introduction

This chapter highlights the role of certain international standards established by and for private entities as they relate to international environmental law.[1] The standards discussed by this chapter are market-oriented and do not originate from intergovernmental agreements. The significance of this type of standards, for environmental goals as in other areas, arises primarily from the influential role that traditional international standardization organizations, such as the International Organization for Standardization (ISO), now play in international business and trade.[2] This and other standard-setting entities have created environmental standards over the last two decades for a variety of reasons, including consumer interest in the environment and the desire of governmental, corporate, and civil society interests to shape the behavior or perception of behavior by transnational corporations. Quite distinct from the evolution of preexisting technical standard-setting bodies, international standards have also proliferated because of increasing interest in the development of non-state market-based approaches to international environmental governance through eco-labeling. This brief chapter provides an overview of the role these types of international standards play in international environmental law and corporate behavior affecting the environment.

II. International Standardization and the Development of Environmental Standards
A. A Brief Primer on Standardization

The ISO, the world's largest and most significant developer of international standards, defines a standard as "a document that provides requirements, specifications, guidelines or characteristics that can be used consistently to ensure that materials, products, processes and services are fit for their purpose."[3] There has been a widespread proliferation of standards as international

995

trade volume has increased in recent decades. ISO alone has developed over 19,000 standards since its inception in 1947.[4] ISO describes many benefits to the use of standards, including improvement in businesses' social and environmental performance, as well as enhancement of global trade.

Although ISO is clearly the dominant standard-setting organization for global commerce, many other general and specialized standard-setting bodies exist at the international level and below. These entities may also serve as representatives of a country in the ISO standard-setting process.[5] In the United States, for example, the American National Standards Institute (ANSI) serves to oversee the creation and use of guidelines impacting U.S. businesses, including the accreditation of programs utilizing ISO standards in the global arena.[6]

A primary motivation for standardization at the global level is the facilitation of international trade. Most standards are aimed at technical aspects of business, such as the specific requirements for products and their performance. Thus, standards are, by and large, favored by and often initiated at the behest of business interests. The development of social and environmental standards is an evolution in the role of standards from their origin as tools for technical coordination. Nonetheless, environmental standards generally serve a similar purpose—facilitating the coordination of business practices across the globe and an indication of quality with regard to products and processes.

Standards no longer play a purely voluntary role in international trade. International agreements now mandate the use of standards as a means of ensuring fairness and consistency in dealings between nations and transnational corporations. The WTO Agreement on Technical Barriers to Trade, for example, mandates that parties base technical regulations on international standards. A related Code of Good Practice specifically references ISO standards and. Although this code does not require states to adopt ISO standards, it arguably elevates ISO standards to the status of international law.[7] The North American Free Trade Agreement (NAFTA) and other regional trade agreements also include requirements that promote reliance on ISO or similar standards. In addition, numerous less comprehensive agreements seek to harmonize standards for particular industries and countries. This further integrates privately developed international standards into governmental regulation. Moreover, major public international organizations, such as the U.N. Economic Commission for Europe (UNECE), maintain standing working groups and committees whose entire purpose is to promote harmonization of international standards in particular industries and regions.[8]

Certification of compliance with international standards has also helped to establish standards as an influential force beyond technical coordination. As the use of standards has evolved to include socially important matters such as environmental impact, a number of different pathways have been created for private entities to demonstrate their compliance. While entities may simply proclaim their voluntary compliance with standards, it is also common for businesses to secure validation of their compliance through outside assessment. ANSI, for example, performs "conformity assessments," which involve "the evaluation of products, processes, systems, services or personnel to confirm adherence to the requirements identified in a specified standard."[9] ISO has also created a system of registration that promotes verification of compliance. Among other reasons, these certification protocols are attractive because they enhance companies' credibility in the market.[10]

B. Environmental Standards

The most globally influential environmental standards are ISO's 14000 series standards. ISO 14000 is a series of environmental management systems (EMS) standards to be implemented on the international level.[11] ISO 14001 and other EMS standards include elements such as policy setting, planning, internal audits, and control of operations.[12] Organizations can either voluntarily and independently declare they are in compliance with the ISO standards or they can be registered through the ISO.[13] There appears to be widespread agreement that the ISO's 14000 standards are the most significant and widely embraced set of general environmental standards.[14]

While ISO standards have clearly moved beyond their technical origins,[15] the standard-setting process employed by ISO does not appear to reflect this shift. Developing countries, civil society, small businesses, and even some significant industrial sectors are underrepresented in ISO's process for environmental standard development.[16] ISO standards are established through a series of meetings throughout the world. The final standards depend upon reaching an informal consensus, which means that no participating entity has mounted sustained opposition to a proposed standard.[17] Environmental non-governmental organizations (NGOs), developing countries, and other potentially interested sectors may not have a significant voice in the process simply because of the resources necessary to be effectively involved in standards development.

In addition to the expansion of general, often technically oriented, standards to include environmental management, a number of sector-specific environmental standards have been created as a result of environmental NGOs' efforts to seek alternatives to public international law for influencing behavior affecting the environment. Among the most important examples of this "eco-labeling" form of standards are the principles and criteria established by the Forest Stewardship Council (FSC).[18] The FSC was formed by a coalition of NGOs in the wake of failed efforts to negotiate a multilateral environmental agreement on forests at the U.N. Conference on the Environment and Development, held in Rio de Janeiro in 1992.[19] The FSC is the most prominent example of efforts to create non-state market-based social and environmental regulation. The core idea behind the FSC and other similar efforts is to provide an easily identifiable indication of environmental stewardship (an "eco-label") in the creation of products that enables consumers to incorporate their concern for the environment into purchasing decisions.

If consumers prefer products bearing eco-labels to a sufficient degree, it will create an incentive for businesses to conform to the standards of the labeling organization. The success of this strategy has varied considerably across sectors and regions. For example, the FSC has enjoyed considerable success in developed countries. But it has only marginally affected the tropical deforestation and degradation that originally motivated its creation. Separately, various forms of "fair trade" labeling, which reflect compliance with social standards, have had success in some sectors (such as coffee).

Other types of environmental standards have also been created at the international level. For example, the United Nations promoted the Global Compact, which seeks to build upon corporate codes of conduct to encourage "good global citizenship" among transnational corporations.[20]

III.   International Standards as Private Governance

Many international standards have reached a degree of prominence and influence that justifies describing them as a form of "private governance." In this context, standards fill a gap in public international law by directly regulating the conduct of transnational corporations and other private actors. Such entities are not directly subject to international law, because international law regulates only the conduct of states. The importance of corporations in affecting environmental and social conditions throughout the world, and especially in developing countries, is immense. Of the 100 largest economies in the world, roughly half are corporations.[21] The effect of corporate behavior on the environment of developing countries, in particular, is often immense. The actions of Shell Oil in Nigeria, for example, have had extensive impacts on not only the environment in that country, but also its legal and other social systems.

International standards are fairly described as private governance because they offer a non-state-based method of regulating activities and behavior. In this sense, they are essentially a new form of "law" that may be understood to compliment, compete with, or otherwise affect traditional international law.[22] The effect of international standards, generally and in specific instances, is widely debated by scholars and others interested in international environmental policy.

One recent assessment of the impact of ISO's 14000 series standards succinctly describes the debate as follows:

> ISO standards have a number of benefits, including promoting international uniformity; elevating environmental issues within an enterprise; promoting international trade; and providing a minimal level of environmental performance in countries with less than adequate regulatory infrastructure. Concerns about ISO standards include the relationship to public regulation; and ISO 14001's essentially procedural, as opposed to performance-based, character. . . . ISO standards may operate either as a sword—a negative standard used to challenge a domestic regulatory

action—or a shield—an internationally agreed reference point that bolsters a national measure.[23]

As this assessment illustrates, international standards cannot be understood in a vacuum. They must be viewed as part of a complex web of regulation that influences corporate behavior affecting the environment. Other elements, such as private contracting, can also play a pivotal role in defining the standards of environmental quality applicable to transnational corporations, but the prominence of international standards in this area cannot be ignored.[24]

IV. Conclusion

International standards now play an important role in international environmental law. This is primarily because they may directly govern private corporate conduct in a way that public international law cannot. They are also important because, through international trade agreements or voluntary adoption, international standards often shape national regulation of transnational corporate behavior.[25]

Notes

1. While there is a rich literature addressing the merits and risks of international standards as private governance, space constraints limit the present chapter to simply identifying some of the key aspects of international standards and providing a context for understanding their operation. Practitioners are encouraged to consult the sources referenced herein for more in-depth treatment of these issues relevant to particular issues that may arise with regard to these standards.

2. *See* http://www.iso.org.

3. Int'l Org. for Standardization, Standards: What Is a Standard?, http://www.iso.org/iso/home/standards.htm (last visited January 14, 2013).

4. Int'l Org. for Standardization: About ISO, http://www.iso.org/iso/home/about.htm (last visited January 14, 2013).

5. The ISO permits each country to participate in standard setting through membership of one entity per country. In developed countries, the members are usually private entities, while developing countries more often establish governmental members. J. Morrison & N. Roht-Arriaza, *Private and Quasi-Private Standard-Setting, in* The Oxford Handbook of International Environmental Law 502 (D. Bodansky, J. Brunee & E. Hey eds., 2007).

6. Am. National Standards Inst., http://www.ansi.org/.

7. Morrison & Roht-Arriaza, *supra* note 5, at 503.

8. *See* http://www.unece.org.

9. *See* http://www.ansi.org. For an overview of the U.S. Standardization System, see http://www.standardsportal.org/usa_en/standards_system.aspx.

10. *Id.*

11. OMNEX, Resource Center, http://www.omnex.com/members/standards/iso14000/iso_14000.aspx.

12. Morrison & Roht-Arriaza, *supra* note 5, at 508.

13. OMNEX, Resource Center, http://www.omnex.com/members/standards/iso 14000/iso_14000.aspx.

14. J. Clapp, *ISO Environmental Standards: Industry's Gift to a Polluted Globe or the Developed World's Competition-Killing Strategy?*, *in* Yearbook of International Co-operation on Environment and Development 2001/2002, at 27–33 (Olav Schram Stokke & Øystein B. Thommessen eds., 2001).

15. Perhaps the best known example illustrating the importance of ISO technical standards are those applicable to photographic film speeds, which have resulted in uniform film speeds for virtually all cameras produced in all countries around the globe.

16. Morrison & Roht-Arriaza, *supra* note 5, at 503.

17. *Id.*

18. *See* https://us.fsc.org.

19. UNCED gave rise to the U.N. Framework Convention on Climate Change and the Convention on Biological Diversity, among other agreements. The effort to create a forest convention at UNCED, however, stands as one of the starkest examples of failure in public international environmental law.

20. David Hunter, James Salzman & Durwood Zaelke, International Environmental Law and Policy 1379, 1398 (4th ed. 2010).

21. *Id.* at 1379.

22. *See, e.g.*, T. M. Roberts, *Innovations in Governance: A Functional Typology of Private Governance Institutions*, 22 Duke Envtl. L. & Pol'y Forum 67 (2011), *available at* http://papers.ssrn.com/sol3/papers.cfm?abstract_id=1690831.

23. D. Wirth, *The International Organization for Standardization: Private Voluntary Standards as Swords and Shields*, 36 B.C. Envtl. Affairs L. Rev. 79 (2009) (abstract).

24. *See* M. Vandenburg, *The New Wal-Mart Effect*, 54 U.C.L.A. L. Rev. 913 (2007).

25. Another important example of standardization in the financial sector is the Equator Principles (EPs). The EPs provide financial institutions with a risk management framework for "determining, assessing and managing environmental and social risk in projects" and provides "a minimum standard for due diligence to support responsible risk decision-making." *See* http://www.equator-principles.com (last visited Feb. 22, 2014). There are currently 79 Equator Principles Financial Institutions in 35 countries, covering over 70 percent of international project finance debt in emerging countries. *Id.* For more information on the EPs and their influence on institutions such as the European Bank for Reconstruction and Development and the Organisation for Economic Co-operation and Development, and the development of the Carbon Principles in the U.S. and Climate Principles worldwide, see http://www.equator-principles.com/index.php/about-ep/about-ep (last visited Feb. 22, 2014). Separately, in the electronics industry, the Electronic Industry Citizenship Coalition has a Code of Conduct that, inter alia, focuses on ensuring environmental responsibility. *See* http://www.eicc.info/documents/EICCCodeofConduct English.pdf (last visited Feb. 24, 2014).

INDEX